to Gary:

after the murials
are are mode – Lets
do positive deals.

With Best Wishes

Sheezy

4/24/86

FOREIGN INVESTMENT IN UNITED STATES REAL ESTATE

A Guide for Buyers, Sellers, Their Agents, and Counsel

Myron Meyers

FOREIGN INVESTMENT IN UNITED STATES REAL ESTATE

A Guide for Buyers, Sellers, Their Agents, and Counsel

DOW JONES-IRWIN
Homewood, Illinois 60430

ISBN 0-87094-204-2

Library of Congress Catalog Card No. 81-68063

Printed in the United States of America

1 2 3 4 5 6 7 8 9 0 K 9 8 7 6 5 4 3 2

To
BARBARA, SUSAN, and STEVEN—
They make it all worthwhile

PREFACE

For the past 25 years as a full-time, practicing real estate attorney, this author has been aware of a number of misconceptions held by the foreign investor in negotiating for, acquiring, developing, and holding U.S. real estate. It is the intent of this book to shed light on the misconceptions and to guide the foreign investor and those brokers, syndicators, investment counselors, trust officers, bankers, accountants, and attorneys who may be called upon to assist the foreign investor in understanding basic principles of real estate investment and taxation in the United States.

Various chapters have been devoted to basic real estate principles and to the ever-increasing limits being placed upon foreigners desiring to invest in various types of U.S. real estate. A working knowledge of the basic principles of current and proposed U.S. tax laws and philosophy as they affect the foreign investor is essential, and thus, there is a basic discussion to aid both the foreign investor and his counselors.

This book is not intended as a text for the professional but rather is written in the hope that it may be of use to a broad spectrum of the public in understanding the various aspects of dealing, investing in, and developing real estate in the United States. A "checklist" approach is used in a number of chapters to raise issues and guide the reader in formulating an investment philosophy and in dealing with the various methods of holding title and their practical effects. While a few citations are set forth to various statutes and, occasionally, Internal Revenue Code sections, the reader will be required to resort to more formal treatises to deal in depth with specific sections or issues that are of concern.

As an example of this latter point, the State Bar of California in cooperation with the University of California, has created a series of books under the title of *Continuing Education of the Bar*. These are practical works drawn by lawyers for lawyers that deal specifically with various subjects that relate directly or indirectly to various aspects of real estate acquisition, ownership, development, and financing. Appendix 5 contains a topical heading of the current publications of the *Continuing Education of the Bar* series, and the reader may desire to obtain copies of specific works that deal with a subject of special interest to him.

As this book is going to press, the regulations dealing with the new Foreign Investment in Real Property Tax Act of 1980 have not been issued. This new Act is creating sweeping and fundamental changes in the method of taxing real estate owned by foreign individuals and entities and creates many new issues which are discussed below. However, the reader is cautioned to seek proper advice and counsel at the time of any specific real estate transaction to assure that no changes have occurred in the laws which may materially affect the method of structuring the acquisition, ownership, or development of this project.

The reader will further note in Appendix 1 that many of the states within the United States have developed a series of restrictive statutes that limit or prohibit, in varying degrees, the ownership of U.S. property by foreigners. The concept of such limitations or restrictions is relatively new, but it is evolving rapidly under continued pressure on state legislatures to further restrict the foreign investor. Again, before undertaking an acquisition or involvement in a real estate transaction in a particular state, the reader should consult with competent, local advisors within that state as to any existing or proposed laws that would affect the transaction in question.

A special word of advice to real estate brokers and investment counselors. It has been the unfortunate experience of this author in dealing with brokers and investment counselors as well as trust officers and title personnel that many of these parties are not sufficiently sensitive to the particular problems of the foreign investor. Further, they seem to assume that since the foreign investor may be sophisticated as a businessman in his country, he is equally as sophisticated and knowledgeable about basic U.S. real estate and tax principles. Don't make such assumptions. Be sure your client understands the ground rules. What is fee ownership? What are the restrictions placed on investment? How do you form a local corporation? What is title insurance? What is an escrow? What is a contract of purchase and sale? How does the financial market work in the United States? What about the availability of long-term financing? What about personal liability? Will the seller "finance" part of the acquisition? Experience has shown that most real estate brokers and investment counselors wrongly assume the foreign investor has basic knowledge of the tools of the real estate profession with which they deal on an everyday basis and which have become second nature to them. Don't make such an assumption. This subject is further expanded in Chapter 6 dealing with some of the special problems that face the foreign investor such as anonymity, freedom from management, currency controls, the use of foreign corporations and trusts, property management agreements, limited partnerships and joint ventures as vehicles for investing, the use of triple-net lease-backs and the advantages of basic tax principles which, as the law now exists, are in many cases more favorable to the foreign investor than to a U.S. citizen or resident.

This author is by training and experience a practicing lawyer not an appraiser, engineer, or investment analyst. Therefore, the approach of this book is directed to the practice of preventive law in the hope that the matters discussed and the checklists developed will aid the reader in avoiding costly pitfalls and errors.

One of the chapters, namely Chapter 11, deals with the formation, operation, and termination of a Netherlands Antilles corporation. The author wishes to express his thanks to Smeets & Smeets, attorneys of Curacao, Netherlands Antilles for their review of the material set forth in that chapter. Chapters 7 and 8, dealing with taxation, and Appendix 3 were prepared with the valuable assistance and advice of Wayne Reiner, CPA, of Price Waterhouse & Company, Los Angeles, California. Wayne's contribution is most gratefully acknowledged. Also, a special thanks to my secretary, Jeannine Frausto, whose dedication and assistance were invaluable.

Myron Meyers

CONTENTS

LIST OF REAL ESTATE AND TAX FORMS

REASONS FOR INVESTING IN UNITED STATES REAL ESTATE

At the outset, the question must be asked as to why the foreign investor should invest in United States real property as distinguished from other types of available investments, such as the stock market, commodities, or simply leaving his money in U.S. banks or other established lending institutions. In this latter regard, the present U.S. tax laws permit the foreign investor to deposit unlimited sums in U.S. financial institutions and enjoy the interest generated by those deposits free of U.S. federal income tax. With present economic conditions, and because U.S. financial institutions are now paying record high interest rates to depositors, a strong argument could be made for the foreign investor to leave his money in such an investment since it is in most cases insured by an instrumentality of the U.S. government and is readily available should any emergency arise. However, in light of current and anticipated inflation and by reason of other factors that will be discussed below, it is this author's opinion that investment in U.S. real estate has in the past and will in the future prove to be the best vehicle for the foreign investor to preserve his capital and enjoy growth.

As will be mentioned elsewhere in this book, when the term *foreign investor* is used, the reader should be careful not to misunderstand its meaning. As used throughout this text, the foreign investor means a *non-U.S.* citizen who is also not *a resident* of the United States for federal tax purposes. The mere fact one is a *non-citizen* of the United States does not exempt that person from U.S. taxation if he is, in fact, a resident.

In addition, when used throughout this text, *foreign investor* also applies to a foreign corporation, the stock of which is owned by non-U.S. citizens and residents. A *foreign corporation* as used throughout this text is a corporation formed and existing under the laws of a nation other than the United States or any of its states or territories.

Some of the primary reasons for investing in U.S. real estate, although not necessarily in order of priority, can be summarized as follows:

1. The best hedge against inflation, especially when coupled with the principle of leverage to be discussed below.
2. Relatively inexpensive prices of U.S. real estate as compared with real property prices in other parts of the world, particularly in Europe and Asia.
3. The relative ease and availability of long-term institutional financing which permits the use of leverage concepts.
4. The willingness of sellers to "finance" real estate acquisitions.
5. The relative ease and lack of restrictions on foreign investors purchasing U.S. real property.
6. The strong political stability of the United States and the ability of foreign investors to be assured of good title and in most instances to be fully insured.
7. The value of the U.S. dollar in relation to foreign currencies has increased, in most instances, the buying power of the foreign investor.
8. The favorable tax benefits given to foreign investors to encourage U.S. investment.
9. A relative freedom from personal liability and downstroke risk associated with real estate investments.

Let us examine some of these factors in more detail. No extended discussion of inflation and its effects on real property is appropriate in a text of this nature. It should, however, be observed that real property prices for both improved and unimproved property have risen dramatically in most areas of the United States in the last 5 to 10 years. This increase has, in most instances, far outstripped the annual rate of inflation during the equivalent period of time. It is this author's opinion that inflation in the United States will continue at double-digit rates for the foreseeable future and that real property prices will continue to keep pace with the inflationary spiral.

It has been my experience that most real estate professionals in the United States have been so accustomed to the availability of long-term fixed-interest rate loans that they do not appreciate the tremendous advantage this produces in the real estate market. The foreign investor, however, is just the opposite. He is accustomed to dealing in cash and is amazed at the ease by which institutional funds can be obtained. Whether or not the U.S. experience will change in the foreseeable future is a question of great debate, but I strongly suggest that the American attitute toward long-term fixed-interest rates will undergo a dramatic change in the near future. In my opinion, more cash will be required for real estate projects, lenders will be reluctant to make long-term commitments at fixed-interest rates, and pressures will be ever increasing for lenders to request "a piece of the deal" either in the form of changing interest rates tied to some objective standard or by actual ownership or participation in the real estate project itself.

In dealing with this entire area of financing, the foreign investor should be made fully aware of the fact that in most instances, the sellers of real property, particularly when unimproved land and agricultural property are involved, are not adverse to carrying back a substantial portion of the purchase price in order to facilitate the sale. Again, this is substantially different from the custom in most foreign countries. There is almost no long-term fixed-interest rate financing available in these countries. The foreign investor should be educated fully as to the various sources of funds. What are some of the traditional sources of funding for real estate projects in the United States?

A.   For short term (temporary loans of not more than two years) banks have been the traditional sources. The amount a bank will loan in relation to the purchase price varies with the area in which the property is located, the financial reputation of the borrower and the amount of equity investment.

B.   For construction funds, banks are the primary sources for funds since they are organized to disburse and administer a construction project. In some instances, savings and loan associations will also grant construction financing, though in most cases such construction lending is tied into a program of ultimate permanent long-term financing of the project in question.

C.   For long-term loans, there are several sources. For larger projects, insurance companies have traditionally been the primary source. Insurance companies are not, however, generally equipped to administer construction funds and prefer to consummate their loan when the project is completed. Savings and loan associations are also the source of long-term financing, but they tend to lend on smaller projects.

D.   Banks, pension funds and trusts, and real estate investment trusts, have in recent times been significant sources of long-term real estate financing and should not be overlooked.

E.   In specialized transactions such as agricultural properties and low-income housing, as an example, instrumentalities of the U.S. federal government can be a significant source for funds and/or loan guaranties to facilitate financing and encourage development.

I wish to emphasize to the foreign investor and his advisors to take advantage of the attitude of many U.S. owners who are willing to self-finance, that is, carry back a note and mortgage (deed of trust). This is contrary to attitudes that foreign investors are used to in their own country. This U.S. attitude, coupled with the U.S. tax laws on installment sales, can be a very useful bargaining tool not to be easily overlooked.

To the knowledge of the author, except in very special circumstances such as leasing of mineral rights and other energy sources, there are no *federal laws* expressly restricting the ownership of real property in the United States by foreign investors. However, the foreign investor must clearly understand that under the U.S. system of law, each state within the United States is a separate jurisdiction and that real property in the United States is in almost every instance affected by local laws which may differ substantially from state to state. In recent years a number of states, particularly those which are highly agricultural in nature, have adopted legislation which in one form or another restricts foreign ownership of real property. Appendix I to this book summarizes on a state-by-state basis the current restrictions in this regard. As before stated, legislators are becoming subject to increasing political and social pressure within the various states to adopt new and more restrictive legislation concerning the ownership by foreigners of U.S. real property. It is therefore urgently suggested that before the foreign investor gets seriously involved in deciding to purchase real property in any particular state, he have a careful examination made of the laws in that jurisdiction which may restrict or limit foreign owner-ship. This is a continuing, evolving problem that should not be overlooked. The foreign investor should not be confused as to the difference between restrictions on ownership and the obligation to disclose and report. The federal statutes have been amended and recent laws adopted requiring disclosure and reporting. Please see Appendixes 2, 3, and 8 for a detailed discussion of this issue. To many foreign investors, the obligation to disclose and report has serious connotations. The counseling of the foreign investor must include a full discussion of these reporting and disclosure requirements.

Little will be served by an extended discussion of the relative political stability of the United States and its attitude toward capital investment and real property ownership by foreigners as compared to other nations. However, in counseling and dealing with the foreign investor and motivating that foreign investor to invest in U.S. real property, several observations can be made. It is possible in almost every instance, except where restricted as discussed above, for the foreign investor to hold absolute fee title to a particular parcel of property and to be insured by a financially stable institution so that he may retain that ownership without restriction or fear of forfeiture. There is readily available to the foreign investor through the escrow process, the use of reputable counsel, and title insurance, an almost foolproof procedure to ensure the validity and stability of title to the property that is being acquired. The concepts of escrow and title insurance as well as other mechanics for acquiring and securing title to property are discussed in more detail below, and the reader is referred to the chapters dealing with each specific subject. It should, however, be emphasized that in this author's experience, these concepts are not sufficiently emphasized to the foreign investor with the result that a substantial inducement for investing is lost.

Though the matter will be discussed in greater detail elsewhere in this text, it should be observed at this time that the United States places few or no restrictions on the influx or removal of capital from the United States. This is contrary to established policy of many foreign countries, particularly those in the underdeveloped areas. Again, elsewhere in this text, the tax aspects of ownership, sale, and development of U.S. real property is discussed at length. However, at this point it can be stated that as the present tax laws of the United States are constituted, there are advantages to the foreign investor which are not enjoyed by U.S. citizens. Further, the foreign investor is not generally penalized merely because he is a non-U.S. citizen or resident, except in the minor area of interest withholding, which is discussed elsewhere in this text.

In most instances, there is little downside risk (beyond his initial capital investment) to the foreign investor in investing in U.S. real property. Most states have adopted the purchase money or no personal liability concept and limit the seller or lender who agrees to finance real property acquisitions to foreclosing upon the real property as its sole remedy, without permitting such seller or lender to seek recovery from the other assets of the foreign investor. If there is no statutory scheme within a particular state limiting personal liability, it has been my experience that with a little careful drafting, in most instances the purchaser (borrower) can negotiate exculpatory clauses in the mortgages to relieve him of personal liability. What is therefore being risked is the initial capital and any additional funds that are invested in carrying the subject property and not his other assets or credit. However, this issue of personal liability is important. Each state has its own laws as to foreclosure, default, and personal liability. The foreign investor must look carefully at the laws in each state to determine the scope of his personal exposure.

Another factor peculiar to foreign investors that cannot be quantitatively evaluated is the question of anonymity. Many foreign investors have a strong desire to avoid their own names being connected with a particular investment. This issue has become very complex and serious due to newly adopted federal and state statutes. Again, see Appendixes 2, 3, and 7 for a detailed discussion.

2

ESTABLISHING
INVESTMENT CRITERIA

I assume at this point that the foreign investor for all the reasons set forth in the previous chapter, or for other reasons peculiar to the needs and goals of the individual investor, has made the decision to get involved in investing in U.S. real property. Since the scope of real estate investment is so broad, how should the foreign investor select the area of real property investment which best meets his needs? There are, of course, enumerable factors that could be considered in answering this question and in counseling and guiding the foreign investor in establishing his real estate portfolio and criteria. Perhaps it would be helpful to list a number of questions or issues that should be addressed by either the foreign investor acting on his own behalf or by his professional counselor. Based upon the experience of this author, some of the issues and criteria are set forth below, again not necessarily in order of priority:

1. Is the investor interested in a cash flow return for either living purposes or other business reasons, or is the investor seeking primarily appreciation of his investment?
2. Does the investor seek a long-term or short-term investment?
3. Does the investor seek a relative short-term quick profit and turnover or is he looking for a method of building up a long-term equity?
4. Does the investor wish to use the investment in real property as an adjunct to an application to obtain permanent residence or to emigrate to the United States. This issue will be discussed in more detail elsewhere in this text?
5. Is the investment to be management-free or does the investor have the desire or ability to actively engage in the operation, development, or management of the real estate investment?
6. How important to the investor is the ability to liquidate the property and realize quick cash therefrom?
7. How much money does the foreign investor have to invest, and what is his financial ability to make future payments to carry the property in the event of cyclical fluctuations in the real estate and financing market?
8. Does the foreign investor have the local contacts for potential joint ventures or investment through the vehicle of a limited or general partnership?

Careful consideration should be given to advising the foreign investor not only of the potential upside advantages from real estate investment but also of the downside risks attendant upon real property ownership. This is particularly true where the leverage concept is maximized resulting in a large debt remaining to be paid and serviced in the future.

Let us now explore in more detail some of the criteria and questions raised at the beginning of this chapter. To many foreign investors, the cash flow return on their investment is not that critical. This is contrary to the attitude that is primarily adopted by most sophisticated American investors in real property. To a large extent, the foreign investor is interested more in risk-free preservation of his capital than in enjoying a cash flow return and is looking primarily for an inflation hedge. Experience has also shown that the foreign investor for various reasons is not primarily concerned with the tax aspects of the acquisition as it relates to creating paper losses to deduct against other income. This latter concept can be used as a successful bargaining tool in dealing with Americans for joint ventures or partnerships. The fact that the foreign investor can, with some restrictions, shift the potential tax losses to the American participants, is a significant inducement and a strong negotiating ploy.

It should be further observed at this point that the foreign investor should be fully apprised of the fact that real property investments do not necessarily retain their liquidity and that it will probably not be possible in an emergency for him to realize immediate cash from his real property investments. The whole question of liquidity seems to be tied in with what I classify as staying power. In this respect, the key to success in real estate in the United States is to have the financial ability to weather the short-term cyclical fluctuations in market conditions, both economic and financial, and to be able to invest, if necessary, additional cash to service the debt on a particular parcel of property when those funds are unavailable from established institutional sources. The foreign investor and his investment counselors should be careful to make detailed cash flow analyses of every property the investor intends to acquire to assure that the investor has the continuing ability to meet the financial obligations anticipated by the investment. See Chapters 3 and 4 where this matter is discussed in more detail.

Long-term versus short-term needs further amplification. When the foreign investor is investing generally in unimproved land, he generally expects a rather rapid appreciation in that land and is looking for a short-term quick gain. Of course, when a quick gain on a short-term is anticipated, the risks are generally increased proportionately. If the investor, however, is looking toward acquiring an existing, highly developed property, such as an apartment house complex or shopping center, the appreciation aspects—the ability to turn a quick profit—are generally nonexistent. Here it is the long-term appreciation from the general increase in the value of the property, the use of leverage, and the gradual reduction of the existing mortgages tied in to a fixed-income stream from long-term leases that attract the investor. Here equity buildup can be anticipated and projected with some degree of accuracy.

Should the foreign investor desire to become actively engaged in the development of the property he seeks to initially purchase, important questions of personal liability as well as adverse tax consequences should be discussed, thoroughly analyzed, and understood before the investment is undertaken. As will be discussed in more detail in another chapter, if the foreign investor is deemed engaged in U.S. trade or business, he losses substantial tax benefits. In addition, once the foreign investor engages in development activity, even through an agent, or as a partner in a partnership or joint venture, he not only loses the capital gains advantage, but may also expose himself or his entity to substantial personal liability. Entering into joint ventures or becoming associated with U.S. developers or contractors is an area of great complexity and cannot be covered in detail in this text. However, some of the criteria and elements to be considered in protecting the foreign investor in this situation are discussed elsewhere in general terms in Chapter 4.

In the experience of this author, many foreign investors and their investment counselors fail to make the necessary detailed careful analyses of the true cash commitments required for a real estate investment and, further, they fail to give full and adequate consideration to the potential downside risk and personal exposure of a project. Nothing courts disaster more than getting two thirds through development of a real estate project and having insufficient funds for its completion. The options then available are painful and expensive, and the bargaining position of the foreign investor deteriorates rapidly at this point. This whole area of cash flow analysis and downside risk is further complicated by the fact that established institutional sources for short-term construction funds and long-term permanent loan financing for real estate projects are undergoing substantial changes in the United States. In this regard, the ground rules that were applicable even a few years ago must be questioned, and adequate provision should be made to obtain necessary funds in the event these old-line established sources are unavailable on realistic terms. It has been the experience of this writer that many foreign investors are now turning to overseas banks and financial institutions for the construction capital and permanent loan financing they were otherwise obtaining in the United States. There seems to be little restriction under U.S. law for foreign banks and financial institutions to engage in real estate financing or indeed joint ventures in the various states in this country. Again, the appendix dealing with restrictions on foreign ownership and investment must be consulted in a specific case.

Should the foreign investor be primarily interested in acquiring a management-free investment, he should be aware, and his investment advisors should counsel him, of the facilities that are available throughout the United States to obtain competent and relatively cheap expertise from established institutions and management companies to manage and operate his property and to fully account to him for all activity. The use of the sale and leaseback to be discussed further in this text is a concept that may be attractive to the foreign investor. The use of professional property management and trust companies with long histories of proven ability and integrity as well as financial stability should be considered by the foreign investor and fully explained and explored by his investment counselors. In most instances, however, for meaningful management-free property to be acquired by the foreign investor, the project must be large enough to generate a sufficient cash flow to give the professional property manager an incentive to get involved in a specific project. Generalities of course are always subject to specific exceptions and each individual project should be analyzed and considered from this viewpoint.

In the opinion of this author agricultural properties in well-located farming areas will undergo rapid appreciation in the near future and should not be overlooked by the foreign investor and his advisors.

For the foreign investor who desires to engage in joint ventures with local developers and contractors, acquiring low-density, well-located, recently constructed apartment complexes for conversion to condominums can potentially produce rapid short-term profits. If proper tax planning is used, these profits can be free of U.S. federal income tax.

PREACQUISITION
CHECKLIST—PART ONE

At this point, I am assuming that the foreign investor has decided to invest in U.S. real property and has further analyzed and established his basic investment goals. The issue as to the method of acquisition now arises in the following context: The foreign investor or his investment counselor wishes to attempt to purchase or enter into negotiations to purchase a particular parcel of real property. What are the factors to consider in analyzing a potential acquisition? We will start out with a parcel of unimproved land since this is usually the simplest of real property acquisitions. Areas for examination and investigation are broken down into three general classes which will be discussed in detail below. The first I call physical conditions. These relate to such items as location, topography, soil conditions, availability of basic utilities, (water, sewer, waste, gas, and electricity), encroachments, and similar and related matters affecting the general, physical condition of the property in question. The second I classify as governmental. This area deals with the existing status of title to the subject project, the local zoning laws, recorded restrictions on use and occupancy, the existing zoning, the attitude of local government toward future development, environmental impact reports, local laws dealing with subdivision and parceling of the property, state and local restrictions on sale and marketing, and the present and potential effect of local laws on the use, occupancy, and development of the property in question such as rent control, condominium conversions, and moratoriums. The third area I designate as economic-financial. This area focuses on appraisal, assumption of existing financing, availability of new loans, subordination, release clauses, local tax laws, assessment procedures, cash flow analyses, development costs, and similar matters of an economic and financial nature.

Let us examine each of the above categories in greater detail. Of course, the three categories outlined above often have areas of overlap, but an attempt will be made to develop an appropriate "checklist approach" to aid the foreign investor and his counselors in analyzing a project and deciding the relative merits of a proposed acquisition. Before we begin a detailed review of each area, the question should be asked—how do you check each item before you

buy or commit the buyer? Won't the property be sold to someone else before
you complete your investigation and analysis? My experience shows that this
dilemma can usually be resolved by the use of an option or a contingent escrow.
The details of acquisition documents will be discussed in Chapter 4. Thus, after
it is determined what to ask for, we can then determine the form and content of
the initial offer to purchase.

Physical conditions

NET VERSUS GROSS ACRES.   Though it seems basic in nature, the
first question to be asked is—what am I buying? When it comes to purchasing
raw land, am I purchasing the property on a gross or net acreage basis. Often
raw land is purchased at a dollar price per acre and the question to be asked is
are you purchasing the acreage on the basis of the total gross acres in the
project without regard to deduction from the acreage calculation for nonuse-
able land, that is net acres? Is there to be excluded from the calculation of
acreage those portions of the real property to be purchased that are subject to
existing easements or public or private roadways? If there are utility easements
or private easements running through the property, are they to be excluded?
These questions should be answered in calculating the initial purchase price.

LOCATION.   Is the property located in unincorporated county territory
or within the boundary lines of an incorporated city or township. This question
becomes important in determining where to proceed to examine local zoning
laws and other similar matters. Is the property located in any special restricted
use or zoning area? As an example, in the state of California, if property is
located within three miles of the Pacific coastline, it falls under the jurisdiction
of the California Coastal Commission which requires all plans, specifications
and details concerning the development of the property to be examined and
approved not only by the local city or jurisdiction within which the property is
located but also compliance with all the rules and regulations of the Coastal
Commission. Throughout the United States there may be numerous, special
jurisdictions of a similar nature which can materially affect the use, occupancy,
value, potential appreciation, and development prospects of a particular parcel
of property.

STATE AND COUNTY.   In what state and county is the property
located? It must again be emphasized that in dealing with real property, the
laws of the local jurisdiction generally control. It is therefore necessary to look
to all of the legislation in a particular state and further to review the legislation
of the county in which the property is located, and should the property be
located within the jurisdiction of an incorporated city, the laws of the city must
also be carefully examined. The foreign investor and his advisors should be
aware that the laws of each state and each county and city vary substantially
throughout the United States and no generalities can be set forth. It is imperative that the foreign investor and his advisors be fully aware of the nuances and
the peculiarities of each particular jurisdiction affecting the subject property.
Again, remember there are restrictions on ownership by foreigners that vary
from state to state. See Appendix 1 for details.

LEGAL DESCRIPTIONS AND SUBDIVISION. Examine the legal description of the property. If the property is described in a form that is commonly referred to as "metes and bounds", that is to say, the property is described by a detailed description in engineering or surveying terminology, as distinguished from being described as "Lot 1 of Tract 12345 in the City of Growth, State of California," this should raise substantial questions in the mind of the purchaser as to whether or not the property being purchased has met the local and state laws relating to subdivision or splitting of property. Most jurisdictions in the United States have local laws which restrict or limit the ability of the seller or developer to transfer property unless there has been compliance with local subdivision or parcel map ordinances. This can be of particular danger to an unsuspecting purchaser who can purchase a parcel of property, even obtain certain types of title insurance, and then attempt to develop, subdivide, or resell the property and discover that local laws restrict or prohibit sale, leasing, or development because the predecessors in title have not complied with the laws of the local jurisdiction. I, again, must emphasize the fact that subdivision is controlled by local law which can vary substantially from place to place even within the same state and county. Thus always verify the fact that that parcel you are looking at when acquired will meet all applicable laws as to its division. In most cases, even dividing one lot into only two parcels requires compliance with local laws. Note further that failure to meet these requirements can prevent development and give rights to your purchaser on a resale to rescind and recover damages. It's a real trap for the unwary, so be careful. There is a further area of concern. If the property must be subdivided, the door is opened to permit the local government to require as a condition to granting the lot split that you, as owner, make costly improvements at your sole expense such as streets, sewers, lights, etc. and expose yourself to the cost of environmental reports and hearings.

TITLE INSURANCE. In almost every jurisdiction in the United States today, it is possible and highly preferable for the foreign investor to obtain from a reputable title insurance company a policy of title insurance that guarantees to him the status of the title to the property he is acquiring, listing all of the exceptions to title, showing the restrictions as to its use and occupancy, and setting forth the mortgages or other encumbrances that affect the property. Most professional real estate counselors are fully acquainted with the concept of title insurance. However, it must be pointed out that this concept is totally alien to the foreign investor. What is title insurance? It is a policy written by a company whose sole or primary business is that of researching and abstracting title to real property and giving written assurances to the purchaser and/or lender as to the current status of its ownership and as to the instruments appearing of record affecting the property.

Who pays for title insurance and how does the procedure work in fact? Further, are there different kinds and types of title insurance? The question of who pays for title insurance is generally a matter of custom and usage in the local jurisdiction where the property is located. For example, in the southern portion of the state of California, it is customary for the seller to bear the cost of a standard coverage policy of title insurance. This procedure is reversed in other portions of the state where the purchaser generally bears such cost. The foreign investor and his counselor should be fully aware of local customs and procedures adopted for the issuance of a title insurance commitment. In many jurisdictions the issuance of title insurance and the sale and transfer of real property is handled solely by local attorneys. This is not the customary procedure in the western part of the United States, and procedures vary substantially from state to state in other portions of this country. It is possible at a relatively nominal cost, before an offer is made to purchase a particular parcel, for the prospective purchaser to go to the local title insurer, whose offices are readily ascertainable from any real estate broker or from the general telephone directory, and obtain a document that is customarily described as a preliminary title report or commitment to insure. Upon request, for a nominal fee in most instances, the title insurer will abstract the title, do a thorough search, and issue to a prospective purchaser a written report showing the current ownership of the property and matters that appear of public record such as easements, restrictions on use, mortgages, and encumbrances, and upon request will furnish the prospective purchaser with copies of each of the recorded instruments. It cannot be emphasized by this author how important it is for the purchaser to obtain a preliminary title report and to examine carefully all of the instruments that appear of record against the subject property before you are committed to close your deal.

As with other types of insurance, there many kinds of title insurance. Generally, insurance of this nature is broken down into two categories—standard coverage and so-called extended coverage or ALTA insurance. ALTA stands for the American Land Title Association which is a group of title insurers who have gotten together with lenders and other interested members of the real estate fraternity and have designed certain forms of title insurance that are generally available throughout the United States. A standard coverage policy of title insurance generally covers only those exceptions to title and encumbrances that affect title to a particular parcel of real property as appear from an examination of the public record. Such a policy, in almost all instances, does not cover matters that a physical inspection or examination or that a full survey of the property would disclose. The experience of the author indicates that if the property is worth buying, it is worth the cost of extended coverage or ALTA-type insurance. In almost all instances in order to be able to obtain this extended coverage insurance, it will be necessary for the title insurer to be furnished with a detailed survey of the subject property. This generally takes three to four weeks to prepare and requires the services of a licensed engineer or surveyor with the assistance of the proposed insuring title insurer. Again, who bears the cost of this survey is a matter of negotiation between the buyer and seller. It is recommended that in each instance the foreign investor insist that his obligation to purchase a particular parcel of property be subject to his approval of an extended coverage preliminary title report and his examination of a survey of the property. The American Land Title Association has also established certain criteria for the preparation of what is commonly referred to as an ALTA survey so that when the insuring title company receives this survey with the appropriate endorsements and certifications thereon, it will be in a position to insure the ownership of the property in favor of the buyer as to those matters that not only appear on the public record (as in a standard coverage policy) but in addition, those matters disclosed by a physical inspection and examination and from the content of the survey. It should be noted that most policies of title insurance do not guarantee the size of the parcel, access to the property from public streets or highways, or insure against the effects of encroachments on the property from improvements on the adjoining land, or any rights of those parties who may be in possession of the property in one form or another. This text does not permit an exhaustive examination of title insurance and its various endorsements. Should the reader be interested in this subject, there is a vast amount of material readily available for further examination and review. Please see Appendix 5 which lists several publications that deal at length with title insurance. When dealing with improved real estate special title insurance endorsements become essential.

INGRESS AND EGRESS. A careful examination of public records should be made to determine that the proposed parcel has adequate and indefeasible access to the property from a fully dedicated, publicly owned street or highway. In most instances, standard coverage insurance does not guaranty to the owner such rights.

SOIL, WATER, GEOLOGY. The prospective purchaser should never assume that there exists on the property or immediately adjacent thereto all of the necessary utilities for the potential development and service of the property. Individual examinations by experts should be made to determine that there are adequate water and sewer facilities and electricity and gas to service the property, not only in its existing condition but in its condition after anticipated development. Whether or not the prospective purchaser wishes to retain the services of various experts to further examine this issue is one that relates peculiarly to the particular characteristics of the potential property to be purchased. When the question of geology arises, this generally requires the services of various experts. The prospective purchaser should never assume that the property has adequate drainage or that the soil is in a condition that can withstand extensive improvements, and a detailed examination of these criteria is recommended in almost every instance unless there are extenuating unusual circumstances surrounding the potential acquisition. If hillside property is involved or the property is of such nature as to require extensive earth-moving procedures, the services of a reputable soils engineer and geologist is imperative. Experience has demonstrated that nothing is to be taken for granted, but that a careful and detailed examination of all of these factors must be made when purchasing a particular parcel of real property. As an example of the gray areas involved, the full exploration of the availability of utilities and the cost of installing or of bringing those facilities to the particular parcel in question can have a dramatic effect on the cash flow analysis and requirements of a particular project. They can, in some instances, cause substantial delays in the developmental process and may, in some extreme cases, prevent the property from ever being developed due to an inability of the local jurisdiction to provide the essential services to the subject property. It has been my experience that a trip to the local city hall and conferences with officials will disclose the problems, if any, in this area and shed light on the city's attitude for future development.

If the property is improved, it will be necessary to consult a further detailed checklist of matters involving existing improvements. This will be discussed further.

Governmental matters

ZONING. In most jurisdictions in the United States, the zoning (i.e., limitations on use) is governed by local laws of the city and/or county in which the property is located. These laws restrict the use, height and density of the potential development on the property in question. Since they vary materially from jurisdiction to jurisdiction, each must be carefully analyzed in light of the potential use of the parcel. Standard coverage policies of title insurance generally have an exception excluding any coverage for zoning matters. Experience has further shown that not only must the prospective purchaser examine the existing ordinances, but a careful examination must also be made of the attitude of the local jurisdiction as to future changes in the zoning laws. In this regard, you should examine general master use plans and have as many discussions with the local authorities as are practical to determine the potential development not only of the property in question but its surrounding area as well. It must be emphasized that, in most states in the United States, there is no vested interest acquired by the buyer in the zoning of a particular property. Thus, even though a purchaser may acquire property and pay a substantial bonus therefore in reliance upon the property being zoned for commercial purposes at the time of its acquisition, he will have no right to turn to the city or his seller for relief if subsequent to his acquisition the city should desire for political or other reasons to change the zoning of the property to residential purposes. The sophistication of zoning varies materially with each local jurisdiction. In some instances, special areas are created to preserve architectural characteristics. All of these areas of potential difficulty should be carefully examined before the property is acquired. See Appendix 5 for publications dealing with zoning matters in depth.

It should be understood that once you apply to a city or county for rezoning or for an exception or variance of existing zoning, you become fair game. The city or county can and will, in most cases, take this opportunity to use their zoning power to require you to do what the city feels is beneficial to your property such as widen and improve an existing street, dedicate an alley, install new street lights and fire hydrants, new water and sewer lines, etc. These potential issues require careful examination. Check them out before you are committed to buy and avoid problems.

PRIVATE RESTRICTIONS. In addition to those limitations on use and construction incorporated into public zoning laws, private restrictions may also exist on the use of property. It is customary throughout the United States for owners of real property to record documents commonly referred to as covenants, conditions, and restrictions or "CC&Rs" that further limit and restrict the use and development of a particular parcel of real property. These instruments must be carefully examined. The law in most jurisdictions is quite clear that if the private restrictions are more stringent than those contained in the zoning laws, then the requirements of the private restrictions will apply. Therefore, both categories must be carefully examined to determine their potential effect on the value, use, occupancy, and development of a particular parcel. In many cases, the existing CC&Rs require the approval by architectural committees of all proposed improvements. This can be costly and time consuming. I urge you to carefully read all CC&Rs before you are committed to buy.

UTILITIES.   The availability of utilities such as water, sewer, gas, electricity, telephone, trash pickup, flood control, and numerous other items vary substantially from jurisdiction to jurisdiction. The local laws in each case must be carefully examined. Many jurisdictions have established extensive criteria for permission to tie in to existing utilities. In many cases, local jurisdictions have placed moratoriums on development due to a lack of capacity in central water or sewer systems to handle further development. Since each of these issues can have a substantial effect on the value and future appreciation of the subject property, they should be carefully explored and examined. In addition, the cost of installing and maintaining these facilities can add a material burden to the true cost of developing a particular parcel and can have damaging effects on the cash flow requirements of a project.

COMMUNITY AND PUBLIC SERVICES.   A careful examination of fire and police protection within the area servicing the property in question is important. This can have a material effect on the rates of fire, theft and casualty insurance, as well as affect lenders' attitudes toward providing adequate funds to improve the subject property and, of course, affect the potential appreciation of the property in question. The availability and capacity of schools, shopping centers and medical facilities should also be examined.

Financial matters

In dealing with financial matters relating to real property acquisition and development, I cannot sufficiently emphasize the necessity for careful planning and examination of the issues involved. It is, of course, quite easy for the prospective foreign investor or his representatives and advisors to calculate the initial purchase price of a particular parcel of property, the down payment, and the immediate closing costs. Where the danger seems to have arisen is in the area of the less obvious or hidden costs relating to real property holding, development, and acquisition. Also, in this area of financial items the question arises as to how extensive the preacquisition research should be.

APPRAISALS AND USE STUDIES.   With the ever-increasing costs of acquiring real property and the ever-increasing expenses involved in maintaining, sustaining and developing real property, the difficult issue arises as to how extensive should be the marketing research for the anticipated project and what examinations should be made before an investor purchases a particular parcel of real property. No firm answers can be given in this area. Rather they depend on the size of the project, the sophisticated nature of the proposed investment, and the business acumen of the foreign investor and his advisors. However, some examination into future trends and projections for the development should be considered. Whether experts, market researchers, accountants, engineers, architects, and appraisers should be hired are matters of individual judgment, but they should not be overlooked. Further, there is an area that is often not considered by the foreign investor and that is the ability to obtain a great deal of useful and well-prepared information from the local jurisdiction. It is common in most parts of the United States that each city or county have chambers of commerce, planning commissions, zoning boards, and similar public departments whose primary function is to gather and disseminate information concerning developmental and population trends and studies, demographic reviews, master plans, and similar data. This information can often be obtained from business organizations and from the local public utility companies. In addition, many of the major banks and universities have departments dealing with urban growth and urban planning. This author has found that a great deal of useful and practical information can be obtained from these sources with minimal effort and expense.

CASH FLOW PROJECTIONS. A careful analysis should be made by the foreign investor and his advisors concerning the potential cash flow obligations in connection with a proposed acquisition. These sums include not only the initial down payment and closing costs which are most obvious, but a number of not so obvious, potentially dangerous areas. What are some of the less obvious cash flow requirements:

1. Real estate taxes and assessments (both as they exist at the time of purchase and how the sale and reassessment will affect cash flow.) In many jurisdictions real estate taxes rise dramatically after the sale. Check this out carefully.
2. Market studies and appraisals.
3. Accounting and legal fees.
4. Architectural, engineering and survey costs.
5. Lender commitment fees and deposits.
6. Interest and carrying costs of existing and future encumbrances.
7. Costs of maintaining adequate insurance on the subject property.
8. The effect of prepayment penalties and acceleration clauses.

We have discussed briefly above market studies and appraisals. Let me add, however, that in dealing with many lenders and with some architectural firms, detailed appraisals and market studies concerning the existing value of the property to be acquired and the effect of potential development is an essential condition precedent to obtaining financing and, in some rare instances, the approval of various governmental bodies for a proposed change in the use of the subject property.

Being a practicing lawyer, this subject of accounting and legal fees is near and dear to my heart. However, realistic budget figures should be established by the foreign investor for the cost of adequate legal and accounting services. It is earnestly observed that the spending of some real dollars at this point can pay substantial dividends in the future to the foreign investor. This will become even more obvious when we discuss in a subsequent chapter the tax aspects of real estate for the foreign investor and how some simple adequate preplanning can avoid potential disastrous tax effects.

We discussed previously in this chapter the use of ALTA surveys. In addition, adequate consideration should be given to the cost of retaining architects and/or engineers, soil analysts, geologists, and other specialists to obtain their advice and counsel in the methods of developing property to be purchased.

Do not overlook the cost of interest payments on either private loans or on the mortgages to be carried back or negotiated with the seller. With respect to existing encumbrances that may be taken over by the foreign investor-buyer, a careful examination of the effect of early prepayment of these obligations and of the so-called due on sale problem should be undertaken. In this regard, most institutional loans in use throughout the United States contain three provisions of concern, the first being a prepayment penalty provision, a so-called lock-in clause, and the latter being an acceleration or due-on-sale clause which permits, in many states, the lender to declare its loan all due and payable should the property in question be transferred or in some cases, further encumbered. In connection with the prepayment penalty, this is generally a provision whereby the borrower agrees that should he desire to pay the loan prior to its normal maturity date, the lender may elect to charge a penalty equal to a number of months of unearned interest for such prepayment. Of course, the amount of the prepayment penalty varies substantially with each lender and with each project. In addition, many states have adopted restrictive legislation either limiting or prohibiting prepayment penalties in certain specific situations. The experience of this author has been that such restrictions are, however, applicable only to the purchase and sale of single-family residences.

A lock-in clause merely prohibits the prepayment for a specified number of years. In most cases, these are enforceable provisions. If you contemplate new development and a pay off of the existing loan, a lock-in clause can be a disaster and can put you in an extremely adverse bargaining position with the holder of the note. Check it out and make a deal with the holder before you are committed to buy.

The acceleration or due-on-sale clause is a matter of greater complexity. Many institutional as well as private notes, mortgages and deeds of trust contain provisions that provide, in substance, that upon the sale or transfer of the property or of an interest therein, that the lender at its election can declare the obligation all due and payable. As the word *lender* is used here, it also, of course, includes a seller who has carried back a note and mortgage as part of the previous sale. There is a great deal of controversy in the law of many states as to whether such a provision is enforceable. For example, in California, a virtual war has been raging between lenders and borrowers for a number of years, and several cases are now pending in the higher courts for a final determination of the issue. The foreign investor should be prudently aware of these problems, particularly in a rising interest rate market where lenders or sellers, having the ability to reinvest their money at a higher interest rate than is contained in the mortgage in question, will generally be aggressive about taking advantage of such a provision. As an example, a buyer may look at a potential purchase and be attracted by the fact that as part of the purchase price he can take over an existing long-term, low-interest loan. The whole deal may turn sour if he lender can call this loan due and require the buyer to refinance at current rates and, of course, at corresponding—higher monthly payments.

A final word about real estate taxes in the preacquisition, planning stage. Experience has shown this author that the real property taxes on a particular parcel that are assessed by and become due and payable to local governmental agencies are substantially affected by a sale and that the purchaser can realistically anticipate that the real estate taxes being enjoyed by the former owner will not be passed on to the new buyer. In most cases, the property will be reappraised for tax purposes based on the sale with a corresponding realistic increase in the taxes. The methods of assessment, the dates of payment, and the attitude toward real estate taxes can be significant in connection with the purchase, ownership, and/or development of real property. A careful examination of all of these aspects should be made by the foreign investor and his counselors before undertaking a purchase.

If the foreign investor intends to syndicate or to raise funds from others or institutions to finance the initial acquisition, then, of course, an additional factor must be added to the cash flow projection for the cost of obtaining these funds, commissions, advertising fees, and similar charges.

The foregoing is a basic outline and checklist for the acquisition of a typical, mythical parcel of real property in its unimproved state. As the sophistication of the property increases, the various matters to be reviewed and considered also increase. If the property contains improvements, a whole additional series of questions should be asked. If the property is agricultural land with growing crops, additional problems should be evaluated. If the property is to be used for potential subdivision or condominium conversion or for some particular commercial or industrial purpose, then, of course, additional issues are raised. In the next chapter, we will attempt to delineate some of these areas to aid the foreign investor in evaluating a particular property. It has been the experience of this writer that if these issues are considered at the beginning, most of them disappear as potential problems. Further, the primary objective in going through such an exhaustive preacquisition checklist is to smoke out the potential problems, understand their scope, nature, and effect on the acquisition and value of the potential property, both present and future, thus enabling the foreign investor to carefully and intelligently evaluate and analyze what he is getting into. If in asking a number of these questions, the investor is met with resistance from a potential seller, that's when he should become concerned. My experience indicates that one should start with the premise that every seller intends to take advantage of the buyer if he can, and that one should then work backward from that point. Take nothing for granted nor assume the honesty of any seller or lender. I believe a prospective purchaser will further discover that most people in dealing in real property will not volunteer information on any item that may be of potential risk or danger. But if they are confronted with a specific question, they will not lie or sandbag but will give a straight answer. The real name of the game is to know what questions to ask and how and when to ask them.

4

PREACQUISITION
CHECKLIST—PART TWO

You will recall in the previous chapters the foreign investor has made the decision to invest in U.S. real estate and established his basic investment goals. Chapter 3 commenced a general approach for analyzing a potential acquisition. The previous chapter separated the analysis into three separate categories: physical conditions, governmental considerations, and economic and financial matters. The purpose of this chapter is to review in more depth each of those catagories as they relate to more sophisticated properties. I started out with the basic assumption that the analysis dealt with unimproved raw land. This chapter will assume that the property being analyzed and considered for acquisition and/or development contains existing improvements or is being acquired for construction of immediate improvements. In discussing more sophisticated properties the reader should keep in mind the use of the forms included as part of this book and in some instances the information contained in the various appendixes. A further matter of insight and caution at this point. In this chapter as in Chapter 3, the preacquisition checklist approach to analyzing a parcel of property is used. Each issue raised must be looked at from both the viewpoint of a prospective seller as well as a prospective buyer. If, as an example, you are the buyer, you want to provide in your purchase instruments a portion of the provisions recited in Form 7 (Escrow Instructions), in the Index of Forms, and obtain affirmative representations and warranties from the seller. Conversely, if you are the seller of the property, ideally you would like to sell the property in its "as is" condition without making warranties or representations to the buyer of any kind or nature. Between these two extremes, depending on which side of the fence you are on, an acceptable document can be negotiated. In analyzing and developing your own personal checklist or analysis criteria for a particular parcel of property, every time an issue is raised you should provide a method of solving the problem and dealing with the potential risk. For example, if the question arises as to the existing zoning on a particular parcel of property, ideally the buyer would like an affirmative covenant in the purchase document whereby the seller warrants to buyer that the property is zoned, as an example R-4, and if the buyer is cautious, he will further provide that his obligation to purchase the property is contingent upon the property remaining zoned R-4 without change as to the scope of R-4 zoning. Conversely, if you are the seller, you would prefer that this whole problem of zoning be at the buyer's risk and that the buyer acknowledge he has made his own independent inspection and investigation of the zoning.

Preventive law is the key. Meeting each problem head on is essential. If the issue is known, it can be solved or the risk shared equitably. Remember only two people generally gain from lawsuits—the seller's lawyer and the buyer's lawyer!

Physical conditions

Let us turn now to a more detailed examination of the three basic areas outlined above and in the prior chapter. At this juncture we are assuming that the property about to be acquired is improved with existing improvements. These improvements can vary from what is commonly referred to in the trade as off-site improvements (streets, curbs, utilities) to a very sophisticated high-rise office building, hotel, restaurant, commercial, or industrial property. With all improvements there are some basic characteristics that apply. Again, this approach necessitates your providing in your purchase agreement as a buyer for an opportunity to investigate and determine whether or not a special issue is a problem. Conversely, if you are the seller, you want to eliminate from your potential exposure any possibility you could be held for warranties, representations, and liability as to any particular physical matter. The first question to be asked in connection with existing improvements is whether or not the improvements meet the minimum standards of the local jurisdiction in which the property is located. In every jurisdiction in the United States, there are extensive local laws, rules, and ordinances relating to the initial installation and construction of improvements as well as their continued maintenance to levels that meet local health and safety standards. Of course, due to different climatic conditions throughout the United States, the variety of soil conditions throughout the United States, and the local politics, the laws differ materially as to these minimum requirements. A detailed analysis of the local laws either by counsel of your choosing or a local engineer or architect is highly recommended. From a drafting standpoint in preparing your documentation, which will be discussed in a future chapter, it's prudent as a buyer to require a seller to make an affirmative representation and warranty that all existing improvements have been built in accordance with all applicable building codes, laws, and ordinances and that there are no pending violations or threatened violations by any governmental authorities concerning the existing improvements. By the use of language of this type, the seller is representing to a buyer that he and his predecessors have complied with all of the local laws relating to all existing improvements. If the property being considered for purchase is a single-family residence or small apartment unit, as distinguished from a more sophisticated commercial or industrial building, this provision can become extremely important. It is not uncommon in the United States for the owner of a house to make extensive improvements without applying for and obtaining a proper building permit from the local jurisdiction in which the property is located. This type of improvement is commonly referred to in the marketplace as "bootlegging". As an example, it is not unusual for an owner to purchase a house with an attached garage and convert the garage into another room. He then adds on a carport or another garage, and in neither case does he obtain the proper permit from the applicable building department. What happens if you purchase a house in which bootlegging has occurred? It is possible that the city, upon determining that the improvements were not built in accordance with code, will revoke your certificate of occupancy and require you to tear down the improvements or spend extensive sums of money to bring these bootlegged improvements up to existing minimum code conditions. Fire insurance policies may provide that if improvements are not built and maintained in accordance with code requirements, that the insurance company can deny liability for a future loss. Further, when it comes time for you to resell the house, should your subsequent buyer be smart enough to ask the right questions, or after the sale, discover that the improvements were bootlegged, you, as a seller, may have extensive personal liability to that purchaser even though you were not the cause of the bootleg improvements to begin with. This whole question of whether or not existing improvements meet code requirements and were built initially in accordance with code, is a matter that can easily be investigated and resolved if you catch the problem at the beginning. Each local city maintains records of all building permits that have been issued. A contact with the city can determine if proper permits were initially obtained and whether or not any investigations are pending.

In this whole area of the status of existing physical improvements and the condition of property being sold, the law in many states is evolving in favor of prospective purchasers. We have to start out with the premise of the buyer beware. That is to say, the seller of property, except in the case of overt fraud or material misrepresentation, has no affirmative duty or obligation, as a general rule, to tell a potential buyer that there is a particular problem with the property. It is up to the buyer to make a reasonable investigation and to determine for himself what he is buying. In other words, a seller doesn't have to volunteer information that a reasonable inspection and examination of a property would disclose. We could, if there were time, get into an extensive discussion as to the difference between a latent and a patent defect. A latent defect is one that cannot be easily seen from a reasonable inspection of the property. A patent defect is one that is ascertainable and discernible from the exercise of reasonable care in connection with the purchase of the property. If we assume, therefore, that the general rule of law is buyer beware, what can the buyer do to protect himself? Do what was discussed above—require the seller to make affirmative representations and warranties to the buyer concerning the physical condition of the property and compliance with laws and incorporate these provisions in the purchase documents. This accomplishes several goals. It makes the seller affirmatively represent to you as a potential buyer the condition of the property and exposes the seller to potential damages should the representations prove untrue. It gives you, as a buyer, the opportunity to examine the property, to check with the various governmental agencies, and to be sure that you are not being led down the garden path. Again, as I mentioned at the end of the previous chapter, always assume in purchasing a parcel of real property that the seller is looking out solely for his interest and not for yours, and don't take anything for granted.

This question of warranties, representations, and examinations of physical improvements can be taken to an extreme depending upon the nature and type of the property in question. I will again use the example of a single-family residence which, of course, can be easily expanded to include more sophisticated properties. In many instances, it is good business practice from the buyer's viewpoint, to require the seller not only to represent and warrant that the minimum code requirements have been met but also that all of the physical improvements are and will remain in good working order. Keep in mind that building departments, building codes, and local laws and ordinances set forth primarily minimum standards for people to follow, which probably do not meet the quality and condition that you as a purchaser of property can reasonably expect. As an example, you intend to buy a single family residence. Is the roof sound and watertight? Are all of the appliances (built-in ovens, air-conditioning systems, electrical systems, plumbing and heating systems) in good working order and will they be in good working order at the time the escrow is closed and you actually become the owner? How do you determine all of these factors? A personal inspection is one way to do it. The hiring of experts is an alternative. In many instances I think the cheapest and best money that can be spent by a potential purchaser is to hire a reputable building contractor, engineer, or architect to make a physical inspection of the house being purchased to determine the level of maintenance of the property, the soundness of the roof and foundation, and the quality of the plumbing and electrical system. Thus, when you close your purchase, you will not be subject to surprises, extensive repairs, or excessive maintenance which can be costly as well as emotionally upsetting. It can thus be readily seen, depending on the nature and type of property, that these representations and warranties as to physical condition, the use of professionals, whether they be building contractors, engineers, or architects, can be valuable and effective. In keeping with the basic approach of this book, these preventive law concepts work. Obviously, if you get into high-rise buildings or other sophisticated property acquisition, the use of these professionals becomes a necessity. In such cases formal reports, certifications, surveys, soil tests, and other specific procedures are required.

We previously discussed the use of surveys and title insurance. We distinguished between the different kinds of title insurance and the fact that some title insurance (standard coverage) insure you only as to matters on the public record while other types of title insurance (extended coverage) also insure your interest as it relates to the physical condition of the property. As the sophistication of the property you are considering for purchase increases, as the value of that property increases, as its potential use and density increase, the issues of encroachments and other problems a survey can uncover become critical. For example, suppose you are buying an industrial property or a property on which you intend to build commercial buildings. In most instances in properties of that class and nature, you are permitted by local building laws to build right up to the boundary line of the property and to intensively use the property both for improvements, parking, and similar matters. Suppose in drafting your plans and in doing all of your analyses you find that the adjoining property encroaches one or two feet over the property line or you find on a careful examination of your property that though the adjoining property seems to be built right up to the lot line, a survey discloses that the foundations of the adjoining property, which hold up the building next to yours, encroach upon your property, below the surface of the ground in such a manner as to affect your ability to develop your property to its fullest extent. If you have not taken the steps to acquire extended coverage title insurance, losses occasioned by an encroachment will not be covered by insurance. Extensive delays may ensue and affect your ability to develop your property. Your financing of the subsequent improvements may be affected, and in some extreme cases, you may have potential liability to tenants or other parties to whom you have made commitments to build or to rent based upon your belief that you had the ability to construct or to rent certain types of improvements. I am not trying to be a harbinger of doom in every case; I merely wish to emphasize as I tried to do in the previous chapter, that extensive and careful investigation before you are committed to buy the property is the key to success in the real estate area. As the value of the property increases, as its extensive use increases, investigation must also increase. Again, each one of these items I have mentioned should create a red flag in your brain. Questions should be asked. What about encroachments? What about ALTA surveys? A contingency factor should be written into your purchase agreement to be sure that your obligation to close the deal is contingent upon your ability to obtain an ALTA survey, to have it analyzed, and to obtain the appropriate title insurance in connection therewith. Again, I refer you to Form 7 which is illustrative of the problem.

Still dealing with questions of physical condition, if you are acquiring property for the purpose of subsequent improvement, subdivision, or development and if that proposed improvement includes such matters as hillside development, or you contemplate the extensive manufacturing of the site which requires extensive movement of earth, I cannot emphasize too strongly obtaining the advice and counsel of learned and sophisticated soil engineers and geologists. This whole area of hillside development and cutting and filling is fraught with danger. The local laws vary substantially and materially from state to state and from city to city and must be examined carefully. Experience has shown this author that getting involved in the extensive manufacturing of land can be a bottomless pit from a money viewpoint and can expose a potential buyer to extreme liability of a personal and even criminal nature depending on the attitude of the local jurisdiction, the type of improvements that are developed, and the subsequent failure of these improvements even many years later.

We touched in the previous chapter upon the availability of utilities and the attitude of local jurisdictions in connection with the ability to tie into existing facilities for gas, water, electricity, sewage disposal, and other similar matters. A careful investigation and examination of each of these items must be made. As an example, in many cities throughout the United States, particularly in those areas of the country that are experiencing rapid development and population shifts, such as the southern part of the United States and the other sunbelt areas of this country, there are extreme pressures on local jurisdictions that can materially affect the value of the property and your ability to develop. I know of an instance in California where moratoriums have been declared on all building permits and all subdivisions because the local city did not have the capacity to accept more sewage. As a result, developments were held up for several years until the city was able to construct a new sewage disposal plant to service the entire community. Answers to the availability of all of these public services can be found by a careful examination of the local situation. Take the time to examine and investigate, and in most cases these problems will go away. If they won't, be forewarned and govern yourself accordingly. Again, you want to provide in your purchase documents if you are the buyer, for contingencies that give you the opportunity to make the necessary inspection. In many areas of the United States there are pumps and wells and other self-contained improvements within the property itself dealing with water and electricity. A careful examination of these existing improvements, water tables, pumping stations, and wells is in order. In many parts of the United States there are allocations of water, and there are agreements dealing with central water districts and private water companies that can have material effects on the value of the property and its use for a particular purpose. Again in each of these instances, representations and warranties by the seller as to the condition of wells and pumps should be carefully set forth in the purchase agreements. When it comes to many areas of the United States, particularly in the west and southwest when water can many times be a critical factor, a careful examination of the district in which the property is located is essential. An examination of the types of water companies that have been created to service an area should also be made. In many instances there is stock in various types of water companies that should pass with a sale of the land which can affect the purchasers ability to obtain water. Reference is made to Form 30, a typical Farm Lease, and to Appendix 5 for the list of *California Continuing Education of the Bar* series for excellent material dealing with farm leasing and acquisition.

Personal property

The whole question of personal property as it relates to a real estate acquisition is something that must be clearly understood by the foreign investor and his various advisors. A short historical note will help clarify this area.

As the U.S. laws have evolved, a clear distinction has been made between real property and personal property. Real property is defined as land and all improvements on the land that are permanently affixed thereto, and personal property is defined as all other kinds of property. Why does the distinction between the two types of property become significant and important in U.S. real estate transactions? The answers are multiple. First, the method of transferring title and interest in real property is handled quite differently from that involving personal property. Secondly, methods of mortgaging and encumbering real and personal property differ substantially. Policies of title insurance relate only to real property, and no insurance is given by the insurer as to title of personal property. You will recall at the very beginning of the preacquisition checklist in the preceding chapter, I said one of the first basic questions you have to ask yourself is what am I buying. Let's see if we can answer this question in light of personal versus real property in an improved property acquisition. Let's assume that you are about to buy a single-family residence. You go out and talk to the seller, or the real estate broker takes you around to look at the property. As you are walking through the house now occupied by the existing seller you see that the house is furnished very handsomely, that there are custom-made drapes on the windows; there is a beautiful crystal chandelier in the dining room; some rooms are fully carpeted; some rooms have area rugs; there is a built-in oven and other appliances; there are a washer and dryer in the service porch; and a series of window air-conditioners in various rooms in the house. You make an offer to purchase the property for a fixed price, let's assume $200,000. You as the buyer then leave the country, and when the sale is consummated and the money has changed hands, you return from an overseas trip and walk into the house. Lo and behold, the only things you find are four bare walls with everything else taken out. Then you start screaming. You turn to your title insurer and ask him to make good on the loss; he turns to you and says, "we only insure real property and these items are not real property." You look for the seller who is now retired and on vacation. Although the foregoing was an extreme example, it's illustrative of the problem. The issue of what is included in the sale of an improved parcel of property is easily resolvable by some careful planning and documentation. First, in the offer to purchase the property, a detailed list of all of the items that you wish included in the sale should be attached to your offer and included as part of the Escrow Instructions (see Form 7). Second, a representation and warranty by the seller that the personal property is included in the sale and that the personal property is free and clear of all liens and encumbrances should be included as part of the purchase documentation. Third, a warranty bill of sale of personal property should be made a part and parcel of the purchase documentation. Fourth, a search should be made of title to the personal property. Let's examine these various aspects of personal and real property a bit further:

WHAT IS PERSONAL PROPERTY? How do you determine what is real property and what is personal property? Established bodies of law have been built up over the years both by case law and by statute to define what is real property and what is personal property. As a general rule, real property is land and all improvements permanently affixed to said land. Where the problem becomes more difficult is defining what is permanently affixed. For example, is carpeting placed on the floor by tackless stripping permanently affixed? Is the crystal chandelier which can be removed from the ceiling by four simple bolts permanently affixed? The answer to these questions varies according to the law of each state and according to the purpose and intent of the parties when they enter into the purchase and sale. The whole problem can be avoided by clearly spelling out in the purchase agreement and in all offers what, in fact, is included in the sale. This way you can be sure what you are buying.

TRANSFER OF TITLE. How do you transfer title to real property and personal property, and how do the transfers differ? In almost all jurisdictions title to real property is transferred by the execution and recordation of a deed of conveyance. These documents are commonly referred to as either grant deeds, warranty deeds, or bargain and sale deeds. The county in which the real property is located maintains public records as to the ownership of all real estate. It is the recording in the office of the county recorder of the deed that has the legal effect of transferring title to the real property from the seller to the buyer. In transferring personal property, generally the rules for transfer are less formal, both because of the physical nature of the personal property and the historical precedent under which the U.S. laws relating to property have evolved. Title to personal property can, in many instances, be transferred merely by physical possession changing hands. It is more prudent to obtain a bill of sale from the seller and to have this bill of sale contain representations and warranties as to the title of the seller.

SEARCHING TITLE.   Finding out who the owner of the real property is and what encumbrances exist against the real property is generally a relatively simple matter. Title insurance companies, title abstractors, and lawyers can make a search of the public records and determine who the recorded owner is of a parcel of real property and what encumbrances, easements, or other restrictions exist concerning the real property. In addition, there are title insurance companies who are willing, for a fee, to give you written assurances as to the status and condition of title. This is not true in the personal property area. Since the method of transfer of personal property is less formal, the methods of determining who is owner of the personal property and whether that personal property is free and clear of any liens or encumbrances becomes more difficult. Most states in the United States have adopted the Uniform Commerical Code (hereinafter for convenience referred to as the UCC). By adopting the UCC, most states have provided a formal procedure whereby those parties who wish to encumber personal property (as distinguished from recording merely changes in ownership) can cause to be filed with the secretary of state of the particular state, and in some cases in the county recorder's office, a document commonly referred to as a financing statement which sets forth the liens and encumbrances against the personal property in question. The UCC further provides a procedure whereby a prospective buyer of the personal property in question can make a search, and the secretary of state will issue a certificate, showing what financing statements are of record against the personal property. Unfortunately, the secretary of state in issuing these certificates issues no insurance and is not responsible for any mistakes or errors. There are many loopholes in the UCC dealing with personal property. These certificates do not deal with the issue of ownership of personal property but only encumbrances. The certificates that are issued by the secretary of state generally run 10 to 15 days behind time, and you have no assurance that from the date the secretary's certificate was issued, the property hasn't been encumbered by your seller. In the case of single-family residences and personal property used for household and family use, in most states there is no requirement that a financing statement be filed by a lender or a vendor of merchandise. Thus, suppose you buy a house with a beautiful crystal chandelier in the dining room that obviously cost many thousands of dollars. You thought when you were buying the house and you received a policy of title insurance, a warranty bill of sale, and even made a UCC search, that that chandelier was free and clear. Three months after you move into the house you get a letter from Sleazy Light Fixture Company. It says that they want their light fixture back, you haven't made your payment, there is a balance due of $3,000, and that if they don't get the $3,000, they are going to come out and take the chandelier back! Who wins—you or Sleazy Light Fixture Company? In most cases, Sleazy would win. Under the existing law, Sleazy is not required to file a financing statement in order to preserve a vendor's lien on the chandelier for the balance of the purchase price payable thereon. Thus, as a practical matter, there is no sure way for you to search the title to personal property or to obtain a title insurance policy thereto. The best thing you can do is to raise the issue. If there is any real question in your mind, insist upon the warranty bill of sale as I set forth above. Make the necessary searches and require the seller to produce for you his original bill of sale for the chandelier and cancelled checks and other evidence of payment. In the extreme case, you may wish to go to the person from whom the light fixure was purchased and verify that the light fixture is paid off. It becomes patently obvious that where personal property is a significant part of a real estate transaction, careful consideration has to be given to describing the personal property, to insuring the personal property, to checking the title and transfer of the personal property, and special investigations have to be made beyond the scope of the search and procedures being taken in connection with real property. As an example, suppose you are buying a hotel or motel that is furnished. The amount of personal property therein can be a significant portion of the value, and detailed inventories are necessary.

INSURANCE. As will be discussed in more detail in another chapter, whether property is real or personal has an effect on the insurance—not only the title insurance as just described but also the so-called fire insurance. It is customary to take out and keep in effect fire insurance from reputable insurance companies insuring you against loss or damage as a result of fire, vandalism, acts of God, etc. Does this fire insurance policy include in its coverage all of the personal property within the house and the light fixtures and all the other matters we have described above? Generally the answer is no. Unless you get specific endorsements to cover the personal property, the loss will be suffered by you without recompense from your insurance carrier.

SUBSEQUENT SALE. All of these concepts concerning real versus personal property are two-edged swords. As an example, suppose you were to buy the house on the terms that I described above, and two years later you decide to sell the house. You are selling the house now for $300,000 and including as part of the sale, all of the fixtures, built-ins, light fixtures, carpeting, drapes, and other extensive improvements you have made in the house while you were the owner. Let's assume your buyer is going to give you a down payment of $100,000, take over an existing loan in favor of the Friendly Savings and Loan Association of $150,000, and you as the seller are going to carry back a second trust deed of $50,000 payable over the next five years. As part of your sale you have the buyer sign a promissory note, and you secure that promissory note by a second deed of trust on the land and the improvements thinking you are fully secure. For some reason unknown to you, your buyer defaults, and you are forced to foreclose on your second deed of trust. After you complete your foreclosure sale, you walk into the house, and it is stripped bare. Do you have any recourse or claim against your buyer? The answer is no. Why? Because the deed of trust you elected to take back to secure your $50,000 note gives you merely a lien against the real property and not against any of the personal property. Thus, in order to protect yourself in this kind of a situation, it would be necessary at the time of the sale that you take back not only a deed of trust, but also a security agreement and file a financing statement with the appropriate state authorities to ensure that you have a lien not only against the real property but against the personal property, the subject of your original sale. If you are careful, you can even include as part of your security for your unpaid balance, the personal property, any replacements of that personal property, or any additional personal property placed in the house subsequent to the sale.

Of course, the whole area of personal property financing and the rights of creditors in the event of bankruptcy is a matter of great complexity. In a text of this type it is not possible to discuss in greater detail the more technical nuances involved in personal property. If the reader is interested, he is again referred to the *California Continuing Education of the Bar* publication which discusses in detail many of the aspects of personal property transfer and financing (See Appendix 5).

TAXES. A word about taxes. In most jurisdictions in the United States, real property is taxed by one method, and personal property is taxed by another. In most jurisdictions in the United States, the local government taxing authority has the ability to cause a lien to be placed on the real property for the payment of local taxes necessary to maintain vital services of city and county government. Personal property is generally taxed in a different manner, and the government does not have the ability to place a lien on it. Thus, a search of the records will not show whether or not there is a lien on personal property at the time you agree to purchase it. A careful examination is required. The problem is further complicated by the fact that in some jurisdictions, the assessing authorities have the option, at their election, to include as part of the real estate taxes which become a lien against the real property the taxes due on the personal property that are inside of it and are used in connection with the real estate in question. In the case of a single-family residence, this is generally not significant. But what if you are buying a large office building or an industrial building occupied by a large manufacturer, who has installed and is using on the premises many complicated machines, computers, or other equipment of high value? Do you want to be charged with paying the taxes on that person's equipment and personal property even though the purchase you are involved in expressly excludes the machinery, equipment, and other personal property of the present occupant? These issues again can be resolved by careful examination of the tax rolls and property documentation at the time your initial offer to purchase is made. The nature and extent of the personal property involved in the transaction will dictate how extensive your search should be and how much care and effort should be devoted to reviewing same. If personal property is a significant portion of a transaction, provisions should also be made for the maintenance of the personal property during the pendency of the escrow and the replacement of worn-out and lost items.

RISK OF DAMAGE. The whole question of damage or destruction and the risk of loss during the pendency of the escrow should be carefully considered. The problem arises this way. Suppose the buyer and seller enter into an agreement to sell and purchase a particular parcel of real estate improved with an existing house. The terms of the agreement require that the purchase be completed in 90 days. Let's assume that all contingencies are removed, that the buyer has placed all the necessary funds in escrow, and that 30 days after the contract is entered into, there is a fire on the property and substantial damage is done to the house. Is the seller obligated to sell, and equally important, is the buyer still obligated to purchase the house even though it is substantially damaged and will not be repaired by the time the escrow is closed? Who bears the risk of loss during the pendency of the contract? The answer to these questions differs under the law from jurisdiction to jurisdiction. The problem can be solved and should be solved by careful documentation. An example of this is contained in Form 7. There are many different ways to handle the situation. It will be discussed in more detail in the discussion of insurance elsewhere in this text. The problem becomes more complex if there is physical damage to the property and there is no insurance to cover it. Is the buyer still obligated to buy? Can the seller force the purchaser to go through with the contract or suffer damages? Can the buyer force the seller to make repairs? Again, the answer to the question depends on the form of the agreement and the laws of each state, and they vary. Careful draftsmanship can avoid the problem completely.

Governmental considerations

Let us turn now to the second general category that was outlined in the preceding chapter, that dealing with what I have classified as governmental matters. This breaks down into issues dealing with existing zoning laws, subdivision and parcelization matters, violations of covenants, conditions and restrictions (which you will recall we previously referred to as CC&Rs), increases in taxes and special assessments, condemnation and eminent domain, licenses and permits required, rent control, political limitation, and moratoriums. Let us examine a number of these subjects in greater detail.

ZONING. As discussed in the prior chapter, zoning is the control and regulation of height, bulk and, use of property. This right is vested in the public and cannot be enforced by private action. It is in almost all instances the sole province of the immediate local jurisdiction. That is to say, if the real property in question is within an incorporated city or town, the zoning is controlled by the town council or city council. If the property is an unincorporated territory, it is almost always controlled by the county board of supervisors or similar political body. If you own a house and your next-door neighbor elects to turn his house into a nightclub that keeps you up until 3 o'clock every morning with jazz music, do you have a private right arising from a violation of the zoning laws to sue your neighbor? In most jurisdictions the answer is generally no. It is only the city that can enforce violations of zoning laws. That is not true in the instance where there is a violation of the CC&Rs or other private restrictions which will be discussed and compared below. The whole question of zoning can be a vexing and dangerous problem. Perhaps the best way to approach the subject is by an example. Let's assume that you as a purchaser enter into a contract with a seller to buy a piece of raw land which we will call Black Acre. You intend to develop on Black Acre a three-story apartment building. At the time you enter into the purchase agreement with the seller and negotiate the purchase price and terms, the property is zoned R-4. Assume also that it is permissible at that time under the R-4 zoning to construct 25 apartment units on Black Acre that require 35 parking spaces in connection with the proposed apartment building. Let's assume that your escrow documents and purchase agreements are silent as to the question of zoning in connection with Black Acre. Let's assume that in reliance on this contract of purchase and sale you hire an architect, cause detailed plans and specifications to be drawn for the property, go to Friendly Savings and Loan Association and negotiate for a large construction and permanent loan for building and financing the proposed improvements, and make application to the city in which Black Acre is located for a permit through the local building department to construct the apartment building and related parking facilities. Let's assume further that after you have made all the necessary applications, obtained all the necessary building permits, paid all of your fees to the lender, paid the architect in full, and you are three days away from closing the escrow and acquiring title to Black Acre, the city council of the city in which Black Acre is located holds an appropriate public hearing and decides to rezone the property from R-4 to R-1 (which rezoning permits only the construction of a single-family residence on the subject property). Or in the alternative, assume that the city council meets and decides that because of public policy and a review of the traffic conditions in the community, 35 parking spaces are no longer sufficient for a property of this kind. The council now requires that there be 60 parking spaces on the premises. You stand up in front of the city hall and say, "you can't do this to me. In reliance on the zoning, I entered into a contract to buy Black Acre. I paid a premium price for the property. I paid thousands of dollars to architects, engineers, and lenders. I put myself in the position of being able to build this property. I have a vested right in this zoning. You can't do this to me." Who wins—you or the city? In most instances, you would lose. In almost all jurisdictions throughout the United States, the law is clear that there is no vested right of a prospective purchaser or present owner of property in existing zoning and that for the public good, the city can cause the property to be rezoned at any time, even though this may cause extreme hardship and economic detriment to a present or prospective owner. In most states the right to keep the existing zoning only becomes fixed when building permits have been issued *and* substantial construction on the property has commenced. Again, as previously mentioned, zoning is a special animal that varies materially from jurisdiction to jurisdiction. In most states, there are no uniform zoning laws that apply throughout the state. There are certainly no federal zoning laws at all, and it is incumbent upon the prospective buyer to make a careful and detailed examination of not only the existing zoning but also the attitudes of the city. Be aware of the possibility that zoning can be changed or that conditions within a particular zoning classification can be modified. Some insight into the problem can be gained by discussing the matter with local city officials, reviewing master plans, monitoring city council meetings, and discussing the matter with local chambers of commerce and financial institutions. However, there is no foolproof way to deal with the political climate in any jurisdiction. In light of the foregoing example and principles, what can you do in connection with your purchase documents? It is suggested that provisions be made in your escrow instructions or other offers and agreements of purchase and sale to deal with the issue of a change in zoning or a change in criteria of the property so that the buyer will have the ability to cancel the transaction and have a refund of any monies deposited should the zoning be changed or should the condition of existing zoning be materially modified. This again illustrates the concept of preventive law. With a little careful thought, you can avoid a great deal of subsequent litigation and financial loss.

   CC&RS AND OTHER PRIVATE RESTRICTIONS. In the previous chapter we discussed briefly CC&Rs and private restrictions. As you will recall, a subdivider of property has the right to cause to be recorded against the property an instrument that will control the use and development of the property, that these restrictions are enforceable and can be material in affecting the use, occupancy, value, and development of the property in question. Suppose the zoning on the property permits a particular use and the recorded CC&Rs prohibit that use. The general rule of law is that you have to look both at the zoning and at the recorded CC&Rs, and whichever document is the most restrictive will control. CC&Rs can be as simple or as complex as the facts dictate. In many instances in larger subdivisions, the CC&Rs are complex and restrictive. The CC&Rs can deal with such matters as architectural approval. They can require that before any improvements are constructed on the property, they must meet both the local zoning laws and building codes and require that the architectural design, the colors, the landscaping, and the material uses be approved by an architectural committee generally composed of other homeowners in the subdivision or the original developer. Violations of these CC&Rs can generally be enforced by private litigation. Thus, in the previous example of the nightclub operating next door, you, as the owner of the adjoining property, would have the right to bring a private action in the courts to enjoin the continued operation of the nightclub in violation of the recorded CC&Rs.

   Suppose there is a recorded CC&R placed on the property 25 years ago when the entire area in which the property was located was solely residential. Suppose that now, due to changing economic circumstances and development patterns, the property is no longer suitable for residential use but logically should be used for commercial purposes or multitenant residential development. Can a change in the circumstances of the property and its economic evolution be a ground for violating or terminating the CC&Rs? Is there a procedure for terminating the CC&Rs should these economic circumstances change? The answer to the question is a complex one. In most cases it is a difficult, costly, and time-consuming procedure to obtain a cancellation of existing CC&Rs. It requires the institution of litigation and of naming all of the surrounding owners within the tract in question as defendants. The courts have to make a substantial, factual determination that the purpose of the original CC&R's no longer exists. In most jurisdictions this will take, at the minimum, several years to resolve. In many cases the CC&Rs have provisions within their terms for their amendment, but generally this requires consent in recordable form of a majority of all of the parties within the tract or subdivision affected by the CC&Rs. CC&Rs can also have material effect not only on the value, but the financability of a particular parcel. As previously mentioned, it is urgently suggested that the prospective purchaser obtain a copy of the recorded CC&Rs and read and analyze them before acquiring the property. Let me give you a word of caution here. In many printed offers to purchase, escrow instructions, and contracts of purchase and sale, there are provisions that the buyer agrees to accept title subject to all of the existing recorded CC&Rs (See Forms 4, 5, and

6). I think these are dangerous clauses, and efforts should be made to strike them from the printed agreements and to give yourself the ability as a buyer to examine a current title report and all easements and other documents of record that affect the subject property. Again, as in other instances, the practice of preventive law is important here. The question of CC&Rs is a two-edged sword. They can enhance the value of the property if they are designed to uphold the integrity of the area, limit and restrict the quality and type of development, and maintain a certain uniformity of architectural design. CC&Rs can be very broad and all-encompassing. They can include restrictions on landscaping; they can include the type of fences you can put up; they can deal with special problems such as equestrian trails, bike paths, signs, lighting, parking, and other areas of use and character of the property. In dealing with industrial and commercial subdivisions, the CC&Rs can go a long way towards preserving a park-like atmosphere in an industrial subdivision; enchance the quality of the development; restrict the density of use; and deal with almost any legitimate subject that is not a violation of established public policy. In this latter regard, any attempt to restrict the use, occupancy, sale or development of the property based upon race, color, creed, or religion is unconstitutional under the laws of the United States and the individual states.

RECORDED EASEMENTS. Other documents that restrict use are recorded easements. What is an easement? An easement is a right given to another person to use your property for a particular purpose. Several examples should illustrate the problem. You grant to the local telephone company the right to use the rear five feet of your property for the purpose of installing telephone lines or wires. Another example would be the agreement between you and your neighbor to share a common driveway from the public street to his property and your property by creating a reciprocal parking and access agreement (See Form 38 for an example of such an agreement). You should carefully examine all of the recorded easements and restrictions. In many rural areas of the country, it was not uncommon for farmers and owners to grant to utility companies and to private parties "blanket" easements across their properties. When a property was an apple orchard, it really wasn't important where the telephone lines ran across a large parcel of acreage. Now, however, the property has become extremely valuable and is being contemplated for division into a series of individual single-family residential lots. Now the exact location of the telephone lines becomes extremely critical, and it may be necessary to renegotiate with the utility company the exact location of their easements as the property is developed. Having the utility company abandon existing easements and create new ones can be, in some instances, very simple. In others it is a matter of extreme difficulty and cost, since the utility lines that now run across the property you have in mind service not only this property but other properties down the line. A careful examination of the existing recorded easements and other restrictions on the property is good preventive law and can avoid a great deal of cost and expense in the future.

REAL ESTATE TAXES AND SPECIAL ASSESSMENTS. As previously mentioned in connection with the personal property versus real property issue described above, there is a distinction between real estate taxes and personal property taxes that need not be further amplified here. A careful examination of the existing tax bill, the existing assessment role, and the potential within a particular city or county for future taxes and assessments is essential to avoid problems. Most real estate taxes are assessed on an annual basis based upon a fixed tax rate usually calculated at so many dollars for each $1,000 of assessed valuation. The tax rate of each jurisdiction can differ materially, since real estate taxes are customarily comprised of a number of assessment districts in which the real property in question is located. As an example, there will be one assessment rate for local schools, one assessment rate for local colleges, one assessment rate for local sewer districts, mosquito abatement districts, and general city taxes, in addition to special assessments that relate to a particular area such as for flood control, new sewer facilities, and a myriad of public and quasi-public endeavors. Also, in some jurisdictions, it is possible by law for an individual subdivider or group of subdividers to create their own assessment districts. For example in California, by following appropriate procedures outlined in the statutes, a subdivider can cause an assessment district to be created and tax-exempt municipal bonds to be created to cover the cost of what is commonly referred to as offsite improvements such as streets, curbs, gutters, all utility facilities, lights, and other public improvements that will be ultimately dedicated and owned by the municipality. In determining what taxes affect the subject property and how the sale will affect the subject property, an analysis of local procedures and customs must be made. Whether the local jurisdiction will increase the taxes based upon the purchase price paid for the property depends on the custom and usage prevalent in each particular jurisdiction. Do not overlook the effect of a sale on increasing the assessed valuation and therefore the amount of property taxes in connection with any particular sale. These increased costs become particularly relevant when coupled with local restrictions as to rent control.

CONDEMNATION AND EMINENT DOMAIN. It is an established principle of U.S. law that public bodies can take all or portions of real property within their jurisdiction for public purposes. U.S. laws further require that should such taking occur, just compensation must be paid to the owner. Thus if it becomes a matter of public necessity and convenience for a portion of a particular parcel of property to be taken in order to widen the street due to changing traffic patterns or to condemn and take a whole parcel of property for some basic public purpose, this is permitted. Whether or not this will affect the development of the balance of the property is a question that has to be examined in each instance. It is suggested, however, that in your preacquisition checklist approach, you carefully discuss the matter with local governmental officials to see what the attitude and potential is for condemnation. Do not confuse this area with the area of subdivision which will be discussed later. As will become evident, when you apply to subdivide or parcel-up a particular parcel of property, the city, as a condition to granting you permission to subdivide or parcel, can require you to dedicate a portion of your land for future streets, street widening, and other public purposes without in such instance paying just compensation for the land conveyed to the city. Many jurisdictions have become very sophisticated in this area and require substantial dedication and substantial improvements as a condition of granting a subdivision map. And in many cases, this is done as a condition for granting rezoning to a particular parcel of property. Keep in mind that whenever you submit yourself to the jurisdiction of a particular city or county for either a rezoning of the property, a variance from existing zoning, or for the right to parcel or subdivide the property, you open a Pandora's box. And you give to the city the right to require, as a condition to granting you the permission you seek, dedication of land to improve streets, to install utilities, and a number of expensive and extensive improvements all at the sole cost and expense of the owner-developer. It could be argued that these costs can be passed along to the purchasers of the houses or renters of the apartments to be constructed. But whether or not this argument holds water depends upon whether or not the economic realities permit you to add these costs to the ultimate product. A detailed economic analysis is necessary for you to determine the answer to this question. Please keep these factors in mind, however, when you are examining a particular property for acquisition and future development. If more information is required in connection with this area, please see Appendix 5 dealing with *Continuing Education of the Bar* publications that deal in great detail with the items of condemnation, eminent domain, and subdivision of property.

SUBDIVISION AND PARCEL MAPS. Again, subdivision and parcelization are the peculiar province of local law and vary materially from state to state, from county to county, and from city to city. The local subdivision, parcel map, and division laws of each jurisdiction must be carefully examined in conjunction with a realistic evaluation of the attitudes of local governments in connection with any subdivision or parcelization. The time factors involved in processing zoning changes, subdivisions, and parcel maps vary again extensively from jurisdiction to jurisdiction. In doing cash flow projections and economic analyses these factors have to be considered. In some states it is required that if the proposed project will materially affect existing conditions, an environment impact report must be made and submitted for approval. This will necessitate the hiring of experts to engage in extensive reports and research for the benefit of the city as a condition to the approval of a proposed subdivision. Do not be lulled into a sense of false security in this area. As previously mentioned, policies of title insurance, even extended coverage policies, often exclude reference to zoning and subdivision. You can thus acquire a home or commercial property with existing improvements and still find that the property has been illegally developed or subdivided in violation of existing laws. Should you purchase a particular parcel and subsequently discover such violation, you could be prevented by the local jurisdiction from getting building permits and have material exposure in the event of a subsequent sale. In most states in the United States, the sale of a property that has been illegally subdivided, even if that subdivision was by your predecessor, can give rise to actions for damages on the part of your subsequent purchaser and to a right of recision of the transaction upon their discovery of the illegal activity. In most cases it is no defense that you as a seller were unaware of the illegal activities of your predecessor. For more information on this subject, see Appendix 5.

MORATORIUMS AND RENT CONTROL. As mentioned briefly elsewhere in this text, each city has the legal authority to declare a moratorium—that is, to prohibit future development—for specific periods of time. In some instances this is done so that the city can have a reasonable opportunity to create a master plan for the entire city. In other cases, moratoriums are declared because of a lack of central facilities to provide basic public services. As an example, there are cases where cities have declared moratoriums on all future building because the local sewer plant was operating to capacity and it was impossible to provide the necessary services for new construction. Whether a moratorium is possible or imminent requires a detailed examination of the local political attitudes and a review by you or your experts of the potential development you have in mind and how it will affect the existing facilities within a particular jurisdiction. In some extreme cases, it becomes necessary as a condition to your ability to develop property, to apply to have the property included within a particular utility district. As an example, in some rural areas, the property may not be presently serviced by a licensed water company. In order for water service to be supplied to the particular property for the purpose of future development as a subdivision, mobile home park, or other development, you may be required to contact a water company and request it to make appropriate applications to a local utility commission for permission to expand its area of service to include your potential development. This can result in costs and expenses which have to be evaluated on an ad hoc basis with each particular project. Do not, however, overlook this problem, and examine carefully all of the local factors. The use of local engineers and architects who are generally familiar with the facts in a particular jurisdiction can often be beneficial.

The questions of rent control are increasingly vexing and important. Social and economic conditions are changing rapidly in the United States. High interest rates, high cost of construction, and the changing age of the population have all exacerbated the existing situation in many jurisdictions resulting in a lack of rentable units at affordable prices and the inability of young people and those on fixed incomes to find affordable housing both as renters and purchasers. As a result of these factors and changing political climates, many local jurisdictions have adopted laws and ordinances restricting the amount of rent that an owner of property can charge. Some have further adopted restrictive laws and ordinances restricting condominium conversions of existing buildings. The breadth and scope of these laws varies materially from city to city and state to state. Such restrictive laws have continually been held to be constitutional by the courts. I cannot emphasize too strongly that if your potential acquisition is an existing apartment complex, being purchased as an investment for future appreciation or for conversion of rental units to condominium, you must make a careful and detailed analysis of the existing laws and ordinances as well as an evaluation of the possibility that new laws and ordinances will be adopted in the foreseeable future. This area of rent control is evolving rapidly in most cities in the United States and is an issue that has to be looked at very carefully as part of a preacquisition analysis by a potential buyer. Again, all of these issues are two-edged swords. What happens if a buyer goes into a firm contract to purchase a particular parcel, hoping that subsequent to the acquisition he will have the ability to raise the rent, and during the term of the escrow, before title is transferred, the local city adopts a rent-control law? Does this action permit the purchaser to rescind the transaction? There are no pat answers in this area. The issue can be resolved by careful forethought and the drafting of appropriate language in the agreements of purchase and sale. A question of who bears this risk is one of negotiation between buyer and seller.

LICENSES AND PERMITS.   In some jurisdictions, if property is to be used for a particular purpose, even though permitted by local zoning laws and private CC&Rs, it is necessary to obtain licenses and permits from a local or state agency. As an example, if you are acquiring a hotel that operates a cocktail lounge and bar, it is generally necessary for you, as purchaser, to make application to a local alcoholic beverage control board and obtain licenses to operate the cocktail lounge and bar. In many instances this requires extensive investigation by local police authorities, and it can present vexing problems to a foreign investor who wishes to maintain anonymity and who is unknown to local authorities. Should the acquisition in question deal with these areas, local counsel and city officials should be consulted. Again this issue can be covered in appropriately drawn agreements of purchase and sale.

SUBDIVIDED LAND ACT AND FEDERAL FULL DISCLOSURE ACT.   Though they vary materially from state to state, most states have laws which require that a permit be obtained from the state as a condition precedent to the right of a developer to sell lots after they have been subdivided in accordance with all local laws. This requires the filing of detailed applications and obtaining a permit to sell subdivided lots and/or condominiums to the general public. In addition to the laws of each state, there are federal statutes dealing with the interstate sale of subdivided lots. Whether or not the compliance with the local state subdivision sales laws will qualify the transaction for federal purposes depends on an analysis of the laws of each state in question. If the acquisition you have in mind is for future subdivision, condominium conversion, or condominium sales, whether residential or commercial, a detailed analysis of the local laws dealing with subdivision is mandatory. Local title insurance companies and local attorneys, as well as many sophisticated real estate brokers, are excellent sources to determine the local requirements as well as compliance with federal statutes in this area. Making necessary applications in compliance with local and federal laws (and the time factor involved) should be considered in the economic evaluation of a project. The best advice I can give is do not take anything for granted. Have the matters checked out carefully by appropriate *experts* in the field. Should the reader desire to delve into this whole question in more depth, there are several excellent publications available. Reference is made in Appendix 5 to the *California Continuing Education of the Bar* publications which deal in depth with this subject.

Economic and financial factors

We have previously had a brief discussion of these matters in the preceding chapter. We will try to examine some of these factors in greater detail. This section deals with the examination of the existing loan documents, the use of beneficiary statements and other lender instruments, prepayment penalties, acceleration clauses, lock-in provisions, the examination of existing books and records, the examination and analysis of leases, the use of offset and estoppel certificates, allocation of costs between improvements and land, the concept of depreciation and a brief discussion about insurance (other than title insurance). Let us now turn to a more specific analysis of each of these topics.

EXAMINATION OF EXISTING LIENS AND ENCUMBRANCES AGAINST THE PROPERTY. It is imperative as part of any careful examination and implementation of a preacquisition checklist that you, as a potential buyer, obtain copies of the existing promissory notes and existing deeds of trust that affect the subject property. Keep in mind that the promissory notes in almost all instances are not recorded, and a receipt of copies of the deed of trust from the public record will not answer, in almost any instance, the important questions dealing with existing loans. Further, because of changing market conditions and the volatile change in interest rates and attitudes of institutional lenders, examining and evaluating the existing encumbrances is imperative. Many loans of record now bear extremely favorable interest rates in light of changing market conditions. There is thus a strong incentive on the part of the holder of these encumbrances to find a way to declare the obligation all due and payable, and by that method either receive back its money which it can lend at much higher rates or force you as a potential purchaser to modify the existing obligation to more closely reflect current market conditions. It is obvious that in many instances, the incentive and the reason for purchasing the property in the first place and its economic terms and values are based to a large extent upon the ability of a buyer to take over the property and enjoy the advantage of the existing loan. Existing loans generally have low interest rates and thus permit a more favorable cash flow from the ownership and operation of the property. We have discussed briefly in previous chapters some of the problems with promissory notes and deeds of trust. These apply equally, of course, to mortgages. Keep in mind in your analysis that the mortgage or deed of trust is merely a security device which gives a lien upon the real property to ensure that the underlying note which is secured by the mortgage or deed of trust is paid pursuant to its terms. The matter is further complicated by the fact that you cannot rely upon the amount of the original mortgage set forth in the recorded instrument. In many cases the lender is permitted to make additional advances and to modify the original loan terms and amount if requested by the borrower. It thus becomes necessary as a matter of prudent practice not only to review the existing documents that are of record but to have a direct contact with the lender to be sure that the obligation you are acquiring is assumable, what the terms of that obligation are, what the interest rate is, what the unpaid balance of the obligation is, and that your predecessor is not in default under the terms and provisions of the note and/or the deed of trust or mortgage securing the note. It is urgently recommended that you obtain what is commonly referred to as a beneficiary statement or offset statement from the lender which verifies:

1. The nature and form of the instruments it holds.
2. That there have been no modifications or amendments or additional advances.

3. That the obligation is current and free of default.
4. That the obligation is assumable.
5. That all requirements of the note and deed of trust have been complied with, such as insurance requirements, tax impounds and matters of a similar nature.

Your agreements of purchase and sale should make provisions for obtaining these beneficiary or offset statements from the lender. Your obligation as a buyer to consummate the transaction is subject to your review and approval of these documents. Further provisions should be made in your agreements of purchase and sale to obligate the seller to keep the commitment current during the pendency of the escrow or purchase agreement so that on consummation the obligation will be current and free of default.

We have already discussed the impact of prepayment penalties, lock-in clauses, acceleration or due-on-sale provision notes, and deeds of trust. Reference is made to the previous chapter in connection with these items. These are serious issues; they have a material impact on a real estate project; they affect the value of the project and can materially affect the cash flow and impede the personal liability on buyer and seller. I cannot overemphasize the necessity of reviewing the existing loan documents in detail. It is possible on specific issues to negotiate a modification of the existing terms with a lender. As an example, most institutional loan documents (see Forms 14–21 for examples) deal with the issue of insurance coverage and disposition of insurance proceeds. Assume there is a fire in an office building secured by a deed of trust in favor of Friendly Savings and Loan and that the lease between you as landlord and your tenant requires you to rebuild the premises in the event of a fire. A careful examination of most typical insurance clauses in standard institutional deeds of trust and mortgages provide that in the event of casualty loss, the lender at its discretion can apply the insurance proceeds received from the insurance company from such loss to the unpaid principal of the loan and not make said proceeds available to you for the purposes of rebuilding and repairs. In my example you are caught on the horns of a dilemma. Your lease obligation to the tenant requires you to rebuild. Your obligation with the lender permits him to take the funds and apply them against the loan. Where are you going to get the money to rebuild? If you don't rebuild, you face the possibility of litigation from your tenant under his lease. These problems can be avoided by careful negotiation and draftsmanship and should not be overlooked as an area of potential risk and danger. Again, since it is an area of great concern, the whole question as to whether or not the lender has the legal right to declare its loan all due and payable upon the sale of the property by the existing seller varies from state to state. A careful examination of the laws of each state by competent counsel (since the current status of those laws is constantly changing) is imperative in making your determination as to whether or not you should acquire the property in question.

EXAMINATION OF EXISTING BOOKS AND RECORDS. Many properties, particularly multiple-unit apartment projects or commercial and industrial properties, are purchased with the expectation that the investment will produce a stipulated income stream to the purchaser. To verify this expectation requires a detailed analysis of the income derived from the

property and the existing expenses in connection with its operation and maintenance. It is urgently suggested that you include in your preacquisition checklist
and purchase documents the right to analyze the books and records of your
seller as they relate to the subject property. How far a period you go back and
whether or not the statements of income and expense should be audited by a
CPA and/or by your own accountants and experts is a matter to be determined
in light of the particular circumstances involving the property in question. At a
very minimum it is urgently suggested that you obtain as part of your agreements of purchase and sale:

1. Firm representations and warranties from the seller as to the income and
   expense in connection with the subject property for a designated and
   specific period of time.
2. Guarantees that you may audit said books and records.
3. Statements that your obligation as buyer to conclude and consummate the
   purchase is subject to and contingent upon your examination and approval
   of the financial data, books, and records supplied to you by the seller.
4. Warranties from the seller concerning the accuracy of all data furnished for
   your review.

**EXAMINATION OF EXISTING LEASES AND ESTOPPEL CERTIF-
ICATES.** In connection with the acquisition of existing commercial and
multiunit residential properties, the examination and review of existing leases
is imperative. As a general rule, a buyer acquiring property purchases subject
to all the terms and provisions of all existing leases and the right of all parties in
possession at the date of title transfer. As the new owner, you are required to
perform all of the terms and provisions of each lease, written or oral. How can
you determine the status of all existing leases and tenancies? The customary
procedure is to require as a condition to the purchase and as part of your
agreement of purchase and sale, that:

1. The present owner furnishes exact copies of all of the existing leases
   affecting the subject property, including all amendments thereto.
2. An affirmative representation and warranty in writing from the seller as to
   the status of each lease.
3. The security deposit of each tenant and the statement from seller that their
   leases are current and free of default both on the part of the tenant and on
   the part of the landlord.

But this covers only half of the problem. In addition to such affirmative covenants and statements from the seller, prudent practice dictates that you obtain
from each tenant in possession a document commonly referred to as an estoppel
certificate whereby each tenant represents and warrants to you as a prospective
purchaser:

1. The current status of lease or tenancy.
2. That same is free of default.
3. That there have been no extensions, written or oral, or other modifications
   of the relationship between seller and the tenant.

A form of potential estoppel certificate for both written and oral tenancies is
included as Forms 31 and 32.

Again, the proper consideration of this area of tenant and landlord rights and the use of estoppel certificates and affirmative representation warranties can avoid many future problems. Also adequate provisions should be made in the agreements of purchase and sale, should the facts so warrant, to set forth criteria for future leasing. That way during the pendency of the escrow and prior to its consummation, new leases cannot be executed and consummated without your consent as a future buyer, which would result in adverse economic effect on the project. Keep in mind that most policies of title insurance exclude from coverage the rights of tenants in possession of the property. It is therefore incumbent upon a future buyer to examine in detail the relationship and terms and provisions under which each tenant occupies all or a portion of the property in question. Special problems can arise in connection with leases where it is incumbent upon the landlord to make certain repairs or to construct improvements. This is common in office leases where the tenant has not yet occupied the suite and where the lease requires the landlord to install certain minimum improvements. Should this be the case, a detailed analysis of the cost factors involved should be made prior to consummation of the purchase in question. Refer to Appendix 5 which describes several excellent publications of the *California Continuing Education of the Bar* series dealing with leases, both residential and commercial, and the rights of landlords and tenants. In addition, you will find a typical office lease (Form 33), a typical commercial lease (Form 34) and a typical farm lease (Form 30), each of which can be used as a checklist for analysis purposes.

ALLOCATION AND DEPRECIATION. As a general rule, the tax laws of the United States impose an income tax based upon profits. Profit is an accounting concept and does not necessarily bear a relationship to the cash received and cash expended in connection with the typical real estate project. A simple example may illustrate the issue. Suppose you acquire our mythical parcel of property, Black Acre, for $1 million. Black Acre consists of 10 acres of land upon which there is constructed a 100,000-square-foot industrial warehouse. Assume further that when you purchased the property there was an existing note and deed of trust in favor of Blank Insurance Company on the property with an unpaid balance of $700,000. Assume further that you made a down payment of $300,000, making up the total purchase price of $1 million. Now assume that the annual expenses in connection with the property such as maintenance, insurance and real estate taxes total $20,000 per year and that these sums are actually expended by you as owner. Assume further that the annual payments of principal and interest on the insurance company note is $60,000 per year. If we total the expenses and the debt service on the insurance company note, we have accounted for $80,000. We have received income of $100,000, thus having a positive cash flow from this property of $20,000. Is that the reportable profit derived from the property for U.S. tax purposes? The answer is no. As a general rule in determining profit, you would start with the income received, deduct from that the annual expenses ($20,000 in our example), deduct from that sum the further amount paid in interest to the lender (excluding that portion of the payment that is *principal*), which I will assume for this example is $50,000 per year, and you may deduct a further sum which is defined as *depreciation.* Let's assume for this example that the depreciation allocable to each year is $30,000. Thus, our total deduction from income is $100,000 (composed of annual expenses of $20,000, interest on the Blank Insurance Company note of $50,000, and depreciation of $30,000). Using this example, for the purposes of U.S. income tax and determination of whether or not there is a profit from the project, the result would be zero, and no tax would be due and payable. However, there is a positive cash flow in my example of $20,000. This cash flow can be enjoyed by the purchaser of the property without immediate income tax ramifications. In determining the amount of depreciation that can be allocated to any particular calendar or fiscal year, there are extensive and complex rules under the U.S. Internal Revenue Code dealing with the amount of depreciation and how much can be deducted in any one particular year. A text of this kind does not permit a detailed analysis of the different methods of depreciation. If more information is required in this connection, the reader should consult his accountant or tax attorney. There are many ramifications to the question of depreciation. There are many elections that can be made to either accelerate the amount of depreciation or to spread that depreciation over a particular period of time.

How depreciation is handled can have a marked effect on the taxable, reportable income derived from a particular project, both during its ownership and operation and at the time of sale. In this regard, the foreign investor is often in conflict with his American counterpart. As a general rule, foreign investors cannot take advantage of paper losses occasioned by the use of accelerated depreciation. However, the American investor can, in many instances, deduct the losses derived from a particular real estate project from income that he earns from other business activities or personal services. Keep in mind, however, that in dealing with this whole area of depreciation, it is not permissible to depreciate land. Thus, in our example, while the purchase price for the whole project was $1 million an allocation has to be made between the value of the land and the value of the improvements. It is only the improvements that can be depreciated. Again, how you allocate value between the land and the improvements depends on the facts in each case and an interpretation of the statutes and regulations promulgated by the U.S. Internal Revenue Service. In preparing your cash flow analysis, and in reviewing a particular parcel for potential acquisition, careful consideration should be given to depreciation and cash flow analysis, and a detailed spread sheet should be prepared for examination and analysis by the foreign investor and his professional advisors. There are further complications in connection with this whole area of depreciation and cash flow as it relates to the foreign investor. Should the lease be a so-called net-net lease, where the tenant pays taxes and debt service directly, arguments can be made that there is a requirement that there be a withholding of these monies equal to 30 percent of the gross amount which can result in a negative cash flow for the investor. This will be discussed further in a subsequent chapter in this book.

Since the foreign investor in many instances cannot take advantage of losses derived from depreciation, he can use this as an important bargaining tool in negotiating partnerships and joint ventures with his U.S. associates. Obviously, the U.S. associates can equally offer to make economic concessions to the foreign investor in exchange for enjoying a larger share of the paper losses. Caution must be used in making depreciation allocations. There are limitations on such allocations imposed by the relevant statutes and regulations of the U.S. Internal Revenue Code.

INSURANCE.   In connection with each improved parcel of real estate, particularly where there are buildings and institutional loans involved, it is necessary for the property to be insured with such companies and in such amounts as shall be approved by the lender. In addition, the ownership of real estate in the United States imposes certain potential liabilities on an owner for injuries that occur on the property by tenants, invitees, and others. Generally speaking, this necessitates the owner of real property to acquire fire, general liability, and property damage insurance for the benefit of the owner and the lender. In addition, the cost of maintaining this insurance becomes increasingly burdensome under present inflationary conditions and changing actuarial experience with insurance companies. The foreign investor is urged to have his advisors make a detailed analysis of the existing potential insurance requirements and their cost as part of the evaluation of a particular project. In addition, it is often advantageous to the foreign investor to be able to take over the existing insurance on the property which enjoys, in some instances, favorable premium notes. The agreements of purchase and sale should make adequate provisions for the foreign investor as purchaser to review all existing insurance policies and to have the opportunity to assume said insurance as part of the purchase. Whether or not insurance is, in fact, assumable and of adequate coverage is a question for detailed analysis by experts in connection with the facts involving each particular acquisition.

PREPARING FOR PURCHASE— (HOW TO MAKE AN OFFER AND METHODS OF ACQUISITION)

In the preceding chapters, I developed criteria for buying property and established a lengthy preacquisition checklist of the various elements and items to be reviewed and considered before purchasing or attempting to purchase a parcel of real property, whether that be desert acreage at one extreme, or a sophisticated high-rise building at the other end of the spectrum. The purpose of this chapter is to examine the method by which we will attempt to purchase a particular parcel of real property and some of the legal and practical aspects in connection therewith. All agreements for the purchase of real property contain certain basic elements and must meet certain minimum criteria. These basic elements can be described as follows:

1. Mutual consent.
2. Capable parties with capacity to contract.
3. Sufficient consideration.
4. A legal object.
5. Contracts for the purchase of real property must be in writing.

With these five elements in mind, let's explore how meeting these requirements can relate to the everyday world of real property acquisition documents. We will take the five elements out of order and dispose of the easy ones first.

A WRITTEN AGREEMENT

Due to historical precedents and statutes that have been adopted throughout the United States, as a general rule, contracts for the purchase and sale of an interest in real property must be in writing. There are, of course, under case law and statute, certain exceptions to this general rule, but these exceptions are created by unusual facts and circumstances. I think it is best to assume for all purposes in dealing with purchasing or optioning real property, that the agreement of purchase and sale, any offers in connection with them, escrow instructions, and other documents that describe an interest in real estate, must be in written form. It should again be noted at this point, that agreements to sell or acquire an interest in personal property, in many instances, do not need to be in written form.

LEGAL OBJECTS AND MISTAKE

This is merely fancy legal terminology which states the principle that the property being purchased or sold must be adequately and reasonably described.   Several of the previous chapters have dealt extensively with this issue. The reader is hereby referred to those chapters which deal with the subjects of what are we buying; net versus gross; whether personal property is included as part of the purchase; an adequate and careful description of what the seller intends to sell and what the buyer intends to buy. Whether or not detailed inventories, surveys, or extensive examination of legal descriptions are in order depends on the facts and circumstances as discussed at length in other chapters.

The question should be raised at this point: What happens if there is a mistake by one or both of the parties relating to the property to be acquired? If the mistake is mutual in nature, for example, the parties place in the document a description of the wrong lot with clear understanding on the part of the potential seller and buyer that they were intending to deal only with another lot, then this frustrates the existing contract. In such circumstances the agreement can be modified either by consent of the parties or by appropriate legal proceedings. The problem of mistake becomes more difficult when it relates not to the specific property in question, but to what is commonly referred to as a collateral issue. For instance, a buyer intends to purchase the property on facts unknown to the seller and uncommunicated to the buyer by the seller. Assume that the buyer has been furnished with information by other than the seller or his agent that the property in question is going to be rezoned or that a new freeway is coming through the area that will make the property in question more valuable. In fact, the rezoning does not take place, or the freeway is abandoned and the buyer now says, "I now want out of the deal because what I expected to happen isn't happening." Under these circumstances of a collateral mistake, it is not a defense, and there is no basis for a buyer to rescind the contract in question. In addition, unilateral mistakes based upon facts peculiarly within the knowledge of the buyer or seller are also not a basis for avoiding the contract.

MUTUAL CONSENT

Mutual consent merely means that the parties have contracted in good faith knowing what they are doing, and the agreement is free of duress. As an extreme example, the buyer can't put a gun to the head of the seller and say, "Sign this contract or I'll blow your brains out," and then attempt to enforce this contract when the seller says, "I really didn't sign it." It's no defense for the buyer to say, "But isn't that your signature on the agreement?" Reference in the previous paragraph to issues of mistake may also be relevant in determining that, in fact, the parties had a general meeting of the minds as to what was being sold and what was being purchased and that they each intended to enter into an agreement binding on its terms between the respective parties.

CAPACITY

Questions of capacity deal with several areas, some of which are purely legal and some of which are of a more practical business nature.

The first question to be asked in the area of capacity is: Are the parties to the agreement capable of entering into a contract? That is to say, are they of legal age and do they have the mental capacity to understand what they are doing. The question as to whether a person signing an agreement has the legal capacity to enter into an agreement varies according to the laws of each particular state. In some states, the legal age for contracting is 21 years of age. In other states, the legal age may be 16 years or 18 years depending on the facts and circumstances. This is common knowledge in most jurisdictions, and a simple contact with a local title insurance company, qualified real estate broker, or attorney can answer this question with little difficulty.

Whether or not the person is of competent mental capacity to enter into a contract can on occasion become a more difficult issue to resolve. Suppose, as an example, you're trying to purchase a single-family residence from an elderly widow. You have reason to believe that this widow has the ability to understand what she is getting into, but you're not sure. The general rule of law is that if a person is senile, or if that person does not have the ability to understand and comprehend, in general terms, the contract that person is entering into, then such contract is void or, in some instances, voidable. As a practical matter, there is no foolproof way of resolving this question. As a matter of law, persons are assumed to be competent until proven otherwise. In extreme cases, I have recommended that other relatives of a potentially senile or older person be contacted and, if required, that an action be instituted in the courts to have a legal guardian or conservator of the estate appointed so that there will be no question of the signing party's legal capacity. Many jurisdictions have adopted new statutes and laws dealing with the question of senility and capacity. Until a few years ago, before a guardian could be appointed for a person with questioned legal capacity, that person had to be declared of unsound mind. This created many psychological problems for relatives who were reluctant to have loved ones declared mentally incompetent. Most states have adopted procedures for the appointment of a representative of an older person without the necessity of having that person declared to be mentally incompetent. A check with local counsel can resolve this question without too much difficulty. Whenever property is owned by more than one party (for example, a single-family residence owned by John and Mary Smith), it is essential that both John and Mary sign the purchase documents. It is insufficient in almost every jurisdiction in the United States for a husband and/or wife to represent that he/she has the power to sign on behalf of his/her spouse. Such agreements in almost all jurisdictions must be in writing, and duly acknowledged for recording purposes. To avoid this whole problem, be sure that all parties who are entitled to the property sign the purchase documents. We will deal with the questions of power of attorney later in this chapter. The question could be raised at this time: How do we know who the present owner of the property is? As previously discussed, a quick search of the title, obtaining a preliminary title report or, in most cases, contact with a local title insurer or title abstractor can, within a matter of a few hours, result in your obtaining a list of all of those parties who, on the public record, are vested in title to the property in question.

Where the contracting parties are a partnership or a corporation, the question of capacity becomes more difficult to resolve.

In dealing with partnerships, the question becomes a bit more complex. There are in the United States several types of partnerships—general partnership, joint venture, and limited partnerships. A general partnership, by definition, is a partnership composed of two or more general partners each of whom have full liability and responsibility on behalf of the partnership and who have authority to sign and bind the partnership. A joint venture is in substance, in most jurisdictions, really a hybrid general or limited partnership. A limited partnership is a partnership in which there are one or more general partners and one or more limited partners. A general partner is the party who has the only authorization, control, and liability in connection with the partnership, and a limited partner, by definition, is a passive investor who merely invests specific sums of money in the partnership and has no authority to act for or on behalf of the partnership, except in rare instances which will be described below. In most jurisdictions in the United States a general partnership can be verbal as can a joint venture involving general partners. A limited partnership, however, must be in writing and must be acknowledged and filed or recorded in accordance with the provisions of local law. Most jurisdictions in the United States have adopted two uniform laws—the Uniform Partnership Act and the Uniform Limited Partnership Act. These particular uniform acts set forth in detail the rights and privileges of partners, both limited and general as the case may be. However, though this is a uniform law adopted by almost all of the states in the United States, each state in adopting its form of these laws has on occasion modified them to meet the specific requirements of that particular state. A careful examination by local counsel is required. In some instances a limited partnership formed under the law of one particular state will not qualify as a limited partnership under the laws of another state. This can create some disasterous legal consequences. As a general rule of law, if a limited partnership does not meet the laws of a particular state, then all of the partners, both general and limited, are treated in substance as general partners resulting in the imposition of personal liability on all of the members of the partnership.

Who can sign for a partnership, and how do you determine this fact? Again, as a general rule of law, any general partner of a partnership has the capacity to sign and bind a general partnership. Also, in most instances, a general partner of a limited partnership has the authority to sign and bind the limited partnership. However, a careful word of caution when dealing with limited partnerships. As you will recall, I previously stated that a limited partnership must be recorded or filed. When such an agreement is recorded or filed, it becomes a matter of public knowledge to all parties dealing with said partnership. Therefore it is incumbent upon you in dealing with the partnership to obtain a copy of the partnership agreement as recorded or filed and to review its contents. In many instances where there is more than one general partner of a limited partnership, the partnership agreement per its terms requires the execution of all agreements by more than one general partner to bind the partnership. In some instances, there are prohibitions upon the acts or actions of the general partner which require a consent in writing of limited partners before a particular act or action can be done. For example, in California there are code provisions in the Uniform Act which grant to a limited partner the right to require the general partner to obtain the limited partner's written consent *before* assets of the partnership can be sold or mortgaged. Should such a provision exist in a partnership agreement, it will be necessary for you as a buyer to obtain the written consent of all of the limited partners (or a majority of them should the agreement so provide) before you have a valid and binding agreement which can be enforced against the partnership. Experience has shown this author that careful examination of the partnership agreement avoids a substantial amount of misunderstanding and litigation in matters of this type. In preparing your agreement of purchase and sale, it is essential that you ask the party signing on behalf of the partnership to make an affirmative representation and warranty that that party has capacity to sign and full authority to execute the agreement for and on behalf of the partnership. (See Form 7). Such a representation and warranty will not protect you against the express provisions of a recorded limited partnership agreement, but in most instances, a party executing such a representation and warranty will be extremely reluctant to sign same if there are prohibitions in the agreement against his acting on behalf of the partnership in question. In dealing with general partnerships in many states in the United States, there are code provisions which provide for the filing of a document that is commonly referred to as a statement of partnership. Such a document deals only with general partnerships and sets forth in substance who the partners of the partnership are and who has authority to sign on behalf of the partnership. Such a document is necessitated by the fact that general partnerships need not be in writing. By recording this statement of partnership, any bona fide person in good faith who deals with the partnership is conclusively presumed to be a bona fide purchaser if the instrument of conveyance or the purchase agreement is executed by those parties who have authority to sign on behalf of the partnership as set forth in the statement of partnership. Again, this instrument can be obtained from the local county recorder's office in almost all jurisdictions.

In dealing with corporations, the question to be asked is: How do I know that the person signing on behalf of the corporation has authority to execute the document and bind the corporation? To answer this question, we must explore several areas. There are, of course, different types of corporations. For the purposes of capacity, we are dealing merely with two types of corporations, so-called local corporations and foreign corporations. For this purpose, a local corporation is a corporation that is incorporated within the state in which the transaction is involved and the real property is located. A foreign corporation is defined as a corporation that is incorporated in a jurisdiction other than the state in which the contract is executed or the real property is located. Perhaps an example will best illustrate the problem. Let's assume that you desire to enter into a purchase agreement to acquire real property in the state of California from a corporation that is originally incorporated in the state of California. For our purposes, this corporation will be a local corporation. Let's change the facts a bit. Let's assume that the real property is located in the state of California, but the owner is a Netherlands Antilles corporation. Or assume that the property is located in the state of California but that the corporation that owns the real property was originally incorporated in the state of Nevada. For our purposes at this point, both of those corporations are deemed to be foreign corporations. If the real property and the state of incorporation are both the same, then the question that has to be asked is: Is this corporation presently in good standing within the state, and does the party executing the agreement have the legal authority to sign and bind the corporation? It is relatively easy to determine whether a corporation incorporated within one of the states of the United States is presently in good standing. The secretary of state of almost all states will, upon request, issue a certificate setting forth the fact that the corporation in question is presently in good standing within that state and has the legal authority and capacity to act. Keep in mind that corporations are peculiar instruments of the state. A corporation can lose its authority and ability to conduct business within the state if it does not comply with all of the local rules and laws of a particular state and pay on a regular basis all taxes due to that state. If the state in which the real property is located is different from the state of incorporation of the corporation, it then becomes necessary to go to the state of incorporation and obtain your certificate of good standing from the secretary of state of said state. In addition, another question arises: Does this foreign corporation have the authority and ability to operate within the state in which the real property is located, and must that corporation qualify to do business within the state where the real estate exists? As a general rule of law, foreign corporations are not permitted to engage in business activities within another state (that is, the state other than its state of incorporation) without having submitted itself to local jurisdiction of the state in question by qualifying to do business therein. Each state within the United States has its own set of laws and regulations as to what is necessary in order to own property within that state and what is required to qualify to do business within that state. An examination of the laws of each state is required in connection with a particular real estate transaction. In most states in the United States, it is not necessary for a foreign corporation to qualify to do business within that state *merely* to own a parcel of real property or to contract within that state for the sale or disposition of that property. Careful examination by local competent counsel can avoid many subsequent problems in this area. When dealing, however, with a corporation that is incorporated under the laws of a country outside of the United States, obtaining certificates of good standing can become more difficult. In fact in most foreign countries the concept of a certificate of good standing doesn't exist. The experience of this author has been, however, it will suffice to obtain a letter from a local magistrate or local counsel in the country of incorporation that the corporation is in fact in good standing and has complied with all of the local laws for its incorporation and maintenance.

All of the foregoing, however, deals only with the entity itself. How do we determine that the actual party signing on behalf of the entity has the authority to act? There is no foolproof answer to this question. With corporations that are formed in the United States, the authority to act on behalf of the corporation is vested in a board of directors, who in turn appoint officers to act on behalf of the corporation. In simplistic form, it works this way. The stock in the corporation is held by its shareholders. The shareholders in turn elect a board of directors, and the board of directors in turn elects officers to act for and on behalf of the corporation. In practice, the actual party signing can be a shareholder, director, and officer, all at the same time. The usual practice therefore, is to require the party signing on behalf of the corporation to present to you a certified resolution of the board of directors of the corporation in question appointing that party as an officer of the corporation, and in turn authorizing that officer by his sole signature to act on behalf of the corporation and to execute documents on its behalf. Whether or not the certified resolution (certified as true and correct and unamended by the secretary of the corporation) is a valid resolution, is an issue that cannot be finitely resolved. In some extreme cases, this author has recommended, in the case of closely held corporations with few shareholders, that signatures of officers who purport to bind the corporation be ratified and acknowledged by all the directors and shareholders of the corporation. In dealing with corporations formed outside of the United States, the concepts of boards of directors and officers may or may not exist. In many countries the corporation is run by the parties who have authority to sign, the managing directors. In those instances, it will normally suffice to obtain appropriate signatures from the managing directors and a representation letter from all of the managing directors, that the party signing has authority to act. When dealing with corporations, both those formed in the United States and those formed overseas, this author has found it very valuable to obtain opinions of counsel. An opinion of counsel is a representation letter addressed to you as buyer or seller, and signed by an attorney representing the corporation. In this letter the attorney states that in his legal opinion, after examining all of the relevant documents of the corporation, the corporation is in good standing and the party signing the agreement on behalf of the corporation has the due power, authority, and capacity to bind the corporation in reference to the purchase agreement in question. The use of opinion letters can be a very important method of avoiding future problems and of bringing potential problems out in the open.

Powers of Attorney

It is acceptable practice in the United States to authorize others to act on your behalf. This is commonly done by the use of an instrument known as a power of attorney. Powers of attorney can, in many instances, also be given by a corporation to an individual to act upon its behalf. Reference to Form 24 for a copy of a typical power of attorney used by an overseas corporation to appoint a U.S. representative to act on its behalf. Caution should be used, however, in dealing with powers of attorney. A power of attorney, to be valid in connection with a real property transaction, must be in writing and should be acknowledged. And if the party granting the power of attorney resides outside of the United States and executes the power of attorney in a foreign country, the power of attorney should be authenticated in front of the U.S. consulate office in the country of execution. Should the party granting the power of attorney die or become incapacitated, as a matter of general law in the United States, the power of attorney becomes void on the date of death or incapacity. When a person uses the power of attorney to act on behalf of another, the method of signing becomes critical. The power of attorney should be signed in a particular manner. As an example, suppose John Smith, residing in England, grants a power of attorney to Myron Meyers to act on his behalf. When Myron Meyers signs the agreement of sale on behalf of John Smith, the document should be signed in Myron Meyers' handwriting—"John Smith by Myron Meyers, his Attorney-in-Fact." The same rules apply if Myron Meyers is acting as the power of attorney for a foreign corporation. In such an event, the instrument should be signed "Real Acre, N.V. by Myron Meyers, its Power of Attorney". In most cases, when a power of attorney is being used, it will be necessary for it to be physically produced and recorded as part of the transaction that consummates the purchase and sale.

SUFFICIENT CONSIDERATION

Sufficient consideration is one of the elements of a valid contract for the purchase and sale of real property. This is a legal concept which should not be confused. Sufficient consideration merely means that there has been an exchange of mutual promises on behalf of a seller to sell and a buyer to buy. The question of sufficient consideration does not speak to the issue of whether or not the business transaction is a reasonable or fair one, and as a practical matter in almost all jurisdictions in the United States, in the absence of fraud or duress, the mere execution by a buyer and seller of an agreement to buy and sell meets the requirements of sufficient consideration.

METHODS OF HOLDING TITLE

There are various classical methods for holding title to real property in the United States that should be explored briefly. Title can be held in an individual name, in joint tenancy, as tenants in common, as community property, as a partnership or joint venture, as a corporation, or in trust. We will explore briefly each of the methods of holding title, with particular emphasis on how the method relates to the foreign investor.

Individual ownership

Of course, title can be taken to real property in the name of a specific individual. As an example, John Smith, a citizen and resident of England, desires to purchase a single-family residence in Los Angeles, California. Title to that residence can be taken in the name of John Smith. However, it is strongly recommended by this author that the foreign investor never take title in his own individual name unless this is part of a plan of emigration and ultimate residency in the United States. What happens if after John Smith takes title, he dies? What if John later desires to make a gift of this house to his children? Under the laws of almost every jurisdiction in the United States, it will be necessary, before Smith's heirs can acquire title to that property, that a probate estate be opened in the United States, within the state where the property is located. And proceedings for the probate must be processed by local counsel. In addition, inheritance taxes must be paid on the full value of the property. This problem can be effectively avoided by forming of an overseas corporation to hold title. In most instances, a corporation formed outside of the United

States permits the issuance of bearer shares in the corporation. Thus John Smith's death will not affect the ownership of real property or its passing by gift. The real estate will continue to be owned by the overseas corporation, and the bearer shares will pass to the successors or assigns of Mr. Smith. In the opinion of this author, no well-counseled foreign investor will hold title to real property in his own name. The foreign investor must also be aware of the U.S. gift tax laws. If property is given to another without consideration, even a family member, a gift tax will be due, and appropriate tax returns must be filed.

Joint tenancy and tenancy in common

Suppose John Smith is married to Mary Smith. John and Mary desire to take title to a particular parcel of real property together. There are two common methods in the United States for accomplishing this end: joint tenancy and tenancy in common. Suppose title to the property is taken in the name of John Smith and Mary Smith, husband and wife as joint tenants. The result of this method of holding title will be that upon the death of either John or Mary, 100 percent ownership of the property will pass to the survivor, whether or not there is a will and whether or not this is the intent of the parties. In most states, upon the death of John, it will be necessary that a probate estate be opened to process the transfer of title from John to Mary, and inheritance taxes will be due and payable as a result. Suppose title is taken to the parcel of property in the name of John Smith and Mary Smith as tenants in common. What happens when John dies? Title to the one-half interest in the property already in the name of Mary is unaffected, of course, by the death of John. The interest of John in the property will pass to his estate. If John has a will, then title to the property will pass in accordance with the will. If John dies without a will (intestate) then you must look to the laws of each local jurisdiction as to the passing of title to the half interest previously owned by John. Again, a probate estate must be opened, and inheritance taxes will be due and payable. In some states, the concept of community property also exists. By historical precedent, community property is a concept that exists primarily on the West Coast of the United States and in states bordering Mexico. If title to the property in question is taken in the name of John Smith and Mary Smith, as community property, then upon the death of John, whether or not title passes to his wife will depend on the laws of each local jurisdiction as to how it treats community property as assets. Again, this method of holding title is not recommended for the reasons set forth above.

Partnership and joint ventures

In most states in the United States, title to property can be taken in the name of a partnership, whether it be general or limited, or in the name of a joint venture. Technically, a joint venture is a partnership, and careful language in connection with vesting of title is imperative. Suppose there is a joint venture composed of A and B, and the name of the joint venture is Abco Development Company. It is not sufficient to take title in the name of Abco Development Company. Proper conveyancing techniques dictate that title should be taken in the name of "Abco Development Company, a joint venture composed of A and B."

Corporations

Title to real property can be vested in the name of a corporation, whether that corporation be local, foreign, or overseas. Again, caution should be exercised as to whether or not, as a condition to taking title to property, the corporation has to qualify to do business within a particular state. Reference to the local laws of each jurisdiction is imperative at this point. Again, keep in mind that many states in the United States have adopted laws restricting in one form or another the ownership by foreign corporations and non-U.S. citizens and residents of real property. Please see Appendix 1 for a summary of the laws of each state in the United States. However, be sure that you have checked with local counsel, since the summary and time factors contained in Appendix 1 may have been amended subsequent to the publication of this book.

Trusts and trustees

Suppose John Smith is the recorded legal owner of a parcel of real property, but John is in fact holding that property for the benefit of his brother, Sam Smith. What if John sells the property to an innocent bonafide buyer and refuses to give Sam the proceeds of the sale? Can Sam upset the sale? Assuming that John's buyer has no knowledge of the fact that John is holding title for Sam, Sam will be unsuccessful in his attempt to upset the sale. Sam, of course, has recourse to John for John's violation of his trust.

Suppose title to the property stands in the name of John Smith, trustee. How should a prospective buyer react? Whenever the term *trustee* appears, a buyer is put on notice that the record owner is acting for someone else. He should make a full investigation of John's status. He should obtain a copy of the trust agreement between John and Sam and satisfy himself that John has the capacity to sell and execute documents. He should submit the trust agreement to local counsel and to the proposed title insurer and obtain assurances that John can act. If any questions arise, the prospective buyer should require Sam to ratify and approve in writing all of the acts of John.

Thus, undisclosed trusts (as in the first example) present no problem to a bonafide innocent buyer. Where title is held in the name of John Smith, trustee or the Blank Bank as trustee of Trust Number 12345, a full evaluation must be made of the terms of the trust and the ability of the trustee to act on its behalf.

Finally, after going through our preacquisition checklist, after considering all of the matters that we have discussed thus far in the book, it is now time to pick up our pencil and make an offer to purchase real property. How do we go about this, and what are the standard procedures and practices involved in doing so? In most states in the United States, the use of standard form offers to purchase, or in California, the use of deposit receipts is the beginning, step. Forms 1 to 4 represent typical deposit receipts, and Forms 5, 6 and 7 typical escrow instructions. Of course, the practice of making an initial offer to purchase varies from state to state and in some cases from county to county. Most competent real estate brokers and local counsel can assist greatly in the preparation of the initial offer. This author cannot emphasize enough the requirement that the initial documents offering to purchase be drafted carefully and specifically. Put all the preacquisition checklist items in the initial agreement and thereby avoid the many pitfalls and problems previously discussed.

Do not allow your representative to make an offer in general terms and "clean the matter up" later on, either when the escrow documents are prepared or when a more formal contract is entered into. In almost all jurisdictions, if an *initial offer* is accepted, it becomes *at that moment,* a binding agreement of purchase and sale between the buyer and the seller. If there are inaccuracies in it or if matters are left to chance and not articulated, they are grounds for litigation. In almost all instances, litigation is counterproductive, expensive, and time-consuming and every step should be taken to attempt to avoid litigation by negotiating and dealing with all of the relevant issues before the buyer and the seller are inexorably bound to buy and sell. The question arises: How do I get a chance as a buyer to tie up a piece of property and have a reasonable opportunity to examine all of the various items that have been set forth on the preacquisition checklist? Experience has shown that the best approach is to make a carefully drawn offer which contains in its body all of the representations and warranties we have discussed and sufficient contingencies to give a reasonable opportunity to the buyer to carefully examine the property before he is committed to conclude a purchase. If a seller becomes reluctant to grant a reasonable time for the buyer to complete his investigation, my experience has been that a buyer should become extremely cautious and assume that there are hidden matters which the seller is trying to conceal from the potential purchaser.

Again, you can obtain preliminary title reports, and binder policies of title insurance which may assist you in your investigatory process and in concluding whether or not you should ultimately purchase a particular parcel of property. Refer to Form 7, Typical escrow instructions for a commercial property, which sets forth in its body a detailed checklist by implication of the matters to be examined in connection with the acquisition of a particular parcel of property.

CHOOSING THE ESCROW HOLDER AND THE BUYER AND SELLER REPRESENTATIVE

Whom you choose to act as escrow holder and whom you choose to be local counsel and representative for either the sale or acquisition of real property can be a problem of some vexation for the foreign investor. I recommend that you avoid the use of private escrow companies. In many cases, private escrow companies are subject to too much influence and control by local real estate brokers since they are dependent on brokers for their day-to-day business activity. I usually recommend a major bank or major title insurance company, or, in the case where local attorneys handle the transaction, counsel who has considerable experience in real property transactions. If you don't know any local attorney to act on your behalf, there is a convenient recognized publication known as *Martindale Hubbell References.* This is a publication sanctioned by the American Bar Association which lists on a state-by-state and city-by-city basis local attorneys who have been rated as to their proficiency and competence. It also contains a brief summary of each attorney's education and experience, and lists representative clients of a particular law firm or individual. This reference is available in any public library. Do not be lulled into a sense of false security. Do not be penny-wise and pound-foolish. The best money you can spend as a prospective buyer or prospective seller is on having the documents prepared by competent, knowledgeable representatives. The money that you will spend at the beginning, will pay great dividends to you in the future and avoid many of the pitfalls that have been implicit in the information set forth in this book to date.

CHOOSING AND DEALING WITH THE REAL ESTATE BROKER _____

To my knowledge, throughout the United States real estate brokers are required to be licensed under the laws of each state. Of course, the qualifications for a real estate broker, the licensing procedure, and the policing of real estate brokers varies materially from state to state. Further, in most jurisdictions in the United States, it is customary for the seller rather than the buyer to pay real estate brokers' commissions. This of course is not always true and is subject to negotiation. Further, the amount of money to be paid to a broker for commissions is in almost all instances a matter of negotiation between the parties. It is not subject to statute or limitation by case law. The seller or buyer should carefully negotiate with the real estate representative as to the amount of fees to be paid and when those fees are due and owing.

Whether or not a seller desires to grant to a particular real estate broker an exclusive listing is a matter of negotiation. In many instances, reputable real estate brokers will refuse to attempt to find a buyer for a particular parcel of property if they are not given a minimum period of time in which they have the exclusive and sole right to deal with that property. Caution should be used in signing an exclusive listing. Pursuant to its terms in most instances, a property is effectively taken off the market for the term of the listing period, and even if the seller himself should decide to sell the property during the period of the exclusive listing, he is obligated to pay a commission. Agreements with real estate brokers are matters of specific negotiation between the parties. There is an excellent publication in the *Continuing Education of the Bar* series dealing brokers in general and with the negotiation of brokers' agreements. Refer to Appendix 5 which gives a list of the relevant publications in this area. Remember that a real estate broker acting, on your behalf is *your agent*, whether you are a buyer or a seller. Thus all representations, warranties, and statements made by the real estate broker are imputed to you and you are bound them. It becomes, therefore, extremely important that you choose as your representative a reputable real estate broker with a proven track record who is if possible, a member of an organization that has financial stability and integrity. Should a problem arise in the future, he can pay damages for any misrepresentations or actions on your behalf. The broker's agreement should be negotiated and completed prior to the acceptance of any offer to buy or sell. Experience has shown that when it comes to larger commercial properties, the amount of commission is highly negotiable, and the method of payment of that commission is equally subject to negotiation. Don't believe it when the broker says "This is our standard form and the only one that we will sign" and, "This is the commission and it's only payable in cash". Each of these items is subject to negotiation. The question is often raised over where you should seek advice—the real estate broker or an attorney? The real estate broker should limit his advice to those matters dealing with the economics and terms of the real estate transaction. You should seek the advice of legal counsel for the drafting of all necessary documents that incorporate the issues that have been set forth in the preacquisition checklist. It has been said to this author on many occasions that whenever a lawyer gets into the picture, he complicates the transaction so that nothing ever gets done. This is not true. In fact when you seek real estate counsel from a knowledgeable and experienced attorney, he can be a catalyst in seeing that the deal is adequately and properly consummated.

The knowledgeable, reputable real estate broker should be cautious not to render legal advice. It exposes him to a great deal of potential liability. His stature can be enhanced by his recognizing the fact that his expertise is limited. Many cases in many jurisdictions hold that if a real estate broker in his exuberance to help the foreign investor renders advice on methods of holding title or other matters of a legal nature, he exposes himself to personal liability for what is in substance malpractice and/or for practicing law without being duly licensed. If you are a lawyer, making your *client* aware of the peculiarities of a foreign investor dealing within your particular state will enhance your stature with the foreign investor. He needs your help. He needs your counsel as a broker. Explain to him what an escrow is. Explain institutional financing and the other matters that have been discussed elsewhere in this book. You will find it will pay dividends in the long run. Tell the foreign investors, that there are many competent, reputable real estate brokers who can provide vital services to him. They have current knowledge of prices, conditions, and the marketplace, of the value of property, and the terms upon which it can be acquired, and the local market for obtaining institutional financing. In addition, many real estate brokerage firms have access to appraisal and current values of property within the area in which they practice and have access to multiple listing services of many other brokerage firms within the community which can supply you and your foreign investor with many alternative properties for acquisition and investment. Take advantage of these services that are readily available and in most instances free of charge. Choose your broker and your counsel carefully. It can pay you dividends and avoid many pitfalls.

METHODS OF RAISING CAPITAL FOR REAL ESTATE INVESTMENT BY THE FOREIGN INVESTOR (OR NOW THAT WE WANT TO BUY, WHERE DO WE GET THE MONEY?)

This chapter deals with methods of raising money for real estate transactions; explores methods of structuring a real estate transaction to limit or avoid raising money; describes participation by foreign investors in general and limited partnerships; explains the use by the foreign investor of domestic and foreign corporations in real estate transactions; explores sources of institutional funds and institutional lending practices; and concludes with brief comments on specialized sources of funds and projects. I have assumed at this stage of the game that the preacquisition checklist has been reviewed, that the property has been tied up by some method of purchase, either an escrow or an option, and we are now proceeding with methods of raising capital to complete the initial acquisition of the land and fund the venture. In addition, a brief review of institutional practices is also set forth. We will, of course, examine each of these topics in greater detail.

The best way to deal with the problem of raising capital is to avoid having to raise it in the first place. How do you avoid rasing money and still consummate your deal? To understand this principal and how it works, we must review various concepts and practices: (1) the concent of leverage—the use of other people's money; (2) seller financing of a portion of the purchase price; (3) the use of subordination; (4) the use of release clauses and its pitfalls; (5) long-term contingent escrows; (6) options and their use; (7) ground leasing with and without subordination; and (8) the use of partnerships, joint ventures and corporations as a financing vehicle. Let us turn now to a review of each concept.

LEVERAGE PRINCIPLES

As previously discussed in other chapters of this book, it has been historically possible in the United States to acquire a real estate property without the necessity of paying all cash for it. As further observed, this traditional concept of borrowing from established institutional sources and using the concept of seller financing and private syndications is changing rapidly. Due to inflation and changing economic and market conditions, more and more cash will be required in the future to acquire real estate projects. In addition, many of the established institutional lenders have become extremely aware of, and sensitive to, the inflationary spiral and are insisting that their loans have shorter maturity dates and interest adjustments to meet current interest conditions. Indeed, in many cases, lenders now insist on becoming active participants in the deal and thus share in the profits, equity, and appreciation of the project. Notwithstanding all of these concepts and economic conditions, the concept of leverage is still valid and is one of the most important concepts in dealing with real property. Leverage really means that you are purchasing a particular parcel for a stipulated sum of money and are able to account for that money either in cash from your own pocket or by borrowing a portion of the money from others. Let's use a simple example: Suppose you wish to purchase a single-family residence for a purchase price of $200,000. You could, of course, pay all cash for the property and avoid the necessity of borrowing anything. Assume, however, that you do not have $200,000 in cash or you wish to take advantage of the concept of leverage. In most instances, should you put down a 30 percent down payment (i.e., $60,000 in my example), you should be able to borrow, historically, from an existing established savings and loan association, savings bank, bank, or insurance company, $140,000, typically on monthly installments amortized over a 20- to 30-year period at a fixed or variable interest rate. This is using the concept of leverage. Expand this concept further. If you have $200,000 in cash to invest, wouldn't you be better off taking that money, and instead of buying one house for $200,000 cash, buying three houses using that same principal of 30 percent down and borrowing in each instance the balance of the purchase price? Why should you do this? If you subscribe to the concept that inflation is here to stay and that real estate will continue to rise in value at a sum equal to the current inflation rate, it makes more sense to take the same $200,000, buy three houses with it, occupy one, and lease out the other two. In the ordinary course of events, the value of the three parcels of property should rise at an average of 10 percent per annum, and you can enjoy the profits from all three houses. This simple concept of leverage has been the basis of amassing huge fortunes in real property in the United States over the last 25 or 30 years. Of course, when you borrow money, there is always a downside risk and exposure to loss of your capital. The concept of personal liability will be discussed at length in the next chapter. Again, the real estate broker and counselor representing the foreign investor should emphasize the concept of leverage. Keep in mind that most brokers and counselors are so aware of this concept of leverage that it is second nature to them. However, this is a strange, novel concept to most foreign investors. The broker and investment counselor must be aware of the fact that in most foreign countries, real property transactions are handled primarily on a cash basis only. If financing is available, it is generally at very high interest rates amortized over a very short period of time. Your advising the foreign investor that this source for purchasing property is available to him will enhance your stature as a broker and will be of material aid and comfort to the foreign investor. It will also, of course, increase your commissions. This leverage concept is even more important when you consider, particularly when dealing with residential property, that there is generally no personal liability imposed upon the foreign investor who borrows money. All of the money you can borrow today and pay back tomorrow with cheaper, inflated dollars should in most instances, enhance your profit margin in the long run. A word of caution at this point: whenever you are purchasing real property, it is essential that you have staying power. That is to say, real estate historically has been subject to cyclical fluctuations in the marketplace. Values go up and down, availability of financing changes from day to day, and laws are adopted that restrict or enhance real estate transactions and their marketability. The foreign investor should always have sufficient funds in reserve to carry institutional mortgages, to withstand the problems of vacancy, slow sales, and bankruptcy which will be discussed elsewhere in this book. You must be in a position to advance funds to a real estate project in bad times, whether those bad times be of a short or protracted nature. Again, as previously mentioned, the use of cash flow projections and cash flow analyses should aid you, the foreign investor, and your counselors in determining how extensively you wish to use this concept of leverage.

SELLER FINANCING

Contrary to established attitudes and practices in most foreign countries, sellers of real estate in the United States have been traditionally willing to finance on behalf of a buyer all or substantial portions of the purchase price. This American attitude should be emphasized and communicated carefully to foreign investors, as it is in most cases, a new concept alien to their thinking. The foreign investor and his counselor should also be aware of U.S. tax laws that, in some instances, encourage the seller to carry back a portion of the purchase price. The United States tax laws dealing with installment sales permit a seller of property to delay reporting the gain made from the sale of real property until the seller has, in fact, received the monies. This is an exception to the general rule of taxing gains in the United States and should be carefully understood by the foreign investor and his counselors. The tax laws dealing with installment sales have recently been amended and made more flexible. This concept creates a valuable negotiating tool that can be of use to the foreign investor and his advisors. Perhaps a simple example will help. Again, assume you wish to purchase a single-family residence of $200,000. Let's assume that there is an existing deed of trust against the property in favor of Friendly Savings and Loan Association in the sum of $100,000, which bears an interest rate of 9 percent per annum payable over 25 years, and further assume that there is no acceleration or due-on-sale clause in that existing deed of trust. Now assume that you wish to make a down payment of $60,000 as part of the purchase price. We still have $40,000 of the total purchase price to account for. It is not unusual for a seller of property in this typical transaction to agree to carry back a second deed of trust securing a promissory note in the sum of

$40,000 at a reasonable interest rate payable over a period of 5 to 10 years. It is possible to further entice a seller to carry back a portion of the purchase price by the use of an all-inclusive promissory note and deed of trust. Copies of a proposed typical form of all-inclusive or wraparound note and deed of trust are contained in Forms 20 and 21. As this book goes to press, the going rate for single-family residence mortgages exceeds 16 percent per annum, and a party who will deposit monies in a bank or savings and loan association can enjoy a short-term interest rate return on his capital of over 15 percent. Is there a method whereby you can entice a seller to carry back paper in light of these present economic conditions? If the sale was constructed in the following manner, it is likely that both the seller and buyer will gain. The purchase price again will be $200,000. The existing deed of trust of record in favor of Friendly Savings and Loan of $100,000 bearing interest at 9 percent remains. The down payment of $60,000 is the same. Instead of the seller taking back a $40,000 second deed of trust bearing interest at, let's say 13 percent, the buyer could offer the seller a transaction whereby the seller carries back an all-inclusive promissory note and deed of trust of $140,000, bearing interest at 11.5 percent per annum. What effect will that have on the seller? The seller will be enjoying a rate of return of 11.5 percent on the $40,000 of equity he has in the all-inclusive note and deed of trust, and an interest spread of 2.5 percent per annum on the difference between the existing note in favor of Friendly Savings and Loan and the interest rate set forth in the all-inclusive promissory note.

Thus, the effective yield to the seller on his $40,000 in equity that the seller is carrying back far exceeds the 15 percent he would otherwise customarily obtain. The buyer is acquiring the subject property with an effective interest rate lower than current market conditions will dictate. Both parties gain. It can readily be seen that the use of all-inclusive notes and deeds of trust can be an important concept in enticing the seller to engage in seller financing. Can the all-inclusive note and deed of trust be used as a basis to avoid an acceleration clause? Unfortunately, the answer is no. The transfer of title from the seller to the buyer is what triggers the due-on-sale or acceleration clause in the first place, and the use of this wraparound or all-inclusive concept will not avoid the problem. This author has found that the use of an all-inclusive note or deed of trust as a financing tool has been successful. It has been used effectively in larger commercial transactions. It is most effective when the seller is an older person who desires a steady income and who can absorb the interest for tax purposes.

SUBORDINATION AS A FINANCING TOOL

What is subordination? In simplest terms, subordination is the right of a buyer to place a new mortgage on property ahead of an existing deed of trust or mortgage of record. Perhaps this can best be illustrated by an example. Suppose you as a buyer desire to purchase from the seller a parcel of raw land upon which you intend to subsequently construct a 20-unit apartment building. Let's assume the purchase price for the property is $300,000. Let's assume further that your down payment for the property is $100,000, and the seller has agreed to carry back a $200,000 note secured by a first deed of trust on the property being purchased payable in equal monthly installments over a period of seven years including interest at 10 percent per annum. Let's assume: (1) you consummate your sale; (2) subsequently you hire an architect who prepares plans and specifications for the construction of this 20-unit apartment building; and (3) you obtain from Blank Bank a construction loan of $1 million. As a matter of practice, the bank will not permit you to record its loan and to use any of the construction proceeds until you can deliver to the bank a policy of title insurance which insures that the bank has a first lien upon the property free and clear of the $200,000 purchase money note and deed of trust carried back by the seller at the time you purchase the property. If, however, the seller has given you permission at the time of the original purchase to place a new loan on the property and permit that it be a new lien and charge upon the real estate superior to the $200,000 trust deed of the sellers, you will be able to complete your construction of the project without having to pay off the seller. The concept for obtaining this permission is called subordination. In order to have an effective subordination provision, it must be very carefully and specifically drawn. Further, it must be drafted and incorporated into the note and mortgage at the time that the initial offer to purchase is negotiated and at the time that the transaction for acquiring the raw land is initially consummated. The proper drafting of a subordination clause requires a great deal of technical skill and the intimate knowledge of the laws and requirements of the particular state and jurisdiction within which the property is located. The nature and sophistication of the subordination clause varies materially from state to state based upon the statutes and cases of each particular jurisdiction. There is attached to this book as Form 19 a deed of trust which contains a subordination provision. It is merely illustrative of the problem, and this author must caution you to obtain competent experienced legal counsel in the preparation of an enforceable subordination provision. Why would a seller be willing to grant you subordination? The best answer I can give is that it's a matter of negotiation and greed. As you are all probably aware, every parcel of real property is for sale at a different price depending, in most cases, on the terms of sale. If the sale is for all cash, you can generally acquire a parcel of real property cheaper than if you are buying property on very favorable terms. Thus, in most cases, if a seller agrees to subordinate, he is getting an increased purchase price for his property. Further, the argument is made that by constructing a 20-unit apartment build-ing on this property, the value of the property as a whole is substantially increased. And since the seller, after the completion of the project, will have a second mortgage on the property, his equity and thus the security value for his second deed of trust is enhanced by the construction of the improvements. It can be readily seen that the use of subordination is a sophisticated concept and, in many instances, frought with danger from the viewpoint of the seller. What happens if, during the course of construction, the purchaser of the property fails to complete the building or defaults in some manner on the construction loan in favor of Blank Bank? In such instance, the bank could foreclose upon the property and wipe out any equity that the seller would have in the second deed of trust. There are methods of limiting the seller's exposure by the use of construction bonds and other procedures that will be fully explored below. Merely because this concept is sophisticated don't be afraid to use it. Subordination can be a valuable tool for the foreign investor and his represent-ative and counselor.

THE USE OF RELEASE CLAUSES AS A FINANCING TOOL _____

What is a release clause? Simply stated, it's the agreement on the part of a holder of a mortgage or deed of trust to release his lien from a portion of the property upon payment of a stipulated sum of money but less than the entire balance due. This again can be best illustrated by an example. Suppose you as a buyer wish to purchase from seller a parcel of unimproved real property. Let's assume further that you intend to take this unimproved parcel of real property and subdivide it into two separate parcels (parcel A and parcel B). You intend to build upon parcel A a 20-unit apartment building and to sell off parcel B for cash. Let's also assume that the purchase price for the total parcel of real property which we will call Black Acre is $400,000. You are paying a down payment of $100,000 cash, and the seller has agreed to carry back a purchase money note secured by a first deed of trust on Black Acre of $300,000 payable in fixed principal and interest payments including interest at 10 percent per annum over a seven-year period of time. Without a release clause, you, as a buyer, must pay off the *entire* sum due on the seller's deed of trust *before* you can record a construction loan on parcel A. If the original deed of trust contained a provision that permitted you as buyer to release parcel A for $150,000, you could pay the seller $150,000 secured now only by parcel B. By use of the concept of a release clause, what has been accomplished? As a buyer, you have reduced your cash flow requirements by $150,000. You enable yourself to develop parcel A without the necessity of paying off the whole balance due to the seller.

There are many factors to consider in drafting a release clause. Let us explore the problem further:

Precise wording. To have a valid and enforceable release clause, the documents must precisely and carefully articulate exactly what portions of the property are to be released. By reviewing the language as drafted, a reasonable person must be able to define and describe the exact area to be released.

Lot split and subdivision. The property, when split, must not create an illegal lot split or illegal subdivision as those terms are defined by local law. Keep in mind that most lot split and subdivision laws cover not only lot division but financing arrangements also. The seller does not want to grant a release of parcel A, then have to foreclose on parcel B and end up with real property he can't use or resell.

Allocation of payments. What happens to the $150,000 paid to release Parcel A? Is it applied to the *next* payments due on the seller's note or the *last* payments due? The release clause should spell out how sums paid to release a parcel are allocated to future sums due to the seller.

Release ratios. How much should a buyer have to pay to a seller to release a portion of the property? Assume that the release clause divides Black Acre into 10 parcels rather than two parcels. Obviously, each of these 10 parcels may have different values. Some of the lots may front on a main street or have a better view. Allocation of value is a matter of negotiation. A buyer will want to release a parcel for as small a price as possible. In turn, a seller wants as much money as he can get and at the minimum a sufficient amount to be sure from an economic viewpoint that the buyer won't release the best lots and then abandon the rest.

Specific performance. If the release clause is not carefully drafted, the buyer will be unable to enforce its provisions by court action. This will result in forcing the buyer to pay off the entire obligation. This can be disastrous to a buyer. It can destroy his cash flow projections.

The use of a release clause is an important concept. It is also technical and sophisticated. It must be prepared by knowledgeable counsel aware of all local requirements. Don't let this scare you. It is a very effective tool used successfully by many investors.

CONTINGENT ESCROWS AS A FINANCING TOOL

We have discussed the issues to be reviewed in the preacquisition checklist chapters. These should be articulated in proper acquisition documents including escrow instructions. See Form 7 for a good example of this concept. What are some of the problems with escrow instructions or similar documents as financing tools?

Negotiation. A seller typically wants to know he has a deal. He does not want his property taken off the market for a long period of time and then find out that the buyer will not complete the purchase. A buyer, on the other hand, wants time to complete his investigation and arrange his financing and, in some cases, commence his predevelopment activities (i.e., zoning, subdivision, plans, etc.). These divergent goals can only be resolved by negotiation.

Title. How can a buyer be sure a seller has the ability to deliver clear title to the property to the buyer? What if the buyer enters into escrow and in reliance on it expends money and time for predevelopment activities? There is no foolproof answer. A buyer can obtain title searches and legal opinions, but these will not cover the problem of subsequent events. What if the seller dies? What if the seller encumbers the property? What if others attain the property for debts owed by the seller? These issues are difficult to resolve. It is possible to record the purchase agreement and take other steps, but they are not foolproof.

Liquidated damages. In many negotiations, a seller will insist on a penalty should the buyer fail to go through with the purchase. If a buyer defaults what are the seller's damages? If a seller defaults, what are the buyer's remedies? To answer these questions, we must look to the local laws of each state. As a general rule, however, subject to local law, a seller is entitled to damages on a buyer's default of the difference in value between the contract terms and the fair market value of the property. A seller can seek only money. A buyer on the other hand, can insist on both damages and specific performance. That is, the buyer can compel the seller to sell him the property by appropriate legal proceedings.

The actual determination of damages requires court action. This is expensive and time consuming. It can take several years in many jurisdictions for a matter to come to trial. In recognition of this fact, many sellers and buyers decide to agree in advance what their respective damages will be should a default occur. Such a provision is a liquidated damage clause. Each state has its own statutes and case law as to the enforceability of a liquidated damage clause and local counsel must be consulted. If properly prepared, such a provision is enforceable.

If the reader desires more information on escrows and damages, he should consult Appendix 5.

OPTIONS

What is an option? It is the right granted by an owner (optionor) to a prospective buyer (optionee) to purchase real property. The buyer is not obligated to buy but merely has the right to buy if he wants to. Why use an option? For generally a relatively small outlay of cash, a prospective purchaser can tie up real property. This gives the prospective buyer time to investigate, and often perform, preacquisition development activity. What are some of the issues in dealing with options?

1. *Drafting.* An option, to be enforceable by the optionee, must be precisely drafted. It must meet all of the requirements of a real estate contract we have previously discussed. The time and method of exercise must be precise. The term of the option must be definite and certain. Provisions for consumating the sale must be clear and precise.
2. *Title.* The optionee must be sure the optionor has good title and has the ability to consumate a sale. This problem can be solved by the buyer recording the option on a Memorandum of Option and obtaining title insurance.
3. *Application of Option Price.* Can the optionee apply the option price as a credit toward the purchase price and down payment if the optionee elects to buy? It's a matter of negotiation. This issue should be carefully articulated in the option agreement.

See Form 27 for a typical option. An option can be a useful tool. It is, however, a sophisticated document. To be of practical value, an option should carefully cover: (1) what is being purchased; (2) the exact economic terms of the purchase; (3) the option term; (4) the method of exercise; (5) the method of transferring title; (6) recordation and title insurance; and (7) allocation of the option price.

Experience has shown me that the option works if carefully drafted. It can also have beneficial tax benefits and give a prospective buyer the practical use of the property for little out of pocket expense. Use it where appropriate.

PARTNERSHIPS

Let us turn now to a new subject: The use of partnerships and joint ventures as financing tools. As the cost of real property increases and the cost of its development rises, it becomes necessary for parties to pool their capital and join together to acquire and/or develop real estate. Partnerships are very complex entities, and the relationship of the members is sensitive and important. Their use is frought with danger, but they are the wave of the future. In many circumstances, their use is the only practical way for the foreign investor to acquire an interest in a large real estate project. When local development, subdivision, or construction is contemplated, it is often the only practical way a foreign investor can participate.

We will review the partnerships and discuss various issues. Each partnership must be tailored to the specific facts of each transaction to meet the goals of each member. Knowledgeable counsel must be employed, and local law must be met. There are, however, basic issues common to most partnerships that we can explore.

Control.   We must, however, before dealing with specifics, set forth some general rules and principals that must be understood by the foreign investor and his advisors. In a general partnership, all of the partners have unlimited personal liability. You will recall that a general partnership, by definition, is a partnership in which there are two or more general partners and no limited partners. In a limited partnership, however, only the general partners, as distinguished from the limited partner-investors, have unlimited general liability. In a limited partnership, the limited partner-investor has no personal liability beyond the extent of his capital investment in the partnership. But in exchange for this the limited partner has no right to take an active part in the management or operation of the partnership and its affairs. Notwithstanding the form of the written documents, should a limited partner, actively engage in the management, control, and operation of the partnership business, he will become a general partner as a matter of law, and thus expose himself to personal liability for all the obligations of the partnership. Let's put these principles in the form of a simple example. A and B form a general partnership. A puts in 90 percent of the capital required, and B puts in 10 percent of the capital required. Both A and B have the right to act on behalf of the partnership and bind the partnership in every respect notwithstanding their disproportionate capitalization and ownership of the partnership. Both A and B are equally liable to third parties for all debts and obligations incurred in the partnership name. Suppose A and B form a limited partnership in which A is the limited partner and puts up 90 percent of the money and B is the general partner and puts up 10 percent of the money. A can take no active part in the management and operation of the partnership. The sole ability to bind and cause the partnership to act is vested in B. If obligations are incurred in the name of the partnership, B has personal liability, and A's liability is limited to the extent of A's capital investment in the partnership. If A exercises management or control of the partnership and its affairs, A will become a general partner. Another important concept must be understood. When you invest and become a partner in a partnership you do not, in fact, own or have an undivided right to the *real property* owned by the partnership. Thus, if a general or limited partnership is formed and the ratio of investment is 90 percent and 10 percent as set forth in the above example, neither A nor B, whether he be a general or limited partner, is entitled to 90 percent or 10 percent of the real property owned by the partnership. The only right that a partner has in a partnership is to participate in its profits and losses and to acquire on dissolution of the partnership an interest in the property in question. This can become an important issue in the event of default of a partner; a dispute between partners; or death of a partner, and the rights of partnership creditors.

Disclosure. Another important concept that must be considered is the concept of disclosure and fiduciary obligation. A general partner is considered a fiduciary. That is to say, a general partner has an absolute obligation to all of the other partners, both general and limited, to make a full, complete, and absolute disclosure of all activities involving the partnership, its acquisition of property, and all matters dealing with the partnership and the property. Thus, if a general partner of a limited partnership is selling property to the partnership, that general partner must make a full, complete, and absolute disclosure of the property being sold, what he paid for the property, and whether or not he is making a profit or gaining any other advantage or benefit from dealing with the partnership. If the general partner is obtaining any commissions, fees, or salaries in connection with the affairs of the partnership, or if the general partner is a contractor and is performing any services for the partnership, these services must be rendered at competitive rates and after a full disclosure of all profits being made by said general partner in dealing with the partnership. Should the general partner fail to make this full and adequate disclosure and act in a fiduciary capacity with the partnership and its partners, he exposes himself to personal liability and to the obligation to repay to the partnership all of the profits and benefits derived from his dealings.

This concept of fiduciary obligation and full disclosure is one that must be carefully understood by the foreign investor and his counselors, and is a basic principle of U.S. partnership law. In the experience of this author, a lot of litigation has been generated from a failure of partners to deal openly and in a forthright manner with each other and to make full and adequate disclosure. Consultation with experts is recommended in this area, and careful drafting of the instrument is essential. A partnership creates a personal relationship. If partners cannot get along, the law will not require these partners to remain together as partners even though the partnership agreement may state otherwise. As a matter of law, any partnership can be dissolved and terminated and the assets distributed or sold if any of the partners do not wish the partnership to continue. This is true even though by the express terms of the partnership agreement, the partners are obligated to remain as partners for a stipulated period of time. This rule of law can sometimes cause difficult problems and adverse tax consequences and must be explored and understood carefully by the foreign investor and his domestic advisors. Should the real estate broker or local U.S. resident or developer desire to create a partnership relationship with the foreign investor, he must become conspicuously aware of his fiduciary duties and obligations, and of the risk and liability he is assuming. This information should be carefully communicated to both the foreign participant and his local associate. The foreign investor is not immune from attack. Even if the laws of a foreign country do not require full disclosure, if the foreign investor brings in other foreign associates and forms an American partnership, he exposes himself to potential liability.

Loss of tax exemption. Prior to the adoption of the Foreign Investment in Real Property Tax Act of 1980, the foreign investor enjoyed substantial tax benefits unavailable to U.S. residents and citizens. If the foreign investor was not engaged in trade or business in the United States as that term was defined by the statutes and regulations of the Internal Revenue Code, gains from the sale of an interest in real property were exempt from federal taxation, if properly documented and conceived. However, participation by a foreign investor as a limited partner in a U.S. limited partnership was not a kind of passive investment anticipated by the revenue code. It resulted in the foreign investor being engaged in trade or business in the United States even though, as a matter of law, the foreign investor had no say in the operation and management of the partnership since he was a limited partner. This concept becomes less important under the terms of the new Foreign Investment in Real Estate Tax Act and will be discussed further in a subsequent chapter.

Protection of capital and loss of control. It becomes obvious that when a foreign investor becomes a limited partner in a U.S. limited partnership, he loses control of the operation and management of the entity and is forced to rely very heavily upon the personal and financial integrity of the general partner or general partners. This concept should not be lost to the foreign investor and should be emphasized by his investment counselor in counseling and advising the foreign investor to participate in a limited partnership. The problem becomes even more complex when the intended purpose of the limited partnership is the development of raw land or involves construction of future improvements. Construction, financing, and lending practices will be discussed elsewhere in this chapter. There is, as in many areas of the law, an exception to the concept just discussed. In some jurisdictions, by virtue of local amendments to the Uniform Limited Partnership Act, limited partners can be given certain essential rights in dealing with management and operation of the partnership that will give them some built-in safeguards without, in turn, making them a general partner. In many states, *before* a general partner can sell or encumber substantially all the assets of a partnership, he must obtain the written consent and approval of the limited partners. This exception is particularly advantageous to a typical real estate project that involves the acquisition of one parcel of property, and contemplates its subsequent development for a particular purpose. The requirement of having the limited partner approve both financing and/or sale gives to the limited partner the effective ultimate control of the type of development to be constructed and its ultimate disposition. The limited partner-investor is cautioned to carefully explore the laws of the state in which the partnership agreement is formed to see if he can take advantage of these particular special rights without thereby becoming a general partner. Again, many general partners in the experience of this author have been reluctant to communicate to a limited partner investor that these special rights and privileges are available to him because they wish to maintain absolute control of the venture. The limited-partner investor should not be reluctant to explore these areas and insist that his ultimate rights be protected if at all possible.

Salaries and expenses. There should be built into every partnership agreement involving the foreign investor (who in most instances is not available in the United States on a day-to-day basis), provisions to protect the foreign investor from excessive expenses incurred on behalf of the partnership. Salaries should be limited. Overhead expenses, entertainment, and general office expenses should be expressly limited and/or eliminated depending on the circumstances. If the general partner is also a real estate broker or general contractor, the fees, charges, and expenses to be enjoyed by the general partner should be carefully and specifically delineated. The limited partner-investor should not be reluctant to raise these issues with any legitimate general partner or coventurer.

Government regulations—public versus private offering. A foreign investor must be aware of a substantial body of law that exists on a federal level, and in many instances on a state level, relating to raising money in connection with a general or limited partnership. Essentially, the law provides that any offering to participate as a limited or general partner in a limited partnership that is classified as a public offering requires a permit from either the federal government or from a particular state therein. The question then arises as to what is a *public offering.* There have been volumes written on the question of public versus private offering, and there is a large body of case law dealing with this issue. For the purposes of this book, the limited partner/foreign investor and his advisors must be aware of this concept. In most instances, a request to participate as a partner in a general or limited partnership will not be a public offering requiring registration and permits if all of the partners are known to each other, all of the partners are sophisticated and are able to understand the nature of the investment they are making, and there is a preexisting relationship between all of the partners in the partnership. Some states have adopted specific statutes and regulations in defining a public or private offering. As an example, in California the regulations provide in substance that if: (a) an offer is made to not more than 25 people; (b) and the ultimate participants in the transaction are not more than 10 in number; (c) and all of these participants are sophisticated business people and have a preexisting relationship with the general partner, then it is presumed that the offering is private in nature not requiring a permit. This presumption, however, is only a preliminary or rebuttable presumption. Thus, should a general partner place an ad in the local newspaper advertising for one investor and consummate a deal after one telephone call from one investor, such an offering would in all probability be a public offering requiring a permit. What is the danger in this area? First, if an offering is determined to be a public offering, the general partner (i.e., the offering party) exposes himself to personal liability and becomes in substance a guarantor of the investment of the limited partner. He may further subject himself in many instances to criminal and civil prosecution for having violated securities regulations of the federal government or of a particular state. If the foreign investor intends to become a promoter and solicits other foreign investors to participate in a U.S. real estate transaction, he is cautioned strongly to obtain the advice and counsel of competent local lawyers who are familiar with laws relating to public and private offerings of this type. He must also be sure that he has qualified for all of the proper exemptions from a public offering. The risk of violating these sections is substantial. In addition, these issues are tested with the value of hindsight since the problem generally only arises when a project gets in trouble—when an investor is about to lose his money, and he is looking for a scapegoat. Again, this is a two-edged sword. Real estate brokers who intend to put together syndications involving foreign investors are cautioned to avoid a violation of the federal and state regulations and statutes relating to public or private issuance of securities. This is a trap for the unwary and can expose the broker to substantial personal liability as well as loss of his professional license.

Restrictions on transfer. There is a general rule of law applicable in the tax field. In substance it states that if a partnership agreement has all of the indicia of a corporation such as central management, continuation after death, and free transferability of shares, it may be treated for tax purposes as if it were a corporation and not a partnership. The Internal Revenue Service is not bound by the form of a partnership agreement, but can look to its substance in evaluating it for tax purposes. This can have disastrous effects on the limited as well as the general partners, and must be avoided. Because of these rules and other practical aspects of limited partnerships, most limited partnership agreements provide for a limitation on the free transferability by a limited or general partner of his interest in the partnership. In the case of a general partner, most partnerships are formed with a strong reliance upon the acumen, integrity, financial stability, and continuation of active participation by the general partner in the business partnership. It is thus essential in most limited partnerships that the original general partner remain as general partner and that he have no ability to transfer or assign his interest in the partnership during its existence. Such provisions can and should be drafted into the body of the limited partnership agreement. The situation is often different with limited partners. They are generally passive investors having put up only a specific sum of money, who take no part in the operation or management of the business. Should a limited partner be permitted to transfer interest in the partnership without the knowledge or consent of the other partners? For tax reasons, obviously no. For practical reasons, it depends on the nature of the partnership. If the partnership requires, per its terms, *additional* contributions from the partners, qualifying the transferee of the limited partnership interest may be essential to be sure that the additional funds are available when needed. In most limited partnership agreements, the question of transferability of the partners is covered by careful documentation. (For example see Forms 11A, 11B, 11C and 12). In substance, most of these provisions provide that before there can be a transfer of a limited partnership interest, this interest must be first offered to all of the other existing limited partners in the partnership who have a right to buy out the limited partner on the same terms and conditions as he is offering to sell his interest to a stranger. In specific circumstances, a more restrictive limitation or transfer may be in order. Consult your local counsel. Keep in mind another concept. Unless there is an expressed prohibition in an agreement, any partner has a right to transfer and assign his interest in a partnership as a matter of general law.

Future Contributions. Many limited or general partnerships are formed anticipating an initial downpayment to acquire a parcel of real property and expecting that subsequent payments will be needed to meet mortgage requirements and/or to cause improvements to be constructed on the property. Adequate provisions must be drafted into the partnership agreement to provide for these additional contributions and, equally important, to cover the situation where a partner obligates himself to put up additional capital but upon being told to do so, fails to perform. There are many different ways to deal with the issue. The best that can be said at this point is that the issue should be carefully explored and drafted into the partnership agreement. There is no foolproof method to solve the problem. Keep in mind that it is an essential element of U.S. law that excessive penalties and forfeitures cannot be placed upon a party for failure to meet his contractual obligations even those of putting up additional money. Thus, a provision that a partner will forfeit all of his initial capital upon failure to make subsequent capital contributions in all probability is not enforceable under the law in most states. Choose your partners carefully. Be sure they have the financial ability to perform. Disastrous economic consequences can arise when partners fail to meet their financial commitments.

Death or disability of the general partner. In most instances, the death or disability of a general partner will cause a dissolution of the partnership as a matter of law. If the partners desire, the agreement can deal with this issue and provide that the partnership will not be dissolved in the event of death or disability (whether physical or economic) of the general partner. You can provide that a new general partner will be elected. Can the limited partners remove a general partner? It depends on the terms of the agreement and local law. In most states, granting the power to the limited partners to remove a general partner is permitted. This raises many issues relating to compensation of the new and old general partners. Competent counsel can assist in drafting appropriate provisions. Practice preventive law here, deal with these issues at the beginning, and avoid substantive problems and litigation later.

It can be readily seen from this brief discussion of partnerships that they are complex documents. They require careful thinking and careful draftsmanship. Don't be lulled into a sense of false security by merely signing that form in front of you, if you are the foreign investor. Insist upon these issues being covered. Obtain adequate, experienced local counsel to prepare and review the terms and provisions of these instruments on your behalf. In the experience of this author, it will be money well spent and can be the basis for avoiding a great number of potential future pitfalls. Do not be afraid to use the limited partnership, general partnership, or joint venture as vehicles to purchase or participate in the ownership of the real property. They are accepted, viable, practical tools that have many advantages if used properly. Use and understand them. They can pay great dividends for the foreign investor, general partner, or real estate broker or counselor.

CORPORATIONS

Let's turn now to another topic: using or participating in a domestic or foreign corporation. We will try to explore briefly the use of foreign and domestic corporations either as a single entity to purchase property, as an entity by itself to purchase property, or as an entity that can participate as a general or limited partner in the partnership or joint venture. How are these corporations formed? How much time does it take? What is the cost? What are the annual maintenance fees? How do you maintain control? Are there any restrictions on the transfer of stock? What happens if shareholders die? How do you handle the raising of additional funds? How do we deal with the question of public versus private offerings? Can you use bearer shares, private trusts, or other methods of dealing with problems of death and anonymity preservation? We will explore each of these areas further.

Forming domestic U.S. Corporations.　The process of forming domestic U.S. corporations in most states in the United States is relatively simple. To the knowledge of this author, there are no restrictions on foreigners owning stock in a U.S. domestic corporation. Refer to Forms 13A, 13B and 13C for a typical set of corporate documents for the formation of a U.S. domestic corporation. Domestic corporations formed within a particular state where no public offering or multiple classes of stock are involved can generally be formed in a matter of days at relatively nominal costs in most jurisdictions in the United States. In most states, stock in the corporation can be issued directly to the shareholders without the necessity of special permissions or permits from any state or federal agency. In some jurisdictions, however, the issuance of stock requires a permit or qualifying exemption from a local state corporations commission or agency. Again, as previously mentioned, the control of United States domestic corporations lies in a board of directors which is controlled by the corporation's shareholders. The board of directors, in turn, appoints officers to act for, and on behalf of, the corporation. In almost all jurisdictions, a U.S. domestic corporation can exist with only one officer and one director. The annual cost of maintaining a local corporation in most jurisdictions is also nominal. There is usually a minimum requirement for holding at least annual meetings of the board of directors and of the shareholders and for filing annual corporate tax returns and informational statements with the appropriate state authorities. The formation of overseas corporations, of course, varies materially with the country involved. Generally, if the foreign overseas jurisdiction has developed an internal policy and industry for the formation of corporations, such as the Cayman Islands and Netherlands Antilles, the formation and maintenance of these corporations is also relatively quick and inexpensive. Refer to Form 29 for typical incorporation documents for a Cayman Island Corporation and Form 22 for typical articles of incorporation of a Netherlands Antilles corporation. In almost all instances in overseas corporations, there are established companies and local counsel who specialize in representing the foreign investor and who can cause the corporations to be formed, hold the annual meetings, and prepare the necessary documents without the necessity of the foreign investor or his advisor ever being present in the country of incorporation. Officers and managing directors as the case may be, will be appointed by a local representative in the country of incorporation. It has been the experience of this author that the representatives in the foreign country are most trustworthy and competent and are generally affiliated or have associations with counsel in other jurisdictions and with major banks and financial institutions. These countries depend heavily on maintaining their integrity and secrecy and are very reliable. If the entity is sophisiticated, has multiple classes of stock, or needs to deal with special requirements of the shareholders, the cost of formation will increase, the time factors will expand, and presence in the county of incorporation will be required.

The maintenance of control. Domestic U.S. Corporations are controlled ultimately by the shareholders. It is not possible to issue bearer shares in domestic U.S. corporations. The issuee of all shares must be a specific individual, corporation, or other recognizable entity. This is not true in many foreign countries where bearer shares are permitted. Of course, you must consult with local counsel to determine the particular laws of each individual jurisdiction. The holder of shares, therefore, in a domestic U.S. corporation votes for the appointment of the board of directors who in turn appoints the officers, who in turn carry out the policies of the corporation. The same general rule is true in foreign corporations although the mechanics may be a little different. The shareholders elect the managing directors who in turn perform services on behalf of the corporation. These managing directors can be changed at any time or the structure of the corporation can be in such form as to require the consent of a certain managing director known specifically to the foreign investor before any action can be taken on behalf of the corporation.

In most instances, when dealing with corporations formed outside the United States, it is not necessary that a bank account for the corporation be opened or maintained in the country of incorporation. Thus, as an example, a corporation can be formed in the Netherlands Antilles, but all bank accounts relating to the Antilles corporation can be maintained within a state in the United States or anywhere else in the world that is convenient for the foreign investor. The signature and control of the funds can be vested in such persons as the foreign investor shall designate. For day-to-day operations of the entity, powers of attorney may be used to designate a representative to act on behalf of the foreign corporation. Refer to Form 24 for a copy of a typical broad form power of attorney. Caution should be exercised in the use of this form or one of a similar nature since it gives to the holder very broad powers to act on behalf of the corporation. A power of attorney may, of course, be drawn for a limited period of time and may be restricted in such manner as fits the particular circumstances. In dealing with domestic U.S. corporations, it is not customary to use powers of attorney. The local U.S. representative is generally designated as an officer of the corporation or as an authorized agent of the corporation and may act on its behalf. In this instance, resolutions of the board of directors are enacted setting forth the scope or limit on the authority of the officer or authorized representative.

Restrictions on transfer—death. In most states in the United States when stock is issued in a privately held, closed domestic U.S. corporation with one class of stock, once the stock is issued, there are no restrictions on the subsequent transfer of stock certificate. This is not true in the state of California and other states that have a more sophisticated corporate regulatory system. The foreign investor is urged to seek advice of local counsel as to a particular law in each jurisdiction. In this regard, it is possible to do some shopping for the place of local incorporation. In various states in the United States there are different rules and regulations regarding the initial formation and maintenance of a closely held corporation. In some jurisdictions, permits are required, minimum amounts are required to be paid annually for local corporate taxes, and the tax rate on corporations varies materially from state to state. Some states in the United States have particularly designed their laws to encourage local incorporation. A careful examination of the laws of each state should be made before a decision is reached in many instances.

In contrast, foreign corporations, that is, those corporations formed outside of the United States, are generally very liberal and place little or no restriction on the transferability of shares. In fact they permit the issuance of bearer shares which really require physical transfer to effect a change of ownership or control. What happens in a U.S. domestic corporation if the shareholder of record dies? The stock passes to his estate. It will be necessary for a probate proceeding to be opened up to transfer the shares to his lawful heirs, and inheritance taxes must be paid. This, of course, does not happen where there are bearer shares, for obvious reasons. It is often customary in forming closely held U.S. corporations for the shareholders to enter into agreements restricting transfer of shares or granting first refusal rights to other shareholders.

Capitalization and raising of additional funds.   In the case of most U.S. domestic corporations, there are no minimum capital requirements to initially form the corporation. This is not generally true in relation to foreign corporations where a certain minimum sum for initial capitalization is a condition for the valid formation of the corporation. As an example, presently in the Netherlands Antilles, as a matter of practice, the minimum capitalization is $6,000 (U.S. money). Though there is no requirement of minimum capitalization in most U.S. corporations, caution should be used in connection with undercapitalization. There is a large body of law dealing with this issue. Should the corporation be inadequately capitalized, substantial questions can arise as to whether or not the officers and shareholders of the corporation have personal liability for the debts and obligations of the corporation. In addition, from a tax-planning viewpoint, undercapitalization can often result in adverse tax consequences for the entity and its shareholders. Time does not permit a detailed discussion of this issue. In most domestic U.S. corporations if additional capital is required for the corporation, that capital can generally be raised by the issuance of additional shares of corporation stock or by loans from the shareholders to the corporation, or a combination of both. Caution again must be used in this area. Should loans be made to the corporation by the individual shareholders, an obligation to withhold up to 30 percent of all interest paid on the loans by foreigners to the corporation may be required. As stated above, the issuance of additional shares in some jurisdictions requires filing for and obtaining a permit from the local state department of corporations.

Anonymity.   Prior to the adoption of the Foreign Real Estate Tax Act of 1980, it was a relatively simple procedure for a foreign investor to maintain complete anonymity. Secrecy laws of most tax-haven jurisdictions, such as the Cayman Islands and the Netherlands Antilles, prevented the United States government or any other party from determining who the true, ultimate owners of a corporation were. This whole problem has been materially changed by the adoption of the new act and other disclosure requirements adopted by the U.S. government. This area is explored in Appendix 7. In addition, refer to Appendix 3 which contains copies of the forms required with a schedule of examples. The problems of anonymity have become vexing and complex. At the time this book goes to press, many of the regulations anticipated under the new act have not yet been promulgated, and there are many unanswered issues in this area. Should the foreign investor be particularly sensitive on the question of anonymity, it is suggested that he contact counsel who has expertise and experience in dealing in this area and consider the various alternatives. In an extreme case, it may be possible to post bonds or other collateral to avoid disclosure.

In the opinion of this author, a foreign investor should, in almost all instances, never take title in his own name. He should take title in the name of a domestic corporation, or in most cases, a corporation formed under the laws of a country other than the United States. There are still substantial tax advantages to this. And it is a practical method to transfer shares and avoid probate. The use of domestic corporations and foreign corporations will become more obvious as the reader explores the new tax act and the chapters and examples relating to tax planning. Refer again to Appendix 4 relating to Netherlands Antilles corporations. Should the reader desire further information concerning a corporation, there are some excellent texts, referred to in Appendix 5 published by the *Continuing Education of the Bar.*

SOURCES OF FUNDS AND INSTITUTIONAL PRACTICES

Let us turn now to the question of sources of institutional funds and institutional practices. Of course, many volumes have been written concerning this subject. In a book of this type, where basic concepts are merely outlined and highlighted, it is not possible to go into a detailed discussion concerning the sources, rules, regulations, and practices of U.S. financial institutions engaged primarily in real estate funding and financing. The reader is directed again to Appendix 5 where there are listed several excellent publications promulgated by the *Continuing Education of the Bar* series dealing in detail in this matter. In addition, refer to Forms 15A, 15B, 16, and 18 dealing with typical notes and deeds of trust with a fixed interest rate and a variable interest rate which may be of interest to the foreign investor. In this section, we will attempt to explore: (1) basic sources for obtaining institutional funds; (2) the practice and use of mortgage bankers and loan brokers; (3) the concept of take-out commitments, (4) loan limitations; (5) interim and permanent financing arrangements; (6) the use of overseas lenders; (7) the effect of lack of local credit and financial history upon the ability of the foreign investor to deal with established institutional lenders; (8) the use of professional appraisers and loan packages; and (9) some brief comments concerning negotiations with lenders. Let us now review these specific topics in more detail.

Before we get to detailed discussions, an observation is necessary for the foreign investor and particularly for the real estate broker, attorney, accountant, or other party who is counseling the foreign investor. Some education of the foreign investor is imperative at this point. In most cases, a sophisticated real estate broker, attorney, or accountant takes for granted the existence of banks, savings and loan associations, insurance companies, savings banks, and pension funds as well as various governmental agencies and programs that make readily available access to long-term or interim real estate funds. Such phenomena are peculiar to the United States. They don't exist in most foreign countries. Advising the foreign investor of these sources of money, of the established institutions such as mortgage bankers, loan brokers, and lender correspondents will materially aid the foreign investor in analyzing his potential investment and in having before him all of the various tools and alternatives needed to make intelligent and successful long-term real estate commitments and investments in the United States. Take the time to examine these areas, explain them to the foreign investor, and deal with the mechanics thereof at a level that the foreign investor can understand. A word of caution, however: the established institutional sources of funds in the experience of this author are changing rapidly. It has been the practice for many years for institutional lenders to make available long-term mortgages secured by real estate at fixed interest rates and amortized over a period of 20 to 30 years. Though a great amount of money is still available on these terms, the marketplace is changing rapidly. Institutional lenders are no longer so willing to grant fixed-interest, 30-year loans. They are changing their lending criteria to granting loans with a 20- or 30-year amortization, requiring that the loan be callable by the lender at the end of the 5th to the 10th year. This, in substance, gives the lender the opportunity to renegotiate the interest rate consistent with then current market conditions. It also creates additional risks and burdens for the borrower. Further, the institutional lenders are becoming more aggressive in enforcing due-on-sale provisions. In addition, institutional lenders, in many instances, insist upon participation in one form or another. As the projects become larger and more sophisticated and as the lenders become more and more aware of the inflationary spiral and changing market conditions on interest rates, they are becoming more aggressive in insisting on participating in the profits derived from a particular project.

Institutional sources.   Traditionally, monies needed to finance real estate projects on a permanent basis, (as distinguished from interim financing which will be discussed below), from life insurance companies, commercial banks, savings banks, savings and loan associations, pension funds, profit sharing funds, (both public and private) and various governmental agencies have been the sources for institutional funding. How do you reach these various sources? When dealing traditionally with banks and savings and loan associations, in most cases, direct contact with the local bank or savings and loan association or a local branch is a sufficient beginning point. You will be directed from a local branch to the main headquarters or to the real estate section in most instances. Insurance companies and major pension funds generally maintain local correspondents either through the use of mortgage bankers or through established loan brokerage agencies. Most of the major insurance companies and major pension funds are located in the eastern portion of the United States. If necessary, they establish local representatives in each state or portion of a state to act on their behalf.

Mortgage bankers, loan brokers, and correspondents. Established institutional lending practices in the United States necessitate the use of local representatives. Since it would be impractical for a major life insurance company to maintain a full staff of agents, appraisers, and technical staff in each major metropolitan area, most of the major life insurance companies and many of the major banks and major pension funds deal through mortgage bankers or loan correspondents. These are generally local, privately owned companies (or in some cases, bank affiliates) who have established relationships with a number of insurance companies, pension funds, and banks. They are generally fully aware of market conditions, the sources of funds, current interest rates, and the current criteria established by the institutional lenders for a particular project. Generally, the mortgage banker or loan correspondent charges a fee for its services which is usually payable only in the event that the correspondent is successful in negotiating a loan on terms mutually acceptable to you as a borrower and the ultimate lender. The use of established mortgage bankers is a very efficacious tool in obtaining financing. Caution, however, should be used in this area. Unfortunately, there are a number of loan correspondents floating around who have no real established relationships with lenders but will merely take your information and shop it all over town. In many cases, they will demand a fee from you in advance. Choose your mortgage banker or loan correspondent, with the same degree of care you use to select a real estate broker, attorney, accountant, or other professional counselor. In negotiating your agreement for a loan commitment with the mortgage banker or correspondent, be careful that you and your counsel review the form and content of the initial engagement agreement. Caution should be used in limiting the authority of the mortgage banker. You, as borrower, should not agree to sign any documents in advance that the lender might put in front of you. Do not agree to pay without limitation all counsel fees, appraisal fees, and other costs and charges that may be required by the ultimate institutional lender. It is customary that all counsel fees, appraisal fees, and other similar charges incurred by the lender be borne by the borrower. The amount of these fees, charges, and expenses should be delineated and limited at the beginning of the negotiations. The borrower must reserve the right to approve the form and substance of all instruments that will be required by the lender before he is obligated to pay fees and charges. As a general rule, the institutional lender will require the payment of certain fees for the privilege of issuing its commitment to make the loan, and the mortgage banker or correspondent will also require the payment of certain fees or charges when he has secured the commitment. In some instances, the mortgage banker or correspondent will require certain funds to be posted as a showing of good faith and economic ability to perform on the part of the potential borrower. Should the lender require those funds, they should be clearly segregated in a trust account, subject to immediate refund and, if possible, be interest-bearing during the period of the length of the agreement entered into between you as borrower and the mortgage banker or correspondent. Again, be cautious in this area. There are a number of smaller or marginal correspondents and loan brokers who will insist on funds being paid to them in advance with no practical assurance on your part that you can have the funds returned to you if the broker is unsuccessful. Each major city or metropolitan area within the United States has established mortgage bankers and loan correspondents whose integrity and track record can be easily checked out through local banking sources or through the use of knowledgeable, sophisticated real estate counsel. In addition, in most states there are established trade associations of mortgage bankers who can easily verify the integrity of the party with whom you propose to do business. Take the time to read the contract and agreement submitted to you by the mortgage banker. Carefully negotiate all of its terms at the beginning of the relationship. Also, be careful to listen to the mortgage banker's recommendations for preparing the financial package for submission to the lender. They can be of great assistance to you in obtaining the type of institutional financing required by your transaction. Traditionally, savings and loan associations, particularly those on the local level, have not availed themselves of the services of the mortgage banker or loan correspondent. Most local savings and loan associations maintain their own lending departments, and you can, in many instances, avoid the additional fees and charges of a mortgage banker or loan correspondent by dealing directly with the savings and loan association. This, of course, is not always true, and a careful examination of local sources and customs is highly recommended. In the experience of this author, the fees and charges paid to a reputable mortgage banker or loan correspondent are money well spent. It can result in a significant saving of time as well as obtaining the best financing available in light of current market conditions.

Take-out commitments. What is a take-out commitment, how is it used, and what are the pitfalls? As mentioned in a previous chapter, traditionally, life insurance companies and pension funds will not get involved in construction financing. This class of lender desires to place permanent loans on a particular project only when all of the contemplated improvements have been fully completed. However, when a potential borrower/developer desires to obtain the funds for constructing a project, he generally seeks the aid of a local commercial bank. This commercial bank is usually only in the business of making temporary loans that mature on completion of construction. The bank desires to have a source of money to pay off its interim construction loan when the project is complete; that is to say, the bank wants to have an established source for it to be "taken out" of this loan upon completion of construction. Thus, the genesis of the term *take-out commitment*. In substance, a take-out commitment is a contractual obligation on the part of a permanent lender, generally a major bank, insurance company, or pension fund, to agree to grant to a borrower a permanent loan, amortizable over a fixed number of years, with generally fixed monthly payments of principal and interest, that will be funded when the project is completed and other conditions set forth in the commitment letter have been fulfilled. This can best be illustrated by an example. Let's assume that the borrower/developer desires to construct a 10-story office building at a cost of $5 million. Assume further that plans and specifications and all necessary building permits have been obtained and the borrower/developer is ready to commence construction. In the typical situation, the proposed borrower will contact a mortgage banker or correspondent of a major life insurance company, present to that correspondent his proposed project and all of his necessary cost breakdowns, contracts, and expenses, and request that the mortgage banker obtain a commitment for a permanent loan from one of the major life insurance companies. When the commitment is obtained from the lender, the necessary fees are paid to the lender and mortgage broker. The borrower/developer, armed with this take-out commitment, will present it to a commercial bank and obtain an interim construction loan, generally assigning all rights under the take-out commitment to the bank, so that the bank will be assured of a source of funds for payment of its construction loan on completion of the project. A book of this nature does not allow for a detailed examination of the terms and conditions of take-out commitments. This author has had considerable experience in negotiating and dealing with institutional lenders and interim construction lenders in all of the ins and outs of take-out commitments. Caution should be exercised by the borrower and his representative in the negotiation concerning the particular terms and provisions of the take-out commitment, so that the commitment is not illusory in nature. Careful examination of all of the terms, provisions and conditions for the funding of the take out commitment should be reviewed, and as many as possible of the contingencies set forth in the commitment resolved at the beginning so that the only practical item left is the completion of construction of the proposed improvements and the granting of the typical certificates of occupancy on completion of the project. Volumes have been written on take-out commitments and their perfection, and there is a vast body of case law interpreting these agreements. If the reader desires more detailed information concerning the use of take-out commitments, he should seek the advice of local, sophisticated real estate counsel dealing in this area. He may also wish to refer to one or more of the excellent publications listed in Appendix 5 of this book. In dealing with lenders, both interim and take-out, the foreign investor and his advisors should be aware that in many jurisdictions, there are loan limitations. In almost all instances, a lender can only make a loan if (1) it is secured by a first mortgage or deed of trust on the property; (2) the amount of the loan does not exceed a certain ratio to the total value of the project; (3) the loan does not bear an interest rate in excess of a stipulated maximum permitted by law; (4) the loan is amortized over a fixed maximum period of time. Loan limitations and criteria vary from state to state. The local mortgage banker or loan correspondent is generally fully familiar with these limitations as is the sophisticated local real estate broker and counsel. The real estate broker and investment counselor should take the time and effort to educate the foreign investor on these loan limitations and the realities as to type of loans that are obtainable in connection with the specific project involved. A more detailed discussion of usury is contained in a subsequent chapter.

Interim and permanent loans. As delineated in this chapter and elsewhere in this book, it is generally established custom that insurance companies and pension funds (and in many cases savings and loan associations and savings banks) do not wish to engage in the practices and pitfalls of construction lending but are concerned only in granting permanent loans upon completion of a project. This practice varies, however, from state to state. Many times local savings and loan associations do have established procedures for granting a combined loan during the course of construction, which upon completion of construction, reverts to a permanent amortized loan payable in fixed installments over a stipulated period of years. Local savings and loan associations' brokers and mortgage bankers can advise the foreign investor of local practices and procedures in this area. Caution should be exercised in negotiating the terms and provisions of interim and combined take-out commitments to be sure that the borrower is paying interest only on funds as they are withdrawn.

Use of overseas lenders. Foreign banks, pension funds, insurance companies, and private lending groups have become an increasing factor in the United States in recent years. The foreign investor may have an advantage in dealing with these foreign lending sources over his U.S. counterpart in that he may have established banking relationships with overseas financial institutions and can use these sources to create direct loans or participation loans with local financial institutions. This avenue should not be overlooked as an imaginative tool for real estate financing, particularly in a tight money market. In many instances, local banks are willing to enter into participation agreements with foreign banks and thus have available a source of funds and a local party to administer the disbursement of construction funds during the course of construction. Most overseas lenders are not equipped to make construction loans. They generally deal with local correspondent banks that have the expertise and personnel to administer construction funds and/or fund permanent loans.

Local credit and financial history. The question is often raised by the foreign investor as to whether or not his lack of local bank credit and a local financial history will be an impediment to his ability to obtain institutional financing. Though it takes a bit of effort, the overseas credit references in almost all instances will be sufficient to allay the fears of the institutional lender. In most cases, the foreign investor is able to obtain from his local bank letters of introduction and interbank credit qualifications that will meet the requirements of the local institutional lender. The problem becomes more complex when the institutional lender requires current financial statements. In most instances foreign investors do not issue financial statements or are reluctant to expose their assets to financial institutions. Each transaction must be handled on an ad hoc basis. Proper consultation with the institutional lender, the loan correspondent, or mortgage banker, coupled with bank references is usually sufficient to meet the requirements of the institutional lender. In addition in most instances, the foreign investor is willing to invest a larger down payment in a real estate project than the average American purchaser. Thus the lender is often requested to grant less of a loan than the maximum permitted by law. The increased down payment of the foreign investor, coupled with references to his local bank and financial sources, is usually sufficient to overcome any reluctance on the part of institutional lenders.

Use of professional appraisers and loan packagers. The question here raised is, "How do I apply for an institution loan?" The answer to the question depends, of course, on how sophisticated the nature of the project is. The larger the project, the more information is required. The mortgage banker, professional appraisers, local counsel, and real estate brokers can generally competently advise the foreign investor as to the requirements for a loan submission. Whether or not private consultants should be hired to make market studies, to assemble the financial and economic data, the construction costs, and other information required for new construction or economic analysis of existing leases and existing cash flow projections, depends on the particular facts and circumstances with each transaction. The foreign investor, however, should be cautious in seeking the advice of so-called professional loan packagers. In some instances, they are extremely competent and aware of market conditions. But since there are no laws or regulations governing their conduct in most states, it is a matter of individual judgment and individual selection as to who the foreign investor turns to for assistance in this area. It is recommended that competent local counsel or local real estate brokers be the parties to initiate the loan submission data supplemented by the loan correspondent or mortgage banker who can generally assist the foreign investor.

Lender Negotiations.   The question is often asked, "Can the foreign investor change the printed form of the lender, the mortgage banker, or the real estate broker?" The answer in most cases is an emphatic yes. The mere fact that the form is printed lends no magic to it. The foreign investor should not be saddled with the attitude that since the form is printed it can't be changed. Experience has shown me that many of the standard forms and provisions in brokerage listing agreements, mortgage banker commission agreements, takeout commitment letters, and the standard form notes, deeds, and trusts and other security instruments of a lender can, in many instances, be renegotiated if careful consideration is given to the necessities and requirements of the project, the institutional lender, and the prospective borrower. Do not be afraid to approach the institutional lender, the broker, the loan correspondent, or mortgage banker, and request reasonable modifications in the documents presented.

Are there special sources of funds that the foreign investor can take advantage of to obtain creative and innovative financing for a proposed real estate acquisition or development? It is incumbent upon the representative of the foreign investor to advise him of changing social and economic conditions in the United States. These conditions, of course, vary materially from jurisdiction to jurisdiction and from locale to locale. For example, there are substantial urban renewal projects now being initiated in most major cities throughout the United States. Under the terms of these urban renewal projects, local cities generally acquire by condemnation large blocks of property which have deteriorated or are underdeveloped and re-offer that property to private developers for the purpose of renewing the business and commercial sections of major cities thus creating new taxing bases for the city. These are complex but innovative concepts and can be the source of large opportunities for the foreign investor. In addition, the federal government has seen fit to create policies and procedures for financing low-income housing. These projects create substantial tax benefits and can be the source of innovative and productive real estate projects. Many cities have created city development bonds as a financing tool to encourage development of local industries and plants. These vary substantially from jurisdiction to jurisdiction but should not be overlooked by the counselor of the foreign investor as a source of real estate funding and as a source of potential projects for development.

7

INTRODUCTION TO U.S. TAXATION OF THE FOREIGN INVESTOR

The tax laws of the United States provide significant incentives for the foreign investor in U.S. real estate. Deductions, credits, and certain methods of accounting can significantly reduce or even eliminate U.S. tax on the annual operating income from the property. The U.S. tax on certain gains from the sale of the investment may be limited to 28 percent; in some cases, the foreigner may avoid completely any U.S. tax on the gain. In addition, U.S. gift and estate taxes may be avoided with proper tax planning.

These benefits do not accrue simply because one is a nonresident alien. A foreigner desiring to secure these benefits will often be required to make certain elections and use certain U.S. tax treaty provisions. Whether a foreigner invests in the property directly or through a corporation, partnership or trust, will also affect ultimate U.S. tax liability. This and the next chapter will discuss the U.S. taxation of foreign investment in U.S. real estate.

In order to better understand the manner in which the U.S. federal government (and in most cases the individual states) taxes foreign investment in U.S. real estate, certain key concepts must be understood by the foreign investor and his advisors.

INCOME.   In general, tax is imposed on *income* not cash flow. Income is generally an accounting concept of income less allowable deductions including depreciation.

U.S.—SOURCE INCOME.   Generally, nonresident alien individuals and foreign corporations are taxed on passive income derived (sourced) in the U.S.

BUSINESS INCOME.   Business income is income arising from the conduct of a trade or business in the United States.

PASSIVE INCOME.   Contrast the business income with passive income which is income attributable to sources other than from the conduct of a U.S. trade or business (such as dividends, interest, royalties, and in certain limited cases, rent).

Why is the distinction important to the foreign investor? Business income (i.e., income which is effectively connected with the conduct of a trade or business in the United States is in some cases taxed at normal graduated rates on *taxable* income (i.e., gross income *less* allowable deductions). Passive income is taxed at a flat rate of 30 percent of the gross income *without* allowance for deduction. This 30 percent rate is reduced as the result of U.S. tax treaties.

TAX TREATIES.   The United States has entered into various tax treaties with foreign governments to avoid both countries' tax of the same income. For example, dividends paid by a U.S. corporation to Canadian shareholders are subject to 15 percent withholding tax rather than 30 percent. The reductions vary from treaty to treaty so that, in some instances, the rate remains at 30 percent (e.g., interest income to Italy), while in others, it is reduced to zero (e.g., interest and royalties to the United Kingdom or the Netherlands); the reductions depend upon how a particular item of income is dealt with in a particular treaty.

WITHHOLDING.   The collection of tax on items of passive or investment income is handled through a system of withholding *tax at the source,* the withholding responsibility falling upon the *payer* of income or his paying agent. In fact, a nonresident alien or foreign corporation whose total tax liability is satisfied by withholding at source is not required to file a U.S. income tax return, with an exception for foreign taxpayers who elect to be taxed on real property income on a net basis.

TAXING RENTAL INCOME.   In order to determine the appropriate method of taxing rental income from real property, it is critical to determine whether the owner is engaged in a U.S. trade or business. If the owner is *not* so engaged, the rental income will not be considered effectively connected with a U.S. trade or business, and the gross rental income will be subject to a withholding tax at a flat rate of 30 percent. However, if the U.S. source rental income is considered effectively connected with the conduct of a U.S. trade or business, such income will be subject to the same progressive tax rates applicable to resident individuals or corporations. These rates are imposed upon *net taxable income,* that is, gross income less deductions for depreciation, interest, and other appropriate expenses allowable to any U.S. corporation or individual. Further, when more than 50 percent of a foreign corporation's income is effectively connected with a U.S. trade or business, the corporation must withhold U.S. tax at a rate of 30 percent on a corresponding portion of the dividends and interest paid to the foreign shareholder.

Initially, rental properties will produce little taxable income as the depreciation and interest deductions will eliminate any taxable income. However, deductions are only allowed against income effectively connected with a U.S. trade or business. Therefore, when rental income is not considered effectively connected with a U.S. trade or business, it will pay a tax of 30 percent on gross rents regardless of the expenses that may be attributable to the rental income. U.S. source income which is effectively connected with the conduct of a U.S. trade or business within the United States and certain types of foreign-source income which are effectively connected are taxed as any other U.S. corporation engaged in U.S. trade or business.

HOW DOES A FOREIGN INVESTOR DETERMINE WHETHER HE IS ENGAGED IN A U.S. TRADE OR BUSINESS?   Certain guidelines have been developed for determining when nonresident alien individual or foreign corporate owners of U.S. real estate are engaged in a trade or business within the United States as a result of the ownership of real property. The mere purchase, investment, or holding of unimproved real estate will not result in the owner being engaged in a trade or business within the United States. However, if the activities of the owners (or their agents) in connection with domestic real estate go beyond the mere receipt of income from rental property and the payment of expenses incidental to the collection of such rents, the owner will be considered to be engaged in a U.S. trade or business, provided that the activities are considerable, contiguous, and regular. Under this test, a foreign investor who hires a U.S. real estate agent to manage his property will be considered to be engaged in a U.S. trade or business (because the management activities of the agent are attributable to the investor). However, if the owner leases property pursuant to a one-tenant net lease, the owner will not be considered to be actively conducting a U.S. trade or business.

ELECTIONS.   Since a 30 percent tax on gross rental income would represent a clearly unacceptable cost to most foreigners investing in U.S. real estate, *special* treatment governs the taxation of real property income derived by a nonresident alien or where the income is not effectively connected with a U.S. business. In accordance with this rule, a foreign taxpayer may *elect* to be taxed *as if* the income were effectively connected with a U.S. business. Such an election affords the taxpayer the opportunity to have the rental income taxed (1) on a net basis, with a deduction for depreciation and interest and taxes, etc., and (2) at the corporate or regular graduated rates, as the case may be, rather than at the flat 30 percent rate.

Statutory election.   There are basically two methods by which a foreign person can elect to be taxed on a net basis; the statutory election or as a treaty election. (Forms 40 and 47). If a drawback exists with the statutory election, it may be that it remains in effect for *all* subsequent taxable years unless permission to revoke is obtained from the commissioner of Internal Revenue or is modified within the three-year period for amending the original year's tax return. If the taxpayer is allowed to revoke the election, a reelection may not be made for another five years without the consent of the commissioner. The election applies to all U.S. real property held for the production of income by an electing individual and to all U.S. real property interests of an electing foreign corporation. As such, the election can not be made on a selective basis with respect to specific properties or various types of income from the same property.

Treaty election. A *treaty* election, if available under the respective treaty, will result in little or no U.S. taxable income as most income will probably be offset by large depreciation and interest deductions (and dividends are limited to earning and profits). Furthermore, the same treaty elections are made annually providing for some flexibility in considering how the operations will be taxed. It can thus be seen that holding title individually by the foreign investor results in loosing flexibility to make elections on a project-by-project basis. This loss of an effective tax planning tool and the added problems of gift tax and estate tax are persuasive arguments for the proposition that the foreign investor should hold title by use of a foreign corporation whenever possible.

INVESTMENT VEHICLES

Let us apply the above principles and explore various investment vehicles. How should the foreign investor hold U.S. real property? There are several ways U.S. property can be held by foreign investors. The principal factor to be considered in determining the most appropriate structure is the character of the contemplated U.S. operations, the possible participation of U.S. citizens or residents in the investment, the intention regarding repatriation of profits, and the character of taxation in the investors' country of residence.

Corporations

DOMESTIC (CORPORATIONS FORMED IN A STATE OF THE UNITED STATES). Domestic corporations are taxed on *worldwide income* at regular U.S. corporate rates. Dividend distributions from *domestic* corporations to *foreign* shareholders are subject to the 30 percent (or lower) treaty rate.

A domestic corporation, although often used in order to comply with state laws which prohibit ownership of land by foreigners, has several disadvantages.

FOREIGN (CORPORATIONS FORMED OUTSIDE OF THE UNITED STATES). As a general statement, most investment in U.S. real estate is done through a foreign corporation rather than the investor holding the property directly or by using a foreign trust or partnership. For example, unimproved real property, U.S. income-producing property, or property acquired for development that is owned directly or through a partnership by a nonresident alien will be subject to the U.S. gift tax if the individual makes a gift of part or all of his interest in the property. His interest in the property also will be subject to U.S. estate tax when he dies. As with U.S. citizens and residents, taxable transfers are determined cumulatively during life and at death. However, nonresident aliens are not allowed the unified gift tax credit nor do they receive credit for the amount of gift tax paid on transfers within three years of death. However, a credit of $3,600 is allowed against the estate tax liability, roughly equivalent to a $60,000 exemption. Further, there is no provision for the marital deduction.

If numerous investments are to be made in U.S. real property, it will generally prove advantageous to have each investment made by a separate and distinct foreign corporation. This is generally advantageous in that an investment considered engaged in a U.S. trade or business will not taint other U.S. investments not so considered. Further, an election to be considered engaged in a U.S. trade or business can be made with respect to each individual property.

Direct Holding

A foreign investor may purchase U.S. real estate directly and hold it in his name because of the simplicity. However, there are several disadvantages to this procedure. The foreign investor may be required to file U.S. returns in his own name, thus losing any desired anonymity. There also exists a potential for unlimited liability with respect to the property. Also, the U.S. situs property will be subject to U.S. estate and gift taxes and the complexities involved in probate of a foreign will.

Trusts

The tax aspects of a domestic trust will depend upon the type of trust used. If the foreign investors use a grantor trust, the tax aspects will generally be the same as holding the property directly.

If a nongrantor trust is utilized by the foreign investor, the foreign beneficiaries of the U.S. trust will be taxed on the amount of the trust's *distributable net income* which is required to be distributed currently, plus any other amounts properly paid or credited or required to be distributed for the taxable year. The trust will be subject to tax on the remainder of its taxable income for the taxable year. Further, if a U.S. trust is used, there will be no withholding imposed on payments made to the trust. However, if distributions are made from income, there will be a 30 percent (or lower) treaty rate withholding tax.

The beneficiary of a trust is not deemed to be engaged in a trade or business in the United States merely because the trustee is so engaged. However, care should be exercised so that the trust itself is not considered engaged in a U.S. trade or business due to its ownership of real property. If the trust is deemed engaged in a U.S. trade or business, its beneficiaries will be considered so engaged. As such, the beneficiary would be subject to the U.S. graduated tax on his share of the net income from the trust.

Partnerships

DOMESTIC OR FOREIGN. Generally, where the requisite U.S. legal characteristics for a partnership exist, the partners of a foreign partnership and a domestic partnership will receive the same U.S. tax treatment.

The use of a partnership may be beneficial where several foreign investors wish to make an investment in U.S. real property, or one or more foreign investors wishes to make a joint investment with one or more U.S. persons. Further, some foreign investors may find a foreign partnership desirable in that it allows them to administer partnership business affairs at home.

The partnership serves only as a conduit. Partnerships are not taxpaying entities under general concepts of U.S. tax law (as distinguished from corporations). As such, each partner is treated as receiving his proportionate share of income gain and loss generated by a partnership, with the respective items retaining their original character. Each partner engaged in a U.S. trade or business through the partnership must file a U.S. tax return, and the statutory or treaty net basis election is to be made by *each* individual partner. A joint return generally cannot be filed by a foreign partner. Therefore, the individual foreign partner may want his partnership interest fragmented among family members, taking advantage of income-splitting benefits. If the partnership is engaged in a U.S. trade or business, the foreign partners will also be considered so engaged.

LIMITED PARTNERSHIPS.   Some investors prefer a limited partnership since primary responsibility rests with the general partner. One might think the limited partner's investment may be considered passive rather than one actively engaged in a U.S. trade or business. However, a foreign partner's status as a limited or general partner is immaterial in determining whether the foreign investor is engaged in a U.S. trade or business. His status will be determined by the *partnership's activities as a whole.* Thus, the limited partner-foreign investor will in all probability be deemed engaged in a U.S. trade or business through the activities of the partnership even though he is totally passive. This can be a trap for the unwary.

OLD LAW REGARDING TAXATION OF REAL ESTATE GAINS

Prior to the new tax act (see Chapter 8) the United States taxed nonresident individuals and corporations on capital gains only if derived from (effectively connected with) a U.S. business activity. But otherwise, a nonresident was exempt from U.S. tax on gains from the disposition of assets in the United States (unless the nonresident was an individual who was physically present in the United States for more than 183 days in the year the gain was realized). Thus, a nonresident who was not engaged in U.S. trade or business who sold U.S. real estate or stock in a corporation owning U.S. real estate, would incur no U.S. tax on the sale gain. This advantage has since been changed. It's a whole new ball game requiring very sophisticated tax planning. This will be discussed in detail in Chapter 8.

This was not an unexpected change. Such a broad exemption of capital gains of nonresidents is unusual. Nearly all other industrial countries tax nonresidents on capital gains from the disposition of real property located in the country as well as on gains derived from business activity there. A small number also tax gains derived by nonresidents on the sale of a *substantial* holding of shares in a domestic corporation. (*Substantial* is typically defined as 25 percent or more of the outstanding shares.) And a few countries tax any sale of shares or other rights when the underlying assets are real property.

If a foreign investor is engaged in a U.S. trade or business by reason of a real estate investment (so that the rental income will be taxed on a net basis), the gain on the sale of the investment would ordinarily be connected with the trade or business and taxable in the United States. Prior to the new act, effective tax planning offered an informed foreign investor several vehicles for reclassifying the sale gain as income which was not effectively connected with a U.S. trade or business, and as such, exempt from U.S. tax. These opportunities that existed before the new tax act for avoiding capital gains tax can be summarized as follows:

AN INSTALLMENT SALE.   By electing an installment sale, the foreign investor can receive most or all of the payments in years following the year of the sale. If his corporation is not actually engaged in a U.S. trade or business in later years when the installment payments are received (and he has not made the election to be treated as if he were so engaged), the gain would not be effectively connected with a trade or business in the later years and, therefore, not subject to U.S. tax.

AN EXCHANGE FOR FOREIGN PROPERTY OF A LIKE KIND.   A foreign investor could exchange his U.S. real property held for productive use or investment for property of a like kind without recognition of gain. Further, if the property was exchanged outside of the U.S., the gain recognized on the ultimate sale of the property received in the exchange would not be subject to U.S. tax because the gain would not be U.S. source income.

SALE OF THE PROPERTY BY A HOLDING COMPANY, COUPLED WITH A COMPLETE LIQUIDATION OF THE COMPANY WITHIN ONE YEAR.   The foreign investor could form a U.S. holding company to receive the rental income. Thereafter, the corporation could sell the property pursuant to a plan of liquidation. As such, the shareholders would generally not recognize a gain when they exchanged their stock and securities in liquidation for the proceeds of the sale of real property because, as foreign investors, they are generally not subject to U.S. capital gains tax. The corporation would be exempt from U.S. tax imposed on the gains derived from the sale of the real property.

SALE OF THE SHARES OF A HOLDING COMPANY.   If the sales price of the stock reflects the appreciated value of the real property, the purchaser of the corporation, even if a U.S. person, could then liquidate the corporation without realizing a gain subject to U.S. tax because the purchaser's basis in the stock for purposes of determining the gain on the liquidation would be the purchase price for the stock. He would also get a stepped-up basis for the real property equal to his purchase price for the stock.

Again, let me emphasize that these structures have generally been made *inoperative* by the new tax law involving foreign investment in the United States. Again, let me refer the reader to the next chapter and to the new act (Appendix 2).

8

TAXING THE FOREIGN INVESTOR TODAY

Prior to the Foreign Investment in Real Property Tax Act of 1980, several model vehicles existed which exempted gain on U.S. real property from U.S. federal income tax. In this book we will not consider taxation by a state in the United States. Each state, of course, has the right, which is exercised in varying degrees, to separately tax each transaction discussed. The reader must consult local tax counsel or his accountant to determine local state tax impact of a transaction. In some states local taxes are significant. Therefore, this issue should not be summarily overlooked. It was once highly unusual that a well-counseled foreign investor in U.S. real estate would pay any U.S. tax on his real estate gains. Congress believed it unfair for foreign investors to be able to avoid tax on their U.S. real estate gains. Initially only farmland was at issue. U.S. farmers believed that foreigners were buying up large parcels of U.S. farmland, and that their ability to avoid U.S. taxes allowed the foreigners to bid the price of U.S. farmland beyond the reach of expanding U.S. farmers. However after several debates, Congress felt that all real estate sold by foreigners should be taxed. As such, Congress enacted and the President signed into law, the *Foreign Investment in Real Property Tax Act of 1980* (hereafter referred to as the Act). A copy of the act and related material are contained in Appendix 2. The reader is encouraged to review the material in this Appendix fully.

The Act introduces a complex scheme of taxation aimed at taxing all real property gains recognized by foreign investors upon disposition of their real property interests located in the United States.

IMPORTANT DEFINITIONS

The act provides that any gain or loss realized by a foreign person from the disposition of a *U.S. real property interest* will be taken into account as if such person were (1) engaged in a trade or business within the United States during the taxable year, and (2) as if such gain or loss were *effectively connected with that trade or business.* Thus, generally, a nonresident alien individual and foreign corporation are taxed in the same manner as a U.S. person in a similar transaction.

U.S. REAL PROPERTY INTEREST. What is a U.S. real property interest and why is it important? The act defines *taxable* U.S. real estate holdings owned by or for foreign investors in terms of a *United States real property interest* (hereafter referred to for brevity as USRPI). The term is broadly drafted to include many forms of real estate. However, the term *USRPI* is specifically defined to include an interest in real property located in the United States, and interests in certain U.S. corporations. In order to understand the scope of USRPI, it is necessary to analyze its components. The first component is defining an interest. What is an interest in real property? An interest in real property includes (1) fee ownership and coownership of land (e.g., tenancies in common, joint tenancies) and (2) leasehold interests and options to acquire real property or a real property leasehold. Real estate is a more obvious component of USRPI, but this too warrants discussion. What is U.S. real estate? Initially you would consider land and buildings as real property. But the act goes even further. It also defines USRPI to include an interest in any *domestic* corporation (except as a creditor) which is or was a *United States real property holding corporation* (hereafter referred to as RPHC) on the date of the sale or at any time during the period the investor held his stock *after June 18, 1980* or the five-year period preceding the disposition, whichever is *shorter*.

U.S. real estate in general includes land and buildings; but more precisely it includes mines, wells, or other natural deposits, movable walls, furnishings, and other personal property associated with the use of real property.

Associated real property is an interesting term the use of which may cause some unexpected results. Associated real property is intended to include property accessory to immovable property (i.e., furnishings in an office building), livestock, and equipment used for agricultural and forestry enterprises. The following example focuses the definition of USRPI.

Example: Mr. Kee, a Hong Kong citizen, owns the following assets:
Raw land in Texas.
A condominium in Beverly Hills.
A producing oil and gas field in Texas.
A cooperative apartment in New York.
An option to acquire a vineyard in Napa Valley.
A hotel in Miami, including the furnishings, all of which are triple-net leased to Hilton Hotel Corporation which operates the hotel.
A farm in Omaha, Nebraska, including the grain storage tower, farmhouse and furnishings, barn, tractors, and livestock.
The stock of a Nevada corporation, the sole asset of which is an office building in San Francisco.

Each of the above assets is a USRPI as defined by the act, and any gain from the sale of any of these assets will give rise to U.S. income tax.

The manner by which the USRPI is held will produce different tax results. Essentially the act addresses itself to individuals and corporations.

Taxation of individuals holding a USRPI

If a nonresident alien individual owns a USRPI in the United States directly, the act provides that any gain or loss arising from the disposition of that property will be treated as if the individual were engaged in a trade or business in the United States and as if the gain were attributable to that trade or business. Thus, individual foreign investors in U.S. real estate will now be treated in substantially the same manner as a similar U.S. investor. As such, for federal U.S. tax purposes, a long-term capital gain (gain from the sale of a capital asset held for more than 12 months) is taxed presently at 40 percent of the total gain. The rate of tax depends on the tax bracket of the individual taxpayer in each case. Therefore, if an individual taxpayer is taxable at a rate of 50 percent, the gain will be taxed at 20 percent. However, if the individual's income tax bracket is lower, the effective rate of tax on the gain will be less than 20 percent. In contrast, if the gain is characterized as short-term or ordinary business income (held 12 months or less) the individual may be taxed at rates up to 50 percent!

Minimum tax on individuals

The intent of the act is to tax foreign investors in a fashion similar to the way U.S. persons were taxed. However, the act does create one important difference between the treatment of an individual U.S. taxpayer and an individual foreign investor. Since foreign income and certain types of U.S.-source income would not be taxed in the United States, the foreign investor as a practical matter may be taxed at a lower effective rate than a U.S. person, particularly if the installment method of reporting income is elected. To cover this issue, the act, therefore, establishes a 20 percent *minimum* tax on the nonresident foreign individual. The amount of this minimum tax is the *lesser* of the following amounts:

a. 20 percent of the foreign investor's alternative, minimum taxable income.
b. 20 percent of the net gain of the foreign investor from all dispositions of his USRPI during the taxable year.
c. $12,000.

A minimum tax will apply where a gain has been recognized. However, the individual will be able to *offset* the gains from the U.S. real estate with *other* business losses and losses from prior years from his U.S. operations.

Taxation of a real property holding company corporation

Now let us focus our attention towards the effect of the act on corporations investing in U.S. real estate. The act identifies the *taxable corporate entity* as a real property holding corporation (RPHC). How does a corporation become an RPHC? Any corporation (foreign or domestic) will be considered an RPHC if at any time during the taxable year the *fair market value* of its USRPI *equals or exceeds 50 percent* of the sum of the *fair market value* of such USRPI, plus its real property interests located *outside* the United States, and the fair market value of *any other assets* used or held for use in a trade or business. For this purpose a corporation's fair market value does not include the value of assets not used or held for use in a business. Excluded would be such assets as marketable securities, notes receivable, certificates of deposit, or other forms of liquid assets.

What is the effect of being classified as an RPHC? The major impact of classifying a *domestic* corporation as an RPHC is that the *stock* of that corporation becomes a *form of USRPI.* Thus, the sale of such stock becomes taxable. (Under prior law the sale would have resulted in no tax to a nonresident alien not engaged in a trade or business in the United States. This is true regardless of whether or not the corporation is an RPHC at the time the stock is sold!. If *at any time during* the preceding five years or during the period after June 18, 1980, that the foreign investor held the stock (whichever period is shorter), the corporation could have been classified as an RPHC, any gains from the sale of stock in the corporation will be subject to tax. A domestic corporation is automatically presumed to be an RPHC unless and until it can prove that less than 50 percent of its assets as USRPI.

We have seen how the stock of a domestic RPHC is treated. Let us examine the effect of a foreign corporation that owns U.S. real estate. The stock in a foreign corporation that owns U.S. real estate is not included in the definition of a USRPI; therefore, the gain from the disposition of stock of a foreign corporation will generally not be subject to tax, but we are not free of tax yet. What happens if a foreign corporation is considered an RPHC and disposes of a USRPI? In this case, any gain from the sale (or other disposition) will be taken into account in determining its tax liability as if the corporation were engaged in a trade or business within the United States during the taxable year of the sale! Again, the result is to treat a foreign corporation in the same manner as a domestic corporation making the same investment.

There are, however, situations where the act treats a foreign corporation differently. Unlike the treatment afforded domestic corporations, certain distributions which would be tax-free to a U.S. corporation are considered taxable. In particular, a disposition of a USRPI to a shareholder as a dividend in kind will result in gain being recognized and a tax imposed upon the distributing foreign corporation. Further, if the foreign corporation distributes the U.S.property in liquidation, it may generate a taxable gain. If the gain constitutes a long-term capital gain, the maximum rate of tax will be 28 percent, essentially the alternative tax afforded U.S. companies for long-term capital gains. However, if the disposition of a USRPI generates a short-term capital gain, such gain will be taxed at regular U.S. corporate tax rates ranging from 17 percent to 46 percent. The minimum corporate rate will be 16 percent in 1982 and 15 percent in 1983.

It should be noted that a significant planning opportunity exists where *foreign real property* can be used in calculating the 50 percent test when determining if the corporation is an RPHC. If the investor has real property located outside the United States, this *can* be used to bring the total percentage of USRPI of the corporation below 50 percent. When a USRPI makes up less than 50 percent of the fair market value of the corporation, the rules as they were in effect *before* the act are applicable, and the sale of a USRPI would not be taxable.

Once a corporation is classified as an RPHC, it carries that label for five years after the U.S. real estate falls below the 50 percent level. If, during that period, the value of the U.S. real estate exceeds 50 percent of total business assets, the five-year period starts again.

The following examples illustrates how the 50 percent test works:

Example: Mr. Alfredo, a Venezuelian citizen, owns all of the shares of XYZ, Inc., a California corporation. XYZ's sole asset is an apartment building which is now worth $2 million and is subject to a $400,000 mortgage. (The stock of XYZ is USRPI.) If Mr. Alfredo sells the shares of stock of XYZ, he will be subject to U.S. income tax on the gain from the sale of those shares.

A year after XYZ acquired the apartment building, it paid $1.8 million for a resort in the Dominican Republic. The test for determining whether XYZ is an RPHC is based upon the *gross* fair market value of its assets, not the net value (therefore, the $400,000 mortgage on the apartment building is not considered). Assuming that the apartment building is still worth $2 million, XYZ would still be an RPHC, because more than 50 percent of its assets are USRPI.

If XYZ has paid $2 million for the land in the Dominican Republic, or the fair market value of the apartment building had dropped to $1.7 million, then less than 50 percent of the assets of XYZ would be real property interests, and the five-year period would begin to run.

One unusual pitfall of the act is presented when a corporation owns U.S. real property which is subject to rapid fluctuation in the market price. For example, a corporation acquires U.S. real property with a fair market value of $1 million. It has one other asset used in its trade or business with a value of $1,250,000. If the value of the U.S. real property appreciates to $1,250,000, the corporation will unexpectedly become an RPHC and subjected to all the rules imposed by the act. This is truly a trap for the unwary investor and indicates that the value of the U.S. real estate should be monitored closely when you are relying on your U.S. assets being less than 50 percent of the total assets of the corporation.

On the other hand, a corporation which is an RPHC will not gain any benefit when the fair market value of its property diminishes to less than 50 percent of the fair market value of all assets. Any disposition of the stock of such a corporation will be taxable for the applicable five-year period.

It should be pointed out that the 50 percent test for an RPHC may be applied at any time during a taxable year theoretically, even if the corporation meets the test for an instant of time.

The look-through approach

In determining whether any corporation in a multiple-tier structure is an RPHC, the act adopts a "look-through" approach. If a corporation owns a controlling interest of another corporation, it is treated as owning a proportionate share of the USRPI owned by such other corporation. The term *controlling interest* is defined as 50 percent or more of the fair market value of all classes of stock of a corporation. If the first corporation owns 50 percent or more but less than 100 percent of the second corporation, only a pro rata portion of each asset of the second corporation will be treated as owned by the first corporation.

This look-through provision may allow a corporation to avoid RPHC status. For example, a corporation with $49 in USRPI and $51 in other assets held for use in trade or business also owns 100 percent of all issued and outstanding stock of a second corporation which, in turn, has $50 of USRPI and $50 of other assets held for use in its trade or business. Pursuant to this provision, the parent would not be an RPHC since less than 50 percent (99/200) of its assets would be treated as USRPI. If the stock of the parent corporation were sold by the foreign shareholders, the old capital gains rules apply, and the foreign shareholder might avoid U.S. taxation even though he sold shares of a U.S. corporation at a gain.

Attribution

The act adopts complicated attribution rules which should be investigated to determine whether a controlling interest exists. When attribution applies, a person is considered to own the stock which is owned by and for another related person (generally family) or entity.

The following example illustrates the application of the attribution rules to an analysis of controlling interest under the act. Corporation X owns 100 percent of the stock of corporation A and 100 percent of the stock of corporation B. Corporation A owns 45 percent of the fair market of all classes of stock of corporation C, and corporation B owns 10 percent of the stock of C. Corporation C owns $1 million of USRPI. Corporation X will be attributed as the owner of 55 percent of the stock of corporation A. Pursuant to the act, corporation X has a controlling interest in corporation C and, therefore, is treated as the owner of $550,000 of USRPI (55 percent of $1 million). If corporation X does not have any other assets, it will be a RPHC.

Exception for publicly traded securities

Stock of a domestic corporation will not be treated as a USRPI, if any class of stock is regularly traded on an established securities market or exchange, provided the shareholder does not own more than 5 percent of the stock during the period after June 18, 1980, or the five-year period ending on the date of the disposition of such interest, whichever is less. In other words, stock of the same publicly traded company may or may not be treated as a USRPI solely on the basis of the size of the block of stock held by a given shareholder.

Sale or liquidation of foreign RPHC

The definition of a USRPI, as discussed previously, is limited to stock of a domestic corporation. Since the act solely taxes dispositions of a USRPI, the gain from the disposition of stock in a foreign corporation is not subject to tax under the act. However, the purchaser of the foreign corporation will be unable to liquidate the foreign corporation on a tax-free basis.

Previously, if properly structured, no gain or loss was recognized by a corporation and no tax incurred on the distribution of its assets in a partial or complete liquidation. Prior to the act, a shareholder could liquidate a foreign corporation without incurring a tax to either the corporation or the distributee shareholder, and the shareholder could attain a step-up in basis for the assets distributed in liquidation. The purchaser will generally want to liquidate the company in order to equate the purchase price of the stock with the depreciable assets of the company (step-up in basis) to generate a larger tax depreciation deduction. As a result, any buyer of foreign corporate stock must, if he is to take actual possession of the property, pay the accumulated capital gains tax which the seller has avoided.

Accordingly, a buyer of the stock of a foreign corporation would in all probability insist on a discount in the purchase price to take into account the potential corporate tax and reduced depreciation deductions attributable to the lower basis of the corporation's real property. However, if the property is not depreciable, the buyer could forego liquidation and the tax could be avoided as long as the property were retained in the foreign corporation.

Although the act provides that the sale or other disposition of the stock of foreign corporation, which would include a liquidation, is not taxable to the shareholder, there is now a new provision which states that gain is recognizable by the foreign corporation on the distribution of a USRPI in an amount equal to the excess of fair market value of the corporation's adjusted basis in such USRPI at the time of the distribution.

However, no tax will apply if the basis or cost of the distributed property in the hands of the distributee shareholder is the same as the basis of the property prior to the distribution increased by any gain recognized by the corporation.

In an effort to bar the use of tax-free exchanges and other nonrecognition provisions by foreign investors as a means of avoiding the impact of the act, specific provisions were enacted which provide that foreign investors in USPRI may no longer use the nonrecognition provisions unless the USRPI is exchanged for an interest which would be subject to U.S. tax if sold. For example, an exchange by a foreign person of U.S. property for foreign real property would generally fail to qualify as a tax-free exchange; instead it would be a taxable event. On the other hand, a foreign person's exchange of U.S. real property for other U.S. real property should qualify as a nontaxable transaction.

Partnerships, trust, and estates

In addition to making direct investments, or investments through the purchase of stock in foreign or domestic corporations, a nonresident individual or corporation may invest in real estate through a foreign or domestic partnership or trust or as part of an estate. The act, in its treatment of these forms of investment effectively disregards the existence of a partnership, trust, or estate and treats the nonresident individual or foreign corporation as owning *directly* its pro rata share of the real property interests owned by the entity. As a consequence, the foreign partner or beneficiary is subject to tax upon the disposition of a real property interest by the partnership, trust, or estate to the extent of its beneficial interest. In addition, the disposition of an interest in a partnership, trust, or estate holding USRPI will be taxable to any foreign partner or beneficiary to the extent that any gain on the disposition is attributable to real property interests held by the entity.

Real estate investment trusts

Distributions by a real estate investment trust (REIT) to a foreign investor will, to the extent attributable to gain from the sale or exchange of a USRPI by the REIT, be treated as gain recognized by the foreign investor from the sale or exchange of a USRPI.

Foreign shareholders of a REIT will not be taxed on the gain derived from the sale of stock in such REIT unless the REIT is a domestically controlled REIT. The term *domestically controlled REIT* means a REIT which during the shortest period five years prior to the disposition, the period the REIT was in existence, or the period between June 19, 1980 and the date of disposition, less than 50 percent in value of the stock was held by foreign persons. In determining foreign ownership, both direct and indirect ownership is relevant, although no attribution rules are specifically referred to. Therefore, USRPI does not include an interest in a domestically controlled REIT which presumably means, but is nowhere stated, that the sale of an interest in any other REIT is the sale of USRPI.

Operations

Even though the act changed the way in which the United States taxes the gains on real estate transactions, the U.S. taxation of operating revenues remains the same. Several of the conventional planning techniques are still effective. For example, even though the Netherlands Antilles no longer provides a mechanism for the avoidance of U.S. tax on the disposition of a U.S. real property interest, it nevertheless provides several key benefits such as:

1. Waiver of U.S. tax on dividends and interest paid by the Antilles company to a non-U.S. person.
2. Exemption of U.S. real estate income from Antilles taxation.
3. Annual net basis election.

In addition, the Netherlands Antilles imposes no tax on:

1. Dividends and interest paid by the Antilles company to nonresidents.
2. Gains on the sale of stock of the Antilles company or liquidation of the corporation.
3. Gifts or bequests of the stock of the Antilles company.

The Netherlands Antilles treaty (see Appendix 4) permits the foreign investor to obtain these benefits without incurring third-country income taxes. Similar benefits were previously available, with proper structuring, in the British Virgin Islands. However, the new treaty with the British Virgin Islands provides no act protection; further withholding taxes will be imposed on dividends paid by a British Virgin Islands corporation that is engaged in a U.S. trade or business. A foreign investor who has no need for these benefits can ignore the treaty and simply use the other relevant provisions of the Internal Revenue Code itself to minimize, or in limited circumstances, even avoid U.S. taxes.

Disclosure

The act provides for extensive reporting requirements in order to identify foreign persons who directly or indirectly own interests in U.S. real estate. These reporting requirements may be considered more onerous by some foreign investors than the tax imposed by the act. Further, when coupled with the reporting requirements under the Agricultural Foreign Investment Disclosure Act and the Commerce Department reporting requirement, the foreign investor has a myriad of forms to fill out.

Different reporting requirements are imposed for:

1. Domestic corporations having foreign shareholders.
2. Foreign corporations and all partnerships, estates, and trusts.
3. Foreign persons owning substantial real property interests who are not engaged in a U.S. trade or business.

In addition to the information required by the statute, the Treasury has the authority to require that other information be reported. These disclosure requirements are discussed in Appendix 7.

Effective date and treaty planning

When did all this take place and when will it affect foreign investors? The act is *retroactive* to dispositions occurring *after June 18, 1980*. What about gain which is attributable to periods before June 18, 1980? Unfortunately, no exemption was made available for such gains. *All* gain is subject to tax even where it can be shown that appreciation was attributable to periods prior to June 18, 1980.

The act provides a *five year grace period* until December 31, 1984, during which time existing income tax treaties would prevail over conflicting provisions of the new legislation. During this five-year period, the Treasury Department hopes to renegotiate conflicting treaties so that they will conform with the new legislation. Certain treaties which have been renegotiated may delay the effective date for up to two years from the date the new treaty is signed. Some treaties will continue to afford certain benefits to those who come within the purview. For example, the current U.S. tax treaty with Canada prohibits the United States from taxing capital gains, including real estate gains realized by residents of Canada.

The use of the Netherlands and the Netherlands Antilles

What tax treaties can provide some help? Several U.S. tax treaties exempt certain capital gains from U.S. tax. One such treaty is the U.S.–Netherlands tax treaty (see Appendix 4). The U.S.–Netherlands tax treaty provides several well-known planning vehicles such as the *Dutch sandwich*. One variant of the Dutch sandwich involves having a Netherlands Antilles Corporation (NV) own a Netherlands corporation (BV) which in turn owns a Netherlands Antilles corporation which in turn owns the U.S. real estate. Dividends from the lower-tier Netherlands Antilles company to the Netherlands corporation may be remitted free of withholding tax. Dividends from the Netherlands corporation to the upper-tier Netherlands Antilles corporation to its shareholders is free from witholding tax. The sale of USRPI is transacted by selling the stock in the lower-tier Netherlands Antilles corporation free from U.S. tax. The gain is not taxed in Holland under the Dutch participation exemption (see Appendix 4).

Another popular vehicle is the Dutch *open face sandwich,* in which the Dutch corporation owns all the stock of a domestic corporation which owns the USRPI. This allows the Dutch corporation to use the treaty capital gains exemption to avoid U.S. tax on the disposition of the stock of the domestic corporation. This exemption is available whether the foreign investor sells the stock of the corporation, or the corporation is liquidated pursuant to the sale of the real property by the corporation within 12 months of such liquidation. The Netherlands corporation could possibly avoid Netherlands tax by means of the Dutch participation exemption. However, there is a 5 percent U.S. withholding tax on dividend remittances to the Netherlands corporation. Perhaps an example of these principles will aid in their understanding:

THE DUTCH SANDWICH

| Netherlands Antilles corporation (NV) |
| Netherlands corporation (BV) |
| Netherlands Antilles corporation (NV) |

U.S. Real Estate

THE DUTCH OPEN FACE SANDWICH

| Netherlands corporation (BV) |
| U.S. Domestic corporation |

U.S. Real Estate

The Netherlands treaty also provides a good example of what *cannot* be accomplished with a treaty with respect to a foreign corporation holding U.S. real property. As noted, the act does not apply to the sale of stock in a foreign corporation but *does* tax the foreign corporation on the disposition of its *directly held U.S. real property interests.* Therefore, U.S. tax could be completely avoided if the Netherlands treaty exempted the foreign corporation from U.S. tax on such gains. However, *no* such exemption is available.

Specifically, since the capital gains exemption in the Netherlands treaty (as well as in most other U.S. treaties containing this exemption) does not apply to the sale of real property, the Dutch corporation cannot use the general treaty exemption on the disposition of directly held U.S. real property (as opposed to shares). The Dutch corporation would also be unable to avoid U.S. tax on a realty disposition by asserting that the treaty prevents the United States from treating foreign corporations differently from U.S. corporations (nondiscrimination clause). In such instance, a special act rule provides an election for the foreign corporation to be treated as a domestic corporation; the sale of its stock would thus be subject to U.S. tax.

Election by foreign corporation

The act provides that a foreign corporation may, under certain circumstances, elect to be treated as a *domestic* corporation for purposes of the act. If the foreign corporation has a permanent establishment in the United States and, under any applicable treaty, that permanent establishment may not be treated less favorably than a domestic corporation carrying on the same activities, the foreign corporation may make this election under conditions to be prescribed by the Internal Revenue Service. Once such an election is made, it will not be revocable without the consent of the Internal Revenue Service. The full impact of the election has not been completely determined at this time. The Internal Revenue Service will undoubtedly elaborate upon this election in the forthcoming regulations.

The act, in a statutory sense, has dealt a formidable blow to the foreign investor who previously was able to escape most, if not all, U.S. tax on U.S. real estate gains. Accordingly, the tax planning for foreign investment in U.S. real estate has simply been elevated to a higher and more complicated plateau than before. As anticipated, more sophisticated situations and transactions have already begun to surface. Some have even termed the act a toothless tiger. This stems from the question as to how the treasury intends to effectively enforce the act, especially when no provisions were made for withholding taxes and enforcement relies on voluntary compliance. Such quandaries as well as several technical considerations may be considered in the forthcoming regulations.

It can be readily seen that the act creates a complex scheme of taxation. Whether there exist practical and reliable tax planning techniques to avoid or minimize U.S. federal income tax depends on (1) a detailed analysis of the act; (2) the extent of future regulations which have not yet been promulgated; (3) the specific facts in each transaction; and (4) the cost of setting up and maintaining various entities. The foreign investor and his advisors are cautioned to look carefully at each interest in U.S. real property they now own or desire to acquire. Only generalities can be used in this chapter. Proper advice and counsel from your accountant or attorney is essential.

RESIDENCE OR NONRESIDENCE: IS IT IMPORTANT? AND IMMIGRATION AND THE FOREIGN INVESTOR: A BRIEF SUMMARY

It is a general rule of federal income taxation in the United States that residents of the United States are treated for tax purposes substantially the same as U.S. citizens even though such residents remain citizens of another country.

Further, the U.S. federal income tax laws tax a person's worldwide income and not just what he earns here in the United States. Additionally, there is a basic difference in the method of taxation toward the foreign taxpayer who is engaged in business in the United States and those not so engaged, as those terms are defined in the Internal Revenue Code. (See Chapters 7 and 8 for a more detailed discussion.)

Various basic concepts must be understood in determining the approach and method of taxation of foreign individuals and corporations. Income derived from engaging in trade or business in the United States will be referred to as class 2 income. Income derived from passive investments such as rents, interests, and dividends is referred to as class 1 income. It can thus be seen that a foreign investor, whether individual or corporate, can have both types of income in any particular taxable year. Generally speaking, corporations are separate taxable entities for U.S. tax purposes. As a general rule, foreign corporations and individuals are taxed at the rate of 30 percent on their class 1 income. The business income of a foreign corporation is subject to taxation similar to that of U.S. domestic corporations in which the tax may be as high as 48 percent. Again, a foreign corporation or individual can receive both types of income in the same year.

What is a foreign corporation? Generally speaking, a foreign corporation is any corporation organized outside the United States regardless of who its shareholders are. Caution should be exercised here that if the entity is not truly a corporation for U.S. tax purposes, certain adverse consequences may accrue.

Nonresident aliens (referred to as NRAs) are taxed on their class 1 and class 2 income derived in the United States or arising from U.S. sources. The 30 percent rate on class 1 income of an NRA may be reduced by certain tax treaties which will be described elsewhere in this text.

It can thus be seen from the foregoing general rules, that it becomes critical to determine if the foreign investor as an individual is a resident or a nonresident of the United States as that term is used and defined in the Internal Revenue Code and the accompanying regulations. If he is a resident, his tax burden becomes substantially more than it would otherwise be, and disasterous tax consequences can flow to the foreign investor under such circumstances.

Further, an NRA, irrespective of the class of income he may generate in the United States, is subject to certain rules relating to tax return exemptions and deductions:

1. Generally, an NRA cannot file a joint return with his spouse.
2. An NRA is not entitled to the standard deduction.
3. He cannot claim certain dependents.
4. If, during a taxable year, his status changes from nonresident to resident, his tax must be computed twice.

It becomes important, therefore, to examine in more detail the meaning of the word *residence* as used in the Internal Revenue Code. Let's review again why it's so important. Assume for a moment that our NRA who has investments in the United States becomes a resident. What happens?

1. All his income from any source becomes subject to U.S. taxation, not just his U.S.-source income.
2. His class 1 income is subject to normal U.S. tax rates which may be higher than the 30 percent maximum on an NRA, or even lower, if the treaty rate applies.
3. Any corporation in which he owns stock or in which his family is involved immediately becomes a controlled foreign corporation which requires the filing of various informational returns.
4. He must disclose all signature rights on all foreign bank accounts.
5. All capital gains are now going to be taxable.
6. Any gifts he makes anywhere in the world will be taxable, and upon his death, his estate will be subject to U.S. estate and probate taxes.
7. Perhaps most devastating of all, if the NRA has made an error in determining his status, he probably has not filed tax returns which may subject him to substantial interest and penalty claims in addition to the tax he may owe. It can thus be seen that the determination of residency is critical.

What are the factors to be considered in analyzing residency?

THE REGULATIONS. The regulations provide that an alien actually present in the United States who is not a mere transient or sojourner is a resident of the United States for purposes of income tax. Thus, to maintain his nonresident status, the alien when present in the United States must maintain his status as a transient.

CASES AND RULINGS.   Several factors are to be considered. U.S. residency requires a union of act and intent, that is, the NRA doesn't intend to remain here as a mere transient.

TIME IN THE UNITED STATES.   The length of time he is here in the United States is a significant factor.

IMMIGRATION STATUS.   Though this is not determinative by law, it is very significant and frequently persuasive. The possession by an alien of a so-called green card is a very persuasive indication of his residency status, but it is not absolute for income tax purposes. The question could be asked at this point: If a person does not have an immigrant visa, is he thereby immune from being determined a resident for tax purposes? No clear answer can be given to this question, unfortunately. And this underlines the requirement for care in reviewing the factors which determine the alien's status.

Other factors to consider.   The location of the taxpayer's family is an important consideration. If the alien brings his family to the United States, this indicates his desire to establish U.S. residency. The social activities of the alien must also be considered. Does he join local clubs, churches, and business organizations?

AVOIDANCE OF RESIDENCY CLASSIFICATION.   These actions can be taken by an alien to avoid being classified as a resident for tax purposes:

1. He should limit his stay in the United States in any one calendar year to not more than 183 days.
2. His abode in the United States should be rented on a short-term basis. If he owns a condominium, it should be treated and cared for as a vacation home—as a second home would be.
3. He should avoid obtaining a green card unless other, nontax factors dictate obtaining such a card. If he obtains one, he should leave the United States as soon afterward as possible and limit his subsequent visits to as short a period as feasible.
4. He should leave his family at home unless they habitually travel with him throughout the world.
5. He should refrain from joining any social, religious, or other group in the United States, and conversely, he should maintain such contacts and memberships elsewhere.
6. He should continually bear in mind that his home is elsewhere and his temporary abode is in the United States.
7. All applications or forms requiring a U.S. address should clearly note that the address is a temporary one and that his permanent home is elsewhere.
8. Where practicable, he should have departing travel plans established with a reservation.
9. He should maintain an office abroad not in the United States. When an office is required, it should be a temporary one at best.
10. He should avoid charge accounts with local merchants. International cards with the statements mailed abroad are to be encouraged, however.
11. He should have an international driver's license not a U.S. license.

12.   Ownership of a car in the United States should be avoided.
13.   He should maintain bank accounts abroad with only short-term accounts in the United States, except to the extent that he needs such a depository.

Where the issue of residency is important, the foreign investor should consult with competent tax counsel. Preplanning of his activities is imperative. His length of stay is critical. Often his plans to emigrate to the United States conflict with sound tax planning. Full coordination between tax and immigration counsel must be observed.

IMMIGRATION LAWS AND VISAS—A BRIEF REVIEW

Why should the foreign investor and his advisors be concerned about the U.S. immigration laws? The immigration status of the foreign investor can bear on his tax status and on his or her ability to conduct business activities in the United States. In addition, many foreign investors desire to use real estate investment and participation in real estate ventures as part of a plan to qualify for entry into the United States and/or for obtaining citizenship. Thus, proper tax planning and investment counseling require an examination of the interrelationship of U.S. tax laws and immigration statutes.

Basic administration

U.S. immigration laws are administered by the U.S. Federal Immigration and Naturalization Service (INS). The INS is part of the Justice Department in the United States and part of the State Department overseas through various U.S. consulates. Aliens are generally placed in two classes—immigrants and nonimmigrants. Nonimmigrants are in the United States on a nonpermanent basis. Immigrants are aliens in the United States with permission to live and work in the United States on a permanent basis. Caution: you can be a nonimmigrant for INS purposes and still be considered a resident for United States income tax purposes.

The procedure involved in obtaining an immigrant visa is often complex and time-consuming (it's called a green card but the card is currently blue!). A green card allows the holder free access in and out of the United States and means the holder will become eligible for United States citizenship within five years.

Nonimmigrant visas

The following summarizes the types of nonimmigrant visas and comments on their use by the foreign investor. These visas are generally obtained at United States consulates outside the United States.

1.   **THE A VISA.** These are generally issued to high government officials and are generally called diplomatic visas. These visas do not prohibit investment in the United States.

2.   **THE B-1 VISA.** This is called a business visitor visa and is issued to nonresident aliens who come to the United States for purposes relating to their

existing business outside the United States. Using this visa, the holder can invest in United States real estate and seek professional advise here.

These visas are usually easy to obtain, but they are generally issued for short durations (not exceeding six months), and extensions are similarly limited. Under a B-1 visa, the foreign investor cannot work in the United States or probably enter into active real estate ventures where he will receive compensation.

3. **THE B-2 VISA.** This is a tourist visa generally limited to 30 days.

4. **THE E-1 VISA—THE TREATY TRADER VISA.** This is an important tool for the foreign investor. It permits a stay up to one year and is readily renewable if the foreign investor's business qualifies. However, such a visa is limited to nationals of countries that have concluded a treaty of friendship, commerce, and navigation with the United States. In addition to this treaty qualification, the alien himself must be involved with an existing enterprise which conducts substantial trade with the United States. This is a popular visa since it generally permits a one-year stay and is readily renewable.

5. **THE E-2 VISA—THE TREATY INVESTOR VISA.** This visa, like the E-1 visa, is limited to nationals of countries that have treaties of friendship, commerce, and navigation with the United States. The alien must be the principal investor or a key employee of the investing entity, and the entity must be owned by nationals of the same country. In addition, the investment must be in an active business. Ownership of undeveloped land will not qualify. This visa does not require the enterprise to involve importation or exportation as does the E-1 visa.

6. **THE F-1 VISA.** This visa is typically given to students, and a spouse of a student can obtain an F-2 visa.

7. **THE L VISA.** This visa is used to transfer aliens employed by an entity to the United States for continued employment by the same entity (or an affiliate). To qualify, the alien must serve in an executive capacity, possess special knowledge and skill, and have been employed by the entity for at least one year.

This visa will work for use by a foreign investor who owns a foreign entity, establishes a U.S. subsidiary, and then transfers himself to the United States. He can work in the United States for the entity and engage in real estate investment if he retains his employement. This visa can be renewed annually. The spouse of the holder of an L visa can qualify for entry into the United States but cannot work.

Immigrant visas

Let us turn now to the types of immigrant visas. These visas are subject to quotas restricting the number of persons who may immigrate each year.

Certain categories of individuals are exempt from the quota system, such as a spouse, minor children, and parents of a U.S. citizen. There are eight categories subject to the quotas.

1. Unmarried sons and daughters of U.S. citizens are allocated the first 20 percent.
2. Spouses and unmarried sons and daughters of lawful U.S. resident aliens are allocated the next 20 percent.
3. The next 10 percent of the quota is allocated to professionals, scientists, and artists.
4. Married sons and daughters of U.S. citizens are allocated the next 10 percent of the quota.
5. Brothers and sisters of U.S. citizens over 21 are allocated the next 24 percent of the quota.
6. The next 10 percent of the quota is allocated to individuals capable of performing specified skilled or unskilled labor for which a shortage of employable and willing persons exists in the United States.
7. Six percent of the quota is allocated to refugees who are likely to encounter political, religious, or racial persecution if returned to their countries of nationality.
8. The final category consists of various other groups, including individuals who are sufficiently financially secure that they will not have to work in the United States and individuals who have invested substantial sums in U.S. business enterprises in which they will act as principal managers. This can aid the financially able foreign real estate investor.

Obtaining a quota number is not enough. The immigrant must pass a security check which requires cooperation by his existing country. Also, quota numbers must be available. In many cases this results in substantial delays. In such an event, the applicant may consider applying for nonimmigrant entry.

To qualify for the sixth preference, the alien must have both a job offer from a U.S. employer and a certification from the U.S. Department of Labor that no qualified and willing U.S. resident can be found to fill the position. Aliens who qualify for the L visa may in many cases qualify for this preference.

The foreign investor who can show he has the economic ability to invest substantial capital in a business enterprise in which he will be the principal investor or who can demonstrate that his income and investments are such that he does not have to work may qualify under the last category set forth above. This is a very fruitful area for counseling the foreign investor. If the foreign investor has over $50,000 to invest, he may meet this requirement.

Where to apply

Applications for immigrant visas may be made in the United States or at a United States consulate overseas. What factors should be considered?

1. Generally if the applicant files in the United States he cannot leave without INS approval. Filing in the United States may delay processing more than filing overseas.
2. If application is made in the United States, this may affect the alien's tax status. This trap should not be overlooked.

As can be seen, the immigration laws are complex and technical. I am not an immigration specialist. The alien should seek the advice of competent immigration counsel who can work with other professionals, such as tax and real estate counselors, to coordinate the tax planning, real estate investment, and immigration goals of the foreign investor.

AVOIDING OR MINIMIZING PERSONAL LIABILITY AND CONSTRUCTION LOANS

This chapter deals with concepts of personal liability and the issue of downside risk inherent in real property investment. Since these risks are an integral part of construction financing, this chapter will also explore typical construction lending practices by institutional lenders and methods of minimizing or avoiding personal liability in that context. We will discuss in this chapter the following topics:

1. The purchase money concept and its limitations.
2. Personal liability and what it really means.
3. Usury—what it means and its limitations.
4. Guarantees—how they work, how they are enforced.
5. Personal liability of a general partner in a partnership.
6. Performance bonds—their use and limitation.
7. Corporations—as an insulation to personal liability and problems attendant with undercapitalization and alter ego.
8. The use of adequate forms of insurance.
9. The mechanics of construction financing, mechanics liens, and relationships with general contractors.

Before we get to a specific discussion of the items just enumerated, it is important to make a general observation. Experience has shown me that many real estate brokers, other financial advisors to the foreign investor, and in some cases attorneys, have been mistaken about the law or at best have been reluctant to advise the foreign investor of the potential exposure for personal liability arising from a real estate transaction. It has been frequently stated, "Oh, there's no personal liability on a real estate loan. The only thing the lender can do is to foreclose upon the property, and you don't have to worry about being stuck for anything personally." This is *not* necessarily a true statement. As you will see, there can be substantial downside risk and liability to the foreign investor. All of us in recent years have been living in an era of rising prices and inflation. Real estate as a general rule has been increasing in value. However, the fact, that this has been true in recent years doesn't necessarily mean that this trend will continue in the future. A prudent foreign investor and his advisors will keep in mind the potential risk attendant in a real estate project. Even in eras of inflation, there have been cyclical fluctuations in the real estate marketplace. Pockets of economic recession or depression in various areas within the United States or in specific industries can expose the foreign investor to personal liability. In representing institutional lenders, I have found that if a loss is imminent, institutional lenders will become extremely aggressive in enforcing their rights. Indeed, it could be argued that it is the obligation of the institutional lender for the protection of its stockholders and depositors to take vigorous action to recover obligations legitimately due even if this means institution of litigation against borrowers whether they be foreign or domestic. Don't be lulled into a sense of false security. Be very cautious before you pick up your pen and sign a promissory note, guarantee, building and loan agreement, or the other instruments that will be discussed in this chapter. Remember, what goes up can also come down, and when it comes down, the lenders are looking for a source of payment. In many instances that best source of payment is the foreign investor since usually at this juncture the foreign investor's local American participant is overextended.

Let us turn now to a more detailed examination of the topics enumerated above.

THE PURCHASE MONEY CONCEPT AND ITS LIMITATIONS

Are there circumstances in real estate acquisitions or financing where there is no personal liability? The answer to the question is a qualified yes. In many states in the United States the legislatures have adopted what is commonly referred to as the *purchase money* concept. Under a purchase money concept, if a seller of real property elects to finance a portion of the total purchase price by agreeing to carry back a note and deed of trust, should there be a default on the part of the buyer, the sole remedy of the seller is to foreclose under the power of sale contained in his deed of trust and reacquire the property. In addition, as a further extension of the purchase money concept, the laws of some of the states provide that, in instances involving personal residences (as distinguished from commercial or industrial property) when a loan is made to facilitate the acquisition of a single-family residence, the lender has no right to seek personal liability against the buyer but must look solely to the real property involved in the sale. These concepts can best be illustrated by an example. Let's assume that a buyer wishes to purchase a single-family residence for a purchase price of $200,000. The buyer has $100,000 cash, the seller is an older person, semiretired, who would like to enjoy monthly payments. The property, let's assume, is free and clear. So the seller agrees to carry back a promissory note secured by a first deed of trust bearing interest at 12 percent per annum amortized over a 20-year period with a 10-year due date. Let's assume further that because of circumstances beyond the control of the buyer, the buyer has to abandon the property and can no longer make the monthly payments. In this instance the sole remedy of the seller would be to foreclose under the power of sale contained in the deed of trust and reacquire the property. Let's change the facts slightly. The same sale for $200,000, but in this situation the seller wants to be cashed out of the deal. The buyer has only $100,000 cash. Therefore, the buyer goes to Friendly Savings and Loan Association and asks for a loan of $100,000. Friendly Savings and Loan agrees to this proposition, and concurrently with closing the purchase escrow between buyer and seller, it grants a $100,000 loan to the buyer secured by a first deed of trust on the house. The proceeds of that loan are paid to the seller who has now been paid in full. On the close of the transaction, the buyer is now the owner of the property subject to a first deed of trust in favor of the savings and loan association. Suppose there is a default on the note in favor of the savings and loan? Under these circumstances the *only* remedy the savings and loan would have would be to foreclose under the power of sale contained in its deed of trust. It can seek no personal liability against the buyer. Suppose that in either of the examples a disaster occurs. Let's assume there is an earthquake or some other casualty loss uninsured by the standard coverage insurance customarily in effect, and as a result of the casualty loss, the house becomes worthless and the fair market value of the land drops to $25,000. Can either the seller or the savings and loan look personally to the buyer to recover the difference between the value of the land after the casualty and the sums still owing? Under the purchase money concept the answer is no. The risk falls upon the seller or the lender as the case may be, and no personal liability is imposed on the buyer/borrower. However, caution should be exercised in this area.

The purchase money concept has *not* been adopted in all of the states of the United States. The local laws of each jurisdiction must be carefully examined to determine whether or not the obligation in question is free of the downside risk of personal liability. You should consult local, experienced real estate counsel to determine your potential liability under the purchase money concept. Let's assume that the state in which you are doing business has not adopted the purchase money concept. Can you still avoid personal liability? Obviously, the answer is yes. Generally there is no public policy or legal requirement in the various states that requires you as a borrower or purchaser to assume the risk of personal liability. You can negotiate with your seller and/or your lender as the case may be for what is commonly referred to as an *exculpatory clause.* An exculpatory clause is merely a provision in which the lender agrees in the event of default that it will look solely and only to the real estate to satisfy the debt and will seek no personal liability or judgment against the borrower. Exculpatory clauses are common in large commercial and industrial transactions. Many sophisticated, financially astute borrowers have taken the position successfully over the years with institutional lenders that under no circumstances will they retain personal liability. Where personal liability is waived there may be adverse tax consequences.

A further word of caution in this whole area of the purchase money concept. In many states where the purchase money concept is in effect, it applies only to residential property actually occupied, and personal liability still exists in many instances where commercial, industrial, or multiunit residential properties are involved. As an example, assume that the buyer wishes to purchase a 20-unit apartment building for $1 million. The seller wants to be cashed out of the transaction, but the buyer only has $300,000 cash. The buyer obtains a loan from Friendly Savings and Loan Association for $700,000 securing that loan by a first deed of trust on the apartment project. Even though that loan closes concurrently with the purchase of the property from the seller, there will be no purchase money exemption. Should an uninsured casualty loss occur, the savings and loan may seek personal liability and recover a judgment against the borrower/purchaser. A careful review of state law and a careful review of insurance requirements will minimize the exposure for downside risk and ultimate personal liability in circumstances of this kind. However, you cannot insure against changing economic conditions. What if the property is vacant? What if there is high unemployment? Personal liability is a factor that must be evaluated.

THE CONCEPT OF USURY

What is usury? Usury is generally defined as charging an interest rate for the use or forebearance of money in excess of the maximum amount permitted by law. In almost all instances, usury is the sole province of each state. The usury laws of each state vary materially. The maximum amount of interest that can be charged is not uniform throughout the United States. The penalties imposed for a usurious transaction vary materially from state to state. In many instances the type of loan determines the usury rate. Thus, in some jurisdictions personal, family, and household loans (i.e., consumer loans) have a maximum rate of, let us assume, 10 percent, while loans made to corporations for industrial, commercial, or business purposes have a maximum interest rate of, let us assume, 20 percent. For example, in some states the maximum interest rate that can be charged by a lender in a commercial transaction is 5 percent over and above that rate charged by the Federal Reserve Bank to local banks within its jurisdiction to borrow funds. In some jurisdictions certain types of real estate transactions have been deemed exempt from the usury statutes permitting a seller of property to charge any interest he can negotiate with a buyer on the reasoning that, instead of raising the interest rate or lowering the interest rate, the amount of the purchase price could be adjusted with the same result. What happens if there is a violation of the local usury laws? In most states interest paid in excess of that permitted by law is refundable. In some states *all* interest paid on the note and not just the excessive portion is refundable. And in other states, not only does the lender lose his right to collect any interest on the obligation, but he also loses his principal, and the borrower may, in fact, recover sums previously paid—both interest and principal. A careful examination of the laws of each state must be made.

A word of caution in this area of usury. It's a complex and technical subject. Suppose the maximum usury rate in a particular state is 12 percent per annum. Suppose the borrower signs a promissory note to pay 12 percent interest on the unpaid balance of the funds he has borrowed, but in addition, the lender charges an initial fee for granting the loan. This initial fee is commonly referred to in the trade as *points*. Let's assume that the lender makes a loan of $100,000 at 12 percent interest per annum and charges two points for granting the loan (i.e., $2,000). Is that loan usurious? In almost all states the loan would be declared usurious. In testing usury all monies paid to the lender for the use of funds are used in calculating the effective interest rate. Suppose the promissory note of the lender contains a prepayment penalty? That is to say that if the note is prepaid by the borrower voluntarily prior to its maturity, the borrower must pay a penalty for the privilege of prepaying the note. Does this make the obligation usurious? In most states the answer to the question is no. Since the prepayment of the obligation is a voluntary act controlled solely by the borrower, the payment by the borrower of a prepayment penalty at the time of early payoff is not used in calculating whether or not an obligation is usurious. In almost all states the question of usury is tested at the time the loan is made.

Time does not permit a more detailed discussion of the whole subject of usury. There are many cases in which the courts have held that they will look to the substance of the transaction and not the form of the documents in testing whether or not a transaction is in fact a loan and whether or not said loan is usurious. Many schemes have been attempted by resourceful lenders to take advantage of needy borrowers and thus avoid the usury statutes. In most states, banks, savings and loan associations, and similar financial institutions are exempt from usury statutes and can charge whatever the traffic will bear. You must analyze the law in each state to determine usury in a specific transaction.

Suppose the promissory note in question contains a variable interest rate provision. As you will recall, a variable interest rate provision allows the lender to increase or decrease the interest rate on the unpaid principal balance based upon some objective criteria such as prime rate, rediscount rate or other object standards. Does that make the loan usurious if at a subsequent time the interest rate exceeds the maximum amount permitted by law at the time the loan was originally granted? In most instances the answer would be no, but again a careful examination of the statutes in cases in each jurisdiction must be reviewed. I must emphasize again that there are no uniform usury laws throughout the United States. The usury laws, the penalties, the procedures, and the statutes of limitations vary substantially from jurisdiction to jurisdiction. Look carefully before you deal. Remember further that if you're a seller, and as a seller you agree to carry back paper as part of the purchase price, you become a lender. Whether or not you are subject to usury laws or exempt from them again depends upon a careful review of the laws of the jurisdiction in question. The issue can even become further complicated if your contract of sale is consummated in one state but the real property exists in another state. Which law do you apply—the law of the state where the contract is drawn or the law of the state where the property is located? No firm answer to this question can be given, but it is illustrative of the technical nature of usury. Suppose you as a borrower feel that the transaction in question is usurious. How do you enforce your rights? A careful examination of state and local laws is required to answer such a question definitively. Each state has different methods of enforcement, each state has a particular statute of limitations (that is to say, a time limit in which the borrower must act). It is suggested that the matter be discussed carefully with competent local counsel before proceeding.

Notwithstanding all I have said on usury, there is now a federal statute that preempts certain types of loans and imposes maximum rates if the statute is applicable. To determine maximum rates a lender can charge, a review must be made of the federal law to see if it applies and then to state law.

GUARANTEES AND THEIR ENFORCEMENT

In the real estate context, what is a guarantee? A guarantee is merely an obligation on the part of the guarantor to agree to pay an obligation or perform an act if the primary borrower fails to pay or perform. Real estate guarantees generally evolve out of two situations—in the construction context and as a general guarantee for borrowed capital. A word of caution about standard form, institutional guarantees. By definition a guarantee is an obligation on the part of the guarantor to perform only if the primary borrower defaults. However, a careful examination of the typical language in an institutional guarantee will reveal that the document being signed by the guarantor is not a true guarantee but is, in fact, a joint and several obligation to pay. Why is this distinction important? Under classic concepts of a guarantee, the lender must proceed first against the primary debtor, exhaust all of his remedies, and, if the lender is still unable to recover all sums owed or performance due, it can then turn to the guarantor. Under a joint and several obligation to pay, however, the lender does not have to exhaust his remedies against the original borrower but can proceed directly against the so-called guarantor. The drafting and enforcement of guarantees is a highly technical and sophisticated area. The law of guarantee differs materially from state to state. Should a guarantee be an instrument relevant to a real estate transaction in which you are involved, either as a borrower or a lender, it is imperative that you consult with local counsel who is facile in this area and obtain his careful advice. See Forms 52 and 53 respectively for a typical guarantee involved in completion of construction and a typical general guarantee. Both of these forms are very broad in nature and have incorporated primarily some specific provisions of California law and should be used only as examples. Should the primary debtor go bankrupt or have other problems with its general creditors, a guarantee can become an important instrument. As a general rule, unless a guarantee is carefully and properly drawn in accordance with all of the applicable statutes and provisions of each local jurisdiction, any modifications or changes in the *primary* obligation by the lender will exonerate (i.e., release) the guarantor. This whole concept can be a trap for the unwary. Experience has shown this author that if a guarantee is truly a material part of the transaction, it should be drafted with great specificity and careful thought. If the reader desires additional information concerning this subject, there is an excellent publication referred to in the *California Continuing Education of the Bar* series. Please refer to Appendix 5 for additional information in this area.

PARTNERSHIP LIABILITY AND EXPOSURE

As discussed in previous chapters in this book, the general partner of a general partnership or the general partner of a limited partnership exposes himself to extensive, personal liability for all of the acts of other general partners and the obligations incurred in the partnership name. In almost all instances the creditor is not limited only to recovering from the assets of the partnership but may, in fact, seek personal liability against the general partner. The problem is exacerbated by the fact that one general partner can bind all of the other general partners to absolute personal liability for all obligations of the partnership incurred in the ordinary course of business. This is true even if the foreign investor is in fact a minority general partner. Care and caution must be used in choosing your cogeneral partner. The foreign investor, in making the decision to become a general partner in a partnership, should consider the possibility of acquiring from his cogeneral partners an indemnity agreement permitting him to look to the other general partners for relief from specific obligations and may in many cases consider securing that indemnity with adequate collateral such as other real estate of the other general partners.

CORPORATIONS AS AN INSULATION AGAINST LIABILITY _____

Under American legal principles, a corporation, whether it be formed in the United States or in a foreign country, is a separate legal entity or person. In contrast, a partnership does not hold such status and is not, in fact, a separate legal entity for liability purposes. Acknowledging the fact that a corporation is a separate, recognized legal entity, all obligations and liabilities incurred in the name of the corporation do not, as a general rule, impose individual liability upon the officers of the corporation, its directors, or shareholders. However, sophisticated sellers and lenders are aware of this legal distinction and in many instances will require personal guarantees of the obligations incurred in the name of and on behalf of the corporation. If a debt is incurred in the name of the corporation only, and there is no personal guarantee of the individual officer, shareholder, or director, can that person still be exposed to personal liability for the debts of the corporation? The answer is a qualified yes. U.S. legal principles also incorporate the doctrine of alter ego. If a corporation is substantially undercapitalized, if the corporation incurs debts and obligations well beyond any possibility of repayment, if the corporation is substantially controlled by an individual, there is a body of case law and statute which in some instances permits creditors to look behind the shield of the corporate entity and seek personal redress against the officers, directors, and shareholders of a particular corporation. In addition, if a party acting as an officer, managing director, or general director of a corporation makes personal statements or misrepresentations, that person can be held personally liable for any damages arising from his acts or actions. It is no defense to say he was acting merely as an officer of the corporation. He may, in addition, be held responsible for his own acts of negligence, misrepresentation, or non-action.

In adequate tax planning for the foreign investor, it is customary to use a series of corporations. The foreign investor is cautioned that in setting up and using a number of different legal entities (which customarily involve the forming of overseas corporations and a series of subsidiary and sister corporations) it is imperative, in order to maintain not only the tax benefits inherent in such plans but also the insulation against personal liability, that: (1) adequate books and records be maintained for each entity; (2) that there be no comingling of funds between entities; (3) each entity be adequately capitalized; (4) adequate minutes and records be kept as to each entity; (5) all of the formal requirements for the formation and maintenance of each entity be strictly observed. Insulation against creditors and the success of a tax plan can fail if proper attention is not paid to the everyday details of business operations of each entity created. Again, this is a highly technical area. Should the reader require additional information concerning the formation of corporations, their maintenance and operation, and the exposure and liability one assumes as an officer or director, he is again referred to Appendix 5. There are several excellent works put out by the *Continuing Education of the Bar* series dealing with liability of corporate officers and directors.

INSURANCE TO AVOID LIABILITY

The ownership of real property in the United States carries with it certain inherent risks. An owner of real property in the United States is obligated to maintain the property in such a manner that it does not create a hazard to the public in general or to those parties who may occupy or use portions of the property. In addition, contrary to the attitudes in many foreign countries, American citizens are generally quite litigation-prone. Thus, even though the foreign investor may be held to have operated and maintained his property in a nonnegligent manner, the cost of defending lawsuits can become prohibitive. In addition, in order to protect property and economic investment, prudent business practice requires that the foreign investor, whether dealing individually or through an entity, maintain broad-form insurance coverage insuring the property against loss arising from: (1) fire, theft, vandalism, and other acts of God; (2) damage to the property of others; (3) injuries suffered by those parties who may have occasion to be physically present on the property even though in some extreme cases those persons would be considered illegal trespassers. Again, the whole area of insurance is a highly technical one. Volumes have been written on the nature and the types of insurance, on types of policies, on liability, and the coverage that can be obtained. As a general rule in the United States, if you are willing to pay enough money, you can insure any risk or eventuality. As a practical matter, the cost of insurance for any possible risk can become prohibitive. Foreign investors should find a reputable, qualified insurance agent, discuss the project fully with him, and obtain a detailed analysis of available coverage. Choosing your insurance agent is as important as choosing your broker, accountant, banker or lawyer.

Setting aside these generalities, we can deal with certain specific items common on many real property acquisitions and transactions. All insurance policies are not alike. Coverage afforded by insurance companies vary. The attitude towards paying claims varies between companies. The cost of insurance for the same coverage can often vary between companies. The use of a skilled, professional insurance counselor can in most instances pay dividends to the foreign investor. How far should the foreign investor go in obtaining coverage, and what limits should he undertake? The question cannot be answered specifically. Obviously the particular facts and circumstances of the property, its physical conditions, its general location, climactic conditions in the area in which the property is located, the amount of insurance that may be carried by tenants, all are factors to be considered. Several thoughts, however, can be set forth at this point that may be of some guidance to the foreign investor and his counselor:

1. Adequate general liability insurance should be carried by the foreign investor insuring against loss occasioned from injuries sustained on the real property and its improvements by tenants, invitees, and trespassers including the obligation to adequately defend any claims that may be raised no matter

how unjust they may seem. Keep in mind that the foreign investor in most cases is a target defendant.

2. The amount of coverage and the limits of liability will depend on the nature of the transaction. The foreign investor, however, should be aware that in most states in the United States the difference in premium between a general liability limit of $1 million and $1.5 million is relatively small. When it comes to the question of the amount of fire insurance, adequate consideration should be given not only to the cost initially incurred in acquiring the property, but what its replacement cost would be in light of present construction costs and inflation. Be sure that the coverage is adequate to rebuild the property based on present market conditions, but do not overinsure. For instance, if the actual value and replacement cost of particular improvements is $500,000, a policy with a limit of $1 million and its attendant premium will give no more coverage to the foreign investor than if the policy had been for $500,000 initially. As a general rule, insurance companies are merely obligated to pay the actual damages suffered notwithstanding the written limits contained in the policy. In many instances, insitutional lenders will require that fire insurance be maintained for an amount equal to the unpaid balance of the lender's loan even though in some cases this amount may exceed the cost of replacing the insured improvements. Should this event occur, negotiations with the lender in most instances will permit modification of the insurance coverage to equal the replacement value of the assets being insured.

3. As previously mentioned elsewhere in this text, most policies of fire insurance do not cover the contents and personal property in the building. To have adequate coverage for the personal property located within real estate improvements generally requires specific endorsements to the policy. Further, should you wish to insure jewelry, objects of art, or other items of special value, most insurance underwriters will require inventories (specifically scheduling each of the items of personal property) and charge an appropriate premium to insure against their loss by the elements, theft, vandalism, and so on. Discuss this adequately and fully with your insurance counselor.

4. If the property involved is income-producing, that is to say, if the property being insured is a commerical building, apartment project, or industrial building, by specific endorsement the insurance company will grant you coverage for loss of rental income. This can become an important concept. Should there be a casualty on the property, in most instances the obligation of a tenant to pay rent ceases. However, your obligation to pay your mortgage, to pay insurance premiums, and to pay real estate taxes continues without abatement. You can cover yourself against this eventuality by obtaining endorsements to your policy for loss of rental income. The scope and nature of that coverage depends on the facts and circumstances in each instance.

5. Shopping for insurance is an important concept. Premiums differ from insurance underwriter to insurance underwriter. The use of professional insurance counselors who have a pulse on the entire insurance marketplace pays you dividends. In addition, when the property in question is large in nature or has a particular, sophisticated, special use, obtaining insurance can sometimes be difficult and expensive. Experience has shown that the larger the project, the more attention should be paid to insurance, its coverage, and its cost. The use of very large insurance agencies who have the economic clout to

negotiate with underwriters can be of benefit to you in placing insurance with adequate limits and at reasonable premium rates.

6. Specialized types of insurance or endorsements can be obtained, again depending on the particular circumstances, and the amount of money you are willing to spend. As an example, do you want flood endorsements? Do you want earthquake and tornado coverage? What about fidelity bonds for loss of income due to embezzlement by employees? What about workers' compensation for injuries incurred by employees working on the property? Each of these items can and should be considered for coverage.

7. Most institutional lenders require that they be furnished periodically with copies of all existing insurance policies concerning the improvements, and further, that the lender be named as a loss payee under the policy and that they be furnished with certificates of insurance and other evidence that the coverage is in effect. Therefore, as a practical matter, when a casualty loss occurs, all insurance proceeds will be made payable in most instances jointly to the lender and to the vested owner of the property. This will require you as the owner to then make your peace with the lender as to the use of the proceeds. This whole issue was discussed in a previous chapter. Careful prenegotiations should be held between a borrower and a lender to be sure that the borrower is able to use these insurance proceeds to repair and rebuild the damaged property.

CONSTRUCTION FINANCING AND PROCEDURES

Let us turn now to a discussion of construction financing and procedure. Of course, whole volumes have been written on construction loans, construction contracts, mechanics liens, and the other areas involved in construction financing. Should the reader desire additional information concerning construction financing and its administration, he should consult Appendix 5 which lists several excellent publications of the *Continuing Education of the Bar* series dealing with these subjects in detail. Refer to Form 51, a typical building loan agreement and Form 54, construction contract. There are, however, certain basic concepts and principles to aid the foreign investor and his advisors in the construction field. We will discuss: an understanding of the basic principles of mechanics liens; the use of performance bonds; labor and material releases; the use of cost breakdowns; the uses of detailed plans and specifications; negotiations with architects and architectural agreements; loan disbursement administration; closing procedures; and points and interest. We will explore each of these subjects in more detail in a moment. It must, however, be emphasized that we can only scratch the surface of this area. Many volumes have been written on construction financing, construction procedure, architectural agreements, from a legal viewpoint, banking viewpoint, accounting viewpoint, administrative and tax planning viewpoint. Obviously a book of this nature does not permit a detailed analysis of each of these items.

Architect's plans and specifications. I am assuming at this point that the foreign investor (or his entity or, of course, a joint venture or partnership in which he is involved) desires to cause improvements to be designed and later constructed on the real property in question. It has been this author's experience over many years in dealing with construction projects that one of the most important decisions the foreign investor can make is choosing a competent architect. In many instances the success or failure of the proposed project will be governed by the quality of the design and the cost savings that a competent architect can build into the product he is creating. I believe that it is penny-wise and pound-foolish to use a planned, checking service or to use any party other than a well-established, competent, knowledgeable architect in conceiving the proposed improvements. Another area to be avoided, in my opinion is the so-called package deal where the general contractor who will ultimately build the project also supplies the plans and specifications for the proposed structures as part of a package arrangement. Except in unusual circumstances, this is an unsatisfactory and costly procedure in the long run. This general rule, of course, has exceptions. When you are dealing with specialized construction such as shopping centers, specialized industrial plants, and hotels, using a contractor who also has architectural capabilities is justified. A competent, reputable architect, in addition to conceiving and designing the actual structures to be built, can have a substantial input in the initial design and layout of the proposed project. He can often effect maximum use of the land, thus maximizing income and reducing costs. Bringing an architect into the initial planning stages of a project is prudent business practice in almost every instance. In addition, it is urgently recommended if the circumstances will permit, to attempt to consult with a knowledgeable and reputable building contractor at the beginning of the planning stages of a construction project and certainly before the plans and specifications are finalized. Generally speaking, knowledgeable building contractors take a practical, everyday approach to the development of a property. In many instances, architects tend to be more artistic and may lose sight of cost factors in development projects. The melding together of the practical approach of a good building contractor with the esthetic and design capabilities of a competent architect generally produces the best finished product.

There are two types of architectural agreements. The first requires the architect to be involved in initial planning of the project, preparing the detailed plans and specifications, processing them through the local governmental offices, and obtaining building permits and intermittent inspections during the course of construction to be sure that the structures being built comply with the final plans and specification. The second type of architectural agreement incorporates all of the matters in the first type of agreement, but in addition, the architect renders substantial additional services and acts as the owner's representative during all of the phases of construction. He certifies all requests for progress billings. He negotiates any modifications or changes during the course of construction. In substance, he becomes the on-the-job supervisor of the project and the day-to-day representative of the owner. Whether or not the foreign investor desires the second category of architectural services, of course, depends on the nature of the transaction, the complexity of the work to be performed, the requirements of the lender, and whether or not the foreign investor through his American associates has sophisticated associates physically present during the course of construction with the experience, expertise, reputation, and financial stability to assume this function.

The foreign investor should keep in mind that the bids he will receive from general contractors or individual subcontractors to construct the proposed improvements will be based upon the plans and specifications prepared by the architect. If the plans and specifications are detailed and specific, the investor will know what he is getting for his money. An example will illustrate my point. Several years ago, I was an arbitrator (under the rules of the American Arbitration Association) in a dispute between a contractor and an owner. The plans and specifications for the project were prepared by the contractor and called for "aluminum doors and an aluminum store front." No other criteria was set forth. The testimony elicited at the arbitration hearing revealed that there were at least six different grades of aluminum doors and store fronts. The contractor, of course, chose the lowest quality and level of aluminum door. These doors constantly required adjustment, and there were numerous complaints by the occupants of the building. The panel was required under the circumstances to rule in favor of the contractor. The whole problem could have been avoided if the plans and specifications spelled out the type and quality of aluminum doors and store front that was to be installed. The American Institute of Architects (AIA) publishes an excellent reference entitled, *Architects Handbook of Professional Practice.* This handbook contains proposed forms of owner-architect agreements, construction documents, general conditions for construction contracts, and numerous other important and valuable materials dealing with insurance, bonds, contract administration, and related subjects. If the reader is interested in further information, he can contact the American Institute of Architects at 1735 New York Avenue, N.V., Washington D.C. 20006. In my experience and opinion, the form AIA agreements should not be taken solely at face value. A number of the provisions may require modification to meet the specific circumstances of the particular project involved and to meet the requirements of local state law, as well as that of the lender in some instances. Again, architectural agreements are subject to negotiation and should be treated merely as a beginning point for defining the relationship between the architect and the owner.

MECHANICS LIENS. In understanding the whole area of architectural agreements, construction contracts, and construction financing, the foreign investor and his advisors should have a basic understanding of the concept of mechanics liens. In substance, a mechanics lien is the granting of a right to a person who furnishes services or materials to a particular construction project to record a lien against the real property (and in some cases the undisbursed funds in the hands of the construction lender) to reimburse him for services rendered or materials furnished to the construction site. The mechanics lien laws of each state differ materially, and of course, the advice of local, competent real estate counsel should be sought by the foreign investor or his advisors when dealing in this area. The problem becomes more complex and dangerous because of the inherent power of the mechanics lien. Perhaps the problem can best be illustrated by an example. Let's assume that you hire a general contractor. In turn, the general contractor hires a subcontractor to install the plumbing in the proposed project. You pay your general contractor for the plumbing work. The general contractor in turn pays the plumbing subcontractor for his services and materials furnished, but the subcontractor fails to pay the supplier who furnished the plumbing fixtures and pipe. By following local procedures, that supplier in most states, has the right to file a mechanics lien against the property. It is no defense to the filing of that lien that you paid the general contractor, and that the subcontractor was supposed to be paid by the general contractor! In most states, should a mechanics lien be filed and not satisfied, the supplier of the plumbing supplies, by filing an appropriate legal action, can cause a foreclosure to be instituted and the real property sold at a foreclosure sale to satisfy the sums due to him! Additional problems arise when there are multiple mechanics liens filed by a number of contractors or suppliers, or when, in addition to filing mechanics liens, suppliers, contractors, or subcontractors also take steps to reach the undisbursed construction proceeds in the hands of the construction lender. Can these potential problems of mechanics liens be minimized or avoided? The answer is a qualified yes. We'll discuss it further below.

CHOOSING THE CONTRACTOR. Basically the foreign investor has several choices in deciding how he will cause the improvements to be constructed. In some instances, particularly where the foreign investor has entered into a partnership agreement with a local American builder or developer, that general partner/ builder/developer will in substance act as a general contractor and sub-out to various trades and subcontractors the elements of the job. As an example, specific subcontracts will be let to plumbing contractors, electrical contractors, roofing contractors, framing contractors, heating and air-conditioning contractors, and similar trades and disciplines. In other instances, there will be one general contract let to a specific general contractor whether that contractor is an associate connected with the project or an independent third party. Which route the foreign investor desires to take obviously depend on the specific facts and circumstances involved in the project in question. Should the foreign investor or one of his American advisors or associates desire to act in substance as the general contractor, the foreign investor should be careful to see that his interests are protected. Will all of the subcontractors be bonded? Will the general partner acting as the general contractor be required to obtain competitive bids for all major components of the project? What will be the percentage of general overhead and supervision charged by the general partner to the partnership or joint venture? How will construction funds be controlled? Can the general partner perform direct construction services, and if so, at what cost? Who will be responsible for contract administration dealing with the lender and coordinating the activities of all of the subcontractors? Will the general partner/developer be personally responsible for any defaults by subcontractors or mechanics liens filed against the project? All of these issues, of course, can be answered by proper consultation with knowledgeable counsel and by incorporating the appropriate safeguards into the partnership agreement or other relevant documents between the foreign investor and his local American associate. These items should be reviewed and addressed at the beginning of the project to avoid misunderstandings and to prevent inordinate and unreasonable expenses being charged against the project which can eat into the profit picture and ultimate equity of the foreign investor.

The American Association of General Contractors has published a series of form contracts and agreements that can be a valuable aide to the foreign investor. In addition, as previously mentioned, the American Institute of Architects has promulgated a series of construction contracts which can form the basis of agreements. Depending on the nature of the project in mind, time should be taken to consult a knowledgeable, real estate attorney familiar with construction agreements to prepare the necessary documents that will be used to form either the general contract or the individual subcontract to be used in connection with a particular project.

There are, of course, different types of contracts. In some cases, if a general contractor is used, he will agree to work either on a cost-plus basis or on a fixed-fee arrangement. From the viewpoint of the foreign investor who does not have association and contact on a day-to-day basis with a local American representative or associate, the use of a so-called turn-key construction contract is advisable. Under this concept, an agreement is entered into between the contractor and the foreign investor whereby the contractor agrees to cause to be constructed the improvements outlined in the plans and specifications for a set maximum price. And he agrees to deliver the improvements at the conclusion of construction in accordance with the plans and specifications and in accordance with all local rules, laws, and ordinances resulting in the issuance of a final certificate of occupancy for the property in question. Of course, the amount of fees to be paid, the nature and extent of the contract, and the obligations of the parties are all subject to negotiation. This again is a complex and sophisticated area. The foreign investor and his advisors are referred to the publications of the American Institute of Architects, the Association of General Contractors, the American Building Institute, and to several excellent publications delineated in Appendix 5 to this book.

Again, let me emphasize that construction contracts or subcontracts are no better than the plans and specifications that are prepared. They should be detailed and specific. In addition, they should incorporate all of the necessary changes required by local building departments. As a matter of procedure, the architect generally prepares plans and specifications. Thereafter, they are submitted by the architect to the local building authorities for their review, comment, and approval. In most instances, building departments will require after inspection and examination of the plans and specifications changes, modifications, or additions. All of these should be incorporated into the final or *permit* set of plans and specifications and all bids received from a general contractor or subcontractor, as the case may be, should incorporate all of these building department changes. This will help the foreign investor and his advisors avoid being charged for substantial extras as part of the construction project and help eliminate cash flow deficits.

BONDING THE JOB.   Keeping in mind the potential problems relating to mechanics liens and the general administration of a construction project, procedures have been adopted to eliminate or minimize the exposure of the owner. In most jurisdictions, a general contractor or subcontractor, as the case may be, can obtain from an independent, financially responsible corporate surety company a performance bond which in substance provides that should the general or subcontractor fail to perform his obligations under his contract, the performance will be guaranteed and made good by the corporate surety. In some jurisdictions, by statute, the proper execution and recordation of a full performance bond will prevent mechanics liens from being filed. This is based on the theory that the financial integrity of the corporate surety is substituted in place of the real property and the claimants are left to look solely to the surety company to recover monies due. Bond forms and requirements differ materially throughout the United States. Consultation with local insurance and surety companies, with local architects and attorneys is essential in this area.

There is another important advantage to the foreign investor from insisting that all construction be fully bonded. In most instances, a corporate surety will not issue a bond either to a general contractor or to a subcontractor unless it has faith in both the financial integrity of the contractor and in his technical competence. Thus, there is a built-in screening device created by the use of performance bonds. There are, of course, additional fees and charges incident to the issuance of performance bonds. The cost usually runs between .75 percent to 2 percent of the total cost of construction. A performance bond is the cheapest form of "insurance" that an owner can acquire. This is particularly relevant to the foreign investor who is normally not present in the United States during the course of construction and has no ability to supervise the day-to-day activities of the contractor, subcontractor, or his American associate or partner. In smaller projects requiring bondable contractors and/or subcontractors, construction costs can increase significantly. The potential cost savings must be compared with potential risk. The smaller the job, the higher the risk, since many small subcontractors are not financially sound.

LOAN ADMINISTRATION. Most construction loans are typically administered by commerical banks and in some instances by savings and loan associations. In almost all instances, as a condition to granting the construction loan, the construction lender will require that it approve the plans and specifications, building permits, construction contract or contracts, and detailed cost breakdowns. In this last regard, the construction lender will require a detailed breakdown and analysis of each of the major elements and components within the project, so that all of the funds to be lent are accounted for and so that there will be sufficient funds left in the undisbursed construction disbursement account to ensure that the project will be fully completed. In addition, most construction lenders will require as a condition for progress payments during the course of construction, that they be furnished by each general and subcontractor with labor and material releases from each contractor, subcontractor, and supplier. By this method, the possibility of mechanics liens being filed is reduced. As a general rule, funds are disbursed on a monthly basis or during certain phases of construction (example: after completion of foundation, after completion of framing, after completion of plumbing, etc.). Whether or not the construction lender or the owner requires that each request for progress payment be certified and approved by an architect is a matter of negotiation in each instance. If more information is required or desired by the reader, there are several excellent publications in the *Continuing Education of the Bar* series outlined in Appendix 5.

INTEREST. The foreign investor should be cautious in dealing with the construction lender to determine whether he is paying interest on the full amount of the construction loan from its beginning or only on funds as they are withdrawn and disbursed to the general or subcontractor. This again, is a matter of negotiation.

Can the foreign investor or his American associate deduct for tax purposes as losses in the year in which expenses are incurred, interest, points, and other sums connected with construction financing? As a general rule, all of these various costs and expenses must be capitalized and cannot be taken as losses during the construction phase of a project. A more detailed analysis of this issue will require you to consult your accountant or attorney.

DEFAULTS AND FORECLOSURE

Let's turn now to another important subject, defaults and foreclosures. The issue raised at this point is what happens if the owner defaults under a note or deed of trust? What are the rights of the lender, and what are the rights of the defaulting borrower? The answer to the question varies materially from state to state. As an example, in California should there be a default under a promissory note secured by a deed of trust, as a matter of law, the defaulting borrower has an absolute right for a period of 90 days from the recording of a notice of default to cure the default and reinstate the loan. This however, is only the rule in one state. The right to cure defaults varies materially from state to state and does not exist at all in certain jurisdictions. Should the foreign investor be concerned about this area, it is strongly recommended that he consult local counsel familiar with real estate transactions. In addition, when a default occurs, in many states the lenders have varying remedies. In some jurisdictions, if the lender elects to foreclose under the power of sale contained in his deed of trust, he waives the right to seek personal liability from the original borrower and any guarantor. In other jurisdictions a lender is required to resort to judicial proceedings in the courts to foreclose. Should a contractor association or subcontractor file a petition in the bankruptcy courts, it is urgently recommended that the foreign investor seek the advice of reputable, knowledgeable bankruptcy counsel immediately. The foreign investor should be aware that under the provisions of United States law, there is automatically incorporated into every contractual agreement all of the provisions of the United States bankruptcy laws which, as a matter of public policy, *cannot* be waived or relinquished in advance by a contractor or subcontractor.

Where income property is involved, foreclosure can be more complex. If a borrower is in default, who is entitled to the rents generated by the property during the foreclosure period? How can these rents be reached? The answer depends on the form of the documents creating the loan and local law. Generally, properly drafted loan documents will permit a lender to demand rents and to constitute appropriate court proceedings to appoint a receiver to collect rents and operate the property. If the defaulting borrower files for protection under the Bankruptcy Act, the issues become more complex. This is not an academic exercise. The foreign investor in all probability will find himself in the status of a lender as a result of a sale pursuant to which he has elected to carry back a note secured by a second deed of trust. In such-instances the foreign investor/seller should be represented by competent counsel. He should secure his note by: (1) a deed of trust (see Forms 17A, 17B, and 18); (2) a security agreement (see Form 49); (3) a financing statement—UCC-1 (see Form 50) and (4) an absolute assignment of rents and profits (see Form 57).

LANDLORD AND TENANTS

What can the foreign investor do if after he purchases U.S. real estate, his tenant defaults? How can he be removed? What are the rights of a landlord? As on most other subjects raised in this book, volumes can be written on each topic. This is another complex area of the law. In addition, the problem has become further complicated due to several factors: (1) changes in local statutes and legal decisions favoring tenants; (2) creation of tenant organizations, legal aid, and public interest law firms militantly advocating tenant rights; (3) local rent control laws which often restrict landlord rights.

The severity of the problem from the landlord's viewpoint varies from place to place and even from city to city. A purchaser of multiunit, residential property must look carefully into the status of existing laws in the jurisdiction controlling the property in question. Eviction procedures vary substantially in each jurisdiction. In my opinion, the problems will only get worse in the next few years, but I must hasten to add, I am landlord-oriented.

If the reader desires more information on this subject, consult Appendix 5.

THE FORMATION, OPERATION, AND TERMINATION OF A NETHERLANDS ANTILLES CORPORATION

This author is not licensed in the Antilles. I do not claim any special expertise as to the formation and operation of a Netherlands Antilles Corporation. The principals and concepts contained in this chapter are derived from general information and my limited practical experience. Form 22 contains typical sample forms of a simple Netherlands Antilles Corporation and related material. Appendix 4 contains copies of the Netherlands and Netherlands Antilles tax treaties, introduction to taxation in the Antilles, and related forms. The reader is encouraged to review the forms and appendix material in detail. With these concepts in hand, we now turn to a general review.

Assuming the foreign investor has decided to take advantage of the benefits intrinsic to the operation of a Netherlands Antilles Corporation, he is faced with the task of forming, operating, and eventually terminating the existence of a Netherlands Antilles Corporation (NAC).

In creating the corporation, certain questions are raised:

1. Who may incorporate the corporation?
2. What documents must be drawn and where must they be filed?
3. How long does it take for the corporation to actively begin doing business?
4. What is the expense involved in forming and maintaining the corporation?

The corporation must be formed by two or more natural or juristic persons. Due to requirements of the Netherlands Antilles (Antilles) Department of Social and Economic Affairs, one of the two persons must be a trust company of the Antilles. As a matter of custom, the second person is often an NAC, wholly owned by the trust company. Since the law of the Antilles requires the incorporators to purchase at least one fifth of the aggregate par value of the corporation's authorized shares, the foreign investor must deposit that amount of money in a corporate bank account for the issuance of shares to the incorporators before an Antilles trust company will agree to act as an incorporator for the purpose of forming an NAC. The trust company and its subsidiary will later assign its shares in the corporation's stock to the foreign investor.

The deed of incorporation, articles of incorporation, or charter is the governing instrument which gives the corporation life. The document sets forth, among other things, the name of the corporation, the place of establishment, its duration, the number of authorized shares and their par value, the distribution of corporate profits, the accounting year, and the authority of the managing directors to transact business on the corporation's behalf. If the articles are in proper form and the minister of justice is satisfied that the incorporators have purchased the requisite number of shares, he will issue a certificate of no objection, whereupon the corporation commences its corporate existence.

Once the trust company has been contacted by the foreign investor and he has placed sufficient funds in a corporate bank account, it normally takes approximately two weeks for the corporation to become properly certified to commence operations. Due to the large increase in Antilles corporations incorporated each year, it is not uncommon to have some difficulty obtaining approval of a corporate name. Proposed corporate names that are misleading or similar to already established names will be rejected by the Antilles minister of justice.

For a corporation with proposed capital in the amount of $30,000 to $50,000, the Antilles trust company charges approximately $2,500 for the drafting and submission of the necessary incorporating documents if standard forms are used. The charge increases for larger capital contributions. Notarial and other miscellaneous incorporation costs may amount to approximately $500. If the foreign investor is in need of a corporate entity able to do business immediately, he may purchase a *shelf corporation* from an Antilles trust company for approximately $3,500. The shelf corporation is no more than a corporation, previously formed, which has never done business. The standardized articles make it suitable for the foreign investor who wishes to avoid the waiting period involved in forming a corporation and who wishes to eliminate any difficulties associated with choosing a new corporate name. For these benefits, he pays approximately $1,000 more and loses the right to name his corporation. In addition, it is customary to pay in advance the first year's "maintenance" fees of approximately $1,500.

After the incorporation process is complete, the foreign investor will want to be apprised on how the corporation operates. The following operational questions will be discussed:

1. What parties have authority to manage the corporation?
2. What corporate actions are required of the corporation under Antilles law?
3. How expensive is it to pay a third party to perform the acts mandated under Antilles law?

The *managing director* is the party in whom the authority to transact corporate business resides. Managing directors are initially appointed by the incorporators and are thereafter elected by the shareholders at the annual meeting. Typically, the foreign investor and the Antilles trust company are managing directors of the corporation. However if anonymity is desired, the foreign investor may wish to name his attorney, accountant, or other agent as managing director rather than himself. In publicly held corporations, the managing directors are professional executives similar to directors of large public U.S. corporations. In such cases, a *controlling shareholder* elected by the shareholders acts as a liaison between the managing directors and the shareholders and oversees, the activities of the managing director to insure that he is acting for the benefit of the shareholders. Because of the power of each managing director to bind the corporation by his word or signature alone, no formal adoption of resolutions of the managing directors is required by the law of the Antilles in order to authorize the conduct of any act. The foreign investor may elect to limit authority of the managing directors by requiring two signatures to bind the corporation.

Since a book of minutes authorizing the managing director to carry on certain activities is often necessary, the two statutory requirements most likely to necessitate the action of a person other than the foreign investor himself are the holding of an annual meeting of shareholders and the filing of an Antilles income tax statement. Both of these functions may be performed by the trust company, along with the keeping of a simple minute book with resolutions required by foreign entities for approximately $2,000 per year. Since the law of the Antilles requires that the mandatory annual meetings of shareholders take place in the Antilles, the meeting of a closely held corporation often takes place by proxy with the trust company handling the details of this procedure without the necessity of the foreign investor ever appearing.

It should be interposed that whereas a single managing director has full authority to transact the corporation's business under Antilles law, in dealing with real property transactions in California (and presumably other states), escrow companies and title insurance companies require resolutions of the NAC's directorate confirming the appointment of the managing director and his authority to act; they also insist upon a letter from Antilles counsel stating that the NAC is in good standing in the Antilles. Such opinions and resolutions are customarily obtainable on reasonable notice without traveling to the Antilles.

Ultimately the time will come when the foreign investor will wish to dissolve the corporation and thereby receive the distribution of the corporation's assets after the corporation's creditors are paid. Of prime importance to the foreign investor wishing to get his capital out of the corporation is how the corporation is dissolved, who may liquidate the corporate assets, how long it will take to distribute the assets, and how much it will cost to liquidate and dissolve.

The corporation may be dissolved by the expiration of its term of existence fixed by the deed of incorporation, insolvency, or a resolution of the shareholders at an annual meeting. If the dissolution occurs by shareholder resolution, then such resolution must be published in the official gazette and filed at the office of the trade register; otherwise third parties acting in the good faith belief that the corporation continues in active business may bind the corporation to its agreements.

The actual winding up of the corporation's affairs is conducted by *liquidators* who, if not named in the instrument of incorporation or by shareholder resolution, are the corporation's managing directors. The liquidators pay off the corporation's creditors and then distribute the remaining assets, if any, to the corporation's shareholders, subject to statutory constraints.

Prior to the distribution of assets to shareholders, the liquidators must publish in the official gazette a notice of the filing of a plan of liquidation setting forth the intended distribution which is filed in the office of the trade register and at the corporation's office. The liquidators must then wait at least two months from the notice date before distributing the assets to the shareholders. The liquidator is personally liable for any distributions made prior to this period resulting in a loss to an unpaid creditor. A creditor may apply for funds at any time within 30 years from the date of the purported debt.

The trust company will handle the entire dissolution process for approximately $2,000.

Must the NAC maintain bank accounts or deposits in the Antilles? Generally, no. Corporate accounts can be maintained by the NAC anywhere. In my experience, U.S. banks accept NAC bank accounts with little formality.

EPILOGUE

A few words about the future. Of course, I have no crystal ball, but here are some of my observations on changing economic conditions that may affect the foreign investor in the future.

CHANGES IN MONEY MARKETS

The attitudes of institutional lenders will change substantially in the immediate future. Long-term fixed interest rate loans will be a thing of the past except in the area of: (1) single-family residences, (2) some types of farm property, (3) government-insured and underwritten loans that meet certain specific social conditions and needs such as urban renewal and low-income housing. An example of this can already be seen. The regulatory authorities that regulate federally chartered savings and loan associations have just recently removed restrictions on these lending institutions. They are now allowed to make variable interest-rate loans without limitation on the increase in interest rates, and change of monthly payments. Institutional lenders will insist upon participating in a project either as a co-owner or in some other manner in the appreciated value of property and its attendant cash flow. Interest rates will continue to remain in the high double-digit range for the foreseeable future, except of course, in specifically underwritten and subsidized government programs. Increased amounts of capital will be required for all future real estate projects. The traditional ability of the American investor to finance substantially all of the costs of his acquisitions and improvements through established institutional sources will be dissipated, and large amounts of equity capital will be required for any substantial real estate project. This will result in the increased use of partnerships, joint ventures, corporations, and similar types of entities that require the pooling of equity capital.

STATE RESTRICTIONS

Increasing pressure will be placed upon state legislatures to limit or restrict investment by foreigners and foreign entities in United States real property of all types. Moves are now under way in a number of state legislatures leading to this end. This activity will accelerate in the foreseeable future.

TAX TREATMENT OF THE FOREIGN INVESTOR

Laws will be adopted and existing tax treaties will be renegotiated to put the foreign investor on equal par with his American counterpart. Of course, some exceptions may continue to exist. The present exemption of foreign investors from the obligations to pay U.S. income tax on interest earned from deposits in U.S. banks and savings and loan associations will continue to exist. The new tax act recently adopted (see Appendix 2) will be further amended to close many of the existing tax loopholes now available to foreign investors, and the regulations to be promulgated under the act will further strengthen this position.

GOVERNMENT ACTIVITY

The federal government will become increasingly involved in the revitalization of major cities in the United States. This will result in an increase in urban renewal-type projects, low-income housing, and in programs that fill existing and future social needs of an increasingly urbanized society in which the average age of the population is rising. This can result in additional opportunities to the foreign investor and his American counterpart for innovative real estate projects.

RENT CONTROL

As the cost of residential housing, whether a single-family residence or condominium, increases, as the cost of financing increases, as the amount of down payment required to purchase residential property increases, the ability of young people and those on fixed incomes to purchase diminishes. As a result of these factors, more and more people will become renters. The portion of society that can afford to be home-owners will diminish, and only those in the higher income brackets will be able to afford to buy. Further, with land cost rising and development costs increasing, the development trend will be away from the single-family residence and away from the suburbs. Increased costs of energy and transportation will result in a return to the cities as distinguished from the trend in recent years to expand into the suburban areas surrounding major metropolitan areas. All of these factors will result in extensive political pressure to control the costs of rental housing. Increased use of rent control and other similar methods will accelerate. Many states will adopt state-wide rent control laws. Whether or not this type of rent control legislation will be materially detrimental to the investor who owns multi-unit properties is difficult to predict. If we can judge the end result from history, the legislation will, in the long run, be devastating to the real estate developer and investor.

SENIOR CITIZENS

The population in the United States is growing increasingly older. More and more people are living longer. There are more retirement funds available than ever before. There will be an increasing demand for housing for senior citizens. This will result in population shifts in the United States to the warmer climates of the deep south and the far west. There will be increased use of and demand for mobile home parks, retirement-type cities, and innovative types of low-cost financing to fill the needs of the retired senior citizen.

INFLATION

Inflation is here to stay. Whether the rate is 6 percent or 13 percent per year, it will continue to rise. The cost of construction will continue to rise. U.S. tax laws will continue to discourage saving money. These factors mitigate in favor of buying all the real estate you can by using as little cash as possible. Real estate can only increase in value.

AGRICULTURE

The need for food throughout the world will increase. The United States will be the prime source for food. The value of good farm land as a result will increase substantially. Buy all the well-located farm land you can, using all the leverage you can.

THE FORMS

CONDITIONS AND STIPULATIONS

1. Definition of Terms

The following terms when used in this policy mean:

(a) "insured": the insured named in Schedule A, and subject to any rights or defenses the Company may have had against the named insured, those who succeed to the interest of such insured by operation of law as distinguished from purchase including, but not limited to, heirs, distributees, devisees, survivors, personal representatives, next of kin, or corporate or fiduciary successors. The term "insured" also includes (i) the owner of the indebtedness secured by the insured mortgage and each successor in ownership of such indebtedness (reserving, however, all rights and defenses as to any such successor who acquires the indebtedness by operation of law as described in the first sentence of this subparagraph (a) that the Company would have had against the successor's transferor), and further includes (ii) any governmental agency or instrumentality which is an insurer or guarantor under an insurance contract or guaranty insuring or guaranteeing said indebtedness, or any part thereof, whether named as an insured herein or not, and (iii) the parties designated in paragraph 2(a) of these Conditions and Stipulations.

(b) "insured claimant": an insured claiming loss or damage hereunder.

(c) "insured lender": the owner of an insured mortgage.

(d) "insured mortgage": a mortgage shown in Schedule B, the owner of which is named as an insured in Schedule A.

(e) "knowledge": actual knowledge, not constructive knowledge or notice which may be imputed to an insured by reason of any public records.

(f) "land": the land described, specifically or by reference in Schedule A, and improvements affixed thereto which by law constitute real property; provided, however, the term "land" does not include any area excluded by Paragraph No. 6 of Part I of Schedule B of this Policy.

(g) "mortgage": mortgage, deed of trust, trust deed, or other security instrument.

(h) "public records": those records which by law impart constructive notice of matters relating to the land.

2. (a) Continuation of Insurance after Acquisition of Title by Insured Lender

If this policy insures the owner of the indebtedness secured by the insured mortgage, this policy shall continue in force as of Date of Policy in favor of such insured who acquires all or any part of the estate or interest in the land described in Schedule A by foreclosure, trustee's sale, conveyance in lieu of foreclosure, or other legal manner which discharges the lien of the insured mortgage; and if such insured is a corporation, its transferee of the estate or interest so acquired, provided the transferee is the parent or wholly owned subsidiary of such insured; and in favor of any governmental agency or instrumentality which acquires all or any part of the estate or interest pursuant to a contract of insurance or guaranty insuring or guaranteeing the indebtedness secured by the insured mortgage. After any such acquisition the amount of insurance hereunder, exclusive of costs, attorneys' fees and expenses which the Company may be obligated to pay, shall not exceed the least of:

(i) the amount of insurance stated in Schedule A;

(ii) the amount of the unpaid principal of the indebtedness plus interest thereon, as determined under paragraph 6(a)(iii) hereof, expenses of foreclosure and amounts advanced to protect the lien of the insured mortgage and secured by said insured mortgage at the time of acquisition of such estate or interest in the land; or

(iii) the amount paid by any governmental agency or instrumentality, if such agency or instrumentality is the insured claimant, in acquisition of such estate or interest in satisfaction of its insurance contract or guaranty.

(b) Continuation of Insurance after Conveyance of Title

The coverage of this policy shall continue in force as of Date of Policy, in favor of an insured so long as such insured retains an estate or interest in the land, or owns an indebtedness secured by a purchase money mortgage given by a purchaser from such insured, or so long as such insured shall have liability by reason of covenants of warranty made by such insured in any transfer or conveyance of such estate or interest; provided, however, this policy shall not continue in force in favor of any purchaser from such insured of either said estate or interest or the indebtedness secured by a purchase money mortgage given to such insured.

3. Defense and Prosecution of Actions—Notice of Claim to be Given by an Insured Claimant

(a) The Company, at its own cost and without undue delay, shall provide for the defense of an insured in litigation to the extent that such litigation involves an alleged defect, lien, encumbrance or other matter insured against by this policy.

(b) The insured shall notify the Company promptly in writing (i) in case of any litigation as set forth in (a) above, (ii) in case knowledge shall come to an insured hereunder of any claim of title or interest which is adverse to the title to the estate or interest or the lien of the insured mortgage, as insured, and which might cause loss or damage for which the Company may be liable by virtue of this policy, or (iii) if title to the estate or interest or the lien of the insured mortgage, as insured, is rejected as unmarketable. If such prompt notice shall not be given to the Company, then as to such insured all liability of the Company shall cease and terminate in regard to the matter or matters for which such prompt notice is required; provided, however, that failure to notify shall in no case prejudice the rights of any such insured under this policy unless the Company shall be prejudiced by such failure and then only to the extent of such prejudice.

(c) The Company shall have the right at its own cost to institute and without undue delay prosecute any action or proceeding or to do any other act which in its opinion may be necessary or desirable to establish the title to the estate or interest or the lien of the insured mortgage, as insured, and the Company may take any appropriate action, whether or not it shall be liable under the terms of this policy, and shall not thereby concede liability or waive any provision of this policy.

(d) Whenever the Company shall have brought any action or interposed a defense as required or permitted by the provisions of this policy, the Company may pursue any such litigation to final determination by a court of competent jurisdiction and expressly reserves the right, in its sole discretion, to appeal from any adverse judgment or order.

(e) In all cases where this policy permits or requires the Company to prosecute or provide for the defense of any action or proceeding, the insured hereunder shall secure to the Company the right to so prosecute or provide defense in such action or proceeding, and all appeals therein, and permit the Company to use, at its option, the name of such insured for such purpose. Whenever requested by the Company, such insured shall give the Company, at the Company's expense, all reasonable aid (1) in any such action or proceeding in effecting settlement, securing evidence, obtaining witnesses, or prosecuting or defending such action or proceeding, and (2) in any other act which in the opinion of the Company may be necessary or desirable to establish the title to the estate or interest or the lien of the insured mortgage, as insured, including but not limited to executing corrective or other documents.

4. Proof of Loss or Damage—Limitation of Action

In addition to the notices required under Paragraph 3(b) of these Conditions and Stipulations, a proof of loss or damage, signed and sworn to by the insured claimant shall be furnished to the Company within 90 days after the insured claimant shall ascertain or determine the facts giving rise to such loss or damage. Such proof of loss or damage shall describe the defect in, or lien or encumbrance on the title, or other matter insured against by this policy which constitutes the basis of loss or damage, and, when appropriate, state the basis of calculating the amount of such loss or damage.

Should such proof of loss or damage fail to state facts sufficient to enable the Company to determine its liability hereunder, insured claimant, at the written request of Company, shall furnish such additional information as may reasonably be necessary to make such determination.

No right of action shall accrue to insured claimant until 30 days after such proof of loss or damage shall have been furnished.

Failure to furnish such proof of loss or damage shall terminate any liability of the Company under this policy as to such loss or damage.

5. Options to Pay or Otherwise Settle Claims and Options to Purchase Indebtedness

The Company shall have the option to pay or otherwise settle for or in the name of an insured claimant any claim insured against, or to terminate all liability and obligations of the Company hereunder by paying or tendering payment of the amount of insurance under this policy together with any costs, attorneys' fees and expenses incurred up to the time of such payment or tender of payment by the insured claimant and authorized by the Company. In case loss or damage is claimed under this policy by the owner of the indebtedness secured by the insured mortgage, the Company shall have the further option to purchase such indebtedness for the amount owing thereon together with costs, attorneys' fees and expenses which the Company is obligated hereunder to pay. If the Company offers to purchase said indebtedness as herein provided, the owner of such indebtedness shall transfer and assign said indebtedness and the mortgage and any collateral securing the same to the Company upon payment therefor as herein provided. Upon such offer being made by the Company, all liability and obligations of the Company hereunder to the owner of the indebtedness

---

CALIFORNIA LAND TITLE ASSOCIATION

STANDARD COVERAGE POLICY 1973

CHICAGO TITLE INSURANCE COMPANY

SUBJECT TO SCHEDULE B AND THE CONDITIONS AND STIPULATIONS HEREOF, CHICAGO TITLE INSURANCE COMPANY, a Missouri corporation, herein called the Company, insures the insured, as of Date of Policy shown in Schedule A, against loss or damage, not exceeding the amount of insurance stated in Schedule A, and costs, attorneys' fees and expenses which the Company may become obligated to pay hereunder, sustained or incurred by said insured by reason of:

1. Title to the estate or interest described in Schedule A being vested other than as stated therein;

2. Any defect in or lien or encumbrance on such title;

3. Unmarketability of such title; or

4. Any lack of the ordinary right of an abutting owner for access to at least one physically open street or highway if the land, in fact, abuts upon one or more such streets or highways;

and in addition, as to an insured lender only:

5. Invalidity of the lien of the insured mortgage upon said estate or interest except to the extent that such invalidity, or claim thereof, arises out of the transaction evidenced by the insured mortgage and is based upon

   a. usury, or

   b. any consumer credit protection or truth in lending law;

6. Priority of any lien or encumbrance over the lien of the insured mortgage, said mortgage being shown in Schedule B in the order of its priority; or

7. Invalidity of any assignment of the insured mortgage, provided such assignment is shown in Schedule B.

In Witness Whereof, CHICAGO TITLE INSURANCE COMPANY has caused this policy to be signed and sealed as of the date of policy shown in Schedule A, the policy to become valid when countersigned by an authorized signatory.

CHICAGO TITLE INSURANCE COMPANY

President

ATTEST:

Secretary

Issued by:
CHICAGO TITLE INSURANCE
COMPANY
3255 Wilshire Boulevard
Los Angeles, California 90010
(213) 380-3940

No.

SCHEDULE   CONTINUED

Chicago Title Insurance Company

Form 3631   R 7/74

SCHEDULE   A

Amount of Insurance $
Charge $

Policy No.
Order No.

Date of Policy

1.   Name of Insured:

2.   The estate or interest in the land described herein and which is covered by this policy is:
      A   Fee

3.   The estate or interest referred to herein is at Date of Policy vested in:

4.   The land referred to in this policy is situated in the County of
      , State of
      , and is described as follows:

This policy valid only if Schedule B is attached.

Chicago Title Insurance Company

FORM 3235 (R1 - 75)

CONDITIONS AND STIPULATIONS, Continued

6. Determination and Payment of Loss

(a) The liability of the Company under this policy shall in no case exceed the least of the insured claimant; or

   (i) the actual loss of the insured claimant; or

   (ii) the amount of insurance stated in Schedule A, or, if applicable, the amount of insurance as defined in paragraph 2(a) hereof; or

   (iii) if this policy insures the owner of the indebtedness secured by the insured mortgage, and provided said owner is the insured claimant, the amount of the unpaid principal of said indebtedness, plus interest thereon, provided such amount shall not include any additional principal indebtedness created subsequent to Date of Policy, except as to amounts advanced to protect the lien of the insured mortgage and secured thereby.

(b) The Company will pay, in addition to any loss insured against by this policy, all costs imposed upon an insured in litigation carried on by the Company for such insured, and all costs, attorneys' fees and expenses in litigation carried on by such insured with the written authorization of the Company.

(c) When the amount of loss or damage has been definitely fixed in accordance with the conditions of this policy, the loss or damage shall be payable within 30 days thereafter.

7. Limitation of Liability

No claim shall arise or be maintainable under this policy (a) if the Company, after having received notice of an alleged defect, lien or encumbrance insured against hereunder, by litigation or otherwise, removes such defect, lien or encumbrance or establishes the title, or the lien of the insured mortgage, as insured, within a reasonable time after receipt of such notice; (b) in the event of litigation until there has been a final determination by a court of competent jurisdiction, and disposition of all appeals therefrom, adverse to the title or to the lien of the insured mortgage, as insured, as provided in paragraph 3 hereof; or (c) for liability voluntarily admitted or assumed by an insured without prior written consent of the Company.

8. Reduction of Insurance; Termination of Liability

All payments under this policy, except payment made for costs, attorneys' fees and expenses, shall reduce the amount of the insurance pro tanto; provided, however, if the owner of the indebtedness secured by the insured mortgage is an insured hereunder, then such payments, prior to the acquisition of title to said estate or interest as provided in paragraph 2(a) of the Conditions and Stipulations, shall not reduce pro tanto the amount of the indebtedness afforded hereunder as to any such insured, except to the extent that such payments reduce the amount of the indebtedness secured by such mortgage.

Payment in full by any person or voluntary satisfaction or release of the insured mortgage shall terminate all liability of the Company to an insured owner of the indebtedness secured by the insured mortgage, except as provided in paragraph 2(a) hereof.

9. Liability Noncumulative

It is expressly understood that the amount of insurance under this policy, as to the insured owner of the estate or interest covered by this policy, shall be reduced by any amount the Company may pay under any policy insuring (a) a mortgage shown or referred to in Schedule B hereof which is a lien on the estate or interest covered by this policy, or (b) a mortgage hereafter executed by an insured which is a charge or lien on the estate or interest described or referred to in Schedule A, and the amount so paid shall be deemed a payment under this policy. The Company shall have the option to apply to the payment

of any such mortgage any amount that otherwise would be payable hereunder to the insured owner of the estate or interest covered by this policy and the amount so paid shall be deemed a payment under this policy to said insured owner.

The provisions of this paragraph 9 shall not apply to an owner of the indebtedness secured by the insured mortgage, unless such insured acquires title to said estate or interest in satisfaction of said indebtedness or any part thereof.

10. Subrogation Upon Payment or Settlement

Whenever the Company shall have paid or settled a claim under this policy, all right of subrogation shall vest in the Company unaffected by any act of the insured claimant, except that the owner of the indebtedness secured by the insured mortgage may release or substitute the personal liability of any debtor or guarantor, or extend or otherwise modify the terms of payment, or release a portion of the estate or interest from the lien of the insured mortgage, or release any collateral security for the indebtedness, provided such act occurs prior to receipt by such insured of notice of any claim of title or interest adverse to the title to the estate or interest or the priority of the lien of the insured mortgage and does not result in any loss of priority of the lien of the insured mortgage. The Company shall be subrogated to and be entitled to all rights and remedies which such insured claimant would have had against any person or property in respect to such claim had this policy not been issued, and the Company is hereby authorized and empowered to sue, compromise or settle in its name or in the name of the insured to the full extent of the loss sustained by the Company. If requested by the Company, the insured shall execute any and all documents to evidence the within subrogation. If the payment does not cover the loss of such insured claimant, the Company shall be subrogated to such rights and remedies in the proportion which said payment bears to the amount of said loss, but such subrogation shall be in subordination to an insured mortgage. If loss should result from any act of such insured claimant, such act shall not void this policy, but the Company, in that event, shall be required to pay only that part of any losses insured against hereunder which shall exceed the amount, if any, lost to the Company by reason of the impairment of the right of subrogation.

11. Liability Limited to this Policy

This instrument together with all endorsements and other instruments, if any, attached hereto by the Company is the entire policy and contract between the insured and the Company.

Any claim of loss or damage, whether or not based on negligence, and which arises out of the status of the lien of the insured mortgage or of the title to the estate or interest covered hereby, or any action asserting such claim, shall be restricted to the provisions and conditions and stipulations of this policy.

No amendment of or endorsement to this policy can be made except by writing endorsed hereon or attached hereto signed by either the President, a Vice President, the Secretary, an Assistant Secretary, or validating officer or authorized signatory of the Company.

No payment shall be made without producing this policy for endorsement of such payment unless the policy be lost or destroyed, in which case proof of such loss or destruction shall be furnished to the satisfaction of the Company.

12. Notices, Where Sent

All notices required to be given the Company and any statement in writing required to be furnished the Company shall be addressed to it at 111 W. Washington Street, Chicago, Illinois 60602 or at any branch office of the Company.

13. Fee

THE FEE CHARGE SPECIFIED IN SCHEDULE A IS THE ENTIRE CHARGE FOR TITLE SEARCH, TITLE EXAMINATION AND TITLE INSURANCE.

CHICAGO TITLE INSURANCE COMPANY

SCHEDULE B

PART I

This policy does not insure against loss or damage, nor against costs, attorneys' fees or expenses, any or all of which arise by reason of the following:

1. Taxes or assessments which are not shown as existing liens by the records of any taxing authority that levies taxes or assessments on real property or by the public records. Proceedings by a public agency which may result in taxes or assessments, or notices of such proceedings, whether or not shown by the records of such agency or by the public records.

2. Any facts, rights, interests or claims which are not shown by the public records but which could be ascertained by an inspection of the land or by making inquiry of persons in possession thereof.

3. Easements, liens or encumbrances, or claims thereof, which are not shown by the public records.

4. Discrepancies, conflicts in boundary lines, shortage in area, encroachments, or any other facts which a correct survey would disclose, and which are not shown by the public records.

5. (a) Unpatented mining claims; (b) reservations or exceptions in patents or in Acts authorizing the issuance thereof; (c) water rights, claims or title to water.

6.* Any right, title, interest, estate or easement in land beyond the lines of the area specifically described or referred to in Schedule A, or in abutting streets, roads, avenues, alleys, lanes, ways or waterways, but nothing in this paragraph shall modify or limit the extent to which the ordinary right of an abutting owner for access to a physically open street or highway is insured by this policy.

7. Any law, ordinance or governmental regulation (including but not limited to building and zoning ordinances) restricting or regulating or prohibiting the occupancy, use or enjoyment of the land, or regulating the character, dimensions or location of any improvement now or hereafter erected on the land, or prohibiting a separation in ownership or a reduction in the dimensions or area of the land, or the effect of any violation of any such law, ordinance or governmental regulation.

8. Rights of eminent domain or governmental rights of police power unless notice of the exercise of such rights appears in the public records.

9. Defects, liens, encumbrances, adverse claims, or other matters (a) created, suffered, assumed or agreed to by the insured claimant; (b) not shown by the public records and not otherwise excluded from coverage but known to the insured claimant either at Date of Policy or at the date such claimant acquired an estate or interest insured by this policy or acquired the insured mortgage and not disclosed in writing by the insured claimant to the Company prior to the date such insured claimant became an insured hereunder; (c) resulting in no loss or damage to the insured claimant; (d) attaching or created subsequent to Date of Policy; or (e) resulting in loss or damage which would not have been sustained if the insured claimant had been a purchaser or encumbrancer for value without knowledge.

F 2938

Form 1: Policy of title insurance—standard coverage—California Land Title Association (CLTA)
Form 2: Policy of title insurance—extended coverage—American Land Title Association (ALTA)

AMERICAN LAND TITLE ASSOCIATION LOAN POLICY-1970 (Amended 10-17-70)
WITH ALTA ENDORSEMENT FORM 1 COVERAGE

CHICAGO TITLE INSURANCE COMPANY

SUBJECT TO THE EXCLUSIONS FROM COVERAGE, THE EXCEPTIONS CONTAINED IN SCHEDULE B AND THE PROVISIONS OF THE CONDITIONS AND STIPULATIONS HEREOF, CHICAGO TITLE INSURANCE COMPANY, a Missouri corporation, herein called the Company, insures, as of Date of Policy shown in Schedule A, against loss or damage, not exceeding the amount of insurance stated in Schedule A, and costs, attorneys' fees and expenses which the Company may become obligated to pay hereunder, sustained or incurred by the insured by reason of:

1. Title to the estate or interest described in Schedule A being vested otherwise than as stated therein;
2. Any defect in or lien or encumbrance on such title;
3. Lack of a right of access to and from the land;
4. Unmarketability of such title;
5. The invalidity or unenforceability of the lien of the insured mortgage upon said estate or interest except to the extent that such invalidity or unenforceability, or claim thereof, arises out of the transaction evidenced by the insured mortgage and is based upon
   a. usury, or
   b. any consumer credit protection or truth in lending law;
6. The priority of any lien or encumbrance over the lien of the insured mortgage;
7. Any statutory lien for labor or material which now has gained or hereafter may gain priority over the lien of the insured mortgage, except any such lien arising from an improvement on the land contracted for and commenced subsequent to Date of Policy not financed in whole or in part by proceeds of the indebtedness secured by the insured mortgage which at Date of Policy the insured has advanced or is obligated to advance; or
8. Any assessments for street improvements under construction or completed at Date of Policy which now have gained or hereafter may gain priority over the insured mortgage; or
9. The invalidity or unenforceability of any assignment, shown in Schedule A, of the insured mortgage or the failure of said assignment to vest title to the insured mortgage in the named insured assignee free and clear of all liens.

In Witness Whereof, CHICAGO TITLE INSURANCE COMPANY has caused this policy to be signed and sealed as of the date of policy shown in Schedule A, the policy to become valid when countersigned by an authorized signatory.

CHICAGO TITLE INSURANCE COMPANY

By: _____ President.

ATTEST: _____ Secretary.

Issued by:
CHICAGO TITLE INSURANCE
COMPANY
3255 Wilshire Boulevard
Los Angeles, California 90010
(213) 380-3940

CALIFORNIA LAND TITLE
ASSOCIATION
STANDARD COVERAGE
POLICY 1973

POLICY
OF
TITLE
INSURANCE

CHICAGO
TITLE INSURANCE
COMPANY

CHICAGO TITLE • INSURANCE COMPANY

CHICAGO TITLE INSURANCE COMPANY
3255 Wilshire Boulevard
Los Angeles, California 90010

FORM 3024 R 10/73

FORM 3581

LOAN FORM

SCHEDULE A

Policy No.
Order No.

Date of Policy

Amount of Insurance $
Fee $

1. Name of Insured:

2. The estate or interest referred to herein is at Date of Policy vested in:

3. The estate or interest in the land described in this Schedule and which is encumbered by the insured mortgage is:

A Fee

4. The mortgage, herein referred to as the insured mortgage, and the assignments thereof, if any, are described as follows:

5. The land referred to in this policy is described as follows:

American Land Title Association

This policy valid only if Schedule B is attached.

Chicago Title Insurance Company

EXCLUSIONS FROM COVERAGE

The following matters are expressly excluded from the coverage of this policy:

1. Any law, ordinance or governmental regulation (including but not limited to building and zoning ordinances) restricting or regulating or prohibiting the occupancy, use or enjoyment of the land, or regulating the character, dimensions or location of any improvement now or hereafter erected on the land, or prohibiting a separation in ownership or reduction in the dimensions or area of the land, or the effect of any violation of any such law, ordinance or governmental regulation.

2. Rights of eminent domain or governmental rights of police power unless notice of the exercise of such rights appears in the public records at Date of Policy.

3. Defects, liens, encumbrances, adverse claims, or other matters (a) created, suffered, assumed or agreed to by the insured claimant; (b) not known to the Company and not shown by the public records but known to the insured claimant either at Date of Policy or at the date such claimant acquired an estate or interest insured by this policy or acquired the insured mortgage and not disclosed in writing by the insured claimant to the Company prior to the date such insured claimant became an insured hereunder; (c) resulting in no loss or damage to the insured claimant; (d) attaching or created subsequent to Date of Policy (except to the extent insurance is afforded herein as to any statutory lien for labor or material or to the extent insurance is afforded herein as to assessments for street improvements under construction or completed at Date of Policy).

4. Unenforceability of the lien of the insured mortgage because of failure of the insured at Date of Policy or of any subsequent owner of the indebtedness to comply with applicable "doing business" laws of the state in which the land is situated.

CONDITIONS AND STIPULATIONS

1. Definition of Terms

The following terms when used in this policy mean:

(a) "insured": the insured named in Schedule A. The term "insured" also includes (i) the owner of the indebtedness secured by the insured mortgage and each successor in ownership of such indebtedness (reserving, however, all rights and defenses as to any such successor who acquires the indebtedness by operation of law as distinguished from purchase including, but not limited to, heirs, distributees, devisees, survivors, personal representatives, next of kin or corporate or fiduciary successors) and further includes (ii) any governmental agency or instrumentality which is an insurer or guarantor under an insurance contract or guaranty insuring or guaranteeing said indebtedness, or any part thereof, whether named as an insured herein or not, and (iii) the parties designated in paragraph 2(a) of these Conditions and Stipulations.

(b) "insured claimant": an insured claiming loss or damage hereunder.

(c) "knowledge": actual knowledge, not constructive knowledge or notice which may be imputed to an insured by reason of any public records.

(d) "land": the land described, specifically or by reference in Schedule A, and improvements affixed thereto which by law constitute real property; provided, however, the term "land" does not include any property beyond the lines of the area specifically described or referred to in Schedule A, nor any right, title, interest, estate or easement in abutting streets, roads, avenues, alleys, lanes, ways or waterways, but nothing herein shall modify or limit the extent to which a right of access to and from the land is insured by this policy.

(e) "mortgage": mortgage, deed of trust, trust deed, or other security instrument.

(f) "public records": those records which by law impart constructive notice of matters relating to said land.

CONDITIONS AND STIPULATIONS (Continued on page below Inserts)

LOAN FORM

FORM 3577

SCHEDULE B

Policy Number _____ Loan _____ Order Number _____

PART II

In addition to the matters set forth in Part I of this Schedule, the title to the estate or interest in the land described or referred to in Schedule A is subject to the following matters, if any be shown, but the Company insures that such matters are subordinate to the lien or charge of the insured mortgage upon said estate or interest:

American Land Title Association

Chicago Title Insurance Company

LOAN FORM

FORM 3566

SCHEDULE B

Policy Number _____ Loan _____ Order Number _____

PART I

This policy does not insure against loss or damage by reason of the following:

Countersigned

_____
Authorized Signatory

Schedule B of this Policy consists of _____ pages.

American Land Title Association

Chicago Title Insurance Company

ENDORSEMENT

Attached to and forming a part of

Policy No. _____

Issued by

CHICAGO TITLE INSURANCE COMPANY

The Company assures the Insured that at the date of this policy there is located on said land

known as

and that the map attached to this policy shows the correct location and dimensions of said land according to those records which under the recording laws impart constructive notice as to said land.

The Company hereby insures the Insured against loss which said Insured shall sustain in the event that the assurance herein shall prove to be incorrect.

The total liability of the Company under said policy and any endorsements therein shall not exceed, in the aggregate, the face amount of said policy and costs which the Company is obligated under the conditions and stipulations thereof to pay.

This endorsement is made a part of said policy and is subject to the exclusions from coverage, schedules, conditions and stipulations therein, except as modified by the provisions hereof.

CHICAGO TITLE INSURANCE COMPANY

_____ President.

ATTEST:

_____ Secretary.

_____
Authorized Signatory

Note: This endorsement shall not be valid or binding until countersigned by an authorized signatory.

F. 3118 (R 9-74) CLTA 116

ENDORSEMENT

Attached to and forming a part of

Policy No. _____

Issued by

CHICAGO TITLE INSURANCE COMPANY

The Company hereby insures against loss which said Insured shall sustain by reason of any of the following matters:

1. Any incorrectness in the assurance which the Company hereby gives:
   (a) That there are no covenants, conditions or restrictions under which the lien of the mortgage referred to in Schedule A can be cut off, subordinated, or otherwise impaired;
   (b) That there are no present violations on said land of any enforceable covenants, conditions or restrictions;
   (c) That, except as shown in Schedule B, there are no encroachments of buildings, structures, or improvements located on said land onto adjoining lands, or any encroachments onto said land of buildings, structures, or improvements located on adjoining lands.

2. (a) Any future violations on said land of any covenants, conditions, or restrictions occurring prior to acquisition of title to said estate or interest by the Insured, provided such violations result in impairment or loss of the lien of the mortgage referred to in Schedule A, or result in impairment or loss of the title to said estate or interest if the Insured shall acquire title in satisfaction of the indebtedness secured by such mortgage;
   (b) Unmarketability of the title to said estate or interest by reason of any violations on said land, occurring prior to acquisition of title to said estate or interest by the Insured, of any covenants, conditions, or restrictions.

3. Damage to existing improvements, including lawns, shrubbery or trees;
   (a) Which are located or encroach upon that portion of the land subject to any easement shown in Schedule B, which damage results from the exercise of the right to use or maintain such easement for the purposes for which the same was granted or reserved;
   (b) Resulting from the exercise of any right to use the surface of said land for the extraction or development of the minerals excepted from the description of said land or shown as a reservation in Schedule B.

4. Any final court order or judgment requiring removal from any land adjoining said land of any encroachment shown in Schedule B.

Wherever in this endorsement any or all of the words "covenants, conditions or restrictions" appear they shall not be deemed to refer to or include the terms covenants and conditions contained in any lease referred to in Schedule A.

The total liability of the Company under said policy and endorsement therein shall not exceed, in the aggregate, the face amount of said policy and costs which the Company is obligated under the conditions and stipulations thereof to pay.

This endorsement is made a part of said policy and is subject to the exclusions from coverage, schedules, conditions and stipulations therein, except as modified by the provisions hereof.

CHICAGO TITLE INSURANCE COMPANY

_____ President.

ATTEST:

_____ Secretary.

_____
Authorized Signatory

Note: This endorsement shall not be valid or binding until countersigned by an authorized signatory.

F. 3120 (R 9-74) CLTA 100

CONDITIONS AND STIPULATIONS (Continued)

2. (a) Continuation of Insurance after Acquisition of Title

This policy shall continue in force as of Date of Policy in favor of an insured who acquires all or any part of the estate or interest in the land described in Schedule A by foreclosure, trustee's sale, conveyance in lieu of foreclosure, or other legal manner which discharges the lien of the insured mortgage, and if the insured is a corporation, its transferee of the estate or interest so acquired, provided the transferee is the parent or wholly owned subsidiary of the insured; and in favor of any governmental agency or instrumentality which acquires all or any part of the estate or interest pursuant to a contract of insurance or guaranty insuring or guaranteeing the indebtedness secured by the insured mortgage; provided that the amount of insurance hereunder after such acquisition, exclusive of costs, attorneys' fees and expenses which the Company may become obligated to pay, shall not exceed the least of:

(i) the amount of insurance stated in Schedule A;

(ii) the amount of the unpaid principal of the indebtedness as defined in paragraph 8 hereof, plus interest thereon, expenses of foreclosure and amounts advanced to protect the lien of the insured mortgage and secured by said insured mortgage at the time of acquisition of such estate or interest in the land; or

(iii) the amount paid by any governmental agency or instrumentality, if such agency or instrumentality is the insured claimant, in the acquisition of such estate or interest in satisfaction of its insurance contract or guaranty.

(b) Continuation of Insurance after Conveyance of Title

The coverage of this policy shall continue in force as of Date of Policy in favor of an insured so long as such insured retains an estate or interest in the land, or holds an indebtedness secured by a purchase money mortgage given by a purchaser from such insured, or so long as such insured shall have liability by reason of covenants of warranty made by such insured in any transfer or conveyance of such estate or interest; provided, however, this policy shall not continue in force in favor of any purchaser from such insured of either said estate or interest or the indebtedness secured by a purchase money mortgage given to such insured.

3. Defense and Prosecution of Actions—Notice of Claim to be given by an Insured Claimant

(a) The Company, at its own cost and without undue delay, shall provide for the defense of an insured in all litigation consisting of actions or proceedings commenced against such insured, or defenses, restraining orders or injunctions interposed against a foreclosure of the insured mortgage or a defense interposed against an insured in an action to enforce a contract for a sale of the indebtedness secured by the insured mortgage, or a sale of the estate or interest in said land, to the extent that such litigation is founded upon an alleged defect, lien, encumbrance, or other matter insured against by this policy.

(b) The insured shall notify the Company promptly in writing (i) in case any action or proceeding is begun or defense or restraining order or injunction is interposed as set forth in (a) above, (ii) in case knowledge shall come to an insured hereunder of any claim of title or interest which is adverse to the title to the estate or interest or the lien of the insured mortgage, as insured, and which might cause loss or damage for which the Company may be liable by virtue of this policy, or (iii) if title to the estate or interest or the lien of the insured mortgage, as insured, is rejected as unmarketable. If such prompt notice shall not be given to the Company, then as to such insured all liability of the Company shall cease and terminate in regard to the matter or matters for which such prompt notice is required; provided, however, that failure to notify shall in no case prejudice the rights of any such insured under this policy unless the Company shall be prejudiced by such failure and then only to the extent of such prejudice.

(c) The Company shall have the right at its own cost to institute and without undue delay prosecute any action or proceeding or to do any other act which in its opinion may be necessary or desirable to establish the title to the estate or interest or the lien of the insured mortgage, as insured, and the Company may take any appropriate action under the terms of this policy, whether or not it shall be liable thereunder, and shall not thereby concede liability or waive any provision of this policy.

(d) Whenever the Company shall have brought any action or interposed a defense as required or permitted by the provisions of this policy, the Company may pursue any such litigation to final determination by a court of competent jurisdiction and expressly reserves the right, in its sole discretion, to appeal from any adverse judgment or order.

(e) In all cases where this policy permits or requires the Company to prosecute or provide for the defense of any action or proceeding, the insured hereunder shall secure to the Company the right to so prosecute or provide defense in such action or proceeding, and all appeals therein, and permit the Company to use, at its option, the name of such insured for such purpose. Whenever requested by the Company, such insured shall give the Company all reasonable aid in any such action or proceeding, in effecting settlement, securing evidence, obtaining witnesses, or prosecuting or defending such action or proceeding, and the Company shall reimburse such insured for any expense so incurred.

4. Notice of Loss—Limitation of Action

In addition to the notices required under paragraph 3(b) of these Conditions and Stipulations, a statement in writing of any loss or damage for which it is claimed the Company is liable under this policy shall be furnished to the Company within 90 days after such loss or damage shall have been determined and no right of action shall accrue to an insured claimant until 30 days after such statement shall have been furnished. Failure to furnish such statement of loss or damage shall terminate any liability of the Company under this policy as to such loss or damage.

5. Options to Pay or Otherwise Settle Claims

The Company shall have the option to pay or otherwise settle for or in the name of an insured claimant any claim insured against or to terminate all liability and obligations of the Company hereunder by paying or tendering payment of the amount of insurance under this policy together with any costs, attorneys' fees and expenses incurred up to the time of such payment or tender of payment by the insured claimant and authorized by the Company. In case loss or damage is claimed under this policy by an insured, the Company shall have the further option to purchase such indebtedness for the amount owing thereon together with all costs, attorneys' fees and expenses which the Company is obligated hereunder to pay. If the Company offers to purchase said indebtedness as herein provided, the owner of such indebtedness shall transfer and assign said indebtedness and the mortgage and any collateral securing the same to the Company upon payment therefor as herein provided.

6. Determination and Payment of Loss

(a) The liability of the Company under this policy shall in no case exceed the least of:

(i) the actual loss of the insured claimant; or

(ii) the amount of insurance stated in Schedule A, or, if applicable, the amount of insurance as defined in paragraph 2(a) hereof; or

(iii) the amount of the indebtedness secured by the insured mortgage as determined under paragraph 8 hereof, at the time the loss or damage insured against hereunder occurs, together with interest thereon.

(b) The Company will pay, in addition to any loss insured against by this policy, all costs imposed upon an insured in litigation carried on by the Company for such insured, and all costs, attorneys' fees and expenses in litigation carried on by such insured with the written authorization of the Company.

(c) When liability has been definitely fixed in accordance with the conditions of this policy, the loss or damage shall be payable within 30 days thereafter.

CONDITIONS AND STIPULATIONS (Continued on Reverse Side)

CONDITIONS AND STIPULATIONS (Continued)

7. Limitation of Liability

No claim shall arise or be maintainable under this policy (a) if the Company, after having received notice of an alleged defect, lien or encumbrance insured against hereunder, by litigation or otherwise, removes such defect, lien or encumbrance or establishes the title, or the lien of the insured mortgage, as insured, within a reasonable time after receipt of such notice; (b) in the event of litigation until there has been a final determination by a court of competent jurisdiction, and disposition of all appeals therefrom, adverse to the title or to the lien of the insured mortgage, as insured, as provided in paragraph 3 hereof; or (c) for liability voluntarily assumed by an insured in settling any claim or suit without prior written consent of the Company.

8. Reduction of Liability

(a) All payments under this policy, except payments made for costs, attorneys' fees and expenses, shall reduce the amount of the insurance pro tanto; provided, however, such payments, prior to the acquisition of title to said estate or interest as provided in paragraph 2(a) of these Conditions and Stipulations, shall not reduce pro tanto the amount of the insurance afforded hereunder except to the extent that such payments reduce the amount of the indebtedness secured by the insured mortgage.

Payment in full by any person or voluntary satisfaction or release of the insured mortgage shall terminate all liability of the Company except as provided in paragraph 2(a) hereof.

(b) The liability of the Company shall not be increased by additional principal indebtedness created subsequent to Date of Policy, except as to amounts advanced to protect the lien of the insured mortgage and secured thereby.

No payment shall be made without producing this policy for endorsement of such payment unless the policy be lost or destroyed, in which case proof of loss or destruction shall be furnished to the satisfaction of the Company.

9. Liability Noncumulative

If the insured acquires title to the estate or interest in satisfaction of the indebtedness secured by the insured mortgage, or any part thereof, it is expressly understood that the amount of insurance under this policy shall be reduced by any amount the Company may pay under any policy insuring a mortgage hereafter executed by an insured which is a charge or lien on the estate or interest described or referred to in Schedule A, and the amount so paid shall be deemed a payment under this policy.

10. Subrogation Upon Payment or Settlement

Whenever the Company shall have settled a claim under this policy, all right of subrogation shall vest in the Company unaffected by any act of the insured claimant, except that the owner of the indebtedness secured by the insured mortgage may release or substitute the personal liability of any debtor or guarantor, or extend or otherwise modify the terms of payment, or release a portion of the estate or interest from the lien of the insured mortgage, or release any collateral security for the indebtedness, provided such act occurs prior to receipt by the insured of notice of any claim of title or interest adverse to the title to the estate or interest or the priority of the lien of the insured mortgage and does not result in any loss of priority of the lien of the insured mortgage. The Company shall be subrogated to and be entitled to all rights and remedies which such insured claimant would have had against any person or property in respect to such claim had this policy not been issued, and if requested by the Company, such insured claimant shall transfer to the Company all rights and remedies against any person or property necessary in order to perfect such right of subrogation and shall permit the Company to use the name of such insured claimant in any transaction or litigation involving such rights or remedies. If the payment does not cover the loss of such insured claimant, the Company shall be subrogated to such rights and remedies in the proportion which said payment bears to the amount of said loss, but such subrogation shall be in subordination to the insured mortgage. If loss of priority should result from any act of such insured claimant, such act shall not void this policy, but the Company, in that event, shall be required to pay only that part of any losses insured against hereunder which shall exceed the amount, if any, lost to the Company by reason of the impairment of the right of subrogation.

11. Liability Limited to this Policy

This instrument together with all endorsements and other instruments, if any, attached hereto by the Company is the entire policy and contract between the insured and the Company.

Any claim of loss or damage, whether or not based on negligence, and which arises out of the status of the lien of the insured mortgage or of the title to the estate or interest covered hereby or any action asserting such claim, shall be restricted to the provisions and conditions and stipulations of this policy.

No amendment of or endorsement to this policy can be made except by writing endorsed hereon or attached hereto signed by either the President, a Vice President, the Secretary, an Assistant Secretary, or validating officer or authorized signatory of the Company.

12. Notices, Where Sent

All notices required to be given the Company and any statement in writing required to be furnished the Company shall be addressed to its principal office at 111 West Washington Street, Chicago, Illinois 60602, or at any branch office of the Company.

13. Fee

The fee, if specified in Schedule A of this policy, is the total fee for title search, examination and title insurance.

American Land Title Association
Loan Policy-1970
(Amended 10-17-70)
With Alta Endorsement Form 1 Coverage

POLICY OF TITLE INSURANCE

CHICAGO TITLE INSURANCE COMPANY

CHICAGO TITLE INSURANCE COMPANY
3255 Wilshire Boulevard
Los Angeles, California 90010

CHICAGO
TITLE INSURANCE
COMPANY

111 WEST WASHINGTON STREET
CHICAGO, ILLINOIS 60602

Form 3614

Chicago Title Insurance Company

Residential Title Insurance Policy

One-to-Four Family Residences

Owner's Coverage Statement

This Policy insures your title to the land described in Schedule A — if that land is a one-to-four family residential lot or condominium unit.

Your insurance, as described in this Coverage Statement, is effective on the Policy Date shown in Schedule A.

Your insurance is limited by the following:

- EXCLUSIONS on page 2
- EXCEPTIONS in Schedule B
- CONDITIONS on page 2 and 3

We insure you against actual loss resulting from:
- any title risks covered by this Policy — up to the Policy Amount, and
- any costs, attorneys' fees and expenses we have to pay under this Policy

Covered Title Risks

This Policy covers the following title risks, if they affect your title on the Policy Date.

1. Someone else owns an interest in your title.
2. A document is not properly signed, sealed, acknowledged, or delivered.
3. Forgery, fraud, duress, incompetency, incapacity or impersonation.
4. Defective recording of any document.
5. You do not have any legal right to access to and from the land.
6. There are restrictive covenants limiting your use of the land.
7. There is a lien on your title because of:
   - a mortgage or deed of trust
   - a judgment, tax, or special assessment
   - a charge by a homeowner or condominium association
8. There are liens on your title, arising now or later, for labor and material furnished before the Policy Date — unless you agreed to pay for the labor and material.
9. Others have rights arising out of leases, contracts, or options.
10. Someone else has an easement on your land.
11. Your title is unmarketable, which allows another person to refuse to perform a contract to purchase, to lease or to make a mortgage loan.
12. You are forced to remove your existing structure—other than a boundary wall or fence—because:
    - it extends on to adjoining land or on to any easement
    - it violates a restriction shown in Schedule B
    - it violates an existing zoning law
13. You cannot use the land for a single-family residence, because such a use violates a restriction shown in Schedule B or an existing zoning law.
14. Other defects, liens, or encumbrances.

Company's Duty to Defend Against Court Cases

We will defend your title in any court case that is based on a matter insured against by this Policy. We will pay the costs, attorneys' fees, and expenses we incur in that defense.

We can end this duty to defend your title by exercising any of our options listed in item 4 of the Conditions.

This policy is not complete without Schedules A and B.

Your Title Insurance Policy is a legal contract between you and Chicago Title Insurance Company.

It applies only to a one-to-four family residential lot or a condominium unit. If your land is not either of these, contact us immediately.

The Policy insures you against certain risks to your land title. These risks are listed on page one of the Policy. The Policy is limited by:

- Exclusions on page 2.
- Exceptions on Schedule B.
- Conditions on page 2 and 3.

You should keep the Policy even if you transfer the title to your land.

If you want to make a claim, see Item 3 under Conditions on page 2.

You do not owe any more premiums for the Policy.

This sheet is not your insurance Policy. It is only a brief outline of some of the important Policy features. The Policy explains in detail your rights and obligations and our rights and obligations. Since the Policy — and not this sheet — is the legal document

YOU SHOULD READ THE POLICY VERY CAREFULLY

If you have any questions about your Policy, contact the issuing office.

Chicago Title Insurance Company

111 West Washington Street
Chicago, Illinois 60602

Issuing Office:
CHICAGO TITLE INSURANCE COMPANY
3255 Wilshire Boulevard
Los Angeles, California 90010
(213) 380-3940

Form 1861

CHICAGO TITLE INSURANCE COMPANY
Residential Title Insurance Policy

SCHEDULE A

Office File Number:	Policy Number:	Policy Date:	Policy Amount:

The Policy Amount will automatically increase by 10% of the amount shown above on each of the first five anniversaries of the Policy Date.

1. Name of Insured:

2. Your interest in the land covered by this Policy is: Fee Simple

3. The land referred to in this Policy is described as follows:

SAMPLE

Form 1861

CHICAGO TITLE INSURANCE COMPANY
Residential Title Insurance Policy

SCHEDULE B

Policy Number: _____

EXCEPTIONS

In addition to the Exclusions, you are not insured against loss, costs, attorneys' fees and expenses resulting from:

SAMPLE

Owner's Policy Endorsements:

Loan Policy Endorsements:

Countersigned: _____

Authorized Signatory

Schedule B of this Policy consists of _____ pages.

Exclusions

In addition to the Exceptions in Schedule B, you are not insured against loss, costs, attorneys' fees, and expenses resulting from:

1. Governmental police power, and the existence or violation of any law or government regulation. This includes building and zoning ordinances and also laws and regulations concerning:
   • land use
   • improvements on the land
   • land division
   • environmental protection

   This exclusion does not limit the zoning coverage described in items 12 and 13 of Covered Title Risks.

2. The right to take the land by condemning it, unless a notice of taking appears in the public records on the Policy Date.

3. Title Risks:
   • that are created, allowed, or agreed to by you
   • that are known to you, but not to us, on the Policy Date—unless they appeared in the public records
   • that result in no loss to you
   • that first affect your title after the Policy Date—this does not limit the labor and material lien coverage in item 8 of Covered Title Risks

4. Failure to pay value for your title.

5. Lack of a right:
   • to any land outside the area specifically described and referred to in item 3 of Schedule A, or
   • in streets, alleys, or waterways that touch your land

   This exclusion does not limit the access coverage in item 5 of Covered Title Risks.

Conditions

1. Definitions:

a. **Easement**—the right of someone else to use your land for a special purpose.

b. **Land**—the land or condominium unit described in Schedule A and any real property improvements on the land which are real property.

c. **Mortgage**—a mortgage, deed of trust, trust deed or other security instrument.

d. **Public Records**—title records that give constructive notice of matters affecting your title—according to the state law where your land is located.

e. **Title**—the ownership of your interest in the land, as shown in Schedule A.

2. Continuation of Coverage: This Policy protects you as long as you:
• own your title, or
• own a mortgage from anyone who buys your land, or
• are liable for any title warranties you make

This Policy protects anyone who receives your title because of your death.

3. How to Make a Claim: If anyone claims a right against your insured title, you must notify us promptly in writing. Send the notice to the issuing office or
Chicago Title Insurance Company
Claims Department
111 West Washington Street
Chicago, Illinois 60602

Please include the Policy number shown in Schedule A, and the county and state where the land is located.

Our obligation to you could be reduced if:
• you fail to give prompt notice and
• your failure affects our ability to dispose of or to defend you against the claim

Continued on page 3

---

d. Pay the amount required by this Policy.
e. Take other action which will protect you.
f. Cancel this Policy by paying the Policy Amount then in force, and only those costs, attorneys' fees and expenses incurred up to that time which we are obligated to pay.

We will repay you for all expenses that we approve in advance.

When we prosecute or defend a court case, we have a right to choose the attorney. We can appeal any decision to the highest court. We do not have to pay your claim until your case is finally decided.

You must cooperate with us in handling any claim or court case and give us all relevant information.

Unless you can show that payment was reasonable and necessary, we will not reimburse you for money you pay or agree to pay:
• to settle disputes, or
• to cover expenses and attorneys' fees

a. We will pay up to your actual loss or the Policy Amount in force when the claim is made—whichever is less.

b. If we remove the claim against your title within a reasonable time after receiving notice of it, we will have no further liability for it.
If you cannot use any of your land because of a claim against your title, and if we place a reasonable substitute land or facility, we will repay you for your actual loss until:
• the cause of the claim is removed, or
• we settle your claim.

When we settle a claim, we have all the rights you had against any person or property related to the claim. You must transfer these rights to us when we ask, and you must not do anything to affect these rights. You must let us use your name in enforcing these rights.

We will not be liable to you if we do not pursue these rights or if we do not recover an amount that might be recoverable.

With the money we recover from enforcing these rights, we will pay whatever part of your loss we have not paid. We have a right to keep what is left.

This Policy, plus all endorsements, is the entire contract between you and Chicago Title Insurance Company. Any title claim you make against us must be made under this Policy and is subject to its terms.

American
Land Title
Association
Residential
Title Insurance
Policy

The fee, if specified in Schedule A of this policy, is the total fee for the title search, examination, and title insurance.

CHICAGO TITLE INSURANCE COMPANY

By
President.

Attest:
Secretary.

Form 20000

BROKER'S COPY

CALIFORNIA ASSOCIATION OF REALTORS® STANDARD FORM

REAL ESTATE PURCHASE CONTRACT AND RECEIPT FOR DEPOSIT

THIS IS MORE THAN A RECEIPT FOR MONEY. IT IS INTENDED TO BE A LEGALLY BINDING CONTRACT. READ IT CAREFULLY.

_____, California, _____, 19____

Received from _____

herein called Buyer, the sum of _____ Dollars $ _____

evidenced by cash ☐, cashier's check ☐, or ☐, personal check ☐ payable to _____,

to be held uncashed until acceptance of this offer, as deposit on account of purchase price of

_____ Dollars $ _____

for the purchase of property, situated in _____, County of _____, California,

described as follows: _____

1.   Buyer will deposit in escrow with _____ the balance of purchase price as follows:

_____

_____

_____

_____

_____

_____

_____

_____

_____

Set forth above any terms and conditions of a factual nature applicable to this sale, such as financing, prior sale of other property, the matter of structural pest control inspection, repairs and personal property to be included in the sale.

2.   Deposit will ☐ will not ☐ be increased by $ _____ to $ _____ within _____ days of acceptance of this offer.

3.   Buyer does ☐ does not ☐ intend to occupy subject property as his residence.

4.   The supplements initialed below are incorporated as part of this agreement.

_____ Structural Pest Control Certification Agreement   _____ Occupancy Agreement

_____ Special Studies Zone Disclosure   _____ VA Amendment

_____ Flood Insurance Disclosure   _____ FHA Amendment

5.   Buyer and Seller acknowledge receipt of a copy of this page, which constitutes Page 1 of _____ Pages.

X _____
BUYER

X _____
BUYER

A REAL ESTATE BROKER IS THE PERSON QUALIFIED TO ADVISE ON REAL ESTATE. IF YOU DESIRE LEGAL ADVICE, CONSULT YOUR ATTORNEY.

For these forms, address California Association of Realtors®
505 Shatto Place, Los Angeles, California 90020
(Revised 1978)   D-11-1 NCR SETS

BROKER'S COPY

REAL ESTATE PURCHASE CONTRACT AND RECEIPT FOR DEPOSIT

The following terms and conditions are hereby incorporated in and made a part of Buyer's Offer

6.   Buyer and Seller shall deliver signed instructions to the escrow holder within _____ days from Seller's acceptance which shall provide for closing within _____ days from Seller's acceptance. Escrow fees to be paid as follows:

7.   Title is to be free of liens, encumbrances, easements, restrictions, rights and conditions of record or known to Seller, other than the following: (1) Current property taxes, (2) covenants, conditions, restrictions, and public utility easements of record, if any, provided the same do not adversely affect the continued use of the property for the purposes for which it is presently being used, unless reasonably disapproved by Buyer in writing within _____ days of receipt of a current preliminary title report furnished at _____ expense, and (3) _____. Seller shall furnish Buyer at _____ expense a standard California Land Title Association policy issued by _____ Company, showing title vested in Buyer subject only to the above. If Seller (1) is unwilling or unable to eliminate any title matter disapproved by Buyer as above, Seller may terminate this agreement, or (2) fails to deliver title as above, Buyer may terminate this agreement, in either case, the deposit shall be returned to Buyer.

8.   Property taxes, premiums on insurance acceptable to Buyer, rents, interest, and _____, shall be pro-rated as of (a) the date of recordation of deed; or (b) _____. Any bond or assessment which is a lien shall be paid ☐ assumed ☐ by _____. transfer taxes, if any, _____ shall pay cost of

9.   Possession shall be delivered to Buyer (a) on close of escrow, or (b) not later than _____ days after close of escrow or (c) _____.

10.   Unless otherwise designated in the escrow instructions of Buyer, title shall vest as follows: _____

(The manner of taking title may have significant legal and tax consequences. Therefore, give this matter serious consideration.)

11.   If Broker is a participant of a Board multiple listing service ("MLS"), the Broker is authorized to report the sale, its price, terms, and financing for the information, publication, dissemination, and use of the authorized Board members.

12.   **If Buyer fails to complete said purchase as herein provided by reason of any default of Buyer, Seller shall be released from his obligation to sell the property to Buyer and may proceed against Buyer upon any claim or remedy which he may have in law or equity; provided, however, that by placing their initials here Buyer: (   ) Seller: (   ) agree that Seller shall retain the deposit as his liquidated damages. If the described property is a dwelling with no more than four units, one of which the Buyer intends to occupy as his residence, Seller shall retain as liquidated damages the deposit actually paid, or an amount therefrom, not more than 3% of the purchase price and promptly return any excess to Buyer.**

13.   If the only controversy or claim between the parties arises out of or relates to the disposition of the Buyer's deposit, such controversy or claim shall at the election of the parties be decided by arbitration. Such arbitration shall be determined in accordance with the Rules of the American Arbitration Association, and judgment upon the award rendered by the Arbitrator(s) may be entered in any court having jurisdiction thereof. The provisions of Code of Civil Procedure Section 1283.05 shall be applicable to such arbitration.

14.   In any action or proceeding arising out of this agreement, the prevailing party shall be entitled to reasonable attorney's fees and costs.

15.   Time is of the essence. All modifications or extensions shall be in writing signed by the parties.

16.   This constitutes an offer to purchase the described property. Unless acceptance is signed by Seller and the signed copy delivered to Buyer, in person or by mail to the address below, within _____ days, this offer shall be deemed revoked and the deposit shall be returned. Buyer acknowledges receipt of a copy hereof.

Real Estate Broker _____   Buyer _____

By _____

Address _____   Address _____

Telephone _____   Telephone _____

ACCEPTANCE

The undersigned Seller accepts and agrees to sell the property on the above terms and conditions. Seller has employed _____ as Broker(s) and agrees to pay for services the sum of _____ Dollars ($ _____), payable as follows: (a) On recordation of the deed or other evidence of title, or (b) if completion of sale is prevented by default of Seller, upon Seller's default or (c) if completion of sale is prevented by default of Buyer, only if and when Seller collects damages from Buyer, by suit or otherwise and then in an amount not less than one-half of the damages recovered, but not to exceed the above fee, after first deducting title and escrow expenses and the expenses of collection, if any. In any action between Broker and Seller arising out of this agreement, the prevailing party shall be entitled to reasonable attorney's fees and costs. The undersigned acknowledges receipt of a copy and authorizes Broker(s) to deliver a signed copy to Buyer.

Dated: _____   Telephone _____   Seller _____

Dated: _____   Seller _____

Broker(s) agree to the foregoing. Broker _____

By _____   Broker _____

Dated: _____   By _____

For these forms, address California Association of Realtors®
505 Shatto Place, Los Angeles, California 90020 (Revised 1978)   D-11-2 NCR SETS

Page _____ of _____ Pages

ESCROW INSTRUCTIONS

TO: **CHICAGO TITLE INSURANCE COMPANY**

Los Angeles, _____ California

Date January 1, 1981   Escrow Officer   E. Ficient   Escrow No. 10000

1. PRIOR TO   March 1, 1981
2. I will hand you One Hundred Thousand ($100,000) Dollars of which sum
3. you are handed Ten Thousand ($10,000) Dollars toward a total purchase
4. price of Five Hundred Thousand ($500,000) Dollars
5.
6.
7.
8.
9. and any additional funds and instruments required from me to enable you to comply with these instructions, which you are to use on or
10. before   March 10 _____ , 19 81 , and when you can issue your Standard coverage
11. Policy of Title Insurance for $ 500,000 _____ on real property in the County of Los Angeles, State of California, viz:
12. Lot 10 of Tract 12345 in the City and County of Los Angeles per
13. Map recorded in Book 100, Page 200 of Official Records of said
14. county. Said property is commonly known as 1500 Maple Street, Los
15. Angeles, California
16.
17.
18.
19.
20.
21.
22.
23.
24.
25. showing title vested in: John Doe and Jane Doe, Husband and Wife as Joint Tenants
26.
27.
28.
29.
30. free from encumbrance EXCEPT: _____
31. (1) _____ all _____ General and Special Taxes for the fiscal year 19 81 - 19 82
32. (2) Covenants, conditions, restrictions, reservations, easements, rights and rights-of-way of record, if any
33. (3) A First Trust Deed and Note in favor of High-Price Savings and
34. Loan Association in the sum of approximately Two Hundred Thousand
35. ($200,000) Dollars, payable in equal monthly installments of Two
36. Thousand, Five Hundred ($2,500) Dollars per month including interest
37. at 12.5% per annum until paid. You are to order current Beneficiary
38. Statements for Buyers' approval.
39.
40. (4) A new Note and Second Deed of Trust on your form in favor of
41. Seller in the approximate sum of One Hundred Thousand ($100,000) Dollars
42. payable interest only monthly at 11% per annum and all due and pay-
43. able five (5) years from the close of escrow. You are to adjust
44. the principal amount to reflect the difference between the first
45. Trust Deed as disclosed by the approved Beneficiary Statement, the
46. cash down payment and the total purchase price.
47.
48. Purchase price includes all carpets, drapes, built-in appliances and
49. light fixtures. Buyer is purchasing the property "as is".
50.
51.
52.
53.
54.
55.
56.
57.
58.
59.
60.
61.
62.
63.
64.
65.
66.
67.
68.
69.
70.
511

(Page One)

The following PRORATIONS/ADJUSTMENTS ARE TO BE MADE IN THIS ESCROW:

Interest on Trust Deeds OF RECORD and any funds shown impounded for future payments of taxes, insurance, etc., or Mortgage Insurance Premium paid FHA during past 12 months, based on Beneficiary's Statement, to ....

City, County and any irrigation district taxes to .... based upon latest information available.

Rentals, on basis of statement furnished by Seller or Broker to...

Premium on .... FIRE INSURANCE Policies to .... on building situated either on property described above or on premises known as No. ....

You are to assume that any such policies are in force and that the premiums thereon are fully paid.

I agree to pay on demand usual Buyer's charges including recording Deed, drawing any Trust Deed executed by me, drawing and recording any other documents necessary on my part, and one-half of Escrow Fee.

THESE AND ALL ADDITIONAL OR AMENDED INSTRUCTIONS SHALL BE SUBJECT TO THE FOLLOWING:

(a)   Make prorations on basis of 30 day month. "Close of escrow" shall mean the day papers are filed for record. Make disbursements by your check. Have fire insurance policies, including coverage, if any, on personal property, assigned to Buyer with mortgage or loss payable clause attached in favor of holder or holders of encumbrances, if any, as shown on page one hereof; and have said policies mailed to holder of first encumbrance, if any, otherwise to Buyer. Mail title policies to holder of first encumbrance being recorded concurrently herewith, if any, otherwise to Buyer. Other documents and checks in my favor to be mailed to my address below.

(b)   If any of the conditions of this escrow are not complied with prior to the date specified on line 10 on page one hereof, any party who has fully complied with his instructions as evidenced by your file may, in writing, subsequent to that date and prior to any transmission by you of irrevocable authority to record or the recording of any instrument provided for herein, demand return of his money, documents and/or property. Upon receipt of such demand, you shall withhold action except to mail copies of such demand to all other parties at their respective address shown below and postpone your decision with respect to compliance with such demand for at least five (5) days after the date of mailing. IF NO SUCH DEMAND IS MADE YOU ARE TO CLOSE THE ESCROW AS SOON AS THE CONDITIONS (EXCEPT AS TO TIME) HAVE BEEN COMPLIED WITH.

(c)   The undersigned agree that in consideration of your acceptance of the within escrow you shall not be liable for the failure of any of the conditions hereof caused by the exercise of your discretion in any particular manner, except gross negligence or wilful misconduct.

(d)   You are not to be held liable for the sufficiency or correctness as to form, manner of execution, or validity of any instrument deposited in this escrow, or as to identity, authority, or rights of any person executing the same, or for failure to comply with any of the provisions of any agreement, or other instrument filed herein or referred to herein, and your duties hereunder shall be limited to the safekeeping of such money, instruments, or other documents received by you as escrow holder and for the disposition of same in accordance with the written instructions accepted by you in this escrow.

(e)   Should any controversy arise between the parties hereto, or any other person, you shall not be liable to take any action of any kind but may withhold all moneys, securities, documents or other things herein deposited until such controversy shall be determined by agreement of the parties, or by proper legal process.

(f)   All parties hereto agree, jointly and severally, to pay on demand, as well as to indemnify and hold you harmless from and against all costs, damages, judgments, attorney's fees, expenses, obligations and liabilities of any kind or nature which, in good faith, you may incur or sustain in connection with, or arising out of this escrow, and you are hereby given a lien upon all rights, titles and interest of each of the undersigned in all escrowed papers and other property or monies deposited in this escrow, to protect your rights and to indemnify and reimburse you under this agreement.

(g)   It is understood that the fees hereunder agreed to be paid for your services are for ordinary and usual services only, and should there be any extraordinary or unusual services rendered by you hereunder, the undersigned agree to pay to you reasonable compensation for such extraordinary or unusual services, together with any costs and expenses which may be incurred by you in connection therewith; and you are hereby given a lien upon all documents, moneys and securities herein deposited until you have been so compensated or reimbursed.

(h)   If any party to these instructions obtain a loan on the land involved, and during the pendency of this escrow, you are authorized to furnish the lender, or any one operating on its behalf, any information concerning this escrow, including, but not limited to, a certified copy of the escrow instructions and any amendments thereto.

(i)   It is understood that no examination will be made of the records pertaining to water rights and contracts, and other matters pertaining thereto.

(j)   Time is of the essence of these and all additional or changed instructions.

(k)   These instructions may be executed in counterparts, each of which so executed, shall, regardless of the date of its execution and delivery be deemed as original, and said counterparts together shall constitute one and the same instrument.

We, jointly and severally, agree that in the event of cancellation, we shall pay you a sum sufficient to pay you for any expenses which you have incurred pursuant to these instructions and a reasonable cancellation fee for services rendered by you, said expenses and fees to be put in escrow before cancellation is effective. We further agree that said charges may be apportioned to us in a manner which you consider equitable and that your decision in that regard will be binding and conclusive upon us. Any funds which have been deposited by a licensed real estate broker for either or both of us shall be returned to such broker.

Signature: ....../S/...   Signature: ..../S/..
            John Doe   Jane Doe

Signature: ....   Signature: ....

Address: ....
                    (Street and Number)

....   Telephone: ....
    (City)   (State)   (Zip Code)

SELLER'S INSTRUCTIONS

                                                            Date: January 1, 1981

THE FOREGOING TERMS, CONDITIONS AND/OR INSTRUCTIONS ARE HEREBY CONCURRED IN, APPROVED AND ACCEPTED, I will hand you all instruments and money necessary for me to comply therewith, including a Deed to the property described, which you are authorized to record and deliver upon payment to you of the sum of $100,000.................. and from which you may pay all Demands for all encumbrances on said property, except as set forth on page one hereof: ....

Attach State Documentary Tax Stamps to Deed in the amount of $..

You will send to me any Promissory Notes in my favor delivered to you and, as my agent, assign any fire and other insurance of mine handed you, or that Beneficiaries inform you they hold, I agree to pay usual Seller's charges, including those for Policy of Title Insurance, one-half of Escrow Fee, drawing of any Deeds or other instruments executed by me or necessary on my part, revenue stamps, recording any Trust Deed in my favor, assignments on insurance policies, and obtaining Offset Statements, Beneficiaries' Statements and/or Demands.

Make check for balance payable to: ....

Said check to be mailed to: ....

Signature: ....../S/...   Signature: ..../S/..

Signature: ....   Signature: ....

Address: ....
                    (Street and Number)

....
    (City)   (State)   (Zip Code)

5-011 1/77

To: Chicago Title Insurance Company   Escrow No.
     Los Angeles, California   Escrow Officer:
                                              _____

THIS AGREEMENT OF PURCHASE AND SALE AND JOINT ESCROW INSTRUC-

TIONS (hereafter referred to as the "Agreement") is made and

entered into as of the 1st day of January, 1981, by and between

AJAX LAND COMPANY (hereafter referred to as the "Seller"), a corpora-

tion and SPEC-LAND, LTD., a Limited Partnership (hereafter referred

to as the "Buyer").

RECITALS AND DEFINITIONS

A. Seller is the owner of the Property, (as hereafter defined)

the subject of this Agreement.

B. This Agreement constitutes an Agreement of Purchase and

Sale pursuant to the terms of which Seller agrees to sell and Buyer

agrees to purchase the Property.

C. "Escrow Holder" or "Escrow" shall mean and refer to CHICAGO

TITLE INSURANCE COMPANY, Los Angeles, California.

D. "Opening Escrow" shall mean and refer to the date as of

which this Agreement is made and entered into.

The terms and conditions of this Agreement and your instruc-

tions with regard thereto, are as follows:

---

1. Purchase and Sale. Seller agrees to sell to Buyer

and Buyer agrees to purchase from Seller, the Property upon

the terms and conditions herein set forth.

2. The Property. The Property being purchased and sold

herein consists of the following:

That certain unimproved real property in the City of

Los Angeles, County of Los Angeles, State of California, described

in Exhibit "A" attached hereto and made a part hereof (hereafter

referred to as the "Property").

3. Purchase Price. The purchase price for the Property shall

be FIVE HUNDRED THOUSAND DOLLARS ($500,000.00).

4. Payment of Purchase Price. The purchase price shall be

all payable in cash on the close of Escrow.

5. Condition of Title. Fee simple title to the Property

shall be conveyed to Buyer (or the Buyer's assignee as hereafter

provided) by the Seller on the close of Escrow by Grant Deed in

the form attached hereto and marked as Exhibit "B" subject only

to the following:

a. Current real property taxes and assessments not then

payable;

b. Such covenants, conditions, restrictions, easements,

rights, rights of way and other exceptions to title of record

that are approved by Buyer as hereafter provided;

-2-

performing all of the terms, covenants and provisions of the Agreement by Seller.

f. That the Property is now, and will on the close of Escrow, be free of all claims and mechanic's liens of any kind or nature and that Seller will hold Buyer free and harmless from all future claims for services rendered and/or materials furnished to the Property prior to the close of Escrow and/or claims of any kind or nature.

7. Conditions to the Close of Escrow. The close of Escrow created hereby, and the purchase and sale contemplated hereby, are subject to and conditioned upon the satisfaction prior to the close of Escrow of the following:

a. Buyer's written approval of an Extended Coverage Preliminary Title Report on the Property to be issued by CHICAGO TITLE INSURANCE COMPANY (hereafter referred to as "CTIC") including copies of all instruments that will appear as exceptions to title. In this connection, the Escrow Holder is hereby directed to order CTIC to prepare and deliver to Buyer an Extended Coverage Preliminary Title Report including copies of said instruments (hereafter referred to as the "Report"). Buyer shall have through and including March 1, 1981, to notify Seller and the Escrow Holder in writing of Buyer's approval or disapproval of the Report and any exceptions to title shown in the Report. In the event of such disapproval, Seller shall, if Buyer so requests, use its best efforts and due diligence

-4-

c. Matters affecting the condition of title suffered or created by or with prior written consent of Buyer.

6. Representations and Warranties of Seller. Seller covenants, agrees, represents and warrants the following, each of which shall survive the close of Escrow and shall be relied upon by Buyer as a material inducement for Buyer entering into this Agreement and consummating the purchase of the Property.

a. That at the present time and at the close of Escrow all improvements have been constructed and are now and will be maintained in accordance with all applicable laws, statutes, building codes and local ordinances and that there are no violations of same existing now or will be on the close of Escrow.

b. There are no structural defects in the improvements at the present time.

c. That there are no contracts or agreements affecting the occupancy, use, operation, management, repaid or maintenance of the Property either written or oral that cannot be terminated without penalty or liability on not more than Thirty (30) days notice by Buyer after the close of Escrow.

d. That Seller is a valid corporation and that _____ has authority and authorization to execute this Agreement and all other relevant documents provided for and contemplated hereby and to bind said corporation.

e. That there are no claims or threats of action now pending against the Property that would limit or prohibit Seller from

-3-

to eliminate such exceptions designated by Buyer and either Seller or Buyer shall have the right by written notice to the other to extend the closing date of this Escrow for an additional period not exceeding ninety (90) days. Buyer's failure to disapprove the Report shall be deemed Buyer's approval thereof.

b. Buyer's written approval prior to March 1, 1981 of an ALTA survey on the Property (to be furnished by Seller to Buyer prior to February 1, 1981).

c. Buyer's written approval of a physical examination by Buyer and Buyer's engineers, contractors and inspectors of all existing improvements. In this connection, Seller hereby consents to Buyer's reasonable access to the Property for the purpose of said examination and agrees to cooperate with Buyer in connection therewith. Seller shall further make available to Buyer a copy of any plans and specifications Seller has in its possession covering the existing improvements on the Property. Buyer shall evidence its approval or disapproval of said inspection by written notice to Seller and the Escrow Holder prior to March 1, 1981.

Buyer's failure to timely disapprove shall be deemed Buyer's approval of said inspection.

d. Verification by Buyer of the zoning on the Property and that Buyer may obtain a building permit to construct upon the Property (or portions thereof) industrial buildings. Seller represents and warrants the foregoing.

-5-

Buyer shall have the right to waive any of the terms and provisions set forth in Subparagraphs a. through d. inclusive. Should the foregoing provisions of this Paragraph 7 remain unsatisfied and not waived within the respective time periods, this Agreement and the rights and obligations of Buyer and Seller hereunder and the Escrow created hereby shall terminate. Provided, however, the parties hereto agree to use their best efforts to satisfy the conditions set forth in this Paragraph 7. In the event of such termination as herein provided, both Buyer and Seller shall pay one-half (1/2) of all Escrow fees and costs, all monies deposited herein and all documents deposited herein shall be refunded and returned to the respective parties depositing same and both Buyer and Seller shall thereafter have no further liability or obligation hereunder.

Both Buyer and Seller shall during the pendency of this Escrow deliver to the other and the Escrow Holder upon request certificates or documents advising Buyer, Seller and the Escrow Holder of the satisfaction, nonsatisfaction or waiver of the foregoing conditions.

8. Prorations. You are to prorate and adjust between Buyer and Seller in cash, to the close of Escrow the following:

a. All property taxes, real and personal, based upon current tax bills affecting the Property.

b. Current special assessments.

-6-

9. _Title Insurance._ On the close of Escrow and as a condition thereto, CTIC shall issue to Buyer at Seller's expense its extended coverage owner's policy of title insurance in form approved in writing by Buyer, with a liability equal to the total purchase price subject only to the following exceptions:

a. Current real property taxes and special assessments, a lien not yet payable.

b. Such covenants, conditions, restrictions, easements, rights, rights of way and other matters of record as are approved by Buyer as provided in this Agreement.

10. _Maintenance and Operation of the Property During the Escrow Period._

a. Should the Property be materially damaged prior to the close of Escrow, Seller shall immediately notify Buyer and the Escrow Holder of such damage. Buyer at election may upon written notice to Seller and the Escrow Holder cancel and terminate this Escrow in which event all monies and documents deposited herein shall be immediately refunded to the respective parties and this Escrow shall terminate, all without further liability of the parties and each shall pay one-half (1/2) of all Escrow fees and charges. Should Buyer elect not to terminate this Escrow after notice of such material damage, the proceeds of any insurance received by Seller shall be made available to repair the Property under the joint direction of Buyer and Seller.

-7-

b. During the pendency of this Escrow, Seller shall continue to maintain the Property in its present physical condition to the end that the Property on the close of Escrow will be in the same state of maintenance and repair as the Property now enjoys on the date hereof.

11. _Costs and Expenses._ The cost and expense of the title insurance policy, documentary transfer taxes and survey shall be pad by the Seller. The Escrow fees of Escrow Holder shall be borne one-half (1/2) by Buyer and one-half (1/2) by Seller. Buyer and Seller shall pay, respectively, the Escrow Holder's customary charges to Buyer and Seller for document drafting, if any, recording and miscellaneous charges.

12. _Close of Escrow._ For purposes of this Agreement, close of Escrow shall be deemed to be the date that the Grant Deed is recorded; provided that Escrow shall close no later than March 15, 1981, (subject to extension of said date as elsewhere provided in this Agreement) unless mutually agreed in writing by Buyer and Seller. In the event Escrow fails to close on or before said date (or any extension thereof) upon the demand of either party hereto and without further notice or authorization, the Escrow Holder shall promptly return to both Buyer and Seller all deeds, documents and monies theretofore deposited with Escrow Holder. Any such action undertaken by Escrow Holder shall in no event relieve the parties hereto from any obligations to Escrow Holder with respect to the Escrow, or waive, release or discharge of any breach of default by any of the parties hereto of

-8-

b. _Successors and Assigns._ This Agreement shall be binding upon and shall inure to the benefit of the heirs, executors, administrators, successors and assigns of the respective parties hereto.

c. _Required Actions of Buyer and Seller._ Buyer and Seller agree to execute all such instruments and documents and to take all actions (including the deposit of funds in addition to such funds as may be specifically provided for herein) as may be required in order to consummate the purchase and sale herein contemplated.

d. _Entire Agreement._ This Agreement contains the entire agreement between the parties hereto and no addition or modification of any terms or provision shall be effective unless set forth in writing, signed by both Seller and Buyer.

e. _Time of Essence._ Time is of the essence of each and every term, condition, obligation and provision hereof.

f. _Counterparts._ This Agreement may be executed simultaneously in counterparts, each of which shall be deemed an original, but all of which, together, shall constitute one and the same instrument.

g. _Legal Fees._ In the event of the bringing of any action or suit by a party hereto against another party hereunder by reason of any breach of any of the covenants, conditions, agreements, or provisions on the part of the other party arising out of

-10-

---

any of their respective covenants, agreements, obligations or duties herein set forth.

13. _Recordation and Disbursement of Monies._ You are instructed to record the Grant Deed from Seller to Buyer (Exhibit "B") when:

a. All of the conditions set forth in Paragraph 7 above have been met or waived as therein provided, and when

b. You can hold for disbursement to Seller the full payment (less prorations, if any, as above provided in Paragraph 8), and when

c. You can issue to Buyer the policy of title insurance as provided in Paragraph 9 above.

14. _Assignment by Buyer._ Buyer may, prior to the close of Escrow, assign all of his rights, title and interest under this Agreement to such person(s) or entity Buyer may designate provided that such assignee (1) expressly assumes all of the Buyer's obligations hereunder as though he was the original signatory hereto and (2) agrees to perform all of the provisions hereof. In such an event, the deed, all other instruments, and title policy shall be issued in the name of such assignee.

15. _Miscellaneous Provisions._

a. _Survival of Conditions._ The covenants, agreements, representations and warranties made in Paragraph 6a., 6b., 6c., 6d., and 6f. hereof shall survive the close of Escrow and the delivery and recordation of the Grant Deed

-9-

this Agreement, then in that event the party in whose favor final judgment shall be entered shall be entitled to have and recover of and from the other party all costs and expenses of suit, including reasonable attorney's fees.

    h. Notices. All notices or other communication required or permitted hereunder shall be in writing and shall be sent registered mail or certified mail, return receipt requested, and shall be deemed received two (2) business days after deposit in the mail in the County of Los Angeles, postage prepaid, addressed to the person to receive such notice at the following address:

TO SELLER: Ajax Land Company

TO BUYER: Spec-Land, Ltd.

WITH A COPY TO: Myron Meyers, Esq.
c/o Meyers, Stevens & Walters
Professional Corporation
Suite 9100
6300 Wilshire Boulevard
Los Angeles, California 90048

Notice of change of address shall be given by written notice in the manner described in Paragraph 15.

16. General Provisions.

    a. You will, as the agent of the respective parties assign any insurance of Seller handed you for use in this Escrow;

    b. Make all adjustments and/or prorations on the basis of a Thirty (30) day month and by credit and/or debit to respective accounts of Seller and Buyer in this Escrow;

    c. The expression "close of Escrow" shall mean the date

-11-

the instruments transferring the title to the properties herein are recorded or registered;

    d. Make disbursements by your check, instruments and check to be mailed to the addresses shown above, unless you are instructed otherwise;

    e. NO NOTICE, DEMAND OR CHANGE OF INSTRUCTIONS SHALL BE OF ANY EFFECT ON THIS ESCROW UNLESS GIVEN IN WRITING BY ALL PARTIES THEREBY. In the event conflicting demands are made or notices served upon you with respect to this Escrow, the parties hereto expressly agree that you shall have the absolute right at your election to do either or both of the following: Withhold and stop all further proceedings in, and performance of, this Escrow or file a suit in interpleader and obtain an order from the court requiring the parties to interplead and litigate in such court their several claims and rights among themselves. In the event such interpleader suit is brought, you shall ipso facto be fully released and discharged from all obligations to further perform any and all duties or obligations imposed upon you in this Escrow, and the parties jointly and severally agree to pay all costs, expenses and reasonable attorney's fees expended or incurred by you, the amount thereof to be fixed and a judgment therefor entered by the court in such suit;

    f. You are not to be held liable for the sufficiency or correctness as to form, manner of execution, or validity of

-12-

any property herein described, or of any profit realized by any person, firm or corporation (broker, agent and parties to this and/or other Escrow included) in connection therewith regardless of the fact that such transaction(s) may be handled by you in this Escrow or in another Escrow;

i. These instructions may be executed in counterparts, each of which so executed shall, irrespective of the date of its execution and delivery, be deemed an original, and said counterparts together shall constitute one and the same instrument;

j. Any amended, supplemental or additional instructions given shall be subject to the foregoing conditions;

k. The parties agree to execute any other and further instructions, not inconsistent herewith, which may be required by the Escrow Holder for its protection or to consummate this transaction.

17. Commissions. It is expressly agreed that Buyer shall have not obligation in connection with the payment of real estate commissions which shall be the sole obligation of the Seller. Seller shall hold Buyer free and harmless from any claim for real estate commissions, finder's fees or similar charges.

SELLER:

AJAX LAND COMPANY,
a corporation

By _____, President

By _____, Secretary

-14-

any instrument deposited in this Escrow, nor as to identity, authority, or rights of any person executing the same, nor for failure to comply with any of the provisions of any agreement contract or other instrument filed herein, and your duties hereunder shall be limited to the safekeeping of such money, instruments, or other documents received by you as Escrow Holder, and for the disposition of same in accordance with the written instructions accepted by you in this Escrow;

g. All parties hereto further agree, jointly and severally, to pay on demand, as well as to indemnify and hold you harmless from and against all costs, damages, judgments, attorney's fees, expenses, obligations, and liabilities of any kind or nature which in good faith you may incur or sustain in connection with or arising out of this Escrow, and you are hereby given a lien upon all rights, titles and interest of each of the undersigned in all Escrowed papers and other property and monies deposited in this Escrow, to protect your rights and to indemnify and reimburse you under this Agreement;

h. It is agreed by the parties hereto that so far as your rights and liabilities are concerned, this transaction is an Escrow and not any other legal relation, and you are an Escrow Holder only on the terms expressed herein, and you shall have no responsibility of notifying any of the parties to this Escrow of any sale, resale, lien, exchange, or other transaction involving

-13-

SCHEDULE OF EXHIBITS

Exhibit "A"   Legal Description of Property

Exhibit "B"   Form of Grant Deed

BUYER:

SPEC-LAND, LTD.,
a Limited Partnership

By _____, General Partner

-15-

AGREEMENT OF PURCHASE
AND
SALE AND ESCROW INSTRUCTIONS

To: Chicago Title Insurance Company
    Los Angeles, California

Escrow No.
Escrow Officer:

THIS AGREEMENT OF PURCHASE AND SALE AND JOINT ESCROW INSTRUCTIONS (hereafter referred to as the "Agreement") is made and entered into as of the 1st day of January, 1981, by and between BLACKACRE COMPANY, a California Limited Partnership, (hereafter referred to as the "Seller"), and WHITEACRE LIMITED, a California Limited Partnership (hereafter referred to as the "Buyer").

RECITALS AND DEFINITIONS

A. Seller is the owner of the Property, (as hereafter defined) the subject of this Agreement.

B. This Agreement constitutes an Agreement of Purchase and Sale pursuant to the terms of which Seller agrees to sell, and Buyer agrees to purchase the Property.

C. "Escrow Holder" or "Escrow" shall mean and refer to CHICAGO TITLE INSURANCE COMPANY, Los Angeles, California.

D. "Opening Escrow" shall mean and refer to the date as of which this Agreement is made and entered into.

The terms and conditions of this Agreement and your instructions with regard thereto, are as follows:

1. Purchase and Sale. Seller agrees to sell to Buyer and Buyer agrees to purchase from Seller, the Property upon the terms and conditions herein set forth.

2. The Property. The Property being purchased and sold herein consists of the following:

a. That certain real property in the City of Los Angeles, County of Los Angeles, State of California, described in Exhibit "A" attached hereto and made a part hereof including all improvements thereto and thereon; and

b. All furniture, fixtures, appliances, equipment, and other personal property owned by the Seller and located and/or used in and about the real property described in Exhibit "A"; and

c. All month-to-month tenancy agreements and/or leases affecting apartments in the property described in Exhibit "A"; and

d. All furniture and/or appliance rental agreements under the terms of which Seller is the lessor.

All of the foregoing is sometimes hereafter referred to as the "Property".

Buyer and Seller agree to cause a detailed inventory of all personal property to be mutually taken and to cause said inventory to be signed and approved by both Buyer and Seller and deposited into Escrow on or before February 1, 1981. Said inventory when deposited into Escrow shall be marked Exhibit "B" and made a part hereof.

-2-

3. Purchase Price. The purchase price for the Property shall be THREE MILLION, ONE HUNDRED FIFTY THOUSAND ($3,500,000.00) DOLLARS.

4. Payment of Purchase Price. Said purchase price shall be payable as follows:

a. A down payment of FOUR HUNDRED THOUSAND ($400,000.00) DOLLARS payable by Buyer to Seller through Escrow on the close of Escrow of which sum TEN THOUSAND ($10,000.00) DOLLARS is handed you herewith for disbursement as hereafter provided. You are to deposit said sum in an interest bearing savings account or purchase an interest bearing certificate of deposit with said monies. All interest thereon shall inure to the benefit of the Buyer.

b. Buyer acquiring the Property subject to an existing First Trust Deed encumbrance in favor of FICTITIOUS SAVINGS & LOAN ASSOCIATION (hereafter referred to as "Lender"), their Loan No. 10000, in the approximate sum of TWO MILLION, TWO HUNDRED NINETY-FIVE THOUSAND ($2,295,000.00) DOLLARS. There is attached hereto as Exhibit "C" and made a part hereof a true and accurate copy of the Promissory Note in favor of Lender, all modifications thereof and all instruments securing said Promissory Note as modified.

c. The balance of the purchase price shall be evidenced by a Purchase Money Promissory Note in the form attached hereto as Exhibit "D" and made a part hereof. Said Promissory Note

-3-

shall be in the approximate sum of FOUR HUNDRED FIFTY-FIVE THOUSAND ($455,000.00) DOLLARS, (subject to adjustment as hereafter provided), shall bear interest at the rate of seven per cent (7%) per annum on the unpaid principal balance, shall be payable interest only monthly commencing thirty (30) days from the close of Escrow for the first five (5) years thereof and thereafter shall be payable in monthly installments of principal and interest equal to one per cent (1%) of the original face amount of said Promissory Note. Said Note may be prepaid in whole or in part without penalty. Said Promissory Note shall be secured by a Purchase Money Deed of Trust in form attached hereto as Exhibit "E" and made a part hereof.

d. Buyer at his election may purchase the Property for cash, all payable on the close of Escrow. Said election shall be by written notice to Seller and Escrow Holder prior to the close of Escrow.

5. Beneficiary Statement and Adjustment of Purchase Money Promissory Note and Deed of Trust. You are instructed hereby to order at once and obtain from Lender a Beneficiary Statement including a copy of Lender's Promissory Note, Deed of Trust and other security instruments securing the Lender obligation, including all amendments and modifications, if any, thereto. Said Beneficiary Statement and said documents are subject to Buyer's approval prior to March 1, 1981. After Buyer has approved said Beneficiary

-4-

Statement, (all all subsequent amendments thereto based upon the fact that additional payments will be made against said obligation during the pendency of this Escrow), you are to adjust the principal amount of the Purchase Money Promissory Note and Deed of Trust (Exhibits "D" and "E") so that the total purchase price and down payment set forth in Paragraph 4 above, remains unchanged and all sums due on Lenders obligation as disclosed by the approved Beneficiary Statements are reflected in the amount of said Purchase Money Note and Deed of Trust by due credit for the unpaid principal amount of the Lender obligation on the close of Escrow.

6. _Condition of Title._ Fee simple title to the Property shall be conveyed to Buyer (or the Buyer's assignee as hereafter provided) by the Seller on the close of Escrow by Grant Deed in the form attached hereto and marked as Exhibit "F" subject only to the following:

a. Current real property taxes and assessments not then payable:

b. Such covenants, conditions, restrictions, easements, rights, rights of way and other exceptions to title of record that are approved by Buyer as hereafter provided;

c. The Lender Deed of Trust and other security instruments securing said obligation;

d. The Purchase Money Deed of Trust (Exhibit "E");

e. Matters affecting the condition of title suffered

-5-

or created by or with prior written consent of Buyer;

f. All existing leases and/or month-to-month tenancy agreements that are approved by Buyer as hereafter provided.

7. _Personal Property._ You are requested hereby at Seller's expense to make immediate personal property search with the Uniform Commercial Code Division of the California Secretary of State under the name BLACKACRE COMPANY, and to obtain the customary certificates from the Secretary of State on said name. Said certificate is subject to Buyer's approval as hereafter provided. You shall have no further obligation as Escrow Holder in connection with the search of title to said personal property. Seller will hand you a Warranty Bill of Sale to the personal property in form attached hereto as Exhibit "G" and made a part hereof. You are to attach to the original Bill of Sale the approved inventory of personal property (Exhibit "D") and deliver the original Bill of Sale to Buyer on the close of Escrow as hereafter provided.

8. _Representations and Warranties of Seller._ Seller covenants, agrees, represents and warrants the following, each of which shall survive the close of Escrow and shall be relied upon by Buyer as a material inducement for Buyer entering into this Agreement and consummating the purchase of the Property.

a. That at the present time and at the close of Escrow all improvements have been constructed and are now and will be maintained in accordance with all applicable laws, statutes,

-6-

f. That there are no other contracts or agreements affecting the occupancy, use, operation, management, repair or maintenance of the Property either written or oral that cannot be terminated without penalty or liability on not more than thirty (30) days notice by Buyer after the close of Escrow.

g. That Seller is a valid Limited Partnership, duly qualified to do business in California and that the General Partner thereof has authority and authorization to execute this Agreement and all other relevant documents provided for and contemplated hereby.

h. That there are no claims or actions or threats of action now pending against the Property that would limit or prohibit Seller from performing all of the terms, covenants, and provisions of the Agreement by Seller.

i. That the Property is now, and will on the close of Escrow, be free of all claims and mechanic's liens of any kind or nature and that Seller will hold Buyer free and harmless from all future claims for services rendered and/or materials furnished to the Property prior to the close of Escrow.

j. That Buyer (or Buyer's assignee) may purchase the Property subject to the Lender's Loan No. 10000 (or assume said loan without personal liability and with a waiver of deficiency judgment) in said loan's present form without further modification, cost or expense on the part of the Buyer. Seller agrees to

-8-

building codes and local ordinances and that there are no violations of same existing now or will be on the close of Escrow.

b. To the best of Seller's knowledge, there are no structural defects in the improvements at the present time.

c. That all personal property to be described in Exhibit "D" and the Bill of Sale (Exhibit "G") is now, and at the close of Escrow will be, free and clear of all claims, liens, and encumbrances of every kind or nature except there may be a prior security interest in favor of Lender given to Lender as additional collateral for Lender's Loan No. 10000.

d. That the statements, schedules and data of income and expenses previously furnished to Buyer by Seller and hereafter furnished to Buyer by Seller are true and accurate and reflect the actual true income and expense relating to the Property. No representation or warranty is given by Seller or Seller's agent as to future income or expenses.

e. That the leases and/or month-to-month tenancy agreements and records of rental payments furnished heretofore or hereafter by Seller to Buyer are true and accurate and reflect all rental income actually received and truly represent the total agreement between Seller as Landlord and each tenant as tenant. Seller has not granted to any tenant any rental concession or rent-free early move-in provision or any similar right or privilege.

-7-

pay all costs or expenses, or fees or charges, if any, required by Lender to obtain the written approval of Lender for Buyer's consummation of this Agreement. Buyer (or Buyer's assignee) agrees consistent with the above provisions, to furnish to Lender upon request, financial statements, loan applications and similar information that may be reasonably requested by Lender and to cooperate with Seller to obtain the requisite consent of Lender as herein provided.

9. Conditions to the Close of Escrow. The close of the Escrow created hereby, and the purchase and sale contemplated hereby, are subject to and conditioned upon the satisfaction prior to the close of Escrow of the following:

a. Buyer's written approval of an Extended Coverage Preliminary Title Report on the Property to be issued by CHICAGO TITLE INSURANCE COMPANY (hereafter referred to as "CTIC") including copies of all instruments that will appear as exceptions to title. In this connection the Escrow Holder is hereby directed to order CTIC to prepare and deliver to Buyer an Extended Coverage Preliminary Title Report including copies of said instruments (hereinafter referred to as the "Report"). Buyer shall have through and including March 1, 1981 to notify Seller and the Escrow Holder in writing of Buyer's approval or disapproval of the Report and any exceptions to title shown in the Report. In the event of such disapproval, Seller shall, if Buyer so requests, use its best

-9-

efforts and due diligence to eliminate such exceptions designated by Buyer and shall have the right by written notice to Buyer to extend the closing date of this Escrow for an additional period not exceeding thirty (30) days. Buyer's failure to disapprove the Report shall be deemed Buyer's approval thereof.

b. Buyer's written approval prior to March 1, 1981 of an ALTA survey on the Property (to be furnished by Seller to Buyer prior to April 1, 1981).

c. Buyer's written approval of a physical examination by Buyer and Buyer's engineers, contractors and inspectors of all existing improvements and all personal property. In this connection, Seller hereby consents to Buyer's reasonable access to the Property for the purpose of said examination and agrees to cooperate with Buyer in connection therewith. Seller shall further make available to Buyer a copy of any plans and specifications Seller has in its possession covering the existing improvements on the Property. Buyer shall evidence its approval or disapproval of said inspection by written notice to Seller and the Escrow Holder prior to March 1, 1981. Buyer's failure to timely disapprove shall be deemed Buyer's approval of said inspection. As part of said inspection, Seller shall make available to Buyer for Buyer's examination, all of Seller's accounts, records, books, agreements and contracts for repairs, renovations and improvement to the Property from June 1, 1980 to date.

-10-

d. Buyer's written approval of all leases and/or month-to-month tenancy agreements affecting the Property and a Certified Rent Roll of all rents, deposits (refundable and non-refundable) and fees as to all existing tenants. In this connection, Seller shall make available to Buyer, its agents and accountants, all books, records, accounts, rental affecting the Property from June 1, 1980 to date and rental agreements and leases currently in effect. Buyer shall evidence its approval or disapproval of said material by written notice to Seller and the Escrow Holder prior to March 1, 1981. Buyer's failure to timely disapprove shall be deemed Buyer's approval thereof.

e. Buyer's written approval of all income and expenses relating to the ownership, operation and maintenance of the Property. In this connection, Seller shall make available to Buyer and Buyer's agents and accountants all books and records from June 1, 1980 to date. Buyer shall evidence its approval or disapproval prior to March 1, 1981. Buyer's failure to timely disapprove shall be deemed Buyer's approval thereof.

f. Buyer's written approval of the form and content of the Lender loan and all security instruments securing same and Buyer's ability to acquire all security instruments securing same and Buyer's ability to acquire the Property subject to the Lender's obligation. Buyer shall evidence its approval or disapproval of the

-11-

foregoing by written notice to Seller and the Escrow Holder prior to March 1, 1981. Buyer's failure to disapprove shall be deemed Buyer's approval of the form and content of same.

g. Seller will furnish a current report from a licensed pest control company (the Report) covering all visible or accessible areas of the Property (including under-areas, garages, and carports). Seller authorizes payment through Escrow for the Report and for the following: (i) elimination of dry rot, fungus and/or active infestation or infection of wood-destroying pests or organisms; (ii) repair of any leaking stall showers and replacement of any tile removed to make such repairs. All other recommendations on the Report will be furnished Buyer and may be performed at the option of Buyer. The Report shall comply with the California Business and Professions Code Section 8519 and California Civil Code Section 1099. The Escrow Holder shall deliver to Buyer upon receipt a copy of the Report and Notice of Work Completed.

Buyer shall have the right to waive any of the terms and provisions set forth in Paragraphs A through G inclusive. Should the foregoing provisions of this Paragraph 9 remain unsatisfied and not waived within the respective time periods, this Agreement and the rights and obligations of Buyer and Seller hereunder and the Escrow created hereby shall terminate. Provided, however, the parties hereto agree to use their best efforts to satisfy the conditions set forth in this Paragraph 9. In the event

-12-

of such termination as herein provided, both Buyer and Seller shall each pay one-half (1/2) of all Escrow fees and costs, all monies deposited herein and all documents deposited herein shall be refunded and returned to the respective parties depositing same and both Buyer and Seller shall thereafter have no further liability or obligation hereunder.

Both Buyer and Seller shall during the pendency of this Escrow deliver to the other and the Escrow Holder upon request, certificates or documents advising Buyer, Seller and the Escrow Holder of the satisfaction, nonsatisfaction or waiver of the foregoing conditions.

10. Prorations. You are to prorate and adjust between Buyer and Seller in cash, to the close of Escrow, the following:

a. All property taxes, real and personal, based upon current tax bills affecting the Property.

b. All sums, if any, held or impounded by Lender based upon Beneficiary Statements furnished to you (and amendments and supplements thereto) by Lender and approved in writing by Buyer.

c. All rents and tenant deposits per Certified Rent Roll to be handed to you by Seller and approved in writing by Buyer. You are not to credit Seller with delinquent rents, which is to be Seller's sole responsibility. You are to credit Buyer with all security deposits and tenant deposits (refundable and non-refundable). Seller will hand you a Certified Rent Roll in the Escrow Holder's

-13-

usual form which is subject to Buyer's written approval prior to the close of Escrow. Seller will immediately, prior to the close of Escrow, update said Rent Roll, which update, shall be subject to Buyer's written approval which shall not be unreasonably withheld. Your prorations shall be based upon said approval and updated Rent Roll.

d. Insurance premiums on existing policies of insurance that have been approved by Buyer only if Buyer elects to assume said insurance policies as more fully set forth in Paragraph 11 below.

11. Insurance. Seller shall deliver to Buyer prior to February 1, 1981, true copies of all existing fire, liability, workers' compensation and other insurance now carried by Seller in connection with the ownership, operation and maintenance of the Property, Buyer shall, prior to the close of Escrow, elect to either assume or not to assume the existing insurance or portions thereof. Should Buyer elect to assume all or any of said insurance policies, the Escrow Holder will prorate the premiums thereon to the close of Escrow based upon paid premium receipts therefor delivered by Seller to Buyer and the Escrow Holder and approved in writing by Buyer. Should Buyer elect not to assume any insurance policy, the Escrow Holder shall not be further concerned therewith. Buyer shall evidence its election to assume or not to assume any insurance policy by written notice prior to the close of Escrow to Seller and the Escrow Holder.

-14-

12. _Title Insurance._ On the close of Escrow and as a condition thereto, CTIC shall issue to Buyer at Seller's expense its extended coverage owner's policy of title insurance in form approved in writing by Buyer, with a liability equal to the purchase price subject only to the following exceptions:

a. Current real property taxes.

b. Such covenants, conditions, restrictions, easements, rights, rights of way and other matters of record as are approved by Buyer as provided in this Agreement.

c. The Lender First Trust Deed and other documents as are approved by Buyer as provided in Paragraph 4b above including any amendment or modification thereof approved by Buyer.

d. The Purchase Money Deed of Trust (Exhibit "E").

13. _Maintenance and Operation of the Property During the Escrow Period._

a. Should the Property be materially damaged prior to the close of Escrow, Seller shall immediately notify Buyer and the Escrow Holder of such damage. Buyer, at its election, may upon written notice to the Seller and the Escrow Holder, cancel and terminate this Escrow in which event all monies and documents deposited herein shall be immediately refunded to the respective parties and this Escrow shall terminate, all without further liability of the parties and each shall pay one-half (1/2) of all Escrow fees and charges. Should Buyer elect not to terminate this

Escrow after notice of such material damage, the proceeds of any insurance received by Seller shall be made available to repair the Property under the joint direction of Buyer and Seller.

b. During the pendency of this Escrow, Seller shall continue to operate the Property in the same manner as Seller has been operating the Property since June 1, 1980, including the continuance of the same level of general maintenance and repairs. Seller shall also continue the same rental policy, level of management, supervision and control. All of the foregoing shall be implemented and executed to the end that the Property on the close of Escrow will be in the same state of operation, maintenance and repair and enjoy the same level of income and expense as the Property now enjoys on the date hereof, acts of God, elements, and other casualty excepted. Seller shall not enter into new rental agreements or leases beyond thirty (30) days in duration.

14. _Costs and Expenses._ The cost and expense of the title insurance policy, documentary transfer taxes and survey shall be paid by the Seller. The Escrow fees and Escrow Holder shall be borne one-half (1/2) by Buyer and one-half (1/2) by Seller. Buyer and Seller shall pay, respectively, the Escrow Holder's customary charges to Buyer and Seller for document drafting, if any, recording and miscellaneous charges.

15. _Liquidated Damages._ Buyer shall use reasonable effort to perform his obligations under this Agreement, but if Buyer fails to perform, Seller should be entitled to compensation therefor. Both Buyer and Seller agree, however, that it is extremely difficult and impractical to determine the extent of Seller's detriment in the event of Buyer's failure to perform. To avoid this problem, the parties agree to liquidate damages as follows:

If Buyer fails to perform, after Buyer has either approved or waived the conditions set forth in Paragraph 9 above, Seller shall be entitled to recover the sum of TEN THOUSAND DOLLARS ($10,000.00) as liquidated damages and shall be entitled to obtain the sum out of any deposit made by Buyer into this Escrow. This sum stated as liquidated damages shall be in lieu of any other relief of which Seller might otherwise be entitled by virtue of this Agreement or by operation of law. In the event of such default by Buyer, you as Escrow Holder shall, without liability to you, pay to Seller the sum of TEN THOUSAND DOLLARS ($10,000.00); Buyer shall pay all of the Escrow Holder's fees and expenses; all other monies and documents shall be returned to the respective parties; and each party shall have no further liability to the other.

Initial_____. Initial_____.

16. _First Refusal Rights._ Seller hereby grants to Buyer the rights of frist refusal to purchase the Purchase Money Promissory

-17-

Note and Deed of Trust as more fully set forth in the letter agreement, a copy of which is attached hereto as Exhibit "H" and made a part hereof.

17. _Close of Escrow._ For purposes of this Agreement, close of Escrow shall be deemed to be the date that the Grant Deed is recorded; provided that Escrow shall close no later than May 15, 1981 (subject to extension of said date as elsewhere provided in this Agreement) unless mutually agreed in writing by Buyer and Seller. In the event Escrow fails to close on or before said date (or any extension thereof), upon the demand of either party hereto and without further notice or authorization, the Escrow Holder shall promptly return to both Buyer and Seller all deeds, documents and monies theretofore deposited with Escrow Holder. Any such action undertaken by Escrow Holder shall in no event relieve the parties hereto from any obligations to Escrow Holder with respect to the Escrow, or waive, release or discharge of any breach or default by any of the parties hereto of any of their respective covenants, agreements, obligations or duties herein set forth.

18. _Recordation and Disbursement of Monies._ You are instructed to record the Grant Deed from Seller to Buyer (Exhibit "F"); to record the Purchase Money Deed of Trust (Exhibit "E"); to deliver to Seller the original Purchase Money Promissory Note (Exhibit "D"); to deliver to Buyer the original Warranty Bill of

-18-

the close of Escrow and the delivery and recordation of the Grant Deed.

b. Successors and Assigns. This Agreement shall be binding upon and shall inure to the benefit of the heirs, executors, administrators, successors and assigns of the respective parties hereto.

c. Required Actions of Buyer and Seller. Buyer and Seller agree to execute all such instruments and documents and to take all actions (including the deposit of funds in addition to such funds as may be specifically provided for herein) as may be required in order to consummate the purchase and sale herein contemplated.

d. Entire Agreement. This Agreement contains the entire agreement between the parties hereto and no addition or modification of any term or provision shall be effective unless set forth in writing, signed by both Seller and Buyer.

e. Time of Essence. Time is of the essence of each and every term, condition, obligation and provision hereof.

f. Counterparts. This Agreement may be executed simultaneously in counterparts, each of which shall be deemed an original, but all of which, together, shall constitute one and the same instrument.

g. Legal Fees. In the event of the bringing of any action or suit by a party hereto against another party hereunder by reason of any breach of any of the covenants, conditions,

-20-

Sale with inventory attached (Exhibits "G" and "B" respectively); deliver to Buyer the Agreement re: First Refusal (Exhibit "H"); deliver to Buyer the original Certified Rent Roll and the original of all leases and month-to-month tenancy agreements; deliver to Buyer a blanket assignment of all leases and month-to-month tenancy agreements in the form of Exhibit "I" attached hereto; when

a. All of the conditions set forth in Paragraph 9 above have been met or waived as therein provided, and when

b. You can hold for disbursement to Seller the down payment (less prorations, if any, as above provided in Paragraph 10), and when

c. You can issue to Buyer the policy of title insurance as provided in Paragraph 6 above.

19. Assignment by Buyer. Buyer may, prior to the close of Escrow, assign all of his rights, title and interest under this Agreement to such person(s) or entity(s) Buyer may designate provided that such assignee (1) expressly assumes all of the Buyer's obligations as though he was the original signatory hereto and (2) agrees to perform all of the provisions hereof. In such an event, the deed, all other instruments and title policy shall be issued in the name of such assignee.

20. Miscellaneous Provisions.

a. Survival of Conditions. The covenants, agreements, representations and warranties made in Paragraph hereof shall survive

-19-

agreements or provisions on the part of the other party arising out of this Agreement, then in that event the party in whose favor final judgment shall be entered shall be entitled to have and recover of and from the other party all costs and expenses of suit, including reasonable attorney's fees.

h. Notices. All notices or other communication required or permitted hereunder shall be in writing and shall be sent registered mail or certified mail, return receipt requested, and shall be deemed received two (2) business days after deposit in the mail in the County of Los Angeles, postage prepaid, addressed to the person to receive such notice at the following address:

To Seller: Blackacre Company,
a California Limited Partnership

To Buyer: Whiteacre Limited,
a California Limited Partnership

Notice of change of address shall be given by written notice in the manner described in this Paragraph 20h.

21. General Provisions.

a. You will, as the agent of the respective parties, assign any insurance of Seller handed you for use in this Escrow;

b. Make all adjustments and/or prorations on the basis of a thirty (30) day month and by credit and/or debit to respective accounts of Seller and Buyer in this Escrow;

-21-

c. The expression "close of Escrow" shall mean the date the instruments transferring the title to the properties herein are recorded or registered;

d. Make disbursements by your check, instruments and check to be mailed to the addresses shown above, unless you are instructed otherwise;

e. NO NOTICE, DEMAND OR CHANGE OF INSTRUCTIONS SHALL BE OF ANY EFFECT ON THIS ESCROW UNLESS GIVEN IN WRITING BY ALL PARTIES THEREBY. In the event conflicting demands are made or notices served upon you with respect to this Escrow, the parties hereto expressly agree that you shall have the absolute right at your election to do either or both of the following: Withhold and stop all further proceedings in, and performance of, this Escrow or file a suit in interpleader and obtain an order from the court requiring the parties to interplead and litigate in such court their several claims and rights among themselves. In the event such interpleader suit is brought you shall ipso facto be fully released and discharged from all obligations to further perform any and all duties or obligations imposed upon you in this Escrow, and the parties jointly and severally agree to pay all costs, expenses and reasonable attorney's fees expended or incurred by you, the amount thereof to be fixed and a judgment therefor entered by the court in such suit;

f. You are not to be held liable for the sufficiency or correctness as to form, manner of execution, or validity of any

-22-

any property herein described, or of any profit realized by any person, firm or corporation (broker, agent and parties to this and/or other Escrow included) in connection therewith regardless of the fact that such transaction(s) may be handled by you in this Escrow or in another Escrow;

i. These instructions may be executed in counter-parts, each of which so executed shall, irrespective of the date of its execution and delivery, be deemed an original, and said counterparts together shall constitute one and the same instrument;

j. Any amended, supplemental or additional instruc-tions given shall be subject to the foregoing conditions;

k. The parties agree to execute any other and further instructions, not inconsistent herewith, which may be required by the Escrow Holder for its protection or to consummate this transaction.

22. Commissions. It is expressly agreed that Buyer shall have no obligation in connection with the payment of real estate commissions which shall be the sole obligation of the Seller. Seller shall hold Buyer free and harmless from any claim for real estate commissions, finder's fees or similar charges.

IN WITNESS WHEREOF the parties have hereto set their hands and seals this date.

Seller:

BLACKACRE COMPANY,
a California Limited Partnership

By _____
    General Partner

-24-

---

instrument deposited in this Escrow, nor as to identify authority or rights of any person executing the same, nor for failure to comply with any of the provisions of any agreement contract or other instrument filed herein, and your duties hereunder shall be limited to the safekeeping of such money, instruments, or other documents received by you as Escrow Holder, and for the disposi-tion of same in accordance with the written instructions accepted by you in this Escrow;

g. All parties hereto further agree, jointly and severally, to pay on demand, as well as to indemnify and hold you harmless from and against all costs, damages, judgments, attorneys' fees, expenses, obligations, and liabilities of any kind or nature which in good faith you may incur or sustain in connection with or arising out of this Escrow, and you are hereby given a lien upon all rights, titles and interest of each of the undersigned in all escrowed papers and other property and monies deposited in this Escrow, to protect your rights and to indemnify and reimburse you under this Agreement;

h. It is agreed by the parties hereto that so far as your rights and liabilities are concerned, this transaction in an Escrow and not any other legal relation, and you are an Escrow Holder only on the terms expressed herein, and you shall have no responsibility of notifying any of the parties to this Escrow of any sale, resale, lien, exchange, or other transaction involving

-23-

SCHEDULE OF EXHIBITS

Exhibit "A"	Legal description of the Property
Exhibit "B"	Inventory of Personal Property
Exhibit "C"	Existing First Trust Deed and Note and all modifications thereof to Fictitious Savings & Loan Association
Exhibit "D"	New Purchase Money Promissory Note
Exhibit "E"	New Purchase Money Deed of Trust
Exhibit "F"	Form of Grant Deed
Exhibit "G"	Form of Warranty Bill of Sale
Exhibit "H"	Form of letter of First Refusal on Sale and Purchase Money Note and Deed of Trust
Exhibit "I"	Form of Blanket Assignment of Leases and month-to-month tenancies

Buyer:

WHITEACRE COMPANY,
a California Limited Partnership

By _____
    General Partner

EXCHANGE ESCROW INSTRUCTIONS

To: _____Escrow Corporation
    _____
    _____

                              January ____, 1981
                              Escrow No. _____

     JOHN SMITH and DON SMITH, jointly and severally hereafter
referred to as "SMITH" and REAL PROP ENTERPRISES, INC., a
California corporation, hereafter referred to as "ENTERPRISE"
hereafter instruct you as follows:

     1.   SMITH is the present owner of Property Number 1 described
in your Escrow No. _____ and commonly known as _____ Money Street,
Growth; Property Number 2 described in your Escrow No. _____ and
commonly known as _____ Dollar Avenue, Growth; and Property Number
3 described in your Escrow No. _____ and commonly known as _____
Speculation Avenue, Growth, California. ENTERPRISE is the owner
of Property Number 4 consisting of two (2) parcels, to wit:

          A.   Parcel 1 - Lots 1 and 2, and the North half of
               Lot No. 3 of Tract No. 6600, in the City of
               Growth, County of Los Angeles, State of Califor-
               nia as per map recorded in Book 1, Page 2 of
               Maps, in the office of the County Recorder of
               said County.

          B.   Parcel 11 - South half of Lot No. 3 and all of
               Lots No. 3 and 4 of Tract No. 6600 in the City
               of Growth, County of Los Angeles, State of
               California as per map recorded in Book 1,
               Page 2 of Maps, in the office of the County
               Recorder of said county.

     2.   Prior to the close of Escrow, SMITH will hand you:

     A.   A Grant Deed to Properties 1, 2 and 3 in favor of
ENTERPRISE or such other party as ENTERPRISE shall direct in
writing to this Escrow.

B. An assignment of all leases in form approved by ENTERPRISE concerning Properties 1, 2 and 3.

C. A rent statement in form approved by ENTERPRISE showing all rents, security deposits, cleaning fees and other deposits, if any, concerning Parcels 1, 2 and 3.

D. A Bill of Sale with inventory attached in form approved by ENTERPRISE of all personal property of SMITH in Properties 1, 2 and 3.

E. A Purchase Money Promissory Note in the form attached hereto as Exhibit "A" and made a part hereof. The principal amount of said Promissory Note shall be calculated as hereafter set forth. You are instructed as Escrow Holder to insert said principal amount on the close of Escrow and to endorse said note to show interest shall accrue from the closing of Escrow.

F. Said Purchase Money Promissory Note shall be secured by:

1. A Deed of Trust in the form attached as Exhibit "B" and made a part hereof.

2. An Absolute Assignment of Rents in the form attached as Exhibit "C" and made a part hereof.

3. A Security Interest in Goods and Chattels in the form attached as Exhibit "D" and made a part hereof.

4. A Financing Statement (UCC-1) in the form attached as Exhibit "E" and made a part hereof.

G. The sum of _____Dollars ($_____ _____.

3. Prior to closing of Escrow, ENTERPRISE will hand you:

A. A Grant Deed to Property Number 4 in favor of SMITH

-2-

as Grantee or such other party as SMITH shall direct in writing
to this Escrow subject to Items 2 through 10 inclusive as shown
on that certain Preliminary Title Report No. _____, dated
_____, 19__, issued by Blank Insurance Company
and ____ - ____ real and personal property taxes.

       B.   An assignment of all leases and rental agreements
concerning Property Number 4.

       C.   A rent statement showing all rents, security deposits,
concerning Property Number 4, and the original of all leases
affecting Property Number 4.

       D.   A Bill of sale of all personal property of ENTERPRISE
in Property Number 4 to SMITH.   In connection with said personal
property, SMITH expressly acknowledges that same is subject to
two (2) chattel mortgages as more fully set forth in the afore-
described Preliminary Title Report, a copy of which report has
been received by SMITH and approved by them.

   4.   SMITH expressly acknowledges and agrees:

       A.   In connection with the rent roll and all existing
leases or month-to-month tenancies and not withstanding the form
of lease or agreement that from time ENTERPRISE has granted to
existing and past tenants rental concessions and/or free or
reduced rentals wherein said tenants have been granted from time
to time free or reduced rentals for various periods of time.

       B.   That prior to the closing of Escrow, ENTERPRISE will
furnish at their expense a Termite Inspection Report dated within
the last thirty (30) days by a state licensed pest control operator,
showing all accessible portions of Property Number 4 to be free and
clear of all visible evidence of infestation of termites, fungi,

-3-

and/or dry rot. Should said report disclose that any curative work is required, same shall be performed at ENTERPRISE'S expense or funds therefor shall be withheld by the Escrow Holder from funds payable to ENTERPRISE with instructions to pay for said work when completed. ENTERPRISE shall not be required to perform any preventative work on said property. Except as to the work to be performed by ENTERPRISE as set forth in this paragraph, SMITH are acquiring the improvements and personal property in Property Number 4 in its "as is" condition without representation or warranty of any kind or nature as to physical condition, fitness for use, quality or quantity.

C. That they are acquiring title to Property Number 4 subject to Items 2 through 9 inclusive as contained in the Preliminary Title Report above referred to. In this regard SMITH expressly agrees to assume the existing first Deeds of Trust and Chattel Mortgages referred to in Items 6, 7, 8 and 9 of said Preliminary Title Report and to execute such documents as Blank Life Assurance Company or its agent, _____ Company, shall request. Said first Deeds of Trust have a present unpaid principal balance of approximately $_____ each and are payable in equal monthly installments of $_____ each including interest at _____ per cent per annum. In addition SMITH acknowledges that each of said Promissory Notes and Deeds of Trust provide for monthly impounds for taxes and insurance.

5. You are to make the following adjustments or prorations:

A. You are to adjust all rents and security deposits on the respective four (4) parcels pursuant to rent statements handed to you by SMITH and ENTERPRISE. Said adjustment is to be in cash and to the closing of Escrow.

-4-

B.   You are to prorate in cash in your usual manner all taxes and premiums on policies of insurance on Properties 1 through 4. In this regard ENTERPRISE has impounded from time to time monies with the _____ Company for the payment of taxes and insurance premiums on Property Number 4. You are instructed to order beneficiary statements on the encumbrances on Property Number 1 through 4 and to prorate taxes and insurance premium in cash as disclosed by said beneficiary statements.

C.   You are to prorate to the closing of Escrow interest and principal on the two first deeds of trust on Property Number 4 as disclosed by the aforesaid beneficiary statements. All of said adjustments as to said principal and interest are to be reflected in the second deed of trust by increasing or decreasing the principal sum thereof so that the cash payment by SMITH to ENTERPRISE shall remain uneffected.

D.   SMITH and ENTERPRISE agree to cause to be handed to you copies of all existing policies of insurance affecting their respective properties. You are instructed to obtain endorsements to the existing policies affecting Property Number 4 on the closing of Escrow showing ENTERPRISE as to second mortgage loss payee thereunder and deliver copies of said policy and endorsements to ENTERPRISE on the closing of Escrow. You are to cause all policies on Properties 1, 2 and 3 to be endorsed to show ENTERPRISE or such other party as enterprise shall designate to you in writing as the owner thereof.

6.   In connection with the Purchase Money Promissory Note to be executed by SMITH in favor of ENTERPRISE, which Promissory Note is to be secured by the second Deed of Trust and other security

-5-

instruments above described, said Promissory Note shall be payable upon the following terms and provisions:

A. The principal sum shall be the sum of $_____ and shall be increased or decreased by any credit or debit from the prorations as provided in Paragraph 5 above. Any reduction in the principal amount of the two first Deeds of Trust on Property Number 4 form and after _____, 19__ shall be credited to ENTERPRISE by increasing the principal of said Note by the amount of such principal reduction.

B. Said Promissory shall bear interest at ____ per cent (____%) per annum and shall be payable in monthly installments equal to three-fourths (3/4) of one per cent (1%) of the original unpaid principal balance on the closing of Escrow with the first payment thirty (30) days from the closing of Escrow and shall be all due and payable five (5) years from the closing of Escrow.

C. Said Promissory Note may be prepaid at any time without penalty. You are instructed to insert in said Promissory Note the principal balance thereof on the closing of Escrow and to endorse interest thereon to accrue from the closing of Escrow.

7. This Escrow is subject to and contingent upon the following:

A. The concurrent closing of your Escrows No. _____, _____, and _____.

B. The concurrent closing of Escrows No. _____, _____, and _____ wherein ENTERPRISE is selling Properties 1, 2 and 3 to _____. If for any reason said Escrows shall fail to close, this Escrow shall not close, it being the express interest of the parties hereto that a substantial inducement for ENTERPRISE entering into this Escrow is the concurrent

-6-

sale of Properties 1, 2, and 3 to _____, and
that ENTERPRISE would not consummate this exchange without concurrently selling said properties to _____
upon the terms set forth in the above referred to Escrows, the
terms of which SMITH acknowledges they are familiar with.

    8. _____ and _____ are licensed real estate brokers
and have performed services for both SMITH and ENTERPRISE in connection with this exchange.   SMITH acknowledges that:

        A.   ENTERPRISE has made no representation or warranties
in connection with Property Number 4 or this exchange by or
through said real estate brokers;

        B.   SMITH have made their own independent investigation
of Property Number 4 and are familiar therewith.

        C.   This is the only agreement between ENTERPRISE and
SMITH.

        D.   That any and all commissions due to said real estate
brokers from this exchange is to be paid by SMITH and that they
agree to save and hold ENTERPRISE free and harmless from any claim
by said brokers.

    9. You are instructed to deliver to SMITH and/or record on
their behalf instruments described in Paragraphs 3 A., B. and C.,
copies of original leases and insurance policies when you hold
for SMITH and ENTERPRISE a Standard Coverage Joint Protection
Policy of Title Insurance with the usual title company printed
exceptions, with a liability of $_____, showing title vested
in SMITH subject to Items 2 through 10 inclusive of the Preliminary
Title Report aforedescribed, ____ - ____ real and personal property
taxes and the second Deed of Trust and Absolute Assignment of Rents

described in Exhibits "B" and "C" attached; and when you hold
and can deliver or record for ENTERPRISE the instruments described
in Paragraph 2 A. through F. inclusive, copies of original leases
and insurance policies and the sum of $_____ less ENTERPRISE'S
portion of your Escrow fees, recording charges and title expenses,
and can comply with all of the terms and provisions of your
Escrows No. _____, _____, _____, _____, _____, and
_____. In this regard, you are requested to file with the
Secretary of State, Uniform Commercial Code Division on the closing
of Escrow the financing statement described in Exhibit "E" attached.

10. If you are unable to comply with these instructions and
to consummate concurrently herewith your Escrows No. _____
through _____ prior to _____, you are to complete
same as soon as possible thereafter unless either SMITH or ENTER-
PRISE shall have notified you in writing to terminate this Escrow
in which event you are to return all documents or funds to the
respective parties hereto and each party shall thereafter have no
liability to you or to each other for any services rendered by
you or any costs, expenses, or title charges incured by you, it
being agreed that in the event any of the aforesaid Escrows fail
to close, that you as Escrow Holder waive any claim against SMITH
or ENTERPRISE.

11. In connection with the Purchase Money Deed of Trust
(Exhibit "B"), said Deed of Trust contains a rider entitled
"Release Clause", which release clause contains two (2) blank
spaces. You are instructed by SMITH and ENTERPRISE to insert in
the first blank space a sum equal to one-half (1/2) of the unpaid
principal balance of the Purchase Money Promissory Note (Exhibit
"A") as determined by you as previously instructed and are to

-8-

insert in the second blank space the same sum you insert in
the first blank space, increased by the sum of ____ Thousand
Dollars ($_____).   You are further instructed to insert
on the first page of the Deed of Trust the unpaid principal
balance of said Purchase Money Promissory Note on the closing
of Escrow.

    12.   GENERAL PROVISIONS.

        A.   You will, as the agent of the respective parties,
assign any insurance of Seller handed you for use in this Escrow;

        B.   Make all adjustments and/or prorations on the basis
of a 30-day month and by credit and/or debit to respective accounts
of Seller and Buyer in this Escrow;

        C.   The expression "Close of Escrow" shall mean the date
the instruments transferring the title to the properties described
herein are recorded or registered;

        D.   Make disbursements by your check, instruments and
checks to be mailed to the addresses shown below, unless you are
instructed otherwise;

        E.   NO NOTICE, DEMAND OR CHANGE OF INSTRUCTIONS SHALL BE
OF ANY EFFECT IN THIS ESCROW UNLESS GIVEN IN WRITING BY ALL PARTIES
AFFECTED THEREBY.   In the event conflicting demands are made or
notices served upon you with respect to this Escrow, the parties
hereto expressly agree that you shall have the absolute right at
your election to do either or both of the following: Withhold and
stop all further proceedings in, and performance of, this Escrow,
or file a suit in interpleader and obtain an order from the court
requiring the parties to interplead and litigate in such court
their several claims and rights among themselves.   In the event
such interpleader suit is brought, you shall ipso facto be fully

-9-

released and discharged from all obligations to further perform
any and all duties or obligations imposed upon you in this
Escrow, and the parties jointly and severally agree to pay all
costs, expenses and reasonable attorney's fees expended or incurred by you, the amount thereof to be fixed and a judgment
therefor to be rendered by the court in such suit;

F.   You are not to be held liable for the sufficiency
or correctness as to form, manner of execution, or validity of
any instrument deposited in this Escrow, nor as to identity,
authority, or rights of any person executing the same, nor for
failure to comply with any of the provisions of any agreement,
contract or other instrument filed herein, and your duties hereunder shall be limited to the safekeeping of such money, instruments, or other documents received by you as Escrow Holder, and
for the disposition of same in accordance with the written instructions accepted by you in this Escrow;

G.   It is agreed by the parties hereto that so far as
your rights and liabilities are concerned, this transaction is
an Escrow and not any other legal relation, and you are an Escrow
Holder only on the terms expressed herein, and you shall have no
responsibility of notifying any of the parties to this Escrow of
any sale, resale, lien, exchange, or other transaction involving
any property herein described, or of any profit realized by any
person, firm or corporation (broker, agent and parties to this
and/or any other Escrow included) in connection therewith regardless of the fact that such transaction(s) may be handled by you
in this Escrow or in another Escrow;

H.   These instructions may be executed in counterparts,
each of which so executed shall, irrespective of the date of its

-10-

execution and delivery, be deemed an original, and said counterparts together shall constitute one and the same instrument;

     I. Any amended, supplemental or additional instructions
given shall be subject to the foregoing conditions:

     J. The parties agree to execute any other and further
instructions, not inconsistent herewith to consummate this transaction;

     K. This is the only agreement between the parties, and
the terms of any offer, deposit receipt, if any, or previous
correspondence between the parties are deemed superseded hereby
and merged into this agreement.

JOHN SMITH ‾‾‾‾‾‾‾‾‾‾‾‾‾‾‾‾‾‾‾‾‾‾‾‾

DON SMITH ‾‾‾‾‾‾‾‾‾‾‾‾‾‾‾‾‾‾‾‾‾‾‾‾‾

REAL PROP ENTERPRISES, INC.

By‾‾‾‾‾‾‾‾‾‾‾‾‾‾‾‾‾‾‾‾‾‾‾‾‾‾
                 , President

By‾‾‾‾‾‾‾‾‾‾‾‾‾‾‾‾‾‾‾‾‾‾‾‾‾‾
                 , Secretary

TO: Blank Insurance & Trust Company

Los Angeles, California
Attention: _____ , Escrow Officer

RE: Escrow No. _____
Date: January ____ , 1981

THIS AGREEMENT TO EXCHANGE PROPERTIES AND ESCROW INSTRUCTIONS (hereinafter "Agreement") is made and entered into this ____ day of January, 1981, by and between ALVIRA STREET CORPORATION, a California corporation (hereinafter "ALVIRA"), and STANFORD, INC., a California corporation (hereinafter "STANFORD"), and said parties mutually agree in accordance with and subject to the terms and provisions of this Agreement to exchange between the parties the properties hereinafter respectively described as the "First Property" and the "Second Property", and each party hereto hereby instructs you in connection with such exchange, as follows:

RECITALS AND DEFINITIONS

A. STANFORD is the present owner of the Second Property which consists, of an unimproved parcel of real property, situated in the County of Los Angeles, State of California,

described as follows:

B. STANFORD desires to exchange the Second Property for the First Property in such manner as to effect a recognized and permitted tax-free exchange which complies with all requirements for such exchange under all applicable statutes and rulings of the United States Internal Revenue Code. STANFORD desires ALVIRA to acquire First Property acceptable to STANFORD and complete the contemplated exchange.

C. At the time this Agreement is entered into, the First Property is undetermined in that STANFORD has not yet designated the First Property it desires to be acquired and exchanged for the Second Property.

D. Notwithstanding the fact that the First Property has not as yet been specifically designated by STANFORD, ALVIRA desires to immediately acquire the Second Property and STANFORD desires to immediately convey the Second Property to ALVIRA in contemplation of this transaction qualifying as a tax-free exchange, as aforesaid.

-2-

E. It is presently the intent of the parties that title to the Second Property will be immediately transferred and conveyed to ALVIRA (first phase of exchange) and that the First Property will be transferred and conveyed by ALVIRA to STANFORD upon the designation thereof by STANFORD and the acquisition thereof by ALVIRA (second phase of exchange).

F. To assure the future performance and obligation on the part of ALVIRA to acquire the First Property, convey the same to STANFORD, and thereby complete the contemplated exchange, the parties hereto have concurrently herewith delivered to the Escrow Holder an Exchange Credit Agreement in form and content attached hereto, marked Exhibit "A" and by this reference made a part hereof.

G. "Escrow" or "Escrow Holder" shall mean and refer to Blank Insurance & Trust Company, _____, Los Angeles, California _____,

Attention: _____, Escrow Officer.

H. "Opening Escrow" shall mean and refer to the date on which this Agreement is made and entered into.

The terms and conditions of this Agreement and the instructions to the Escrow Holder are as follows:

1. Recitals and Definitions. Each and all of the foregoing recitals and definitions are hereby incorporated herein and made a part hereof as though set forth hereat at length.

-3-

2. Exchange. STANFORD hereby agrees to transfer and convey the Second Property to ALVIRA, and ALVIRA agrees to transfer and convey the First Property to STANFORD, as an exchange of each of said properties for the other.

3. Exchange Values. The parties hereto have placed an agreed value on the Second Property of $_____.
In addition thereto, taxes with respect to the Second Property shall be prorated between the parties at the close of escrow as below set forth. While the First Property is presently undetermined, the parties hereto acknowledge and agree that STANFORD shall be credited against the value thereof said sum of $_____, plus or minus the results of the tax prorations, as aforesaid.

4. Obligations of the Parties.

A. STANFORD will hand to you as Escrow Holder prior to close of escrow:

(1) A Grant Deed to the Second Property in favor of ALVIRA;

(2) Sufficient monies to pay (i) all fees and costs of the escrow holder in this transaction, (ii) the cost of such title insurance as more specifically hereinbelow set forth, and (iii) the cost of all documentary stamps to be affixed to the aforesaid Grant Deed.

B. STANFORD and ALVIRA will jointly hand to you as Escrow Holder prior to close of escrow:

-4-

(1) Two (2) copies of the Exchange Credit Agreement in form and content as attached hereto as Exhibit "A", fully executed by each of said parties;

(2) Two (2) copies of a Stock Pledge Agreement in form and content as attached as Exhibit 1 to the aforesaid Exchange Credit Agreement, fully executed by each of said parties.

5. Title Insurance. On the close of Escrow and as a condition thereof, Blank Insurance & Trust Company shall issue to ALVIRA its standard coverage California Land Title Association policy of title insurance, with a liability equal to the agreed value of the Second Property in the sum of $_____, showing title to the Second Property to be vested in ALVIRA subject only to the following:

A. Current real property taxes and assessments;

B. Such covenants, conditions, restrictions, easements, rights-of-way and other exceptions of record to title to the Second Property as follows: Items 1, 2, 3., and 4. of Paragraph 4, Schedule A, of that Interim Binder Form A issued by Blank Insurance & Trust Company as Order No. _____, dated _____, 19___, a copy of which Interim Binder Form A is attached hereto as Exhibit "B" and by this reference made a part hereof.

6. Contingency. This exchange is subject to and contingent upon the concurrent close herewith of that certain

-5-

escrow, dated _____, 19__, bearing Blank Insurance and Trust Company Escrow No. _____, and the recording of the Grant Deed to the Second Property herein from ALVIRA to the Buyer in said Escrow No. _____.

7. Prorations. The Escrow Holder is to prorate and adjust between STANFORD and ALVIRA in cash to the close of escrow all current real property taxes and assessments, if any, per current tax bills.

8. Recordation and Delivery of Documents. You as Escrow Holder are hereby instructed to record and/or deliver the documents herein to the parties hereto, as follows:

WHEN:

A. All contingencies herein, as hereinabove set forth, have been met or waived; and

B. You can issue to ALVIRA your standard coverage policy of title insurance as more specifically set forth in paragraph 5., above;

THEN, you are to do each and all of the following:

A. Record the Grant Deed from STANFORD to ALVIRA of the Second Property (Exhibit "C");

B. Deliver to STANFORD:

(1) One (1) executed copy of Exchange Credit Agreement (Exhibit "A");

(2) One (1) executed copy of Stock Pledge Agreement (Exhibit "1" to Exhibit "A");

C. Deliver to ALVIRA:

(1) One (1) executed copy of Exchange Credit Agreement (Exhibit "A");

-6-

(2) One (1) executed copy of Stock Pledge Agreement (Exhibit "1" to Exhibit "A");

(3) The policy of title insurance as above provided in paragraph 5.

9. Close of Escrow. For the purpose of this Agreement, close of Escrow shall be deemed to be the date that the Grant Deed to ALVIRA of the Second Property is recorded (Exhibit "C"). In the event that Escrow is not closed prior to _____, 19___, upon the demand of either party hereto, and without further notice or authorization, the Escrow Holder shall promptly return to both STANFORD and ALVIRA, respectively, all deeds, documents and monies theretofore deposited with the Escrow Holder. Any such action undertaken by Escrow Holder shall in no event relieve the parties from any obligation to the Escrow Holder with respect to the Escrow, or waive, release or discharge any breach of any of the parties of any of their respective covenants, agreements, obligations or duties herein set forth.

10. Commissions. The parties hereto shall hold each other free and harmless from any claim for real estate commissions, finder's fees or similar charges by any party claiming to represent either such party.

11. Miscellaneous Provisions.

A. Successors and Assigns. This Agreement shall be binding on and shall inure to the benefit of the heirs, executors, administrators, successors and assigns of the respective parties hereto.

-7-

B. Required Actions of Parties. The parties hereto agree to execute all such instruments and document, and to take all such action (including the deposit of funds in addition to such funds as may be specifically provided for herein) as may be required in order to consummate the exchange herein contemplated.

C. Entire Agreement. This Agreement contains the entire Agreement between the parties hereto and no addition or modification of any term or provision shall be effective unless set forth in writing, signed by both of the parties hereto.

D. Time of Essence. Time is of the essence of each and every term, condition, obligation and provision hereof.

E. Counterparts. This Agreement may be executed simultaneously in counterparts, each of which shall be deemed an original, but all of which, together, shall constitute one and the same instrument.

F. Notice. All notices or other communication required or permitted hereunder including the service of any summons and complaint or other legal process shall be in writing and shall be sent by registered mail or certified mail, return receipt requested, and shall be deemed received two (2) business days after deposit in the mail in the County of Los Angeles, postage prepaid, addressed to the persons to receive such notice at the following addresses:

-8-

TO ALVIRA: Alvira Street Corporation
6300 Wilshire Boulevard
Suite 9100
Los Angeles, California 90048

WITH A COPY TO:

TO STANFORD:

Service of such notices when made in accordance with the procedure set forth above shall be deemed full and complete service for all jurisdictional and other purposes.

12. General Provisions.

A. Escrow Holder will, as the agent of the respective parties, make all adjustments and/or prorations on the basis of a thirty (30) day month and by credit and/or debit to the respective accounts of the parties in this Escrow.

B. The expression "close of Escrow" shall mean the date the instruments transferring the title to the property herein to ALVIRA are recorded and registered.

C. Escrow Holder shall make disbursement by its own check, instruments and checks to be mailed to the addresses as shown above unless Escrow Holder is instructed otherwise.

D. ALL NOTICES, DEMANDS, OR CHANGES OF INSTRUCTIONS SHALL BE OF NO EFFECT ON THIS ESCROW UNLESS GIVEN IN WRITING BY ALL PARTIES THEREBY. In the event conflicting demands are made and notices are served upon Escrow Holder with respect to this Escrow, the parties hereto expressly agree that the Escrow Holder shall have the absolute right at her election to do

-9-

either or both of the following: withhold and stop all the proceedings in, and performance of, this Escrow or file a suit in interpleader and obtain an order from the Court requiring the parties to interplead and litigate in such Court their several claims and rights among themselves. In the event such interpleader suit is brought, Escrow Holder shall ipso facto be fully released and discharged from all obligations imposed upon it in this Escrow, and the parties jointly and severally agree to pay all costs, expenses and reasonable attorney's fees expended or incurred by Escrow Holder, the amount thereof to be fixed and a judgment therefor entered by the Court in such suit.

E. The Escrow Holder is not to be held liable for the sufficiency or correctness as to form, manner of execution, or validity of any instrument deposited in Escrow, nor for the identity, authority or rights of any person executing the same, nor for failure to comply with any of the provisions of this Agreement, or other instruments filed herein, and the duties of the Escrow Holder hereunder shall be limited to the safekeeping of such money, instruments, or other documents received in its capacity as Escrow Holder, and for the disposition of same in accordance with the written instructions accepted by the Escrow Holder in this Escrow.

F. The Escrow Holder is not to be held liable for the sufficiency or correctness as to form, manner of execution, validity, handling, processing or other dissemination of any instrument or monies which directly relate to the documentation of the consideration for the conveyance of the

-10-

property from STANFORD to ALVIRA or which form all or any part of said consideration. The Grant Deed which appears at Exhibit "C" is not addressed by this Paragraph 12. F.

G. All parties hereto further agree, jointly and severally, to pay on demand, as well as to indemnify and hold the Escrow Holder harmless from and against all costs, damages, judgments, attorney's fees, expenses, obligations, and liabilities of any kind and nature which in good faith the Escrow Holder may incur or sustain in connection with or arising out of this Escrow, and the Escrow Holder is hereby given a lien upon all right, title and interest of each of the undersigned and all escrowed papers and other property and monies deposited in this Escrow, to protect the rights of the Escrow Holder and to indemnify and reimburse the Escrow Holder under this Agreement.

In the event that Escrow fails to close for any reason, each of the parties hereto shall pay one-half of all costs, fees, expenses and obligations of any kind and nature which in good faith the Escrow Holder has incurred or sustained in connection with or arising out of this Escrow.

H. It is agreed by the parties hereto that so far as the rights and liabilities of the Escrow Holder are concerned, this transaction is an Escrow and not any other legal relation, and the Escrow Holder shall serve in said capacity only on the terms expressed herein, and the Escrow Holder shall have no responsibility of notifying any of the parties to this Escrow of any sale, resale, exchange or

-11-

other transaction involving any property herein described, or of any profit realized by any person, firm or corporation (broker, agent and parties to this and/or other Escrow included) in connection therewith regardless of the fact that such transaction(s) may be handled by the Escrow Holder in this Escrow or in another Escrow.

I. These Escrow Instructions may be executed in counterparts, each of which executed shall, irrespective of the date of its execution and delivery, be deemed an original, and said counterparts together shall constitute one and the same instrument.

J. Any amended, supplemental or additional instructions shall be subject to the foregoing conditions.

K. The parties agree to execute any other and further instructions, not inconsistent herewith, which may be required by the Escrow Holder for its protection or to consummate this transaction.

IN WITNESS WHEREOF, the parties have hereunto set their hands and seals this date.

ALVIRA:

ALVIRA STREET CORPORATION, a California corporation

By: MYRON MEYERS, President

STANFORD:

STANFORD, INC., a California corporation

By: _____ President

By: _____ , Secretary

-12-

EXCHANGE CREDIT AGREEMENT

THIS EXCHANGE CREDIT AGREEMENT (hereinafter "Agreement") is made and entered into this ___ day of January, 1981, by and between ALVIRA STREET CORPORATION, a California corporation (hereinafter "ALVIRA") AND STANFORD, INC., a California corporation (hereinafter "STANFORD") with respect to the following recitals:

A. The parties hereto have concurrently herewith entered into an Agreement to Exchange Properties and Escrow Instructions (hereinafter "Exchange Agreement") such Exchange Agreement being directed to Blank Escrow Company, _____, Los Angeles, California under its Escrow No. ___ ;

B. By the terms of said Exchange Agreement, STANFORD has agreed to exchange its real property, as described in said Exchange Agreement and therein designated as "the Second Property" for certain real property to be hereafter designated by STANFORD and to be hereafter acquired by ALVIRA for conveyance thereof to STANFORD:

C. Notwithstanding the fact that STANFORD has not as yet specifically designated the property to be acquired and conveyed to it by ALVIRA in exchange for the Second Property, ALVIRA desires to immediately acquire, and STANFORD desires to immediately convey to ALVIRA, the Second Property, in

contemplation of the transaction effecting a recognized and permitted tax free exchange complying with all requirements for such exchange under all applicable statutes and rulings of the United States Internal Revenue Code;

D. It is presently the intent of the parties that title to the Second Property will be transferred and conveyed to ALVIRA pursuant to the terms of the Exchange Agreement and that, in exchange thereof, ALVIRA will acquire and convey to STANFORD such real property as is hereafter designated by STANFORD, all in accordance with the terms and provisions of this Agreement.

E. The parties hereto now enter into this Agreement to delineate their respective rights and obligations with respect to the future designation of properties by STANFORD, the acquisition thereof by ALVIRA and the conveyance thereof to STANFORD, to complete the exchange as contemplated by the Exchange Agreement, and to assure the performance of the obligations of the respective parties hereto in connection therewith.

NOW, THEREFORE, in consideration for the mutual covenants and agreements as herein set forth, and for other good, valid, valuable consideration, it is hereby agreed by and between the parties hereto, as follows:

1. Term. The term of this Agreement shall be for a period of eighteen (18) months commencing upon the consummation of the Exchange Agreement and close of escrow as therein provided, unless sooner terminated as hereinafter set forth; provided, however, that in the event said Exchange Agreement

-2-

(2) That the value of such monthly increase shall be increased at the rate of $_____ for each $100.00 of net proceeds received by ALVIRA from the Note commencing upon the date of each $100.00 increment of receipt by ALVIRA of such net proceeds;

b. In the event of the default by the obligor under the terms of the Note, the value of the exchange credits shall be deemed reduced by an amount equal to the then unpaid principal balance of the Note until the defaults are cured or the Trust Deed is foreclosed upon as more specifically hereinafter set forth;

c. In the event ALVIRA forecloses upon the Trust Deed, and is not the purchaser of the Second Property at such foreclosure sale, then the value of the exchange credits (having been reduced pursuant to the terms of sub-paragraph b, above) shall be increased by an amount equal to the net proceeds received by ALVIRA from such foreclosure sale after deducting therefrom all Trustee's fees and costs in connection with such sale and all attorney's fees and court costs as may be incurred and/or paid by ALVIRA for legal counsel and any litigation relating to such foreclosure sale;

d. In the event ALVIRA forecloses upon the Trust Deed and acquires the Second Property as the purchaser at the foreclosure sale thereof, the value of the exchange credits shall continue at the reduced value pursuant to sub-paragraph b, above and be further reduced by the amount of Trustor's

-4-

is not consummated, and the escrow as therein provided has not closed, by no later than April 6, 1981, or any extension thereof as the parties hereto shall mutually agree in writing, then this Agreement shall be of no further force or effect and neither of the parties hereto shall thereafter have any obligation or liability to the other hereunder.

2. Exchange Credits. Upon consummation of the Exchange Agreement and close of escrow as therein provided, ALVIRA shall be deemed as holding for STANFORD and to the use and benefit of STANFORD exchange credits of a value equal to the sum of $_____. Said exchange credits are derived, in part, from the anticipated proceeds of that certain promissory note, dated _____, 1981, executed by Development Co., a California corporation, to ALVIRA in the sum of $_____, together with the deed of trust securing same and encumbering the aforesaid Second Property. Said promissory note is hereafter referred to as the Note, and the deed of trust as the Trust Deed. The value of the exchange credits held by ALVIRA for and on behalf of the use and benefit of STANFORD shall be adjusted upon the happening of each of the events, and in the amounts, as follows:

a. The value of the exchange credits shall be increased at the rate of $_____ for each calendar month during the term of this Agreement; provided

(1) That the value of such monthly increase for any period less than a calendar month shall be in pro rate proportion to such increase for each calendar month;

-3-

consummate the sale of the property to the third party offeror upon the terms and conditions as set forth in such party's offer.

e. In the event of the acquisition of any real property by ALVIRA pursuant to the designation thereof by STANFORD in accordance with the provisions of paragraphs 3. and 4., below, and the application of exchange credits to such acquisition and ultimate transfer and exchange of such real property to STANFORD, in accordance with the provisions of paragraph 5., below, the value of such exchange credits shall be deemed reduced by the value thereof applied to such exchange to STANFORD. In like manner, the increase in such exchange credits for each calendar month, as provided by the terms of sub-paragraph a., above, shall be reduced in such proportion as the value of the exchange credits available for the acquisition and exchange of properties after any application thereof pursuant to the provision of paragraph 5., bears to the value of the exchange credits available for such application prior to any such application thereof.

3. Designation by STANFORD of Properties to be Acquired. At any time, and from time to time during the term of this Agreement, STANFORD shall, at its sole option, designate in writing to ALVIRA such real property it desires ALVIRA to acquire and to convey and transfer to STANFORD in order

-6-

fees and costs paid by ALVIRA upon such foreclosure, until such time as ALVIRA shall sell the Second Property at which time the value of the exchange credits shall be increased, from such reduced value, in an amount equal to the net sales price for the Second Property received by ALVIRA upon such sale. In the event ALVIRA shall re-acquire the property encumbered by the Trust Deed and shall desire to re-sell the same, it shall, upon receiving an offer to purchase said property which it deems acceptable, immediately notify STANFORD in writing of the terms and conditions of such offer, enclosing a copy thereof, and STANFORD shall have seven (7) days from and after the effective date of such notification to exercise a right of first refusal to re-acquire the property in consideration for the cancellation of exchange credits of a value equal to the then unpaid principal remaining unpaid under the terms of the Note, notwithstanding the same had theretofore been foreclosed, and disregarding the amount bid by ALVIRA upon the foreclosure sale held pursuant to the Trust Deed. Such right of first refusal shall be exercised, if at all by STANFORD notifying ALVIRA in writing, within said seven (7) day period of its exercise of said right of first refusal and in such event, ALVIRA shall immediately thereupon transfer and convey the property to STANFORD, with title thereto subject only to those matters of record as upon the original acquisition of the property by ALVIRA, plus Note and Deeds of Trust. In the event STANFORD fails to exercise such rights of first refusal, ALVIRA shall be free to

-5-

acquisition thereof by ALVIRA. In such event, ALVIRA shall complete the acquisition of the designated property, transfer and exchange the same to STANFORD, and retain the balance of the exchange credits to the use and benefit of STANFORD, as hereinbelow set forth.

5. Application of Exchange Credits. Upon the acquisition by ALVIRA of each parcel of real property as designated by STANFORD, and the transfer and exchange thereof to STANFORD, as aforesaid, there shall be deemed to have been applied to each such acquisition, exchange credits held to the use and benefit of STANFORD herein, as aforesaid, of a value equal to all cash sums expended by ALVIRA upon each such acquisition including, without limitation, all cost sums expended upon the purchase price, for commissions, and for all costs and expenses, incident to each such acquisition, transfer and exchange to STANFORD, and the value of the exchange credits held by ALVIRA to the use and benefit of STANFORD after each such acquisition shall be deemed reduced by the value of such credits so applied.

Notwithstanding anything to the contrary in this Agreement set forth, in no event shall the value of exchange credits available from time to time, for application to the acquisition of real property by ALVIRA and the transfer and exchange thereof to STANFORD, exceed the total value of such exchange credits as calculated pursuant to the terms of paragraph 2., above, less the unpaid balance of principal remaining unpaid,

-8-

to complete the exchange for the Second Property as contemplated by the Exchange Agreement. Such real property as shall be designated by STANFORD may consist of one or more parcels and may be acquired and exchanged in separate increments. Such property to be acquired and exchanged by ALVIRA may be subject to existing encumbrances or be purchased by ALVIRA upon condition that it place new encumbrances thereon.

4. Acquisition and Exchange of Properties by ALVIRA. ALVIRA shall use its best efforts to acquire and exchange to STANFORD those parcels of real property as designated by STANFORD within sixty (60) days of notification to ALVIRA by STANFORD of each parcel so designated; provided, however, that the acquisition of each such parcel by ALVIRA and transfer and exchange thereof to STANFORD shall, in all events, occur concurrently. At STANFORD's election, it may designate a parcel or parcels of real property for ALVIRA to acquire and exchange which requires consideration in excess of exchange credits then available for the acquisition thereof by ALVIRA, as more specifically hereinbelow set forth. In such event, STANFORD shall contribute all additional sums as shall be required to complete the acquisition of the contemplated parcel or parcels concurrently with the completion of the exchange and conveyance thereof to STANFORD. Further, at STANFORD's election, it may designate a parcel or parcels of real property for ALVIRA to acquire and exchange which requires consideration less than the exchange credits then available for the

-7-

from time to time, under the terms of the Note, whether or not the Trust Deed has been foreclosed upon and the property encumbered thereby has been acquired by ALVIRA.

6. Exchange of Property in "As Is" Condition. All parcels of real property acquired by ALVIRA pursuant to the designation thereof by STANFORD, and transferred and exchanged to STANFORD, shall be so transferred and exchanged in its "as is" and "where is" condition without representation or warranty of any kind or nature whatsoever, either as to title, condition, or fitness for use, or in any other respect whatsoever, on the part of ALVIRA to STANFORD, and STANFORD hereby waives as against ALVIRA and releases and discharges ALVIRA and each of its shareholders, directors, officers, agents, employees, and attorneys, of and from any and all claims, actions, obligations and liabilities based upon any such representation or warranty.

7. Hold Harmless and Indemnity by STANFORD. STANFORD hereby agrees to hold harmless and indemnify ALVIRA and its shareholders, directirs, officers, agents, employees, and attorneys, from and against any and all claims, actions, damages, obligations, and liabilities, of and every kind and nature whatsoever, of any and all persons whomsoever, in connection with or arising from, whether directly or indirectly, the acquisition and exchange by ALVIRA of any and all parcels of real property pursuant to the designation thereof by STANFORD in accordance with the terms of this Agreement including, without limitation, any and all obligations under the terms of any promissory notes, deeds of trust, or other

-9-

evidences or indebtedness executed or assumed by ALVIRA in connection with its acquisition of any and all such parcels of real property. In this regard, the parties hereto agree that ALVIRA's sole responsibility with respect tc the acquisition and exchange of parcels of real property as designated by STANFORD pursuant to the terms of this Agreement shall be the application of exchange credits upon such acquisition and the exchange of such parcels to STANFORD in the same condition as to title, physical condition, and in all other respects, as obtained upon the acquisition thereof by ALVIRA.

8. Security for ALVIRA's Performance. To secure the due, prompt, and diligent performance of ALVIRA under the terms of this Agreement, the shareholders of ALVIRA shall, concurrent with the commencement of the terms of this Agreement, execute and deliver to STANFORD a Pledge Agreement in form and content as attached hereto as Exhibit "1" and by this reference made a part hereof.

9. Termination of Agreement. This Agreement shall terminate upon the earliest to occur of the following events:

a. Upon the date which is eighteen (18) months from and after the commencement of the term of this Agreement or, in the event of the extension of the term by mutual agreement

-10-

of the parties hereto, then upon the last day of the term hereof as so extended upon such termination, ALVIRA shall deliver to STANFORD cash in a sum equal to all exchange credits held by ALVIRA on the date of termination which are otherwise available for the acquisition of property designated by STANFORD, together with the Note and Trust Deed or, in the event the same has been theretofore foreclosed upon and the property encumbered thereby purchased by ALVIRA, then either the property previously encumbered thereby or any evidences of indebtedness and security therefor in the event ALVIRA has re-sold such property.

b. At such time as ALVIRA has applied all of the exchange credits to the use and benefit of STANFORD. In this latter regard, and notwithstanding anything to the contrary in this Agreement set forth, ALVIRA shall pay over to STANFORD, at any time or times as STANFORD shall request, cash in a sum equal to all or any portion of the exchange credits available for the acquisition of properties upon STANFORD's designation, as hereinabove set forth, to-gether with the Note and Trust Deed or, in the event the same has theretofore been foreclosed upon and the property encumbered thereby purchased by ALVIRA, then ALVIRA shall deliver to STANFORD either the property previously encumbered thereby or any evidences of indebtedness and security therefor in the event ALVIRA has re-sold such property; all as STANFORD shall request.

-11-

10. Notices. All notices or other communications required or permitted hereunder shall be in writing and shall be sent by registered or certified mail, return receipt requested, and shall be deemed received two (2) business days after deposit in the mail in the County of Los Angeles, postage prepaid, addressed to the persons to receive notices at the following addresses:

TO ALVIRA: Alvira Street Corporation
              6300 Wilshire Boulevard, Suite 9100
              Los Angeles, California 90048

TO STANFORD: Stanford, Inc.

The address of either party hereto may be changed by notice thereof by either such party to other in accordance with the provisions hereof.

11. Arbitration. Either party hereto may require the arbitration of any matter arising under or in connection with this Agreement. Arbitration shall be initiated by either party giving notice to the other specifying the matter to be arbitrated. The arbitration shall be in conformity with ard subject to applicable rules and procedure of the American Arbitration Association at Los Angeles, California. The arbitrators shall be bound by the terms of this Agreement. STANFORD shall pay all costs of arbitration including fees of the arbitrators. Any award issued upon such arbitration shall be final, binding and conclusive upon the parties hereto, and judgment may be entered theron by any Court of competent jurisdiction upon petition of either of the parties hereto.

-12-

PLEDGE AGREEMENT

THIS PLEDGE AGREEMENT (hereinafter "Pledge") is entered into this ___ day of ___, 1981, by and between ___ (hereinafter jointly and severally referred to as "Pledgors") and STANFORD, INC., a California corporation (hereinafter "Secured Party"). Pledgors and Secured Party are hereinafter from time to time referred to as "the Parties".

RECITALS

A. Pledgors are the sole shareholders, officers and directors of ALVIRA STREET CORPORATION, a California corporation (hereinafter "ALVIRA").

B. ALVIRA and Secured Party have concurrently herewith entered into a certain written agreement entitled Exchange Credit Agreement.

C. To secure the due and timely performance of ALVIRA under the terms of said Exchange Credit Agreement, Pledgors desire to grant to Secured Party a security interest in and to all of the shares of stock issued by ALVIRA now owned or hereafter owned by Pledgors and each of them, and Secured Party desires to accept such security interest.

NOW, THEREFORE, it is hereby agreed by and between Pledgors and Secured Party as follows:

SECURITY INTEREST

1.1 In order to secure Pledgors' obligations to Secured Party under this Pledge and any and all other agreements

---

12. Entire Agreement. This Agreement contains the entire agreement between the parties hereto and no addition or modification of any term or provision hereof shall be effective unless set forth in writing and signed by both of the parties hereto.

13. Amendments. This Agreement may be amended only in writing signed by each of the parties hereto.

14. Successors and Assigns. This Agreement shall be binding upon and inure to the benefit of the successors and assigns of the respective parties hereto.

IN WITNESS WHEREOF, the parties hereto have entered into this Agreement the day and year first above written.

ALVIRA STREET CORPORATION,
a California corporation

By _____

STANFORD, INC.,
a California corporation

By _____

By _____

-13-

between Pledgors and Secured Party ("Pledgors' Obligations"), Pledgors hereby grant to Secured Party a security interest in and to all of Pledgors' now owned and hereafter owned shares of stock of ALVIRA, which are presently, as follows:

a. _____ shares of stock of ALVIRA issued to _____ pursuant to Certificate No. 1, dated _____, 1981, by ALVIRA;

b. _____ shares of stock of ALVIRA issued to _____ pursuant to Certificate No. 2, dated _____, 1981, of ALVIRA;

all the above shares being hereinafter referred to as "Pledged Stock", together with all distributions and payments whether in cash or in kind upon or in connection with Pledged Stock whether such distributions are dividends or in partial or complete liquidation, or as a restructure of the capital structure of ALVIRA or otherwise, and any and all substitutions, warrants and options of the Pledged Stock, and any and all other property of ALVIRA in which Pledgors, and each of them, have or hereafter acquire an interest; including, without limitation, evidences of indebtedness of ALVIRA to either of Pledgors or which Pledgors, or either of them, shall hold as Payees, and all proceeds of the foregoing. The foregoing is all hereinafter referred to as the "Collateral".

1.2 In connection with the Collateral, Pledgors agree to forthwith deliver to Secured Party any such distribution in payments in the form in which the distribution was received

-2-

by Pledgors, and Secured Party shall hold any such distribution as additional Collateral pledged to secure Pledgors' Obligations. Any share of capital stock or evidences of indebtedness so distributed to Pledgors shall be delivered to Secured Party with irrevocable stock powers relating thereto or assignments thereof duly executed by Pledgors in the form acceptable to Secured Party.

1.3 Pledgors shall deliver to Secured Party all such stocks, warrants, options and such other rights, and upon delivery, Secured Party shall hold such securities as additional Collateral to secure Pledgors' Obligations; provided, however, that if Secured Party determines in its sole discretion that the value of such distributions and other rights shall terminate, expire or be materially reduced in value by holding the same as pledged Collateral, Secured Party shall have the rights in its sole discretion to hold or sell or exercise the same, and if exercised, then the monies disbursed by Secured Party shall be deemed to be a loan by Secured Party to Pledgors, and become a part of Pledgors' Obligations.

1.4 Until default by Pledgors under this pledge, Pledgors shall have the right to vote the Pledged Stock or, if any of the Pledged Stock is registered in the name of Secured Party, Pledgors shall have the right in writing to direct Secured Party how to vote by written proxy. Secured Party shall not be required to attend meetings requiring any physical presence of the registered owner of stock; provided, however, in the event of any such default, Secured

-3-

Party shall have the right to vote the Pledged Stock and attend meetings.

1.5   Concurrently with Pledgors' execution of this Pledge, Pledgors shall deliver to Secured Party the Pledged Stock together with properly executed irrevocable assignments thereof or stock powers therefor, endorsed in blank. Pledgors' signatures at the request of Secured Party shall be guarantied by a national or other banking institution.

1.6   Pledgors hereby warrant, relinquish and release Secured Party from any and all duties which Secured Party may have, whether or not such duties arise by statute, contract or otherwise, to in any way care for, protect or preserve any rights and interests of Pledgors or Secured Party in the collateral. Without in any way affecting the generality of the foregoing, Secured Party shall not be required to take any affirmative action with respect to said stock or any rights or interest derived therefrom and any loss or damage to said stock or securities shall be at the risk of Pledgors. Pledgors further agree that they will at all times keep themselves fully informed as to any and all facts concerning said stock and securities, including, but not limited to any and all rights, duties and obligations of the stockholders or security holders of said stock and securities, and advise Secured Party of all such facts immediately upon Pledgors becoming aware thereof.

-4-

1.7   Pledgors shall execute and deliver to Secured Party concurrently with Pledgors executing this Pledge, and at any time or times hereafter at the request of Secured Party, all documents that Secured Party may request, in a form satisfactory to Secured Party in order to perfect, and maintain perfected, Secured Party's secured interests in the Collateral and in order to fully consummate the transactions contemplated under this Pledge.

PLEDGOR'S WARRANTIES AND REPRESENTATIONS

2.1   Pledgors warrant, represent, and agree as follows:

a.   Pledgors shall cause ALVIRA to duly and timely perform each and all of the acts to be performed by ALVIRA under the terms of the aforesaid Exchange Credit Agreement.

b.   The Pledged Stock is validly issued, fully paid and non-assessable, and Pledgors are the lawful owners thereof and have the right to grant to Secured Party a security interest therein free and clear of all liens, encumbrances, claims or demands whatsoever.

c.   Pledgors will not suffer or permit any lien or encumbrance of any nature to attach to the Collateral.

DEFAULT

3.1   Any one or more of the following events shall constitute a default by Pledgors under this Agreement: (a) Pledgors' failure to perform any term, provision, condition, covenant, warranty or representation on Pledgors' part to be performed

-5-

as contained in this Pledge or in any other agreements which may exist between Pledgors and Secured Party; (b) Pledgors' failure to pay when due and payable any of Pledgors' obligations; (c) ALVIRA's default under the terms and conditions of any agreements between ALVIRA and Secured Party including, without limitation, the aforesaid Exchange Credit Agreement; (d) the entry of a decree or order for relief by a court having jurisdiction in the premises in respect of Pledgors or ALVIRA in an involuntary case under the federal bankruptcy laws, as now or hereafter constituted, or any other applicable federal or state bankruptcy, insolvency or other similar law, or appointing a receiver, liquidator, assignee, custodian, trustee, sequestrator (or similar official) of Pledgors or ALVIRA or for any substantial part of their property and the continuance of any such decree or order unstayed and in effect for a period of 60 days; (e) the commencement by Pledgors or ALVIRA of voluntary proceedings under the federal bankruptcy laws, as now constituted or hereafter amended, or any other applicable federal or state bankruptcy, insolvency or other similar law, or the consent by them to the appointment of or taking possession by a receiver, liquidator, assignee, trustee, custodian, sequestrator (or other similar official) of Pledgors or ALVIRA or for any substantial part of their property, or the making by Pledgors or ALVIRA of any assignment for the benefit of creditors; (f) if all or any part of the

-6-

Collateral is attached, seized, subjected to a writ or distress warrant, or levied upon, or a charge order is decreed thereon or on any part thereof and not removed within 60 days.

3.2 In the event of a default by Pledgors under this Pledge, Secured Party may, at its election, without notice of its election and without demand, do any one or more of the following, all of which are authorized by Pledgors:

(a) declare all of Pledgors' Obligations immediately due and payable; (b) exercise any or all of the rights accruing to a Secured Party under the Uniform Commercial Code and any other applicable law upon default by a debtor; (c) sell or otherwise dispose of the Collateral at public or private sale as Secured Party deems advisable for cash or in installments (on credit) with Secured Party retaining a security interest therein; provided, however, that Pledgors shall be credited with the net proceeds of such sale only when such proceeds are actually received by Secured Party, and Pledgors shall remain liable to Secured Party for any deficiency after said proceeds have been credited Pledgors' Obligations; it being specifically agreed that because the precise amount of Pledgors Obligations may not be know at the time of a sale of the Collateral, Secured Party may retain all of proceeds from the sale as Secured Party in its sole discretion deems advisable.

Because the Collateral consists of stock and other interests for which there is not a recognized market by which the value

-7-

of public sale shall also be given by publication in a newspaper of general circulation published in Los Angeles County, California, at least once not earlier than twenty-one (21) days nor later than fourteen (14) days prior to the date fixed for such sale, and again at least once not earlier than thirteen (13) days nor later than seven (7) days prior to the date fixed for such sale. The notice to be provided to Pledgor and to the secured parties who have filed a written request for notice, and the notice to be published, all as aforesaid, shall additionally provide a description of the Collateral to be sold, merely stating the certificate number, the number of shares, the name of the corporation, and the state of incorporation, and a notification that all documents as shall be relevant to the Collateral to be sold shall be available for inspection at the address of Secured Party, or in the alternative, at the address of Secured Party's attorney (with his name and address set forth) on Monday through Friday of each week, during reasonable business hours, commencing with the date upon which the notice is originally either personally delivered to or deposited in the United States mail addressed to Pledgors as aforesaid, through the end of the business day immediately preceding the date of sale. In this connection, Pledgors agree to make the books and records of ALVIRA and the most recent financial statements of ALVIRA, certified by Pledgors, available for inspection by

-9-

of the Collateral is easily determinable, Pledgors hereby agree that Secured Party shall be conclusively deemed as having acted in good faith and in a commercially reasonable manner with respect to any sale of the Collateral held pursuant to and in accordance with the following: If Pledgors have not signed after default a statement renouncing or modifying their right to notification of sale, Secured Party shall give to Pledgors, and to any other person who has a security interest in the Collateral and who has filed with Secured Party a written request for notice giving his address (before Secured Party sends its notification to Pledgors or before Pledgors' renunciation of their rights), a notice in writing of the time and place of any public sale or of the time on or after which any private sale or other intended disposition is to be made. Such notice shall be delivered personally or be deposited in the United States mail, postage prepaid, addressed to Pledgors at their address as set forth in this Pledge or at such other address as may have been furnished to Secured Party in writing for this purpose, or, if no address has been so set forth or furnished, at their last known address, and to any other secured party at the address set forth in his request for notice, at least twenty-one (21) days before the date fixed for any public sale or before the day on or after which any private sale or other disposition is to be made. Notice of the time and place

-8-

potential purchasers at the places and times designated for inspection. Any public sale shall be held at the then place of business of Secured Party, or at the address of its attorney, in the County of Los Angeles, State of California. Any public sale may be postponed from time to time by public announcement at the time and place last scheduled for the sale. Secured Party may become a purchaser at any such public or private sale if permissible under applicable law. All of Secured Party's aforesaid rights and remedies are cumulative and non-exclusive.

3.3 For the purposes hereinafter set forth, Pledgors hereby irrevocably make, constitute, designate and appoint Secured Party (and any of Secured Party's employees or agents designated by Secured Party) as Pledgors' true and lawful attorney-in-fact and agent. In the event of any default hereunder by Pledgors, such agent shall have full power and authority for and in the name of Pledgors to arrange for the transfer of the Pledged Stock on the books of ALVIRA to the name of Secured Party, or any purchaser from or nominee of Secured Party. Pledgors hereby ratify and confirm all that said agent may do or cause to be done in connection with any power or authority herein conferred.

3.4 Except as above provided in sub-paragraph 3.2, any notice required to be given by Secured Party of any intended action by Secured Party, deposited in the United

-10-

States mail, first class mail, postage prepaid and duly addressed to Pledgors at least ten (10) calendar days prior to such proposed action, shall constitute reasonable and fair notice to Pledgors of any such action and will be deemed to have been received by Pledgors two (2) days after the date such notice is deposited in the United States mail.

3.5 If at any time or times hereafter Secured Party employs counsel for representation (i) with respect to any of the Collateral or this Pledge, (ii) to represent Secured Party in any litigation or proceeding (whether instituted by Secured Party, Pledgors, or any other party) in any respect relating to any of the Collateral, this Pledge, or any other agreements, (iii) to protect, collect, sell, take possession of or liquidate any of the Collateral, (iv) to attempt to enforce any security interest of Secured Party in any of the Collateral, or (v) to enforce any rights of Secured Party against Pledgors or against any other person who may be obligated to Secured Party by virtue of this Pledge then in any of the foregoing events, all of the reasonable attorneys' fees arising from such services and all expenses, costs and charges in any way or respect arising in connection therewith or relating thereto shall constitute a part of Pledgors' Obligations and be payable on demand.

3.6 Any waiver by Secured Party of any default by Pledgors under this Agreement or the other agreements shall not waive or affect any other default by Pledgors hereunder.

-11-

feminine and neuter shall include one another, and the singular and plural shall include one another.

5.7 This Pledge may be prepared and executed in more than one counterpart. All counterparts, taken together, shall constitute one agreement only.

IN WITNESS WHEREOF, the Parties have executed this Agreement as of the date first above written.

PLEDGORS:

SECURED PARTY:

STANFORD, INC.,
a California corporation

By _____

-13-

4.0 Upon full and complete performance and discharge of each and all of the obligations of Pledgors pursuant to this Pledge, all rights of Secured Party in and to the Collateral shall cease and terminate, and this Pledge shall be of no further force or effect.

MISCELLANEOUS PROVISIONS

5.1 This Pledge shall be binding upon, and shall inure to the benefit of, the Parties, and their respective heirs, personal representatives, successors and assigns.

5.2 No delay or omission on the part of the Secured Party in exercising any rights or remedies hereunder shall operate as a waiver of any such rights or remedies hereunder or elsewhere.

5.3 If any provision of this Pledge or the application thereof to any Party or circumstance is held invalid or unenforceable, the remainder of this Pledge and the application of such provision to the other Party or to other circumstances will not be affected thereby, the provisions of this Pledge being severable in any such instance.

5.4 This Pledge shall be governed, as to validity, interpretation, effect and all other aspects, by the laws of the State of California.

5.5 As to each and every term or provision hereof, time is of the essence.

5.6 Where the context hereof so requires, the masculine,

-12-

CAUTION AND CAVEAT:
THE LEGAL AND TAX CONSEQUENCES

CAUTION AND CAVEAT:

THE LEGAL AND TAX CONSEQUENCES IMPLICIT IN THE CONCEPTS

EMBODIED IN THIS FORM ARE SUBJECT TO CONTROVERSY AND

DEBATE. ITS USE MAY RESULT IN CHALLENGE BY THE UNITED

STATES INTERNAL REVENUE SERVICE. YOU ARE CAUTIONED TO

SEEK ADVICE OF COMPETENT CPAS AND ATTORNEYS BEFORE ITS

USE.

-14-

ESCROW CLOSING STATEMENT

STATEMENT OF ESCROW NO. _____ OFFICE

TO   DOCUMENTS RECORDED _____

PROPERTY:	CHARGES	CREDITS
CONSIDERATION OR SALES PRICE	$	$
Paid outside of Escrow		
Deposits		
By First Trust Deed in Favor of		
By Second Trust Deed in Favor of		
PRORATIONS MADE AS OF		
Taxes for one-half year $ From To		
$ From To		
From To		
Rent @ $ per mo. From To		
COMMISSION PAID TO		
POLICY OF TITLE INSURANCE		
Sub-Escrow Fee		
Documentary Transfer Tax		
Recording Deed		
Recording Trust Deed (2)		
Recording Reconveyance		
Recording Partnership Agreement		
New Fire Insurance		
Tax Service		
Reconveyance Fee		
Taxes Paid		
ESCROW FEE		
Drawing Deed		
Drawing Trust Deed		
Loan Tie-in Fee		
PRINCIPAL OF ENCUMBRANCE PAID TO		
Interest @ % From To		
Prepayment charges		
Beneficiary's Fee		

	CHARGES	CREDITS
PRINCIPAL OF ENCUMBRANCE PAID TO	$	$
Interest @ % From To		
Prepayment charges		
Beneficiary's Fee		
NEW LOAN CHARGES		
Credit Report		
Interest @ % From To		
IMPOUNDS—Taxes		
Insurance		
MMI Premium		
Balance due UNITED STATES ESCROW		
Balance due you for which our check is enclosed		
TOTALS	$	$

REVIEW THIS STATEMENT CAREFULLY. We will rely upon your acceptance of this statement as your approval of the closing of escrow accordance with your instructions, unless we are notified immediately.

PARTNERSHIP AGREEMENT
OF
GREEN ACRE ASSOCIATES

This Partnership Agreement is entered into and effective this 1st day of January, 1981, by and between JOHN SMITH, RICHARD ROWE, and THE GOTROCKS COMPANY, a corporation.

All of the parties to this Agreement desire to constitute themselves as a Partnership for the purposes and upon the terms, covenants and conditions hereinafter set forth.

The parties hereby agree to become partners in business together, and therefore agree between them as follows:

1. NAME AND PRINCIPAL PLACE OF BUSINESS
The name of this Partnership shall be GREEN ACRES ASSOCIATES. Upon the execution of this Agreement or a subsequent change in the membership of this Partnership, the Partners shall sign, cause to be filed, and published in Los Angeles County, a Certificate of Fictitious Name as required by law. The principal place of business of the Partnership shall be 6300 Wilshire Boulevard, Suite 9100, Los Angeles, California 90048, in the County of Los Angeles, State of California, or at such other place in the County of Los Angeles or the County of Orange as the Managing Partner shall hereafter determine. In addition, the Partners shall sign and cause to be recorded in the office of the County Recorder of Los Angeles, a Statement of Partnership in accordance with California Corporations Code Section 15010.5. Should the Managing Partner change the principal place of business of this Partnership, he shall give prompt written notice to all of the Partners of this Partnership.

2. TERM OF PARTNERSHIP
This Partnership shall commence on the date above written and shall continue until the first of the following events:
1. The expiration of THIRTY (30) years from the date hereof; or
2. Until such time as the Partners holding EIGHTY-FIVE (85%) PER CENT of interest in distributions of profits and losses shall give SIXTY (60) day's written notice of termination.

It is understood and agreed, however, that no dissolution or termination of this Partnership shall release or relieve any of the parties hereto of their contractual obligations to the others under this agreement.

Winding up of the affairs of the Partnership, the distribution of Partnership assets and the liquidation of the Partnership business shall be conducted in accordance with the provisions of this agreement upon such termination. Under no circumstances shall the death, bankruptcy or incapacity of any Partner terminate this Partnership. Upon the death, legal incapacity or adjudication of bankruptcy of, or assignment for the benefit of creditors, or admission in writing of an act or insolvency by a Partner, the remaining partners shall form a new partnership on

the same terms and conditions as are contained herein, and if appropriate designate a new Managing Partner.
3. In the event of the dissolution of this Partnership, whether by voluntary agreement, expiration of the term provided for herein pursuant to the provisions of any of the preceding paragraphs, or for any other reason, a proper accounting shall be made of the capital and income accounts of each Partner and of the net profit or net loss of this Partnership to the date of dissolution, the Partnership liabilities and obligations to creditors shall be paid; and the Partnership assets, or the proceeds of their sale, shall then be distributed as hereafter provided.

3. PURPOSE AND NATURE OF BUSINESS
The purpose, nature and character of the business of this Partnership is to acquire, lease and hold for investment, improved real property in the City of Los Angeles, described in Exhibit "A" attached hereto, and refinance and/or hold for investment and sell, or otherwise dispose of, the said real property, together with any improvements thereto. In this connection, the Managing Partner is authorized by his sole signature on behalf of and in the name of this Partnership to consummate the purchase by this Partnership of the real property described in Exhibit "A" and all personal property incidental thereto and to execute any and all documents that said Managing Partner shall in his sole discretion determine including, but not limited to, Escrow Instructions and amendments, Promissory Notes, Deeds of Trust, Loan applications, Loan Modification Agreements, and Management Contracts. The Partnership is to initially acquire the property described in Exhibit "A" from the Green Acre Trust for an approximate purchase price of FIVE MILLION, TWO HUNDRED SIXTY THOUSAND ($5,260,000) DOLLARS. As part of the terms of purchase, this Partnership may acquire new mortgage financing on subject property.

4. CAPITAL CONTRIBUTIONS, CAPITAL ACCOUNTS, PROFITS AND LOSSES AND CASH FLOW

A. Partnership Capital Contributions
On the execution hereof, each of the Partners, agrees to contribute to the capital of this Partnership, the sum set forth opposite his name below:

John Smith $
Richard Rowe $
The Gotrocks Company $

On or before May 15, 1981, each of the Partners agrees to contribute to the capital of this Partnership the additional sum set forth opposite his name below:

John Smith $
Richard Rowe $
The Gotrocks Company $

B. Capital Accounts, Profits and Losses and Cash Flow

The capital accounts and profits and losses of this Partnership shall be kept and maintained in accordance with generally accepted and recognized accounting principles and practices consistently applied, and profits and losses shall be determined in accordance therewith by accountants of this Partnership. The share of the losses to be borne and suffered by each such Partner, is as follows:

John Smith _____%
Richard Rowe _____%
The Gotrocks Company _____%

C. Cash Flow

"Cash flow" as used herein is defined as monies, interests, credits, notes and Deed of Trust derived from any source available for distribution.

D. Additional Contributions

Each Partner shall be required to contribute additional capital to this Partnership upon the unanimous vote of all Partners. No interest shall be paid on any contribution made by any Partner.

E. Withdrawal of Capital

No Partner shall have the right to withdraw his capital contribution or to demand or receive return of his contribution and in this regard the Partners specifically waive all of the provisions of the Uniform Partnership Act which under certain circumstances permits a Partner to demand the return of his contribution.

5. ACQUISITION FEE TO MANAGING PARTNER

There shall be due and payable by this Partnership to the Managing Partner, JOHN SMITH, a sum equal to THREE (3%) PER CENT of the gross purchase price paid by this Partnership for the property described in Exhibit "A," for the services performed by him in the acquisition of the property decribed in Exhibit "A."

A. No sums shall be payable by this Partnership to Smith, if for any reason this Partnership fails to purchase the property described in Exhibit "A."

B. The sums shall be paid to Smith from time to time solely from the assets and cash flow of this Partnership and the obligation for said payment shall not be the personal obligation of any of the Partners.

C. When, after due consideration is given to the business requirements and obligations of this Partnership and the effective operation of Partnership assets, there are funds available to pay Smith, Smith shall receive from time to time a portion of said sum due him without interest.

D. The obligation to Smith is not an absolute obligation and the payment thereof is expressly contingent upon the availability of monies by this Partnership as above provided.

6. CASH FLOW AND DISTRIBUTION THEREOF

The Cash Flow of this Partnership shall be distributed from time to time, but not less than semi-annually, in the following manner:

FIRST: To pay the current debts of this Partnership.

SECOND: To pay such reasonable reserves as the Managing Partner shall determine is in the best interests of this Partnership. In this connection, the Managing Partner shall furnish to the Partners no later than February 1 of each year, an annual projection of the budget, cash flow and recommended operating reserve for the following year. The proposed reserve shall be subject to approval by the majority in interest of the Partners, provided however, that such reserve may not be established at less than one month's scheduled rental income without the Managing Partner's consent.

THIRD: The balance of the cash flow shall be divided among the Partners in accordance with their percentage of profits and losses as provided in Paragraph 4B above.

7. SALE AND TRANSFER OF A PARTNERSHIP INTEREST

Except as hereafter provided respecting the transfer of all or part of a Partner's interest by Will or by intestacy, neither the whole nor any portion of a Partner's interest shall be sold, hypothecated, assigned or transferred, directly or indirectly, without complying with the following:

(i) The interest proposed to be sold, transferred or hypothecated shall first be offered in writing to the Partners, at the price and on the terms on which it is proposed to be sold, or transferred or hypothecated ("proposed price" and "proposed terms" respectively herein), and the Partners shall have a period of FORTY-FIVE (45) days to accept or reject such offer, in full, at the proposed price, and on the proposed terms.

(ii) The Partners shall have the right to purchase such interest in the same ratio as their respective percentage of profits and losses bears to one another. If all of the remaining interest is not disposed of under such apportionment, each Partner desiring to purchase a portion of the remaining interest in excess of his proportionated share thereof, as above provided, shall be entitled to purchase such proportion of the remaining interest in this Partnership, determined as set forth above bears to the respective interest of any other Partners desiring to exercise such option in excess of their proportionate share thereof, as above provided.

(iii) If the entire interest of the Partner desiring to sell, hypothecate, assign or transfer is not purchased in accordance with the provisions of (i) and (ii) above, then after said TWENTY (20) day period has elapsed, the Partner may sell, transfer, or hypothecate his interest upon the proposed terms and at the proposed price. Such sale, transfer or hypothecation must be completed during the SIXTY (60) day period next following the expiration of said FORTY-FIVE (45) day period, or no portion of his interest shall be sold, transferred, or hypothecated without first being re-offered to the Partners, in accordance with (i) and (ii) above.

8. FISCAL YEAR, BOOKS, REPORTS, AUDITS, RETURNS

A. The Partnership hereby adopts a fiscal year ending on the 31st day of December of each year for the purposes of both the Partnership and income tax reporting.

B. The Partnership shall maintain full and accurate books in accordance with standard accounting procedures at its principal place of business, and all partners or their duly authorized agents shall have the right to inspect and examine such books at reasonable times. The books shall be kept on a cash basis. The books shall be closed and balanced at the end of each fiscal year. This Partnership shall maintain a bank account or accounts at such banks in the County of Los Angeles as the Managing Partner shall determine from time to time. All monies received by this Partnership shall be deposited into the Partnership bank accounts. Funds may be withdrawn therefrom upon the sole signature of the Managing Partner.

C. The Managing Partner shall deliver to each Partner within NINETY (90) days after expiration of each fiscal year of the Partnership, a balance sheet and a profit and loss statement, together with a statement showing the capital accounts of each Partner, the distribution to each Partner, and all amounts reportable by each Partner for State and Federal tax purposes.

D. A copy of all Partnership tax returns for each fiscal year shall be supplied to all Partners within NINETY (90) days from the end of such fiscal year.

E. A copy of all financial reports and income tax returns of the Partnership shall be supplied to any withdrawn Partner so long as he is entitled to receive a portion of the net profits of the Partnership.

F. An individual capital account shall be maintained for each Partner.

G. The Managing Partner shall cause to be prepared and distributed to all Partners quarterly an interim statement of income, expenses, profits and losses of this Partnership.

9. DRAWS AND INTEREST ON CAPITAL ACCOUNT

Except as herein otherwise provided, none of the Partners shall receive any salary or drawings for services rendered on behalf of the Partnership or in their capacity as Partners. No Partner shall receive any interest on his contribution to the Partnership capital. Any advance of money to the Partnership by any Partner in excess of his respective agreed capital contribution to the Partnership shall not be deemed a capital contribution, but a debt due from the Partnership and shall be repaid with interest at such rates and times as may be agreed upon at the time of such advance but not to exceed TEN (10%) PER CENT per annum.

10. RIGHTS, DUTIES AND OBLIGATIONS OF PARTNERS AND MANAGEMENT BY MANAGING PARTNER

A. JOHN SMITH shall be the Managing Partner and as such shall have the primary responsibility and obligation for the day-to-day operation and management of the property to be acquired by this Partnership. Smith shall devote such time to the conduct of the affairs of this Partnership as shall be necessary to operate and manage the property of this Partnership in an efficient manner, to maximize the income therefrom, and enhance and preserve the value thereof. Smith shall not be required to devote his full time and effort to the affairs of this Partnership it being fully understood and agreed by all the Partners that Smith shall exercise overall supervision, management and control of the Partnership and its assets and affairs, but that he may from time to time contract with and/or employ a professional manager and others as hereafter provided.

B. Except as expressly set forth below, the Managing Partner shall have full charge of the management, conduct and operation of the Partnership business in all respects and in all matters, and shall from time to time in the event of extraordinary or substantial occurrences and not less often than quarterly, render a report to the Partners of the status of this Partnership and its assets and shall have the power on behalf of the Partnership to:

(i) Deal in any Partnership asset and to enter into contracts and agreements of every kind or nature;

(ii) Employ from time to time persons, firms, or corporations to render direct and reasonable services to this Partnership including without limitation, accountants and attorneys;

(iii) Execute, acknowledge and deliver all instruments and agreements of every kind or nature in connection with the initial acquisition of the property described in Exhibit "A" by this Partnership.

(iv) Upon the eventual disposal of the property, use his best endeavor to sell or otherwise dispose of the property without payment by the Partnership of any brokerage fee or commission. It is expressly agreed that the Managing Partner is to receive no additional fee or compensation in connection with such sale or disposition.

PROVIDED, HOWEVER, that notwithstanding the foregoing except as to the provisions of Paragraph (iii) just above, the Managing Partner shall not (a) sell or encumber the real property assets of this Partnership, or (b) enter into any contract of agreement binding this Partnership to any single obligation in excess of the sum of TWENTY-FIVE THOUSAND ($25,000.00) DOLLARS, without the prior written consent of the majority in interest of the Partners.

(v) Execute, acknowledge and deliver any and all instruments to effectuate the foregoing.

C. Any of the Partners, and the officers, directors and shareholders thereof, may engage in, or possess an interest in, other business ventures of every nature and description independently or with others, including, but not limited to, the ownership, financing, leasing, operation, management, syndication, brokerage, and development of real property, and neither the Partnership nor the Partners shall have the right by virtue of this agreement in or to such independent ventures or to the income, benefits, or profits thereof.

D. The Managing Partner shall be reimbursed for all reasonable direct out-of-pocket expenses relating to the affairs of this Partnership only and, in addition thereto, shall receive from this Partnership, a management fee of _____ DOLLARS per month.

E. Upon the death, resignation or other disability of the Managing Partner, a new Managing Partner shall be elected by the vote of the remaining Partners who hold more than half of the remaining right to receive profits and losses of this Partnership.

11. ASSIGNMENT OF PARTNER'S INTEREST

A Partner shall not assign, pledge, encumber, sell or otherwise dispose of his interest as a Partner in this Partnership, or enter into any agreement as a result of which any individual shall obtain his Partnership interest in the Partnership, without first complying with the conditions set forth below:

(a) All applicable terms of Article 7 hereof shall be adhered to;

(b) Notification in writing to the Partners of the name, address, social security number, occupation of the assignee at least THIRTY (30) days prior to the contemplated assignment;

(c) The transfer shall be only by an instrument in writing in form and substance satisfactory to the Managing Partner; and

(d) A counterpart of the instrument of transfer, executed and acknowledged by the transferring Partner, shall be filed with this Partnership.

12. SUBSTITUTED PARTNERS

A. A Partner shall have the right to transfer his Partnership interest after complying with Articles 7 and 11, hereof. No such proposed purchaser of a Partner's interest in this Partnership shall have the right to become a substituted Partner in the place of his assignor, unless:

(i) His assignor shall designate such intention in the instrument of assignment;

(ii) The assignor and assignee named in the assignment instrument shall execute and acknowledge such other instruments as the Managing Partner may deem necessary or desirable to effectuate such admission;

(iii) The assignee accepts and adopts in writing all of the terms and provisions of this agreement, as the same may have been amended; and

(iv) Such assignee pays or obligates himself to pay, as the Managing Partner may determine, all reasonable expenses connected with such admission, including, but not limited to, the cost of preparing, filing and publishing any amendments to this agreement which may be required.

B. Notwithstanding the foregoing, no assignment by any Partner of all or any part of his interest in this Partnership, whether or not in compliance with the terms of this agreement, shall cause or constitute a dissolution of this Partnership.

C. In the event that a substitution of a new Partner is permitted, as hereinabove provided, the Managing Partner shall prepare a new or amended Certificate of Partnership which sets forth the respective interests of the continuing and substituted Partners. No new Partnership interest shall be created except with the consent of the majority in interest of the Partners.

13. DEATH OF A PARTNER

A. On the death of a Partner, his executor or administrator shall have all rights of a Partner for the purpose of settling the estate, and such power as the deceased had to constitute his assignee a substantial Partner. Any sale of the deceased Partner's interest by his executor or administrator shall be subject to all the terms and provisions of Paragraphs 7 and 12 hereof. The estate of a deceased Partner shall be liable for all his liabilities as a Partner.

B. Notwithstanding anything to the contrary contained in this Agreement, the restrictions contained in Article 7 shall not apply to a transfer by Will or by intestacy of all or any part of a Partner's interest in the Partnership. Subject to compliance with subparagraphs A (ii) and A (iii) and A (iv) of Article 12 and such transferee executing such documents as the Managing Partner may deem desirable or necessary, any such transferee shall be entitled to admission to this Partnership, as a substituted Partner, and all other Partners hereby authorize jointly and severally the Managing Partner to execute on their behalf an amended Certificate of Partnership which will reflect the admission of such substituted Partner. Any such substituted Partner, however, shall hold his Partnership interest subject to all of the other provisions, authorizations, conditions and restrictions of this Agreement.

14. NOTICES

Notices under this Agreement shall be in writing, and shall be given to all Partners by United States mail, postage prepaid, and shall be addressed to each Partner at the address set opposite his name on the signature pages below, or at such other place as provided herein.

15. VOTE AND AMENDMENT TO THIS AGREEMENT

This Partnership Agreement is subject to amendment only by a vote of the majority in interest of the Partners, unless specifically provided otherwise in this Agreement, and such amendment shall be effective as of such date as may be determined by them.

16. ARTICLE HEADINGS

The Article headings in no way define, limit, extend or interpret the scope of this Agreement or of any particular provision thereof.

17. ADDITIONAL DOCUMENTS

Each party hereto agrees to execute with acknowledgement or affidavit, any and all documents and writings which may be necessary or expedient in the creation of this Partnership and the achievement of its purpose, specifically including, without limitation, the Certificate of Partnership, all amendments thereto and any cancellation thereof.

18. ARBITRATION

In the event of any disagreement between any of the Partners and/or the Partnership, such dispute or disagreement may be arbitrated pursuant to the rules and regulations of the American Arbitration Association (AAA) then in effect. An Arbitrator shall be immediately appointed, who shall head and adjudicate the matter pursuant to said rules and regulations of the AAA and the award of said Arbitrator shall be final and binding on all parties and may be entered as a Judgment in any court of competent jurisdiction. The cost of said arbitration shall be borne by the Partnership.

19. INTERPRETATION

When the context in which words are used in this Agreement indicates that such is the intent, the singular and plural number shall each be deemed to include the other, and the masculine and feminine and neuter gender shall each be deemed to include the others. For the purpose of this Agreement, whenever an action of the Partnership requires approval of "a majority in interest," this phrase shall be interpreted as meaning that individuals or entities holding interests in this Partnership representing the aggregate more than FIFTY (50%) PER CENT of the share of profits and losses of the Partnership must vote affirmatively for such action.

20. VALIDITY

In the event that any provision of this Agreement shall be held to be invalid, the validity of the remainder of the terms and provisions of this Agreement shall not be effected thereby in any respect. This Agreement is made and entered into in the State of California and shall be interpreted in accordance with the laws of the State of California.

21. COUNTERPARTS AND EXECUTION

A copy of this Agreement, or any amendment thereto may be executed in multiple counterparts by each of the parties hereto. All executed and acknowledged signature pages shall be attached to one filled-out copy of this Agreement including all Exhibits by the Managing Partner, and thereafter said copy shall be deemed the original Partnership Agreement.

22. EXHIBITS

Exhibits "A" and "B" attached hereto, are incorporated into this Agreement by reference. Whenever the word "agreement" is used herein, it shall be deemed to also refer to and include said Exhibits "A" and "B."

23. LIMITATIONS OF PARTNER'S AUTHORITY

No Partner except as expressly provided elsewhere in this Agreement, shall engage in any of the following acts on behalf of the Partnership or its property without written consent of all of the Partners:

1. Sign, pledge, hypothecate or mortgage any asset belonging to this Partnership, or execute any bond or lease;
2. Pledge credit;
3. Make an assignment for the benefit of creditors;
4. Release, assign or transfer a claim, security or other property;
5. Make, draw or accept any notices or obligation for the payment of money;
6. Become a surety, guarantor, endorser, or accommodation endorser for any other person or firm;
7. Borrow or lend any money.

24. SUCCESSORS AND ASSIGNS

Subject to prohibitions against assignments and transfer, this Agreement shall inure to the benefit of and be binding upon the parties, their legal representatives and successors.

IN WITNESS WHEREOF, we have hereunto set our hands and seals on the date indicated.

Dated: January _____, 1981.

Address: _____ JOHN SMITH

Address: _____ RICHARD ROWE

Address: _____ THE GOTROCKS COMPANY,
a Corporation

By _____

3.   PRINCIPAL PLACE OF BUSINESS.   The principal place of business of the Partnership shall be 933 South White- acre Avenue, Los Angeles, California, or at such other place as the partners shall hereafter jointly determine.

4.   FICTITIOUS BUSINESS NAME.   In compliance with Sections 17900, et. seq. of the California Business and Pro- fessions Code, the partners shall draft, sign and cause to be filed, recorded and published in Los Angeles County, a Certifi- cate of Fictitious Business Name upon the execution of this Agreement, or upon a subsequent change in the membership of this Partnership.

5.   NAME AND ADDRESSES OF PARTNERS.   The name and addresses of the partners are as follows:

Con Structor

The Whiteacre Corporation N.V.
c/o Myron Meyers, Esq.
Meyers, Stevens & Walters
Professional Corporation
6300 Wilshire Boulevard, Suite 9100
Los Angeles, California 90048

6.   TERM OF PARTNERSHIP.   This Partnership shall com- mence on the date of this Agreement and shall continue until such time as the first of the following shall occur:

(a) Thirty (30) years from the date hereof;

and/or

-2-

PARTNERSHIP AGREEMENT

OF

WHITEACRE DEVELOPERS

This Partnership Agreement is entered into and effec- tive this 1st day of January, 1981, by and between CON STRUCTOR and THE WHITEACRE CORPORATION N.V. (hereinafter "Corporation").

Both parties to this Agreement desire to constitute themselves a Partnership for the purposes and upon the terms, covenants and conditions hereinafter set forth.

The parties hereby agree to become partners in business together, and therefore agree between them as follows:

1.   NAME.   The firm name of this Partnership shall be WHITEACRE DEVELOPERS.

2.   PURPOSE.   The purpose of this Partnership shall be to purchase, own as an investment, lease, improve, hypothecate and encumber real property, improved or unimproved, with the power to sell, exchange or transfer said real property if it is in the Partnership's best interests to do so.   The specification of particular business shall not be deemed a limitation upon the general powers of the Partnership, and this Partnership may engage in any other business that the partners shall jointly determine. This Partnership further contemplates initially purchasing and developing the unimproved real property described in Exhibit "A" attached hereto and made a part hereof.

(b) The mutual agreement of the partners.

7. CAPITAL CONTRIBUTIONS.

(a) Initial Capital Contributions. Corporation shall contribute One Hundred Twenty-Five Thousand Dollars ($125,000.00) as its initial capital contribution to the Partnership. Con Structor shall contribute the land located at 933 South Whiteacre Avenue, Los Angeles, California, free and clear of all encumbrances plus all plans, specifications, documents or materials of any kind held by him in connection with such land. The parties hereby agree that the value of Con Structor's capital contribution is One Hundred Twenty-Five Thousand Dollars ($125,000.00).

(b) Additional Capital Contributions. In the event that the partners agree that the Partnership requires additional funds to accomplish the purpose set forth in Paragraph 2 above, and they agree additional capital contributions would best supply that need for additional funds, Corporation shall contribute up to One Hundred Seventy-Five Thousand Dollars ($175,000.00) as an additional capital contribution.

8. PROFITS AND LOSSES, NET CASH FLOW, AND THE ALLOCATION AND DISTRIBUTION THEREOF.

(a) "Profits and losses" shall mean those profits and losses determined by the use of generally accepted accounting principals consistently applied for the purpose of determing

-3-

state and federal income taxes. The profits and losses to be received by each partner shall not necessarily bear any relationship to the distribution of net cash flow defined below.

(b) "Net cash flow" shall mean all monies received by the Partnership from any source including, but not limited to, cash received from operations, borrowings, sales of real or personal property or refinancing, after the deduction of all necessary Partnership cash expenditures, less such reasonable reserves determined by the General Partner, as set forth in Paragraph 13 below, to be required for working capital, or unforeseen contingencies.

(c) Allocation of Profits and Losses. The percentage of profits to be received and losses to be borne by each partner shall be equal to that partner's initial capital contribution and additional capital contribution, if any, divided by the total initial and additional capital contributions made to the Partnership.

(d) Allocation of Net Cash Flow. The allocation of net cash flow shall be in the following order and amounts:

(i) Ratably to the partners in an amount euqal to their initial and additional capital contributions set forth in Paragraph 7 above, less any capital contribution previously returned to the partners;

(ii) As to the remainder of the net cash flow, that amount set forth in Paragraph (c) above.

-4-

(e) Distribution of Cash Flow. Distributions of cash flow to the partners shall be made at reasonable intervals during the accounting year, as determined by the General Partners, but in any event, not less than a quarterly basis. Such distributions shall be made in compliance with Section 15516 of the California Corporations Code.

9. CAPITAL ACCOUNTS. Capital accounts shall be kept and maintained for each partner in accordance with generally accepted accounting principles consistently applied. Such capital accounts shall be adjusted from time to time to reflect additional contributions to capital, if any, allocation of profits and losses and distributions of Partnership assets, including the distribution of net cash flow.

10. SOURCE OF ADDITIONAL FUNDS. In the event that the capital contributions set forth in Paragraph 7 above are insufficient to meet necessary Partnership expenditures, the General Partners may, but without the obligation to do so, loan from time to time, such monies to the Partnership. These loans shall be evidenced by promissory notes and shall bear interest at the rate equal to the then prime rate charged by The Bank of America to its most credit-worthy borrowers for 90-day commercial loans, and they shall be repaid from the first Partnership funds available after the payment of non-partner creditors.

11. TIME FOR RETURN OF CAPITAL. If (prior to eighteen (18) months from the date hereof) each of the partners have not

-5-

received from any source their initial capital contribution or additional capital contributions made pursuant to Paragraph 7 above, a sum equal to ten per cent (10%) per annum from and after that date shall be paid to the partners on the then remaining portion of their capital contribution until that remaining portion of their capital contribution, plus accrued interest, has been returned to the partner.

12. WITHDRAWAL OF CAPITAL. Either partner shall have the right to withdraw his or its entire capital contribution prior to the submission and approval of the final plans and specifications, the award of contract bids, the hiring of a supervising architect as set forth in Paragraph 14 below, and the recordation of a construction loan. Notwithstanding anything to the contrary herein, in the event that a partner exercises his or its right to withdraw his contributed capital, the Partnership shall immediately dissolve and distribute the remaining Partnership assets to the partners in the amount and kind of their capital contributions, except that the partner so withdrawing for the Partnership shall bear any and all costs expended in the Partnership prior to his or its withdrawal. Except as otherwise provided, the partner shall have the right to withdraw his or its capital from the Partnership.

13. MANAGEMENT. Management and control of Partnership operations shall be exercised on the basis of the respective capital contributions of the partners, as follows:

-6-

is proceeding in compliance with the plans and specifications for the improvements.

15. ACCOUNTS AND RECORDS.

(a) Establishment of and Authorized Signatures for Bank Account. The partners shall jointly open one or more Partnership bank accounts, and all Partnership funds shall be deposited therein. All checks drawn against said accounts, or any other form of withdrawal of funds, shall require the signature of one or both of the partners, as determined by Paragraph 13 above.

(b) Partnership Records. Partnership books and records shall be kept at the principal office of the Partnership and each partner, or his or its duly authorized representative, shall have access thereto for the purposes of inspecting and photocopying said books and records or having an independent audit of such books and records performed.

(c) Partnership Tax Returns. The partners shall cause to be prepared, within a reasonable period after the close of each fiscal year (not exceeding ninety (90) days) and upon the termination of the Partnership, at the expense of the Partnership, a report of the Partnership's operation, containing a balance sheet and an income statement, and an informational tax return in the name of the Partnership. Within a reasonable period after the close of the period covered by the report (not exceeding

(a) In the event that the initial and capital contributions, if any, made by the partners are of an equal amount, all Partnership acts including, but not limited to, the signing of contracts, mortgaging of Partnership assets, assigning of duties, and approval of construction vouchers must be signed by both partners to bind the Partnership.

(b) In the event that the initial and additional capital contributions, if any, made by one partner is greater than that of the other partner, all Partnership acts, including but not limited to those specified in Subparagraph (a) above, must be signed only by the partner making the greater capital contribution. Such partner shall exercise his or its best efforts to consult with and obtain the consent of the other partner prior to performing such act.

14. CONSTRUCTION OF IMPROVEMENTS. The construction of improvements on the property shall be carried out under the supervision and responsibility of a duly-licensed contractor who will be selected by virtue of his submission of the lowest of two or more competitive sealed bids tendered by said licensed builders.

Contractor must obtain a completion bond on the project as a condition precedent to his employment hereunder. Prior to the commencement of construction, the Partnership shall enter into a written contract with an architect for the oversight and supervision of such construction in order to assure that the construction

ninety (90) days), a copy of the report and of the Partnership information tax return shall be furnished to each partner at the expense of the Partnership.

16. ASSIGNABILITY OF A PARTNER'S INTEREST.

(a) Each of the partners agrees that they will not sell, transfer, assign, pledge, encumber, mortgage or otherwise hypothecate the whole or any part of their interest in this Partnership without complying with the provisions of Subparagraph (b) of this paragraph. The transfer of an interest hereunder shall not cause a termination of the Partnership.

(b) In the event that any partner shall desire to sell, assign, pledge, encumber, mortgage, or otherwise hypothecate his interest in this Partnership, which offer is acceptable to such partner (hereinafter referred to as "selling partner") may do so only in compliance with the following requirements and limitations:

(i) The selling partner shall send a copy of such offer by certified mail to the other partner. Such offer shall thereupon be deemed to be an offer by the selling partner to so transfer his Partnership interest to the other partner (hereinafter called "purchasing partner"), upon the same terms and conditions as contained in that offer. The purchasing partner shall then notify the selling partner in writing by certified mail, within ten (10) days after mailing of the offer to him, as

-9-

to whether he accepts such offer. Such offer shall be deemed to have been rejected if acceptance thereof is not mailed by the purchasing partner by the end of the ten (10) day period.

(ii) If purchasing partner desires to acquire less than the entire interest offered, he shall set forth in his letter of acceptance the amount of interest that he is willing to acquire. In this event, the selling partner shall have the right to transfer his entire Partnership interest to the third party offeror within thirty (30) days of the date of mailing of the original offer; provided that such transaction is consummated strictly in accordance with the terms of the offer originally submitted to the purchasing partner.

(iii) In the event that the aggregate Partnership interest accepted by the purchasing partner is equal to the interest offered by the selling partner, the selling partner shall transfer, and the purchasing partner shall acquire, the Partnership interest in accordance with the terms and conditions of the third party offer.

(c) Notwithstanding the above provisions, the interest of an individual partner may be transferred or disposed of by will or intestacy, subject to the provisions herein set forth below in this Agreement.

(d) No conveyance of a partner's interest, though otherwise permitted hereunder, shall be valid and effective, and

-10-

19. REMUNERATION AND REIMBURSEMENT OF EXPENSES. The partners shall not be entitled to any salaries under this Agreement. Any direct expenses including overhead incurred by any of the partners for or on behalf of the Partnership shall be reimbursed by the Partnership to said partner. No expense or overhead shall be incurred by a partner without the consent of the other partners.

Notwithstanding the above, Con Structor shall be given an exclusive listing for the sale of the property after the completion of the construction of the improvements thereon. Said listing shall provide for a commission of five per cent (5%) of the sales price, and shall continue for a period of six (6) months from the date a certificate of occupancy is issued for the building. In the event that the building remains unsold after the six (6) month period, Con Structor shall place the property with a multiple listing service, and he agrees to share his above-designated commission in the customary manner.

20. DEATH OR DISSOLUTION OF A PARTNER. The death or disability of a partner shall not work a dissolution of the Partnership, but the business shall continue without interruption and without any break in continuity. In the event of death or dissolution, the legal representative of a deceased partner and the successor in interest to the dissolved partner, shall be deemed to be the assignee of the partner's Partnership

-12-

the Partnership shall not recognize the same for the purposes of making payment of profits, cash flow, return of contribution, or other distributions with respect to such interest or any part thereof or with respect to other rights herein contained, unless transferred in accordance with the terms of this paragraph, and the transferee agrees to be bound in writing by the terms of this Partnership Agreement and executes an appropriate written amendment to this Partnership Agreement.

17. FISCAL YEAR. The fiscal year of the Partnership shall be the calendar year.

18. RIGHT TO ENGAGE IN OTHER ACTIVITIES. Each of the partners may engage in other business ventures exclusively for their own account, and may acquire, operate, and sell real and personal property without liability of any nature therefor to the Partnership or to the other partner. No partner shall have any obligation or liability or duty to offer to the Partnership any business or investment or venture or other opportunity which may be presented to him even though it may be presented by reason of being one of the partners thereof. Each partner shall have the right to engage in other business ventures or other business opportunities, even though in competition herewith. None of the partners shall devote their full time and energy to the business affairs of the Partnership, but only shall devote so much of his time and attention to the Partnership business as he thinks necessary or available.

-11-

interest, and may become a substituted partner upon the terms and conditions set forth below. The estate of the deceased partner shall be liable for all of his liabilities and obligations to the Partnership. Such Partnership interest may be transferred upon death or dissolution, notwithstanding the provisions of Paragraph 16 above.

21. SUBSTITUTED PARTNER. The partners must admit as substituted partners, persons, firms or corporations who acquire a Partnership interest or any part thereof of a partner, provided the provisions of Paragraph 16 above have been complied with. The admission of an assignee as a substituted partner shall be conditioned upon the assignee's agreement to pay or a payment of all sums due the Partnership by his assignor relating to the Partnership interest being acquired, and his acceptance and adoption of all of the terms and provisions of this Agreement in form satisfactory to all of the other partners. Any costs required, any filing fees incurred, including reasonable attorney's fees in effectuating such transfer and substitution as a partner shall be paid by the assuming partner. An amended Agreement of Partnership shall be prepared and executed by all partners.

22. VOLUNTARY DISSOLUTION. Upon the agreement of both partners, the Partnership may be dissolved and the assets liquidated forthwith. The Partnership shall engage in no further business thereafter other than that necessary to wind-up the

-13-

business and sitribute the assets. The maintenance of offices shall not be deemed a continuation of the business for purposes of this provision. The partners shall continue to divide profits and losses and net cash flow during the winding-up period in the same ratio as profits and losses were divided prior to dissolution. The proceeds from the liquidation of Partnership assets shall be divided in the following order:

(a) The expenses of liquidation and the debts of the Partnership, other than debts owing to the partners, shall be paid.

(b) Such debts as are owing to the partners, including loans and advances made to or for the benefit of the Partnership, shall be computed.

(c) As provided in Paragraph 8 above.

The partners shall cause to have published a Notice of Dissolution as required by law.

After all of the debts of the Partnership have been paid, the partners may elect by mutual agreement of all partners to distribute the assets of the Partnership in kind.

23. NOTICES. All notices, demands or other communication hereunder shall be in writing and shall be deemed to have been given when the same are:

(a) Deposited in the United States mail and sent by certified or registered mail, postage prepaid; or,

-14-

(b) Delivered in each case to the parties at the addresses of each of the partners set forth in Paragraph 5 above.

24. COOPERATION. The partners shall execute and deliver such further instruments and so such further acts and things as may be required to carry out the intent and purpose of this Agreement.

25. AGREEMENT IN COUNTERPARTS. This Agreement may be executed in counterparts, and all so executed shall constitute one Agreement binding on all of the parties hereto, notwithstanding that all of the parties are not signatories to the original, or the same, counterpart.

26. CAPTIONS. Captions contained in this Agreement are inserted only as a matter of convenience, and in no way define, limit, extend or describe the scope of this Agreement or the intent of any provision thereof.

27. CONSTRUCTION. None of the provisions of this Agreement shall be for the benefit of or enforceable by any creditor of the Partnership.

28. APPLICABLE LAW. This Agreement shall be construed exclusively in accordance with the laws and decisions of the State of California.

29. SUCCESSORS AND ASSIGNS. Subject to prohibitions against assignment and transfer, this Agreement shall

-15-

inure to the benefit of and be binding upon the parties, their legal representatives and successors.

30. ARBITRATION. Any dispute or controversy arising under, out of, or in connection with, or in relation to this Certificate and Agreement amy, at the sole election of either partner, be determined by arbitration in Los Angeles, California, pursuant to the rules then obtaining of the American Aribration Association, and judgment may be entered upon the award in any court having jurisdiction thereof, which award shall be final and binding on all partners.

CON STRUCTOR

THE WHITEACRE CORPORATION N.V.,
a corporation

By: CHEN WONG
President-Secretary

-16-

CONTRIBUTION OF LAND AND MONIES - FUTURE CONSTRUCTION

AGREEMENT, CERTIFICATE AND ARTICLES OF

LIMITED PARTNERSHIP

OF

FUTURE DEVELOPMENT, LTD.

This Certificate, Agreement and Articles of Limited Partnership, hereinafter called the "Agreement", is made this 1st day of January, 1981, by and amont FUTURE INVESTMENTS, INC. (hereinafter referred to as the "Limited Partner", and BRIGHT FUTURE (hereinafter referred to as the "General Partner".

W I T N E S S E T H

WHEREAS, the undersigned are desirous of forming a Limited Partnership pursuant to Title 2, Chapter 2 of the California Corporations Code by this Agreement; and

WHEREAS, the undersigned are desirous of entering into this Agreement for the purpose of setting forth the rights, duties and obligations of the General Partner as well as the rights and limits of liability of the Limited Partner; and

WHEREAS, the undersigned are desirous of stating the rights of the undersigned with respect to the assets of the Partnership and the receipt of profits of the undersigned by reason of being a party to this Agreement; and

WHEREAS, the undersigned are desirous of forming this Limited Partnership for the purposes as hereinafter described in Paragraph 4;

For good and valuable consideration, and the mutual covenants, promises and agreements contained herein,

IT IS HEREBY AGREED AS FOLLOWS:

1. FORMATION. The parties hereto hereby form a Limited Partnership, hereinafter called "the Partnership", pursuant to Chapter 2, Title 2 of the California Corporations Code, known and referred to herein as the "Uniform Limited Partnership Act". It is agreed that in executing this Agreement, the parties are executing a Certificate of Limited Partnership, which shall be duly recorded forthwith in the office of the count recorder of each county in which is situated a place of business of the Partnership or in which real property of the Partnership is located, all in accordance with the provisions of the Uniform Limited Partnership Act.

2. PRINCIPAL PLACE OF BUSINESS. The principal place of business of the Partnership shall be 6300 Wilshire Boulevard, Suite 9100, Los Angeles, California 90048, or at such other place or places in the County of Los Angeles, State of California as the General Partner may, from time to time, determine. The General Partner shall give with reasonable promptness written notice of any such change to the Limited Partner.

3. NAME. The name under which the Partnership business shall be conducted is FUTURE DEVELOPMENT, LTD. The parties hereto may execute a Certificate of Fictitious Firm Name and

-2-

cause such Certificate to be published and filed with the County Clerk in the county where the principal place of business of the Partnership is located.

4. PURPOSE. The sole purpose of this Partnership shall be to purchase, own as an investment, lease, improve, hypothe-cate and encumber, or sell, exchange or transfer the real property described in Exhibit "A" attached hereto and made a part hereof.

5. TERM OF PARTNERSHIP. The Partnership shall commence on the date of this Agreement and shall continue until such time as the General and Limited Partner shall give sixty (60) days written notice of termination or for five (5) years from the date hereof, whichever date is first to occur.

6. PARTNERSHIP CAPITAL CONTRIBUTIONS. On the execution hereof, each of the Partners, both Limited and General, agrees to contribute to the capital of the Partnership forthwith those sums set forth in Exhibit "B" of the Agreement, which total amounts shall be the capital contribution of such partner.

7. CAPITAL ACCOUNTS, PROFITS AND LOSSES AND CASH FLOW.

A. The capital accounts and profits and losses of the Partnership shall be kept and maintained in accordance with gen-erally accepted and recognized accounting principles and practices consistently applied, and profits and losses shall be determined in accordance therewith by the accountants of the Partnership.

-3-

The share of the profits which each partner, both Limited and General, shall receive, and the share of the losses to be borne and suffered by each partner, both Limited and Gen-eral, is as follows:

Bright Future 40%

Future Investments, Inc. 60%

The profits to be received, the losses to be suffered and borne by each partner shall not necessarily bear any relation-ship to the distribution of cash flow as hereinafter provided or to the capital accounts of each partner.

B. "Cash Flow" as herein used, is hereby defined as monies from any source in the Partnership available for distribution to the Limited and General Partner after all deductions therefrom as determined by the General Partner without regard to profits and losses. Cash flow shall be distributed from time to time as set forth below.

8. FUTURE CONTRIBUTIONS TO CAPITAL.

A. Except as expressly set forth in Exhibit B and below in Paragraphs B and C, no Limited or General Partner shall be required to contribute additional capital to the Partnership, and no interest shall be paid on any contribution made by any Limited or General Partner.

B. The General Partner may, from time to time, at his sole discretion, have the right in addition to those contribu-tions set forth in Exhibit "B" hereof to demand additional

-4-

capital contributions from the General and Limited Partner in an amount proportionate to their initial capital contribution set forth in Exhibit "B" and their share of profit and loss in order to provide the Partnership with reasonable funds to carry out the business purposes of the Partnership and to preserve Partnership assets. Such additional capital contributions shall only be made on the following conditions:

1. At least fifteen (15) days written notice of such contribution shall be given to the Limited Partner by the General Partner by registered or certified mail addressed to the address set forth in this Agreement or where the least tax return of this Partnership was mailed to each partner.

2. Said written notice shall specify the nature, purpose and proposed use of the funds requested and shall be accompanies by proof that the General Partner has deposited with the Partnership his proportionate share (which may be withdrawn by him if the Limited Partner fails to timely contribute its proportionate share).

3. Any additional capital contribution will not alter the Partnership status of any partner from a General Partner to a Limited Partner or from a Limited Partner to a General Partner.

4. The provisions hereof are for the sole benefit of the partners and shall not inure or give rights of any kind to the present and/or future creditors or third party claimants

-5-

of this Partnership.

5. Except as expressly otherwise set forth in this Agreement, no partner shall have the right to withdraw his capital contribution(s) or to demand or receive the return of his contribution(s) and each of the partners expressly waive any provisions of California law to the contrary.

9. CASH FLOW AND DISTRIBUTION THEREOF. The cash flow of the Partnership shall be distributed in the following manner:

A. First, to pay the just debts of the Partnership, including the amortization of secured and unsecured loans, mortgages or deeds of trust on real property owned by the Partnership;

Second, to such reasonable reserves as the General Partner shall determine is in the best interests of the Partnership;

Third, to each partner, a sum equal to their initial capital contribution plus any additional capital contributions set forth in Paragraph 8 above, less any capital contributions previously returned to said partners;

Fourth, to the partners in accordance with their then allocated percentage of profits and losses at the date of said distribution.

B. Distributions to the partners of cash flow of the Partnership shall be made at reasonable intervals during the fiscal year, and in any event, shall be made within ninety (90)

-6-

days after the close of each fiscal year.

10. ACCOUNTS AND RECORDS.

A. All funds of the Partnership shall be deposited in one or more bank accounts in the name of the Partnership. Partnership books shall be maintained at the principal office of the Partnership, and each partner or his duly authorized representative shall have access thereto at all reasonable times.

B. The General Partner shall cause to be prepared, within a reasonable period after the close of the fiscal year (not exceeding 90 days) and upon the termination of the Partnership, at the expense of the Partnership, a report of the Partnership's operation, containing a balance sheet and an income statement, and an informational tax return in the name of the Partnership. Within a reasonable period after the close of the period covered by the report (not exceeding 90 days), a copy of or a condensed version of the report and of the Partnership information tax return shall be furnished to each member of the Partnership at the expense of the Partnership.

C. In the event of a transfer of a Partnership interest during any calendar year, generally accepted accounting principles shall apply in making any allocation of profits or losses or rendering any interim accounting to the transferor and transferee.

11. ASSIGNABILITY OF A PARTNER'S INTEREST.

A. Each of the partners agree that they will not sell,

-7-

transfer, assign, pledge, encumber, mortgage or otherwise hypothecate the whole or any part of their interest in this Partnership without complying with the provisions of subparagraph B of this Paragraph. The transfer of an interest hereunder shall not cause a termination of the Partnership.

B. In the event that any partner shall desire to sell, assign, pledge, encumber, mortgage or otherwise hypothecate his interest in this Partnership, which offer is acceptable to such partner, such partner (hereinafter referred to as "selling party") may do so only in compliance with the following requirements and limitations:

1. The selling party shall send a copy of such offer by certified mail to the other Partner. Such offer shall thereupon be deemed to be an offer by the selling party to deal with his interest in the Partnership to the other Partner (hereinafter called "purchasing party"), upon the same terms and conditions as contained in the offer received by the selling party which he is willing to accept. Thereupon, the purchasing party shall notify the other Partner in writing by certified mail, within fifteen (15) days after mailing of the offer to them, as to whether he accepts such offer. Such offer shall be deemed to have been rejected if acceptance thereof is not mailed by the Partner by the end of said fifteen day period.

-8-

2. Upon such rejection, the selling party shall be free to deal with his interest so offered with the person named in the notice communicated to the other Partner; provided such transaction is consummated in strict accordance with the terms originally submitted by the selling party.

3. Upon acceptance by the purchasing party he (or it) shall be bound to comply with the terms of the offer in strict accordance with its terms.

C. Notwithstanding the above provisions, the interest of an individual partner may be transferred or disposed of by Will or intestacy, subject to the provisions herein set forth below in this Agreement.

D. No conveyance of a partner's interest, though otherwise permitted hereunder, shall be valid and effective, and the Partnership shall not recognize the same for the purposes of making payment of profits, cash flow, return of contribution, or other distributions with respect to such interest or any part thereof or with respect to other rights herein contained, unless transferred in accordance with the terms of this Paragraph, and the transferee agrees to be bound in writing by the terms of this Partnership Agreement and executes an appropriate written amendment to this Partnership Agreement.

12. ACCOUNTING YEAR. The accounting year of the Partnership shall be the calendar year.

-9-

13. RIGHTS, DUTIES AND OBLIGATIONS OF PARTNERS.

A. The General Partner shall have the control over the business of the Partnership, including the power to assign duties, to sign all contracts, to execute promissory notes, to execute leases and agreements, to assume all direction of business operations, to cause improvements to be constructed and to execute all agreements of every known nature in connection therewith or otherwise. Provided, however, the General Partner may not sell or encumber the property owned by the Partnership without the prior written consent of the Limited Partner.

B. Each of the Partners may engage in other business ventures exclusively for their own account, and may acquire, operate, and sell real and personal property without liability of any nature therefor to the Partnership or to the other Partner. No partner shall have any obligation or liability or duty to offer to the Partnership any business or investment or venture or other opportunity which may be presented to him even though it may be presented by reason of its connection with this Partnership, or by reason of being one of the partners thereof. Each partner shall have the right to engage in other business ventures or other business opportunities, even though in completion herewith. None of the partners shall devote their full-time and energy to the business affairs of the Partnership, but only shall devote so much of his time and attention to the Partnership business as he

-10-

thinks necessary or advisable. Bright Future, being a general contractor, shall be responsible for carrying out all those duties customarily performed by a general contractor including, but not limited to, the supervision and construction of improvements in accordance with approved plans and specifications. Furthermore, he shall devote all time necessary to let bids, obtain permits and perform all required services to supervise and coordinate all improvements to be constructed and supervise disbursement of construction funds.

C. The partners shall not be entitled to any salaries under this Agreement. Any construction of improvements shall be built for the Partnership at cost, and Bright Future shall gain no profit, and he shall not be reimbursed for any general overhead expenses incurred in the construction of said improvements.

14. RETIREMENT. The Partners shall have the right to retire from the Partnership at the end of any fiscal year upon mailing written notice of his intention to retire to the remaining Partner. Said notice shall be mailed at least ninety (90) days prior to the close of the fiscal year. The death or retirement of a General or Limited Partner shall not work dissolution of the Partnership, but the business shall continue without interruption and without any break in continuity. In the event of death, the legal representative of a deceased partner's Partnership interest,

-11-

and may become a substituted partner upon the terms and conditions set forth below. The Estate of the deceased Partner shall be liable for all of his liabilities and obligations to the Partnership. Such Partnership interest may be transferred upon death, notwithstanding the provisions of Paragraph 9 above. Upon the death of the General Partner, the Limited Partner shall elect a new General Partner.

15. SUBSTITUTED PARTNER. The partners must admit as substituted partners, persons, firms or corporations who acquire a Partnership interest or any part thereof of a partner provided the provisions of Paragraph 11, above, have been complied with. The admission of an assignee as a substituted partner shall be conditioned upon the assignee's agreement to pay or a payment of all sums due the Partnership by his assignor relating to the Partnership interest being acquired, and his acceptance and adoption of all of the terms and provisions of this Agreement in form satisfactory to all of the other partners. Any costs required, any filing fees incurred, including reasonable attorney's fees in effectuating such transfer and substitution as a partner, shall be paid by the assuming partner. An amended Agreement of Partnership shall be prepared and executed by all partners.

16. VOLUNTARY DISSOLUTION. Upon the unanimous agreement of all of the Partners, the Partnership may be dissolved and the assets liquidated forthwith. The Partnership shall engage in

-12-

no further business thereafter other than that necessary to wind up the business and distribute the assets. The maintenance of offices shall not be deemed a continuation of the business for purposes of this provision. The partners shall continue to divide profits and losses during the winding up period in the same ratio as profits and losses were divided prior to dissolution. The proceeds from the liquidation of Partnership assets shall be divided in the following order:

1. The expenses of liquidation and the debts of the Partnership, other than debts owing to the Partners, shall be paid;

2. Such debts as are owing to the Partners, including loans, and advances made to or for the benefit of the Partnership, shall be computed;

3. As provided in Paragraph 9, above.

The Partners shall cause to have published a Notice of Dissolution as required by law.

After all of the debts of the Partnership have been paid, the Partners may elect by mutual agreement of all Partners to distribute the assets of the Partnership in kind.

17. AMENDMENT OF PARTNERSHIP ARTICLES. These Articles may be amended by an agreement of the Limited and General Partner at any time during the continuance of the Partnership. All such amendments shall be in writing and signed by all of the said Partners.

-13-

18. LIMITATIONS ON PARTNER'S AUTHORITY. Notwithstanding Paragraph 13 above, no partner, General or Limited, without the written consent of the other Partner, shall engage in any of the following acts:

1. Sign, pledge, hypothecate, or mortgage any asset belonging to the Partnership, or execute any bond or lease in the Partnership name or sell the assets of the Partnership;

2. Pledge the credit of the Partnership in any way;

3. Make an assignment for the benefit of creditors;

4. Release, assign, or transfer a Partnership claim, security, or any other asset belonging to the Partnership;

5. Make, draw, or accept any notice or obligation for the payment of money;

6. Become a surety, guarantor, endorser, or accommodation endorser for any other person or firm;

7. Borrow any money in the name of the Partnership or lend any money belonging to the Partnership.

19. RIGHTS, POWERS AND RESTRICTIONS ON THE LIMITED PARTNER.

A. Notwithstanding anything to the contrary herein contained, the Limited Partner shall not become liable for any obligations or losses of this Partnership beyond the amounts of his respective capital contribution.

B. The Limited Partner shall not take part in the management of the business or transact any business for the Partnership and shall have no power to sign for or to bind the Partnership.

-14-

all of the parties are not signatories to the original, or the same counterpart.

23. CAPTIONS. Captions contained in this Agreement are inserted only as a matter of convenience, and in no way define, limit, extend or describe the scope of this Agreement or the intent of any provision thereof.

24. CONSTRUCTION. None of the provisions of this Agreement shall be for the benefit of or enforceable by any creditor of the Partnership.

This Agreement shall be construed exclusively in accordance with the laws and decisions of the State of California.

25. SUCCESSORS AND ASSIGNS. Subject to prohibitions against assignment and transfer, this Agreement shall inure to the benefit of and be binding upon the parties, their legal representatives and successors.

26. ARBITRATION. Any dispute or controversy arising under, out of, or in connection with, or in relation to this Certificate and Agreement, may, at the sole election of any partner, be determined by arbitration in Los Angeles, California, pursuant to the rules then obtaining of the American Arbitration Association, and judgment may be entered upon the award in any court having jurisdiction thereof which award shall be final and binding on all partners.

-16-

C. The General Partner shall not be liable, responsible or accountable in damages or otherwise to the Limited Partner for any act performed by them or for any nonaction or failure to act within the scope of the authority conferred on them by this Agreement or by law, except for acts of malfeasance or misfeasance. Without limiting the generality of the foregoing, it is expressly agreed that the General Partner shall not be personally liable for the return of the capital or any other contribution of the Limited Partner, or any portion thereof, but that, on the contrary, any such return shall be made solely from Partnership assets.

20. NOTICES. All notices, demands or other communication hereunder shall be in writing and shall be deemed to have been given when the same are:

1. Deposited in the United States mail and sent by certified or registered mail, postage prepaid; or

2. Delivered in each case to the parties at the addresses of each of the partners as set forth below.

21. COOPERATION. The partners shall execute and deliver such further instruments and do such further acts and things as may be required to carry out the intent and purpose of this Agreement.

22. AGREEMENT IN COUNTERPARTS. This Agreement may be executed in counterparts, and all so executed shall constitute one Agreement binding on all of the parties hereto, notwithstanding that

-15-

EXHIBIT "B"

GENERAL PARTNER	CAPITAL CONTRIBUTION - LAND	CAPITAL CONTRIBUTION - CASH	PERCENTAGE OF PROFIT AND LOSS
Bright Future	An undivided interest in and to the real property described in EXHIBIT "A" of this Agreement which the Partners agree has an agreed upon fair market value of $88,000	$20,000	40%
Future Investments, Inc.	An undivided 60% interest in and to the real property described in EXHIBIT "A" of this Agreement which the Partners agree has an agreed upon fair market value of $132,000	$30,000	60%

IN WITNESS WHEREOF, the parties hereto have executed and delivered this Agreement the day and year first above written.

BRIGHT FUTURE
_____
1000 - 1st Street
Los Angeles, California

FUTURE INVESTMENTS, INC.
c/o Meyers, Stevens & Walters
Professional Corporation
Suite 9100
6300 Wilshire Boulevard
Los Angeles, California 90048

By _____
   President

By _____
   Secretary

-17-

STATE OF CALIFORNIA } SS.
COUNTY OF Los Angeles

On January 1, 1981 before me, the undersigned, a Notary Public in and for said County and State, personally appeared ~~xxxxxxxxxx~~ ~~xxxxxxxx~~ JOHN SMITH, known to me to be the Secretary of the corporation that executed the within Instrument, and acknowledged to me that such corporation executed the within instrument pursuant to its by-laws or a resolution of its board of directors.

Signature _____

Name (Typed or Printed)
1-118   Notary Public in and for said County and State

(This area for official notarial seal)

STATE OF CALIFORNIA } SS.
COUNTY OF Los Angeles

On January 1, 1981 before me the undersigned, a Notary Public in and for said County and State, personally appeared BRIGHT FUTURE, known to me to be the person whose name is subscribed to the within instrument and acknowledged that he executed the same.

Signature _____

Name (Typed or Printed)
1-117   Notary Public in and for said County and State

FOR NOTARY SEAL OR STAMP

CHICAGO TITLE INSURANCE COMPANY

EXHIBIT "A"

LEGAL DESCRIPTION OF PROPERTY
TO BE ACQUIRED BY THE PARTNERSHIP

PARCEL 1:

The North 1/2 of Lot 39 and all of Lot 40, Block 40 of the Resubdivision of Blocks H and I of TERALTA, City and County of San Diego, State of California, according to Map thereof No. 1036, filed in the Office of the County Recorder of San Diego County, March 8, 1907.

PARCEL 2:

Lots 38 and the South 1/2 of Lot 39 in Block 40 of the Resubdivision of Blocks H and I of TERALTA, in the City of San Diego, County of San Diego, State of California, according to Map thereof No. 1036, filed in the Office of the County Recorder of San Diego County, March 8, 1907.

CERTIFICATE OF LIMITED
PARTNERSHIP OF SUPER
HOTEL LIMITED

This Certificate is executed this 1st day of January, 1981, between HOTEL DEVELOPERS, INC., a California corporation (hereinafter referred to as the "General Partner") and HOTEL INVESTORS, INC., a California corporation (hereafter referred to as the "Limited Partner").

W I T N E S S E T H:

WHEREAS, the Partners desire to form a limited partnership pursuant to Title 2, Chapter 2 of the California Corporations Code, known as the Uniform Limited Partnership Act, to hold real property, and for such other purposes and upon the terms and conditions hereinafter set forth:

NOW, THEREFORE, it is mutually agreed as follows:

1. Formation. The parties do hereby form a limited partnership pursuant to Title 2, Chapter 2 of the California Corporations Code for the purposes hereinafter provided.

2. Name. The name of this limited partnership shall be "SUPER HOTEL LIMITED".

3. Principal Place of Business. The principal place of business shall be located at 6300 Wilshire Boulevard, Suite 9100, Los Angeles, California 90048, or at such other place or places as the General Partner shall hereafter determine from time to time. Notice of any change shall be given by the General Partner to the Limited Partner.

4. Certificate of Limited Partnership. The General Partner shall cause this Certificate to be recorded in the office of the County Recorder of the county in which the principal place of business of the partnership is situated. If the partnership has places of business situated in different counties or holds property in different counties, a copy of this Certificate shall be recorded in compliance with the laws of the state in which such property is situated.

5. Certificate of Fictitious Name. Upon execution of this Certificate and any subsequent change in the membership of this limited partnership, the parties shall sign and cause to be filed and published in the county in which the principal place of business is situated, a certificate of fictitious name setting forth the name and residence of each partner.

6. Purpose. The purpose of this limited partnership shall be to manage, improve, hold, resell, exchange, lease and otherwise transfer that certain real property commonly known as 1000 South Wilshire Boulevard, Los Angeles, California, which is more particularly described in Exhibit "A" attached hereto and incorporated by reference herein, (hereafter described as "the Property"), and to carry on any and all activities, and to do any and all things necessary, related or incidental thereto, as the General Partner shall determine. The specific purposes hereinabove set forth do not limit the General Partner's authority or ability to act in any manner.

7. Term of Partnership. The partnership shall terminate upon the first of the following to occur:

(a) Twenty (20) years from the date hereof;

(b) Upon the affirmative vote of all of the partners;

(c) Upon the insolvency, retirement, death or insanity of the General Partner.

8. Contributions of the Limited Partner.

(a) Initial Contributions of the Limited Partner. The following will constitute the initial capital contributions of the Limited Partner to the Partnership:

(i) Title to the entire Property.

The Partners stipulate that the agreed value of this contribution is Six Hundred Twenty-Five Thousand Dollars ($625,000.00).

(ii) Twenty Thousand Dollars ($20,000.00).

(b) Subsequent Contributions of the Limited Partner. Except as expressly set forth below in this paragraph (b), the Limited Partner shall not be required to contribute additional capital to the

(i) The Selling Party shall send a photocopy of such offer, by certified mail, to the other partner. Such offer shall thereupon be deemed to be an offer by the Selling Party to sell to the other partner (hereinafter called the "Purchasing Party") the interest offered upon the same terms and conditions as contained in the offer received by the Selling Party. Thereafter, Purchasing Party shall notify the Selling Party, in writing, by certified mail within ten (10) days after receipt of the offer, as to whether he rejects or accepts such offer. Such offer shall be deemed to have been rejected by Purchasing Party whose acceptance of same is not received by the Selling Party by the end of the aforesaid ten (10) day period. If the Purchasing Party desires to purchase less than the entire interest offered, he shall set forth in his letter of acceptance the amount of interest that such Purchasing Party is willing to purchase, if available.

(ii) In the event that the aggregate total of partnership interests accepted, as aforesaid, by the Purchasing Party is less than the entire interest offered by the Selling Party, the Selling Party shall have the right to sell the said entire interest so offered to the person or persons named in the offer communicated to the Purchasing Party within forty-five (45) days from the date of mailing of the original offer to Purchasing Party, provided that such sale is made strictly in accordance with the terms of the offer originally submitted to the Purchasing Party and provided the requisite consent, if any, of all regulatory bodies is obtained.

(iii) In the event that the aggregate total of the partnership interest accepted as aforesaid by the Purchasing Party is equal to the entire interest offered by the Selling Party, the Selling Party shall be deemed bound to sell the entire interest offered, and the Purchasing Party shall be deemed bound to purchase the amount of partnership interest which each of them has accepted, in accordance with the terms and conditions set forth in the offer submitted to the Purchasing Party.

(c) No conveyance of a partner's interest or any part thereof, though otherwise permitted hereunder, shall be valid and effective, and the partnership shall not recognize the same for the purpose of making payment of profits, income, return of contribution or other distribution with respect to such interest or part thereof, unless transferred in accordance with the terms of this paragraph, or by a separate written agreement between the partners herein and the transferee agrees to be bound by the terms of this Certificate and any such separate written agreement and such transferee executes such documents as the General Partner shall

partnership. The General Partner may, from time to time, in his sole discretion and at his sole election, demand additional capital contributions from the Limited Partner in order to provide the partnership with reasonable funds to carry out the business purposes of the partnership and to preserve Partnership assets. Such additional capital contributions shall only be made on the following conditions: (i) At least thirty (30) days' written notice of said contribution if it exceeds Fifty Thousand Dollars ($50,000.00), or at least fifteen (15) days' written notice of said contribution if it does not exceed Fifty Thousand Dollars ($50,000.00), shall be given to the Limited Partner by the General Partner requesting said contributions as aforesaid and setting forth the date by which said contribution is to be made; (ii) The General Partner requesting such additional contribution shall post with the partnership a sum equal to one-hundred percent (100%) of the total contribution then requested of the Limited Partner, said sum to become the additional capital contribution of the General Partner. Said sum must be so posted on or before the date on which the Limited Partner is required to post his additional contribution.

9. Limited Partner's Share of Profits or Other Compensation by Way of Income. The share of profits or other compensation by way of income that the Limited Partner shall receive by reason of his initial contribution is fifty percent (50%) of the profits of the Partnership.

10. Assignability of Limited Partner's Rights and Interest.

(a) The Partners agree that the Limited Partner will not sell, transfer, assign, pledge, encumber, mortgage or otherwise hypothecate the whole or any part of his interest in the Partnership prior to the completion of the construction of improvements on the Partnership's Property set forth in Paragraph 6 above and thereafter agree that the Limited Partner may so assign such interest only in compliance with the provisions of subparagraph (b) below. The transfer of an interest hereunder shall not cause a dissolution of the partnership. As used below in this Paragraph 10, the word "sell" shall mean "sell, transfer, assign, pledge, encumber, mortgage or otherwise hypothecate."

(b) In the event that the Limited Partner shall desire to sell, and shall receive a written offer for the whole or any part of his interest in the Partnership, which offer is acceptable to such partner, such partner (hereinafter referred to as the "Selling Party") may sell the whole or any part of such interest, as the case may be, only in compliance with the following requirements and limitations:

reasonably request. Any costs and expenses or attorneys' fees incurred in connection with an invalid transfer of a partnership interest pursuant to this paragraph shall be borne by the partner attempting to make such a transfer.

(d) Only upon an assignment of Partnership interest as hereabove provided may a new Limited Partner be admitted to the Partnership.

11. Multiple Counterparts. This Certificate may be signed in multiple counterparts.

IN WITNESS WHEREOF, the parties have executed and delivered this Certificate the day and year first above written.

GENERAL PARTNER:
(Address)

    HOTEL DEVELOPERS, INC.,
    a corporation

    By _____

LIMITED PARTNER:
(Address)

    HOTEL INVESTORS, INC.,
    a corporation

    By _____

-5-

TO 449 CA (5-73)
(Corporation)

STATE OF CALIFORNIA
COUNTY OF LOS ANGELES } SS.

On _____ before me, the undersigned, a Notary Public in and for said State, personally appeared _____ President, and _____ known to me to be the _____ known to me to be the _____ Secretary of the corporation that executed the within Instrument, known to me to be the persons who executed the within Instrument on behalf of the corporation therein named, and acknowledged to me that such corporation executed the within instrument pursuant to its by-laws or a resolution of its board of directors.

WITNESS my hand and official seal.

Signature _____

Name (Typed or Printed)

(This area for official notarial seal)

STAPLE HERE

TO 449 CA (5-73)
(Corporation)

STATE OF CALIFORNIA
COUNTY OF LOS ANGELES } SS.

On _____ before me, the undersigned, a Notary Public in and for said State, personally appeared _____ President, and _____ known to me to be the _____ known to me to be the persons who executed the within Secretary of the corporation that executed the within Instrument, known to me to be the persons who executed the within Instrument on behalf of the corporation therein named, and acknowledged to me that such corporation executed the within instrument pursuant to its by-laws or a resolution of its board of directors.

WITNESS my hand and official seal.

Signature _____

Name (Typed or Printed)

(This area for official notarial seal)

STAPLE HERE

AGREEMENT AND ARTICLES OF LIMITED PARTNERSHIP OF SUPER HOTEL LIMITED

For good and valuable consideration, the receipt of which is hereby acknowledged, HOTEL DEVELOPERS, INC., a corporation (hereinafter "General Partner") and HOTEL INVESTORS, INC., a corporation (hereinafter "Limited Partner") hereby enter into this Agreement and Articles of Limited Partnership of Super Hotel Limited, a California limited partnership, (hereinafter "Agreement") this _____ day of _____, 1981. The Limited Partner and the General Partner are hereinafter referred to jointly as the "Partners". This Agreement incorporates herein by reference the Certificate of Limited Partnership of Super Hotel Limited (hereinafter "Certificate") executed by the General Partner and the Limited Partner concurrently herewith, a copy of which is attached as Exhibit "A" hereto. Super Hotel Limited is hereinafter referred to as the "Partnership".

WITNESSETH:

WHEREAS, the Partners desire to form a limited partnership pursuant to the provisions of the California Corporation Code, Title 2, Chapter 2, known as the Uniform Limited Partnership Act, to hold real property, and for such other purposes and upon the terms and conditions hereinafter set forth:

NOW THEREFORE, it is mutually agreed as follows:

1. Formation. The parties do hereby form a limited partnership pursuant to Title 2, Chapter 2 of the Corporations Code of the State of California for the purpose hereinafter provided.

2. Name. The name of this limited partnership shall be SUPER HOTEL LIMITED.

3. Principal Place of Business. The principal place of business shall be located at 6300 Wilshire Boulevard, Suite 9100, Los Angeles, California 90048, or at such other place or places as the General Partner shall hereafter determine from time to time. Notice of any change shall be given by the General Partner to the Limited Partner.

4. Certificate of Limited Partnership. The General Partner shall cause the Certificate to be recorded in the office of the County Recorder of the county in which the

principal place of business of the partnership is situated. If the partnership has places of business situated in different counties or holds property in different counties, a copy of the Certificate shall be recorded in compliance with the laws of the state in which such property is situated.

5. Certificate of Fictitious Name. Upon execution of this Agreement and any subsequent change in the membership of this Limited Partnership, the parties shall sign and cause to be filed and published in the county in which the principal place of business is situated a certificate of fictitious name setting forth the name and residence of each partner.

6. Purpose. The purpose of this Limited Partnership shall be to manage, improve, hold, resell, exchange, lease, and otherwise transfer that certain real property commonly known as 1000 South Wilshire Boulevard, Los Angeles, California, which is more particularly described in Exhibit "B" attached hereto and incorporated by reference herein, (hereafter described as "the Property"), and to carry on any and all activities, and to do any and all things necessary, related or incidental thereto, as the General Partner shall determine. The specific purposes hereinabove set forth do not limit the General Partner's authority to perform any and all acts he deems necessary.

7. Term of Partnership. The partnership shall terminate upon the first of the following to occur:

(a) Twenty (20) years from the date hereof;

(b) Upon the affirmative vote of all of the partners;

(c) Upon the insolvency, retirement, death or insanity of the General Partner.

8. Put Agreement.

(a) The Purpose. The purpose of this Put Agreement (as contained in this Article 8) is to create a power with an irrevocable interest in the General Partner to sell and an affirmative obligation in the Limited Partner and his successors to buy the property described in Paragraph 8 (b) according to the terms and conditions hereinafter described notwithstanding any other collateral agreement of the parties hereto including but not limited to the "Agreement", this Put Agreement and the "Certificate".

-2-

(b) The Put Property. The Put Property (hereinafter "Put Property") which is the subject of this Put Agreement is the General Partner's general partnership interest in the Partnership.

(c) The Sale Price. Subject to the fulfillment of the conditions precedent to the General Partner's exercise of his put set forth in Paragraph 8 (d) below, the exercise price of the sale of the Put Property described in Paragraph 8 (b) above shall be a sum equal to One Million Two Hundred Fifty Thousand Dollars ($1,250,000), plus all cash contributions plus loans made by the General Partner to the Partnership over and above the initial cash contributions of Six-Hundred Twenty-Five Thousand Dollars ($625,000), including (by way of illustration and not as a limitation) any and all costs concerning permanent financing, less all distributions made by the Partnership to the General Partner pursuant to Paragraph 11 (e) below.

(d) Conditions Precedent to Exercise of Put. The General Partner may exercise his put when and only when the following has occurred:

(i) The improvements to be constructed on the Property have been completed in substantial compliance with the plans, specifications and working drawings approved by the City of Los Angeles, and a Notice of Completion has been recorded.

(ii) The General Partner has procured a commitment for a long-term loan from a bank, savings and loan association, insurance company or correspondent thereof, real estate investment trust or pension plan in an amount not less than Three Million Dollars ($3,000,000.00) at the then prevailing interest rate and terms and in form used by said lender to be amortized in equal monthly installments of principal and interest over a period of not less than twenty (20) years, with a maturity date of not less than ten (10) years. Said loan shall be executed by and in the name of the Limited Partner or a party designated by him, but in no event shall the loan be made or be in the name of the General Partner or impose any personal liability on the General Partner. All fees, costs and expenses of said loan are to be paid by the Limited Partner.

(iii) The General Partner is not in default under this Agreement.

(e) Procedure for Exercise of Put. The General Partner shall notify the Limited Partner of his intention to exercise this Put by registered or certified mail, return receipt requested, addressed to the Limited Partner at the location set forth in the signature page herein, or at such location as is requested in writing by the Limited Partner. Within six (6) months from his receipt of the General Partner's notice and concurrently with the General Partner's tender, without recourse, of his entire, and unencumbered, interest in the Partnership, the Limited Partner shall transfer to the General Partner a certified check in the amount set forth in Paragraph 8 (c) above. The transfer of the General Partner's interest to the Limited Partner shall be in the form of an assignment by the General Partner to the Limited Partner of said General Partner's partnership interest in the Partnership. The General and Limited Partners agree to execute all instruments necessary to consummate said transfer, including but not limited to an amendment of the Agreement and of the Certificate and a revised Certificate of Fictitious Name.

(f) Term of This Put Agreement. This Put Agreement shall remain in full force and effect for a period of five (5) years from the date hereof, at which time the Put Agreement shall continue for successive six (6) month periods thereafter unless one of the Partners gives the other party three (3) months prior written notice of his intent thereafter to terminate the Put Agreement.

(g) Indemnification of General Partner Subsequent to Exercise of Put. Upon the conveyance of the General Partner's entire interest in the Partnership, pursuant to Paragraph 8 (e) above, the Limited Partner agrees hereby to indemnify the General Partner and hold him harmless from all claims of any kind or nature and the resulting costs, expenses, attorneys' fees and damages, if any, arising in connection with the General Partner's status as the former General Partner of the Partnership. This indemnification shall survive said conveyance by the General Partner and the dissolution of this Partnership and be binding upon the successors and assigns of the Limited Partner. The Limited Partner hereby authorizes the General Partner to formally dissolve the Partnership after the conveyance of the General Partner's interest in the Partnership unless an Amendment to the Agreement is promptly made removing the General Partner's name as a Partner in the Partnership.

(h) _Entire Agreement_. This Put Agreement (Paragraph 8) embodies the full and complete Put Agreement of the Partners and no changes or modifications shall be effective unless made in writing and signed by both of the Partners.

(i) _Attorneys' Fees_. In any action at law or in equity to enforce any of the provisions or rights under this Put Agreement, the unsuccessful party to such litigation, as determined by the Court in final judgment or decree, shall pay to the successful party or parties all costs, expenses and reasonable attorneys' fees incurred therein by such party or parties (including without limitation such costs, expenses and fees on any appeals), and if such successful party shall recover judgment in any such action or proceeding such costs, expenses and attorneys' fees shall be included in as part of such judgment.

(j) _General Partner's Rights upon Default by Limited Partner_. In the event that the Limited Partner fails to comply with the provisions of Paragraph 8 (e) above (time being of the essence), the General Partner shall have the following additional rights to be exercised by the General Partner at his option within one year from said default by the Limited Partner:

(i) The right to require the Limited Partner to sell to the General Partner all of the Limited Partner's limited partnership interest in the Partnership, for a price equal to (I) Six Hundred Forty-Five Thousand Dollars ($645,000.00), plus (II) all subsequent contributions and/or loans made by the Limited Partner to the Partnership (III) less distributions which the Partnership has made to the Limited Partner other than that distribution expressly provided by Paragraph 11 (e) below to be made on _____, _____; or

(ii) The right to sell all of the assets of the Partnership and to distribute the proceeds from such sale as follows:

(I) First, to the General Partner, an amount equal to One-Million Two Hundred Seventy Thousand Dollars ($1,270,000.00) plus all contributions and/or loans which were made by the General Partner to the Partnership other than the initial contributions of the General Partner as set forth in Paragraph 10 (a) of the Agreement, less all distributions which were made by the Partnership to the General Partner pursuant to Paragraph 11 (e) of the Agreement.

-5-

balance of the proceeds.

(II) Secondly, to the Limited Partner, the

9. Option to Purchase.

(a) _The Purpose_. The purpose of this Option Agreement (as contained in this Paragraph 9) is to create a power with an irrevocable interest in the Limited Partner to buy the property described in Paragraph 9 (b) according to the terms and conditions hereinafter described notwithstanding any other collateral agreement of the parties hereto including but not limited to the "Agreement", this Option Agreement and the "Certificate".

(b) _The Option Property_. The Option Property (hereinafter "Option Property") which is the subject of this Option Agreement is the General Partner's general partnership interest in the Partnership.

(c) _The Sale Price_. Subject to the fulfillment of the conditions precedent to the Limited Partner's exercise of his option set forth in Paragraph 9 (d) below, the exercise price of the sale of the Option Property described in Paragraph 9 (b) above shall be a sum equal to One Million Two Hundred Fifty Thousand Dollars ($1,250,000.00), plus all cash contributions and/or loans by the General Partner to the Partnership over and above the initial cash contributions of Six-Hundred Twenty-Five Thousand Dollars ($625,000.00), including (by way of illustration and not as a limitation) any and all costs concerning permanent financing, less all distributions made by the Partnership to the General Partner pursuant to Paragraph 11 (e) below.

(d) _Conditions Precedent to Exercise of Option_. The Limited Partner may exercise his option when and only when the following has occurred:

(i) The improvements to be constructed on the Property have been completed in substantial compliance with the plans, specifications and working drawings approved by the City of Los Angeles, and a Notice of Completion has been recorded;

(ii) The General Partner has procured a commitment for a long-term loan from a bank, savings and loan association, insurance company or correspondent thereof, real estate investment trust or pension plan in an amount not less than Three Million Dollars ($3,000,000.00) at the then prevailing interest rate and terms and in form used by said lender to be amortized in equal monthly installments of principal and

-6-

interest over a period of not less than twenty (20) years, with a maturity date of not less than ten (10) years;

(iii) The Limited Partner obtains a full release from the interim construction lender and permanent lender releasing the General Partner from all liability thereunder; and

(iv) The Limited Partner is not in default under the Agreement.

(e) Procedure for Exercise of Option and Term of Option.

(i) The Limited Partner shall notify the General Partner of his intent to exercise his option to purchase by registered or certified mail, return receipt requested, at the location set forth in the signature page herein or at such other location as is requested in writing by the General Partner.

(ii) Such notice shall be made within ninety (90) days from the recording by the General Partner of a Notice of Completion and shall be accompanied by a cashier's check for Sixty-Five Thousand Dollars ($65,000.00), payable to the General Partner. Should the Limited Partner timely conclude the purchase of the Option Property said sum shall be applied to the Option price. Should the limited Partner fail to timely consummate the purchase of the Option Property, upon consideration of the anticipated damage accruing to the General Partner due to the Limited Partner's failure to so consummate said purchase, and in recognition of the cost and difficulty involved in establishing the cause, foreseeable consequences and actual damages attendant to such a breach of obligations, the Partners agree that the following conditions for the imposition of and the amount of liquidated damages are reasonable under the circumstances at the date hereof. The General Partner shall be entitled to retain the above sum of Sixty-Five Thousand Dollars ($65,000.00) as liquidated damages.

By their signatures below, the Partners acknowledge that they have read and understood the above paragraph covering the imposition of liquidated damages.

_____

_____

-7-

than ninety (90) days from the date of the notice by the Limited Partner to the General Partner as provided in Paragraph 9 (e) (i) above, time being of the essence.

(iv) The transfer of the General Partner's interest to the Limited Partner shall be in the form of an assignment by the General Partner to the Limited Partner of said General Partner's partnership interest in the Partnership. The General and Limited Partners agree to execute all instruments necessary to consummate said transfer, including but not limited to an amendment of the Agreement and of the Certificate and a revised Certificate of Fictitious Name.

(f) Indemnification of General Partner Subsequent to Exercise of Option. Upon the conveyance of the General Partner's entire interest in the Partnership, pursuant to Paragraph 9 (e) above, the Limited Partner agrees hereby to indemnify the General Partner and hold him harmless from all claims of any kind or nature and the resulting costs, expenses, permanent financing, attorneys' fees or damages, if any, arising in connection with the General Partner's status as the former General Partner of the Partnership. This indemnification shall survive said conveyance by the General Partner and the dissolution of this Partnership and be binding upon the successors and assigns of the limited Partner. The Limited Partner hereby authorizes the General Partner to formally dissolve the Partnership after the conveyance of the General Partner's interest in the Partnership unless an Amendment to the Agreement is promptly made removing the General Partner's name as a Partner in the Partnership.

(g) Entire Agreement. This Option Agreement (Paragraph 9) embodies the full and complete Option Agreement of the Partners and no changes or modifications shall be effective unless made in writing and signed by both of the Partners.

(h) Attorneys' Fees. In any action at law or in equity to enforce any of the provisions or rights under this Option Agreement, the unsuccessful party to such litigation, as determined by the Court in final judgment or decree, shall pay the successful party or parties all costs, expenses and reasonable attorneys' fees incurred therein by such party or parties (including without limitation such costs, expenses and fees on any appeals), and if such successful party shall recover judgment in any such action or proceeding such costs, expenses and attorneys' fees shall be included in as part of such judgment.

-8-

Partner. (i) General Partner's Rights upon Default by Limited Partner. In the event that the Limited Partner fails to comply with the provisions of Paragraph 9 (e) above, the General Partner shall have the following additional rights to be exercised by the General Partner at his option within one year from said default by the Limited Partner:

(i) The right to retain the sum of Sixty-Five Thousand Dollars ($65,000.00) as liquidated damages as set forth above; and

(ii) The right to require the Limited Partner to sell to the General Partner all of the Limited Partner's limited partnership interest in the Partnership, for a price equal to (I) Six Hundred Forty-Five Thousand Dollars ($645,000.00), plus (II) all subsequent contributions and/or loans made by the Limited Partner to the Partnership (III) less distributions which the Partnership has made to the Limited Partner other than that distribution expressly provided by Paragraph 11 (e) below to be made on March 1, 1981; or

(iii) The right to sell all of the assets of the Partnership and to distribute the proceeds from such sale as follows:

(I) First, to the General Partner, an amount equal to One-Million Two-Hundred Seventy Thousand Dollars ($1,270,000.00) plus all contributions and/or loans which were made by the General Partner to the Partnership other than the initial contributions of the General Partner as set forth in Paragraph 10 (a) of the Agreement, less all distributions which were made by the Partnership to the General Partner pursuant to Paragraph 11 (e) of the Agreement.

(II) Secondly, to the Limited Partner, the balance of the proceeds.

10. Contributions of the Partners.

(a) Initial Contributions of the Partners.

(i) By the General Partner. The total initial capital contribution of the General Partner to the Partnership shall be in the sum of Six-Hundred Forty-Five Thousand Dollars ($645,000.00), which sum shall be paid by the General Partner and shall be allocated as follows:

-9-

(A) By the General Partner taking subject to approximately Two-Hundred Ninety-Thousand Dollars ($290,000.00) of principal plus accrued interest which is owing on a Note secured by a Deed of Trust on the Property. Copies of said Note and Deed of Trust are attached hereto as Exhibit "C" and incorporated herein by this reference. The total sums owing to the beneficiary shall be determined from a Beneficiary Statement to be obtained from the present holder of said Note. While the Partnership is to take title to said Property subject to said Note and Deed of Trust, as between the Partners, all payments to be made on said Note after the date on which title to said Lots is recorded in the name of the Partnership, are to be made by the General Partner from his own funds as part of his contribution as General Partner. All sums paid on said Note and to remove the lien against the Property, including all interest, penalties, costs and fees, shall be credited toward the General Partner's initial capital contribution.

(B) Payment by the General Partner on _____ or before _____, of approximately _____ Thousand Dollars. The precise amount of said contribution will be determined by subtracting the total of the General Partner's contributions made pursuant to Paragraph 10 (a) (i) immediately above from the General Partner's total contribution of Six-Hundred Forty-Five Thousand Dollars ($645,000.00). Notwithstanding any other provisions of this Agreement, said sum shall be distributed by the Partnership to the Limited Partner on or before _____. Said distribution shall have no effect on the provisions of Paragraph 11, below.

(ii) By the Limited Partner. The following will constitute the initial capital contributions of the Limited Partner to the Partnership:

(A) Title to the entire Property. The Limited Partner's contribution to the Partnership shall be his interest in the Property. It is agreed between the Partners that the Property, if free and clear of all liens and encumbrances, has a current fair market value of One-Million Two-Hundred Fifty Thousand Dollars ($1,250,000.00). In reaching this agreed-upon fair market value, the Partners believe that said sum represents the current true value thereof and is based in part on an appraisal, a copy of which is attached hereto as Exhibit "_" and made a part hereof. However, the Property is subject to various liens and in part is to be acquired by the Partnership as provided elsewhere in this Agreement. In addition, the Limited Partner is sharing in the profits, losses and cash flow as provided elsewhere in this

-1C-

Agreement. In addition, the Limited Partner is sharing in the profits, losses and cash flow as provided in this Agreement. It is thus agreed that the agreed value of the Limited Partner's contribution of his interest in the Property is Six Hundred Twenty-Five Thousand Dollars ($625,000.00). The obligation of the General Partner to make his initial capital contributions is conditioned upon: (1) The conveyance of the Property to the Partnership; (2) The issuance of an ALTA owner's policy of title insurance in form approved by the General Partner; and (3) the General Partner's approval of the General Beneficiary Statement on all encumbrances of record against the Property.

(B) Payment concurrently herewith of Twenty Thousand Dollars ($20,000.00) which will be placed in the Partnership bank account. Said sum will be used for the operation and the administration of the Partnership.

(iii) Simultaneous Contributions. All of the initial contributions as specified in this Paragraph 10 (a) shall be made simultaneously, except that:

(A) The contributions to be made by the General Partner pursuant to Paragraph 1C(a)(i)(A), may, in the sole discretion and at the sole election of the General Partner, be paid in installments pursuant to the terms of the respective Notes or may be prepaid in whole or in part at any time.

(B) The contribution to be made by the General Partner pursuant to Paragraph 10 (a) (i) (b) may be made at any time on or before March 1, 1981.

(b) Subsequent Contributions of Partners. Except as expressly set forth below in this Paragraph (b), no Partner shall be required to contribute additional capital to the Partnership. The General Partner may, from time to time, in his sole discretion and at his sole election, demand additional capital contributions from the Limited Partner in order to provide the Partnership with reasonable funds to carry out the business purposes of the Partnership and to preserve Partnership assets. Such additional capital contributions shall only be made on the following conditions:

(i) Written notice of said contribution shall be given to the Limited Partner by the General Partner requesting said contribution as aforesaid and setting forth the date by which said contribution is to be made. If the amount so demanded of the Limited Partner does not exceed Fifty-Thousand Dollars ($50,000.00), at least fifteen (15)

-11-

days' written notice must be given as aforesaid. If the amount so demanded of the Limited Partner exceeds Fifty-Thousand Dollars ($50,000.00), at least thirty (30) days' written notice must be given as aforesaid.

(ii) The General Partner requesting such additional contribution shall post with the Partnership a sum equal to one-hundred percent (100%) of the total contribution then requested of the Limited Partner, said sum to become the additional capital contribution of the General Partner. Said sum must be so posted on or before the date on which the Limited Partner is required to post his additional contribution.

(iii) In the event that either Partner, hereafter referred to as the "defaulting Partner", fails to pay his allocable portion of the additional capital within the time set forth in the notice described above in (i), time being of the essence, the following shall apply:

(A) The capital account of the defaulting Partner shall not be credited with the additional contribution.

(B) The General Partner, in his sole discretion and at his sole election, may engage in any of the following four activities or any combination of the first three thereof, provided that the total of additional funds provided to the Partnership pursuant to Paragraphs (1), (2) and (3) below shall not exceed the amount demanded of the defaulting Partner pursuant to Paragraph (i) above.

(1) The General Partner may make a further capital contribution and/or may solicit and receive a further capital contribution from the Limited Partner. The capital account of each Partner and his respective interest in the profits and losses of the Partnership shall be adjusted in order to correspond to the percentage of the total capital contributions, initial and subsequent, which he has contributed.

(2) The General Partner may loan money to the Partnership pursuant to Paragraphs 14 and 15 hereinbelow.

(3) The General Partner may borrow money from third parties on behalf of the Partnership, pledging, encumbering or otherwise hypothecating any partnership property, to the extent required (as determined by the General Partner) to secure any such loan.

-12-

the defaulting Partner.   (4) The General Partner may buy out the defaulting Partner. In order to buy out the defaulting Partner, the General Partner must pay him a sum which equals Six-Hundred Forty-Five Thousand Dollars ($645,000.00) plus all subsequent contributions which the defaulting partner has made to the Partnership, less all distributions which the Partnership has made to the defaulting Partner other than that distribution expressly provided by Paragraph 11 (e) below to be made on March 1, 1981. In the event of such buy-out, the Limited Partner shall, concurrently with payment to him, assign his Limited Partnership interest to the General Partner and execute all documents to consummate such a transfer.

(C) The only penalties imposed upon a defaulting Partner for failure to pay his contribution shall be as provided immediately above in Paragraphs (A) and (B).

(D) The provisions hereof are for the sole benefit of the Partners and shall not inure or give rights of any kind or nature to the present and/or future creditors or claimants of the Partnership.

11. Profits and Losses, Net Cash Flow, and the Allocation and Distribution Thereof.

(a) "Profits and Losses" shall mean those profits and losses determined by the use of generally accepted accounting principles consistently applied for the purpose of determining state and federal income taxes. The profits and losses to be received by each Partner shall not necessarily bear any relationship to the distribution of net cash flow defined below.

(b) "Net Cash Flow" shall mean all monies received by the Partnership from any source including but not limited to cash received from operations, borrowings, sales of real or personal property or refinancing, after the deduction of all necessary Partnership cash expenditures less such reasonable reserves as determined by the General Partner to be required for working capital, or unforseen contingencies.

(c) Allocation of Profits and Losses. The allocation of profits to be received and losses to be borne by each Partner is as follows:

HOTEL DEVELOPERS, INC.   50%
HOTEL INVESTORS, INC.   50%

-13-

(d) Allocation of Net Cash Flow. The allocation of net cash flow shall be in the following order and amounts:

(i) Ratably to the Partners in an amount equal to their capital contributions set forth in Paragraph 10 above; less any capital contribution previously paid to the Partners;

(ii) As to the remainder of the net cash flow, fifty percent (50%) to the General Partner and fifty percent (50%) to the Limited Partner.

(e) Distribution of Cash Flow. Distributions of cash flow to the Partners shall be made at reasonable intervals during the accounting year, as determined by the General Partner, but in any event shall be made within ninety (90) days after the close of the Partnership's accounting year. Such distributions shall be made in compliance with Section 15516 of the California Corporations Code.

12. Capital Accounts. Capital accounts shall be kept and maintained for each Partner in accordance with generally accepted accounting principles consistently applied. Such capital accounts shall be adjusted from time to time to reflect additional contributions to capital, if any, allocation of profits and losses and distributions of Partnership assets including the distribution of net cash flow.

13. Withdrawal of Capital. Except as otherwise provided in this Agreement, no Partner may withdraw his capital from the Partnership without the consent of all Partners, Limited and General.

14. Source of Additional Funds. In the event that the capital contributions set forth in Paragraph 10 above are insufficient to meet necessary Partnership expenditures, the General Partner may, but without the obligation to do so, loan from time to time such monies to the Partnership. Each such loan shall be evidenced by a promissory note and shall bear interest at a rate as determined by the General Partner, not to exceed the maximum legal rate, and each such loan shall be repaid from the first Partnership funds available after the payment of non-partner creditors.

15. Loans. If any Partner, in addition to this contribution to his respective capital account of the Partnership, should advance monies to the Partnership on behalf of the Partnership, such advance shall not entitle such Partner to any increase in the share of the distribution of the profits

-14-

and losses and/or cash flow of the Partnership. Any such advance shall be deemed an obligation of the Partnership to such Partner and shall bear interest at a rate as determined by the General Partner, not to exceed the maximum legal rate. Notwithstanding the provisions of this Agreement, no Limited Partner shall advance monies on behalf of the Partnership without the approval of the General Partner, provided, however, that the General Partner may advance monies to the Partnership to meet the expenses and obligations of the Partnership although the General Partner is not required to do so.

16. Management.

(a) The General Partner shall have exclusive control over the business of the Partnership and shall have authority to act on behalf of the Partnership in all matters respecting the Partnership, its business, and its property, unless limited expressly hereafter. The General Partner shall have authority to employ, at the expense of the Partnership, such agents, employees, independent contractors, attorneys, and accountants as he deems reasonably necessary; to create by grant or otherwise, easements and servitudes; to improve and repair Partnership property; to effect necessary insurance for the property protection of the Partnership and any of the Partners; to pay, collect, compromise, arbitrate, or otherwise adjust any and all claims or demands of or against the Partnership. The General Partner shall devote such time to the business of the Partnership as he shall deem reasonably necessary. The General and the Limited Partner may engage in other business ventures exclusively for their own account and may acquire, operate and sell real property for their own account. The Partnership shall indemnify and hold harmless the General Partner on account of loss, damage or liability for any and all acts done in good faith on behalf of the Partnership.

(b) The General Partner shall be responsible for the development of the Property and shall have the right to enter into contracts with the Partnership (in his individual capacity or with a corporation in which he has an interest) concerning any and all aspects of the development, design, financing and construction on the Property. The General Partner shall provide the following services concerning said development: supervision of the architect, mechanical engineering, structural engineering, electrical engineering, supervision of soil tests and surveys, and on-site supervision during the course of construction. For such enumerated services, the General Partner shall receive a sum equal to fifteen percent (15% of the total costs of construction (including financing

-15-

costs) of the improvements ultimately constructed on the Property. Said compensation shall be in payment for the enumerated services of the General Partner, shall have no affect on any other right which the General Partner has according to the terms of this Agreement or at law to receive funds related to the Partnership for his personal benefit, and shall have no affect on the distribution of profits and losses (and/or cash flow) of the Partnership. The General Partner shall use his best efforts to cause the Partnership to construct on the Property a "completed building", herein defined to mean a building which has received a Notice of Completion and which includes tacked-down carpets, drapes and light fixtures, but does not include other fixtures or articles of personal property. This obligation of the General Partner shall not impose any additional financial or personal obligation on the General Partner.

(c) The General Partner shall be compensated by the Partnership for his out-of-pocket expenses for the benefit of the Partnership, including (by way of example and not limitation) accountants fees and attorneys fees. Said compensable out-of-pocket expenses shall not include expenses for the overhead of any office which the General Partner does not use exclusively for the Partnership, for business driving, or for business entertaining.

(d) Except as provided in this Agreement, the General Partner shall not be entitled to receive from the Partnership any salary or other compensation.

17. Limited Partner's Activities and Liabilities. The Limited Partner shall take no part in the conduct or control of the partnership business, including (by way of illustration and not as a limitation) construction of the contemplated improvements on the Property, and shall have no right or authority to act for or bind the Partnership. The Limited Partner shall not be personally liable for any of the debts of the Partnership or any of the losses thereof beyond the amount contributed by him to the capital of the Partnership.

18. Books of Account and Records.

(a) The General Partner shall keep or cause to be kept books of account fully and accurately detailing each Partnership transaction.

(b) The books of account, Certificate, Agreement, and fictitious business name statement shall be kept at the principal office of the Partnership, and shall be open for inspection and examination by the Partners or their representative during reasonable business hours.

-16-

such offer, by certified mail, to the other Partner. Such offer shall thereupon be deemed to be an offer by the Selling Party to sell to the other Partner (hereinafter called the "Purchasing Party") the interest offered upon the same terms and conditions as contained in the offer received by the Selling Party. Thereupon, Purchasing Party shall notify the Selling Party, in writing, by certified mail within ten (10) days after receipt of the offer, as to whether he rejects or accepts such offer. Such offer shall be deemed to have been rejected by Purchasing Party whose acceptance of same is not received by the Selling Party by the end of the aforesaid ten (10) day period. If the Purchasing Party desires to purchase less than the entire interest offered, he shall set forth in his letter of acceptance the amount of interest that such Purchasing Party is willing to purchase, if available.

(ii)   In the event that the aggregate total of Partnership interests accepted, as aforesaid, by the Purchasing Party is less than the entire interest offered by the Selling Party, the Selling Party shall have the right to sell the said entire interest so offered to the person or persons named in the offer communicated to the Purchasing Party within forty-five (45) days from the date of mailing of the original offer to Purchasing Party, provided that such sale is made strictly in accordance with the terms of the offer originally submitted to the Purchasing Party and provided the requisite consent, if any, of all regulatory bodies is obtained.

(iii)   In the event that the aggregate total of the Partnership interest accepted as aforesaid by the Purchasing Party is equal to the entire interest offered by the Selling Party, the Selling Party shall be deemed bound to sell the entire interest offered, and the Purchasing Party shall be deemed bound to purchase the amount of Partnership interest which each of them has accepted, in accordance with the terms and conditions set forth in the offer submitted to the Purchasing Party.

(c)   No conveyance of a Partner's interest or any part thereof, though otherwise permitted hereunder, shall be valid and effective, and the Partnership shall not recognize the same for the purpose of making payment of profits, income, return of contribution or other distribution with respect to such interest or part thereof, unless transferred in accordance with the terms

-13-

(c)   Within ninety (90) days after the close of the Partnership accounting year, and upon the Partnership's termination, the General Partner shall prepare or cause to be prepared by a public accountant an annual balance sheet and profit and loss statement and Partnership information tax return as of the close of each accounting year. Within a reasonable time thereafter, said financial statements shall be furnished to each member of the Partnership.

(d)   The books of account shall be kept according to generally accepted accounting principles consistently applied.

19.   Banking.   The General Partner shall have the right to open one or more checking accounts and/or savings accounts at such bank or banks or savings and loan associations, or similar institutions, that the General Partner deems appropriate. Any person or persons so designated by the General Partner shall be authorized to perform those duties with respect to said account or accounts as specified by the General Partner. The signature power of any person with respect to the signing of checks or carrying on said account transactions may be terminated by the General Partner upon giving written notice to the financial institution or institutions involved, and to the person to whom the signature power is being terminated. The General Partner shall also have the right to utilize a bank as a collection and/or disbursing agent of the Partnership.

20.   Assignability of Partner's Rights and Interest.

(a)   The Partners agree that they will not sell, transfer, assign, pledge, encumber, mortgage or otherwise hypothecate the whole or any part of their interest in the Partnership prior to the completion of the construction of improvements on the Partnership's property set forth in Paragraph 6 above and thereafter they agree to so assign such interest only in compliance with the provisions of Subparagraph (b) below. The transfer of an interest hereunder shall not cause a dissolution of the Partnership. As used below in this Paragraph 20, the word "Sell" shall mean "sell, transfer, assign, pledge, encumber, mortgage or otherwise hypothecate".

(b)   In the event that any Partner shall desire to sell, and shall receive a written offer for the whole or any part of his interest in the Partnership, which offer is acceptable to such Partner, such Partner (hereinafter referred to as the "Selling Party") may sell the whole or any part of such interest, as the case may be, only in compliance with the following requirements and limitations:

-17-

of this paragraph, and the transferee agrees to be bound by the terms of this Limited Partnership Agreement and such transferee executes such documents as the General Partner reasonably request. Any costs and expenses or attorneys' fees incurred in connection with an invalid transfer of a Partnership interest pursuant to this paragraph shall be borne by the Partner attempting to make such a transfer.

(d) If the General Partner desires to transfer his interest in the Partnership, the foregoing procedures shall be followed, provided, however, that such interest shall become a Limited Partnership interest upon such transfer, and if the entire interest of the General Partner is transferred, a new General Partner shall be selected by the affirmative vote or written consent of Partner(s) having a simple majority interest in the total capital of the Partnership. The former General Partner shall send written notice to all the other Partner(s) either calling a meeting of Partner(s) or seeking their written consent to the election of a new General Partner pursuant to this provision.

(e) Only upon an assignment of Partnership interest as hereabove provided in this Paragraph 20 may a new Limited Partner be admitted to the Partnership.

21. Proceeds from Sale and/or Financing of Partnership Property. The proceeds from the sale and/or financing of the Partnership real property shall be distributed to all Partners within thirty (30) days from said sale and/or financing. Any such proceeds distributed shall be divided and distributed in the following order:

(a). The expenses of sale and/or financing and the debts of the Partnership other than any debts owing to the Partners shall be paid.

(b) Such debts of the Partnership as are owing to the Partners, including any loans and advances and reimbursement for expenses of the Partnership, shall be paid.

(c) The remaining proceeds shall be distributed among the Partners to the same extent and in the same manner that the Partners share in the cash flow.

22. Voluntary Dissolution and Distribution of Partnership Property.

(a) Upon the affirmative vote of all of the Partners, both General and Limited, the Partnership shall be dissolved and its assets liquidated. The Partnership shall engage in no further business thereafter, other than that necessary to wind

-19-

up the business and distribute the assets. The maintenance of offices shall not be deemed a continuance of the business for purposes of this section. The Partners shall continue to divide profits and losses during the winding up period in the same ratio as profits and losses were divided immediately prior to dissolution. The proceeds from the liquidation of Partnership assets shall be divided in the same manner as set forth in Paragraph 21 above.

(b) Upon dissolution, and at the Partnership's expense, the General Partner shall cause to be performed those acts necessary to formally dissolve the Partnership.

23. Amendments. This Agreement shall be amended whenever:

(a) There is a change in the name of the Partnership or the amount or character of the contribution of any Partner;

(b) A person is substituted as a Limited Partner;

(c) An additional Limited Partner is admitted;

(d) A person is admitted as a General Partner;

(e) There is a change in the character of the business of the Partnership;

(f) There is a false or erroneous statement contained herein; or,

(g) There is a change in the time as stated in this Agreement for dissolution of the Partnership or for the return of a contribution.

24. Notices. Unless otherwise specified in writing sent to the General Partner, all notices required by this Agreement shall be sent by registered or certified mail to the addresses of the Partners as set forth on the signature page hereof. The General Partner shall be notified in writing of any change of address by the Limited Partner.

25. Captions. Any section or paragraph titles or captions contained in this Agreement are for convenience only, and shall not be deemed part of the context of this Agreement.

26. Variations in Pronouns and Gender. All pronouns and any variations thereof shall be deemed to refer to the masculine, feminine, neuter, singular or plural as the identity of the person or persons, firm or firms, corporation or corporations, may require.

-20-

(b) The tax consequences that will be obtained from the formation, operation, and ultimate distribution of Partnership assets.

34. Arbitration. Any dispute or controversy arising under, out of, or in connection with, or in relation to the Certificate and/or the Agreement may, at the election of the General or Limited Partner, be determined by arbitration in Los Angeles, California, pursuant to the rules then obtaining of the American Arbitration Association and judgment may be entered upon the award. The cost of arbitration shall be borne by the unsuccessful party. The arbitrators may award reasonable attorneys' fees to the prevailing party.

35. Applicable Law. All the terms and provisions of this Agreement shall be interpreted under the law of the State of California.

IN WITNESS WHEREOF, the parties have executed and delivered this Agreement the day and year first above written.

GENERAL PARTNER: HOTEL DEVELOPERS, INC.
(Address)

        By _____

LIMITED PARTNER: HOTEL INVESTORS, INC.
(Address)

        By _____

---

27. Validity. In the event that any provision of this Agreement shall be held to be invalid, the same shall not affect in any respect whatsoever the validity of the remainder of this Agreement.

28. Further Acts. Each Partner agrees to perform any further acts and execute and deliver any documents which may reasonably be necessary to carry out the provisions of this Agreement.

29. Binding. This Agreement shall be binding upon the heirs, personal representatives, assigns and successors in interest of the Partners. The Partners agree for themselves and for their heirs, personal representatives, assigns, and successors in interest to execute any instrument in writing which may be necessary or property carry out the purposes and intent of this Agreement.

30. Agreements. This Agreement contains the entire understanding between the Partners. There are no representations, agreements, arrangements or understanding, oral or written, between or among the Partners relating to the subject matter of this Agreement, which are not fully expressed herein. This Agreement may be amended from time to time by the written agreement of the Partners holding a simple majority in interest in the total capital account of the Partnership from time to time existing.

31. Multiple Counterparts. This Agreement may be signed in multiple counterparts.

32. Other Activity. Each Partner, both Limited and General, may engage in other business activity and business ventures exclusively for his own account, and may acquire, operate and sell real and personal property without liability or obligation of any kind or nature to this Partnership or the Partners thereof. No Partner shall have any obligation or duty to offer to this Partnership or any Partner thereof any business or investment or other opportunity of any kind or nature even though in competition herewith.

33. Business Results. The General Partner makes no representations or warranties as to:

(a) The success of the Partnership, nor does he guaranty that this Partnership will make a profit. The Partners recognize that their investment herein is speculative in nature.

JOINT VENTURE AGREEMENT

THIS JOINT VENTURE AGREEMENT ("Agreement") is made and entered into this ——— day of March, 1981, at Los Angeles, California, by and between PERFECT REAL ESTATE INVESTMENTS, a California partnership (hereinafter "PREI"), and ABC PROPERTIES, a California general partnership (hereinafter "ABC"), with respect to the recitals as follows:

RECITALS

A. PREI hereby represents and warrants unto ABC that PREI is a California partnership, that John Smith is the sole managing partner thereof, and that PREI is authorized and empowered to enter into this Agreement and that the same is, in all respects, binding upon it;

B. ABC hereby represents and warrants unto PREI that ABC is a California general partnership, that Sam Jones, Jack Jones, and Robert Doe are all of the general partners thereof, and that ABC is authorized and empowered to enter into this Agreement and that the same is, in all respects, binding upon it;

C. PREI is the fee owner of that certain real property situated in the County of Los Angeles, State of California, described as follows:

-1-

Parcel 1 in the County of Los Angeles, State of California, as shown on Parcel Map No. 12345, filed in Book 10 Pages 1 to 7 inclusive of Parcel Maps in the office of the County Recorder of said County.

Said real property is subject only to such matters of record as set forth in that certain title policy dated January 1, 1981, issued by Blank Insurance Company under its No. 60 00 00, is unimproved, and is hereinafter referred to as "the Valuable property".

D. ABC is the fee owner of that certain real property situated in the County of Los Angeles, State of California, described as follows:

Lot 2 of Tract No. 10000, as per map recorded in Book 11, pages 3 to 5, inclusive, of Maps, in the office of the County Recorder of said County.

ABC represents and warrants unto PREI that upon commencement of the term of this joint venture, said real property shall be subject only to items 1 through 5 of such matters of record as set forth in that certain Preliminary Report, dated January 1, 1981, issued by Blank Insurance Company under its No. 60 00 00.

Among such matters of record, said real property is presently encumbered by a deed of trust securing a promissory note, dated October 1, 1979 in the original principal sum of $140,000.00, said note and deed of trust being hereinafter

-2-

referred to as the "Champion note and trust deed". A copy of the Champion note and deed of trust is attached hereto as Exhibit "A". ABC represents and warrants unto PREI that the Champion note and trust deed are in full force and effect in accordance with the terms thereof, that the same have not been modified or amended in any particular, that each and all of the parties thereto have, to the date hereof, fully performed each and all of the terms thereof on their respective parts to be performed, and that the present unpaid principal balance thereof is in the sum of $_____. Said real property is improved with an industrial building consisting of approximately 10,000 square feet, and related improvements, and is hereinafter referred to as the "Champion property".

E. PREI and ABC desire to enter into a joint venture for the purpose of owning, developing, leasing, managing, and holding for investment purposes for long-term appreciation, the valuable property and the Champion property, all as more fully set forth below;

NOW THEREFORE, in consideration of the foregoing, and the mutual promises, covenants, undertakings and agreements contained herein, the parties hereto hereby agree as follows:

-3-

ARTICLE I

FORMATION, PURPOSES AND TERM

Section 1.01. Formation.

(a) PREI and ABC hereby agree to become joint venturers together in a joint venture (hereinafter "Venture") for the purposes, and pursuant to the terms and provisions, set forth in this Agreement and for the term commencing on the date set forth in Section 1.03. The Venture shall be governed, except as otherwise herein provided, by the Uniform Partnership Act of the State of California, as from time to time amended.

(b) The business of the Venture shall be conducted under the name of Valuable Industrial Properties.

(c) In connection with the acquisition of the Valuable and Champion properties by the Venture, the parties hereto shall execute, acknowledge and verify a Statement of Partnership pursuant to the provisions of Section 15010.5 of the Corporation Code of the State of California and cause such statement to be recorded in the official records of Los Angeles County, California on or about the date this Agreement is executed. At such time, the parties shall also execute a Fictitious Business Name Statement and shall cause such Statement to be published and filed in accordance with Sections 17900-17930 of the Business and Professions Code of the State of California. The parties shall execute, acknowledge, verify, file and record all such other instruments and statements as may be required by this Agreement, any amendments hereto, or by law.

-4-

(d) The principal place of business of the Venture shall be 6300 Wilshire Boulevard, in the City of Los Angeles, California 90048. The principal place of business may at any time be changed by the written agreement of the parties.

Section 1.02. Purposes and Business.

The purposes for which the Venture is formed are, and the business of the Venture shall be, to acquire the Valuable and Champion properties, to own, lease to others, manage and hold for investment purposes for long-term appreciation, the Champion properties, to own, lease to others, manage and hold for investment purposes for long-term appreciation, the Champion property, to own the Valuable property, and to construct, develop, and then to operate and lease to others an industrial building on the Valuable property of approximately 25,000 square feet, and to hold the same for investment purposes for long-term appreciation, and to conduct such other business as may be necessary or incidental thereto. The Venture shall have the power to take such actions as may be necessary and appropriate to accomplish such purposes and conduct such business and shall not engage in any other business without the prior written consent of both parties hereto.

Section 1.03. Term.

The term of the Venture shall commence on the date of execution of this Agreement and shall continue until the first to occur of the events specified in Section 5.01 or until

-5-

terminated in accordance with the terms and provisions of this Agreement.

ARTICLE II

OPERATION OF THE PARTNERSHIP

Section 2.01. Liability of Parties.

Neither of the parties hereto shall incur any obligations for which the other shall be liable except for obligations incurred in the name of the Venture and subject to the provisions of Section 2.03 below set forth with respect to the right of the general partner of PREI, in the event of disagreement between the parties hereto, to alone make all final determinations and decisions regarding the business of the Venture and to alone perform all acts and execute all documents on behalf of the Venture as may be incidental to such business, and subject to each and all of the other terms and provisions of this Agreement. Notwithstanding the foregoing, the parties acknowledge that PREI has heretofore incurred and expended the sum of $_____ in connection with the potential development of the Valuable property and the parties hereby agree that the Venture shall reimburse PREI the full sum of said expenditures from the first funds available therefor.

Section 2.02. Protection of Third Parties.

Any person or entity dealing with the Venture may rely upon a certificate executed by PREI on behalf of the Venture, as to the authority of PREI to bind and otherwise act on

behalf of the Venture or as to any other fact pertaining to the Venture.

Section 2.03. Management of the Partnership and Authority of Partners.

(a) The parties hereto shall consult and counsel with each other with respect to all decisions and determinations to be made by and on behalf of the Venture, and they shall keep each other apprised of all relevant facts and circumstances relating thereto, and shall make every reasonable attempt to mutually agree upon such decisions and determinations to be so made; provided, however, that in the event the parties hereto cannot so mutually agree as to any such decision and determination, then the final decision of PREI, acting by and through its general partner, shall alone prevail and its decision and determination shall be conclusive and binding upon the Venture; provided further, that after completion of the industrial building to be constructed on the Valuable property, PREI, as managing joint venturer, shall not expend or incur expenses on behalf of the Venture of more than $10,000.00, in the aggregate, in any six (6) months calendar period without the prior consent thereto of ABC. Further, the signature of PREI, by its general partner, on behalf of the Venture shall alone be required for the execution of all instruments and documents of whatsoever kind or nature on behalf of the Venture and shall bind the Venture in all respects including, without limitation, all contracts, loan applications, loan commitments, loan documents, and deeds.

(b) PREI agrees to use its best efforts to perform all acts as shall reasonably be required to fulfill the purposes of this Venture including, without limitation, the development of the Valuable property and leasing to others of an industrial building thereon of approximately 25,000 square feet; provided, however, that in the event PREI is unable to perform, or subsequently deems impractical, such development of the Valuable property or any other purpose of this Venture, PREI shall have no liability or obligation to ABC in connection therewith, and ABC hereby waives, releases and relinquishes as to PREI, and its partners, agents, representatives, and attorneys, any and all claims, demands, actions, and causes of action it may have as against any such person being released, arising from or relating to the failure of the Venture to accomplish any of its purposes, except for acts performed other then in good faith. In the event the Venture is unable to develop the industrial building to be constructed upon the Valuable property as aforesaid, or in the event such development is subsequently determined to be impractical under conditions then prevailing, PREI or ABC may, at their respective opion, cancel this Venture, whereupon the parties will return to each other their respective real properties contributed thereto, and thereafter the parties hereto shall have no claim, demand,

-8-

action, or cause of action, of any kind or nature against each other or their respective partners, agents, representatives, or attorneys, with respect to the Venture.

Section 2.04. Business Opportunity Doctrine.

Nothing contained herein shall be construed to require either party to offer to the other or the Venture any business opportunity, whether or not similar or related to the Venture business, which any party may wish to enter into with persons or parties not a party hereto. Either party hereto may enter any business activities, whether similar or related to the activities contemplated by this Agreement, or into any other business activity, without first offering participation in any such business activity to the other party hereto or the Venture. The parties acknowledge that they are each involved in other ventures and projects, including other real estate projects, and recognize that they will devote only such time as is reasonably necessary to the business of the Venture. In this connection, the parties hereto acknowledge the PREI is the owner of real property adjacent to the Valuable property and hereby consent to all acts as PREI may perform in connection with said adjacent real property.

ARTICLE III

PARTNERSHIP CAPITAL, LOANS, PROFITS AND LOSSES.
DISTRIBUTIONS AND PAYMENT OF MANAGEMENT FEES

Section 3.01. Initial Capital Contributions.

Concurrently with the execution of this Agreement, PREI

-9-

shall execute all documents and perform all acts as shall be necessary and/or incidental to transfer and convey the Valuable property to the Venture subject only to those matters of record set forth in that certain title policy described above.

Concurrently with the execution of this Agreement, ABC shall execute all documents and perform all acts as shall be necessary and/or incidental to transfer and convey the Champion property, together with all improvement thereon and all rights and interests of ABC therein, to the Venture subject only to those matters of record set forth as items 1 through 5 in that certain Preliminary Report, dated January 1, 1981, issued by Blank Insurance Company under its Order No. 60 00 00. ABC shall further provide the Venture, concurrently with the execution of this Agreement, with a beneficiary statement with regard to the Champion note and trust deed.

The parties hereto hereby acknowledge and agree that the fair market value of the equity in each of the Valuable and Champion properties, subject only to such matters of record, is in the sum of Two Hundred Fifty Thousand Dollars ($250,000.00) and that, therefore, PREI and ABC shall each be deemed to have actually contributed the sum of $250,000.00 to the Venture as their respective original capital contributions thereto.

The parties hereto hereby further acknowledge that a real estate brokerage commission of $ _____ shall be owed to Happy Industrial Real Estate upon the Venture's acquisition of

-10-

the Champion property and that such commission expense shall be borne and paid by the Venture and shall not reduce the value of said property contributed to the Venture as herein provided.

Section 3.01.1 Loans by PREI.

Subsequent to the formation of this Venture and the original contributions by the parties of the property set forth in Paragraph 3.01., above, it is anticipated that the Venture will be in need of additional funds to pay for costs and expenses incident to the contemplated development of the Valuable property in excess of sums which may be borrowed by the Venture for such purposes.

To provide the Venture with funds for the forgoing purposes, PREI agrees to lend to the Venture up to the sum of $100,000.00 until the time of completion of the improvements to be constructed on the Valuable property.

All such loans shall bear interest from the date thereof at the same rates as payable, as of the dates of such loans, by Security Pacific Bank on 90-day certificates of deposit, provided that such interest rate shall, in no event, exceed the maximum rate of interest permitted by law, and shall be secured by such assets of the Venture as PREI shall determine. The signature of PREI alone, on behalf of the Venture, shall bind the Venture in all respects in connection with said loans and the security therefor. Said loans will be repaid from

-11-

the first monies available to the Venture for the repayment of same, whether from cash flow or refinance or sale of any of its assets; provided, however, that said loans shall be repaid in any event within three (3) years from the date of the making of the first of such loans.

Section 3.02. Subsequent Contributions.

In addition to the contributions of the parties set forth in Section 3.01. above, and the loans referred in paragraph 3.01.1, above, the parties hereto may, in their respective discretion, thereafter and from time to time contribute to the Venture, either in the form of loans or additional contributions to capital, such additional sums as shall be reasonably required for the continued operation of the business affairs of the Venture. All such additional loans shall be repayable on the same terms as set forth in Section 3.01.1, above, and shall bear interest at the same rate as therein provided. In the event either party hereto shall desire not to contribute any portion of such additional funds, such party shall bear no penalties or sanctions by reason thereof except for the payment of any interest by the Venture on those funds contributed as loans by the other party.

Section 3.03. Allocation of Net Profits and Net Losses.

The Net Profits and Losses of the Venture shall be allocated fifty percent (50%) to each of the parties hereto.

Section 3.04. Net Profits and Net Losses: Definitions.

The terms "Net Profits" and "Net Losses" for each fiscal year of the Venture shall mean the net profits and net losses

-12-

of the Venture as determined after the close of the fiscal year in accordance with the accounting principles employed in the federal income tax return filed by the Venture for that year, but without any special provision for tax exempt or partially tax exempt income.

Section 3.05. Partnership Distributions - Operation of Property.

All cash available to the Venture from its operations, excluding the sale or refinancing of its property, after the establishment of such reserves as PREI shall determine, and except as otherwise provided in this Agreement, shall be distributed not less frequently than semi-annually to the parties in accordance with their respective interests in the Net Profits and Losses of the Venture.

Section 3.06. Sale or Refinancing of Improved Property.

Upon sale or refinance of either or both the Champion property and the Valuable property, the net proceeds therefrom shall be distributed in the following order:

(a) First, to pay all existing trust deeds and loan balances owed by the Venture and then required to be paid, secured by the property so sold or refinanced, other than loans from one of the parties hereto;

(b) Second, to pay the obligations of the Venture not secured by any remaining property of the Venture, other than loans from either of the parties hereto;

-13-

Section 3.08. Withdrawals of Capital.

Except as expressly set forth in this Agreement, no portion of the capital of the Venture may be withdrawn at any time without the express written consent of both of the parties hereto.

Section 3.09. Management Fees and Construction Fees.

Commencing one (1) year following completion of the improvements to be constructed on the Valuable property, the Venture may retain a management company for the purpose of managing either or both of the properties of the Venture. Such management company may receive an annual management fee in an amount equal to not more than five percent (5%) of the gross annual rentals from the Venture's property which is so managed. Either party hereto, or any partner of any such party, may be an owner, member of, or participant in, anu such management company and may share in and receive, to its or his own use and benefit, and for its or his own account, such share of such management fee as it or he is entitled by reason of participation in such management company.

In addition to the management fee above provided, the parties hereto approve and consent to PREI, or any of the partners thereof, owning, sharing or participating in, any entities which may engage in the construction and development of improvements upon property of the Venture, and further approve and consent to PREI, or any partner thereof, sharing and participating in, obtaining and receiving, for its or his own account

-15-

(c) Third, to repay any loans made to the Venture by either party hereto;

(d) Fourth, to the parties hereto in the amount of their remaining capital contributions after retaining a reasonable reserve for anticipated obligations and known contingencies of the Venture;

(e) Fifth, the remainder of funds or assets shall be distributed to the parties hereto in such shares as they are entitled to share in the Net Profits and Losses of the Venture.

Section 3.07. Capital Accounts of the Parties.

An individual Capital Account shall be maintained for each party hereto to which shall be credited (i) each such party's actual contributions to the capital of the Venture and (ii) such party's share of the Net Profits of the Partnership pursuant to the provisions of Section 3.03, and to which shall be debited (i) all amounts distributed to such Partner pursuant to the provisions of Sections 3.05. and 3.06 and (ii) such party's share of the Net Losses of the Venture pursuant to the provisions of Section 3.03. Each such party's Capital Account Balance shall, at any given time, be equal to the sum total of (i) such party's actual contributions and (ii) such party's share of the Net Profits of the Venture, less the sum total of (i) all amounts distributed to such party pursuant to the provisions of Sections 3.05 and 3.06 and (ii) such party's share of the Net Losses of the Partnership. Neither contributions to the capital of the Venture nor the Capital Account Balances shall bear interest.

-14-

and to it or his own use and benefit, the share of any and all contractor's fees paid to such entities for services rendered to the Venture to the extent PREI, or any partner thereof, is entitled thereto by reason of its or his interest in such entitled. In this regard, it is agreed that any such fees shall not exceed ten percent (10%) of the cost of construction of any such improvements.

Except as hereinabove set forth, neither party hereto shall receive any fees or salaries for services rendered to the Venture. However, all other costs and expenses related to the Venture or its property, including, without limitation, general and administrative expenses and fees for outside services by persons hired by the Venture, will constitute expenses of the Venture and will be paid by and charged to the Venture.

Section 3.10. Rights of First Refusal Upon Sale.

(a) In the event that PREI determines that all market conditions dictate the liquidation of some or all of the investment real estate of the Venture, then upon PREI receiving an offer from a third party to purchase any real property of the Venture which is acceptable to PREI, PREI shall immediately notify ABC in writing of the terms and conditions of such offer, enclosing a copy of said offer, and ABC shall have seven (7) days from and after the effective date of such notification to exercise its right of first refusal to purchase

-16-

the property on the same terms and conditions; provided, however, that in the event ABC shall exercise its right of first refusal, there shall be deducted from the purchase price payable by ABC for the property such sum as would otherwise be payable as and for brokerage commissions had the property been sold to the third party offeror. Such right of first refusal shall be exercised, if at all, by ABC notifying PREI in writing within such seven (7) day period of its exercise of said right of first refusal. In the event ABC exercises its right of first refusal, this Venture, as Seller, and ABC, as Buyer, shall immediately thereupon enter into escrow for the sale and purchase of the property in accordance with the terms of the offer therefor, as aforesaid, subject to the reduction in the purchase price thereof as set forth above.

(b) In the event PREI is not notified by ABC of the latter's exercise of its right of first refusal within said seven (7) day period, as set forth in subparagraph (a) above, PREI shall, immediately upon expiration of said seven (7) day period, or sooner, if ABC shall agree, enter into escrow with the third party offeror for the sale to such party of the property in accordance with the terms of its offer therefor, and shall timely execute all documents and perform all acts as are necessary and incidental to consummate such escrow.

-17-

ARTICLE IV

ACCOUNTING

Section 4.01. Books and Records.

At all times during the term of the Venture, PREI shall maintain at the Venture's principal place of business the Venture's books and records of account in which shall be entered all financial matters relating to its business and affairs, including all income, expenditures, assets and liabilities thereof, in accordance with the customary and usual accounting methods applicable to a real estate holding venture. Such books and records shall be adequate and appropriate for the Venture's business and shall be open to inspection and copying by either of the parties hereto or their authorized representatives at any reasonable time during normal business hours. Within thirty (30) days after the end of each calendar quarter, the Venture shall submit to each of the parties hereto a statement of operations of the Venture for the preceding calendar quarter. PREI may retain, at the expense of the Venture, the services of such accountants as it may desire for the purposes as set forth in this Section 4.01.

The parties hereto by mutual agreement may, from time to time, elect to cause a certified public accountant to conduct an examination of the books and records of the Venture in accordance with generally accepted accounting principles and issue or cause to be issued financial statements at the cost and expense of the Venture.

-18-

Section 4.02. Fiscal Year.

The fiscal year of the Venture shall be the calendar year.

Section 4.03. Tax Returns.

PREI shall designate a certified public accountant to prepare for filing on or before the due dates thereof (including any extensions thereof) annual federal and California Partnership Returns of Income and any other federal, state or local tax returns required to be filed by or on behalf of the Venture; all of such returns may be signed on behalf of the Venture by PREI.

Section 4.04. Banking.

PREI shall open and maintain accounts for the Venture in such bank or banks in the State of California as it shall determine in its sole discretion. All funds of the Venture shall be deposited in such accounts or in such certificates or other interest-bearing accounts as determined by PREI. No funds other than funds of the Venture shall be deposited in such accounts. Venture funds shall be used solely for the business of the Venture and withdrawals therefrom shall be made only by checks signed by PREI on behalf of the Venture or by the representatives of PREI as may be designated from time to time.

ARTICLE V

DISSOLUTION

Section 5.01. Causes of Dissolution.

The Venture shall be dissolved upon the first to occur

-19-

of the following events:

(a) The sale of all or substantially all of the Venture's assets;

(b) Fifteen (15) years from and after the date of this Agreement;

(c) Such date as the parties hereto may agree upon in writing.

Section 5.02. Procedure Upon Dissolution.

Upon dissolution of the Venture for any reason, all its assets to the extent possible shall be liquidated in an orderly fashion over a reasonable period of time in accordance with established real estate practices in the County of Los Angeles, and the Venture shall engage in no further business except as may be necessary to liquidate its assets and wind up its affairs. An accounting shall be made to the date upon which the affairs of the Venture are wound up. The proceeds from the liquidation of the assets of the Venture, to the extent that they are sufficient, shall be distributed in the order and priority as set forth in Section 3.06. above.

ARTICLE VI

MISCELLANEOUS

Section 6.01. Creation of a Limited Partnership and Transfer of Interest in Venture Upon Stated Events.

Upon the bankruptcy, insolvency, assignment for the benefit of creditors, or dissolution of either of the parties

hereto, or in the event a trustee or receiver is appointed with respect to the interest of any party hereto, or in the event a charging order is issued against the interest of any party hereto in the Venture and is not released within forty-five (45) days, or in the event an attachment or execution is levied against the interest of a party hereto and is not released within forty-five (45) days, that party, or its successor(s) in interest (herein called a "Substituted Limited Partner") shall become a Limited Partner in a Limited Partnership to be formed, the terms of which shall be substantially the same as set forth herein except for the changes inherent in the conversion of this entity from a Joint Venture to a Limited Partnership. In addition thereto, the Substituted Limited Partner shall pay a transfer fee to the Venture which is sufficient to cover all reasonable expenses connected with such transfer of interest, or change in status, including, without limitation, legal fees and the costs of drafting and recording a Certificate and/or Agreement of Limited Partnership.

Section 6.02. No Assignment.

Except as otherwise expressly provided in this Agreement, neither party hereto shall have the right to sell, mortgage, hypothecate or assign all or any portion of its interest in the Venture other than to the other party hereto on such terms as may be agreed, nor shall any party hereto have the right to substitute anyone in its place, or assign or otherwise transfer this Agreement or any of its rights, duties, obligations or interests hereunder without the prior written consent of the other party hereto, which consent may be withheld in the sole and absolute discretion of such other party. Any attempted assignment or transfer without such consent shall be null and void. Subject to the foregoing and to the other provisions of this Agreement, this Agreement shall be binding upon, enforceable by, and shall inure to the benfit of, the successors and assigns of the parties hereto.

Section 6.02. Arbitration.

All disputes between the parties hereto concerning the interpretation or performance of this Agreement shall be promptly submitted for decision to an arbitrator to be mutually agreed upon by the parties hereto from a list of arbitrators furnished by the American Arbitration Association (A.A.A.) or, if they cannot mutually agree, then to be selected by the head or acting head of the office of the A.A.A. in Los Angeles, California. The rules and regulations of the A.A.A. shall govern any such arbitration and a judgment upon the award of such arbitrator may be rendered in accordance with the laws of the State of California. The arbitrator's decision shall be binding and conclusive upon the parties hereto and shall be rendered with due consideration for the furtherance and best interests of the purposes and business of this Venture under all relevant circumstances as may then exist.

-22-

The arbitrator is authorized and directed to award such sums as may be proper to compensate for time and expense incidental to the proceedings, including but not limited to the cost of arbitration, the arbitrator's fees which the arbitrator shall fix, and reasonable attorney's fees for the prevailing party.

Section 6.04. Legal Fees.

If any action, suit or proceeding is brought by either party hereto against the other arising out of this Agreement, such party in whose favor final award or judgment shall be entered shall be entitled to recover from the other all costs and expenses of suit, including reasonable attorneys' fees.

Section 6.05. Severability.

In the event any portion of this Agreement shall be declared by any court of competent jurisdiction to be invalid, illegal, or unenforceable, such portion shall be deemed severed from this Agreement, and the remaining parts thereof shall remain in full force and effect, as fully as though such portion had never been part of this Agreement.

Section 6.06. Headings.

The Article and Section headings contained in this Agreement are for purposes of reference and convenience only and shall not limite or otherwise affect the meaning of this Agreement.

-23-

Section 6.07. Entire Agreement.

This Agreement contains the entire agreement between the parties hereto and no addition or modification of any term or provision shall be effective unless set forth in writing and signed by both parties hereto.

Section 6.08. Required Actions.

The parties hereto agree to execute all such instruments and documents and to take all actions as may be necessary or desirable to carry out the purposes of the Venture.

Section 6.09. Notices.

All notices or other communications required or permitted hereunder shall be in writing, and shall be personally delivered or sent by registered or certified mail, return receipt requested, and shall be deemed received upon personal delivery or three (3) business days after deposit in the United States mail in the County of Los Angeles, postage prepaid, addressed to the person to receive same at the following addresses:

To PREI   12345 Development Avenue
               Valuable, California 99999

               With a copy to:

               Myron Meyers, Esq.
               Meyers, Stevens & Walters
               Professional Corporation
               6300 Wilshire Boulevard
               Suite 9100
               Los Angeles, California 90048

To ABC   12345 Owner Way
               Champion, California 99999

               With a copy to:

               John Law, Esq.
               00000 Venture Blvd, Suite 000
               Equity, California 99999

-24-

Notice of change of address shall be given by written notice in the manner detailed in this Section.

Section 6.10. Construction.

Whenever the context of this Agreement requires same, the singular shall include the plural and the masculine shall include the feminine. This Agreement shall not be construed as if it had been prepared by one of the parties, but rather as if both parties had prepared the same. Unless otherwise indicated, all references to Recitals, Sections and Articles are to Recitals, Sections and Articles in this Agreement.

This Agreement is executed and delivered in the State of California and shall be construed and enforced in accordance with, and governed by, the laws of the State of California.

Section 6.11. Waiver of Action for Partition.

Each of the parties hereto irrevocably waives, during the term of the Venture and during the period of its liquidation following any dissolution, any right that such party may have to maintain any action for partition with respect to any of the properties or other assets of the Venture.

Section 6.12. Financing.

Notwithstanding the right grated to PREI in Section 2.03 above, to alone execute on behalf of this Venture all documents in connection with the purposes of this Venture, each of the parties hereto shall execute all documents and instruments and perform all acts necessary and/or incidental to the effectuation of the purposes of this Venture, including, without limitation,

-25-

ARTICLES OF INCORPORATION

OF

WHITEACRE INVESTMENTS, INC.

I

The name of this corporation is:

WHITEACRE INVESTMENTS, INC.

II

The purpose of this corporation is to engage in any lawful act or activity for which a corporation may be organized under the General Corporation Law of California other than the banking business, the trust company business or the practice of a profession permitted to be incorporated by the California Corporations Code.

III

The name and address in the State of California of this corporation's initial agent for service of process is:

Myron Meyers
Suite 9100
6300 Wilshire Boulevard
Los Angeles, California 90048

IV

This corporation is authorized to issue only one class of shares of stock; the total number of shares which this

---

the execution of building loan agreements, promissory notes, deeds of trust, and such other documents as may be required by any lender or surety for the securing of financing incident to the purposes of this Venture.

SecSection 6.13. Counterparts.

This Agreement may be executed in counterparts, each of which shall be deemed an original, but all of which together shall constitute one and the same instrument.

IN WITNESS WHEREOF, the parties hereto have executed this Agreement on the day and year first above written.

PERFECT REAL ESTATE INVESTMENTS,
a California partnership

By _____
   John Smith,
   General Partner

ABC PROPERTIES,
a California general partnership

By _____
   Sam Jones

By _____
   Jack Jones

By _____
   Robert Doe

CAUTION: THIS IS A FORM ONLY - IT MAY REQUIRE SUBSTANTIAL REVISION - CONSULT YOUR OWN COUNSEL.

-26-

MINUTES OF THE FIRST
ORGANIZATIONAL MEETING OF
WHITEACRE INVESTMENTS, INC.,
A California Corporation

The undersigned, being the Incorporator of this corporation, held the first meeting of the corporation at 6300 Wilshire
Boulevard, Suite 9100, Los Angeles, California on the 2nd day
of November, 1980 at 12:00 o'clock noon.

Present at this session of the meeting was Myron Meyers,
being the Incorporator of said corporation named in its Articles of Incorporation. Also present was Melvin Walters.

On motion duly made, seconded and unanimously carried,
Myron Meyers was elected temporary Chairman and Melvin Walters
was elected temporary Secretary of the meeting.

The temporary Chairman stated that the corporation had been
formed by the filing of the original Articles of Incorporation
in the Office of the California Secretary of State by the Incorporator acting pursuant to Section 210 of the General Corporation
Law, and the Articles of Incorporation had been assigned the
following filing date and State Corporation Number:

Official Filing Date: January 1, 1981

Official Filing Number: 000000

corporation is authorized to issue is 1,000.

Dated: January 1, 1981.

Myron Meyers, Incorporator

I hereby declare that I am the person who executed the
foregoing Articles of Incorporation, which execution is my
act and deed.

Myron Meyers

-2-

WAIVER OF NOTICE AND CONSENT TO HOLDING
OF FIRST MEETING OF DIRECTORS OF

WHITEACRE INVESTMENTS, INC.,

A California Corporation

We, the undersigned, being all of the directors elected at the first organizational meeting of this corporation, desiring to hold the first meeting of the Board of Directors of said corporation for the purpose of completing the organization of its affairs, DO HEREBY waive notice of said meeting and consent to the holding thereof, at the time, on the day and at the place set forth as follows:

TIME: 10:00 a.m.

DATE: January 15, 1981

PLACE: 6300 Wilshire Boulevard, Suite 9100
         Los Angeles, California 90048

Said meeting is to be held for the purpose of adopting By-Laws, electing officers, adopting a form of corporate seal and share certificate, selecting an accounting year, establishing a bank account, authorizing issuance of shares in accordance with the provisions of the California Corporations Code and the filing of a statement of non-necessity for a permit with the California Commissioner of Corporations, and transacting such other business as may be brought before said meeting; and do further agree that any business transacted at said meeting shall be as valid and legal and of the same force and effect as though said meeting were held after notice duly given.

WITNESS our signatures this 15th day of January, 1981.

_____
GEORGE GOTROCKS

_____
JOSE RIVAS

The Temporary Chairman then presented to the meeting a certified copy of said Articles of Incorporation, showing filings as stated, and the temporary Secretary was directed to insert said copy in the Minute Book of the corporation.

Acting pursuant to the power vested in him by Section 210 of the General Corporation Law, and in anticipation of a By-Law provision providing for a two person Board of Directors, the Incorporator proceeded to elect George Gotrocks and Jose Rivas as Directors of the corporation to further complete the organization of the corporation. Said persons had previously communicated to the Temporary Chairman their acceptance of the office to which they were so elected respectively.

The Incorporator next announced his intention to submit his resignation.

By this signature, the undersigned Incorporator hereby signifies his resignation.

_____
MYRON MEYERS

There being no further business to come before the meeting, upon motion duly made, seconded and unanimously carried, the meeting was adjourned.

_____
Temporary Chairman MYRON MEYERS

ATTEST:

_____
Temporary Secretary MELVIN WALTERS

-2-

MINUTES OF FIRST MEETING OF
BOARD OF DIRECTORS OF

WHITEACRE INVESTMENTS, INC.,

A California Corporation

The Directors elected at the first organizational meeting
of the above named corporation, constituting the Board of Directors of said corporation, held their first meeting at the time,
on the day and at the place set forth as follows:

TIME: 10:00 a.m.

DATE: January 15, 1981

PLACE: 6300 Wilshire Boulevard, Suite 9100
            Los Angeles, California 90048

There were present at the meeting the following Directors,
constituting the full board:

GEORGE GOTROCKS

JOSE RIVAS

On motion and by unanimous vote, the following named persons
were elected Chairman and Secretary of the first meeting:

Chairman: George Gotrocks

Secretary: Jose Rivas

The Chairman announced that the meeting was held pursuant
to written waiver of notice thereof and consent thereto signed
by all of the directors of the corporation; such waiver and consent was presented to the meeting and upon motion duly made,
seconded and unanimously carried was made a part of the records
of the meeting and now precedes the minutes of this meeting in
the Book of Minutes of the corporation.

RESIGNATION OF INCORPORATOR

Upon motion duly made, seconded and unanimously carried, the
Incorporator's resignation was accepted by the Directors.

ADOPTION OF BY-LAWS

So that the corporation would have a comprehensive set
of rules and regulations for the operations of its affairs,
the adoption of By-Laws was next considered. The Chairman
presented to the meeting a form of By-Laws which he believed
was in the best interests of the corporation to adopt. On
motion duly made, seconded and unanimously carried, the following resolutions were adopted:

RESOLVED: That the copy of proposed By-Laws presented to this meeting and hereby adopted as the
official By-Laws of this corporation.

RESOLVED FURTHER: That the Secretary of this corporation be and hereby is authorized and directed
to execute a certificate of the adoption of said
By-Laws and to insert said By-Laws as so certified
in the Minute Book of this corporation, and to see
that a copy of said By-Laws, similarly certified,
is kept at the principal office for the transaction
of business of this corporation, in accordance with
Section 213 of the California General Corporation
Law.

AGENT FOR SERVICE OF PROCESS

The matter of the appointment of an agent for service of
process was next presented. On motion duly made, seconded and
unanimously carried, the following resolution was adopted:

RESOLVED: That Myron Meyers, whose address is 6300
Wilshire Boulevard, Suite 9100, Los Angeles, California 90048 named as the initial agent for service of
process in the Articles of Incorporation is hereby
confirmed as the corporation's agent for the purpose
of service of process.

-2-

PRINCIPAL OFFICE LOCATION

After some discussion, the location of the principal office of the corporation for the transaction of the business of the corporation was fixed pursuant to the following resolution, adopted on motion duly made, seconded and unanimously carried:

RESOLVED: That 6300 Wilshire Boulevard, Suite 9100, Los Angeles, California 90048 be and the same hereby is, designated and fixed as the principal office for the transaction of business of the corporation.

ELECTION OF OFFICERS

The meeting then proceeded to the election of officers.

After discussion, and upon motion duly made, and seconded, the following resolution was unanimously adopted:

RESOLVED: That the following persons are elected to the offices indicated after their names:

George Gotrocks   President and Chief Financial Officer

Jose Rivas   Vice President and Secretary

Each officer so elected and thereafter the President presided at the meeting as Chairman and the Secretary acted as Secretary of the meeting.

CORPORATE SEAL

The Secretary presented for approval of the meeting a proposed seal of the corporation, consisting of two concentric circles

-3-

with the name of the corporation in one circle and the words and figures "Incorporated - January 1, 1981" and "California" in the form and figures as follows:

On motion duly made, seconded and unanimously carried, the following resolution was adopted:

RESOLVED: That the form of the corporate seal presented to this meeting be, and the same is hereby adopted, as the seal of this corporation.

SHARE CERTIFICATE

The Secretary presented to the meeting a proposed form of the share certificate for use by the corporation. On motion duly made, seconded and unanimously carried, the following resolution was adopted:

RESOLVED: That the form of stock certificate presented to ths meeting be, and the same is, hereby adopted as the stock certificate of this corporation.

FURTHER RESOLVED: That the Secretary insert a copy of said stock certificate in the Minute Book immediately following the Minutes of this meeting.

ORGANIZATIONAL EXPENSES

In order to provide for the payment of expenses of incorporation and organization of the corporation, on motion duly made, seconded and unanimously carried, the following resolution was adopted:

-4-

for payment of money issued in the name of this corporation against any funds deposited in any of such accounts, and to revoke any such designation.

(e) to authorize the use of facsimile signatures for the signing or countersigning of checks, drafts or other orders for the payment of money, and to enter into such agreements as banks and trust companies customarily require as a condition for permitting the use of facsimile signatures;

(f) to make such general and special rules and regulations with respect to such accounts as they may deem necessary or advisable; and

(g) to complete, execute and/or certify any customary printed blank signature card forms in order to conveniently exercise the authority granted by this resolution and any resolutions printed therefrom shall be deemed adopted as a part hereof.

RESOLVED FURTHER: That the form resolution of the bank as presented to this meeting is hereby adopted in such form utilized by that bank, and the Secretary of this corporation is hereby authorized to certify such resolution as having been adopted at this meeting and is directed to insert the form of such resolution in the Minute Book immediately following the Minutes of this meeting.

RESOLVED FURTHER: That any such depository to which a copy certified by the Secretary or any assistant Secretary of this corporation of these resolutions shall have been delivered shall be entitled to rely thereon for all purposes until it shall have received written notice of the revocation or amendment of these resolutions by the Board of Directors of this corporation.

ACCOUNTING YEAR

The Chairman suggested that the meeting consider the adoption of an accounting year, either fiscal or calendar, so its taxable year would be established. On motion duly made, seconded

-6-

RESOLVED: That the President or Secretary of this corporation is hereby authorized and directed to pay the expenses of incorporation and organization of this corporation.

BANK RESOLUTIONS

The Chairman expressed the need for a corporate bank account and other depositories for the corporation's funds. He also indicated that enabling resolutions should be considered to empower designated persons to act for the corporation in dealing with such depositories. On motion duly made, seconded and unanimously carried, the following resolutions were adopted:

RESOLVED: That the President and Chief Financial Officer and the Secretary, and each of them are hereby authorized:

(a) to designate Blank Bank and one or more other banks, trust companies or similar institutions as depositories of the funds, including without limitation, cash and cash equivalents, of this corporation;

(b) to open, keep and close general and special bank accounts, including general deposit accounts, payroll accounts and working fund accounts, with any such depositor;

(c) to cause to be deposited in such accounts with any such depository, from time to time, such funds including without limitation, cash and cash equivalents of this corporation as such officers deem necessary or advisable, and to designate or change the designation of the officer or officers and agent or agents of this corporation who will be authorized to make such deposits and to endorse checks, drafts or other instruments for such deposit.

(d) from time to time to designate or change the designation of the officer or officers and agent or agents of this corporation who will be authorized to sign or countersign checks, drafts or other orders

-5-

and unanimously carried, the following resolution was adopted:

RESOLVED: That this corporation hereby adopts an accounting year as follows:

Date accounting year ends: June 30

AUTHORITY OF OFFICERS

In order to provide for the day-to-day operations of the corporation on motion duly made, seconded and unanimously carried, the following resolutions were adopted:

RESOLVED: That George Gotrocks, the President-Chief Financial Officer and Secretary, and Jose Rivas, the Vice-President and Secretary, and each of them, ("Designated Persons"), are hereby authorized, directed and empowered now and from time to time hereafter to make, execute, deliver and enter into for and on behalf of the corporation, without further authorization of any other person or entity, such agreements, instruments and documents, including, without limitation, notes, security agreements, real estate mortgages, trust deeds, bills of sale, leases, certificates, reports, assignments and contracts ("Agreements") as they in their sole discretion deem necessary, advisable, expedient, convenient or proper.

BE IT FURTHER RESOLVED: That the Agreements may contain such provisions, terms, conditions, covenants and representations as Designated Persons may in his or her sole discretion deem necessary, advisable, expedient or proper.

BE IT FURTHER RESOLVED: That any and all acts and things that Designated Persons have done or may do on behalf of corporation and in connection with these resolutions, are hereby ratisfied, approved and confirmed.

ISSUANCE OF SHARES UNDER CLOSE CORPORATION EXEMPTION

As the next order of business, the Chairman suggested that the meeting consider the issuance of the capital stock

-7-

of the corporation. He was informed that Section 25102(h) of the California Corporations Code provides for a close corporation exemption if certain qualifications are met and set forth in the notice form required by the Commissioner of Corporations together with an opinion of legal counsel based thereon.

He was advised that while this would exempt the initial stock issuance, the Commission's regulations would require a Legend Condition restricting subsequent transfer of shares.

Upon motion duly made, seconded and unanimously carried, the following resolutions were adopted:

RESOLVED: That immediately after the sale and issuance of the shares hereinafter proposed to be issued, the issuer will be owned beneficially by no more than ten (10) persons, and all of the certificates evidencing such stock will contain the Legend required by Section 260.102.6 of Title 10 of the California Administrative Code as contained in Section 260.141.11(c) of said Code.

RESOLVED FURTHER: That the offer and sale of such shares will not be accompanied by the publication of any advertisement and that neither selling expenses nor promotional considerations were or will be given in connection therewith.

RESOLVED FURTHER: That the consideration received or to be received by the issuer for the stock to be issued consisted of or will consist of one of the kinds described in Section 25102(h) of the General Corporation Law.

SALE OF SHARES

In order to obtain working capital for the corporation, the sale of shares was discussed. The meeting was informed

-8-

RESOLVED: That the corporation adopts the following plan intended to qualify under Internal Revenue Code Section 1244, effective as of the date of this meeting:

(a) The maximum number of common shares to be issued under this plan shall not exceed 300 shares, and the aggregate consideration, which shall consist only of cash or property, to be received for these shares shall not exceed $30,000.00;

(b) This plan shall expire no later than two years from the date of this meeting, and all stock to be issued under it shall be issued within this period, provided that the board may in its discretion terminate the plan at an earlier date;

(c) The share to be issued to the proposed shareholders named in the above resolutions adopted at this meeting are part of the shares to be issued under this plan; and

(d) No stock other than that sold and issued under this plan shall be offered or sold during the period of this plan.

RESOLVED FURTHER: That the officers of the corporation are authorized and directed to do or cause to be done all acts required or appropriate to carry out the above resolution.

The board next considered the advantages of electing to be taxed as a small business corporacion under Internal Revenue Code sub-chapter S. On motion, the following resolutions were adopted:

RESOLVED: That the corporation elects to be taxed under Internal Revenue Code sub-chapter S as a small business corporation;

RESOLVED FURTHER: That the officers of the corporation are authorized and directed to prepare, execute,

-10-

---

that the Articles of Incorporation had authorized the issuance of 1,000 shares of corporate stock. After a brief discussion concerning to whom and in what manner the shares should best be issued, the following resolutions were adopted upon motion duly made and seconded and unanimously carried.

RESOLVED: It is in the best interests of the corporation to sell its stock to the following persons for the described consideration:
George Gotrocks 200 shares and Jose Rivas 100 shares in consideration for cash in the sum of $30,000.00.

RESOLVED FURTHER: That the President and Secretary of this corporation be, and they hereby are, authorized and instructed to issue and sell the shares of stock of this corporation above authorized to be issued and sold hereby, for the consideration stated and in compliance with all of the terms and conditions of Section 25102(h) of the California General Corporation Law.

RESOLVED FURTHER: That the directors and officers of this corporation be, and they hereby are, authorized and directed to prepare, or cause to be prepared, verify and file, or cause to be filed, on behalf of this corporation, a Notice to the California Commissioner of Corporations notifying said Commissioner of Corporations as required by law, with a copy of said Notice to be inserted in the Minute Book of this corporation.

The board next considered the advisability of adopting a plan under Internal Revenue Code Section 1244 to qualify the corporation's Common stock as Section 1244 stock to enable each shareholder to obtain ordinary loss treatment if the stock becomes worthless. After discussion, on motion, the following resolutions were unanimously adopted:

-9-

BY-LAWS OF

WHITEACRE INVESTMENTS, INC.

A California Corporation

ARTICLE I
PLACE OF BUSINESS

The principal office for the transaction of the business of the corporation shall be located at such place or places within the County of Los Angeles, State of California, as the Board of Directors shall from time to time determine.

ARTICLE II
DIRECTORS - MANAGEMENT

Section 1. POWERS. Subject to the limitation of the Articles of Incorporation, of the By-Laws and of the Laws of the State of California as to actions to be authorized or approved by the shareholders, all corporate powers shall be exercised by or under authority of, and the business and affairs of this corporation shall be controlled by, a Board of Directors.

Notwithstanding the provisions of Section 1 above, in the event that this corporation shall elect to become a close corporation, its shareholders may enter into a Shareholders' Agreement. Said Agreement may provide for the exercise of corporate powers and the management of the business and affairs of this corporation by the shareholders, provided, however, such Agreement shall, to the extent and so long as the discretion or the powers of the Board in its management of corporate affairs is controlled by such Agreement, impose upon each shareholder who is a party thereof liability for managerial acts performed or omitted by such person pursuant thereto otherwise imposed upon Directors.

Section 2. NUMBER OF DIRECTORS AND QUALIFICATION. The authorized number of Directors of the corporation shall be until changed by amendment to the Articles of Incorporation or by an amendment to this Section 2, Article II of these By-Laws, adopted by the majority of the voting power of the corporation.

---

and file, Internal Revenue Service Form 2553, together with a statement by each shareholder consenting to this election, and to do all other acts that may be required to make this election effective.

ADJOURNMENT

There being no further business to come before the meeting, upon motion duly made, seconded and unanimously carried, the meeting was adjourned.

_____
President and Chairman
GEORGE GOTROCKS

ATTEST:

_____
Secretary
JOSE RIVAS

-11-

Section 3. ELECTION AND TENURE OF OFFICE. The Directors shall be elected by ballot at the annual meeting of the shareholders, to serve for one year and until their successors are elected and have qualified. Their term of office shall begin immediately after election.

Section 4. VACANCIES. Vacancies in the Board of Directors may be filled by a majority of the remaining Directors, though less than a quorum, or by a sole remaining Director, and each Director so elected shall hold office until his successor is elected at an annual meeting of shareholders or at a special meeting called for that purpose.

The shareholders may at any time elect a Director to fill any vacancy not filled by the Directors, and may elect the additional Directors at the meeting at which an amendment of the By-Laws is voted authorizing an increase in the number of Directors.

A vacancy or vacancies shall be deemed to exist in case of the death, resignation or removal of any Director, or if the shareholders shall increase the authorized number of Directors but shall fail at the meeting at which such increase is authorized, or at an adjournment thereof, to elect the additional Director so provided for, or in case the shareholders fail at any time to elect the full number of authorized Directors.

If the Board of Directors accepts the resignation of a Director tendered to take effect at a future time, the Board, or the shareholders, shall have power to elect a successor to take office when the resignation shall become effective.

No reduction of the number of Directors shall have the effect of removing any Director prior to the expiration of his term of office.

The entire Board of Directors or any individual Director may be removed from office as provided in the Corporations Code. In such case, the remaining Board members may elect a successor Director to fill such vacancy for the remaining unexpired term of the Director so removed.

Section 5. NOTICE, PLACE AND MANNER OF MEETINGS. Meetings of the Board of Directors may be called by the Chairman of the Board, or the President, or any Vice President, or the Secretary, or any two (2) Directors, and shall be held at the principal executive office of the corporation in the State of California, unless some other place is designated in the notice of the

meeting. Members of the Board may participate in a meeting through use of a conference telephone or similar communications equipment so long as all members participating in such a meeting can hear one another. Accurate minutes of any meeting of the Board or any committee thereof shall be maintained as required by the Corporations Code, by the Secretary or any other officer designated for that purpose.

Section 6. SPECIAL MEETINGS - NOTICES - WAIVERS. Special meetings of the Board may be called at any time by the President or, if he is absent or unable or refuses to act, by any Vice President, or the Secretary, or by any two (2) Directors, or by one Director if only one is provided.

At least forty-eight (48) hours' notice of the time and place of special meetings shall be delivered personally to the Directors or personally communicated to them by a corporate officer by telephone or telegraph. If the notice is sent to a Director by letter, it shall be addressed to him at his address as it is shown upon the records of the corporation, or if it is not so shown on such records or is not readily ascertainable, then it should be mailed to the place in which the meetings of the Directors are regularly held. In case such notice is mailed, it shall be deposited in the United States mail, postage prepaid, in the place in which the principal executive office of the corporation is located, at least four (4) days prior to the time of the holding of the meeting. Such mailing, telegraphing, telephoning or delivery as above provided shall be due, legal and personal notice to such Director.

When all of the Directors are present at any Directors meeting, however called or noticed, and either (i) sign a written consent thereto on the records of such meeting, or (ii) if a majority of the Directors are present and if those not present sign a waiver of notice of such meeting or a consent to holding the meeting or an approval of the minutes thereof, whether prior to or after the holding of such meeting, which said waiver, consent or approval shall be filed with the Secretary of the corporation, or (iii) if a Director attends a meeting without notice but, without protesting, prior thereto or at its commencement, the lack of notice to him, then the transactions thereof are as valid as if had at a meeting regularly called and noticed.

Section 7. SOLE DIRECTOR PROVIDED BY ARTICLES OF INCORPORATION. In the event only one Director is required by the By-Laws or Articles of Incorporation, then any reference

Section 12. COMMITTEES. Committees of the Board may be appointed by resolution passed by a majority of the whole Board. Committees shall be composed of two (2) or more members of the Board, and shall have such powers of the Board as may be expressly delegated to it by resolution of the Board of Directors, except those powers expressly made non-delegable by the Corporations Code.

Section 13. ADVISORY DIRECTORS. The Board of Directors from time to time may elect one or more persons to be Advisory Directors who shall not by such appointment be members of the Board of Directors. Advisory Directors shall be available from time to time to perform special assignments specified by the President, to attend meetings of the Board of Directors upon invitation and to furnish consultation to the Board. The period during which the title shall be held may be prescribed by the Board of Directors. If no period is prescribed, the title shall be held at the pleasure of the Board.

Section 14. RESIGNATIONS. Any Director may resign effective upon giving written notice to the Chairman of the Board, the President, the Secretary of the Board of Directors of the corporation, unless the notice specifies a later time for the effectiveness of such resignation. If the resignation is effective at a future time, a successor may be elected to take office when the resignation becomes effective.

ARTICLE III
OFFICERS

Section 1. OFFICERS. The officers of the corporation shall be a Chairman of the Board or a President, or both, a Secretary and a Chief Financial Officer. The corporation may also have, at the discretion of the Board of Directors, one or more Vice Presidents, one or more Assistant Secretaries, and such other officers as may be appointed in accordance with the provisions of Section 3 of this Article. One person may hold two or more offices.

Section 2. ELECTION. The officers of the corporation, except such officers as may be appointed in accordance with the provisions of Section 3 or Section 5 of this Article, shall be chosen annually by the Board of Directors, and each shall hold his office until he shall resign or shall be removed or otherwise disqualified to serve, or his successor shall be elected and qualified.

herein to notices, waivers, consents, meetings or other actions by a majority or quorum of the Directors shall be deemed to refer to such notice, waiver, etc., by such sole Director, who shall have all the rights and duties and shall be entitled to exercise all of the powers and shall assume all the responsibilities otherwise herein described as given to a Board of Directors.

Section 8. DIRECTORS ACTING BY UNANIMOUS WRITTEN CONSENT. Any action required or permitted to be taken by the Board of Directors may be taken without a meeting and with the same force and effect as if taken by a unanimous vote of Directors, if authorized by a writing signed individually or collectively by all members of the Board. Such consent shall be filed with the regular minutes of the Board.

Section 9. QUORUM. A majority of the number of Directors as fixed by the Articles of Incorporation or By-Laws shall be necessary to constitute a quorum for the transaction of business, and the action of a majority of the Directors present at any meeting at which there is a quorum, when duly assembled, is valid as a corporate act; provided that a minority of the Directors, in the absence of a quorum, may adjourn from time to time, but may not transact any business. A meeting at which a quorum is initially present may continue to transact business, notwithstanding the withdrawal of Directors, if any action taken is approved by a majority of the required quorum for such meeting.

Section 10. NOTICE OF ADJOURNMENT. Notice of the time and place of holding an adjourned meeting need not be given to absent Directors if the time and place be fixed at the meeting adjourned and held within twenty four (24) hours thereof. If adjourned more than twenty four (24) hours, notice shall be given to all Directors not present at the time of the adjournment.

Section 11. COMPENSATION OF DIRECTORS. Directors, as such, shall not receive any stated salary for their services, but by resolution of the Board, a fixed sum and expense of attendance, if any, may be allowed for attendance at each regular and special meeting of the Board, provided that nothing herein contained shall be construed to preclude any Director from serving the company in any other capacity and receiving compensation therefor.

Section 3. SUBORDINATE OFFICERS, ETC. The Board of Directors may appoint such other officers as the business of the corporation may require, each of whom shall hold office for such period, have such authority and perform such duties as are provided in the By-Laws or as the Board of Directors may from time to time determine.

Section 4. REMOVAL AND RESIGNATION. Any officer may be removed, either with or without cause, by a majority of the Directors at the time in office, at any regular or special meeting of the Board, or, except in case of an officer chosen by the Board of Directors, or, by any officer upon whom such power of removal may be conferred by the Board of Directors.

Any officer may resign at any time by giving written notice to the Board of Directors, or to the President, or to the Secretary of the corporation. Any such resignation shall take effect at the date of the receipt of such notice or at any later time specified therein; and, unless otherwise specified therein, the acceptance of such resignation shall not be necessary to make it effective.

Section 5. VACANCIES. A vacancy in any office because of death, resignation, removal, disqualification or any other cause, shall be filled in the manner prescribed in the By-Laws for regular appointments to such office.

Section 6. CHAIRMAN OF THE BOARD. The Chairman of the Board, If there shall be such an officer, shall, if present, preside at all meetings of the Board of Directors, and exercise and perform such other powers and duties as may be from time to time assigned to him by the Board of Directors or prescribed by the By-Laws.

Section 7. PRESIDENT. Subject to such supervisory powers, if any, as may be given by the Board of Directors to the Chairman of the Board, if there be such an officer, the President shall be the Chief Executive Officer of the corporation and shall, subject to the control of the Board of Directors, have general supervision, direction and control of the business and officers of the corporation. He shall preside at all meetings of the shareholders and, in the absence of the Chairman of the Board, or if there be none, at all meetings of the Board of Directors. He shall be ex officio a member of all the standing committees, including the Executive Committee, if any, and shall have the general powers and duties of management usually vested in the office of President of a corporation, and shall have such other powers and duties as may be prescribed by the Board of Directors or the By-Laws.

Section 8. VICE PRESIDENT. In the absence or disability of the President, the Vice Presidents, in order of their rank as fixed by the Board of Directors or, if not ranked, the Vice President designated by the Board of Directors, shall perform all the duties of the President, and when so acting shall have all the powers of and be subject to all the restrictions upon, the President. The Vice Presidents shall have such other powers and perform such other duties as from time to time may be prescribed for them respectively by the Board of Directors or the By-Laws.

Section 9. SECRETARY. The Secretary shall keep, or cause to be kept, a book of minutes at the principal office, or at such other place as the Board of Directors may order, of all meetings of Directors and shareholders, with the time and place of holding, whether regular or special and, if special, how authorized; the notice thereof given; the names of those present at Directors' meetings; the number of shares present or represented at shareholders' meetings; and the proceedings thereof.

The Secretary shall keep, or cause to be kept, at the principal office or at the office of the corporation's transfer agent, a share register, or duplicate share register, showing the names of the shareholders and their addresses; the number and classes of shares held by each; the number and date of certificates issued for the same; and the number and date of cancellation of every certificate surrendered for cancellation.

The Secretary shall give, or cause to be given, notice of all the meetings of the shareholders and of the Board of Directors required by the By-Laws or by law to be given, and he shall keep the seal of the corporation in safe custody, and shall have such other powers and perform such other duties as may be prescribed by the Board of Directors or the By-Laws.

Section 10. CHIEF FINANCIAL OFFICER. This officer shall keep and maintain, or cause to be kept and maintained, in accordance with generally accepted accounting principles, adequate and correct accounts of the properties and business transactions of the corporation, including accounts of its assets, liabilities, receipts, disbursements, gains, losses, capital, earnings (or surplus) and shares. The books of account shall be open to inspection by any Director at all reasonable times.

This officer shall deposit all monies and other valuables in the name and to the credit of the corporation with such depositories as may be designated by the Board of Directors. He shall disburse the funds of the corporation as may be ordered by the Board of Directors; shall render to the President and Directors, whenever they request it, an account of all of his transactions and of the financial condition of the corporation; and shall have such other powers and perform such other duties as may be prescribed by the Board of Directors or the By-Laws.

ARTICLE IV
SHAREHOLDERS MEETINGS

Section 1. PLACE OF MEETINGS. Meetings of the shareholders shall be held at the principal executive office of the corporation, in the State of California, unless some other appropriate and convenient location be designated for that purpose from time to time by the Board of Directors.

Section 2. ANNUAL MEETINGS. The annual meetings of the shareholders shall be held each year as follows: The first day of November. If this day shall be a legal holiday, then the meeting shall be held on the next succeeding business day, at the same hour. At the annual meeting, the shareholders shall elect a Board of Directors, consider reports of the affairs of the corporation, and transact such other business as may be properly brought before the meeting.

Section 3. SPECIAL MEETINGS. Special meetings of the shareholders may be called at any time by the Board of Directors, the Chairman of the Board, the President, a Vice-President, the Secretary, or by one or more shareholders holding not less than one tenth (1/10th) of the voting power of the corporation. Except as next provided, notice shall be given as for the annual meeting.

Upon receipt of a written request addressed to the Chairman, President, Vice President or Secretary, mailed or delivered personally to such officer by any person (other than the Board) entitled to call a special meeting of shareholders, such officer shall cause notice to be given to the shareholders entitled to vote that a meeting will be held at a time requested by the person or persons calling the meeting, not less than twenty five (25) nor more than sixty (60) days after the receipt of such request. If such notice is not given within twenty (20) days after receipt of such

request, the persons calling the meeting may give notice thereof in the manner provided by these By-Laws or apply to the Superior Court as provided in the Corporations Code.

Section 4. NOTICE OF MEETINGS - REPORTS. Notice of meetings, annual or special, shall be given in writing not less than ten (10) nor more than sixty (60) days before the date of the meeting, to shareholders entitled to vote thereat by the Secretary or the Assistant Secretary, or, if there be no such officer, or in the case of his neglect or refusal, by any Director or shareholder.

Such notices or any reports shall be given personally or by mail or other means of written communications as provided in the Corporations Code and shall be sent to the shareholder's address appearing on the books of the corporation, or supplied by him to the corporation for the purpose of notice, and in the absence thereof, as provided in the Corporations Code.

Notice of any meeting of shareholders shall specify the place, the day and the hour of meeting, and (1) in case of a special meeting, the general nature of the business to be transacted and no other business may be transacted; or (2) in the case of an annual meeting, those matters which the Board at date of mailing intends to present for action by the shareholders. At any meetings where Directors are to be elected, notice shall include the names of the nominees, if any, intended at date of notice to be presented by management for election.

If a shareholder supplies no address, notice shall be deemed to have been given to him if mailed to the place where the principal executive office of the company, in California, is situated, or published at least once in some newspaper of general circulation in the County of said principal office.

Notice shall be deemed given at the time it is delivered personally or deposited in the mail or sent by other means of written communication. The officer giving such notice or report shall prepare and file an affidavit or declaration thereof.

When a meeting is adjourned for forty five (45) days or more, notice of the adjourned meeting shall be given as in case of an original meeting. Except as aforesaid, it shall not be necessary to give any notice of adjournment or of the business to be transacted at an adjourned meeting other than by announcement at the meeting at which such adjournment is taken.

Section 5. VALIDATION OF SHAREHOLDERS' MEETINGS. The transactions of any meeting of shareholders, however called and noticed, shall be valid as though had at a meeting duly held after regular call and notice, if a quorum be present either in person or by proxy, and if, either before or after the meeting, each of the shareholders entitled to vote who will not be or were not present in person or by proxy, sign a written waiver of notice, a consent to the holding of such meeting or an approval of the minutes thereof. All such waivers, consents or approvals shall be filed with the corporate records or made a part of the minutes of the meeting. Attendance shall constitute a waiver of notice, unless objection shall be made as provided in the Corporations Code.

Section 6. SHAREHOLDERS ACTING WITHOUT A MEETING - DIRECTORS. Any action which may be taken at a meeting of the shareholders may be taken without a meeting or notice of meeting if authorized by a writing signed by all of the shareholders entitled to vote at a meeting for such purpose and filed with the Secretary of the corporation, provided further that while ordinarily Directors can only be elected by unanimous written consent as provided in the Corporations Code, if the Directors fail to fill a vacancy, then a Director to fill that vacancy may be elected by the written consent of persons holding a majority of shares entitled to vote for the election of Directors.

Section 7. OTHER ACTIONS WITHOUT A MEETING. Unless otherwise provided in the Corporations Code or the Articles, any action which may be taken at any annual or special meeting of shareholders may be taken without a meeting and without prior written consent of shareholders to hold said meeting setting forth the action to be taken, shall be signed by the holders of outstanding shares having not less than the minimum number of votes that would be necessary to authorize or take such action at a meeting at which all shares entitled to vote thereon were present and voted.

Unless the consents of all shareholders entitled to vote have been solicited in writing,

(1) Notice of any shareholder approval pursuant to the Corporations Code without a meeting by less than unanimous written consent shall be given at least ten (10) days before the consummation of the action authorized by such approval; and

(2) Prompt notice shall be given of the taking of any other corporate action approved by shareholders without a meeting by less than unanimous written consent, to each of those shareholders entitled to vote who have not consented in writing.

Any shareholder giving a written consent, or the shareholder's proxyholders, or a transferee of the shares or a personal representative of the shareholder or their respective proxyholders, may revoke the consent by a writing received by the corporation prior to the time that written consents of the number of shares required to authorize the proposed action have been filed with the Secretary of the corporation, but may not do so thereafter. Such revocation is effective upon its receipt by the Secretary of the corporation.

Section 8. QUORUM. The holders of a majority of the shares entitled to vote thereat, present in person or represented by proxy, shall constitute a quorum at all meetings of the shareholders for the transaction of business except as otherwise provided by law, by the Articles of Incorporation, or by these By-Laws. If, however, such majority shall not be present or represented at any meeting of the shareholders, the shareholders entitled to vote thereat, present in person or by proxy, shall have the power to adjourn the meeting from time to time, until the requisite amount of voting shares shall be present. At such adjourned meeting at which the requisite amount of voting shares shall be represented, any business may be transacted which might have been transacted at a meeting as originally notified.

If a quorum be initially present, the shareholders may continue to transact business until adjournment, notwithstanding the withdrawal of enough shareholders to leave less than a quorum, if any action taken is approved by a majority of the shareholders required to initially constitute a quorum.

Section 9. VOTING RIGHTS - CUMULATIVE VOTING. Only persons in whose names shares entitled to vote stand on the stock records of the corporation on the day of any meeting of shareholders, unless some other day be fixed by the Board of Directors for the determination of shareholders of record, and then on such other day, shall be entitled to vote at such meeting.

Provided the candidate's name has been placed in nomination prior to the voting and one or more shareholders has given notice at the meeting prior to the voting of the shareholder's intent to cumulate the shareholder's votes, every shareholder entitled to vote at any election for Directors may cumulate his votes and give one candidate

are appointed, the chairman of any such meeting may, and on the request of any shareholder or his proxy shall, make such appointment at the meeting, in which case the number of inspectors shall be either one (1) or three (3) as determined by a majority of the shareholders represented at the meeting.

Section 13. SHAREHOLDERS' AGREEMENTS. Notwithstanding the above provisions in the event this corporation elects to become a close corporation, an agreement between two or more shareholders thereof, if in writing and signed by the parties thereof, may provide that in exercising any voting rights the shares held by them shall be voted as provided therein or as provided by the Corporations Code, and may otherwise modify these provisions as to shareholders meetings and actions.

ARTICLE V
CERTIFICATE AND TRANSFER OF SHARES

Section 1. CERTIFICATES FOR SHARES. Certificates for shares shall be of such form and device as the Board of Directors may designated and shall state the name of the record holder of the shares represented thereby; its number; date of issuance; the number of shares for which it is issued; a statement of the rights, privileges, preferences and restrictions, if any; a statement as to the redemption or conversion, if any; a statement of liens or restrictions upon transfer or voting, if any; if the shares be assessable or, if assessments are collectible by personal action, a plain statement of such facts.

Every certificate for shares must be signed by the President or a Vice President and the Secretary or an Assistant Secretary or must be authenticated by facsimiles of the signatures of the President and Secretary or by a facsimile of the signature of its President and the written signature of its Secretary or an Assistant Secretary.

Section 2. TRANSFER ON THE BOOKS. Upon surrender to the Secretary or transfer agent of the corporation of a certificate for shares duly endorsed or accompanied by proper evidence of succession, assignment or authority to transfer, it shall be the duty of the corporation to issue a new certificate to the person entitled thereto, cancel the old certificate and record the transaction upon its books.

Section 3. LOST OR DESTROYED CERTIFICATES. Any person claiming a certificate of stock to be lost or destroyed shall

---

a number of votes equal to the number of Directors to be elected multiplied by the number of votes to which his shares are entitled, or distribute his votes on the same principle among as many candidates as he thinks fit.

The candidates receiving the highest number of votes up to the number of Directors to be elected are elected.

The Board of Directors may fix a time in the future not exceeding thirty (30) days preceding the date of any meeting of shareholders or the date fixed for the payment of any dividend or distribution, or for the allotment of rights, or when any change or conversion or exchange of shares shall go into effect, as a record date for the determination of the shareholders entitled to notice of and to vote at any such meeting, or entitled to receive any such dividend or distribution, or any allotment of rights, or to exercise the rights in respect to any such change, conversion or exchange of shares. In such case, only shareholders of record on the date so fixed shall be entitled to notice of and to vote at such meeting, or to receive such dividends, distribution or allotment of rights, or to exercise such rights, as the case may be, notwithstanding any transfer of any share on the books of the company after any record date fixed as aforesaid. The Board of Directors may close the books of the company against transfers of shares during the whole or any part of such period.

Section 10. PROXIES. Every shareholder entitled to vote, or to execute consents, may do so, either in person or by written proxy executed in accordance with the provisions of the Corporations Code and filed with the Secretary of the corporation.

Section 11. ORGANIZATION. The President, or in the absence of the President, any Vice President, shall call the meeting of the shareholders to order, and shall act as chairman of the meeting. In the absence of the President and of the Vice Presidents, shareholders shall appoint a chairman for such meeting. The Secretary of the company shall act as Secretary of all meetings of the shareholders, but in the absence of the Secretary at any meeting of the shareholders, the presiding officer may appoint any person to act as Secretary of the meeting.

Section 12. INSPECTORS OF ELECTION. In advance of any meeting of shareholders, the Board of Directors may, if they so elect, appoint inspectors of election to act at such meeting or any adjournments thereof. If no inspectors of election

Section 6. LEGEND CONDITION. In the event any shares of this corporation are issued pursuant to a permit or exemption therefrom requiring the imposition of a legend condition, the person or persons issuing or transferring said shares shall make sure said legend appears on the certificate and on the stub relating thereto in the stock record book and shall not be required to transfer any shares free of such legend unless an amendment to such permit or a new permit be first issued so authorizing such a deletion.

Section 7. CLOSE CORPORATION CERTIFICATES. All certificates representing shares of this corporation, in the event it shall elect to become a close corporation, shall contain the legend required by the Corporations Code.

ARTICLE VI
CORPORATE RECORDS AND REPORTS - INSPECTION

Section 1. RECORDS. The corporation shall maintain, in accordance with generally accepted accounting principles, adequate and correct accounts, books and records of its business and properties. All of such books, records and accounts shall be kept at its principal executive office in the State of California, as fixed by the Board of Directors from time to time.

Section 2. INSPECTION OF BOOKS AND RECORDS. All books and records provided for in the Corporations Code shall be open to inspection of the Directors and Shareholders from time to time and in the manner provided in said Corporations Code.

Section 3. CERTIFICATION AND INSPECTION OF BY-LAWS. The original or a copy of these By-Laws, as amended or otherwise altered to date, certified by the Secretary, shall be kept at the corporation's principal executive office and shall be open to inspection by the shareholders of the company, at all reasonable times during office hours, as provided in the Corporations Code.

Section 4. CHECKS, DRAFTS, ETC. All checks, drafts or other orders for payment of money, notes or other evidences of indebtedness, issued in the name of or payable to the corporation, shall be signed or endorsed by such person or persons and in such manner as shall be determined from time to time by resolution of the Board of Directors.

---

make an affidavit or affirmation of that fact and shall, if the Directors so require, give the corporation a bond of indemnity, in form and with one or more sureties satisfactory to the Board, in at least double the value of the stock represented by said certificate, whereupon a new certificate may be issued in the same tenor and for the same number of shares as the one alleged to be lost or destroyed.

Section 4. TRANSFER AGENTS AND REGISTRARS. The Board of Directors may appoint one or more transfer agents or transfer clerks, and one or more registrars, which shall be an incorporated bank or trust company, either domestic or foreign, who shall be appointed at such times and places as the requirements of the corporation may necessitate and the Board of Directors may designate.

Section 5. CLOSING STOCK TRANSFER BOOKS - RECORD DATE. In order that the corporation may determine the shareholders entitled to notice of any meeting or to vote or entitled to receive payment of any dividend or other distribution or allotment of any rights or entitled to exercise any rights in respect of any other lawful action, the Board may fix, in advance, a record date, which shall not be more than sixty (60) nor less than ten (10) days prior to the date of such meeting nor more than sixty (60) days prior to any other action.

If no record date is fixed:

(1) The record date for determining shareholders entitled to notice of or to vote at a meeting of shareholders shall be at the close of business on the business day next preceding the day on which notice is given or, if notice is waived, at the close of business on the business day next preceding the day on which the meeting is held.

(2) The record date for determining shareholders entitled to give consent to corporate action in writing without a meeting, when no prior action by the Board is necessary, shall be the day on which the first written consent is given.

(3) The record date for determining shareholders for any other purpose shall be at the close of business on the day on which the Board adopts the resolution relating thereto, or the sixtieth day prior to the date of such other action, whichever is later.

in Section 1 of this Article VIII, and the limitations of the Corporations Code, the Board of Directors may adopt, amend or repeal any of these By-Laws other than a By-Law or amendment thereof changing the authorized number of Directors.

Section 3. RECORD OF AMENDMENTS. Whenever an amendment or new By-Law is adopted, it shall be copied in the book of By-Laws with the original By-Laws, in the appropriate place. If any By-Law is repealed, the fact of repeal with the date of the meeting at which the repeal was enacted or written assent was filed shall be stated in said book.

ARTICLE IX
SEAL

The corporation shall adopt and use a corporate seal setting forth the name of the corporation and showing the State and date of incorporation.

ARTICLE X
INDEMNIFICATION OF DIRECTORS, OFFICERS,
EMPLOYEES, AND OTHER AGENTS

Section 1. AGENTS, PROCEEDINGS AND EXPENSES. For the purposes of this Article, "agent" means any person who is or was a Director, officer, employee, or other agent of this corporation, or is or was serving at the request of this corporation as a Director, officer, employee or agent of another foreign or domestic corporation, partnership, joint venture, trust or other enterprise, or was a Director, officer, employee, or agent of a foreign or domestic corporation which was a predecessor corporation of this corporation or of another enterprise at the request of such predecessor corporation; "proceeding" means any threatened, pending or completed action or proceeding, whether civil, criminal, administrative, or investigative; and "expenses" includes, without limitation, attorneys' fees and any expenses of establishing a right to indemnification under Section 4 or Section 5(c) of this Article.

Section 2. ACTIONS OTHER THAN BY THE CORPORATION. This corporation shall indemnify any person who was or is a party, or is threatened to be made a party, to any proceeding (other than an action by or in the right of this corporation) by reason of the fact that such person is or was an agent of this corporation, against expenses, judgments,

---

Section 5. CONTRACTS, ETC. - HOW EXECUTED. The Board of Directors, except as otherwise provided in the By-Laws, may authorize any officer or officers, agent or agents, to enter into any contract or execute any instrument in the name of and on behalf of the corporation. Such authority may be general or confined to specific instances. Unless so authorized by the Board of Directors, no officer, agent or employee shall have any power or authority to bind the corporation by any contract or agreement, or to pledge its credit, or to render it liable for any purpose or to any amount, except as provided in the Corporations Code.

ARTICLE VII
ANNUAL REPORTS

Section 1. DUE DATE, CONTENTS. The Board of Directors shall cause an annual report or statement to be sent to the shareholders of the corporation not later than 120 days after the close of the fiscal or calendar year in accordance with the provisions of the Corporations Code. Such report shall be sent to shareholders at least fifteen (15) days prior to the annual meeting of shareholders. Such report shall contain a balance sheet as of the end of the fiscal year, an income statement and a statement of report thereon of independent accountant or, if there is no such report, a certificate of the Chief Financial Officer or President that such statements were prepared without audit from the books and records of the corporation.

Section 2. WAIVER. The foregoing requirement of an annual report may be waived by the Board so long as this corporation shall have less than 100 shareholders.

ARTICLE VIII
AMENDMENTS TO BY-LAWS

Section 1. BY SHAREHOLDERS. New By-Laws may be adopted or these By-Laws may be repealed or amended at their annual meeting, or at any other meeting of the shareholders called for that purpose, by a vote of shareholders entitled to exercise a majority of the voting power of the corporation, or by written assent of such shareholders.

Section 2. POWER OF DIRECTORS. Subject to the right of the shareholders to adopt, amend or repeal By-Laws, as provided

fines, settlements and other amounts actually and reasonably incurred in connection with such proceeding if that person acted in good faith and in a manner that person reasonably believed to be in the best interests of this corporation and, in the case of a criminal proceeding, had no reasonable cause to believe the conduct of that person was unlawful. The termination of any proceeding by judgment, order, settlement, conviction, or upon a plea of nolo contendere or its equivalent shall not, of itself, create a presumption that the person did not act in good faith and in a manner which the person reasonably believed to be in the best interests of this corporation or that the person had reasonable cause to believe that the person's conduct was unlawful.

Section 3. ACTIONS BY THE CORPORATION. This corporation shall indemnify any person who was or is a party, or is threatened to be made a party, to any threatened, pending or completed action by or in the right of this corporation to procure a judgment in its favor by reason of the fact that the person is or was an agent of this corporation, against expenses actually and reasonably incurred by that person in connection with the defense or settlement of that action if that person acted in good faith, in a manner that person believed to be in the best interests of this corporation and with such care, including reasonably inquiry, as an ordinarily prudent person in a like position would use under similar circumstances. No indemnification shall be made under this Section 3:

(a) In respect of any claim, issue or matter as to which that person shall have been adjudged to be liable to this corporation in the performance of that person's duty to this corporation, unless and only to the extent that the court in which that action was brought shall determine upon application that, in view of all the circumstances of the case, that person is fairly and reasonably entitled to indemnity for the expenses which the court shall determine;

(b) Of amounts paid in settling or otherwise disposing of a threatened or pending action, with or without court approval; or,

(c) Of expenses incurred in defending a threatened or pending action which is settled or otherwise disposed of without court approval.

Section 4. SUCCESSFUL DEFENSE BY AGENT. To the extent that an agent of this corporation has been successful on the merits in defense of any proceeding referred to in Sections 2 or 3 of this Article, or in defense of any claim, issue, or matter therein, the agent shall be indemnified against expenses actually and reasonably incurred by the agent in connection therewith.

Section 5. REQUIRED APPROVAL. Except as provided in Section 4 of this Article, any indemnification under this Article shall be made by this corporation only if authorized in the specific case on a determination that indemnification of the agent is proper in the circumstances because the agent has met the applicable standard of conduct set forth in Sections 2 or 3 of this Article, by:

(a) A majority vote of a quorum consisting of directors who are not parties to the proceeding;

(b) Approval by the affirmative vote of a majority of the shares of this corporation entitled to vote represented at a duly held meeting at which a quorum is present or by the written consent of holders of a majority of the outstanding shares entitled to vote. For this purpose, the shares owned by the person to be indemnified shall not be considered outstanding or entitled to vote thereon; or

(c) The court in which the proceeding is or was pending, on application made by this corporation or the agent or the attorney or other person rendering services in connection with the defense, whether or not such application by the agent, attorney, or other person is opposed by this corporation.

Section 6. ADVANCE OF EXPENSES. Expenses incurred in defending any proceeding may be advanced by this corporation before the final disposition of the proceeding on receipt of an undertaking by or on behalf of the agent to repay the amount of the advance unless it shall be determined ultimately that the agent is entitled to be indemnified as authorized in this Article.

Section 7. OTHER CONTRACTUAL RIGHTS. Nothing contained in this Article shall affect any right to indemnification to which persons other than directors and officers of this corporation or any subsidiary hereof may be entitled by contract or otherwise.

Section 8. LIMITATIONS. No indemnification or advance shall be made under this Article, except as provided in Section 4 or Section 5(c), in any circumstance where it appears:

NOTE SECURED BY DEED OF TRUST – INSTALLMENT NOTE – INTEREST EXTRA

DO NOT DESTROY THIS NOTE: When paid, this note, with Deed of Trust securing same, must be surrendered to Trustee for cancellation, before reconveyance will be made.

$ 100,000   Los Angeles   , California,   January 1   , 19 81

In installments as herein stated, for value received, I promise to pay to   Sam Seller

_____, or order,

at Los Angeles, California   the sum of   One Hundred Thousand   DOLLARS,

with interest from   Date   on unpaid principal at the rate of   12   per cent

per annum, payable   monthly commencing February 1, 1981

principal payable in installments of   One Thousand   DOLLARS

on the   1st   day of each.

February   on the   1st   day of each.   month, beginning on the   1st   day of

February   , 19 81 and continuing until December 31, 1985

when all unpaid principal and accrued interest shall become all due

and payable.

and continuing until said principal and interest have been paid.

Should interest not be so paid it shall thereafter bear like interest as the principal, but such unpaid interest to be compounded shall not exceed an amount equal to simple interest on the unpaid principal at the maximum rate permitted by law. Should default be made in payment of any installment of principal or interest when due the whole sum of principal and interest shall become immediately due at the option of the holder of this note. Principal and interest payable in lawful money of the United States. If action be instituted on this note I promise to pay such sum as the Court may fix as attorney's fees. This note is secured by a DEED OF TRUST to CHICAGO TITLE INSURANCE CO., a corporation, as Trustee.

_____

     /S/
_____
     Burton Buyer

1-123

(a) That it would be inconsistent with a provision of the articles, a resolution of the shareholders, or an agreement in effect at the time of the accrual of the alleged cause of action asserted in the proceeding in which the expenses were incurred or other amounts were paid, which prohibits or otherwise limits indemnification; or

(b) That it would be inconsistent with any condition expressly imposed by a court in approving a settlement.

Section 9. INSURANCE. Upon and in the event of a determination by the Board of Directors of this corporation to purchase such insurance, this corporation shall purchase and maintain insurance on behalf of any agent of the corporation against any liability asserted against or incurred by the agent in such capacity or arising out of the agent's status as such whether or not this corporation would have the power to indemnify the agent against that liability under the provisions of this Section.

Section 10. FIDUCIARIES OF CORPORATE EMPLOYEE BENEFIT PLAN. This Article does not apply to any proceeding against any trustee, investment manager, or other fiduciary of an employee benefit plan in that person's capacity as such, even though that person may also be an agent of the corporation as defined in Section 1 of this Article. Nothing contained in this Article shall limit any right to indemnification to which such a trustee, investment manager, or other fiduciary may be entitled by contract or otherwise, which shall be enforceable to the extent permitted by law other than this Article.

NOTE SECURED BY DEED OF TRUST, Installment Note, Interest Included, Balance Due Date

DO NOT DESTROY THIS NOTE: When paid, this note, with Deed of Trust securing same, must be surrendered to Trustee for cancellation, before reconveyance will be made.

$100,000   Los Angeles   California, January 1 , 19 81

In installments as herein stated, for value received, Sam Seller promise to pay to

One Hundred Thousand   or order, at Los Angeles, California principal sum of dollars,

with interest from Date on unpaid principal at the rate of 12 per cent

per annum: principal and interest payable in installments of One Thousand dollars or more on the 1st day of

each month, beginning on the 1st day of February , 19 81

and continuing until the 31st day of December , 19 85, on which day the unpaid balance of said principal sum, the unpaid interest due thereon, shall become due and payable.

Each payment shall be credited first on interest then due; and the remainder on principal; and the interest shall thereupon cease upon the principal so credited. Should default be made in payment of any installment of principal and interest, the whole sum of principal and interest shall at the option of the holder of this note, become immediately due. Principal and interest payable in lawful money of the United States. If action be instituted on this note, the undersigned promise to pay such sum as the Court may adjudge as attorney's fees. This note is secured by a DEED OF TRUST to CHICAGO TITLE INSURANCE COMPANY, a corporation.

/S/ Burton Buyer

1-112 (1-67)

PAYMENTS

DATE PAID M D Y	AMOUNT PAID	INTEREST PAID	PRINCIPAL PAID	INTEREST PAID TO M D Y	BALANCE PRINCIPAL UNPAID	TO WHOM PAID

NOTE SECURED BY DEED OF TRUST, Straight Note

DO NOT DESTROY THIS NOTE: When paid, this note, with Deed of Trust securing same, must be surrendered to Trustee for cancellation, before reconveyance will be made.

$ 100,000 _____ Los Angeles _____ , California, __January 1__ , 19 81 , after date, for value received

_____ promise $ ____ to pay to

_____ Sam Seller _____

_____ , or order, at

Los Angeles, California

the sum of __One Hundred Thousand__ _____ dollars,

with interest from __Date__ until paid, at the rate of __12__ per cent per annum, payable __interest only monthly commencing thirty (30) days from the date hereof.__

Should default be made in payment of principal or interest, the whole sum of principal and interest shall, at the option of the holder of this note, become immediately due. Principal and interest payable in lawful money of the United States. If action be instituted on this note, the undersigned promise—to pay such sum as the Court may adjudge as attorney's fees. This note is secured by a DEED OF TRUST to CHICAGO TITLE INSURANCE COMPANY, a corporation.

on or before three (3) years
Burton Buyer

/S/ _____
        Burton Buyer

_____

1-111

PAYMENTS

DATE PAID M D Y	AMOUNT PAID	INTEREST PAID	PRINCIPAL PAID	INTEREST PAID TO M D Y	BALANCE PRINCIPAL UNPAID	TO WHOM PAID

INSTALLMENT NOTE

(Interest only for a definite period and thereafter Principal and Interest Payable in Installments)

$ _____   San Gabriel, California _____

In installments and at the times hereinafter stated, for value received, I/we or either of us promise — to pay to

SAVINGS AND LOAN ASSOCIATION,

a corporation or order, at its office in the City of San Gabriel, California, or at such other place, either within or without the State, as the owner

of this note may from time to time designate, the principal sum of _____ (_____) Dollars

with interest from date on principal unpaid at the rate of _____ per cent per annum, payable.

and monthly thereafter, and with interest from and after maturity at the rate of eight per cent (8%) per annum. Principal and interest

accruing after _____ shall be due and payable in installments of _____ (_____) Dollars each, on the _____ day of each and every

month beginning _____, and continuing to and including _____

balance of principal and interest then unpaid to be due and payable on _____

Each payment shall be credited first, on interest then due; and the remainder on principal; the interest shall thereupon cease upon the principal so credited. Should default be made in payment of interest or of any installment when due, or in the performance of any agreement in the deed of trust securing the payment of this note, then the whole sum of principal and interest shall become immediately due at the option of the holder of this note and shall, at the option of such holder, bear interest during the period of such default at the rate of 8 per cent per annum. Holder may charge and the maker also agrees to pay up to one-fifth of one per cent on the unpaid balance for each default, with a minimum of $5.00 for each default. Principal and interest payable in lawful money of the United States. If action be instituted on this note, I promise to pay such sum as the Court may fix as attorney's fees. This note is secured by DEED OF TRUST to _____, a California corporation.

The makers, endorsers, guarantors and sureties of this note and each of them hereby waive diligence, demand, presentment for payment, notice of non-payment, protest and notice of protest and specifically consent to and waive notice of any renewals or extensions of this note, whether made to or in favor of the makers or any other person or persons. The pleading of any statute of limitations as a defense to any demand against makers, endorsers, guarantors and sureties, is expressly waived by each and all of said parties.

On or after six months from date, on three months written notice to the obligor, the holder may increase the above interest rate by a maximum of ⅜ of 1% per annum for each ¼ of 1% per annum by which Prudential Savings and Loan Association has increased the interest rate payable to its certificate holders on investment certificate accounts over the now existing rate, provided within said three months period, the obligor may pay in full the balance due plus all accrued interest without any prepayment penalty.

If the obligor shall sell, convey or alienate the property described in the deed of trust securing this note, or any part thereof, or any interest therein, or shall be divested of his title, or any interest therein, in any manner or way, whether voluntary or involuntary, any indebtedness or obligation secured thereby, irrespective of the maturity dates expressed in any note evidencing the same, at the option of the holder hereof, and without demand or notice, shall immediately become due and payable.

PAYMENTS

DATE PAID M D Y	AMOUNT PAID	INTEREST PAID	PRINCIPAL PAID	INTEREST PAID TO M D Y	BALANCE PRINCIPAL UNPAID	TO WHOM PAID

DO NOT DESTROY THIS NOTE: When paid, this note, with Deed of Trust securing same, must be surrendered to the Trustee for cancellation before reconveyance will be made.

Loan No.

PROMISSORY NOTE

$_____   _____, California

_____ 19___

FOR VALUE RECEIVED, the undersigned, jointly and severally, promise(s) to pay to the order of _____ SAVINGS AND LOAN ASSOCIATION at its office in _____, California, or at any other place designated by the holder, the principal sum of ($_____)_____ Dollars, with interest from the date hereof on the unpaid principal at the rate of _____ per cent per annum, payable in installments as hereinafter provided.

The principal and interest shall be payable in installments of ($_____)_____ Dollars each, the first installment due and payable on the _____ day of _____, 19___ and subsequent installments on the _____ day of each succeeding month until _____, 19___, when any balance remaining shall become due and payable. Each installment payment shall be applied first to accrued interest and any balance remaining shall be applied in reduction of principal. Should default be made in the payment of any installment when due, or in the performance of any agreement in the Deed of Trust securing the payment of this note, the holder hereof may, at its option, declare any portion or the entire amount of principal and interest to be immediately due and payable.

Should interest not be paid when due, at the option of the holder, it shall be added to the unpaid principal and thereafter bear like interest as the principal.

In the event any payment hereunder is not made when due, the undersigned agree(s) to pay a late charge equal to one-twelfth of an additional 2% per annum on the unpaid principal for each month or portion thereof that the payment remains delinquent, with a minimum late charge of $5.00 for each default. The undersigned further agree(s) to pay reasonable attorney's fees and expenses of collection and servicing that may be incurred by the holder hereof. Principal and interest are payable in lawful money of the United States.

If the property described in the Deed of Trust securing this note is or becomes income property, the undersigned agree(s) to furnish to the holder hereof an annual statement of income and expense with respect to the property. Such statement of income and expense shall be furnished within sixty days after the end of each calendar year and shall be prepared in such detail as to present fairly the operating results of the property during the calendar year then ended. The statement shall be accompanied by a certificate executed by the undersigned to the effect that the statement of income and expense has been prepared in accordance with generally accepted accounting principles, consistently applied. In the event the undersigned shall fail to provide any such statement of income and expense, the holder hereof may, at its option, declare any portion or the entire amount of principal and interest to be immediately due and payable.

If the undersigned shall sell, convey or alienate the property described in the Deed of Trust securing this note, or any part thereof, or any interest therein, or shall be divested of title, or any interest therein in any manner or way, whether voluntary or involuntary, the holder hereof may, at its option, declare any portion or the entire amount of principal and interest to be immediately due and payable.

Each of such options may be exercised separately, or may be exercised concurrently with any other option or options. Failure to exercise any option shall not constitute a waiver of the right of the holder hereof to exercise such option in the event of any subsequent default.

The undersigned and endorsers hereof hereby severally waive demand, presentment for payment, protest, notice of nonpayment and notice of dishonor.

This note is secured by a Deed of Trust of even date herewith to Financial Federation, Inc., a Delaware corporation.

The undersigned shall have the privilege of prepaying the principal of this note either in full or in part on any installment date; provided, however, that when the aggregate amount of prepayments, together with required payments of principal and interest, in any calendar year exceeds 20% of the original principal amount of this note, the undersigned agree(s) to pay 180 days interest on such amount prepaid in excess of said 20%.

PROMISSORY NOTE

NOTICE TO BORROWER: THIS DOCUMENT CONTAINS PROVISIONS FOR A VARIABLE INTEREST
RATE

US $ 250,000.00   LOAN NO.

TORRANCE, California   19

1. For value received, I promise to pay to   a
corporation, or order, at WHITTIER   or at such other
offices as the holder hereof may from time to time designate, the principal sum of TWO HUNDRED
FIFTY THOUSAND AND NO\100——
    DOLLARS, with interest from the date hereof on the unpaid principal balance at the initial rate
of 11.25 percent per annum ("Initial Interest Rate"), principal and interest payable in monthly installments
of TWO THOUSAND
    FOUR HUNDRED THIRTY AND NO\100 ($2,430.00) Dollars each, beginning on the
    day of   , 19   , and continuing on the 15TH day of each and every month thereafter
until said principal and interest have been paid in full.

Each payment shall be credited first on interest then due and the remainder on principal; and interest
thereupon ceases upon the principal so credited.

2. I agree that the Initial Interest Rate shall be increased and decreased from time to time in accordance
with increases and decreases in the weighted average cost of savings, borrowings, and Federal Home
Loan Bank advances to California members of the Federal Home Loan Bank of San Francisco, as computed
from statistics tabulated and published by the Federal Home Loan Bank of San Francisco (such weighted
average cost being hereinafter referred to as the "Standard"), or such other Standard as may be approved
by the California Savings and Loan Commissioner. Subject to the following provisions, such increases
and decreases shall be effected in such manner as to maintain the same margin above or below the
Initial Interest Rate as the last published Standard is above or below the last published Standard on the
date of this Note:

(a) Any change in the interest rate shall not exceed 1/4 of 1% per annum in any semiannual period
and shall not result in an interest rate more than 2.5 percentage points greater than the Initial Interest
Rate.

(b) No increase or decrease in the interest rate in any semiannual period shall be less than 1/10 of
1% per annum except for increases or decreases not previously invoked in full by reason of the 1/4 of
1% per annum maximum limitation set forth above.

(c) No change in the rate of interest shall be made during the first seimannual period; after the first
semiannual period there shall be only one change in any one semiannual period and at least six months
shall elapse between each change. As used in this Note, "semiannual period" means each of the successive
periods of six calendar months commencing with the first day of the calendar month in which this Note
is dated.

(d) Each change in the interest rate shall become effective commencing on the date the monthly
installment becomes due during the second month following the first publication of the Standard in each
semiannual period, provided, however, that the first change in interest rate (if there has then been a
sufficient change in the Standard) shall become effective with the first loan installment falling due more
than 30 days after the first publication of the Standard following expiration of the first semiannual period
of the loan.

(e) Decreases in the interest rate shall be mandatory and increases shall be optional with the holder,
but the fact that the holder may not have invoked a permissible increase, in whole or in part, shall not
be deemed a waiver of the holder's right to invoke said increase at any time thereafter within the limits
herein provided.

(f) When there is a change in the interest rate, at the option of the holder of this Note, (i) the amount
of each monthly installment payable hereon may be decreased or increased to an amount which, when
paid in equal monthly installments rounded to the next highest dollar amount, would result in full payment
of the then unpaid principal balance together with interest thereon at the changed interest rate by the
end of the amortization period in effect just prior to such change, or (ii) with the consent of the undersigned,
such amortization period may be reduced or extended, or (iii) a combination of (i) or (ii) may be made.
Notwithstanding the foregoing, if the purpose of the loan evidenced by this Note is to finance the purchase
or construction of real property containing four or fewer residential units, then upon any increase in the
interest rate, at the option of the undersigned the amortization period of this Note may be extended for
such additional period as may be required to amortize this Note without increasing the then existing
monthly installment payable hereon, but not to exceed a maximum amortization period of 40 years from
the due date of the first installment.

(g) Notices of any change in interest rate or amount of the monthly installment shall be deemed given
by the holder when deposited in the United States mail, postage prepaid, addressed to the current owner

of the property described in the Deed of Trust securing this Note and any other person personally liable on this Note, as those persons' names and addresses appear on the holder's records at the time of giving notice.

3. Should default be made in the payment of any installment when due, or in the performance of any provision or condition contained in the Deed of Trust securing this Note, the whole sum of principal and interest shall become immediately due at the option of the holder.

4. If any installment is not paid within 10 days after its due date, Borrower shall pay the Note holder a late charge equal to 10% of the amount of the installment, or $10, whichever is greater. Since it would be impracticable or extremely difficult to fix the actual damage resulting from the failure to make payment when due, the damage shall be presumed to be an amount calculated as aforesaid, and shall be in lieu of all other money damage remedies.

If the Deed of Trust securing the Note is on real property containing only a single-family, owner-occupied dwelling (as defined by California law), then if any installment is not paid within 10 days after its due date, the amount of the late charge shall be 6% of the amount of the installment, or $5, whichever is greater.

5. The indebtedness created hereby may be prepaid at any time, provided, that if the aggregate amount prepaid in any twelve month period exceeds 20% of the original amount of this Note, I agree to pay the holder hereof an amount equal to six months advance interest, at the interest rate then in effect, on the amount prepaid in excess of 20% of the original principal amount. Such interest shall be paid whether prepayment is voluntary or involuntary, including any prepayment effected by the exercise of any acceleration provision contained in this Note or the Deed of Trust securing it. However, the charges and limitations contained in this paragraph are not applicable (a) within the 90 day period immediately following notice of any increase in interest rate, or (b) to any prepayment made more than five years after the date of execution of the Deed of Trust securing this Note if the real property covered by said Deed of Trust is a single family owner occupied dwelling.

6. Principal, interest, and charges payable in lawful money of the United States.

7. Presentment, notice of dishonor, and protest are hereby waived by all makers, sureties, guarantors and endorsers hereof. This Note shall be the joint and several obligation of all makers, sureties, guarantors and endorsers, and shall be binding upon them and their successors and assigns.

8. The indebtedness evidenced by this Note is secured by a Deed of Trust, and reference is made to the Deed of Trust for rights as to acceleration of the indebtedness evidenced by the Note, including paragraph 16 which provides as follows:

"(16) Acceleration Clause: Right of Beneficiary to Declare All Sums Due on any Transfer, Etc. Beneficiary shall have the right, at its option, to declare any indebtedness and obligations secured hereby, irrespective of the maturity date specified in any note or agreement evidencing the same, due and payable within 30 days after such declaration if (a) Trustor or any successor in interest to Trustor of such property sells, enters into a contract of sale, conveys or alienates such property or any part thereof, or suffers his title or any interest therein to be divested, whether voluntarily or involuntarily, or leases such property or any part thereof for a term of 5 years or more, or changes or permits to be changed the character or use of the property, or drills or extracts or enters into a lease for the drilling for or extracting oil, gas or other hydrocarbon substance or any mineral of any kind or character on such property, or (b) Trustor is a partnership and the interest of a general partner is assigned or transferred, or (c) Trustor is a trust and there is a change of beneficial interest with respect to more than 25% of such property, or (e) Trustor has made any material misrepresentation or failed to disclose any material fact, in those certain financial and other written representations and disclosures made by Trustor in order to induce Beneficiary to enter into the transaction evidenced by the Promissory Note or notes or agreements which this Deed of Trust secures."

9. Except as provided in Section 2(g) above, any notice to Borrower provided for in this Note shall be given by mailing such notice by certified mail addressed to Borrower at the address of the Property securing this note, or to such other address as Borrower may designate by notice to the Note holder. Any notice to the Note holder shall be given by mailing such notice by certified mail, return receipt requested, to the Note holder at the address stated in the first paragraph of this Note, or at such other address as may have been designated by notice to Borrower.

10. In the event any provision of the Note or the Deed of Trust securing it is held to be invalid, this shall not invalidate any of the remaining provisions of the Note or Deed of Trust.

*   *   *   *   *   *   *

DATE:

LOAN NO.

....
—Borrower

....
—Borrower

....
—Borrower

....
—Borrower

DO NOT DESTROY THIS NOTE: When paid, this Note, with the Deed of Trust securing it, must be surrendered to Trustee for cancellation, before reconveyance will be made.

RECORDING REQUESTED BY

Sam Seller

AND WHEN RECORDED MAIL TO

Name ⌜Sam Seller
c/o Meyers, Stevens & Walters
Street Address 6300 Wilshire Blvd., #9100
City & State Los Angeles, California 90048⌟

——— SPACE ABOVE THIS LINE FOR RECORDER'S USE ———

LONG FORM DEED OF TRUST AND ASSIGNMENT OF RENTS
THIS FORM FURNISHED BY TICOR TITLE INSURERS

TO 1942 CA (8-74) (OPEN END)　　　　　　　　　　　　　　　　　　A. P. N._____

This Deed of Trust, made this　1st　　　day of　January, 1981　　　, between

Burton Buyer
, herein called TRUSTOR,

whose address is　12345 Main Street　　　Los Angeles　　California　　90000 ,
　　　　　　　　　　(number and street)　　　　　(city)　　　(state)　　　(zip)

TITLE INSURANCE AND TRUST COMPANY, a California corporation, herein called TRUSTEE, and

Sam Seller
, herein called BENEFICIARY,

Witnesseth: That Trustor IRREVOCABLY GRANTS, TRANSFERS AND ASSIGNS to TRUSTEE IN TRUST, WITH POWER OF SALE,
that property in　City of Los Angeles, Los Angeles　　　　　County, California, described as:

Lot 1 of Tract 12345 per Map recorded in Book 100, Page 200 of Official
Records, Los Angeles County, California

TOGETHER WITH the rents, issues and profits thereof, SUBJECT, HOWEVER, to the right, power and authority hereinafter given to and conferred upon Beneficiary to collect and apply such rents, issues and profits.

For the Purpose of Securing:
　1. Performance of each agreement of Trustor herein contained. 2. Payment of the indebtedness evidenced by one promissory note of even date herewith, and any extension or renewal thereof, in the principal sum of $ 100,000.00 executed by Trustor in favor of Beneficiary or order. 3. Payment of such further sums as the then record owner of said property hereafter may borrow from Beneficiary, when evidenced by another note (or notes) reciting it is so secured.

To Protect the Security of This Deed of Trust, Trustor Agrees:
　(1) To keep said property in good condition and repair; not to remove or demolish any building thereon; to complete or restore promptly and in good and workmanlike manner any building which may be constructed, damaged or destroyed thereon and to pay when due all claims for labor performed and materials furnished therefor; to comply with all laws affecting said property or requiring any alterations or improvements to be made thereon; not to commit or permit waste thereof; not to commit, suffer or permit any act upon said property in violation of law; to cultivate, irrigate, fertilize, fumigate, prune and do all other acts which from the character or use of said property may be reasonably necessary, the specific enumerations herein not excluding the general.
　(2) To provide, maintain and deliver to Beneficiary fire insurance satisfactory to and with loss payable to Beneficiary. The amount collected under any fire or other insurance policy may be applied by Beneficiary upon any indebtedness secured hereby and in such order as Beneficiary may determine, or at option of Beneficiary the entire amount so collected or any part thereof may be released to Trustor. Such application or release shall not cure or waive any default or notice of default hereunder or invalidate any act done pursuant to such notice.
　(3) To appear in and defend any action or proceeding purporting to affect the security hereof or the rights or powers of Beneficiary or Trustee; and to pay all costs and expenses, including cost of evidence of title and attorney's fees in a reasonable sum, in any such action or proceeding in which Beneficiary or Trustee may appear, and in any suit brought by Beneficiary to foreclose this Deed.
　(4) To pay: at least ten days before delinquency all taxes and assessments affecting said property, including assessments on appurtenant water stock; when due, all incumbrances, charges and liens, with interest, on said property or any part thereof, which appear to be prior or superior hereto; all costs, fees and expenses of this Trust.
　Should Trustor fail to make any payment or to do any act as herein provided, then Beneficiary or Trustee, but without obligation so to do and without notice to or demand upon Trustor and without releasing Trustor from any obligation hereof, may: make or do the same in such manner and to such extent as either may deem necessary to protect the security hereof, Beneficiary or Trustee being authorized to enter upon said property for such purposes; appear in and defend any action or proceeding purporting to affect the security hereof or the rights or powers of Beneficiary or Trustee; pay, purchase, contest or compromise any incumbrance, charge or lien which in the judgment of either appears to be prior or superior hereto; and, in exercising any such powers, pay necessary expenses, employ counsel and pay his reasonable fees.
　(5) To pay immediately and without demand all sums so expended by Beneficiary or Trustee, with interest from date of expenditure at the amount allowed by law in effect at the date hereof, and to pay for any statement provided for by law in effect at the date hereof regarding the obligation secured hereby any amount demanded by the Beneficiary not to exceed the maximum allowed by law at the time when said statement is demanded.

(6) That any award of damages in connection with any condemnation for public use of or injury to said property or any part thereof is hereby assigned and shall be paid to Beneficiary who may apply or release such moneys received by him in the same manner and with the same effect as above provided for disposition of proceeds of fire or other insurance.

(7) That by accepting payment of any sum secured hereby after its due date, Beneficiary does not waive his right either to require prompt payment when due of all other sums so secured or to declare default for failure so to pay.

(8) That at any time or from time to time, without liability therefor and without notice, upon written request of Beneficiary and presentation of this Deed and said note for endorsement, and without affecting the personal liability of any person for payment of the indebtedness secured hereby, Trustee may: reconvey any part of said property; consent to the making of any map or plat thereof; join in granting any easement thereon; or join in any extension agreement or any agreement subordinating the lien or charge hereof.

(9) That upon written request of Beneficiary stating that all sums secured hereby have been paid, and upon surrender of this Deed and said note to Trustee for cancellation and retention and upon payment of its fees, Trustee shall reconvey, without warranty, the property then held hereunder. The recitals in such reconveyance of any matters or facts shall be conclusive proof of the truthfulness thereof. The grantee in such reconveyance may be described as "the person or persons legally entitled thereto." Five years after issuance of such full reconveyance, Trustee may destroy said note and this Deed (unless directed in such request to retain them).

(10) That as additional security, Trustor hereby gives to and confers upon Beneficiary the right, power and authority, during the continuance of these Trusts, to collect the rents, issues and profits of said property, reserving unto Trustor the right, prior to any default by Trustor in payment of any indebtedness secured hereby or in performance of any agreement hereunder, to collect and retain such rents, issues and profits as they become due and payable. Upon any such default, Beneficiary may at any time without notice, either in person, by agent, or by a receiver to be appointed by a court, and without regard to the adequacy of any security for the indebtedness hereby secured, enter upon and take possession of said property or any part thereof, in his own name sue for or otherwise collect such rents, issues and profits, including those past due and unpaid, and apply the same, less costs and expenses of operation and collection, including reasonable attorney's fees, upon any indebtedness secured hereby, and in such order as Beneficiary may determine. The entering upon and taking possession of said property, the collection of such rents, issues and profits and the application thereof as aforesaid, shall not cure or waive any default or notice of default hereunder or invalidate any act done pursuant to such notice.

(11) That upon default by Trustor in payment of any indebtedness secured hereby or in performance of any agreement hereunder, Beneficiary may declare all sums secured hereby immediately due and payable by delivery to Trustee of written declaration of default and demand for sale and of written notice of default and of election to cause to be sold said property, which notice Trustee shall cause to be filed for record. Beneficiary also shall deposit with Trustee this Deed, said note and all documents evidencing expenditures secured hereby.

After the lapse of such time as may then be required by law following the recordation of said notice of default, and notice of sale having been given as then required by law, Trustee, without demand on Trustor, shall sell said property at the time and place fixed by it in said notice of sale, either as a whole or in separate parcels, and in such order as it may determine, at public auction to the highest bidder for cash in lawful money of the United States, payable at time of sale. Trustee may postpone sale of all or any portion of said property by public announcement at such time and place of sale, and from time to time thereafter may postpone such sale by public announcement at the time fixed by the preceding postponement. Trustee shall deliver to such purchaser its deed conveying the property so sold, but without any covenant or warranty, express or implied. The recitals in such deed of any matters or facts shall be conclusive proof of the truthfulness thereof. Any person, including Trustor, Trustee, or Beneficiary as hereinafter defined, may purchase at such sale.

After deducting all costs, fees and expenses of Trustee and of this Trust, including cost of evidence of title in connection with sale, Trustee shall apply the proceeds of sale to payment of: all sums expended under the terms hereof, not then repaid, with accrued interest at the amount allowed by law in effect at the date hereof; all other sums then secured hereby; and the remainder, if any, to the person or persons legally entitled thereto.

(12) Beneficiary, or any successor in ownership of any indebtedness secured hereby, may from time to time, by instrument in writing, substitute a successor or successors to any Trustee named herein or acting hereunder, which instrument, executed by the Beneficiary and duly acknowledged and recorded in the office of the recorder of the county or counties where said property is situated, shall be conclusive proof of proper substitution of such successor Trustee or Trustees, who shall, without conveyance from the Trustee predecessor, succeed to all its title, estate, rights, powers and duties. Said instrument must contain the name of the original Trustor, Trustee and Beneficiary hereunder, the book and page where this Deed is recorded and the name and address of the new Trustee.

(13) That this Deed applies to, inures to the benefit of, and binds all parties hereto, their heirs, legatees, devisees, administrators, executors, successors and assigns. The term Beneficiary shall mean the owner and holder, including pledgees, of the note secured hereby, whether or not named as Beneficiary herein. In this Deed, whenever the context so requires, the masculine gender includes the feminine and/or neuter, and the singular number includes the plural.

(14) That Trustee accepts this Trust when this Deed, duly executed and acknowledged, is made a public record as provided by law. Trustee is not obligated to notify any party hereto of pending sale under any other Deed of Trust or of any action or proceeding in which Trustor, Beneficiary or Trustee shall be a party unless brought by Trustee.

The undersigned Trustor requests that a copy of any Notice of Default and of any Notice of Sale hereunder be mailed to him at his address hereinbefore set forth.

Signature of Trustor

/S/
_____
Burton Buyer

STATE OF CALIFORNIA
COUNTY OF __Los Angeles__ } SS.
On__January 1, 1981__ before me
the undersigned, a Notary Public in and for said County and State,
personally appeared __Burton Buyer__

_____,
_____, known to me
to be the person___whose name __is__ subscribed to the within
instrument and acknowledged that __he__ executed the same.

Signature_____

_____
Name (Typed or Printed)
Notary Public in and for said County and State

1-117

FOR NOTARY SEAL OR STAMP

Staple
Staple

—— DO NOT RECORD ——

FOR RECONVEYANCE OR FORECLOSURE SEND TO THE NEAREST OFFICE OF THE TITLE INSURANCE AND TRUST COMPANY

REQUEST FOR FULL RECONVEYANCE

To be used only when note has been paid.

Dated_____

To TITLE INSURANCE AND TRUST COMPANY, Trustee:

The undersigned is the legal owner and holder of all indebtedness secured by the within Deed of Trust. All sums secured by said Deed of Trust have been fully paid and satisfied; and you are hereby requested and directed, on payment to you of any sums owing to you under the terms of said Deed of Trust, to cancel all evidences of indebtedness, secured by said Deed of Trust, delivered to you herewith together with the said Deed of Trust, and to reconvey, without warranty, to the parties designated by the terms of said Deed of Trust, the estate now held by you under the same.

MAIL RECONVEYANCE TO:

(By)_____

(By)_____

Do not lose or destroy this Deed of Trust OR THE NOTE which it secures. Both must be delivered to the Trustee for cancellation before reconveyance will be made.

Long Form Deed of Trust WITH POWER OF SALE

Title Insurance and Trust Company AS TRUSTEE

COMPLETE STATEWIDE TITLE SERVICE WITH ONE LOCAL CALL

RECORDING REQUESTED BY

Sam Seller

AND WHEN RECORDED MAIL TO

NAME ⌐Sam Seller
ADDRESS c/o Meyers, Stevens & Walters
CITY & 6300 Wilshire Blvd., #9100
STATE Los Angeles, California
         90048 ⌐

Title Order No. _____ Escrow No. _____

—— SPACE ABOVE THIS LINE FOR RECORDER'S USE ——

DEED OF TRUST AND ASSIGNMENT OF RENTS

By This Deed of Trust, made this 1st   day of   January   , 19 81   , between

Burton Buyer

, herein called Trustor,

whose address is 12345 Main Street   Los Angeles   California   90000
                 (number and street)   (City)   (State)   (Zip Code)

and **CHICAGO TITLE INSURANCE COMPANY**, a Missouri corporation, herein called Trustee, and

Sam Seller

, herein called Beneficiary,

Trustor grants, transfers, and assigns to trustee, in trust, with power of sale, that property in City of Los Angeles, Los
County, California, described as: Angeles

Lot 1 of Tract 12345 per Map recorded in Book 100, Page 200 of
Official Records, Los Angeles County, California

Trustor also assigns to Beneficiary all rents, issues and profits from said real property reserving, however, the right to collect and use the same so long as there is no existing default hereunder and does hereby authorize Beneficiary to collect and recover the same in the name of Trustor or his successor in interest by use of any lawful means.

FOR THE PURPOSE OF SECURING: (1) Payment of the indebtedness evidenced by one promissory note of even date herewith in the principal sum of $100,000.00   , payable to Beneficiary or order; (2) Payment of any additional sums and advances hereafter made by Beneficiary or his assignee to Trustor or his successor in ownership of the real property encumbered hereby; (3) Performance of each agreement of Trustor herein contained.

TO PROTECT THE SECURITY OF THIS DEED OF TRUST, TRUSTOR AGREES that all of the provisions of Section A, Paragraphs 1 through 5, and IT IS MUTUALLY AGREED that all of the provisions of Section B, Paragraphs 1 through 10, both of that certain Fictitious Deed of Trust recorded on the date, as the instrument number and in the book and at the page of Official Records in the office of the county recorder of the county where said property is located, noted below opposite the name of such county, viz.:

COUNTY	RECORDING DATE	INST. NO.	BOOK	PAGE	COUNTY	RECORDING DATE	INST. NO.	BOOK	PAGE
Kern	5-20-68	30035	4162	480	Santa Barbara	5-20-68	16024	2232	955
Los Angeles	1-12-67	1159	T-5220	910	San Diego	1-12-67—Series 8		1967	5000
Orange	1-12-67	6275	8151	422	San Luis Obispo	5-20-68	9567	1476	459
Riverside	1-12-67	3020	6757	41	Ventura	1-12-67	1498	3092	378
San Bernardino	1-12-67	453							

(which provisions, identical in all counties, are printed on the reverse side hereof) are hereby incorporated herein and the parties hereto agree to be bound thereby as though fully set forth herein. All references to property, obligations and parties in the provisions of said Fictitious Deed of Trust are the property, obligations and parties set forth in this deed of Trust.
The undersigned Trustor requests that a copy of any notice of default and any notice of sale hereunder be mailed to him at the address set forth above.

Signature of Trustor

STATE OF CALIFORNIA
COUNTY OF_____   } SS.

On_____ before me, the under-
signed, a Notary Public in and for said County and State, personally
appeared_____

_____
_____, known to me
to be the person___ whose name_____ subscribed to the within
instrument and acknowledged that_____ executed the same.

/S/ _____

   Burton Buyer

_____

_____

_____

_____ Name (Typed or Printed) _____
Notary Public in and for said County and State

FOR NOTARY SEAL OR STAMP

CHICAGO TITLE FORM 1-106

DO NOT RECORD

The following is a copy of provisions (1) to (5), inclusive, of Section A and (1) to (10), inclusive, of Section B of the fictitious deed of trust referred to in the foregoing deed of trust and made a part thereof:

A. TO PROTECT THE SECURITY OF THIS DEED OF TRUST, TRUSTOR AGREES:

(1) To keep said property in good condition and repair, not to remove or demolish any building thereon, to complete or restore promptly and in good and workmanlike manner any building which may be constructed, damaged or destroyed thereon and to pay when due all claims for labor performed and materials furnished therefor; to comply with all laws affecting said property or requiring any alterations or improvements to be made thereon, not to commit or permit waste thereof; not to commit, suffer or permit any act upon said property in violation of laws; to cultivate, irrigate, fertilize, fumigate, prune and do all other acts which from the character or use of said property may be reasonably necessary, the specific enumerations herein not excluding the general.

(2) Trustor shall at all times, at the cost and expense of Trustor, keep all of the encumbered property of an insurable nature constantly insured against loss or damage by fire, lightning, explosion, tornado, wind storm, and against such other risks and hazards as is customarily required by Beneficiary under deeds of trust covering similar properties in this locality, and against such other risks as the Beneficiary may reasonably request, in an amount at least sufficient to pay all unpaid indebtedness secured hereby. Such insurance shall be in companies satisfactory to the Beneficiary, and all such policies of insurance shall be so written as to make any loss occurring thereunder payable by standard mortgage clause attached thereto to the Beneficiary, irrespective of, and which may not be invalidated by, any act or default of the Trustor. Trustor shall also maintain, at the cost and expense of the Trustor, such public liability, workmen's compensation, and other insurances as Beneficiary may reasonably request, insuring the Trustor and the Beneficiary against liabilities, claims, damages, and losses to persons and property arising by reason of construction on, or the use of, the encumbered property, or arising by reason of the conduct and operation of the Trustor on said property.

(3) To appear in and defend any action or proceeding purporting to affect the security hereof or the rights or powers of Beneficiary or Trustee; and to pay all costs and expenses, including cost of evidence of title and attorney's fees in a reasonably sum, in any such action or proceeding in which the Beneficiary or Trustee may appear, and in any suit brought by Beneficiary to foreclose this Deed of Trust.

(4) To pay, at least ten days before delinquency, all taxes and assessments affecting said property, including assessments on appurtenant water stock; when due, all encumbrances, charges and liens, with interest, on said property or any part thereof, which appear to be prior or superior hereto; all costs fees and expenses of this Trust.

Should Trustor fail to make any payment or to do any act as herein provided, then Beneficiary or Trustee, but without obligation so to do and without notice to or demand upon Trustor and without releasing Trustor from any obligation hereof, may: make or do the same in such manner and to such extent as either may deem necessary to protect the security hereof, Beneficiary or Trustee being authorized to enter upon said property for such purposes; appear in and defend any action or proceeding purporting to affect the security hereof, or the rights or powers of Beneficiary or Trustee; pay, purchase, contest or compromise any encumbrance, charge or lien which in the judgment of either appears to be prior or superior hereto; and, in exercising any such powers, pay necessary expenses, employ counsel and pay his reasonable fees.

(5) To pay immediately and without demand all sums so expended by Beneficiary or Trustee, with interest from date of expenditure at seven per cent per annum.

B. IT IS MUTUALLY AGREED THAT:

(1) Any award of damages in connection with any condemnation for public use of or injury to said property or any part thereof is hereby assigned and shall be paid to Beneficiary who may apply or release such moneys received by him in the same manner and with the same effect as above provided for disposition of proceeds of fire or other insurance.

(2) By accepting payment of any sum secured hereby after its due date, Beneficiary does not waive his right either to require prompt payment when due of all other sums so secured or to declare default for failure so to pay.

(3) That at any time or from time to time, without liability therefor, and without notice, upon written request of Beneficiary and presentation of this Deed and said note for endorsement and without affecting the personal liability of any person for payment of the indebtedness secured hereby, Trustee may: reconvey any part of said property; consent to the making of any map or plat thereof; join in granting any easement thereon; or join in any extension agreement or any agreement subordinating the lien or charge hereof.

(4) That upon written request of Beneficiary stating that all sums secured hereby have been paid, and upon surrender of this Deed and said note to Trustee for cancellation and retention and upon payment of its fees, Trustee shall reconvey without warranty, the property then held hereunder. The recitals in such reconveyance of any matters or facts shall be conclusive proof of the truthfulness thereof. The grantee in such reconveyance may be described as "the person or persons legally entitled thereto." Five years after issuance of such full reconveyance, Trustee may destroy said note and this Deed, unless directed in such request to retain them.

(5) As additional security, Trustor hereby gives to and confers upon Beneficiary the right, power and authority, during the continuance of these Trusts, to collect the rents, issues and profits of said property, reserving unto Trustor the right, prior to any default by Trustor in payment of any indebtedness secured hereby or in performance of any agreement hereunder; to collect and retain such rents, issues and profits as they become due and payable. Upon any such default, Beneficiary may at any time without notice, either in person by agent, or by a receiver to be appointed by a court, and without regard to the adequacy of any security for the indebtedness hereby secured, enter upon and take possession of said property or any part thereof, in his own name sue for or otherwise collect such rents, issues and profits, including those past due and unpaid, and apply the same, less costs and expenses of operation and collection, including reasonable attorney's fees, upon any indebtedness secured hereby and in such order as Beneficiary may determine. The entering upon and taking possession of said property, the collection of such rents, issues and profits and the application thereof as aforesaid, shall not cure or waive any default or notice of default hereunder or invalidate any act done pursuant to such notice.

(6) Upon default by Trustor in payment of any indebtedness secured hereby, or in performance of any agreement hereunder, Beneficiary may declare all sums secured hereby immediately due and payable by delivery to Trustee of written declaration of default and demand for sale and of written notice of default and of election to cause said property to be sold, which notice Trustee shall cause to be filed for record. Beneficiary also shall deposit with Trustee this Deed of Trust, said note and all documents evidencing expenditures secured hereby.

After the lapse of such time as may then be required by law following the recordation of said notice of default and notice of sale having been given as then required by law, Trustee, without demand on Trustor shall sell said property at the time and place fixed by it in said notice of sale, either as a whole or in separate parcels, and in such order as it may determine, at public auction to the highest bidder for cash in lawful money of the United States, payable at time of sale. Trustee may postpone sale of all or any portion of said property by public announcement at such time and place of sale, and from time to time thereafter may postpone such sale by public announcement at the time fixed by the preceeding postponement. If the sale is so postponed, or is postponed in any other manner, or if the sale for any reason is not held within one year from the time set for the first sale, the Trustee, at his election, shall have the right to again give notice of sale as then required by law for an original sale. Trustee shall deliver to such purchaser its deed conveying the property so sold, but without any covenant or warranty, express or implied. The recitals in such deed of any matters or facts shall be conclusive proof of the truthfulness thereof. Any person, including Trustor, Trustee, or Beneficiary as hereinafter defined, may purchase at such sale.

After deducting all costs, fees and expenditures of Trustee and of this Trust, including cost of evidence of title in connection with sale, Trustee shall apply the proceeds of sale to payment of all sums expended under the terms hereof, not then repaid, with accrued interest at seven percent per annum; all other sums then secured hereby; and the remainder, if any, to the person or persons legally entitled thereto.

(7) Trustor, or if said property shall have been transferred, the then record owner, together with Beneficiary, may from time to time by instrument in writing substitute a successor or successors to any Trustee named herein or acting hereunder, which instrument, executed and acknowledged by each and recorded in the office of the recorder of the county or counties where said property is situated, shall be conclusive proof of proper substitution of such successor Trustee or Trustees who shall, without conveyance from the Trustee predecessor, succeed to all its title, estate, rights, powers and duties. Said instrument must contain the name of the original Trustor, Trustee, and Beneficiary hereunder, the book and page where this Deed is recorded and the name and address of the new Trustee. If notice of default shall have been recorded, this power of substitution cannot be exercised until after the costs, fees and expenses of the then acting Trustee shall have been paid to such Trustee, who shall endorse receipt thereof upon such instrument of substitution. The procedure herein provided for substitution of Trustee shall not be exclusive. Such substitution may be made in any other manner then permitted by law.

(8) Beneficiary or his successor in interest is hereby empowered to recover from Trustor or the person so requesting those amounts provided for in Section 2954 Civil Code for a statement regarding the obligation or obligations secured by this Deed of Trust, in the manner provided for in said Section.

(9) This Deed of Trust applies to, inures to the benefit of, and binds all parties hereto, their heirs, legatees, devisees, administrators, executors, successors and assigns. The term Beneficiary shall mean the owner and holder, including pledgees, of the note secured hereby, whether or not named as Beneficiary herein. In this Deed of Trust, whenever the context so requires, the masculine gender includes the feminine and/or neuter, and the singular number includes the plural.

(10) Trustee accepts this Trust when this Deed of Trust, duly executed and acknowledged, is made a public record as provided by law. Trustee is not obligated to notify any party hereto of pending sale under any other Deed of Trust or of any action or proceeding in which Trustor, Beneficiary or Trustee shall be a party unless brought by Trustee.

DO NOT RECORD

REQUEST FOR FULL RECONVEYANCE – To be used only when note has been paid.

Date ______________________________, 19____

TO CHICAGO TITLE INSURANCE COMPANY, TRUSTEE

The undersigned is the legal owner and holder of all indebtedness secured by the within Deed of Trust. All sums secured by said Deed of Trust have been fully paid and satisfied; and you are hereby requested and directed, on payment to you of any sums owing to you under the terms of said Deed of Trust, to cancel all evidences of indebtedness, secured by said Deed of Trust, delivered to you herewith together with the said Deed of Trust, and to reconvey, without warranty, to the parties designated by the terms of said Deed of Trust, the estate now held by you under the same.

MAIL RECONVEYANCE TO:

____

____

DO NOT LOSE OR DESTROY THE DEED OF TRUST AND NOTE WHICH IT SECURES. BOTH MUST BE DELIVERED TO THE TRUSTEE FOR CANCELLATION BEFORE RECONVEYANCE WILL BE MADE.

DEED OF TRUST

AND ASSIGNMENT OF RENTS

CHICAGO TITLE INSURANCE COMPANY

WESTERN REGIONAL HEADQUARTERS
3255 WILSHIRE BOULEVARD
LOS ANGELES, CALIFORNIA 90010
(213) 380-3940

VENTURA	(805) 642-4151
RIVERSIDE	(714) 784-2464
SAN BERNARDINO	(714) 884-0448
SAN DIEGO	(714) 232-8921
TUSTIN	(714) 832-7222
FOUNTAIN VALLEY	(714) 964-1751
COVINA	(213) 966-0536
SHERMAN OAKS	(213) 986-5611
SANTA MONICA	(213) 451-8021

RECORDING REQUESTED BY

WHEN RECORDED, PLEASE MAIL
THIS INSTRUMENT TO:

SAVINGS AND
LO^N ASSOCIATION

ORDER NO.
ESCROW OR LOAN NO.

─────SPACE ABOVE THIS LINE FOR RECORDER'S USE─────
DEED OF TRUST WITH ASSIGNMENT OF RENTS

This Deed of Trust, made this   day of   19   , between

herein called TRUSTOR,

whose address is

(Street and Number)   (City)   (State)

a   corporation, herein called TRUSTEE, and

SAVINGS AND LOAN ASSOCIATION, a corporation, herein called BENEFICIARY,

WITNESSETH: That Trustor irrevocably GRANTS, TRANSFERS and ASSIGNS to TRUSTEE, IN TRUST, WITH POWER OF SALE, the property in the County of   , State of California, described as:

Together with the improvements now or hereafter placed thereon and the easements, hereditaments and appurtenances thereunto belonging, including water rights benefiting said property whether represented by shares of a company or otherwise, and the rents, issues and profits therefrom, SUBJECT, HOWEVER, to the right, power and authority hereinafter given to and conferred upon Beneficiary to collect and apply such rents, issues and profits;

For the purpose of Securing: 1. Payment of the sum of $..with interest thereon according to the terms of a promissory note or notes of even date herewith, made by Trustor, payable to the order of the Beneficiary and extensions or renewals thereof. 2. Payment of such additional sums, with interest thereon, as may be borrowed hereafter from the Beneficiary by the then record owner or owners of said property and evidenced by another promissory note or notes. 3. Payment, with interest thereon, of any other indebtedness or obligation of the Trustor (or of any successor in interest of the Trustor to said property) to the Beneficiary, whether created directly or acquired by assignment, whether absolute or contingent, whether matured or unmatured, whether otherwise secured or not, and whether existing at the time of the execution of this deed of trust or arising thereafter. 4. Performance of each agreement of Trustor herein contained.

To Protect the Security of This Deed of Trust, Trustor Agrees: By the execution and delivery of this deed of trust and the note or notes secured hereby, that provisions (1) to (26), inclusive, of the fictitious deed of trust recorded on the date, in the book and beginning at the page of Official Records in the office of the county recorder of the county where said property is located noted below opposite the name of such county, viz.:

COUNTY	BOOK	PAGE	COUNTY	BOOK	PAGE	COUNTY	BOOK	PAGE	COUNTY	BOOK	PAGE
Recorded 11-27-61			Kings	795	264	Placer	899	136	Sierra	30	45
Alameda	460	157	Lake	364	90	Plumas	152	100	Siskiyou	469	248
Alpine	1	274	Lassen	172	448	Riverside	3026	555	Solano	1110	507
Amador	105	143	Los Angeles	T2109	167	Sacramento	4349	301	Sonoma	1858	672
Butte	1151	52	Madera	812	518	San Benito	272	370	Stanislaus	1724	62
Calaveras	146	249	Marin	1519	154	San Bernardino	5595	58	Sutter	575	126
Colusa	297	501	Mariposa	77	633	San Diego	S-2-61	205051	Tehama	403	108
Del Norte	79	179	Mendocino	582	527	San Francisco	A-347	127	Trinity	94	129
El Dorado	572	409	Merced	1551	309	San Joaquin	2482	361	Tulare	2300	656
Fresno	464	47	Modoc	184	1180	San Luis Obispo	1157	176	Tuolumne	135	436
Glenn	424	37	Mono	53	143	San Mateo	4100	662	Ventura	2076	294
Humboldt	662	145	Monterey	2206	53	Santa Barbara	1886	904	Yolo	657	85
Imperial	1094	211	Napa	641	273	Santa Clara	5376	209	Yuba	337	358
Inyo	148	337	Nevada	307	254	Santa Cruz	1438	135	Recorded 12-7-61		
Kern	3437	22	Orange	5923	794	Shasta	688	160	Contra Costa	4010	283

shall be and they hereby are adopted and incorporated herein and made a part hereof as fully as though set forth herein at length; that Trustor will observe and perform said provisions; that the references in said provisions to property and obligations shall be construed to refer to the property affected and the obligations secured by this deed of trust, respectively; and that the references in said provisions to "Trustor," "Beneficiary" and "Trustee" shall be construed to refer to Trustor, Beneficiary and Trustee, respectively, under this deed of trust. Trustor acknowledges that a full copy of said provisions is set forth on the reverse hereof and that he has read and is familiar therewith.

The undersigned Trustor requests that a copy of any Notice of Default and of any Notice of Sale hereunder be mailed to him at his address hereinbefore set forth.

Signature of Trustor

....

....

....

STATE OF CALIFORNIA, COUNTY OF..ss. On..
before me, the undersigned, a Notary Public in and for said County and State, personally appeared..

................known to me to be the person........whose name................subscribed to the within instrument and acknowledged that............ executed the same. Witness my hand and official seal..

My Commission Expires..

Title Order No..

Escrow or Loan No..

If executed by a Corporation the Corporation Form of Acknowledgment must be used.   S.V.   FORM 122-9

DO NOT RECORD

The following is a copy of provisions (1) to (26), inclusive, of the fictitious deed of trust recorded in several counties in California, as stated in the foregoing Deed of Trust, and incorporated by reference in said Deed of Trust as being a part thereof as though set forth therein at length.

To Protect the Security of This Deed of Trust, Trustor Agrees:

(1) To keep said property in good condition and repair; not to remove, demolish or substantially alter (except as such alteration may be required by laws, ordinances or regulations) any building or structure thereon; to complete or restore promptly and in good and workmanlike manner any building or structure which may be constructed, damaged or destroyed thereon, and to pay when due all claims for labor performed and materials furnished therefor; to comply with all laws affecting said property or requiring any alterations or improvements to be made thereon; not to commit or permit waste thereof; not to commit, suffer or permit any act upon said property in violation of law; to cultivate, irrigate, fertilize, fumigate, prune and do all other acts which from the character or use of said property may be reasonably necessary, the specific enumerations herein not excluding the general.

(2) To provide, maintain, and deliver to Beneficiary fire, and if required by Beneficiary other, insurance satisfactory to and with loss payable to Beneficiary. If said insurance policies have not been delivered to the Beneficiary thirty days before the expiration of any of the said insurance, with evidence of the premium having been paid, the Beneficiary shall have the right, but is not obligated, to obtain said insurance on behalf of the Trustor and pay the premium thereon. Neither Trustee nor Beneficiary shall be responsible for such insurance or for the collection of any insurance moneys, or for any insolvency of any insurer or insurance underwriter. The amount collected under any policy of insurance may, at the option of the Beneficiary, be applied by Beneficiary upon any obligation secured hereby and in such order as Beneficiary may determine, or said amount or any portion thereof may, at the option of the Beneficiary, either be used in replacing or restoring the improvements partially or totally destroyed to a condition satisfactory to said Beneficiary, or be released to the Trustor, in either of which events neither the Trustee nor the Beneficiary shall be obligated to see to the proper application thereof; nor shall the amount so released or used be deemed a payment on any obligation secured hereby. Such application, use, and or release shall not cure or waive any default or notice of default hereunder or invalidate any act done pursuant to such notice. Any unexpired insurance and all returnable insurance premiums shall inure to the benefit of, and pass to, the purchaser of the property covered thereby at any trustee's sale held hereunder or at any foreclosure sale of said property.

(3) To appear in and defend any action or proceeding purporting to affect the security hereof or the rights or powers of Beneficiary or Trustee; and to pay all costs and expenses, including cost of evidence of title and attorney's fees in a reasonable sum, in any such action or proceeding in which Beneficiary or Trustee may appear, or in any action or proceeding instituted by Beneficiary or Trustee to protect or enforce the security of this Deed of Trust or the obligations secured hereby.

(4) To pay (a) at least ten days before delinquency, all taxes and assessments affecting the property, and not permit any improvement bond to issue for any special assessments for public improvements, all assessments upon water company stock, and all rents, assessments and charges for water appurtenant to or used in connection with the property; (b) when due, all encumbrances, charges and liens on the property or any part thereof, which appear to be prior or superior hereto, with interest; and (c) all costs, fees and expenses of this trust.

(5) That should Trustor fail to make any payment or to do any act as herein provided, then Beneficiary or Trustee, but without obligation so to do and without notice to or demand upon Trustor and without releasing Trustor from any obligation hereof, may: (a) make or do the same in such manner and to such extent as either may deem necessary to protect the security hereof, Beneficiary or Trustee being authorized to enter upon said property for such purposes; (b) appear in, commence or defend any action or proceeding purporting to affect the security hereof or the rights or powers of Beneficiary or Trustee; (c) pay, purchase, contest or compromise any encumbrance, charge or lien which in the judgment of either appears to be prior or superior hereto; and (d) in exercising any such powers, or in enforcing this Deed of Trust by judicial foreclosure, pay necessary expenses, employ counsel and pay his reasonable fees.

(6) To insure the payment of taxes and assessments affecting the property described at least ten days before the delinquency thereof as provided for in paragraph (4) hereinabove, and to pay such premiums upon policies of insurance which may be required by the Beneficiary as provided for in paragraph (2) hereinabove, the Trustor agrees to pay to the Beneficiary each month, in addition to any other payments required hereunder, an installment of the taxes and special assessments levied or to be levied against the hereinabove described premises and an installment of the premium or premiums that will become due and payable to renew the insurance on the premises covered hereby and required by the Beneficiary, Trustor agreeing to deliver promptly to Beneficiary all bills and notices therefor. Such installments shall be equal to the estimated premium or premiums for such insurance and taxes and assessments next due (as estimated by Beneficiary) less all installments already paid therefor, divided by the number of months that are to elapse before one month prior to the date when such premium or premiums and taxes and assessments will become delinquent. If the amounts paid to the Beneficiary under the provisions of this paragraph are insufficient to discharge the obligation of the Trustor to pay such premium or premiums, taxes and assessments as the same became due, Trustor shall pay to Beneficiary upon its demand such additional sums as it may require to discharge Trustor's obligation to pay premium or premiums, taxes and assessments. At the option of Beneficiary, all moneys paid to Beneficiary under the terms of this paragraph shall be held by Beneficiary in trust to pay such premium or premiums, taxes and assessments before the same become delinquent, or may be credited directly to interest and principal due under the terms of the obligation secured hereby: if said moneys are so credited to interest and principal, then upon payment by the Beneficiary of taxes, assessments and insurance premiums, the amount so paid shall be charged to the principal due upon the obligation secured hereby. If the Trustor shall fail to pay the installments provided for in this paragraph, such failure shall constitute a default under this Deed of Trust.

(7) That in the event of default in the payment of any of the moneys to be paid under the terms of the obligation secured hereby or this Deed of Trust or in the performance of any of the covenants and obligations of this Deed of Trust, then any funds in the possession of the Beneficiary under the provisions of paragraph (6) may, at the option of the Beneficiary, be applied to the payment of principal and or interest upon the obligation secured hereby in lieu of being applied to any of the purposes for which the fund established under paragraph (6) is established.

(8) To pay immediately and without demand all sums expended by Beneficiary or Trustee pursuant to the provisions hereof, with interest from date of expenditure at the rate specified in the obligation secured hereby.

(9) That if the loan secured hereby or any part thereof is being obtained for the purpose of construction of improvements on said property, Trustor also agrees, anything in this Deed to the contrary notwithstanding: (a) to complete same in accordance with plans and specifications satisfactory to Beneficiary; (b) to allow Beneficiary to inspect said property at all times during construction; (c) to replace any work or materials unsatisfactory to Beneficiary, within fifteen (15) calendar days after written notice from Beneficiary of such fact, which notice may be given to the Trustor by registered mail, sent to his last known address, or by personal service of the same; (d) that work shall not cease on the construction of such improvements for any reason whatsoever for a period of fifteen (15) calendar days. The Trustee, upon presentation to it of an affidavit signed by Beneficiary, setting forth facts showing a default by Trustor under this paragraph, is authorized to accept as true and conclusive all facts and statements therein, and to act thereon hereunder.

(10) That any award of damages made in connection with the condemnation for public use of or injury to the property or any part thereof is hereby assigned and shall be paid to Beneficiary, who may apply or release such moneys received therefor in the same manner and with the same effect as above provided for the disposition of proceeds of fire or other insurance, and Trustor will execute such further assignment of any such award as Beneficiary or Trustee requires.

(11) That the acceptance by Beneficiary of any payment less than the amount then due shall be deemed an acceptance on account only and shall not constitute a waiver of the obligation of Trustor to pay the entire sum then due or of Beneficiary's right either to require prompt payment of all sums then due or to declare default. The acceptance of payment of any sum secured hereby after its due date shall not constitute a waiver of the right of Beneficiary either to require prompt payment when due of all other sums so secured or to declare default for failure so to pay, and no waiver of any default shall be a waiver of any preceding or succeeding default of any kind, nor shall the consent to any transaction or occurrence be a consent to, or a waiver of the right to require a consent to, any other transaction or occurrence whether or not similar in nature.

(12) That if the Trustor shall sell, convey, or alienate, or further encumber said property, or any part thereof, or any interest therein, or shall be divested of his title or any interest therein in any manner or way, whether voluntary or involuntary, all obligations secured hereby, irrespective of the maturity date expressed in any note evidencing the same, at the option of the Beneficiary and without demand or notice, shall immediately become due and payable.

(13) That at any time, or from time to time, without liability therefor and without notice, upon written request of Beneficiary and presentation of this Deed of Trust and the note or notes secured hereby for endorsement, and without affecting the personal liability of any person for payment of the obligation secured hereby or the effect of this Deed of Trust upon the remainder of said property in securing the full amount of the indebtedness then or thereafter secured hereby Trustee may: Reconvey any part of said property; consent in writing to the making of any map or plat thereof; join in granting any easement thereon; or join in any extension agreement or any agreement subordinating the lien or charge hereof.

(14) That upon written request of Beneficiary stating that all sums secured hereby have been paid, and upon surrender of this Deed of Trust and said note to Trustee for cancellation and retention and upon payment of its fees, Trustee shall reconvey, without warranty, the property then held hereunder. The recitals in such reconveyance of any matters or facts shall be conclusive proof of the truthfulness thereof. The grantee in such reconveyance may be described as "the person or persons legally entitled thereto." Five years after issuance of such full reconveyance, Trustee may destroy said note and this Deed (unless directed in such request to retain them). Such request and reconveyance shall operate as a re-assignment of the rents, issues and profits hereinafter assigned to Beneficiary.

(15) That as additional security, Trustor hereby gives to and confers upon Beneficiary the right, power and authority, during the continuance of these Trusts, to collect the rents, royalties, issues and profits of said property, reserving unto Trustor the right, prior to any default by Trustor in payment of any obligations secured hereby or in performance of any agreement hereunder, to collect and retain such rents, royalties, issues and profits as but not before they become due and payable. Upon any such default, Beneficiary may at any time without notice, either in person, by agent, or by a receiver to be appointed by a court, and without regard to the adequacy of any security for the obligations hereby secured, (a) enter upon and take possession of said property or any part thereof, and (b) with or without taking possession, in his own name sue for or otherwise collect such rents, royalties, issues and profits, including those past due and unpaid, and apply the same less costs and expenses of operation and collection, including reasonable attorney's fees, upon any obligations secured hereby, and in such order as Beneficiary may determine. The entering upon and taking possession of said property, the collection of such rents, royalties, issues and profits and the application thereof as aforesaid shall not cure or waive any default or notice of default hereunder or invalidate any act done pursuant to such notice.

(16) That upon default by Trustor in payment of any obligation secured hereby or in performance of any agreement hereunder, or upon default under any prior lien or encumbrance on all or any part or said property, Beneficiary may declare all sums secured hereby immediately due and payable by delivery to Trustee of written declaration of default and demand for sale and of written notice of default and of election to cause to be sold said property, which notice Trustee shall cause to be filed for record. Beneficiary also shall deposit with Trustee this Deed, said note and all documents evidencing expenditures secured hereby.

(17) That after the lapse of such time as may then be required by law following the recordation of said notice of default, and notice of sale having been given as then required by law, Trustee, without demand on Trustor, shall sell said property at the time and place fixed by it in said notice of sale, either as a whole or in separate parcels, and in such order as it may determine, at public auction to the highest bidder for cash in lawful money of the United States, payable at time of sale. Trustee may postpone sale of all or any portion of said property by public announcement at such time and place of sale, and from time to time thereafter may postpone such sale by public announcement at the time fixed by the preceding postponement. Trustee shall deliver to such purchaser its deed conveying the property so sold, but without any covenant or warranty, express or implied. The recitals in such deed of any matters or facts shall be conclusive proof of the truthfulness thereof. Any person, including Trustor, Trustee, or Beneficiary may purchase at such sale. After deducting all costs, fees and expenses of Trustee and of this Trust, including costs of evidence of title in connection with sale, Trustee shall apply the proceeds of sale to payment of: (a) all sums expended under the terms hereof, not then repaid, with accrued interest at the rate specified in the obligation secured hereby; (b) all other sums then secured hereby; and (c) the remainder, if any, to the person or persons legally entitled thereto.

(18) That Trustee and Beneficiary, and each of them, shall be entitled to enforce payment and or performance of any obligations secured hereby and to exercise all rights and powers under this Deed of Trust or under any other agreement or any laws now or hereafter in force, notwithstanding some or all of the obligations secured hereby are now or shall hereafter be otherwise secured, whether by mortgage, deed of trust, pledge, lien, assignment or otherwise. Neither the acceptance of this Deed of Trust nor its enforcement whether by court action or pursuant to the power of sale or other powers herein contained, shall prejudice or in any manner affect Trustee's or Beneficiary's right to realize upon or enforce any other security now or hereafter held by Trustee or Beneficiary, it being agreed that Trustee and Beneficiary, and each of them, shall be entitled to enforce this Deed of Trust and any other security now or hereafter held by Beneficiary or Trustee in such order and manner as they or either of them may in their uncontrolled discretion determine.

(19) That without affecting the liability of Trustee or of any other party now or hereafter bound by the terms hereof for any obligation secured hereby, Beneficiary from time to time and with or without notice may release any person now or hereafter liable for the performance of such obligation, extend the time for payment or performance, accept additional security, and alter, substitute or release any security.

(20) That if this Deed or any note secured hereby provides for any penalty for prepayment of any obligation secured hereby, Trustor agrees to pay such penalty if any such obligation be paid prior to the due date thereof, notwithstanding that all sums or obligations secured hereby shall have become immediately due and payable by reason of any provision herein contained.

(21) That no remedy hereby given to Beneficiary or Trustee is exclusive of any other remedy hereunder or under any present or future law.

(22) That Beneficiary may, from time to time, by instrument in writing, substitute a successor or successors to any Trustee named herein or acting hereunder, which instrument, executed and acknowledged by Beneficiary and recorded in the office of the recorder of the county or countries where said property is situated, shall be conclusive proof of proper substitution of such successor Trustee or Trustees, who shall, without conveyance from the Trustee predecessor, succeed to all its title, estate, rights, powers and duties. Said instrument must contain the name of the original Trustor, Trustee and Beneficiary hereunder, the book and page where this Deed is recorded, and the name and address of the new Trustee. If notice of default shall have been recorded, this power of substitution cannot be exercised until after the costs, fees and expenses of the then acting Trustee shall have been paid to such Trustee who shall endorse receipt thereof upon such instrument of substitution. The procedure herein provided for substitution of Trustee shall be exclusive of all other provisions for substitution, statutory or otherwise.

(23) That Trustor waives the right to assert at any time any statute of limitations as a bar to any action brought to enforce any obligation hereby secured.

(24) That this Deed shall inure to and bind the heirs, legatees, devisees, administrators, executors, successors, and assigns of the parties hereto. All obligations of Trustor hereunder are joint and several. The term "Beneficiary" shall mean the owner and holder, including pledgees of the indebtedness secured hereby, whether or not named as Beneficiary herein, and whether by operation of law or otherwise. Whenever used, the singular number shall include the plural, the plural the singular, and the use of any gender shall include all genders.

(25) That Trustee accepts this Trust when this Deed, duly executed and acknowledged, is made a public record as provided by law. Trustee is not obligated to notify any party hereto of pending sale under any other Deed of Trust or of any action or proceeding in which Trustor, Beneficiary or Trustee shall be a party unless brought by Trustee. The Trustee shall not be obligated to perform any act required of the Trustee hereunder unless the Trustee is requested in writing and is reasonably indemnified against loss, cost, liability and expense.

(26) To pay $15 for each statement requested by Trustor, or on his behalf, which contains only information that is among the matters specified in Chapter 1561, California Statutes 1961, and to pay the reasonable charges of Beneficiary for any other service rendered Trustor, or on his behalf, connected with this Deed of Trust or the loan secured hereby including, without limiting the generality of the foregoing, the delivery to an escrow holder of a request for full or partial reconveyance of this Deed of Trust; transmitting to an escrow holder moneys secured hereby; changing its records pertaining to this Deed of Trust and the loan secured hereby to show a new owner of said property; replacing an existing policy of fire insurance or other casualty insurance held by Beneficiary hereunder, with another such policy, Any such charge shall be secured hereby and Trustor agrees to pay the same, together with interest from the date of such charge at the rate specified in the obligation secured hereby, immediately and without demand.

The undersigned Trustor requests that a copy of any Notice of Default and of any Notice of Sale hereunder be mailed to him at his address hereinbefore set forth.

DO NOT RECORD

REQUEST FOR FULL RECONVEYANCE

To be used only when note has been paid.

TO TRUSTEE: Dated ____________

The undersigned is the legal owner and holder of all indebtedness secured by the within Deed of Trust. All sums secured by said Deed of Trust have been fully paid and satisfied; and you are hereby requested and directed, on payment to you of any sums owing to you under the terms of said Deed of Trust, to cancel all evidences of indebtedness secured by said Deed of Trust and delivered to you herewith together with said Deed of Trust, and to reconvey, without warranty, to the parties designated by the terms of said Deed of Trust, the estate now held by you under the same.

MAIL RECONVEYANCE TO:

____________ ____________

____________ ____________

____________ BY ____________

____________ BY ____________

Do not lose or destroy this Deed of Trust OR THE NOTE which it secures. Both must be delivered to the Trustee for cancellation before reconveyance will be made.

RECORDING REQUESTED BY

Title Insurance & Trust
Company

AND WHEN RECORDED MAIL TO

Name ⌐Real Property N.V.
Street c/o Myron Meyers, Esq.
Address Suite 9100
City & 6300 Wilshire Boulevard
State ⌊Los Angeles, California 90048

DEED OF TRUST WITH RELEASE CLAUSES

AND SUBORDINATION - FUTURE SUBDIVISION

———— SPACE ABOVE THIS LINE FOR RECORDER'S USE ————

SHORT FORM DEED OF TRUST AND ASSIGNMENT OF RENTS (CORPORATION)   A.P.N.

This Deed of Trust, made this   day of   , between
SPEC LAND COMPANY

a corporation organized under the laws of the State of   **California**   , herein called TRUSTOR,
whose address is **6300 Wilshire Boulevard,Suite 9100, Los Angeles, Ca. 90048** ,
                  (number and street)   (city)   (state)   (zip)

Title Insurance and Trust Company, a California corporation, herein called TRUSTEE, and

REAL PROPERTY N.V., a Netherlands Antilles corporation, herein called BENEFICIARY,

Witnesseth: That Trustor IRREVOCABLY GRANTS, TRANSFERS AND ASSIGNS to TRUSTEE IN TRUST, WITH POWER OF SALE,
that property in   County, California, described as:

See Exhibit "A" attached and made a part hereof.

See also Rider attached hereto and made a part hereof.

TOGETHER WITH the rents, issues and profits thereof, SUBJECT, HOWEVER, to the right, power and authority given to and conferred upon Beneficiary by paragraph (10) of the provisions incorporated herein by reference to collect and apply such rents, issues and profits.
For the Purpose of Securing: 1. Performance of each agreement of Trustor incorporated by reference or contained herein. 2. Payment of the indebtedness evidenced by one promissory note of even date herewith, and any extension or renewal thereof, in the principal sum of $_____ executed by Trustor in favor of Beneficiary or order. 3. Payment of such further sums as the then record owner of said property hereafter may borrow from Beneficiary, when evidenced by another note (or notes) reciting it is so secured.
To Protect the Security of This Deed of Trust, Trustor Agrees: By the execution and delivery of this Deed of Trust and the note secured hereby, that provisions (1) to (14), inclusive, of the fictitious deed of trust recorded in Santa Barbara County and Sonoma County October 18, 1961, and in all other counties October 23, 1961, in the book and at the page of Official Records in the office of the county recorder of the county where said property is located, noted below opposite the name of such county, viz.:

COUNTY	BOOK	PAGE	COUNTY	BOOK	PAGE	COUNTY	BOOK	PAGE	COUNTY	BOOK	PAGE
Alameda	435	684	Kings	792	833	Placer	895	301	Sierra	29	335
Alpine	1	250	Lake	362	39	Plumas	151	5	Siskiyou	468	181
Amador	104	348	Lassen	171	471	Riverside	3005	523	Solano	1105	182
Butte	1145	1	Los Angeles	T2055	899	Sacramento	4331	62	Sonoma	1851	689
Calaveras	145	152	Madera	810	170	San Benito	271	383	Stanislaus	1715	456
Colusa	296	617	Marin	1508	339	San Bernardino	5567	61	Sutter	572	297
Contra Costa	3978	47	Mariposa	77	292	San Francisco	A332	905	Tehama	401	289
Del Norte	78	414	Mendocino	579	530	San Joaquin	2470	311	Trinity	93	366
El Dorado	568	456	Merced	1547	538	San Luis Obispo	1151	12	Tulare	2294	275
Fresno	4626	572	Modoc	184	851	San Mateo	4078	420	Tuolumne	135	47
Glenn	422	184	Mono	52	429	Santa Barbara	1878	860	Ventura	2062	386
Humboldt	657	527	Monterey	2194	538	Santa Clara	5336	341	Yolo	653	245
Imperial	1091	501	Napa	639	86	Santa Cruz	1431	494	Yuba	334	486
Inyo	147	598	Nevada	305	320	Shasta	684	528			
Kern	3427	60	Orange	5889	611	San Diego	Series 2 Book 1961, Page 183887				

(which provisions, identical in all counties, are printed on the reverse hereof) hereby are adopted and incorporated herein and made a part hereof as fully as though set forth herein at length; that he will observe and perform said provisions; and that the references to property, obligations, and parties in said provisions shall be construed to refer to the property, obligations, and parties set forth in this Deed of Trust.
The undersigned Trustor requests that a copy of any Notice of Default and of any Notice of Sale hereunder be mailed to him at his address hereinbefore set forth.

STATE OF CALIFORNIA,   }SS.
COUNTY OF_____
On_____, before me, the
undersigned, a Notary Public in and for said State, personally
appeared_____

_____
known to me to be the_____President, and

_____
known to me to be the_____Secretary of the
corporation that executed the within instrument, and known to me
to be the persons who executed the within instrument on behalf of
the corporation therein named, and acknowledged to me that such
corporation executed the within instrument pursuant to its by-laws
or a resolution of its board of directors.

WITNESS my hand and official seal.

Signature_____

Signature of Trustor

SPEC LAND COMPANY
                                    a corporation

By _____
                                    President

By _____
                                    Secretary

(This area for official notarial seal)

Title Order No._____   Escrow or Loan No._____

TO 1938 CA (7-75) (OPEN END)

── DO NOT RECORD ──

The following is a copy of provisions (1) to (14), inclusive, of the fictitious deed of trust, recorded in each county in California, as stated in the foregoing Deed of Trust and incorporated by reference in said Deed of Trust as being a part thereof as if set forth at length therein.

To Protect the Security of This Deed of Trust, Trustor Agrees:

(1) To keep said property in good condition and repair; not to remove or demolish any building thereon; to complete or restore promptly and in good and workmanlike manner any building which may be constructed, damaged or destroyed thereon and to pay when due all claims for labor performed and materials furnished therefor; to comply with all laws affecting said property or requiring any alterations or improvements to be made thereon; not to commit or permit waste thereof; not to commit, suffer or permit any act upon said property in violation of law; to cultivate, irrigate, fertilize, fumigate, prune and do all other acts which from the character or use of said property may be reasonably necessary, the specific enumerations herein not excluding the general.

(2) To provide, maintain and deliver to Beneficiary fire insurance satisfactory to and with loss payable to Beneficiary. The amount collected under any fire or other insurance policy may be applied by Beneficiary upon any indebtedness secured hereby and in such order as Beneficiary may determine, or at option of Beneficiary the entire amount so collected or any part thereof may be released to Trustor. Such application or release shall not cure or waive any default or notice of default hereunder or invalidate any act done pursuant to such notice.

(3) To appear in and defend any action or proceeding purporting to affect the security hereof or the rights or powers of Beneficiary or Trustee; and to pay all costs and expenses, including cost of evidence of title and attorney's fees in a reasonable sum, in any such action or proceeding in which Beneficiary or Trustee may appear, and in any suit brought by Beneficiary to foreclose this Deed.

(4) To pay: at least ten days before delinquency all taxes and assessments affecting said property, including assessments on appurtenant water stock; when due, all incumbrances, charges and liens, with interest, on said property or any part thereof, which appear to be prior or superior hereto; all costs, fees and expenses of this Trust.

Should Trustor fail to make any payment or to do any act as herein provided, then Beneficiary or Trustee, but without obligation so to do and without notice to or demand upon Trustor and without releasing Trustor from any obligation hereof, may: make or do the same in such manner and to such extent as either may deem necessary to protect the security hereof, Beneficiary or Trustee being authorized to enter upon said property for such purposes; appear in and defend any action or proceeding purporting to affect the security hereof or the rights or powers of Beneficiary or Trustee; pay, purchase, contest or compromise any incumbrance, charge or lien which in the judgment of either appears to be prior or superior hereto; and, in exercising any such powers, pay necessary expenses, employ counsel and pay his reasonable fees.

(5) To pay immediately and without demand all sums so expended by Beneficiary or Trustee, with interest from date of expenditure at the amount allowed by law in effect at the date hereof, and to pay for any statement provided for by law in effect at the date hereof regarding the obligation secured hereby any amount demanded by the Beneficiary not to exceed the maximum allowed by law at the time when said statement is demanded.

(6) That any award of damages in connection with any condemnation for public use of or injury to said property or any part thereof is hereby assigned and shall be paid to Beneficiary who may apply or release such moneys received by him in the same manner and with the same effect as above provided for disposition of proceeds of fire or other insurance.

(7) That by accepting payment of any sum secured hereby after its due date, Beneficiary does not waive his right either to require prompt payment when due of all other sums so secured or to declare default for failure so to pay.

(8) That at any time or from time to time, without liability therefor and without notice, upon written request of Beneficiary and presentation of this Deed and said note for endorsement, and without affecting the personal liability of any person for payment of the indebtedness secured hereby, Trustee may: reconvey any part of said property; consent to the making of any map or plat thereof; join in granting any easement thereon; or join in any extension agreement or any agreement subordinating the lien or charge hereof.

(9) That upon written request of Beneficiary stating that all sums secured hereby have been paid, and upon surrender of this Deed and said note to Trustee for cancellation and retention and upon payment of its fees, Trustee shall reconvey, without warranty, the property then held hereunder. The recitals in such reconveyance of any matters or facts shall be conclusive proof of the truthfulness thereof. The grantee in such reconveyance may be described as "the person or persons legally entitled thereto." Five years after issuance of such full reconveyance, Trustee may destroy said note and this Deed (unless directed in such request to retain them).

(10) That as additional security, Trustor hereby gives to and confers upon Beneficiary the right, power and authority, during the continuance of these Trusts, to collect the rents, issues and profits of said property, reserving unto Trustor the right, prior to any default by Trustor in payment of any indebtedness secured hereby or in performance of any agreement hereunder, to collect and retain such rents, issues and profits as they become due and payable. Upon any such default, Beneficiary may at any time without notice, either in person, by agent, or by a receiver to be appointed by a court, and without regard to the adequacy of any security for the indebtedness hereby secured, enter upon and take possession of said property or any part thereof, in his own name sue for or otherwise collect such rents, issues and profits, including those past due and unpaid, and apply the same, less costs and expenses of operation and collection, including reasonable attorney's fees, upon any indebtedness secured hereby, and in such order as Beneficiary may determine. The entering upon and taking possession of said property, the collection of such rents, issues and profits and the application thereof as aforesaid, shall not cure or waive any default or notice of default hereunder or invalidate any act done pursuant to such notice.

(11) That upon default by Trustor in payment of any indebtedness secured hereby or in performance of any agreement hereunder, Beneficiary may declare all sums secured hereby immediately due and payable by delivery to Trustee of written declaration of default and demand for sale and of written notice of default and of election to cause to be sold said property, which notice Trustee shall cause to be filed for record. Beneficiary also shall deposit with Trustee this Deed, said note and all documents evidencing expenditures secured hereby.

After the lapse of such time as may then be required by law following the recordation of said notice of default, and notice of sale having been given as then required by law, Trustee, without demand on Trustor, shall sell said property at the time and place fixed by it in said notice of sale, either as a whole or in separate parcels, and in such order as it may determine, at public auction to the highest bidder for cash in lawful money of the United States, payable at time of sale. Trustee may postpone sale of all or any portion of said property by public announcement at such time and place of sale, and from time to time thereafter may postpone such sale by public announcement at the time fixed by the preceding postponement. Trustee shall deliver to such purchaser its deed conveying the property so sold, but without any covenant or warranty, express or implied. The recitals in such deed of any matters or facts shall be conclusive proof of the truthfulness thereof. Any person, including Trustor, Trustee, or Beneficiary as hereinafter defined, may purchase at such sale.

After deducting all costs, fees and expenses of Trustee and of this Trust, including cost of evidence of title in connection with sale, Trustee shall apply the proceeds of sale to payment of: all sums expended under the terms hereof, not then repaid, with accrued interest at the amount allowed by law in effect at the date hereof; all other sums then secured hereby; and the remainder, if any, to the person or persons legally entitled thereto.

(12) Beneficiary, or any successor in ownership of any indebtedness secured hereby, may from time to time, by instrument in writing, substitute a successor or successors to any Trustee named herein or acting hereunder, which instrument, executed by the Beneficiary and duly acknowledged and recorded in the office of the recorder of the county or counties where said property is situated, shall be conclusive proof of proper substitution of such successor Trustee or Trustees, who shall, without conveyance from the Trustee predecessor, succeed to all its title, estate, rights, powers and duties. Said instrument must contain the name of the original Trustor, Trustee and Beneficiary hereunder, the book and page where this Deed is recorded and the name and address of the new Trustee.

(13) That this Deed applies to, inures to the benefit of, and binds all parties hereto, their heirs, legatees, devisees, administrators, executors, successors and assigns. The term Beneficiary shall mean the owner and holder, including pledgees, of the note secured hereby, whether or not named as Beneficiary herein. In this Deed, whenever the context so requires, the masculine gender includes the feminine and/or neuter, and the singular number includes the plural.

(14) That Trustee accepts this Trust when this Deed, duly executed and acknowledged, is made a public record as provided by law. Trustee is not obligated to notify any party hereto of pending sale under any other Deed of Trust or of any action or proceeding in which Trustor, Beneficiary or Trustee shall be a party unless brought by Trustee.

── DO NOT RECORD ──

REQUEST FOR FULL RECONVEYANCE
To be used only when note has been paid.

To TITLE INSURANCE AND TRUST COMPANY, Trustee: Dated _____

The undersigned is the legal owner and holder of all indebtedness secured by the within Deed of Trust. All sums secured by said Deed of Trust have been fully paid and satisfied and you are hereby requested and directed, on payment to you of any sums owing to you under the terms of said Deed of Trust, to cancel all evidences of indebtedness, secured by said Deed of Trust, delivered to you herewith together with said Deed of Trust, and to reconvey, without warranty, to the parties designated by the terms of said Deed of Trust, the estate now held by you under the same.

MAIL RECONVEYANCE TO:

_____
_____
_____
_____

Do not lose or destroy this Deed of Trust OR THE NOTE which it secures. Both must be delivered to the Trustee for cancellation before reconveyance will be made.

**Short Form
Deed of Trust**
WITH POWER OF SALE
(CORPORATION)

**Title Insurance
and
Trust Company**
AS TRUSTEE

**TITLE INSURANCE
AND TRUST**
A TICOR COMPANY

COMPLETE STATEWIDE TITLE SERVICE
WITH ONE LOCAL CALL

RIDER TO DEED OF TRUST

Trustor: SPEC LAND COMPANY

Trustee: TITLE INSURANCE AND TRUST COMPANY

Beneficiary: REAL PROPERTY N.V.

NOTICE: THIS SUBORDINATION AGREEMENT RESULTS IN YOUR SECURITY INTEREST IN THE PROPERTY BECOMING SUBJECT TO AND OF LOWER PRIORITY THAN THE LIEN OF SOME OTHER OR LATER SECURITY INSTRUMENT.

The above referenced Deed of Trust is supplemented as follows and in addition the Trustor and Beneficiary agree as follows:

Real Property N.V., a Netherlands Antilles corporation (hereafter "Beneficiary"), and its successors and Spec Land Company, a California corporation (hereafter "Trustor") and its successors agree:

1. PROVIDED Trustor, or its successors, is not then in default under the terms and provisions of this Deed of Trust and the Promissory Note secured hereby, Beneficiary or its successors agree, from time to time, to grant to Trustor or its successors partial reconveyances from the lien and charge of this Deed of Trust.

A. Trustor may obtain a full reconveyance (release) of any one or more of the lawfully subdivided lots comprising a portion of the real property secured by this Deed of Trust. A lawfully subdivided lot for this purpose shall be a numbered lot or parcel designated on a recorded subdivision or parcel map describing all or a portion of the real proeprty described in Exhibit "A" to this Deed of Trust, containing not less than 20 acres.

B. A lawfully subdivided lot (hereafter "Lot") shall be released (reconveyed) from the lien and charge of this Deed of Trust when the following terms and conditions have been met:

(1) The gross sales price of each Lot shall be not less than a sum equal to Four Thousand Dollars ($4,000) per acre times the number of acres in the Lot so released. Thus, by way of example, should a Lot contain 40 acres and the per acres price is $4,000, the gross sales price shall be not less than $160,000.

The number of acres shall be designated on the tract or parcel map or in lieu thereof, a letter signed by a California registered engineer or surveyor certifying the acres in each parcel so released shall be binding on all parties.

(2) The cash received from the sale of the Lot (including principal and/or interest) at the time of the initial sale of said Lot shall not be less than One Thousand Dollars ($1,000) for each acre in said Lot. If a Lot contains a portion of an acre, said $1,000 shall be prorated.

(3) The balance of the gross sales price shall be evidenced by a Purchase Money Promissory Note that provides for the following minimum terms (in addition to other terms and provisions Trustor or its successors shall require):

(i) it shall bear interest at not less than ten per cent (10%) per annum on the unpaid balance;

(ii) principal payments (and/or principal and interest) shall be payable not less often than semiannually with a principal reduction equal to Two Hundred Dollars ($200) for each acre released;

(iii) the entire unpaid balance of principal and interest shall be all due and payable no later than eight (8) years from the date of the Note;

(iv) interest and/or principal may be prepaid in whole or in part at any time without penalty.

(4) The Promissory Note shall be secured by a First Deed of Trust on the Lot in question free and clear of the underlying obligations. The issuance by a title insurance company of title insurance insuring said Deed of Trust to be a first lien on the Lot shall be conclusive evidence that said Deed of Trust is a first Deed of Trust on the Lot in question.

(5) Concurrently with the release of the lien and charge of this Deed of Trust on a Lot, the Promissory Note and Deed of Trust described in Paragraphs 3 and 4 above, Trustor (or its successors) as the Beneficiary of said Deed of Trust (and Payee of the said Promissory Note) shall assign said Note and Deed of Trust without recourse to _____, the Escrow Holder of the escrow, under which Beneficiary and Trustors are parties (the "Escrow"). The creation of said Escrow, the partial releases contemplated hereby and the individual Notes and Deeds of Trust assigned to Real Property as collateral for the Note secured by this Deed of Trust

-2-

TO 1945 CA (8-74)
(Corporation)

STATE OF CALIFORNIA
COUNTY OF   LOS ANGELES   } SS.

On   April , 1981   before me, the undersigned, a Notary Public in and for said State, personally appeared

known to me to be the   President, and
known to me to be the   Secretary
of the corporation that executed the within Instrument, known to me to be the persons who executed the within Instrument on behalf of the corporation therein named, and acknowledged to me that such corporation executed the within instrument pursuant to its by-laws or a resolution of its board of directors.

WITNESS my hand and official seal.

Signature _____

(This area for official notarial seal)

TI

TO 444 C
(Attorney in Fact)

STATE OF CALIFORNIA
COUNTY OF   LOS ANGELES   } SS.

On   April , 1981   before me, the undersigned, a Notary Public in and for said State, personally appeared

known to me to be the person   whose name   subscribed to the within instrument, as the Attorney   in fact of
and acknowledged to me that   subscribed the name
_____ thereto as principal
_____ and _____ own name _____ as Attorney _____ in fact.

WITNESS my hand and official seal.

Signature _____

Name (Typed or Printed)

(This area for official notarial seal)

STAPLE HERE

---

shall be without recourse to the Trustor or its successors. Real Property and its successors agree to look solely to the collateral of said individual Notes and Deeds of Trust and expressly hereby waive any right to a claim or judgment against Trustor or its successors or their respective officers, directors, agents or shareholders.

C. All monies received by Beneficiary (or its successors) under the Escrow shall be disbursed as set forth in the Escrow.

D. All of the terms and provisions of the Escrow are incorporated herein and made a part hereof.

E. Trustor or its successor may cause to be created and recorded Covenants, Conditions and Restrictions (CC&R's) and easements for water lines and pumps and for ingress and egress ("Easements") which will affect the property secured by this Deed of Trust. Beneficiary and its successors agree (1) to subordinate the lien and charge of this Deed of Trust to said CC&R's and Easements; and (2) to join in the recordation of said CC&R's and Easements; and (3) execute such documents as Trustor or its successor or any insuring title company shall request to the end that CC&R's and Easement shall be at all times superior to the lien and charge of this Deed of Trust.

NOTICE: THIS SUBORDINATION AGREEMENT CONTAINS A PROVISION WHICH ALLOWS THE PERSON OBLIGATED ON OUR REAL PROPERTY SECURITY TO OBTAIN A LOAN, A PORTION OF WHICH MAY BE EXPENDED FOR OTHER PURPOSES THAN IMPROVEMENT OF THE LAND.

APPROVED:

Trustor: SPEC LAND COMPANY,
          a California corporation

          By _____

Beneficiary: REAL PROPERTY N.V.;
          a Netherlands Antilles corporation

          By _____

-3-

DO NOT DESTROY THIS ORIGINAL NOTE: When paid, said original note, together with the Deed of Trust securing same, must be surrendered to Trustee for cancellation and retention before reconveyance will be made.

ALL-INCLUSIVE PURCHASE MONEY PROMISSORY NOTE SECURED BY LONG FORM ALL-INCLUSIVE PURCHASE MONEY DEED OF TRUST
(INSTALLMENT NOTE, INTEREST INCLUDED)

$_____   _____, California, _____, 19____

In installments as herein stated, for value received, I/We ("Maker") promise to pay to_____

_____

("Payee") or order, at _____

the principal sum of_____

_____DOLLARS($_____) with interest from

_____on unpaid principal at the rate of _____per cent per annum; principal

and interest payable in installments of _____

_____DOLLARS($_____)

or more on the _____ day of each _____ month, beginning on the _____

day of _____ 19_____, and continuing until said principal and interest have been paid.

Each installment shall be applied first on the interest then due and the remainder on principal; and interest shall thereupon cease upon the principal so credited.

The total principal amount of this Note includes the unpaid principal balance of the promissory note(s) ("Underlying Note(s)") secured by Deed(s) of Trust, more particularly described as follows:

1. (A) PROMISSORY NOTE:

 Maker:_____

 Payee:_____

 Original Amount:_____

 Date:_____

 (B) DEED OF TRUST:

 Trustor:_____

 Beneficiary:_____

 Original Amount:_____

 Recordation Date:_____

 Document No. _____ Book _____ Page_____

 Place of Recordation: _____, County, California

2. (A) PROMISSORY NOTE:

 Maker:_____

 Payee:_____

 Original Amount:_____ _____

 Date:_____

 (B) DEED OF TRUST:

 Trustor:_____

 Beneficiary:_____

 Original Amount:_____

 Recordation Date:_____

 Document No. _____ Book _____ Page _____

 Place of Recordation: _____, County, California

By Payee's acceptance of this Note, Payee covenants and agrees that, provided Maker is not delinquent or in default under the terms of this Note, Payee shall pay all installments of principal and interest which shall hereafter become due pursuant to the provisions of the Underlying Note(s) as and when the same become due and payable. In the event Maker shall be delinquent or in default under the terms of this Note, Payee shall not be obligated to make any payments required by the terms of the Underlying Note(s) until such delinquency or default is cured. In the event Payee fails to timely pay any installment of principal or interest on the Underlying Note(s) at the time when Maker is not delinquent or in default hereunder, Maker may, at Maker's option, make such payments directly to the holder of such Underlying Note(s), in which event Maker shall be entitled to a credit against the next installment(s) of principal and interest due under the terms of this Note equal to the amount so paid and including, without limitation, any penalty, charges and expenses paid by Maker to the holder of the Underlying Note(s) on account of Payee failing to make such payment. The obligations of Payee hereunder shall terminate upon the earliest of (i) foreclosure of the lien of the All-Inclusive Purchase Money Deed of Trust securing this Note, or (ii) cancellation of this Note and reconveyance of the All-Inclusive Purchase Money Deed of Trust securing same.

Should Maker be delinquent or in default under the terms of this Note, and Payee consequently incurs any penalties, charges or other expenses on account of the Underlying Note(s) during the period of such delinquency or default, the amount of such penalties, charges and expenses shall be immediately added to the principal amount of this Note and shall be immediately payable by Maker to Payee.

Notwithstanding anything to the contrary herein contained, the right of Maker to prepay all or any portion of the principal of this Note is limited to the same extent as any limitation exists in the right to prepay the principal of the Underlying Note(s). If any prepayments of principal of this Note shall, by reason of the application of any portion thereof by Payee to the prepayment of principal of the Underlying Note(s), constitute such prepayment for which the holders of the Underlying Note(s) are entitled to receive a prepayment penalty or consideration, the amount of such prepayment penalty or consideration shall be paid by Maker to Payee upon demand, and any such amount shall not reduce the unpaid balance of principal or interest hereunder.

At any time when the total of the unpaid principal balance of this Note, accrued interest thereon, all other sums due pursuant to the terms hereof, and all sums advanced by Payee pursuant to the terms of the All-Inclusive Purchase Money Deed of Trust securing this Note, is equal to or less than the unpaid balance of principal and interest then due under the terms of the Underlying Note(s), Payee, at his option, shall cancel this Note and deliver same to Maker and execute a request for full reconveyance of the Deed of Trust securing this Note.

Should default be made by Maker in payment of any installments of principal, interest, or any other sums due hereunder, the whole sum of principal, interest and all other sums due from Maker hereunder, after first deducting therefrom all sums then due under the terms of the Underlying Note(s), shall become immediately due at the option of the holder of this Note. Principal, interest and all other sums due hereunder payable in lawful money of the United States. If action be instituted of this Note, I/we promise to pay such sums as the Court may fix as attorney's fees. This Note is secured by a LONG FORM ALL-INCLUSIVE PURCHASE MONEY DEED OF TRUST to **TITLE INSURANCE AND TRUST COMPANY**, a California corporation, as Trustee.

_____   _____
      (Maker)   (Maker)

_____   _____
      (Maker)   (Maker)

The undersigned hereby accept(s) the foregoing All-Inclusive Purchase Money Promissory Note and agree(s) to perform each and all of the terms thereof on the part of Payee to be performed.

Executed as of the date and place first above written.

_____   _____
      (Payee)   (Payee)

_____   _____
      (Payee)   (Payee)

(THIS NOTE IS FOR USE ONLY IN PURCHASE MONEY TRANSACTIONS. IT IS RECOMMENDED THAT, PRIOR TO THE EXECUTION OF THIS NOTE, THE PARTIES CONSULT WITH THEIR ATTORNEYS WITH RESPECT THERETO.)

CAUTION - THIS FORM CONTEMPLATES A SOPHISTICATED TRANSACTION WITH MANY RAMIFICATIONS - OBTAIN LOCAL COUNSEL BEFORE USING.

RECORDING REQUESTED BY

AND WHEN RECORDED MAIL TO

Name

Street
Address

City &
State

——————————— SPACE ABOVE THIS LINE FOR RECORDER'S USE ———————————

LONG FORM ALL-INCLUSIVE PURCHASE MONEY DEED OF TRUST AND ASSIGNMENT OF RENTS

This All-Inclusive Purchase Money Deed of Trust, made this _____ day of, _____
between_____,
herein called TRUSTOR, whose address is _____,
  (number and street) (city) (state) (zip)
TITLE INSURANCE AND TRUST COMPANY, A California corporation, herein called TRUSTEE, and
_____, herein called BENEFICIARY,
Witnesseth: That Trustor IRREVOCABLY GRANTS, TRANSFERS AND ASSIGNS TO TRUSTEE IN TRUST, WITH POWER OF SALE,
that property in _____County, California described as:

TOGETHER WITH the rents, issues and profits thereof, SUBJECT, HOWEVER, to the right, power and authority hereinafter given to and conferred upon Beneficiary to collect and apply such rents, issues and profits.

For the Purpose of Securing:

1. Performance of each agreement of Trustor herein contained. 2. Payment of the indebtedness evidenced by one all-inclusive purchase money promissory note of even date herewith, and any extension or renewal thereof, in the principal sum of $_____ executed by Trustor in favor of Beneficiary or order.

Underlying Obligations:

This is an all-inclusive purchase money deed of trust, securing an all-inclusive purchase money promissory note in the original principal amount of _____ Dollars ($_____) (the "Note") which includes within such amount the unpaid balance of the following:

(a) A promissory note in the original principal sum of _____ Dollars ($_____) in favor of _____ as Payee, secured by a deed of trust recorded _____, 19____, as Document No. _____, in Book _____, Page _____, Official Records of _____ County, California, and

(b) A promissory note in the original principal sum of _____ Dollars ($_____) in favor of _____ as Payee, secured by a deed of trust recorded _____, 19____, as Document No. _____, in Book _____, Page _____, Official Records of _____ County, California.

(The Promissory Notes secured by such deeds of trust are hereinafter called the "Underlying Notes").

To Protect the Security of This Deed of Trust, Trustor Agrees:

(1) To keep said property in good condition and repair; not to remove or demolish any building thereon; to complete or restore promptly and in good and workmanlike manner any building which may be constructed, damaged or destroyed thereon and to pay when due all claims for labor performed and materials furnished therefor; to comply with all laws affecting said property or requiring any alterations or improvements to be made thereon; not to commit or permit waste thereof; not to commit, suffer or permit any act upon said property in violation of law; to cultivate, irrigate, fertilize, fumigate, prune and do all other acts which from the character or use of said property may be reasonably necessary, the specific enumerations herein not excluding the general.

(2) To provide, maintain and deliver to Beneficiary fire, vandalism and malicious mischief insurance satisfactory to and with loss payable to Beneficiary. The amount collected under any fire or other insurance policy may be applied by Beneficiary upon any indebtedness secured hereby and in such order as Beneficiary may determine, or at option of Beneficiary the entire amount so collected or any part thereof may be released to Trustor.

Such application or release shall not cure or waive any default or notice of default hereunder or invalidate any act done pursuant to such notice. The provisions hereof are subject to the mutual agreements of the parties as below set forth.

(3) To appear in and defend any action or proceeding purporting to affect the security hereof or the rights or powers of Beneficiary or Trustee; and to pay all costs and expenses, including cost of evidence of title and attorney's fees in a reasonable sum, in any such action or proceeding in which Beneficiary or Trustee may appear, and in any suit brought by Beneficiary to foreclose this Deed.

(4) To pay: at least ten days before delinquency all taxes and assessments affecting said property, including assessments on appurtenant water stock; subject to the mutual agreements of the parties as below set forth, to pay when due, all incumbrances, charges and liens, with interest, on said property or any part thereof, which appear to be prior or superior hereto; all costs, fees and expenses of this Trust.

Should Trustor fail to make any payment or to do any act as herein provided, then Beneficiary or Trustee, but without obligation so to do and without notice to or demand upon Trustor and without releasing Trustor from any obligation hereof, may: make or do the same in such manner and to such extent as either may deem necessary to protect the security hereof, Beneficiary or Trustee being authorized to enter upon said property for such purposes; appear in and defend any action or proceeding purporting to affect the security hereof or the rights or powers of Beneficiary or Trustee; pay, purchase, contest or compromise any incumbrance, charge or lien which in the judgment of either appears to be prior or superior hereto; and, in exercising any such powers, pay necessary expenses, employ counsel and pay his reasonable fees.

(5) To pay immediately and without demand all sums so expended by Beneficiary or Trustee, with interest from date of expenditure at the amount allowed by law in effect at the date hereof, and to pay for any statement provided for by law in effect at the date hereof regarding the obligation secured hereby any amount demanded by the Beneficiary not to exceed the maximum allowed by law at the time when said statement is demanded.

(6) That any award of damages in connection with any condemnation for public use of or injury to said property or any part thereof is hereby assigned and shall be paid to Beneficiary who may apply or release such moneys received by him in the same manner and with the same effect as above provided for disposition of proceeds of fire or other insurance. The provisions hereof are subject to the mutual agreements of the parties as below set forth.

(7) That by accepting payment of any sum secured hereby after its due date, Beneficiary does not waive his right either to require prompt payment when due of all other sums so secured or to declare default for failure so to pay.

(8) That at any time or from time to time, without liability therefor and without notice, upon written request of Beneficiary and presentation of this Deed and said note for endorsement, and without affecting the personal liability of any person for payment of the indebtedness secured hereby, Trustee may: reconvey any part of said property; consent to the making of any map or plat thereof; join in granting any easement thereon; or join in any extension agreement or any agreement subordinating the lien or charge hereof.

(9) That upon written request of Beneficiary stating that all sums secured hereby have been paid, and upon surrender of this Deed and said note to Trustee for cancellation and retention and upon payment of its fees, Trustee shall reconvey, without warranty, the property then held hereunder. The recitals in such reconveyance of any matters or facts shall be conclusive proof of the truthfulness thereof. The grantee in such reconveyance may be described as "the person or persons legally entitled thereto." Five years after issuance of such full reconveyance, Trustee may destroy said note and this Deed (unless directed in such request to retain them).

(10) That as additional security, Trustor hereby gives to and confers upon Beneficiary the right, power and authority, during the continuance of these Trusts, to collect the rents, issues and profits of said property, reserving unto Trustor the right, prior to any default by Trustor in payment of any indebtedness secured hereby or in performance of any agreement hereunder, to collect and retain such rents, issues and profits as they become due and payable. Upon any such default, Beneficiary may at any time without notice, either in person, by agent, or by a receiver to be appointed by a court, and without regard to the adequacy of any security for the indebtedness hereby secured, enter upon and take possession of said property or any part thereof, in his own name sue for or otherwise collect such rents, issues and profits, including those past due and unpaid, and apply the same, less costs and expenses of operation and collection, including reasonable attorney's fees, upon any indebtedness secured hereby, and in such order as Beneficiary may determine. The entering upon and taking possession of said property, the collection of such rents, issues and profits and the application thereof as aforesaid, shall not cure or waive any default or notice of default hereunder or invalidate any act done pursuant to such notice.

(11) That upon default by Trustor in payment of any indebtedness secured hereby or in performance of any agreement hereunder, Beneficiary may declare all sums secured hereby immediately due and payable by delivery to Trustee of written declaration of default and demand for sale and of written notice of default and of election to cause to be sold said property, which notice Trustee shall cause to be filed for record. Beneficiary also shall deposit with Trustee this Deed, said note and all documents evidencing expenditures secured hereby.

After the lapse of such time as may then be required by law following the recordation of said notice of default, and notice of sale having been given as then required by law, Trustee, without demand on Trustor, shall sell said property at the time and place fixed by it in said notice of sale, either as a whole or in separate parcels, and in such order as it may determine, at public auction to the highest bidder for cash in lawful money of the United States, payable at time of sale. Trustee may postpone sale of all or any portion of said property by public announcement at such time and place of sale, and from time to time thereafter may postpone such sale by public announcement at the time fixed by the preceding postponement. Trustee shall deliver to such purchaser its deed conveying the property so sold, but without any covenant or warranty, express or implied. The recitals in such deed of any matters or facts shall be conclusive proof of the truthfulness thereof. Any person, including Trustor, Trustee, or Beneficiary as hereinafter defined, may purchase at such sale.

After deducting all costs, fees and expenses of Trustee and of this Trust, including cost of evidence of title in connection with sale, Trustee shall apply the proceeds of sale to payment of: all sums expended under the terms hereof, not then repaid, with accrued interest at the amount allowed by law in effect at the date hereof; all other sums then secured hereby; and the remainder, if any, to the person or persons legally entitled thereto.

(12) Beneficiary, or any successor in ownership of any indebtedness secured hereby, may from time to time, by instrument in writing, substitute a successor or successors to any Trustee named herein or acting hereunder, which instrument, executed by the Beneficiary and duly acknowledged and recorded in the office of the recorder of the county or counties where said property is situated, shall be conclusive proof of proper substitution of such successor Trustee or Trustees, who shall, without conveyance from the Trustee predecessor, succeed to all its title, estate, rights, powers and duties. Said instrument must contain the name of the original Trustor, Trustee and Beneficiary hereunder, the book and page where this Deed is recorded and the name and address of the new Trustee.

(13) That this Deed applies to, inures to the benefit of, and binds all parties hereto, their heirs, legatees, devisees, administrators, executors, successors and assigns. The term Beneficiary shall mean the owner and holder, including pledgees, of the note secured hereby, whether or not named as Beneficiary herein. In this Deed, whenever the context so requires, the masculine gender includes the feminine and/or neuter, and the singular number includes the plural.

(14) That Trustee accepts this Trust when this Deed, duly executed and acknowledged, is made a public record as provided by law. Trustee is not obligated to notify any party hereto of pending sale under any other Deed of Trust or of any action or proceeding in which Trustor, Beneficiary or Trustee shall be a party unless brought by Trustee.

The Undersigned Trustor requests that a copy of any Notice of Default and of any Notice of Sale hereunder be mailed to him at his address hereinbefore set forth.

Trustor and Beneficiary Mutually Agree:

(A) By Beneficiary's acceptance of this All-Inclusive Purchase Money Deed of Trust, Beneficiary covenants and agrees that provided Trustor is not delinquent or in default under the terms of the Note secured hereby, Beneficiary shall pay all installments of principal and interest which shall hereafter become due pursuant to the provisions of the Underlying Note(s) as and when the same become due and payable. In the event Trustor shall be delinquent or in default under the terms of the Note secured hereby, Beneficiary shall not be obligated to make any payments required by the terms of the Underlying Note(s) until such delinquency or default is cured. In the event Beneficiary fails to timely pay any installment of principal or interest on the Underlying Note(s) at the time when Trustor is not delinquent or in default under the terms of the Note secured hereby, Trustor may, at Trustor's option make such payments directly to the holder of such Underlying Note(s), in which event Trustor shall be entitled to a credit against the next installment(s) of principal and interest due under the terms of the Note secured hereby equal to the amount so paid and including, without limitation, any penalty, charges and expenses paid by Trustor to the holder of the Underlying Note(s) on account of Beneficiary's failing to make such payment. The obligations of Beneficiary hereunder shall terminate upon the earliest of (i) foreclosure of the lien of this All-Inclusive Purchase Money Deed of Trust, or (ii) cancellation of the Note secured hereby and reconveyance of this All-Inclusive Purchase Money Deed of Trust.

Should Trustor be delinquent or in default under the terms of the Note secured hereby, Beneficiary consequently incurs any penalties, charges, or other expenses on account of the Underlying Note(s) during the period of such delinquency or default, the amount of such penalties, charges and expenses shall be immediately added to the principal amount of the Note secured hereby and shall be immediately payable by Trustor to Beneficiary.

If at any time the unpaid balance of the Note secured hereby, accrued interest thereon, and all other sums due pursuant to the terms thereof and all sums advanced by beneficiary pursuant to the terms of this Deed of Trust, is equal to or less than the unpaid principal balance of the Underlying Note(s) and accrued interest thereon, the Note secured hereby, at the option of Beneficiary, shall be cancelled and said property shall be reconveyed from the lien of this Deed of Trust.

(B) Trustor and Beneficiary agree that in the event the proceeds of any condemnation award or settlement in lieu thereof, or the proceeds of any casualty insurance covering destructible improvements located upon said property, are applied by the holder of the Underlying Note(s) in reduction of the unpaid principal amount thereof, the unpaid principal balance of the Note secured hereby shall be reduced by an equivalent amount and be deemed applied to the last sums due under the Note.

(C) At such times as the Note secured hereby becomes all due and payable, the amount of principal and interest then payable to Beneficiary thereunder shall be reduced by the then unpaid balance of principal and interest due on the Underlying Note(s).

(D) Any demand hereunder delivered by Beneficiary to Trustee for the foreclosure of the lien of this Deed of Trust may be not more than the sum of the following amounts:

(i) The difference between the then unpaid balance of principal and interest on the Note secured hereby and the then unpaid balance of principal and interest on the Underlying Note(s); plus

(ii) The aggregate of all amounts theretofore paid by Beneficiary pursuant to the terms of this Deed of Trust prior to the date of such foreclosure sale, for taxes and assessments, insurance premiums, delinquency charges, foreclosure costs, and any other sums advanced by Beneficiary pursuant to the terms of this Deed of Trust, to the extent the same were not previously repaid by Trustor to Beneficiary; plus

(iii) The costs of foreclosure hereunder; plus attorneys fees and costs incurred by Beneficiary in enforcing this Deed of Trust or the Note secured hereby as permitted by law.

(E) Notwithstanding any provision to the contrary herein contained, in the event of a Trustee's sale in furtherance of the foreclosure of this Deed of Trust, the balance then due on the Note secured hereby, for the purpose of Beneficiary's demand, shall be reduced, as aforesaid, by the unpaid balance, if any, of principal and interest then due on the Underlying Note(s), satisfactory evidence of which unpaid balances must be submitted to Trustee prior to such sale. The Trustee may rely on any statements received from Beneficiary in this regard and such statements shall be deemed binding and conclusive as between Beneficiary and Trustor, on the one hand, and the Trustee, on the other hand, to the extent of such reliance.

Signature of Trustor

_____   _____

_____   _____

Signature of Beneficiary

_____   _____

_____   _____

STAPLE APPROPRIATE ACKNOWLEDGMENTS HERE

(THIS DEED OF TRUST FOR USE ONLY IN PURCHASE MONEY TRANSACTIONS. IT IS RECOMMENDED THAT, PRIOR TO THE EXECUTION OF THIS DEED OF TRUST, THE PARTIES CONSULT WITH THEIR ATTORNEYS WITH RESPECT TO SAME).

Title Order No._____   Escrow or Loan No._____

S T A T U T E N:

NAAM EN ZETEL

Artikel **1**
----
1. De vennootschap is genaamd:
2. De vennootschap is gevestigd op Curacao.
DOEL

Artikel **2**
----
   1. Het doel van de vennootschap is:
a. het beleggen van haar middelen in effecten, zoals aandelen
   en andere bewijzen van deelgerechtigdheid en obligaties,
   alsmede in andere rentedragende schuldvorderingen onder
   welke naam en in welke vorm ook;
b. het verkrijgen van:
(1) opbrengsten, voortvloeiende uit de vervreemding of het
   afstaan van het recht tot het gebruik maken van
   auteursrechten, octrooien, modellen, geheime procede's
   of recepten, handelsmerken en soortgelijke zaken;
(ii) royalties, daaronder begrepen huren, met betrekking **tot**
   films of terzake van het gebruik van nijverheids-,
   handels-, of wetenschappelijke installaties, alsmede
   met betrekking tot de exploitatie van een mijn of groeve
   of enige andere natuurlijke hulpbron en andere onroerende zaken;
(iii) vergoedingen voor het verlenen van technische hulp;
c. het direct of indirect beleggen van haar middelen in
   onroerende goederen en rechten, het verkrijgen, bezitten,
   huren, verhuren, pachten, verpachten, verkavelen, droogleg-
   gen, ontwikkelen, verbeteren, bewerken, bebouwen, verkopen,
   of anderzins vervreemden, verhypothekeren of anderzins bezwaren van onroerende goederen en het aanleggen **van**
   infrastructurele werken als wegen, leidingen en soortgelijke werken op onroerende goederen.
   2. De vennootschap is bevoegd tot alles wat tot het berei-
ken van haar doel nuttig of nodig kan zijn of daarmede **in de**
ruimste zin des woords verband houdt, daaronder begrepen **het**
deelnemen in enige andere onderneming of vennootschap.

```
                              - 2 -


                              DUUR
                              ----
                           Artikel  3
                           ----------
     De vennootschap is aangegaan voor onbepaalde tijd.
                       KAPITAAL EN AANDELEN
                       --------------------
                           Artikel  4
                           ----------
        1. Het maatschappelijk kapitaal van de vennootschap be-
    draagt dertigduizend United States Dollars (US$ 30.000,--),
    verdeeld in dertigduizend (30.000) aandelen van een United
    States Dollar (US$ 1,--) elk, waarvan zesduizend (6.000)
    aandelen zijn geplaatst.
        2. Onderaandelen kunnen worden uitgegeven.
                           Artikel  5
                           ----------
        1. De aandelen luiden op naam.
        2. Door de directie zal een aandeelhoudersregister worden
    aangelegd en bijgehouden.
        3. Uitgifte van aandelen geschiedt door de directie.
        4. Op verzoek van een aandeelhouder kunnen aandeelbewijzen
    worden uitgegeven voor zijn aandelen. Aandeelbewijzen
    worden getekend door of namens de directie.
        5. De levering van aandelen geschiedt, hetzij door de
    betekening van een akte van overdracht aan de vennootschap
    hetzij door een schriftelijke erkenning van de overdracht
    door de vennootschap, hetgeen slechts kan geschieden door
    een aantekening op het aandeelbewijs, indien aandeelbewijzen
    uitgegeven zijn.
        6. Het vorig lid is ook van toepassing ingeval van toe-
    wijzing van aandelen bij de scheiding en deling van enige ge-
    meenschap.
        7. De vennootschap mag volgestorte aandelen in haar eigen
    kapitaal voor eigen rekening onder bezwarende titel verwerven
    tot een zodanig bedrag, dat tenminste een/vijfde gedeelte van
    het maatschappelijk kapitaal geplaatst blijft bij anderen dan
    de vennootschap zelf. De bevoegdheid tot zodanige verwerving
    berust bij de directie.
        8. De vennootschap kan geen rechten ontlenen aan aandelen
    in haar eigen kapitaal. Zodanige aandelen zullen niet meetellen
    bij de berekening van het geplaatste kapitaal.
                            BESTUUR
                            -------
                           Artikel  6
                           ----------
        1. Het bestuur van de vennootschap is opgedragen aan een
    directie, bestaande uit een of meer directeuren.
        2. De directeuren worden door de algemene vergadering van
    aandeelhouders benoemd en kunnen te allen tijde door haar wor-
    den geschorst en ontslagen.
        3. De vennootschap wordt in en buiten rechte vertegenwoor-
    digd door ieder van de directeuren, ook in geval van tegen-
    strijdig belang tussen de vennootschap en een of meer directeu-
    ren, hetzij in prive, hetzij qualitate qua.
        4. De directie is bevoegd om procuratiehouders aan te stel-
    len en regelt hun bevoegdheden en de wijze waarop zij de ven-
    nootschap zullen vertegenwoordigen en voor haar tekenen en in
    het algemeen de voorwaarden van hun aanstelling.
```

- 3 -

5. De directie kan overeenkomsten als bedoeld in artikel
60 van het Wetboek van Koophandel van de Nederlandse Antillen
aangaan, zonder voorafgaande machtiging van de algemene vergadering van aandeelhouders.

6. Bij belet of ontstentenis van een of meer directeuren,
berust het bestuur geheel bij de overblijvende directeuren of
directeur.

7. Bij belet of ontstentenis van alle directeuren zal een
persoon, jaarlijks aangewezen door de algemene vergadering van
aandeelhouders, met het bestuur van de vennootschap zijn
belast.

ALGEMENE VERGADERINGEN VAN AANDEELHOUDERS

Artikel 7

1. Algemene vergaderingen van aandeelhouders worden gehouden op Curacao.

2. De jaarlijkse algemene vergadering van aandeelhouders
moet gehouden worden binnen negen maanden na afloop van het
boekjaar van de vennootschap.

3. In genoemde vergadering:

a. zal de directie verslag uitbrengen over de gang van zaken
   van de vennootschap en het gevoerde beheer gedurende het
   afgelopen boekjaar;
b. zal de balans en de winst- en verliesrekening worden vast-
   gesteld, na te zijn overgelegd tezamen met een toelichting,
   waarin vermeld wordt naar welke maatstaf de roerende en
   onroerende zaken van de vennootschap zijn gewaardeerd;
c. zal de persoon bedoeld in lid 7 van artikel 6 worden aangewezen;
d. zullen die voorstellen worden behandeld, welke in de agenda
   opgenomen in de oproeping voor de vergadering, zijn vermeld.

Artikel 8

1. Algemene vergaderingen van aandeelhouders worden bijeen-
geroepen door middel van luchtpostbrieven aan het adres van
iedere aandeelhouder, zoals dit vermeld is in het aandeelhou-
dersregister.

2. De luchtpostbrieven zullen tenminste tien dagen voor de
dag van de vergadering worden verzonden. In dringende gevallen
kan die termijn worden verminderd tot vijf dagen, de dag van
verzending van de brieven aan aandeelhouders en die van de vergadering niet meegerekend.

3. De te behandelen onderwerpen moeten in de oproeping voor
de vergadering worden vermeld of daarin moet worden meegedeeld
dat de aandeelhouders er ten kantore van de vennootschap kennis
van kunnen nemen.

4. Algemene vergaderingen zullen worden voorgezeten door
een persoon die daartoe telkenmale door de vergadering zal
worden aangewezen.

5. Alle besluiten van jaarlijkse en buitengewone algemene
vergaderingen van aandeelhouders zullen worden genomen met vol-
strekte meerderheid van stemmen, voorzover in deze statuten
niet anders is bepaald.

6. Aandeelhouders kunnen zich op een vergadering doen ver-
tegenwoordigen door een schriftelijk of telegrafisch gevol-
machtigde.

7. Directeuren en in het algemeen personen in dienst van
de vennootschap mogen niet als gemachtigden van aandeelhouders

- 4 -

optreden in een algemene vergadering van aandeelhouders.
   8. Elk aandeel geeft recht op het uitbrengen van een stem.
   9. Geldige stemmen kunnen ook worden uitgebracht voor de
aandelen van hen, aan wie, uit anderen hoofde dan als aandeelhouders van de vennootschap, door het te nemen besluit enig
recht jegens de vennootschap zou worden toegekend, of van hen,
die daardoor van enige verplichting jegens de vennootschap zou-
den worden ontslagen.
   10. Voorstellen te doen door aandeelhouders voor onderwerpen
te behandelen, zowel op jaarlijkse als op buitengewone algemene
vergaderingen, kunnen alleen dan in behandeling worden genomen,
indien zij zo tijdig en schriftelijk bij de directie zijn inge-
diend, dat zij met inachtneming van de voor de bijeenroeping
van algemene vergaderingen vastgestelde termijn op de wijze
als voor bijeenroeping bepaald kunnen worden aangekondigd.
   11. Indien het gehele geplaatste kapitaal ter algemene vergadering van aandeelhouders vertegenwoordigd is, kunnen geldige
besluiten worden genomen, zelfs wanneer de voorschriften van de
statuten omtrent oproeping, bekendmaking van de punten van behandeling of plaats van vergadering, niet of slechts ten dele
in acht zijn genomen, mits deze besluiten met algemene stemmen
worden genomen.

BOEKJAAR

Artikel 9
----

   1. Het boekjaar van de vennootschap loopt van een januari
tot en met eenendertig december van ieder jaar.
   2. Het eerste boekjaar van de vennootschap loopt van de
aanvang van de vennootschap tot en met eenendertig december
negentienhonderd eenentachtig.
BALANS EN WINST- EN VERLIESREKENING

Artikel 10
----

   1. Binnen acht maanden na afloop van het boekjaar zullen
een balans en een winst- en verliesrekening, met de toelichting
als genoemd in lid 3 van artikel 7, door de directie worden
overgelegd aan de aandeelhouders.
   2. De balans en de winst- en verliesrekening zullen door de
jaarlijkse algemene vergadering van aandeelhouders worden vast-
gesteld.
   3. De vaststelling van de balans en de winst- en verliesrekening strekt de directie tot acquit en decharge voor het
gevoerde bestuur gedurende het desbetreffende boekjaar.
WINSTVERDELING

Artikel 11
----

   1. De winst, waaronder is te verstaan de netto-winst ingevolge de winst- en verliesrekening, kan ter beoordeling van de
algemene vergadering van aandeelhouders worden gereserveerd of
als dividend uitgekeerd.
   2. Indien en voorzover de winst van de vennootschap het
toelaat, kan de directie besluiten tot uitkering van een of
meer interimdividenden, als vooruitbetaling op het te verwach-
ten dividend.
   3. Indien blijkens de vastgestelde winst- en verliesrekening over enig jaar verlies geleden is, hetwelk niet uit een

- 5 -

reserve bestreden of op andere wijze gedelgd wordt, geschiedt
in volgende jaren winstuitkering niet voordat zodanig verlies
weer is aangezuiverd.
        STATUTENWIJZIGING EN ONTBINDING VAN DE VENNOOTSCHAP

                        Artikel 12
                        ----
    1. Een besluit tot wijziging van de statuten of tot ontbin-
ding van de vennootschap kan slechts genomen worden in een
algemene vergadering van aandeelhouders, waarin tenminste drie/
vierde gedeelte van het geplaatste kapitaal vertegenwoordigd
is.
    2. Indien in die vergadering niet het vereiste kapitaal
vertegenwoordigd is, wordt een tweede vergadering bijeengeroe-
pen, te houden binnen twee maanden na de eerste, in welke tweede vergadering alsdan, ongeacht het vertegenwoordigde kapitaal,
geldige besluiten over die onderwerpen kunnen worden genomen.
    3. In geval van ontbinding van de vennootschap zal de li-
quidatie geschieden onder zulke bepalingen als de algemene vergadering van aandeelhouders zal besluiten.

```
ARTICLES OF INCORPORATION
-------------------------



                          NAME AND DOMICILE
                          -----------------
                             Article 1
                             ---------
     1. The name of the company is:
     2. The company is established in Curacao.
                             PURPOSE
                             -------
                             Article 2
                             ---------
       1. The purpose of the company is:
  a. to invest its assets in securities, including shares
     and other certificates of participation and bonds, as
     well as other claims for interestbearing debts however
     denominated and in any and all forms;
  b. to acquire:
  (  i) revenues, derived from the alienation or leasing of
        the right to use copyrights, patents, designs, secret
        processes or formulae, trademarks and other analogous
        property;
  ( ii) royalties, including rentals, in respect of motion
        picture films or for the use of industrial, commercial
        or scientific equipment, as well as relating to the
        operation of a mine or a quarry or of any other natural
        resources and other immovable properties;
  (iii) considerations paid for technical assistance.
  c. to invest its assets directly or indirectly in real
     property, to acquire, own, hire, let, lease, rent, divide,
     drain, reclaim, develop, improve, cultivate, build on, sell
     or otherwise alienate, mortgage or otherwise encumber real
     property and to construct infrastructural works like
     roads, pipes and similar works on real estate.
       2. The company is entitled to do all that may be useful
  or necessary for the attainment of its object or that is
  connected therewith in the widest sense, including the partici-
  pation in any other venture or company.
```

- 2 -

DURATION

Article 3

The company is constituted for an indefinite period of time.

CAPITAL AND SHARES

Article 4
----

1. The authorized capital of the company amounts to thirty thousand United States Dollars (US$ 30,000.--) divided into thirty thousand (30,000) shares of one United States Dollar (US$ 1.--) each, of which six thousand (6,000) shares are subscribed for.

2. Fractional shares may be issued.

Article 5
----

1. The shares of stock are registered shares.

2. The Managing Board will make and keep a register of shareholders.

3. Shares are issued by the Managing Board.

4. On the request of a shareholder, share certificates may be issued for his shares. Share certificates shall be signed by or on behalf of the Managing Board.

5. The transfer of shares is effected either by serving a deed of conveyance upon the company, or by written acknowledgement of the transfer by the company, which latter can only take place by an annotation on the sharecertificate if sharecertificates have been issued.

6. The foregoing paragraph shall also apply in the case of an allocation resulting from a division and partition of any community.

7. The company may acquire for its own account for a valid consideration fully paid up shares in its own capital stock up to such an amount that at least one/fifth part of the authorized capital remains outstanding with others than the company itself. The authority to such acquisition is vested in the Managing Board.

8. The company may not derive any rights from its treasury shares. For the purpose of determining the issued capital such shares shall not be included as part of such capital.

MANAGEMENT

Article 6
----

1. The management of the company is commissioned to a Managing Board, consisting of one or more managing directors.

2. The managing directors are appointed by the general meeting of shareholders and may be suspended and removed by it at all times.

3. The company is represented at law and otherwise by any one of the managing directors, also in case of a conflict of interests between the company and one or more managing directors, either acting in private or ex officio.

4. The Managing Board is entitled to appoint attorneys-in-fact. It regulates their powers and the manner in which they will represent the company and sign for it and in general the conditions of their appointment.

- 3 -

5. The Managing Board is authorized to enter into such contracts as referred to in Article 60 of the Commercial Code of the Netherlands Antilles without previous authorization by the general meeting of shareholders.

6. In case one or more managing directors are prevented from or are incapable of acting as such, the management shall be left entirely to the remaining managing directors or remaining managing director.

7. In case all managing directors are prevented from or are incapable of acting as such, a person yearly appointed by the general meeting of shareholders will be in charge of the management of the company.

GENERAL MEETING OF SHAREHOLDERS

Article 7

1. General meetings of shareholders shall be held on Curacao.

2. The annual general meeting of shareholders shall be held within nine months after the close of the company's financial year.

3. In said meeting:

a. the Managing Board shall render a report on the business of the company and the conduct of its affairs during the preceding financial year;

b. the balance sheet and the profit and loss account shall be determined, after having been submitted together with an explanatory statement, stating by which standards the movable and immovable property of the company have been appraised;

c. the person, referred to in article 6, paragraph 7, shall be appointed;

d. the proposals included in the agenda specified in the notice of the meeting shall be dealt with.

Article 8

1. General meetings of shareholders shall be convoked by means of airmail letters, mailed to the addresses of shareholders as stated in the register of shareholders.

2. The airmail letters shall be mailed not less than ten days prior to the date of the meeting. In urgent cases the term mentioned may be shortened to five days, not including the day upon which the letters to shareholders were mailed and excluding the day of the meeting.

3. The agenda for the meeting shall be specified in the notice of the meeting or it shall be stated that the shareholders may take cognizance thereof at the office of the company.

4. General meetings shall be presided over by a person designated each time thereto by the meeting.

5. All resolutions of annual and special general meetings of shareholders shall be taken by absolute majority of votes, except where otherwise provided by these articles of incorporation.

6. Shareholders may be represented at the meeting by proxy designated by letter or telegram.

7. Managing directors or in general persons employed by the company may not act as proxies of shareholders at a meeting.

8. One vote may be cast for each share.

9. Valid votes may also be cast for the shares of those

- 4 -

who (otherwise than as shareholders of the company) would
acquire any right or be discharged from any obligation towards
the company, by the resolution to be adopted.
     10. Proposals of items for an agenda to be made by share-
holders , either for the annual or for the special general
meetings can only be dealt with if presented to the Managing
Board in writing at such time that they can be announced within the period of time and in the manner prescribed for the
convocation of general meeting.
     11. However, when the entire issued share capital is repre-
sented at any general meeting of shareholders ,valid resolutions may be adopted, even when the provisions of these articles of incorporation with respect to convocation , specification of the agenda or place of the meeting have not or have
only partially been observed , provided that such a resolution
is unanimously adopted.

FINANCIAL YEAR

Article 9

     1. The financial year of the company runs from January
first up to and including December thirty-first of each year.
     2. The first financial year of the company runs from the
date of the company's incorporation until the thirty-first
day of December nineteenhundred and eighty-one inclusive.

BALANCE SHEET AND PROFIT AND LOSS ACCOUNT

Article 10

     1. Within eight months after the close of the company's
financial year, the balance sheet and profit and loss account
covering the preceding year, with the explanatory statement
referred to in article 7, paragraph 3, shall be submitted to
the shareholders by the Managing Board.
     2. The balance sheet and profit and loss account shall be
determined by the annual meeting of shareholders.
     3. The determination of the balance sheet and profit and
loss account shall acquit and discharge the Managing Board
for its management during the relevant financial year.

DISTRIBUTION OF PROFITS

Article 11

     1. The profit, by which is to be understood the net profit
according to the profit and loss account, may be reserved or
paid out as dividend, at the discretion of the general meeting
of shareholders.
     2. If and to the extent that the profits of the company
permit same, the Managing Board may resolve to declare one or
more interim-dividends as an advance payment of expected
dividends.
     3. In the event that the profit and loss account shows a
loss for any given year, which loss cannot be covered by the
reserves or compensated in another manner, no profit shall be
distributed in any subsequent year, as long as the loss has not
been recovered.

- 5 -

AMENDMENT OF THE ARTICLES OF INCORPORATION
AND LIQUIDATION OF THE COMPANY

Article 12

1. Resolutions to amend the articles of incorporation or to dissolve the company may only be passed in a general meeting of shareholders at which at least three/fourths of the issued capital is represented.

2. If the required issued capital is not represented at said meeting, a second meeting shall be convoked, to be held within two months after the first one, at which second meeting valid resolutions may then be taken with respect to the foregoing, irrespective of the capital represented.

3. In the event of dissolution of the company, the liquidation shall take place under such provisions as the general meeting of shareholders shall determine.

Handelsregister van de Kramer van Koophandel en Nijverheid in Curaçao

In te vullen door
het Handelsregister

Jaarletter }
Opgaafnummer }   No.
Dossiernummer

Datumstempel

Talonnummer
Akteletter

TOELICHTING

1. Betreft de opgaaf een gehuwde vrouw of weduwe, dan worden mede opgegeven de naam en de voornamen van de echtgenoot of van de overleden echtgenoot.
2. In te vullen „procuratiehouder" eventueel met vermelding van de bijzondere titel als adjunct-directeur onder-directeur, enz.
3. Ligt de geboorteplaats of de woonplaats buiten het Staatsdeel Curaçao dan wordt mede opgegeven de naam van het land waar die plaats ligt.
4. Onder vestiging wordt verstaan, vestiging in de zin van P.B. 1937 No. 58, of de algemene verordening die deze later eventueel vervangt.

NIET BESCHRIJVEN

Behoort bij de opgaaf van

Opgaaf van _____ (Handelsnaam) _____ N.V.

(1)   (2)

Name

a. Naam . . . .
   (Zie toelichting 1)
b. Voornamen (voluit) . . . .
   Christian names in full
c. Welke functie bekleedt hij? . .
   capacity
d. Woonplaats, straat huisnummer en
   residence
   district. . . . .
e. Geboorteplaats . . . . . .
   Place of birth
   (Zie toelichting 3)
f. Datum en jaar van geboorte . .
   date and yearof birth
g. Nationaliteit . . . .
   nationality
h. Vestiging . . . .
   not applicable
   (Zie toelichting 4)
i. Handtekening   } die door de betrokkene
   signature   } onder de stukken, de
                   } zaak betreffende, ge-
                   } steld wordt, of de re-
j. Paraaf   } dem van verhindering.
   initials
k. Aard van de beperkende bepalingen
   der volmacht . . . .

Model K. (Afzonderlijke opgaaf betreffende *procuratiehouders* of *andere dergelijke gevolmachtigden*). (2e lid van art. 13 der Handelsregister-verordening).

POWER OF ATTORNEY

FOR _____

KNOW ALL MEN BY THESE PRESENTS:

That _____, a limited liability company established in _____ (hereafter referred to as the "Company") hereby constitutes and appoints _____ residing in _____ County, U.S.A., its true and lawful attorney and agent for it and in its name and in any capacity which it has at present or may acquire in the future to exercise any and all of the following powers:

(a) To ask, demand, sue for, recover, collect and receive each and every sum of money, debt, account, legacy, bequest, interest, dividend, annuity and demand (which now is or hereafter shall become due, owing or payable) belonging to or claimed by the Company and to use and take any lawful means for the recovery thereof by legal process or otherwise, and to execute and deliver a satisfaction or release therefor, together with the right and power to compromise or compound any claim or demand;

(b) To exercise any or all of the following powers as to real property, any interest therein and/or any building thereon: To contract for, purchase, receive and take possession thereof and of evidence of title thereto; to lease the same for any term or purpose, including leases for business, residence, and/or mineral development; to sell, exchange, grant or convey the same with or without warranty; and to mortgage, transfer in trust, or otherwise encumber or hypothecate the same to secure payment of a negotiable or non-negotiable note or performance of any obligation or agreement;

(c) To exercise any or all of the following powers as to all kinds of personal property and goods, wares and merchandise, choses in action and other property in possession or in action: To contract for, buy, sell, exchange, indorse, transfer and in any legal manner deal in and with the same; and to mortgage, transfer in trust, or otherwise encumber or hypothecate the same to secure payment of a negotiable or non-negotiable note or performance of any obligation or agreement;

(d) To borrow money and to execute and deliver negotiable or non-negotiable notes therefor with or without security; and to loan money and receive negotiable or non-negotiable notes therefor with such security as he shall deem proper;

(e) To transact business of any kind or class and as the act of the Company to sign, execute, acknowledge and deliver any deed, lease, assignment of lease, covenant, indenture, indemnity, agreement, mortgage, deed of trust, assignment of mortgage or of the beneficial interest under deed of trust, extension or renewal of any obligation, subordination or waiver of priority, hypothecation and note, whether negotiable or non-negotiable, receipt, evidence of debt, full or partial release or satisfaction of mortgage, judgment and other debt, request for partial or full reconveyance of deed of trust and such other instruments in writing of any kind or class as he may deem necessary or proper in the premises.

GIVING AND GRANTING unto _____ full power and authority to do and perform all and every act and thing whatsoever requisite, necessary or appropriate to be done in and about the premises as fully to all intents and purposes as the Company might or could do if present, hereby ratifying all that _____ shall lawfully do or cause to be done by virtue of these presents. The powers and authority hereby conferred upon _____ shall be applicable to all real and personal property or interests therein now owned or hereafter acquired by the Company.

_____ is empowered hereby to determine at his sole discretion the time when, purpose for and manner in which any power herein conferred upon him shall be exercised, and the condition, provisions and covenants of any instrument or document which may be executed by him pursuant hereto; and in the acquisition or disposition of real or personal property, _____ shall have power to fix the terms thereof for cash, credit and/or property, and if on credit with or without security.

All of the above powers are without the right of substitution.

Signed in _____ on _____, 19____ .

By _____
Managing Director

By _____

-2-

)
) SS:
)
CONSULATE GENERAL OF THE)
UNITED STATES OF AMERICA)

I _____, Consul of the United States of America
at _____, duly commissioned
and qualified, do hereby certify that _____
the true signature and official seal are, respectively, subscribed
and affixed to the attached certificate, was on the date thereof,
the _____ day of _____, 19____,
_____ in _____, to which official
acts, faith and credit are due.

IN WITNESS WHEREOF I have hereunto set my hand and affixed the
seal of the Consulate General of the United States of America at
_____, _____, day of
_____, 19____.

                                   _____
                                   Consul of the United States of
                                   America

Seen for legalization the signatures appearing on the attached
document, of Messrs. _____ and _____
both residing in _____ and acting in their capacity
of managing director and attorney-in-fact respectively of the
limited liability company _____ established in
_____, which company in its turn acts as managing
director of the limited liability company _____,
established in _____, by me, _____, acting for
_____, a civil-law notary, residing in _____
candidate-notary, residing in _____
_____, on this _____ day of _____, 19____

PUT AGREEMENT

FOR GOOD AND VALUABLE CONSIDERATION, the receipt of which is hereby acknowledged, REAL PROPERTY INVESTMENT LIMITED, a corporation (hereinafter "Seller") and JOHN SMITH and DON SMITH, both jointly and severally (hereinafter collectively "Buyers"), hereby enter into this agreement (hereinafter "Put Agreement") dated January 1, 1981 for the purpose of creating a power in the Seller to sell, and an obligation of the Buyers to purchase, all of the outstanding stock of THE ZERO CORPORATION, based upon terms and conditions set forth below.

RECITALS

A. JOHN SMITH and DON SMITH are the General Partners of SPEC LAND, LTD., a California limited partnership (hereinafter "Limited").

B. THE ZERO CORPORATION, a California corporation (hereinafter "A" Corp.") is the limited partner of Limited.

C. "A" Corp. is wholly owned by REAL PROPERTY INVESTMENT LIMITED, a corporation.

D. Limited formed and is the sole shareholder of SPEC WEST, INC., a California corporation (hereinafter "B" Corp.").

E. "B" Corp. shall build approximately _____ ( ) condominiums on the real property located at _____ Money Street, Growth City, California (hereinafter "the Real Property").

NOW, THEREFORE, the parties hereto agree as follows:

1. PURPOSE. The purpose of this Put Agreement is to create a power with an irrevocable interest in the Seller to sell, and an affirmative obligation in the Buyers, jointly and severally, to buy the property described in Paragraph 2 according to the terms and conditions hereinafter described, notwithstanding any other collateral agreement of the parties hereto, including but not limited to "The Agreement, Certificate, and Articles of Limited Partnership of SPEC LAND LIMITED" made December ____, 1980, a copy of which is attached hereto, marked Exhibit "A" and incorporated by reference herein.

2. PUT PROPERTY. The property (hereinafter "Put Property"), which is the subject of the Put Agreement, shall be all of the issued and outstanding common stock of "A" Corp.

3. PUT PRICE. The Seller shall sell, and the Buyers shall purchase, the Put Property for the sum of FIVE HUNDRED THOUSAND DOLLARS ($500,000) pursuant to the terms set forth in Paragraph 6 below.

4. PUT TERM. The Seller may exercise its Put only upon the occurrence of the earlier of the following events:

(a) The completion of the construction of improvements, the receipt of a certificate of occupancy, and the issuance of a final public report in connection with the Real Property; or

-2-

Buyers, either jointly or severally, shall deliver to Seller, or its designated agent, a certified check made payable to Seller or its agent, in the sum equal to five per cent (5%) of the amount set forth in Paragraph 3 above.

(b) Concurrent with the tender of the certified check described above, Buyers shall jointly execute:

(i) a Promissory Note for the balance of the Put price, in the form attached hereto, marked Exhibit "B" and incorporated herein by reference;

(ii) a security and pledge agreement securing said Promissory Note in the form attached hereto, marked Exhibit "C" and incorporated by reference herein.

(c) Concurrent with the Buyers' performance of Subparagraphs (a) and (b) above, Seller shall transfer title to the Put Property to the Buyers in the name of JOHN SMITH and DON SMITH, except as otherwise instructed in writing by the Buyers.

(d) The execution of documents and delivery of monies and stock certificates contemplated by this paragraph shall take place at the offices of Meyers, Stevens & Walters Professional Corporation, 6300 Wilshire Bouelvard, Suite 9100, Los Angeles, California. The parties further agree that such meeting shall take place during normal business hours, and should

-4-

(b) January 1, 1982, or

(c) The recordation of a Notice of Default under the terms of any Deed of Trust encumbering the Real Property which Deed of Trust secures a loan approved primarily to construct improvements in the Real Property.

The Buyers hereby further agree to notify Seller or its designated agent of the occurrence of all the events described in Subparagraph (a) above within ten (10) days from the happening of such events. The Put shall expire at 11:59 p.m. on January 1, 1990.

5. NOTIFICATION OF EXERCISE OF PUT. The Seller shall notify each Buyer of its intention to exercise its Put by personal service or by registered or certified mail, return receipt requested, addressed to each Buyer at the location set forth in the signature page herein or at such location as is requested in writing by the Buyers. Each Buyer will be deemed to have received the Seller's statement of intent to exercise its Put within two (2) days after the date of mailing of such statement.

6. PROCEDURE FOR PAYMENT OF PUT PRICE. The Put price set forth in Paragraph 3 above shall be payable upon the following terms:

(a) Within thirty (30) days from Buyers' receipt of Seller's exercise of its Put pursuant to Paragraph 5 above, the

-3-

all of its properties, real and personal, including its limited partnership interest in Limited, undiminished and unassessed, free and clear of all liens, encumbrances or charges of any kind or character.

(e) There will be no actions, suits, claims or proceedings pending or threatened against, by or affecting "A" Corp. in any court or before any arbitrator or governmental agency, domestic or foreign, which might prevent or impede the sale of such capital stock, or in the event there are such claims, Seller agrees to indemnify Buyers from any damages and/or loss resulting therefrom.

(f) Seller will have received all consents and other approvals of all applicable governmental agencies for the transfer of its "A" Corp. stock to Buyers, except Buyers shall agree to execute the Statement of Transferee as may be required under California law.

(g) The paid-in and contributed capital of "A" Corp. shall be not less than _____ (_____).

(h) "A" Corp. shall have initially contributed capital of not less than _____ (_____) to Limited.

-6-

the specified closing date be on a Saturday, Sunday or other legal holiday, the meeting shall be held the first business day thereafter.

7. REPRESENTATIONS AND WARRANTIES. Seller hereby represents and warrants to Buyers that, as of the specified closing date set forth in Paragraph 6 above, the following will be true:

(a) "A" Corp. will be a duly organized, validly existing corporation in good standing under the laws of the State of California.

(b) All of the issued and outstanding capital stock of "A" Corp. will be owned by Seller and these shares will be free of all liens, charges, encumbrances or claims of any kind whatsoever, except this Put Agreement. All of the shares are validly issued, fully paid and nonassessable, and none of such shares was issued in violation of the preemptive rights of any shareholder.

(c) "A" Corp. will not have any debts, liabilities or obligations of any kind, whether accrued, absolute, contingent or otherwise including, without limitation, any liability or obligation on account of any governmental charges or penalties, interest or fines, and employment agreements of every nature and kind.

(d) "A" Corp. will have good and marketable title to

-5-

and consents, the written resignations of all officers, directors and employees of "A" Corp., and all such other corporate papers and documents as Buyers may reasonably request regarding "A" Corp.

(b) A certificate of Seller or its designated agent that the representations and warranties set forth in Paragraph 7 are true and correct as of the date of the closing meeting.

9. REMEDIES FOR BREACH OF AGREEMENT. Each party's obligation under this Agreement is unique. If any party should default in its obligations under this Agreement, the parties each acknowledge that it would be extremely impracticable to measure the resulting damages; accordingly, the non-defaulting party, in addition to any other available legal rights or remedies, may sue in equity for specific performance, and the parties each expressly waive the defense that a remedy in damages will be adequate.

10. APPLICABLE LAW. All the terms and provisions of the Put Agreement shall be interpreted under the laws of the State of California.

11. PARTIAL INVALIDITY. If any term, provision or condition of the Put Agreement shall be held invalid, void or unenforceable, by a court of competent jurisdiction, the remainder of this Put Agreement shall remain in full force and effect.

-8-

(i) "A" Corp. shall not have disbursed any sums received from Limited to any shareholder, officer, director or employee.

(j) "A" Corp. shall not have amended its Articles of Incorporation or By-Laws or filed any consent pursuant to the Internal Revenue Code of 1954, as amended, or the California Revenue and Taxation Code, without the prior notification and consent of the Buyers.

8. ADDITIONAL DOCUMENTS TO BE DELIVERED TO BUYERS. In the event Seller exercises its Put to Buyers as herein provided, Seller shall deliver the following documents to Buyers at the time of the meeting set forth in Paragraph 6 above:

(a) The corporate minute books of "A" Corp., including the Articles of Incorporation, By-Laws, Directors' Minutes and Shareholders' Minutes, the corporate seal, the share certificate or certificates representing all outstanding capital stock of "A" Corp. duly endorsed by Seller for transfer or accompanied by an assignment of the shares duly executed by Seller (except as otherwise provided in the security and pledge agreement attached hereto as Exhibit "D"), all permits, orders and consents issued by any applicable governmental authority with respect to "A" Corp. or any security of it, all applications for such permits, orders

-7-

IN WITNESS WHEREOF, the parties hereto have executed this Put Agreement as of the day and year first above written.

BUYER:

_____
JOHN SMITH
12345 Dollar Way
Growth, California

BUYER:

_____
DON SMITH
12345 Dollar Way
Growth, California

SELLER:

REAL PROPERTY INVESTMENT LIMITED,
a corporation

By _____, Its Attorney in Fact
c/o Myron Meyers, Esq.
6300 Wilshire Boulevard, Suite 9100
Los Angeles, California 90048

-10-

---

12. ENTIRE AGREEMENT. This Put Agreement embodies the full and complete agreement of the parties hereto and no changes or modifications shall be effective unless made in writing and signed by both Buyers and Seller herein.

13. BINDING ON SUCCESSORS. This Put Agreement shall be binding upon the parties hereto, their heirs, successors, assigns, and legal representatives.

14. ATTORNEYS' FEES. In any action at law or in equity to enforce any of the provisions or rights under this Agreement, the unsuccessful party to such litigation, as determined by the court in final judgment or decree, shall pay the successful party or parties all costs, expenses and reasonable attorneys' fees incurred therein by such party or parties (including, without limitation, such costs, expenses and fees on any appeals), and if such successful party shall recover judgment in any such action or proceeding, such costs, expenses, and attorneys' fees shall be included in as part of such judgment.

15. COUNTERPARTS. This Agreement may be executed in counterparts, and all such counterparts shall constitute one agreement, binding upon the parties hereto.

16. PARAGRAPH HEADINGS. The headings and subdivisions hereof have been inserted as a matter of convenience and shall not affect the construction hereof.

-9-

PUT AGREEMENT

This Put Agreement ("this Agreement") is entered into this 1st day of January, 1981 by and between DEVELOPMENT CORP., a California corporation ("DC"), NATIONAL ENTERPRISES, INC., a Nevada corporation ("Parent"), and MEDICAL ASSOCIATES, a California general partnership ("Associates").

W I T N E S S E T H:

On this date in accordance with a certain Memorandum of Closing and Agreement ("Purchase Agreement") between DC, Parent and Associates, a medical office building and related improvements and the site on which they are located were purchased by Associates from DC. In accordance with the Purchase Agreement, the parties agreed that this Put Agreement would be entered into.

In implementation thereof and in consideration of the mutual agreements herein contained and intending to be legally bound hereby, and subject to the conditions and on the terms set forth herein, the parties hereby agree as follows:

1. Grant of Option. DC hereby grants to Associates and Associates shall have the irrevocable right and option (the "Put Option") during the Option Period (herein defined) to sell the Improvements and the Site to DC at the sale price and upon the terms and conditions set forth in this Agreement. The Option Period shall be the period commencing on the date hereof and ending on the fifth anniversary of the date hereof. If not timely exercised, the Put Option shall lapse. As used herein, "Site" and "Improvements" shall mean the "site and improvements acquired by Associates from DC this date and legally described in Exhibit "A" attached hereto and incorporated herein by this reference.

2. Exercise of Option. The Put Option shall be exercised, if at all, by notice of option exercise to DC from Associates on or prior to expiration of the Option Period. The notice of the Put Option exercise shall be deemed timely given if delivered or sent to DC by 12:00 p.m. on the last day of the Option Period, in the manner provided in Section 13.1. Upon timely exercise of the Put Option, Associates shall sell the Improvements and Site to DC and DC shall purchase the Improvements and Site from Associates, on the Closing Date, at the sale price determined pursuant to Sections 3 and 4.

If prior to the expiration of the Option Period, some other person, firm or corporation (a "Third Party") shall acquire the Site from Associates, the Third Party shall succeed, without further action by any party hereto, ipso facto, to all the rights of Associates hereunder, with respect to the Site as if the Put Option were granted initially to the Third Party and Associates. In such case, the Put Option may only be exercised by Associates and Third Party jointly and DC shall have no obligation hereunder unless so jointly exercised.

3. Improvements Sale Price. The sale price of the Improvements shall equal Associates' net (depreciated) book value of the Improvements, including any capital additions, improvements or alterations thereto, on the Closing Date, as determined and certified to in writing by Associates' regularly employed certified public accountants from the books and records of Associates. At least 10 days prior to the Closing Date, the accountants' determination shall be delivered to Associates and DC, together with such other information as the accountants shall deem necessary or appropriate to adequately inform them of the manner by which such determination was made. The accountant's determination of the sale price of the Improvements shall be binding and conclusive on the parties.

4. Site Sale Price. The sale price of the Site shall be the Site Purchase Price pursuant to the Purchase Agreement.

5. Closing Date/Escrow. The Closing Date shall be the first business day of the second calendar month following the date of the Put Option exercise. The sale shall be consummated through an Escrow with Blank Title Insurance Company, Growth, California (the "Escrow Holder") by Associates, and DC, who shall severally execute and deliver all customary and reasonable Escrow Instructions, using the Escrow Holder's standard form with such changes as are deemed necessary to incorporate all of the terms, conditions, and provisions of this Agreement in such Escrow Instructions. In the event of any conflict between the terms of this Agreement and those of the Escrow Instructions, the provisions of this Agreement shall prevail. The Escrow Holder shall be instructed to make all of the

-2-

affect the merchantability of title. Associates and any Third Party, respectively, shall deliver through the Escrow, quit claim deeds in recordable form conveying their rights, title and interest only in Parcel 2. The Escrow shall be deemed closed and the deeds shall be recorded on the Closing Date.

8. Title Insurance/Possession. On the Closing Date, Associates and any Third Party shall respectively deliver to DC, at their expense, an owner's policy or policies of title insurance in standard CLTA form in the amount of the respective sales prices of the Improvements and the Site issued by Blank Title Insurance Company covering Parcel 1, and containing as exceptions only the customary printed exceptions in such policies and the exceptions for the matters to which the conveyances are subject, provided in Section 7. Possession of the Site and Improvements shall be delivered to DC on the Closing Date. The cost of recording the grant deeds and quitclaim deeds and any documentary taxes shall be borne by the respective grantors. The cost of recording any reconveyances of any deeds of trust on the Site or on the Improvements shall be borne by DC.

9. Damage to Improvements. If the Improvements should be destroyed or substantially damaged prior to the Closing Date, Associates and DC shall each have the right, exercisable by giving notice thereof to the other, to cancel and terminate the sales of the Improvements and the Site, without any cost or further liability on the part of any of the parties hereto. In the event of such termination, Associates shall cause the funds deposited in Escrow to be returned to DC. Associates shall pay 50% of the costs relating to the cancellation of the Escrow, and DC shall pay the other 50% of such costs.

10. Warranties and Representations by Associates. Associates represents and warrants to DC that as of the Closing Date:

10.1. The sale of the Improvements and the Site will not result in any breach of, or constitute a default under, or result in the creation of any lien, charge or encumbrance upon the Improvements or the Site under any mortgage, deed of trust or any other instrument to which Associates is a party.

10.2. Associates has full powe and authority to enter into, perform and consummate this Agreement in accordance with its terms.

-4-

---

standard Escrow charges and prorations on the Closing Date including, but not limited to, those for taxes, prepaid rents, rents, security deposits, utility charges, assessments, insurance and interest on the existing deeds of trust, if any. In addition, except as provided in Section 10, Associates shall assign any existing leases to DC.

6. Method of Payment. The sales price shall be paid in cash at the Close of Escrow to Associates and the Third Party, if any, respectively, provided that:

6.1. If there is an existing first deed of trust on the Improvements and the Site, DC shall be given credit against the sale price of the Improvements in the amount of the principal balance of the note (and accrued interest thereon) secured by such first deed of trust and, if DC is the holder thereof, such first deed of trust shall be cancelled as paid.

6.2. If there is an existing second deed of trust on the Improvements and Site, DC shall be given credit against the sale price of the Site in the amount of the principal balance of the note (and accrued interest thereon) secured by such second deed of trust, and if DC is the holder thereof, such note shall be cancelled as paid.

7. Title to Site and Improvements. Except with respect to Parcel 2, Associates and any Third Party, respectively, shall deliver, through the Escrow, executed grant deeds in recordable form conveying the Improvements and Site, respectively, free and clear of all liens and encumbrances except current taxes, the lien of which is not yet delinquent, those portions of current assessments not yet due and payable, any existing first deed of trust, any existing second deed of trust to secure the original purchase price under the Purchase Agreement, all covenants, conditions, restrictions, easements and rights of way of record on the date of this Agreement, leases and other tenancy agreements (other than as provided in Section 10) and any other matters of record which do not adversely

-3-

10.3. Through the Closing Date, Associates assumes full responsibility and liability for any and all damage or other injury of any kind whatsoever to any and all persons, whether employees of Associates or otherwise, and to all property arising or connection with the Improvements, and Associates hereby indemnifies DC, its successors and assigns, against and shall hold DC and its successors and assigns free and harmless from any and all loss, damage, liability and expense, including costs and reasonable attorney fees, arising out of or connected with any such damage or injury; provided that the assumption and indemnification of Associates herein given shall not extend to, or release DC from any loss, damage, liability or expenses arising out of or connected with any damage or injury caused by negligence of DC, or its employees, agents or representatives.

10.4. There is no pending or threatened litigation affecting the Site or the Improvements.

11. Warranties and Representations of DC and Parent. DC and Parent jointly and severally represent and warrant to Associates that now and as of the Closing Date:

11.1. Each has full power, authority and capacity to enter into, perform and consummate this Agreement in accordance with its terms.

11.2. There is no action, proceeding or investigation pending or threatened which questions DC or Parent's ability to consummate the transactions contemplated hereby.

12. Entire Agreement. This Agreement is being entered into after full investigation, neither party relying upon any statement or representation not embodied in this Agreement made by the other. This Agreement, the Purchase Agreement, and the other agreements entered into pursuant to the Purchase Agreement and to which they are also parties (together the "other agreements") constitute the entire agreement of the parties and the same may not be amended or modified orally. All understandings and agreements heretofore made between the parties are merged into this Agreement and the other agreements, which together fully and completely express their understanding.

13. Miscellaneous.

13.1. All notices (including but not limited to the notice of Put Option exercise), consents, demands or other communications

-5-

required or desired to be given hereunder shall be in writing. Any such notice, demand or other communication by one party to the other shall be deemed given delivered to such party, if by hand, or when either if sent when mailed via United States mail, registered or certified, with return receipt requested, properly addressed to the party for whom intended with postage prepaid. Until otherwise notified in writing of a change of address, all such notices, demands or communications to the respective parties shall be addressed as appears below:

    to DC:

    to Parent:

    to Associates:

    to Escrow Holder:

Copies of all such communications to any one or both of DC and Parent shall be sent to:

    Meyers, Stevens & Walters
    Professional Corporation
    6300 Wilshire Boulevard, Suite 9100
    Los Angeles, California 90048
    Attention Myron Meyers, Esq.

Copies of all such communications to any one of both of Associates and the Escrow Holder shall also be sent to:

13.2. The waiver by one party of the performance of any covenant, condition or promise shall not invalidate this Agreement nor shall it be considered a waiver of any other covenant, condition or promise. The waiver by either or both parties of the time

-6-

for performing any act shall not constitute a waiver of the time for performing any other act or an identical act required to be performed at a later time.

13.3.   This Agreement shall be construed as a whole and in accordance with its fair meaning. Captions and organizations are for convenience only and shall not be used in construing meaning.

13.4.   If either party to this Agreement brings an action to enforce the terms hereof or declare rights hereunder, the prevailing party in any such action shall be entitled to reasonable attorneys' fees as fixed by the court.

13.5.   Each of the parties represents and warrants to the others that it has not dealt with any finder or real estate broker in connection with the transaction contemplated by this Agreement and each party agrees to hold the others harmless from any loss or damage which either party may suffer by reason of the breach of this representation and warranty.

13.6.   The provisions of this Agreement are severable, and if one or more provisions are determined to be unenforceable, in full or in part, by a court of competent jurisdiction, the validity of the remaining provisions, including any partially unenforceable provisions, to the extent enforceable, shall not be affected in any respect whatsoever.

13.7.   All matters pertaining to the validity, construction, effect and enforcement of this Agreement shall be governed by and construed in accordance with the laws of the State of California.

13.8.   All of the terms, covenants, conditions, representations and warranties contained in this Agreement shall survive any closings of the sales hereunder upon exercise of the Put Option, and shall inure to the benefit of and be binding on the parties to this Agreement, their respective heirs, personal representatives, permitted assigns and successors in interest.

13.9.   Time is of the essence of this Agreement.

13.10.   Associates shall not assign this Agreement or its rights hereunder without the prior written consent of DC, except as provided in Section 2.

14.   Parent's Guaranty.

14.1.   Parent hereby unconditionally and absolutely guarantees the due and punctual performance, observance and compliance by DC of all the terms, covenants, representations, warranties and conditions (together "DC's Obligations") to be kept, observed, complied with or performed by DC under this Agreement, whether according to its present terms or pursuant to any extension of time or to any changes therein, now or any time hereafter made or granted.

14.2.   Parent waives notice of any and all indulgences, notices and formalities of every kind and consents to any and all forebearances and extensions of time for performance, and to any and all changes in DC's Obligations hereafter made or granted, it being the intent hereof, that Parent shall remain liable as a principal until all of DC's Obligations have been fully kept, observed, complied with and performed, notwithstanding any act, omission or thing which might otherwise operate as a legal or equitable discharge of Parent.

IN WITNESS WHEREOF, the parties have executed this Agreement as of the day and year first above written.

DC:
                              DEVELOPMENT CORP.,
                              a California corporation

                              By _____

ASSOCIATES: MEDICAL ASSOCIATES,
                              a California general partnership

                              By _____

PARENT: NATIONAL ENTERPRISES, INC.,
                              a Nevada corporation

                              By _____

STOCK PURCHASE AGREEMENT

THIS AGREEMENT, made in Curaco, Netherlands Antilles, on _____, between N.V., a Netherlands Antilles corporation (hereinafter called "Seller") and COMPANY N.V., a Netherlands corporation (hereinafter called "Purchaser").

WITNESSETH:

In consideration of the premises and the mutual agreements hereinafter contained, Seller and Purchaser agree as follows:

1. Representations and Warranties. Seller represents and warrants to Purchaser, and this agreement is made in reliance upon, the following:

(a) SUPER HOTEL, INC. (the "Company") has been duly incorporated and is validly existing and in good standing as a corporation under the laws of the State of California, U.S.A.

(b) The Company has a total of _____ shares of capital stock, $_____ par value (the "Shares"), outstanding and no more; all of the Shares have been legally and validly issued and are fully paid and nonassessable; and the Company has no outstanding obligations, understandings, or commitments regarding the issuance of any additional shares, or any options, rights, or warrants concerning the issuance of any additional shares or securities convertible into shares.

(c) Seller owns beneficially and of record all the Shares of the Company, and has all right, title and interest in and to the Shares, and has good and marketable title thereto, free and clear of any claims, liens or encumbrances of any nature whatsoever. Seller has good, marketable and indefeasible title to and full power of disposition over and has full right to sell and transfer to the Purchaser the Shares; and the Shares are free of all liens, claims, debts or other encumbrances upon their transfer to the Purchaser under this Agreement.

(d) Seller delivered to Purchaser financial statements of the Company and statements of profit and loss. Such financial statements fairly present the financial conditions of the Company as of the date and the results of its operations for the periods indicated in accordance with generally accepted principles consistently applied; since said date, there has not been any material adverse change in the financial condition

or operations of the Company from that shown on said financial statements, nor have there been any other changes in such condition except changes occurring in the ordinary course of the Company's business; and since said date, there have been no dividends or other distributions made by the Company to its shareholders, nor has it purchased, redeemed, or otherwise acquired any shares of its outstanding stock.

(e) The Company is not subject to any material liability or liabilities of any kind, absolute or contingent, not disclosed in said statement of condition, except liabilities (none of which is material) incurred after said date in the ordinary course of business and those set forth in Exhibit "A" attached hereto and incorporated herein by this reference.

(f) The Company is not a party to any material contracts or commitments of any kind, except that certain Lease with option to purchase dated _____ between Seller, as Landlord, and the Diplomat, as Tenant.

(g) The execution and performance of this Agreement, and the consummation of the transactions contemplated hereby, have been duly and validly authorized by all requisite corporate action on the part of Seller and Purchaser and does not and will not violate any provision of either Seller or Purchaser's Articles of Incorporation or By-Laws, or any material agreement or other instrument to which either is bound, or any law, regulation, or order applicable to Seller or Purchaser's business. This Agreement constitutes a valid and binding agreement on the part of Seller and Purchaser, enforceable in accordance with its terms.

2. Sale of Shares. At the Closing, Seller shall sell, transfer and deliver to Purchaser all the Shares outstanding, consisting of _____ Shares of stock of the Company, for a purchase price per share of $_____, or an aggregate sum of $_____ payable as per Exhibit "B" attached hereto and incorporated herein by reference.

3. Closing. The sale and purchase of the Shares shall be consummated at Curaco, Netherlands Antilles, on or before _____, by delivery to Purchaser of certificates for the Shares duly endorsed for assignment and transfer, or accompanied by duly executed stock powers, with signatures guaranteed by a bank or trust company or otherwise as approved by Purchaser, against payment by bank cashiers' or certified check(s) by Purchaser of the full purchase price for the Shares. The time of delivery and payment is herein called the "Closing Date".

-2-

8. _Assignment._ This Agreement shall be binding upon, inure to the benefit of, and be enforceable by the heirs, administrators, executors, and assigns of Seller and of Purchaser.

9. _Governing Law._ This Agreement shall be construed in accordance with the laws of the State of California, U.S.A.

10. _Entire Agreement._ This Agreement contains the entire agreement of the parties hereto, and supersedes any prior written or oral agreements between them concerning the subject matter contained herein. There are no representations, agreements, arrangements, or understandings, oral or written, between and among the parties hereto, relating to the subject matter contained in this Agreement, which are not fully expressed herein.

11. _Notices._ All notices, requests, demands and other communications hereunder shall be in writing and shall be deemed to have been duly given if delivered or mailed by United States certified or registered mail, prepaid, to the parties at the following addresses:

To Seller:
N.V.

Curaco, Netherlands Antilles

with a copy to:

Myron Meyers, Esq.
6300 Wilshire Boulevard
Suite 9100
Los Angeles, CA   90048

To Purchaser:

N.V.

Curaco, Netherlands Antilles

with a copy to:

John Law, Esq.
1234 South Wilshire Street
Los Angeles, CA 99999

The parties hereto may change said addresses by giving written notice thereof to the other parties hereto in accordance with the provisions hereof.

-4-

---

4. If the sale of the Shares is made on a deferred basis, then notwithstanding anything contained in paragraph 3 of this Agreement to the contrary, the certificates for the Shares as endorsed for assignment and transfer shall be delivered at Closing to Seller or a party mutually agreeable to Seller and Purchaser, to be held by said party until Purchaser shall have paid the entire purchase price of the Shares. The parties hereto shall enter into a pledge agreement with respect to the Shares and that the Purchaser shall be entitled to vote the Shares so pledged; subject, however, to the Seller's approval with respect to the sale, transfer, assignment, hypothecation or any other disposition of all or substantially all of the assets of the Company, which approval shall not be unreasonably withheld.

5. _Conditions of Purchaser's Obligations._ Purchaser's obligation to purchase the Shares from Seller is subject to the following conditions:

(a) The representations and warranties of Seller stated in paragraph l shall be true as of the Closing Date, and there shall have been no material adverse changes in the financial condition or affairs of the Company between the date of this Agreement and the Closing Date; and a certificate to all of such effects signed by Seller shall be delivered to Purchaser on the Closing date.

(b) Seller shall deliver to Purchaser on the Closing Date the resignations of all directors and officers of the Company.

(c) All of the Shares shall be concurrently sold to Purchaser.

6. _Survival of Representations and Warranties._ The representations, warranties and covenants of Seller herein shall remain in full force regardless of any investigation or approval by Purchaser, and shall survive the delivery of the Shares to Purchaser.

7. _Indemnification._ Seller shall indemnify and hold harmless Purchaser from any and all losses, costs, damage or other liabilities of any nature whatsoever (including, but not limited to, reasonable attorneys' fees) arising out of or attributable to a breach by Seller of any of its respective agreements, promises, representations, warranties and/or undertakings herein contained. Purchaser shall indemnify and hold harmless Seller from any and all losses, costs, damage or other liabilities (including, but not limited to, reasonable attorneys' fees) arising out of or attributable to a breach by Purchaser of any of its agreements, promises, representations, warranties, and/or undertakings herein contained.

-3-

EXHIBIT "A"

SCHEDULE OF MATERIAL LIABILITIES

The Company is indebted to Monetary Inc in the sum of $1,500,000.00 (U.S.). Said indebtedness bears interest at 10% per annum; is secured by a first lien on Company's real property in Los Angeles, California; and is due and payable with accrued interest and costs prior to _____.

12. Rights and Remedies Cumulative. No remedy conferred to any of the specific provisions of this Agreement is intended to be exclusive of any other remedy, and each and every remedy shall be cumulative and shall be in addition to every other remedy given hereunder or now or hereafter existing at law or in equity or by statute or otherwise. The election of any one or more remedies by Seller or the Company shall not constitute a waiver of the right to pursue other available remedies.

13. Counterparts. This Agreement may be executed in one or more counterparts, each of which shall be deemed an original, but all of which together shall constitute one and the same instrument.

14. Captions and Paragraph Headings. Captions and paragraph headings used herein are used for convenience only and are not a part of this Agreement and shall not be used in construing it.

15. Miscellaneous. Feminine or neuter pronouns shall be substituted for those of masculine form or vice versa, and the plural shall be substituted for the singular numer or vice versa in any place or places herein in which the context requires such substitution.

IN WITNESS WHEREOF, this Agreement has been executed by the parties hereto on the date first above written in Curacao, Netherlands Antilles.

N.V.

By: _____

By: _____

N.V.

By: _____

By: _____

-5-

EXHIBIT "B"

PAYMENT SCHEDULE

The total purchase price of $ _____ shall be payable as follows:

1. _____ ($ _____) U.S. Dollars shall be paid at Closing (prior to _____).

2. The balance of $ _____ shall be paid as follows:

(a) _____ ($ _____) U.S. Dollars on or before _____ ;

(b) _____ ($ _____) U.S. Dollars on or before _____ ;

(c) _____ ($ _____) U.S. Dollars on or before _____ ; and

(d) The balance plus accrued interest at the rate of _____ percent (__ %) per annum on the remaining unpaid principal balance on or before _____ .

Purchase shall have the right to repay all or any portion thereof without penalty.

All sums paid by Purchaser on the obligation described in Exhibit "A" shall be deducted from the sums due pursuant to this Exhibit "B".

THIS OPTION, made and granted this _____1st_____ day of January, 1981, by FRIENDLY SAVINGS AND LOAN ASSOCIATION, a corporation, hereinafter sometimes referred to as "FRIENDLY," or "Optionor," and SPECULATION, INC. a California corporation, hereinafter sometimes referred to as "SI" or "Optionee," is as follows:

FOR AND IN CONSIDERATION of the entering into by and between the parties hereto of this Option Agreement and the payment to FRIENDLY by SI of the sum of TEN THOUSAND DOLLARS ($10,000.00) receipt of which is hereby acknowledged, as consideration to FRIENDLY for the granting of this Option, the parties hereto agree as follows:

I. FRIENDLY does herein and hereby grant to SI the sole and exclusive right and option for a term commencing with the date of the execution of this option by all of the parties hereto and terminating on midnight of the _____ day of _____ , _____ , to purchase that certain real property more particularly described hereinafter upon the terms and conditions hereinafter set forth.

II. DESCRIPTION OR PROPERTY: The property, the subject of this Option, consists of that certain real property in the City of Future, County of Growth, State of California, containing approximately 9.5 acres, more particularly described in Exhibit "A" attached hereto, incorporated herein by reference and made a part hereof.

III. PURCHASE PRICE AND TERMS OF PAYMENT: The total purchase price for subject property shall be ONE MILLION DOLLARS ($1,000,000.00) payable all cash upon the close of Excrow, more fully described below.

A. Said sum of $1,000,000 shall be payable as follows:

(i) ONE HUNDRED THOUSAND DOLLARS ($100,000.00) upon the exercise of the option by the Optionee as hereinafter provided. Said sum of $100,000.00 shall be deposited into the Escrow to facilitate the purchase and sale which escrow is hereafter described.

(ii) The balance of the purchase price shall be payable in cash through Escrow upon the close of Escrow.

(iii) Should Optionee timely exercise this Option and thereafter timely complete the purchase Escrow hereafter described, Optionee shall receive concurrently with the close of Escrow credit in the sum of TEN THOUSAND DOLLARS ($10,000.00) and the total purchase price shall be reduced by that sum. Should Optionee fail to timely exercise this Option and timely close the Escrow hereafter described, the $10,000.00 paid by Optionee to FRIENDLY concurrently with the execution of this Option Agreement shall be retained by FRIENDLY as consideration for the granting to Optionee of this Option.

IV. TITLE:

A. The parties hereto agree that FRIENDLY shall deliver title to the property, the subject of this Option, at the close of Escrow in the nature of a Grant Deed subject to all matters of record set forth in that certain preliminary title report No. _____ , dated _____ day of _____ , _____ , issued by _____ Title Insurance Company, and in addition thereto current real and personal property taxes and assessments and all matters arising from any acts of the Optionee occurring hereafter.

B. Except as expressly set forth in sub-paragraph A of this paragraph IV, the property which is the subject of this Option shall, upon the exercise thereof, be purchased in an "as is and where is" condition without representation or warranty of any kind or nature on the part of FRIENDLY with respect thereto. In this regard, Optionee shall make their own independent investigation concerning the property in question, its zoning, its usability for any particular purpose, and the physical condition thereof, and shall in no manner rely upon FRIENDLY in connection therewith.

V. METHOD OF EXERCISE OF OPTION: The Option granted herein shall be exercised, if at all, at any time prior to midnight of the _____ day of _____, _____ by Optionee, giving written notice of their intention to exercise same by registered or certified mail, by personal delivery or by telegram, addressed to FRIENDLY at 100 Dollar Drive, Money, California, Attention of Hy Cost, President. Said notice shall be accompanied by a cashier's check or certified check in the sum of ONE HUNDRED THOUSAND DOLLARS ($100,000.00) payable to FRIENDLY, and unless so accompanied, shall not constitute sufficient notice of intent to exercise said option. In the event said option shall not be exercised as herein provided before the said date, the terms of this Option Agreement shall be of no further force and effect. The $100,000.00 to be delivered to FRIENDLY as aforesaid shall be deposited by FRIENDLY into the Escrow hereafter described.

VI. ASSIGNMENT OF OPTION: Optionee shall have the right to assign this Option to any and all persons as FRIENDLY may approve, and FRIENDLY agrees not to unreasonably withhold such approval. Upon any such assignment, this Option and each and all of the terms hereof, shall be binding upon said assignee. In addition thereto, Optionee may exercise said option in its own name but designate, any time prior to the close of Escrow, the name of the party actually purchasing the same; except that in such an event any such persons must, prior to the close of said Escrow, be approved by FRIENDLY and FRIENDLY agrees not to unreasonably withhold such approval.

VII. ASSIGNEE OR NOMINEE: In the event of any assignment or nomination as provided for hereinabove, the Optionee herein, his assignee or nominee, shall prior to the approval by FRIENDLY deliver to FRIENDLY the following additional information:

A. A writing evidencing the name and address of the assignee or nominee, together with a summarization of his or its business history for the past five (5) years;

B. Financial statements, credit information, and other evidence required by FRIENDLY, evidencing the assets, liabilities and net worth of the assignee or nominee which financial information and other information shall be not more than ninety (90) days old and be in form required by FRIENDLY. All financial statements shall be certified by a Certified Public Accountant approved by FRIENDLY.

VIII. ESCROW AND POSSESSION: To facilitate the transfer of title and to carry out the executory provisions of this Agreement, an Escrow shall be opened within five (5) days from the exercise, as aforesaid, of this Option at _____ Bank or at such title company as shall be approved by FRIENDLY and the Optionee. Said Escrow instructions shall embody each and all of the terms and provisions hereof but shall be subordinate to this Agreement in the event of ambiguity or conflict. Said Escrow instructions shall provide that any party may waive any term, provision or condition for its benefit, or that FRIENDLY may waive, at its option, any of the terms and provisions to be performed by the Optionee. Said Escrow shall close on or before ten (10) days from the date of its opening and at such time the documents herein mentioned entitled to be recorded shall be recorded, and all monies disbursed. Each party shall pay half of all Escrow charges. All taxes and insurance, if any, shall be prorated to the close of Escrow. FRIENDLY shall pay for the cost of a standard coverage owner's policy of title insurance with a liability of $1,000,000.00, which policy shall be written in the usual form of the title insurer, with all the usual printed exceptions, and further subject to all of the matters previously described in the preliminary title report set forth in paragraph IV above. Said escrow shall further provide that possession shall be delivered on the close of Escrow and that FRIENDLY shall execute a Grant Deed to subject property in favor of the ultimate purchaser.

IX. TIME IS OF THE ESSENCE: Time is of the essence in this Agreement as to all of the acts to be performed by the respective parties hereto including that certain Escrow to be opened pursuant to the terms hereof.

X. ATTORNEY'S FEES: Should suit be instituted to enforce any of the terms hereof, or of the Escrow entered into pursuant hereto, the prevailing party in said action shall be entitled to reasonable attorney's fees in addition to any other award made by the court.

XI. ARBITRATION: In the event any dispute arises hereunder regarding the terms of this option as herein granted, the parties hereto agree that an arbitrator of the Los Angeles office of the American Arbitration Association shall arbitrate such dispute. In the event the parties are unable to agree upon an impartial arbitrator approved by such office of the American Arbitration Association, the parties hereto shall each select an arbitrator from a list of approved arbitrators submitted to them by such office of the American Arbitration Association. The two arbitrators so selected shall then agree upon a third arbitrator and said third arbitrator, acting alone, shall arbitrate such dispute. The fees of such arbitration shall be shared by the parties equally; provided, however, that each party shall pay its own legal fees. The decision of such arbitrator shall be binding and conclusive upon the parties, and the parties agree to abide thereby.

XII. ASSIGNS: This Option Agreement shall be binding upon and shall inure to the benefit of the assigns and successors in interest of the respective parties hereto.

XIII. NO ORAL REPRESENTATIONS: Optionee hereby attests that this Option Agreement constitutes the full and complete transaction between the parties. No oral representations of any kind have been made to Optionee or anyone in connection with this transaction. Further, no oral representations of any nature have induced Optionee to enter into this transaction.

XIV. EXTENSION OF OPTION: Optionee shall have the additional right and option to extend the term of this Option Agreement for additional periods of time not to exceed an additional period of sixty (60) days in total, by payment to FRIENDLY prior to the expiration of the original option period, or any extended period as provided in this paragraph, of a sum equal to THREE HUNDRED FIFTY ($350) DOLLARS for each day's extension. Such extensions shall be for periods of not less than five (5) days at a time and each such extension shall be accompanied by a written notice of FRIENDLY, addressed in the same manner as an exercise of the option would be addressed, accompanied by a cashier's or certified check of not less than SEVENTEEN HUNDRED FIFTY DOLLARS ($1,750.00) made payable to FRIENDLY, and setting forth the number of days of extension requested. If additional requests are made, same shall and must be made to be effective prior to the expiration of the original option period or any extension thereof previously timely exercised and paid for. Should the Option ultimately be exercised as provided in this Option Agreement, all sums paid to FRIENDLY to obtain extensions of said option is not ultimately exercised duly and timely as herein provided, all sums paid for any extensions shall be retained by FRIENDLY for and in consideration of the granting of any such extensions.

XV. BROKER'S COMMISSIONS: Should the Optionee duly and timely exercise the Option and should as a result thereof an Escrow be in fact consummated and FRIENDLY receives the total sum of $1,000,000.00 as and for the property in question, in such an event, FRIENDLY acknowledges that it will cause to be paid through escrow from the proceeds thereof the sum of SIXTY THOUSAND DOLLARS ($60,000.00) to AGGRESSIVE REALTY CO. as commissions earned at that time. Nothing herein contained shall, however, be deemed any agreement on the part of FRIENDLY to pay any commissions to AGGRESSIVE REALTY CO. or any other person, firm or entity, or be deemed an admission that any commission has in fact been earned, it being expressly understood that said commission will be paid solely and only in the event of a consummation of a sale, pursuant to a valid exercise of option and processing of the Escrow herein described, and if for any reason whatsoever such sale shall not be consummated, FRIENDLY shall have no duty or obligation of any kind or nature to any party to pay a commission or incur any liability of any kind or nature to AGGRESSIVE REALTY CO. or any other person.

Optionee further agrees that this Option may not be modified except and unless such modification be in writing signed by the parties. They acknowledge that they understand no one has authority to modify the terms of this Agreement and Option orally.

IN WITNESS WHEREOF, the parties have hereto set their hands and seals this date.

OPTIONOR: FRIENDLY SAVINGS AND LOAN
ASSOCIATION, a corporation
By _____
       Title _____

By _____
       Title _____

OPTIONEE: SPECULATION, INC, a California corporation
By _____
             President

By _____
             Secretary

The provisions of Paragraph XV are hereby approved and accepted.

DATED: _____
AGGRESSIVE REALTY CO.
By _____

STATE OF CALIFORNIA   )
) SS.
COUNTY OF LOS ANGELES)
On _____, 19_____, before me, the undersigned, a Notary Public in and for
said State, personally appeared _____, known to me to
be the _____ and _____, known to be
the _____ of the corporation that executed the within Instrument,
known to me to be the persons who executed the within Instrument on behalf of the corporation therein
named, and acknowledge to me that such corporation executed the within instrument pursuant to its by-
laws or a resolution of its board of directors.
    WITNESS my hand and official seal.

_____
_____
Print or type name

STATE OF CALIFORNIA   )
) SS.

COUNTY OF LOS ANGELES)

On _____, 19 _____, before me, the undersigned, a Notary Public in
and for said State, personally appeared _____, known to me to
be the _____ and _____, known to me to
be the _____ of the corporation that executed the
within Instrument, known to me to be the persons who executed the within Instrument on behalf of the
corporation therein named, and acknowledge to me that such corporation executed the within instrument
pursuant to its by-laws or a resolution of its board of directors.
    WITNESS my hand and official seal.

_____
         Print or type name

BORROWER'S SECURITY AND PLEDGE AGREEMENT

THIS SECURITY AND PLEDGE AGREEMENT (this "Agreement") is entered into at Curacao, Netherlands Antilles, as of this _____ day of _____, 19__, by and between _____ N.V. ("Borrower"), a Netherlands Antilles corporation with its principal place of business located at _____, Curacao, Netherlands Antilles, and _____ N.V. ("Lender"), a Netherlands Antilles corporation, with its principal place of business located at _____, Curacao, Netherlands Antilles.

I

THE COLLATERAL

1.1 "Borrower's liabilities," wherever used in this Agreement, shall mean all liabilities and indebtedness of any and every kind and nature heretofore, now or hereafter owing, arising, due or payable from Borrower to Lender, howsoever evidenced, created, incurred, acquired or owing, whether primary, secondary, direct, contingent, fixed or otherwise, or arising under any security agreements, stock purchase agreement, mortgages, leases, instruments, documents, contracts or similar agreements heretofore, now or hereafter executed by Borrower and delivered to Lender (all such loan and security agreements, riders, security agreements, mortgages, leases, instruments, documents, contracts and similar agreements being hereinafter individually and collectively referred to as "the Financing Agreements"), or by oral agreement or operation of law, and whether evidenced by instruments or other evidences of indebtedness. The provisions of the Financing Agreements are incorporated herein by this reference thereto.

1.2 To secure the payment of Borrower's liabilities, Borrower grants Lender a security interest in and to the shares of stock, and all proceeds thereof, described in Exhibit "A" attached hereto and made a part hereof, and in and to all of Borrower's rights, titles and interests therein and thereto, which stock, together with any additional stock, securities, evidences of indebtedness or other collateral in which Borrower has granted to Lender a security interest hereunder is hereinafter referred to as "the Pledged Stock."

1.3 To secure payment of Borrower's Liabilities, Borrower grants Lender a security interest in and to any and all distributions and payments, whether in cash or in kind, upon or in connection with the Pledged Stock, whether such distributions or payments are dividends, or in partial or complete liquidation, or the result of reclassification, readjustment or other changes in the capital structure of the corporations which have issued the Pledged Stock, or otherwise. Borrower shall forthwith deliver to Lender any such distribution and payment in the form in which that distribution or payment is received by Borrower and thereupon Lender shall hold any such distribution, except for cash, as additional collateral pledged to secure Borrower's Liabilities. Any cash distribution so received by Borrower shall, upon receipt by Borrower and delivery thereof to Lender, be applied on account of Borrower's Liabilities. Any shares of capital stock, securities or evidences of indebtedness so distributed to Borrower shall be delivered to Lender accompanied with irrevocable stock powers relating thereto or assignments thereof duly signed by Borrower in form acceptable to Lender. Borrower's signature on such stock powers or assignments shall be guaranteed by a national banking institution.

1.4 To secure payment of Borrower's Liabilities, Borrower grants Lender a security interest in and to any and all subscriptions, warrants, options and any other rights issued upon or in connection with the Pledged Stock, and Borrower shall forthwith deliver to Lender all such subscriptions, warrants, options and all such other rights, and upon delivery to Lender,

2

Lender shall hold such subscriptions, warrants, options and other rights as additional collateral pledged to secure Borrower's Liabilities; provided, however, that if Lender determines in its sole discretion that the value of any of such subscriptions, warrants, options or other rights shall terminate, expire or be materially reduced by holding the same as pledged collateral, Lender shall have the right in its sole discretion to sell or exercise the same, and if exercised, then the monies disbursed by Lender in connection therewith shall be deemed a loan by Lender to Borrower, the repayment of which loan shall be secured by all of the security interests now or hereafter granted by Borrower to Lender, and by all of the stock, securities or evidences of indebtedness so acquired which shall be deemed the property of Borrower pledged to Lender hereunder.

1.5 Lender may at any time, and from time to time, transfer any or all of the Pledged Stock into the name of Lender, or into the name of Lender's nominee without disclosing that such Pledged Stock so transferred is pledged or hypothecated, and without any indication on any new certificate or other document issued to evidence such Pledged Stock, that such stock is pledged or hypothecated and any issuer of such Pledged Stock, or its transfer agent, shall not be bound to inquire in the event that Lender or said nominee makes any other transfer of the Pledged Stock, as to whether Lender or its nominee has the right to make such further transfer, and any such issuer, or its transfer agent, shall not be liable for transferring the same.

1.6 Until default by Borrower under this Agreement, Borrower shall have the right to vote the Pledged Stock, or if any or all of the Pledged Stock is registered in the name of Lender, with respect to such Pledged Stock so registered in the name of Lender, Borrower shall have the right to direct Lender how to vote the stock; provided, however, in the event of any such default,

3

Lender shall have the right to vote the Pledged Stock.

1.7 Concurrently with Borrower's execution of this Agreement, Borrower shall deliver to Lender the Pledged Stock, together with properly executed irrevocable assignments thereof or stock powers therefor, endorsed in blank. Borrower's signature on each such assignment and stock power shall be guaranteed by a national or other banking institution.

II
WARRANTIES

2.1 Borrower warrants and represents to Lender as follows:

(a) The Pledged Stock is validly issued, fully paid and non-assessable and Borrower is the lawful owner thereof and has the right to grant Lender a security interest therein free and clear of all liens, encumbrances, claims or demands whatsoever; and,

(b) Borrower will not suffer or permit any lien or encumbrance of any nature to attach to the Pledged Stock.

III
DEFAULT

3.1 Any one of the following events shall constitute a default hereunder by Borrower:

(a) Failure of Borrower promptly to pay when due or declared due any of Borrower's Liabilities;

(b) Failure of Borrower to perform and observe any of the terms, conditions and provisions contained in this Agreement or in any of the Financing Agreements; or

(c) A default by Borrower under the Financing Agreements.

4

3.2 In the event of a default by Borrower hereunder, Lender may, at its election, without notice of such election to and without demand upon Borrower, do any one or more of the following:

(a) Declare Borrower's Liabilities immediately due and payable;

(b) Sell or cause to be sold the Pledged Stock or any part thereof and all of Borrower's right, title and interest therein at public auction or private sale in accordance with the applicable laws of the United States or of any state; such sale may be made for cash or credit at the election of Lender and Borrower shall be credited with the amounts of any such sale only when the proceeds thereof are actually received by Lender; to the extent permitted by applicable law, Borrower hereby waives and releases Lender of and from any and all liabilities or penalties for failure of Lender to comply with statutory or other requirements imposed on Lender relating to notices of sale, holding of sale, reporting of any sale and all rights of redemption from any such sale; Lender, or its nominee, may become the purchaser at such sale and may, in its discretion, continue or postpone any sale from time to time without notice to Borrower; or

(c) Exercise all of the rights and remedies of a Secured Party under the Uniform Commercial Code.

3.3 For the purposes hereinafter set forth, Borrower does hereby irrevocably make, constitute, designate and appoint Lender (and any of Lender's officers, employees or agents designated by Lender) as Borrower's true and lawful attorney-in-fact and agent. In the event of any default hereunder by Borrower, such agent shall have the full power and authority for and in the name of Borrower to arrange for the transfer of the Pledged Stock on the books of issuing companies thereof to the name of Lender, or any purchaser from nominee of Lender. Borrower does hereby ratify and confirm all that said agent

5

may do or cause to be done in connection with any of the power or authority herein conferred.

3.4 In the event that Lender elects to exercise any of the remedies provided for in this Article, there shall be included as part of Borrower's Liabilities attorneys' fees, as hereinafter provided for, expenditures which may be paid or incurred by or on behalf of Lender for publication and advertising costs, transfer taxes, and any other costs and expenses incurred or paid in connection with any sale, transfer or foreclosure of the Pledged Stock (including, without limiting the generality of the foregoing, all monies, if any, paid by Lender to any party on account of such party's asserted, claimed or actual prior security interest in the Pledged Stock, it being agreed by Borrower that Lender, in connection with any such payment, may consider any statement rendered by any such party to Lender on account thereof as true and accurate, and Lender shall not be responsible for an error or mistake therein or misrepresentation thereof, and Borrower shall look only to such other party on account thereof), and all such expenditures shall be immediately due and payable and bear interest at the rate provided in the Financing Agreements and shall be secured by the Pledged Stock.

3.5 If at any time or times hereafter Lender employs counsel for advice or other representation (i) with respect to this Agreement or the Financing Agreement, (ii) to represent Lender in any litigation, contest, dispute, suit or proceeding (whether instituted by Lender, Borrower or any other party) in any way or respect relating to this Agreement or the Financing Agreements, or (iii) to collect or enforce Borrower's Liabilities, then, in any of the foregoing events, all of the reasonable attorneys' fees arising from such services and all expenses, costs and charges in any way or respect arising in connection therewith or relating thereto shall be paid by Borrower to Lender,

6

on demand, shall bear interest at the rate provided in the Financing Agreements, and shall be secured by the Pledged Stock.

3.6 In the event any notice is required to be given to Borrower with respect to any sale or liquidation of the Pledged Stock, or any other action by Lender, any notice addressed to Borrower at its address set forth at the beginning of this Agreement, postage prepaid, deposited in the United States mail, five (5) days prior to the date of any such intended action, shall be deemed to be a sufficient and commercially reasonable notice.

3.7 Borrower is obligated, pursuant to the terms of the Stock Purchase Agreement between Borrower and Lender, to pay to Lender prior to

the sum of $ (U.S.) Time is made expressly of the essence in reference to said payment. Should Borrower fail to timely make said payment, then, notwithstanding the other provisions of this Pledge Agreement, the following shall occur:

(a) Lender shall return by re-endorsement and delivery to Borrower the shares described in Exhibit "A" attached.

(b) Lender shall return to Borrower the sum of $ (U.S.) paid by Borrower to Lender pursuant to the Stock Purchase Agreement. Said sum shall be returned without interest.

(c) The Pledge Agreement and the Stock Purchase Agreement shall thereafter be deemed null and void and of no further effect.

All sums paid by Borrower on the indebtedness described in Exhibit "A" of the Stock Purchase Agreement shall be credited against sums due pursuant to this paragraph 3.7.

IV

MISCELLANEOUS

4.1 If any provision of this Agreement or the application thereof to

7

any party or circumstance is held invalid or unenforceable, the remainder of this Agreement and the application of such provision to other parties or circumstances will not be affected thereby, the provisions of this Agreement being severable in any such instance.

4.2 No remedy or right of Lender shall be exclusive of any other remedy or right now or hereafter existing at law or equity, but shall be in addition thereto; no delay in exercising, or omission to exercise, any remedy or right accruing on any default shall impair any such remedy or right, or shall be construed to be a waiver of any such default, or acquiescence therein, nor shall it affect any subsequent default of the same or a different nature. Every such right or remedy may be exercised concurrently or independently, and so often as may be deemed expedient by Lender.

4.3 All covenants, warranties and representations contained herein shall be true as of the date hereof and shall survive the execution and delivery of this Agreement.

4.4 This Agreement and all the provisions hereof shall be binding upon and inure to the benefit of the successors and assigns of Borrower and Lender, and shall be construed in accordance with the laws and decisions of the State of California, U.S.A.

IN WITNESS WHEREOF, this Agreement has been duly executed as of the day and year at the beginning hereof.

                                                                N. V.

                                        By: _____

                                        By: _____

                                                                N. V.

                                        By: _____

                                        By: _____

8

LEASE

THIS LEASE is entered into and effective as of this 1st day of January, 1981, by and between BLACKACRE PROPERTIES, INC., a California corporation (hereinafter called "Landlord") and WHITEACRE DEVELOPMENT, INC., a California corporation (hereinafter called "Tenant").

SECTION 1. PREMISES AND RENTAL AGREEMENTS.

1.1 Premises. In consideration of the agreements herein expressed, Landlord leases to Tenant and Tenant leases from Landlord that certain real property, as hereinafter described, together with all improvements presently located thereon, and all rights, privileges, easements and appurtenances to such real property, all of which, together with all buildings, structures, fixtures, paving, landscaping, and other physical improvements, hereafter constructed or installed in or upon said real property by Tenant, are herein referred to as the "premises".

Said real property is located in the County of Los Angeles, State of California, and is legally described as follows:

Lots 1, 2, 3 and 4, Block 5, of tract 10000 in the City of Los Angeles, County of Los Angeles, State of California per Map recorded in Book 100, Pages 10 through 50, inclusive, of Maps in the Office of the County Recorder of Los Angeles County, California.

EXHIBIT "A" TO BORROWER'S SECURITY AND PLEDGE AGREEMENT DATED THE _____ DAY OF _____ BETWEEN _____ N. V. (BORROWER) AND _____ N. V. (LENDER)

ISSUER	CERTIFICATE NUMBER	NAME OF STOCKHOLDER	NUMBER OF SHARES
	1		

BORROWER'S RIGHT OF SUBSTITUTION

Borrower, at its election, may, upon written notice to Lender, substitute for the above stock certificate a certificate of the outstanding and issued stock of _____ a California corporation (" _____ "), that represents not less than _____ percent ( ) out of all issued and outstanding shares of Diplomat. Borrower represents and warrants that Diplomat has only one class of shares, and all shares outstanding are owned by Borrower.

1.2. Additional Lot. Landlord intends to acquire in addition to the parcels described in Paragraph 1.1 above, Lot 6 of the same tract. Should Landlord acquire said Lot, concurrently with such acquisition said Lot shall be deemed included as a portion of the premises and all of the other terms and provisions of this Lease shall apply to such additional Lot.

1.3 Rental Agreements. As additional consideration for the agreements herein expressed, Landlord sells, assigns, transfers and conveys to Tenant all of Landlord's right, title and interest in and to all leases and rental agreements existing in connection with the premises at the commencement of the term of this Lease, together with all rents and security deposits with respect thereto; all rents assigned hereunder shall be prorated between Landlord and Tenant assumes and agrees to perform all of Landlord's obligations and liabilities under the terms of said leases and rental agreements accruing after the commencement of the term of this Lease, and agrees to indemnify and hold Landlord free and harmless therefrom, including, without limitation, all attorneys' fees, expenses and court costs in the defense thereof.

SECTION 2. TERM, POSSESSION, OPTIONS TO EXTEND.

2.1 Initial Term. The initial term of this Lease shall be fifty-five (55) years, commencing January 1, 1981, and expiring December, 31, 2036.

2.2. Possession. Possession of the premises shall be delivered to Tenant on or about the 1st day of January, 1981; and as to the additional Lot, when Landlord acquires title thereto.

3.2 Options to Extend Term. Tenant is granted the option to extend the initial term of this Lease for three (3) additional consecutive periods of five (5) years each, subject to all provisions of this Lease, including but not limited to provisions for adjustment to and variations in rent. Failure to exercise the option for any period shall nullify the option for all subsequent periods. Tenant may, at Tenant's election, assign these options, or any of them, at any time and from time to time to any one or more leasehold mortgagees, or trust deed beneficiaries permitted by this Lease, and may give any such mortgage, or trust deed beneficiary, with or without such assignment, power of attorney to exercise any such option. After the exercise of any option to extend, all references in this Lease to the term shall be considered to mean the term as extended, and all reference to termination or to the end of the term shall be considered to mean the termination or end of the term as extended. Tenant's right to the option is subject to:

A. The following conditions precedent;

(1) The Lease shall be in effect at the time notice of exercise is given and on the last day of the term.

(2) Tenant shall not be in default under any provision of this Lease at the time notice of exercise is given or on the last day of the term.

B. Compliance with the following procedure for exercising the option:

(1) Lessee shall give Lessor notice irrevocably exercising the option prior to the last day of the term.

(2) In lieu of executing a new Lease, each party shall, at the request of the other, endorse on the original Lease or signatures, the date the option was exercised, and the words "option exercised". Alternatively, each party shall, at the request of the other, execute a memorandum, in recordable form, acknowledging the fact that the option has been exercised and otherwise complying with the requirements of law for an effective memorandum or abstract of lease.

SECTION 3.   RENT

3.1. Basic Annual Rent. Tenant shall pay to Landlord as basic annual rent the sum of Two Hundred Fifty Thousand Dollars (($250,000.00) per Lease year for the duration of the term of this lease; provided, however, that when the additional Lot described in Paragraph 1.2 is acquired by Landlord and possession thereof is delivered to Tenant, said annual rental shall be increased by the sum of Fifty Thousand Dollars ($50,000.00) per annum prorated from the date of such possession and shall be payable with the other basic annual rent herein defined. "Lease year" is defined as that period commencing with the commencement of the initial term of this Lease and expiring twelve (12) months thereafter. Said basic annual rent shall be payable at the end of the lease year for the first least year, and monthly thereafter. The rental above specified shall be subject to adjustment at the times and in the manner below set forth in paragraph 3.2. All rent hereunder shall be paid in lawful money of the United States.

3.2 Rent Adjustments The rent above specified shall be adjusted as of the first day of every fourth lease year during the term hereof, the first such adjustment to be made on January 1, 1984, according to the following computation: The base for computing the adjustment is the Consumer Price Index (all terms) for the Los Angeles - Long Beach Metropolitan area, published by the Unites States Department of Labor, Bureau of Labor Statistics ("Index"). On the first rent adjustment date, if the Index which is published for the most recent month next preceding such first adjustment date ("First Adjusted Index") has increased over the Index published for the most recent month next preceding the commencement of the term of this Lease ("Initial Index"), the monthly rental rate for the following three (3) year period shall be computed by multiplying the basic annual rent set forth in paragraph 3.1 above, by a fraction the numerator of which is the First Adjusted Index and the denominator of which is the Initial Index. On each adjustment date thereafter, if the Index which is published for the most recent month next preceding such new adjustment date exceeds the Index published for the most recent month next preceding the last adjustment date, the annual rental rate for the following three (3) year period shall be computed by multiplying the annual rental rate payble during the preceding three (3) years by a fraction, the numerator of which is the Index published for the most recent month next preceding the new adjustment date and the denominator of which is the Index published for the most recent month next preceding the last adjustment date.

The Index for each rent adjustment date shall be the one recorded in the United States Deaprtment of Labor's most comprehensive official Index then in use and most nearly answering the foregoing description of the Index to be used. If the

note (s) and trust deed (s) that affect said additional Lot. Tenant agrees to pay said obligations promptly when due and to save and hold Landlord free and harmless from the payment of all sums hereafter due thereon. Proveded, however, Tenant shall not be obligated to pay any "balloon" payment that may hereafter be due on said obligations the payment of which shall be Landlord's obligation. Tenant's obligation under this paragraph shall be limited to the monthly payments of interest and/or principal and interest only.

SECTION 4. TAXES.

4.1 Tenant to Pay Taxes. In addition to the rentals hereinabove provided Tenant shall pay and discharge all real and personal property taxes, general and special assessments, and other charges of every description levied on or assessed against the land, improvements located on the land, personal property located on or in the land or improvements, the lease-hold estate, or any subleasehold estate, to the full extent of installments falling due during the term, whether belonging to or chargeable against Landlord or Tenant. Tenant shall make all such payments directly to the charging authority before delinquency and before any fine, interest, or penalty shall become due or be imposed by operation of law for their nonpayment. If, however, the law expressly permits the payment of any or all of the above items in installments (whether or not interest accrues on the unpaid balance), Tenant may, at Tenant's election, utilize the permitted installment method, but shall pay each installment with any interest before delinquency. Landlord shall take all reasonable steps to have future tax bills sent directly to Tenant.

Index is changed so that the base year differs from that used as of the date immediately preceding the month in which the term of this Lease commences, the Index shall be converted in accordance with the conversion factor published by the United States Department of Labor, Bureau of Labor Statistics.

If the Index is discontinued or revised during the term of this Lease, such other government index or other computation with which it is replaced will be used in order to obtain sub- stantially the same result as would be obtained if the Index had not been discontinued or revised.

Notwithstanding anything to the contrary herein contained, in no event shall the annual rent payable under paragraph 3.2 of this Lease be less than the basic annual rent set forth in paragraph 3.1 above. Further, in no event shall the adjusted rent payable for any three (3) year period exceed by more than ten percent (10%) the rent payable for the immediately preceding three year period.

3.3. Additional Rent - Payment of Encumbrance. In addition to the basic annual rent, Tenant shall cause to be paid each month as same becomes due and payable the monthly payments of principal and/or principal and interest due on each of the notes secured by deeds of trust on one or more of the lots comprising the premises including the additional Lot when same is acquired by Landlord and possession thereof is delivered to Tenant. Landlord has furnished to Tenant copies of each of the notes and deeds of trust that now encumber any of the lots comprising the premises and will deliver to Tenant when Landlord acquires the additional Lot copies of the

All payments of taxes or assessments or both, except permitted installment payments, shall be prorated for the initial Lease year and for the year in which the Lease terminates. Tenant may elect to reduce or not to reduce the assessments or charges to installments but shall pay the required percentage before expiration of the term.

4.2 Other Property of Landlord. If the land is assessed with other property of Landlord for purposes of property taxes, assessments or other ad valorem or improvement levies (collectively referred to in this paragraph as taxes), all taxes imposed on the entire parcel of which the land is a part shall, until the land is separately assessed, be prorated and Tenant shall pay that fraction of the entire tax computed upon the proportion which the square footage of the land bears to the entire parcel so taxed.

4.3 Tenant's Right to Contest. Tenant may contest the legal validitiy or amount of any taxes, assessments, or charges for which Tenant is responsible under this Lease, and may institute such proceedings as Tenant considers necessary. If Tenant contests any such tax, assessment or charge, Tenant may withhold or defer payment or pay under protest but shall protect Landlord and the premises from any lien by adequate surety bond or other appropriate security. Landlord appoints Tenant as Landlord's attorney-in-fact for the purpose of contesting any taxes, assessments, or charges, conditioned on Tenant's preventing any liens from being levied on the premises or on Landlord (other than the statutory lien of Revenue and Taxation Code Section 2187). Landlord agrees to join in any proceeding or contest brought by Tenant to the extent any

provision of law requires that the proceeding or contest be brought in the Landlord's or owner's name.

4.4 Exemptions. Tenant's obligation to pay taxes or assessments levied or charged against the premises or against specified personal property shall not include the following, whatever they may be called: business, income or profits taxes levied or assessed against Landlord by federal, state, or other governmental agency; estate, succession, inheritance, or transfer taxes of Landlord; or corporation, franchise, or profits taxes imposed on the corporate owner of the fee title of the land.

SECTION 5. USE.

5.1 Agreed Uses. Tenant shall have the right to use the premises for any lawful use. Tenant may enter into agreements restricting use of, and granting easements over the premises, and may obtain zoning changes or conditional use permits. Landlord shall, upon receipt of Tenant's request, join with Tenant in such applications and proceedings to obtain necessary use or zoning changes, permit or approvals, and in granting easements over the premises, but without cost or expense to Landlord.

5.2 Tenant's Intended Use. Tenant represents that it intends to construct a residential condominium development upon the subject real property and further warrants that it will use its best efforts to diligently prosecute such development to completion. Nothing contained in this paragraph 5.2 shall in any manner limit or prescribe the uses which Tenant is permitted to make of the premises as above set forth in paragraph 5.1.

SECTION 6. IMPROVEMENTS, DEMOLITION, CONSTRUCTION

6.1 Ownership of Existing Improvements. The parties agree that during the term of this Lease, title to all improvements existing on the premises at the commencement of the term hereof are and will be vested in Landlord. The word "improvements" as used in this Lease includes, without limitation, all buildings, structures, fixtures, paving, landscaping, and other physical improvements on the premises.

6.2 Construction and Alteration. At any time and from time to time during the term of this Lease, Tenant may, but is not obligated to, construct or otherwise make new improvements on any part or all of the premises and may demolish, remove, replace, alter, relocate, reconstruct, or add to any existing improvement on the premises in while or in part, and may modify or change the contour or grade, or both, of the land. All salvage shall belong to Tenant. In this regard, as aforesaid, Landlord and Tenant acknowledge that Tenant presently intends to demolish the present improvements on the subject real property and to construct, at its own cost and expense, a residential condominimum development on the real property which development shall be of such design and construction as Tenant shall determine. Landlord agrees that it will, immediately upon request of Tenant perform all acts and execute all documents (i) including without limitation all convenants, conditions, restrictions, easements, rights and rights of way and all dedications as may be required of Landlord by any and all governmental agencies having jurisdiction thereof, (ii) for all permits, authorizations, and approvals as

may be required for such construction, or any other construction, upon such terms as Tenant shall deem reasonable. In addition, Landlord shall, immediately upon request of Tenant, execute all documents and perform all acts as may reasonably be required by any lender in connection with the financing by Tenant of the construction of any improvements upon the subject real property.

In addition to Tenant bearing the cost and expense of demolition and construction in connection with any improvements to be constructed by Tenant upon the subject real property, Tenant shall, at its sole cost and expense, construct and install all off-site improvements which may be incident thereto as shall be reasonable required by any and all governmental agencies having jurisdiction thereof.

6.3 Notice of Demoliton or Construction. Tenant shall give written notice to Landlord or Tenant's intention to commence any major demolition or major construction, as hereinafter defined, upon the subject real property thirty (3) days prior to commencement of any such work or delivery of any materials therefor. Landlord shall have the right to post and maintain on the premises any notices of non-responsibility proveded for under applicable law.

6.4 Bonds. Notwithstanding anything to the contrary in this Lease otherwise set forth, Tenant shall not commence any work of major demolition or major construction ("major demolition" being defined as the demolition of more than ten (10%) percent of the improvements then existing upon the premises, and "major construction" being defined as new construction of a cost exceeding ten (10%) percent of the value

or demolition.

Landlord may, but shall not unreasonably, disapprove the bond. The bond shall be deemed approved unless notice of disapproval is given within seven (7) working days after receipt of the proposed bond.

6.5 Builder's Risk and Other Insurance. Further to the foregoing, prior to Tenant entering upon any work of major demolition or major construction, as above defined, Tenant shall deliver to Landlord (1) certificates of insurance evidencing coverage for "builder's risk", (2) evidence of workmen's compensation insurance covering all persons employed in connection with the work and with respect to whom death or bodily injury claims could be asserted against Landlord or the premisesm abd (3) evidence that Tenant has paid or caused to be paid all premiums for the coverage described above in this paragraph and any increase in premiums on insurance provided for in the section on insurance, sufficient to assure maintenance of all insurance above during the anticipated course of the work. Tenant shall maintain keep in force, and pay all premiums required to maintain and keep in force all insurance above at all times during which such work is in progress.

6.6 Completion of Construction and Alteration. Once any work of construction, alteration, improvement, or demolition has begun, Tenant shall with reasonable diligence prosecute the same to conclusion. All construction, alteration and work of improvement shall be performed in a good and workmanlike manner, and shall comply with all applicable

of the last improvement existing upon the subject real property prior to demolition thereof) unless Tenant shall promptly furnish to Landlord, after Landlord gives notice of demand therefore to Tenant, a bond a hereinafter described. The bond shall be that of a responsible surety company licenses to do business in California, in an amount not less than the contract price of the demolition or construction to be entered upon by Tenant, and shall remain in effect until the entire cost of the work shall have been paid in full and the new improvements shall have been insured as provided in this Lease. The bond shall state the following:

(a) That it is conditioned to secure completion of the proposed demolition or construction, free from all liens and claims of contractors, subcontractors, mechanics, laborers, and materialmen.

(b) That the construction work shall be effected by Tenant, the general contractor, or, on their default, the surety.

(c) That in the event of default of such completion and payment, such part of the amount of the bond as shall be required to complete the work shall be paid to Landlord as liquidated and agreed damages for the nonperformance of Tenant's agreements, it being agreed that the exact amount of Landlord's damages is difficult and impractical to ascertain; and,

(d) That the surety will defend and indemnify Landlord against all loss, cost, damage, expense, and liability arising out of or connected with the work of improvement

governmental permits and laws.

6.7 Mechanics' Liens. Tenant shall pay and discharge all expenses incurred by it for all works of improvement, including without limitation, the services of mechanics, and the cost of goods and material delivered by materialmen, and shall save and hold harmless Landlord and the premises from any claims by such mechanics or materialmen for labor or services performed and goods delivered at the instance or request of the Tenant. Tenant shall have the right to contest the validity or amount of any asserted lien, claim, or demand, and in such case Tenant shall defend, at its own expense, any such suits, and shall discharge and satisfy and judgments taken on account of claims of lien filed by mechanics or materialmen for work ordered by Tenant, and shall indemnify Landlord against all liability and loss on account thereof together with reasonable attorneys' fees in defending against any such claims.

6.8 Tenant's Right to Grant Easements. Landlord grants to Tenant the right to grant to public entities or public service corporations, for the purpose of serving only the premises, rights of way or easements on or over the premises for poles or conduits or both for telephone, electricity, water, sanitary or storm sewers or both, and for other utilities and municipal or special district services.

6.9. Ownership of New Improvements. All improvements caused to be constructed by Tenant shall at all times be and remain the property of Tenant and may be removed by Tenant upon termination of this Lease.

6.10 Landlord's Representations. Landlord represents and warrants to tenant that Landlord is not aware of any factor intrinsic in the subject real property, whether as to title, zoning, buildability, or in any other respect, which would prevent the development by Tenant of the intended condominium project.

6.11 Landlord's Waiver of Interest. Landlord hereby waives all right, title and interest in and to any and all improvements, furniture, fixtures, trade fixtures, equipment, appliances and personalty hereafter constructed, placed or installed in or upon the subject real property, and shall execute, upon request, of Tenant, any and all documents and instruments as shall be required by any lessors, sellers, lenders, or others to evidence such waiver by Landlord.

SECTION 7. MAINTENANCE AND REPAIRS.

7.1 Tenant's Responsibility. Throughout the term of this Lease, Tenant shall, at Tenant's sole cost and expense, maintain the premises and all improvements in good condition and repair, ordinary wear and tear excepted, and in accordance with all applicable laws, rules, ordinances, orders, and regulations of all governmental agencies having jurisdiction thereof.

7.2 Contest of Governmental Orders. Tenant has the right to contest by appropriate judicial or administrative proceedings, without cost to Landlord, the validity or application of any law requiring that Tenant repair, maintain, alter or replace the improvements now or hereafter located on the premises in while or in part, and Tenant shall not be in default for failing to do such work until a reasonable time

Except as otherwise provided in this Section 9, Tenant shall have no right, at any time, to assign, sell or otherwise transfer (hereinafter referred to collectively as "assignment") Tenant's interest, in whole or in part, in this Lease without the prior written consent of Landlord first obtained.

9.2 Tenant May Sublet. Tenant shall have the right at any time and from time to time during the term to sublet all or any part or parts of the premises and to assign, encumber, extend, or renew any sublease, provided that:

(a) Tenant remains primarily obligated to perform Tenant's obligations hereunder.

(b) Tenant shall use reasonable efforts to ensure that each sublease entered into after the term of this Lease commences shall contain a provision requiring the sublessee, so long as the terms of such sublease are recognized and honored, to attorn to Landlord or, in the event of any proceeding to foreclose any leasehold mortgage, to the leasehold mortgage, or any person designated in a notice from such leasehold mortgagee, if Tenant defaults under this Lease, and if the subtenant is notified of Tenant's default and instructed to make subtenant's rental payments to Landlord or such mortgagee or designated persona as in this paragraph provided.

9.3 Mortgaging Tenant's Leasehold Estate. Tenant shall have the right at any time or times and from time to time during the term, without being required to obtain Landlord's consent, to mortgage or hypothecate all or any portion (s) of the leasehold estate of Tenant created under this Lease. In the

---

following final determination of Tenant's contest.

7.3. This Paragraph Not in Limitation of Right to Modify Improvements. Nothing in this Section 7 defining the duty of maintenance shall be construed as limiting any right given elsewhere in this Lease to alter, modify, demolish, remove, or replace any improvement, or as limiting provisions relating to condemnation or to damage or destruction during the final year or years of the term. No deprivation, impairment, or limitation of use resulting from any event or work contemplated by this paragraph shall entitle Tenant to any offset, abatement, or reduction in rent nor to any termination or extension of the term.

7.4 Landlord's Non-Responsibility. During the term of this Lease, Landlord shall not be required to maintain or make any reapirs or replacements of any nature or description whatsoever to the improvements located on the premises. Tenant hereby expressly waives the righ to make repairs at the expense of Landlord, as provided for in any statute or law in effect at the time of execution of this Lease, or in any other statute or law which may hereafter be enacted.

SECTION 8. UTILITIES.

Tenant shall pay all charges and expenses for all water, sewerage, gas electricity, telephone, and other similar services furnished to the premises during the term of this Lease.

SECTION 9. ASSIGNMENT, SUBLETTING, AND ENCUMBERING LEASEHOLD.

9.1 Tenant May Not Assign Without Consent of Landlord.

event that Tenant, either pursuant to a mortgage, deed of trust, or other instrument of security (hereafter a mortgage, deed of trust, and other instrument of security shall be referred to as "mortage", and a mortgagee, beneficiary under a deed of trust, or secured party under a security instrument shall be referred to as "mortgagee"), encumbers the leasehold estate of Tenant created hereby, the leasehold mortgagee becomes the owner of the leasehold estate pursuant to foreclosure, or otherwise, and thereafter said leasehold mortgage, its successors, or assigns, shall remain liable for such obligations only so long as such mortgagee, its successors or assigns, remain the owner of the leasehold estate, it shall be entitled to all rights and privileges granted to Tenant pursuant to this Section 9.

Should a leasehold mortgagee obtain possession of the premises either under the terms of the leasehold mortgage or this Lease, the leasehold mortgagee and any successor (s) shall have the right of assignment of all or any part of the leasehold interest without Landlord's prior consent.

9.4 Landlord's Encumbrances. During the term of this Lease, Landlord shall not encumber or hypothecate in any manner whatsoever all or any portion of Landlord's interest in this Lease or Landlord's fee interest in the land which comprises the premises.

SECTION 10. INDEMNITY; LIABILITY INSURANCE.

10.1 Indemnity. Tenant shall hold harmless Landlord from all damages arising out of any damage to any person or property occurring in, on or about the premises, except those resulting from the negligent or wilful acts of Landlord or any of its agents, servants, representatives or employees as to which Landlord shall hold Tenant free and harmless.

10.2 Public Liability Insurance. Throughout the term of this Lease, Tenant shall at its sole cost, keep or cause to be kept in force, for the mutual benefit of Landlord and Tenant, combined bodily injury and property damage liability insurance with a minimum coverage of $500,000.00 per occurrence.

Such insurance shall be issued by a company or companies licensed to do business in California. On commencement of the term, Tenant shall deliver to Landlord certificates of insurance indicating that Tenant has complied with the provisions of this paragraph. Such policies shall also provide that they will not be cancelled or materially changed except after ten (10) days' notice to Landlord.

SECTION 11. FIRE AND EXTENDED COVERAGE INSURANCE.

11.1 Fire Insurance. Tenant at its cost shall maintain on the improvements on the premises a policy or policies of standard fire and extended coverage insurance, with vandalism and malicious mischief endorsements, to the extent required by the holders of existing encumbrances affecting the premises. The insurance policy or policies shall be issued in the names of Landlord, Tenant and any lender, as their interest appear. The insurance policy or policies shall provide that any proceeds shall be made payable to Tenant, and Tenant shall apply and use such proceeds as required by this Section 11, subject to the right of any lender. Such insurance shall be issued by a company or companies licensed to do business in California

On commencement of the term, Tenant shall deliver to Landlord certificates of insurance indicating that Tenant has complied with the provisions of this paragraph. Such policies shall also provide that they will not be cancelled or materially changed except after ten (10) days' notice to Landlord.

11.2 Insured Casualty - Proceeds Available. If the improvements on the premises are damaged or destroyed totally or partially by a risk which is insured against the insuranc referred to in paragraph 11.1, Tenant shall repair and rebuild the damaged or destroyed improvements within a reasonable time after Tenant receives the insurance proceeds payble as a result of the damage or destruction.

11.3 Uninsured Casualty. If the improvements on the premises are damaged or destroyed by a risk not insured against by the insurance referred to in paragraph 11.1, Tenant shall repair and rebuild the damaged or destroyed improvements within a reasonable time at its sole cost and expense.

11.4 Effect of Damage on Rent. There shall be no abatement or reduction of rent under the terms of this Lease by reason of any damage or destruction of the improvements on the premises.

SECTION 12. CONDEMNATION.

12.1 Definitions. The following words and phrases shall have the following meanings for the purposes of this paragraph:

(a) "Condemnation" means (i) the exercise of any governmental power, whether by legal proceedings or otherwise, by a condemnor, and (ii) a voluntary sale or transfer by Landlord to any condemnor, either under threat of condemnation or while legal proceedings are pending.

(b) "Date of taking" means the date the condemnor has the right to possession of the property being condemned.

(c) "Award" means all compensation, sums, or anything of value awarded, paid, or received on a total or partial condemnation.

(d) "Condemnor" means any public or quasi-public authority, or private corporation or individual, having the power of condemnation.

12.2 Rights and Obligations of Parties. If, during the term, there is any condemnation of all or any part of the premises or any interest in this Lease, the rights and obligations of the parties shall be determined pursuant to this Section 12.

12.3 Total Taking - Effect on Lease. If the total premises are taken by condemnation, this Lease shall terminate on the date of taking.

12.4 Partial Taking - Effect on Lease. If any portion of the premises is taken by condemnation, this Lease shall remain in effect, except that Tenant shall have the election to terminate this Lease if Tenant reasonably determines that the remaining portion of the premises will be uneconomical for Tenant's continued use, operation and management. Tenant must make such elections within sixty (60) days after the date of taking.

12.6 Restoration of Premises. If there is a partial taking of the premises and this Lease remains in full force and effect pursuant to paragraph 12.4, Tenant shall restore any partially taken improvements so as to render the same a complete architectural unit to the extent permitted by the severance damages Tenant shall receive. Rent shall not be abated or reduced during the period of restoration and all other obligations of Tenant under this Lease shall remain in full force and effect.

12.7 Distribution of Award. The condemnation award shall be apportioned between Landlord and Tenant as follows: (1) for Tenant: that amount of said award attributable to the value for the improvements constructed by Tenant then existing on the premises, the value of Tenant's leasehold interest in the premises, and severance damages; (2) for Landlord: the remainder of said award.

SECTION 13.   TITLE OF LANDLORD.

Landlord represents and warrants that on the commencement of the term of this Lease, the premises and every part thereof, shall be free and clear of all covenants, conditions, restrictions, easements, rights of way, rights, liens and encumbrances, except those as follows:

A. Such covenants, conditions, restrictions and easements as were recorded in the Official Records of the County Recorder of Los Angeles County, California, prior to January 1, 1981.

B. Such deeds of trust now of record and such deeds of trust on the additional Lot when said Lot is

acquired by Landlord and possession thereof is delivered to Tenant.

C. All existing leases and rental agreements and affecting the additional Lot.

Tenant may, at its own expense, obtain an extended coverage of Lessee's policy of title insurance, with such endorsements and in such amount as Tenant shall require, insuring the priority and superiority of Tenant's interest in the subject real property under the terms of this Lease, over all matters as customarily contained in such policy of title insurance, except the matters as in this Section 13 set forth.

SECTION 14.   JOINER BY LANDLORD IN DOCUMENTS.

Landlord agrees that within seven (7) days after receipt of written request from Tenant so to do, Landlord shall:

A. Execute any and all releases referred to in paragraph 6.11.

B. Join in and execute any and all documents of any nature whatsoever in connection with Tenant's dealings with Assessment Districts.

C. Join in and execute any and all applications for permits, licenses or other authorizations or documents required by an governmental or other body claiming jurisdiction in connection with any construction and/or demolition work which Tenant may perform on the premises.

D. Join in any reasonable grants for easements

for electric, telephone, gas, water, sewer and such other public utilities and facilities as may be reasonably necessary in the use, operation and management of the premises or of any improvements that may be erected thereon. And,

E. Execute any and all grants and other documents necessary to effectuate dedications of portions of the premises for public use which dedications shall be required by any governmental or other body claiming jurisdiction in connection with Tenant's development of the premises.

If, at the expiration of such seven (7) day period, Landlord shall not have performed its obligations as hereinabove provided, Tenant shall have the right to execute such documentation and grants in the anme of Landlord, and, for that purpose, Landlord hereby irrevocably appoints Tenant as its attorney-in-fact to execute same on behalf of Landlord.

SECTION 15. TENANT'S DEFAULTS; NOTICES, LANDLORD's REMEDIES.

15.1 Tenant's Defaults. Each of the following events shall be a default by Tenant and a breach of this Lease:

(a) Abandonment or surrender of the premises or of the leasehold estate, or failure or refusal to pay when due any installment of rent or any other sum required by this Lease to be paid by Tenant, or to perform as required or conditioned by any other covenant or condition of this Lease subject to the provisions of paragraph 15.2 below.

(b) The subjection of any right or interest of Tenant to attachment, execution, or other levy, or to seizure under legal process, if not released within ten (10) days, provided that the foreclosure of any mortgage permitted by provisions of this Lease relating to purchase or construction of improvements shall not be construed as a default within the meaning of this paragraph.

(c) The appointment of a receiver to take possession of the premises or improvements or of Tenant's interest in the leasehold estate or of Tenant's operations on the premises for any reason, including but not limited to, assignment for benefit of creditors or voluntary or involuntary bankruptcy proceedings, but not including receivership (i) pursuant to any mortgage permitted by provisions of this Lease relating to purchase or contruction of improvements, or (ii) instituted by Landlord, the event of default being not the appointment of a receiver at Landlord's instance but the event justifying the receivership, if any.

(d) An assignment by Tenant for the benefit of creditors or the filing of a voluntary or involuntary petition by or against Tenant under any law for the purpose of adjudicating Tenant a bankrupt; or for extending time for payment, adjustment, or satisfaction of Tenant's liabilities; or for reorganization, dissolution, or arrangement on account of or to prevent bankruptcy or insolvency; unless the assignment or proceeding, and all consequent orders, adjudications, custodies, and supervisions are dismissed, vacated, or otherwise permanently stayed or terminated within sixty (60) days after the assignment, filing, or other initial event.

15.2 Notice of Default - Cure Periods. In the event Tenant shall fail to perform any of the provisions contained herein on Tenant's part to be performed, Tenant shall not be deemed to be in breach or default hereunder unless Landlord shall first have given Tenant thirty (30) days' notice of any alleged breach or default, and Tenant shall have such period of time within which to remedy or cure any such alleged breach or default. Any such written notice shall specify the alleged breach or default. If any default, other than non-payment of rent, cannot reasonably be cured within thirty (30) days, the commencement of the cure of such default within such thirty (30) day period shall be deemed to be a cure of such default, provided such cure is diligently prosecuted to completion.

15.3 Notice of Default to Lender; Lender's and Landlord's Right to Cure Defaults. Landlord agrees, if and so long as the real property comprising the premises and/or the leasehold estate of Tenant is encumbered by a leasehold mortgage(s), to give the holder(s) of such mortgage(s) at such address or addresses as may be specified by the mortgagee(s) to Landlord in writing, written notice of any default of Tenant hereunder, simultaneously with the giving of such notice to Tenant, as provided in subparagraph 15.2 above, and the holder(s) of any such mortgage(s) shal have the right, within the period Tenant has to cure said default and to the same extent and with the same effect as though done by Tenant, to take such action or to make such payment

as may be necessary or appropriate to cure any such default or contingency so specified, it being the intention of the parties hereto that Landlord shall not exercise its right to terminate this Lease or Tenant's right to possession of the premises without first affording to the holder(s) of any such mortgage(s) the same rights and the same notices with respect to any such default or contingency and the period of time herein set forth within which to cure the same, including the right to enter into possession of the premises.

15.4 Remedies of Landlord. In the event Tenant shall at any time be in default and in breach of this Lease, then in addition to any or all other rights or remedies of the Landlord hereunder and by law provided, it shall be at the option of the Landlord, without further notice or demand of any kind to Tenant or to any other person:

(a) The right of the Landlord to declare the term hereof ended and to reenter the premises and take possession thereof and remove all persons therefrom, and the Tenant shall have no further claim thereon or hereunder; or,

(b) The right of the Landlord without declaring this Lease ended to reenter the premises and occupy the whole or any part thereof for and on account of the Tenant and to collect said rent and any other rent that may thereafter become payable; or,

(c) The right of the Landlord, even though it may have reentered the premises, to thereafter elect to terminate this Lease and all of the rights of the Tenant in or to the premises.

Should the Landlord have reentered the premises under the provision of subparagraph (b) above, the Landlord shall not be deemed to have terminated this Lease, or the liability of the Tenant to pay rent thereafter to accure, or its liability for damages under any of the provisions hereof by any such reentry or by any action in unlawful detainer, or otherwise, to obtain possession of the premises, unless the Landlord shall have notified the Tenant in writing that it has so elected to terminate this Lease, and the Tenant further covenants that the service by the Landlord of any ntoice pursuant to the unlawful detainer statues of the State of California and the surrender of possession pursuant to such notice shall not (unless the Landlord elects to the contrary at the time of or at any time subsequent to the serving of such notices and such election is evidenced by a written notice to the Tenant) be deemed to be a termination of this Lease. In the event of any entry or taking possession of the premises as aforesaid, the Landlord shall have the right, but not the obligation, to remove therefrom all or any part of the personal property located therein and may place the same in storage at a public warehouse at the expense and risk of the owner or owners thereof.

should the Landlord elect to terminate this Lease under the provisions of subparagraph (a) or (c) above, the Landlord may recover from the Tenant as damages:

(i) the worth at the time of any award of any unpaid rent which had been earned at the time of such termination; plus

(ii) the worth at the time of award of the amount by which the unpaid rent which would have been earned after termination until the time of award exceeds the amount of such rental loss Tenant proves could have been reasonably avoided; plus

(iii) the worth at the time of award of the amount by which the unpaid rent for the balance of the term after the time of award exceeds the amount of such rental loss that Tenant proves could be reasonably avoided; plus

(iv) any other amount necessary to compensate Landlord for all detriment proximately caused by Tenant's failure to perform his obligations under this Lease or which in the ordinary course of things would be likely to result therefrom, including, but not limited to any costs or expenses incurred by Landlord (a) in retaking possession of the premises, including reasonable attorneys' fees therefor, (b) maintaining or preserving the premises after such default, (c) preparing the premises for reletting to a new tenant, including repairs or alterations to the premises for such reletting, (d) leasing commissions, or (e) any other costs necessary or appropriate to relet the premises; plus

(v) at Landlord's election, such other amounts in addition to or in lieu of the foregoing as may be permitted from time to time by the laws of the State of California.

As used in subparagraphs (i) and (ii) above, the "worth at the time of award" is computed by allowing interest at the rate of ten (10%) percent per annum. As used in subparagraph

or renewal of the Lease or revocation of any notice or other act by Landlord. No covenant, term, or condition of this Lease shall be deemed to have been waived by Landlord unless such waiver be in writing signed by Landlord.

15.5 New Lease. If this Lease shall terminate by reason of the occurrence of any default of Tenant, and if Landlord shall obtain possession of the premises, Landlord agrees that the holder of any mortgage upon the leasehold estate of Tenant in the premises shall have the right, for a period of two (2) months subsequent to said termination of this Lease, to elect to demand a new lease of the premises of the character and, when executed and delivered and possession of the premises is taken thereunder, having the effect hereinafter set forth. Such new lease shall be for a term to commence at the date of termination of this Lease, and shall have as the date for the expiration thereof the same expiration date stated in this Lease. The rent thereof shall be at the same rate as would have been applicable under the provisions of this Lease, and all other provisions of the new lease shall be the same as the provisions of this Lease. If any such holder of any such mortgage as aforesaid shall elect to demand such new lease within said two (2) month period, such holder shall give written notice to Landlord of such election; and, thereupon, within ten (10) days thereafter, Landlord and such holder shall execute and deliver such new lease upon the terms above set forth, and such holder of any such mortgage shall, at the time of the execution and delivery of such new lease, pay to Landlord

(iii) above, the "worth at the time of award" is computed by discounting such amount at the discount rate of the Federal Reserve Bank situated nearest to the location of the premises at the time of award plus one (1%) percent.

In the event of default, all of the Tenant's fixtures, furniture, equipment, improvements, additions, alterations and other personal property shall remain on the premises and in that event, and continuing during the length of said default, Landlord shall have the right to take exclusive possession of same and to use same, rent or charge free, until all defaults are cured or, at its option, at any time during the term of this Lease, to require Tenant to forthwith remove same.

The remedies given to the Landlord in this paragraph shall be in addition and supplemental to all other rights or remedies which the Landlord may have under the laws then in force.

The waiver by Landlord of any breach of any term, covenant or condition herein contained shall not be deemed to be a waiver of such term, covenant or condition or any subsequent breach of the same or any other term, covenant or condition herein contained. The subsequent acceptance of rent hereunder by Landlord shall not be deemed to be a waiver of any preceding breach by Tenant of any term, covenant or condition of this Lease, other than the failure of Tenant to pay the particular rental so accepted, regardless of Landlord's knowledge of such preceding breach at the time of acceptance of such rent, nor shall acceptance of rent or any other payment after termination constitute a reinstatement, extension or

with any convenant or condition imposed on Tenant under this Lease or any such note or document, and the amount so paid plus the reasonable cost of any such performance or compliance, plus interest on such sum at the rate of ten (10%) percent per year from the date of payment, performance, or compliance (herein called act), shall be deemed to be additional rent payable by Tenant with the next succeeding installment of rent. No such act shall constitute a waiver of default or of any remedy for default or render Landlord liable for any loss or damage resulting from any such act.

SECTION 16. ESTOPPEL CERTIFICATES.

Tenant and Landlord shall, at any time and from time to time during the term hereof and upon not less than ten (10) days' prior request by the other party, execute, acknowledge, and deliver to each other, as the case may be, a statement in writing certifying that this Lease is un-modified, and in full force and effect (or if there have been any modifications, that the same is in full force and effect as modified, and stating the modifications) and, if so, the dates to which the fixed rent and other charges have been paid in advance, it being intended that any such statement delivered pursuant to this paragraph may be relied upon by any prospective purchaser, encumbrancer, or assignee of the premises.

If, at the expiration of such ten (10) day period, a party shall not have performed its obligations as hereinabove provided ("defaulting party"), the other party shall have the right to execute such statement in the name of the defaulting party, and, for the purpose, each of the parties hereto irre-vocably appoints the other as its attorney-in-fact to exercise

all rent and other sums owing by Tenant to Landlord under the terms of this Lease immediately prior to the termination of this Lease as well as all rent and other sums which would have become payable hereunder by Tenant to Landlord to the date of the execution and delivery of such new lease, had this Lease not terminated, and which remain unpaid at the time of the execution of such new lease. Any holder of such mortgage shall be given credit for any net rents and income actually collected in the meantime by Land-lord from the subtenants of the premises. Any such new lease as in this paragraph contemplated may, at the option of the mortgagee, be executed to a nominee of such holder, or to a corporation, without the mortgagee assuming the burdens and obligations of Tenant thereunder, beyond the period of its occupancy.

Upon the executin and delivery of such new lease in accordance with the provision of this subparagraph 15.5, all subleases which theretofore may have been assigned and transferred to Landlord, and all deposits being held there-under, shall thereupon be assigned and transferred without recourse by Landlord to the mortgagee, as the new tenant.

15.6 Landlord's Right to Cure Defaults. After expiration of the applicable time for curing a particular default, or before the expiration of that time in the event of emergency, Landlord may at Landlord's election, but is not obligated to, make any payment required of Tenant under this Lease or under any note or other document pertaining to the financing of improvements or fixtures on the premises, or perform or comply

execute same on its behalf.

SECTION 17. APPROVAL BY FINANCIAL INSTITUTION.

The provisions of this Lease must be approved by the financial institutions which make the mortgages herein provided for. If any such institution should require as a condition of such financing any modifications of the provisions of this Lease, Landlord will approve and execute any such modifications, provided no such modification shall relate to the rent payable hereunder, the length of the term, or materially change the rights and obligations of Landlord and Tenant.

SECTION 18. NON-MERGER.

There shall be no merger of this Lease, or of the leasehold estate created thereby, with the fee estate in and to the premises by reason of the fact that this Lease, or the leasehold estate created hereby, or any interest in either thereof, may be held directly or indirectly by or for the account of any person who shall own the fee estate in and to the premises, or any portion thereof, and no such merger shall occur unless and until all persons at the time having any interest in the fee estate and all persons having any interest in this Lease or the leasehold estate, including the leasehold mortgagee and the holder or any mortgage upon the fee estate in and to the premises, shall join in a written instrument effecting such merger.

SECTION 19. NOTICES.

Wherever this Lease provides for notices, communications or demands between the parties, or by Landlord or Tenant to any mortgagee, or wherever the law requires or gives the right of serving a notice, the same shall be served by registered or certified mail, addressed to Landlord as follows:

and addressed to Tenant as follows:

and addressed to any leasehold mortgagee as directed at the address specified in a leasehold mortgage or at such other address as may be specified by a leasehold mortgage in writing by notice addressed to the Landlord and Tenant in the manner prescribed by this paragraph; provided, however, that Landlord, Tenant and any mortgagee may, at any time, change the place of receiving notice by written notice of such change of address to the other.

SECTION 20. COST OF SUIT.

If legal action shall be brought by either of the parties hereto for the unlawful detainer of the premises, for the recovery of any rent due under the provisions of this Lease, or because of the breach of any provision hereof, the party prevailing in said action shall be entitled to recover from the party not prevailing costs of suit and a reasonable attorneys' fee which shall be fixed by the judge of the court.

SECTION 21. OPTION TO PURCHASE PREMISES.

21.1 Grant of Option. Landlord grants to Tenant the option to purchase the premises in accordance with the provisions of this Lease, as long as Tenant is not in default at the time it exercises the option.

21.2 Option Periods; Option Notice. Tenant shall have the right to exercise the option to purchase at any time during the period September 1, 1981 through April 30, 1982.

Tenant shall exercise the option by giving notice ("Option notice") to Landlord in accordance with the provisions of Section 19.

21.3 Purchase Price. The purchase price for the premises shall be as follows:

(a) If the option is exercised at any time from September 1, 1981 through October 1, 1981, the purchase price shall be $_____ if the additional Lot is included in the premises and $_____ if said additional Lot is not a part of the premises.

(b) If the option is exercised at any time from October 2, 1981 through November 1, 1981, the purchase price shall be $_____ if the additional Lot is included in the premises and $_____ if said additional Lot is not a part of the premises.

(c) If the option is exercised at any time from November 2, 1981 through December 1, 1981, the purchase price shall be $_____ if the additional Lot is included in the premises and $_____ if said additional Lot is not a part of the premises.

(d) If the option is exercised at any time from December2, 1981 through January 1, 1981, the purchase price shall be $_____ if the additional Lot is included in the premises and $_____ if said additional Lot is not a part of the premises.

(e) If the option is exercised at any time from January 2, 1981 through February 1, 1981, the purchase price shall be $_____ if the additional Lot is included in the premises and $_____ if said additional Lot is not a part of the premises.

(f) If the option is exercised at any time from February 2, 1981 through March 1, 1981, the purchase price shall be $_____ if the additional Lot is included in the premises and $_____ if said additional Lot is not a part of the premises.

(g) If the option is exercised at any time from March 2, 1981 through April 1, 1981, the purchase price shall be $_____ if the additional Lot is included in the premises nad $_____ is said additional Lot is not a part of the premises.

(h) If the option is exercised at any time from April 2, 1981 through May 1, 1981, the purchase price shall be $_____ if the additional Lot is inlcuded in the premises and $_____ if said additional Lot is not part of the premises.

(i) If the option is exercised at any time from May 2, 1981 through June 1, 1981, the purchase price shall be $_____ if the additional Lot is included in the

(j) If the option is exercised at any time from June 2, 1981 through July 1, 1981, the purchase price shall be $ _____ if the additional Lot is included in the premises and $ _____ if said additional Lot is not a part of the premises.

(k) If the option is exercised at any time from July 2, 1981 through August 1, 1981, the purchase price shall be $ _____ if the additional Lot is included in the premises and $ _____ if said additional Lot is not a part of the premises.

(l) If the option is exercised at any time from August 2, 1981 through September 1, 1981, the purchase price shall be $ _____ if the additional Lot is included in the premises and $ _____ if said additional Lot is not a part of the premises.

(m) If the option is exercised at any time from September 2, 1981 through October 1, 1981, the purchase price shall be $ _____ if the additional Lot is included in the premises and $ _____ if said additional Lot is not a part of the premises.

(n) If the option is exercised at any time from October 2, 1981 through November 1, 1981 the purchase price shall be $ _____ if the additional Lot is included in the premises and $ _____ if said additional Lot is not a part of the premises.

(o) If the option is exercised at any time from November 2, 1981 through December 1, 1981, the purchase price shall be $ _____ if the additional Lot is

included in the premises and $ _____ if said additional Lot is not part of the premises.

(p) If the option is exercised at any time from December 2, 1981 through January 1, 1982, the purchase price shall be $ _____ if the additional Lot is included in the premises and $ _____ if said additional Lot is not a part of the premises.

(q) If the option is exercised at any time from January 2, 1982 through February 1, 1982, the purchase price shall be $ _____ if the additional Lot is included in the premises and $ _____ if said additional Lot is not a part of the premises.

(r) If the option is exercised at any time from February 2, 1982 through March 1, 1982, the purchase price shall be $ _____ if the additional Lot is included in the premises and $ _____ if said additional Lot is not a part of the premises.

(s) If the option is exercised at any time from March 2, 1982 through May 1, 1982, the purchase price shall be $ _____ if the additional Lot is included in the premises and $ _____ if said additional Lot is not a part of the premises.

21.4 Payment of Purchase Price. The purchase price shall be payable in cash in lawful money of the United States to Landlord by Tenant at close of escrow (the date the grant deed is recorded) as provided in paragraph 21.6.

21.5 Title to Premises. Landlord shall deliver to Tenant an executed grant deed in recordable form conveying premises vested in Tenant subject to the matters set forth in paragraph 21.5.

21.8 _Proration of Rent; Costs._ Rent, except taxes, and insurance premiums, shall be prorated as of close of escrow.

Transfer taxes and recording fees on the grant deed shall be paid by Landlord. The cost of the title policy referred to in paragraph 21.7 shall be paid by Tenant. Charges of escrow and all other closing costs shall be paid in accordance with the custom of such purchases and sales in Los Angeles County, California.

21.9 _Damage and Destruction._ If the improvements on the premises are totally or partially destroyed between the date Tenant exercises its option to purchase and the date set for the close of escrow, such destruction shall not affect this option, the date set for the close of escrow, or the purchase price of the premises.

21.10 _Termination of Lease on Close of Escrow._ As of close of escrow this Lease shall terminate, and the parties shall be released from all liability and obligations under this Lease which would otherwise thereafter accrue.

SECTION 22. SURRENDER OF PREMISES: TITLE TO IMPROVEMENTS. At the expiration or earlier termination of this Lease, unless such termination is effected by Tenant's purchase of the premises, Tenant shall surrender to Landlord possession of the premises. Any improvement constructed by Tenant, fixtures, and trade fixtures of Tenant or any subtenant then remaining on the premises shall thereupon, at Landlord's election,

the premises. Title to the premises shall be conveyed by Landlord to Tenant free and clear of all liens, encumbrances, covenants, conditions, restrictions, easements, and rights of way of record, leases or other tenancy agreements, and other matters of record, except (i) current taxes, a lien not yet delinquent, (ii) those portions of current assessments not yet due and payable, (iii) anything of record or not of record that in any way affects title to the premises resulting from the acts or omissions of Tenant; (iv) those matters referred to in Section 13 above, (v) any liens and encumbrances placed on the premises by Tenant pursuant to the provisions of subparagraph 9.3 above, (vi) leases or other tenancy agreements existing at the commencement of the term of this Lease, and (vii) subleases covering portions of the premises executed by Tenant during the term. All of the foregoing shall include the additional Lot when it becomes a part of the premises.

21.6 _Escrow._ The sale shall be consummated through an escrow with a title company selected by Tenant designated in the option notice, to be opened within fifteen (15) days from the date the option notice is given to Landlord. Escrow shall close within ninety (90) days thereafter. Escrow shall be deemed to be closed pursuant to this paragraph on the date the grant deed is recorded.

21.7 _Title Insurance._ At the close of escrow, the title company referred to in paragraph 21.6 must be prepared to issue a CLTA Standard Coverage Policy of Title Insurance in the amount of the purchase price insuring title to the

to arbitration as they stand amended at the time of the notice. The arbitrator shall be bound by this Lease and the ruling of the arbitrator shall be final and binding on all parties and may be entered as a judgement in any court of competent jurisdiction. Each party shall pay half the cost of arbitration including arbitrator's fees. Attorneys' fees shall be awarded as separately provided in this Lease.

SECTION 24. CONSTRUCTION LOANS, RELEASE PROVISIONS, ENCUMBRANCE OF LANDLORD'S FEE INTEREST.

24.1 Provided Tenant is not in default under this Lease, and provided Tenant shall have given to Landlord the option notice described in paragraph 21.2 above, Tenant may encumber the fee of the Landlord on the terms and provisions hereafter provided.

24.2 Landlord agrees to join in the execution of any deed of trust or other security instrument requested by a lender procured by Tenant, to the end that Landlord will permit said lender to acquire a first lien upon the Landlord's fee interest inthe premises and that said lien shall be superior to the rights of Landlord under this Lease.

24.3 The proposed lender shall be a licensed bank, savings and loan association, insurance company, mortgage banker, or similar institutional lender.

24.4 Landlord recognizes that the lender and/or any insuring title insurance company may request Landlord to

become the property of Landlord. Tenant shall have the surrendered premises and any other property in good and broom-clean condition. If Tenant fails to surrender the premises at the expiration or sooner termination of this Lease, Tenant shall defend and indemnify Landlord from all liability and expense resulting from the delay or failure to surrender, including, without limitation, claims made by any succeeding tenant founded on or resulting from Tenant's failure to surrender.

SECTION 23. ARBITRATION.

Either party may require the arbitration of any matter arising der or in connection with this Lease, except any matters which involve the payment of rent by Tenant to Landlord. Arbitration is initiated and required by giving notice specifying the matter to be arbitrated. If action is already pending on any matter concerning which the notice is given, the notice is ineffective unless given before the expiration of ten (10) days after service of process on the person giving the notice.

Except as provided to the contrary in these provisions on arbitration, the arbitration shall be in conformity with and subject to applicable rules and procedures of the American Arbitration Association and there shall be a single arbitrator selected by said Association in accordance with its rules and procedures. If the American Arbitration Association is not then in existence or for any reason fails or refuses to act, the arbitration shall be in conformity with and subject to provisions of the California Code of Civil Procedure relating

execute specific documents in connection with the proposed loan to finance proposed improvements on the premises, and Landlord agrees to execute all documents promptly upon presentment, provided that any such document does not impose personal liability on Landlord.

24.5 The proposed loan shall be for the purpose of construction of improvements on the premises and include all interest, finance charges, title fees, appraisal costs and other usual and customary charges, fees and costs.

24.6 The deed of trust and other security instruments of the lender may also contain release clauses for the release of specific condominium units on terms required by Tenant and said lender. All sums received by Tenant from the sale of a condominium unit (less sums due the lender) shall be paid to Landlord, if at the time of such sale Tenant has not consummated its option to purchase the premises as provided in this Lease. Any such sums received by Landlord from such sales shall be applied by Landlord toward the purchase price of the premises.

SECTION 25. CREDITS AGAINST ANNUAL RENT

It is acknowledged by Landlord and Tenant that Tenant will expend substantial sums during the first two (2) Lease years in connection with the steps necessary to commence construction of the proposed condominium project on the property. It is in Landlord's best interest that Tenant

be encouraged to take all steps necessary to commence construction and to encourage Tenant to exercise the option to purchase herein contained. In the event Tenant has given Landlord notice of its election to exercise its option to purchase, and only in such an event, Tenant may, upon furnishing Landlord with reasonable evidence thereof, deduct from the annual rental due for the first two (2) Lease years, a sum equal to seventy-five per cent (75%) of all sums Tenant has expended in connection with the proposed construction of improvements and matters incident thereto.

SECTION 24. MISCELLANEOUS PROVISIONS.

24.1 Recordation. This Lease shall not be recorded; only an abstract of this Lease shall be recorded in the form as set forth in Exhibit "A" attached hereto, upon execution of this Lease.

24.2 Time of Essence. Time is of the essence of each provision of this Lease.

24.3 California Law. This Lease shall be construed and interpreted in accordance with the laws of the State of California.

24.4 Integrated Agreement; Modification. This Lease contains all the agreements of the parties with respect to the tenancy created by this Lease and cannot be amended or modified except by a written agreement.

24.5 Captions. The captions of the various articles and paragraphs of this Lease are for convenience and ease of reference only and do not define, limit, augment, or describe the scope, content, or intent of this Lease or of any part or parts of this Lease.

24.6 Binding Effect. Subject to any provisions hereof restricting assignment by Tenant, this Lease shall inure to the benefit of, and be binding upon, the parties, and their respective heirs, personal representatives, successors, and assigns.

24.7 Severability. The invalidity of any provision of this Lease shall in no way affect the validity of any other provision hereof.

IN WITNESS WHEREOF, the parties hereto have executed this Lease as of the day and year first above written.

LANDLORD:

BLACKACRE PROPERTIES, INC.,
a California corporation

By: _____

By: _____

TENANT:

WHITEACRE DEVELOPMENT, INC.,
a California corporation

By: _____

By: _____

THIS LEASE is made and entered into as of the 1st
day of January, 1981, by and between REAL ACRE N.V. ("Landlord")
and FARMCO OPERATIONS, INC., a California corporation ("Tenant").

R E C I T A L S:

WHEREAS, Landlord is the owner of that certain real
property and all improvements and appurtenances thereto (the
"Premises") situated in the County of Growth, State of
Appreciation, consisting of approximately One Thousand (1,000)
acres, more or less, more particularly described in Exhibit
"A" attached hereto and hereby made a part hereof, and known
as the "Fertile Farms"; and

NOW, THEREFORE, in consideration of their mutual
covenants hereunder, Landlord and Tenant agree as follows:

A G R E E M E N T:

I. LEASE AND TERM.

1.01. Lease. Landlord hereby leases to Tenant and Tenant
hereby leases from Landlord the Premises upon the terms and
conditions set forth below.

1.02. Term. The term of this Lease shall commence on
January 1, 1981, and end on December 31, 1981, unless this
Lease is sooner terminated under its terms.

II. RENTAL

2.01. Basic Rental. The basic rental to be paid by
Tenant to Landlord for each year of the term of this Lease
shall be One Hundred Fifty Thousand Dollars ($150,000.00)
The rental for less than a full period shall be prorated on
the basis of a thirty (30) day month and a three hundred
sixty (360) day year.

2.02. <u>Payment of Rental</u>. The rental required by this
Lease for each year of the term hereof shall be payable in
cash in advance in two equal installments on June 30, and
December 31, each year for the ensuing six (6) month period,
except that the rental for the period from commencement of
the term hereof to June 30, 1981, shall be payable at or
before commencement of the term hereof. All rental and other
payments hereunder shall be made to Landlord at the place
provided for notice to Landlord in this Lease, except as
otherwise specified pursuant hereto.

2.03. <u>Security Deposit</u>. Landlord shall receive from
Tenant at or before commencement of the term hereof a security
deposit in the sum of _____Thousand Dollars
($_____) which sum shall be held by Landlord as partial
security for performance of Tenant's obligations hereunder.
Landlord shall deposit said amount in an interest bearing pass-
book account, in the name of Landlord, provided that any interest
thereon shall be paid or caused to be paid by Landlord to Tenant
quarterly, as accrued, and provided further that Landlord
shall have the full right to resort to said deposit to defray
costs and/or damages arising from any default of Tenant, and
in the event thereof Tenant shall, within ten (10) days of
demand therefor, restore any portion of said security deposit
so applied. At termination of this Lease, if Tenant is not
then in default, Landlord shall return to Tenant any remaining
part of said sum not utilized by Landlord to defray costs and
damages, if any, arising from any default of Tenant.

2.04. <u>Taxes, Utilities and Insurance</u>. It is the intent
of Landlord and Tenant that the rental set forth above shall
be a "net net net rental", as those terms are used and
understood in connection with the leasing of real property.
Accordingly, as additional rental hereunder, Tenant shall pay
prior to delinquency all taxes and assessments (whether made

-2-

against Tenant in the first instance or against Landlord as
the owner of the Premises) assessed for or during the term
hereof against the Premises or any portion thereof and any
personal property, equipment and improvements and trade or
business fixtures in possession of Tenant, or installed by
or for Tenant, in, upon or about the Premises. Additionally,
Tenant will, at its own cost and expense, furnish all light,
heat, electricity, telephone and other utility services,
including electrical demand charges for itself and its employees,
which may be required for the Premises during the term hereof,
and shall pay all surface water charges and ground water
assessments or any other charge for water with respect to
the Premises for or during the term hereof. Tenant shall also
pay all insurance premiums applicable to the term hereof with
respect to the Premises, all expenses of occupying, operating,
altering, maintaining and repairing the Premises (including
but not limited to any soil improvements and additions) during
said term, and any other expenses or charges which shall be
levied, assessed or imposed for or during the term of this
Lease by any governmental authority upon or with respect to,
or incurred in connection with, the possession, occupation,
operation, alteration, maintenance, repair and use of the
Premises, it being intended that this Lease shall result in
a rental to be paid to Landlord in the amounts specified in
Section 2.01 above without additional cost to Landlord in
the amounts specified in Section 2.01 above without additional
cost to Landlord or diminution or offset thereto. If any of
the foregoing taxes, assessments or other charges shall constitute a lien on the Premises, Landlord shall have the right,
in the event that Tenant fails to pay said taxes or assessments,
to make said payment together with any accrued penalties and
interest, and to recover said sums from Tenant upon demand.

-3-

III. POSSESSION AND USE.

    3.01. Use. The Premises are leased to Tenant for the
sole purpose of planting, growing and harvesting and processing
of agricultural row crops. Tenant shall not use, or permit
to be used, any part of the Premises for any other purpose
without the written consent of Landlord.

    3.02. Occupancy. Tenant will enter into possession of
the Premises on commencement of the term of this Lease, and
thereafter during the term hereof will remain in possession
and charge and give its supervision and direction to the farming
operations to be conducted upon the Premises pursuant to the
terms and provisions hereof.

    3.03 Tenant's Acceptance of Present Condition. Tenant
accepts the occupancy and possession of the Premises in their
condition at commencement of the term hereof without any
warranties of Landlord as to the condition of the land or any
improvements thereon at the time of the execution of this Lease,
and Tenant acknowledges that it is familiar with the Premises
and the drainage and irrigation systems and all other improvements
on the Premises.

    3.04. Cultivation.

        (a) Tenant shall maintain and conduct all farming
operations on the Premises in good farmerlike manner, in
accordance with generally approved practices and the usual
methods of farming in the neighborhood, and in a manner to
preserve and enhance the value of the Premises. Specifically,
but without limitation:

            (i) Tenant shall maintain and protect
against pollution and any other damage from Tenant's operations
any and all wells, springs and other water sources and all
existing or appropriate irrigation systems on the Premises, by
all necessary or appropriate means. Tenant shall maintain
all existing and appropriate fencing around and within the
Premises for security and other appropriate purposes.

-4-

(ii) Tenant shall take all reasonable precautions
to eliminate from the Premises and exterminate all pests and all
noxious grasses, weeds and plants, and to keep the Premises
free of rubbish.

(iii) Tenant shall take all reasonable precautions to protect the Premises from fire.

(iv) Tenant shall not commit or suffer
to be commited any waste on the Premises. Tenant shall not
remove or permit to be removed from the Premises or any part
thereof any soil, rock, sand, gravel or manure.

(v) Tenant shall not make or suffer to
be made any structural alterations to the improvements on the
Premises, or conduct any grading of the Premises which would
alter the basic contour of the land or would result in flood
or erosion hazards, without the prior written consent of Landlord.

(vi) No hunting or taking of game shall
be permitted upon the Premises.

(vii) Tenant shall do all things reasonably
necessary or desirable to maintain and enhance the quality
and fertility of the soil of the Premises and, should blight
or disease of any character appear in growing crops, to check
and eliminate said blight or disease.

(b) Tenant shall inform Landlord in reasonable
detail with respect to its farming operations on the Premises
and all receipts therefrom, not less frequently than on each
rental payment date under this Lease.

(c) Tenant shall obtain Landlord's prior
written approval of the crops and rotation program for the
Premises for the last two years of the stated term of this
Lease, which consent shall not be unreasonably withheld.

3.05. Title to Crops; Encumbrances. The legal title
of any crops on the Premises at the execution of this Lease
or subsequently grown on the Property by Tenant shall remain

and be vested in Tenant during the term of this Lease, and
Tenant may mortgage or encumber said crops; provided, that
all financing instruments therefor shall require that Landlord
be given at least thirty (30) days' prior written notice of
any default by Tenant thereunder. Except as expressly permitted in this Section 3.05, Tenant shall not voluntarily or
involuntarily permit any liens of any kind or nature upon
the Premises, or the crops or appurtenances thereon or any
part thereof (other than liens created by Landlord), or
execute any crop or chattel mortgage in connection therewith,
without the prior written consent of Landlord. If Tenant
shall fail to discharge any such lien at its sole cost and
expense, then, in addition to any other right or remedy of
Landlord, Landlord may, but shall not be obligated to, discharge the same either by paying the amount claimed to be due
or by procuring the discharge of said lien, by depositing in
court or by giving security or in such other manner as is or
may be prescribed by law. Any amounts paid by Landlord for
any of the aforesaid purposes and all reasonable expenses
of Landlord, including attorney fees, with interest thereon
at the maximum legal rate from the date of payment, shall be
repaid by Tenant to Landlord on demand and if unpaid may be
treated as additional rental.

   3.06. <u>Oil, Gas and Mineral Rights</u>. All rights in all
mineral, oil, gas and other hydrocarbons located on or under
the Premises, and all rights of exploitation or attempted
exploitation thereof, are particularly reserved to Landlord
and are particularly excepted from the Premises covered by
the terms of this Lease. Tenant expressly grants to Landlord,
and to lessees from Landlord of oil, gas and mineral rights,
and to Landlord's agents and licensees, a right of entry and
a right-of-way for ingress and egress in and to, over and on
the Premises during the term of this Lease for the exploration,

drilling and mining of minerals, oil, gas and other hydrocarbons on the Premises; provided, that Landlord shall reimburse
Tenant for any reasonable damages that Tenant sustains as a
result of any interference with the agricultural operations
conducted on the Premises under the terms of this Lease arising
from said exploration, drilling or mining operations.

    3.07. Future Improvements. Any under or below ground
improvements or alterations or additions made on or to the
Premises shall become at once the property of Landlord and
none shall be removed by Tenant.

    3.08. Compliance with Restrictions and Laws. Tenant
shall occupy, farm and use the Premises subject to and in
compliance with all recorded or non-recorded easements,
servitudes, licenses, covenants, conditions, restrictions,
encumbrances and other rights affecting the Premises or any
portion thereof, and all applicable statutes, laws ordinances
and health, sanitation and safety regulations and requirements
of any governmental authority or entity having jurisdiction
or purporting to have jurisdiction over or with respect to the
Premises, or the operations thereon or hereunder, which are
now or hereafter effective.

IV. INSURANCE AND MAINTENANCE.

    4.01. Insurance. Tenant agrees to purchase and maintain
during the term of this Lease at its own expense and with
companies acceptable to Landlord (a) public liability
insurance for protection against liability to persons or property arising as an incident to the use of or resulting from
any accident or event occurring in or about the Premises,
and (b) such comprehensive fire and extended coverage insurance
for protection against risks of physical loss or damage to
the Premises as is prudent for agricultural property such as
the Premises and is approved by Landlord in writing. The

-7-

limits of liability under said public liability insurance
are to be amounts not less than One Million Dollars
($1,000,000) for any one person injured, One Million Dollars
($1,000,000) for any one accident, and One Million Dollars
($1,000,000) for property damage.   These policies shall
insure any contingent or other liability of Landlord.
Tenant shall furnish to Landlord, prior to commencement of
the term hereunder, certificates of all said insurance for
its files, and Tenant shall obtain a written obligation
imposed on the insurance carriers to notify Landlord in
writing thirty (30) days before any cancellation of said
insurance.   Tenant further agrees to take out and keep in
force during the term of this Lease at its own expense
proper and adequate workmen's compensation insurance covering
all employees of Tenant and insuring and indemnifying both
Landlord and Tenant against any and all liability of every
kind and nature arising out of or existing by virtue of the
provisions of the Labor Code of the State of California or
any similar federal or state law, to obtain and furnish
evidence to Landlord of the waiver by said insurance carrier
of any right of subrogation against Landlord, and upon
Landlord's request to exhibit said insurance policy to
Landlord.   If Tenant does not keep all insurance agreed upon
pursuant hereto in force, Landlord may take out the necessary
insurance and pay the premiums therefor, and the repayment
of said premium (or Tenant's portion thereof) shall be part
of the rental owed to Landlord and shall be made on the next
day on which rental becomes due.

    4.02. <u>Waiver and Indemnity</u>. Tenant, as a material part
of the consideration to be rendered to Landlord, hereby waives
all claims against Landlord for damage to any and all property
upon or about the Premises and for injuries to persons on or
about said Premises from any cause arising at any time, and

-8-

Tenant will hold Landlord exempt and harmless from any damage
or injury to any person or to the property of any person arising
from the use or occupancy of the Premises (including but not
limited to the spraying of agricultural crops on the Premises
by aircraft) by Tenant, its employees, servants, licensees
or agents.

    4.03. <u>Maintenance</u>. Throughout the term of this Lease,
Tenant shall maintain all improvements and appurtenances
on the Premises in as good condition, save ordinary wear, as
on deliver to Tenant (or as that in which thereafter placed,
if better) and at all events in good order, repair and
operating condition, without expense to Landlord. However,
Tenant shall not be responsible for damage from fire not due
to fault or neglect of Tenant or its employees or agents, so
long as Tenant maintains fire insurance in accordance with
Section 4.01 above. Owner shall not be obligated to make
any repairs (whether for fire damage or otherwise), alterations
or improvements to the Premises or any improvements thereon,
nor to erect any new or additional building or improvements.

    4.04. <u>Occupancy of Buildings</u>. If Tenant occupies,
uses or permits to be occupied all or any part of any buildings
now or hereafter located on the Premises, or any other
buildings owned by Landlord whether or not on the Premises,
said occupancy or use shall be permissible only without
consideration and no relation of landlord and tenant shall
be created between Landlord and Tenant with respect thereto
by virtue of the same and Tenant hereby acknowledges that it
has no right to require Landlord to put or maintain any of
said buildings in a habitable condition or otherwise to make
any repairs thereto or replacements or reconstructions
thereof, and Landlord owes no duty to Tenant respecting any
of said buildings. Tenant further agrees to hold Landlord

-9-

harmless from any loss or liability from any cause resulting
from any such occupancy or use.

    4.05. <u>Quality and Quantity of Water and Other Services</u>.
Landlord shall not be responsible for any damage to crops or
other property of Tenant which may be caused through lack of
water, electricity or other utility services, and likewise
shall not be responsible for any failure in the quality of
water or other utilities.

V. <u>DEFAULT BY TENANT</u>.

    5.01. The occurrence of any of the following shall
constitute a material default and breach of this Lease by
Tenant:

        (a) Any failure by Tenant to pay the rental
or to make any other payment required to be made by Tenant
hereunder.

        (b) The abandonment or vacation of the Premises
by Tenant.

        (c) A failure by Tenant to observe and perform
any other provision of this Lease to be observed or performed
by Tenant, where said failure continues for ten (10) days
after written notice thereof by Landlord to Tenant; provided,
that if the nature of said default is such that the same
cannot reasonably be cured within said ten (10) day period,
Tenant shall not be deemed to be in default if Tenant shall
within said period commence said cure and thereafter diligently
prosecute the same to completion.

        (d) The making by Tenant of any general assignment
for the benefit of creditors; the filing by or against Tenant
or any such person or entity of a petition to have it or him
adjudged a bankrupt or of a petition for reorganization or
arrangement under any law relating to bankruptcy (unless, in
the case of a petition filed against such person, the same is
dismissed within sixty (60) days); the appointment of a trustee

-10-

or receiver to take possession of substantially all of Tenant's assets located at the Premises or of Tenant's interest in this Lease, where possession is not restored to Tenant within thirty (30) days; or the attachment, execution or other judicial seizure of substantially all of Tenant's assets located at the Premises or of Tenant's interest in this Lease, where said seizure is not discharged within thirty (30) days.

(e) Any breach or default by Tenant under the Agreement.

5.02. In the event of any such default, then in addition to any other remedies available to Landlord at law or in equity, Landlord shall have the immediate option to terminate this Lease and all rights of Tenant hereunder by giving written notice of said intention to terminate. In the event that Landlord shall elect to so terminate this Lease, then Landlord may recover from Tenant:

(a) the worth at the time of award of any unpaid rent which had been earned at the time of said termination; plus

(b) the worth at the time of award of the amount by which the unpaid rent which would have been earned after termination until the time of award exceeds the amount of said rental loss Tenant proves could have been reasonably avoided; plus

(c) the worth at the time of award of the amount by which the unpaid rent for the balance of the term after the time of award exceeds the amount of said rental loss that Tenant proves could be reasonably avoided; plus

(d) any other amount necessary to compensate Landlord for all the detriment proximately caused by Tenant's failure to perform his obligations under this Lease or which in the ordinary course of things would be likely to result therefrom, having regard particularly to the recitals in this Lease; plus

-11-

(e)   such other amounts in addition to or in lieu
of the foregoing as may be permitted from time to time by
applicable California law.

As used in Sections 5.02(a) and (b) above, the "worth
at the time of the award" shall be computed by allowing
interest at the maximum lawful rate from time to time. As
used in Section 5.02(c) above, the "worth at the time of
award" shall be computed by discounting said amount at the
discount rate of the Federal Reserve Bank of San Francisco
at the time of award plus one percent (1%).

5.03. In the event of any such default by Tenant,
Landlord shall also have the right, with or without terminating
this Lease, to reenter the Premises and remove all persons
and personal property from the Premises; said personal property
may be removed and stored in a public warehouse or elsewhere
at the cost and risk of Tenant, and shall be deemed abandoned
by Tenant under Section 7.06 below unless reclaimed by Tenant
together with payment of said cost within thirty (30) days.

5.04. In the event of the vacation or abandonment
of the Premises by Tenant or in the event that Landlord
shall elect to reenter as provided in Section 5.03 above or
shall take possession of the Premises pursuant to legal
proceeding or pursuant to any notice provided by law, then
if Landlord does not elect to terminate this Lease as provided
in Section 5.02 above, Landlord may from time to time,
without terminating this Lease, either recover all rental as
it becomes due or relet the Premises or any part thereof for
such term or terms and at such rentals and upon such other
terms and conditions and with the right to make such alterations and repairs to the Premises as Landlord in its sole
discretion may deem advisable. In the event that Landlord
shall elect to so relet, then rentals received by Landlord

-12-

from said reletting shall be applied: first, to the payment
of any indebtedness other than rent due hereunder from
Tenant to Landlord; second, to the payment of any cost of
said reletting; third, to the payment of the cost of any
alterations and repairs to the Premises; fourth, to the
payment of rent due and unpaid hereunder; and the residue,
if any, shall be held by Landlord and applied in payment of
future rent as the same may become due and payable hereunder.
If that portion of said rental received from said reletting
during any month, which is applied to the payment of rent
hereunder, is less than the rent payable during that month
by Tenant hereunder, then Tenant shall pays said deficiency
to Landlord immediately upon demand therefor by Landlord.
Said deficiency shall be calculated and paid monthly.
Tenant shall also pay to Landlord, as soon as ascertained,
any costs and expenses incurred by Landlord in said reletting
or in making said alterations and repairs not covered by
the rentals received from said reletting.

5.05. No reentry or taking possession of the Premises
by Landlord pursuant to Section 5.03 or Section 5.04 above
shall be construed as an election to terminate this Lease
unless a written notice of said intention be given to Tenant
or unless the termination thereof be decreed by a court of
competent jurisdiction. Notwithstanding any reletting
without termination by Landlord because of any default by
Tenant, Landlord may at any time after said reletting elect
to terminate this Lease for any such default.

5.06. Landlord's rights and remedies hereunder are
cumulative to each other and those provided by law, and the
exercise or enforcement of any thereof shall not preclude
Landlord from concurrent or later enforcement of any others.

-13-

No acceptance of rent hereunder shall constitute a waiver by
Landlord of any breach of this Lease, and no waiver by
Landlord of any provision of this Lease shall be deemed to
be a waiver of any other provision hereof or of any subsequent
breach of the same or any other provision. Landlord shall
be entitled to specific performance of each obligation of
Tenant hereunder, including but not limited to those under
Section 3.04 above, and to damages for any delay in said
performance. Every covenant of Tenant hereunder is agreed
to be a condition of Landlord's performance hereunder. Any
sum payable by Tenant hereunder shall bear interest at the
maximum lawful rate from time to time, from the date payable
hereunder until paid. Tenant shall pay Landlord's reasonable
expenses, including counsel fees, in any action or proceeding,
either by Landlord against any other party hereto based on
default hereunder or to which they shall otherwise be party
based on any obligation or asserted obligation devolving on
Tenant hereunder, which expenses may be included in the
judgment in said action or separately recovered.

VI. CONDEMNATION.

        If during the term hereof the whole or any part of
the Premises, or any improvements thereon or appurtenances
thereto, are taken under process of eminent domain, or any
transfer in contemplation or in avoidance thereof, then
this Lease shall terminate as to said part of the Premises
as of the date of said appropriation and the basic rental
hereunder shall be reduced for the period thereafter by the
fraction which the acreage so taken bears to the original
acreage subject to this Lease; provided, that if said
appropriation renders impossible the farming of the remainder
of the Premises, Landlord or Tenant shall have the option to
terminate this Lease immediately by written notice to the

-14-

other party. Landlord shall be entitled to the entire
compensation awarded therefor (both for its interest and
that of Tenant in what is so taken, and for any resultant
damange to the remainder of the Premises), any interest
therein which Tenant would otherwise have had being hereby
assigned to Landlord; except that Tenant shall be entitled
to that portion of any such award specifically identified by
the condemning authority as made on account of Tenant's
actual expenses, exclusive of rental value, of preparing for
crops and planting any portion of the Premises so taken.

VII. MISCELLANEOUS.

7.01. Landlord's Right to Enter. Landlord and its
agents and employees may at all times enter upon the Premises
to inspect the same, to post such notices as Landlord may
reasonably desire to protect its interest, to perform such
work as in Landlord's judgment is required, to determine
that all terms and conditions hereof upon the part of Tenant
are being faithfully kept and performed, and for such other
purposes as Landlord shall deem appropriate for business
purposes. Landlord shall also have the right to post "For
Sale" or "For Lease" or similar notices and to show the
Premises to prospective purchases or lessees.

7.02. Sale or Exchange or Premises; Subordination;
Estoppel Certificates. Landlord reserves the right to sell
or exchange all or any portion of the Premises during the
term of this Lease, in which event Landlord may either (a)
assign its rights and obligations hereunder, with or without
recourse, in which event Tenant agrees to attorn to any such
purchaser or assignee as Landlord hereunder, or (b) at
Landlord's option, upon written notice to Tenant, terminate
this Lease at the end of the lease year in which the sale or
exchange occurs as to the portion of the Premises sold or

-15-

exchanged (and "lease year" for this purpose shall mean each
period beginning January 1, and ending December 31, in each
calendar year during the term hereof, or any applicable
portion of the same at the commencement or termination of
this Lease). This Lease, at Landlord's option, shall be
subordinate to any ground lease, mortgage, deed of trust, or
any other hypothecation for security now or hereafter placed
upon the real property of which the Premises are a part and
to any and all advances made on the security thereof and to
all renewals, modifications, consolidations, replacements
and extensions thereof provided that notwithstanding such
subordination, Tenant's right to quiet possession of the
Premises shall not be disturbed if Tenant is not in default
and so long as Tenant shall pay the rent and observe and
perform all of the provisions of this Lease, unless this
Lease is otherwise terminated pursuant to its terms. If any
mortgagee, trustee or lessor shall elect to have this Lease
prior to the lien of its mortgage, deed of trust or ground
lease, and shall give written notice thereof to Tenant, this
Lease shall be deemed prior to such mortgage, deed of trust,
or ground lease, whether this Lease is dated prior or subsequent
to the date of said mortgage, deed of trust or ground lease
or the date of recording thereof. Tenant agrees to execute
any documents required to effectuate such subordination
or to make this Lease prior to the lien of any mortgage,
deed of trust or ground lease, as the case may be,
and failing to do so within ten (10) days after written
demand, does hereby make, constitute and irrevocably appoint
Landlord as Tenant's attorney in fact and in Tenant's name,
place and stead, to do so.

   Tenant shall execute and deliver such estoppel
certificates as Landlord may request, and such amendments

-16-

hereto as may be required (and which shall not materially adversly affect Tenant's interest hereunder) in connection with existing or future financing, sale or exchange of all or any portion of the Premises.

7.03. <u>Conservation Programs</u>. The determination to participate in any soil or other conservation, proration, allocation or allotment program under the Agricultural Adjustment Administration or similar federal or state agency or law or statute relative thereto, or otherwise, may be made only by written agreement of Landlord, provided that Tenant shall, if Landlord shall so request, cooperate with any such program and do such things as may be necessary or appropriate to qualify therefor.

7.04. <u>Relationship of Landlord and Tenant</u>. Nothing contained in this Lease shall be construed to create the relationship of principal and agent, employer and employee, or of partnership or joint venture or any association between Landlord and Tenant or any other party hereto.

7.05. <u>Assignment</u>. Tenant shall not assign, encumber or otherwise transfer any interest in this Lease, nor permit any other person (the employees and agents of Tenant excepted) to occupy or use any portion of the Premises, nor shall any interest of Tenant hereunder be assignable by operation of law. Notwithstanding the foregoing, Tenant may sublease the Premises or portions thereof upon the prior written consent of Landlord, which shall not be unreasonably withheld; provided, that Tenant shall remain liable for all of its obligations hereunder, and shall not delegate its responsibility for supervision and direction of all farming operations upon the Premises. If Tenant hereunder is a corporation, unincorporated association, partnership or other entity, the

-17-

cumulative transfer, conveyance, assignment or hypothecation of any stock or interest as the case may be, in such corporation, association, or entity partnership exceeding in the aggregate, twenty-five percent (25%) of the total amount of such stock or interests therein shall be deemed an assignment of this Lease for the purpose hereof. A consent by Landlord to one assignment, subletting, occupation or use by any other person whether by operaion of law or otherwise, shall not be deemed to be a consent to any subsequent assigment, subletting, occupation or use. Any assignment or subletting, whether by operation of law or otherwise, without Landlord's prior written consent, shall be void and shall, at the option of Landlord, terminate this Lease.

7.06. <u>Surrender</u>. Tenant, upon expiration of the term hereof or the sooner termination hereof, shall promptly and peaceably quit and surrender possession of the Premises and all improvements thereon, in the condition required under Section 4.03 of this Lease. All personal and other property of Tenant which is not removed by Tenant upon the expiration or sooner termination of this Lease shall be deemed to have been abandoned and Landlord is authorized to deal with or dispose of the same in any manner without liability or notice to Tenant.

7.07. <u>Holding Over</u>. Any holding over after the expiration of the term hereof shall require the written consent of Landlord, and shall be construed to be a tenancy from month to month at a basic monthly rental of twice the rental provided hereunder payable to Landlord monthly in advance, and otherwise on the terms and conditions herein specified.

-18-

7.08. <u>Notices</u>. For the purpose of this Lease and any notice to be given hereunder, the address of Landlord shall be:

c/o Myron Meyers
Meyers, Stevens & Walters
Professional Corporation
6300 Wilshire Blvd, Suite 9100
Los Angeles, California 90048

and the address of Tenant shall be:

12345 Corn Crop Drive
Growth, California 90000

Either party may change its respective address by written notice thereof to the other. Notices shall be given in writing and either personally delivered or mailed by registered mail, postage fully prepaid and addressed as herein provided, and shall be deemed given when so personally delivered or deposited in the United States mail.

7.09. <u>Governing Law, Headings, Severability and Parties</u>. This Lease and the rights and obligations of the parties hereunder shall be construed in accordance with the internal law (and not the law of conflice of laws) of the State of California. The headings herein are for convenience only and shall not be used to interpret this Lease. If any provision hereof is held invalid in any jurisdiction, the remaining provisions hereof shall remain in full force and effect between the parties, and said invalidity shall not affect the validity of said provisions in any other jurisdiction. The provisions of this Lease shall bind and inure to the benefit of the respective heirs, executors, assigns and successors of Landlord and Tenant, except as provided elsewhere in this Lease.

7.10. <u>Time of the Essence</u>. Time is of the essence of every provision of this Lease.

7.11. <u>Entire Understanding</u>. This Lease contains the entire understanding between Landlord and Tenant respecting the matters referred to herein, there are no representations,

-19-

promises or agreements in connection therewith which are not
expressly set forth herein, and this Lease may be amended or
supplemented only by a writing executed subsequent hereto by
all parties hereto.

7.12. <u>Counterparts</u>. This Lease may be executed in
one or more counterparts, each of which shall be deemed an
original copy hereof and all of which shall together constitute one agreement.

7.13. <u>Recording</u>. Tenant shall not record this Lease
without Landlord's prior written consent, and such recordation
shall, at the option of Landlord, constitute a non-curable
default of Tenant hereunder. Tenant shall, upon request
of Landlord, execute, acknowledge and deliver to Landlord
a "short form" memorandum of this Lease for recording purposes.

IN WITNESS WHEREOF, the parties hereto have executed
this Lease as of the date first above written.

<u>TENANT</u>:

FARMCO OPERATIONS, INC.,
a California corporation

By _____
                   President

By _____
                   Secretary

<u>LANDLORD</u>:

REAL ACRE N.V.,
a Netherlands Antilles corporation

By _____
        Its Power of Attorney

-20-

3. Owner holds your security deposit of $_____ and the next payment of $_____ is due _____.

4. You paid your rent due _____.

5. You have no actual knowledge that the Owner has in any manner sold, transferred, or hypothecated the Lease.

Please fill in the relevant information and return a signed copy.

Thank you for your cooperation.

Very truly yours,

DEVELOPERS, INC.

By _____

ALL OF THE ABOVE IS CONFIRMED, ACKNOWLEDGED AND AGREED TO THIS _____ DAY OF _____, 1981

_____
(to be added by Owner after Tenant signs)

ALL OF THE FOREGOING IS TRUE AND ACCURATE AND THE UNDERSIGNED CONCURS THEREIN.

DATED _____.

REALPROP N.V.

By _____

-2-

ESTOPPEL CERTIFICATE - WRITTEN LEASE

Developers, Inc.
12345 Builders Way
Growth, California

To: _____

Tenants in possession of
Money Street,
Growth, California

ESTOPPEL CERTIFICATE

DEVELOPERS, INC. ("Buyer") is in the process of purchasing from your present landlord, REALPROP N.V. ("Owner") the real property which includes the space you occupy under the lease described below. Buyer will rely upon the information set forth herein and by signing below you acknowledge such reliance.

You confirm the following:

1. The only agreement between you as Tenant and Owner is that certain written lease dated _____. A copy of the written lease and all amendments, if any, is attached as Exhibit "A" (the "Lease").

2. The Lease has not been amended or changed and there are no other agreements between you and the Owner except as set out in the Lease.

Developers, Inc.
12345 Builders Way
Growth, California

To: The Tenant(s) in possession
    of Apt.# _____ at _____ South
    Money Street, Growth, California

DEVELOPERS, INC. ("Buyers") are purchasing the building in which your apartment is located from Mr. and Mrs. John Smith.

As part of the purchase, the Buyers wish you to verify the following. Please be accurate as the Buyers will rely upon what you say:

1. You occupy your apartment as a month-to-month Tenant under a verbal month-to-month agreement.

2. Your monthly rent is $_____ payable in advance on the _____ day of each month. The Landlord pays for water and you pay all other utilities.

3. Rent has been paid to _____, 1981, with the next payment due _____, 1981. The Landlord holds no security deposit.

4. You have no options to revew or extend your month-to-month occupancy.

Thank you for your cooperation.

Very truly yours,
DEVELOPERS, INC.

By _____

WE APPROVE AND VERIFY THE ABOVE:
Dated: January _____, 1981.

_____
NAME

_____
ADDRESS

_____
NAME

_____
TELEPHONE NUMBER

-2-

STANDARD OFFICE LEASE

TABLE OF CONTENTS

SUBWAY TERMINAL BUILDING
STANDARD OFFICE LEASE

THIS LEASE dated _____, 19 _____,
is made between THE SUBWAY TERMINAL BUILDING ("Landlord"), and

_____, Tenant.

PREMISES

Landlord hereby leases to Tenant and Tenant hereby hires from Landlord, subject to all terms and conditions of this Lease, those certain premises (the "Premises") shown as Suite No. _____ in the drawing attached hereto as Exhibit "A", located on the _____ floor(s) of that certain office building commonly known as _____ Los Angeles, California_____. Said building, together with the underlying real property, is sometimes hereinafter referred to as the "Building."

Article 1.   **TERM**

The term of this Lease, unless sooner terminated as provided herein, shall be _____ years and _____ months, commencing on the "Commencement Date" which shall be the first to occur of (i) the date Tenant occupies the Premises for purposes other than construction and decorating and (ii) _____, 19 _____. If Landlord, for any reason whatsoever, cannot deliver possession of the Premises to Tenant on or before the date specified in (ii) above, this Lease shall not be void or voidable nor shall Landlord be liable to Tenant for any loss or damage resulting therefrom, but in such event, Tenant shall not be liable for any rent until such time as Landlord delivers possession of the Premises to Tenant.

Article 2.   **RENT**

Tenant shall pay as total basic rent the sum of _____
_____ ($_____).
Beginning with the Commencement Date, Tenant shall pay a basic monthly rent for the Premises in the amount of _____ Dollars ($ _____), payable on the first day of each month in advance, except that if the Commencement Date occurs on a day other than the first day of a month, then the basic rent for the fraction of the month starting with the Commencement Date shall be paid on said Commencement Date, prorated on the basis of the actual number of days in said month. If the term hereof ends on a day other than the last day of a month, then the basic rent for the month during which said expiration occurs shall be prorated on the basis of the actual number of days in said month. In addition to the basic rent, Tenant shall pay, all as additional rent, other amounts as and when hereinafter provided in this Lease. The basic rent and additional rent are sometimes hereinafter collectively referred to as the "rent." The rent shall be payable to Landlord, without further notice or demand and without deduction or offset, in lawful money of the United States of America at the address for Landlord set forth on the signature page hereof, or to such other person or at such other place as Landlord may from time to time designate in writing.

Article 3.   **RENT ADJUSTMENT**

3.1 If, in any Fiscal Year (as hereinafter defined) during the term of this Lease, Landlord's annual "Operating Costs" (as hereafter defined) shall be higher than such Costs for the Fiscal Year 19 _____ (the "base year"), the rent payable by Tenant for such Fiscal Year shall be increased over that payable for the base year by an amount equal to "Tenant's Proportionate Share" (as hereafter defined) of such increase in Operating Costs.

3.2 If, in any Fiscal Year during the term of this Lease, Landlord's "Real Estate Taxes" (as hereafter defined) shall be higher than such Taxes for the base year, the rent payable by Tenant for such Fiscal Year shall be increased over that payable for the base year by an amount equal to Tenant's Proportionate Share of such increase in Real Estate Taxes.

3.3 For purposes of this Article 3:

(i) "Operating Costs" shall mean all costs, expenses and disbursements of every kind and nature which Landlord shall pay or be obligated to pay in respect of a Fiscal Year because of or in connection with the ownership, insuring, management, maintenance and operation of the Building; excluding, however: (a) the capitalized costs of alterations to any tenant's premises; (b) capitalized costs of improvements (except depreciation and interest with respect to machinery, equipment, systems, property or facilities first installed in or used in connection with the Building after the Commencement Date if one of the principal purposes of such installation or use was to reduce other items of Operating Costs, or with respect to costs incurred by Landlord in complying with any requirement imposed after the Commencement Date by any statute, ordinance, regulation, or order of any governmental body); (c) depreciation (except on wall coverings and carpeting in public corridors and common areas); (d) interest and principal payments on mortgages and other debt costs; (e) brokerage commissions; and (f) state and federal income and excess profit taxes, if any. Landlord may, in a reasonable manner, allocate insurance premiums for so-called "blanket" insurance policies which insure other properties as well as the Building. Except as otherwise provided herein, the determination of Operating Costs and their allocation shall be in accordance with generally accepted accounting principles consistently applied.

(ii) "Real Estate Taxes" shall mean all real and personal property taxes and assessments incurred during any Fiscal Year, including, without limitation, special and extraordinary assessments (computed as though paid in permitted installments regardless of whether actually so paid) and other governmental levies imposed upon or with respect to the Building, together with any tax on or measured by gross rentals received from rentals of space in the Building. The determination of real estate taxes and their allocation shall be in accordance with generally accepted accounting principles consistently applied.

(iii) "Fiscal Year" shall mean a year commencing January 1 and ending December 31 provided, however, that Landlord reserves the right to change from time to time the Fiscal Year and, in such event, the calculation of additional rent payable under this Article 3 shall be equitably adjusted in accordance with such new Fiscal Year.

(iv) "Tenant's Proportionate Share" shall be _____.

3.4 During the last calendar month of each Fiscal Year or as soon thereafter as practical, Landlord shall give Tenant written notice of the amounts reasonably estimated by Landlord to be payable by Tenant under Sec-

1

tions 3.1 and 3.2 hereof for the ensuing Fiscal Year. On or before the first day of each month during such ensuing Fiscal Year, Tenant shall pay to Landlord one-twelfth (1/12) of the amount of such estimate; provided, however, that until such notice is given, Tenant shall continue to pay additional rent on the basis of the estimate of such amounts given by Landlord with respect to the preceding Fiscal Year.

3.5 Within ninety (90) days after the close of each Fiscal Year or as soon thereafter as practical, Landlord shall deliver to Tenant a reasonably detailed statement of the amount of additional rent actually payable under Sections 3.1 and 3.2 hereof for such Fiscal Year. If such statement shows additional rent owing by Tenant in an amount less than the aggregate payments previously made by Tenant on account of additional rent, such statement shall be accompanied by a refund of the excess from Landlord to Tenant. If such statement shows an amount owing by Tenant that is more than the aggregate payments previously made by Tenant on account of additional rent, Tenant shall pay the deficiency to Landlord within ten (10) days after delivery of such statement.

3.6 If, for any reason other than a default by Tenant, this Lease shall terminate on a day other than the last day of a Fiscal Year, the amount of the increase, if any, in rental payable by Tenant applicable to the Fiscal Year, in which such termination occurs shall be prorated on the basis for which the number of days from the commencement of such Fiscal Year to and including such termination date bears to 365.

Article 4.   **SECURITY DEPOSIT**

Tenant has deposited with Landlord the sum of .

_____ Dollars ($_____

as security for the full and faithful performance of every provision of this Lease to be performed by Tenant. If Tenant defaults with respect to any provision of this Lease, including, without limitation the provisions relating to the payment of rent, the repair of damage to the Premises and/or cleaning the Premises upon termination of this Lease, Landlord may use, apply or retain all or any part of this security deposit for the payment of any rent or other sum in default, the repair of such damage to the Premises, the cost of such cleaning or the payment of any other amount which Landlord may spend or become obligated to spend by reason of Tenant's default or to compensate Landlord for any other loss or damage which Landlord may suffer by reason of Tenant's default to the full extent permitted by law. If any portion of said deposit is so used, applied, or retained, Tenant shall, within ten (10) days after written demand therefor, deposit cash with Landlord in an amount sufficient to restore the security deposit to its original amount and Tenant's failure to do so shall be a material default and breach of this Lease. Landlord shall not be required to keep any security deposit separate from its general funds, and Tenant shall not be entitled to interest on any such deposit. If Tenant shall fully and faithfully perform every provision of this Lease to be performed by it, the security deposit or any balance thereof shall be returned to Tenant or to the last assignee of Tenant's interest hereunder at the expiration of the term of this Lease.

Article 5.   **UTILITIES AND SERVICES**

5.1 Landlord shall furnish to the Premises such amounts of air conditioning, heating and ventilation as may be reasonably necessary for the comfortable use and occupation of the Premises. Subject to the provisions set forth below, Landlord shall at all times furnish the Premises with elevator service and reasonable amounts of electric current for normal lighting by Landlord's building standard overhead fluorescent and incandescent fixtures and for fractional horsepower office machines and furnish the common areas of the Building with water for lavatory purposes. Landlord may impose a reasonable charge for any utilities or services, including, without limitation, electric current, required to be provided by Landlord by reason of any excessive use of any thereof or by reason of any substantial recurrent use of the Premises at any time other than reasonable hours of generally recognized business days. Landlord shall provide janitor service equivalent to that furnished in comparable office buildings and window washing as reasonably required; provided, however, that Tenant shall pay for any additional or unusual janitorial services required by reason of any non-building standard improvements in the Premises, including without limitation wall coverings and floor coverings, installed by or for Tenant. Landlord shall replace fluorescent tubes and ballasts in Landlord's building standard overhead fluorescent fixtures as required. Tenant shall pay for replacement of all other bulbs as required. Landlord shall not be liable for any failure to furnish any of such services or utilities when such failure is caused by accidents, strikes, lockouts, acts of God, or other casualty, other labor troubles or other conditions beyond Landlord's reasonable control, including, without limitation, any governmental water, energy, other conservation program, or regulation. No such failure shall entitle Tenant to any damages, relieve Tenant of the obligation to pay the full rent reserved herein or constitute or be construed as a constructive or other eviction of Tenant.

5.2 Tenant will not without the prior written consent of Landlord use any apparatus or device in the Premises, including, without limitation, electronic data processing machines, punch card machines and machines requiring current in excess of one hundred ten (110) volts which will in any way increase the amount of electricity or water usually furnished or supplied for use of the Premises as general office space; nor connect any apparatus, machine or device with water pipes or electric current (except through existing electrical outlets in the Premises), for the purpose of using electric current or water. If Tenant shall require electric current in excess of that which Landlord is obligated to furnish under Section 5.1 above, Tenant shall first obtain the consent of Landlord, which Landlord may refuse, to the use thereof and Landlord may cause an electric current meter to be installed in the Premises to measure the amount of electric current consumed for any such other use. The cost of any such meter and of installation, maintenance and repair thereof shall be paid for by Tenant and Tenant shall reimburse Landlord promptly upon demand therefor by Landlord for all such electric current consumed for any such other use as shown by said meter, at the rates charged for such services by the local public utility furnishing the same, plus any additional expense incurred in keeping account of the electric current so consumed. If any lights, machines or equipment (including without limitation electronic data processing machines) are used by Tenant in the Premises which materially affect the temperature otherwise maintained by the air conditioning system, or generate substantially more heat in the Premises than would generated by the building standard lights and usual fractional horsepower office equipment, Landlord shall have the right to install any machinery and equipment which Landlord reasonably deems necessary to restore temperature balance, including without limitation modifications to the standard air conditioning equipment, and the cost thereof, including the cost of installation and any additional cost of operation and maintenance occasioned thereby, shall be paid by Tenant to Landlord upon demand by Landlord.

Article 6.   **USE OF PREMISES**

Tenant shall use and occupy the Premises only for _____

_____

and shall not use or occupy the Premises for any other purpose, including without limitation any medical or dental office, clinic, laboratory or similar business, without the prior written consent of Landlord. Tenant shall not

2

use or occupy the Premises in violation of law and shall discontinue any use of the Premises which is declared by any governmental authority to be a violation of law. Tenant, at its sole cost and expense, shall comply with any directive of any governmental authority which shall impose any duty upon Tenant or Landlord with respect to the Premises or the use or occupation thereof, by reason of the nature of Tenant's use or occupancy of the Premises. Tenant shall not commit, or suffer to be committed, any waste, nuisance or other act which may disturb the quiet enjoyment of any other tenant or other occupant of the Building, or any act which may increase the cost of public liability or any other insurance Landlord elects to carry in connection with the ownership, management, maintenance and operation of the Building or which is otherwise in contravention of insurance underwriting regulations, guidelines and practices.

Article 7.   **ACCEPTANCE OF PREMISES**

Tenant acknowledges that neither Landlord nor any agent of Landlord has made any representation or warranty with respect to the Premises or the Building or with respect to the suitability or fitness of either for the conduct of Tenant's business or for any other purpose. The taking of possession or use of the Premises by Tenant for any purpose other than construction shall conclusively establish that the Premises and the Building were at such time in satisfactory condition and in conformity with the provisions of this Lease in all respects, except as to any items required to be accomplished by Landlord under the Work Letter referred to in Article 29 hereof as to which Tenant shall give Landlord written notice in reasonable detail within fifteen (15) days after Tenant takes such possession or commences such use of the Premises. Nothing contained in this Article 7 shall affect the commencement of the term of this Lease or the obligation of Tenant to pay rent hereunder as provided in Article 2 hereof.

Article 8.   **ALTERATIONS AND EQUIPMENT**

Tenant shall make no alterations or improvements to the Premises without the prior written consent of Landlord, and Landlord may impose as a condition to such consent such requirements as Landlord in its sole discretion may deem necessary or desirable, including, without limitation, requirements as to posting by Tenant with Landlord of appropriate bonds and the manner in which or the time or times at which such work shall be done, and Landlord shall have the right to approve the contractor selected by Tenant to perform such work. All such alterations, additions or improvements shall become the property of Landlord and shall be surrendered with the Premises, as a part thereof, at the end of the term of this Lease, except that Landlord may, by written notice to Tenant given at least thirty (30) days prior to the end of such term, require Tenant to remove all or certain designated partitions, counters, railings and the like installed by Tenant, and repair any damage to the Premises caused by such installation or removal, all at Tenant's sole expense.

Article 9.   **LIENS**

Tenant shall keep the Premises and the Building free from any mechanics' liens arising out of any work performed, materials furnished or obligations incurred by or on behalf of Tenant. Tenant shall indemnify and hold harmless Landlord from and against any such lien or claim or action thereon, and reimburse Landlord promptly upon demand therefor by Landlord for costs of suit and reasonable attorneys' fees incurred by Landlord in connection with any such claim or actions.

Article 10.   **TAX ON TENANT'S PROPERTY**

10.1 Tenant shall be liable for and shall pay at least ten (10) days before delinquency, all taxes levied against any personal property or trade fixtures placed by Tenant in or about the Premises. If any such taxes on Tenant's personal property or trade fixtures are levied against Landlord or Landlord's property and if Landlord, after written notice to Tenant, pays the same (which Landlord shall have the right to do regardless of the validity of such levy, but only under proper protest if requested by Tenant), or if the assessed value of Landlord's property is increased by the inclusion therein of a value placed upon such personal property or trade fixtures of Tenant and if Landlord, after written notice to Tenant, pays the taxes based upon such increased assessment (which Landlord shall have the right to do regardless of the validity thereof, but only under proper protest if requested by Tenant), Tenant shall pay to Landlord the taxes so levied against Landlord or the proportion of such taxes resulting from such increase in the assessment; provided, however, that in any such event Tenant shall have the right, in the name of Landlord and with Landlord's full cooperation, but at not cost to Landlord, to bring suit in any court of competent jurisdiction to recover the amount of any such tax so paid under protest, and any amount so recovered shall belong to Tenant.

10.2 If the tenant improvements in the Premises, whether installed and/or paid for by Landlord or Tenant and whether or not affixed to the real property so as to become a part thereof, are assessed for real property tax purposes at a valuation higher than the valuation at which tenant improvements conforming to Landlord's building standards in other space in the Building are assessed, then the real property taxes and assessments levied against Landlord or Landlord's property by reason of such excess assessed valuation shall be deemed to be taxes levied against personal property of Tenant and shall be governed by the provisions of Section 10.1 hereof.

Article 11.   ·   **MAINTENANCE AND REPAIR**

11.1 Subject to the provisions of Section 11.2 hereof, Tenant shall maintain in good condition and repair the Premises and the fixtures therein and reimburse Landlord for all repairs thereto or to the Building which are made necessary as a result of any misuse or neglect by (i) Tenant or any of its officers, agents, employees, contractors or licensees, or (ii) any visitors, guests or invitees of Tenant while in the Premises.

11.2 Subject to the provisions of Section 5.1 and Article 17 hereof, Landlord shall maintain in good condition and repair the Building structure and public areas and the plumbing, air conditioning and electrical systems serving the Premises. Landlord shall not be liable for any failure to make any repairs or to perform any maintenance unless such failure shall persist for an unreasonable time after written notice of the need for such repairs or maintenance is given to Landlord by Tenant. Except as provided in Article 17 hereof, there shall be no abatement of rent and no liability of Landlord by reason of any injury to or interference with Tenant's business arising from the making of any repairs, alterations or improvements in or to any portion of the Building, including the Premises, or in or to the fixtures, appurtenances and equipment therein; provided, however, that in making such repairs, alterations or improvements, Landlord shall interfere as little as reasonably practicable with the conduct of Tenant's business in the Premises. As a material inducement Landlord entering into this Lease, Tenant waives and releases its right to make repairs at Landlord's expense under Section 1942 of the California Civil Code and the provisions of Section 1932(1) of the California Civil Code. Landlord shall not be liable for any

3

failure to maintain or repair when such failure is caused by accidents, strikes, lockouts, Acts of God or other casualty, other labor troubles or other conditions beyond Landlord's reasonable control, including, without limitation, any governmental water, energy, other conservation program or regulation. No such failure shall entitle Tenant to any damages, relieve Tenant of the obligation to pay the full rent reserved herein, or constitute or be construed as a constructive or other eviction of Tenant.

Article 12.   **ENTRY AND INSPECTION**

Tenant will permit Landlord and its agents at all reasonable times during normal business hours and at any time in case of emergency, in such manner as to cause as little disturbance to Tenant as reasonably practicable, (i) to enter into and upon the Premises for the purpose of inspecting the same, or for the purpose of protecting the interest therein of Landlord, or to post notices of non-responsibility, and (ii) to take all required materials and equipment into the Premises, and perform all required work therein, including the erection of scaffolding, props, or other mechanical devices, for the purpose of making alterations, repairs or additions to the Premises or to any other portion of the Building or maintaining any service provided by Landlord to Tenant hereunder, including window cleaning and janitor service, without any rebate of rent to Tenant for any loss of occupancy or quiet enjoyment of the Premises, or damage, injury or inconvenience thereby occasioned. Tenant shall also permit Landlord and its agents, upon request, to enter and/or pass through the Premises or any part thereof, at reasonable times during normal business hours to show the Premises to the fee owners, lessors of superior leases, holders of encumbrances on the interest of Landlord, or prospective purchasers, mortgagees, lessors or tenants of the Building or a portion thereof. Landlord shall also have the right to enter and/or pass through the Premises, or any part thereof, at such times as such entry shall be required by circumstances of emergency affecting the Premises or any other portion of the Building. If during the last month of the term hereof Tenant shall have removed substantially all of Tenant's property and personnel from the Premises, Landlord may enter the Premises and repair, alter and redecorate the same, without abatement of rent and without liability to Tenant, and such acts shall have no effect on this Lease.

Article 13   **HOLD HARMLESS AND NON-LIABILITY**

13.1 As a material part of the consideration for this Lease, Tenant hereby (a) assumes all risk of damage to property or injury to persons, in, on or about the leased premises and on the building arising from any cause, and Tenant hereby waives all claims in respect thereof against Landlord; (b) agrees to indemnify, defend and hold Landlord harmless from and against any and all claims, loss, damage or liability arising from Tenant's use, occupation, or alteration of the leased premises, from the conduct of Tenant's business therein, or from any other activity, work or things done, permitted or suffered by Tenant in or about the leased premises or elsewhere; (c) any and all claims, loss, damage, or liability arising from any breach or default in the performance of any of Tenant's obligations hereunder, or arising from any negligence of Tenant, or any of Tenant's agents, contractors, employees or invitees; and (d) all costs, attorney's fees, expenses and liabilities incurred in the defense of any claim, loss, damage or liability for which Tenant has agreed to indemnify Landlord or any action or proceeding brought thereon, whether or not an action or proceeding is brought and whether or not it is prosecuted to judgment. In the event that Landlord is ever made a party to any action or proceeding by reason of any matter for which Tenant has hereby agreed to indemnify Landlord, then Tenant, upon notice from Landlord, shall defend such action or proceeding on behalf of Landlord at Tenant's expense by counsel satisfactory to Landlord. If Landlord commences an action against Tenant to enforce any of the terms hereof or because of the breach by Tenant of any of the terms hereof, or for the recovery of any rent or other sum due hereunder, or for any unlawful detainer of said premises, Tenant shall pay to Landlord reasonable attorney's fees and expenses, and the right to such attorney's fees and expenses shall be deemed to have accrued on the commencement of such action and shall be enforceable whether or not such action is prosecuted to judgment. If Tenant breaches any term of this Lease, Landlord may employ an attorney or attorneys to protect Landlord's rights hereunder, and in the event of such employment following any breach by Tenant, Tenant shall pay Landlord reasonable attorney's fees and expenses incurred by Landlord, whether or not an action is actually commenced against Tenant by reason of breach. If Landlord breaches any term of this Lease, Tenant may employ an attorney or attorneys to protect Tenant's rights hereunder, and in the event of such employment following any breach by Landlord, Landlord shall pay Tenant's reasonable attorney's fees and expenses incurred by Tenant, whether or not an action is actually commenced against Landlord by reason of the breach.

13.2 Tenant hereby agrees that Landlord shall not be liable for injury to Tenant's business or any loss of income therefrom or for damage to the goods, wares, merchandise or other property of Tenant, Tenant's employees, invitees, customers, or any other person in or about the leased premises, nor shall Landlord be liable for injury to the person of Tenant, Tenant's employees, agents, or contractors, whether such damage or injury is caused by or results from fire, steam, electricity, gas, water or rain, or from the breakage, leakage, obstruction or other defects of pipes, sprinklers, wires, appliances, plumbing, air conditioning or lighting fixtures, or from any other cause, whether the said damage or injury results from conditions arising upon the leased premises or upon other portions of the building of which the leased premises are a part, or from other sources or places, and regardless of whether the cause of such damage or injury or the means of repairing the same is inaccessible to Tenant. Landlord shall not be liable for any damages arising from any act or neglect of any other tenant, if any, of the building in which the leased premises are located. Landlord shall have the right to replace, at the expense of Tenant, any and all plate and other glass damaged or broken from any cause whatsoever in or about demised premises. There shall be no allowance to Tenant for a diminution of rental value, and no liability on the part of Landlord by reason of inconvenience, annoyance or injury to business arising from the making of any repairs, alterations, decorations, additions or improvements in or to any portion of the building or the leased premises, or in or to fixtures, appurtenances or equipment, and there shall be no liability upon Landlord for failure to make any repairs, alterations, decorations, additions, or improvements in or to any portion of the building or the leased premises, or in or to fixtures, appurtenances or equipment or by reason of any act or neglect of any other tenant or occupancy of the building.

13.3 Tenant, at its own expense, shall provide and keep in force with companies acceptable to Landlord public liability insurance for the benefit of Landlord and Tenant jointly against liability for bodily injury and property damage in the amount of not less than Two Hundred Fifty Thousand Dollars ($250,000.00) in respect to injuries to or death of any person, and in an amount of not less than Five Hundred Thousand Dollars ($500,000.00) in respect to injuries to or death of more than one person in any one occurrence, and in the amount of not less than Fifty Thousand Dollars ($50,000.00) per occurrence in respect to damage to property, such limits to be for any greater amounts as may be reasonably indicated by circumstances from time to time existing. Tenant shall furnish Landlord with a certificate of such policy and whenever required shall satisfy Landlord that such policy is in full force and effect. Such policy shall name Landlord as additional insured and shall be primary and non-contributing with any insurance carried by Landlord. The policy shall further provide that it shall not be cancelled or altered without thirty (30) days' prior notice to Landlord. Insurance required hereunder shall be written by companies rated A to AAA or better in "Best's Insurance Guide".

4

13.4 In the event Tenant fails to provide or maintain the required insurance as provided under this Lease, or to deliver to Landlord the required proof thereof, Landlord, at its option, but without obligation so to do, may upon five (5) days' notice to Tenant of its intention so to do, procure such insurance, and any sums expended by it to procure such insurance shall be repaid by Tenant as additional rent. Tenant shall promptly notify Landlord of all claims in excess of $1,000.00 made under any policy required to be maintained by Tenant under the terms of this Lease.

Article 14.   **WAIVER OF SUBROGATION**

Tenant and Landlord each hereby waive any and all rights of recovery against the other, or against the officers, employees, agents and representatives of the other, for loss of or damage to such waiving party or its property or the property of others under its control to the extent that such loss or damage is insured against under any insurance policy in force at the time of such loss or damage. The insuring party shall, upon obtaining the policies of insurance required hereunder, give notice to the insurance carrier or carriers that the foregoing mutual waiver of subrogation is contained in this Lease.

Article 15.   **ASSIGNMENT AND SUBLETTING**

15.1 Tenant shall not either voluntarily or by operation of law assign, encumber, pledge or otherwise transfer or hypothecate all or any part of Tenant's leasehold estate hereunder, or permit the Premises to be occupied by anyone other than Tenant or Tenant's employees or sublet the Premises or any portion thereof without Landlord's prior written consent in each instance. Subject in each instance to all the provisions of this Article 15, including without limitation the recapture options of Landlord set forth in Section 15.3 hereof, Landlord's consent to any assignment or subletting shall not be unreasonably withheld if:

(i) Tenant or the proposed subtenant or assignee shall agree to pay Landlord, upon demand, as additional rent, a sum equal to the additional costs, if any, incurred by Landlord for maintenance and repair as a result of any change in the nature of the occupancy caused by any such subletting or assignment; and

(ii) the occupancy resulting from such subletting or assignment will be consistent with the general character of the businesses carried on by the tenants of the Building, will conform to the use restrictions set forth in Article 6 hereof and will not violate any rights or options held by any other tenant of the Building.

No collection or acceptance of rent by Landlord from any person other than Tenant shall be deemed a waiver of any provision of this Article 15 or the acceptance of any assignee or subtenant as the tenant hereunder, or a release of Tenant from any obligation under this Lease, whether theretofore or thereafter accruing.

15.2 If Tenant desires at any time to assign this Lease or to sublet the Premises or any portion thereof, it shall first notify Landlord of its desire to do so and shall submit in writing to Landlord (a) the name of the proposed subtenant or assignee; (b) the nature of the proposed subtenant's or assignee's business to be carried on in the Premises; (c) the terms and provisions of the proposed sublease or assignment; and (d) such financial information as Landlord may reasonably request concerning the proposed subtenant or assignee.

15.3 At any time within thirty (30) days after Landlord's receipt of the information specified in Section 15.2 hereof, Landlord may by written notice to Tenant elect to (a) sublease the Premises or the portion thereof so proposed to be subleased by Tenant, or to take an assignment of Tenant's leasehold estate hereunder, or such part thereof as shall be specified in said notice, upon the same terms as those offered to the proposed subtenant or assignee, as the case may be; or (b) terminate this Lease as to the portion (including all) of the Premises so proposed to be subleased or assigned, with a proportionate abatement in the rent payable hereunder. If Landlord does not exercise any option set forth in this Section 15.3 within said thirty (30) day period, Tenant may thereafter within ninety (90) days after the expiration of said thirty (30) day period enter into a valid assignment or sublease of the Premises or portion thereof, upon the terms and conditions set forth in the information furnished by Tenant to Landlord pursuant to Section 15.2 hereof, subject, however, in each instance, to Landlord's consent pursuant to Section 15.1 hereof.

15.4 No consent by Landlord to any assignment or subletting by Tenant shall relieve Tenant of any obligation to be performed by Tenant under this Lease, whether accruing before or after such assignment or subletting. The consent by Landlord to any assignment or subletting shall not relieve Tenant from the obligation to obtain Landlord's express written consent to any other assignment or subletting. Any assignment or subletting which is not in compliance with this Article 15 shall be void and, at the option of Landlord, shall constitute a material default by Tenant under this Lease.

15.5 Each assignee or transferee, other than Landlord, shall assume all obligations of Tenant under this Lease and shall be and remain liable jointly and severally with Tenant for the payment of the rent, and for the due performance of all the terms, covenants, conditions and agreements herein contained on Tenant's part to be performed for the term of this Lease; provided, however, that the assignee or transferee shall be liable to Landlord for rent only in the amount set forth in the assignment or transfer. No assignment shall be binding on Landlord unless such assignee or Tenant shall deliver to Landlord a counterpart of such assignment and an instrument in recordable form which contains a covenant of assumption by the assignee satisfactory in substance and form to Landlord, consistent with the requirements of this Section 15.5, but the failure or refusal of the assignee to execute such instrument of assumption shall not release or discharge the assignee from its liability as set forth above.

Article 16.   **TRANSFER OF LANDLORD'S INTEREST**

In the event of any transfer or transfers of Landlord's interest in the Premises or the building, other than a transfer for security purposes only, the transferor shall be automatically relieved of any and all obligations and liabilities on the part of Landlord accruing from and after the date of such transfer, including, without limitation, the obligation of Landlord under Article 4 hereof to return the security deposit as provided herein.

Article 17.   **DAMAGE OR DESTRUCTION**

17.1 In the event of (a) a partial destruction of the leased premises or the building during the term which requires repairs to either the leased premises or the building, or (b) the leased premises or the building being declared unsafe or unfit for occupancy by any authorized public authority for any reason other than Tenant's act, use or occupation which declaration requires repairs to either the leased premises or the building, Landlord shall forthwith make such repairs, provided (i) such repairs can be made within ninety (90) days under the laws and regulations of authorized public authorities, and (ii) provided further, such partial destruction results from a cause insured under the standard fire insurance policy or policies Landlord shall have in effect on the leased premises and/or the building and such insurance proceeds are made available to Landlord to make such repairs.

5

Such partial destruction (including any destruction necessary in order to make repairs required by any declaration) shall in no wise annul or void this Lease, except that Tenant shall be entitled to a proportionate reduction of rent while such repairs are being made. The proportionate reduction is to be based upon the extent to which the making of said repairs shall interfere with the business carrried on by Tenant in the leased premises. In making said repairs, Landlord shall be obligated to replace only such glazing as shall have been damaged by fire or other insured casualty, and other damaged glazing shall be replaced by Tenant. If said repairs cannot be made within ninety (90) days, or the other conditions above set forth to making said repairs have not been met, Landlord may, at its option, and at its sole discretion, make same within a reasonable time, this Lease continuing in full force and effect and the rent shall be proportionately abated as provided in this paragraph. In the event that Landlord does not so elect to make repairs as above provided, or repairs cannot be made under current laws and regulations, this Lease may be terminated at the option of either party upon written notice to the other party. In respect to any partial destruction (including any destruction necessary in order to make repairs required by any declaration) which Landlord is obligated to repair or may elect to repair under the term of this paragraph, the provisions of Section 1932, Subdivision (2), and Section 1933, Subdivision (4), of the Civil Code of the State of California, are waived by Tenant. A total destruction (including any destruction required by an authorized public authority) of either the leased premises or the building, shall terminate this Lease. In the event of any dispute between Landlord and Tenant relative to the provisions of this paragraph, they may each select an arbitrator, the two arbitrators so selected shall select a third arbitrator, and the three arbitrators so selected shall hear and determine the controversy and their decision thereon shall be final and binding on both Landlord and Tenant, who shall bear the cost of such arbitration equally between them. Landlord shall not be required to repair any property installed in the leased premises by Tenant. Notwithstanding the foregoing, if the leased premises are partially destroyed or damaged during the last six (6) months of the term of this Lease, the Landlord may, at Landlord's option, cancel and terminate this Lease as of the date of occurrence of such damage by giving written notice to Tenant of Landlord's election to do so within thirty (30) days after the date of occurrence of such damage.

17.2 Landlord shall not be required to carry insurance of any kind on Tenant's property and, except by reason of the breach by Landlord of any of its obligations hereunder (subject to the provisions of Article 14 hereof), shall not be obligated to repair any damage thereto or replace the same.

Article 18. EMINENT DOMAIN

18.1 If the whole of the Premises or so much thereof as to render the balance unusable by Tenant shall be taken under power of eminent domain, this Lease shall automatically terminate as of the date of such condemnation, or as of the date possession is taken by the condemning authority, whichever is earlier. No award for any partial or entire taking shall be apportioned, and Tenant hereby assigns to Landlord any award which may be made in such taking or condemnation, together with any and all rights of Tenant now or hereafter arising in or to the same or any part thereof; provided, however, that nothing contained herein shall be deemed to give Landlord any interest in or to require Tenant to assign to Landlord any award made to Tenant for its relocation expenses, the taking of personal property and fixtures belonging to Tenant, the interruption of or damage to Tenant's business and/or for Tenant's unamortized cost of leasehold improvements.

18.2 In the event of a partial taking which does not result in a termination of this Lease, rent shall be abated in proportion to that part of the Premises so made unusable by Tenant.

18.3 No temporary taking of the Premises and/or of Tenant's rights therein or under this Lease shall terminate this Lease or give Tenant any right to any abatement of rent hereunder; any award made to Tenant by reason of any such temporary taking shall belong entirely to Tenant and Landlord shall not be entitled to share therein.

Article 19. RELOCATION

If the Premises contain less than six thousand (6,000) square feet of rentable area, Landlord shall have the right, at its option, upon at least thirty (30) days' written notice to Tenant to relocate Tenant and to substitute for the Premises other space in the Building containing at least as much rentable area as the original Premises. Such substituted Premises shall be improved by Landlord at its expense, with decorations and improvements at least equal in quantity and quality to those in the original Premises. Landlord shall pay the expenses reasonably incurred by Tenant in connection with such substitution of Premises, including but not limited to costs of moving, door lettering, telephone relocation and reasonable quantities of new stationery.

Article 20. DEFAULTS AND REMEDIES

20.1 The occurrence of any one or more of the following shall constitute a default by Tenant:

(i) The failure by Tenant to pay the rent or make any other payment required to be made by Tenant hereunder as and when due where such failure continues for three (3) days.

(ii) The abandonment or vacation of the Premises by Tenant;

(iii) The failure by Tenant to observe or perform any other provision of this Lease to be observed or performed by Tenant, where such failure continues for thirty (30) days after written notice thereof by Landlord to Tenant; provided, however, that if the nature of such default is such that the same cannot reasonably be cured within such thirty (30) day period, Tenant shall not be deemed to be in default if Tenant shall within such period commence such cure and thereafter diligently prosecute the same to completion; and, provided further, that such thirty (30) day notice shall be in lieu of and not in addition to any notice required under Section 1161 of the California Code of Civil Procedure;

(iv) The entry of a decree or order for relief by a court having jurisdiction in the premises in respect of the Tenant in an involuntary case under the federal bankruptcy laws, as now or hereafter consituted, or any other applicable federal or state bankruptcy, insolvency or other similar law, or appointing a receiver, liquidator, assignee, custodian, trustee, sequestrator (or similar official) of the Tenant or for any substantial part of Tenant's property, or ordering the winding-up or liquidation of Tenant's affairs.

(v) The commencement by the Tenant of a voluntary case under the federal bankruptcy laws, as now constituted or hereafter amended, or any other applicable federal or state bankruptcy, insolvency or other similar law, or the consent by Tenant to the appointment of or taking possession by a receiver, liquidator, assignee, trustee, custodian, sequestrator (or other similar official) of the Tenant, or for any substantial part of Tenant's property, or the making by Tenant of any assignment for the benefit of creditors, or the failure of the Tenant generally to pay its debts as such debts become due, or the taking of action by the Tenant in furtherance of any of the foregoing.

(vi) Failure of Tenant to pay Tenant's debts as they mature.

6

20.2 In the event of any such default, then, in addition to any other remedies available to Landlord at law or in equity, Landlord shall have the immediate option to terminate this Lease and all rights of Tenant hereunder by giving Tenant written notice of such election to terminate. In the event Landlord shall elect to so terminate this Lease, Landlord may recover from Tenant:

(i) the worth at the time of award of any unpaid rent which has been earned at the time of such termination; plus

(ii) the worth at the time of award of any amount by which the unpaid rent which would have been earned after termination until the time of award exceeds the amount of such rental loss Tenant proves could have been reasonably avoided; plus

(iii) the worth at the time of award of the amount by which the unpaid rent for the balance of the term after the time of the award exceeds the amount of such rental loss that Tenant proves could be reasonably avoided; plus

(iv) any other amount necessary to compensate Landlord for all the detriment proximately caused by Tenant's failure to perform its obligations under this Lease or which in the ordinary course of things would be likely to result therefrom; and

(v) at Landlord's election, such other amounts in addition to or in lieu of the foregoing as may be permitted from time to time by applicable law.

The term "rent" as used herein shall be deemed to be and to mean the basic rent and all other sums required to be paid by Tenant pursuant to the terms of this Lease. All such sums, other than the basic annual rent, shall be computed on the basis of the average monthly amount thereof accruing during the 12-month period immediately prior to default, except that if it becomes necessary to compute such rental before such 12-month period has occurred, then on the basis of the average monthly amount during such shorter period. As used in subparagraphs (i) and (ii) above, the "worth at the time of award" shall be computed by allowing interest at the rate of ten percent (10%) per annum. As used in subparagraph (iii) above, the "worth at the time of award" shall be computed by discounting such amount at the discount rate of the Federal Reserve Bank of San Francisco at the time of award plus one percent (1%).

20.3 If Landlord terminates this Lease by reason of any such default, Landlord shall also have the right to re-enter the Premises and remove all persons and property from the Premises.

20.4 If Landlord does not elect to terminate this Lease on account of any such default as provided in Section 20.2 hereof, Landlord may from time to time, without terminating this Lease, enforce all of its rights and remedies under this Lease, including the right to recover all rent as it becomes due.

20.5 Landlord shall have the right, at Landlord's option, to suspend or discontinue the services specified in Article 5 hereof, or any thereof, during the continuance of any such default and any such suspension or discontinuance shall not be deemed or construed to be an eviction or ejection of Tenant.

20.6 If Tenant fails to make any payment of rent or other amount required to be made by Tenant hereunder as and when due, then, in addition to any other amounts recoverable by Landlord hereunder, Tenant shall pay Landlord a late charge in an amount equal to the greater of (i) Five Cents ($0.05) for each dollar past due, or (ii) Twenty-Five Dollars ($25.00) for each billing or additional billing on account of the past due amount, for the purpose of defraying the administrative costs and expenses incident to handling any delinquent payment hereunder, and the cost to Landlord of borrowed funds. Such late charge represents a fair and reasonable estimate by Landlord and Tenant of the fair average compensation for the loss that may be sustained by Landlord due to the failure of Tenant to make timely payments, the parties hereto recognizing that the exact amount of such extra costs and expenses is impossible or extremely impracticable to ascertain. Such late charge shall be due and payable on demand and the acceptance thereof by Landlord shall in no event constitute a waiver of Tenant's default with respect to any such overdue amount, nor prevent Landlord from exercising any of the other rights and remedies contained herein.

Article 21.   SURRENDER OF PREMISES; REMOVAL OF PROPERTY

21.1 The voluntary or other surrender of this Lease by Tenant, or a mutual termination thereof, shall not work a merger, and shall at the option of Landlord, operate as an assignment to it of any or all subleases or subtenancies affecting the Premises.

21.2 Upon the expiration of the term of this Lease, or upon any earlier termination of this Lease, Tenant shall quit and surrender possession of the Premises to Landlord in as good order and condition as the same are now or hereafter may be improved by Landlord or Tenant, reasonable wear and tear and repairs which are Landlord's obligation excepted, and shall, without expense to Landlord, remove or cause to be removed from the Premises all debris and rubbish, all furniture, equipment, business and trade fixtures, free-standing cabinet work, movable partitions and other articles of personal property owned by Tenant or installed or placed by Tenant at its expense in the Premises, and all similar articles of any other persons claiming under Tenant unless Landlord exercises its option to have any subleases or subtenancies assigned to it, and Tenant shall repair all damage to the Premises resulting from such removal.

21.3 Whenever Landlord shall re-enter the Premises as provided in Article 20 hereof, or as otherwise provided in this Lease, any property of Tenant not removed by Tenant upon the expiration of the term of this Lease (or within forty-eight (48) hours after a termination by reason of Tenant's default), as provided in this Lease, shall be considered abandoned and Landlord may remove any or all of such items and dispose of the same in any manner or store the same in a public warehouse or elsewhere for the account and at the expense and risk of Tenant, and if Tenant shall fail to pay the cost of storing any such property after it has been stored for a period of thirty (30) days or more, Landlord may sell any or all of such property at public or private sale, in such manner and at such times and places as Landlord, in its sole discretion, may deem proper, without notice to or demand upon Tenant for the payment of all or any part of such charges or the removal of any such property. Landlord shall apply the proceeds of such sale first, to the cost and expense of such sale, including reasonable attorneys' fees actually incurred; second, to the payment of the cost of or charges for storing any such property; third, to the payment of any other sums of money which may then or thereafter be due to Landlord from Tenant under any of the terms hereof; and fourth, the balance, if any, to Tenant.

21.4 All fixtures, equipment, alterations, additions, improvements and/or appurtenances attached to or built into the Premises prior to or during the term hereof, whether by Landlord at its expense or at the expense of Tenant or both, shall be and remain part of the Premises and shall not be removed by Tenant at the end of the term hereof unless otherwise expressly provided for in this Lease or unless such removal is required by Landlord pursuant to the provisions of Article 8 hereof. Such fixtures, equipment, alterations, additions, improvements and/or appurtenances shall include, without limitation, floor coverings, drapes, paneling, molding, doors, vaults (exclusive of vault doors), plumbing systems, electrical systems, lighting systems, silencing equipment, communication systems, all fixtures and outlets for the systems mentioned above and for all telephone, radio, telegraph and television purposes, and any special flooring or ceiling installations.

Article 22.   **WAIVER OF DAMAGES FOR RE-ENTRY**

Tenant hereby waives all claims for damages that may be caused by Landlord's re-entering and taking possession of the Premises or removing and storing the property of Tenant as herein provided, and Tenant shall indemnify and hold harmless Landlord therefrom, and no such re-entry shall be considered or construed to be a forcible entry.

Article 23.   **COSTS OF SUIT**

23.1 If Tenant or Landlord shall bring any action for any relief against the other, declaratory or otherwise, arising out of or under this Lease, including any suit by Landlord for the recovery of rent or possession of the Premises, the losing party shall pay the successful party a reasonable sum for attorneys' fees in such suit and such attorneys' fees shall be deemed to have accrued on the commencement of such action and shall be paid whether or not such action is prosecuted to judgment.

23.2 Should Landlord, without fault on Landlord's part, be made party to any litigation instituted by Tenant or by any third party against Tenant, or by or against any person holding under or using the Premises by license of Tenant, or for the foreclosure of any lien for labor or material furnished to or for Tenant or any such other person or otherwise arising out of or resulting from any action or transaction of Tenant or of any such other person, Tenant shall indemnify and hold harmless Landlord from and against any judgment rendered against Landlord or the Premises or any part thereof, and all costs and expenses, including reasonable attorneys' fees, incurred by Landlord in or in connection with such litigation.

Article 24.   **HOLDING OVER**

If Tenant holds over after the term hereof, without the express written consent of the Landlord, such tenancy shall be from month to month only, and not a renewal hereof or an extension for any further term, and in such case basic monthly rent shall be payable at the rate of one hundred fifty percent (150%) of the rent specified in Article 2 hereof, additional rent shall be payable in accordance with Article 3 hereof, and such month to month tenancy shall be subject to every other term, covenant and agreement contained herein. Nothing contained in this Article 24 shall be construed as consent by Landlord to any holding over by Tenant and Landlord expressly reserves the right to require Tenant to surrender possession of the Premises to Landlord as provided in Article 21 hereof upon the expiration of the term of this Lease or other termination of this Lease.

Article 25.   **SUBORDINATION**

This Lease is and at all times shall be subject and subordinate to any ground or underlying leases, mortgages, trust deeds or like encumbrances, which may now or hereafter affect the real property of which the Premises are a part, and to all renewals, modifications, consolidations, replacements and extensions of any such lease, mortgage, trust deed or like encumbrance. This clause shall be self-operative and no further instrument of subordination shall be required by any ground or underlying lessee or by any mortgagee or beneficiary, affecting any lease or the real property of which the Premises are a part. In confirmation of such subordination, Tenant shall execute promptly any certificate that Landlord may request. The subordination of this Lease to any such lease, mortgage, trust deed or like encumbrance shall, however, be subject to the following:

(i) In the event of the sale of the Building upon foreclosure or upon the exercise of a power of sale, or by transfer in lieu of foreclosure or such exercise, Tenant will upon written request attorn to the purchaser and recognize the purchaser, or transferee, as the Landlord under this Lease.

(ii) Notwithstanding such subordination, Tenant's right to quiet possession of the Premises shall not be disturbed so long as Tenant shall pay the rent and observe and perform all of the provisions of this Lease to be observed and performed by Tenant unless this Lease is terminated pursuant to specific provisions relating thereto contained herein.

Article 26.   **ESTOPPEL CERTIFICATES**

Tenant shall at any time and from time to time upon not less than twenty (20) days' prior notice by Landlord, execute, acknowledge and deliver to Landlord a statement in writing certifying that this Lease is unmodified and in full force and effect (or if there have been modifications, that the same is in full force and effect as modified and stating the modifications), and the dates to which the basic rent, additional rent and other charges have been paid in advance, if any, and stating whether or not to the best knowledge of Tenant, Landlord is in default in the performance of any covenant, agreement or condition contained in this Lease and, if so, specifying each such default of which Tenant may have knowledge. Any such statement delivered pursuant to this Section may be relied upon by any prospective purchaser of the fee of the Building or any mortgagee, ground lessor or other like encumbrancer thereof or any assignee of any such encumbrancer upon the Building.

Article 27.   **ACCESS; CHANGES IN BUILDING FACILITIES; NAME**

27.1 All portions of the Building except the inside surfaces of all walls, windows and doors bounding the Premises (including exterior building walls, core corridor walls and doors and any core corridor entrance), and any space in or adjacent to the Premises used for shafts, stacks, pipes, conduits, fan rooms, ducts, electric or other utilities, sinks or other building facilities, and the use thereof, as well as access thereto through the Premises for the purposes of operation, maintenance, decoration and repair, are reserved to Landlord.

27.2 Tenant shall permit Landlord to install, use and maintain pipes, ducts and conduits within the demising walls, bearing columns and ceilings of the Premises.

27.3 Landlord reserves the right, at any time, without incurring any liability to Tenant therefor, to make such changes in or to the Building and the fixtures and equipment thereof, as well as in or to the street entrances, halls, passages, concourse, elevators, escalators, stairways and other improvements thereof, as it may deem necessary or desirable.

27.4 Landlord may adopt any name for the Building and Landlord reserves the right to change the name and/or address of the Building at any time.

8

Article 28.   **RULES AND REGULATIONS**

The Rules and Regulations attached hereto as Exhibit "B" are by this reference incorporated herein and made a part hereof. Tenant shall abide by and comply with, and cause its employees, agents and invitees to abide by and comply with, said Rules and Regulations and any reasonable and non-discriminatory amendments, modifications and/or additions thereto as may hereafter be adopted by Landlord. Landlord shall not be liable to Tenant for any violation of such Rules and Regulations by any other tenant.

Article 29.   **WORK LETTER**

If Landlord or Tenant is required to perform work in connection with this Lease, the Premises shall be finished in accordance with a separate agreement of the parties executed contemporaneously herewith, which such agreement is entitled and is referred to herein as the "Work Letter."

Article 30.   **RIGHT OF LANDLORD TO PERFORM**

All covenants and agreements to be performed by Tenant under any of the terms of this Lease shall be performed by Tenant at Tenant's sole cost and expense and without any abatement of rent. If Tenant shall fail to pay any sum of money, other than rent, required to be paid by it hereunder or shall fail to perform any other act on its part to be performed hereunder, and such failure shall continue beyond any applicable grace period set forth in Article 20 hereof, Landlord may, but shall not be obligated so to do, and without waiving or releasing Tenant from any obligations of Tenant, make any such payment or perform any such other act on Tenant's part to be made or performed hereunder. Tenant shall, promptly and upon demand therefor by Landlord, reimburse Landlord for all sums so paid by Landlord and all necessary incidental costs, together with interest thereon at the rate of ten percent (10%) per annum from the date of such payment by Landlord, and Landlord shall have the same rights and remedies in the event of the failure by Tenant to pay such amounts as Landlord would have in the event of a default by Tenant in the payment of rent.

Article 31.   **NOTICES**

All notices which Landlord or Tenant may be required, or may desire, to serve on the other may be served, as an alternative to personal service, by mailing the same by registered or certified mail, postage prepaid, addressed to Landlord at the address for Landlord set forth on the signature page hereof and to Tenant at the address for Tenant set forth on the signature page hereof, or, from and after the Commencement Date, to Tenant at the Premises whether or not Tenant has departed from, abandoned or vacated the Premises, or addressed to such other address or addresses as either Landlord or Tenant may from time to time designate to the other in writing.

Article 32.   **QUIET ENJOYMENT**

Tenant, upon paying the basic rent, additional rent and other charges herein provided for and observing and keeping the covenants, agreements and conditions of this Lease on its part to be kept, shall lawfully and quietly hold, occupy and enjoy the Premises during the term of this Lease without hindrance or molestation of anyone lawfully claiming by, through or under Landlord, subject, however, to all of the other terms and provisions of this Agreement.

Article 33.   **BROKERS**

Unless otherwise agreed in writing, if Tenant has dealt with any person or real estate broker in respect to leasing or renting space in the Building, Tenant shall be solely responsible for the payment of any fee due said person or firm and Tenant shall hold Landlord free and harmless from and against any liability in respect thereto.

Article 34.   **INTERPRETATION**

34.1 The words "Landlord" and "Tenant," as used herein, shall include the plural as well as the singular. Words used in neuter gender include the masculine and feminine and words in the masculine or feminine gender include the neuter. The headings or titles to the articles of this Lease are not a part of this Lease and shall have no effect upon the construction or interpretation of any part thereof.

34.2 If there be more than one Tenant, the obligations hereunder imposed upon Tenant shall be joint and several.

34.3 Subject to the provisions of Article 15 hereof relating to assingment and subletting, this Lease is intended to and does bind the heirs, executors, administrators, successors and assigns of any and all of the parties hereto.

34.4 Time is of the essence of this Lease.

34.5 This Lease shall be governed by and interpreted in accordance with the laws of the State of California.

34.6 If any term or provision of this Lease, the deletion of which would not adversely affect the receipt of any material benefit by either party hereunder, shall be held invalid or unenforceable to any extent, the remainder of this Lease shall not be affected thereby and each term and provision of this Lease shall be valid and enforceable to the fullest extent permitted by law.

34.7 The waiver by Landlord or Tenant of any breach of any term, covenant or condition herein contained shall not be deemed to be a waiver of such term, covenant or condition as to any subsequent breach of the same or any other term, covenant or condition herein contained. The subsequent acceptance of rent by Landlord shall not be deemed to be a waiver of any preceding breach by Tenant of any term, covenant or condition of this Lease, other than the failure of Tenant to pay the particular rent so accepted, regardless of Landlord's knowledge of such preceding breach at the time of acceptance of such rent.

34.8 This instrument along with any exhibits and attachments or other documents affixed hereto or referred to herein constitutes the entire and exclusive agreement between Landlord and Tenant relating to the Premises, and this agreement and said exhibits and attachments and other documents may be altered, amended or revoked only by an instrument in writing signed by the party to be charged thereby. All prior or contemporaneous oral agreements, understandings and/or practices relative to the leasing of the Premises are merged in or revoked by this agreement.

34.9 This Lease may be executed in one or more counterparts, each of which shall constitute an original and all of which shall be one and the same agreement.

Submission of this Lease for examination, even though executed by Tenant, shall not bind Landlord in any manner and no lease or other obligation on the part of Landlord shall arise, until this Lease is executed and delivered by Landlord to Tenant.

IN WITNESS WHEREOF, the parties hereto have executed this Lease as of the date first above written.

Landlord: Tenant:

SUBWAY TERMINAL BUILDING   _____

                                                             _____

                                                             _____

                                                             _____

By _____   By _____

By _____   By _____

Address: Address:

417 South Hill Street   _____
Los Angeles, California   _____
90013   _____

EXHIBIT B

RULES AND REGULATIONS ATTACHED

TO AND MADE A PART OF OFFICE SPACE LEASE

1

The sidewalks, entrances, passages, courts, elevators, vestibules, stairways, corridors or halls shall not be obstructed or used for any purpose other than ingress or egress. The halls, passages, entrances, elevators, stairways, balconies and roof are not for the use of the general public, and Landlord shall in all cases retain the right to control or prevent access thereto by all persons whose presence in the judgment of Landlord shall be prejudicial to the safety, character, reputation or interests of the Building and its tenants, provided that nothing herein contained shall be construed to prevent such access by persons with whom the tenant normally deals in the ordinary course of its business unless such persons are engaged in illegal activities. Tenant shall not enter the mechanical rooms, air handler rooms, electrical closets, janitorial closets, or go upon the roof of the Building without the prior written consent of Landlord.

2

No awnings or other projections shall be attached to the outside walls of the Building and no window shades, blinds, drapes or other window coverings shall be hung in the Premises (other than as specified in the Work Letter, if any), without the prior written consent of Landlord. Except as otherwise specifically approved by Landlord, all electrical ceiling fixtures hung in offices or spaces along the perimeter of the Building must be fluorescent, of a quality, type, number, design and bulb color approved by Landlord.

3

No sign, picture, advertisement or notice shall be inscribed, exhibited, painted or affixed by any tenant on any part of, or so as to be seen from the outside of, the Premises or the Building without the prior written consent of Landlord. No obstructions or advertising devices of any kind whatsoever shall be placed in front of or in the passageways, hallways, lobbies or corridors of the Building by Tenant. In the event of the violation of the foregoing by any tenant, Landlord may remove the same without any liability, and may charge the expense incurred in such removal to the tenant violating this rule. Interior signs on doors and directory tablet shall be inscribed, painted or affixed for each tenant by Landlord at the expense of such tenant, and shall be of a size, color and style acceptable to Landlord.

4

The toilets, wash basins and other plumbing fixtures shall not be used for any purpose other than those for which they were constructed, and no sweepings, rubbish, rags or other substances shall be thrown therein. All damage resulting from any misuse of such fixtures shall be borne by the tenant who, or whose servants, employees, agents, visitors or licensees, shall have caused the same.

5

No tenant shall mark, paint, drill into, or in any way deface any part of the Premises or the Building. No boring, cutting or stringing of wires or laying of linoleum or other similar floor coverings shall be permitted without the prior written consent of Landlord and then only as Landlord may direct.

6

No bicycles, vehicles or animals of any kind shall be brought into or kept in or about the Premises and no cooking shall be done or permitted by any tenant on the Premises without the prior written consent of Landlord except that the preparation of coffee, tea, hot chocolate and similar items for the tenant and its employees and business visitors shall be permitted. No tenant shall cause or permit any unusual or objectionable odors to escape from the Premises.

7

The Premises shall not be used for manufacturing or for the storage of merchandise except as such storage may be incidental to the use of the Premises for general office purposes. No tenant shall occupy or permit any portion of the Premises to be occupied as an office for a public stenographer or typist, or for the manufacture or direct sale of liquor, narcotics, or tobacco in any form, or as a medical office, or as a barber shop, manicure shop or employment agency. No tenant shall engage or pay any employees on the Premises except those actually working for such tenant on the Premises nor advertise for laborers giving an address at the Premises. The Premises shall not be used for lodging or sleeping or for any immoral or illegal purposes.

8

No tenant shall make, or permit to be made, any unseemly or disturbing noises, sounds or vibrations, or otherwise disturb or interfere with occupants of this or neighboring buildings or premises or those having business with them whether by the use of any musical instrument, radio, phonograph, unusual noise, or in any other way.

9

No tenant shall throw anything out of doors or down the public corridors, stairways or other common areas of the Building.

10

No tenant shall at any time bring or keep in the Premises any inflammable, combustible or explosive fluid, chemical or substance. No tenant shall do or permit anything to be done in the Premises, or bring or keep anything therein, which shall in any way increase the rate of fire insurance on the Building or on the property kept therein, or obstruct or interfere with the rights of other tenants, or in any way injure or annoy them, or conflict with the regulations of the Fire Department or the fire laws, or with any insurance policy upon the Building or any part thereof, or with any rules and ordinances established by the Board of Health or other governmental authority.

B-1

11

No additional locks or bolts of any kind shall be placed upon any of the doors or windows by any tenant, nor shall any tenant make any changes in existing locks or the mechanisms thereof. Each tenant must, upon the termination of its tenancy, give Landlord the combination to all combination locks on safes, safe cabinets and vaults and restore to Landlord all keys of stores, offices, and toilet rooms, either furnished to, or otherwise procured by such tenant, and in the event of the loss of any key so furnished, such tenant shall pay to Landlord the cost of replacing the same or of changing the lock or locks opened by such lost key if Landlord shall deem it necessary to make such change.

12

All removals, or the carrying in or out of any safes, freight, furniture, or bulky matter of any description must take place at the time and in the manner which Landlord may determine from time to time. The moving of safes or other fixtures or bulky matter of any kind must be made upon previous notice to the manager of the Building and under his supervision, and the persons employed by any tenant for such work must be acceptable to Landlord. Landlord reserves the right to inspect all safes, freight or other bulky articles to be brought into the Building and to exclude from the Building all safes, freight or other bulky articles which violate any of these Rules and Regulations or the lease of which these Rules and Regulations are a part. Landlord reserves the right to prohibit or impose conditions upon the installation in the Premises of heavy objects which might overload the Building floors.

13

No tenant shall purchase or otherwise obtain for use in the Premises water, ice, towel, vending machine, barbering, bootblacking, or other like services, or purchase or otherwise obtain janitorial, maintenance or other like services, except from persons authorized by Landlord, and at hours and under regulations fixed by Landlord.

14

No tenant shall engage in advertising which, in Landlord's opinion, tends to impair the reputation of the Building or its desirability as an office building.

15

Landlord reserves the right to exclude from the Building at all times other than the reasonable hours of generally recognized business days determined by Landlord all persons who do not present a pass to the Building signed by Landlord. Landlord shall furnish passes to persons for whom any tenant requests the same in writing. Each tenant shall be responsible for all persons for whom he requests passes and shall be liable to Landlord for all acts of such persons.

16

All doors opening onto public corridors shall be kept closed, and, during non-business hours, locked, except when in use for ingress or egress.

17

The requirements of tenants will be attended to only upon application to the Office of the Building or to such other place as Landlord shall from time to time direct.

18

Canvassing, soliciting and peddling in the Building are prohibited and each tenant shall cooperate to prevent the same.

19

All office equipment and any other device of any electrical or mechanical nature shall be placed by tenant in the Premises in settings approved by Landlord, to absorb or prevent any vibration, noise or annoyance.

20

No air conditioning unit, engine, boiler, machinery, heating unit or other similar apparatus shall be installed or used by any tenant without the prior written consent of Landlord, and then only as Landlord may direct.

21

There shall not be used in any space, or in the public halls of the Building, either by any tenant or others, any hand trucks except those equipped with rubber tires and side guards.

22

Landlord will direct electricians as to where and how telephone and telegraph wires are to be introduced. No boring or cutting for wires or stringing of wires will be allowed without the prior written consent of Landlord, and then only as Landlord may direct. The location of telephones, call boxes and other office equipment affixed to the premises shall be subject to the approval of Landlord.

23

No person shall be allowed to transport or carry beverages, food, food containers, etc., on any passenger elevators except in such manner as Landlord may from time to time prescribe.

24

Tenants shall cooperate with Landlord in obtaining maximum effectiveness of the cooling system by closing drapes and other window coverings when the sun's rays fall on windows of the Premises. Tenant shall not obstruct, alter or in any way impair the efficient operation of Landlord's heating, ventilating and air conditioning, electrical, fire, safety or lighting systems. Tenant shall not tamper with or change the setting of any thermostats or temperature control valves.

25

No explosives or firearms shall be brought into the Premises or the Building without the prior written consent of Landlord.

B-2

26

The work necessary to do any repairs or maintenance required pursuant to Article 11 or to make any alterations, improvements or additions to the Premises to which Landlord may consent pursuant to Article 8 shall be done by employees or contractors employed by Landlord. No person or contractor not employed by Landlord shall be used to perform window washing, cleaning, decorating, repair or any other work in the Premises without the prior written consent of Landlord.

27

Subject to the provisions of the Lease, heat and air conditioning will be provided from 8 a.m. until 6 p.m., Monday through Friday (holidays excepted) whenever such heat or air conditioning shall, in Landlord's judgment, be required for the comfortable occupation of the building. Should Tenant desire heat or air conditioning at other times, Landlord will endeavor, at Tenant's expense, to accommodate Tenant's request to the extent that Landlord, in his sole discretion, deems feasible. Requests for such service must be submitted to Landlord by 1:00 p.m. of the business day prior to the date on which service is to be provided.

28

The bulletin board or directory of the building will be provided exclusively for the display of the name and location of tenants only; and Landlord reserves the right to exclude any other names therefrom, and also to make a charge of $3.50 for each and every name in addition to the name of Tenant placed upon such bulletin board or directory.

29

On weekends and legal holidays, and on other days between the hours of 6 p.m. and 8 a.m. the following day, access to the building, or to the halls, corridors, elevators or stairways in the building, or to the Premises may be refused unless the person seeking access is known to the person or employee of the building in charge and has a pass or is properly identified. The Landlord shall in no case be liable for damages for any error with regard to the admission to or exclusion from the building of any person. In case of invasion, mob, riot, public excitement, or other commotion, the Landlord reserves the right to prevent access to the building during the continuance of the same by closing the door or otherwise, for the safety of the Tenant and protection of property in the building and the building. Tenant agrees that all of its employees, officers and guests shall comply with all security regulations established from time to time by Landlord.

30

Landlord reserves the right to exclude or expel from the Building any person who, in the judgment of Landlord, is intoxicated or under the influence of liquor or drugs, or who shall in any manner do any act in violation of any of the rules and regulations of the Building.

31

All parking ramps and areas, pedestrian walkways, and plaza and other public areas forming a part of the Building, if any, shall be under the sole and absolute control of Landlord, who shall have the exclusive right to regulate and control these areas.

STANDARD INDUSTRIAL LEASE

THIS LEASE, is executed at Los Angeles, California, this day of , 19 by and between

and

(herein called the "Landlord") (herein called the "Tenant").

1. **DESCRIPTION OF PREMISES.** Landlord hereby leases to Tenant and Tenant hires from Landlord for the term, at the rental and upon all of the terms, covenants and conditions set forth herein, those premises situated in the City of , County of , State of California, commonly known as , which premises are more fully described in Exhibit "A" attached hereto (hereinafter referred to as the "Leased Premises"), located in the building, indicated on Exhibit "A" attached hereto, consisting of approximately square feet (hereinafter referred to sometimes as the "Building").

2. **TERM.** 2.1 The term of this Lease shall be for commencing on the day of , 19 , and ending on the day of , 19

2.2 **Delay in Commencement.** Notwithstanding said commencement date, if for any reason Landlord cannot deliver possession of the Leased Premises to Tenant on said date, Landlord shall not be subject to any liability therefor, nor shall such failure affect the validity of this Lease or the obligations of Tenant hereunder or extend the term hereof, but in such case Tenant shall not be obligated to pay rent until possession of the Leased Premises is tendered to Tenant. If Tenant occupies the Leased Premises prior to said commencement date, such occupancy shall be subject to all provisions hereof, and such occupancy shall not advance the termination date. Provided, however, notwithstanding all of the foregoing, if possession is not delivered by the Landlord to Tenant within six (6) months from said commencement date, either party may at its option within ten (10) days thereafter, by written notice to the other, terminate this Lease, all without liability each unto the other.

3. **RENT.** 3.1 Tenant agrees to pay as rent to Landlord at such place as Landlord may designate, without offset, deduction, prior notice or demand of any kind or nature, and Landlord agrees to accept as rent for the Leased Premises, the total sum of Dollars ($), lawful money of the United States, payable in equal monthly installments of Dollars ($), payable in advance on the first day of each month during the term of this Lease. The sum of Dollars ($) is hereby acknowledged as received by the Landlord concurrently with the execution of this Lease as rent for the first months' rental. Rent for any period during the term hereof which is for less than one month shall be a prorata portion of the monthly installment.

3.2 In addition to the rent payable under paragraph 3.1 above, the rental payable during each calendar year of the term hereof, subsequent to the 31st day of December of the calendar year in which the lease term commences as above provided (the base year), shall be increased by an amount equal to any increase in direct expenses, as hereinafter defined, paid or incurred by Landlord with respect to the Leased Premises for the ensuing calendar year, over the direct expenses incurred for the base year based upon that ratio which the square footage of the Leased Premises bears to the total square footage of the Building. Landlord shall endeavor to give Tenant, on or before the first day of March of each year after the base year, and on or before the first day of March of each year thereafter, statements of the increase in rent payable by Tenant hereunder, but failure to give such statements by said dates shall not constitute a waiver by Landlord of its right to require an increase in rent. In the event of an increase in direct expenses, the amount thereof shall be divided into twelve (12) equal monthly installments and Tenant shall pay to Landlord, concurrently with the regular monthly rent payment next due following the receipt of such statement, an amount equal to one (1) monthly installment multiplied by the number of months from January in the calendar year to the month of such payment, both inclusive. Subsequent installments shall be payable concurrently with the regular monthly rent payments for the balance of that calendar year. In the event this Lease shall terminate or come to an end on any date other than the last day of a calendar year, the amount of increase in rent by Tenant in the calendar year in which the Lease terminates or comes to an end shall be prorated.

3.3 The term "direct expenses" as used herein shall include any and all direct costs of operation and maintenance as determined by standard accounting practices and shall include the following costs by way of illustration but not limitation: Property management fees and costs, real property taxes and assessments and other governmental charges of any kind or nature assessed or imposed upon the Leased Premises or portions thereof, rent taxes, gross receipt taxes (whether assessed against the Landlord or the Tenant and collected by the Landlord, or both), water and sewer charges, insurance premiums, utilities, janitorial services, labor, air conditioning and heating (including maintenance and repair of said systems), supplies, materials, equipment, tools, elevator maintenance and repairs, common parking area maintenance (if any, including repairs, insurance and regulation), landscaping area maintenance, and maintenance of all other common areas. The term "direct expenses" shall not include depreciation on the Building or equipment therein, interest, executive salaries or real estate brokers' commissions.

3.4 In addition, Tenant agrees to pay, as rental for the Leased Premises, within ten (10) days of Landlord's demand therefor unless otherwise provided herein, all other amounts which Tenant shall be obliged to pay Landlord by reason of the provisions of this Lease.

4. **SECURITY DEPOSIT.** Tenant shall deposit with Landlord upon execution hereof Dollars ($) as security for Tenant's faithful performance of Tenant's obligations hereunder. If Tenant fails to pay rent or other charges due hereunder, or otherwise defaults with respect to any provision of this Lease, Landlord may use, apply or retain all or any portion of said deposit for the payment of any rent or other charge in default or for the payment of any other sum to which Landlord may become obligated by reason of Tenant's default, or to compensate Landlord for any loss or damage which Landlord may suffer thereby. If Landlord so uses or applies all or any portion of said deposit, Tenant shall within ten (10) days after written demand therefor deposit cash with Landlord in an amount sufficient to restore said deposit to the full amount hereinabove stated and Tenant's failure to do so shall be a material breach of this Lease. Landlord shall not be required to keep said deposit separate from its general accounts. If Tenant performs all of Tenant's obligations hereunder, said deposit, or so much thereof as has not theretofore been applied by Landlord, shall be returned, without payment of interest or other increment for its use, to Tenant (or, at Landlord's option, to the last assignee, if any, of Tenant's interest hereunder) at the expiration of the term hereof, and after Tenant has vacated the premises.

IGL 74-1

5. **USE OF PREMISES.** 5.1 Use of the Leased Premises and all portions thereof shall be used and occupied solely and only for and for no other purpose or purposes without Landlord's prior written consent. Further, Tenant's use of the Leased Premises or any portion thereof shall be in full compliance with all covenants, conditions or restrictions affecting all or any portion of the Leased Premises.

5.2 **Compliance With Law.** Tenant shall, at Tenant's expense, comply promptly with all applicable statues, ordinances, rules, regulations, orders and requirements in effect during the term hereof regulating the use by Tenant of the Leased Premises. Tenant shall not use or permit the use of the Leased Premises in any manner that will tend to create waste or a nuisance or, if there shall be more than one tenant of the building containing the Leased Premises, which shall tend to disturb such other tenants. Tenant shall not do or permit anything to be done in or about the Leased Premises, or bring ot keep anything in the Leased Premises that will in any way increase the fire insurance upon the Building. Tenant shall not cause, maintain or permit any outside storage on or about the Leased Premises.

5.3 **Condition of Leased Premises.** Tenant hereby accepts the Leased Premises in their condition existing as of the date of the execution hereof, subject to all applicable zoning, municipal, county and state laws, ordinances and regulations governing and regulating the use of the Leased Premises, and accepts this Lease subject thereto and to all matters disclosed thereby and by any exhibits attached hereto. Tenant acknowledges that neither Landlord nor Landlord's agent has made any representation or warranty as to the suitability of the Leased Premises for the conduct of Tenant's business.

6. **UTILITIES.** Tenant shall pay for all water, gas, heat, light, power, trash and refuse removal, telephone service and all other services furnished the Leased Premises. If such items are not separately metered or charged to the Leased Premises, tenant shall pay its proportionate share as determined by the Landlord. Landlord further reserves the right to install separate meters for any public utility servicing the Leased Premises for which a meter is not presently installed, in which event Tenant shall make payments when due directly to the public utility involved. When water service is not separately metered, Tenant shall pay to Landlord for restroom water service the sum of Dollars ($) per month as additional rent. If Tenant uses the water service for other than restroom purposes, the monthly water charge may, at the option of the Landlord, be increased accordingly.

7. **MAINTENANCE, REPAIRS AND ALTERATIONS.** 7.1 **Tenant's Obligations.** Tenant shall during the term of this Lease keep in good order, condition and repair, the Leased Premises and every part thereof, structural or non-structural, and all adjacent sidewalks, landscaping, driveways, parking lots, fences and signs located in the areas which are adjacent to and included with the Leased Premises. Landlord shall incur no expense nor have any obligation of any kind whatsoever in connection with maintenance of the Leased Premises, and Tenant expressly waives the benefits of any statute now or hereafter in effect which would otherwise afford Tenant the right to make repairs at Landlord's expennse or to terminate this Lease because of Landlord's failure to keep the Leased Premises in good order, condition and repair. Landlord agrees to keep and maintain at Landlord's sole expense the exterior walls and roofs of the Building. Tenant shall, at its sole cost, keep and maintain all heating and air conditioning, utilities, fixtures and mechanical equipment used by Tenant in good order, condition and repair and furnish all expendables (lights, bulbs, paper goods, soap, etc.) used in the Leased Premises during the term of this Lease.

7.2 **Landlord's Rights.** If Tenant fails to perform Tenant's obligations under this Paragraph 7, Landlord may at its option (but shall not be required to) enter upon the Leased Premises, after ten (10) days' prior written notice to Tenant, and put the same in good order, condition and repair, and the cost thereof, together with interest thereon at the rate of 10 percent per annum shall become due and payable as additional rental to Landlord, together with Tenant's next rental installment.

7.3 **Surrender.** On the last day of the term hereof, or on any sooner termination, Tenant shall surrender the Leased Premises to Landlord in the same condition as when received, broom clean, ordinary wear and tear excepted. Tenant shall repair any damage to the Leased Premises occasioned by the removal of Tenant's trade fixtures, furnishings and equipment which repair shall include the patching and filling of holes and repair of structural damage.

7.4 **Alterations and Additions.** (a) Tenant shall not, without Landlord's prior written consent, make any alterations, improvements, additions, or utility installations in, on or about the Leased Premises.

(b) Tenant shall pay, when due, all claims for labor or materials furnished or alleged to have been furnished to or for Tenant at or for use in the Leased Premises, which claims are or may be secured by any mechanics' or materialmen's lien against the Leased Premises or any interest therein. Tenant shall give Landlord not less than ten (10) days' notice prior to the commencement of any work in the Leased Premises, and Landlord shall have the right to post notices of non-responsibility in or on the Leased Premises as provided by law.

7.5 Notwithstanding any of the foregoing, Tenant may, upon written consent of Landlord, install trade fixtures, machinery or other trade equipment in the Leased Premises.

8. **FIRE INSURANCE AND HAZARDS.** 8.1 No use shall be made or permitted to be made of the Leased Premises, nor acts done, which will increase the existing rate of insurance upon the Building or cause the cancellation of any insurance policy covering the Building, or any part thereof, nor shall Tenant sell, or permit to be kept, used or sold, in or about the Leased Premises, any article which may be prohibited by the standard form of fire insurance policies. Tenant shall, at its sole cost and expense, comply with any and all requirements pertaining to the Leased Premises of any insurance organization or company necessary for the maintenance of reasonable fire

and public liability insurance covering the Leased Premises, Building and appurtenances. Tenant agrees to pay to Landlord as additional rent any increase in premiums on policies which may be carried by Landlord on the Leased Premises covering damages to the Building and loss of rent caused by fire and the perils normally included in extended coverage above the rates for the least hazardous type of occupancy for industrial warehousing, office and distribution operations.

8.2 Tenant shall maintain in full force and effect on all of its fixtures and equipment in the Leased Premises a policy or policies of fire and extended coverage insurance with standard coverage endorsement to the extent of at least eighty percent (80 percent) of their insurable value. During the term of this Lease the proceeds from any such policy or policies of insurance shall be used for the repair or replacement of the fixtures and equipment so insured. Landlord shall have no interest in the insurance upon Tenant's equipment and fixtures and will sign all documents necessary or proper in connection with the settlement of any claim or loss by Tenant. Landlord will not carry insurance on Tenant's possessions. Tenant shall furnish Landlord with a certificate of such policy and whenever required shall satisfy Landlord that such policy is in full force and effect.

9. **LIABILITY INSURANCE.** 9.1 Tenant, at its own expense, shall provide and keep in force with companies acceptable to Landlord public liability insurance for the benefit of Landlord and Tenant jointly against liability for bodily injury and property damage in the amount of not less than Two Hundred Fifty Thousand Dollars ($250,000) in respect to injuries to or death of any person, and in an amount of not less than Five Hundred Thousand Dollars ($500,000) in respect to injuries to or death of more than one person in any one occurence, and in the amount of not less than Fifty Thousand Dollars ($50,000) per occurance in respect to damage to property, such limits to be for any greater amounts as may be reasonably indicated by circumstances from time to time existing. Tenant shall furnish Landlord with a certificate of such policy and whenever required shall satisfy Landlord that such policy is in full force and effect. Such policy shall name Landlord as an additional insured and shall be primary and non-contributing with any insurance carried by Landlord. The policy shall further provide that it shall not be cancelled or altered without 30 days' prior notice to Landlord. Insurance required hereunder shall be written by companies rated AAA or better in "Best's Insurance Guide".

9.2 In the event Tenant fails to provide or maintain the required insurance as provided under this Lease, or to deliver to Landlord the required proof thereof, Landlord at its option, but without obligation so to do, may upon five (5) days' notice to Tenant of its intention so to do, procure such insurance, and any sums expended by it to procure such insurance shall be repaid by Tenant as additional rent. Tenant shall promptly notify Landlord of all claims in excess of $1,000 made under any policy required to be maintained by Tenant under the terms of this Lease.

9.3 **Waiver of Subrogation.** Tenant and Landlord each hereby waive any and all rights of recovery against the other, or against the officers, employees, agents and representatives of the other, for loss of or damage to such waiving party or its property or the property of others under its control to the extent that such loss or damage is insured against under any insurance policy in force at the time of such loss or damage. The insuring party shall, upon obtaining the policies of insurance required hereunder, give notice to the insurance carrier or carriers that the foregoing mutual waiver of subrogation is contained in this Lease.

10. **INDEMNIFICATION.** 10.1 As a material part of the consideration for this Lease, Tenant hereby (a) assumes all risk of damage to property or injury to persons, in, on or about the Leased Premises and on the building arising from any cause and Tenant hereby waives all claims in respect thereof against Landlord; (b) agrees to indemnify, defend and hold Landlord harmless from and against any and all claims, loss, damage or liability arising from Tenant's use, occupation, or alteration of the Leased Premises, from the conduct of Tenant's business therein, or from any other activity, work or things done, permitted or suffered by Tenant in or about the Leased Premises or elsewhere; (c) any and all claims, loss, damage or liability arising from any breech or default in the performance of any of Tenant's obligations hereunder, or arising from any negligence of Tenant, or any of Tenant's agents, contractors, employees or invitees; and (d) all costs, attorney's fees, expenses and liabilities incurred in the defense of any claim, loss, damage or liability for which Tenant has agreed to indemnify Landlord or any action or proceeding brought thereon, whether or not an action or proceeding is brought and whether or not it is prosecuted to judgement. In the event that Landlord is ever made a party to any action or proceeding by reason of any matter for which Tenant has hereby agreed to indemnify Landlord, then Tenant, upon notice from Landlord, shall defend such action or proceeding on behalf of Landlord at Tenant's expense by counsel satisfactory to Landlord. If Landlord commences an action against Tenant to enforce any of the terms hereof or because of the breach by Tenant of any of the terms hereof, or for the recovery of any rent or other sum due hereunder, or for any unlawful detainer of said premises, Tenant shall pay to Landlord reasonable attorneys' fees and expenses, and the right to such attorneys' fees and expenses shall be deemed to have accrued on the commencement of such action and shall be enforceable whether or not such action is prosecuted to judgment. If Tenant breaches any term of this Lease, Landlord may employ an attorney or attorneys to protect Landlord's rights hereunder, and in the event of such employment following any breach by Tenant, Tenant shall pay Landlord reasonable attorney's fees and expenses incurred by Landlord, whether or not an action is actually commenced against Tenant by reason of breach. If Landlord breaches any term of this Lease, Tenant may employ an attorney or attorneys to protect Tenant's rights hereunder, and in the event of such employment following any breach by Landlord, Landlord shall pay Tenant's resonable attorneys' fees and expenses incurred by Tenant, whether or not an action is actually commenced against Landlord by reason of the breach.

10.2 **Exemption of Landlord From Liability.** Tenant hereby agrees that Landlord shall not be liable for injury to Tenant's business or any loss of income therefrom or for damage to the goods, wares, merchandise or other property of Tenant, Tenant's employees, invitees, customers, or any other person in or about the Leased Premises, nor shall Landlord be liable for injury to the person of Tenant, Tenant's employees, agents or contractors, whether such damage or injury is caused by or results from fire, steam, electricity, gas, water or rain, or from the breakage, leakage, obstruction or other defects of pipes, sprinklers, wires, appliances, plumbing, air conditioning or lighting fixtures, or from any other cause, whether the said damage or injury results from conditions arising upon the Leased Premises or upon other portions of the Building of which the Leased Premises are a part, or from other sources or places, and regardless of whether the cause of such damage or injury or the means of repairing the same is inaccessible to Tenant, Landlord shall not be liable for any damages arising from any act or neglect of any other tenant, if any, of the Building in which the Leased Premises are located. Landlord shall

IGL 74-2

have the right to replace, at the expense of Tenant, any and all plate and other glass damaged or broken from any cause whatsoever in or about demised premises. There shall be no allowance to Tenant for a diminution of rental value, and no liability on the part of Landlord by reason of inconvenience, annoyance or injury to business arising from the making of any repairs, alterations, decorations, additions or improvements in or to any portion of the Building or the Leased Premises, or in or to fixtures, appurtenances or equipment, and there shall be no liability upon Landlord for failure to make any repairs, alterations, decorations, additions, or improvements in or to any portion of the Building or the Leased Premises, or in or to fixtures, appurtenances or equipment or by reason of any act or neglect of any other tenant or occupant of the Building.

11. **AUCTIONS, SIGNS, LANDSCAPING.** Tenant shall not conduct or permit to be conducted any sale by auction on the Leased Premises. Landlord shall have the right to control landscaping and to approve the placing of signs and the size and quality of the same. Tenant shall make no alterations or additions to the Leased Premises or landscaping and shall place no exterior signs on the Leased Premises without the prior written consent of Landlord.

12. **ENTRY BY LANDLORD.** Tenant shall permit Landlord and Landlord's agents to enter the Leased Premises at all reasonable times for the purpose of inspecting the same or for the purpose of maintaining the Building, or for the purpose of making repairs, alterations or additions to any portion of the Building, including the erection and maintenance of such scaffolding, canopies, fences, and props as may be required, or for the purpose of posting notices of non-responsibility for alterations, additions, or repairs, or for the purpose of placing upon the Building any usual or ordinary "for sale" signs, without any rebate of rent and without any liability to Tenant for any loss of occupation or quiet enjoyment of the Leased Premises thereby occasioned; and shall permit Landlord at any time within thirty (30) days prior to the expiration of this Lease, to place upon the Leased Premises any usual or ordinary "to let" or "to lease" signs. For each of the aforesaid purposes, Landlord shall at all times have and retain a key with which to unlock all of the doors in, upon and about the Leased Premise, excluding Tenants vaults and safes. The Tenant shall not alter any lock or install a new or additional lock or any bolt on any door of the Leased Premises without prior written consent of the Landlord. If Landlord shall give its consent, the Tenant shall in each case furnish the Landlord with a key for any such lock.

13. **TAXES.** 13.1 Tenant shall pay before delinquency any and all taxes, assessments, license fees, and public charges levied, assessed or imposed and which become payable during the Lease upon Tenant's fixtures, furniture, appliances and personal property installed or located in the Leased Premises.

13.2 Tenant shall pay to Landlord upon demand as additional rent, that portion of all real estate taxes assessed during the term of this Lease in excess of the real estate taxes assessed for the fiscal year in which the Lease term commences. Tenant's liability shall be an equitable proportion of the real property taxes for all of the land and improvements included within the tax parcel containing the Leased Premises, such proportion to be determined by Landlord from the valuations assigned by the Assessor based upon the percentage which the square footage of the Leased Premises bears to the total square footage of buildings located on the land.

14. **ABANDONMENT.** Tenant shall not vacate nor abandon the Leased Premises at any time during the term of this Lease, nor permit the Leased Premises to remain unoccupied for a period longer than fifteen (15) consecutive days during the term of this Lease; and if Tenant shall abandon, vacate or surrender the Leased Premises, or be dispossessed by process of law, or otherwise, any personal property belonging to Tenant and left on the Leased Premises shall, at the option of the Landlord, be deemed abandoned.

15. **RIGHTS OF LENDERS.** 15.1 This Lease, in the event Landlord so notifies Tenant in writing, shall be subordinate to any deed of trust or other hypothecation for security now or hereafter placed upon the Leased Premises and/or other property of which the Leased Premises is a part and to any and all advances made on the security thereof and to all renewals, modifications, replacements and extensions thereof. Tenant agrees to promptly execute any documents which may be required to effectuate such subordination.

15.2 Notwithstanding such subordination, Tenant's right to quiet possession of the Leased Premises shall not be disturbed if Tenant is not in default and so long as Tenant shall pay the rent and observe and perform all of the provisions of this Lease.

16. **RECONSTRUCTION.** In the event of (a) a partial destruction of the Leased Premises or the Building during the lease term which requires repairs to either the Leased Premises or the Building, or (b) the Leased Premises or the Building being declared unsafe or unfit for occupancy by any authorized public authority for any reason other than Tenant's act, use or occupation which declaration requires repairs to either the Leased Premises or the Building, Landlord shall forthwith make such repairs, provided (i) such repairs can be made within sixty (60) days under the laws and regulations of authorized public authorities, and (ii) provided further, such partial destruction results from a cause insured under the standard fire insurance policy or policies Landlord shall have in effect on the Leased Premises and-or the Building and such insurance proceeds are made available to Landlord to make such repairs. Such partial destruction (including any destruction necessary in order to make repairs required by any declaration) shall in no wise annul or void this Lease, except that Tenant shall be entitled to a proportionate reduction of rent while such repairs are being made. The proportionate reduction is to be based upon the extent to which the making of said repairs shall interfere with the business carried on by Tenant in the Leased Premises. In making said repairs, Landlord shall be obligated to replace only such glazing as shall have been damaged by fire and other damaged glazing shall be replaced by Tenant. If said repairs cannot be made within sixty (60) days, or the other conditions above set forth to making said repairs have not been met, Landlord may, at its option, and at its sole discretion, make same within a reasonable time, this Lease continuing in full force and effect and the rent shall be proportionately abated as provided in this paragraph. In the event that Landlord does not so elect to make repairs as above provided, or repairs cannot be made under current laws and regulations, this Lease may be terminated at the option of either party upon written notice to the other party. In respect to any partial destruction (including any destruction necessary in order to make repairs required by any declaration) which Landlord is obligated to repair or may elect to repair under the term of this paragraph, the provisions of Section 1932, Subidivision (2), and Section 1933, Subdivision (4), of the Civil Code of the State of California, are waived by Tenant. A total destruction (including any destruction required by an authorized public authority) of either the Leased Premises or the Building shall terminate this Lease. In the event of any dispute between Landlord and Tenant relative to the provisions of this paragraph, they may each select an

arbitrator, the two arbitrators so selected shall select a third arbitrator and the three arbitrators so selected shall hear and determine the controversy and their decision thereon shall be final and binding on both Landlord and Tenant who shall bear the cost of such arbitration equally between them. Landlord shall not be required to repair any property installed in the Leased Premises by Tenant. Notwithstanding the foregoing, if the Leased Premises are partially destroyed or damaged during the last six (6) months of the term of this Lease, the Landlord may at Landlord's option cancel and terminate this Lease as of the date of occurance of such damage by giving written notice to Tenant of Landlord's election to do so within thirty (30) days after the date of occurrence of such damage.

17. **ASSIGNMENT AND SUBLETTING.** 17.1 **Landlord's Consent Required.** Tenant shall not voluntarily or by operation of law assign, transfer, mortgage, sublet or otherwise transfer or encumber all or any part of Tenant's interest in this Lease or in the Leased Premises without Landlord's prior written consent, which Landlord shall not unreasonably withhold. Any attempted assignment, transfer, mortgage, encumbrance or subletting without such consent shall be void, and shall constitute a breach of this Lease.

17.2 **No Release of Tenant.** Regardless of Landlord's consent, no subletting or assignment shall release Tenant of Tenant's obligation or alter the primary liability of Tenant to pay the rent and to perform all other obligations to be performed by Tenant hereunder. The acceptance of rent by Landlord from any other person shall not be deemed to be a waiver by Landlord of any provision hereof. Consent to one assignment or subletting shall not be deemed consent to any subsequent assignment or subletting.

17.3 **Attorney's Fees.** In the event that Landlord shall consent to a sublease or assignment under Paragraph 17.1, Tenant shall pay Landlord's reasonable attorneys' fees not to exceed $100 incurred in connection with giving such consent.

18. **DEFAULTS AND REMEDIES.** 18.1 The occurrence of any of the following shall constitute a material default and breach of this Lease by Tenant:

(a) Any failure by Tenant to pay the rental or to make any other payment required to be made by Tenant hereunder.

(b) The abandonment or vacating of the Leased Premises by Tenant.

(c) A failure by Tenant to observe and perform any other provision of this Lease to be observed or performed by Tenant, where such failure continues for three (3) days after written notice thereof by Landlord to Tenant; provided, however, that if the nature of the default is such that the default cannot reasonably be cured within the three (3) day period, Tenant shall not be deemed to be in default if Tenant shall, within such period, commence to cure the default and thereafter diligently prosecute to completion within a reasonable period of time whatever action is necessary to cure said default and any other default thereby occasioned.

(d) The making by Tenant of any general assignment for the benefit of creditors; the filing by or against Tenant of a petition to have Tenant adjudged a bankrupt or of a petition for reorganization or arrangement under any law relating to bankruptcy unless, in the case of a petition filed against Tenant, the same is dismissed within 60 days; the appointment of a trustee or receiver to take possession of substantially all of Tenant's assets located at the Leased Premises or of Tenant's interest in this Lease, where possession is not restored to Tenant within 30 days; or the attachment, execution or other judicial seizure of substantially all of Tenant's assets located at the Leased Premises or of Tenant's interest in this Lease, where such seizure is not discharged within 30 days.

18.2 (a) In the event of any such default by Tenant, then in addition to any other remedies available to Landlord at law or in equity, Landlord shall have the immediate option to terminate this Lease and all rights of Tenant hereunder by giving written notice of such intention to terminate in the manner specified in Article 20 of this Lease.

(b) In the event that Landlord shall elect to terminate this Lease, then Landlord may recover from Tenant (i) the worth at the time of award of any unpaid rent which had been earned at the time of such termination; plus (ii) the worth at the time of award of the amount by which the unpaid rent which would have been earned after termination until the time of award exceeds the amount of such rental loss Tenant proves could have been reasonably avoided; plus (iii) the worth at the time of award of the amount by which the unpaid rent for the balance of the term after the time of award exceeds the amount of such rental loss that Tenant proves could be reasonably avoided; plus (iv) any other amount necessary to compensate Landlord for all the detriment proximately caused by Tenant's failure to perform his obligations under this Lease or which in the ordinary course of things would be likely to result therefrom; and (v) such other amounts in addition to or in lieu of the foregoing as may be permitted from time to time by applicable California law.

As used in subparagraphs (i) and (ii) above, the "worth at the time of award" is computed by allowing interest at the rate of ten percent per annum. As used in subparagraph (iii) above, the "worth at the time of award" is computed by discounting such amount at the discount rate of the Federal Reserve Bank of San Francisco at the time of award plus one percent, (but in no event more than 10 percent).

18.3 In the event of any such default by Tenant, Landlord shall also have the right, with or without terminating this Lease, to reenter the Leased Premises and remove all persons and property from the Leased Premises, and to store such property in a public warehouse or elsewhere at the cost of and for the account of Tenant.

18.4 (a) In the event of the vacation or abandonment of the Leased Premises by Tenant or in the event that Landlord shall elect to reenter as provided in this section 18 above or shall take possession of the Leased Premises pursuant to legal proceedings or pursuant to any notice provided by law, then, if Landlord does not elect to terminate this Lease as provided in this section 18, the Lease shall remain in full force and effect, and Landlord may from time to time recover all rental as it becomes due and enforce any and all other rights and remedies afforded by this Lease.

(b) No reentry or taking possession of the Premises by Landlord pursuant to this section 18 shall be construed as an election to terminate this Lease unless a written notice of such intention be given to Tenant or unless the termination thereof be decreed by a court of competent jurisdiction.

(c) Notwithstanding any reentry or taking possession by Landlord pursuant to this section 18 of this Article, Landlord may at any time thereafter terminate this Lease and recover from Tenant an amount computed in accordance with the provisions of section 18.2 (b) of this Article.

18.5 **Default by Landlord.** Landlord shall not be in default unless Landlord fails to perform obligations required of Landlord within a reasonable time, but in no event later than thirty (30) days after written notice by Tenant to Landlord and to the holder of any first mortgage or deed of trust covering the Leased Premises whose name and address shall have theretofore been furnished to Tenant in writing, specifying wherein Landlord has failed to perform such obligations; provided, however, that if the nature of Landlord's obligation is such that more than thirty (30) days are required for performance then Landlord shall not be in default if Landlord commences performance within such 30-day period and thereafter diligently prosecutes the same to completion.

18.6 **Surrender of Lease Not Merger.** The voluntary or other surrender of this Lease by Tenant, or a mutual cancellation thereof, shall not work a merger, and shall, at the option of Landlord terminate all or any existing subleases, and/or subtenancies, or may, at the option of Landlord, operate as an assignment to it of any or all of such subleases or subtenancies.

19. **EMINENT DOMAIN.** If any part of the Leased Premises shall be taken or condemned for a public or quasi public use, and a part thereof remains which is susceptible of occupation hereunder, this Lease shall, as to the part so taken, terminate as of the date title shall vest in the condemnor, and the rent payable hereunder shall be adjusted so that the Tenant shall be required to pay for the remainder of the term only such portion of such rent as the number of square feet in the part remaining after the condemnation bears to the number of square feet in the entire Leased Premises at the date of condemnation; but in such event Landlord shall have the option to terminate this Lease as of the date when title to the part so condemned vests in the condemnor. If all the Leased Premises, or such part thereof be taken or condemned so that there does not remain a portion susceptible for occupation hereunder, this Lease shall thereupon terminate. If a part or all of the Leased Premises be taken or condemned, all compensation awarded upon such condemnation or taking shall go to the Landlord and the Tenant shall have no claim thereto, and the Tenant hereby irrevocably assigns and transfers to the Landlord any right to compensation or damages to which the Tenant may be entitled during the term hereof by reason of the condemnation of all or a part of the Leased Premises. Any dispute between Lessor and Lessee concerning the provisions of this paragraph may be submitted to arbitration in accordance with the procedure set forth in Paragraph 16.

20. **NOTICES.** 20.1 All communications, notices and demands of any kind which either party may be required or desire to give to or serve upon the other party ("notices") shall be made in writing and delivered by personal service or sent by certified mail, postage prepaid, return receipt requested, to the following addresses:

To Landlord:

To Tenant:

or to the Leased Premises.

20.2 Either party may change the address to which notices are to be delivered by giving the other party written notice of its new address as herein provided.

21. **WAIVER.** The waiver by Landlord of any breach of any term, covenant, or condition herein contained shall not be deemed to be a waiver of such term, covenant, or condition or any subsequent breach of the same or any other term, covenant, or condition herein contained. The subsequent acceptance of rent hereunder by Landlord shall not be deemed to be a waiver of any preceding breach by Tenant of any term, covenant, or condition of this Lease, other than the failure of Tenant to pay the particular rental so accepted, regardless of Landlord's knowledge of such preceding breach at the time of acceptance of such rent.

22. **EFFECT OF HOLDING OVER.** If Tenant should remain in possession of the Leased Premises after the expiration of the Lease term and without executing a new Lease, then such holding over shall be construed as a tenancy from month to month, subject to all the conditions, provisions, and obligations of this Lease insofar as the same are applicable to a month-to-month tenancy.

23. **PARKING.** Tenant shall be entitled to park in common with other tenants of Landlord. Tenant agrees not to over burden the parking facilities and agrees to cooperate with Landlord and other tenants in the use of parking facilities. Landlord reserves the right in its absolute discretion to determine whether parking facilities are becoming crowded and, in such event, to allocate parking spaces among Tenant and other tenants. Tenant shall comply with all rules and regulations promulgated from time to time for the use of the parking facilities as said rules and regulations are promulgated by the Landlord or by the local jurisdiction.

24. **ESTOPPEL CERTIFICATE.** 24.1. Tenant shall at any time upon not less than ten (10) days prior written notice from Landlord execute, acknowledge and deliver to Landlord a statement in writing (i) certifying that this Lease is unmodified and in full force and effect (or, if modified, stating the nature of such modification and certifying that this Lease, as so modified, is in full force and effect) and the date to which the rent and other charges are paid in advance, if any, and (ii) acknowledging that there are not, to Tenant's knowledge, any uncured defaults on the part of Landlord hereunder, or specifying such defaults if any are claimed. Any such statement may be conclusively relied upon by any prospective purchaser or encumbrancer of the Leased Premises.

24.2 Tenant's failure to deliver such statement within such time shall be conclusive upon Tenant (i) that this Lease is in full force and effect, without modification except as may be represented by Landlord, (ii) that there are no uncured defaults in Landlord's performance, and (iii) that not more than one month's rent has been paid in advance.

24.3 If Landlord desires to finance or refinance the Leased Premises, or any part thereof, Tenant hereby agrees to deliver to any lender designated by Landlord such financial statements of Tenant as may be reasonably required by such lender. Such statements shall include the past three years' financial statements of Tenant. All such financial statements shall be received by Landlord in confidence and shall be used only for the purposes herein set forth.

25. **TENANT IMPROVEMENTS.** Attached hereto as Exhibit "B" and made a part hereof is a schedule of improvements to be supplied by the Landlord at its sole cost and expense in connection with the Leased Premises and the Building thereon. All other improvements except those expressly set forth on Exhibit "B" shall be at the sole cost and expense of the Tenant.

26. **ASSIGNMENT OF LANDLORD'S INTEREST.** The term "Landlord" as used herein shall mean only the owner or owners at the time in question of the fee title affecting the Leased Premises. In the event of any transfer of such title

IGL 74-3

or interest, Landlord herein named (and in case of any subsequent transfers the then grantor) shall be relieved from and after the date of such transfer of all liability as respects Landlord's obligations thereafter to be performed. The obligations contained in this Lease to be performed by Landlord shall be binding on Landlord's successors and assigns only during their respective periods of ownership.

27. MISCELLANEOUS PROVISIONS.

(a) Whenever the singular number is used in this Lease and when required by the context, the same shall include the plural, and the masculine gender shall include the feminine and neuter genders, and the word "person" shall include corporation, firm or association. If there be more than one Tenant, the obligations imposed upon Tenant under this Lease shall be joint and several.

The headings or titles to paragraphs of this Lease are not a part of this Lease and shall have no effect upon the construction or interpretation of any part of this Lease.

(c) This instrument contains all of the agreements and conditions made between the parties to this Lease and may not be modified orally or in any other manner than by agreement in writing signed by all parties to this Lease.

(d) Time is of the essence of each term and provision of this Lease.

(e) Except as otherwise expressly stated, each payment required to be made by Tenant shall be in addition to and not in substitution for other payments to be made by Tenant.

(f) Subject to Paragraph 17, the terms and provisions of this Lease shall be binding upon and inure to the benefits of the heirs, executors, administrators, successors, and assigns of Landlord and Tenant.

(g) All covenants and agreements to be performed by Tenant under any of the terms of this Lease shall be performed by Tenant at Tenant's sole cost and expense and without any abatement of rent.

(h) Tenant shall not use the name of the Building or of the development in which the Building is situated for any purpose other than as an address of the business to be conducted by the Tenant in the Leased Premises.

28. INTEREST ON PAST DUE OBLIGATIONS. Except as expressly herein provided, any amounts due to Landlord not paid when due shall bear interest at 10 percent per annum from the date due. Payment of such interest shall not excuse or cure any default by Tenant under this Lease.

29. LATE CHARGES. Tenant acknowledges that late payment by Tenant to Landlord of rent or other sums due hereunder will cause Landlord to incur costs not contemplated by this Lease, the exact amount of which would be extremely difficult and impractical to ascertain. Such costs include, but are not limited to, processing and accounting charges, and late charges which may be imposed on Landlord by the terms of any mortgage or trust deed covering the Premises. Therefore, in the event Tenant should fail to pay any installment of rent or any other sum due hereunder within ten (10) days after such amount is due, Tenant shall pay to Landlord as additional rent a late charge equal to 5 percent of each such installment or other sum or $25.00 per month, whichever is greater. A $5.00 charge will be paid by the Tenant to the Landlord for each returned check.

30. SPECIAL PROVISIONS. Special provisions of this Lease (if any) numbered _____ through _____ are attached hereto and made a part hereof. If none, so state in the following space:

31 CORPORATE AUTHORITY. If Tenant is a corporation, each individual executing this Lease on behalf of said corporation represents and warrants that he is duly authorized to execute and deliver this Lease on behalf of said corporation in accordance with a duly adopted resolution of the Board of Directors of said corporation or in accordance with the Bylaws of said corporation and that this Lease is binding upon said corporation in accordance with its terms. If Tenant is a corporation, Tenant shall, within thirty (30) days after the execution of this Lease, deliver to Landlord a certified copy of a resolution of the Board of Directors of said corporation authorizing or ratifying the execution of this Lease.

32. DISCRIMINATION. The Tenant herein covenants by and for himself, his heirs, executors, administrators and assigns, and all persons claiming under or through him, and this Lease is made and accepted upon and subject to the following conditions: That there shall be no discrimination against or segregation of any person or group of persons on account of race, color, creed, national origin, or ancestry, in the leasing, subleasing, transferring, use, or enjoyment of the Leased Premises herein leased nor shall the Tenant himself, or any person claiming under or through him, establish or permit any such practice or practices of discrimination or segregation with reference to the selection, location, number, use or occupancy, of tenants, lessees, sublessees, subtenants or vendees in the premises herein leased.

33. CALIFORNIA LAWS. This Lease is executed in the County of Los Angeles, State of California and the laws of California shall apply in all respects in interpreting this Lease or any of the terms and provisions thereof.

IN WITNESS WHEREOF, landlord and Tenant have executed this Lease of the day and year first above written.

THIS LEASE IS SUBJECT TO ACCEPTANCE BY LANDLORD.

Executed at
on
Address

By _____   By _____
           "Landlord"

Executed at
on
Address

By _____   By _____
                "Tenant"

GUARANTY

WHEREAS, Tenant is desirous of entering into the Lease set forth above, and

WHEREAS, Landlord is willing to lease the Leased Premises described in the above Lease to Tenant if, but only if, performance of all covenants, terms and conditions of the Lease is guaranteed, jointly and severally, by _____ ("Guarantors"), and

WHEREAS, Guarantors, stockholders in Tenant corporation, are willing to furnish such a guarantee to Landlord as a condition precedent to said Lease.

1. NOW, THEREFORE, in consideration of Landlord's agreement to enter into said Lease with Tenant following execution of this Guaranty by Guarantors, evidenced by Landlord's signature hereafter, Guarantors, jointly and severally, guarantee faithful and complete performance of all covenants, terms and conditions of the Lease during its Term, including but not limited to payment of rent as defined and on the terms set forth in the Lease and the accuracy of warranties contained therein. Guarantors also agree to pay Landlord reasonable attorneys' fees and all costs and other expenses incurred by Landlord in enforcing its rights under this guaranty whether or not suit is brought thereon and, if brought, whether or not prosecuted to judgment. Guarantors waive notice of acceptance of this Guaranty and notice of Tenant's default under the Lease.

2. This is a continuing guaranty which shall remain in force during the term of the Lease, and thereafter until Tenant's obligations under the Lease are fully satisfied. This agreement shall inure to the benefit of Landlord, its successors and assigns, and shall be binding on Guarantors and their legal representatives.

3. Guarantors acknowledge and represent that this Guaranty and the Guarantors' execution thereof was and has been solicited by Tenant and not by Landlord.

4. Guarantors warrant, represent and agree to furnish to Landlord quarterly, or more frequently as Landlord shall require, all pertinent facts relating to the ability of Tenant to pay and to perform Tenant's liabilities, and all pertinent facts relating to Guarantors' abilities to pay and to perform Guarantors' obligations, and Guarantors further warrant, represent and agree to keep informed with respect to all such facts. Guarantors acknowledge and agree that Landlord will and will continue to rely upon the facts and information to be furnished to it by Guarantors, as aforesaid. Guarantors further warrant, represent and agree that, in executing this Guaranty and at all times hereafter, Guarantors rely and will continue to rely upon Guarantors' own investigation and upon sources other than Landlord for all information and facts relating to the ability of Tenant to pay and to perform Tenant's liabilities, and Guarantors do not and will not hereafter rely upon Landlord for any such information or facts. Guarantors waive any and all right to assert against Landlord any claims or defenses based upon any failure of Landlord to furnish to Guarantors any information or facts relating to the ability of Tenant to pay and to perform Tenant's liabilities.

5. Guarantors further acknowledge, warrant, represent and agree:

(a) Guarantors have independently reviewed all instruments and documents executed by Tenant and Guarantors have made an independent determination as to the validity and enforceability thereof upon the advice of Guarantors' own counsel, and in executing and delivering this Guaranty to Landlord, Guarantors are not in any manner relying upon Landlord as to the validity and/or enforceability of any security interest of any kind or nature granted by the Tenant to the Landlord.

(b) That Guarantors waive all defenses, counterclaims and offsets of any kind or nature, in connection with the validity and/or enforceability of this Guaranty, arising directly or indirectly from the perfection, sufficiency, validity and/or enforceability of any rider, instrument or document acquired by Landlord from Tenant.

6. Guarantors waive any and all rights to assert against Landlord any claim or defense based upon any election of remedies by Landlord, which, in any manner impairs, affects, reduces, releases or extinguishes Guarantors' subrogation rights or Guarantors' rights to proceed against Tenant for reimbursement, or any other rights of Guarantors against Tenant, or against any other person or security, including, but not limited to, any defense based upon an election of remedies by Landlord under the terms of Section 580(d) of the Code of Civil Procedure of the State of California and any similar provision of other laws of any state, governmental entity, or country. Section 580(d) of the California Code of Civil Procedure provides as follows:

"No judgment shall be rendered for any deficiency upon a note secured by a deed of trust or mortgage upon real property hereafter executed in any case in which the real property has been sold by the mortgagee or trustee under power of sale contained in such a mortgage or deed of trust.

The provisions of this section shall not apply to any deed of trust, mortgage, or other lien given to secure the payment of bonds or other evidences of indebtedness authorized or permitted to be issued by the Commissioner of Corporations, or which is made by a public utility subject to the provisions of the Public Utilities Act."

IN WITNESS WHEREOF, Guarantors have executed this Guaranty the _____ day of _____, 19___

GUARANTORS:

Name

Address

Name

Address

WHEN RECORDED RETURN TO:

Myron Meyers, Esq.
6300 Wilshire Boulevard, Suite 9100
Los Angeles, California 90048

DECLARATION OF

COVENANTS, CONDITIONS AND RESTRICTIONS

ESTABLISHING A PLAN OF CONDOMINIUM OWNERSHIP

ARTICLE I

STATEMENT OF PURPOSE

THIS DECLARATION, made by Earth Galaxy, Inc., a California corporation, hereinafter referred to as "Declarant," is made this 10th day of February, 1982, with reference to the following facts:

A. Declarant is the owner of a certain tract of land located in the City of Los Angeles, County of Los Angeles, State of California, more particularly described in Article III of this Declaration and incorporated by reference herein.

B. Declarant intends to improve said property by constructing thereon a high-rise condominium structure containing a total of nineteen (19) levels. The uppermost fifteen (15) levels will house seventy-five (75) condominium units with five (5) units per level. The level directly below the lowest level of condominiums will consist of recreational facilities, storage facilities, and maids' rooms. There will be three (3) levels of parking, having a minimum of one hundred sixty-nine (169) parking spaces. Two (2) of the three (3) parking levels will be totally subterranean, while the third level will be partially subterranean. This high-rise structure will complement existing buildings in the area along Clam Row in Santa Gertrudes Shores.

TYPICAL COVENANTS, CONDITIONS AND RESTRICTIONS - CONDOMINIUM

PROJECT - MULTI-STORY STRUCTURE - RESIDENTIAL ONLY.

C. Declarant intends to utilize said improvements as a "Project" (as defined in Article II, Paragraph 27 of this Declaration) in conformity with the provisions of the California Condominium Act. Declarant further intends to sell and to convey the condominiums therein subject to the covenants, conditions and restrictions set forth in this Declaration.

D. Declarant desires that the covenants, conditions and restrictions set forth in this Declaration shall be enforceable equitable servitudes which shall inure to and bind all owners of condominiums in the Project for their mutual benefit in effectuating the enhancement, maintenance, and protection of the value and the attractiveness of the Project. Declarant further intends that all such servitudes shall run with the land and shall be binding on the grantor, its successors and assigns, all subsequent owners of all or any part of said real property and improvements, together with their grantees, successors, heirs, executors, administrators, devisees and assigns, and all other persons having or acquiring any right, title or interest in or to any part of the Project.

F. Declarant desires that the provisions of this Declaration shall be liberally construed to implement a uniform plan for the development of a condominium project.

G. Declarant intends that all the Condominium Documents (as defined in Article II, Paragraph 13 of this Declaration) conform to the requirements of any governmental agency which is empowered to regulate mortgages, their purchases, their guarantees, their insurance or their subsidization, including, without limitation, the Federal Home Loan Mortgage Corporation, the Government National Mortgage Association, the Federal Housing Administration, and the Veterans Administration.

NOW, THEREFORE, Declarant hereby declares that the hereinafter-described property shall be held, conveyed, mortgaged, encumbered, leased, rented, used, occupied, sold, and improved, subject to the following declarations, limitations, covenants, conditions, restrictions and easements, all of which are for the purpose of enhancing and protecting the value and attractiveness of the property, and the Project, and every part thereof, in accordance with the Plan for the improvement of the property and the division thereof into condominiums. All of the limitations, covenants, conditions, restrictions and easements shall constitute covenants which shall run with the land and shall be binding upon Declarant and its successors and assigns, and all parties having or acquiring any right, title or interest in or to any part of the property or the Project.

ARTICLE II

DEFINITIONS

1. The "Articles" mean the Association's Articles of Incorporation, as amended from time to time.

2. "Assessment" means an assessment levied or charged against an Owner or his Condominium as established by the Association as representing that portion of the cost of maintaining, improving, repairing, operating and managing the property, which is to be paid by said Owner.

3. The "Association" means the Homeowners' Association, a California mutual benefit non-profit corporation, its successors and assigns. The Association consists of all Owners of Units in the Project.

4. The "Board" means that Board of Directors of the Association.

5. The "Bylaws" mean the Association's Bylaws, as amended from time to time.

6. "Capital Assessment" means an assessment levied by the Association in any fiscal year, as provided in Article VIII, Paragraph D.2.(a) of this Declaration, for the purpose of defraying, in whole or in part, the cost of any new construction, or unanticipated repair or replacement of a capital improvement in or upon the Common Area, including any incidental fixtures and chattels.

7. "Common Area" means the entire Project, excepting all Units therein granted or reserved, as defined in this Declaration or as shown on the Condominium Plan.

8. "Common Expenses" means and includes the actual and estimated expenses of operating the Project and any reasonable reserve for such purposes as found and determined by the Board and all sums designated Common Expenses by or pursuant to the Condominium Documents. Common Expenses do not include the cost of capital improvements or repairs thereto, including incidental fixtures and chattels.

9. "Common Funds" means all funds collected or received by the Association in order to satisfy Common Expenses.

10. "Common Interest" means an undivided one-(1/) interest as a tenant-in-common in and to the Common Area, which is appurtenant to each Unit as set forth in this Declaration.

11. "Condominium" means a freehold estate in fee in real property consisting of an undivided interest held by a tenancy in common in the Common Area, together with a fee interest in a Unit shown and described on the Condominium Plan, together with such easements as provided in the grant deed to each owner.

12. "Condominium Building" means the residential structure, containing Condominium Units to be erected as a part of the Project.

13. "Condominium Documents" mean and include this Declaration, as it may be amended from time to time, the exhibits, if any, attached hereto, the Articles of Incorporation, the Bylaws, and the Rules and Regulations.

14. "Condominium Plan" means the Condominium Plan prepared and recorded pursuant to California Civil Code Section 1351 respecting the Project, and any amendments to said Plan.

15. "Declarant" means _____, its successors and assigns, if such successors and assigns acquire or hold record title to any portion of the Project for development purposes.

16. "Declaration" means this Declaration of Covenants, Conditions and Restrictions, as amended from time to time.

17. "Individual Assessment" means an Assessment made against a particular Owner and his Condominium, as provided in Article VIII, Paragraph D.2.(b).

18. "Institutional Mortgagee" is a Mortgagee that is a bank, savings and loan association, insurance company, established mortgage company, or other financial institution or other institution not disenabled by statute from being a Mortgagee, which holds a recorded Mortgage.

19. "Map" means and refers to that subdivision map entitled _____ recorded the ____ day of _____, 19__, in Book ____ of Maps at Page ____, in the Official Records of Los Angeles County.

20. "Member" means and refers to any person entitled to membership in the Association as provided herein.

21. "Mortgage" means a mortgage or deed of trust made in good faith and for value encumbering a Condominium, or other portion of the Project.

22. "Mortgagee" means the record owner of a beneficial interest under a Mortgage.

23. "Mortgagor" means one who, having all or some part of title to a Condominium, by written instrument, pledges that interest or a portion thereof as security for a debt represented by a Mortgage.

24. "Occupant" means any person who is within a Condominium Unit with the approval of the Owner or Owners or the agent of the Owner or Owners, including, by way of illustration and not by way of limitation, the Owner or Owners and the families, guests, tenants, servants, agents, employees, and invitees, of the Owner or Owners, while within the Condominium Unit.

25. "Owner" means any person holding a record ownership interest in a Condominium Unit, including Declarant. "Owner" does not include any person who holds an interest in a Condominium merely as security for the performance of an obligation or as a contract purchaser.

26. "Person" means a natural person, a corporation, a partnership, a trustee or other legal entity.

27. "Project" means the entire parcel of real property described in Article III divided, or to be divided, into Condominiums, including all structures thereon.

28. "Restricted Common Area" means any portion of the Common Area set aside for the exclusive use of any Owner, which may include (by way of illustration and not limitation) balconies, patios, garage parking spaces, and storage compartments.

29. "Rules and Regulations" means those Rules and Regulations, adopted from time to time by the Association or its Board, including any amendments thereto.

30. "Special Assessment" means a Capital Assessment or an Individual Assessment.

31. "Unit" means the elements of a Condominium that are not owned in common with the other Owners of Condominiums in the Project. The boundaries of a Unit are shown and described in the Condominium Plan. In interpreting deeds and plans, the existing physical boundaries of a Unit or of a Unit reconstructed in substantial accordance with the original Plans, shall be conclusively presumed to be its boundaries rather than the description expressed in the deed or plans, regardless of minor variance between boundaries shown on the Plan or in the deed or those of the Condominium Building, or regardless of settling or lateral movement of the Condominium Building. Whenever reference is made in this Declaration, in the Condominium Plan, in any deed or elsewhere, to a Unit, it shall be assumed that such reference is made to such Unit as a whole, including each of its component elements and to all exclusive easements, if any, appurtenant to such Unit over the Common Area.

ARTICLE III

DESCRIPTION OF THE PROJECT

The Project consists of the underlying real property with Condominium Units and all other improvements located thereon. Declarant will construct upon the Project a high-rise condominium building containing a total of nineteen (19) levels. The uppermost fifteen (15) levels will house seventy-five (75) condominium Units with five (5) Units per level. The level directly below the lowest level of condominiums will consist of recreational facilities, storage facilities, and maids' rooms. There will be three (3) levels of parking, having a minimum of one hundred sixty-nine (169) parking spaces. Two (2) of the three (3) parking levels will be totally subterranean, while the third level will be partially subterranean.

Reference is made to the Plan referred to in the Condominium Plan to supply further details concerning the Project.

LEGAL DESCRIPTION:

Lot 1 of Tract No. 72818 in the City of Los Angeles, County of Los Angeles, as per Map recorded on July 6, 1981, in Book 409, Pages 5 and 6 inclusive of Maps, in the Office of the Los Angeles County Recorder.

ARTICLE IV

DIVISION OF THE PROPERTY AND
THE CREATION OF PROPERTY RIGHTS

The interests in real property in the Project are hereby divided in accordance with the provisions of this Article.

A.   Units: Each of the Units as separately shown, numbered and designated in the Condominium Plan consists of the space bounded by and contained within the interior unfinished surfaces of the perimeter walls, floors, ceilings, windows, and doors of each Unit, each of said spaces being defined and referred to herein as a "Unit". Each Unit includes both the portions of the Condominium Building so described and the airspace so encompassed. The Unit does not include those areas and those things which are defined as "Common Areas" in Article II, Paragraph 7, with the exception of exclusive easements appurtenant thereto. Each Unit is subject to such encroachments as are contained in the Condominium Building, whether the same now exist or may be later caused or created in any manner, referred to in Article IV, Paragraph D. In interpreting deeds and plans, the then-existing physical boundaries of a Unit, whether in its original state or reconstructed in substantial accordance with the original plans thereof, shall be conclusively presumed to be its boundaries rather than the boundaries expressed in the deed or Plan, regardless of settling or lateral movement of the Condominium Building and regardless of minor variance between boundaries shown on the Plan or deed and those of the Condominium Building.

The right of each Owner to the quiet enjoyment of his respective Unit shall be subject to the following rights and restrictions:

(1)   The right of Declarant or its designees to enter on the Project to construct the Project and to make such repairs and remedy construction defects with a minimum of inconvenience to any Owner in the use of his Unit.

(2)   The right of the Association, or its agents, to enter any Unit upon reasonable notice to its Owner, to perform its obligations under this Declaration, including obligations with respect to construction, maintenance or repair for the benefit of the Common Area or the Owners in common, or to make necessary repairs that said Owner has failed to perform. The right shall be immediate and without prior notice in case of an emergency originating in or threatening such Unit, and the obligation can be performed whether or not the Owner is present.

to improve the Common Area.

(3) The right of the Association to borrow money

(4) The right of the Association to assign, rent, license or otherwise designate and control use of unassigned parking spaces, if any, within the Common Area.

(5) The right of Declarant or its designees to enter on the Common Area to construct the Project and to make repairs and remedy construction defects with minimum inconvenience to any Owner in the use of the Common Area.

(6) The right of the Association, or its agents, to enter the Common Area to perform its obligations under this Declaration, including obligations with respect to construction, maintenance or repair for the benefit of the Common Area or the Owners in common, or to make necessary repairs that said Owner has failed to perform.

C. Restricted Common Areas: Those portions of the Common Area which are set aside and allocated for the restricted use of the respective Units are Restricted Common Areas. Restricted Common Areas are defined in Article II, Paragraph 28. To complete each Condominium at the time of its conveyance, Declarant, or its successor, shall designate and describe in the document of conveyance for the Condominium two (2) designated parking spaces to be used solely in conjunction with the use of the respective Unit; the document of conveyance must also set forth all other exclusive easements thereby conveyed. The grant of use of the Restricted Common Areas shall be an easement appurtenant to the respective Unit for the exclusive uses and purposes as set forth herein, and shall be subject to an easement in favor of the Association for support and minor encroachment of the Common Areas and an easement in favor of Owners of adjoining Restricted Common Areas for minor variances between parking space designations and the actual painted striping thereof. The exclusive right of use of Restricted Common Area granted to an Owner does not entitle such Owner to alter, to change, or to add to, in any way, the surfaces or structural parts of said Restricted Common Area. No easement of a Restricted Common Area may be separately conveyed from the Unit to which said easement is appurtenant.

D. Easements for Minor Encroachments: Each Condominium within the Property is hereby declared to have an easement over all adjoining Condominiums and Common Area for the purpose of accommodating any encroachment due to engineering errors, errors

(3) The right of any Owner, or his representatives, to enter the Unit of any other Owner to perform permissible installations, alterations or repairs to mechanical or electrical services, cables, if requests for entry are made in advance and such entry is at a time convenient to the Owner whose Unit is being entered. In case of emergency, such right of entry shall be immediate and without prior notice to the Owner.

B. Common Areas: The remaining portion of the Property referred to herein as "Common Area" or Common Areas," shall include, without limitation, all of the elements set forth in Article II, Paragraph 7. Each Unit Owner shall have, as appurtenant to his Unit, an undivided one- (1/) interest as a tenant-in-common in the Common Area. The ownership of each Condominium shall include a Unit and such undivided interest in the Common Area. The common interest appurtenant to each Unit is declared to be permanent in character and cannot be altered without the consent of all the Owners affected, and seventy-five (75%) percent of the first Mortgagees of such Owners, as expressed in an amended Declaration. Such common interest cannot be separated from the Unit to which it is appurtenant. Each Owner may use the Common Areas in accordance with the purposes for which they are intended without hindering the exercise of or encroaching upon the rights of any other Owners.

Every Owner of a Condominium shall have a non-exclusive easement of use and enjoyment in, to and throughout the Common Area of the Project and for ingress, egress and support over and through the Common Area. However, such non-exclusive easements shall be subordinate to, and shall not interfere with, exclusive easements appurtenant to Units over the Common Area, if any. Each such easement shall be appurtenant to and pass with the title to every Unit, subject to the following rights and restrictions:

(1) The right of the Association to limit the number of guests, and to adopt Association Rules and Regulations, as defined in Article II, Paragraph 29, regulating the use and enjoyment of the Common Area.

(2) The right of the Association to charge reasonable admission and other fees for the use of any unassigned parking spaces and recreational facilities situated on the Common Area, if any.

No Owner shall be entitled to sever his Unit from his undivided interest in the Common Area for any purpose. None of the component interests can be separately sold, transferred, conveyed, encumbered or hypothecated, and any violation or attempted violation of this provision shall be void. Similarly, no Owner can sever any exclusive easement appurtenant to his Unit over the Common Area from his Condominium, and any attempt to do so shall be void.

J. Parking: In addition to the parking spaces assigned to Units on the Condominium Plan, each of which is a Restricted Common Area, there are ( ) unassigned parking spaces. These may be used by all Owners, their tenants and guests. The Board may, from time to time, assign the exclusive right to use said spaces to particular Units. Reassignment of said spaces shall be based upon mutual consent of the Owners, whose assignments are to be changed, and failing such consent, shall be after notice to such Owners and hearing before the Board.

ARTICLE V

USE RESTRICTIONS

1. Residential Use: Except as provided in Article V, Paragraph 2 hereof, no Condominium shall be occupied or used except for residential purposes by the Owners, their tenants, and social guests, and no trade or business shall be conducted therein.

Nothing in this Declaration shall prevent an Owner from leasing or renting his Condominium as provided in Article V, Paragraph 21 hereof.

2. Commercial Use: Except for the management, operation and maintenance of the Project, including, but not limited to, valet and garage parking, cable television, laundry and cleaning pick-up and delivery, repair work, doorman, athletic instruction, security facilities and security guards, and the leasing of Units, no part of the Project shall ever be used or caused, allowed, or authorized to be used in any way, directly or indirectly, for any business, commercial, manufacturing, mercantile, storing, vending, or other such non-residential purpose; provided, however, that Declarant,

---

in original construction, settlement or shifting of the Condominium Building, or due to any other cause. There shall be valid easements for the maintenance of said encroachments as long as they shall exist, and the rights and obligations of Owners shall not be altered in any way by said encroachment, settlement, or shifting; provided, however, that in no event shall a valid easement for encroachment be created in favor of an Owner or Owners if said encroachment occurred due to the willful conduct of said Owner or Owners. In the event the Condominium Building is partially or totally destroyed, and then repaired or rebuilt, the Owners of each Condominium agree that minor encroachments over adjoining Condominiums or Common Area shall be permitted and that there shall be valid easements for the maintenance of said encroachments so long as they shall exist.

E. Easements for Maintenance of Utilities. There shall exist easements for the maintenance of utilities as provided by Article IX.

F. Declarant's Easements for Construction. Declarant shall have the right to use whatever easements are necessary to effectuate the provisions of Article XX, Paragraph A.

G. Easements Reserved and Granted. Any easement referred to in this Declaration shall be deemed either reserved or granted, as appropriate, by reference to this Declaration in a deed to any Condominium.

H. No Dedication Implied. Nothing contained in this Declaration shall be deemed to be a gift or dedication of all or any portion of the Project to the general public or for any public use or purposes whatsoever.

I. Prohibition Against Partition and Severance: The Common Area shall remain undivided as set forth hereinabove. Except as provided by Article XV, no Owner shall bring an action for partition, it being agreed that this restriction is necessary in order to preserve the rights of the Owners with respect to the operation and management of the Project. Judicial partition by sale of a single Unit owned by two (2) or more persons and division of the sales proceeds are not prohibited hereby. The partition of title to a single Unit is prohibited. Upon the recordation of the certificate not to rebuild pursuant to the provisions of Article XIII, the right of any Owner to partition his Unit through legal action shall forthwith revive.

No such animal may be kept if it is kept, bred or raised for a commercial purpose. The total number of cats and dogs in any Unit cannot exceed two (2). All animals must have current inoculations and licenses as prescribed by law. No animal may be kept on the Project if its presence violates any zoning ordinance or other applicable law. The Board can prohibit maintenance of any animal that constitutes, in the sole and exclusive opinion of the Board, a nuisance to any other Owner. Each person bringing or keeping an animal on the Project shall be absolutely liable to other Owners, their family members, guests, invitees, and tenants, and their respective family members, guests, and invitees for any damage to persons or property caused by an animal brought on or kept on the Project by such person or by members of his family, his guests or invitees.

    No pets shall be allowed in the Common Area except as may be permitted by rules of the Board. No dog shall enter the Common Area except while on a leash which is held by a person capable of controlling it. Declarant or any Owner may cause any unleashed dog found within the Common Area to be removed by Declarant or any Owner to a pound or animal shelter under the jurisdiction of the City of Los Angeles, the County of Los Angeles, or other authority, by calling the appropriate authorities. No dog whose barking disturbs other Owners shall be permitted to remain on the Project.

    Owners shall prevent their pets from soiling any portion of the Common Area where other persons customarily walk and shall promptly clean up any mess left by their pets. The Board is empowered to assess a penalty of up to One Hundred ($100.00) Dollars against any Owner who fails promptly to clean up any mess left by his pet within the Common Area.

    4. Nuisances: No noxious, illegal or offensive activity shall be carried on or upon any Condominium, or in any part of the Project, nor shall anything be done thereon which may be or may become an annoyance or a nuisance to or which may in any way interfere with the quiet enjoyment of each of the Owners of his respective Unit, or which will impair the structural integrity of the Condominium Building. Unless otherwise permitted by the Association, no Owner shall serve food or beverages, cook, barbeque, or engage in similar activities except within such Owner's Unit or within those portions of the Common Area subject to exclusive easements appurtenant to such Owner's Unit. Exterior fires and barbequing are further limited by Paragraph 12 of this Article.

its successors or assigns, may use any Unit or Units in the Project which it owns for a model home site or sites and display and sales office. In any event, no model home site may be maintained by Declarant, its successors and assigns, more than three years after the date of the issuance of the Final Public Report by the Department of Real Estate regarding the Project. The right to maintain a model home site or sites is further subject to the requirement that no such usage may unreasonably interfere with any Owner's use of the Common Areas.

    3. Animals: No animals, including, without limitation, insects, reptiles, rodents, birds, fish, livestock and poultry, shall be kept in any Condominium or elsewhere within the Project, except that domestic dogs, domestic cats, domestic fish, domestic turtles and domestic birds inside suitable bird cages, may be kept as household pets within any one Unit, subject to the terms and conditions of this Declaration.

5. Increasing Insurance Risk: Nothing shall be done which shall in any way increase the rate of insurance for the Project, cause any insurance policy to be cancelled, or cause a refusal to renew the same, where such insurance is on the Project, or any portion of the Project, without prior written consent of the Board.

6. Maintenance of Unit: Each Owner of a Condominium shall be responsible for maintaining his Unit, including the equipment and fixtures in the Unit and its interior walls, ceilings, windows and doors, in a clean, sanitary, habitable and attractive condition. In the event that any Owner fails to maintain his Unit, the Board may perform any necessary maintenance or repairs as provided by Article VII, Paragraph A9.

However, unless otherwise specifically provided in this Declaration, each Owner has complete discretion as to the choice of furniture, furnishings, and interior decorating. Notwithstanding anything to the contrary contained herein, windows can be covered only by drapes or shades and cannot be painted or covered by metal foil, cardboard, plywood, paper, or other similar material. Each Owner shall be responsible for repair and replacement of the glass in the windows of his Unit with a glass of a similar color, thickness and quality to that supplied originally with the Unit. Unless otherwise provided in this Declaration, each Owner shall clean and maintain the exclusive easements appurtenant to his Unit over the Common Area.

7. Structural Alterations. Exterior Alterations, and Architectural Control. No structural alterations to the interior of any Unit shall be made and no plumbing or electrical work within any bearing or common wall shall be made by any Owner without the prior written consent of the Board.

No Owner shall at his expense or otherwise make any alterations or modifications to the exterior of the Condominium Building, fences, railings, or walls situated within the Project, without the prior written consent of the Board and the holder of any Mortgage or deed of trust then of record whose interest may be affected.

No landscaping visible from the street or from a Common Area which does involve the use of synthetic materials, or of concrete, rock, or similar materials, shall be undertaken by any Owner until plans and specifications showing the nature, kind, shape and location of the materials shall have been submitted to and approved in writing by the Board or by the Architectural Control Committee. (Provisions relative to the establishment, impanelment, and operation of the Architectural Control Committee are found in Article XVI).

8. Signs. No signs of any kind shall be displayed to the public view or to the Common Area on or from any Condominium without the approval of the Board, except such signs as may be used by the Declarant or its agents for a period of three (3) years from the date of recordation of this Declaration for the purpose of selling the Condominiums, and for the purpose of developing, selling and improving real property owned by Declarant or its designees and situated in the vicinity of the Project.

Notwithstanding any of the above provisions of this Paragraph 8, the right of each Owner to post a "for sale" sign concerning his Unit shall be implemented as follows:

(a) The Association shall maintain on the Project a sign, legible from the sidewalk immediately in front of the Project, which shall announce, as appropriate, "Condominium for Sale," "No Condominium for Sale," or other such message.

(b) In proximity to the main entrance to the Condominium Building, and in a place which is accessible to the public, the Association shall maintain an announcement board detailing any current offer of sale of a Condominium. The Association shall be empowered to develop and to effect Rules and Regulations with respect to (i) the use and specific location of any such announcement board, and (ii) procedures which an Owner must follow in order to notice on such announcement board his offer of sale of a Condominium.

9. Antennae, External Fixtures and Equipment. No television or radio poles, antennae, flag poles, or other external fixtures other than those originally installed by Declarant or approved by the Board, or replacements thereto, shall be constructed, erected or maintained on or within the Common Area or any structures on it. No wiring, insulation, air conditioning, or other machinery, equipment or display

other than that originally installed by Declarant or approved by the Board, or replacements thereto, shall be constructed, erected, or maintained on or within the Common Area, including any structures on it. Each Owner shall have the right to maintain television or radio antennae within completely enclosed portions of his Unit.

10. Fences, Walls, Screens and Awnings. No fences, awnings, ornamental screens, screen doors, sunshades or walls of any nature shall be erected or maintained on or around any portion of the Condominium Building or elsewhere within the Project, except as those that are installed in accordance with the original construction of the Project, and replacements thereto, or as are authorized and approved by the Architectural Control Committee.

11. Outside Drying and Laundering. No exterior clothes lines shall be erected or maintained and there shall be no exterior drying or laundering of clothes.

12. Exterior Fires. There shall be no exterior fires within the Project whatsoever except for barbeque fires in confined receptacles which are adequately designed for such purposes and approved by the Association. The Association shall have the authority to limit and to proscribe exterior fires and barbequeing.

13. Personal Property Remaining in Common Areas. No Owner shall allow furniture, furnishings, or other personalty belonging to such Owner to remain within any portion of the Common Area, except portions subject to exclusive easements over Common Area appurtenant to such Owner's Unit and except as may otherwise be permitted by the Board. This paragraph shall not serve to proscribe the delivery of nonnoxious items or packages to the doorway of a Unit or to a part of the Common Area designated by the Board for such deliveries, provided that (i) such a delivered item or package is removed by the Owner within a reasonable period of time; (ii) said item or package does not materially interfere with the use of the Common Area for the purpose for which it was intended, including, but not limited to, its usage as a passageway; (iii) said item or package does not serve as an attractive nuisance, and (iv) said item or the contents of such package do not spoil, decay, melt, exude odors, or in any other way become noxious or hazardous.

14. Trash and Garbage Disposal. All rubbish, trash and garbage shall be regularly removed from the Project and shall not be allowed to accumulate thereon. Trash, garbage, and other waste shall not be kept except in sanitary containers. All equipment for the storage or disposal of such material shall be kept in a clean and sanitary condition. All related equipment (other than trash chutes) shall be kept screened and concealed from view of other Units, streets, and Common Areas, except on those days scheduled for trash pick-up.

15. Parking Restrictions; Use of Garage. Unless otherwise permitted by the Board, no motor vehicles shall be parked or left on the Project, other than on or within the garage or assigned or appurtenant parking stall or space. No boat, trailer, recreational vehicle, camper, truck, or commercial vehicle shall be parked or left on the Project, other than in a parking area designated by the Board for the parking and storage of such vehicles. However, parking by commercial vehicles for the purpose of making deliveries shall be permitted in accordance with the Rules and Regulations. No inoperable motor vehicles shall be stored on the Project. No off-road, unlicensed motor vehicle shall be operated upon the Project.

16. Restricted Use of Recreational Vehicles. No boat, trailer, recreational vehicle, camper, truck, or other vehicle, or tent or similar structure, shall be used as a place of habitation while on the Project. However, trailers or temporary structures for use incidental to the initial construction or subsequent reconstruction of the Project or the initial sales of Units may be maintained within the Project, but shall be promptly removed on completion of all initial construction and all initial sales or on completion of said subsequent reconstruction.

17. Power Equipment and Car Maintenance. No power equipment, hobby shops, or motor vehicle maintenance (other than emergency work) shall be permitted on the Project, except with prior written approval from the Board. Approval shall not be unreasonably withheld and, in deciding whether to grant approval, the Board shall consider the effects of noise, air pollution, dirt or grease, fire hazard, interference with radio or television reception, and similar possible deleterious side effects.

said lease must be filed with the Board within five (5) work days of the day on which the lessee comes into possession of the Condominium.

[The following space can be used for additional use restrictions reflecting the particular character of the condominium project. Typical paragraphs address such subjects as replacement and maintenance of drapes, flooring and windows; the cleaning of windows; the helipad; maids' rooms; occupation by children; tennis court; and the swimming pool.]

18. Oil Drilling, Quarrying and Mining Operations. No oil drilling, oil development operations, oil refining, quarrying, or mining operations of any kind shall be permitted on or in the Project, and no oil wells, tanks, tunnels, or mineral excavations or shafts shall be permitted on the surface of the Project or within five hundred (500) feet below the surface of the Project. No derrick or other structure designed for use in boring for water, oil or natural gas shall be erected, maintained or permitted on the Project.

19. Future Construction. Nothing in this Declaration shall limit the right of Declarant to complete construction of improvements to the Common Area and to Units owned by Declarant or to alter them or to construct additional improvements as Declarant deems advisable before completion and sale of the entire Project. The rights of Declarant in this Declaration may be assigned by Declarant to any successor to all or any part of Declarant's interest in the Project, as developer, by an express assignment incorporated in a recorded deed that transfers an interest to a successor.

20. Compliance with Laws. Each Owner shall promptly and fully comply with any and all applicable laws, rules, ordinances, statutes, regulations and requirements of any governmental agency or authority with respect to the occupancy and use of his Condominium.

21. Right to Lease. The respective Condominiums shall not be rented by the Owners thereof for transient or hotel purposes, which shall be defined as:

(a) Rental for any period under thirty (30) days;

or,

(b) Any rental if the occupants of the Unit are provided customary hotel service, such as room service for food and beverage, maid's service (not otherwise provided to that Unit), the provisioning of laundry and linens, and bellboy service.

Subject to the foregoing restrictions, the Owners of the respective Condominiums shall have the absolute right to lease same, provided that the lease is made subject to the covenants, conditions, restrictions, limitations and uses contained in this Declaration and the Bylaws. Said lease must be in writing, and must be duly executed. A copy of

ARTICLE VI

THE ASSOCIATION: ADMINISTRATION, MEMBERSHIP
AND VOTING RIGHTS AND ELECTIONS

A. ADMINISTRATION.

1. Nonprofit Corporation. _____ is a nonprofit corporation formed under the Nonprofit Mutual Benefit Corporations Law of California (enacted by Stats.1978, Chapters 567 and 1305, and amended by Stats. 1979, Chapters 681 and 724). The Association shall be charged with the duties and invested with the powers set forth in the Articles, the Bylaws, and this Declaration, including, but not limited to, control and maintenance of the Common Area and any Common Area facilities.

2. Implementation of Association. On the close and recording of the first Condominium sale to an Owner (other than Declarant), the Association shall begin its existence. The members of the Association shall hold an organizational meeting as provided by the Bylaws and by section 5 hereinbelow.

3. Officers and Directors. The Association shall have such Directors (who shall compose the Board of Directors) and officers as provided by the Bylaws. At the organizational meeting, a Board of Directors shall be elected, as provided by the Bylaws. At the time the Association comes into existence, Declarant shall appoint all Board members and any replacements until those Board members elected at the organizational meeting shall be installed.

4. Non-liability of Officers and Directors. No member of the Board, or of any committee of the Association, or any officer of the Association, or any manager or Declarant, or any agent of Declarant, shall be personally liable to any Owner or any other party, including the Association, for any damage, loss or prejudice suffered or claimed on account of any act, omission, error or negligence of any such person or entity while serving in any capacity hereinabove stated, if such person or entity has, on the basis of such information as may be possessed by him or it, acted in good faith, without wilful or intentional misconduct. All members of the Board, and of any committee of the Association, and any officer of the Association, and any manager, and Declarant, and any agent of Declarant, shall be indemnified by the Association against all reasonable costs, expenses and liabilities (including attorneys' fees and court costs) actually and necessarily incurred by or imposed upon said individuals, in connection with any claim, action, suit, proceeding, investigation or inquiry of whatever nature in which he or it may be involved as a party or otherwise by reason of his having been an officer or director of member of the Association, or of any committee of the Association, whether he continues, in said capacity at the time of the incurring or imposition of such costs, expenses or liabilities, except in relation to matters to which he or it shall be finally adjudged in such action, suit, proceeding, investigation or inquiry to be liable for wilful misconduct or negligence towards the Association, any Owner, or other party in the performance of his duties.

The Association shall maintain errors and omissions insurance coverage for all members of the Board, and committees of the Association, and all officers of the Association, and all managers, as provided in Article XI of this Declaration.

5. Meetings. An organizational meeting shall be held as soon as practicable after incorporation of the Association, and the Directors elected then shall hold office until the first annual meeting. All offices of the Board of Directors shall be filled at the organizational meeting. Directors shall be elected in accordance with the provisions of Paragraph C. of this Article VI.

The first annual meeting of Members of the Association shall be held within forty-five (45) days after the closing of the sale of the Condominium that represents the 51st percentile interest authorized for sale under the first final subdivision public report issued for the Development for the California Commissioner of Real Estate, but in no case later than six (6) months after the closing and recording of the sale of the first Condominium within the Development. Thereafter, regular meetings of members of the Association shall be held at least once in each calendar year at a time and place as prescribed in the Bylaws. Special meetings may be called as provided for in the Bylaws.

(a) Notice. Notice of all member's meetings, regular or special, shall be given by regular mail, personal delivery or telegram to all Owners and to any mortgagee who has requested in writing that such notice be sent to it, and shall be given not less than ten (10) days nor more than thirty (30) days before the time of the meeting, and shall set forth the place, date, and hour of the meeting, and the nature of the business to be undertaken.

(b) Quorum Requirements. The presence at any meeting in person or by proxy of members entitled to cast at least (%) percent of the total votes of all members of the Association shall constitute a quorum. If any meeting cannot be held because a quorum is not present, members representing a majority of the votes present, either in person or by proxy, may adjourn the meeting to a time not less than five (5) days or more than thirty (30) days from the date of such meeting by members representing a majority of the votes present in person or by proxy. If a time and place for the adjourned meeting is not fixed by those in attendance at the original meeting or if for any reason a new date is fixed for the adjourned meeting after adjournment, notice of the time and place of the adjourned meeting shall be given to members in the manner prescribed for regular meetings.

(c) Attendance. In addition to members, any mortgagee, through its designated representative, shall be entitled to attend any such meeting, but except as provided in C.2.d. of this Article, shall not be entitled to vote.

(d) Special Meetings. A special meeting of the Members shall be promptly called by the Board upon a written request for a special meeting signed by Members representing at least five percent (5%) of the total voting power of the Association, or upon the vote for such a meeting by a quorum of the Board of Directors.

B. MEMBERSHIP.

1. Qualifications for Membership. Each Owner of a Condominium, including Declarant, shall be a member of the Association. Ownership of a Condominium or an interest in it shall be the sole qualification of membership in the Association. Each Owner shall remain a member of the Association until his Ownership Interest in all Condominiums ceases, at which time his membership in the Association shall automatically cease.

(a) Transfer of Membership. Any transfer of title to a Condominium or to an interest in it shall operate automatically to transfer the appurtenant membership rights in the Association to the new Owner.

(b) Security Holders and Mortgagees. Persons or entities who hold an interest in a Condominium merely as security for performance of an obligation are not to be regarded as Members.

2. Non-severability of Membership. Membership in the Association shall not be assigned, transferred, pledged, hypothecated, conveyed or alienated in any way except on a transfer of title to each such Condominium or interest in it, and then only to the transferee. Any attempt to make a prohibited transfer shall be void.

3. Member's Rights and Duties. Each Member shall have the rights, duties and obligations set forth in this Declaration, the Articles, the Bylaws, and the Rules and Regulations, including amendments to the foregoing.

C. VOTING RIGHTS AND ELECTIONS.

1. Classes of Votes. The Association shall have two (2) classes of voting membership:

(a) Class A: Class A members are all Owners with the exception of Declarant. Each Class A member shall be entitled to one (1) vote for each Condominium in which such member owns an interest. However, when more than one Class A member owns an interest in a Condominium, the vote for such Condominium shall be exercised as they themselves determine, but in no case shall more than one vote be cast with respect to any one Condominium.

(b) Class B: The Class B member shall be the Declarant, who shall be entitled to three (3) votes for each Condominium owned. The Class B membership shall cease and be converted to Class A membership on the happening of one of the following events, whichever occurs earlier:

(i) When the total votes outstanding in the Class A membership equal the total votes outstanding in the Class B membership or,

(ii) On the second anniversary of the original issuance of the Final Public Report for the Project by the Commissioner of Real Estate of California.

or removed, or any two or more of them. The candidates receiving the highest number of votes up to the number of Board members to be elected shall be deemed elected. A Member shall be entitled to cumulate his vote for one or more candidates for the Board if the candidate's name has been placed in nomination prior to voting and if the Member has given notice at the meeting prior to the voting of his intention to cumulate votes.

As to removal (other than by expiration of term), unless the entire Board is removed by a vote of Association members, an individual Director shall not be removed unless the number of votes in favor of removal satisfies the requirements of California Corporations Code §303 (a) (1).

(c) Proxies. Every person entitled to vote or execute consents shall have the right to do so in person or by an agent duly authorized by written proxy executed by such person or his duly authorized agent or agents and filed with the Secretary of the Association prior to commencement of the meeting at which the proxy is to be exercised. Every proxy shall be revocable and revoked upon the receipt of notice by the Secretary of the meeting at which it would otherwise be exercised prior to the exercise thereof, and shall automatically cease upon sale or conveyance by the person granting the proxy of his interest in the Condominium.

(d) Vote by Mortgagee. A Mortgagee can exercise the voting rights of his defaulting Mortgagor/Owner only if (i) the Mortgagee acquires fee title to the Condominium which is subject to the Mortgage or (ii) the Owner gives the Mortgagee his proxy.

(e) Secret Written Ballot. Voting for the Board shall be by secret written ballot.

3. Specially Elected Directors. As long as a majority of the voting power of the Association resides in the Declarant, or as long as there are two outstanding classes of membership in the Association, the election of 20% of the Directors (hereinafter referred to as the "Specially Elected Directors") shall be determined at a special election held immediately before the regular election of Directors (except in the case of the election of a Specially Elected Director following removal of his predecessor, which election shall take place as soon after removal as practicable and in accordance with the Declaration). At a duly constituted meeting of members, nominations for the Specially Elected Directors shall be made from the floor. When nominations have been

As long as two classes of members of the Association exist, no action by the Association that must have the prior approval of the Association members, shall be deemed approved by the members unless approved by the appropriate percentage of both classes of members, except as provided in Article XII, Completion Bond. As long as there are two classes of membership, except where expressly set forth in the Condominium Documents differently, approval of any action shall require a simple majority of the voting power of a quorum of each class.

Where any of the Condominium Documents prescribe two classes of voting membership and require the vote or written assent of a prescribed percentage of each class of membership for the initiation of action by or in the name of the Association, any requirement (except as expressly provided below in this Paragraph C.1. of Article VI) that the vote of Declarant shall be excluded in any such determination shall be applicable only if there has been a conversion of Class B to Class A shares and only for so long as the Declarant holds or directly controls twenty-five percent or more of the voting power of the Association. Notwithstanding the above, the vote of Declarant shall be excluded on matters concerning (i) the enforcement of bonded obligations (as set forth hereinbelow in Article XII, Completion Bond), and (ii) amendment of any of the Condominium Documents to the extent expressly set forth therein.

2. Voting Rights.

(a) Joint Owner Votes. The voting rights for each Condominium cannot be cast on a fractional basis. If the joint Owners of a Condominium are unable to agree among themselves as to how their voting rights shall be cast, their one joint vote shall be cast as their majority chooses. If any Owner exercises the voting rights of a particular Condominium, it will be conclusively presumed for all purposes that he was acting with the authority and consent of all other Owners of the same Condominium. If more than one person or entity exercises the voting rights for a particular Condominium, their one joint vote shall count as their majority choose.

(b) Cumulative Voting. Election to and removal from the Board shall be by cumulative voting, as defined in California Corporations Code §708. Each member shall be entitled to vote, in person or by proxy, as many votes as such member is entitled to exercise as provided in this Declaration, multiplied by the number of Directors to be elected or removed, and he may cast all of such votes for or against any single candidate or director, or he may distribute them amont the number of candidates or Directors to be elected

ARTICLE VII

DUTIES AND POWERS OF THE BOARD OF DIRECTORS

A. DUTIES AND POWERS.

The Association shall have all the powers of a nonprofit mutual benefit corporation organized under the Nonprofit Mutual Benefit Corporation Law, subject only to such limitations on such powers as are set forth in the Condominium Documents. The Association shall have the duty to conduct all business affairs of common interest to all Owners. All duties and powers of the Association shall be exercised by and through the Board. Without limiting the generality of the foregoing, the duties and powers of the Board shall include, but shall not be limited to, the following:

1. Enforcement of the Condominium Documents and Other Instruments for the Ownership, Management and Control of the Project. The Board, on behalf of the Association and in the name of the Association, or on behalf of any Owner who consents, can commence and maintain actions for damages or to restrain or enjoin any actual or threatened breach of any provisions of this Declaration, or of the Articles or Bylaws, or of the Association Rules and Regulations, or any resolutions of the Board, or of any other instrument relating to the management and control of the Project, and to enforce by mandatory injunction, by other equitable means, or otherwise, all of those provisions.

2. Payment of Taxes and Assessments. The Board shall pay all real and personal property taxes and assessments and all other taxes levied against the Common Area, personal property owned by the Association, or against the Association, provided that any such tax or assessment to be paid could otherwise become a lien against all or a part of the Common Area.

3. Insurance. The Board shall obtain, from reputable insurance companies which are admitted to do business in California, and to maintain insurance coverage as described in Article XI of this Declaration.

closed, the special election shall take place. Declarant shall not have the right to participate in or vote in such special election (although Declarant or Declarant's representative may be present), and the candidates receiving the highest number of votes up to the number of Specially Elected Directors, and their term shall be the same of any other Director. Unless members (excluding Declarant) holding a majority of all voting rights (excluding any voting rights held by Declarant) consent, by vote or written consent, such Specially Elected Directors cannot be removed. In case of the death, resignation or removal of a Specially Elected Director, his successor shall be elected at a special meeting of the members, and the provisions set forth in this section respecting the election of a Specially Elected Director shall apply as to the election of a successor. Except as provided in this Declaration, the provisions of this Declaration and of the Articles and Bylaws applicable to Directors, including their election and removal, shall apply to a Specially Elected Director.

4. Special Elections. Except as otherwise expressly provided in this Declaration, special elections will be conducted in accordance with the provisions of the Bylaws.

6. Financial Statements and Budgets of the Association. The Board shall prepare, or cause to be prepared, budgets and financial statements of the Association for distribution to the Members as hereinbelow set forth. The Association's fiscal year shall be a calendar year unless the Board adopts a different fiscal year.

Financial statements for the Association shall be regularly prepared and distributed to all Members regardless of the number of Members or the amount of assets of the Association as follows:

A pro forma operating statement (budget) for each fiscal year shall be distributed not less than sixty (60) days before the beginning of the fiscal year.

A balance sheet, as of an accounting date which is the last day of the month closest in time to six months from the date of closing of the first sale of an interest in the subdivision, and an operating statement for the period from the date of the first closing to the said accounting date, shall be distributed within sixty (60) days after the accounting date. This operating statement shall include a schedule of assessments received and receivable identified by the number of the subdivisions interest and the name of the entity assessed.

An annual report consisting of the following shall be distributed within one hundred twenty (120) days after the close of the fiscal year: a balance sheet as of the end of the fiscal year, an operating (income) statement for the fiscal year, a statement of changes in financial position for the fiscal year, and any information required to be reported under Section 8322 of the Corporations Code. Ordinarily such an annual report shall be prepared by an independent accountant for any fiscal year in which the gross income to the Association exceeds seventy five thousand dollars ($75,000.00). If said annual report is not prepared by an independent accountant, it shall be accompanied by the certificate of any authorized officer of the Association that the statements were prepared without audit from the books and records of the Association.

4. Operation and Maintenance of Common Areas. The Board shall operate, maintain, or otherwise manage or provide for the operation, maintenance and management of the Common Area, (including all Restricted Common Areas but not including cleaning of Restricted Common Areas which are storage compartments, patios or balconies) and all its facilities, improvements, and landscaping, including any private driveways, and any other property acquired by the Association, including personal property, in a first-class condition and in a good state of repair. In this connection, the Association may enter into contracts for services or materials for the benefit of the Association or the Common Area, including contracts with Declarant. The term of any such service contract shall not exceed one (1) year and shall be terminable by either party with or without cause and without payment of a termination fee upon thirty (30) days' written notice.

5. Delegation of Powers. The Board can delegate its power, duties, and responsibilities to committees, officers of the Association or employees, including a professional managing agent (manager). Any agreement for professional management of the Condominium Project shall be terminable by either party with or without cause and without payment of a termination fee on thirty (30) days' written notice. The term of any such agreement shall not exceed one year, although such agreement may be renewed from year to year by the Board. If the Project is professionally maintained or managed, the Board shall not terminate professional management and assume self-management of the Project without the consent of all first Mortgagees.

10. Election of Officers. The Board shall be responsible for the election of officers of the Association as set forth in the Bylaws.

11. Filling of Vacancy on the Board. The Board shall be responsible for filling vacancies on the Board except for any vacancy created by the removal of a Board member. The Board may fill a vacancy on the Board created by the removal of a Board member, provided that such replacement is approved by the vote or written assent of at least fifty-one percent of the voting rights of the Association residing in Members other than Declarant.

12. Inspection of Association's Books and Records. The Board shall make available for inspection and copying by any Member of the Association, or his duly appointed representative, or any mortgagee, at any reasonable time and for a purpose reasonably related to his interest as a Member or mortgagee, at the office of the Association or at such other place within the Project as the Board prescribes, any membership register, books of account, minutes of meetings of the Members, minutes of meetings of the Board, and minutes of meeting of committees of the Board.

The Board shall establish by resolution reasonable rules with respect to:

Notice to be given to the custodian of records of the Association by the members, representatives, or Mortgagees desiring to make an inspection;

Hours and days of the week when an inspection may be made;

Payment of the cost of reproducing copies of documents requested by a member or a representative or mortgagee.

Every Director of the Association shall have the absolute right at any reasonable time to inspect all books, records and documents of the Association and the physical properties owned or controlled by the Association. The right of inspection by a Director includes the right to make extracts and copies of documents.

Any of the documents referred to above to Paragraph 6. shall be mailed to any Mortgagee who has requested in writing that such copies be sent to it.

7. Association Rules and Regulations. The Board shall adopt, amend and repeal Rules for the Association as it deems reasonable. The Association Rules shall govern the use of the Common Area including, but not limited to, any recreational facilities and private driveways, by the Owner or his family, guests, invitees, or tenants or their respective family members, guests or invitees. However, the Association Rules will not be inconsistent with or materially alter any other provisions of this Declaration, the Articles or the Bylaws. A copy of the Association Rules as adopted, amended or repealed shall be mailed or otherwise delivered to each Owner, and a copy shall be posted in a conspicuous place within the Project. In case there is any conflict between any Association Rules and any other provisions of this Declaration, the Articles, or Bylaws, the provisions of the Association Rules shall be deemed to be superseded by the provisions of this Declaration, the Articles or the Bylaws to the extent of any inconsistency.

8. Disciplinary Proceedings. In addition to the provisions of Paragraph A. 1. of this Article VII, the Board can suspend use privileges of the Common Area facilities, and can assess monetary penalties against any Owner or other person entitled to exercise such right or privileges for any violation of this Declaration, or the Articles, Bylaws, Rules and Regulations, or Board resolutions. However, any such suspension of use privileges cannot exceed a period of seven (7) days for each violation and any such assessment cannot exceed forty ($40.00) dollars for any such violation, except as provided in Article V. Paragraph 3. In determining to impose a disciplinary measure upon a Member, the Board is bound to act in good faith and in a fair and reasonable manner.

The imposition of any disciplinary measure must be undertaken in conformity with the procedure therefor set forth in the Bylaws.

9. Entry into Units and Restricted Common Areas for Construction, Maintenance or Emergency Repair. The Board, through its appropriate agent, may enter upon any privately-owned or privately-controlled subdivision interest as necessary in connection with construction, maintenance or emergency repair for the benefit of the Common Area or the Owners in common. Where reasonably possible, notice shall be given prior to such entry. Entry shall be made with as little inconvenience to the Owner as possible and any damage caused thereby shall be repaired by the Board at the expense of the Association.

of the Association who hold certain prescribed percentages of the voting rights of the Association.

1. Fifty-One (51%) Percent of the Voting Rights. Except with the vote or written assent of members of the Association holding fifty-one (51%) percent of the voting rights of the Association residing in Members other than Declarant, the Board shall not take any of the following actions:

(a) Incur aggregate expenditures for capital improvements to the Common Area in any fiscal year in excess of 5% of the budgeted gross expenses of the Association for that fiscal year; or

(b) Sell, during any fiscal year, property of the Association having an aggregate fair market value greater than 5% of the budgeted gross expenses of the Association for that fiscal year; or

(c) Pay compensation to members of the Board or to officers of the Association for services performed in the conduct of the Association's business. However, the Board may cause a member of the Board or an officer to be reimbursed for expenses incurred in carrying on the business of the Association; or

(d) Fill a vacancy on the Board created by the removal of a Board member; or

(e) Enter into a contract with a third person wherein the third person will furnish goods or services for the Common Areas or the Association for a term longer than one year with the following exceptions:

(i) A management contract, the terms of which have been approved by the Federal Housing Administration or Veterans Administration;

(ii) A contract with a public utility company if the rates charged for the materials or services are regulated by the Public Utilities Commission provided, however, that the term of the contract shall not exceed the shortest term for which the supplier will contract at the regulated rate; and

13. Levying Assessments. The Board shall have the powers to establish, fix, and levy against the Owners and to enforce payment of such assessments in accordance with the provisions of this Declaration.

14. Utilities. The Board shall acquire, provide, and pay for water, sewer, garbage disposal, refuse and rubbage collection, electrical, telephone, gas, and any other necessary utility services for the Common Area, and for Condominiums when the Condominiums are not separately billed. The term of any contract to supply any of the listed services shall not exceed one year or, if the supplier is a regulated public utility, the shortest term not to exceed one year for which the supplier will contract at the applicable regulated rate.

15. Utility Easements. The Board shall have authority to grant easements where necessary for utilities and sewer facilities over the Common Area to serve the Common Area and Condominium Units.

16. Discharge of Lien and Assessment to Member. The Board shall have the power to discharge, by payment if necessary, any lien against the Common Area, or any assessment that could become a lien, and assess the cost thereof to the member or members responsible for the existence of said lien.

17. Personal Property of Association. The Board may acquire and hold tangible and intangible personal property and may dispose of the same by sale or otherwise. Upon dissolution of the Association, if no other plan of distribution has been adopted, each Owner shall be deemed to own a beneficial interest in any such property which is in the same ratio to all such property as the square footage of said Owner's Unit is to the square footage of all of the Units.

18. Other Acts. The Board shall be authorized to perform such other acts, whether or not expressly authorized by this Declaration, as may be reasonably necessary to enforce any of the provisions of this Declaration, the Bylaws, or the Rules and Regulations.

B. LIMITATIONS ON AUTHORITY.

As hereinbelow set forth, certain specified actions may be undertaken by the Board only with the assent of members

(iii) Prepaid casualty and/or liability insurance policies of not to exceed three years duration provided that the policy permits short rate cancellation by the insured.

2. Seventy-five (75%) Percent of the Voting Rights. Except with the vote or written assent of members of the Association holding seventy-five (75%) percent of the voting rights of each class of members, the Board shall not take any of the following actions: mortgage, pledge, deed in trust, or hypothecate any or all of the Association's real or personal property as security for money borrowed or debts incurred.

ARTICLE VIII

ASSESSMENTS

A. COVENANT AND AGREEMENT TO PAY. The Declarant for each Condominium owned by it in the Project that is expressly made subject to assessment as set forth in this Declaration, covenants and agrees, and each purchaser of a Condominium by his acceptance of a deed or other instrument of title, covenants and agrees, for each Condominium which he owns, to pay to the Association regular assessments and special assessments, such assessments to be established, made and collected as provided in this Declaration.

B. PERSONAL OBLIGATIONS. Each assessment or installment, together with any late charge, interest, collection costs and reasonable attorneys' fees, shall be the personal obligation of the person that was an Owner at the time such assessment, or installment, became due and payable. If more than one person was the Owner of a Condominium, the personal obligation to pay such assessments or installments, respecting such Condominium, shall be both joint and several. The personal obligation for delinquent assessments, or delinquent installments, and other such sums, shall not pass to an Owner's successors in interest unless expressly assumed by them. No Owner of a Condominium may exempt himself from payment of assessment, or installment, by waiver of the use or enjoyment of all or any portion of the Common Area or by waiver of the use or enjoyment of, or by abandonment of, his Condominium.

C. PURPOSE OF ASSESSMENT. The assessments levied by the Association shall be used exclusively to promote the recreation, health, safety, and welfare of the members of the Association, the improvement, replacement, repair, operation and maintenance of the Common Area and the performance of the duties of the Association set forth in this Declaration.

D. CATEGORIES OF ASSESSMENTS.

1. Regular Assessments.

(a) Basis for Determination. Not more than sixty (60) days nor less than thirty (30) days before the beginning of each fiscal year, the Board shall estimate the total amount of funds necessary to defray the common expenses of the Association for the next fiscal year. If the amount is approved by a majority vote of the Board, without a vote of the members of the Association, the estimate shall become the regular assessment for such year. However, the Board may not increase the amount of the regular assessment for any fiscal year of the Association by more than twenty percent (20%) above the amount of the prior year's assessment, except the first such year if it shall be less than twelve (12) months, without the approval by vote or written consent of a majority of the voting power of the Association residing in Members other than Declarant. The assessment shall be uniform and shall be determined as provided in §F of this Article. The regular assessment shall be payable in regular installments as provided in this Declaration and shall include adequate reserve funds for contingencies and for maintenance, repairs, and replacement of the Common Area improvements that must be replaced on a periodic basis sufficient to satisfy the requirements of any mortgagee. Unless the Association is exempt from federal or state taxes, all reserves shall be accounted for as contributions to the capital of the Association and as trust funds segregated from the regular income of the Association or in any other manner authorized by law or regulation of the Internal Revenue Service and the California Franchise Tax Board that will prevent such funds from being taxed as income of the Association.

(b) Assessment Period. The regular assessment period shall commence on January 1 of each year and shall terminate on December 31 of each year. However, the initial regular assessment period shall commence on the first day of the calendar month following the date on which the sale of the first Condominium to a purchaser is closed and recorded and shall terminate on December 31 of the year in which the initial sale is closed and recorded. Voting rights attributable to subdivision interests shall not be vested until assessments against those interests have been levied by the Association.

(c) Monthly Payments. Regular assessments shall be payable in equal monthly installments unless the Board adopts some other basis for collection.

2. Special Assessments. In addition to regular assessments, the Board is empowered to impose Capital Assessments and Individual Assessments as provided hereinafter:

(a) Capital Assessments. The Association may levy during any fiscal year a capital assessment, applicable to

that fiscal year only, for the purpose of defraying the costs of an action or undertaking on behalf of the Association; provided, however, that no such Capital Assessment which in the aggregate exceeds five percent (5%) of the budget gross expenses of the Association for that fiscal year may be levied without the vote or written assent of a majority of the voting power of the Association held by Owners other than Declarant.

Where a Capital Assessment is levied to raise funds for the rebuilding or major repair of the structural common area housing units of the Project it shall be levied upon the basis of the ratio of the square footage of floor area of each Unit to be assessed to the square footage of all Units to be assessed.

A Capital Assessment shall be levied by written notification by the Board to each Owner at least thirty (30) days in advance of the first payment due under such Capital Assessment, and shall be payable in the manner specified in such notice.

(b) Individual Assessments. Individual assessments may only be levied against Owners and their respective Condominiums in the following circumstances:

(i) Insurance Proceeds Unavailable. If the proceeds of any insurance obtained by the Association are paid to a Mortgagee of a Unit, and by reason of such payment such insurance proceeds are not made available to the Association as trustee or otherwise to affect any repairs, reconstruction or restoration of any damage or destruction to all or any portion of the Project as provided in Article XIII of this Declaration, then the amount not made available shall be levied against the Owner of such Unit and his Condominium as an individual assessment. Such individual assessment shall be levied by written notification from the Board to the Owner or Owners against whom made and shall be payable in full within thirty (30) days following such notice.

(ii) Owner's Failure to Maintain Unit. In the event any Owner fails to maintain the interior of his Unit and make repairs thereto, and the Board causes such maintenance or repair to be performed as provided in Article VII, Paragraph A.9., all costs and expenses incurred in connection with such work, maintenance or repairs shall be immediately assessed and levied against such Owner and his Condominium as an individual assessment. Such individual assessment shall be made by written notification from the Board to the Owner and shall be payable in full within ten (10) days following such notice.

debt of each Owner against whom the same is levied, and notwithstanding anything herein contained to the contrary, shall not exceed an amount equal to the assessed fair market value of the Condominium against which such individual assessment is levied, as determined from the latest tax bill for real property taxes attributable to such Condominium.

E. NOTICE AND ADOPTION OF ANY ACTION AUTHORIZED UNDER ARTICLE VIII, PARAGRAPH D. Any action authorized under Article VIII, Paragraph D. which requires a vote of the membership, shall be taken at a meeting called for that purpose, written notice of which shall be sent to all members not less than thirty (30) days nor more than sixty (60) days in advance of the meeting, specifying the place, day and hour of the meeting and, in the case of a special meeting, the nature of the business to be undertaken. If a quorum is present and the proposed action is favored by a majority vote of the members present at such meeting, but such vote is less than the requisite majority of each class of members, members who were not present in person or by proxy may give their assent in writing, provided that the same is obtained by the appropriate officers of the Association not later than thirty (30) days from the date of such meeting.

F. DIVISION OF ASSESSMENTS AT UNIFORM RATE. Except as expressly provided in this Declaration, the Owner or Owners of each Condominium shall pay the proportionate share of regular assessments and Capital Assessments attributable to said Condominium, which equals (   ) of the total of any such assessment.

G. UNALLOCATED TAXES. In the event that any taxes are assessed against the Common Area, or the personal property of the Association rather than against the Units, said taxes shall be included in the assessment made under the provisions of Article VIII, Section D.2(a), and if necessary, a special assessment may be levied against the Units in an amount equal to said taxes, to be paid in two installments, thirty (30) days prior to the due date of each tax installment.

H. ASSESSMENT ROLL. Each assessment against an Owner and his Condominium shall be set forth and recorded upon an assessment roll maintained by the Board and available for inspection at all reasonable times by an Owner or his duly-authorized representative, provided such representative is an attorney or accountant. Such assessment roll shall indicate for each Condominium, the name and address of the Owner thereof, and the amount of all assessments paid and unpaid.

(iii) Damage to Common Area. In the event an Owner is liable for any damage or destruction to any portion of the Common Area as provided in Article XIII of this Declaration, the Board shall immediately cause same to be repaired or replaced, and all costs and expenses incurred in connection therewith (to the extent not covered or reduced by insurance proceeds paid to or received by the Association) shall be assessed or levied against such Owner and his Condominium as an individual assessment. Such individual assessment shall be made by written notification from the Board to the Owner and shall be payable in full within ten (10) days following such notice.

(iv) Acts Increasing Insurance Premium. If any act or omission of any Owner or occupant of his Unit shall increase the premiums for any insurance policy purchased or obtained by the Association for the benefit of the Project and the residents thereof, the amount of such increase shall be assessed and levied against such Owner and his Condominium as an individual assessment. Such individual assessment shall be made by written notification from the Board to such Owner and shall be payable in full at least ten (10) days in advance of the date or dates for the payment of such increased insurance premiums, or within ten (10) days following such notice, whichever is later.

(v) Other Individual Assessments. In addition to the individual assessments hereinabove authorized, whenever in this Declaration it is provided that the Association shall have the right to assess and levy a cost or expense against an Owner and his Condominium as an individual assessment, an individual assessment may be levied against such Owner by written notification by the Board, and such individual assessment shall be payable in full within thirty (30) days from such notice, or within such extended period as the Board may permit. Also, the Board may levy and assess against the Owner and his Condominium any costs incurred and other charges deemed appropriate as an individual assessment to enforce compliance by such Owner with any provisions of the Bylaws, Rules and Regulations and this Declaration, and to deter violation thereof, and such individual assessment shall be payable in full within ten (10) days following notice thereof to the Owner from the Board.

(vi) Limitations. Any individual assessment made in accordance with this Declaration shall be the separate

I. COLLECTION OF ASSESSMENTS.

1. Due Dates; Effect of Nonpayment of Assessments; Creation of Delinquency. Due dates for the payments of assessments or installments thereon shall be determined by the Board as provided by this Article VIII and the Bylaws. Any assessment not paid within thirty (30) days after the due date shall be deemed delinquent and shall bear interest at the rate of ten percent (10%) per annum, or at such other rate permitted by applicable law and adopted by the Board, from the due date until paid. Such interest shall be termed "the late charge". On becoming delinquent in the payment of any assessment or installment thereon, each delinquent Owner shall be deemed to have absolutely assigned all rent, issues and profits of his Condominium to the Association and shall further be deemed to have consented to the appointment of a receiver. The Board shall be empowered to appoint such a receiver.

2. Creation of Lien. By recording a notice of assessment In the Office of the County Recorder of Los Angeles as provided by California Civil Code §1356, the Board may create a lien against the Condominium to recover a delinquency in the payment of any assessment or installment thereon. The amount of the lien shall be the total of the payments delinquent, the late charge described in Section I.1. of this Article, and all collection costs and expenses incurred by the Board, or its authorized representative, including reasonable attorneys' fees.

3. Priorities; Enforcement; Remedies. Each lien recorded pursuant to paragraph I.2. of this Article shall be prior and superior to all other liens, except (a) all taxes, bonds, assessments and other levies which, by law, would be superior thereto, and (b) the lien or charge of any first institutional Mortgagee.

The right to collect and to enforce assessments is vested in the Board acting by and on behalf of the Association. The Board or its authorized representatives, including any manager, can enforce the obligations of the Owners to pay assessments provided for in this Declaration by commencement and maintenance of a suit at law or in equity, or the Board may foreclose by judicial proceedings or through the

exercise of the power of sale pursuant to Paragraph I.4. of this Article to enforce the lien rights created. Suit to recover a money judgment for unpaid assessments together with all other amounts described in Paragraph I.2. of this Article shall be maintainable without foreclosing or waiving the lien rights.

The Board may temporarily suspend the voting rights and the right to use recreational facilities of a member who is in default in payment of any assessment or installment thereon after notice and hearing as provided by 10 California Administrative Code §2792.26 and the Bylaws.

4. Notice of Default; Foreclosure by Board. Not more than one (1) year nor less than ten (10) days after the recording of the notice of assessment as provided in Paragraph I.2. of this Article, the Board or its authorized representative can record a notice of default and can cause the Condominium to be sold in the same manner as a sale is conducted under California Civil Code §§2924 et seq. or their successor statutes applicable to the exercise of powers of sale in mortgages and deeds of trust, or through judicial foreclosure. In connection with any such sale, the Board is authorized to appoint its attorney, any officer or director, or any title insurance company authorized to do business in California as trustee for purposes of conducting the sale. The Association, acting on behalf of the Owners, shall have the power to bid on the Condominium at the foreclosure sale and to acquire, hold, lease, mortgage and convey the Condominium.

During the pendency of any foreclosure proceeding, whether judicial or by power of sale, the Condominium Owner shall be required to pay to the Association reasonable rent for the Condominium and the Association shall be entitled to the appointment of a receiver to collect the rent.

5. Transfer of Unit by Sale or Foreclosure. Sale or transfer of any Condominium shall not affect an assessment lien. However, the sale or transfer of any Condominium pursuant to mortgage foreclosure shall extinguish the lien of such assessments as to payments which become due prior to such sale or transfer, except for assessment liens recorded prior to the Mortgage. The obligation which the lien had represented shall continue as provided by Paragraph B. of this Article. No sale or transfer shall relieve such Condominium from liability for any assessments thereafter becoming due or from the lien thereof.

if any. The prospective purchaser or lender may conclusively rely on the written statement as to the payment of assessments, but the Association warrants all other matters only to the extent of its then actual knowledge.

L. WAIVER OF EXEMPTIONS WITH RESPECT TO LIENS.

To the extent permitted by law, and with respect to any liens created pursuant to this Article VIII, each Owner waives the benefit of any homestead or exemption laws of California in effect at the time any assessment or installment thereon becomes delinquent or any lien is imposed.

M. CONTROL.

All assessments collected under the provisions of this Article VIII, together with any other Common Funds or other funds, fees, levies, charges, and monies elsewhere provided for in this Declaration, shall be controlled by Declarant prior to the organizational meeting of the Association and shall thereafter be controlled by the Board.

ARTICLE IX.

UTILITIES

A. OWNERS' RIGHTS AND DUTIES.

The rights and duties of the Owners of Condominiums within the Project with respect to sanitary sewer, water, electricity, television, gas and telephone lines and facilities, and heating and air conditioning facilities, shall be as follows:

1. Whenever sanitary sewer, water, electricity, gas, television, telephone lines or connections, heating or air conditioning conduits, ducts, or flues are installed within the Project, which connections, or any portion thereof lie in or upon Condominiums owned by other than the Owner of a Condominium served by said connections, those Owners served thereby shall have the right, and are hereby granted an easement to the full extent necessary therefor, to enter upon the Condominiums or to have the utility companies enter upon the Condominiums in or upon which said connections, or any portion thereof, lie, to repair, replace and generally maintain said connections as and when necessary.

6. Curing of Default. If any default, including interest, late charges and a fifteen ($15.00) dollar charge for release, is cured before sale, or before completing a judicial foreclosure, the Board or its authorized representative shall cause to be recorded in the Office of the County Recorder of Los Angeles County a certificate setting forth the satisfaction of such claim and release of such lien on payment of actual expenses incurred, including reasonable attorneys' fees.

7. Cumulative Remedies. The assessment lien and the rights with respect to foreclosure and sale thereunder, as particularly described hereinabove, shall be in addition to, and not in substitution of, all other rights and remedies which the Association and its assigns may have hereunder, or by law, including, but not limited to, a suit to recover a money judgment for unpaid assessments. Further, each Owner hereby vests in, and delegates to, the Board, or its duly authorized representatives, the right and the power to bring all actions at law or in equity, or lien foreclosures, whether judicially, by power of sale, or otherwise, against any and all Owners for the collection of delinquent assessments.

J. CERTIFICATE OF PAYMENT.

The Association shall, upon demand, furnish to any Owner liable for assessments, a certificate in writing signed by an officer of the Association, setting forth whether the assessments on his Unit or Condominium have been paid and the amount of any delinquency, if any.

A standard charge for the issuance of each such certificate may be made by the Board. The Board shall be empowered to determine such a standard charge and may readjust that charge from time to time in response to changes in administrative costs.

K. ESTOPPEL CERTIFICATE.

Upon fourteen (14) days' prior written request, the Board or manager shall issue a written statement to a designated prospective purchaser or lender declaring whether or not the particular Owner is in default under any provisions of this Declaration. The statement shall further set forth the regular and special assessments due on the Condominium in question, the installment payments made, and those installments due and unpaid,

A. OWNER'S RIGHT TO ENCUMBER BY MORTGAGE.

Any Owner may encumber his Condominium with a Mortgage. Within ten (10) days of the execution of such Mortgage, the Owner shall give written notice to the Board of the name and address of the Mortgagee and the amount secured by the Mortgage. The Owner shall notify the Board in the same manner of any release, discharge, or novation of the Mortgage.

B. VALIDITY OF LIEN OF FIRST MORTGAGE.

No breach of any of the covenants, conditions and restrictions herein contained, nor the enforcement of any lien provisions herein, shall render invalid the lien of any first Mortgage (meaning a Mortgage with first priority over any other Mortgage) on any Unit made in good faith and for value, but all of said covenants, conditions and restrictions shall be binding upon and effective against any Owner whose title is derived through foreclosure or trustee's sale, or otherwise.

C. NOTICE OF DEFAULT BY CONDOMINIUM MORTGAGOR.

Any Mortgagee that has filed with the Association a request for notice of default shall be entitled to receive written notice from the Association of any default in the performance by a Mortgagor of any obligation arising under this Declaration or by Bylaws which is not cured within thirty (30) days.

D. SUBORDINATION.

Any lien created or claimed under the provisions of this Declaration is expressly made subject and subordinate to the rights of any first mortgage made in good faith and for value, and no such lien shall in any way defeat, invalidate, or impair the obligation or priority of such first Mortgage unless the first Mortgagee expressly subordinates his interest, in writing, to such lien.

2. Whenever sanitary sewer, water, electricity, gas, television, or telephone lines or connections, heating or air conditioning conduits, ducts, or flues are installed within the Project, which connections serve more than one Condominium, the Owner of each Condominium served by said connection shall be entitled to the full use and enjoyment of such portions of said connections as service his Condominium.

3. In the event of a dispute between Owners with respect to the repair or rebuilding of said connections, or with respect to the sharing of the cost thereof, then, upon written request of one of such Owners addressed to the Association, the matter shall be submitted to the Board of Directors, who shall decide the dispute, and the decision of the Board shall be final and conclusive on the parties.

B. EASEMENTS FOR MAINTENANCE OF UTILITIES.

Easements within the Project for the installation, repair, and maintenance of electric, telephone, water, gas, and sanitary sewer lines and facilities, heating and air conditioning facilities, cable or master television antenna lines, drainage facilities, walkways, and landscaping as shown on the recorded map of the Project, and as may be hereafter required or needed to service the Project, are hereby reserved by Declarant and its successors and assigns, including the Association, together with the right to grant and transfer the same.

C. ASSOCIATION'S DUTIES.

The Association shall maintain all utility installations located in the Common Area, except for those installations maintained by utility companies, public, private, or municipal. The Association shall pay all charges for utilities supplied to the Project, except those metered or charged separately to the Units.

ARTICLE X

PROTECTION OF THE RIGHTS OF
MORTGAGEES AND INSTITUTIONAL LENDERS

POSSESSION OF PRIOR CLAIM.

E. APPLICABILITY TO LIENHOLDER THAT COMES INTO POSSESSION OF PRIOR CLAIM.

Each holder of a first Mortgage lien on a Unit who comes into possession of the Unit by virtue of foreclosure of the Mortgage, or any purchaser at a foreclosure sale, will take the Unit free of any claims for unpaid assessments and charges against the Unit which accrue prior to the time such holder comes into possession of the Unit, except for claims for a pro rata share of such assessments or charges resulting from a pro rata reallocation of such assessments or charges to all Project Units including the mortgaged Unit and except for assessment liens recorded prior to the Mortgage.

F. NON-CURABLE BREACH.

Any Mortgagee who acquires title to a Condominium by foreclosure or by deed in lieu of foreclosure or assignment in lieu of foreclosure shall not be obligated to cure any breach of this Declaration that is non-curable. A "non-curable breach" shall not include any breach that can be remedied in full by the payment of delinquent assessments.

G. VOTING RIGHTS ON DEFAULT.

In case of default by the Owner of any Condominium in any payment due under the terms of any first Mortgage (meaning a Mortgage with priority over other Mortgages) encumbering such Condominium or the promissory note secured by the Mortgage, said Mortgagee, or his representative, may only exercise the voting rights of said Owner only (1) upon taking title to said Condominium or (2) upon receiving the proxy of said Owner.

H. LOAN TO FACILITATE.

Any Mortgage given to secure a loan to facilitate the resale of a Condominium after acquisition by foreclosure or by deed in lieu of foreclosure or by assignment in lieu of foreclosure shall be deemed to be a loan made in good faith and for value and entitled to all of the rights and protections of this Article X.

I. EXEMPTION FROM RIGHT OF FIRST REFUSAL.

Any first Mortgagee that comes into possession of a Condominium pursuant to the remedies provided in the Mortgage, or by foreclosure of the Mortgage or by deed or assignment in lieu of foreclosure, shall be exempt from any requirements of a right of first refusal which shall appear in the Condominium Documents as amended from time to time, except where such a right of first refusal is required by law.

J. MORTGAGEE'S RIGHT TO ACCESS TO INFORMATION CONCERNING THE ASSOCIATION'S OPERATIONS.

Upon timely request any Mortgagee shall be entitled to:

1. Inspect the books and records of the Association during normal business hours;

2. Receive an annual audited financial statement of the Association within one-hundred twenty days (120) following the end of the Association's fiscal year;

3. Receive written notice of all meetings of the Association;

4. Designate a representative to attend meetings of the Association, who may vote only as provided in Paragraph G. of this Article X.

K. NOTICE TO MORTGAGEE OF LOSS OR TAKING.

Upon timely request, any Mortgagee shall be entitled to written notice from the Association of any loss or taking:

1. To any Condominium covered by its Mortgage where the loss or taking exceeds one-thousand dollars ($1,000.00); or

2. To the Common Area, where the loss or taking exceeds ten-thousand dollars ($10,000.00).

L. PRIORITY OF RIGHTS OF FIRST MORTGAGEES CONCERNING DISTRIBUTIONS COMPENSATING FOR LOSSES OR TAKINGS.

b. Determining the pro rata share of ownership of each Condominium in the Common Area;

3. Partition or subdivide any Condominium Unit;

4. By act or omission, seek to abandon, partition, subdivide, encumber, sell or transfer the Common Area or any portion thereof. (The granting of easements for public utilities or for other public purposes consistent with the intended use of the Common Area shall not be deemed a transfer or other act within the meaning of this clause.);

5. Use hazard insurance proceeds for losses to any Condominium property (whether to Units or to Common Area) for other than the repair, replacement or reconstruction of such Condominium property, except as provided by statute in case of substantial loss to the Units and/or Common Area of the Condominium Project;

6. Effectuate any decision by the Association to terminate professional management and assume self-management;

7. Make any material amendment to the Declaration or to the Bylaws; "material amendment" shall mean any amendment governing the following subjects:

a. The percentage of interest of the Unit Owners in the common elements of the Project;

b. The fundamental purpose for which the Project was created (such as a change from residential use to a different use);

c. Voting;

d. Assessments, assessment liens and subordination thereof;

e. The reserve for repair and replacement of common elements;

f. Property maintenance obligations;

No provision of the Condominium Documents shall give a Condominium Owner or any other party priority over any rights of first Mortgagees of Condominiums pursuant to their Mortgages in the case of a distribution to Condominium Owners of insurance proceeds or condemnation awards for losses to or takings of Condominium Units or common elements.

All applicable fire and physical loss or extended coverage insurance policies shall contain loss-payable clauses acceptable to the affected Mortgagees, naming the Mortgagees as their interests may appear.

M. LIENS HAVING PRIORITY UNDER LOCAL LAW.

All taxes, assessments and charges which become liens prior to any first Mortgage under local law shall relate only to individual Condominiums and not to the Project as a whole.

N. MORTGAGEE'S RIGHT TO FURNISH INFORMATION TO THE ASSOCIATION. Any Mortgagee may furnish information to the Board concerning the status of any Mortgage.

O. ACTIONS REQUIRING APPROVAL OF MORTGAGEES. Unless at least seventy-five percent (75%) of the combined total of holders of first Mortgages (based upon one (1) vote for each first Mortgage owned) and of Owners of Condominium Units which are not subject to first Mortgages (based upon one (1) vote for each such Unit so owned) give their prior written approval, the Association shall not be entitled to:

1. By act or omission, seek to abandon or to terminate the Condominium Project;

2. Change the pro rata interest or obligations of any individual Condominium Unit for the purpose of:

a. Levying assessments or charges or allocating distributions of hazard insurance proceeds or condemnation awards, or

T. CONFLICT.

If there is any conflict between any provision of this Article X and any other provision in this Declaration or other Condominium Document, the provisions of this Article X shall control.

ARTICLE XI

INSURANCE

A. DUTIES AND POWERS OF THE BOARD.

As authorized by Article VII, Paragraph A.3., the Board shall have the following duties and powers:

1. Authority to Purchase Insurance. All insurance provided for herein (except where otherwise specifically provided) shall be purchased and maintained by the Association acting through the Board, and the premiums thereon shall be part of the common expenses and paid of the common funds (except where otherwise specifically provided). For the purposes of the provisions of this Article XI, the Board shall be deemed the Agent, coupled with an interest, of all of the Owners and Occupants.

2. Assumption of Insurance Acquired by Declarant. Prior to the time of the initial installation of the Board as provided in Article VI, Paragraph A.3., the Declarant may, in the exercise of its prudent judgment, contract for various forms of insurance coverage to benefit all or part of the Project for some or all of these persons having any insurable interests in any aspect of the Project. Once the Board is initially installed, the Board shall automatically assume the responsibility to maintain such insurance, except to the extent that any such insurance is solely for the benefit of Declarant or of any successor of Declarant where said successor intends to develop the Project. The maintenance of this Article XI, and any inconsistencies between insurance coverage acquired by the Declarant and any requirement of this Article XI shall be remedied by the Board as soon after its initial installation as reasonably possible.

---

g. Casualty and liability insurance;

h. Reconstruction in the event of damage or destruction;

i. Rights to use the common elements;

j. Annexation;

k. Any provision which by its terms is specifically for the benefit of First Mortgagees or specifically confers rights on first Mortgagees.

P. AMENDMENT.

No amendment to this Declaration, the Articles or Bylaws shall affect the rights of any Mortgagee under any Mortgage made in good faith and for value recorded before the recordation of any such amendment.

Q. AGREEMENT FOR PROFESSIONAL MANAGEMENT.

Any agreement for professional management of the Condominium Project may not exceed one (1) year. Any such agreement must provide for termination by either party without either cause or payment of a termination fee upon thirty (30) days written notice. Any decision to terminate such an agreement shall be made pursuant to Paragraph 0.6 of this Article X, to the extent that said section is relevant.

R. CONTRACTS WITH DECLARANT.

Any agreement between the Association and Declarant pursuant to which the Declarant agrees to provide services shall provide for termination by either party without any cause or payment of a termination fee upon thirty (30) days written notice and may not exceed one (1) year.

S. RESERVE FUNDS FOR COMMON AREA.

Regular Assessments shall include an adequate reserve fund for maintenance, repairs and replacement of those Common Area improvements that must be replaced on a periodic basis, as provided in Article VIII, Paragraph D.1.(a).

3. Triennial Review. The Board is empowered to review and revise all types of insurance coverage which it maintains. Such review and revision may occur at any time (provided that a meeting of Members is convened to discuss proposed changes, subject to the various requirements concerning notice and quorum for a meeting set forth in Article VI of this Declaration), but in no event shall more than three (3) years lapse without a review of each type of insurance policy in force and each category of insurance provided for in this Article XI.

4. Assessments. Except where otherwise specifically provided, premiums for insurance maintained by the Board shall be a common expense to be included in the monthly assessments levied by the Association. The Owner or Owners of each Condominium shall be responsible for the one-seventy-fifth interest of his or their Condominium for such insurance.

5. Exclusive Power to Adjust Losses on Behalf of Insureds. The Board is appointed attorney-in-fact by each Owner to negotiate and to agree on the value and on the extent of any loss under any policy carried by the Board. The Board is granted full right and authority to enforce any claim by legal action or otherwise and to execute releases in favor of any insurer. The Board shall have the power to distribute proceeds of insurance obtained under the provisions of Paragraph B. of this Article.

6. Selection of Trustee for Insurance Proceeds. A commercial bank which maintains a full service office in the Los Angeles County and which agrees in writing to serve as a trustee for insurance proceeds may be selected by the Board to serve as such a trustee. All insurance proceeds payable under any policy of insurance which is maintained by the Board, and subject to the rights of Mortgagees as provided in Paragraph D.1 of this Article XI, may be paid to said trustee, to be held and expended for the benefit of the Owners, Mortgagees, and others, as their respective interests shall appear in the respective insurance policies.

7. Notwithstanding any other provision of this Article XI, the Board is empowered to consider the acquisition of types of insurance or of insurance coverage not expressly provided for in this Article XI, and to acquire any such further insurance as the Board shall deem prudent.

8. Consultations with Insurance Services' Office. The Board is empowered to consult with the Insurance Services' Office, directly or through any appropriate intermediary, in order to gain information concerning the development and availability of particular insurance forms or insurance package policies which shall be developed specifically for condominiums. (The Insurance Services' Office is a non-profit unincorporated association doing business nationally and concerned with the promulgation of information concerning forms and contents of insurance policies.)

B.   TYPES OF INSURANCE TO BE MAINTAINED BY BOARD.

The Board has the duty to maintain the following types of insurance coverage. Except as otherwise specifically stated in this Paragraph B., there shall be no requirements that the policies by which such insurance coverages are maintained include any of the listed types of insurance coverage in any prescribed combination or specifically by any endorsement to any policy.

1. Casualty Insurance.

a. Fire and Extended Coverage. The Board shall obtain and maintain insurance against casualties, including fire, earthquake, and such other casualties as are commonly found in extended coverage policies, special form endorsements and difference-in-conditions endorsements. The Board may also obtain and maintain insurance against vandalism and malicious mischief.

b. Full Insurable Replacement Value. All such casualty insurance shall be for the full insurable replacement value of all of the improvements upon the Project, excluding any improvements added by an Owner and excluding all personal property of any Owner including (by way of illustration and not by way of limitation) furniture, furnishings, and decorations. The Board shall determine the full insurable replacement value of the improvements to be insured under the provisions of Paragraph A.3. of this Article XI. The Board is also empowered to determine deductible amounts with respect to any casualty insurance.

c. Authority of Association to Decide With Respect to Reconstruction. All policies of casualty insurance shall include a provision stating that the insurer issuing said policy agrees to abide by the decision of the Association whether to repair, reconstruct or restore all or any damaged or destroyed portion of the Common Area.

d. Other Provisions. Any policy of casualty insurance may include a stipulated amount clause, a determinable cash adjustment clause, or any clause similar to either of these two clauses, an endorsement for contingent liability from operation of building laws, and such other provisions as the Association deems prudent.

2. Comprehensive Public Liability and Property Damage. Comprehensive public liability and property damage coverage shall be obtained and maintained as herein provided. Such coverage may be provided by means of an umbrella policy, a combination of primary liability and excess policies, by endorsements, or by any combination of the above.

a. Minimum Amounts of Coverage.

(i) Initial Coverage. Initial coverage shall be: one million dollars ($1,000,000.00) for bodily injury, personal injury, or death of any one person; three million dollars ($3,000,000.00) for personal injury, bodily injury, or deaths of more than one person arising from one occurrence; and five hundred thousand dollars ($500,000.00) for property damage in any one occurrence.

(ii) Adjustment. The amounts stated above in Paragraph B.2.a.(i). of this Article XI shall be subject to adjustment whenever the casualty insurance needs of the Project are reviewed as provided in Paragraph A.3. of this Article XI.

The base for computing any such adjustment shall be the Consumer Price Index for All Urban Consumers for the Standard Metropolitan Statistical Area which includes the Project, published by the United States Department of Labor, Bureau of Labor Statistics (hereinafter referred to as "the Bureau"), most immediately prior to one-hundred twenty (120) days prior to the "adjustment date (hereinafter referred to as "the Adjustment Index"). The adjustment date of any such insurance which is so reviewed shall be the date on which such insurance is replaced or renewed.

Each of the amounts stated above in Paragraph B.2.a.(i) shall be adjusted by multiplying it by a fraction of which the numerator shall equal the Adjustment Index and the denominator shall equal the Consumer Price Index for All Urban Consumers as of the date of recordation of this Declaration for the Standard Metropolitan Statistical Area which did include the Project on the date of the recordation of this Declaration.

If the Index is discontinued, made subject to a conversion factor, or in any other manner revised, such other government index or computation with which it is replaced or by which it is revised shall be used in order to obtain substantially the same result as would be obtained if the Index had not been discontinued, made subject to a conversion factor, or in any other manner revised.

The amounts stated above in subsection (i) as adjusted by the provisions of the subsection (ii) which appear above, shall represent the respective minimum amounts of coverage to be obtained pursuant to the review, as provided in Paragraph A.3. of this Article XI, for which the Adjustment Index was applied. Such adjusted minimum amounts may be rounded off by the Board in order to make said amounts commercially practicable, but in no event shall any such adjusted minimum amount be reduced more than two (2%) percent.

b. Intentional Torts. Coverage shall be provided against intentional torts.

c. Supplemental Coverages. To the extent germane to the operations of the Association, the Association shall obtain liability coverage for hired automobiles, non-owned automobiles, collisions, off-premise employees, elevators, and theft and embezzlement.

3. Demolition Insurance. The Board may obtain and maintain demolition insurance in an amount adequate to cover demolition in case of total or partial destruction of the Condominium Building and a decision not to rebuild.

4. Workers' Compensation. The Board shall obtain and maintain workers' compensation insurance and employers' liability insurance to the extent required by law.

5. Officers' and Directors' Liability Insurance. The Board shall obtain and maintain officers' and directors' liability insurance. Such insurance may be obtained in whole or in part by bond; such insurance shall include coverage for errors and omissions. The insureds under such a policy shall include the Association, the Board, their officers and directors, and anyone serving on a duly constituted committee of the Association or of the Board, and such coverage shall apply with respect to any act or omission in the performance of their obligation while acting in their capacities hereinabove stated or resulting from their membership on the Board or any committee thereof.

6. Other Customary Insurance. The Board may obtain and maintain any other insurance which is or does become customary for projects similar to the Project with respect to location, size, and purpose.

C. INSURANCE RESPONSIBILITIES OF OWNERS.

1. Insurance Acquired by Owners. Each Owner has the responsibility, at his option, to obtain and to maintain at his sole expense, such casualty, liability, property damage, or other insurance covering his personal property, furniture, furnishings, decorations within his Unit, any improvements added by an Owner or occupant, or otherwise protecting his Unit or his own insurable interests.

2. Personal Liability Insurance. In addition to liability insurance which the Association shall carry, and notwithstanding any of the provisions of Paragraph C.1. of this Article XI, each Owner shall carry personal liability insurance covering damage to property or injury to the person of others within the Project resulting from the negligence of the Owner or his agents, in an amount not less than one-quarter of the amount of insurance coverage in force at the same time which has been obtained and maintained by the Board with respect to property damage per occurrence as implemented under the provisions of Paragraph B.2.a. of this Article XI.

3. Duplication of Coverage. No Owner shall duplicate insurance obtained and maintained by the Board. Any diminution in the amount of insurance proceeds otherwise payable pursuant to the provisions of Paragraph B. of this Article XI as a result of the existence of separate insurance purchased by an Owner as provided in this Paragraph C. shall be assessed and levied against such Owner as an individual assessment to the extent of such diminution.

4. Act Increasing Insurance Risk. As provided in Article V, Paragraph 5, of this Declaration, no Owner shall do anything which shall in any way increase the rate of insurance for the Project, cause any insurance policy to be cancelled, or cause a refusal to renew the same, where such insurance is on the Project, or any common portion of the Project, without the prior written consent of the Board. Any Owner doing any such act or causing any such act to occur shall be liable in damages to the Association.

5. Facilitation of the Procurement and Maintenance of Insurance. Each Owner shall provide in a timely fashion all information requested of him and reasonably related to any of his common interests with other Owners, as sought by the Board or, at the direction of the Board, an insurer with whom the Board has contracted or is attempting to contract for insurance. Each Owner shall abide by the requirements of Article VIII of this Declaration with respect to the payment of his assessment for insurance. Each Owner shall further perform all acts reasonably required of him in order to facilitate the procurement and maintenance of insurance as provided by this Article XI.

D.   PROTECTION OF THE RIGHTS OF INSTITUTIONAL LENDERS AND MORTGAGEES.

The provisions of this Paragraph D. apply to any insurance obtained or maintained under the provisions of Paragraphs B. or C. of this Article XI.

1. Distributions to Mortgagees. Any Mortgagee has the option to apply insurance proceeds either payable on account of a Condominium or payable to him, in reduction of the obligation secured by the Mortgage of such Mortgagee.

2. Maximum Requirements of First Mortgagees of Record. The form, contents and terms of any insurance policy and its endorsements and the issuing company must be satisfactory to all first Mortgagees of record. If more than one such first Mortgagee has a loan of record against the Project, or any part of it, the policies and endorsements shall meet the maximum standards of the various institutional Mortgagees represented in the Project. Any insurance policies must adhere to the requirements for Condominium Projects established by the Federal National Mortgage Association and the Government National Mortgage Association, so long as either is a Mortgagee or Owner of a Condominium within the Project, except to the extent that such coverage is not available or has been waived in writing by the Federal National Mortgage Association or the Government National Mortgage Association.

E.   CONDITIONS AND INFORMATION TO BE INCLUDED IN ALL INSURANCE POLICIES.

The provisions of this Paragraph E. pertain to any policy of insurance obtained or maintained under the provisions of Paragraph B. or Paragraph C. of this Article XI.

1. Waiver by Insurer of Right of Subrogation Against Insureds. A waiver by insurer of the right of subrogation against insureds shall be contained in each insurance policy, where relevant.

2. Cross-liability or Severability of Interest. Each insurance policy shall contain a provision for cross-liability or severability of interest, where relevant.

3. Designation of Named Insureds. Each policy of insurance shall designate all of the following as insureds (or as additional insureds, as appropriate): the Association, the Board, and their officers, directors, and committee members; the professional manager (if there is one) of the Project and his staff members; Declarant (so long as any Condominiums remain unsold); any other employees of this Association; and all of the Owners, occupants, and their guests and invitees.

4. No "Other Insurance" Clause Voiding Coverage. There shall be no "other insurance" clause, or similar clause, voiding insurance coverage, in whole or in part, under any policy of insurance.

5. No Right of Cancellation Without Prescribed Prior Procedures. Each policy of insurance shall include the following provisions and shall state that no policy of insurance may be cancelled unless these procedures have first been followed:

a. The insurer must demand in writing that the Association, Declarant, or an Owner, as appropriate, cure any breach that serves as the grounds for cancellation of any policy of insurance;

b. The insurer must give thirty (30) days written notice to the Association, Declarant, and to any Owner or Mortgagee who files a written request with such insurer for such notice of impending cancellation.

6. Satisfaction of All First Mortgagees of Record as Their Interests Appear. To the extent relevant, any policy of insurance shall contain a provision stating that, for the respective liability insured against, each first mortgagee of record will receive satisfaction as and to the extent that its interests may appear under Paragraph E.3. of this Article XI or as recorded.

ARTICLE XII

COMPLETION BOND

In the event that the Project is not completed prior to the issuance of the Final Public Report by the California Department of Real Estate and the Association is obligee under a bond or other arrangement (hereinafter "Bond") to secure performance of the commitment of Declarant to complete the improvements, the following provisions shall apply with respect to the initiation of action by the Association to enforce the obligations of the subdivider and the surety of the Bond:

ARTICLE XIII

DESTRUCTION, RECONSTRUCTION AND REPAIR
OF COMMON AREA IMPROVEMENTS

In the event of a total or partial destruction of the improvements situated in the Common Area, the provisions of this Article XIII shall govern the effectuation of decisions with respect to reconstruction. Where no time requirements are expressly set forth, the procedures set forth below in this Article XIII shall be followed as soon as practicable after total or partial destruction of the improvements.

A. SPECIAL MEETING. A special meeting of the Association shall be called within sixty (60) days of said destruction.

1. Insurance Proceeds Not Exceeding 85% of Reconstruction Costs. If the proceeds of insurance carried pursuant to Article XI do not exceed eighty five percent (85%) of the costs of repair, reconstruction may nevertheless take place if a majority of the total voting power of each class of members entitled to vote and present, in person or by proxy, determine that such repair and reconstruction shall take place.

2. Insurance Proceeds Exceeding 85% of Reconstruction Costs. If the available proceeds of the insurance carried pursuant to Article XI are sufficient to cover more than eighty five percent (85%) of the costs of repair and construction, the improvements shall be promptly rebuilt unless Members holding at least seventy five percent (75%) of the total voting power of each class of members entitled to vote and present, in person or by proxy, determine that such repair and construction shall not take place.

3. Insurance Proceeds. The Board may appoint a trustee to receive insurance proceeds. In the event that the total of insurance proceeds exceeds all reconstruction costs, any excess insurance proceeds may be deposited into the general funds of the Association.

B. RECONSTRUCTION PROCEDURES.

1. Solicitation of Bids and Acceptance of Contract. If the Members determine to rebuild, the Board or its authorized representative shall obtain bids from reputable, licensed California contractors. If the Board reasonably believes that all such costs shall total two hundred thousand dollars ($200,000.00) or less, the Board shall obtain at least two such bids. If the Board reasonably believes that all such costs shall total more than two hundred thousand dollars ($200,000.00) but less than one million five hundred thousand dollars ($1,500,000.00), the Board shall obtain at least three such bids. If the Board reasonably believes that all such

tion of action by the Association to enforce the obligation of action by the Association to enforce the obligations under the Bond with respect to any improvements for which a notice of completion has not been filed within sixty (60) days after the completion date specified for that improvement in the Planned Construction Statement appended to the Bond. If the Association has given an extension in writing for the completion of any Common Area improvement, the Board shall be directed to consider and vote on the aforesaid question if a notice of completion has not been filed within thirty (30) days after the expiration of the extension.

b. A special meeting of Members for the purpose of voting to override a decision by the Board not to initiate action to enforce the obligations under the Bond or on the failure of the Board to consider and vote on the question shall be held not less than thirty-five (35) days or more than forty-five (45) days after receipt by the Board of a petition for such a meeting signed by Members representing five percent (5%) of the total voting power of the Association.

c. The Bond shall be enforced against Declarant, the surety, or both of them upon the affirmative vote of a majority of Members of the Association, excluding Declarant, at the special meeting called for the purpose set forth in (b) above.

d. A vote of the majority of the voting power of the Association residing, in Members other than Declarant, to take action to enforce the obligations under the Bond shall be deemed to be the decision of the Association and the Board shall thereafter implement this decision by initiating and pursuing appropriate action in the name of the Association.

shall be made final and binding on all Owners, as modified, by a majority of the total voting power of each class of Members. If no adjustments are recommended by the Board, the decision of the Board shall be final and binding on all Owners, including any Owner filing written objections.

C. DECISION NOT TO REBUILD.

1. Distribution of Insurance Proceeds. If the Association decides not to rebuild, any insurance proceeds then or subsequently available for reconstruction or repair of the structural Common Area shall be distributed by the Association among Owners and their respective Mortgagees according to the respective fair market values of their Units at the time of the destruction as determined by an independent appraisal.

Such an independent appraisal shall be conducted as hereinafter set forth. As soon as practicable after the date of damage or destruction, the Board shall hire an independent real estate appraiser (the "Appraiser") to conduct such an appraisal according to the customary procedures of his profession. The Appraiser must either hold the professional designation of M.A.I. (as a member of the American Institute of Real Estate Appraisers), hold the professional designation of S.R.A. (as certified by the Society of Real Estate Appraisers), or hold another professional designation which, at the date he is so hired, has professional stature and recognition similar to the two above-cited designations on the date of this Declaration. The Appraiser may not be an Owner; may not be a partner in a partnership which is an Owner; may not be an officer or director of a corporation which is an Owner; may not have any pecuniary interest in the Project (other than his right to a fee for his services to be rendered pursuant to this paragraph, and any lien rights thereunder); may neither be related to any of the above-described persons more closely than third degree nor may be the spouse of any person so related; and may not be an employee, officer, or director of any Mortgagee.

2. Revival of Right to Partition. On recordation of a declaration of intent not to rebuild pursuant to Paragraph D. of this Article XIII, the right of any Owner to partition through legal action as provided by Article XV shall be revived.

D. RECORDATION OF DECLARATION OF INTENT WITH RESPECT TO REPAIR AND RECONSTRUCTION. Within one hundred twenty (120) days from the date of destruction, the Board shall execute, acknowledge and record in the office of the Los Angeles County Recorder a certificate which declares the intent of the Association with respect to repair and reconstruction.

---

costs shall total at least one million five hundred thousand dollars ($1,500,000.00), the Board shall obtain at least four such bids.

The dollar limitation hereinabove set forth shall be subject to adjustment by the same formula, applying the Consumer Place Index for All Urban Consumers, as appears in Article XI, Paragraph B.2.a.(ii), of this Declaration. For the purposes of this section, the applicable index shall be the one most recently published prior to the date of destruction.

The Board shall have the authority to enter into a written agreement with the contractor that submits the lower bid. The Board shall have the authority to distribute the insurance proceeds for such repair or reconstruction as provided in Article XI of this Declaration. The Board shall take all necessary actions to assure (a) the commencement of such repair or reconstruction within one hundred twenty (120) days after damage or destruction and (b) the diligent progress of such repair or reconstruction to completion.

2. Pro Rata Contribution of Owners. Each Owner shall be obligated to pay as a Capital Assessment such funds as shall be necessary to pay his pro rata share of the costs of reconstruction over and above any insurance proceeds. Each Owner's pro rata share of such a Capital Assessment shall be of the same proportion to the total costs of reconstruction as the square footage of his Unit is to the total square footage of all Units to be assessed.

Nothing in this Paragraph B.2 shall be deemed to supersede the Board's power to levy individual assessments for damage to the Common Area in the event of liability of any Owner as provided in Article VIII, Paragraph D.2.(b)(iii).

3. Board's Power to Make Adjustments. If any Owner disputes the amount of his pro rata obligation under Paragraph B.2. of this Article XIII, such Owner may contest the amount of his obligation by submitting to the Board, within ten (10) days after notice to the Owner of his pro rata share of the expenses for reconstruction, a written objection supported by cost estimates or other information that the Owner deems to be material. The Owner may request a hearing before the Board at which he may be represented by counsel. Following such a hearing (or, in the absence of a request for a hearing and of a hearing, within twenty (20) days after the filing of a written objection by such Owner) the Board shall give written notice of its decision to all Owners, including any recommendations that any adjustment be made with respect to the obligation of any Owner. If such adjustments are recommended, the notice shall schedule a special meeting of Members for the purpose of acting on the Board's recommendation, including any other adjustments if deemed by the Members to be necessary or appropriate. All adjustments

E. NOTICE TO INSTITUTIONAL MORTGAGEE. Notice to each concerned Institutional Mortgagee shall be given under the provisions of Article X, Paragraph K. No provision of the Declaration or Bylaws will entitle the Owner of the Condominium or other party to priority over such Institutional Mortgagee with respect to the distribution to such Condominium of any insurance proceeds.

F. MINOR REPAIR AND RECONSTRUCTION. Notwithstanding any other provision of this Declaration, the Board shall have the duty to repair and reconstruct improvements without the consent of the Members and irrespective of the amount of available insurance proceeds, in all cases of partial destruction when the estimated cost of repair and reconstruction does not exceed twenty thousand dollars ($20,000.00). The Board is expressly empowered to levy a Capital Assessment for the cost of repairing and reconstructing improvements to the extent insurance proceeds are unavailable, such assessment to be levied as described in Paragraph D.2.(a) of Article VIII, but without the consent or approval of Members despite any contrary provisions in this Declaration.

G. DAMAGE TO UNITS. Any repairs or reconstruction undertaken pursuant to the foregoing provisions of this Article XIII shall cover only the Common Area. Restoration and repair of any damage to the personal property, furniture, furnishings and decorations contained within a Unit, or any improvements added to a Unit by an Owner or occupant, shall be made by and at the expense of the Owner of such Unit and, in the event of a determination to repair or reconstruct after partial or total destruction, shall be completed as promptly as practical and in a lawful and workmanlike manner.

ARTICLE XIV
CONDEMNATION

A. EMINENT DOMAIN. If an eminent domain action against all or a portion of the Project has been commenced by any governmental agency having the right of eminent domain, or if such a governmental agency has informed the Board in writing of its intention to take all or any portion of the Project by eminent domain, the Board shall then take the following measures.

1. Participation of Board in Negotiations. The Board shall participate in negotiations with the condemning authority and shall propose the method of division of the proceeds of condemnation where Units are not valued separately by the condemning authority or the court.

2. Sale in Contemplation of Eminent Domain. The Board shall inform each Owner in writing of said action or intention. Any such notice may request the written consent of the Owner authorizing the Board to sell that portion of the Project which has been designated for a taking in eminent domain. Upon receipt of such written consents from Owners of seventy-five percent (75%) of the Condominiums the Board shall provide written notice to all Mortgagees of record, and may then sell such portion of the Common Area of the Project.

B. INVERSE CONDEMNATION. When it deems appropriate, the Board is authorized to bring an action for inverse condemnation of all or any portion of the Project and to enter into any negotiations concerning such an alleged inverse condemnation.

C. DISTRIBUTION OF FUNDS. Any funds received by the Association as an award for a taking in eminent domain, a sales price for a sale made in contemplation concerning an inverse condemnation action shall be disbursed as provided in this Paragraph C. The Board may appoint a trustee to administer the distribution of any such award.

1. Common Area. A condemnation award affecting all or a part of the Project, which is not apportioned among the Owners by court judgment or by agreement between the condemning authority and each of the affected Owners, shall be distributed among the affected Owners according to the relative fair market values of their Units determined by independent appraisal.

Such an independent appraisal shall be conducted as hereinafter set forth. As soon as practicable after the date of condemnation, the Board shall hire an independent real estate appraiser (the "Appraiser") to conduct such an appraisal according to the customary procedures of his profession. The Appraiser must either hold the professional designation of M.A.I. (as a member of the American Institute of Real Estate Appraisers), hold the professional designation of S.R.A. (as certified by the Society of Real Estate Appraisers), or hold another professional designation which, at the date he is so hired, has professional stature and recognition similar to the two above-cited designations on the date of this Declaration. The Appraiser may not be an Owner; may not be a partner in a partnership which is an Owner; may not have any pecuniary interest in the Project (other than his right to a fee for his services to be rendered pursuant to this paragraph, and any lien rights thereunder); may neither be related to any of the above-described persons more closely than third degree nor may be the spouse of any person so related; and may not be an employee, officer or director of any Mortgagee.

ARTICLE XV

PARTITION

A. PARTITION OF COMMON AREAS.

1. Circumstances. Except as provided in this Paragraph A.1. the Common Areas shall remain undivided, and there shall be no judicial partition thereof. Partition may occur under any of these circumstances:

a. Destruction. Where there has been a decision not to repair or rebuild following damage or destruction, as provided in Article XIII, Paragraph C.2.

b. Condemnation. Where there has been a taking or a transfer of title of more than fifty percent (50%) of the Condominiums, as provided in Article XIV, Paragraph G.

c. Statutory Right. Where there is a statute expressly conferring a right to partition a condominium project; such a right may be exercised as provided by such a statute.

2. Power of Attorney. Each Owner gives an irrevocable power of attorney to the Board to sell the entire Project for the benefit of all of the Owners thereof. Said power shall:

a. Be exercisable only upon entry by a court duly so empowered of a final judgment of partition;

b. Be binding upon all Owners;

c. Be exercisable by the Board only upon the affirmative vote of sixty percent (60%) or more of the Board members; and

d. Be exercisable only after recordation in the Office of the County Recorder of the County of Los Angeles of a certificate by those who have the power to exercise it that said power is properly exercisable hereunder, which certificate shall be conclusive evidence thereof in favor of any person relying thereon in good faith.

B. PARTITION OF CONDOMINIUM. Nothing in this Article XV shall be deemed to prevent partition of a contenancy in a Condominium.

---

be subject to the rights of his Mortgagees and all unpaid assessments against said Owner with any interest and other charges attributable thereto.

2. Unit. Any such funds paid with respect to any Unit shall be payable to the Owner of the respective Unit, subject to (i) the rights of Mortgagees under Mortgages encumbering said Unit and (ii) all unpaid Assessments of said Owner together with interest and other charges attributable thereto.

D. DIVESTMENT OF INTEREST IN PROJECT. Upon acceptance by the Owner of all funds with respect to any one Unit received and disbursed under the provisions of Paragraph C.2. of this Article XIV, where such funds have been determined, either by agreement of the Owner with the assent of all of his Mortgagees, by final adjudication, or by independent appraisal as hereinabove set forth to represent the total value of the Unit, the Owner and all his Mortgagees of said Unit shall be divested of all interest in the Project related to said Unit or to appurtenant rights of said Owner related to said Unit or to appurtenant rights if said Owner shall vacate his Unit as a result of said acceptance of funds.

E. DISPOSITION OF PORTION OF PROJECT REMAINING. After there has been a taking or sale as provided in the foregoing provisions of this Article XIV, including the disbursement of all funds therefor, the remaining Owners shall decide by a vote of the Owners of a majority of the remaining Condominiums whether to rebuild or to repair the Project, or to take any other action. The remaining portion of the Project shall be resurveyed, if necessary, and the Declaration shall be amended to reflect such taking or sale and to readjust proportionately the percentages of the undivided interest of the remaining Owners in the Project.

F. REVIVAL OF RIGHT TO PARTITION. Upon transfer of title to any governmental agency or agencies, under the provisions of this Article XIV, of more than fifty percent (50%) of the Units, the rights of any Owner to partition through legal action as provided in Article XV of this Declaration shall revive immediately.

G. PROTECTION OF THE RIGHTS OF INSTITUTIONAL MORTGAGEES. In addition to any other provisions of this Declaration, the provisions of this Paragraph G shall apply for the protection of Institutional Mortgagees with respect to the operation of this Article XIV. Each respective first Mortgagee shall have a right superior to that of his Mortgagor to receive the respective condemnation award or applicable portion thereof to satisfy said Mortgage.

ARTICLE XVI

ARCHITECTURAL CONTROL COMMITTEE

A committee for the control of structural and landscaping architecture and design within the Project, hereinafter referred to as the "Architectural Control Committee", shall be established, consisting of three natural persons. Declarant may, at its sole option, appoint all of the original committee members to the Architectural Control Committee and all replacements until the first anniversary of the most recently issued or amended public report. Thereafter, Declarant may, at its sole option, appoint a majority of said committee persons until (i) 90% of the Units have been sold, or (ii) until the fifth anniversary of the original issuance of the Final Public Report, whichever occurs first. Notwithstanding the above, after one year from the date of the issuance of the original Final Public Report the Board shall have the power to appoint one member of the Architectural Control Committee, retaining said power until (i) 90% of the Units have been sold, or (ii) until the fifth anniversary of the original issuance of the Final Public Report, whichever occurs first. Thereafter, the Board shall appoint all of said committee members. Architectural Control Committee members appointed by the Board shall be Members, but those appointed by Declarant need not be Members.

No addition, alterations, repairs or restorations to the exterior or structural portions of any Unit nor changes in nor additions of fences, hedges, patio covers, garages, awnings, walls or other structures visible from any Common Area shall be commenced, erected or maintained by any person, other than the Declarant (through its officers, agents or employees), until the plans and specifications showing the nature, kind, shape, height, materials, color, locations and approximate cost of the same shall have been submitted to and approved in writing by the Architectural Control Committee as to conformity and harmony of external color, design and location with existing structures in the Project. If the Architectural Control Committee fails to approve or disapprove such design and location within eighty (80) days after said plans and specifications have been submitted to it, such approval will not be required and this paragraph will be deemed to have been fully complied with.

C. SEVERANCE. As stated in Article IV, Paragraph I., there shall be no severance of any element of a Condominium from any other such element, including those elements set forth in Article IV. Any violation or attempted violation of this Paragraph C. shall be void and of no effect. Any conveyance or encumbrance of a Unit shall be deemed also to convey or encumber all of the other elements of the Condominium of which the conveyed or encumbered Unit is an element, even though the description in the instrument of conveyance or encumbrance may refer only to an interest in the Unit.

ARTICLE XVII

AMENDMENT AND REVISION OF CONDOMINIUM DOCUMENTS

A. AMENDMENT AND REVISION OF CONDOMINIUM DOCUMENTS OTHER THAN DECLARATION.

Any amendment or revision of any Condominium Documents, other than the Declaration, shall be subject to those provisions of the Bylaws which set forth the requirements and conditions of amendment of said documents. Any amendment or revision of the Articles of Incorporation shall also be subject to those provisions of the Articles which set forth the requirements and conditions of amendment of the Articles.

B. AMENDMENT AND REVISION OF DECLARATION.

1. "Amendment". As used in this Paragraph B, the word "amendment" shall include revocation as well as change or alteration.

2. Before Close of Escrow of First Sale. Before the close of escrow on the sale of the first Unit to a purchaser other than Declarant, Declarant may amend this Declaration with the consent of the Department of Real Estate.

3. After Close of Escrow of First Sale. After the close of escrow on the sale of the first Unit to a purchaser other than Declarant, the Declaration may be amended by the written consent or vote (in person or by proxy) of the holders of not less than seventy-five percent (75%) of the voting rights of each class of members. As a further requirement, in a single-class voting structure, after close of escrow of the first sale, the Declaration may only be amended by the written consent or vote (in person or by proxy) of a bare majority of the votes of Members other than Declarant. Nothing in this Paragraph 3 shall be deemed to limit Declarant's authority as provided by Paragraph C.1. of this Article XVII.

The percentage of the voting power necessary to amend a specific clause or provision shall not be less than the percentage of affirmative votes prescribed for action to be taken under that clause.

4. Recordation. Any amendment shall be ineffective unless and until it is acknowledged and recorded in the County Recorder's Office of the County of Los Angeles.

5. Approval of City. Any amendment to the Declaration which would defeat the obligation of the Association to maintain the Common Area in a first-class condition and in a good state of repair, or which would defeat the assessment procedure to insure said maintenance, shall be ineffective unless and until it is approved in writing by the City of Los Angeles.

C. AMENDMENT AND REVISION OF ALL CONDOMINIUM DOCUMENTS.

Any amendment or revision of any Condominium Document shall be subject to the provisions of this Paragraph C.

1. Amendment to Conform with Requirements of Mortgagee. Declarant expressly reserves the right and shall be entitled to amend the Condominium Documents unilaterally as long as Declarant owns more than twenty-five percent (25%) of the Condominiums in the Project in order to incorporate into the Condominium Documents the requirements of any governmental agency which is empowered to regulate mortgages, their purchases, their guarantees, their insurance or their subsidization, including without limitation, the Federal Home Loan Mortgage Corporation, the Government National Mortgage Association, the Federal Housing Administration, and the Veterans Administration. Subject to the same conditions, Declarant is unilaterally empowered to execute, on behalf of the Association, any regulatory agreement between the Association and the Federal Housing Commissioner. Any such amendment or agreement shall gain the approval of the California Department of Real Estate prior to its submission to such a governmental agency as hereinabove stated. Each Owner of a Unit and each Mortgagee, by acceptance of a deed or encumbrance of a Unit, consents to the incorporation in the Declaration of any such provisions and to the execution of any such regulatory agreement and agrees to be bound by any such provision as if it were incorporated in the Declaration. The Board and each Owner shall take any action, and the Board shall adopt any resolution required by Declarant or any Mortgagee to conform the Declaration to any such requirement.

ARTICLE XVIII

DECLARATION: TERM, BINDING NATURE & ENFORCEMENT

The covenants, conditions and restrictions of the Declaration shall run with the land, and shall inure to the benefit of, and shall be enforceable by, the Association, any Owner, and his devisees, grantees, lessees, successors and assigns, for the term of forty-five years from the date on which the Declaration is recorded. At the end of said forty-five year term, the covenants, conditions and restrictions of the Declaration shall be automatically extended for one term of ten years, unless an instrument, signed by at least sixty percent (60%) of those who are Owners on the date of recordation hereinbelow specified, has been recorded within the last eight months of the forty-five year term, by which the signatories have agreed to change the Declaration, in whole or in part, or to terminate it. Any such termination or change shall come into force upon the end of said forty-five year term.

The Declaration may be subsequently extended, or a new Declaration, binding the Association, the Owners, and their devisees, successors and assigns, may be subsequently effectuated, for a term as specified in the instrument which extends or effectuates said Declaration, upon the recordation of an instrument, extending or effectuating said Declaration, which has been signed by a majority of those Owners on the date of recordation hereinbelow specified. Said recordation must take place within the eight months immediately preceding the date on which either the Declaration is to commence its extended term or the new Declaration is to come into effect.

ARTICLE XIX

OBLIGATIONS OF OWNERS

In addition to any obligations which are imposed upon any Owner by law or under any other provision of this Declaration, each Owner must perform the following obligations:

---

2. Reliance on Amendments. Any amendments made pursuant to this Article XVII shall be presumed valid by anyone relying on them in good faith.

3. Approval of Real Estate Commissioner, Re: Material Change of Owner's Rights. To the extent stipulated by law, no amendment or modification of any provision of any of the Condominium Documents which would materially change the rights of an Owner concerning his ownership, possession, or use of interests in the Project, whether such a change would be direct or as a Member of the Association, shall be submitted for a vote of Owners or Members or by any other means become valid without the prior written consent of the Real Estate Commissioner during the period of time that the Declarant holds or directly controls as many as one-fourth of the votes that may be cast to effect such change.

To the extent stipulated by law, there shall be no official meeting of Owners or Members nor any written solicitation of them for the purpose of effectuating a change referred to in this Paragraph C.3. except in accordance with a procedure approved by the Real Estate Commissioner; provided, however, that the Board may meet and vote on the question of submission of the proposed change to the Commissioner.

4. No Adverse Effect on Prior Recorded Mortgage. No amendment shall adversely affect the rights of the holder of any Mortgage of record against any portion of the Project, where such mortgage has been recorded prior to the recordation of such amendment.

D. DAMAGE, DESTRUCTION OR CONDEMNATION OF PROJECT.

In the event of damage, destruction or condemnation of any portion of the Project, the Board shall, as soon as practicable, cause to be prepared and duly filed any amendments to any of the Condominium Documents necessary to reflect the altered status of the Project, including (by way of illustration and not by way of limitation) the elimination of all or a part of one or more of the Units as a result of such damage, destruction or condemnation.

REPAIR.

A. OWNER'S RIGHT AND OBLIGATION TO MAINTAIN AND REPAIR.

Except for those portions of the Project which the Association or Declarant is required to maintain and repair, each Unit Owner shall, at his sole cost and expense, maintain and repair his Unit (and shall maintain the landscaping within any exclusive easement appurtenant thereto which is part of the Restricted Common Area), keeping the same in good condition. Each Owner shall have the exclusive right to paint, plaster, panel, tile, wallpaper, or otherwise refinish and decorate the inner surfaces of the walls, ceilings, floors, and doors bounding his Unit. In the event an Owner fails to maintain the interior of his Unit (or the landscaping within his appurtenant exclusive easement) in a manner which the Board deems necessary to preserve the appearance and value of the Property, the Board may notify said Owner of the work required and request it be done within sixty (60) days from the giving of such notice. In the event Owner fails to carry out such maintenance within said period, the Board may cause such work to be done and may specially assess the cost thereof to such Owner and, following notice and hearing, if necessary, impose a lien against his Condominium for the amount thereof.

B. OWNER'S COMPLIANCE.

Each Owner, tenant or occupant of a Condominium shall comply with the provisions of the Condominium Documents and resolutions of the Board or its duly authorized representative, giving priority in such compliance to the provisions of the Declaration. Failure to comply with the Condominium Documents or such resolutions shall be grounds for an action to recover sums due, for damages, or for injunctive relief, as appropriate.

All agreements and determinations lawfully made by the Association in accordance with the voting percentages established in the Condominium Documents shall be deemed to be binding on each Owner, his successors and assigns.

C. JOINT AND SEVERABLE LIABILITY OF OWNERS.

In the case of joint ownership of a Condominium, the obligations of each of the Owners thereof in connection with the obligations set forth in the Declaration shall be joint and several.

D. RIGHT OF ENTRY FOR EMERGENCY REPAIRS OR ABATEMENT OF NUISANCE.

Each Owner gives to the Board, acting through its agents, the right to enter upon and within his Condominium in order to make emergency repairs, to abate nuisances, and to protect the property rights and collective best interests of the Owners. To the extent practicable, said right shall be exercised with the knowledge and in the presence of the Owner or tenant of the Condominium so entered.

E. LIABILITY OF OWNERS FOR DAMAGE TO COMMON AREA: INDEMNIFICATION.

The Owner of each Unit shall be liable to the Association for all damages to Common Area or improvements thereon caused by such Owner or any occupant of his Unit or guest, except for that portion of said damage, if any, fully covered by insurance. Each Owner, by acceptance of his deed, agrees for himself and for the members of his family, tenants, guests and invitees, to indemnify each and every other Owner and to hold him and them harmless from, and to defend him and them against any claim of any person for personal injury or property damage occurring within the Unit of that particular Owner and any exclusive easements over the Common Area apurtenant to that Unit.

F. OWNER'S OBLIGATION FOR TAXES.

To the extent allowed by law, all Units, including their pro rata undivided interest in the Common Area and the membership of an Owner in the Association, shall be separately assessed and taxed so that all taxes, assessments and charges which may become liens having priority over first Mortgages by operation of law shall relate only to the individual Unit and not to the Project as a whole. Each Owner shall be obligated to pay any taxes or assessments assessed by the Assessor of Los Angeles County against his Condominium and against his personal property.

G. NOTIFICATION OF SALE OF CONDOMINIUM.

Within five business days of the date of transfer of title to a Condominium, the new Owner shall notify the Board in writing of said transfer. Said notification shall set forth the names of the transferor, the transferee, and their respective Mortgages (if any); the common address of the Condominium so transferred, the mailing addresses of the transferee and his Mortgagee, and the date on which title was transferred. Prior to the receipt of such notification, the Association, the Board and their agents shall be deemed to have satisfied the notice requirement of Article XXI which sets forth the method of determining the address to be used in order to notify the Owner, if they send all notices concerning said Condominium to the address for notices most recently provided by the transferring Owner to the Association.

H. LEGAL DUTY TO PROVIDE NEW OWNER WITH COPY OF DECLARATION.

Each Owner who sells or otherwise transfers title to his Condominium must acquaint himself with any provision of law in effect at the time of said conveyance which requires that said Owner furnish the buyer with a copy of the Declaration or other Condominium Documents.

ARTICLE XX

OBLIGATIONS OF DECLARANT

In addition to any obligations which are imposed upon the Declarant and limitations thereon under any other provision of this Declaration or which exist by law, the Declarant is subject to the following obligations and limitations thereon.

A. LIMITATION OF RESTRICTIONS ON DECLARANT.

Declarant is undertaking the work of construction of residential Condominiums and incidental improvements upon the Project. The completion of that work and the sale, rental, and other disposal of said Condominiums are essential to the establishment and welfare of the Project as a residential community. In order that said work may be completed and the Project be established as a fully occupied residential community as rapidly as possible, nothing in this Declaration shall be understood or construed to:

1. Prevent Declarant, its contractors, of subcontractors from doing on the Project or any Unit whatever is reasonably necessary or advisable in connection with the completion of said work; or

2. Prevent Declarant or its representatives from erecting, constructing, and maintaining on any part or parts of the Project such structures as may be reasonable and necessary for the conduct of its business of completing said work and establishing the Project as a residential community and disposing of the same in parcels by sale or otherwise; or

3. Prevent Declarant from conducting on any part of the Project its business of completing said work and of establishing a plan of Condominium ownership and of disposing of said Project as Condominiums by sale or otherwise; or

4. Prevent Declarant from maintaining such sign or signs on any part of the Project as may be necessary for the sale or other disposition therof.

The foregoing limitations on the application of the restrictions to Declarant shall terminate upon the sale of Declarant's entire interest in the Project.

Declarant shall make every reasonable effort to avoid disturbing the use and enjoyment of the Units and the Common Area by the Owners while completing any work necessary to said Units or Common Area.

B. TERMINATION OF ANY RESPONSIBILITY OF DECLARANT.

In the event Declarant shall convey all of its right, title and interest in and to the property to any partnership, individual or individuals, corporation or corporations, then and in such event, Declarant shall be relieved of the performance of any further duty or obligation hereunder, and such partnership, individual or individuals, corporation or corporations, shall be obligated to perform all such duties and obligations of the Declarant.

For the purposes of this Paragraph B. only, "Declarant" shall mean only Earth Galaxy, Inc.

ARTICLE XXI

GENERAL PROVISIONS

A. VIOLATION OF DECLARATION AS NUISANCE.

Every act or omission in violation of any provision of the Declaration shall constitute a nuisance and, in addition to any other remedies available to any injured party, such nuisance may be enjoined or judicially abated by the Association, the Board, their agents, and any Owner.

B. VIOLATION OF LAW AS VIOLATION OF DECLARATION.

Any violation of any federal, state, municipal, or local law, regulation, or ordinance, pertaining to the ownership, occupation or use of the Project or any part thereof shall be a violation of the Declaration.

C. ENFORCEMENT OF DECLARATION.

The Association or any Owner shall have the right to enforce, by any proceeding at law or in equity, all restrictions, conditions and covenants now or hereafter imposed by the provisions of the Declaration, and in such action shall be entitled to recover reasonable attorneys' fees as ordered by the Court. Failure by the Association or by any Owner to enforce any covenant, condition and restriction of the Declaration shall in no event be deemed a waiver of the right to do so thereafter.

D. CUMULATIVE REMEDIES.

Each remedy provided for in the Declaration shall be cumulative and shall not preclude the exercise of any other remedy provided for in the Declaration or otherwise available.

E. NOTICES.

Any written notice or other document relating to, required by, or permitted by the Declaration may be delivered either personally or by mail. If by mail, such notice or document shall be deemed to have been delivered seventy-two (72) hours after it has been deposited in the United States mail, postage prepaid, addressed to the address most recently provided by the addressee.

Following are the initial addresses to be used for all such communication. Any of said addresses may be changed by delivering a notice of said change as provided by this Paragraph E. No change of address shall be deemed to be an amendment of the Declaration.

Declarant's address shall be 202 Jennifer Drive East, Suite A-45, Los Angeles, California 90067. A copy of any such communication addressed to Declarant must be delivered to Declarant's legal counsel, Meyers, Stevens & Walters Professional Corporation, 6300 Wilshire Boulevard, Suite 9100, Los Angeles, California 90048, in order to satisfy the requirement of delivery imposed by this Paragraph E.

The address of each Owner shall be the address of his respective Unit in the Project.

The address of the Association and of the Board shall be the address which is placed on file with the California Secretary of State for the Association.

F. FAIR HOUSING.

No Owner shall, directly or indirectly, forbid or restrict the conveyance, encumbrance, leasing, or mortgaging of his Unit to any person on account of race, color, religion, ancestry, or national origin.

K. GENDER.

Unless the context clearly requires otherwise, as used in the Declaration, the neuter, feminine, and masculine shall include one another.

G. SEVERABILITY AND PARTIAL INVALIDITY.

The provisions of the Declaration are deemed severable, so that a legal determination that any provision of the Declaration is either invalid or in conflict with an applicable law, shall not affect the validity, full force, or effect of any other provision or portion of the Declaration.

H. HEADINGS.

The headings used in the Declaration are for convenience only and are not to be used to interpret the meaning of any of the provisions of the Declaration. However, each subsection of the Declaration shall be deemed to refer to the section of which it is a subsection.

I. - EXHIBITS.

All exhibits referred to in the Declaration are attached to the Declaration and are incorporated by this reference.

J. NUMBER.

Unless the context clearly requires otherwise, as used in the Declaration, the singular shall include the plural, and the plural shall include the singular.

ARTICLES OF INCORPORATION

OF

THE LATAKIA COTILLION HOMEOWNERS' ASSOCIATION

I

The name of this corporation is the Latakia Cotillion Homeowners' Association.

II

A. This corporation is a nonprofit mutual benefit corporation organized under the Nonprofit Mutual Benefit Corporation Law. The purpose of this corporation is to engage in any lawful act or activity for which a corporation may be organized under such law.

B. The specific purpose of this corporation is to provide for the common interest in the condominium project located at 3600 Vandenberg Boulevard, Naranja, California, of all persons who are owners of any portion of said project. Such provisions may be accomplished by agents and must include all undertakings required of said Homeowners' Association by law. Such provisions must include (by way of illustration and not by way of limitation) maintenance and repair of the common area of said project and the collection and payment of property taxes assessed against said common area.

III

The name and address in the State of California of this corporation's initial agent for service of process is:

H. Clark Hoover
Villandry Development Company
2049 Sutter Street, Suite 2930
Naranja, California

DATED _____, 19__.

_____
Signature of Incorporator

-1-

_____
Name of Incorporator

I hereby declare that I am the person who executed the foregoing Articles of Incorporation, which execution is my act and deed.

_____
Signature of Incorporator

-2-

BYLAWS OF

THE BERGAMOT CONDOS HOMEOWNERS' ASSOCIATION, INC.

A California Nonprofit Mutual Benefit Corporation

ARTICLE I

NAME

The name of this Corporation shall be the Bergamot Condos Homeowners' Association, Inc., (hereinafter referred to as the "Association").

ARTICLE II

OFFICES

The principal office of the Association shall be in San Diego County, California. Meetings of the members shall be held at 620 Bergamot Avenue, La Jolla, California. In the event of the destruction of or substantial damage to the Condominium Project, the Board of Directors shall have the full authority and power to designate such other location, in reasonable proximity to the Condominium Project, for meetings of members.

ARTICLE III

DEFINITIONS

A. Declaration. The "Declaration" means the Declaration of Covenants, Conditions and Restrictions, and any amendments thereto, once recorded, applicable to that Condominium Project located in San Diego County, California, legally described as Lot 1 of Tract 8460 as per Map recorded in Book 317, Pages 32 through 33, inclusive of Maps in the Office of the County Recorder of San Diego County, State of California.

B. Other Definitions. Each and every definition appearing in the Declaration shall have in these Bylaws the same meaning therein set forth.

-1-

ARTICLE IV

OBJECTIVES AND PURPOSES

The objectives and purposes of this Corporation shall be to provide for the common interests of the members in the Condominium Project, including (by way of illustration and not as a restriction):

A. The maintenance and repair of the common area;

B. The payment of taxes on the common area;

C. The determination and collection of assessments from the members for all common expenses;

D. The protection of the interest of Mortgagees in the Project;

E. Such other acts and enterprises which are reasonably necessary for the harmonious and orderly administration of the Condominium Project.

ARTICLE V

MEMBERSHIP

A. Qualifications for Membership. Each Owner of the Condominium, including Declarant, shall be a member of the Association. Ownership of a Condominium or an interest in it shall be the sole qualification of membership in the Association. Each Owner shall remain a member of the Association until his Ownership Interest in all Condominiums ceases, at which time his membership in the Association shall automatically cease.

1. Transfer of Membership. Any transfer of title to a Condominium or to an interest in it shall operate automatically to transfer the appurtenant membership rights in the Association to the new Owner.

2. Security Holders and Mortgagees. Persons or entities who hold an interest in a Condominium merely as security for performance of an obligation are not to be regarded as members.

B. Non-severability of Membership. Membership in the Association shall not be assigned, transferred, pledged, hypothecated, conveyed or alienated in any way except on a transfer of title to each such condominium or interest in it, and then only to a transferee. Any attempt to make a prohibited transfer shall be void.

-2-

C. Members Rights and Duties. Each member shall have the rights, duties and obligations set forth in the Declaration, the Articles, the Bylaws, and the Rules and Regulations, including amendments to the foregoing.

ARTICLE VI

CLASSES OF MEMBERSHIP

The Association shall have two (2) classes of voting membership:

A. Class A. Class A members are all Owners, with the exception of Declarant. Each Class A member shall be entitled to one (1) vote for each Condominium in which such members owns an interest. However, when more than one Class A member owns an interest in a Condominium, the vote for such Condominium shall be exercised as they themselves determine, but in no case shall more than one vote be cast with respect to any one Condominium.

B. Class B. The Class B member shall be Declarant, which shall be entitled to three (3) notes for each Condominium owned. The Class B membership shall cease and be converted to Class A membership on the happening of one of the following events, whichever occurs earlier:

1. When the total votes outstanding in the Class A membership equal the votes outstanding in the Class B membership, or;

2. On the second anniversary of the original issuance of the Final Public Report for the Project by the Commissioner of Real Estate of California.

As long as two classes of members of the Association exist, no action by the Association that must have the prior approval of the Association members, shall be deemed approved by the members unless approved by the appropriate percentage of both classes of members, except as provided in Article XII of the Declaration.

Where any of the Condominium Documents prescribe two classes of voting membership and require the vote or written assent of a prescribed percentage of each class of membership for the initiation of action by or in the name of the Association, any requirement (except as expressly provided below in this Paragraph B) that the vote of Declarant shall be excluded in any such determination shall be applicable only if there has been a conversion of Class B to Class A shares and only for so long as Declarant holds or directly controls twenty-five

percent or more of the voting power of the Association. Notwithstanding the above, the vote of Declarant shall be excluded on matters concerning (i) the enforcement of bonded obligations (as set forth in Article XII of the Declaration, and (ii) amendment of any of the Condominium Documents to the extent expressly set forth therein.

ARTICLE VII

MEETINGS OF MEMBERS

A. Organizational Meeting. An organizational meeting shall be held as soon as practicable after incorporation of the Association, and the Directors elected then shall hold office until the first annual meeting. All offices of the Board of Directors shall be filled at the organizational meeting.

B. Annual Meetings. The first, whether annual or special, meeting of Members of the Association shall be held within forty-five (45) days after the close of the sale of the Condominium that represents the 51st percentile interest authorized for sale under the first final subdivision public report issued for the Project by the California Commissioner of Real Estate, but in no case later than six (6) months after the closing and recording of the sale of the first Condominium within the Project. Thereafter, regular meetings of members of the Association shall be held at least once annually.

C. Special Meetings. A special meeting of the Association shall be promptly called by the Board upon either the vote for such a meeting by a majority of a Quorum of the Board or receipt of a written request for a special meeting signed by Members representing at least five percent of the total voting power of the Association.

D. Notice of Members' Meetings. Notice of all members' meetings, regular or special, shall be given by regular mail, personal delivery or telegram to all Owners and to any mortgagee who has requested in writing that such notice be sent to it, and shall be given not less than ten (10) days nor more than thirty (30) days before the time of the meeting, and shall set forth the place, date, and hour of the meeting, and the nature of the business to be undertaken. Except in an emergency situation, the ten-day minimum shall apply.

If action is proposed to be taken at any meeting for approval of any of the following proposals, the notice shall also state the general nature of the proposal. Member action on such items is invalid unless the notice or written waiver of notice states the general nature of the proposal(s):

(i) Removing a Director without cause;

(ii) Filling vacancies on the Board of Directors by the members;

(iii) Amending the Articles of Incorporation;

(iv) Approving a contract or transaction in which a Director has a material financial interest;

(v) Approving a plan of distribution of assets, other than cash, in liquidation when the Association has more than one class of memberships outstanding.

E. Quorum Requirements. The presence at any meeting in person or by proxy of members entitled to case at least fifty percent (50%) of the total votes of all members of the Association shall constitute a quorum. If any meeting cannot be held because a quorum is not present, members representing a majority of the votes present, either in person or by proxy, may adjourn the meeting to a time not less than five (5) days or more than thirty (30) days from the date the original meeting was called. No other business may be conducted at such adjourned original meeting.

F. Action of Members Without Meeting. Any action which may be taken by the vote of Members at a regular or special meeting except the election of Board Members where cumulative voting is a requirement may be taken without a meeting if done in compliance with the provisions of Section 7513 of the Corporations Code.

ARTICLE VIII

VOTING RIGHTS

A. Joint Owner Votes. The voting rights for each Condominium cannot be cast on a fractional basis. If the joint Owners of a Condominium are unable to agree among themselves as to how their voting rights shall be cast, their one (1) joint vote shall be cast as their majority chooses. If any Owner exercises the voting rights of a particular Condominium, it will be conclusively presumed for all purposes that he was acting with the authority and consent of all other Owners of the same Condominium. If more than one person or entity exercises the voting rights for a particular Condominium, their one joint vote shall count as their majority chooses.

B. Cumulative Voting. Election to and removal from the Board shall be by cumulative voting, as defined in California Corporations Code §708. Each member shall be entitled to vote in person or by proxy, as many votes as such member is entitled to exercise as provided in the Declaration, multiplied by the

number of Directors to be elected or removed, and he may cast all of such votes for or against any single candidate or Director, or he may distribute them among the number of candidates or Directors to be elected or removed, or any two or more of them. The candidates receiving the highest number of votes up to the number of Board members to be elected shall be deemed elected. A Member shall be entitled to cumulate his vote for one or more candidates for the Board if the candidate's name has been placed in nomination prior to voting and if the Member has given notice at the meeting prior to the voting of his intention to cumulate votes.

As to removal (other than by expiration of term), unless the entire Board is removed by a vote of Association members, an individual Director shall not be removed unless the number of votes in favor of removal satisfies the requirements of California Corporations Code §303(a)(1).

C. Proxies. Every person entitled to vote or execute consents shall have the right to do so in person or by an agent duly authorized by written proxy executed by such person or his duly authorized agent or agents and filed with the Secretary of the Association prior to commencement of the meeting at which the proxy is exercised. Every proxy shall be revocable and revoked upon the receipt of notice by the Secretary of the meeting at which it would otherwise be exercised prior to the exercise thereof, and shall automatically cease upon sale or conveyance by the person granting the proxy of his interest in the Condominium.

D. Vote by Mortgagee. A Mortgagee can exercise the voting rights of his defaulting Mortgagor/Owner only if (i) the Mortgagee acquires fee title to the Condominium which is subject to the Mortgage or (ii) the Owner gives the Mortgagee his proxy.

E. Suspension of Voting Rights. The voting rights of any member may be suspended as provided by the Declaration and by Article XVII of these Bylaws.

F. Secret Written Ballot. Voting for the Board shall be by secret written ballot.

ARTICLE IX

ELECTION OF DIRECTORS

A. Number and Membership Status. The Association shall have three (3) Directors. Except when a majority of the voting power of the Association resides in Declarant or when there are two (2) outstanding classes of membership in the

Association, any person elected a Director must be a member of the Association. A Director may also be an Officer.

B. Nomination. Any member may nominate any member as a candidate for election to the Board of Directors. Such nomination shall be made by written notice, signed by the nominator, and sent to the Board of Directors pursuant to the notice provisions of the Declaration, at least thirty (30) days prior to the date on which the meeting for the election of Directors is to take place. In addition, at any meeting to elect Directors, any member present at the meeting, in person or by proxy, may place a name or names in nomination.

C. Campaigning. Any candidate for election to the Board of Directors may campaign in any manner that he chooses, provided that no funds of the Association are expended on behalf of his campaign, and provided further that his campaign does not intrude upon the quiet enjoyment of any Condominium Unit by its Owner.

D. Election and Term of Office. Directors shall be elected at the organizational meeting and at each annual meeting of the members, but if any such annual meeting is not held or the Directors are not elected thereat, the Directors may be elected at any special meeting of members held for that purpose. Each Director shall serve until the next annual meeting of members and until a successor has been elected and qualified.

E. Specially Elected Directors. Notwithstanding any other provisions of these Bylaws, as long as a majority of the voting power of the Association resides in Declarant or as long as there are two (2) outstanding classes of membership in the Association, the elections of twenty percent (20%) of the Directors (herein referred to as the "Specially Elected Directors") shall be determined at a special election held immediately before the regular election of Directors (except in the case of the election of a Specially Elected Director, following removal of his predecessor, which election shall take place as soon after removal as practicable in accordance with the provisions hereinbelow). At a duly constituted meeting of members, nominations for the Specially Elected Directors shall be made from the floor. When nominations have been closed, the special election shall take place. Declarant shall not have the right to participate in or vote in such special election (although Declarant or its representative may be present), and the candidates receiving the highest number of votes up to the number of Specially Elected Directors shall be deemed elected as Specially Elected Directors, and their term shall be the same as any other Director. Unless members (excluding any voting rights held by Declarant) consent, by vote or written consent, such Specially Elected Directors cannot be removed. In case of the death, resignation or removal of a Specially Elected Director,

-7-

his successor shall be elected at a special meeting of the members, and the provisions set forth in this section respecting the election of Specially Elected Director shall apply as to the election of a successor.

F. Change in Authorized Number of Directors. Once members have been admitted to the Association, any Bylaws changing the fixed number of Directors may only be adopted by approval of the Members.

ARTICLE X

POWERS OF DIRECTORS

A. General Corporate Powers. Subject to the provisions of the California Nonprofit Corporation Law and any limitations in the Declaration of Covenants, Conditions and Restrictions, the Articles of Incorporation and these Bylaws relating to action required to be approved by the members, the business and affairs of the corporation shall be managed, and all corporate powers shall be exercised, by or under the direction of the Board of Directors.

B. Specific Powers. Without prejudice to these general powers, and subject to the same limitations, the Directors shall have the power to:

1. Select and remove all Officers, Agents, and Employees of the Association; prescribe any powers and duties for them that are consistent with law, with the Declaration of Covenants, Conditions and Restrictions, with the Articles of Incorporation, and with these Bylaws; and fix their compensation.

2. Fill vacancies on the Board except for any vacancy created by the removal of a Board member. The Board may fill a vacancy on the Board created by the removal of a Board member, provided that such replacement is approved by the vote or written assent of at least fifty-one percent (51%) of the voting rights of the Association residing in Members other than Declarant.

3. Adopt, make, and use a corporate seal, prescribe the forms of membership certificates, if any; and alter the form of the seal and certificate.

4. Subject to the Declaration of Covenants, Conditions and Restrictions and to the requirements of the California Department of Real Estate, borrow money and incur indebtedness on behalf of the Association and cause to be executed and delivered for the Association's purposes, in the Association's name,

-8-

promissory notes, bonds, debentures, pledges, hypothecations, and other evidences of debt and securities.

ARTICLE XI

MEETINGS OF THE BOARD OF DIRECTORS

A. Frequency. Meetings of the Board of Directors shall be held at least once every two months.

B. Place. Meetings of the Board of Directors shall occur within the Project and at a time and place to be determined by the Board.

C. Notice. Notice of the time and place of each Board meeting shall be posted at a prominent place or places within the Project. Except for emergency situations, such notice or notices must be posted during the full four-day period immediately prior to the meeting. Such notice must also be communicated to Board members (absent an emergency) not less than four days prior to the meeting unless the time and the place of meeting is fixed by the Bylaws provided, however, that notice of meeting need not be given to any Board member who has signed a waiver of notice or a written consent to holding of the meeting.

D. Special Meetings. A special meeting of the Board may be called by written notice signed by either the President or by any two members of the Board. Said notice shall specify the time and place of the meeting, and the nature of any special business to be considered. Said notice shall be sent to all members of the Board and shall further conform to all of the requirements of Paragraph C., above.

E. Access to Meetings. Regular and special meeting of the Board shall be open to all Members of the Association, provided, however, that Members who are not on the Board may not participate in any deliberation or discussion unless expressly authorized by the vote of a majority of a quorum of the Board.

F. Executive Session. The Board may, with the approval of a majority of its members, adjourn a meeting and reconvene in executive session (absent Members of the Association who are not on the Board), to discuss and to vote upon personal matters, litigation in which the Association is or may become involved, and orders of business of a similar nature. The nature of any and all business to be considered in executive session shall first be announced in the open session.

-9-

G. Quorum. Except as provided in Article XVII of these Bylaws, a quorum of the Board of Directors shall equal eighty percent (80%) of its members then in office.

H. Action Without Meeting. The Board may take actions without a meeting if all of its members' consent in writing to the action to be taken. If the Board resolves by unanimous written consent to take action, an explanation of action taken shall be posted at a prominent place or places within the common area within three days after the written consents of all Board members have been obtained.

-10-

ARTICLE XII

COMMITTEES

Consonant with the requirements of law, the Board shall be empowered to create Committees, composed of Members of the Association, and to invest in those Committees such powers as permitted by law.

A. Architectural Control Committee. The Board shall make appointments to the Architectural Control Committee in accordance with Article XVI of the Declaration.

B. Other Committees. The Board, in its discretion, may create other Committees and assign appropriate powers to said Committees.

ARTICLE XIII

OFFICERS

The Officers of the Association shall be a President, a Secretary, and a Chief Financial Officer. The Association may also have, at the discretion of the Board of Directors, a Chairman of the Board, one or more Vice Presidents, one or more Assistant Secretaries, one or more Assistant Treasurers, and such other Officers as may be appointed in accordance with the provisions of Paragraph B of this Article XIII. Any number of offices may be held by the same person, except that neither the Secretary nor the Chief Financial Officer may serve concurrently as either the President or the Chairman of the Board.

A. Election of Officers. The Officers of the Association, except those appointed in accordance with the provisions of Paragraph B of this Article XIII, shall be chosen by the Board of Directors, and each shall serve at the pleasure of the Board, subject to the rights, if any, of an Officer under any contract of employment.

B. Subordinate Officers. The Board of Directors may appoint, and may authorize the Chairman of the Board or the President, or another Officer to appoint, any other Officers that the business of the Association may require, each of whom shall have the title, hold office for the period, have the authority, and perform the duties specified in the Bylaws or determined from time to time by the Board of Directors.

-11-

C. Removal of Officers. Subject to the rights, if any, of an Officer under any contract of employment, any Office may be removed, with or without cause, by the Board of Directors, at any regular or special meeting of the Board.

D. Resignation of Officers. Any Officer may resign at any time by giving written notice to the Association. Any resignation shall take effect at the date of the receipt of that notice or at any later time specified in that notice; and, unless otherwise specified in that notice, the acceptance of the resignation shall not be necessary to make it effective. Any resignation is without prejudice to the rights, if any, of the Association under any contract to which the Officer is a party.

E. Vacancies in Offices. A vacancy in any office because of death, resignation, removal, disqualification, or any other cause shall be filled only in the manner prescribed in these Bylaws for regular appointments to that office.

F. Responsibilities of Officers.

1. Chairman of the Board. If such an Officer be elected, the Chairman of the Board shall preside at meetings of the Board of Directors and exercise and perform such other powers and duties as may be from time to time assigned to him by the Board of Directors or prescribed by the Bylaws. If there is no President, the Chairman of the Board shall, in addition, be the Chief Executive Officer of the Association and shall have the powers and duties prescribed in Paragraph 2, below.

2. President. Subject to such supervisory powers as may be given by the Board of Directors to the Chairman of the Board, if any, the President shall, subject to the control of the Board of Directors, generally supervise, direct, and control the business and the Officers of the Association. He shall preside at all meetings of the members and, in the absence of the Chairman of the Board, or if there be none, at all meetings of the Board of Directors. He shall have such other powers and duties as may be prescribed by the Board of Directors or the Bylaws.

3. Vice Presidents. In the absence or disability of the President, the Vice Presidents, if any, in order of their rank as fixed by the Board of Directors or, if not ranked, a Vice President designated by the Board of Directors, shall perform all the duties of the President, and when so acting shall have all the powers of, and be subject to all the restrictions upon, the President. The Vice Presidents shall have such other powers and perform such other duties as from time to time may be prescribed for them respectively by the Board of Directors or the Chairman of the Board.

-12-

the following:

4. **Secretary.** The Secretary shall attend to the following:

(a) *Book of Minutes.* The Secretary shall keep or cause to be kept, at the principal executive office or such other place as the Board of Directors may direct, a book of minutes of all meetings and actions of Directors, Committees of Members, and Members, with the time and place of holding, whether regular or special, and, if special, how authorized, the notice given, the names of those present at such meetings, the number of members present or represented at members' meetings, and the proceedings of such meetings.

(b) *Membership Records.* The Secretary shall keep, or cause to be kept, at the principal executive office, as determined by resolution of the Board of Directors, a record of the Association's members, showing the names of all members, their addresses, and the class of membership held by each.

(c) *Notices, Seal and Other Duties.* The Secretary shall give, or cause to be given, notice of all meetings of the members and of the Board of Directors required by the Bylaws to be given. He shall have such other powers and perform such other duties as may be prescribed by the Board of Directors or the Bylaws.

5. **Chief Financial Officer.** The Chief Financial Officer shall attend to the following:

(a) *Books of Account.* The Chief Financial Officer shall keep and maintain, or cause to be kept and maintained, adequate and correct books and records of accounts of the properties and business transactions of the Association, including accounts of its assets, liabilities, receipts, disbursements, gains, losses, capital, retained earnings, and other matters customarily included in financial statements. The Books of account shall be open to inspection by any Director at all reasonable times.

(b) *Deposit and Disbursement of Money and Valuables.* The Chief Financial Officer shall deposit all money and other valuables in the name and to the credit of the Association with such depositories as may be designated by the Declaration or the Board of Directors; shall disburse the funds of the Association as may be ordered by the Board of Directors; shall render to the President and Directors, whenever they request it, an account of all of his transactions as Chief Financial Officer and of the financial condition of the Association; and shall have other powers and perform such other duties as may be prescribed by the Board of Directors or the Bylaws.

-13-

(c) *Bond.* If required by the Board of Directors, the Chief Financial Officer shall give the Board a bond in the amount and with the surety or sureties specified by the Board for faithful performance of the duties of his office, and for restoration to the Association of all its books, papers, vouchers, money, and other property of every kind in his possession or under his control on his death, resignation, retirement, or removal from office.

ARTICLE XIV

INDEMNIFICATION

No member of the Board, or of any Committee of the Association, or any Officer of the Association, or any manager of Declarant or any agent of Declarant, shall be personally liable to any Owner or any other party, including the Association, for any damage, loss, or prejudice suffered or claimed on the account of any act, omission, error or negligence of any such person or entity while serving in any capacity hereinabove stated, if such person or entity has, on the basis of such information as may be possessed by him or it, acted in good faith, without wilful or intentional misconduct. All members of the Board, and of any Committee of the Association, and any Officer of the Association, and any manager and Declarant, and any agent of Declarant, shall be indemnified by the Association against all reasonable costs, expenses and liabilities (including attorney's fees and court costs) actually and necessarily incurred by or imposed upon said individuals, in connection with any claim, action, suit, proceeding, investigation or inquiry of whatever nature in which he or it may be involved as a party or otherwise by reason of his having been an officer or director or member of the Association, or of any Committee of the Association, whether he continues in said capacity at the time of the incurring or imposition of such costs, expenses or liabilities, except in relation to matters to which he or it shall be finally adjudged in such action, suit, proceeding, investigation or inquiry to be liable for wilful misconduct or negligence toward the Association, any Owner, or other party in the performance of his duties.

The Association shall maintain errors and omissions coverage for all members of the Board, and Committees of the Association, and all Officers of the Association, and all managers as provided in Article XI of the Declaration.

-14-

ARTICLE XV

COMPENSATION OF DIRECTOR OR OFFICER

No Officer or Director shall receive any compensation for his service as an Officer or Director, except as provided in the Declaration. This proscription on compensation does not bar (a) the reimbursement to any Officer or Director for any expenses personally incurred for the benefit of the Association at the request and with the authority of the Board of Directors; or (b) the payment to and the receipt of compensation from the Association to any person serving as an Officer or Director, if the compensation is for any goods or services received from said Officer or Director in a capacity other than as an Officer or Director.

ARTICLE XVI

CONSTRUCTION AND DEFINITIONS

Unless the context requires otherwise, the general provisions, rules of construction, and definitions in the California Non-profit Corporation Law shall govern the construction of these Bylaws. Without limiting the generality of the above, the masculine gender includes the femine and neuter, the singular number includes the plural, the plural number includes the singular, and the term "person" includes both the Homeowners Association and a natural person.

ARTICLE XVII

AMENDMENTS

A. Amendment by Members. New Bylaws or Articles may be adopted or these Bylaws or the Articles may be amended or repealed by approval of the members or their proxies, or by written assent of these persons. The vote to amend the Bylaws or Articles must be at least a bare majority of the voting power of the Association, and must be at least a bare majority of the votes of members other than Declarant. However, if the Association has two classes of voting members, any amendment of the Articles or the Bylaws must be approved by at least a bare majority of the Members of each class. Further, where any provision of these Bylaws requires the vote of a larger proportion of the members than otherwise required by law, such provision may not be altered, amended or repealed except by vote of such larger number of members. No amendment may extend the term of a Director beyond that for which such Director was elected.

-15-

B. Amendment by Declarant. Declarant expressly reserves the right and shall be entitled to amend the Condominium Documents unilaterally as long as Declarant owns more than twenty-five percent (25%) of the Condominiums in the Project in order to incorporate into the Condominium Documents the requirements of any governmental agency which is impowered to regulate mortgages, their purchases, their guarantees, their insurance or their subsidization, including without limitation, the Federal Home Loan Mortgage Corporation, the Government National Mortgage Association, the Federal Housing Administration, and the Veterans Administration. Subject to the same conditions, Declarant is unilaterally empowered to execute, on behalf of the Association, any regulatory agreement between the Association and the Federal Housing Commissioner. Any such amendment or agreement shall gain the approval of the California Department of Real Estate prior to its submission to such a governmental agency as hereinabove stated. Each Owner of a Unit and each Mortgagee, by acceptance of a deed or encumbrance of any such provisions and to the execution of any such regulatory agreement and agrees to be bound by any such provision as if it were incorporated in the Declaration. The Board shall adopt any resolution required by Declarant or any Mortgagee to conform the Declaration to any such requirement.

C. Approval of Real Estate Commissioner, Re: Material Change of Owner's Rights. To the extent stipulated by law, no amendment or modification of any provision of any of the Condominium Documents which would materially change the rights of an Owner concerning his ownership, possession, or use of interests in the Project, whether such a change would be direct or as a Member of the Association, shall be submitted for a vote of Owners or Members or by any other means become valid without the prior written consent of the Real Estate Commissioner during the period of time that the Declarant holds or directly controls as many as one-fourth (1/4) of the votes that may be cast to effect such change.

To the extent stipulated by law, there shall be no official meeting of Owners or Member nor any written solicitation of them for the purpose of effectuating a change referred to in this Paragraph except in accordance with a procedure approved by the Real Estate Commissioner; provided, however, that the governing body of the Owner's Association may meet and vote on the question of submission of the proposed change to the Commissioner.

-16-

D. No Adverse Effect on Prior Recorded Mortgage. No amendment shall adversely affect the rights of the holder of any Mortgage recorded against any portion of the Project, where such a Mortgage has been recorded prior to the recordation of such amendment.

ARTICLE XVII

DISCIPLINARY MEASURES AGAINST MEMBERS

The Board may exercise its authority to impose disciplinary measures against a Member only in accordance with this Article XVII. Delinquent assessments and any and all late charges shall not be deemed to be disciplinary measures.

A. Fines. The Board may fine any Member subject to the limitations set forth in the Declaration and hereinbelow. From the date of notice of the imposition of said fine, the Owner so fined must, within fifteen (15) days, either (a) pay the entire amount of the fine, or (b) file a written objection to the fine with the Board. If the Owner fails to take either action, interest shall commence to run on the unpaid portion of the fine from the fifteenth day after notification, said interest to be established by the Board prior to the date that the Board levies such fine. Said interest rate shall be timely paid, the Board may exercise any other right given by included in the Rules and Regulations. Concerning a fine not the Condominium Documents or by law.

If the fined Owner files a written objection as hereinabove provided, the fine shall be suspended pending the completion of the Board review procedure set forth below. Upon receipt of said written objection, the Board shall schedule a special Board meeting within twenty (20) days to review the objection. The Board shall make a good faith effort to schedule said special meeting at a time convenient for the fined Owner. At said special meeting, a quorum will equal sixty percent (60%) of the Directors then in office. At said special meeting, the Board may consider any oral or written evidence submitted to it, and the fined Owner may be represented by an attorney or another representative. Within five (5) days of said special meeting, the Board shall notify the fined Owner of the amount of the fine which remains levied against him. The fined Owner must pay said sum within fifteen (15) days. There shall be no right to petition the Board for a second special meeting to review said fine. Interest, as set forth above, shall commence to run on the fifteenth day of after the Board notifies the fined Owner regarding the imposition of the fine.

-17-

B. Suspension of Votings. The Board may suspend the right of any Member to vote in any Association balloting subject to the limitations set forth in the Declaration and hereinbelow. Any suspension must be done in good faith and in a fair and reasonable manner. The Board must give the subject Owner fifteen (15) days' prior written notice, stating the reasons for suspension and listing the elements of the suspension. The Board shall give the subject Owner an opportunity to object to the contemplated suspension, orally or in writing, not less than five days before the effective date of the suspension. The Board shall convene a special Board meeting to review any objection which is made. At said special meeting, a quorum will equal sixty percent (60%) of the Directors then in office. At said special meeting, the Board may consider any oral or written evidence submitted to it, and the subject Owner may be represented by an attorney or other representative. The Board shall notify the subject Owner of its decision regarding suspension no less than two (2) days before the scheduled suspension.

C. Forfeiture or Abridgement of Rights. There can be no purported power in the Board to cause a forfeiture or abridgement of an Owner's rights to the full use and enjoyment of his individually owned subdivision interest on account of a failure by the Owner to comply with provisions of the Condominium Documents, except where the loss or forfeiture is the result of the judgment of a court or a decision arising out of arbitration or on account of a foreclosure or sale under a power of sale for failure of the Owner to pay assessments levied by the Association.

CERTIFICATE OF SECRETARY

I, the undersigned, certify that I am the presently elected and acting Secretary of the Bergamot Condos Homeowners' Association, a California nonprofit mutual benefit corporation, and the above Bylaws, consisting of eighteen (18) pages including this Certificate, are the Bylaws of this Association as adopted at a meeting of the Board of Directors held on _____, 19___.

DATED: _____ at _____, California.

_____
Secretary

-18-

(MULTI-UNIT RESIDENTIAL PROPERTY)

Careful Management Company
Los Angeles, California

PROPERTY MANAGEMENT AGREEMENT

This agreement is made and entered into this ____ day of ____, 19__, by and between _____ (hereinafter referred to as "Owner") and CAREFUL MANAGEMENT COMPANY, a general partnership (hereinafter referred to as "Agent").

Owner is the present owner of the real property located at _____.

consisting of a ____ unit apartment building and related facilities (hereinafter referred to as "Property"). Owner desires to employ Agent to manage the Property and Agent desires to enter into this Agreement of employment and to perform the services hereinafter set forth.

In consideration of the mutual promises and other good and valuable consideration, it is hereby agreed as follows:

1. Owner hereby employs the Agent as the sole and exclusive management agent of the Property to rent, lease, operate and manage the Property upon the terms hereinafter set forth for a period of ____ months beginning on the ____ day of ____, 19__, and ending on the ____ day of ____, 19__; and thereafter on an annual basis unless on or before sixty (60) days

prior to the expiration of any renewal period, either party hereto notifies the other in writing of an intention to terminate this Agreement, in which event this Agreement shall thereby be deemed terminated.

2. Agent accepts the employment and agrees:

A. To manage and operate the Property to the best of his ability in a faithful and diligent manner; however, Agent shall not be required to devote himself exclusively to the management of the Property. Agent agrees to furnish the services of his organization for the renting, leasing, operation, management, and maintenance of the Property.

B. Agent shall keep accurate books of account with correct entries therein of all receipts and expenditures with respect to the Property and have such books of account open to the inspection of Owner during usual business hours during the term of this Agreement and for a reasonable time thereafter. Agent shall render to Owner on or before the 15th of each month a detailed statement in writing detailing all receipts and disbursements by Agent during the preceding month and shall remit to the Owner any excess sums in possession of the Agent, reserving, however, a reasonable sum to be mutually agreed upon between the Owner and Agent as a reserve for repairs and maintenance, and for the payment of anticipated expenses including debt service and taxes.

C. Agent agrees to deposit all receipts collected with reference to the Property in a trust account, separate from Agent's

-2-

and/or leases and all rental checks may be made in the name of the Agent and may be payable to the Agent.

C. To employ, discharge and pay (from funds advanced by Owner, if required) all servants, employees or contractors necessary or desirable to be employed or engaged in the care, maintenance, repair, management and operation of the Property. To make the usual and ordinary repairs and to purchase all necessary supplies for the operation of the Property and to pay all bills so incurred from receipts received from the Property or from funds advanced by the Owner, if required. To pay from receipts received from the Property or funds advanced by the Owner, if required, all charges for water, gas, electricity, trash removal, elevator maintenance or other services or commodities necessary or desirable in the operation, repair, care or maintenance of the Property, including advertising material if required. To supervise repairs and alterations and to do decorating on the Property. In this connection the Agent agrees to secure the approval of the Owner on all expenditures in excess of $2,500 for any one item, except monthly, or recurring operating charges or emergency repairs in excess of the maximum, if in the opinion of the Agent, such repairs are necessary to protect the Property from damage or to maintain services to tenants as called for in any agreement in existence at that time.

-4-

other accounts in a national or state banking institution and to cause all disbursements, when practicable, to be disbursed by check and retain vouchers and other evidence of obligations and disbursements for examination at the request of the Owner from time to time as above provided in this Agreement.

Owner hereby gives to Agent the following authority and powers and agrees to assume all expenses in connection therewith:

A. To procure tenants and negotiate leases and/or monthly rental agreements for portions of the Property. To advertise the availability of the Property for rental and to sign, renew and/or cancel leases or tenancy agreements, either written or oral; to terminate tenancies and to sign and serve in the name of the Owner or in the name of the Agent at the Agent's election, such notices as are deemed appropriate by Agent; to institute and prosecute actions to evict tenants, and/or collect sums due, and/or to recover possession of portions of the Property and to bring actions in connection therewith in the name of the Agent acting on behalf of the Owner or the Agent's own behalf to recover rents and other sums due, and where expedient to settle, compromise and release such actions or suit, or reinstate such tenancies or take such other action as Agent shall deem appropriate.

B. To collect all rentals and other income arising from the Property and endorse and deposit all checks or drafts in payment thereof in Agent's trust account. All tenancy agreements

-3-

such of them as the Agent shall deem advisable. The Owner agrees to assume the obligation of any contracts or agreements so entered into at the termination of this agreement. Agent agrees to exercise sound business judgment in entering into all purchase and service contracts, and agreements as to price and terms, and that the Agent will not directly or indirectly receive any discount or other benefit for their own account.

4. Owner agrees to save and hold the Agent free and harmless from all damages, suits, actions, or claims arising in connection with this Agreement and the management and operation of the Property, and from liability for injuries suffered by any employee or other person whomsoever. In the event any lawsuits or other legal proceedings are instituted in which Agent is made a part by reason of Agent's management and operation of the Property and/or the performance of the Agent's obligations as provided in this Agreement, Owner shall provide at Owner's expense legal counsel for Agent's defense and indemnify Agent from any loss, cost or damage which may result from such lawsuit or legal proceedings. It is specifically understood, however, the Owner's obligation in this regard shall not extend to any occurrence or matter in which Agent or any of his employees have been guilty of willful misconduct or gross negligence.

In furtherance of the foregoing, Owner agrees to cause to be carried at Owner's expense, public liability insurance, fire and

-6-

D. To hire, discharge and supervise all labor and employees required for the operation, repair and maintenance of the Property. In this connection it is agreed that all employees, including any resident manager, shall be deemed employees of the Agent and Agent agrees to deduct all social security, unemployment and other similar taxes due to the United States government, the State of California, or any other local government for the wages of each employee whose wages are chargeable to the operation and maintenance of the Property. Any direct or indirect expenses in connection with the maintenance and employment of said employees shall be an expense of the Owner, including but not limited to, employer contributions, workers' compensation insurance, fidelity bonds and fringe benefits. The Agent may perform any of his duties through his attorneys, agents, or employees, and shall not be responsible for their acts, defaults or negligence if the Agent has used reasonable care and has exercised due diligence in their appointment and retention. The Agent shall not be liable for errors of judgment or for any mistake of fact or law, or for anything which they may do or refrain from doing hereafter, except in cases of willful misconduct or gross negligence.

E. To make contracts for electricity, gas, fuel, water, telephone, window cleaning, rubbish hauling and other services or

-5-

extended coverage insurance and other insurance if required by Agent, in such amounts and with such companies as shall be mutually approved by Owner and Agent, and to cause all such policies of insurance now in existence, or that hereafter may be in existence, to provide that the Agent shall be named as an additional insured party therein, and to cause said policies of insurance to be maintained at all times during the term of this Agreement and to cause copies thereof to be made available to the Agent. At the request of the Owner, Agent will assist in procuring all insurance and review from time to time the insurance requirements in connection with the Property.

5. Owner shall advise Agent of existing mortgage payments (trust deed payments), real property taxes, fire and liability insurance premiums and other fixed payments and obligations presently in existence or hereafter incurred in connection with the Property, and the Agent shall be authorized from the receipts derived from the Property or other monies deposited by the Owner with the Agent to cause to be paid duly and timely all of said obligations.

For the services to be rendered by the Agent in connection with the terms and provisions of this Agreement, all of which Agent hereby agrees to duly and timely perform, Owner agrees to pay to Agent as compensation for services rendered hereunder ___ per cent of all gross receipts actually collected from the

-7-

premises from time to time. Said amount shall be due and payable monthly and may be deducted by the Agent from the first receipts collected monthly from the Property. In addition, Agent may elect to perform repairs and/or maintenance and in such event Agent will be reimbursed therefor at competitive rates.

6. In the event Owner or Agent is notified by any governmental agency of any alleged violation or violations pertaining to the Property, each shall promptly notify the other and immediate action shall be taken at Owner's expense to cure the conditions complained of or to contest the requirements of said governmental agency. Should said conditions not be immediately cured or a bona fide contest be instituted, Agent shall have the right at his option to terminate this Agreement by giving thirty (30) days prior written notice to the Owner.

7. This agreement shall be binding upon and inure to the benefit of the heirs, executors, administrators, successors and assigns of Owner and Agent.

8. Agent shall consult with the Owner from time to time on all major policy decisions concerning the operation, repair, maintenance and rental policy affecting the Property.

9. Should suit be instituted to enforce any of the terms and provisions of this Agreement, the prevailing party in said action shall be entitled to recover his attorney's fees and such

-8-

costs as shall be fixed by any court of competent jurisdiction.

This agreement is made and entered into in the County of Los Angeles, State of California, and the laws of the State of California shall govern this agreement in every respect.

IN WITNESS WHEREOF, the parties hereto have affixed their signatures the day and date above written.

CAREFUL MANAGEMENT COMPANY

By _____
    AGENT

By _____
    OWNER

-9-

COMMON DRIVEWAY PRIVATE OWNERSHIP

WHEN RECORDED RETURN TO:
PERFECT REAL ESTATE INVESTMENTS
c/o MEYERS, STEVENS & WALTERS
PROFESSIONAL CORPORATION
6300 Wilshire Boulevard, Suite 9100
Los Angeles, California 90048

------------SPACE ABOVE THIS LINE FOR RECORDER'S USE------------

RECIPROCAL EASEMENT AGREEMENT

This Reciprocal Easement Agreement (hereinafter "Agreement") is made and entered into this _____ day of January, 1981, by and between the PERFECT REAL ESTATE INVESTMENTS, a California partnership (hereinafter "PREI") and CHAMPION DEVELOPERS, a California partnership (hereinafter "CD").

1. RECITALS:

   A.   PREI is a fee owner of the real property in the County of Los Angeles, State of California, described in Exhibit "B" attached hereto and made a part hereof (hereafter referred to as "Parcel 2").

   B.   CD is the fee owner of the real property in the County of Los Angeles, State of Californis described in Exhibit "A" attached hereto and made a part hereof (hereafter referred to as "Parcel 1").

   C.   Parcels 1 and 2 are continguous to each other. The common boundaries between the two said Parcels is hereinafter referred to as being oriented along a line running northwesterly

easement for vehicular and pedestrian ingress, egress and passage over and through, to, from, upon and across the most northwesterly thirteen (13) feet of Parcel 1, excepting therefrom the most northwesterly twenty (20) feet, for the purpose of providing access, ingress and egress to and from Parcel 2.

5. The term of this Agreement shall commence on the date hereof and terminate fifty (50) years from the date hereof.

6. Each of the parties hereto shall maintain their respective parcels at their own cost and expense and each shall defend, hold harmless and indemnify the other from all claims, demands, actions and liability arising out of the use of the other's property for the purposes herein set forth.

7. The easements herein granted by each party to the other are each for the mutual benefit of each and every parcel described in Exhibits "A" and "B", respectively, and for the respective parties hereto and their respective successors and assigns.

8. It is the intent of this Agreement that the easements granted herein and the terms and provisions herein contained inure to and pass with the fee land as to each parcel and apply to and bind the parties hereto and their respective successors ans assigns and, further, that same shall run with the land as to each parcel, and inure and pass with each conveyance of each parcel. Insofar as each parcel is benefited by the terms and provisions herein contained such parcel shall be deemed the dominant estate and insofar as each parcel is burdened thereby it shall be deemed the servient estate.

and southeasterly. The parties desire to enter into a non-exclusive agreement pursuant to which each party will grant to the other a non-exclusive easement for vehicular and pedestrian ingress and egress, to, from, upon and across said common boundary, excepting therefrom the most northwesterly twenty (20) feet, for the purpose of providing access, ingress and egress to, from, upon and across each of said Parcels 1 and 2.

NOW THEREFORE, it is agreed as follows:

2. Each recital is incorporated herein and made a part hereof.

3. PREI does hereby grant and convey to CD and its successors and assigns and its tenants and sub-tenants and to their respective agents, servants, employees, guests and invitees and their successors and assigns, a non-exclusive easement for vehicular and pedestrian ingress, egress and passage over and through, to, from, upon and across the most southwesterly thirteen (13) feet, of Parcel 2, excepting therefrom the most northwesterly twenty (20) feet, for the purpose of providing access, ingress and egress to and from Parcel 1.

4. CD does hereby grant and convey to PREI and its successors and assigns and to its tenants and sub-tenants and to their respective agents, servants, employees, guests and invitees and their successors and assigns a non-exclusive

said action, which sums shall be included in any judgment or decree entered in such action in favor of the prevailing party.

13.   If any clause, sentence or other portion of the terms, conditions and/or covenants of this agreement shall become illegal, null or void for any reason or be held by any court of competent jurisdiction to be so, the remaining portion will remain in full force and efect.

14.   All notices, statements, demands, approvals or other communications to be given under and pursuant to this Agreement will be in writing and may be served personally or by registered or certified mail, return receipt requested, postage prepaid, addressed to the parties at their respective addresses as provided below:

PERFECT REAL ESTATE INVESTMENTS,
a California partnership
0000 Development Way
Valuable, California   99999

CHAMPION DEVELOPERS,
a California partnership
0000 Ownership Avenue
Chamption, California   99999

15.   Each and all of the easements and rights granted or created hereunder are appurtenances to each parcel and none of the easements and rights may be transferred, assigned or encumbered except as appurtenances thereto.

-5-

9.   In the event of any violation or threatened violation by any party hereto, or by any tenant or sub-tenant of any such party, or by any successor or assign of any such party, of any portion of this Agreement, each of the parties hereto, or their respective successors and assigns, will have the right to enjoin such violation or threatened violation in any court of competent jurisdiction, in addition to the right to recover damages therefor.

10.   Except as hereinabove otherwise set forth, this Agreement and any provision, covenant, condition or restriction contained within it may be terminated, extended, modified or amended as to the whole thereof or any portion of it only with the consent of all the parties hereto in writing.

11.   Nothing contained in this Agreement will be deemed to be a gift or dedication of any portion of land above described, or of any interest therein, to the general public or for the general public or for any public purpose whatsoever, it being the intention of the parties that this agreement will be strictly limited to and for the purposes expressed herein.

12.   If any party to this Agreement, or his successor or assign in interest thereto shall bring an action in any court of competent jurisdiction to enforce any provision of this Agreement, the prevailing party shall be entitled to reasonable attorneys' fees and all costs and expenses in connection with

-4-

EXHIBIT "A"

TO RECIPROCAL EASEMENT AGREEMENT

PARCEL 1 IN THE COUNTY OF LOS ANGELES, STATE
OF CALIFORNIA, AS SHOWN ON PARCEL MAP NO.
00000, FILED IN BOOK 10 PAGES 1 TO 10 INCLUSIVE
AS PARCEL MAPS, IN THE OFFICE OF THE COUNTY
RECORDER OF SAID COUNTY.

IN WITNESS WHEREOF the parties hereto have hereto set their
hands and official seals this date.

PERFECT REAL ESTATE INVESTMENTS,
a California partnership

By _____

CHAMPION DEVELOPERS,
a California partnership

By _____

-6-

THE COMPANIES LAW
COMPANY LIMITED BY SHARES
MEMORANDUM OF ASSOCIATION
OF
INVESTMENTS S. A.

1. The name of the Company is   INVESTMENTS S.A.

2. The Registered Office of the Company shall be at the offices of
P.O. Box   , George Town, Grand Cayman, Cayman
Islands, British West Indies or at such other place as the Directors
may from time to time decide.

3. The objects for which the Company is established are as follows:

(i) (a) To carry on the business of an investment company and to carry
on business as financiers, capitalists, concessionaires and merchants and to
undertake and carry on and execute all kinds of investment, financial, commercial,
trading and other operations.

(b) To carry on in any part of the world whether as principals, agents
or otherwise howsoever the business of realtors, developers, consultants, estate
agents or managers, builders, contractors, engineers, manufacturers, dealers in
or vendors of all types of property including services, and to act as promoters
and entrepreneurs.

(ii) To exercise and enforce all rights and powers conferred by or incidental
to the ownership of any shares, stock, obligations, or other securities including
without prejudice to the generality of the foregoing all such powers of veto or
control as may be conferred by virtue of the holding by the company of some
special proportion of the issued or nominal amount thereof to provide managerial
and other executive supervisory and consultant services for or in relation to
any company in which the Company is interested upon such terms as may be thought
fit.

(iii) To purchase or otherwise acquire, to sell, exchange, surrender, lease,
mortgage, charge, convert, turn to account, dispose of and deal with real and
personal property and rights of all kinds and in particular, mortgages, debentures, produce, concessions, options, contracts, patents, annuities, licenses,
stocks, shares, bonds, policies, book debts, business concerns, undertakings,
claims, privileges and choses in action of all kinds.

- 2 -

EXHIBIT "B"

TO RECIPROCAL EASEMENT AGREEMENT

PARCEL 2 IN THE COUNTY OF LOS ANGELES, STATE
OF CALIFORNIA, AS SHOWN ON PARCEL MAP NO.
00000, FILED IN BOOK 10 PAGES 1 TO 10 INCLUSIVE
AS PARCEL MAPS, IN THE OFFICE OF THE COUNTY
RECORDER OF SAID COUNTY.

(iv)   To subscribe for, conditionally or unconditionally, to underwrite, issue on commission or otherwise, take hold, deal in and convert stocks, shares and securities of all kinds and to enter into partnership, or into any arrangement for sharing profits, reciprocal concessions or co-operation with any person, or company and to promote and aid in promoting, constitute, form or organize any company, syndicate or partnership of any kind, for the purpose of acquiring and undertaking any property and liabilities of the Company, or of advancing directly or indirectly, the objects of the Company, or for any other purpose which the Company may think expedient.

(v)   To stand surety for or to guarantee, support or secure the performance of all or any of the obligations of any person, firm or company whether or not related or affiliated to the Company in any manner and whether by personal covenant or by mortgage, charge or lien upon the whole or any part of the undertaking, property and assets of the Company both present and future, including its uncalled capital or by any such method whether or not the Company shall receive valuable consideration therefore.

(vi)   To engage in or carry on any other lawful trade, business or enterprise which may at any time appear to the Director of the Company capable of being conveniently carried on in conjunction with any of the aforementioned businesses or activities or which may appear to the Directors or the Company likely to be profitable to the Company.

IT BEING HEREBY DECLARED that in the interpretation of this Memorandum of Association in general and of this Clause 3 in particular no object, business or power specified or mentioned shall be limited or restricted by reference to or inference from any other object, business or power, or the name of the Company, or by the juxtaposition of two or more objects, businesses or powers and that in the event of any ambiguity in this clause or elsewhere in this Memorandum of Association, the same shall be resolved by such interpretation and construction as will widen and enlarge and not restrict the objects, businesses and powers of and exercisable by the Company.

4.   Except as prohibited or limited by the Companies Law (Cap. 22), the Company shall have and be capable of from time to time and at all times exercising any and all of the powers at any time or from time to time exercisable by a natural person or body corporate in doing in any part of the world whether as principal, agent, contractor, or otherwise whatever may be considered by it necessary for the attainment of its objects and whatever else may be considered by it as incidental

- 3 -

or conducive thereto or consequential thereon, including, but without in any way restricting the generality of the foregoing, the power to make any alterations or amendments to this Memorandum of Association and the Articles of Association of the Company considered necessary or convenient in the manner set out in the Articles of Association of the Company and the power to do any of the following acts or things, viz. to pay all expenses of and incidental to the promotion formation and incorporation of the Company; to sell, lease or dispose of any property of the Company; to draw, make, accept, endorse, discount, execute and issue promissory notes, debentures, Bills of Exchange, Bills of Lading, warrants and other negotiable or transferable instruments; to lend money or other assets and to act as guarantors; to borrow or raise money on the security of the undertaking or on all or any of the assets of the Company including uncalled capital or without security; to invest monies of the Company in such manner as the directors determine; to promote other companies; to sell the undertaking of the Company for cash or any other consideration; to distribute assets in specie to members of the Company; to carry on any trade or business and generally to do all acts and things which, in the opinion of the Company or the Directors, may be conveniently or profitably or usefully acquired and dealt with, carried on, executed or done by the Company in connection with the business aforesaid PROVIDED THAT the Company shall only carry on the businesses for which a license is required under the Banks and Trust Companies Regulations Law 1966 when licenced to do so under the terms of that Law.

5.   The liability of each member is limited to the amount from time to time unpaid on such member's shares.

6.   The share capital of the Company is U. S.   divided into   shares of a nominal or par value of U. S. $1.00   each with power for the Company insofar as is permitted by law, to redeem any of its shares and to increase or reduce the said capital subject to the provisions of the Companies Law (Cap. 22) and the Articles of Association and to issue any part of its capital, whether original, redeemed or increased with or without any preference, priority or special privilege or subject to any postponement of rights or to any conditions or restrictions and so that unless the conditions of issue shall otherwise expressly declare every issue of shares whether declared to be preference or otherwise shall be subject to the powers hereinbefore contained.

- 4 -

THE COMPANIES LAW

COMPANY LIMITED BY SHARES

ARTICLES OF ASSOCIATION

OF

INVESTMENTS S.A.

1.   In these Articles Table A does not apply and, unless there be something in the subject or context inconsistent therewith:-

"Articles" means these Articles as originally framed or as from time to time altered by Special Resolution.

"The Auditors" means the persons for the time being performing the duties of auditors of the Company.

"Bearer Holder" means the bearer for the time being of a Bearer Share certificate issued pursuant to Article 4 hereof.

"Bearer Share" means a share transferable by delivery of the relevant Bearer Share certificate.

"The Company" means the above-named Company.

"Debenture" includes debenture stock, mortgages, bonds and any other such securities of the Company whether constituting a charge on the assets of the Company or not.

"The Directors" means the directors for the time being of the Company.

"Dividend" includes bonus.

"Member" shall have the meaning ascribed to it in the Statute and shall include a Bearer Holder.

"Month" means calendar month.

"Paid-up" means paid-up and/or credited as paid-up.

"Registered Office" means the registered office for the time being of the Company.

"Register" means the register of members required to be maintained pursuant to Article 4 hereof.

"Registered Holder" means a member other than a Bearer Holder.

"Registered Share" means any share other than a Bearer share.

---

7.   The operations of the Company will be carried on subject to the provisions of Section 190 of the Companies Law Cap. 22.

WE the several persons whose names and addresses are subscribed are desirous of being formed into a company in pursuance of this Memorandum of Association and we respectively agree to take the number of shares in the capital of the Company set opposite our respective names.

Dated the   9th   day of   May   A.D. 1979

SIGNATURE, ADDRESSES and DESCRIPTION OF SUBSCRIBERS	NUMBER OF SHARES TAKEN BY EACH
	one
	one
	one

I,   Registrar of Companies in and for the Cayman Islands DO HEREBY CERTIFY that this is a true and correct copy of the Memorandum of Association of this Company duly incorporated on the   day of   197

REGISTRAR OF COMPANIES

-5-

—2—

"Seal" means the common seal of the Company and includes every official seal.

"Secretary" includes an Assistant Secretary and any person appointed to perform the duties of Secretary of the Company.

"Special Resolution" has the same meaning as in the Statute.

"Statute" means The Companies Law of the Cayman Islands as amended and every statutory modification or re-enactment thereof for the time being in force.

"Written" and "in writing" include all modes of representing or reproducing words in visible form.

Words importing the singular number only include the plural number and vice-versa.

Words importing the masculine gender only include the feminine gender.

Words importing persons only include corporations.

2. The business of the Company may be commenced as soon after incorporation as the Directors shall see fit, notwithstanding that part only of the shares may have been allotted.

3. The Directors may pay, out of the capital or any other monies of the Company, all expenses incurred in or about the formation and establishment of the Company including the expenses of registration.

ISSUE OF SHARES

4. (i) Certificates representing shares of the Company shall specify the shares to which they relate and the amount paid thereon and otherwise shall be in such form as shall be determined by the Directors. Such certificates shall be under the Seal. All certificates for shares shall be consecutively numbered or otherwise identified. The name and address of the person to whom the shares represented thereby are issued or the fact that the same is issued to bearer with the number of shares and date of issue shall be entered in the Register provided that in respect of a share or shares held jointly by several persons the Company shall not be bound to issue more than one certificate for any one share and delivery of a certificate or a share to one of the several joint holders shall be sufficient delivery to all such holders. All certificates surrendered to the Company for transfer shall be cancelled and no new certificate shall be issued until the former certificate for a like number of shares shall be issued to bearer unless it is fully paid up and non-assessable so that no amount shall after the issue of the share remain due to the Company whether on account of the nominal value of the share or on account of premium.

(ii) The Company shall cause to be kept a Register of its Registered Holders.

5. (i) Notwithstanding Article 4 of these Articles, if a share certificate be defaced, lost or destroyed, it may be replaced upon evidence satisfactory to the Directors having been adduced and on such terms as to indemnity and the payment of the expenses incurred by the Company in investigating evidence as the Directors may prescribe.

—3—

(ii) If after replacement of a share certificate as aforesaid both the original share certificate and its replacement or the coupon attached thereto shall be presented to the Company for any purpose whatsoever the Directors may recognise the bearer of such of the certificates as it thinks fit as the person entitled to the rights attaching thereto and shall be under no liability whatsoever to the bearer of the other share certificate or certificates.

6. (i) Subject to the provisions, if any, in that behalf in the Memorandum of Association and to any direction that may be given by the Company in general meeting and without prejudice to any special rights previously conferred on the holders of existing shares, the Directors may dispose of shares of the Company with or without preferred, deferred or other special rights or restrictions, whether in regard to dividend, voting, return of capital or otherwise and whether to bearer or otherwise.

(ii) Every member shall be entitled without payment to receive within two months after allotment or registration of a transfer as the case may be (or within such other period as the conditions of issue shall provide) one certificate for all his shares or several certificates each for one or more of his shares provided that no one certificate shall be issued for both Bearer Shares and Registered Shares.

(iii) There may, if the Directors so resolve, be attached to each Bearer Share certificate upon issue a coupon in such form as the Directors may determine, such coupon to specify the number of shares to which such certificate relates and to bear a distinguishing number to the intent that to each dividend declared by the Directors there shall correspond one and only one distinguishing number.

BEARER SHARES

7. (i) Except as is otherwise provided in these Articles the only person capable of being recognised as a Bearer Holder shall be the bearer of a Bearer Share certificate in respect of those shares.

(ii) No person as bearer of any Bearer Share certificate shall be entitled to exercise any of the rights of a member (save as hereinafter provided with regard to general meetings) without not less than 24 hours before exercising such rights delivering such Bearer share certificate as and where the Directors so require and permitting an endorsement to be made thereon of the date and purpose of its production.

TRANSFER OF SHARES

8. The instrument of transfer of any Registered Share shall be in writing and shall be executed by or on behalf of the Transferor and if partly paid by the Transferee and the Transferor shall be deemed to remain the holder of a share until the name of the Transferee is entered in the Register in respect thereof. A Bearer Share shall be transferable by delivery of the Bearer Share certificate representing the same.

-4-

9.   The Directors may in their absolute discretion decline to register any transfer of Registered Shares without assigning any reason therefor. If the Directors refuse to register a transfer they shall notify the Transferee within two months of such refusal.

10.   The registration of transfers may be suspended at such time and for such periods as the Directors may from time to time determine; Provided always that such registration shall not be suspended for more than forty-five days in any year.

REDEEMABLE SHARES

11.   Subject to the provisions of the Statute and the Memorandum of Association, shares may be issued on the terms that they may, or at the option of the Company may, be redeemed on such terms and in such manner as the Company, before the issue of the shares, may determine.

VARIATION OF RIGHTS OF SHARES

12.   (i)   If at any time the share capital of the Company is divided into different classes of shares, the rights attached to any class (unless otherwise provided by the terms of issue of the shares of that class) may, whether or not the Company is being wound-up, be varied with the consent in writing of the holders of all of the issued shares of that class, or with the sanction of a Special Resolution passed at a general meeting of the holders of the shares of that class.

(ii)   The provisions of these Articles relating to general meetings shall apply to every such general meeting of the holders of one class of shares except that the necessary quorum shall be two persons holding or representing by proxy at least one-third of the class present in person or by proxy.

(iii)   The rights conferred upon the holders of the shares of any class issued with preferred or other rights shall not, unless otherwise expressly provided by the terms of issue of the shares of that class, be deemed to be varied by the creation or issue of further shares ranking pari passu therewith.

13.   (i)   Any Registered Holder may upon delivery to the Directors of a request in writing and the Registered Share certificate registered in his name surrender his share certificate and receive in its stead a Bearer Share certificate for some or all of his shares and a Registered Share certificate for the remainder (if any).

(ii)   Any Bearer Holder may upon delivery to the Directors of a request in writing and a Bearer Share certificate surrender his Bearer Share certificate and be registered as a Registered Holder in respect of some or all of his shares and receive a Registered Share certificate for those of his shares in respect of which he wishes to become a Registered Holder and a Bearer Share certificate for the remainder (if any).

-5-

COMMISSION ON SALE OF SHARES

14.   The Company may in so far as the Statute from time to time permits pay a commission to any person in consideration of his subscribing or agreeing to subscribe whether absolutely or conditionally for any shares of the Company. Such commission may be satisfied by the payment of cash or the lodgement of fully or partly paid-up shares or partly in one way and partly in the other. The Company may also on any issue of shares pay such brokerage as may be lawful.

NON-RECOGNITION OF TRUSTS

15.   No person shall be recognised by the Company as holding any share upon any trust and the Company shall not be bound by or be compelled in any way to recognise (even when having notice thereof) any equitable, contingent, future or partial interest in any share, or any interest in any fractional part of a share, or (except only as is otherwise provided by these Articles or the Statute) any other rights in respect of any share and the Company shall not be bound by any allegations or proceeding concerning the ownership of any share except an absolute right to the entirety thereof in the Registered Holder or Bearer Holder as the case may be. The Company shall not recognize any more than one person as being the bearer of a Bearer Share or entitled thereto.

LIEN ON SHARES

16.   The Company shall have a first and paramount lien and charge on all shares (whether fully paid-up or not) registered in the name of a member (whether solely or jointly with others) for all debts, liabilities or engagements to or with the Company (whether presently payable or not) by such member or his estate, either alone or jointly with any other person, whether a member or not, but the Directors may at any time declare any share to be wholly or in part exempt from the provisions of this Article. The registration of a transfer of any such share shall operate as a waiver of the Company's lien (if any) thereon. The Company's lien (if any) on a share shall extend to all dividends or other monies payable in respect thereof.

17.   The Company may sell, in such manner as the Directors think fit, any shares on which the Company has a lien but no sale shall be made unless a sum in respect of which the lien exists is presently payable, nor until the expiration of fourteen days after a notice in writing stating and demanding payment of such part of the amount in respect of which the lien exists as is presently payable, has been given to the Registered Holder or Holders for the time being of the share, or the person, of which the Company has notice entitled thereto by reason of his death or bankruptcy.

18.   To give effect to any such sale the Directors may authorise some person to transfer the shares sold to the purchaser thereof. The purchaser shall be registered as the holder of the shares comprised in any such transfer and he shall not be bound to see to the application of the purchase money nor shall his title to the shares be affected by any irregularity or invalidity in the proceedings in reference to the sale.

-6-

CALL ON SHARES

19. The proceeds of such sale shall be received by the Company and applied in payment of such part of the amount in respect of which the lien exists as is presently payable and the residue, if any, shall (subject to a like lien for sums not presently payable as existed upon the shares before the sale) be paid to the person entitled to the shares at the date of the sale.

20. (a) The Directors may from time to time make calls upon the members in respect of any monies unpaid on their shares (whether on account of the nominal value of the shares or by way of premium or otherwise) and not by the conditions of allotment thereof made payable at fixed terms, provided that no call shall exceed one-fourth of the nominal value of the share or be payable at less than one month from the date fixed for the payment of the last preceding call, and each member shall (subject to receiving at least fourteen days notice specifying the time or times of payment) pay to the Company at the time or times so specified the amount called on the shares. A call may be revoked or postponed as the Directors may determine. A call may be made payable by instalments.

(b) A call shall be deemed to have been made at the time when the resolution of the Directors authorising such call was passed.

(c) The joint holders of a share shall be jointly and severally liable to pay all calls in respect thereof.

21. If a sum called in respect of a share is not paid before or on a day appointed for payment thereof, the persons from whom the sum is due shall pay interest on the sum from the day appointed for payment thereof to the time of actual payment at such rate not exceeding ten per cent per annum as the Directors may determine, but the Directors shall be at liberty to waive payment of such interest either wholly or in part.

22. Any sum which by the terms of issue of a share becomes payable on allotment or at any fixed date, whether on account of the nominal value of the share or by way of premium or otherwise, shall for the purposes of these Articles be deemed to be a call duly made, notified and payable on the date on which by the terms of issue the same becomes payable, and in the case of non-payment all the relevant provisions of these Articles as to payment of interest, forfeiture or otherwise shall apply as if such sum had become payable by virtue of a call duly made and notified.

23. The Directors may, on the issue of shares, differentiate between the holders as to the amount of calls or interest to be paid and the times of payment.

24. (a) The Directors may, if they think fit, receive from any member willing to advance the same, all or any part of the monies uncalled and unpaid upon any shares held by him, and upon all or any of the monies so advanced may (until the same would but for such advances, become payable) pay interest at such rate not exceeding (unless the Company in general meeting shall otherwise direct) seven (7%) per cent per annum, as may be agreed upon between the Directors and the member paying such sum in advance.

-7-

(b) No such sum paid in advance of calls shall entitle the member paying such sum to any portion of a dividend declared in respect of any period prior to the date upon which such sum would, but for such payment, become presently payable.

FORFEITURE OF SHARES

25. (a) If a member fails to pay any call or instalment of a call or to make any payment required by the terms of issue on the day appointed for payment thereof, the Directors may, at any time thereafter during such time as any part of the call, instalment or payment remains unpaid, give notice requiring payment of so much of the call, instalment or payment as is unpaid, together with any interest which may have accrued, and all expenses that have been incurred by the Company by reason of such non-payment. Such notice shall name a day (not earlier than the expiration of fourteen days from the date of giving of the notice) on or before which the payment required by the notice is to be made, and shall state that, in the event nonpayment, at or before the time appointed the shares in respect of which such notice was given will be liable to be forfeited.

(b) If the requirements of any such notice as aforesaid are not complied with, any share in respect of which the notice has been given may at any time thereafter, before the payment required by the notice has been made, be forfeited by a resolution of the Directors to that effect. Such forfeiture shall include all dividends declared in respect of the forfeited share and not actually paid before the forfeiture.

(c) A forfeited share may be sold or otherwise disposed of on such terms and in such manner as the Directors think fit and at any time before a sale or disposition the forfeiture may be cancelled on such terms as the Directors think fit.

26. A person whose shares have been forfeited shall cease to be a member in respect of the forfeited shares, but shall, notwithstanding, remain liable to pay to the Company all monies which, at the date of forfeiture were payable by him to the Company in respect of the shares together with interest thereon, but his liability shall cease if and when the Company shall have received payment in full of all monies whenever payable in respect of the shares.

27. A certificate in writing under the hand of one Director and the Secretary of the Company that a share in the Company has been duly forfeited on a date stated in the declaration shall be conclusive evidence of the fact therein stated as against all persons claiming to be entitled to the share. The Company may receive the consideration given for the share on any sale or disposition thereof and may execute a transfer of the share in favour of the person to whom the share is sold or disposed of and he shall thereupon be registered as the holder of the share and shall not be bound to see to the application of the purchase money, if any, nor shall his title to the share be affected by any irregularity or invalidity in the proceedings in reference to the forfeiture, sale or disposal of the share.

28. The provisions of these Articles as to forfeiture shall apply in the case of non-payment of any sum which, by the term of issue of a share, becomes payable at a fixed time, whether on account of the nominal value of the share or by way of premium as if the same had been payable by virtue of a call duly made and notified.

-8-

REGISTRATION OF EMPOWERING INSTRUMENTS

29.   The Company shall be entitled to charge a fee not exceeding one dollar (US$1.00) on the registration of every probate, letters of administration, certificate of death or marriage, power of attorney, notice in lieu of distringas or other instrument.

TRANSMISSION OF SHARES

30.   In case of the death of a Registered Holder, the survivor or survivors where the deceased was a joint holder, and the legal personal representatives of the deceased where he was a sole holder, shall be the only persons recognised by the Company as having any title to his interest in the shares, but nothing herein contained shall release the estate of any such deceased holder from any liability in respect of any share which had been held by him solely or jointly with other persons.

31.   (a) Any person becoming entitled to a Registered Share in consequence of the death or bankruptcy of a member (or in any other way than by transfer) may, upon such evidence being produced as may from time to time be required by the Directors and subject as hereinafter provided, elect either to be registered himself as holder of the share or to make such transfer of the share to such other person nominated by him as the deceased or bankrupt person could have made and to have such person registered as the transferee thereof, but the Directors shall, in either case, have the same right to decline or suspend registration as they would have had in the case of a transfer of the share by that member before this death or bankruptcy as the case may be.

       (b) If the person so becoming entitled shall elect to be registered himself he shall deliver or send to the Company a notice in writing signed by him stating that he so elects.

32.   A person becoming entitled to a Registered Share by reason of the death or bankruptcy of the holder (or in any other case than by transfer) shall be entitled to the same dividends and other advantages to which he would be entitled if he were the Registered Holder of the share, except that he shall not, before being registered as a member in respect of the share, be entitled in respect of it to exercise any right conferred by membership in relation to meetings of the Company PROVIDED HOWEVER that the Directors may at any time give notice requiring any such person to elect either to be registered himself or to transfer the share and if the notice is not complied with within ninety days the Directors may thereafter withhold payment of all dividends, bonuses or other monies payable in respect of the share until the requirements of the notice have been complied with.

CONVERSION OF SHARES AND STOCK

33.   (a) The Company may by ordinary resolution convert any paid-up shares into stock and re-convert any stock into paid-up shares of any denomination.

-9-

       (b) The holders of stock may transfer the same, or any part thereof, in the same manner, and subject to the same regulations as and subject to which, the shares from which the stock arose might previously to conversion have been transferred, or as near thereto as circumstances admit; the Directors may from time to time fix the minimum amount of stock transferable, but so that such minimum shall not exceed the nominal amount of the shares from which the stock arose.

       (c) The holders of stock shall, according to the amount of stock held by them, have the same rights, privileges and advantages as regards dividends, voting at meetings of the Company and other matters as if they held the shares from which the stock arose, but no such privilege or advantage (except participation in the dividends and profits of the Company and in the assets on winding up) shall be conferred by an amount of stock which would not if existing in shares have conferred that privilege or advantage.

34.   Such of these Articles as are applicable to paid up shares shall apply to stock and the words "share" and "shareholder" herein shall include "stock" and "stockholder".

AMENDMENT OF MEMORANDUM OF ASSOCIATION, CHANGE OF LOCATION OF REGISTERED OFFICE & ALTERATION OF CAPITAL

35.   (a) Subject to and in so far as is permitted by the provisions of the Statute, the Company may from time to time by ordinary resolution alter or amend its Memorandum of Association otherwise than with respect to its name and objects and may, without restricting the generality of the foregoing:

            (i) increase the share capital by such sum to be divided into shares of such amount or without nominal or par value as the resolution shall prescribe and with such rights, priorities and privileges annexed thereto, as the Company in general meeting may determine;

            (ii) consolidate and divide all or any of its share capital into shares of larger amount than its existing shares;

            (iii) by subdivision of its existing shares or any of them divide the whole or any part of its share capital into shares of smaller amount than is fixed by the Memorandum of Association or into shares without nominal or par value;

            (iv) cancel any shares which at the date of the passing of the resolution have not been taken or agreed to be taken by any person.

       (b) All new shares created hereunder shall be subject to the same provisions with reference to the payment of calls, liens, transfer, transmission, forfeiture and otherwise as the shares in the original share capital.

       (c) Subject to the provisions of the Statute the Company may by Special Resolution change its name or alter its objects.

       (d) Subject to the provisions of the Statute the Company may by Special Resolution redeem any of its shares, or reduce its share capital, any capital Redemption Reserve Fund, or any share Premium Account.

-10-

(e)   Subject to the provisions of the Statute the Company may by resolution of the Directors change the location of its registered office.

CLOSING TRANSFER BOOK OR FIXING RECORD DATE

36.   For the purpose of determining Registered Holders entitled to notice of or to vote at any meeting of shareholders or any adjournment thereof, or Registered Holders entitled to receive payment of any dividend, or in order to make a determination of Registered Holders for any other proper purpose, the Board of Directors of the Company may provide that the share or stock transfer books shall be closed for a stated period but not to exceed in any case fourteen (14) days. If the share or stock transfer books shall be closed for the purpose of determining Registered Holders entitled to notice of or to vote at a meeting of shareholders such books shall be closed for at least ten (10) days immediately preceding such meeting.

37.   In lieu of or apart from closing the share or stock transfer books, the Board of Directors may fix in advance a date as the record date for any such determination of Registered Holders, such date in any case to be not more than fourteen (14) days and, in the case of a meeting of shareholders, not less than ten(10) days prior to the date on which the particular action, requiring such determination of Registered Holders, is to be taken.

38.   If the said transfer books are not closed and no record date is fixed for the determination of Registered Holders entitled to notice of or to vote at a meeting of shareholders, or shareholders entitled to receive payment of a dividend, the date on which notice of the meeting is mailed or the date on which the resolution of the Board of Directors declaring such dividend is adopted, as the case may be, shall be the record date for such determination of Registered Holders. When a determination of shareholders entitled to vote at any meeting of shareholders has been made as provided in this section, such determination shall apply to any adjournment thereof.

GENERAL MEETING

39.   (a)   The Company may in each year of its existence hold a general meeting as its Annual General Meeting and shall specify the meeting as such in the notices calling it. The Annual General Meeting shall be held at such time and place as the Directors shall appoint.

(b)   At these meetings the Directors shall be elected, the report of the Directors shall be presented and the general business of the Company transacted.

40.   (a)   The Directors may whenever they think fit, and they shall on the requisition of members of the Company holding at the date of the deposit of the requisition less than one-tenth of such of the paid-up capital of the Company as at the date of the deposit carries the right of voting at general meetings of the Company, proceed to convene a general meeting of the Company.

(b)   The requisition must state the object of the meeting and must be signed by the requisitionists and deposited at the Registered Office of the Company and may consist of several documents in like form each signed by one or more requisitionists.

-11-

the deposit of the requisition duly proceed to convene a general meeting, the requisitionists, or any of them representing more than one-half of the total voting rights of all of them, may themselves convene a general meeting, but any meeting so convened shall not be held after the expiration of three months after the expiration of the said twenty-one days.

(d)   A general meeting convened as aforesaid by requisitionists shall be convened in the same manner as nearly as possible as that in which general meetings are to be convened by Directors.

(e)   If at any such general meeting a resolution requiring confirmation at another meeting is passed, the Directors shall forthwith convene a further general meeting to be held not less than ten days nor later than one month after the passing of the first resolution for the purpose of considering the resolution and if the Directors do not give notice of so convening such further general meeting within seven days from the date of the passing of the first resolution the requisitionists or any of them representing more than one-half of the total voting rights of all the requisitionists may themselves give notice and convene the general meeting.

(f)   No Bearer Holder shall be entitled to attend or vote or exercise in respect of his Bearer Shares any of the rights of a member at any general meeting unless he produces for inspection by the Company the relevant Bearer Share certificate at the commencement of such meeting.

NOTICE OF GENERAL MEETINGS

41.   (i)   At least 5 days' notice shall be given of an Annual General Meeting or any other general meeting and a general meeting at which consideration is to be given confirmation of any Special Resolution passed at a previous general meeting shall be held only at an interval of not less than ten days nor more than one month from the date of the meeting at which the Special Resolution was first passed. Every notice shall be exclusive of the day on which it is given or deemed to be given and of the day for which it is given and shall specify the place, the day and the hour of the meeting and, in case of special business, the resolutions to be proposed and shall be given, in manner hereinafter mentioned or in such other manner if any as may be prescribed by the Company PROVIDED that a general meeting of the Company shall be deemed to have been duly called notwithstanding that it is called by shorter notice than that specified in this regulation or that no notice of such meeting shall have been given if it is so agreed by all the members entitled to attend and vote thereat or their proxies.

(ii)   Notwithstanding the foregoing, in the case of notice to be given to Bearer Holders such notice need not specify in case of special business the resolutions to be proposed but shall state that copies of such resolutions shall be available on demand to any Bearer Holder at the Registered Office or such other place or places specified in such notice.

42.   The accidental omission to give notice of a general meeting to, or the non-receipt of notice of a meeting by any person entitled to receive notice shall not invalidate the proceedings of that meeting.

-12-

43.   In every notice calling a meeting of the Company there shall appear with reasonable prominence a statement as to which members are entitled to attend and vote and that Registered Holders are entitled to appoint proxies to attend and vote instead of them and that those proxies need not also be members.

PROCEEDINGS AT GENERAL MEETINGS

44.   No business shall be transacted at any general meeting unless a quorum of members is present at the time when the meeting proceeds to business; one (1) member present in person or by proxy shall be a quorum.

45.   Subject and without prejudice to any provisions of the Statute, a resolution in writing signed by all members for the time being entitled to receive notice of and to attend and vote at general meetings (or being corporations by their duly authorised representatives) shall be as valid and effective as if the same had been passed at a general meeting of the Company duly convened and held.

46.   If within half an hour from the time appointed for the meeting a quorum is not present, the meeting, if convened, upon the requisitions of members, shall be dissolved any other case it shall stand adjourned to the same day in the next week at the same time and place or to such other time or such other place as the Directors may determine and if at the adjourned meeting a quorum is not present within half an hour from the time appointed for the meeting the members present shall be a quorum.

47.   The Chairman, if any, of the Board of Directors shall preside at every general meeting of the Company or if there is no such Chairman, or if he shall not be present within fifteen minutes after the time appointed for the holding of the meeting, or if he shall be unwilling to act, the Directors present shall elect one of their number to be Chairman of the meeting.

48.   If at any general meeting no Director is willing to act as Chairman or if no Director is present within fifteen minutes after the time appointed for holding the meeting, the members present shall choose one of their number to be Chairman of the meeting.

49.   The Chairman may, with the consent of any general meeting duly constituted hereunder, and shall if so directed by the meeting, adjourn the meeting from time to time and from place to place, but no business shall be transacted at any adjourned meeting other than the business left unfinished at the meeting from which the adjournment took place. When a general meeting is adjourned for thirty days or more, notice of the adjourned meeting shall be given as in the case of an original meeting; save as aforesaid it shall not be necessary to give any notice of an adjournment or of the business to be transacted at an adjourned general meeting.

50.   At any general meeting a resolution put to the vote of the meeting shall be decided on a show of hands unless a poll is, before or on the declaration of the result of the show of hands, demanded by the Chairman or any other member present in person or by proxy.

51.   Unless a poll be so demanded a declaration by the Chairman that a resolution has on a show of hands been carried, or carried unanimously, or by a particular majority, or lost, and an entry to that effect in the Company's

-13-

Minute Book containing the Minutes of the proceedings of the meeting shall be conclusive evidence of that fact without proof of the number or proportion of the votes recorded in favour of or against such resolution.

52.   The demand for a poll may be withdrawn.

53.   Except as provided in Article 55, if a poll is duly demanded it shall be taken in such manner as the Chairman directs and the result of the poll shall be deemed to be the resolution of the general meeting at which the poll was demanded.

54.   In the case of an equality of votes, whether on a show of hands or on a poll the Chairman of the Meeting shall have a second or casting vote.

55.   A poll demanded on the election of a Chairman or on a question of adjournment shall be taken forthwith. A poll demanded on any other question shall be taken at such time as the Chairman of the general meeting directs and any business other than that upon which a poll has been demanded or is contingent thereon may be proceeded with pending the taking of the poll.

VOTES OF SHAREHOLDERS

56.   Subject to any rights or restrictions for the time being attached to any class or classes of shares, on a show of hands every member present in person at a general meeting shall have one vote and on a poll every member shall have one vote for each share held by him.

57.   In the case of joint members the vote of the senior who tenders a vote, whether in person or by proxy, shall be accepted to the exclusion of the votes of the other joint holders; and for this purpose seniority shall be determined by the order in which the names stand in the register of members.

58.   A member of unsound mind, or in respect of whom an order has been made by any court, having jurisdiction in lunacy, may upon production of evidence of their appointment satisfactory to the Directors, vote whether on a show of hands or on a poll, by his committee, receiver, curator bonis, or other person in the nature of a committee, receiver or curator bonis appointed by that court, and any such committee, receiver, curator bonis or other persons may on a poll, vote by proxy.

59.   No member shall be entitled to vote at any general meeting unless all calls presently payable or other sums presently payable by him in respect of shares in the Company have been paid.

60.   No objection shall be raised to the qualification of any voter except at the general meeting or adjourned general meeting at which the vote objected to is given or tendered and every vote not disallowed at such general meeting shall be valid for all purposes. Any such objection made in due time shall be referred to the Chairman of the general meeting whose decision shall be final and conclusive.

61.   On a poll votes may be given either personally or by proxy, and if a member shall exercise his vote in respect of any share his proxy shall be precluded from voting in respect of such share in the same resolution.

-14-

PROXIES

62.   The instrument appointing a proxy shall be in writing and shall be executed under the hand of the appointor or of his attorney duly authorised in writing, or, if the appointor is a corporation, either under seal, or under the hand of an officer, or under the hand of an attorney duly authorised in that behalf. A proxy need not be a member of the Company.

63.   The instrument appointing a proxy and, if the Directors so require, the power of attorney or other authority, if any, under which it is executed or a notarially certified copy of that power or authority, shall be deposited at that Registered Office of the Company or at such other place as is specified for that purpose in the notice convening the general meeting not less than 2 hours before the time for holding the meeting, or adjourned meeting.

64.   The instrument appointing a proxy may be in any form acceptable to the Directors and may be expressed to be for a particular meeting and/or any adjournment thereof.

65.   An instrument appointing a proxy shall be deemed to include the power to demand or join or concur in demanding a poll.

66.   A vote given in accordance with the terms of an instrument of proxy shall be valid notwithstanding the previous death or insanity of the principal or revocation of the proxy or of the authority under which the proxy was executed, or the transfer of the share in respect of which the proxy is given provided that no intimation in writing of such death, insanity, revocation or transfer as aforesaid shall have been received by the Company at the Registered Office before the Commencement of the general meeting, or adjourned general meeting at which it is sought to use the proxy.

67.   Any corporation which is a member of record of the Company may in accordance with its Articles or in the absence of such provision by resolution of its Directors or other governing body authorise such person as it thinks fit to act as its representative at any meeting of the Company or of any class of members of the Company, and the person so authorised shall be entitled to exercise the same powers on behalf of the corporation which he represents as the corporation could exercise if it were an individual member of record of the Company.

DIRECTORS

68.   There shall be a Board of Directors consisting of not less than one or more than ten persons (exclusive of Alternate Directors) PROVIDED HOWEVER that the Company may from time to time by ordinary resolution increase or reduce the limits in the number of Directors. The first Directors of the Company shall be determined in writing by the subscribers of the Memorandum of Association or a majority of them.

69.   The remuneration to be paid to the Directors shall be such remuneration as the Directors shall determine. Such remuneration shall be deemed to accrue from day to day. The Directors shall also be entitled to be paid their travelling, hotel and other expenses properly incurred by them in going to, attending and returning from meetings of the Directors, or any committee of the Directors, or general meetings of the Company, or to receive a fixed allowance in respect thereof as may be determined by the Directors from time to time, or a

-15-

combination partly of one such method and partly the other.

70.   The Directors may by resolution award special remuneration to any Director of the Company undertaking any special work or services for, or undertaking any special mission on behalf of, the Company other than his ordinary routine work as a Director. Any fees paid to a Director who is also counsel or solicitor to the Company, or otherwise serves it in a professional capacity shall be in addition to his remuneration as a Director.

71.   A Director or Alternate Director may hold any other office or place of profit under the Company (other than the office of auditor) in conjunction with his office of Director for such period and on such terms as to remuneration and otherwise as the Directors may determine.

72.   A Director or Alternate Director may act by himself or his firm in a professional capacity for the Company and he or his firm shall be entitled to remuneration for a professional services as if he were not a Director or Alternate Director.

73.   A shareholding qualification for Directors may be fixed by the Company in general meeting, but unless and until so fixed no qualification shall be required.

74.   A Director or other officer of or otherwise interested in any Company promoted by the Company or in which the Company may be interested as shareholder or otherwise and no such Director or Alternate Director shall be accountable to the Company for any remuneration or other benefits received by him as a Director or officer of, or from his interest in such other Company.

75.   No Director or Alternate Director shall be prevented by such office from contracting with the Company, either as vendor, purchaser or otherwise nor shall any such contract or any contract or transaction entered into by or on behalf of the Company in which any Director or Alternate Director so contracting or being so interested be liable to account to the Company for any profit realised by any such contract or transaction by reason of such Director holding office or of the fiduciary relation thereby established. A Director (or his Alternate Director in his absence) shall be at liberty to vote in respect of any contract or transaction in which he is so interested as aforesaid PROVIDED HOWEVER that the nature of the interest of any Director or Alternate Director in any such contract or transaction shall be disclosed by him or the Alternate Director appointed by him at or prior to its consideration and any vote thereon.

76.   A general notice that a Director or Alternate Director is a shareholder of any specified firm or company and is to be regarded as interested in any transaction with such firm or company shall be sufficient disclosure under Article 75 and after such general notice it shall not be necessary to give special note relating to any particular transaction.

ALTERNATE DIRECTORS

77.   Subject to the exception contained in Article 85, a Director who expects to be unable to attend Directors' Meetings because of absence, illness or otherwise may appoint any person to be an Alternate Director to act in his stead and such appointee whilst he holds office as an Alternate Director shall, in the event of absence therefrom of his appointor, be entitled to attend meetings of the Directors and to vote thereat and to do, in the place and stead of his appoin-

tor, any other act or thing which his appointor is permitted or required to do by virtue of his being a Director as if the Alternate Director were the appointor, other than appointment of an Alternate to himself, and he shall ipso facto vacate office if and when his appointor ceases to be a Director or removes the appointee from office. Any appointment or removal under this Article shall be effected by notice in writing under the hand of the Director making the same.

POWERS AND DUTIES OF DIRECTORS

78. The business of the Company shall be managed by the Directors who may pay all expenses incurred in promoting, registering and setting up the Company, and may exercise all such powers of the Company as are not, from time to time by the Statute, or by these Articles, or such regulations, being not inconsistent with the aforesaid, as may be prescribed by the Company in general meeting required to be exercised by the Company in general meeting PROVIDED HOWEVER that no regulations made by the Company in general meeting shall invalidate any prior act of the Directors which would have been valid if that regulation had not been made.

79. The Directors may from time to time and at any time by powers of attorney appoint any company, firm, person or body of persons, whether nominated directly or indirectly by the Directors, to be the attorney or attorneys of the Company for such purpose and with such powers, authorities and discretions (not exceeding those vested in or exercisable by the Directors under these Articles) and for such period and subject to such conditions as they may think fit, and any such powers of attorney may contain such provisions for the protection and convenience of persons dealing with any such attorney as the Directors may think fit and may also authorise any such attorney to delegate all or any of the powers, authorities and discretions vested in him.

80. All cheques, promissory notes, drafts, bills of exchange and other negotiable instruments and all receipts for monies paid to the Company shall be signed, drawn, accepted, endorsed or otherwise executed as the case may be in such manner as the Directors shall from time to time by resolution determine.

81. The Directors shall cause Minutes to be made in books provided for the purpose:-

(a) of all appointments of officers made by the Directors;

(b) of the names of the Directors (including those represented thereat by an Alternate or by proxy) present at each meeting of the Directors and of any committee of the Directors;

(c) of all resolutions and proceedings at all meetings of the Company, and of the Directors, and of Committees of Directors.

82. The Directors on behalf of the Company may pay a gratuity or pension or allowance on retirement to any Director who has held any other salaried office or place of profit with the Company or to his widow or dependents and may make contributions to any fund and pay premiums for the purchase or provision of any such gratuity, pension or allowance.

-16-

83. The Directors may exercise all the powers of the Company to borrow money and to mortgage or charge its undertaking, property and uncalled capital or any part thereof, and to issue debentures, debenture stock and other securities whether outright or as security for any debt, liability or obligation of the Company or of any third party.

LOCAL MANAGEMENT

84. (a) The Directors may from time to time provide for the management of the affairs of the Company abroad in such manner as they shall think fit and the provisions contained in the three next following paragraphs shall be without prejudice to the general powers conferred by this paragraph.

(b) The Directors from time to time and at any time may establish any committees, local boards or agencies for managing any of the affairs of the Company abroad and may appoint any persons to be members of such committees or local boards or any managers or agents and may fix their remuneration.

(c) The Directors from time to time and at any time may delegate to any such committee, local board, manager or agent any of the powers, authorities and discretions for the time being in the Directors and may authorise the members for the time being of any such local board, or any of them to fill up any vacancies therein and to act notwithstanding vacancies and any such appointment or delegation may be made on such terms and subject to such conditions as the Directors may think fits the Directors may at any time remove any person so appointed and may annul or vary any such delegation, but no person dealing in good faith and without notice of any such annulment or variation shall be affected thereby.

(d) Any such delegates as aforesaid may be authorised by the Directors to sub-delegate all or any of the powers, authorities, and discretions for the time being vested in them.

MANAGING DIRECTORS

85. The Directors may, from time to time, appoint one or more of their body (but not an Alternate Director) to the office of Managing Director for such term and at such remuneration (whether by way of salary, or commission, or participation in profits, or partly in one way and partly in another) as they may think fit and a Director so appointed shall not, while holding that office be subject to retirement in accordance with Article 98 nor be subject to the provisions of Article 102 relating to the removal of a Director; but his appointment shall be subject to determination ipso facto if he ceases from any cause to be a Director and no Alternate Director appointed by him can act in his stead as a Director or Managing Director.

86. The Directors may entrust to and confer upon a Managing Director any of the powers exercisable by them upon such terms and conditions and with such restrictions as they may think fit and either collaterally with or to the exclusion of their own powers and may from time to time revoke, withdraw, alter or vary all or any of such powers.

-17-

–18–

PROCEEDINGS OF DIRECTORS

87.   Except as otherwise provided by these Articles, the Directors shall meet together for the despatch of business, convening, adjourning and otherwise regulating their meetings as they think fit. Questions arising at any meeting shall be decided by a majority of votes of the Directors and Alternate Directors present at a meeting at which there is a quorum; the vote of an Alternate Director not being counted if his appointor be present at such meeting. In case of an equality of votes, the Chairman shall have a second or casting vote.

88.   A Director or Alternate Director may, and the Secretary on the requisition of a Director or Alternate Director shall, at any time summon a meeting of the Directors by at least five days' notice in writing to every Director and Alternate Director to which notice the provisions of Articles 41 and 42 shall mutatis mutandis apply as if it were a notice to members of a general meeting unless notice is waived by all the Directors (or their Alternates) either at before or after the meeting is held and PROVIDED FURTHER if notice is given in person, by telegram, telex cablegram or wireless the same shall be deemed to have been given on the day it is delivered to the Directors or transmitting organisation as the case may be.

89.   The quorum necessary for the transaction of the business of the Directors may be fixed by the Directors and unless so fixed shall be at least half of the number of persons comprising the Board of Directors, a Director and his appointed Alternate Director being considered only one person for this purpose.

90.   The continuing Directors may act notwithstanding any vacancy in their body, but if and so long as their number is reduced below the number fixed by or pursuant to these Articles as the necessary quorum of Directors the continuing Directors or Director may act for the purpose of increasing the number of Directors to that number, or of summoning a general meeting of the Company, but for no other purpose.

91.   The Directors may elect a Chairman of their Board and determine the period for which he is to hold office; but if no such Chairman is elected, or if at any meeting the Chairman is not present within five minutes after the time appointed for holding the same, the Directors present may choose one of their number to be Chairman of the meeting.

92.   The Directors may delegate any of their powers to committees consisting of such member or members of the Board of Directors (including Alternate Directors in the absence of their appointors) as they think fit; any committee so formed shall in the exercise of the powers so delegated conform to any regulations that may be imposed on it by the Directors.

93.   A committee may meet and adjourn as it thinks proper. Questions arising at any meeting shall be determined by a majority of votes of the members present, and in the case of an equality of votes the Chairman shall have a second or casting vote.

94.   All acts done by any meeting of the Directors or of a committee of Directors (including any person acting as an Alternate Director) shall, notwithstanding that it be afterwards discovered that there was some

–19–

defect in the appointment of any Director or Alternate Director, or that they or any of them were disqualified, be as valid as if every such person had been duly appointed and qualified to be a Director or Alternate Director as the case may be.

95.   A resolution in writing, signed by all the Directors for the time being (an Alternate Director being entitled to sign such resolution on behalf of his appointor) shall be as valid and effectual as if it had been passed at a meeting of the Directors duly convened and held.

96.   (a)   A Director may be represented at any meetings of the Board of Directors by a proxy appointed by him in which event the presence or vote of the proxy shall for all purposes be deemed to be that of the Director.

(b)   The provisions of Articles 62 - 65 shall mutatis mutandis apply to the appointment of proxies by Directors.

VACATION OF OFFICE OF DIRECTOR

97.   The office of a Director shall be vacated:

(a)   if he gives notice in writing to the Company that he resigns the office of Director;

(b)   if he absents himself (without being represented by proxy or an Alternate Director appointed by him) from three consecutive meetings of the Board of Directors without special leave of absence from the Directors, and they pass a resolution that he has by reason of such absence vacated office;

(c)   if he dies, becomes bankrupt or makes any arrangement or composition with his creditors generally;

(d)   if he is found a lunatic or becomes of unsound mind.

RETIREMENT OF DIRECTORS

98.   Subject to Article 85, at the first and every subsequent Annual General Meeting of the Company all of the Directors constituting the Board of Directors immediately prior to such meeting shall be automatically retired from office and a new Board of Directors shall be elected. All Directors so retired from office automatically shall be eligible for re-election as Directors at the Annual General Meeting.

99.   The Company, at the Annual General Meeting at which a Director is automatically retired in the manner aforesaid, may fill the vacated office by electing a person thereto, and in default the retiring Director shall, if offering himself for re-election, be deemed to have been re-elected unless at such Annual General Meeting it is expressly resolved not to fill such vacated office or unless a resolution for the re-election of such Director shall have been put to the Annual General Meeting and lost.

-21-

the Company required to be authenticated by the Company under seal.

OFFICERS

105. The Company may have a President and shall have a Secretary or Secretary-Treasurer appointed by the Directors who may also from time to time appoint such other officers as they consider necessary, all for such terms, at such remuneration and to perform such duties, and subject to such provisions as to disqualification and removal as the Directors from time to time prescribe.

106. A provision of the Statute or these Articles requiring or authorising a thing to be done by a Director and an officer shall not be satisfied by its being done by the one person acting in the dual capacity of Director and officer.

DIVIDENDS AND RESERVE

107. Subject to the Statute, the Directors may for any Accounting Year declare and pay dividends on shares of the Company outstanding and may from time to time declare and pay such interim dividends as appear to the Directors to be justified by the profits of the Company.

108. The Directors may, before declaring any dividends set aside such sums as they think proper as a reserve or reserves which shall at the discretion of the Directors, be applicable for any purpose of the Company and pending such application may, at the like discretion, be employed in the business of the Company. The Directors may also without placing the same to reserve carry forward any profits which they may think prudent not to divide.

109. Without prejudice to the provisions of Article 107 no dividend shall be payable except out of the profits of the Company.

110. Subject to the rights of persons, if any, entitled to shares with special rights as to dividend, all dividends shall be declared and paid according to the amounts paid or credited as paid on the shares in respect whereof the dividend is paid but no amount paid or credited as paid on a share in advance of calls shall be treated for the purposes of the regulation as paid on the share. All dividends shall be apportioned and paid proportionately to the amounts paid or credited as paid on the shares during any portion or portions of the period in respect of which the dividend is paid; but if any share is issued on terms providing that it shall rank for dividend as from a particular date such share shall rank for dividend accordingly.

111. The Directors may deduct from any dividend payable to any member all sums of money (if any) presently payable by him to the Company on account of calls or otherwise.

112. The Directors may declare that any dividend be paid wholly or partly by the distribution of specific assets and in particular of paid up shares, debentures, or debenture stock or of any other company or in any one or more ways and where any distribution the Directors may settle the same as they think expedient and in particular may issue fractional certificates and fix the value for distribution of such specific assets or any part thereof and may determine that cash payments shall be made to any members upon the

-20-

100. No person other than a Director so retired from office automatically at the Annual General Meeting shall, unless approved by the Directors, be eligible for election to the office of Director at any general meeting unless not less than ten nor more than twenty-one days before the date appointed for the general meeting there shall have been left at the Registered Office of the Company notice in writing signed by a member only qualified to attend and vote at the general meeting for which such notice is given, of his intention to propose such person for election, and also notice in writing signed by that person of his willingness to be elected.

101. The Directors shall have power at any time and from time to time to appoint any person to be a Director, either to fill a casual vacancy or as an addition to the existing Directors but so that the total amount of Directors (exclusive of Alternate Directors) shall not at any time exceed the number fixed in accordance with these Articles. Any Director appointed under this Article shall hold office only until the next following Annual General Meeting and then shall be eligible for re-election.

102. Subject as provided by Article 85, the Company may by ordinary resolution remove any Director before the expiration of his period of office and may by ordinary resolution appoint another person in his stead; the person so appointed shall be subject to retirement at the same time as if he had become a Director on the day on which the Director in whose place he is appointed was last elected a Director.

PRESUMPTION OF ASSENT

103. A Director of the Company who is present at a meeting of the Board of Directors at which action on any Company matter is taken shall be presumed to have assented to the action taken unless his dissent shall be entered in the Minutes of the meeting or unless he shall file his written dissent from such action with the person acting as the Secretary of the meeting before the adjournment thereof or shall forward such dissent by registered mail to the Secretary of the Company immediately after the adjournment of the meeting. Such right to dissent shall not apply to a Director who voted in favour of such action.

SEAL

104. The seal shall only be used by the authority of the Directors or of a committee of the Directors authorised by the Directors in that behalf and every instrument to which the seal has been affixed shall be signed by one person who shall be a Director and counter-signed by another person who shall be either the Secretary or Secretary-Treasurer or another Director or some other person appointed by the Directors for the purpose but no instrument may be validly signed if bearing only the signatures of a Director and an Alternate Director appointed by him.

PROVIDED THAT the Company may have for use in any territory district or place not situate in the Cayman Islands, an official seal which shall be a facsimile of the common seal of the Company with the addition on its face of the name of every territory, district or place where it is to be used.

PROVIDED FURTHER THAT a Director, Secretary, other officer or authorised person may affix the seal of the Company over his signature alone to any document of

-22-

footing of the value so fixed in order to adjust the rights of all members and may vest any such specific assets in trustees as may seem expedient to the Directors.

113. (a) Any dividend, interest or other monies payable in cash in respect of Registered Shares may be paid by cheque or warrant sent through the post directed to the registered address of the holder or, in the case of joint holders, to the holder who is first named on the register of members or to such person and to such address as such holder or first named joint holder may in writing direct. Every such cheque or warrant shall be made payable to the order of the person to whom it is sent. Any one or more joint holders may give effectual receipts for any dividend, or other assets or monies payable in respect of the share held by them as joint holders;

(b) Any dividend, interest or other monies payable in cash in respect of Bearer Shares shall be payable only on delivery of the relevant coupon (where coupons have been issued) or otherwise upon production of the relevant Bearer Share certificate in the manner specified in the advertisement thereof as set out in paragraph (c) of this Article and may be paid by cheque or warrant sent through the post directed to such address as may be specified in writing by the Bearer Holder on the relevant coupon or upon production of the relevant certificate as the case may be. When coupons have been issued there shall be sent in like manner with such payment a coupon as referred to in Article 6 bearing the next consecutive distinguishing number;

(c) Upon any dividend being declared to be payable upon Bearer Shares the Directors shall publish an advertisement thereof in two consecutive editions of the International Herald Tribune or, if the International Herald Tribune shall cease to be published, in such other newspaper or magazine of international circulation, and in such other publication, if any, as the Directors may deem expedient and such advertisement shall state:-

(i) the date of declaration of the dividend;
(ii) the place or places to which the coupon or certificate shall be delivered or produced as the case may be;
(iii) the time within which the coupon or certificate shall be delivered or produced as the case may be; and
(iv) where appropriate, the distinguishing number of the relevant coupon.

114. No dividend shall bear interest against the Company.

115. The Company may, upon the recommendation of the Directors by ordinary resolution authorise the Directors to capitalise any sum standing to the credit of any of the Company's reserve accounts (including Share Premium Account and Capital Redemption Reserve Fund) or any sum standing to the credit of profit and loss account or otherwise available for distribution and to appropriate such sum to members in the proportions in which such sum would have been divisible amongst them had the same been a distribution of profits by way of dividend and to apply such sum on their behalf in paying up in full unissued shares (not being redeemable shares) for allotment and distribution credited as fully paid up to and amongst them in the proportion aforesaid. In such event the Directors shall do all acts and things required to give effect to such capitalisation, with full power to the Directors to make such provisions as they think

-23-

fit for the case of shares becoming distributable in fractions (including provisions whereby the benefit of fractional entitlements accrue to the Company rather than to the members concerned). The Directors may authorise any person to enter on behalf of all the members interested into an agreement with the Company providing for such capitalisation and matters incidental thereto and any agreement made under such authority shall be effective and binding on all concerned.

BOOKS OF ACCOUNT

116. The Directors shall cause proper books of account to be kept with respect to:

(a) all sums of money received and expended by the Company and the matters in respect of which the receipt or expenditure takes place;
(b) all sales and purchases of goods by the Company;
(c) the assets and liabilities of the Company.

Proper books shall not be deemed to be kept if there are not kept such books of account as are necessary to give a true and fair view of the state of the Company's affairs and to explain its transactions.

117. The Directors shall from time to time determine whether and to what extent and at what times and places and under what conditions or regulations the accounts and books of the Company or any of them shall be open to the inspection of members not being Directors and no member (not being a Director) shall have any right of inspecting any account or book or document of the Company except as conferred by Statute or authorised by the Directors.

118. The Directors shall from time to time cause to be prepared and to be laid before the Company in general meeting Profit and Loss accounts, Balance Sheets, group accounts (if any) and such other reports and accounts as may be required by law.

AUDIT

119. The Company may at an Annual General Meeting appoint an auditor or auditors of the Company who shall hold office until the next Annual General Meeting and fix his or their remuneration.

120. The Directors may before the first Annual General Meeting appoint an auditor or auditors of the Company who shall hold office until the first Annual General Meeting unless previously removed by a resolution of the shareholders in general meeting in which case the shareholders at that meeting may appoint auditors. The Directors may fill any casual vacancy in the office of auditor but while any such vacancy continues the surviving or continuing auditor or auditors, if any, may act. The remuneration of any auditor appointed by the Directors under this Article may be fixed by the Directors.

121. Every auditor of the Company shall have a right of access at all times to the books of account and vouchers of the Company and shall be entitled to require from the Directors and Officers of the Company such information and explanation as may be necessary for the performance of the duties of the auditors.

-24-

122.   Auditors shall at the next Annual General Meeting following their appointment and at any other time during their term of office upon request of the Directors or any general meeting of the shareholders, make a report on the accounts of meeting of the shareholders, make a report on the account of the Company in general meeting during their tenure of office.

NOTICES

123.   Notices to Registered Holders shall be in writing and may be given by the Company to any such member either personally or by sending it by post, cable or telex to him or to his address as shown in the register of members, such notice, if mailed, to be forwarded airmail if the address is outside the Cayman Islands. Notices to Bearer Holders shall be deemed to have been given upon publication in two successive editions of the International Herald Tribune or, if the International Herald Tribune shall cease to be published, in such other newspaper or magazine of international circulation, and in such other publication, if any, as the Directors may deem expedient.

124.   (a)   Where a notice is sent by post, service of the notice shall be deemed to be effected by properly addressing, pre-paying and posting a letter containing the notice and to have been effected at the expiration of three days after the letter containing the same is posted as aforesaid;

         (b)   Where a notice is sent by cable or telex, service of the notice shall be deemed to be effected by properly addressing, pre-paying and sending through a transmitting organisation the notice, and to have been effected at the expiration of two days after the same is sent as aforesaid.

125.   A notice may be given by the Company to the joint holders of Registered Shares by giving the notice to the joint holder first named on the register of members in respect of the share.

126.   A notice may be given by the Company to the person or persons which the Company has been advised are entitled to a Registered Share or Registered Shares in consequence of the death or bankruptcy of a Registered Holder by sending it through the post as aforesaid in a pre-paid letter addressed to them by name, or by the title of representatives of the deceased, or trustee of the bankruptcy, or by any like description at the address supplied for that purpose by the persons claiming to be so entitled, or at the option of the Company by giving the notice in any manner in which the same might have been given if the death or bankruptcy had not occurred.

127.   Notice of every general meeting shall be given in any manner hereinbefore authorised to -

         (a)   every person shown as a member in the register of members as of the record date for such meeting except that in the case of joint holders the notice shall be sufficient if given to the joint holder first named in the register of members;

         (b)   every person upon whom the ownership of a Registered Share devolves by reason of his being a legal personal representative or a trustee in bankruptcy of a Registered Holder where such member but for his death or bankruptcy would be entitled to receive notice of the meeting; and

-25-

         (c)   every Bearer Holder in manner hereinbefore set out;

         (d)   the Company's auditors for the time being, if any.

No other person shall be entitled to receive notices of general meetings.

WINDING UP

128.   If the Company shall be wound up the liquidator may, with the sanction of a Special Resolution of the Company and any other sanction required by the Statute, divide amongst the members in specie or kind the whole or any part of the assets of the Company (whether they shall consist of property of the same kind or not) and may for such purpose set such value as he deems fair upon any property to be divided as aforesaid and may determine how such division shall be carried out as between the members or different classes of members. The liquidator may with the like sanction, vest the whole or any part of such assets in trustees upon such trusts for the benefit of the contributories as the liquidator, with the like sanction think fit, but so that no member shall be compelled to accept any shares or other securities whereon there is any liability.

129.   If the Company shall be wound up, and the assets available for distribution amongst the members as such shall be insufficient to repay the whole of the paid-up capital, such assets shall be distributed so that, as nearly as may be, the losses shall be borne by the members in proportion to the capital paid up, or which ought to have been paid up, at the commencement of the winding up on the shares held by them respectively. And if in a winding up the assets available for distribution amongst the members shall be more than sufficient to repay the whole of the capital paid up at the commencement of the winding up, the excess shall be distributed amongst the members in proportion to the capital at the commencement of the winding up paid up on the shares held by them respectively. This Article is to be without prejudice to the rights of the holders of shares issued upon special terms and conditions.

INDEMNITY

130.   The Directors, auditors, Secretary and other officers for the time being of the Company and any trustee for the time being acting in relation to any of the affairs of the Company and their heirs, executors, administrators and personal representatives respectively shall be indemnified out of the assets of the Company from and against all actions, proceedings, costs, charges, losses, damages and expenses which they or any of them shall or may incur or sustain by reason of any act done or omitted in or about the execution of their duty in their respective offices or trusts except such (if any) as they shall incur or sustain by or through their own wilful neglect or default respectively and no such Director, officer or trustee shall be answerable for the acts, receipts, neglects or defaults of any other Director, officer or trustee or for joining in any receipt for the sake of conformity or for the solvency or honesty of any bankers or other persons with whom any monies or effects belonging to the Company may be lodged or deposited for safe custody or for any insufficiency of any security upon which any monies of the Company may be invested or for any other loss or damage due to any such cause as aforesaid or which may happen in or about the execution of his office or trust

-26-

unless the same shall happen through the wilful neglect or default of such Director, officer or trustee.

ACCOUNTING YEAR

131.   The Accounting Year of the Company shall begin on the date of incorporation of the Company and the anniversary date of incorporation of the Company and the anniversary date thereof in each year ending the day prior to the anniversary date each year unless the Directors prescribe some other period therefor.

AMENDMENTS TO ARTICLES

132.   Subject to the Statute, the Company may at any time and from time to time by Special Resolution alter or amend these Articles in whole or in part.

-27-

DATED the   day of   19

I,   Registrar of Companies in and for the Cayman Islands DO HEREBY CERTIFY that this is a true and correct copy of the Articles of Association of this company duly incorporated on the day of   19

_____

Registrar of Companies

Form 959 (Rev. 1-78)   Page 2

Part III   **To be completed by shareholders**

1 Internal Revenue Service Center where shareholder filed his most recent income tax return. (If new corporation, where return will be filed.)

2 Country under laws of which the foreign corporation was incorporated.

3 Country where the foreign corporation's principal place of business is located.

4 Date the foreign corporation was organized.

5 Date of each reorganization of the foreign corporation, if any, after 1959, while shareholder(s) filing return owned 5% or more in value of the stock.

6 Name and address of the foreign corporation's statutory or resident agent in the country of incorporation.

7 Name, address, and identifying number of the U.S. agent or U.S. branch office for the foreign corporation.

8 For each of the 3 calendar or fiscal years preceding the date on which liability arises to file this return, enter the year(s) for which the foreign corporation filed a U.S. income tax return or a consolidated return (including the name of the corporation filing the consolidated return), the type of form used, the Internal Revenue Service Center where filed, and the amount of tax paid, if any.

9 Name and address of the person having custody of the foreign corporation's books and records.

10 Location of the books and records if different from the location shown in item 9.

11 The following information is required. Indicate for each item whether you have attached it.

	Yes	No
a. Name, address, and social security number of all U.S. persons who are principal officers (for example, president, vice president, secretary, treasurer, controller, or persons performing comparable functions) or members of the board of directors on the date liability arises to file this return.		
b. A complete statement of the principal business activities in which the corporation is actually engaged. Do not quote from the articles of incorporation or the by-laws.		
c. (1) Is the foreign corporation a member of a group constituting a chain of ownership?		
(2) If "Yes," have you attached a chart indicating each unit of which the shareholder owns 5% or more in value of the stock showing the foreign corporation's position in the chain of ownership and the percentages of ownership?		
d. A copy of the corporation's profit and loss statement for the most recent complete annual accounting period and a copy of the balance sheet as of the end of the most recent complete annual accounting period. (All amounts must be in U.S. currency with a statement of the exchange rates used.)		
e. A statement showing, as of the date liability arises to file this return, the amount and type of any indebtedness of the foreign corporation to (1) any U.S. person owning 5% or more in value of its stock or (2) any other foreign corporation owning 5% or more in value of the stock of the foreign corporation, with respect to which the return is filed provided the shareholder filing the return owns 5% or more in value of the stock of such other foreign corporation, together with the name, address, and identifying number of each such shareholder or entity. (All amounts must be in U.S. currency with a statement of the exchange rates used.)		
f. A statement showing, as of the date liability arises to file this return, the name, address, and identifying number of each person who is, on the date on which liability arises to file this return, a subscriber to the stock of the foreign corporation and the number of shares subscribed to by each.		
g. A statement showing the number of shares of each class of stock of the foreign corporation owned by each shareholder filing the return and (1) if the stock was acquired after 1953, the dates of acquisitions, the amounts paid or value given for the stock, the method of acquisition (i.e., by original issue, purchase on open market, direct purchase, gift, inheritance, etc.), and from whom acquired or (2) if the stock was acquired before 1954, a statement that the stock was acquired before that date and the value at which the stock is carried on the books of the shareholder.		
h. A statement showing, as of the date liability arises to file this return, the name, address, and identifying number of each U.S. person who owns 5% or more in value of the outstanding stock of the foreign corporation, the classes of stock held, the number of shares of each class held (including the name, address, and identifying number of each actual owner if such person is different from the shareholder of record), and a statement of the nature and amount of the interests of each actual owner.		
i. A statement showing the total number of shares of each class of outstanding stock of the foreign corporation (or other information indicating the shareholder's percentage of ownership).		

FORM 40

959

Form (Rev. January 1978)

Department of the Treasury
Internal Revenue Service

Return by an Officer, Director, or Shareholder
With Respect to the Organization or Reorganization
of a Foreign Corporation and Acquisition of Its Stock

(Under section 6046 of the Internal Revenue Code)

Part I   **To be completed by officers, directors, or shareholders**

(1) Name and address of person filing return (Number and street, city or town, State and ZIP code or country)

(2) Check applicable box.			(3) Identifying number
(a) Officer	(b) Director	(c) Shareholder	

(4) Name of foreign corporation

(5) Employer identification number, if any

(6) Foreign address of foreign corporation

(7) Date of liability to file this return

Part II   **To be completed by officers and directors (See Specific Instructions)**

(1) Name and address of shareholder (Number and street, city or town, State and ZIP code or country)

(2) Date	(3) Date	(4) Identifying number

Form **959** (Rev. 1-78)

Form 1001. Ownership, Exemption, or Reduced Rate Certificate. (cont'd)

(3) A nonresident alien individual or fiduciary, foreign partnership, or foreign corporation, engaged in a trade or business in the United States during the taxable year, if the income is effectively connected with the conduct of a trade or business within the United States by such person and is exempted from withholding under section 1441 or section 1442 by reason of section 1.1441–4(a) of the Regulations (File Form 4224).

(4) A nonresident alien individual or fiduciary, a foreign corporation, or a foreign partnership composed wholly of nonresident alien individuals and foreign corporations, if the interest is treated under section 861(a)(1) and the regulations thereunder as income not from sources within the United States, or

(5) A foreign partnership or foreign corporation engaged in trade or business in the United States during the taxable year, with respect to income which is exempted from withholding under section 1441 or section 1442 by reason of section 1.1441–4(f) of the Regulations.

C. Where and When to File.—A signed copy of this form must be filed with the withholding agent—

(1) In the case of interest on coupon bonds (including tax-free covenant bonds), each time a coupon is presented for payment (a separate Form 1001 must be used for each issue of bonds);

(2) In the case of income other than coupon bond interest when claiming the benefit of an income tax convention, as soon as practicable for any successive three-

calendar-year period during which such income is expected to be received. (A separate Form 1001 must be used for each type of income checked in line 1, except in the case of an owner claiming the benefit of an income tax convention for income received from a trust, estate, or investment account. In the case of income received from a trust, estate, or investment account, a separate Form 1001 must be used for each different trust, estate, or investment account.)

If, after filing such form, the owner ceases to be eligible for the benefits of the convention for such income, he shall promptly notify the withholding agent by letter. When any change occurs in the ownership of the income as recorded on the books of the payer, the exemption from, or reduction in the rate of, withholding of United States tax shall no longer apply unless the new owner of record is entitled to a reduced or exempt rate of tax under a convention and does properly file Form 1001 with the withholding agent.

D. Release of Withheld Tax.—This form may be used by an owner claiming the benefit of an income tax convention to claim a release of tax withheld at source. In preparing Form 1001, complete lines 1, 2, (if applicable) and 4 and file the signed copy with the withholding agent. Identify income tax convention and rate of tax for items 1(a), (c)–(i), on line 4.

E. Line 2. Coupon Bond Information.—Use the table below to enter the applicable rate, if any, on line 2(g). If the rate of tax is exempt, write the word "None."

Classes of Interest Payments on Bonds	Nontreaty Countries and Unknown Owners (Coupon ONLY)	Treaty Countries [1] (Coupon ONLY)				
		Bel-gium [1]	Canada	France	Japan	Switzer-land
1. Issued by corporation before January 1, 1934, and over 2% of the tax assumed by obligor.	2%	2%	2%	2%	2%	2%
2. Issued by corporation before January 1, 1934, and not over 2% of the tax assumed by obligor.	30%	15%	15%	10%	10%	5%
3. Issued by corporation without tax-free covenant on or on or after January 1, 1934, with a tax-free covenant.	30%	15%	15%	10%	10%	5%
4. Issued by corporation before January 1, 1934, maturity date extended on or after that date, and over 27½% of the tax assumed by obligor	27½%	15%	15%	15%	10%	5%
5. Issued by the United States or any agency or instrumentality thereof	30%	15%	15%	15%	10%	5%

[1] Australia, Italy, New Zealand, Pakistan, Republic of South Africa, Trinidad and Tobago are subject to a tax rate of 30%, unless affected by the withholding rates applicable to tax-free covenant bonds. The remaining treaty countries are exempt.

[1] These rates also apply to the Republic of Rwanda and Republic of Burundi.

Instruction to Withholding Agent

The withholding agent is not required to forward Form 1001 to Internal Revenue Service. He shall retain Form 1001 for at least 4 years after the end of the last calendar year in which income subject to the form is paid, and will use Form 1001 for preparing Form 1042S. A Form 1042S must be prepared for each separate payment of any item of income including coupon bond interest made during the calendar

year. When more than one Form 1001 is received from an owner during the calendar year, the withholding agent may prepare only one Form 1042S to show the total amount of any item paid to that owner for such calendar year.

Additional Information

For withholding rates as well as other information, see Publication 515, "Withholding of Tax on Nonresident Aliens and Foreign Corporations."

☆ U.S. GOVERNMENT PRINTING OFFICE: 1979—O—285-482 2)–1738428

page 725.092
7/79

Form 1001. Ownership, Exemption, or Reduced Rate Certificate.

FORM 41

Form 1001 (Rev. Nov. 1978)
Department of the Treasury
Internal Revenue Service

Ownership, Exemption, or Reduced Rate Certificate

(Please type or print)

Owner of income

Name | U.S. identifying number, if any

Address (Number and street)

City | Country

1 Check type of income for which this certificate applies. (If you check box (a), you are not required to check any other box.)

(a) ☐ Income from a trust, estate, or investment account
(b) ☐ Coupon bond interest (including tax-free covenant bonds)
(c) ☐ Interest, other than coupon bond interest
(d) ☐ Rents
(e) ☐ Natural resource royalties and income from real property
(f) ☐ Royalties from use of patents, secret processes, etc.
(g) ☐ Royalties from use of films, television tapes, etc.
(h) ☐ Annuities
(i) ☐ Other income (specify)

If you checked box (b), complete line 2 and, if applicable, line 4.
If you checked any box other than (b), complete either line 3 or line 4, whichever is applicable.
Note: Before completing line 4, see Instruction D.

2 Information on coupon bonds.

(a) Name and address of obligor of bonds.

(b) Name of bond

(c) Date of issue

(d) Date interest due | (e) Date interest paid | (f) Gross amount of interest paid | (g) Rate of tax (see instr. E) | (h) Amount of tax withheld

$ | $ | % | $

3 Calendar years for which the reduced or exempt rate of tax applies to other than coupon bond interest.

First year | Second year | Third year

4 Withheld tax requested to be released (see Instruction D).

$

I certify that the information entered hereon is correct; and, if a reduced or exempt rate of tax applies, I further certify that I have complied with all requirements to qualify for such a reduced or exempt rate of tax.

Sign Here ▶ _____ _____
(Signature of owner, fiduciary, trustee, or agent) (Date)

(If trust or estate, enter name)

_____
(Address of fiduciary, trustee, or agent)

Instructions

(References are to the Internal Revenue Code and Income Tax Regulations)

A. Who Must File.—Except as set forth in paragraph B, this form must be filed by an owner, his trustee, or agent in cases where the owner is either a:

(1) Nonresident alien-individual or fiduciary,
(2) Foreign partnership,
(3) Foreign corporation or other foreign entity,
(4) Nonresident foreign partnership composed in whole or in part of nonresident aliens (applies to section 1451 only), or
(5) Nonresident foreign corporation (applies to section 1451 only),

receiving income subject to withholding under section 1441, 1442, or 1451 of the Internal Revenue Code. **Note:** The form

must also be filed by a payee who does not know the identity of the owner.

B. Exceptions to "Who Must File".—This form is not required to be filed by:

(1) An owner, trustee, or agent described in paragraph A who receives only dividends (the withholding agent may generally rely on the address of record of an owner as the basis for allowing the benefit of an income tax convention, if applicable, to the dividends being paid such owner).

(2) An owner, trustee, or agent described in paragraph A who receives only income other than coupon bond interest, and does NOT claim the benefit of an income tax convention,

Form 1040NR (1980)   Page 2

Tax Computation

34	Amount from line 33 (adjusted gross income)	34	
35	Enter itemized deductions (from page 3, line 68)	35	
	Enter: $3,400 if qualifying widow(er). $2,300 if single. $1,700 if married filing separately. } (estates and trusts enter zero)	36	
37	If line 35 is larger than line 36, subtract line 36 from line 35 and enter excess itemized deductions	37	
38	If line 36 is larger than line 35, subtract line 35 from line 36 and enter difference	38	
39	Tax table income. If an amount appears on line 37, subtract it from line 34 OR if an amount appears on line 38, add it to line 34	39	
40	Exemptions (see instructions)	40	
41	Taxable income. Subtract line 40 from line 39	41	
42	Tax. Check if from ☐ Tax Tables (see instructions below line 39) or if figured on the amount on line 41 by using ☐ Tax Rate Schedule W, X, Y, or Z, OR ☐ maximum tax from Form 4726	42	
43	Additional taxes. (See page 6 of instructions.) Enter here and check if from ☐ Form 4970, ☐ Form 4972, ☐ Form 5544, ☐ Form 5405, or ☐ Section 72(m)(5) penalty tax.	43	
44	**Total. Add lines 42 and 43**	44	

Credits

45	Credit for contributions to candidates for public office	45	
46	Credit for child and dependent care expenses (attach Form 2441)	46	
47	Investment credit (attach Form 3468)	47	
48	Foreign tax credit (attach Form 1116)	48	
49	Work incentive (WIN) credit (attach Form 4874)	49	
50	Jobs credit (attach Form 5884)	50	
51	Residential energy credits (see page 6 of instructions)	51	
52	**Total credits. Add lines 45 through 51**	52	
53	Balance. Subtract line 52 from line 44 and enter difference (but not less than zero)	53	

Other Taxes

54a	Minimum tax. Attach Form 4625 and check here ▶ ☐	54a	
54b	Alternative minimum tax. Attach Form 6251 and check here ▶ ☐	54b	
55	Tax from recomputing prior-year investment credit (attach Form 4255)	55	
56	Tax on income not connected with U.S. trade or business (from page 4, line 101)	56	
57	Social security (FICA) tax on tip income not reported to employer (attach Form 4137)	57	
58	Uncollected employee FICA and RRTA tax on tips (from Form W-2)	58	
59	Tax on an IRA (attach Form 5329)	59	
60	Advance earned income credit (EIC) payments received (from Form 1040C)	60	
61	**Total Tax. Add lines 53 through 60**	61	

Payments

62	Total Federal income tax withheld (attach Forms W-2, W-2G, and W-2P to front)	62	
63	1980 estimated tax payments and amount applied from 1979 return	63	
64	Earned income credit (see page 9 of instructions)	64	
65	Amount paid with Form 4868	65	
66	Excess FICA and RRTA tax withheld (two or more employers)	66	
67	Credit for Federal tax on special fuels and oils (attach Form 4136 or 4136-T)	67	
68	Regulated Investment Company credit (attach Form 2439)	68	
69	Credit for amount paid with Form 1040C	69	
70	U.S. tax withheld at source (from page 4, line 98)	70	
71	**Total. Add lines 62 through 70**	71	

Refund or Balance Due

72	If line 71 is larger than line 61, enter amount **OVERPAID**	72	
73	Amount of line 72 to be **REFUNDED TO YOU**	73	
74	Amount of line 72 to be applied to your 1981 estimated tax	74	
75	If line 61 is larger than line 71, enter **BALANCE DUE**. Attach check or money order for full amount payable to "Internal Revenue Service." Write your social security number on check or money order.	75	

Please Sign Here
Under penalties of perjury, I declare that I have examined this return, including accompanying schedules and statements, and to the best of my knowledge and belief, it is true, correct, and complete. Declaration of preparer (other than taxpayer) is based on all information of which preparer has any knowledge.

▲ Your signature   Date

Paid Preparer's Use Only
Preparer's signature and date — Check if self-employed ☐ — Preparer's social security no.
Firm's name (or yours, if self-employed) and address — E.I. No. — ZIP code

---

Form **1040NR**
Department of the Treasury — Internal Revenue Service

FORM 42
U.S. Nonresident Alien Income Tax Return

19**80**

For the year January 1–December 31, 1980, or other tax year beginning _____, 1980, and ending _____, 19___

Please print or type

Your first name and initial — Last name — Identifying or social security no.

Present home address (Number and street, including apartment number, or rural route) — Occupation in the U.S.

City, town or post office, State and ZIP code

Check whether ☐ Individual ☐ Fiduciary

Of what country were you a citizen or national during the tax year? ▶

Give address to which you want any refund check mailed — Give address in the country where you are a permanent resident

Filing Status and Exemptions for Individuals — Filing status (Check only one box)

| | | Regular | | | Age 65 or over | | Blind | | Enter total |
| | | Yourself | Spouse | | Yourself | Spouse | Yourself | Blind | |

1 ☐ Single resident of Canada or Mexico, or a national of the U.S.
2 ☐ Other single nonresident alien.
3 ☐ Married resident of Canada or Mexico, or a national of the U.S.
4 ☐ Married resident of Japan (Spouse must live in the U.S.)
5 ☐ Other married nonresident alien
6 ☐ Qualifying widow(er) with dependent child (Year spouse died ▶ 19___). See page 3 of instructions.

Personal exemption for spouse is not allowable if spouse is filing a return.

7 List first names of dependent children (applies to residents of Canada, Mexico and Japan and to nationals of the U.S.) Japanese children must live with parent in U.S.   Enter Number ▶

8 Other dependents (applies to residents of Canada and Mexico, and to nationals of the U.S.). Give full name, relationship, and months lived with you.   Enter Number ▶

9 Total number of exemptions claimed (add lines 1 through 8)

Income Effectively Connected with U.S. Trade or Business
Please attach Copy B of your Forms W-2 here
Please attach Check or Money Order here

10	Wages, salaries, tips, etc.	10	
11	Interest income	11	
12a	Dividends (see Instructions)	12c	
c	Subtract line 12b from line 12a	13	
12b	Exclusion		
13	Refunds of State and local income taxes (see page 3 of instructions)	13	
14	Awards and prizes	14	
15	Business income or (loss) (attach Schedule C (Form 1040))	15	
16	Capital gain or (loss) (attach Schedule D (Form 1040))	16	
17	40% of capital gain distributions not reported on line 16 (see page 3 of instructions)	17	
18	Supplemental gains or (losses) (attach Form 4797)	18	
19	Scholarships and fellowships (attach explanation)	19	
20	Pensions, annuities, rents, royalties, partnerships, estates or trusts, etc. (attach Schedule E (Form 1040))	20	
21	Farm income or (loss) (attach Schedule F (Form 1040))	21	
22a	Unemployment compensation (insurance). Total received	22b	
b	Taxable amount, if any, from worksheet on page 4 of instructions	23	
23	Other income (state nature and source)	24	
24	**Total effectively connected income. Add amounts in column for lines 10 through 23**	24	

Adjustments

25	Moving expense (attach Form 3903)	25	
26	Employee business expenses (attach Form 2106)	26	
27	Payments to an IRA (enter code from page 5 _____)	27	
28	Payments to a Keogh (H.R. 10) retirement plan	28	
29	Interest penalty on early withdrawal of savings	29	
30	Scholarships and fellowships excluded	30	
31	Disability income exclusion (attach Form 2440)	31	
32	**Total adjustments. Add lines 25 through 31**	32	

33 Adjusted gross income. Subtract line 32 from line 24. Enter here and on line 34 | 33 | |

Form **1040NR** (1980)

Form 1040NR (1980)   Page 4

Computation of Tax on Income Not Connected With U.S. Trade or Business
(On an attachment, please show names and addresses of withholding agents and payers of income.)

Nature of income	U.S. tax withheld at source	Enter amount of income under the appropriate rate of tax					
		(a) 2%	(b) 5%	(c) 10%	(d) 14%	(e) 15%	(f) 27½%	(g) 30%

89 Dividends paid by:
  a U.S. corporations
  b Foreign corporations
90 Interest:
  a Mortgage
  b Paid by foreign corporations
  c Others
91 Copyrights
92 Industrial royalties
93 Natural resources
94 Real property income
95 Pensions and annuities
96 Capital gains (enter gain from line 102 below)
97 Other (specify)

98 Total tax withheld at source. Enter here and on Form 1040NR, line 70

99 Total income (add lines 89 through 97 for each column)

100 Tax on income (multiply yearly income on line 99 by rate of tax)

101 Total tax on income not connected with U.S. trade or business (total of amounts on line 100). Enter here and on Form 1040NR, line 56.

Gains and Losses from Sales or Exchanges of Property

(a) Kind of property and description (if necessary, attach statement of descriptive details not shown below)	(b) Date of acquisition (mo., day, yr.)	(c) Date of sale (mo., day, yr.)	(d) Gross sales price less expense of sale	(e) Depreciation allowed (or allowable) since acquisition	(f) Cost or other basis, cost of later improvements (if not bought, attach explanation)	(g) Add columns (d) and (e); then subtract column (f)

Enter only the gains and losses from property sales or exchanges that are from sources within the U.S. and not connected with a U.S. business. (Include all amounts listed in the instructions for page 4, except amounts described in paragraph 1.)

Report property sales or exchanges that are connected with a U.S. business on Schedule D (Form 1040), Form 4797, or both.

102 Net gain. Enter on line 96 above.

U.S. GOVERNMENT PRINTING OFFICE: 1970—313—079

Form 1040NR (1980)   Page 3

Itemized Deductions

In this schedule list your deductions from income connected with a U.S. trade or business.

76a State income taxes
  b Local income taxes
77 Total State and local income taxes. Enter here and on line 84.
78 Contributions (Itemize)

79 Total contributions. Enter here and on line 85.

80a Personal casualty or theft loss of more than $100 after insurance reimbursement
   If you had more than one loss, omit lines 80a and b and see instructions.
  b Subtract $100.
81 Casualty or theft loss. Enter here and on line 86.
82 Miscellaneous deductions (Itemize)

83 Total miscellaneous deductions. Enter here and on line 87
84 Taxes (from line 77)
85 Contributions (from line 79)
86 Casualty or theft loss (from line 81)
87 Miscellaneous deductions (from line 83)
88 Total deductions. Enter here and on page 2, line 35.

Please Answer All Questions
(Enter "N/A" for questions that do not apply to you.)

A What country issued your passport?

B Were you ever a U.S. citizen? ☐ Yes ☐ No

C Give the purpose of your visit to the U.S.

D Type of entry visa and visa number

E Did you abandon your permanent residence as an immigrant in the U.S. this year? ☐ Yes ☐ No

F Dates you entered and left the U.S. during the year. (Residents of Canada or Mexico entering and leaving the U.S. at frequent intervals, give name of country only.)

G For nonresident aliens from tax treaty countries. Give number of days (including vacation and non-work days) you were in the U.S. during 1980.

H For residents of Canada, Mexico, or Japan, or a national of the United States. Did your spouse contribute to the support of any children claimed on Form 1040NR, line 7? ☐ Yes ☐ No

I Did you file a U.S. income tax return for any year before 1980? ☐ Yes ☐ No
  If "Yes," give the latest year and form number

  To which Internal Revenue Service Center was it sent?

J To which Internal Revenue office did you pay any amounts claimed on Form 1040NR, lines 63, 65, and 69?

K Have you excluded from gross income in this return any amount other than foreign source income not effectively connected with a U.S. trade or business? ☐ Yes ☐ No
  If "Yes," attach statement showing amount, nature, and source of each item of this income and the reason it was excluded from gross income.

L If you claimed the benefits of a U.S. income tax convention with a foreign country, please give the following information:
  Country
  Kind and amount of exempt income you claim. Also identify the applicable tax treaty:
  for 1980
  for earlier years

  Were you subject to tax in that country on any of the income you claim is entitled to the convention benefits? ☐ Yes ☐ No

  Did you have a permanent establishment (as defined by the tax convention) in the U.S. at any time during 1980? ☐ Yes ☐ No

M If you file this return to report community income, give spouse's name, address, and social security number. Also, show the address of the Internal Revenue Service Center where his or her return was filed

N Did you file Form 1040C or Form 2063 during the tax year? ☐ Yes ☐ No
  If "Yes," show the address of the Internal Revenue Service Office where you filed.
  Date filed ►

Form **1042**
Department of the Treasury
Internal Revenue Service

U.S. Annual Return of Income Tax To Be Paid at Source (Under Chapter 3, Internal Revenue Code)

1980

Name of withholding agent | Employer identification number of withholding agent

Address (number and street)

City, State, and ZIP code

PART I.—Record of Federal Tax Deposits

Deposit period ending		Tax liability for period	Amount deposited	Date of deposit	Deposit period ending		Tax liability for period	Amount deposited	Date of deposit
Jan.	7				July	7			
	15					15			
	22					22			
	31					31			
1 Jan. total					7 July total				
Feb.	7				Aug.	7			
	15					15			
	22					22			
	29					31			
2 Feb. total					8 Aug. total				
Mar.	7				Sept.	7			
	15					15			
	22					22			
	31					30			
3 Mar. total					9 Sept. total				
Apr.	7				Oct.	7			
	15					15			
	22					22			
	30					31			
4 Apr. total					10 Oct. total				
May	7				Nov.	7			
	15					15			
	22					22			
	31					30			
5 May total					11 Nov. total				
June	7				Dec.	7			
	15					15			
	22					22			
	30					31			
6 June total					12 Dec. total				

13 Total for year (add lines 1 through 12)

14 Final deposit made for year. (Enter zero if final deposit is included in line 12)

15 Total deposits for year (add lines 13 and 14)—enter here and in line 19 below

PART II.—Due or Overpayment

16 Form 1042S: 16a Number filed .... 16b Gross amount paid $............ 16c Tax withheld ▶

17 Form 1000: 17a Number filed .... 17b Gross amount paid $............ 17c Tax assumed ▶

18 Total of lines 16c and 17c

19 Total paid by federal taxes deposited with Form 512 for 1980 (from line 15 above)

20 Overpayment allowed as a credit on Form 1042 for 1979

21 Total (add lines 19 and 20)

22 If line 18 is larger than line 21, enter BALANCE DUE here. (If over $200 use depositary system.)

23 If line 21 is larger than line 18, enter OVERPAYMENT here

24 Apply overpayment on line 23 to ☐ Credit on 1981 Form 1042; ☐ Refund

25 If you expect this to be your final return, write "Final Return" here ▶

Please Sign Here

Under penalties of perjury, I declare that I have examined this return, including accompanying schedules and statements, and to the best of my knowledge and belief it is true, correct, and complete. Declaration of preparer (other than withholding agent) is based on all information of which preparer has any knowledge.

▶ Your signature | Date | ▶ Capacity in which acting

Paid Preparer's Use Only

Preparer's signature and date ▶ | Check if self-employed ▶ ☐ | Preparer's social security no.

Firm's name (or yours, if self-employed), and address ▶ | E.I. No. ▶ | ZIP code ▶

Instructions

United States Withholding Agents

Purpose of Form

Use Form 1042 to transmit information items (Forms 1042S) and to report withheld taxes.

(References are to the Internal Revenue Code.)

Who Must File.—This return is required to be made by all individuals, corporations, and partnerships, in whatever capacity acting, having the control, receipt, custody, disposal, or payment of interest, dividends, rent, royalties, annuities, salaries, wages, premiums, compensations, remunerations, emoluments, or other fixed or determinable annual or periodical income, and of gains described in sections 402(a)(2), 403(a)(2), or 631 (b) or (c), amounts subject to tax under section 871(a)(1)(C) or 881(a)(3), gains subject to tax under section 871 (a)(1)(D) or 881(a)(4), and gains on transfer described in section 1235 made on or before October 4, 1966, to the extent that any of such items constitute gross income from sources within the United States (see sections 638 and 861 through 864) of nonresident alien individuals, foreign partnerships, or foreign corporations.

This return must be filed whether or not any tax is withheld or is required to be withheld if you are required to make an information return on Form 1042S. Form 1042S must be filed to report all classes of income described above which is withheld on or is not withheld on due to treaty exemptions or in the situation described below. The gross amount paid as shown on Form 1042S should be reported on line 16b.

Form 1042 must also be filed by all withholding agents who pay gross investment income to foreign private foundations which are subject to the tax imposed by section 4948(a).

The payers of such income are required to withhold and deduct a tax therefrom at the rate in effect when the payment is made. Form 1042S must be filed to report such income paid, except income paid to such persons and required to be shown on Form W–2.

No deduction or withholding of tax by the payers is required for any of the above income (other than compensation for personal services) which is effectively connected with the conduct of a trade or business within the United States and which is includible in the gross income of the recipient under section 871(b)(2), 842, or 882(a)(2) for the taxable year. Form 4224 or a written statement by the recipient reflecting the information shown on Form 4224, must be filed in duplicate with the withholding agents, to obtain at the time of payment of such income an exemption from withholding of tax for the taxable year. A duplicate copy of each statement or form must be attached to the appropriate Form 1042S required for the calendar year.

Where an amount of tax withheld has been released by the withholding agent under the authority of any Treasury regulation, ruling or procedure of the Commissioner, the amount of tax withheld should be reduced by the amount of tax released and only the net tax withheld shown on Form 1042. Details of the amount withheld and released must be reported on Form 1042S.

The tax paid at the source upon tax-free covenant bond interest payable to a domestic or resident fiduciary and allocable to any nonresident alien beneficiary under section 652 or 662 is allowable, pro rata, as a credit against the tax required to be withheld by the fiduciary from the income of the beneficiary.

Deposit Requirements.—Generally, you must deposit the tax withheld under Chapter 3 of the Code with an authorized financial institution or a Federal Reserve Bank or Branch (FRB) using Federal Tax Deposit Form 512. Please follow the instructions on the back of that form. Please do not use anybody else's forms. If you don't have your forms when a deposit is due, mail your payment to the Internal Revenue Service Center where you file your return. Make it payable to IRS, and show on it: Your name, employer identification number, address, kind of tax, and period covered. The following rules show how often you must make deposits.

(1) If at the end of any quarter-monthly period the cumulative amount of undeposited taxes for the year is $2,000 or more, you must deposit the taxes within three banking days after the end of the quarter-monthly period. (A quarter-monthly period ends on the 7th, 15th, 22nd, and last day of the month.) In determining banking days exclude any local banking holidays observed by authorized commercial banks, as well as Saturdays, Sundays, and legal holidays. The deposit requirements are considered met if: (a) you deposit at least 90 percent of the actual tax liability for the deposit period, and (b) if the quarter-monthly period occurs in a month other than December, you deposit any underpayment with your first deposit that is required to be made after the 15th day of the following month. Any underpayment for a quarter-monthly period that occurs during December that is $200 or more must be deposited on or before January 31.

(2) If at the end of any month the cumulative amount of undeposited taxes for the year is $200 or more and less than $2,000, you must deposit the taxes within 15 days after the end of the month. (This does not apply if you made a deposit for a quarter-monthly period that occurred during the month under the $2,000 rule in (1) above.)

(3) If at the end of the year, the total amount of undeposited taxes is less than $200, you are not required to make a deposit. You must, however, pay the taxes directly to Internal Revenue along with your Form 1042 or you may make a deposit if you so desire.

Computation of Balance Due or Overpayment.—If during 1980 a withholding agent: (a) withholds more than the tax required to be withheld, and (b) makes a payment or deposit of the overwithholding as provided in section 1.1461–3 or 1.6302–2 of the Regulations you may repay such amount at any time before filing Form 1042 for such year. Any amounts repaid (i.e. tax released) should be entered on Form 1042S, column "e," and only the net tax withheld, column "f," Form 1042S, should be entered on line 16c of Form 1042.

Line 16c is, therefore, the sum of all Forms 1042S, column "d" (when no tax released) plus column "f" (in those cases where tax released). If line 16c differs from the total of Forms 1042S (column "d" and column "f," if applicable), attach a statement explaining the difference.

Withholding taxes paid during 1980 by federal taxes deposited with Form 512 should be shown on line 19 of Form 1042.

Amounts shown as overpayments on line 23 for 1980 may be claimed on line 24 as a refund under section 301.6402–3 or as a credit under section 1.6414–1(b) for 1981. If claimed as a credit, it may serve to reduce your deposits of the tax required to be withheld during 1981.

Accompanying Forms Required.—The original copies of Forms 1042S and Forms 1000 must be summarized on lines 16 and 17, respectively, and forwarded with this return, even though the income is exempt from withholding of tax.

When a Form 1042S is prepared for an item of income upon which tax has not been withheld under Chapter 3 of the Code (for example, salaries of certain visiting professors, teachers, etc.), a brief statement as to the authority for not withholding must be made on that form or in a separate statement attached thereto.

In determining tax withheld under Chapter 3 of the Code on remuneration paid for labor or personal services performed within the United States by a nonresident alien, the benefit of the deduction for personal exemptions, to the extent allowable under section 873(b)(3), shall be allowed prorated upon the basis of $2.74 per day for each exemption for the period during which labor or personal services are performed within the United States by such alien. A statement as to the amount of compensation allocable to labor or personal services performed within the United States, together with the amount of the exemptions thus prorated, must be attached to the applicable Form 1042S.

Wages paid to a nonresident alien employee which are subject to withholding under section 3402 must be reported on Form 941. See section 31.3402 (f)(6)–1 of the Employment Tax Regulations for exemptions allowable to such employees.

Magnetic Tape Reporting.—You may use magnetic tape to furnish information required by Form 1042S. To do so, see Rev. Proc. 79–20, available from any Internal Revenue Service Center.

Tax Conventions.—Residents of certain foreign countries may be entitled to reduced rates of, or exemptions from, tax under an applicable tax convention between the country in which they are a resident and the United States. The procedures by which the recipient must establish qualifications with the withholding agent are set forth in Treasury Decisions or Revenue Procedures issued under the respective tax conventions. For additional information, get **Publication 515,** Withholding of Tax on Nonresident Aliens and Foreign Corporations.

Time and Place for Filing.—Form 1042, accompanied by Forms 1042S and 1000, must be filed by withholding agents with the Internal Revenue Service Center, Philadelphia, PA 19255, on or before March 16, 1981. The balance of tax due, if any, for calendar year 1980, must be paid in full with this return. Check or money order should be made payable to "Internal Revenue Service."

Sign and Date Your Return.—Form 1042 is not considered a return unless you sign it.

Did You Have Someone Else Prepare Your Return?—If you fill in your own return, the Paid Preparer's space should remain blank.

If someone prepares your return and **does not charge you,** that person **should not sign** your return.

Generally, anyone who is paid to prepare your tax return must sign your return and fill in the other blanks in the Paid Preparer's Use Only area of your return.

If the preparer is self-employed (that is, is not employed by any person or business entity to prepare the return), he or she should **check the "self-employed" box.** A partner who prepares your income tax return as a member of a partnership should **not** check the self-employed box in the preparer's section of Form 1042. However, the partners are still considered self-employed for self-employment tax purposes.

If you have questions about whether a preparer is required to sign your return, please contact an IRS office.

The person required to sign your return MUST complete the required preparer information and:

- Sign it, by hand, in the space provided for the preparer's signature. (Signature stamps or labels are not acceptable.)
- Give you a copy of your return in addition to the copy to be filed with IRS.

Tax return preparers should be familiar with their responsibilities. **Publication 1045,** Information and Order Blanks for Preparers of Federal Income Tax Returns, lists some of the preparers' other responsibilities and penalties for which they may be liable. The publication also contains the regulation citations which govern their work.

Canadian Withholding Agents

This return is to be made by persons in Canada who receive dividends from sources within the United States for the account of any person who is not entitled to the reduced rate applicable to a resident of Canada or to a corporation organized under the laws of Canada.

Any nominee, representative, fiduciary, or partnership in Canada through whom the dividends are received by a person who is not entitled to the reduced rate of 15 percent granted by the tax convention between the United States and Canada, becomes in turn a withholding agent and is to withhold the additional tax due on such income. However, see section 7.511 of Treasury Decision 5532, 1946–2 C.B. 73 and instructions issued by Canadian Revenue Authority.

This annual withholding return should be forwarded to the Internal Revenue Service Center, Philadelphia, PA 19255, on or before March 16, 1981, accompanied by the tax shown to be due in United States currency.

☆ U.S. GOVERNMENT PRINTING OFFICE : 1980– 36-2726430

FORM 45

Form **1120F**

Department of the Treasury
Internal Revenue Service

U.S. Income Tax Return of a Foreign Corporation

For calendar year 1980 or other tax year beginning .... , 1980, and ending .... , 19....

Employer identification number

Name

Number and street

City or town, State and ZIP code, or country

NOTE: Complete Section I to compute tax on income from U.S. sources that is NOT effectively connected with the conduct of a trade or business within the U.S.
Complete Section II to compute tax on income effectively connected with the conduct of a trade or business within the U.S.
Corporations having both income effectively connected and income not effectively connected must complete both Sections I and II.
Corporations having only income that is NOT effectively connected need file only pages 1 and 2.

A Country of incorporation ....

B Foreign country under whose laws the income reported on this return is subject to tax ....

C Date incorporated ....

D The corporation's books are in care of ....
located at ....

E Were you at any time during the taxable year engaged in a trade or business within the U.S.? . . . . . ☐ Yes ☐ No

F Did you have a permanent establishment in the U.S. at any time during the taxable year within the meaning of section 894(b) and any applicable tax convention between the U.S. and a foreign country? . . . . . ☐ Yes ☐ No
If "Yes," name the foreign country ....

G (1) Did you at the end of the taxable year own, directly or indirectly, 50% or more of the voting stock of a U.S. corporation? (For rules of attribution, see section 267(c).) . . ☐ Yes ☐ No
If "Yes," attach a schedule showing: (a) name, address and identifying number, (b) percentage owned, (c) taxable income or (loss) from line 28, page 1, Form 1120 for the taxable year ending with or within your taxable year, (d) highest amount owed by you to such corporation during the year, and (e) highest amount owed to you by such corporation during the year.

(2) Did any corporation, individual, partnership, trust, or association at the end of the taxable year own, directly or indirectly, 50% or more of your voting stock (For rules of attribution, see section 267(c).) . . ☐ Yes ☐ No
If "Yes," attach a schedule showing: (a) name, address and identifying number, (b) percentage owned, and
(c) Enter highest amount owed by you to such owner during the year ....
(d) Enter highest amount owed to you by such owner during the year ....
Note: For purposes of G(1) and G(2), "highest amount owed" includes loans and accounts receivable/payable.

H Have you filed a U.S. income tax return for the preceding taxable year? . . . . . ☐ Yes ☐ No

I. If you had an agent in the U.S. at any time during the year, enter the following: Kind of agent
Name ....
Address ....

J Are you a foreign personal holding company under Section 552? . . . . . ☐ Yes ☐ No
If "Yes," have you filed Forms 957 and 958? (Sec. 6035.) . ☐ Yes ☐ No
K Are you a personal holding company? (See instruction K.) ☐ Yes ☐ No
L Are you a controlled foreign corporation? (Sec. 957.) . ☐ Yes ☐ No

1 Tax from Section I (line 14, page 2) . . . .
2 Tax from Section II (line 20, Schedule J—Tax Computation, page 5) . . . .
3 Personal holding company tax (attach Schedule PH (Form 1120)) . . . .
4 Minimum tax (see instructions) . . . .
5   TOTAL tax—Add lines 1 through 4 . . . .
6 Credits: (a) Overpayment from 1979 allowed as a credit . .
(b) 1980 estimated tax payments . . . .
(c) Less refund of 1980 estimated tax applied for on Form 4466 . .
(d) 1980 estimated tax payments . . . .
(e) Tax deposited with Form 7004 . . . .
(f) Tax deposited with Form 7005 (attach copy) . . . .
(g) Credit from regulated investment companies (attach Form 2439) . .
(g) U.S. tax on special fuels, nonhighway gas, and lubricating oil (attach Forms 4136 and 4136-T) . .
(h) U.S. income tax paid or withheld at the source . . . .
7 Total (add lines 6(a) through 6(h)) . . . .
8 TAX DUE (subtract line 7 from line 5). See instruction C for depositary method of payment . . . . .
9 OVERPAYMENT (subtract line 5 from line 7) . . . .
10 Enter amount of line 9 you want: Credited to 1981 estimated tax .... Refunded ....

Please Sign Here
Under penalties of perjury, I declare that I have examined this return, including accompanying schedules and statements, and to the best of my knowledge and belief, it is true, correct, and complete. Declaration of preparer (other than taxpayer) is based on all information of which preparer has any knowledge.

▲ Signature of officer   Date   ▲ Title

Paid Preparer's Use Only
Preparer's signature and date
Check if self-employed ☐
Preparer's social security no.
Firm's name (or yours, if self-employed) and address
E.I. No. ▲
ZIP code ▲

Form **1042S**

FORM 44
Income Subject to Withholding Under Chapter 3, Internal Revenue Code

1980

Copy A for Internal Revenue Service

Line	a. Income code (see instr.)	b. Gross amount of income paid	c. Rate of tax %	Check if exemption based on income effectively connected	e. Amount of tax released	f. Amount of net tax withheld (column d less e)	g. Country codes
1							
2							
3							
4	Total						

Type of recipient code (see instructions) . . ▲
Recipient's U.S. tax identifying no. ▲
Recipient's country of legal residence ▲

Withholding agent's employer identification no. ▲

PAID TO Name of recipient, street address, city, province, country, and postal zone.

PAID BY Name of withholding agent, address and ZIP code.
Department of the Treasury—Internal Revenue Service

Instructions

Indicate in column "a" the appropriate income code.

Enter in the box provided in the middle left-hand side of Form 1042S the appropriate code for type of recipient.

Type of Income

Code	Type of Income
01	Interest paid by U.S. obligors—general
02	Interest on real property mortgages
03	Interest paid to a controlling foreign corporation
04	Interest paid by foreign corporation (U.S. agent)
05	Interest on tax-free covenant bond
06	Dividends paid by U.S. corporation—general
07	Dividends paid by U.S. subsidiary to foreign parent corporation
08	Dividends paid by foreign corporation
09	Capital gains
10	Industrial royalties
11	Motion picture or television copyright royalties
12	Other royalties (e.g. copyright, recording, publishing, etc.)
13	Real property income and natural resources royalties
14	Pensions or annuities
15	Scholarship or fellowship grant
16	Compensation for independent personal services
17	Compensation for dependent personal services
18	Compensation for teaching
19	Compensation during training
20	Other income (e.g. alimony, insurance premium)
	(specify) ....

Type of Recipient

Code	Type of Recipient
1	Individual
2	Corporation
3	Partnership
4	Fiduciary
5	Nominee
6	Government or International Organization
7	"Tax Exempt" Organization (Section 501(a), IRC)
8	Private Foundation
9	Other (specify) ....
10	Type of recipient unknown

For country codes see last page.

Form 1120F (1980)   Page 3

SECTION II — To Be Completed for Income Effectively Connected With the Conduct of a Trade or Business Within the U.S.

IMPORTANT—Fill in all applicable lines and schedules. If the lines on the schedules are not sufficient, see instruction U.

GROSS INCOME

1 (a) Gross receipts or sales $ .... 1(b) Less returns and allowances $ .... 1(c) Balance ▶		
2 Cost of goods sold (Schedule A) and/or operations (attach schedule)		
3 Gross profit (subtract line 2 from line 1(c))		
4 Dividends (Schedule C)		
5 Interest on obligations of the U.S. and its instrumentalities		
6 Other interest		
7 Gross rents		
8 Gross royalties		
9 (a) Capital gain net income (attach Schedule D (Form 1120))		
(b) Net gain or (loss) from line 11, Part II, Form 4797 (attach Form 4797).		
10 Other income (see instructions—attach schedule)		
11 TOTAL income—Add lines 3 through 10		

DEDUCTIONS

12 Compensation of officers (Schedule E)		
13 (a) Salaries and wages	13(b) Less Jobs and WIN credits	13(c) Balance ▶
14 Repairs (see instructions)		
15 Bad debts (Schedule F if reserve method is used)		
16 Rents		
17 Taxes		
18 Interest		
19 Contributions (not over 5% of line 30 adjusted per instructions—attach schedule)		
20 Amortization (attach schedule)		
21 (a) Depreciation (from attached Form 4562)		
(b) Depreciation claimed in Schedule A and elsewhere on return		
(c) Balance (subtract line 21(b) from line 21(a)) ▶		
22 Depletion		
23 Advertising		
24 Pension, profit-sharing, etc. plans (see instructions)		
25 Employee benefit programs (see instructions)		
26 Other deductions (total from page 5)		
27 TOTAL deductions—Add lines 12 through 26		
28 Taxable income before net operating loss deduction and special deductions (subtract line 27 from line 11)		
29 (a) Net operating loss deduction (see instructions—attach schedule)		
(b) Special deductions (Schedule I)		
30 Taxable income or (loss) (subtract line 29 from line 28)		

Schedule A   Cost of Goods Sold   (See instructions for Schedule A)

1 Inventory at beginning of year.		
2 Merchandise bought for manufacture or sale.		
3 Salaries and wages.		
4 Other costs (attach schedule).		
5 Total (add lines 1 through 4).		
6 Subtract: Inventory at end of year.		
7 Cost of goods sold—Enter here and on line 2, Section II.		

8 (a) Check all methods used for valuing closing inventory:
□ Cost   □ Lower of cost or market as described in regulations section 1.471–4 (see instructions)
□ Writedown of "subnormal" goods as described in regulations section 1.471–2(c) (see instructions)

(b) Did you use any other method of inventory valuation not described above?   □ Yes   □ No
If "Yes," specify method used and attach explanation ▶

(c) Check if this is the first year LIFO inventory method was adopted and used
If checked, attach Form 970.

(d) If the LIFO inventory method was used for this taxable year, enter percentage (or amounts) of closing
inventory computed under LIFO.

(e) Is the corporation engaged in manufacturing activities? ▶   □ Yes   □ No
If "Yes," are inventories valued under regulations section 1.471–11 (full absorption accounting method)?   □ Yes   □ No

(f) Was there any substantial change in determining quantities, cost, or valuations between opening and closing
inventory?   □ Yes   □ No
If "Yes," attach explanation.

Form 1120F (1980)   Page 2

SECTION I — To Be Completed for Income From U.S. Sources That Is Not Effectively Connected With the Conduct of a Trade or Business Within the U.S.

If you are required to complete Section II or are using the form as a claim for refund of tax withheld at the source, include in this section ALL income from U.S. sources that is effectively connected with the conduct of a trade or business in the U.S. Otherwise, you may include only those items of income on which the U.S. income tax was not fully paid at the source. The rate of tax on each item of income listed below is 30% unless limited by tax treaty. Fill in treaty rates where applicable.

Name of treaty country, if any ▶

Nature of income	Amount	Rate of tax (%)	Amount of tax
1 Interest			
2 Dividends			
3 Rents			
4 Royalties			
5 Annuities			
6 Gains from disposal of timber, coal, or domestic iron ore with a retained economic interest (attach statement of details)			
7 Gains from certain evidences of indebtedness issued after September 28, 1965 and before April 1, 1972			
8 Gains from certain evidences of indebtedness issued after May 27, 1969 and before April 1, 1972			
9 Gains from certain evidences of indebtedness issued after March 31, 1972			
10 An amount equal to the original issue discount accrued since the last payment of interest on gains from certain evidences of indebtedness issued after March 31, 1972 (but not in excess of the interest less the tax imposed on the interest)			
11 Gains from sale or exchange of patents, copyrights, etc.			
12 Fiduciary distributions (attach a statement showing the kind of income and rate)			
13 Other fixed or determinable annual or periodical income (specify):			
14 Total—Enter here and on line 1, page 1 ▶			

Explanation of Lines 1 Through 13 Above (Enter each individual item of income)

1. Payer of income and, if known, withholding agent (name and address) (Show owner of record if other than taxpayer)	2. Nature of income (such as interest, dividends, etc.)	3. Gross amount of income	4. Date of payment	5. Amount of U.S. income tax paid or withheld at the source
Total of column 3. Enter here and on line 6(b), page 1		▶		
Total of column 5.			▶	

Form 1120F (1980) Page 5

Schedule J Tax Computation

1 Taxable income (line 30, page 3)
2 Enter line 1 or $25,000, whichever is less. (Members of a controlled group, see instructions)
3 Subtract line 2 from line 1
4 Enter line 3 or $25,000, whichever is less. (Members of a controlled group, see instructions)
5 Subtract line 4 from line 3
6 Enter line 5 or $25,000, whichever is less. (Members of a controlled group, see instructions)
7 Subtract line 6 from line 5
8 Enter line 7 or $25,000, whichever is less. (Members of a controlled group, see instructions)
9 Subtract line 8 from line 7
10 17% of line 2
11 20% of line 4
12 30% of line 6
13 40% of line 8
14 46% of line 9
15 Income tax. (Total of lines 10 through 14 or alternative tax from separate Schedule D (Form 1120), whichever is less)
16 (a) Foreign tax credit (attach Form 1118)
   (b) Investment credit (attach Form 3468)
   (c) Work incentive (WIN) credit (attach Form 4874)
   (d) Jobs credit (attach Form 5884)
17 Total of lines 16(a), (b), (c) and (d)
18 Subtract line 17 from line 15
19 Tax from recomputing a prior year investment credit (attach Form 4255)
20 Add lines 18 and 19. Enter here and on line 2, page 1

Schedule K Record of Form 503 Federal Tax Deposits (List deposits in order made—See instruction C)

Date of deposit	Amount	Date of deposit	Amount	Date of deposit	Amount

Other Deductions

Explanation	Amount	Explanation	Amount
	TOTAL—Enter here and on line 26, page 3		

Additional Information Required

M Business description (see page 8 of instructions)
  (1) Business code number
  (2) Principal business activity
  (3) Principal product or service

N Taxable income or (loss) from line 28, page 3 for your taxable year beginning in:
  1977
  1978
  1979

O Were you a member of a controlled group subject to the provisions of section 1561?   Yes   No
  If "yes," check type of relationships:
  (1) ☐ Parent-subsidiary
  (2) ☐ Brother-sister
  (3) ☐ Combination of (1) and (2) (see section 1563)

	Yes	No
P Did you file all required Forms 1042, 1087, 1096, and 1099?		
Q Did you claim a deduction for expenses connected with:		
(1) Entertainment facility (boat, resort, ranch, etc.)?		
(2) Living accommodations (except for employees on business)?		
(3) Employees attending conventions or meetings outside the U.S. or its possessions?		
(4) Employees' families at conventions or meetings?		
If "Yes," were any of these conventions or meetings outside the U.S. or its possessions?		
(5) Employee or family vacations not reported on Form W-2?		

R Enter total amount claimed on Form 1120F for entertainment, entertainment facilities, gifts, travel, and conventions, of the type for which substantiation is required under section 274(d) of the Internal Revenue Code ▶ $

S During the tax year was any part of your tax accounting records maintained on a computerized system?

Form 1120F (1980) Page 4

Schedule C Dividends (See instruction 4)

1 Domestic corporations subject to the 85% deduction
2 Certain preferred stock of public utilities
3 Foreign corporations subject to the 85% deduction
4 Other dividends from foreign corporations
5 Foreign dividend gross-up (section 78)
6 Taxable dividends from a DISC or a former DISC not included in line 1 (section 246(d))
7 Other
8 Total—Enter here and on line 4, Section II, page 3

Schedule E Compensation of Officers (See instruction 12)

1. Name of officer	2. Social security number	3. Time devoted to business	Percent of corporation stock owned		6. Amount of compensation	7. Expense account allowances
			4. Common	5. Preferred		

Total compensation of officers—Enter here and on line 12, Section II, page 3

Schedule F Bad Debts—Reserve Method (See instruction 15)

1. Year	2. Trade notes and accounts receivable outstanding at end of year	3. Sales on account	Amount added to reserve		6. Amount charged against reserve	7. Reserve for bad debts at end of year
			4. Current year's provision	5. Recoveries		
1975						
1976						
1977						
1978						
1979						
1980						

Schedule I Special Deductions (See instructions for Schedule I)

1 Dividends received: (a) 85% of line 1, Schedule C
  (b) 59.13% of line 2, Schedule C
  (c) 85% of line 3, Schedule C
2 Total—May not exceed 85% of line 28, page 3. The 85% limitation does not apply to a year in which a net operating loss occurs
3 Deduction for dividends paid on certain preferred stock of public utilities (see instructions)
4 Total special deductions—Add lines 2 and 3. Enter here and on line 29(b), Section II, page 3

Sample Netherlands Antilles Annual Treaty Election
to Be Taxed on a Net Basis

The Taxpayer hereby elects to be subject to tax on a net income basis as provided in Article X of the Income Tax Convention between the United States and the Netherlands as extended by Protocol to the Netherlands, Antilles. The only real property which the Taxpayer owns is located at _____ ; the Taxpayer is the (fee) owner of that property; the property is improved by a _____ .

(NOTE: This is attached to the corporation's tax return when filed.)

Form 1120F (1980)   Page 6

Schedule L   Balance Sheets

ASSETS	Beginning of tax year (A)	(B)	End of tax year (C)	(D)
1 Cash				
2 Trade notes and accounts receivable				
(a) Less allowance for bad debts				
3 Inventories				
4 Govt obligations: (a) U.S. and instrumentalities				
(b) State, subdivisions thereof, etc.				
5 Other current assets (attach schedule)				
6 Loans to stockholders				
7 Mortgage and real estate loans				
8 Other investments (attach schedule)				
9 Buildings and other fixed depreciable assets				
(a) Less accumulated depreciation				
10 Depletable assets				
(a) Less accumulated depletion				
11 Land (net of any amortization)				
12 Intangible assets (amortizable only)				
(a) Less accumulated amortization				
13 Other assets (attach schedule)				
14 Total assets				
LIABILITIES AND STOCKHOLDERS' EQUITY				
15 Accounts payable				
16 Mtges, notes, bonds payable in less than 1 year				
17 Other current liabilities (attach schedule)				
18 Loans from stockholders				
19 Mtges, notes, bonds payable in 1 year or more				
20 Other liabilities (attach schedule)				
21 Capital stock: (a) Preferred stock				
(b) Common stock				
22 Paid-in or capital surplus				
23 Retained earnings—Appropriated (attach schedule)				
24 Retained earnings—Unappropriated				
25 Less cost of treasury stock				
26 Total liabilities and stockholders' equity				

Schedule M-1   Reconciliation of Income Per Books With Income Per Return

1 Net income per books

2 Federal income tax

3 Excess of capital losses over capital gains

4 Income subject to tax not recorded on books this year (itemize)

5 Expenses recorded on books this year not deducted in this return (itemize)
(a) Depreciation . $
(b) Depletion . $

6   Total of lines 1 through 5

7 Income recorded on books this year not included in this return (itemize)
(a) Tax-exempt interest $

8 Deductions in this tax return not charged against book income this year (itemize)
(a) Depreciation . . $
(b) Depletion . . $

9   Total of lines 7 and 8

10 Income (line 28, page 3)—line 6 less line 9

Schedule M-2   Analysis of Unappropriated Retained Earnings Per Books (line 24 above)

1 Balance at beginning of year

2 Net income per books

3 Other increases (itemize)

4   Total of lines 1, 2, and 3

5 Distributions: (a) Cash
(b) Stock
(c) Property

6 Other decreases (itemize)

7   Total of lines 5 and 6

8 Balance at end of year (line 4 less line 7)

WARRANTY BILL OF SALE

For and in consideration of the sum of One Hundred Thousand and no/100 Dollars ($100,000.00) and other good and valuable consideration, receipt of which is hereby acknowledged, the undersigned does hereby sell, assign, convey and transfer to REAL ACRE N.V., a corporation, and its successors and assigns, that certain personal property described in Exhibit "A" hereto, which exhibit is incorporated by reference herein as though set forth in full hereat. Said personal property is now located on or about that certain real property described in Exhibit "B" hereto, which exhibit is incorporated by reference herein as though set forth in full hereat, and in or about the buildings and improvements thereon.

In connection with said sale of the personal property described in Exhibit "A", the undersigned warrants, represents and agrees as follows:

1. The undersigned is the present owner of the personal property being sold, assigned, and transferred hereby.

2. No person, corporation or other entity (other than the undersigned) has any interest in said personal property whatsoever.

The Taxpayer hereby elects to be subject to tax on a net income basis as provided under Code Section _____.*

The only real property which the taxpayer owns is located at _____; the Taxpayer is the (fee) owner of that property; the property is improved by a _____.

* "871 (d)" if election is by an individual and insert "882 (d)" if election is by a corporation.

3. This Bill of Sale sells, assigns, conveys and transfers to REAL ACRE N.V., a corporation, good and complete title to said personal property, free and clear of any liens, encumbrances or charges.

4. The undersigned will defend REAL ACRE N.V., a corporation, its successors and assigns against any and all claims which may be made to or against said personal property, or any portion thereof, and pay for any defense against such claims.

5. The undersigned agrees to and does hereby indemnify and hold REAL ACRE N.V., a corporation, its successors and assigns, free and harmless against and from any claims of any kind or nature which may be made to or against said personal property or any portion thereof, or against REAL ACRE N.V., a corporation, its successors and assigns, by virtue of their exercise of dominion and control over and to said personal property or any portion thereof, including but not limited to costs of defense, including reasonable attorney's fees, of any such claims.

6. The undersigned will and does hereby indemnify and hold REAL ACRE N.V., a corporation, its successors and assigns, harmless against and from any direct, indirect, or consequential damage, loss or detriment of any kind, nature or description which may be suffered by REAL ACRE N.V., a corporation, its successors or assigns, by reason of any and all claims, whether

2

valid or invalid, which may be made to or against said personal property or any portion thereof, including but not limited to:

A. Loss of rentals or sales of said personal property, or any part thereof, or any premises in which said personal property, or any part thereof may be placed or is placed;

B. Liability to any other person, corporation, or entity who claims any interest in or to said personal property, or any portion thereof, under or through REAL ACRE N.V., its assigns or successors, whether direct, indirect or consequential;

C. Loss of use of said personal property, or any portion thereof; and

D. Costs of defense to or settlement of any claim or action resulting in or which could or might have resulted in such damage, loss or detriment.

Solely and exclusively in connection with this numbered Paragraph 6, and not in connection with any of the other portions or provisions of this agreement, it is agreed as follows:

i. As to claims of persons who have leased or purchased said personal property or any portion thereof from REAL ACRE N.V., or its successors or assigns, the provisions of Paragraph 6 shall apply only if the lease or document of transfer of said personal property to said claimants contains a provision giving said REAL ACRE N.V., or its successors or

3

assigns, the right to substitute for said personal property or any portion thereof covered by said lease or bill of sale similar personal property of substantially the same type, quality and condition.

ii. The undersigned shall not have any liability under the provisions of this Paragraph 6 until after ten (10) days' written notice from REAL ACRE N.V., its successors or assigns, of any claim referred to in this Paragraph 6.

iii. The undersigned shall have the right within ten (10) days after receiving the aforesaid written notice of any claim to either replace the item or items of personal property upon which a claim has been made; and if it so does, it shall be released from further liability under this Paragraph 6.

iv. REAL ACRE N.V., its successors or assigns, shall not be entitled to any claim for damages resulting from acts which occur or claims which are made more than four (4) years from the date hereof.

v. The provisions of this Paragraph 6 shall only remain effective as to each item of personal property so long as REAL ACRE N.V., its successors or assigns, keep and maintain said item of personal property on the premises described in Exhibit "B", attached hereto and incorporated by reference herein, provided, however, that temporary removal of an item of person property from the premises for the purpose of

4

---

repair, maintenance, cleaning, or similar purposes, shall not be deemed as a removal of said item of personal property so as to eliminate the effect of this Paragraph 6 as to such item.

7. By acceptance of this Bill of Sale, REAL ACRE N.V. acknowledges that it has received the personal property referred to in Exhibit "A".

In addition, the undersigned hereby sells, assigns and transfers to REAL ACRE N.V., a corporation, all of its right, title and interest in and to any and all personal property now located on or about that certain real property described in Exhibit "B" hereto, which exhibit is incorporated by reference herein as though set forth in full hereat, and in or about the buildings and improvements thereon.

Any and all sales or use taxes accruing because of this transaction are to be paid by the undersigned.

In the event REAL ACRE N.V. shall incur any costs of enforcing any of the provisions of this Bill of Sale, whether by suit or otherwise, including but not limited to attorney's fees, the undersigned shall pay to REAL ACRE N.V. an amount equal to such costs.

DATED: _____

SELLER, INC.,
a corporation

By _____
Title _____

5

STATE OF _____)
) ss.
COUNTY OF _____)

On _____, before me, the under-
signed, a Notary Public in and for said State, personally
appeared _____,
known to me to be the _____ of the
corporation that executed the within instrument on behalf
of the corporation therein named, and acknowledged to me
that such corporation executed the within instrument pursuant to its By-Laws or a resolution of its Board of
Directors.

WITNESS my hand and official seal.

            _____
            Notary Public in and for said
            County and State.

(SEAL)

6

SECURITY AGREEMENT

Friendly Savings & Loan Association   April ___, 1981
1200 Profit Way
Growth, California 90000   Loan No. _____

Gentlemen:

1. We hereby grant you a continuing security interest in all goods (as defined in Division 9 of the Uniform Commercial Code of the State of California) and chattels, including, but not limited to, all furniture, furnishings, fixtures, machinery, tools and equipment of every kind, nature or description, presently or hereafter owned by us, or in which we have any interest of any type, kind, description or nature, and presently or hereafter located at or upon that certain real property described in Exhibit "A," attached hereto and incorporated by reference as though set forth in full hereat, together with all additions, substitutions, replacemens, improvements and repairs to same and the increase or increment thereof, all of which shall herein be referred to collectively as "Collateral."

2. The security interest hereby granted is to secure the payment of all principal and interest and the true, faithful, full and exact performance and observance of all of the covenants and conditions of those certain promissory notes and deeds of trust, and such other agreements as may be described in Exhibit "B," attached hereto and incorporated by reference herein as though set forth in full hereat, and all of the covenants and conditions contained in any other agreement to which you are a party and which affects, directly or indirectly, the obligations secured hereby, the real property described in Exhibit "A," or the collateral, whether such agreement was executed by us or our predecessors in interest in said real property or collateral, including, but not limited to, all fees, charges, expenses and attorney's fees chargeable and/or secured under and by said promissory notes, deeds of trust, or this agreement, or any of them, (all herein referred to as "obligations").

3. We represent, warrant and covenant that: (a) we are the lawful owner of the collateral which is and will be free and clear of all security interests, liens and encumbrances (except as provided in Exhibit "C," attached hereto and incorporated by reference herein as though set forth in full hereat, and have the sole right and authority to deliver this instrument; (b) we will defend title to the collateral and your security interest therein against the claims and demands of all persons; (c) we will keep the collateral free and clear of all attachments, levies, taxes, liens, security interests, and encumbrances of every kind and nature and we will, at our own cost and expense, keep the collateral in good state of repair and will not waste or destroy the same or any part thereof and will not be negligent in the care and use thereof; (d) we will not, without your prior written consent, sell, assign, mortgage, lease or otherwise dispose of the collateral; (e) we will insure the collateral in your name against loss or damage by fire, theft, burglary, pilferage, loss in transit and such other hazards as you shall specify, in amounts and under policies by insurers acceptable to you, and all premiums thereon shall be paid by us and the policies delivered to you (if we fail to do so, you may procure such insurance, the cost of which shall be and is hereby deemed to be a cost of maintenance and preservation of the real property described in Exhibit "A" and the collateral); (f) we will not remove the collateral from its present location without your prior written consent and we will at all times allow you or your representatives free access to and right of inspection of the collateral; (g) we shall comply with the terms and conditions of any orders, ordinances, laws or statutes of any city, state or governmental department having jurisdiction with respect to such premises where the collateral is located or the conduct of business thereon and, when requested by you, we will execute any written instruments and do any other acts necessary to effectuate more fully the purposes and provisions of this agreement; and (h) we will indemnify and save you harmless from all loss, cost, damage, liability or expense including reasonable attorney's fees that you may sustain or incur by reason of defending or protecting this security interest or the priority thereof, or enforcing payment of the indebtedness hereby secured, or in the prosecution or defense of any action or proceeding concerning any matter growing out of or connected with this agreement and/or the obligation and/or the collateral.

4. You may, at your option, pay, purchase, contest, compromise or discharge any taxes, claims, debts, liens, charges, security interests or emcumbrances, which in your judgment may affect or appear to affect the collateral or your right hereunder. In addition, you may pay for the maintenance and preservation of the collateral. The amount of any payments made by you under any provisions of this agreement, together with all costs and expenses, including a reasonable attorney's fee, are all to be repaid to you, together with interest thereon at the rate charged upon the obligations, are all secured hereby and shall be, and is hereby deemed to be, a cost of maintenance and preservation of the real property described in Exhibit "A" and the collateral.

5. We shall be in default hereunder if: (a) we shall fail to pay, when due, or punctually perform any of the obligations; or (b) any warranty, representation or statement made or furnished to you by us or on our behalf was false in any material respect when made or furnished; or (c) any event shall occur which results in the acceleration of the maturity of any debt of ours to others secured by a security interest, lien or encumbrance described in Exhibit "C" hereto; or (d) any of the collateral shall be lost, stolen, or damaged; or (e) there shall be a levy upon, seizure or attachment of any of the collateral; or (f) we shall become insolvent; or (g) we shall make an assignment of our property for the benefit of creditors or suffer the appointment of a receiver of any part of our property; or (h) any proceedings under any provision of the Bankruptcy Act or any insolvency law shall be commenced by or against us.

6. Upon our default hereunder all obligations secured hereby shall, at your option and without notice or demand, become immediately due and payable then and thereafter you shall have all the rights and remedies of a secured party under the Uniform Commercial Code. In addition: (a) you shall thereupon have the right to take immediate possession of the collateral or any portion thereof, and for that purpose, may enter any of the premises described in Exhibit "A," or any other premises, with or without force or process of law, wherever this mortgaged property might be, and search for the same and take possession of and keep and store the same on said premises until sold and delivered (and we shall not charge you for storage of the collateral during foreclosure, sale or other disposal of the collateral); and/or remove the collateral or any part thereof to such other places as you may desire; (b) if you exercise your right to take possession of the collateral, we shall, upon your demand, assemble the collateral and make it available to you at a place convenient to you; (c) you may sell and dispose of all or part of the collateral at public auction or private sale, for cash or for credit, upon such terms as you may elect, after giving such notice as is required by the Uniform Commercial Code of the State of California, and we shall be credited with the amounts of any such sale only when the cash proceeds thereof are actually received by you. The requirements of notice shall be met if such notice is mailed, postage prepaid, to us at our address as set forth herein, at least five days before the time of sale or other disposition; (d) none of the collateral subject to the security interest created hereby need be in view of those attending the sale and you need not take or have the same in your physical possession at or as a condition to selling or otherwise disposing thereof; (e) you may sell same or such other collateral as you may have securing said obligations (including real property collateral) in such order, priority and lots as you in your sole discretion may designate, and we shall not have the right to direct in what order or priority the collateral may be sold; (f) all expenses of retaking, holding, preparing for sale, selling or the like shall include, without limitation, your reasonable attorney's fees and other legal expenses and disbursements.

7. No delay or failure on your part in exercising any right, privilege, remedy or option hereunder shall operate as a waiver of such or of any other right, privilege, remedy or option and no waiver whatever shall be valid unless in writing, signed by you, and then only to the extent therein set forth. You may have and may exercise one or more or all of the foregoing remedies and rights and any one and/or more of all the rights and remedies provided for in any and all contracts now or hereafter existing between us and in such order and priority and/or successively, alternatively or concurrently and in such manner as you in your sole discretion may direct. All of your rights and remedies are specifically hereby made cumulative; we agree to join with you in executing financing statements or other instruments pursuant to the Uniform Commercial Code, in form satisfactory to you and in executing such other documents or instruments as may be required or deemed necessary by you for purposes of effecting or continuing your security interest in the collateral.

8. This agreement cannot be changed or terminated orally. All of the rights, privileges, remedies and options given to you hereunder shall inure to the benefit of your successors and assigns; and all of the terms, conditions, promises, covenants, provisions and warranties of this agreement shall inure to the benefit of and shall bind the representatives, successors and assigns of each of us.

9. This agreement is cumulative to and not in derogation of any prior security agreements, deeds of trust, or other security devices, between you and us heretofore executed and shall not be construed to affect or vary any of the terms or provisions of such prior security agreements, deeds of trust, or other security devices.

10. The address to which all notices hereunder may be sent is:

11. Whenever the word "we" is used herein, it shall mean "we and each of us"; and whenever the word "us" is used herein it shall mean "us and each of us." Whenever the words "notes" and "Deeds of Trust" are used it shall also include the singular.

REAL ACRE N.V.

By_____

EXHIBIT "A"

(Legal Description)

EXHIBIT "B"

1.   A Promissory Note of even date in the original sum of
$700,000 executed by REAL ACRE N.V., a corporation, as Maker,
to FRIENDLY SAVINGS & LOAN ASSOCIATION, as Payee.

2.   A Deed of Trust of even date securing the above Promissory
Note executed by REAL ACRE N.V. as Trustor to BLANK TITLE INSUR-
ANCE COMPANY, as Trustee, for the benefit of FRIENDLY SAVINGS &
LOAN ASSOCIATION as Beneficiary.

EXHIBIT "C"

(PRIOR SECURITY INTERESTS, LIENS AND ENCUMBRANCES)

None

FRIENDLY SAVINGS AND LOAN ASSOCIATION

BUILDING LOAN AGREEMENT

THIS AGREEMENT is executed by the undersigned owner(s), hereinafter jointly and severally called "Owner", for the purpose of obtaining a loan from FRIENDLY SAVINGS AND LOAN ASSOCIATION, hereinafter called "Association", which loan is to be evidenced by a promissory note of Owner for $_____ in favor of Association and secured by, among other things, a deed of trust affecting real property in the County of _____, State of California, described as:

In consideration of the making of the loan, Owner agrees as follows:

1. In order to consummate such loan, Owner will hand Association the following, all of which shall be in a form acceptable to, and approved by, Association:

(a) Loan application, financial statement form, signature cards, and any other instruments

---

This FINANCING STATEMENT is presented for filing pursuant to the California Uniform Commercial Code.

1. DEBTOR   (LAST NAME FIRST—IF AN INDIVIDUAL)
REAL ACRE N.V., a corporation

1A. SOCIAL SECURITY OR FEDERAL TAX NO.

1B. MAILING ADDRESS   1C. CITY, STATE   1D. ZIP CODE
6300 Wilshire Boulevard, Suite 9100   Los Angeles, California   90048

2. ADDITIONAL DEBTOR   (IF ANY)   (LAST NAME FIRST—IF AN INDIVIDUAL)

2A. SOCIAL SECURITY OR FEDERAL TAX NO.

2B. MAILING ADDRESS   2C. CITY, STATE   2D. ZIP CODE

3. DEBTOR'S TRADE NAMES OR STYLES   (IF ANY)

3A. FEDERAL TAX NUMBER

4. SECURED PARTY
NAME Friendly Savings & Loan Association
MAILING ADDRESS 1200 Profit Way
CITY Growth,   STATE California   ZIP CODE 90000

4A. SOCIAL SECURITY NO. FEDERAL TAX NO.
OR BANK TRANSIT AND A.B.A. NO.

5. ASSIGNEE OF SECURED PARTY   (IF ANY)
NAME
MAILING ADDRESS
CITY   STATE   ZIP CODE

5A. SOCIAL SECURITY NO. FEDERAL TAX NO.
OR BANK TRANSIT AND A.B.A. NO.

6. This FINANCING STATEMENT covers the following types or items of property (**include description of real property on which located and owner of record when required by instruction 4).**

Assignment of all proceeds, including but not limited to escrow proceeds, in connection with the sale of the real property described herein. The term collateral shall also include, but not be limited to, plumbing and plumbing material and supplies, concrete, lumber, hardware, electrical wiring and electrical materials and supplies, heating and air conditioning material and supplies, roofing material and supplies, window material and supplies, flooring, carpeting, fixtures, fencing, landscaping and other materials, supplies and property of every kind and nature now or hereafter delivered to or located at, upon or about or attached to the real property described herein, together with the proceeds of any insurance policy issued with respect to said project and property.

7. □ 7A. □ PRODUCTS OF COLLATERAL ARE ALSO COVERED   [X]

8. □ DEBTOR IS A "TRANSMITTING UTILITY" IN ACCORDANCE WITH UCC § 9105 (1) (n)

7B. DEBTOR(S) SIGNATURE NOT REQUIRED IN ACCORDANCE WITH INSTRUCTION 5 (a) ITEMS:
□(1) □(2) □(3) □(4)

9. ▲
SIGNATURE(S) OF DEBTOR(S)

REAL ACRE N.V.
TYPE OR PRINT NAME(S) OF DEBTOR(S)

▲
SIGNATURE(S) OF SECURED PARTY(IES)

FRIENDLY SAVINGS & LOAN ASSOCIATION
TYPE OR PRINT NAME(S) OF SECURED PARTY(IES)

10. THIS SPACE FOR USE OF FILING OFFICER
(DATE, TIME, FILE NUMBER AND FILING OFFICER)

C O D E
1
2
3
4
5
6
7
8
9
0

DATE:

11. Return copy to:
NAME   Myron Meyers, Esq.
ADDRESS Meyers, Stevens & Walters
         Professional Corporation
CITY   6300 Wilshire Boulevard, Suite 9100
STATE   Los Angeles, California 90048
ZIP CODE

(1) FILING OFFICER COPY

FORM UCC-1—FILING FEE $3.00
Approved by the Secretary of State

required by Association properly completed and executed by Owner.

(b) Promissory note payable to the order of Association in the principal amount of $_____, dated as written, bearing interest at the rate of _____% per annum; principal and interest payable in monthly installments of $_____ each on the _____ day of each month beginning _____; provided, however, that until regular monthly installments begin, interest shall be payable monthly on the principal sum at the rate above stated.

_____

(c) First deed of trust executed by Owner, covering the above described real property and securing the aforesaid promissory note.

(d) Absolute and specific assignment of rents, issues and profits, security agreement in goods and chattels, financing statement and any other security or other instruments executed by Owner.

(e) Detailed plans and specifications for the construction of improvements on said property executed by Owner and bearing the written approval

-2-

of Association.

(f) Cost breakdown(s) for onsite and offsite improvements, setting forth the estimated cost of construction, on Association's form, and bearing written approval of Association.

(g) A recordable completion and performance bond in the amount of the estimated cost of completion of the onsite and offsite improvements running in favor of, among others, Association, in a form and with a surety approved by Association.

(h) A labor and materials bond insuring lien-free completion of the onsite and offsite improvements in the amount of the estimated cost of completion of said improvements running in favor of, among others, Association, in a form and with a surety approved by Association.

(i) Fire insurance policy in amount and form and written by an insurance company acceptable to Association.

(j) In the event the amount available for construction purposes, as hereinafter defined, is less than the estimated cost of construction as shown on the cost breakdown(s), Owner will hand Association a sum equal to such difference, to be disbursed in the manner specified in Para-

-3-

graph 2 hereof before disbursement of any loan funds.

(k) Copies of the following contracts:

_____

_____

_____

(l) _____

(m) _____

Association is authorized to use the foregoing and to consummate the loan when it has obtained an ALTA lender's extended coverage policy of title insurance in the full amount of the loan and satisfactory to Association, with liability of not less than the principal amount of the loan and insuring Association that the above described deed of trust is a first lien and charge on the above described property; excepting only such items as shall have been approved in writing by Association.

2. Association, when it shall have accepted the Owner's application, and when it holds the items specified in Paragraph 1, shall consummate the loan and make payments on account thereof, as follows:

(a) To pay loan costs and expenses, as follows:

(i) $ _____ Commission and service fee

-4-

(ii) $ _____ Escrow fee and charge for drawing loan instruments

(iii) $ _____ Charge for title insurance policy

(iv) $ _____ Tax reporting service

(v) $ _____ Premium on $ _____ fire insurance policy

(vi) $ _____ Performance and completion bond premium

(vii) $ _____ Labor and materials bond premium

(viii) $ _____ Recording fees

(ix) $ _____ _____

_____

_____

In the event the actual charge for any of the above items should differ from the amount above set forth, Association shall make payment for Owner's account of the actual charge when determined.

(b) To pay the amount available for construction purposes for the completion of onsite and offsite improvements as set forth in the plans

-5-

and specifications, such payment to be in the manner and to the persons and entities specified in Paragraph 3 hereof. The balance of said loan, after payment of the items specified in part (a) of this Paragraph, shall constitute the amount available for construction purposes.

Except as otherwise herein provided, this agreement and the rights created hereunder shall not be assigned or transferred. Any such assignment or transfer, whether voluntary or involuntary, of this agreement or any right created hereunder shall not be binding upon, nor shall the same in any way affect, Association without its prior written consent, and Association may pay out the moneys herein provided for, as herein set forth, notwithstanding any such assignment or transfer.

3. Ninety per cent (90%) of the amount available for construction purposes as defined in Paragraph 2 shall be disbursed to pay for items listed in the cost breakdown(s) furnished Association pursuant to Paragraph 1, the amount to be disbursed for each item not to exceed the amount specified therefor in such cost breakdown(s); provided, however, that pior to the installation of building foundations in the construction project pursuant to the plans and specifications, no more than $_____ (including disbursements made pursuant to Paragraph 2(a) shall be disbursed on amount of the entire loan). Said amount to be disbursed pursuant to this paragraph shall be

-6-

paid to persons or entities who have furnished labor, services and/or materials theretofore used in, or related to, the construction project, upon submission to Association by such persons or entities of written non-negotiable vouchers in a form customarily used by, and approved by, Association. In this regard, Owner acknowledges receipt of a copy of the form of such non-negotiable voucher customarily used by Association and further acknowledges that no payment shall be made respecting any such non-negotiable voucher to Owner or such persons or entities unless and until each and all of the conditions and requirements of payment as set forth therein have been met. The following are hereby designated as persons authorized to sign written non-negotiable vouchers on behalf of Owner in accordance with the terms of this agreement, and Owner, with the consent of Association, shall have the sole right to revoke such designation, and substitute any other person as the person authorized to sign such vouchers on behalf of Owner: _____.

Notwithstanding any provision hereof to the contrary, Association may require, prior to disbursement of any funds hereunder, on forms supplied by it: (1) Submission of proof of the delivery to and/or incorporation into the work of improvement of all labor and/or materials, as well as such other supporting affidavits and/or statements as Association may require. (2) Submission by Owner to Association of the names and addresses of all persons and entities who have or will perform or furnish any work, labor or materials in connection

-7-

cable governmental approvals respecting the improvements constructed, including, but not limited to, acceptances, certificates of use and occupancy and releases and exonerations of all bonds, together with a written certification by a licensed engineer or architect that all work per the plans and specifications hereinabove described has been fully completed.

6. Owner agrees to commence construction of the proposed improvements promptly after the recordation of the aforesaid deed of trust and to continue such construction with reasonable speed and in a workmanlike manner. Owner will complete such improvements promptly, in accordance with the said plans and specifications, including any specifications prescribed by Association, and will pay the cost thereof. If there is any difference between any such prescribed specifications and the plans and specifications furnished Association pursuant hereto, then the requirements of whichever thereof are the higher shall be met in constructing said improvements. Owner further agrees to furnish Association, at its request, immediately upon completion of the building foundations on the proejct, a survey made and certified by a licensed engineer or surveyor, showing that said foundations are located entirely within the property lines and do not encroach upon any easement, or breach or violate any covenant, condition or restriction of record, or any building or zoning ordinance.

7. No materials, equipment, fixtures, carpets, appli-

-9-

with the work of improvement. (3) Submission of proof that a period of 20 days has expired after the performing or furnishing of the labor, services and/or materials for which each voucher is presented and that no preliminary notice describing such labor, services and/or materials has been served upon Association or Owner except by the person or entity named in the voucher as the "voucher payee."

4. The remaining balance of the amount available for construction and any other amounts not otherwise disbursed shall be disbursed when said improvements have been completed and when Owner has deposited with Association an affidavit stating that all bills for labor and/or materials used in, or related to, such construction have been paid or ordered to be paid pursuant to Paragraph 3 hereof together with such proof as, in the sole uncontrolled judgment of the Association, establishes that the amount available for construction has been used for the direct cost of the proposed construction. Any excess, at the sole option of Association, shall constitute a reduction in the amount of the loan, or shall be paid to Owner.

5. For purposes hereof, completion is defined as either of the following, whichever last occurs:

(a) Seventy-five (75) days after the recording of a valid Notice of Completion (as determined solely by Association); or

(b) Upon submission to Association by Owner of satisfactory evidence of receipt of all appli-

-8-

to stop said work and order its replacing whether or not said unsatisfactory work has theretofore been incorporated in said improvements, and to withhold all further disbursements until such work is satisfactory to it. If said work is not made satisfactory to Association within fifteen (15) calendar days from the date of stoppage by Association, such failure to do so shall constitute a default by the Owner under the terms of this agreement. Owner agrees that Association is under no obligation to construct or supervise construction of said improvements and that the inspection by Association of the construction of said improvements is for the sole purpose of protecting the security of the Association, and that such inspection is not to be construed as a representation that there will be a strict compliance on the part of Owner with plans and specifications, or that construction will be free from faulty material or workmanship, Owner agrees to make or cause to be made such further and other independent inspections as Owner may desire for Owner's protection.

11. In the event of a default by Owner in the performance of any of the terms, covenants and/or conditions contained in this agreement, or any other joint and/or several obligation or obligations of Owner to Association, all sums disbursed or advanced by Association shall immediately become due and payable and Association shall have no obligation to disburse any further funds and shall be released from any and all obligations to Owner under the terms of this agreement.

-11-

ances, or any other part of said improvements shall be purchased or installed under conditional sales agreements or under other arrangements wherein the right is reserved or accrues to anyone to remove or to repossess any such items, or to consider them as personal property. It is expressly agreed that all such items are a part of the real property.

8. In the event of the filing with Association of a notice to withhold or the recording of a mechanics lien Association may summarily refuse to honor any orders for payment pursuant to this loan, and in the event Owner fails to furnish Association a bond causing such notice or lien to be released, within 10 days of such filing or recording, such failure shall at the option of the Association constitute a default under the terms of this Agreement.

9. If and whenever Association shall determine and notify Owner that the amount of the loan after deduction of amounts therefore paid out pursuant hereto is less than the amount required fully to complete any pay for said improvements, and Association shall demand that Owner deposit with Association an amount equal to such deficiency as estimated by Association, then, and in that event, Owner shall comply with such demand within ten (10) days from the date thereof, and the judgment of Association shall be final and conclusive in this respect.

10. Association and its agents shall have the right at all times to enter upon the said property during the period of construction and, if said work is not in conformance with the plans and specifications, Association shall have the right

-10-

related costs incurred, including fees of counsel, in any way relating to, pertaining to, concerning, or arising out of, the construction of the above described improvements.

15. Should work cease on the improvements, specifically including stoppage by Association in accordance with Paragraph 10 hereof, or for any reason whatsoever not progress continuously in a manner satisfactory to Association, it being the sole judge as to this requirement, then Association may, at its option, without notice, declare Owner to be in default hereunder and/or may take possession of said premises and let contracts for or proceed with the finishing of said improvements and pay the cost thereof, plus a fee of fifteen percent (15%) for supervision of construction, disbursing all or any part of the loan for such purposes; and should the cost of finishing said improvements plus such fee amount to more than the undisbursed balance of the loan then such additional costs may be expended at its option by Association, in which event it shall be considered and be an additional loan to the Owner and the repayment thereof, together with interest thereon at the rate provided in the above loan, shall be secured by the aforesaid deed of trust and shall be repaid within thirty (30) days after the completion of said improvements, and Owner agrees to pay the same within said thirty (30) days. Owner further hereby authorizes Association at its option at any time, whether default exists or not, either in its option at any time, whether default exists or not, either

-13-

12. Owner does hereby irrevocably appoint, designate, empower and authorize Association Owner's agent, coupled with an interest, to sign and file for record any notices of completion, notices of cessation of labor or any other notice or written document that Association may deem necessary to file or record to protect its interests. Owner acknowledges that Owner is not the agent of Association.

13. Association may conclusively assume that the statements, facts, information and representations contained in any affidavits, vouchers, receipts or other written instruments which are filed with Association or exhibited to it are true and correct and mayb rely thereon without any investigation or inquiry, and any payment made by Association in reliance thereon shall be a complete release in its favor of all sums so paid.

14. Association shall in no way be liable for any agreements, acts or omissions of Owner, or any agent of Owner, or any contractor or other person or entity furnishing labor and/or materials used in or related to such construction. In this regard, Owner does hereby agree to indemnify, save, protect and forever hold harmless, and defend (by counsel satisfactory to Association) Association, and all directors, shareholders, officers, agents and employees of Association, and said real property and the subject construction loan funds, of, from and against any and all claims, demands, liabilities, damages, costs, expenses, fees, charges, covenants, agreements, lien claims, stop notices and equitable liens, together with

-12-

in its own name or in the name of Owner, to do any and all things necessary or expedient in the opinion of Association to secure the performance of the construction contracts and to secure the erection and completion of the improvements substantially in accordance with the plans and specifications, and to accept the improvements as completed or substantially completed, and to do any and every act or thing pertaining to or arising out of the construction or completion of such improvements or any contract therefor, disbursing all or any part of the loan proceeds for such purposes. In addition to the specific rights and remedies hereinabove mentioned, Association shall have the right to avail itself of any other rights or remedies to which it may be entitled under any existing law or laws.

16. Owner agrees that copies of all preliminary notices delivered pursuant to Section 1193 of the California Code of Civil Procedure (a) to Owner and (b) to the property, addressed to Association or to "Construction Lender" shall be promptly delivered to Association. Owner further agrees that Association and its agents shall have the right at all times to enter upon the said property and post such notices and other written or printed material thereon as it may deem necessary or desirable for its protection as lender.

17. In the event that Association shall be a party to any legal proceedings instituted in connection with or arising out of the construction of said improvements, or the loans herein provided for, Owner agrees to pay to Association all sums paid and/or incurred by it as costs in said legal

-14-

proceedings, together with such reasonable sums as may be paid or incurred by it in the employment of counsel to represent it in such legal proceedings. Further, should suit be instituted hereon, or involve this agreement, Association shall be entitled to recover reasonable fees of counsel incurred by it.

18. Time is of the essence of this agreement, of each and every provision and of all acts to be performed hereunder.

19. The waiver by Association of any breach or breaches hereof shall not be deemed, nor shall the same constitute, a waiver of any subsequent breach or breaches.

20. This agreement is made for the sole benefit and protection of Owner and Association, its successors and assigns, and no other person shall have any right of action or right to rely hereon. This agreement and said promissory note and deed of trust and the other documents specifically referred to herein contain all of the terms and conditions agreed upon between the parties respecting the real property hereindescribed, and no other agreement regarding the subject matter thereof shall be deemed to exist or bind any party unless in writing and signed by the party to be charged. In any event, there are no oral agreements of any nature whatsoever between the parties, all thereof being written.

21. Owner has made certain statements and disclosures in order to induce Association to make said loan and enter into this agreement, and in the event Owner has made material mis-

-15-

24. The obligations of any and all persons and entities comprising "Owner" hereunder shall be both joint and several.

NO MODIFICATION OR CHANGE IN THIS INSTRUMENT SHALL BE VALID UNLESS APPROVED BY AN EXECUTIVE OFFICER OF ASSOCIATION AND SUCH APPROVAL ENDORSED HEREON.

Executed by Owner this ___ day of _____, 19___.

_____
Owner

_____
Owner

Accepted _____, 19___.

FRIENDLY SAVINGS AND LOAN ASSOCIATION

By _____

-17-

representations or failed to disclose any material fact, Association may treat such misrepresentation or omission as a breach of this agreement. Such action shall not affect any remedies Association may have under its deed of trust for such misrepresentation or concealment.

22. If payment of the indebtedness secured by said deed of trust is to be insured or guaranteed by the Federal Housing Administrator, or the Veterans' Administration, or by any other government agency, then Owner agrees to conform to and abide by all of the rules, regulations and requirements of said Federal Housing Administrator, Veterans' Administration, or other governmental agency, and to do all things necessary, convenient and proper to cause said indebtedness to be so insured or guaranteed, and Owner shall furnish Association with proper evidence that all requirements of such agency, or agencies, as to the construction of said improvements, and otherwise, have been fully met; and if, for any reason, said requirements are not fully met or said indebtedness not so insured or guaranteed on or before _____, 19___, such failure shall constitute a default under the terms hereof (if date not filled in, the same shall be deemed to be one (1) year from the date of acceptance thereof).

23. A default hereunder shall constitute a default under said promissory note and said deed of trust. A default under said deed of trust and/or said promissory note shall constitute a default hereunder.

-16-

FORM - GUARANTY OF COMPLETION - CONSTRUCTION LOAN

GUARANTY OF COMPLETION

For and in consideration of the execution by NATIONAL BANK, herein called the "Bank", of the Building Loan Agreement with REAL ACRE N.V., a corporation, and for and in further consideration of said Bank's making any of the loans referred to in said Agreement and waiving the requirement of a Lien and Completion Bond in connection therewith, the undersigned, jointly and severally hereby unconditionally guarantee to complete to Bank's satisfaction all improvements in said Project and warrant and guarantee to said Bank, its successors or assigns, the full, prompt, and faithful performance, payment, discharge, and completion of each of the provisions, agreements, obligations, and conditions contained in the said Agreement or in any modification thereof, supplement thereto, substitute therefore, or in any rider or exhibit now or hereafter thereto attached, or in any other written instrument executed by Borrower to carry out the provisions of said Agreement.

Further, the undersigned, and each of them, hereby agree and do subordinate to the loan or loans referred to in said Agreement and to any obligation or Borrower therein contained the payment by the Borrower to the undersigned, or

---

(To be signed where contractor is not the owner and to be physically attached to Building Loan Agreement)

Undersigned is the general contractor for the project which the attached and foregoing Building Loan Agreement covers.

It is Undersigned's understanding that Friendly Savings and Loan Association will not make the loan referred to therein, the net proceeds of which are to be used pursuant to such agreement in the construction of such project, unless Undersigned agrees to be bound by, and perform, all of the obligations of "Owner" as set forth herein.

Undersigned has read said Building Loan Agreement and has been furnished with a copy thereof as well as a copy of the non-negotiable voucher described therein. Undersigned understands the provisions of said agreement. In order to induce Friendly Savings and Loan Association to make the loan, and for other good and valuable consideration, receipt of which is hereby acknowledged, Undersigned agrees to be bound by the provisions of said agreement in its construction of the project, and to perform all of the obligations of Owner as set forth therein.

Contractor _____

License No. _____

Tax I.D. No. _____

-18-

any of them, of any indebtedness of the Borrower to the undersigned, or any of them, whether existing now or hereafter, direct or indirect, contingent or determined; and, further, the undersigned, and each of them, agree to forebear and not to ask, demand, or make claim for any such indebtedness unless and until any and all indebtedness of the Borrower to the Bank arising under said loan or said Agreement shall have been paid in full. The undersigned, and each of them, further agree not to transfer or assign any such indebtedness while this Agreement remains in effect, except after first notifying the Bank and making such assignment or transfer expressly subject to this Guaranty Agreement.

In the event of a breach of or failure or refusal to observe any of the covenants, warranties, or guarantees of the undersigned, or any of them, herein set forth, it is agreed that the Bank shall have a direct cause of action against each of those, jointly and severally, of the under-signed whose liability is stated or indicated in this Agreement and to the full extent of such liability as herein expressed for all loss, damage, injury and expense sustained or incurred by the Bank as a consequence of such breach or failure or refusal to perform, including reasonable fees of Bank's attorneys in such action or actions, it being agreed that the Bank shall have no duty or responsibility to pursue the Borrower or anyone else primarily or otherwise liable or responsible for

-2-

the improvement, development, or other handling of said Lots, and that the Bank may at its election, from time to time look to and require performance by any one or more of those of the undersigned who are liable or have assumed liability as herein stated without first proceeding or attempting to enforce any of its rights against the Borrower or any of said property, or instituting or conducting any foreclosure or sale proceedings under (any of) its Deed of Trust or otherwise realizing upon or enforcing any security for (any of) its said loan.

If any indebtedness of Debtor to Bank is secured by a deed of trust or other interest in real property, the undersigned expressly waives any defenses to recovery by Bank of a deficiency after nonjudicial sale of said real property and further expressly waives any defenses or benefits available to the undersigned under Section 580a and 580d of the California Code of Civil Procedure, or under similar laws of other jurisdictions.

IN WITNESS WHEREOF, we have hereunto set our hands and seals on this _____ day of _____, 19____.

_____

-3-

CORPORATE GUARANTY

April   , 1981

Friendly Savings & Loan Association
1200 Profit Way
Growth, California 90000

Gentlemen:

The undersigned, Real Acre Holdings B.V. ("Guarantor"), a Netherlands corporation, whose address is set forth beneath its signature herein, is financially interested in Real Acre N.V. ("Debtor"), a Netherlands Antilles corporation.

By reason of the foregoing, it will be to Guarantor's direct interest and financial advantage to enable Debtor to procure now and from time to time hereafter funds, credits and other financial assistance from you, Friendly Savings & Loan Association ("Lender"), a corporation duly organized, existing and in good standing under the laws of the State of California and whose principal place of business is located at the address set forth above. Upon the solicitation of Debtor, and not Lender, Guarantor hereby requests of Lender that Lender give such financial assistance to Debtor. Lender has refused to give such financial assistance to Debtor unless Guarantor executes and delivers this Guaranty to Lender.

1. In order to induce Lender to give such financial assistance to Debtor, Guarantor unconditionally, absolutely, continuingly, and irrevocably guarantees to Lender "Debtor's Liabilities." Guarantor's obligations to Lender under this Guaranty are hereinafter referred to as "Guarantor's Obligations." For all purposes of this Guaranty, "Debtor's Liabilities" means: (a) Debtor's prompt payment in full, when due or declared due and at all times thereafter, of all indebtedness, liability or liabilities of any and every kind and nature, heretofore, now or at any time or times hereafter owing, arising, due or payable from Debtor to Lender, howsoever evidenced, created, incurred, acquired, or owing, whether primary, secondary, direct, contingent, fixed or otherwise, and whether arising under any financing agreements, security agreements, riders to financing agreements and security agreements, agreements, instruments, documents, leases, mortgages, assignments or contracts heretofore, now

-2-

or at any time or times hereafter executed by Debtor and delivered to Lender (all of the foregoing described financing agreements, security agreements, riders, contracts, leases, mortgages, assignments, agreements, instruments and documents being hereinafter individually and collectively referred to as the "Financing Agreements"), or by oral agreement or operation of law and whether evidenced by instruments or other evidences of indebtedness; and (b) Debtor's prompt, full and faithful performance, observance and discharge of each and every term, condition, agreement, representation, warranty, undertaking, covenant, guaranty and provision to be performed, observed or discharged by Debtor under the Financing Agreements. Guarantor agrees that Guarantor is directly and primarily liable, jointly and severally with Debtor, for Debtor's Liabilities.

2. Guarantor acknowledges, warrants, represents and agrees:

a. that Guarantor has independently reviewed all instruments and documents executed by Debtor, and Guarantor has made an independent determination as to the validity and enforceability thereof upon the advise of Guarantor's own counsel, and in executing and delivering this Guaranty to Lender, Guarantor is not in any manner relying upon Lender as to the validity and/or enforceability of any security interest of any kind or nature granted by the Debtor to Lender or granted to Lender by any other guarantors of Debtor's Liabilities ("other guarantor").

b. Guarantor waives all defenses, counterclaims and offsets of any kind or nature, in connection with the validity and/or enforceability of this Guaranty, arising directly or indirectly from the perfection, sufficiency, validity and/or enforceability of any of the Financing Agreements.

3. Guarantor further warrants, represents and agrees to furnish, to Lender quarterly, or more frequently as Lender shall require, all pertinent facts relating to the ability of Debtor to pay and to perform Debtor's Liabilities, and all pertinent facts relating to Guarantor's or any other guarantor's ability to pay and to perform Guarantor's obligations, and Guarantor further warrants, represents and agrees to keep informed with respect to all such facts. Guarantor acknowledges and agrees that Lender is and will continue to rely upon the facts and information to be furnished to it by Guarantor, as aforesaid. Guarantor further warrants, represents and agrees that, in executing this Guaranty and at all times hereafter, Guarantor relies and will continue to rely upon Guarantor's own investigation and upon sources other than Lender for all information and facts relating to the ability of Debtor to pay and to perform Debtor's Liabilities, and Guarantor does not and will not hereafter

-3-

rely upon Lender for any such information or facts. Guarantor waives any and all right to assert against Lender any claims or defenses based upon any failure of Lender to furnish to Guarantor any information or facts relating to the ability of Debtor to pay and to perform Debtor's Liabilities.

4. In the event that bankruptcy, insolvency, liquidation, receivership, conservatorship or other similar or related proceedings are instituted by or against Guarantor, any other guarantor, or Debtor or in the event Guarantor, any other guarantor, or Debtor becomes incompetent, insolvent, makes an assignment for the benefit of creditors, attempts to effect a composition with creditors, or in the event of the death of any guarantor, that Debtor commits a default under the Financing Agreements, then in any such event, notwithstanding any collateral that Lender may possess from Debtor, Guarantor, other guarantor, or any other party, at Lender's election and without notice thereof or demand therefor, Guarantor's Obligations shall become due and payable and enforceable against Guarantor, whether Debtor's Liabilities are then due and payable or not. Guarantor from time to time shall pay to Lender, on demand, at Lender's principal place of business, Guarantor's Obligations as they become or are declared due and in the event such payment is not made forthwith, Lender may proceed to suit against Guarantor and/or realize upon any security for Guarantor's Obligations. At Lender's election, one or more and successive or concurrent suits may be brought hereon by Lender against Guarantor, whether or not suit has been commenced against Debtor, and in any such suit Debtor may be joined as a party with Guarantor.

5. Guarantor waives any right to assert against Lender as a defense, counterclaim, set-off or crossclaim, any defense (legal or equitable), set-off, counterclaim or claim (a) which Guarantor may now or at any time or times hereafter have against Debtor or any other party liable to Lender in any way or manner, or (b) which is based upon any election of remedies by Lender, which, in any manner impairs, affects, reduces, releases or extinguishes Guarantor's subrogation rights or Guarantor's right to proceed against Debtor for reimbursement, or any other rights of Guarantor against Debtor, or against any other person or party or security, including, but not limited to, any defense based upon an election of remedies by Lender under the terms of Section 580d of the Code of Civil Procedure of the State of California and any similar provision of other laws of any state, governmental entity, or country. Section 580d of the California Code of Civil Procedure provides as follows:

"No judgment shall be rendered for any deficiency upon a note secured by a deed of trust or mortgage

-4-

upon real property hereafter executed in any case in which the real property has been sold by the mortgagee or trustee under power of sale contained in such a mortgage or deed of trust.

"The provisions of this section shall not apply to any deed of trust, mortgage or other lien given to secure the payment of bonds or other evidences of indebtedness authorized or permitted to be issued by the Commissioner of Corporations, or which is made by a public utility subject to the provisions of the Public Utilities Act."

6. If at any time or times hereafter Lender employs counsel for advice or other representation (a) with respect to this Guaranty, (b) to represent Lender in any litigation, contest, dispute, suit or proceeding (whether instituted by Lender, Guarantor, Debtor or any other party) in any way or respect relating to this Guaranty, or (c) to enforce Guarantor's Obligations, then, in any of the foregoing events, all of the reasonable attorneys' fees arising from such services and all expenses, costs and charges in any way or respect arising in connection therewith or relating thereto shall be paid by Guarantor to Lender, on demand.

7. As security for Guarantor's Obligations, Guarantor agrees that: (a) all security interests, liens and encumbrances heretofore, now and at any time or times hereafter granted by Guarantor to Lender shall secure Guarantor's Obligations; (b) all indebtedness, liability or liabilities now and at any time or times hereafter owing by Debtor to Guarantor are hereby subordinated to Debtor's Liabilities; (c) in the event Guarantor fails to pay Guarantor's Obligations when due and payable under this Guaranty, any of Guarantor's assets of any kind, nature or description in the possession, control or custody of Lender may, without notice to Guarantor, be reduced to cash or the like and applied by Lender in reduction or payment of Guarantor's Obligations; (d) all security interests, liens and encumbrances which Guarantor now has and from time to time hereafter may have upon any of Debtor's assets are hereby subordinated to all security interests, liens and encumbrances which Lender now has and from time to time hereafter may have thereon; and (e) all indebtedness, liability or liabilities now and at any time or times hereafter owing to Guarantor by any party who is also liable to Debtor are hereby subordinated to all indebtedness, liability or liabilities owed by such party to Debtor, if Lender has a security in such parties' indebtedness, liability or liabilities.

-5-

8. Guarantor hereby waives notice of the following events or occurrences: (a) Lender's acceptance of this Guaranty; (b) Lender's heretofore, now or from time to time hereafter loaning monies or giving or extending credit to or for the benefit of Debtor, whether or not pursuant to the Financing Agreements or any amendments, modifications or additions thereto or alterations or substitutions thereof, heretofore made, now made or at any time or times hereafter made; (c) Debtor's heretofore, now or at any time or times hereafter granting to Lender security interests, liens, or encumbrances in any of Debtor's assets or Lender's heretofore, now or from time to time hereafter obtaining, amending, substituting for, releasing, waiving or modifying any such security interests, liens or encumbrances; (d) Lender's heretofore, now or at any time or times hereafter obtaining, releasing, waiving or modifying any other party's guaranty of Debtor's Liabilities or any security interest, lien or encumbrance in any other party's assets given to Lender to secure such other party's guaranty of Debtor's Liabilities; (e) Lender's heretofore, now or at any time or times hereafter obtaining, amending, substituting for, releasing, waiving or modifying, any of the Financing Agreements; (f) presentment and demand, notices of default, non-payment, partial payment and protest, and all other notices or formalities to which Guarantor may be entitled; (g) Lender's heretofore, now or at any time or times hereafter granting to Debtor (and any other party liable to Lender on account of Debtor's Liabilities) of any indulgences or extensions of time of payment of Debtor's Liabilities; (h) Lender's heretofore, now or at any time or times hereafter paying in satisfaction or settlement any other liens or security interests on any of Debtor's assets, whether or not such liens and security interest are superior to Lender's, with the result that such payments become part of Debtor's Liabilities guaranteed hereby; and (i) Lender's heretofore, now or at any time or times hereafter accepting from Debtor or any other party any partial payment or payments on account of Debtor's Liabilities or any collateral securing the payment thereof or Lender's settling, subordinating, compromising, discharging or releasing the same. Guarantor agrees that Lender may heretofore, now or at any time or times hereafter do any or all of the foregoing events or occurrences in such manner, upon such terms and at such times as Lender, in its sole and absolute discretion, deems advisable, without in any way or respect impairing, affecting, reducing or releasing Guarantor from Guarantor's Obligations and Guarantor hereby consents to each and all of the foregoing events or occurrences.

9. As a condition to payment or performance by Guarantor under this Guaranty, Lender is not required to (a) prosecute collection of or seek to enforce or resort to any remedies

-6-

against Debtor or any other party liable to Lender on account of Debtor's Liabilities or any guaranty thereof, or (b) seek to enforce or resort to any remedies with respect to any security interest, liens or encumbrances granted to Lender by Debtor or any other party liable to Lender on account of Debtor's Liabilities or any guaranty thereof. Lender shall have no obligation to protect, secure or insure any of the foregoing security interests, liens or encumbrances or the properties or interests in properties subject thereto. Guarantor's Obligations shall in no way be impaired, affected, reduced or released by reason of (a) Lender's failure or delay to do or take any of the acts, actions or things described in this Guaranty, including, without limiting the generality of the foregoing, those acts, actions and things described in this paragraph and Paragraph 8, or (b) the invalidity, unenforceability, loss of or change in priority or reduction in or loss of value of any of the aforesaid security interests, liens and encumbrances.

10. This Guaranty shall continue in full force and effect until Debtor's Liabilities are fully paid, performed and discharged and Lender gives Guarantor written notice of that fact at Guarantor's address specified below. This Guaranty shall be binding upon and inure to the benefit of Guarantor and Lender and their respective successors and assigns. Guarantor agrees, and expressly consents, that Lender may at its election and in its sole discretion, without notices whatsoever to Guarantor, assign, hypothecate, or transfer this Guaranty and/or the Financing Agreements and/or the Collateral securing the payments of Debtor's Liabilities and/or this Guaranty, in whole or in part. Any claim or claims which Lender may, at any time or times hereafter have against Guarantor under this Guaranty shall be asserted by Lender against Guarantor by written notice directed to Guarantor at the Guarantor's address specified below.

11. THIS GUARANTY IS SUBMITTED TO LENDER AT LENDER'S PRINCIPAL PLACE OF BUSINESS STATED AFORESAID AND SHALL BE DEEMED TO HAVE BEEN MADE THEREAT. THIS GUARANTY SHALL BE GOVERNED AND CONTROLLED AS TO INTERPRETATION, ENFORCEMENT, VALIDITY, CONSTRUCTION, EFFECT AND IN ALL OTHER RESPECTS BY THE LAWS, STATUTES AND DECISIONS OF THE STATE OF CALIFORNIA. GUARANTOR, IN ORDER TO INDUCE LENDER TO ACCEPT THIS GUARANTY AND FOR OTHER GOOD AND VALUABLE CONSIDERATION, THE RECEIPT AND SUFFICIENCY OF WHICH IS HEREBY ACKNOWLEDGED, AGREES THAT ALL ACTIONS OR PROCEEDINGS ARISING DIRECTLY, INDIRECTLY OR OTHERWISE IN CONNECTION WITH, OUT OF, RELATED TO OR FROM THIS GUARANTY SHALL BE LITIGATED, AT LENDER'S SOLE DISCRETION AND ELECTION, ONLY IN COURTS HAVING SITUS WITHIN THE STATE OF CALIFORNIA. GUARANTOR HEREBY CONSENTS AND SUBMITS TO THE JURISDICTION OF ANY LOCAL, STATE OR FEDERAL COURT LOCATED WITHIN THE STATE OF CALIFORNIA. GUARANTOR HEREBY WAIVES ANY RIGHT GUARANTOR MAY HAVE TO TRANSFER OR CHANGE THE VENUE OF ANY LITIGATION BROUGHT AGAINST GUARANTOR BY LENDER IN ACCORDANCE WITH THIS PARAGRAPH.

TO 444 C
(Attorney in Fact)

STATE OF CALIFORNIA } ss.
COUNTY OF _____

On _____ before me, the undersigned, a Notary Public in and for said State, personally appeared _____ known to me to be the person_ whose name_ subscribed to the within instrument, as the Attorney_ in fact of _____ subscribed the name _____ thereto as principal and acknowledged to me that _____ own name_ as Attorney_ in fact. of _____ and _____

WITNESS my hand and official seal.

Signature _____

_____
Name (Typed or Printed)

(This area for official notarial seal.)

← STAPLE HERE →

-7-

13. Guarantor warrants and represents to Lender that Guarantor has read this Guaranty and understands the contents hereof and this Guaranty is enforceable against Guarantor in accordance with its terms.

REAL ACRE HOLDINGS B.V.,
a Netherlands corporation
c/o Myron Meyers, Esq.
Meyers, Stevens & Walters
Professional Corporation
Suite 9100
6300 Wilshire Boulevard
Los Angeles, California 90048

By _____
Its Attorney in Fact

NOTE: This form can easily be adapted to be an Individual Guaranty.

CAUTION. THIS IS A VERY BROAD FORM OF GUARANTY. IT IS TAILORED TO CALIFORNIA LAW ONLY. CONSULT LOCAL COUNSEL IN USING ANY GUARANTY.

FORM - CONSTRUCTION CONTRACT

MULTI-STORY RESIDENTIAL GUARANTEED MAXIMUM PRICE

CONSTRUCTION CONTRACT

THIS CONTRACT is entered into this _____ day of April, 1981 by and between CALIFORNIA REAL ACRE, a California corporation, hereafter referred to as "Owner", whose address is 6300 Wilshire Boulevard, Suite 9100, Los Angeles, California 90067, and BUILDCO, INC., a California licensed contractor, with California License No. _____, whose address is 1000 First Avenue, Growth, California 90000, hereafter referred to as "Contractor".

RECITALS

A. Owner owns that certain real property commonly known as _____ Growth, California (hereinafter referred to as "said real property"). Said real property is legally described as set forth upon Exhibit "A" attached hereto and made a part hereof.

B. Owner desires to have constructed upon said real property an apartment complex containing _____ units, indoor community recreation facilities, a swimming and therapy pool, and parking facilities for vehicles (all hereinafter referred to as "the improvements") in strict accordance with the plans and specifications therefor which have been signed by both the Owner and Contractor and are

1.

made a part hereof (hereinafter referred to as "said plans and specifications").

C. Owner and Contractor desire that Contractor furnish all labor, materials, building permits, equipment, and services necessary to complete the improvements, all in accordance with the terms and conditions of this Agreement.

NOW, THEREFORE, in consideration of the mutual agreements herein, and for other good and valuable consideration, it is hereby agreed between the parties hereto, as follows:

1. Contractor agrees to furnish all labor, materials, building permits, equipment and services necessary to diligently perform and complete the improvements upon said real property in a good and workmanlike manner in strict accordance with said plans and specifications and all governmental laws, ordinances, regulations and the like applicable thereto. Contractor further agrees to pay as a cost of the work all applicable governmental taxes, fees, charges or licenses, pertaining to the construction of the improvements.

2. Contractor acknowledges having fully examined said plans and specifications which have been approved by the local governmental Building Department having jurisdiction over the construction of the improvements. Contractor will, prior to the commencement of work, bring any conflict in said plans and specifications, insofar as any such conflict is known to Contractor, to the attention of Owner, and Contractor will follow Owner's instructions respecting the resolution of any such conflict.

2.

3. Construction of the improvements is being financed by a construction loan to be made by a bank or savings and loan association (hereinafter referred to as the "Lender"). Contractor agrees, after its independent review, to comply with the loan documents of the Lender insofar as applicable to the Contractor and, notwithstanding any other terms of this Agreement, to abide by, comply with, and accept payment in accordance with all of said loan documents, including, without limitation, the building loan agreement. If after Contractor's independent review, Contractor cannot agree to comply with the terms of the loan documents, Owner shall attempt to have said loan documents modified. If Owner is unable to have said loan documents modified, then either party can terminate this Contract without liability to either party. Contractor shall not start construction until after the loan documents have been recorded and the loan has been funded and Contractor has verified same.

4. All materials supplied by Contractor shall be new, of acceptable quality, and in accordance with said plans and specifications. Contractor shall furnish, exclusive of independent testing, at its own cost and expense, reasonable verification of the grade or quality of materials he is using in his work, if requested by Owner.

5. Owner is employing V. Bright, AIA (hereinafter referred to as the "Architect") to be Owner's agent and representative in connection with this Agreement and the construction of the improvements.

6. The Owner agrees to reimburse Contractor for the cost of the work as defined in paragraph 8 of this Agreement,

3.

(hereinafter referred to as the "cost of the work"), and in addition, pay to the Contractor a fee of $_____ (hereinafter referred to as the "Contractor's Fee").

7. Unless otherwise agreed by Owner, Contractor shall obtain 3 competitive bids for all work which will be subcontracted by Contractor. Said bids will be obtained from individuals and entities approved by Owner and Architect. All subcontracts shall conform to said plans and specifications. Owner and Architect shall review all bids, and may, in their sole discretion and at their election, request a fourth competitive bid from a party mutually acceptable to Owner, Architect and Contractor. Owner, upon the advice of Architect and Contractor, shall designate which bids shall be accepted. Based upon said bids which are to be accepted, Contractor shall submit a guaranteed maximum price (excluding the Contractor's fee) which, when accepted by Owner, will be the Guaranteed Maximum Cost. Any modifications, alterations and changes resulting in a change in cost will change the guaranteed maximum cost accordingly. Upon completion of the construction of the improvements, the final actual cost will be determined. If the final actual cost is less than the guaranteed maximum cost, the difference between the final actual cost and the guaranteed maximum cost shall be divided ___% to Owner, ___% to Contractor.

8. The term Cost of the Work shall mean costs necessarily incurred in the proper performance of the Work and paid by the Contractor. Such costs shall be at rates not higher than

4.

of all materials, supplies, equipment, temporary facilities, and hand tools not owned by the Workers, which are consumed in the performance of the Work, and cost less salvage value on such items used but not consumed which remain the property of the Contractor.

(g) Rental charges of all necessary machinery and equipment, exclusive of hand tools, used at the site of the Work, including installation, minor repairs and replacements, dismantling, removal, transportation and delivery costs thereof, at rental charges consistent with those prevailing in the area.

(h) Cost of premiums for all bonds and insurance which the Contractor is required by the Contract Documents to purchase and maintain.

(i) Sales, use, gross receipts or similar taxes which are directly attributable and which taxes are imposed by any governmental authority.

(j) Permit fees, royalties, damages for infringement of patents and costs of defending suits therefor, and deposits lost for causes other than the Contractor's negligence.

(k) Losses and expenses, not compensated by insurance or otherwise, sustained by the Contractor in connection with the Work, provided they have resulted from causes other than the fault or neglect of a principal or managing representative, including superintendents, of the Contractor. Such losses shall include settlements made with, the written

6.

the standard paid in the locality of the Work except with prior consent of the Owner, and shall include the following:

(a) Wages paid for labor in the direct employ of the Contractor in the performance of the Work under applicable collective bargaining agreements, or under a salary or wage schedule agreed upon by the Owner and Contractor, and including such welfare or other benefits, if any, as may be payable with respect thereto.

(b) Salaries of Contractor's personnel when stationed at the field office, in whatever capacity employed. Personnel engaged, at shops or on the road, in expediting the production or transportation of materials or equipment, shall be considered as stationed at the field office and their salaries paid for that portion of their time spent on this Work.

(c) Cost of contributions, assessments or taxes incurred during the performance of the Work for such items as unemployment compensation, social security, safety engineering accruals insofar as such cost is based on wages, salaries, or other remuneration paid to employees of the Contractor as set forth in Subparagraphs (a) and (b).

(d) Cost of all materials, supplies and equipment incorporated in the Work, including costs of transportation thereof.

(e) Payments made by the Contractor to Subcontractors for Work performed pursuant to subcontracts under this Agreement.

(f) Cost, including transportation and maintenance

5.

consent and approval of the Owner. No such losses and expenses shall be included in the Cost of the Work for the purpose of determining the Contractor's Fee. If, however, such loss requires reconstruction and the Contractor is placed in charge thereof, he shall be paid for his services a Fee proportionate to that stated in Paragraph 6.

(1) Minor expenses such as telegrams, long distance telephone calls, telephone service at the site, and similar petty cash items in connection with the Work.

(m) Cost of removal of all debris.

(n) Costs incurred due to an emergency affecting the safety of persons and property.

(o) Other costs incurred in the performance of the Work if and to the extent approved in advance in writing by the Owner.

(p) Cost of warranty (pickup) Work not to exceed the sum of $ _____ .

9. The term Cost of the Work shall not include any of the following items:

(a) Salaries or other compensation of the Contractor's personnel at the Contractor's principal office and branch offices.

(b) Expenses of the Contractor's principal and branch offices other than the field office.

(c) Any part of the Contractor's capital expenses, including interest on the Contractor's capital employed for the Work.

7.

(d) Except as specifically provided for in Subparagraph 8(g) or in modifications thereto, rental costs of machinery and equipment.

10. Owner reserves the right to in any way revise the drawings, plans, specifications and/or general conditions and any completed portions of such improvements. With respect thereto:

(a) Contractor shall, but only upon written order of Owner, comply with such revisions and/or make such changes, which writing shall constitute an amendment to this Agreement.

(b) The consideration for performance of such revisions or changes shall be on the basis of the Cost of the Work as defined in Paragraph 7, provided no consideration shall be required as to which there shall be no additional cost to the Contractor.

(c) The Contractor's Fee shall be adjusted by agreement in writing between Owner and Contractor.

(d) The time for performance of this Contract shall be increased for any delay resulting from any revisions in the drawings, plans, specifications or the general conditions or causes set forth in the general conditions.

(e) If any revisions in the drawings, plans, specifications or general conditions change the cost of the project, the guaranteed maximum cost will be adjusted accordingly.

11. All cash discounts shall accrue to the Contractor unless the Owner deposits funds with which to make payments, in which case the cash discounts shall accrue to the Owner. All trade discounts, rebates and refunds, and all returns from sale of surplus materials and

8.

equipment shall accrue to the Owner, and the Contractor shall make provisions so that they can be secured.

12. Owner will pay Contractor on a monthly basis as follows:

(a) Contractor will make an application for payment which will be submitted to the Architect and Owner on the first day of each month. Said application will include releases for all labor and materials, and such other documents and information as required by lender.

(b) Within five (5) business days after receipt of Contractor's application, the Architect based upon the information supplied to him by the Contractor, the Architect's observations and inspections of the Work, and other information brought to the Architect's attention, shall certify the amount of payment due to Contractor, provided that:

(i) all work including all subcontracted work, has been done in strict compliance with said plans and specifications; and

(ii) that all Work has been inspected, tested, and approved by all governmental authorities as required under any and all applicable laws, ordinances, rules and regulations.

(c) The issuance of a Certificate shall constitute a representation by the Architect that the Work has progressed to the point indicated, that the quality of the Work is in

9.

accordance with said plans and specifications and that the Contractor is entitled to payment in the amount certified.

(d) If the Architect withholds his Certificate in whole or in part, the Architect shall notify the Contractor and Owner of the reasons for withholding the Certificate within five (5) business days of receipt by the Architect of the Contractor's application. If the Contractor, the Architect and Owner cannot agree on a revised amount, the Architect will promptly issue a Certificate for Payment for the Amount for which he is able to make such representations to the Owner.

(e) The Architect may also decline to certify payment or, because of subsequently discovered evidence or subsequent observations, he may nullify the whole or any part of any Certificate for Payment previously issued, to such extent as may be necessary in his opinion to protect the Owner from loss because of:

(i) defective work not remedied;

(ii) third party claims filed or reasonable evidence indicating probable filing of such claims, provided, however, that if contractor elects to provide a bond against any said third party claim, which bond is in a form and an amount acceptable to Owner and Lender, then in such event payment is not to be withheld;

10.

contained herein or in any of Lender's documents, and except as provided in subparagraphs 12 (i) and 12 (j), ten percent (10%) of any amounts which would otherwise be due and payable from time to time to Contractor shall be retained, which retention shall be paid upon full and final completion of the improvements. For purposes hereof, "full and final completion of the improvements" shall occur when all of the following events have taken place:

(i) The improvements have been fully and finally completed as determined by said Lender and Owner;

(ii) All labor and materials have been furnished pursuant to said plans and specifications;

(iii) The improvements have been fully and finally accepted as completed by all governmental authorities having jurisdiction thereof and all written acceptances have been issued, including, if applicable, a temporary Certificate of Use and Occupancy.

(iv) The time period for the filing of any and all mechanic's lien claims and stop notices have, in the judgment of the Owner, Lender, and insuring title company, expired; and

12.

(iii) failure of the Contractor to make payments properly to Subcontractors on for labor, materials or equipment,

(iv) reasonable evidence that the Work cannot be completed for the unpaid balance of the Guaranteed Maximum Cost;

(v) damage to the Owner or another contractor;

(vi) reasonable evidence that the Work will not be completed within the Contract Time, or

(vii) persistent failure to carry out the Work in accordance with the Contract Documents. When the above grounds are removed, payment shall be made for amounts withheld because of them.

(f) Within five (5) business days of the delivery of the Certificate by the Architect to the Owner and the Lender, Owner shall request the Lender to immediately pay the certified amount to the Contractor.

(g) Notwithstanding anything to the contrary contained in this Paragraph, and in addition to all other conditions contained herein, no payment will be made until all conditions for payment which are imposed by the Lender have been met, which shall be determined in the Lender's sole discretion.

(h) Notwithstanding anything to the contrary

11.

(v) Contractor has performed all the terms of this Agreement.

(i) Notwithstanding anything to the contrary contained herein, payment for structural steel material will be paid when the material is received by the fabricator, provided that the Lender's security interests therein are fully protected in the Lender's sole discretion, and that the material is fully covered by insurance.

(j) Notwithstanding anything to the contrary contained herein, Owner, in his sole discretion, and at his election, may release a portion or all of the 10% retained on account of any subcontract, provided that:

(i) the Lender consents; and,

(ii) the payments from which 10% has been retained have been fully certified by the Architect; and

(iii) there have been no applications for payment which have not been certified, and

(iv) the Contractor is not otherwise in default under this Agreement.

(k) If Lender so elects, in its sole discretion, Lender may make payments jointly to Contractor and his suppliers of material and/or labor.

13. Based upon the Foundation Report No. _____ prepared by _____ dated _____ Contractor has inspected the job site (being said real property) and acknowledges that there will be no extras

13.

---

attributable to grade, excavations, soil condition, utilities, drainage, or otherwise, and Contractor accepts the conditions of the job site as they presently exist.

14. Contractor shall commence work within five (5) days after notification by Owner and shall complete the improvements not more than _____ ( ) months after commencement. Estimated date of commencement is _____ Owner shall have the right to cancel and terminate this Agreement at any time prior to commencement of work by Contractor, without liability of any kind or nature.

15. Contractor shall make no alterations or deviations from said plans and specifications. It is conclusively presumed that all work performed by Contractor is included in the aforementioned Guaranteed Maximum Cost and Contractor's Fee unless Owner has signed a written extra work order specifying additional consideration to be paid. The only person authorized to sign extra work orders on behalf of Owner is Steve Elghanayan or such other persons as he shall designate in writing. No oral order will be considered as a waiver of this or any other provision of this contract.

16. Contractor shall protect the improvements as work progresses and shall complete same in broom-clean condition. If Contractor fails to do so, Owner or the Lender may withhold payment until the same has been accomplished or, in the alternative, Owner may contract such work to be done and hold Contractor responsible for the costs thereof.

14.

17. Notwithstanding that any labor or material furnished and installed by Contractor shall have been approved or accepted by Owner or any governmental agency, Contractor expressly warrants all labor, material and fixtures to be free of any defects whatsoever, and further:

(a) Contractor covenants he will promptly replace or repair, as Owner in its sole judgment shall direct, any and all such labor and/or material and/or fixtures which shall evidence defects at any time within one (1) year after (i) completion of improvements or (ii) that such improvements shall be put to use by the Owner or its successor, whichever date shall later occur, but in no event more than _____ ( ) months after completion of improvements (except as to air-conditioning units which shall be limited to one (1) year), and Contractor will pay any inspection fees imposed by any governmental agency in connection therewith.

(b) The warranties and covenants of the Contractor herein are expressly made for, and shall inure to the benefit of, the Owner and its successors in interest.

(c) The warranties of the Contractor herein shall not limit or otherwise affect other warranties or guarantees made by the Contractor or any of its subcontractors or materialmen and shall not be deemed to waive or limit such remedies as may be afforded by law.

Provided, however, that if the plans and specifications, or either thereof, call for a longer period of guarantee, then said longer period shall control.

18. (a) The Contractor shall purchase and maintain such insurance as will protect him from claims set forth below which

15.

may arise out of or result from the Contractor's operations under this Agreement, whether such operations be by himself or by any Subcontractor or by anyone directly or indirectly employed by any of them, or by anyone for whose acts any of them may be liable:

(i) claims under worker's or workmen's compensation, disability benefit or other similar employee benefit acts;

(ii) claims for damages because of bodily injury, occupational sickness or disease, or death of his employees;

(iii) claims for damages because of bodily injury, sickness or disease, or death of any person other than his employees;

(iv) claims for damages insured by usual personal injury liability coverage which are sustained (1) by any person as a result of an offense directly or indirectly related to the employment of such person by the Contractor, or (2) by any other person;

(v) claims for damages, other than to the Work itself, because of injury to or destruction of tangible property, including loss of use resulting therefrom; and

(vi) claims for damages because of bodily injury or death of any person or property

16.

amounts as may be agreed upon by Owner and Contractor, with
the consent of Lender.

(b) Owner shall purchase and maintain earthquake and flood insurance for the Work. Said insurance shall
be in such amounts as Owner and Contractor may agree upon,
with the consent of Lender.

(c) The Contractor, the Lender, the Architect
and all Subcontractors and/or materialmen shall be named as
additional insureds, as their interests may appear, only under
the policy of insurance required by this paragraph 19.

(d) Owner shall have the power to adjust and
settle any losses covered by the insurance provided under this
paragraph 19, on such terms and conditions as Owner may decide
in his sole discretion. All deductible requirements under the
policies of insurance shall be at Owner's expense.

(e) Owner shall file a copy of all policies
with the Contractor before an exposure to loss may occur.

(f) Owner may, in his sole discretion, purchase
such other insurance for the Work and Project as Owner desires
Said insurance shall be in such amounts as Owner may decide in
his sole discretion.

18.

---

damage arising out of the ownership,
maintenance or use of any motor vehicle.

(b) The insurance required by this paragraph
18 shall be written for not less than limits of liability as
agreed upon by Owner and Contractor with the consent of Lender.

(c) The Owner, the Lender, and the Architect
shall be named as additional insureds, as their interests may
appear, under the policies of insurance required by this paragraph 18.

(d) Certificates of Insurance acceptable to
the Owner shall be filed with the Owner prior to commencement
of the Work. These Certificates shall contain a provision that
coverages afforded under the policies will not be cancelled until at least thirty (30) days' prior written notice has been
given to the Owner and Lender.

(e) The Contractor shall purchase and maintain
such other insurance in such form and amounts as may be required
by Lender.

19. (a) Owner shall purchase and maintain property
insurance upon the entire Work at the site. This insurance shall
insure against the perils of fire and extended coverage and shall
include "all risk" insurance for physical loss or damage, including, without duplication of coverage, theft, vandalism and
malicious mischief, but shall not include any coverage for any
property of the Contractor or any Subcontractor whether said
property is at or off the site. This insurance shall be in such

17.

20. Contractor shall be responsible for loss or damage to materials or fixtures until full and final completion of the improvements (as defined herein) and shall at all times be responsible for all loss or damage to Contractor's own tools and equipment, and for all damage done by Contractor or Contractor's workmen or employees to property or work of others on the job.

21. Contractor agrees to indemnify, hold harmless, and forever defend Owner, Owner's directors, officers, agents, employees, heirs, personal representatives, successors and assigns, and said real property. from and against any and all claims, liabilities, loss, damages, mechanic's liens, other liens, stop notices, causes of action, costs, expenses, attorney's fees. and any other matters, which in any way relate to or arise out of, directly or indirectly, the execution and delivery of this Agreement or the performance by Contractor hereunder. Any defense provided by Contractor pursuant to this Paragraph 22 shall be by counsel satisfactory to Owner, provided, however, such approval by Owner shall not be arbitrarily or unreasonably withheld. If Owner rejects any proposed Counsel, Owner shall give Contractor written notice thereof, with the reasons therefor. Contractor agrees that within two (2) days notice from Owner of the filing of any mechanic's liens or stop notices to have the same discharged and released and, in the event of the failure of Contractor to do so, Owner may cause the same to be discharged and

19.

released and, in the event of the failure of Contractor do so so, Owner may cause the same to be discharged and the expense thereof, and Owner's reasonable attorneys' fees in connection therewith, shall be charged to and paid by Contractor, provided, however, in the event that Contractor has provided a bond against any mechanic's lien and stop notices in such form and amount acceptable to Owner and lender, then in such event Owner shall have no right to cause the same to be discharged and released.

22. Whenever reasonably requested by Owner, Contractor shall file with Owner or the Lender a verified statement in writing, in form satisfactory to Owner, certifying the amounts then due and owing from Contractor for labor and materials furnished hereunder, stating the names of the persons whose charges and/or claims are unpaid and the amount due to each. Before final payment is made, Contractor will execute such general release and waiver of lien and submit such evidence that no unpaid claims exist for labor, material, or other obligations incurred by Contractor, as Owner shall require.

If Contractor fails to meet and pay all of his just obligations incurred in performance of this Contract, or if any liens, claims or demands arising out of or in connection with the work of his performance shall be outstanding, Owner shall have the right to withhold out of any payments, final or otherwise, such sums as Owner may deem ample to protect it against loss and, at Owner's option, to apply such sums as

20.

Owner deems proper to secure protection and/or to satisfy such claims. Such application shall be deemed payments for Contractor's account.

23. If Contractor fails to perform any of its obligations hereunder, or if Contractor fails to proceed with the construction with all reasonable diligence and without interruption, Owner may, at Owner's option, give Contractor written notice to correct such defect or default, and if Contractor shall fail to make such correction within five (5) business days after receipt of said notice, Owner may terminate this Contract five (5) days after giving Contractor written notice of Owner's intention to do so, and Owner shall have no further obligation to Contractor hereunder. In such event, Owner may cause another licensed contractor to complete the improvements and Contractor shall be liable for the cost of such completion and for any other costs, damages or liabilities suffered by Owner as a result of said default on the part of Contractor. All determinations by Owner as to the existence of a default hereunder entitling Owner as to the existence of a default hereunder entitling Owner to terminate this Contract or take any other action shall be conclusive upon Contractor.

24. If any proceedings are instituted by or against the Contractor under the Bankruptcy Act, which proceedings are not terminated within seven (7) days after the institution thereof, or if Contractor makes an assignment for the benefit of creditors, or if a receiver is appointed to take possession

21.

of all or any portion of the assets of Contractor and said receiver does relinquish possession within seven (7) days after the taking thereof, then, and in any such event, Owner shall have the option to terminate this Agreement by giving twenty-four (24) days' prior written notice of termination to Contractor. In such event, Owner shall have the same rights and remedies as set forth in paragraph 15 above. If the Work is stopped for a period of ninety (90) days under an order of any court or other public authority having jurisdiction, or as a result of an act of government, such as a declaration of a national emergency making materials unavailable, through no act or fault of the Contractor or a Subcontractor or their agents or employees or any other persons performing any of the Work under a contract with the Contractor, or if the Work should be stopped for a period of thirty (30) days by the Contractor because the Architect has not issued, except for just cause, a Certificate for Payment, or because the Owner has not made, except for just cause, payment thereon, then the Contractor may, upon seven (7) additional days' written notice to the Owner and the Architect, terminate the Contract and recover from the Owner payment for all Work executed and for any proven loss sustained upon any materials, equipment, tools, construction equipment and machinery, including reasonable profit and damages.

25. The Contractor shall check all materials, equipment and labor entering into the Work and shall keep such full and detailed accounts as may be necessary for proper and financial management under this Agreement, and the system shall be

22.

Contractor hereunder. Any attempt by Contractor to do so shall be a nullity and shall constitute a default hereunder giving Owner the right to terminate this Contract by the giving of written notice of termination, as aforesaid.

30. Owner shall not be liable to Contractor for any delay or loss or damage to Contractor's work from any cause whatsoever, unless such delay, loss or damage is attributable solely to acts or omissions of Owner.

31. The parties agree Owner is not acting as a Contractor as defined under the laws of the State of California.

32. Time is of the essence of each term of this Agreement.

33. Owner and Contractor recognize that the plans and specifications contain general conditions of the Contract for construction, and supplementary general conditions. To the extent that the plans and specifications and other documents are in conflict with any provision or terms of this Contract, Owner and Contractor agree that the terms of this Contract shall control and be binding on Owner and Contractor. There are no oral agreements and all prior negotiations are superseded hereby.

34. Whenever used in this Agreement, words in the singular include the plural, and those in the plural the singular, as the case may be; words in the masculine, feminine or neuter gender shall mean one of the other, as the case may be.

35. Owner's waiver of any provision of this Agreement shall not operate as a future or further waiver by Owner,

24.

---

satisfactory to the Owner. The Owner shall be afforded access to all the Contractor's records, books, correspondence, instructions, drawings, receipts, vouchers, memoranda and similar data relating to this Contract, and the Contractor shall preserve all such records for a period of three (3) years, or for such longer period as may be required by law, after the final payment.

26. If any dispute should arise between the parties hereto as to any matter herein referred to, Contractor shall continue to perform such work as directed by Owner notwithstanding such dispute is not then settled. Notwithstanding anything to the contrary contained herein, if the subject of the disputes is monies due to Contractor for performance under this Contract, and if such sum in dispute shall exceed $_____ then Contractor shall not be required to continue performance under this Contract until said dispute has been settled.

27. Any notice under this Contract may be given by certified mail, return receipt requested, at the addresses above set forth. Such addresses may be changed by written notice given by one party to the other. Notice shall be deemed given one (1) day after mailing, as aforesaid, postage prepaid.

28. If either party shall employ counsel to enforce any of the provisions hereof, the prevailing party shall be entitled to reasonable attorneys' fees.

29. Contractor may not transfer, assign or hypothecate this Contract or any rights granted or payments due

23.

(d)   The Arbitrator shall determine which party shall bear the costs of arbitration.

(e)   The rules of arbitration of the American Arbitration Association shall apply and be binding upon Owner and Contractor.

(f)   Pendency of hearing of arbitration proceedings and/or the arbitration award shall not authorize Contractor to suspend or delay performance of its obligations hereunder, except as provided in Paragraph 27 of the Contract.

41.   This Agreement shall be binding upon, and shall inure to the benefit of, the respective heirs, personal representatives, successors and assigns, of the parties hereto; provided nothing herein shall permit Contractor to enter into any assignment hereof or of the rights granted or payments due Contractor hereunder.

IN WITNESS WHEREOF, the parties hereto have executed this Agreement as of the date first above written.

OWNER: CALIFORNIA REAL ACRE,
                a California corporation

                By: _____

CONTRACTOR: BUILDCO, INC.,
                a California corporation

                By: _____

26.

---

nor a waiver of any remedy reserved to Owner.

36.   This Agreement may be executed in counterparts, and each counterpart shall be deemed to be an original.

37.   Contractor represents and warrants to Owner that Contractor is duly licensed to perform all obligations of the Contract to be performed. Breach hereof shall constitute a default entitling Owner to terminate this Contract as hereinabove provided. Contractor shall be entitled to no compensation hereunder for any period during which Contractor is not licensed to perform its obligations hereunder.

38.   Should a dispute arise between Owner and Contractor concerning the interpretation or performance of this Agreement, said dispute may be settled by arbitration as hereinafter provided:

(a)   Either Owner or Contractor may, by five (5) days' notice to the other, elect arbitration. In the event of such election, the matter shall be submitted to the Los Angeles office of the American Arbitration Association, which Association shall appoint one (1) arbitrator within ten (10) days from notice to it by either Owner or Contractor.

(b)   Said arbitrator shall, at his election, take relevant evidence and, in any event, shall rule and settle all disputes within thirty (30) days from his appointment.

(c)   The award of the arbitrator shall be final and binding upon all parties and may be entered as judgment in any competent court.

25.

ABSOLUTE AND SPECIFIC ASSIGNMENT OF RENTS AND PROFITS

THIS INDENTURE, made this..................................day of..., 19........., by the undersigned Owner. whose address is hereinafter set forth, is collectively and individually hereinafter referred to as "Owner," for the benefit of referred to hereinafter as "Lender." Lender has heretofore loaned to owner or Owner's predecessor-in-interest certain sums more fully set forth in the promissory notes and deeds of trust described in Exhibit "B," attached hereto, and which promissory notes are secured by said deeds of trust, which deeds of trust constitute first liens on the real property described in Exhibit "A," attached hereto.

WITNESSETH:

1. For good and valuable consideration, the undersigned owner of the real property described in Exhibit "A," attached hereto, which is encumbered or to be encumbered by the afore-described deeds of trust, hereby sells, assigns and transfers absolutely to Lender, its successors and assigns, all rents, issues and profits due, or to become due, crops and produce of, on and from the said real property, and hereby transfers and sets over unto Lender, its successors and assigns, all leases, tenancies and contracts, oral and written, now or hereafter existing, in connection with said real property, the improvements now or hereafter placed or constructed thereon, and/or any existing or future leases, tenancies, royalties, and/or any other monies, income, rents, issues or profits arising therefrom. Lender is hereby given full power and authority to operate, maintain, manage and lease said premises, to compromise, modify or enforce the terms, covenants and conditions of all existing and/or future leases on said premises, or any part thereof, to take possession of said premises, or any part thereof, in its own name, or in the name of an agent, or in the name of Owner, collect all of the rents, issues and profits, and apply any sums realized as hereinafter set out. Owner expressly authorizes tenants, lessees, and all others having any interest in the said premises to pay to Lender, or its agent or order, all sums due, or to become due, under leases, contracts and agreements, heretofore or hereafter made, and Lender is hereby authorized to give, for and in behalf of Owner, full receipt and acquittance for any payment so made.

2. Lender is further authorized, but shall not be obligated to pay taxes, assessments and charges on the premises, insure, repair and/or improve the buildings located thereon, and expend such sums as may be necessary to defend title, or property, or use thereof, or recover rents and profits, or protect rental rights, and/or make such other expenditures for said property as it may in its sole discretion deem necessary, proper, or expedient. Lender may, but shall not be obligated to, advance funds for any of the above purposes, and any amount so advanced shall be a first and prior claim on the rents and profits realized from the said property, and shall be repaid to Lender before any distribution, as hereinafter set out. Should the rents and profits be insufficient to pay advances so made by Lender, any unpaid balance shall become a part of the debt secured by the afore-described deeds of trust and shall bear interest at the maximum legal rate from date of advancement; and in the event such advancments are made after the deed of trust debt has been reduced to judgment, Owner shall pay advancements, with interest, to Lender in addition to any amount necessary to pay and satisfy the judgment, interest and costs or to redeem the property from foreclosure sale, either private or judicial. However, nothing contained herein shall give Owner any right to redeem not heretofore given to Owner or allowed by law.

Lender shall be entitled to retain possession of the property until such advancements and inte rest are fully paid.

The Lender shall be required to account for only such rentals and payments as are actually collected by it. Nothing herein contained shall be deemed to create any liability on the part Lender for failure to rent the premises, or any part thereof, or for failure to make collection of rentals, or for failure to do any of the things which are authorized herein. This instrument is an absolute grant of rights and privileges to Lender and shall not be held to create any duties or liabilities except as herein expressly set out. For the purpose of accounting the books and records of Lender shall be deemed prima facie correct.

3. Unless the Lender gives Owner written notice to the contrary, the Lender shall in the exercise of its control and management of the premises be deemed the agent of Owner. Lender shall not be liable for any damage to any person or property where such damage arises out of the operation of, or in connection with, the said premises.

4. The acceptance by Lender of any payment or performance under any lease or other contract with reference to the said premises, from any tenant or other person, shall not bar nor abridge any of the rights of Lender under its deed of trust against such tenant or person.

5. This agreement, and the rights given to and for the Lender thereunder, shall remain in full force and effect so long as the indebtedness secured by the above-described deeds of trust or any other security agreements, or any extension or renewal thereof, or any sums secured thereby, including, but not limitd to, additional sums advanced or loaned to Owner, whether or not evidenced by another promissory note or notes, remain unpaid and, in the event of foreclosure, whether by private sale or court action, during any period of redemption and until the recording of the deed issued under such foreclosure proceedings and until delivery of actual and complete possession of the premises to the grantee in such deed. This agreement shall not affect Owner's right to redeem from foreclosure sale; but such redemption shall not terminate this agreement unless and until said debts secured by the said deeds of trust or other security agreement or any judgment rendered thereon, plus interest, costs, attorney's fees and expenses and any advancements made by Lender, with interest as above mentioned, have been fully paid. In the event of termination of this agreement, Owner shall approve and accept any and all outstanding leases made by Lender or its agent.

6. The provisions of this agreement are a covenant running with the land herein described and shall bind all persons hereafter acquiring any interest in the said premises; and it is expressly agreed that the within assignment and grant of rights and powers is coupled with an interest.

7. Any amount received or collected by Lender by virtue of this agreement shall be applied as follows, (but not necessarily in the order stated); the priority of payment of such items to be within the sole discretion of Lender:

7.1. To the repayment to Lender of any and all amounts advanced by it under the terms of this agreement, the said deeds of trust or other security agreement, together with interest at the highest legal rate on the respective advancements from the date of the same.

7.2. To the payment of taxes, assessments and charges and the expense of insurance, repairs to and improvements on the property; but Lender shall not be obligated to keep insurance on, make repairs to and/or improvements on the property.

7.3. To the payment of all other necessary expenses of management, protection and/or preservation of the property.

7.4. To the payment of all amounts due, or to become due, under the said deeds of trust, or any sums secured thereby, including, but not limited to, additional sums advanced or loaned to Owner, whether or not evidenced by another promissory note or notes, or any extension or renewal thereof and/or to the payment of any judgment rendered thereon, together with interest, costs and expenses.

7.5. The surplus, of any, after full payment of the above, shall be paid to the then Owner of record of the said premises.

8. It is understood that this agreement shall not be deemed payment of the afore-described obligations secured by said deeds of trust, or other security agreement, except as to money actually received by Lender for its sole use and is applied as such payment; nor shall this agreement be deemed a waiver of any default occurring hereafter in the full performance of the conditions of the said deeds of trust or promissory notes; nor shall the application of any money received by Lender under this agreement toward curing such default in any manner waive such default or prevent foreclosure because of the same, there being hereby reserved to Lender all its rights and privileges under the said promissory notes and deeds of trust as fully as though this agreement had not been entered into.

9. Lender shall not be liable for any act or failure to act under the terms of this agreement, except for wilfull misconduct or gross negligance, nor shall Lender be liable for the act or omission of any agent.

10. This instrument is a present and executed assignment of rents, issues and profits and a present and executed grant of the powers hereinbefore granted to Lender. It is agreed that if the Owner is permitted to collect any of said rents, issues or profits (which permission is not granted or conferred by this paragraph) that the same is at the sufferance of Lender, at its discretion, and that such sufferance shall in no way be deemed a waiver by Lender of any of its rights hereunder and may be revoked at any time; provided, however, that in no event shall Owner have authority to collect any rents, issues or profits for more than forty-five days in advance, and; provided further, that if a petition in bankruptcy, or any other proceedings under the jurisdiction of the Bankruptcy Act or related statutes of the United States is filed by or against Owner, or if any proceeding is instituted for the reorganization of Owner or the adjustment of the obligations of Owner, or if Owner makes any assignment for the benefit of creditors, or if an application for a Receiver is filed against Owner which will or may affect the said premises, then upon the happening of any one or more of such events, Lender shall be deemed to have then and at that time terminated such sufferance and agency without notice or other action and may thereafter manage and control and be deemed in possession of said real estate and improvements and collect the rents, issues and profits to the full extent of all rights given it under this agreement. The exercise of any and all of the rights of Lender is not conditional upon the default by Owner of any of the terms, covenants and conditions contained in the promissory notes and/or the deeds of trust, or other instruments executed by Owner in favor of Lender.

11. This agreement shall not be termintaed, except as herein provided, nor shall it be altered, modified or amended, except by written agreement.

12. This agreement shall be binding on and shall inure to the benefit of the parties hereto and their respective heirs, personal representatives, successors and assigns.

13. Where the terms "foreclosure" or "foreclosure sale" or "redemption from foreclosure," or similar words are used in this instrument, same shall mean the rights of private sale authorized under the terms and provisions of the deeds of trust above referred to and/or any sale by judicial foreclosure under the applicable provisions of the laws of the State of California.

14. The words "premises" or "property," or similar words used in this instrument, shall be deemed to include the real property described in Exhibit "A" attached, all improvements now or hereafter existing thereon, and all leases, rents, issues and profits arising or accruing therefrom, or from the use and/or occupancy thereof.

15. This agreement is made for and on behalf of Lender and for its use and benefit. It is acknowledged that Lender is relying on this agreement and the execution of same is a material inducement to Lender.

16. Should suit be instituted to enforce any of the provisions hereof the Lender, in addition to any other sums awarded, shall be entitled to reasonable costs and attorney's fees.

17. In this instrument, whenever the context so requires, the masculine gender includes the feminine and/or neuter, and the singular number includes the plural.

IN WITNESS WHEREOF, the parties have executed this instrument the day and year first above written.

OWNER: ....
ADDRESS: ....
....

OWNER: ....
ADDRESS: ....
....

Author's Note: The information contained in this Appendix was abstracted from two articles published in the September/October 1978 and the November/December 1979 issues of the Lawyer's Supplement to the GUARANTOR, published by Chicago Title. The information contained was printed with the permission of the GUARANTOR. The cooperation of Hugh A. Brodkey, Esq., Vice President and Associate General Counsel of Chicago Title Insurance Company is gratefully acknowledged.

Caveat: The information contained is current only to legislation adopted prior to July 1, 1979. Since activity in this area is increasing, a review of the current laws of each state must be made and the reader should not rely upon the information contained in this Appendix.

SUMMARY BY STATE
(Alphabetical)

1. Alabama.

A. Aliens: Bona fide resident aliens are constitutionally authorized to possess, enjoy and inherit "property" on same basis as native born citizens. Ala. Const., art. 1, §34. Non-resident aliens are statutorily authorized to take and hold, by purchase, descent or devise and to similarly dispose of real and personal property on same basis as native citizens. Ala. Code §34-1-1 (1975).

B. Corporations: No express restrictions on alien corporations or alien-controlled corporations. Statutory definition of foreign corporation may be broad enough to include alien corporation. See, Ala. Code §10-2-2(2) (definition of foreign corporation), §10-2-160(4) (powers of domestic corporation), §§10-2-230 et.seq. 256 (foreign corporation code) (1975).

2. Alaska.

A. Aliens: No express restrictions, except with respect to exploration and mining rights in state-owned lands. Alienage no bar to inheritance. Alas. Stats. §13.11.060 (1977).

District judges and magistrates are required to file with the Commissioner of Commerce a copy of each recorded conveyance which states that the property is conveyed to or for the benefit of a nonresident alien. Alas. Stat. §22.15.110(4) (1977).

Territorial laws concerning ownership of land by aliens appear to have been terminated on June 30, 1961. Alaska Statehood Act, Pub. L. 85-508, §8(d), 72 Stat. 339 (1958) and Alaska Omnibus Act, Pub. L. 86-70, §3, 73 Stat. 141 (1959).

B. Corporations: Alien corporations statutorily treated as foreign corporations. Alas. Stat. §10.05.597 (reference to foreign "country"). Upon qualification, foreign corporations enjoy same rights and privileges as domestic corporations, including powers to buy and sell real property. Alas. Stat. §10.05.009 (powers of domestic corporation), §10.05.603 (powers of foreign corporation) (1962). Alien corporations and alien-controlled corporations restricted in ownership of exploration and mining rights in state-owned lands.

C. Exploration and Mining Rights in State-Owned Lands: May be acquired or held only by U.S. citizens at least 19 years of age (or their guardians or trustees), persons at least 19 years of age who have declared their intention to become U.S. citizens, aliens at least 19 years of age whose home country grants reciprocal treatment, associations of the above persons, and certain corporations. To be qualified, a corporation must be organized under the laws of a State or territory of the United States, and no more than 50 percent of its stock may be owned or controlled by aliens who could not own directly. Alas. Stats. §38.05.190 (1973).

3. Arizona.

A. Aliens: No express restrictions. Alienage is no bar to inheritance. Ariz. Rev. Stat. §14-2112 (1974).

B. Corporations: Statutory definition of foreign corporation may be broad enough to include alien corporation. Ariz. Rev. Stat. §10-002(11) (definition of foreign corporation) (1974). See also Ariz. Const. art. 14, §15 (reference to the "country" of a foreign corporation). Upon qualification, foreign corporations enjoy same rights and privileges as domestic corporations, including powers to buy and sell real property. Id., §10-004(4) (powers of domestic corporation), §10-107 (powers of foreign corporation).

4. Arkansas.

A. Aliens: No distinction can constitutionally be made between resident aliens and citizens in regard to the possession, enjoyment or descent of property. Ark. Const. art. 2, §20. "All aliens" are statutorily authorized to take, hold, alienate and devise real property interests and alienage is no bar to descent. Ark. Stat. Ann. §50-301 (1971). Ark. Stat. Ann. §61-143 (1971) (alienage no bar to inheritance).

B. Corporations: Alien corporations are statutorily treated as foreign corporations. Ark. Stat. Ann. §64-102(B) (reference to foreign corporation), §64-1201 (reference to foreign "country") (1971). Foreign corporations are not expressly granted or denied the power to acquire and deal with real property.

C. Public Lands: Alien is not eligible to obtain a deed to tax-forfeited agricultural land from the state until naturalized. Ark. Stat. Ann. §10-926 (Replacement 1976).

D. Arkansas Agricultural Foreign Investment Act (Act 1096 of 1979): Effective April 19, 1979, acquisition of any interest in "agricultural land" in Arkansas by a "foreign party" must be registered with the Circuit Clerk of the county where the land is located. Special records are kept by the Circuit Clerk and by the Secretary of State. "Foreign party" includes nonresident aliens, foreign governments, entities created under the laws of a foreign government and domestic entities in which a "significant interest" or "not insubstantial control" is directly or indirectly held by any of the proscribed foreign parties. Failure to report may result in an action by the Attorney General resulting in an order requiring divestiture

-3-

within 2 years and a penalty of up to 25% of the value of the property. The Act does not apply to agricultural land already owned by "foreign parties" prior to the effective date of the Act nor to aliens who are bona fide residents of the United States. Section 9 of the Act confirms the right of all aliens to own real estate "except agricultural land."

5. California.

A. Aliens: "Noncitizens have the same property rights as citizens." Cal. Const. art. 1, §20 (Deering's Supp. 1978). (An earlier constitutional provision granting more restricted rights to resident foreigners was repealed on November 5, 1974, the same date as the adoption of Section 20. See, Cal. Const. art. 1, §17 (Deering's 1974).) By statute, any person "whether citizen or alien" is authorized to take, hold and dispose of real property. Cal. Civ. Code §671 (Deering's 1954). But see reference below to Public Lands.

B. Corporations: Statutory definition of foreign corporation may be broad enough to include alien corporation. Cal. Corp. Code §171 (Deering's 1977). The power of foreign corporations to deal with real estate is recognized. Id., §08(e) (possible compiler's misprint for §208(c)). But see reference below to Public Lands.

C. Public Lands: Leases and prospecting permits on public lands can be issued only to and held by persons and associations of persons who are citizens of the U.S. or who have declared the intention of becoming citizens or whose country grants such rights by reciprocity or who are granted the right by treaty. Alien corporations are not eligible unless 90% or more of the shares owned by eligible persons or corporations. Cal. Public Resources Code §6801 (Deering's 1976).

6. Colorado.

A. Aliens: Bona fide resident aliens are authorized to acquire, inherit, possess, enjoy and dispose of real property the same as native born citizens. Colo. Const. art. II, §27. "No person" is disqualified to take as an heir, devisee, grantee, lessee, mortgagee, assignee or "other transferee" because he or a person through whom he claims is or has been an alien. Colo. Rev. Stat. §15-11-112 (as amended 1977).

-4-

B. Corporations: Alien corporations statutorily treated as foreign corporations. Colo. Rev. Stat. §7-9-107(a) (reference to foreign "country"). Upon qualification, foreign corporations enjoy same rights and privileges as domestic corporations, including powers to buy and sell property. Id., §7-3-101(d) (powers of domestic corporation), §7-9-104 (powers of foreign corporation).

7. Connecticut.

A. Aliens: Those aliens "resident in the United States" are authorized to purchase, hold, inherit or transmit real estate. Conn. Gen. Stats. Rev. §47-58 (Supp. 1978). French citizens enjoy same rights as U.S. citizens so long as France grants reciprocal right. Id. Non-resident aliens are only authorized to acquire and hold real estate for quarrying and mining and developing products of such quarries and mines subject to forfeiture if not used for 10 years. Id., §47-57; Pavlick v. Meriden Trust & Safe Deposit Co., 141 Conn. 471, 107 A.2d 262 (1954). Where a legatee, distributee, cestui or beneficiary is not resident within the U.S. and would not have the benefit or use or control of property due him, it may be subject to control by order of the probate court. Conn. Gen. Stats. Rev., §45-278 (Supp. 1977-78). Unless otherwise specified by treaty, real estate devised to or which would be inherited by an alien not a resident of the U.S. shall be ordered sold and the net proceeds of the sale distributed to the alien. Conn. Gen. Stats. Rev. §45-249 (Supp. 1978).

B. Corporations: Alien corporations statutorily treated as foreign corporations. Conn. Gen. Stats. Rev. §33-284(j) (definition of foreign corporation), §33-284(u) (definition of "state" includes foreign country) (Supp. 1978). Upon qualification, foreign corporations enjoy same rights and privileges as domestic corporations. §33-401 (powers of foreign corporation) (1958). A domestic corporation has the power to acquire and exercise rights of ownership in and to real property "except to the extent otherwise provided in, and subject to the limitations contained in, its certificate of incorporation or in any law affecting it . . ." Id., §33-291(e). Additionally, a foreign corporation is authorized to purchase, hold, mortgage, lease, sell and convey real estate "for its lawful uses and purposes" without having to qualify to transact business. Id., §33-397 (Supp. 1977).

8. Delaware.

A. Aliens: Aliens are authorized to take, acquire, hold and dispose of real property in the same manner as a citizen of the

-5-

state. Del. Code tit. 25, §306 (1974). Alienage no bar to title by descent. Id., tit. 25 §307.

B. Corporations: Alien corporations are treated as foreign corporations. Del. Code tit. 8, §371(a) (definition of foreign corporation), and deeds made by alien corporations and foreign corporations are specifically declared to be valid to same extent as deeds of lawfully created and existing domestic corporations. Foreign corporations may exercise same rights and privileges of ownership as domestic corporations. Id., tit. 25, §305.

9. District of Columbia.

A. Aliens: Aliens are authorized to acquire, hold, own and dispose of real estate in the District of Columbia to the extent authorized to do so in U.S. territories. D.C. Code Ann. §45-1501 (1973). See also, 48 USC §1508. These territorial rights are defined by 48 U.S.C. §§1501-1507, but §1502 states that these sections "shall not be construed to prevent any persons not citizens of the United States from acquiring or holding lots or parcels of lands in any incorporated or platted city, town or village." This section was specifically applied to property in the District of Columbia. Larkin v. Washington Loan and Trust Co., 31 F2d 635 (D.C. Cir. 1929). Alienage of an ancestor is no bar to title by descent. D.C. Code Ann. §19-321 (1973).

B. Corporations: Alien corporations statutorily treated as foreign corporations. D.C. Code Ann. §29-902(b) (definition of foreign corporation), §29-902(o) (definition of "state" includes foreign country) (1973). Upon qualification, foreign corporations enjoy same rights and privileges as domestic corporations. Id. §29-933(a). Domestic corporations may not be organized specifically "to buy, sell, or deal in real estate, except corporations to transact the business ordinarily carried on by real estate agents or brokers." Id., §29-201. An alien corporation is a "person" for purposes of acquiring and holding real property in D.C. under §1502 quoted above. Larkin v. Washington Loan and Trust Co., 31 F.2d 635 (D.C. Cir. 1929).

C. Legations: The ownership of legations and residences by representatives of foreign governments or attaches was specifically permitted at a time when prior law restricted foreign ownership; this permission still appears in the D.C. Code Ann. §45-1505 (1973).

-6-

10. **Florida.**

A. *Aliens:* The Florida constitution states that "aliens ineligible for citizenship" may be subjected to regulation or prohibition in their ownership, inheritance, disposition and possession of real property. Fla. Const. art. 1, §2 (1968 Rev.). No statutory restriction presently exists, however. Alienage no bar to inheritance. Fla. Stats. Ann. §732.1101 (Supp. 1977).

B. *Corporations:* Alien corporations statutorily treated as foreign corporations. Fla. Stats. Ann. §607.004(2) (definition of foreign corporation), §607.34(1) (reference to foreign "country") (1977). Upon qualification, foreign corporations enjoy same rights and privileges as domestic corporations, including powers to buy and sell real property. Id., §607.011(2)(b) (powers of domestic corporation), §607.307 (powers of foreign corporation).

11. **Georgia.**

A. *Aliens:* Aliens are specifically accorded privilege of purchasing, holding and conveying real estate, so long as their government is at peace with the United States. Ga. Code Ann. §§79-302, -303 (1973). Aliens may receive and enforce liens on real estate. Ga. Code Ann. §79-304 (1973).

B. *Corporations:* Statutory definition of foreign corporation may be broad enough to include alien corporation. Ga. Code Ann. §22-102(b) (1973). Upon qualification, foreign corporations enjoy same rights and privileges as domestic corporations, including powers to buy and sell real property. Id., §22-202(b) (5) (powers of domestic corporation), §22-1402 (powers of foreign corporation).

12. **Hawaii.**

A. *Aliens:* No express restrictions. Alienage is no bar to inheritance. Haw. Rev. Stat. §560:2-107 (1976).

B. *Corporations:* Alien corporations statutorily treated as foreign corporations. Haw. Rev. Stat. §418-1 (reference to foreign "country") (1976). Upon qualification, foreign corporations have power to hold, take and convey real property. Id., §418-7.

C. *Public Lands:* Purchase or lease of residence lots on Oahu from the Board of Land and Natural Resources is restricted to citizens or declarant aliens. Haw. Rev. Stat. §206-9 (1976).

NOTE: Prior restrictions on alien ownership contained in Territorial Laws terminated automatically two years after admission of Hawaii to statehood. Hawaii Statehood Act of 1959, Publ. L. 86-3, §15, 73 Stat. 4 (1959). Restrictions related to public lands may not have been so affected. Atty. Gen. Op. 61-68.

13. **Idaho.**

A. *Aliens:* Aliens are authorized to take, hold and dispose of real property. Ida. Code §55-103 (1957). But see reference below to Public Lands. Alienage no bar to inheritance. Id., §15-2-112 (Supp. 1975).

B. *Corporations:* Alien corporations constitutionally treated as foreign corporations. Ida. Const. art. 11, §10. See also, Ida. Code §30-101(2) (definition of foreign corporation) (1957). Upon qualification, foreign corporations enjoy same rights and privileges as domestic corporations, including powers to buy and sell real property. Id., §30-510 (powers of foreign corporations), §30-114(2)(d) (powers of domestic corporations).

C. *Public Lands:* Sale of State lands restricted to U.S. citizens and those who shall have declared their intention to become such. Ida. Code §58-313 (1976).

14. **Illinois.**

A. *Aliens:* "All aliens" are authorized to acquire, hold, inherit, alienate, sell, assign, incumber, devise and convey lands, but they must dispose of such lands within six years (or, if under age of 21, within 6 years of reaching 21), unless during the interim the alien obtains U.S. citizenship. Ill. Rev. Stats. ch. 6, §§1, 2 (Smith-Hurd Supp. 1978). Penalty is sale by state with proceeds going to the state. Id., §2. Aliens affirmatively authorized to acquire and hold personal property to same extent as natural born citizens. Id., §7 (Smith-Hurd 1975). Alien landlords are prohibited from including the payment of taxes as part of the direct or indirect rent due on lease of farmlands. Id., §9.

B. *Corporations:* Alien corporations statutorily treated as foreign corporations. Ill. Rev. Stats. ch. 32, §157.2-2 (definition of foreign corporation), §157.106 (reference to foreign "country") (Smith-Hurd, 1975). Upon qualification, foreign corporations enjoy same rights and privileges as domestic corporations.

Id., §157.103, §157.5(d) (powers of domestic corporation, including powers to buy and sell property), §157.7 (dealing in real estate a valid corporate purpose).

C. Agricultural Foreign Investment Disclosure Act (Public Act 81-187, 1979): This act requires the filing of a report with the Illinois Director of Agriculture as to any holding and any acquisition or transfer of any interest in agricultural land by a "foreign person." The definition of a "foreign person" and many of the provisions of the act are similar to those in the federal Agricultural Foreign Investment Disclosure Act of 1978 (AFIDA). A copy of the report required by the federal act will satisfy the requirements of the Illinois Act (P.A. 81-187 Section 6). The penalty for failure to file a proper report is coordinated with AFIDA so that aggregate penalties under the two acts does not exceed 25% of the fair market value of the property. While AFIDA requires reports concerning leaseholds of 10 years or more, the Illinois statute applies to leaseholds of more than 5 years. Regulations for carrying out the act are to be promulgated by the Director of Agriculture no later than 90 days after the date of enactment (August 14, 1979) and reporting requirements become effective at that date.

15. Indiana.

A. Aliens: Natural persons who are either resident or non-resident aliens are authorized to acquire by purchase, devise or descent and to hold, enjoy, convey, devise, transmit or encumber real estate with same effect as state or U.S. citizens. Ind. Code Ann. §32-1-8-1 (1973). Unless the alien becomes a citizen, property in excess of 320 acres must be disposed of within 5 years (or within 5 years of alien reaching age 18) under penalty of escheat. Id., §32-1-8-2. All real property acquired by an alien through enforcement of a lien or debt may have to be divested within 5 years. See, Id., §32-1-7-1 and §32-1-7-3. Alienage of an ancestor is no bar to inheritance. Id., §32-1-8-1.

B. Corporations: Alien corporations statutorily treated as foreign corporations. Ind. Code Ann. §23-1-1-1(b) (definition of foreign corporation), §23-1-11-4(1) (reference to foreign "country") (1974). Upon qualification, foreign corporations enjoy same rights and privileges as domestic corporations. Id., §23-1-11-2, §23-1-2-2(b) (4) (powers of domestic corporation, including powers to buy and sell real property). In dealing with alien corporations and alien-controlled corporations, consideration should be given,

-9-

however, to the provision which limits corporate powers to those possessed by "natural persons" and to such purposes as are "not repugnant to law". Id., §23-1-2-2(a) and (b).

16. Iowa.

A. Aliens - Ownership: Effective January 1, 1980, the basic Iowa law concerning the right of aliens to acquire and deal with land - Chapter 567 of the Iowa Code - is amended in its entirety. House File 148 (approved June 10, 1979, but effective January 1, 1980) sets out the following rights for a nonresident alien, a foreign government and a "foreign business" (defined as including a corporation formed under the laws of a foreign country or any business entity "in which a majority interest is owned directly or indirectly by nonresident aliens"). A nonresident alien, foreign business or foreign government may acquire real property except "agricultural land" by grant, purchase, devise or descent and may own, hold, devise or alienate the property. Id., §3. These entities "or an agent, trustee or fiduciary thereof" are prohibited from acquiring agricultural land in the state beyond what is held on the effective date of the statute. Id., §4(1). Agricultural land not exceeding 320 acres may be acquired "for an immediate or pending use other than farming." (Id., §4(2)) and such conversion of use must take place within 5 years. Id., §5. During that time, farming can take place only by leasing the property to a person or entity not under a disability created by this statute or by the Corporate Farming statute, §172C.4 of the Iowa Code. Id., §3. Land acquired by a nonresident alien, foreign business or foreign government or an agent, trustee or fiduciary thereof by devise or descent after the effective date of the act must be divested within 2 years. Id., §6. If an alien or business entity acquires agricultural land after the effective date of the statute and later becomes a "nonresident alien" or a "foreign business," the land must be divested within 2 years. Id., §7. Ownership and acquisition of agricultural land by the proscribed persons and entities must be registered with the Secretary of State (Id., §8) and land acquired for an immediate or pending use other than farming is subject to periodic reports. (Id., §9). Holding land in violation of the act may result in a proceeding to declare an "escheat" of the property to the state with the land being sold through judicial sale and the proceeds of the sale in excess of court costs being paid to the person divested of the property "but only in an amount not exceeding the actual cost paid by the person for that property"; excess proceeds go to the county. Id., §§10, 11. Penalty for failure to file the registration or reports when required is a fine of not more than $2,000.

-10-

B. Corporations: Section 491.67 of the Iowa Code, dealing with the right of alien corporations and corporations formed in the U.S. with alien stockholders has been repealed (House File 148, §13, effective January 1, 1980). Note, however, the references to corporations in the other parts of this updated Iowa summary.

C. Corporations and Trusts - Moratorium on Acquisition or Lease of Agricultural Land (House File 451, Approved April 20, 1979): Effective January 1, 1980, the temporary moratorium on acquisition or leasing of agricultural land by corporations or trusts (established by Sec. 172C.4, of the Iowa Code and due to expire August 15, 1980) is made permanent. Only designated kinds of corporations and trusts may acquire agricultural land; the list of exempt transactions remains the same. The wording of §172C.7, requiring a report to be filed by every person acting in a fiduciary capacity or as trustee on behalf of "any corporation, limited partnership or nonresident alien individual; holding agricultural land, was amended to strike the word "individual" (House File 451, Section 2).

17. Kansas.

A. Aliens: State constitution provides that "(t)he rights of aliens in reference to the purchase, enjoyment or descent of property may be regulated by law." Kan. Const. Bill of Rights §17(1889). There is now no express right of ownership granted to aliens except in the area of will and descent. By statute, aliens "eligible to citizenship under the laws of the United States" may "transmit and inherit" real estate in the same manner and to the same extent as citizens of the U.S. "All other aliens" may "transmit and inherit" only as provided by federal treaty. Kans. Stat. Ann. §59-511(1977).

B. Corporations: Alien corporations are statutorily treated as foreign corporations. Kans. Stat. Ann. §17-7301(a) (Supp. 1977) (definition of foreign corporation), §17-7305(c) (1974) (reference to "foreign country"). Upon qualification, foreign corporations are "subject to the same provisions, judicial control, restrictions and penalties ... as corporations organized under the laws of this state." Id., §17-7305(c). See restrictions below on Corporate Farming.

C. Corporate Farming: Agricultural and horticultural business cannot be carried on by corporations other than domestic corporations meeting certain requirements as to the number and type of stockholders. The incorporators must be natural persons

residing in the state and the ownership and control of land is limited to 5,000 acres. Foreign and domestic corporations organized for mining purposes can engage in agricultural and horticultural activity on land used for coal strip mining. Kans. Stat. Ann. §17-5901 (1974). Certain annual reports are required. Id., §17-5902.

18. Kentucky.

A. Aliens: Alien declaring intention to become citizen of U.S. and who is not an enemy may recover, inherit, hold and pass real property by descent, devise or otherwise as if he were a citizen of the state. Ky. Rev. Stats. Ann. §381.290 (Baldwin 1970). If citizenship not acquired 8 years from property's acquisition, property may escheat. Id., §381.300. "Any alien, not an enemy" may take and hold any personal property except chattels real; resident aliens may take and hold lands for residence for business, trade or manufacture purposes, and then only for a period not exceeding 21 years. Id., §381.320. Special rules apply for the alien spouse or child of a U.S. citizen. Id., §381.310. Nonresident aliens can hold property acquired by descent or devise for only 8 years. Id., §381.330. Alienage is no bar to disposition of property by conveyance, descent or devise. Id., §381.340, §381.300(2).

B. Corporations: Alien corporations statutorily treated as foreign corporations. Ky. Rev. Stat. Ann. §271A.010(2) (definition of foreign corporation). Upon qualification, foreign corporations enjoy same rights and privileges as domestic corporation. Id., §271A.525; §271A.020(4) (powers of domestic corporation, including powers to buy and sell real property). No corporation may hold real estate, except such as is "proper and necessary for carrying on its legitimate business" for longer than 5 years, under penalty of escheat. The escheat action is preceded by a notice requiring disposition of the property by the corporation within two years. Id., §271A.705 (Supp. 1976).

19. Louisiana.

A. Aliens: No express restrictions. See, La. Const. of 1921, art. 19, §21, not carried forward in La. Const. of 1974.

B. Corporations: Alien corporations statutorily treated as foreign corporations. La. Stat. Ann. §12:1(k) (definition of foreign corporation), §12:301 (reference to foreign "country") (1969). Upon qualification, foreign corporations enjoy same rights and privileges as domestic corporations, including powers to buy and sell real property. Id., §12:41(B)(4) (powers of domestic corporation), §12:306(2) (powers of foreign corporation).

20. Maine.

A. Aliens: Aliens are authorized to "take, hold, convey and devise" real estate. Me. Rev. Stat. Ann. tit. 33, §451 (1978). If a person dies intestate while "not an inhabitant" of Maine, the decedent's real estate descends "according to the laws of (Maine)," and the personal estate descends according to the laws of the country of which he was an inhabitant. Id., tit. 18 §901.

B. Corporations: Statutory definition of foreign corporation may be broad enough to include alien corporation. Me. Rev. Stat. Ann. tit. 13A, §102(11) (1978). Upon qualification, foreign corporations enjoy same rights and privileges as domestic corporations, including powers to buy and sell real property. Id., tit. 13A, §202(I) (powers of domestic corporation), §1204 (powers of foreign corporation).

21. Maryland.

A. Aliens: Any alien who is not an enemy is authorized to own, sell, devise, dispose of and deal with "property" the same as citizens of the state by birth. Md. Real Prop. Code, §14-101 (1975).

B. Corporations: Alien corporations statutorily treated as foreign corporations. Md. Corp. Code, §1-101(1) (1975). Foreign corporations are not expressly granted or denied the power to acquire and deal with real property.

22. Massachusetts.

A. Aliens: Aliens are authorized to take, hold, transmit and convey real property and no title to real property is invalid on account of the alienage of a former owner. Mass. Gen. Law Ann. ch. 184, §1 (1970). Payments of a "legacy or distributive share" to a person domiciled in a country where there is not a reasonable assurance that the distributee will actually receive payment in substantially full value, may be subject to certain restrictions. Id., ch. 206, &27B (1958).

B. Corporations: Statutory definition of foreign corporation may be broad enough to include alien corporation. Mass. Gen. Law Ann. ch. 181, §1 (1977). The power of foreign corporations to own real estate is recognized. Id., ch. 181, §3.

-13-

23. Michigan.

A. Aliens: Resident aliens are constitutionally accorded the same rights and privileges in property as state citizens. Mich. Const. art. X, §6. "Any alien" is statutorily authorized to acquire, hold, purchase, inherit, convey, mortgage and devise land the same as state or U.S. citizens. Mich. Comp. Laws Ann. §§26.1105, .1106 (1970). Alien status is no bar to dower. Mich. Comp. Laws Ann. §26.237 (1970).

B. Corporations: Alien corporations statutorily treated as foreign corporations. Mich. Comp. Laws Ann. §21.200 (107)(2) (definition of foreign corporation), §27.200 (1016)(1) (reference to "foreign language") (1974). Upon qualification, foreign corporations enjoy same rights and privileges as domestic corporations, including powers to buy and sell real property. Id., §21.200 (26i) (f) (powers of domestic corporation), §21.200 (1002) (powers of foreign corporation).

24. Minnesota.

A. Aliens: No natural person shall acquire directly or indirectly any interest in agricultural land unless he be a citizen of the U.S. or a permanent resident alien. Minn. Stat. Ann. §500.221(2) (Supp. 1977-78). An "interest in agricultural land" is defined as including a leasehold interest. Id. §500.221(1). Agricultural land acquired by someone other than a citizen or permanent resident alien by devise, inheritance or through collection of debts or enforcement of a lien or claim must be disposed of within 3 years after acquisition. The general prohibition is expressly inapplicable where contrary to treaty rights. Agricultural land used for transportation purposes or acquired for mining purposes or research or experimental purposes is exempt from the prohibition. Id., §500.221(2). Penalty for noncompliance is forced divestiture of the land or, if not divested within one year from date of divestiture order, forced public sale. A prospective or threatened violation may be enjoined on petition of the attorney general. Id., §500.221 (3). Prestatute acquisitions unaffected, except for certain reporting requirements. Id., §500.221(4). Alienage of a former owner is no obstacle to title. Id., §500.221(3). (Note that former section 500.221(1), containing 90,000 square foot limitation, was repealed by laws 1977, ch. 269, §2.)

B. Corporations: Alien corporations statutorily treated as foreign corporations. Minn. Stat. Ann. §300.02(6) (definition

-14-

C. Public Lands: Nonresident aliens, corporations (except certain banks) and "any association of persons composed in whole or in part of nonresident aliens" cannot, directly or indirectly, purchase or own public lands. Miss. Code Ann. §29-1-75 (1972).

26. Missouri.

A. Aliens: Nonresident aliens can acquire "real estate except agricultural land" by grant, purchase, devise and descent and can own, hold, devise, or alienate as if they were citizens of the U.S. and residents of the state. Mo. Rev. Stat. §442.560(1) (1978), §474.100 (1969). "Agricultural Land" is defined as a tract more than 5 acres whether inside or outside corporate limits, capable of supporting an agricultural enterprise. Id., §442.560(2) (1) (1978). Agricultural land now owned can be held by present owners. Id., §442.560(6). Additional agricultural land acquired by nonresident alien or land converted from nonagricultural use must be divested within 2 years or land will be subjected to public sale. Id., §442.560(4). Resident alien who ceases to be a bona fide resident of U.S. must similarly divest agricultural lands Id., §442.560(6). §442.566. §442.506(6) should read: §442.560. §442.586. §442.560(1) should read: §442.576. §442.560(6) should read: §442.560(4) should read: §442.586.

B. Corporations: Alien corporations are specifically authorized to acquire, own, hold and alienate "real estate except agricultural land". Mo. Rev. Stat. §442.560(1) (1978). A "Foreign Business", defined as any business entity regardless of form in which a controlling interest is owned by aliens, is prohibited from acquiring "agricultural land" after the effective date of the statute (August 13, 1978) and must divest any such land "within the minimum time required by Art. XI, Section 5 of the Missouri Constitution (10 years). Id., §442.560(4). Foreign business may retain agricultural lands already owned. Id., §442.560 (6). See also restriction on Corporate Farming. §442.560(1) should read: §442.566(4) and §442.576. §442.560(4) should read: §442.586. §442.560(6) should read: §442.586.

C. Corporate Farming: No corporation other than those specified by statutes can hold a direct or indirect interest in agricultural land or engage in farming. Mo. Rev. Stat. §360.010

of foreign corporation), §303.06(1) (reference to foreign "country"), §303.08(2) (reference to foreign "country") (1969). Upon qualification, foreign corporations enjoy same rights and privileges as domestic corporations, including powers to buy and sell real property. Id., §300.08(4) (powers of domestic corporation), §303.09 (powers of foreign corporation). No corporation, partnership, limited partnership, trustee or other business entity shall acquire, directly or indirectly, any legal or beneficial interest in "agricultural land", any legal or beneficial interest in "agricultural land", unless 80 per cent of each class of stock issued or of the ultimate beneficial interest is held directly or indirectly by U.S. citizens or permanent resident aliens. Minn. Stat. Ann. §500.221(2). This restriction is subject to the same exceptions noted above.

C. Corporate Farming: All corporations are prohibited from engaging in farming and from acquiring real estate capable of being used for farming, subject to certain exceptions. Minn. Stat. Ann. §500.24 (Supp. 1977-78). Among the exceptions are certain "Family farm corporations" and "Authorized farm corporatons" involving a requirement that some portion of the stockholders reside on the property. Id., §500.24(1)(c) and (d). Reports must be filed disclosing the names and addresses of all shareholders. Id., §500.24(3).

25. Mississippi.

A. Aliens: Constitution requires that the legislature "shall enact laws to limit, restrict, or prevent the acquiring and holding of land in (Mississippi) by nonresident aliens...". Miss. Const. art. 4, §84(19). By statute, resident aliens may acquire and hold land and may dispose of it and transmit it by descent as citizens of the state may. Nonresident aliens may not acquire or hold land except through the enforcement of a lien, in which case it can be held by the alien for no more than 20 years. Penalty for noncompliance is escheat. Miss. Code Ann. §89-1-23 (1974). Nonresident aliens who are citizens of Syria or the Lebanese Republic may inherit property from citizens or residents of Mississippi. Id. See also, Public Land below.

B. Corporations: Alien corporations statutorily treated as foreign corporations, Miss. Code Ann. §79-3-3(b) (definition of foreign corporation), §79-3-211 (reference to foreign "country") (1973). Upon qualification, foreign corporations enjoy same rights and privileges as domestic corporations. Id., §79-3-213; §79-3-7(d) (powers of domestic corporation, including powers to buy and sell real property).

et. seq. .030 (1975). Violations may result in a court-ordered sale of the interest. Id., §350.030. Annual reports are required. Id., §350.020.

D. *Aliens - Reports of Ownership, Acquisitions and Sales of Agricultural Land*: Senate Bill 34 of 1979 added Section 442.592 to the Revised Statutes of Missouri requiring that individual nonresident aliens, foreign governments, entities organized outside the U.S. or domestic entities "substantially controlled" by any of the described foreign persons, governments or entities, must report to the Director of Agriculture any interest held in agricultural land (including leaseholds of 10 years or more and beneficial interests under contracts). Similar reports must be filed for every acquisition and transfer. There is a civil penalty for failure to report, not to exceed 25% of the value of the interest.

27. Montana.

A. *Aliens*: Aliens are constitutionally authorized to acquire, purchase, possess, enjoy, convey, transmit and inherit mining property. Mont. Const. art. III, §25. A prior act defining the rights and disabilities of aliens with respect to land was declared unconstitutional by the Montana Supreme Court, but the legislature has not subsequently repealed the act or passed additional legislation defining the rights of aliens. State v. Oakland, 129 Mont. 347, 287 P. 2d 39 (1955). However, alienage is no bar to inheritance unless the country in which the heir resides does not allow reciprocity. Mont. Rev. Code Ann. §91A-2-111 (Spec. Pamphlet 1977).

B. *Corporations*: Alien corporations statutorily treated as foreign corporations. Mont. Rev. Code Ann. §15-2202(b) (definition of foreign corporation), §15-2299 (reference to foreign "country") (1974). §15-22-103(a) (reference to foreign "country") (1974). Upon qualification, foreign corporations enjoy same rights and privileges as domestic corporations. Id., §15-22-100, §15-2204(d) (powers of domestic corporation, including powers to buy and sell real property).

28. Nebraska.

A. *Aliens*: State constitution permits the regulation of the rights of aliens with respect to property. Neb. Const. art.1, §25 (1970). Aliens are prohibited from acquiring, title or holding interests in land except for land which lies within the corporate limits of a city or village or within 3 miles thereof and leases on any land for no more than 5 years. Neb. Rev. Stat. §§76-402, 76-414 (1976). Aliens are also permitted to purchase or lease

-17-

(as lessor or lessee) real estate necessary for the erection of manufacturing and industrial establishments or erecting and maintaining petroleum filling stations or bulk stations. Id., §§76-413, 76-414. Resident aliens may acquire real property by devise or descent but must dispose of it within 5 years under Penalty of escheat. Id., §76-405. The "escheat" involves a judicial forfeiture but requires a payment to the alien. Id., §76-408. The alien has the option of having a partition sale. Id., §76-409. Nonresident aliens may take by devise or descent only if under the law of the alien's home country, a reciprocal right exists for U.S. citizens, a U.S. citizen would receive payment in money from estates of persons dying in such country, and the alien would otherwise receive the benefit of the property or estate proceeds without confiscation by the foreign government. Id., §4-107. Land acquired through the enforcement of a lien or debt must be sold within 10 years under penalty of escheat. Id., §§76-411, 76-408. Neb. Rev. Stat. §30-2312 (1976) (limitation on right of nonresident alien to inherit, similar to §4-197).

B. *Corporations*: Corporations organized outside Nebraska are generally prohibited from land ownership, except for lands within city or village limits or within three miles thereof and leases on any lands for up to 5 years. Neb. Rev. Stat. §§76-402, 76-414 (1976). Any corporation, domestic or foreign, which is doing business in the state and which has aliens comprising a majority of the board of directors, or a majority of the capital stock of which is owned by aliens or which has an alien as an executive officer or manager will be treated as an alien individual for purposes of landholding. Id., §76-406, 76-407. Corporations of other states can own oil and gas leases for limited period. Id., §76-404. Restrictions do not apply to erecting of manufacturing and industrial establishments or erecting and maintaining petroleum filling stations or bulk stations. Id., §76-413. See Corporate Farming below.

C. *Corporate Farming*: In order to protect "the family farm against potential monopolization of the agriculture industry, and to protect against alien ownership of Nebraska agricultural land" corporations owning any interest in agricultural land must file an annual report with the Secretary of State disclosing the identity of officers, board members and shareholders owning 10% and specifically identifying those who are aliens. Id., §§76-1501 et. seq. 76-1506.

-18-

29. Nevada.

A. Aliens: Nonresident aliens are authorized to take, hold and enjoy real property on same terms as resident citizens. Nev. Rev. Stat. §111.055 (1973). Nonresident aliens' right to take by will or descent is dependent on reciprocal right in alien's country to take and receive payment. Id., §134.230.

B. Corporations: Any nonresident corporation may take, hold and enjoy real property on same terms as a domestic corporation. Nev. Rev. Stat. §111.055 (1973). (For broad powers of domestic corporations in relation to real property, see Id., §78.060 (2)(d).) Alien corporations statutorily treated as foreign corporations. Id., §80.010(1) (reference to foreign "country"), §80.040 (corporate documents in foreign language must be translated).

30. New Hampshire.

A. Aliens: An alien resident in the state may take, purchase, hold, convey or devise real estate; and it may descend in the same manner as if he were a citizen. N. H. Rev. Stat. Ann. §477.20 (1968). The New Hampshire Supreme Court has expressed the view that the Common Law restrictions apply to nonresident aliens and this statute would not be extended to permit nonresident aliens to inherit the property. Hanafin v. McCarthy, 95 N.H. 36, 37, 57 A.2d 148; 149 (1948); Lazarou v. Moraros, 101 N.H. 383, 143 A.2d 669 (1958).

B. Corporations: Alien corporations statutorily treated as foreign corporations. N.H. Rev. Stat. Ann §300:4(a) (reference to foreign "country") (1968). Foreign corporations are not expressly granted or denied the power to acquire and deal with real property other than a provision granting foreign manufacturing corporations the power to acquire, hold and convey real and personal property. Id., §300:1. The power of a corporation of another state to acquire property in New Hampshire has been recognized. Lumbard v. Aldrich, 8 N.H. 31 (1835).

31. New Jersey.

A. Aliens: "Alien friends" accorded same rights as native-born citizens with respect to real estate. N. J. Rev. Stat. §46:3-18 (Supp. 1975). Where it shall appear that legatee, heir or trust beneficiary would not have benefit, use or control of property due him, the court may order such property to be paid into the court and held for the benefit of such person. Id., §3A:25-10(1953). This statute could be applied in the case of nonresident alien heirs or devisees. See, In re Kish's Estate, 52 N.J. 454, 246 A.2d 1 (1968).

as foreign corporations. N.J. Rev. Stat. §14A:13-4(2) (reference to "foreign corporation). §14A:1-2(j), (definition of foreign corporation), §14A:1-2(j) (reference to "foreign language") (1953). Upon qualification, foreign corporations enjoy same rights and privileges as domestic corporations, including powers to buy and sell real property. Id., §14A:3-1(1)(d) (powers of domestic corporation), 14A:13-1 (powers of foreign corporation specifically relative to real estate).

32. New Mexico.

A. Aliens: State constitution prohibits aliens "ineligible to citizenship under the laws of the United States" from acquiring title, leasehold or other interest in real estate "unless otherwise provided by law." N. Mex. Const. art. 11, §22 as amended in 1921. By statute passed in 1975, "aliens" are authorized to acquire real estate by deed, will, inheritance or otherwise, to hold and to alienate, sell, assign and transfer real estate to heirs or other persons regardless of citizenship. N. Mex. Stat. Ann §45-2-112 (1978).

B. Corporations: Alien corporations statutorily treated as foreign corporations. N. Mex. Stat. Ann §53-11-1 (definition of foreign corporation), §53-17-1 (reference to foreign "country"), §53-17-5 (reference to foreign "country") (1978). Upon qualification, foreign corporations enjoy same rights and privileges as domestic corporations. Id., §§53-17-2, 53-11-4 (powers of domestic corporation including powers to buy and sell real property.) Constitutionally, no corporation, co-partnership or association, a majority of the stock or interest in which is owned or held by aliens "ineligible to citizenship" can acquire title, leasehold or other interest in real estate "until otherwise provided by law." N. Mex Const. art. 11, §22, as amended in 1921.

33. New York.

A. Aliens: Aliens are authorized to take, hold, transmit, and dispose of real property in the same manner as citizens. N.Y. Real Prop. Law §§10(2),11 (McKinney, 1968). Alienage of prior holder does not affect title. Id., §15. Foreign governments are empowered to hold, transmit and dispose of real property for the purpose of maintaining offices and places of residence for their ambassadors and consular officials. Id., §10(3). In appropriate circumstances a court may direct that the money or property due an alien beneficiary be paid into the court for the benefit of such beneficiary or other persons who may later become entitled to it. N.Y. Surr. Court Proc. Act §2218 (McKinney, Supp. 1975).

B. Corporations: Alien corporations statutorily treated as foreign corporations. N.Y. Bus. Corp. Law §1304(b) (corporate documents in foreign language must be translated) (McKinney, 1963). Foreign corporations authorized to acquire, hold and convey real property "in furtherance of its corporate purposes" the same as domestic corporations. Id., §1307.

34. North Carolina.

A. Aliens: Aliens are authorized to take by purchase and descent and to hold and convey lands as fully as state citizens. N.C. Gen. Stat. §64-1 (1975). The right of a nonresident alien to inherit real estate is dependent upon existence of reciprocal right of U.S. citizen in alien's resident country. Id. §64-3. In the absence of eligible heirs, the property escheats. Id., §64-5. N.C. Gen. Stat. §29-11 (1975) (limitation on right to nonresident alien to inherit, similar to §64-3).

B. Corporations: Alien corporations statutorily treated as foreign corporations. N.C. Gen. Stat. §55-2(4) (definition of foreign corporation), §55-138(a) (1) (reference to foreign "country"), §55-139(a) (reference to foreign "country") (1975). Upon qualification, foreign corporations enjoy same rights and privileges as domestic corporations, including powers to buy and sell real property. Id., §55-17(b) (1) (powers of domestic corporation), §55-132(a) (powers of foreign corporation).

C. Public Reports of Alien Ownership: Chapter 610, House Bill 1306 (1979) adds G.S. 64-1.1 directing the Secretary of State to collect and maintain a public file of "all information obtainable from reports by aliens made to agencies of the federal government on ownership of real property interests in North Carolina."

35. North Dakota.

A. Aliens: Aliens are authorized to take, hold and dispose of real property. N.D. Cent. Code Ann §47-01-11 (1960). Alienage is no bar to inheritance. Id., §30.1-04-12.

B. Aliens - Ownership of Agricultural Land: Aliens are now authorized to take, hold and dispose of real property with exceptions. N.D. Cent. Code Ann §47-01-11 (1960) as amended by HB 1209 enacted 1979. Under the 1979 Act (effective July 1, 1979), no interest in "agricultural land" (including a leasehold but not a mineral interest) may be acquired directly or indirectly by any person who is not a citizen of the U.S. or a citizen of Canada or a permanent resident alien. A partnership, limited partnership,

trustee, "or other business entity" may not obtain such an interest in any title to agricultural land unless the "ultimate beneficiary interest in the entity" is held directly or indirectly by citizens of the U.S. or permanent resident aliens. Agricultural property acquired by devise, inheritance or the enforcement of a debt or lien must be disposed of within 3 years. The register of deeds is prohibited from recording any deed in violation of the Act. The attorney general is empowered to bring an action to declare a violation at which point the non-qualified owner has one year to divest itself of the property. Failure to do so results in a public sale. Ineligible individuals and entities owning titles prior to July 1, 1979 may retain ownership but must file annual public reports. A violation of the Act is also a misdemeanor.

C. Corporations: Alien corporations statutorily treated as foreign corporations. N. Dak. Cent. Code Ann §10-19-02(2) (definition of foreign corporation), §10-22-05(1) (reference to foreign "country") (1976). Upon qualification, foreign corporations enjoy same rights and privileges as domestic corporations, including powers to buy and sell real property. Id., §10-19-04(4) (powers of domestic corporation), §19-22-02 (powers of foreign corporation). But see restriction below on Corporate Farming.

D. Corporate Farming: All corporations, domestic and foreign, are prohibited from engaging in farming and agriculture, N.D. Cent. Code Ann. §10-06-01 (1976). Statute exempts cooperative corporations 75% of whose members or stockholders are actual farmers residing on farms or depending principally on farming for their livelihood. Id., §10-06-04. Land used or usable for such purposes must be divested or be subjected to public sale with proceeds returned to corporation. Id., §§10-06-02, 10-06-03, 10-06-05, 10-06-06.

36. Ohio.

A. Aliens: Aliens are authorized to hold, possess and enjoy real property by descent, devise, gift or purchase as fully as U.S. or state citizens. O. Rev. Code Ann §2105.16 (1968).

B. Aliens - Reports of Acquisitions and Sales: O. Rev. Code Ann §5301.254, effective March 19, 1979, requires that non-resident aliens acquiring an interest in Ohio property in excess of 3 acres or that has a market value in excess of $100,000 or any mineral or mining rights must file a report with the Secretary of State. Sale of the interest must also be reported and the reports are to be made public. The statute requires that a similar report must be filed by each corporation "or other business entity" created or organized under the laws of any state or of a foreign nation or that has its principal place of business in a foreign nation and in which a nonresident alien acquires at least 10% of the stock in which an aggregate of 40% or more of the stock is owned by nonresident aliens. The penalty for failure to report is a fine of not less than $5,000 nor more than 25% of the market value of the property. Id., §5301.99(A).

C. Corporations: Alien corporations statutorily treated as foreign corporations. O. Rev. Code Ann. §1703.01(B) (definition of foreign corporation), §1703.01(C) (definition of "state" includes foreign country). Foreign corporations are not expressly granted or denied the power to acquire and deal with real property.

37. Oklahoma.

A. Aliens: State Constitution declares that aliens who are not U.S. citizens or bona fide Oklahoma residents are prohibited from acquiring or owning land and requires that the state legislature enact laws whereby nonresident aliens and their nonresident alien heirs must dispose of all property acquired by devise, descent or otherwise within 5 years under penalty of escheat. Okla. Const. art. 22, §1. Such statutes have been enacted. Okla. Stat. Ann tit. 60 §§121 et. seq. 127 (1971). The statutes assure resident aliens of the right to acquire and hold land on the same terms as citizens of the state provided that on ceasing to be a bona fide resident of the state, the alien must alienate the land within 5 years. Id., tit. 60, §122. A nonresident U.S. citizens has such rights to hold personal property as are accorded U.S. citizens by the laws of the nation to which the alien belongs or by treaty. Id., tit. 60, §121.

B. Corporations: By constitution and statute all corporations are prohibited from owning or holding real property other than that located in any incorporated city or town or any addition thereto. Corporations can hold such additional real estate as is "necessary and proper" for carrying on the business "for which it was chartered or licensed." Okla.Const. art. 22, §2 (Supp. 1977-78). See also, Okla. Stat. Ann tit. 18, §1.20(b) (1) (Supp. 1977-78), granting such power to carry on the business "for which any corporation has been lawfully formed or domesticated." However, "buying, acquiring, trading or dealing in real estate" outside cities and towns and their additions is not a lawful corporate purpose. Okla. Const. art. 22, §2. Farming and ranching is a legitimate

corporate purpose. LeForce v. Bullard, 454 P. 2d 297 (Okla. S. Ct. 1969). But see limitation on Corporate Farming noted below. "Any corporation" may, however, acquire real estate for sale or lease to any other corporation which is eligible to acquire such real estate. Okla. Const. art. 22, §2 (Supp. 1977-78); Okla. Stat. Ann. tit. 18, §1.20(b) (5) (Supp. 1977-78). Property acquired by a corporation outside an incorporated city or town or addition through foreclosure or the enforcement of a debt may be held for only 7 years. Id., and Okla. Stat. Ann tit. 18, §1.20(C) (Supp. 1977-78). Statutory definition of foreign corporation may be broad enough to include alien corporation. Okla. Stat. Ann tit. 18, §1.2(3) (1975). Upon qualification, foreign corporations enjoy same rights and privileges, but no greater, than a domestic corporation. Id., §1.199(d) (1953). Caution: The present Attorney General of Oklahoma has taken the position that corporations organized in another country are subject to the same limitations on land ownership as individual aliens. He has also expressed concern as to the ownership of land by U.S. corporations which are controlled by nonresident aliens. Opinion 79-286 (Sept. 12, 1979) withdrawing Opinion 74-211 (Jan. 30, 1974).

C. Corporate Farming and Ranching: Subsequent to June 1, 1978, the only entities which are permitted to own or lease any interest in land to be used for farming or ranching besides natural persons and the described corporations are certain types of trusts, partnerships and limited partnerships described by statute. Okla. Stat. Ann. tit 18, §955 A (Supp. 1978). Violation may result in enforcement of a fine or may constitute a misdemeanor. Id., §955 B. It is also ground for an action to require disposing of the land. Id., §956.

38. Oregon.

A. Aliens: No express restriction, except with respect to Public Lands.

B. Corporations: Alien corporations statutorily treated as foreign corporations. Ore. Rev. Stat. §57.004(7) (definition of foreign corporation), §57.655(1) (reference to foreign "country"). §57.675(1)(a) (reference to foreign "country") (1974). Upon qualification, foreign corporations enjoy same rights and privileges as domestic corporations, including powers to buy and sell real property. Id., §57.030(4) (powers of domestic corporation), §57.660 (powers of foreign corporation). See Corporate Farming Reports.

C. Public Lands: Applications for purchase of state land and the making of mining claims are limited to persons who are citizens of the U.S. or who have declared the intention to become a citizen. Ore. Rev. Stat. §§273.255, 517.010, 517.044 (1977).

D. Corporate Farming Reports: Corporations that engage in farming activities or that own or lease farmland must file additional information with their annual corporate reports disclosing, among other things, the name and address of each owner of 10% or more of voting shares. Id., §57,757 (1977). The requirement is effective January 1, 1978, and is repealed July 1, 1981. Oregon Laws 1977, ch. 49, §§13,14. The annual report required by Ore. Rev. Stat. §57.757 (1977) also requires disclosure of the name of each country other than the U.S. in which the corporation conducts farming or owns or leases farmland.

39. Pennsylvania.

A. Aliens: Aliens are authorized to purchase and hold real estate not exceeding 5,000 acres nor exceeding a net income of $20,000.00. Pa. Stat. Ann tit. 68, §32 (1965). Alienage no bar to inheritance. Id., tit. 20, §2104(8). Foreign governments are specifically prohibited from directly or indirectly acquiring or holding real estate. Id., tit. §21. Alienage is also no bar to testamentary disposition. Pa. Stat. Ann tit. 20, §218 (1975).

B. Corporations: Alien corporations statutorily treated as "Foreign Business Corporations." Pa. Stat. Ann tit. 15, §1002(8) (definition of Foreign Business Corporation), tit. 15, §2001(A) (reference to foreign "country") (Supp. 1977-78). "Foreign Business Corporations" are a type of "corporation for profit" and the acreage and earnings restrictions applicable to aliens were specifically repealed in so far as they relate to corporations for profit. Id., tit. 15, §203. Foreign business corporations, the activities of which do not constitute doing business in the Commonwealth, are also specifically empowered to acquire, hold, mortgage, lease and transfer real property. Id., tit. 15, §2012.

40. Rhode Island.

A. Aliens: Aliens are authorized to take, hold, transmit and convey real estate in the same way as if they were citizens of the U.S. R.I. Gen. Laws §34-2-1 (1956).

B. Corporations: Alien corporations statutorily treated as foreign corporations. R.I. Gen. Laws §7-1.1-2(b) (definition of foreign corporation), §7-1.1-99 (reference to foreign "country"), §7-1.1-103 (reference to foreign "country") (1956). Upon qualification, foreign corporations enjoy same rights and privileges as domestic corporations, including powers to buy and sell real property. Id., §7-1.1-4(d) (powers of domestic corporation), §7-1.1-100 (powers of foreign corporation).

41. South Carolina.

A. Aliens: Constitution requires General Assembly to enact laws limiting the number of acres which any alien or any corporation controlled by aliens may own within the state. S.C. Const. art. 3, §35. Legislation authorizes aliens to acquire, hold and dispose of real and personal property in the same manner as a natural born citizen, provided the alien may not own or control more than 500,000 acres. S.C. Code §27-13-10, §27-13-30 (1976). Property in excess of 500,000 acres acquired through foreclosure must be disposed of within 5 years unless additional period is granted. Id., §27-13-40.

B. Corporations: Alien corporations statutorily treated as foreign corporations. S.C. Code §33-1-20(c) (definition of foreign corporation), §33-1-20(u) (definition of "state" includes foreign country) (1976). Foreign corporations and corporations controlled by aliens authorized to deal with land to same extent as an alien. Id., §§27-13-10, 27-13-30.

42. South Dakota.

A. Aliens: Aliens are authorized to take, hold and dispose of real property. S. Dak. Comp. Laws Ann §43-2-9 (1967). Alienage no bar to inheritance. Id., §29-1-17.

B. Aliens - Ownership of Agricultural Land: Senate Bill 90 enacted in 1979 prohibits the acquisition of "agricultural land" exceeding 160 acres by any nonresident alien or foreign government, unless such right is granted by treaty. Agricultural land in excess of 160 acres acquired by such parties through the collection of debts must be disposed of within 3 years and a resident alien who ceases to be a bona fide resident of the U.S. has 3 years to dispose of agricultural land over 160 acres. Nonresident aliens acquiring agricultural land by devise or descent must alienate the land within 3 years. The penalty for violation of the Act is forfeiture of the land to the state through a proceeding by the Attorney General.

The Act confirms that alienage of a former owner does not affect the validity of a title.

The Act also mandates the Department of Agriculture to look for violations of the Act by monitoring the reports available under the United States Agricultural Foreign Investment Disclosure Act of 1978.

C. Corporations: Alien corporations statutorily treated as foreign corporations. S. Dak. Comp. Laws Ann §47-2-1(2) (definition of foreign corporation), §47-8-3 (reference to foreign "country"), §47-8-7(1) (reference to foreign "country") (1967). Upon qualification, foreign corporations enjoy same rights and privileges as domestic corporations, including powers to buy and sell real property. Id., §47-2-58(4) (powers of domestic corporation), §47-8-4 (powers of foreign corporation). But see restrictions below on Corporate Farming.

D. Corporate Farming: Subject to certain exemptions, no corporation is allowed to own, directly or indirectly, an interest in real estate used for farming or capable of being used for farming. S. Dak. Comp. Laws Ann §47-9A (Supp. 1977). Among the exemptions are corporations which owned or leased lands prior to July 1, 1974, Id., §47-9A05 "family farm corporations" and "authorized farm corporations" Id., §47-9A-13. Reports must be filed and may require disclosure of the names and address of all shareholders. Id., §§47-9A-16 and 17.

43. Tennessee.

A. Aliens: Aliens are authorized to take, hold, dispose of and transmit real property the same as native citizens. Tenn. Code Ann §64-201 (1976). Alienage no bar to devise or descent. Id., §64-202. There is, however, a special statute dealing with distribution of property when heirs or next of kin are aliens. Id., 31-401 (compare Id., §31-204).

B. Corporations: Alien corporations statutorily treated as foreign corporations. Tenn. Code Ann §48-102(m) (definition of foreign corporation), §48-1101(1) (reference to foreign "country") (Supp. 1977). Upon qualification, foreign corporations enjoy same rights and privileges as domestic corporations, including powers to buy and sell real property. Id., §48-402(c) (powers of domestic corporation), §48-103(3) (domestic corporate code applies to foreign corporations).

44. Texas.

A. Aliens: Aliens have same rights to real property as U.S. citizens. Tex. Rev. Civ. Stat. Ann art. 166a (Vernon's 1969). Tex. Probate Code §41(c) (Vernon's 1978 Supp.) (Alienage is no bar to inheritance).

B. Corporations: Private corporations are authorized to purchase only such lands as are "necessary to enable such corporations to do business" or to secure payment of debt. Surplus lands and lands acquired in payment of debt must be disposed of within 15 years from date of acquisition. Tex. Rev. Civ. Stat. Ann art. 1302-4.01, 4.02 (Vernon's Supp. 1978). Corporation whose main business purpose is the acquisition or ownership of land is prohibited from acquiring land. Id., art. 1302-4.04. But land within incorporated or unincorporated towns, cities and villages, or in their suburbs, can be leased, purchased, sold or subdivided by corporations chartered for that purpose. Id., art. 1302-4.05. Lands held contrary to any of these provisions are subject to "escheat" involving a condemnation sale with proceeds held for the benefit of the stockholders or person who owned the corporation. Id., art. 1302-4.06, 4.07.

45. Utah.

A. Aliens: No express restriction on alien land ownership. Alienage no bar to inheritance. Utah Code Ann §75-2-112 (1975).

B. Corporations: Alien corporations statutorily treated as foreign corporations. Utah Code Ann §16-10-2(b) (definition of foreign corporation), §16-10-102 (reference to foreign "country"), §16-10-106(a) (reference to foreign "country") (1975). Upon qualification, foreign corporations enjoy same rights and privileges as domestic corporations, including powers to buy and sell real property. Id., §16-10-4(d) (powers of domestic corporation), §16-10-103 (powers of foreign corporation).

46. Vermont.

A. Aliens: Right to acquire, hold and transfer land is granted by Constitution to persons who settle in the state having taken an oath of allegiance. Vt. Const. §66 (Supp. 1978). There is no express statutory restriction on land ownership by nonresident aliens and the Vermont Supreme Court has expressed an unwillingness to so construe the constitutional provision or to enforce any claim against the land of nonresident aliens. State v. Boston, Concord & Montreal R.R. Co., 25 Vt. 170 (1853).

B. Corporations: Alien corporations are included in the definition of foreign corporations. Vt. Stat. Ann, tit. 1, §114 (1972). Upon qualification, foreign corporations enjoy same rights and privileges as domestic corporations, including powers to buy and sell real property. Id., tit. 11, §1852 (powers of domestic corporation), tit. 11, §2102 (powers of foreign corporation) (1958).

47. Virginia.

A. Aliens: "Any alien not an enemy" may acquire, inherit, hold and transmit real estate the same as citizens. Va. Code Ann §55-1 (1974). Alienage of an ancestor is no bar to inheritance. Va. Code Ann §64.1-4 (1974).

B. Corporations: Alien corporations statutorily treated as foreign corporations. Va. Code Ann §13.1-2(d) (definition of foreign corporation), §13.1-102 (refernce to foreign "country") (1974). Qualification does not permit a foreign corporation to exercise any power "forbidden by law". Id., §13.1-103. The buying and selling of real property is not specifically forbidden to foreign corporations.

C. Foreign Agricultural Investment Disclosure Act - (Chapter 289 of 1979): Chapter 4.4 is added to Title 3.1 of the Code of Virginia (§§3.1-22.22 through 3.1-22.27) requiring any "foreign person" owning, acquiring or transferring any interest in "agricultural land" to report that fact to the Commissioner of Agriculture and Consumer Service. The Act covers nonresident aliens, foreign governments, entities organized under the laws of a foreign country or which have their principal place of business in a foreign country and domestic entities which are "substantially controlled" by the described foreign persons, governments, or entities. The penalty for failure to report is a civil penalty not to exceed $500.

48. Washington.

A. Aliens: Aliens are authorized to acquire and hold lands by purchase, devise or descent and to convey, mortgage and transfer by devise or descent as native citizen of the state or of the U.S. Wash. Rev. Code Ann §64.16.005 (Supp. 1976).

-29-

B. Corporations: Alien corporations statutorily treated as foreign corporations. Wash. Rev. Code Ann. §23A.04.010 (2) (definition of foreign corporation). §23A.32.050(1) (reference to foreign "country") (1968). Upon qualification, foreign corporations enjoy same rights and privileges as domestic corporations, including powers to buy and sell real property. Id., §23A.08.020 (4) (powers of domestic corporation), §23A.32.020 (powers of foreign corporation).

C. Public Lands: Substantial restrictions on aliens purchasing or leasing interests in public lands were dropped by Laws 1967, ch. 163, §§1 et. seq. 9, pursuant to Amendment 42 to the Washington Constitution. (See, Wash. Rev. Code Ann §64.16.005 (annotation following)).

44. West Virginia.

A. Aliens: "Any alien" is authorized to take land by devise, inheritance, gift, or purchase and to hold, convey and dispose of land by devise or descent "as if he were a citizen." W.Va. Code §36-1-21 (1966). W.Va. Code §42-1-4 (1966). (Alienage no bar to inheritance).

B. Corporations: Alien corporations statutorily treated as foreign corporations. W.Va. Code §31-1-6(j) (definition of foreign corporation) (1975), §31-1-53(a) (1) (reference to foreign "country"), §31-1-54(a) (reference to foreign "country") (Supp. 1976). Upon qualification, foreign corporations enjoy same rights and privileges as domestic corporations, including powers to buy and sell real property. Id., §31-1-8(d) (powers of domestic corporation), §31-1-50 (powers of foreign corporation). Every corporation holding more than 10,000 acres of land in West Virginia must apply to the Secretary of State for a special certificate authorizing such holding and pay a tax. Id., §11-12-75.

50. Wisconsin.

A. Aliens: Constitution and statute give resident aliens same rights as citizens with respect to possession, enjoyment and descent of property. Wisc. Const. art. 1, §15. Wisc. Stat. Ann §710.01. Alien not a resident of some state or territory of the U.S. or of the Dist. of Columbia cannot acquire or hold more than 640 acres, except by devise or inheritance of pursuant to the collection of debt. Wisc. Stat. Ann §710.02 (Spec. Pamphlet 1977).

-30-

Sec. 897 [1954 Code]. (a) GENERAL RULE.—

(1) TREATMENT AS EFFECTIVELY CONNECTED WITH UNITED STATES TRADE OR BUSINESS.—For purposes of this title, gain or loss of a nonresident alien individual or a foreign corporation from the disposition of a United States real property interest shall be taken into account—

(A) in the case of a nonresident alien individual, under section 871(b)(1), or

(B) in the case of a foreign corporation, under section 882(a)(1), as if the taxpayer were engaged in a trade or business within the United States during the taxable year and as if such gain or loss were effectively connected with such trade or business.

(2) 20-PERCENT MINIMUM TAX ON NONRESIDENT ALIEN INDIVIDUALS.—

(A) IN GENERAL.—In the case of any nonresident alien individual, the amount determined under section 55(a)(1)(A) for the taxable year shall not be less than 20 percent of whichever of the following is the least:

(i) the individual's alternative minimum taxable income (as defined in section 55(b)(1)) for the taxable year,

(ii) the individual's net United States real property gain for the taxable year, or

(iii) $60,000.

(B) NET UNITED STATES REAL PROPERTY GAIN.—For purposes of subparagraph (A), the term "net United States real property gain" means the excess of—

(i) the aggregate of the gains for the taxable year from dispositions of United States real property interests, over

(ii) the aggregate of the losses for the taxable year from dispositions of such interests.

(b) LIMITATION ON LOSSES OF INDIVIDUALS.—In the case of an individual, a loss shall be taken into account under subsection (a) only to the extent such loss would be taken into account under section 165(c) (determined without regard to subsection (a) of this section).

(c) UNITED STATES REAL PROPERTY INTEREST.—For purposes of this section—

(1) UNITED STATES REAL PROPERTY INTEREST.—

(A) IN GENERAL.—Except as provided in subparagraph (B), the term "United States real property interest" means—

(i) an interest in real property (including an interest in a mine, well, or other natural deposit) located in the United States, and

(ii) any interest (other than an interest solely as a creditor) in any domestic corporation unless the taxpayer establishes (at such time and in such manner as the Secretary by regulations prescribes) that such corporation was at no time a United States real property holding corporation during the shorter of—

(I) the period after June 18, 1980, during which the taxpayer held such interest, or

(II) the 5-year period ending on the date of the disposition of such interest.

(B) EXCLUSION FOR INTEREST IN CERTAIN CORPORATIONS.—

The term "United States real property interest" does not include any interest in a corporation if—

Penalty is forfeiture to the state. Id., If it appears that a legatee of distributee of an estate or trust will not receive his payment, the court may order funds deposited in the state school fund until a proper claim is made. Id., §863.37 (1971).

B. Corporations: No alien corporation and no corporation or association in which more than 20% of the stock is owned by non-resident aliens can acquire or hold more than 640 acres other than through the good faith collection of debts by judicial process. Penalty is forfeiture to the state. Prohibitions do not apply to railroad or pipeline corporations. Wisc. Stat. Ann §710.02 (Spec. Pamphlet 1977). See also restrictions on Corporate Farming.

C. Corporate Farming: Corporations generally prohibited from owning land on which to carry on farming operations with certain exceptions. Wisc. Stat. Ann §182.001 (Supp. 1977-78). Effective May 27, 1978, the restriction on corporate ownership of farm land contained in Wisc. Stat. Ann. §182.001 applies to trusts also. Id., (March 1979 Pamphlet).

51. Wyoming.

A. Aliens: By constitution, resident aliens have the same rights as citizens as to possession, taxation, enjoyment and descent of property. Wyo. Const. art. 1, §29. "Nonresident aliens not eligible to citizenship under the laws of the United States" are prohibited from acquiring, possessing, enjoying, using, leasing, transferring, transmitting or inheriting real property, except to the extent that a reciprocal right exists for U.S. citizens in the alien's country of citizenship. Wyo. Stat. §34-15-101 (1977). Transfers in violation of this provision are stated to be absolutely void, and both parties may be subjected to criminal penalties. Id., §§34-15-102, 103. Nonresident aliens cannot take by inheritance or testamentary disposition unless reciprocal right exists in the alien's country of citizenship. Id., §2-3-107 (1977).

B. Corporations: Alien corporations statutorily treated as foreign corporations. Wyo. Stat. §17-1-102(ii) (definition of foreign corporation), §17-1-701 (reference to foreign "country"). Upon qualification, foreign corporations enjoy same rights and privileges as domestic corporations. Id., §17-1-702, §17-1-104 (iv) (powers of domestic corporation, including powers to buy and sell real property).

(i) as of the date of the disposition of such interest, such corporation did not hold any United States real property interests, and

(ii) all of the United States real property interests held by such corporation at any time during the shorter of the periods described in subparagraph (A)(ii)—

(I) were disposed of in transactions in which the full amount of the gain (if any) was recognized, or

(II) ceased to be United States real property interests by reason of the application of this subparagraph to 1 or more other corporations.

(2) UNITED STATES REAL PROPERTY HOLDING CORPORATION.—The term "United States real property holding corporation" means any corporation if—

(A) the fair market value of its United States real property interests equals or exceeds 50 percent of

(B) the fair market value of—

(i) its United States real property interests,

(ii) its interests in real property located outside the United States, plus

(iii) any other of its assets which are used or held for use in a trade or business.

(3) EXCEPTION FOR STOCK REGULARLY TRADED ON ESTABLISHED SECURITIES MARKETS.—If any class of stock of a corporation is regularly traded on an established securities market, stock of such class shall be treated as a United States real property interest only in the case of a person who, at some time during the shorter of the periods described in paragraph (1)(A)(ii), held more than 5 percent of such class of stock.

(4) INTERESTS HELD BY FOREIGN CORPORATIONS AND BY PARTNERSHIPS, TRUSTS, AND ESTATES.—For purposes of determining whether any corporation is a United States real property holding corporation—

(A) FOREIGN CORPORATIONS.—Paragraph (1)(A)(ii) shall be applied by substituting "any corporation (whether foreign or domestic)" for "any domestic corporation".

(B) INTERESTS HELD BY PARTNERSHIPS, ETC.—United States real property interests held by a partnership, trust, or estate shall be treated as owned proportionately by its partners or beneficiaries.

(5) TREATMENT OF CONTROLLING INTERESTS.—

(A) IN GENERAL.—Under regulations, for purposes of determining whether any corporation is a United States real property holding corporation, if any corporation (hereinafter in this paragraph referred to as the "first corporation") holds a controlling interest in a second corporation—

(i) the stock which the first corporation holds in the second corporation shall not be taken into account,

(ii) the first corporation shall be treated as holding a portion of each asset of the second corporation equal to the percentage of the fair market value of the stock of the second corporation represented by the stock held by the first corporation, and

(iii) any asset treated as held by the first corporation by reason of clause (ii) which is used or held for use by the second corporation in a trade or business shall be treated as so used or held by the first corporation.

Any asset treated as held by the first corporation by reason of the preceding sentence shall be so treated for purposes of applying the preced-

ing sentence successively to corporations which are above the first corporation in a chain of corporations.

(B) CONTROLLING INTEREST.—For purposes of subparagraph (A), the term "controlling interest" means 50 percent or more of the fair market value of all classes of stock of a corporation.

(6) OTHER SPECIAL RULES.—

(A) INTEREST IN REAL PROPERTY.—The term "interest in real property" includes fee ownership and co-ownership of land or improvements thereon, leaseholds of land or improvements thereon, options to acquire land or improvements thereon, and options to acquire leaseholds of land or improvements thereon.

(B) REAL PROPERTY INCLUDES ASSOCIATED PERSONAL PROPERTY.—The term "real property" includes movable walls, furnishings, and other personal property associated with the use of the real property.

(C) CONSTRUCTIVE OWNERSHIP RULES.—For purposes of determining under paragraph (3) whether any person holds more than 5 percent of any class of stock and of determining under paragraph (5) whether a person holds a controlling interest in any corporation, section 318(a) shall apply (except that paragraphs (2)(C) and (3)(C) of section 318(a) shall be applied by substituting "5 percent" for "50 percent").

(d) TREATMENT OF DISTRIBUTIONS, ETC., BY FOREIGN CORPORATIONS.—

(1) DISTRIBUTIONS.—

(A) IN GENERAL.—Except to the extent otherwise provided in regulations, notwithstanding any other provision of this chapter, gain shall be recognized by a foreign corporation on the distribution (including a distribution in liquidation or redemption) of a United States real property interest in an amount equal to the excess of the fair market value of such interest (as of the time of the distribution) over its adjusted basis.

(B) EXCEPTION WHERE THERE IS A CARRYOVER BASIS.—Subparagraph (A) shall not apply if the basis of the distributed property in the hands of the distributee is the same as the adjusted basis of such property before the distribution increased by the amount of any gain recognized by the distributing corporation.

(2) SECTION 337 NOT TO APPLY.—Section 337 shall not apply to any sale or exchange of a United States real property interest by a foreign corporation.

(e) COORDINATION WITH NONRECOGNITION PROVISIONS.—

(1) IN GENERAL.—Except to the extent otherwise provided in subsection (d) and paragraph (2) of this subsection, any nonrecognition provision shall apply for purposes of this section to a transaction only in the case of an exchange of a United States real property interest for an interest the sale of which would be subject to taxation under this chapter.

(2) REGULATIONS.—The Secretary shall prescribe regulations (which are necessary or appropriate to prevent the avoidance of Federal income taxes) providing—

(A) the extent to which nonrecognition provisions shall, and shall not, apply for purposes of this section, and

(B) the extent to which—

(i) transfers of property in reorganization, and

(ii) changes in interests in, or distributions from, a partnership, trust, or estate,

shall be treated as sales of property at fair market value.

(i) ELECTION BY FOREIGN CORPORATION TO BE TREATED AS DOMESTIC CORPORATION.—

(1) IN GENERAL.—If—

(A) a foreign corporation has a permanent establishment in the United States, and

(B) under any treaty, such permanent establishment may not be treated less favorably than domestic corporations carrying on the same activities,

then such foreign corporation may make an election to be treated as a domestic corporation for purposes of this section and section 6039C.

(2) REVOCATION ONLY WITH CONSENT.—Any election under paragraph (1), once made, may be revoked only with the consent of the Secretary.

(3) MAKING OF ELECTION.—An election under paragraph (1) may be made only subject to such conditions as may be prescribed by the Secretary.

.01 Added by P. L. 96-499.

Committee Report on P. L. 96-499.

General rule

25 *House bill.*—Nonresident aliens and foreign corporations ("foreign investors") would be subject to tax on the disposition of U. S. real property. Real property is intended to have the same meaning for this purpose that it has in the U. S. Treasury's model income tax treaty and thus it includes personal property associated with real property. Foreign investors would also be taxed on gain from the disposition of an interest in a U. S. real property holding organization (RPHO). The tax would be imposed regardless of whether or not the gain was effectively connected with a U. S. business or the seller was present in the United States.

Senate amendment.—Substantially the same as House bill.

Conference agreement.—The conference agreement follows the House bill and the Senate amendment.

Rate of tax

House bill.—All gains and losses from the disposition of U. S. real property interests would be treated as if they were effectively connected with a U. S. trade or business. Losses attributable to the U. S. real property from years prior to the year of sale would be allowed as deductions against the foreign investor's effectively connected U. S. gross income (including gains from real property sales) if the foreign investor elects under section 871(d) or 882(d) to be taxable on a net basis on its U. S. real property investment income.

Senate amendment.—Same as House bill, except that net gains from disposition of U. S. real property interests would be subject to tax at a minimum rate of 28 percent if that tax would be higher than the tax under the generally applicable rules. No tax would be due if net gains during the taxable year from the sale of U. S. real property interests do not exceed $3,000.

Conference agreement.—Same as House bill. However, certain aspects of the Senate amendment were retained in modified form so that the tax on foreign investors would be more comparable to the tax imposed on U. S. investors in similar circumstances. The impact of the Senate amendment on foreign investors would have been greater than the tax imposed on similarly situated U. S. investors because the 28-percent minimum rate of the Senate amendment is higher than the capital gains rate imposed on long-term capital gains of U. S. investors who are not in the highest marginal tax brackets. In addition, the Senate amendment, in computing the tax, did not permit the use against U. S. effectively connected net losses which are effectively connected with another U. S. trade or business of the foreign investor or net losses from holding the U. S. real property interest which were attributable to prior years. The House bill, on the other hand, in many situations would have imposed a tax at rates lower than those imposed on similarly situated U. S. investors since the rate of tax would be determined with reference only to the foreign investor's income which was effectively connected with a U. S. trade or business. Since any other U. S. source investment income and all foreign source income of the foreign investor would not be taken into account, the rate of tax on the U. S. real estate gains of foreign investors (particularly if an installment sale were used to spread the gain over several years) would generally be lower than that imposed on U. S. investors in similar circumstances. Consequently, the conferees decided, in the case of individuals, to impose the U. S. tax at a minimum rate of 20 percent of property gains (net of U. S. effectively connected losses) but otherwise to follow the approach of the House bill and generally to treat U. S. real property gains as gains effectively connected with a U. S. trade or business subject to the U. S. graduated capital gains rates and with full use of effectively connected losses against those gains.

Real property holding organizations (RPHOs)

House bill.—Corporation, partnership or trust would be an RPHO if, during the taxable year, the fair market value of its (i) U. S. real property interests was at least 50 percent of the sum of the values of its (i) U. S. real property interests, (ii) other real property, and (iii) other assets used in its trade or business. "Look through" rules would apply where the entity had a controlling interest in another entity, and attribution rules would apply to determine whether a controlling interest existed.

(3) NONRECOGNITION PROVISION DEFINED.—For purposes of this subsection, the term "nonrecognition provision" means any provision of this title for not recognizing gain or loss.

(f) DISTRIBUTION BY DOMESTIC CORPORATIONS TO FOREIGN SHAREHOLDERS.—If a domestic corporation distributes a United States real property interest to a nonresident alien individual or a foreign corporation in a distribution to which section 301 applies, notwithstanding any other provision of this chapter, the basis of such United States real property interest in the hands of such nonresident alien individual or foreign corporation shall not exceed—

(1) the adjusted basis of such property before the distribution, increased by

(2) the sum of—

(A) any gain recognized by the distributing corporation on the distribution, and

(B) any tax paid under this chapter by the distributee on such distribution.

(g) SPECIAL RULE FOR SALES OF INTEREST IN PARTNERSHIPS, TRUSTS, AND ESTATES.—Under regulations prescribed by the Secretary, the amount of any money, and the fair market value of any property, received by a nonresident alien individual or foreign corporation in exchange for all or part of its interest in a partnership, trust, or estate shall, to the extent attributable to United States real property interests, be considered as an amount received from the sale or exchange in the United States of such property.

(h) SPECIAL RULES FOR REITS.—For purposes of this section—

(1) LOOK-THROUGH OF DISTRIBUTIONS.—Any distribution by a REIT to a nonresident alien individual or a foreign corporation shall, to the extent attributable to gain from sales or exchanges by the REIT of United States real property interests, be treated as gain recognized by such nonresident alien individual or foreign corporation from the sale or exchange of a United States real property interest.

(2) SALE OR STOCK IN DOMESTICALLY-CONTROLLED REIT NOT TAXED.—The term "United States real property interest" does not include any interest in a domestically-controlled REIT.

(3) DISTRIBUTIONS BY DOMESTICALLY-CONTROLLED REITS.—In the case of a domestically-controlled REIT, rules similar to the rules of subsection (d) shall apply to the foreign ownership percentage of any gain.

(4) DEFINITIONS.—

(A) REIT.—The term "REIT" means a real estate investment trust.

(B) DOMESTICALLY-CONTROLLED REIT.—The term "domestically-controlled REIT" means a REIT in which at all times during the testing period less than 50 percent in value of the stock was held directly or indirectly by foreign persons.

(C) FOREIGN OWNERSHIP PERCENTAGE.—The term "foreign ownership percentage" means that percentage of the stock of the REIT which was held (directly or indirectly) by foreign persons at the time during the testing period during which the direct and indirect ownership of stock by foreign persons was greatest.

(D) TESTING PERIOD.—The term "testing period" means whichever of the following periods is the shortest:

(i) the period beginning on June 19, 1980, and ending on the date of the disposition or of the distribution, as the case may be,

(ii) the 5-year period ending on the date of the disposition or of the distribution, as the case may be, or

(iii) the period during which the REIT was in existence.

In general, all gains from the disposition of an interest in an RPHO would be subject to tax. However, no tax would be imposed on sale of publicly traded stock in a corporation by a person who owned 5 percent or less.

Senate amendment.—Corporation, partnership or trust would be an RPHO if (a) at least a 50 percent interest in the entity is held by 10 or fewer persons, and (b) the fair market value of its U. S. real property interests is at least 50 percent of the value of all its assets (other than liquid assets).

U. S. tax treaties generally provide for a reduced rate of tax on dividends which might make it advantageous for a domestic corporation to distribute a U. S. real property interest to a shareholder in dividend form. To prevent this, the bill denies the recipient a basis step-up except to the extent that the corporation recognizes gain and the recipient pays U. S. income tax on the distribution. "Look-through" and attribution rules similar to the House bill would apply. All gains from disposition of an interest in an RPHO would be subject to tax.

Conference agreement.—The conference agreement generally follows the House bill with respect to domestic corporate RPHOs but adopts different rules for other entities as set forth below. Attribution rules similar to the House bill apply to determine whether there is a controlling interest in another entity but the "look through" rules apply to such an interest only with respect to assets actually held downward through the chain of ownership. U. S. corporations would be treated as RPHOs unless they elect to file returns establishing that less than 50 percent of their assets are U. S. real property interests.

(i) *Foreign corporations.*—Gain on the disposition of stock in a foreign corporation would not be subject to the tax imposed under the bill. Instead, the foreign corporation would be taxed on any distribution (whether or not in liquidation) of appreciated U. S. real property interests to its shareholders. Also, tax would be imposed if the property is sold in connection with a liquidation.

If the application of the provisions of section 897 or section 6039C to any foreign corporation would be barred by a treaty obligation of the United States which provides that a permanent establishment of a foreign corporation in the United States may not be treated less favorably than a domestic corporation carrying on the same activities, then that foreign corporation may elect, subject to such terms and conditions as are specified by the IRS, to be treated as a U. S. corporation for purposes of sections 897 and 6039C. The election may be revoked only with the consent of the Secretary.

Conditions imposed by the IRS on the making of the election might, for example, include a requirement that the foreign corporation notify its shareholders that the election was being made or a requirement that the IRS be satisfied that treaty relief was applicable. Ordinarily, the election would be made before the first disposition of stock in a foreign corporation which would be taxable if the election had been made before that first disposition. Where it deemed it to be appropriate, however, the IRS could permit the election to be made after the first disposition, provided satisfactory arrangements were made for the payment of an amount equal to the tax on any dispositions made prior to the election which would have been owing on the dispositions (if the election had been made prior to the first disposition) and an appropriate interest charge for the period since the time at which that tax would have been required to have been paid. In the case of dispositions of stock in foreign corporations made prior to the conference committee's action, it is contemplated that the election may be made retroactively, provided satisfactory arrangements are made for the payment of tax on the stock sale. (For example, if amounts were withheld by the buyer on the purchase of the foreign corporation's stock or were deposited in an escrow account for the satisfaction of the seller's tax liability on the stock sale, the election might be permitted if those funds were made available to satisfy the seller's tax liability.)

(ii) *Partnership, trusts, and estates.*—Gain on the disposition of an interest in these entities also would not be subject, in its entirety, to tax. Instead, a foreign investor in such an entity would be taxable on the disposition of his interest to the extent that the gain represented his pro rata share of appreciation in the value of U. S. real property interests of the entity.

(iii) *REITs.*—Distributions by a real estate investment trust (REIT) to foreign shareholders would be treated as gain on the sale of U. S. real property to the extent of the shareholders' pro rata share of the net capital gain of the REIT. In the case of REITs which are controlled by U. S. persons, sales of the REIT shares by foreign shareholders would not be subject to tax (other than in the case of distribution by the REIT).

Nonrecognition rules

House bill.—The Secretary would be authorized to prescribe regulations providing the extent to which nonrecognition rules would (or would not) apply under the bill. Pending the issuance of these regulations, nonrecognition provisions of the Code would apply, but only in the case of an exchange of a U. S. real property interest for an interest the disposition of which would be taxable under the Code (as modified by any treaty pursuant to sections 894 and 7852(d)).

Senate amendment.—Similar to the House bill, but without a rule prescribing treatment prior to the issuance of regulations.

Conference agreement.—Follows the House bill, but also allows prescription of regulations determining the extent to which transfers of property in reorganizations are to be treated as sales at fair market value. Similar rules apply in the case of partnerships, trusts, and estates.

Withholding

House bill.—No provision.

Senate amendment.—The withholding requirement would apply only if the purchaser knows or has received a notice that the seller is a foreign person. The seller is required to notify the purchaser that the seller is a foreign person. The seller's agent is also required to notify the purchaser that the seller is a foreign person if the agent has reason to believe that the seller may be a foreign person. The amount to be withheld is the smallest of (i) 28 percent of the sales price, (ii) the "seller's maximum tax liability" (discussed below), or (iii) the fair market value of that portion of the sale proceeds which is within the withholder's control. The "seller's maximum tax liability" is the maximum amount which the Treasury determines that the seller could owe on his gain on the sale plus any unsatisfied prior withholding tax liabilities of prior foreign owners with respect to that property.

A purchaser would not be required to withhold if: (i) the property being sold is a single family residence which is to be used by the purchaser as his principal residence and the amount realized by the seller on the sale is $150,000 or less, (ii) the property being sold is stock of a corporation and the sales transaction takes place on an established securities market or (iii) the seller obtains a "qualifying statement" from the Treasury that he is exempt from tax or he has provided adequate security or has otherwise made arrangements with Treasury for the payment of the tax. The Treasury may prescribe a reduced amount to be withheld under similar procedures.

Conference agreement.—The conference agreement follows the House bill. The Senate conferees had proposed that the tax imposed under the conference agreement be enforced by the withholding provisions contained in the Senate bill, modified in several respects.[1] The House conferees refused to agree to the withholding provisions in the conference agreement. The conferees agreed it would be necessary to structure withholding provisions carefully to ensure that they would not inadvertently disrupt the U. S. real estate market or expose U. S. buyers or U. S. agents of foreign sellers of U. S. real estate to liability where such liability would not be appropriate. Given this potential, the House conferees took the position that withholding provisions should not be adopted until they could be more fully considered by the committees and the public had adequate opportunity to consider and comment on the proposed withholding mechanism. The conferees agreed that, until and unless withholding provisions were adopted by a subsequent Congress, the tax should be enforced through information reporting as discussed below.

Reporting

a. Returns to identify whether an entity is an RPHO

House bill.—If, at any time during a calendar year, (i) an entity beneficiary owns U. S. real property interests which constitute more than 40 percent of the fair market value of the assets taken into consideration in determining whether or not it is an RPHO and (ii) at least one foreign person has an interest (other than a portfolio interest in publicly-traded stock) in the entity, the entity is required to file an information return for the year. The return is to set forth the name and address of any foreign person who held an interest, whether the entity is an RPHO at any time during the calendar year, and other information which the Treasury may prescribe by regulations.

Senate amendment.—If, at any time during a calendar year, (i) an entity has U. S. real property interests which constitute more than 40 percent of the fair market value of its assets, (ii) 10 or fewer persons have a controlling interest in the entity, and (iii) at least one foreign person has an interest in the entity, the entity is required to file an information return for the year. The information required is similar to the information required under the House bill.

Conference agreement.—The conference agreement deletes the requirement that entities file returns establishing whether or not they are RPHOs. Under the conference agreement, an entity (or a person owning an interest in the entity) may on a voluntary basis file a return, containing such information as may be required by the IRS, establishing that the entity is not an RPHO.

b. Returns to identify foreign owners

House bill.—Foreign owners of U. S. real estate who are not subject to the return requirements described above the generally required to file returns showing (i) the name and address of the person, (ii) a description of all U. S. real property interests held by such person, and (iii) such other information as the Treasury may prescribe by regulations.

Senate amendment.—No provision.

Conference agreement.—The conference agreement generally follows the House bill with several modifications.

U. S. corporations which are U. S. real property holding corporations or which were U. S. real property holding corporations at any time during the preceding 4 years will be required to file annual returns setting forth the name and the address (if known by the corporation) of each foreign shareholder (other than shareholders owning stock which is publicly traded, any information required by the Secretary with respect to transfers of stock in the corporation

[1] The withholding provisions of the Senate amendment would be modified to provide that neither the purchaser nor any settlement agent would be required to withhold unless he has actual knowledge that the seller is foreign or has received a notice from a seller's agent. The seller's agent would be relieved of any responsibility to give such a notice if he relies in good faith on a statement from the seller (or, in the case of a seller's agent retained by another seller's agent, from the seller's agent who retained him) that the seller is a U. S. person or, if the seller is foreign, that the seller notified the purchaser. A second modification proposed to the Senate bill withholding provisions was that if the purchaser assumes a debt of the seller or took the property subject to a debt of the seller, which was incurred within one year prior to the sale, that amount of the consideration would also be subject to withholding. A final modification would have set forth in greater detail the circumstances under which withholding might be reduced or waived. The taxpayer would be permitted to reduce (or eliminate) the amount of withholding by filing a return stating the basis for the property and the character of the contemplated gain. The IRS would be required to accept that basis and character for withholding purposes unless the IRS responded within 30 days specifying a lower (or zero) basis or different character if the IRS were not satisfied that the amount to be withheld would be sufficient to cover the taxpayer's underlying liability.

by such foreign shareholders and any other information which the Secretary may prescribe by regulations. Any nominee holding stock in a U. S. corporation was unable to supply a U. S. corporation is required to file a return in the same manner as the corporation, for example, its stock is in bearer form or was held by publicly traded stock is imposed because information with respect to foreign shareholders holding more than 5 percent of any publicly traded class of stock in a U. S. corporation (less than 5 percent shareholders are not taxable on the disposition of their stock) should be readily available from the SEC.

Foreign corporations and partnerships, trusts, or estates (whether foreign or domestic) are required to file annual returns setting forth the name and address of each foreign person who has a substantial indirect investment in U. S. real property through the entity, such information with respect to the assets of the entity, and such other information as the Secretary may prescribe by regulations. For this purpose, a foreign person having a substantial share of the U. S. real property interests held by the entity exceeds $50,000 at any time during the calendar year. Any entity required to make such a return is also required to furnish each of the foreign persons holding a substantial investment in U. S. real property through that entity a statement showing the name and address of the entity, the substantial investor's pro rata share of the U. S. real property held by the entity and such other information as is required by regulations. In determining whether the pro rata share of any foreign person's beneficial interest in the real property held by the entity exceeds $50,000, the entity's pro rata share of any real property interest held by any other such entity in which the first entity holds a beneficial interest, and interests in the first entity held by the person's family, shall also be taken into account.

These reporting requirements will not apply to any entity for any calendar year where the entity furnishes the IRS with such security as the IRS determines to be necessary to ensure that any U. S. tax with respect to U. S. real property interests held by such entity will be paid. It is expected that the security which the IRS would consider to be satisfactory would depend upon the circumstances. Thus, for example, in the case of a foreign corporation the only asset of which is a tract of undeveloped U. S. real estate, the IRS might require a recorded security interest in the real estate, a guarantee by a person from whom the IRS could reasonably certain it could collect the unpaid tax, or some similar type of security. On the other hand, in the case of a foreign corporation engaged in a U. S. trade or business with a variety of U. S. assets and wherethe circumstances indicated that it was improbable that the foreign corporation would attempt to liquidate and remove its assets from the United States without satisfying its U. S. tax liability, the IRS might only require an understaking by the foreign corporation to pay the tax in a closing agreement or some similar security. Where an arrangement is reached with the IRS, the entity is not required to report the identity of its foreign persons holding interests in the entity and in addition, the foreign person is not required to take its pro

rata interest in the entity into account in determining its own reporting requirements. Where the foreign corporation was unable to supply the necessary information on behalf of the identity of its shareholders because, for example, its stock is in bearer form or was held by the beneficial owner, it would be required to provide security satisfactory to the IRS.

A separate reporting requirement applies to foreign persons owning U. S. real property who are not required to file a return under section 6038C(b) for the year. Where such a foreign person did not engage in a trade or business in the United States would be allowed with respect to a disposition made to a related U. S. real property interests held by the foreign person at any time during the year equals or exceeds $70,000, the foreign person is required to file a return setting forth his (or its) name and address, a description of all U. S. real property interests held at any time during the calendar year and such other information as is required by regulations. "Look through" and family attribution rules apply to determine whether a person is a substantial investor.

c. Failure to make a return or furnish a statement

House bill.—A penalty for failure to file a tax return or to furnish a statement required under the rules described above will be imposed in an amount equal to the greater of (i) $25 a day during which the failure continues but not to exceed $25,000. Also, in the case of a failure by a foreign person to file a return required by the rules set forth in (b) above, the penalty for any calendar year cannot exceed 5 percent of the aggregate of (i) the fair market value of the U. S. real property interests owned by that person at any time during the year and (ii) the face amount of the fair market value of the U. S. real property interests held by the person at any time during the year.

Senate amendment.—A penalty for failure to file a return or to furnish a statement required under the rules described above will be imposed in an amount equal to the greater of (i) $25 a day during which the failure continues, but not to exceed $25,000 or (ii) the amount of the tax under the bill which is not paid and which is attributable to transfers (other than those made in an established securities market) occurring during the calendar year for which the return or statement was required.

Conference agreement.—The conference agreement generally follows the House bill.

In the case of each failure to file a return containing the information required, or those information reporting requirements or to furnish the statement to a beneficial owner of an interest of its property assets held by the entity, a penalty is imposed of $25 for each day during which the failure continues (but not to exceed $25,000 for each calendar year) unless it is shown that the failure is due to reasonable cause and not to willful neglect. A further limitation, in the case of a failure of a foreign person to disclose his U. S. real property interests (sec. 6038C(c)). In the case of such a failure, the penalty is not to exceed 5 percent of the aggregate fair market value of the U. S. real property interests held by the person at any time during the year.

Effective date

a. General rule

House bill.—The bill would apply to dispositions after June 18, 1980.

Senate amendment.—The Senate amendment would apply to dispositions after December 31, 1979, except those made pursuant to a contract binding at all times after December 6, 1979.

Conference agreement.—The conference agreement generally follows the House bill and the Senate amendment, but no step-up in basis would be allowed with respect to a disposition made to a related party which is exempt from the tax imposed by the bill solely because of delays of the effective date attributable to conflicting treaty obligations. In situations where a treaty is renegotiated to resolve conflicts between the treaty and the effective date of the conference agreement, the delay in the effective date of the conference agreement can be extended in the revised treaty or an accompanying exchange of notes for a period of up to two years after the signing of the revised treaty in order to permit the Senate adequate time to consider the revised treaty.—Conference Committee Report.

b. Tax treaties

House bill.—Until January 1, 1985, gain would not be taxed to the extent required by treaty

obligations of the U. S. On and after that date, the provision would prevail over any conflicting treaty provisions remaining in effect.

Senate amendment.—Same as House bill.

REPORTING REQUIREMENTS

Form Number	Title of Form	Who Must File	Exemptions
BE-13A & B	Report on a Foreign Person's Establishment, Acquisition or Purchase of the Operating Assets of a U.S. Business Enterprise, including Real Estate.	1. Form BE-13A "Form for a U.S. Business Enterprise, Business Segment, or Operating Unit that has been Established or Acquired by a Foreign Person or Existing U.S. Affiliate or Existing U.S. Affiliate of a Foreign Person," must be completed either: a. by a U.S. business enterprise when a foreign person establishes or acquires directly, or indirectly through an existing U.S. affiliate, a 10 percent or more voting interest in that enterprise, including an enterprise that results from the direct or indirect acquisition by a foreign person of a business segment or operating unit of an existing U.S. business enterprise that is then organized as a separate legal entity; or b. by the existing U.S. affiliate of a foreign person when it acquires a U.S. business enterprise, or a business segment or operating unit of a U.S. business enterprise, that the existing U.S. affiliate merges into its own operations rather than continuing or organizing as a separate legal entity.	1. TOTAL EXEMPTIONS (BE-13A) a. Real estate held exclusively for personal use and not for profit making purposes is exempt from being reported. A residence that is leased by an owner who intends to reoccupy it is considered real estate held for personal use. b. An existing U.S. affiliate is totally exempt from reporting the acquisition of a U.S. business enterprise, or a business segment or operating unit of a U.S. business enterprise, that it then merges into its own operations, if the total cost of the acquisition was $1,000,000.00 or less. 2. PARTIAL EXEMPTION (BE-13A) For periods prior to January 1, 1981, a new U.S. affiliate, as consolidated, is partially exempt, if: (a) the new U.S. affiliate's total assets (not the foreign parent's or existing U.S. affiliate's share) at the time of acquisition or immediately after being established, were $500,000.00 or less and (b) the new affiliate does not own 200 acres or more of U.S. land, it must report regardless of the value of total assets).

REPORTING REQUIREMENTS

Form Number	Title of Form	Who Must File	Exemptions
BE-13A & B (Cont)		2. Form BE-13B "Form for Foreign Person, or Existing U.S. Affiliate of a Foreign Person, that Establishes or Acquires a U.S. Business Enterprise, or a Business Segment or Operating Unit of a U.S. Business Enterprise", must be completed either:	A partially exempt new U.S. affiliate must still file a Form BE-13A, but only Part 1 and items 1 through 19 of Part 2 need be completed, and a notation made giving the value of assets and the number of acres of U.S. land owned (items 39, 47-60).
		a. by a foreign person when it establishes or acquires a direct voting interest in a U.S. business enterprise that becomes its U.S. affiliate, or by the new U.S. affiliate for the foreign parent to the extent it has or can secure the information; or	For transactions subsequent to December 12, 1980, a U.S. affiliate that was partially exempt from filing Form BE-13A and which had to complete only items 1 and 5 through 19 will now be considered totally exempt and rather than filing a partially completed Form BE-13A should file an "Exemption Claim, Form BE-13A".
		b. by an existing U.S. affiliate of a foreign person when it establishes or acquires a direct voting interest in a U.S. business enterprise of such a magnitude that the established or acquired enterprise becomes a U.S. affiliate of the foreign person, i.e., the foreign person thereby acquires an indirect (or direct and indirect) voting interest of 10% or more in the established or acquired U.S. business enterprise; or	3. TOTAL EXEMPTION (BE-13B): The foreign parent or existing U.S. affiliate is exempt from filing a BE-13B if: a. The new U.S. affiliate consists of real estate held exclusively for personal use and not for profit making purposes. A residence that is leased by an owner who intends to reoccupy it is considered real estate held for personal use.

Form Number

BE-13A & B
(Cont)

Title of Form

REPORTING REQUIREMENTS

Who Must File

c. by an existing U.S. affiliate of a foreign person when it acquires a U.S. business enterprise, or a business segment or operating unit of a U.S. business enterprise, and merges it into its own operations.

A separate Form BE-13B must be completed by or for each foreign parent, or by each existing U.S. affiliate, that has secured a direct voting interest in a new U.S. affiliate.

DUE DATE

BE-13A & BE-13B: 45 days after each covered direct investment transaction which occurs on or after January 1, 1979

PENALTY

A fine not exceeding $10,000 or commanding such person to file the form, or both. Its failure to file results from the willful neglect of an individual, he/she may be imprisoned for not more than one year or be fined not more than $10,000, or both.

Exemptions

b. The U.S. business enterprise, or business segment or operating unit of a U.S. business enterprise, that is acquired by an existing U.S. affiliate and merged into its own operations, is acquired at a total cost of $1,000,000.00 or less.

c. The new U.S. affiliate, as consolidated (a) has total assets (not the foreign parent's or existing U.S. affiliate's share), at the time of acquisition or immediately after being established, of $1,000,000.00 or less and (b) does not own 200 acres or more of U.S. land if the new U.S. affiliate owns 200 acres or more of U.S. land, the foreign parent or existing U.S. affiliate must report regardless of the value of the new U.S. affiliate's total assets).

Note: For period prior to January 1, 1981 the dollar exemptions in Bond C were $500,000.

OTHER CONSIDERATIONS

BE-607, Industry Classification Questionnaire must be completed and returned with Form BE-13A.

PRIOR TO 1981, FORM BE-13 REQUIRED DISCLOSURE OF THE IDENTITY OF FOREIGN INDIVIDUALS IF SUCH PERSONS WERE THE ULTIMATE BENEFICIAL OWNER OF THE U.S. INVESTMENT. THE BEA NO LONGER REQUIRES THE NAMES OF INDIVIDUALS BUT ONLY THEIR COUNTRY OF LOCATION. WHILE THIS CHANGE IN POLICY IS NOT EXPRESSLY SET FORTH IN THE REGULATIONS, THE BEA HAS INDICATED THAT IT WILL BE SET FORTH IN THE INSTRUCTIONS TO THE REVISED FORM-13.

REPORTING REQUIREMENTS

Form Number	Title of Form	Who Must File	Exemptions
BE-14	Report by a U.S. Person who Assists or Intervenes in the Acquisition of a U.S. Business Enterprise by, or who enters into a Joint Venture with a Foreign Person.	This report is to be completed either by: a. a U.S. person - including, but not limited to, an intermediary, a real estate broker, business broker, business broker and a brokerage house - who assists or intervenes in the sale to, or purchase by, a foreign person or a U.S. affiliate of a foreign person, of a 10 percent or more voting interest in a U.S. business enterprises, including real estate; or b. a U.S. person who enters into a joint venture with a foreign person to create a U.S. business enterprise. A U.S. person is required to report only when such a foreign involvement is known; it is not incumbent upon the U.S. person to ascertain the foreign status of a person involved in an acquisition unless the U.S. person has reason to believe the acquiring party may be a foreign person. If a U.S. person required to file a Form BE-14 files either Form BE-13A or Form BE-13B relating to the acquisition of the U.S. business enterprise by a foreign person, then form BE-14 is not required. PENALTY A fine not exceeding $10,000 or commanding such person to file the form, or both. If failure to file results from the willful neglect of an individual, he/she may be imprisoned or not more than one year or be fined not more than $10,000, or both.	Real Estate - Real estate held exclusively for personal use and not for profit making purposes is exempted from being reported. A residence that is leased by an owner who intends to reoccupy it is considered real estate held for personal use. Dollar Value - If the U.S. business enterprise acquired has total assets of, or if the capitalization (including loans from the joint venturers) of the joint venture to be established is, $1,000,000.00 or less, then no report is required, provided the enterprise does not own 200 acres or more of U.S. land. (If it owns 200 acres or more of U.S. land, a report is required regardless of the value of total assets.) OTHER CONSIDERATIONS The BE-14 merely identifies the transaction sufficiently to enable the BEA to obtain a BE-13 from the proper parties. If a BE-13 is filed, a BE-14 need not be filed.

REPORTING REQUIREMENTS

Form Number	Title of Form	Who Must File	Exemptions

BE-15	Interim Survey of Foreign Direct Invest-ment in the U.S. (Approved as annual report).	Each U.S. affiliate, except a bank, i.e., for each U.S. business enterprise in which a foreign person owned or controlled, directly or indirectly, 10% or more of the voting securities if an incorpo-rated U.S. business enterprise, or an equivalent interest if an unincorporated U.S. business enterprise, at any time during a calendar or fiscal year.	Exemption – A U.S. affiliate as consolidated, is not required to file a report if:
			
			a. Each of the following three items for the U.S. affiliate (not the foreign parent's share) was between –$5,000,000 and +$5,000,000 during the reporting period:
			
			  1. Total assets,
			  2. sales or gross operating revenues excluding sales taxes, and
			  3. Net income after provision for U.S. income taxes;
			
			and
			
			b. The U.S. affiliate did not own 200 acres or more of U.S. land during the reporting period (if the U.S. affiliate owned 200 acres or more of U.S. land, it must report regardless of the value of the three items listed above);
			
			or
			
			c. The U.S. affiliate is a bank, i.e., a business enterprise in which over 50 percent of its total revenues are generated by activities classified in industry code 600.

DUE DATE

Annual Form for:
1977–due 1/31/79
1978–due 10/31/79
1979–due 5/15/80

PENALTY

A fine not exceeding $10,000 or commanding such person to file the form, or both. It failure to file results from the willful neglect of an individual, he/she may be imprisoned for not more than one year or be fined not more than $10,000, or both.

OTHER CONSIDERATIONS

BE-12, instead of BE-15 would be used to report 1980 financial and operating data

REPORTING REQUIREMENTS

Form Number	Title of Form	Who Must File	Exemptions
BE-12	Benchmark Survey of Foreign Direct Investment in the U.S. - 1980.	Each U.S. affiliate, except a bank, i.e., for each U.S. business enterprise in which a foreign person owned or controlled, directly or indirectly, 10% or more of the voting securities if an incorporated U.S. business enterprise, or an equivalent interest if an unincorporated U.S. business enterprise, at any time during a calendar year or fiscal year.	Exemption - A U.S. affiliate is not required to file a report if:

a. Each of the following three items for the U.S. affiliate (not the foreign parent's share) was between -$1,000,000 and +$1,000,000 during the reporting period:

1. Total assets,
2. sales or gross operating revenues excluding sales taxes, and
3. Net income after provision for U.S. income taxes;

and

b. The U.S. affiliate did not own 200 acres or more of U.S. land during the reporting period (if the U.S. affiliate owned 200 acres or more of U.S. land, it must report regardless of the value of the three items listed above);

or

c. The U.S. affiliate is a bank, i.e., business enterprise in which over 50 percent of its total revenues are generated by activities classified in industry code 600.

OTHER CONSIDERATIONS

1. BE-12 should be filed instead of BE-13 every fifth year.

2. No BE-607 requires with BE-12 since the BE-607 form is incorporated into BE-12, Part I

DUE DATE

August 15, 1981

PENALTY

A fine not exceeding $10,000 or commanding such person to file the form, or both. If failure to file results from the willful neglect of an individual, he/she may be imprisoned for not more than one year or be fined not more than $10,000, or both.

REPORTING REQUIREMENTS

Form Number	Title of Form	Who Must File
BE-605	Transactions of a U.S. Corporation with Foreign Parent	Every U.S. corporation in which a foreign person had a direct and/or indirect ownership interest of 10% or more of the voting stock at any time during the reporting period, provided that there are direct transactions or positions between the U.S. Corporation (U.S. affiliate) and the foreign parent.

DUE DATE

Quarterly, within 30 days after the close of each quarter for all calendar or fiscal quarters, except for the final quarter of the calendar or fiscal year when the form may be filed within 45 days.

PENALTY

A fine not exceeding $10,000 or commanding such person to file the form, or both. If failure to file results from the willful neglect of an individual, he/she may be imprisoned for not more than one year or be fined not more than $10,000, or both.

Exemptions

All directly owned U.S. affiliates(fully consolidated) must file BE-605 unless exempt because a U.S. affiliate is not required to report if each of the following three items for the U.S. affiliate(not the foreign parent's share) is between -$5,000,000 and +$5,000,000.

1. Total assets,
2. Annual sales or gross operating revenues, excluding sales taxes, and
3. Annual net income after provision for U.S. income taxes

OTHER CONSIDERATIONS

1. May be required retroactively when it is determined that the exemption level has been exceeded. If a U.S. affiliate's total assets, sales, or net income exceed the exemption level in a given year, it is deemed that the exemption level will also be exceeded in the following year.

2. Reports are also required for the reporting period even though the U.S. affiliate may have been acquired, liquidated, sold or inactivated during the reporting period.

3. File with Form BE-607 if there is a change in the industry classification since the last filing of this form.

REPORTING REQUIREMENTS

Form Number	Title of Form	Who Must File	Exemptions
BE-607	Industry Classification Questionnaire	1. Each U.S. affiliate newly established or acquired by a foreign person; or 2. An existing U.S. affiliate whose industry classification changed since the last filing of BE-607 or BE-12	Filing is required only if the affiliate must file one of the other reports.

DUE DATE

Periodic filing of BE-607 is not necessary. It is to be submitted with initial filing of related reports, or whenever a change from one BEA 3-digit industry classification to another has occurred.

PENALTY

A fine not exceeding $10,000 or commanding such person to file the form, or both. If failure to file results from the willful neglect of an individual, he/she may be imprisoned for not more than one year or be fined not more than $10,000, or both.

OTHER CONSIDERATIONS

Generally filed with BE-13A or BE-13B.

REPORTING REQUIREMENTS

Form Number	Title of Form	Who Must File	Exemptions
ASCS-153	Agricultural Foreign Investment Disclosure Act Report	A "foreign person" owning, acquiring or transferring agricultural land. A "foreign person" includes a foreign individual, corporation or other entity, and also includes a U.S. corporation in which a significant interest is directly or indirectly held by a "foreign person".	Land held for personal use of under one acre where the agricultural products are produced for personal use. Leaseholds of under ten years, future interests, easements unrelated to agricultural production, and security interests in agricultural land are also exempt from reporting.

DUE DATE

90 days after date of acquisition or transfer; foreign persons holding an interest in agricultural land before February 2, 1979 were required to submit ASCS-153 by August 1, 1979.

PENALTY

Late reports will be assessed a penalty of one-tenth of one percent of the fair market value of the foreign person's interest in the reportable property, as determined by the ASCS for each week or portion thereof that the violation continues. However, the late filing penalty is not to exceed 25%.

OTHER CONSIDERATIONS

The information on this form is available for public inspection in the Washington, D.C. and the local Agricultural Stabilization and Conservation Service Office.

See Reiner. "The Agricultural Foreign Investment Disclosure Act and its Regulation", The Agricultural Law Journal, Winter 1981.

FORM BE-12
(REV. 12-80)

U.S. DEPARTMENT OF COMMERCE
BUREAU OF ECONOMIC ANALYSIS (BEA)

MANDATORY – CONFIDENTIAL

**BENCHMARK SURVEY OF
FOREIGN DIRECT INVESTMENT IN THE U.S.**

1980

| RETURN REPORTS TO | U.S. Department of Commerce Bureau of Economic Analysis BE-50 (IN) Washington, D.C. 20230 |

Important Read *Instruction Booklet*

before completing form. The instructions given below are only a brief summary of certain ones relating to this form.

BANKS – See page   of *Instruction Booklet* regarding special instructions and report forms for reporting by banks and bank holding companies.

● **DEFINITIONS**

1. **Foreign direct investment in the United States** means the ownership or control, directly or indirectly, by one foreign person of 10 per centum or more of the voting securities of an incorporated U.S. business enterprise or an equivalent interest in an unincorporated U.S. business enterprise, including a branch.

2. **Business enterprise** means any organization, association, branch, or venture which exists to profitmaking purposes or to otherwise secure economic advantage, and any ownership of any real estate.

3. **Affiliate** means a business enterprise located in one country which is directly or indirectly owned or controlled by a person of another country to the extent of 10 per centum or more of its voting securities for an incorporated business enterprise or an equivalent interest for an unincorporated business enterprise, including a branch.

4. **U.S. affiliate** means an affiliate located in the United States in which a foreign person has a direct investment.

5. **U.S. affiliate's 1980 fiscal year** is the affiliate's financial reporting year that has an ending date in calendar year 1980.

● **REPORTING REQUIREMENTS**

1. **Who must report** – A BE-12 report is required for each U.S. affiliate, i.e., for each U.S. business enterprise in which one foreign person owned or controlled, directly or indirectly, 10 percent or more of the voting securities if an incorporated U.S. business enterprise, or an equivalent interest if an unincorporated U.S. business enterprise, at anytime during the business enterprise's 1980 fiscal year.

2. **Consolidated reporting** – A U.S. affiliate shall file on a fully consolidated basis, including in the full consolidation all other U.S. affiliates in which it directly or indirectly owns more than 50 percent of the outstanding voting securities. Hereinafter, the fully consolidated entity is considered to be one U.S. affiliate. See Instruction Booklet, page   . Exemption criteria are applied to the consolidated entity.

3. **Aggregation of real estate investments** – A foreign person holding real estate investments must aggregate all such holdings for the purpose of applying the exemption level tests. If the aggregate of such holdings exceeds one or more of the exemption levels, then the holdings must be reported even if they individually would be exempt.

4. **Exemption** – A U.S. affiliate as consolidated, or aggregated in the case of real estate investments, is not required to file a report, if:

   (a) Each of the following three items for the U.S. affiliate (not the foreign parent's share) was between –$1,000,000 and +$1,000,000 during the reporting period:
   (1) Total assets,
   (2) Sales or gross operating revenues, excluding sales taxes, and
   (3) Net income after provision for U.S. income taxes;

   and

   (b) The U.S. affiliate did not own 200 acres or more of U.S. land during the reporting period (if the U.S. affiliate owned 200 acres or more of U.S. land, it must report regardless of the value of the three items listed above).

   A U.S. affiliate that is not required to file a completed Form BE-12 because it falls below the exemption levels, must complete and file a Claim for Not Filing a Form BE-12, with Item 5 of the Claim marked, and furnish the information requested in Item 5. (The Claim is on the last page of Form BE-12 and should be detached for filing.)

5. **Response required** – A person or their agent who is sent a report form by BEA and who claims to not be subject to the reporting requirements must file a completed "Claim for Not Filing a Form BE-12" which is printed on the last page of Form BE-12. The Claim must be filed within 30 days of the date the BE-12 was sent by BEA.

6. **Due Date** – A completed report on the BE-12 is due no later than

● **ASSISTANCE** – Telephone (202) 523–0547.

● **GENERAL NOTES**

1. Number of acres, number of employees, hours worked, and other non-monetary amounts must be reported to the nearest whole unit.

2. Monetary amounts must be reported in U.S. dollars rounded to the nearest thousand (omitting 000). Do not enter amounts in the shaded portions of any line.
EXAMPLE: If amount is $1,334,615.00, report as:

Bil.	Mil.	Thous.	Dols.
	1	335	/////

3. If an item is between +$500,000 and –$500,000 enter "0."

4. Use parentheses to indicate negative numbers.

5. All questions must be answered in the context of the reporting period delineated in items 8, 9, and 10.

Part I IDENTIFICATION OF U.S. AFFILIATE

1. Name and principal mailing address

A mailing label, if affixed, shows, among other things, the name and address of this U.S. affiliate, as known to BEA. If there are no changes to the name and address, write "same" in space below. If there are any changes in name or address, enter correct name and address below in full.

If no mailing label is affixed, or if there is a change in the name and address as given on the mailing label, print name and address in blocks; skip a single block between words.

BEA USE ONLY

Name of U.S. Affiliate

Street or P.O. Box

City and State   ZIP Code

2. Is more than 50 percent of the ownership interest in this U.S. affiliate owned by another U.S. affiliate of your foreign parent?

   1 ☐ Yes   2 ☐ No

If the answer is "Yes," do not complete this report unless this affiliate qualifies for filing separately and has obtained permission from BEA to do so. Otherwise, the report must reflect information and data for, and be filed in the name of, the fully-consolidated U.S. business enterprise meeting the definition of U.S. affiliate. Please forward this BE-12 survey packet to the U.S. business enterprise owning your company to the extent of more than 50 percent, notify BEA of the action taken, and provide to BEA the name and address of the U.S. business enterprise that is required to file for the fully-consolidated U.S. business enterprise.

(WHEREVER THE INSTRUCTION "MARK ONE" IS GIVEN BELOW, IF IT IS NECESSARY TO MARK MORE THAN ONE ANSWER, GIVE AN EXPLANATION.)

3. Form of organization of U.S. affiliate (Mark one):

   1 ☐ Incorporated in U.S.

   2 ☐ U.S. partnership

   3 ☐ U.S. branch of a foreign person

   4 ☐ Real property not in 1–3 above

   5 ☐ Business enterprise incorporated abroad, but whose head office is located in the United States and whose business activity is conducted in, or from, the United States

   6 ☐ Other – Specify:

4. Enter primary Employer Identification Number used by U.S. affiliate to file U.S. income and payroll taxes.

   ☐☐–☐☐☐☐☐☐☐ ◄── E.I. Number

5. U.S. affiliates fully consolidated in this report:

If this report is for a single unconsolidated U.S. affiliate enter "1" in the box. If more than one U.S. affiliate is fully consolidated in this report, enter the number of U.S. affiliates fully consolidated. (Hereinafter, they are considered to be one U.S. affiliate.) Exclude all minority-owned U.S. business enterprises, and all foreign business enterprises owned by this U.S. affiliate, from full consolidation; such affiliates must be included in this report on the equity basis, or cost basis if less than 20 percent owned. See consolidation instruction, page   of the *Instruction Booklet*. (Note that all-more-than-50-percent-owned U.S. affiliates must be fully consolidated in this report unless permission has been received from BEA to do otherwise; those not fully consolidated must file a separate Form BE-12.)

   ☐ ◄── Number   If number is greater than one, Supplement A must be completed.

6. U.S. affiliates not fully consolidated:

Number of U.S. affiliates in which this U.S. affiliate has an ownership interest that ARE NOT fully consolidated in this report.

   ☐ ◄── Number   If figure is not zero, Supplement B must be completed. The U.S. affiliate named in Item I must include data for such U.S. affiliates in this report on an equity basis, and must notify such other U.S. affiliates of their obligation to file a BE-12 in their own name.

7. Does this U.S. affiliate have an equity interest in a foreign business enterprise or conduct operations outside the United States?

   1 ☐ Yes   2 ☐ No   If "Yes," do not fully consolidate such enterprises in this report; include them in data on an equity basis, or cost basis if less than 20 percent owned.

MANDATORY – This survey is being conducted pursuant to the International Investment Survey Act of 1976 (P.L. 94–472, 90 Stat. 2059, 22 U.S.C. 3101 to 3108 – hereinafter "the Act"), and the filing of reports is mandatory pursuant to Section 5(b)(2) of the Act (22 U.S.C. 3104).

PENALTIES – Whoever fails to report may be subject to a civil penalty not exceeding $10,000 and to injunctive relief commanding such person to comply, or both. Whoever willfully fails to report shall be fined not more than $10,000 and, if an individual, may be imprisoned for not more than one year, or both. Any officer, director, employee, or agent of any corporation who knowingly participates in such violations, upon conviction, may be punished by a like fine, imprisonment, or both. (See Section 6 of the Act, 22 U.S.C. 3105.)

CONFIDENTIALITY – The information filed in this report may be used only for analytical and statistical purposes and access to the information shall be available only to officials and employees (including consultants and contractors and their employees) of agencies designated by the President to perform functions under the Act. The President may authorize the exchange of the information between agencies or officials designated to perform functions under the Act, but only for analytical and statistical purposes. No official or employee (including consultants and contractors and their employees) shall publish or make available any information collected under the Act in such a manner that the person to whom the information relates can be specifically identified. Reports and copies of reports prepared pursuant to the Act are confidential and their submission or disclosure shall not be compelled by any person without the prior written permission of the person filing the report and the customer of such person where the information supplied is identifiable as being derived from the records of such customer (22 U.S.C. 3104).

Print name and address

U.S. PERSON FOR BEA TO CONSULT ABOUT THIS REPORT:	U.S. TELEPHONE NUMBER		
	Area Code	Number	Extension

► **CERTIFICATION**   The undersigned official certifies that the information contained in this report is correct and complete to the best of his/her knowledge.

Authorized Official's Signature	Type Name and Title	Date

18 U.S.C. 1001 (Crimes and Criminal Procedure) makes it a criminal offense to make a willfully false statement or representation to any department or agency of the United States as to any matter within its jurisdiction. Any officer, director, employee, or agent of any corporation who knowingly participates in a willful failure to report, upon conviction, may be punished by a fine, imprisonment, or both (22 U.S.C. 3105). For a further citation of applicable statutes, see the *Instruction Booklet* to this form.

Part I – IDENTIFICATION OF U.S. AFFILIATE (Continued)

8. This U.S. affiliate's 1980 fiscal year ends on:

	Month	Day	Year

NOTE: For a U.S. business enterprise that was a U.S. affiliate for all of FY 1980 – Data for the reporting period should be for the U.S. affiliate's 1980 fiscal year; data for close FY 1980 should be for the U.S. affiliate as it existed at the ending date of the 1980 fiscal year; and data for close FY 1979 should be for the U.S. affiliate as it existed one year prior to the 1980 fiscal year date. (Close FY 1979 data must not be restated due to changes in the entity during FY 1980.)

For a U.S. business enterprise that was a U.S. affiliate for only part of FY 1980 – If the enterprise became a U.S. affiliate during the reporting period, the Close FY 1979 data columns should all be zero. If the enterprise ceased to be an affiliate during the reporting period, the Close FY 1980 data columns should all be zero.

9. Was the U.S. business enterprise a U.S. affiliate for only part of FY 1980?

1 ☐ Yes
2 ☐ No

10. If the answer to item 9 is yes, complete one of the following:

	Month	Day	Year
Date U.S. business enterprise became a U.S. affiliate.			
OR			
Date U.S. business enterprise ceased to be a U.S. affiliate.			

11. Was there a change in the entity during FY 1980 that caused prior year data to be restated?

1 ☐ Yes   If "Yes," please note that all close FY 1979 data must be before restatement due to a change in the entity, unless otherwise specified. The effect of restatement on retained earnings of an incorporated affiliate or owners' equity for an unincorporated affiliate, must be entered in item 70, and the effect of restatement on property, plant, and equipment accounts must be entered in item 99.

2 ☐ No

Ownership – Enter percent of ownership, to a tenth of one percent, based on voting stock if an incorporated affiliate or an equivalent interest if an unincorporated affiliate, in this U.S. affiliate held directly by –

	Close FY 1980 (1)	Close FY 1979 (2)
12. All foreign parents of this affiliate – Give name of each (if more than 4, continue on separate sheet):	. %	. %
a.	/////	/////
b.	/////	/////
c.	/////	/////
d.	/////	/////
13. All U.S. affiliates of the foreign parents included in item 12	. %	. %
14. All other U.S. persons	. %	. %
15. All other foreign persons	. %	. %
16. TOTAL – Sum of items 12 through 15 ⟶	100. 0 %	100. 0 %

If there is an entry in item 13, column 1 or column 2, give the information requested for each U.S. affiliate holding a direct ownership interest in this U.S. affiliate (if more than 4, continue on separate sheet).

U.S. affiliate holding direct ownership interest in this U.S. affiliate		Percent direct ownership in this U.S. affiliate (For the close of each year the sum of these percents for all direct owners must equal item 13)		U.S. affiliate in ownership chain which is directly owned by a foreign parent	
Name	BEA Identification Number	Close FY 1980	Close FY 1979	Name	BEA Identification Number
(1)	(2)	(3)	(4)	(5)	(6)
17.		. %	. %		
18.		. %	. %		
19.		. %	. %		
20.		. %	. %		

21. Major activity of fully consolidated U.S. affiliate (Mark one)
(For inactive affiliate, indicate the activity pertinent to the last active period; for "start-up," show the intended activity.)

Extracting oil or minerals (including exploration and development) (BEA codes in the 100 series, except 070 and 138)   1 ☐

Manufacturing (fabricating, assembling, processing) (BEA codes in the 200–300 series)   2 ☐

Selling or distributing goods (BEA codes in the 500 series)   3 ☐

Real estate (investing in or engaging in as an operator, manager, developer, lessor, agent, or broker) (BEA codes 640, 650, and 652)   4 ☐

Providing a service (BEA codes in the 400–800 series, and 070 and 138; exclude 640, 650, and 652)   5 ☐

Other – Specify: 6 ☐

22. What is the major product or service involved in this activity? If a product, also state what is done to it; i.e., whether it is mined, manufactured, sold at wholesale, transported, packaged, etc.

BEA USE ONLY

FORM BE-12 (REV. 12-80)   Page 2

Part I – IDENTIFICATION OF U.S. AFFILIATE (Continued)

Industry classification of fully consolidated U.S. affiliate (based on sales or gross operating revenues) –
Enter the appropriate 3-digit industry code(s) and the sales (as defined in item 56) associated with each code.
For a full explanation of each code, see the _Industry Classifications and Export and Import Trade Classifications Booklet._ If you use fewer than eight codes you must account for total sales. For an inactive affiliate, show the industry classification(s) pertinent to the last active period; for "start-ups" with no sales, show the intended activity(ies).

	Industry code (1)	Sales (2) Bil. Mil. Thous. Dols.
23. Enter code with largest sales	1	2
24. Enter code with second largest sales	1	2
25. Enter code with third largest sales	1	2
26. Enter code with fourth largest sales	1	2
27. Enter code with fifth largest sales	1	2
28. Enter code with sixth largest sales	1	2
29. Enter code with seventh largest sales	1	2
30. Enter code with eighth largest sales	1	2
31. Sales accounted for (Sum of items 23 through 30)		2
32. Sales not accounted for above		2
33. Total sales – Sum of items 31 and 32 and must equal item 56. ⟶		2
BEA USE ONLY ▶		2

Summary of Industry Classifications

AGRICULTURE, FORESTRY, AND FISHING

010 Agricultural production – crops
020 Agricultural production – livestock, except beef cattle feedlots
021 Agricultural production – beef cattle feedlots
070 Agricultural services
080 Forestry
090 Fishing, hunting, and trapping

MINING

101 Iron ore
102 Copper, lead, zinc, gold, and silver ores
103 Bauxite and other aluminum ores
109 Other metallic ores and metal mining services
110 Coal and other nonmetallic minerals, except oil and gas
133 Crude petroleum extraction (no refining) and natural gas
138 Oil and gas field services

CONSTRUCTION

150 Construction

MANUFACTURING

201 Meat products
202 Dairy products
203 Canned and preserved fruits and vegetables
204 Grain mill products
205 Bakery products
208 Beverages
209 Other food and kindred products
210 Tobacco manufactures
220 Textile mill products
230 Apparel and other finished products made from fabrics and similar materials
240 Lumber and wood products, except furniture
250 Furniture and fixtures
262 Pulp, paper, and board mills
264 Miscellaneous converted paper products
265 Paperboard containers and boxes
270 Printing, publishing, and allied industries
281 Industrial chemicals, plastics materials, and synthetics
283 Drugs
284 Soap, cleaners, and toilet goods
285 Paints and allied products
287 Agricultural chemicals
289 Chemical products, n.e.c.
291 Integrated petroleum refining and extraction
292 Petroleum refining without extraction
299 Petroleum and coal products, n.e.c.
305 Rubber products
307 Miscellaneous plastics products
310 Leather and leather products
321 Glass products
329 Stone, clay, cement, and concrete products

MANUFACTURING – Continued

331 Primary metal products, ferrous
335 Primary metal products, non-ferrous
341 Metal cans and shipping containers
342 Cutlery, hand tools, and hardware
343 Metal plumbing fixtures and heating equipment, except electric and warm air
344 Fabricated structural metal products
345 Screw machine products, bolts, nuts, screws, rivets, and washers
346 Metal stampings and forgings
349 Fabricated metal products, n.e.c.; ordnance; and coating, engraving, and allied services
351 Engines and turbines
352 Farm and garden machinery and equipment
353 Construction, mining, and materials handling machinery and equipment
354 Metalworking machinery and equipment
355 Special industry machinery
356 General industrial machinery and equipment
357 Office, computing, and accounting machines
358 Refrigeration and service industry machinery
359 Machinery, except electrical, n.e.c.
363 Household electrical appliances
364 Electric lighting and wiring equipment
366 Radio, television, and communication equipment
367 Electronic components and accessories
369 Electrical machinery, n.e.c.
371 Motor vehicles and equipment
379 Other transportation equipment, n.e.c.
381 Scientific instruments and measuring and controlling devices
383 Optical and ophthalmic goods
384 Surgical, medical, and dental instruments and supplies
386 Photographic equipment and supplies
387 Watches, clocks, and watchcases
390 Miscellaneous manufactured products, n.e.c.

TRANSPORTATION, COMMUNICATIONS, ELECTRIC, GAS, AND SANITARY SERVICES

441 Petroleum tanker operations
449 Other water transportation
450 Transportation by air
461 Pipeline transportation, including natural gas transmission
470 Petroleum storage for hire
479 Transportation, warehousing, terminal facilities, travel agents, and related services, n.e.c.
480 Communications
490 Electric, gas, and sanitary services

WHOLESALE TRADE

501 Motor vehicles and automotive parts and supplies
503 Lumber and other construction materials
504 Farm and garden machinery, equipment, and supplies
505 Metals and minerals, except petroleum
506 Electrical goods
507 Hardware, plumbing and heating equipment and supplies
508 Machinery, equipment, and supplies, except farm and garden machinery and equipment
509 Miscellaneous durable goods, n.e.c.
511 Paper and paper products
512 Drugs, proprietaries, and sundries
513 Apparel, piece goods, and notions
514 Groceries and related products
515 Farm-product raw materials
517 Petroleum and petroleum products
519 Miscellaneous nondurable goods, n.e.c.

RETAIL TRADE

540 Food stores and eating and drinking places
554 Gasoline service stations
590 Retail trade, except gasoline service stations, food stores, and eating and drinking places

FINANCE, INSURANCE, AND REAL ESTATE

600 Banking, including bank holding companies
610 Finance, except banking
630 Insurance carriers, agents, brokers, and services
640 Lessors of gasoline service stations and sites
650 Real estate, except agricultural and forestry and except lessors of gasoline service stations and sites
652 Real estate, agricultural and forestry
660 Combinations of real estate, insurance, loans, and law offices
671 Holding companies, excluding bank holding companies
672 Individuals, estates, and trusts holding investments

SERVICES

700 Hotels, rooming houses, camps, and other lodging places
731 Advertising
780 Motion pictures, including television tape and film
891 Engineering, architectural, and surveying services
893 Accounting, auditing, and bookkeeping services
894 Religious, charitable, and other groups, associations or organizations operating on a noncommercial, nonprofit basis
899 Other personal business services, n.e.c., provided on a commercial basis

Part II – FINANCIAL AND OPERATING DATA OF U.S. AFFILIATE

- Use U.S. generally accepted accounting principles unless otherwise specified. All data must represent a full consolidation of domestic majority-owned U.S. affiliates only; include other U.S. and foreign business enterprises on the equity basis, or cost basis if less than 20 percent owned.

- Close FY 1979 balances should not be restated due to changes in the entity.

- U.S. AFFILIATES THAT ARE INSURANCE COMPANIES OR IN REAL ESTATE – See the special instructions in the Instruction Booklet, page

- IMPORTANT NOTE – UNINCORPORATED U.S. AFFILIATES – A change in method of reporting has been instituted for unincorporated U.S. affiliates commencing with this survey. Before proceeding, see discussion of change as given in the Instruction Booklet, page

IMPORTANT EXAMPLE: Report all dollar figures below in thousands of U.S. dollars, as illustrated:

	Bil.	Mil.	Thous.	Dols.
EXAMPLE: If figure is $2,125,628,000.00	2	125	628	

SECTION A — BALANCE SHEET

UNINCORPORATED U.S. AFFILIATE: All asset and liability items should be disaggregated in the detail shown; in particular, receivables and payables between the affiliate and the foreign parent should be shown in the proper asset and liability accounts of the affiliate rather than being included only as a net amount in total owners' equity. Include asset and liability items of the U.S. affiliate that are carried only on an owners' books.

	Balances							
	Close FY 1980 (1)				Close FY 1979 (unrestated) (2)			
	Bil.	Mil.	Thous.	Dols.	Bil.	Mil.	Thous.	Dols.
• ASSETS								
34. Cash items – Deposits in financial institutions and other cash items. Do NOT include overdrafts here as negative cash.	1 / $				2 / $			
35. Trade accounts and trade notes receivable, current, net of allowances for doubtful items.	1				2			
36. Other current receivables, net of allowances for doubtful items.	1				2			
37. Inventories – Land development companies should exclude land held for resale (include in item 38); finance and insurance companies should exclude inventories of marketable securities (include it item 38 or item 42, as appropriate).	1				2			
38. Other current assets, including current marketable securities.	1				2			
39. Property, plant, and equipment, net – Land, timber, mineral rights, structures, machinery, equipment, special tools, deposit containers, construction in progress, and capitalized tangible and intangible exploration and development costs of the affiliate, at historical cost net of accumulated depreciation, depletion, amortization, and like charges. Include items on capital leases from others, per FASB 13. Exclude all other types of intangible assets, and land held for resale. (An unincorporated affiliate should include items owned by its foreign parent but which are in the affiliate's possession whether or not carried on its own books or records.)	1				2			
40. Equity investment in other U.S. affiliates that are not fully consolidated – For those owned 20 percent or more, show on the equity basis to include equity in undistributed earnings since acquisition; for those owned less than 20 percent, show at cost.	1				2			
41. Equity investment in foreign business enterprises owned 20 percent or more – Show on the equity basis to include equity in undistributed earnings since acquisition.	1				2			
42. Noncurrent investments not shown in items 40 and 41 – Noncurrent marketable securities, other equity investments whether carried at cost or on equity basis, and other investments.	1				2			
43. Trade accounts and trade notes receivable, noncurrent, net of allowances for doubtful items	1				2			
44. Other noncurrent assets – Intangible assets, net of amortization, and other noncurrent assets not included above.	1				2			
45. TOTAL ASSETS – Sum of items 34 through 44. ⟶	1 / $				2 / $			
• LIABILITIES								
46. Trade accounts and trade notes payable, current	1				2			
47. Other current liabilities – Current portion due of long-term debt, overdrafts, and other current liabilities not included in item 46; having an original maturity of one year or less.	1				2			
48. Long-term debt – Debt with an original maturity of more than one year or with no stated maturity, and debt with an original maturity of one year or less that has been renewed, or with respect to which there is the intention and the means to renew, extend or refinance for more than one year. Include capitalized lease obligations; exclude current portion due of long-term debt.	1				2			
49. Other noncurrent liabilities – Items other than those identifiable as long-term debt, such as deferred taxes and underlying minority interest in consolidated U.S. subsidiaries. Specify major items:	1				2			
50. TOTAL LIABILITIES – Sum of items 46 through 49 ⟶	1 / $				2 / $			
• OWNERS' EQUITY (INCORPORATED AFFILIATE ONLY, ITEMS 51–54)								
51. Capital stock – Common and preferred, voting and non-voting.	1				2			
52. Additional paid-in capital.	1				2			
53. Retained earnings (deficit).	1				2			
54. Treasury stock.	1 ( )				2 ( )			
• TOTAL OWNERS' EQUITY (INCORPORATED OR UNINCORPORATED U.S. AFFILIATE)								
55. Items 51 + 52 + 53 + 54 for incorporated U.S. affiliate. For an unincorporated U.S. affiliate, give no breakdown in items 51–54, but enter total owners' equity in this item. For both incorporated and unincorporated affiliates, total owners' equity must equal item 45 minus item 50.	1 / $				2 / $			

FORM BE-12 (REV. 12-80)

Page 4

Part II – FINANCIAL AND OPERATING DATA OF U.S. AFFILIATE (Continued)

SECTION B   **INCOME STATEMENT**
(Net income must be calculated in accordance with the "all inclusive" concept of the income statement.)

	Amount (I)			
	Bil.	Mil.	Thous.	Dols.

● INCOME

56. Sales or gross operating revenues, excluding sales taxes — Gross sales minus returns, allowances, and discounts, or gross operating revenues, both exclusive of sales or consumption taxes levied directly on the consumer and excise taxes levied directly on manufacturers, wholesalers and retailers.

57. Income from other U.S. affiliates for which investment is shown in item 40 — For those owned 20 percent or more, report equity in earnings during the reporting period; for those owned less than 20 percent, report dividends received.

58. Equity in net income of foreign business enterprises owned 20 percent or more, for which investment is shown in item 41 — Equity in earnings during the reporting period.

59. Income from other equity investments — Income from equity investments included in item 38 or item 42. For those business enterprises owned 20 percent or more, report equity in earnings during the reporting period; for those owned less than 20 percent, report dividends received. Do not include any interest income.

60. Net realized and unrealized capital gains (losses) — Include gains (losses) resulting from the sale or disposition of investment securities, property, plant, and equipment, or other assets; those resulting from changes in the dollar value of the affiliate's foreign currency denominated assets and liabilities due to changes in foreign exchange rates during the reporting period; and all other recognized capital gains (losses), including those resulting from revaluation of assets, whether or not realized.

61. Other income — Non-operating and other income not included above. *Specify*

62. TOTAL INCOME – Sum of items 56 through 61. ⟶

● COSTS AND EXPENSES

63. Costs of goods sold — Operating expenses (other than selling, general and administrative expenses) that relate to sales or gross operating revenues, item 56. Include production royalty payments to governments, their subdivisions and agencies, and to other persons. Include depletion charges representing the amortization of the actual cost of capital assets, but exclude all other depletion charges.

64. Selling, general, and administrative expenses.

65. Income taxes — Provision for U.S. Federal, State, and local income taxes. Exclude production royalty payments.

66. Other costs and expenses not included above, including underlying minority interest in profits that arises out of consolidation. — *Specify major items:*

67. TOTAL COSTS AND EXPENSES – Sum of items 63 through 66 ⟶

● NET INCOME

68. Net income after provision for U.S. Federal, State, and local income taxes (item 62 minus item 67).

SECTION C   **CHANGE IN RETAINED EARNINGS OF INCORPORATED U.S. AFFILIATE, OR IN TOTAL OWNERS' EQUITY OF UNINCORPORATED U.S. AFFILIATE**

	Amount (I)			
	Bil.	Mil.	Thous.	Dols.

69. Balance, close FY 1979 before restatement due to a change in the entity, if any — Incorporated affiliate, enter amount from item 53, column 2; unincorporated affiliate, enter amount from item 55, column 2.

70. Increase (decrease) to FY 1979 closing balance resulting from restatement due to a change in the entity. *Specify reasons for change.*

71. FY 1979 closing balance as restated — Item 69 plus item 70.

72. Net income — Enter amount from item 68.

73. Dividends or remitted earnings — Incorporated affiliate, enter amount of dividends declared, inclusive of withholding taxes, out of current or prior period income, on common and preferred stock, excluding stock dividends. Unincorporated affiliate, enter amount of current or prior period net income distributed to owners.

74. Net realized and unrealized capital gains (losses) that were not included in the determination of net income and therefore excluded from item 60, but that were taken directly to retained earnings or to a surplus account for an incorporated affiliate, or to owners' equity for an unincorporated affiliate. Report amount after giving effect to income tax liability (benefit) if any, on the gains (losses). *Specify —*

75. Other increases (decreases) in retained earnings of an incorporated affiliate, including stock or liquidating dividends, or in total owners' equity of an unincorporated affiliate, including capital contributions (return of capital). *Specify —*

76. FY 1980 closing balance — Sum of items 71, 72, 74, and 75 minus item 73. For incorporated affiliate, must equal item 53, column 1; and for an unincorporated affiliate, must equal item 55, column 1.

SECTION D   **CHANGE IN ADDITIONAL PAID-IN CAPITAL OF INCORPORATED AFFILIATE**

	Amount (I)			
	Bil.	Mil.	Thous.	Dols.

77. Increase (decrease) in all additional paid-in, or contributed, capital, in addition to or in excess of capital stock items, causing difference between close FY 1980 and close FY 1979 balances of item 52. *Specify —*

Part II – FINANCIAL AND OPERATING DATA OF U.S. AFFILIATE (Continued)

SECTION E — COMPOSITION OF EXTERNAL FINANCES OF U.S. AFFILIATE

	Total (1)	Foreign parent(s) and its (their) foreign affiliates (2)	Other foreign persons, including foreign business enterprises owned by this U.S. affiliate (3)	U.S. persons (4)
	Bil. Mil. Thous. Dols.	Bil. Mil. Thous. Dols.	Bil. Mil. Thous. Dols.	Bil. Mil. Thous. Dols.

● CLOSE FY 1980:

Current liabilities — Sum of items 78 and 79, column I, must equal sum of Items 46 and 47, column I

78. To banks

79. To other than banks

Long-term debt — Sum of items 80 and 81, column I must equal item 48, column I

80. To banks

81. To other than banks

82. Current receivables — Column I must equal sum of items 35 and 36, column I

83. Noncurrent financial investments and noncurrent receivables — Column I must equal sum of item 43 and that part of item 42 that is financial investments, column I

84. Total owners' equity — For incorporated U.S. affiliate, column I must equal sum of items 51, 52, and 53, column I; for unincorporated U.S. affiliate, column I must equal item 55, column I

● CLOSE FY 1979, before restatement due to a change in the entity:

Current liabilities — Sum of items 85 and 86, column I, must equal sum of items 46 and 47, column 2

85. To banks

86. To other than banks

Long-term debt — Sum of items 87 and 88, column I, must equal item 48, column 2

87. To banks

88. To other than banks

89. Current receivables — Column I must equal sum of items 35 and 36, column 2

90. Noncurrent financial investments and noncurrent receivables — Column I must equal sum of item 43 and that part of item 42 that is financial investments, column 2

91. Total owners' equity — For incorporated U.S. affiliate, column I must equal sum of items 51, 52, and 53, column 2; for unincorporated U.S. affiliate, column I must equal item 55, column 2

► BEA USE ONLY ►

SECTION F — LAND AND OTHER PROPERTY, PLANT, AND EQUIPMENT

Land and other property, plant, and equipment includes all land and other property, plant, and equipment carried anywhere on the U.S. affiliate's balance sheet, whether or not the intent is to hold and actively use the asset in the operating activity of the business. Land refers to any part of the earth's surface; other property, plant, and equipment includes timber, mineral and like rights owned, all structures, machinery, equipment, special tools, and other depreciable property, construction in progress, and capitalized tangible and intangible exploration and development costs, but excludes other types of intangible assets. In addition to items carried in property, plant, and equipment (item 39), such items may be carried in noncurrent investments (item 42), or in other current or noncurrent assets.

Items, including land, being acquired from others pursuant to capital leases are to be considered as owned by the affiliate; items which the affiliate has sold on a capital lease basis are not to be considered as owned by the affiliate. The capitalized value of timber, mineral, and like rights leased by the affiliate from others is to be included.

Expenditures cover all acquisitions by, or transfers to, the U.S. affiliate of the items detailed above, irrespective of where carried on the balance sheet. Exclude from expenditures all changes in land and in other property, plant, and equipment accounted for by a change in the entity (i.e., due to mergers, acquisitions, divestitures, etc.) during your 1980 fiscal year; such changes are separately accounted for in item 99.

	Number of acres (1)	Land — Gross book value (historical cost) (2)	Other property, plant, and equipment — Gross book value (historical cost) (3)	Other property, plant, and equipment — Net book value (4)
		Bil. Mil. Thous. Dols.	Bil. Mil. Thous. Dols.	Bil. Mil. Thous. Dols.

● Land and other property, plant, and equipment at close of FY 1980:

92. Carried in property, plant, and equipment accounts — Column 2 plus column 4 must equal item 39, column I.

93. Carried in noncurrent investments — that part of item 42 that is land or other property, plant, and equipment.

94. Carried elsewhere on balance sheet (Specify where):

95. Total — Sum of items 92 through 94 ►

	Amount (1)
	Bil. Mil. Thous. Dols.

● Schedule of change from FY 1979 closing balances to FY 1980 closing balances:

Balances at close FY 1979, before restatement due to a change in the entity:

96. Gross book value (historical cost) of all land and other property, plant, and equipment, wherever carried on balance sheet

97. Accumulated depreciation and depletion applicable to assets included in item 96

98. Net book value of assets included in item 96 — item 96 minus item 97

Changes during FY 1980:

99. If answer to item 11 was "Yes," give amount by which the net book value in item 98 would be restated due to a change in the entity. If a decrease, put amount in parentheses.

Expenditures by the U.S. affiliate for, or transfers into the U.S. affiliate of:

100. Land

101. Mineral rights

102. New* plant, equipment and property other than land and mineral rights

103. Used* plant, equipment, and property other than land and mineral rights.

104. Depreciation and like charges applicable to assets defined for inclusion in this section

105. Depletion and like charges applicable to assets defined for inclusion in this section

106. Net book value of sales, retirements, or transfers out of assets defined for inclusion in this section. Other increases (decreases)— Specify:

Balances at close of FY 1980:

107. Net book value — Equals sum of items 98, 99, 100, 101, 102, and 103, minus sum of items 104, 105, and 106; and must also equal item 95, column 2 plus column 4

108. Accumulated depreciation, depletion, and like charges applicable to assets included in item 107

109. Gross book value (historical cost) of all land and other property, plant, and equipment, wherever carried on balance sheet — Sum of items 107 and 108 and also must equal item 95, column 2 plus column 4

* If it would be burdensome to exclude all used plant, equipment, etc., from new, then minor used items may be included in item 102 and only major items of used reported in 103.

Part II – FINANCIAL AND OPERATING DATA OF U.S. AFFILIATE (Continued)

SECTION G — INTEREST, TAXES, AND SUBSIDIES

	Amount (1)
	Bil. Mil. Thous. Dols.
110. Interest received by U.S. affiliate from, or credited to U.S. affiliate by, all payors (including foreign parents and affiliates), net of tax withheld at the source. Do not net against interest paid (item 111).	
111. Interest paid or credited to all payees (including foreign parents and affiliates), by U.S. affiliate, gross of tax withheld by the affiliate. Do not net against interest received (item 110).	
112. Production royalty payments — Include amounts paid or accrued for the year to U.S. Federal, State, or local governments, their subdivisions and agencies for production royalties for natural resources.	
113. Taxes (other than income and payroll taxes) and non-tax payments (other than production royalties) — Amount paid or accrued for the year, net of refunds or credits, to U.S. Federal, State, or local governments, their subdivisions and agencies for sales, consumption and excise taxes; property and other taxes on the value of assets and capital; any remaining taxes (other than income and payroll taxes); and all payments and accruals of non-tax liabilities (other than for purchases of goods and services and payments of production royalties), such as import and export duties, license fees, fines, penalties, and similar items.	
114. Subsidies and grants received — Monetary and other grants received or accrued from U.S. Federal, State, or local governments, their subdivisions and agencies, that are not payments for property, goods, or services purchased from this affiliate, whether such subsidies or grants are reflected in income of the affiliate, or are used for investment or are to cover losses of property, plant, and equipment.	

SECTION H — RESEARCH AND DEVELOPMENT (R & D)

	Amount (1)
	Bil. Mil. Thous. Dols.
115. Research and development expenditures, calculated in accordance with FASB-2. All R & D costs incurred, including depreciation, amortization, wages and salaries, taxes, cost of materials and supplies, allocated overhead, indirect R & D costs, and the costs of R & D conducted by others on behalf of the U.S. affiliate. Exclude costs incurred in R & D activities conducted for others under a contractual arrangement (such as those reported in item 116).	
116. Federally-funded R & D expenditures — R & D expenditures not included in item 115, but conducted under a contractual arrangement for the Federal government, its subdivisions and agencies.	

SECTION I — EMPLOYMENT AND EMPLOYEE COMPENSATION

Employment and compensation data should be based on payroll records. They should relate to activities during the reporting period regardless of whether such activities were charged as an expense on the income statement, charged to inventories, or capitalized. Do NOT include data related to activities of a prior period, such as those capitalized or charged to inventories in prior periods. See Instruction Booklet, page

	Number of employees (1)
● EMPLOYMENT — Report the average of the number of persons on the payroll at the end of each pay period, month, or quarter, during the reporting period. Include part-time employees.	
117. Research and development managers, scientists, and engineers, and other professional and technical employees engaged in research and development	
118. All other employees	
119. TOTAL NUMBER OF EMPLOYEES - Sum of items 117 and 118. ———————➤	
120. Number of employees in item 119 covered by collective bargaining agreements	

	Total, for all employees (1)
	Bil. Mil. Thous. Dols.
● EMPLOYEE COMPENSATION — All expenditures made by employer in connection with the employment of workers, including cash payments, payments in-kind, and employer expenditures for employee benefit plans.	
121. Wages and salaries — Employee's gross earnings (before payroll deductions), and all direct and in-kind payments by the employer to employees	
122. Employee benefit plans — Employer expenditures for all employee benefit plans, including those required by statute, such as employer's social security taxes, those resulting from collective bargaining contracts, and those that are voluntary.	
123. TOTAL EMPLOYEE COMPENSATION - Sum of items 121 and 122 ———————➤	

● Employment and wage and salary data by industry	Industry Code – Enter respective industry codes from items 23 through 30 (1)	Number of employees engaged in activities encompassed in each industry code in column 1 (2)	To be completed only for the industry codes listed in column 1 that fall within manufacturing — BEA codes 201 through 390		
			Number of production workers engaged in activities encompassed in each manufacturing industry code in column 1 (3)	Number of hours of work for which the production workers in column 3 were paid (4)	Wages and salaries paid to production workers in column 3 (5) Bil. Mil. Thous. Dols.
124. Code of industry with largest sales					
125. Code of industry with second largest sales					
126. Code of industry with third largest sales					
127. Code of industry with fourth largest sales					
128. Code of industry with fifth largest sales					
129. Code of industry with sixth largest sales					
130. Code of industry with seventh largest sales					
131. Code of industry with eighth largest sales					
132. Employees in central administrative offices and headquarters	/////		//////	////	////////////
133. Amount accounted for above - Sum of items 124 through 132	/////				
134. Employees not accounted for above	/////		//////	////	////////////
135. TOTAL EMPLOYMENT - Column 2 must equal item 119 ——————➤	/////		//////	////	////////////
BEA USE ONLY ▶					

Part II – FINANCIAL AND OPERATING DATA OF U.S. AFFILIATE (Continued)

SECTION J   EXPORTS AND IMPORTS OF U.S. AFFILIATE – GOODS ONLY, DO NOT INCLUDE SERVICES

IMPORTANT NOTES: This section requires data on U.S. merchandise trade for the U.S. affiliate's reporting period. The data must be reported on a "shipped" basis, irrespective of to or from whom the shipments were billed or "charged." The value of merchandise exports or imports shipped by or to the U.S. affiliate is not the same as the affiliate's sales to, or purchases from, foreign persons. Thus, data for Section J usually cannot be obtained from your financial or accounting records, but must be derived from documents of your shipping and receiving department showing when, where, and to whom goods actually were sent.

Data in this section cover all goods which physically left or entered the U.S. customs area in the reporting period, including capital goods but excluding the value of ships, planes, railroad rolling stock, and trucks that are temporarily outside the United States transporting people or merchandise. Consigned goods must be included in the trade figures when shipped or received, even though not normally recorded as sales or purchases when initially consigned. (See page   of the *Instruction Booklet* for additional details of data requirements.

Please indicate source of your data for this Section J (Mark "X")

  ¹ 1 ☐ Accounting records

  ¹ 2 ☐ Documents of your shipping and receiving department

  ¹ 3 ☐ Other – Specify

The certification on page 1 of this BE-12 includes a certification that the trade data supplied in this Section J are on a shipment basis.

MERCHANDISE TRADE OF U.S. AFFILIATE WITH ALL FOREIGNERS	BEA USE ONLY (1)	EXPORTS – Shipped by U.S. affiliate to foreigners (valued f.a.s. U.S. port)			IMPORTS – Shipped to U.S. affiliate by foreigners (valued f.a.s. foreign port)		
		TOTAL (2)	To foreign parent(s) and its (their) foreign affiliates (3)	To all other foreigners (4)	TOTAL (5)	By foreign parent(s) and its (their) foreign affiliates (6)	To all other foreigners (7)
		BIL. MIL. THOUS.	BIL. MIL. THOUS.	BIL. MIL. THOUS.	BIL. MIL. THOUS.	BIL. MIL. THOUS.	BIL. MIL. THOUS.
136. Merchandise trade of U.S. affiliate with foreigners, total – Equals sum of items 137 through 148; sum of items 149 and 150; sum of items 151 through 154; and, beginning with item 155, the sum of data for all countries with entries.	1	2	3	4	5	6	7
BY PRODUCT (See the "Export and Import Trade Classifications" portion of the *Industry Classifications and Export and Import Trade Classifications Booklet*)							
137. Raw and prepared foods and live animals (SITC 0)	1	2	3	4	6	6	7
138. Beverages and raw and manufactured tobacco (SITC 1)	1	2	3	4	5	6	7
139. Inedible crude materials, except fuels (SITC 2)	1	2	3	4	5	6	7
140. Petroleum and products, mineral waxes, natural and manufactured gas (Part of SITC 3)	1	2	3	4	5	6	7
141. Coal, coke, and briquets (Part of SITC 3)	1	2	3	4	5	6	7
142. Chemicals (SITC 5)	1	2	3	4	5	6	7
143. Machinery, electrical and non-electrical (SITC 71–77)	1	2	3	4	5	6	7
144. Road motor vehicles and parts) (SITC 78) – Include all parts that are shipped with the vehicles. Parts that are shipped separately may be in this or another classification*	1	2	3	4	5	6	7
145. Other transportation equipment (SITC 79) – Include all parts that are shipped with the equipment. Parts that are shipped separately may be in this or another classification*	1	2	3	4	5	6	7
146. Metal manufactures (SITC 67, 68, and 69)	1	2	3	4	5	6	7
147. Other manufactures (SITC 61 through 66, and 8) Specify –	1	2	3	4	5	6	7
148. All other products (SITC 4 and 9) Specify –	1	2	3	4	5	6	7
BY WHOSE PRODUCTS:							
149. Products of shipper – That part of item 136 that is products grown, extracted, processed, assembled, or manufactured by the U.S. affiliate (for exports), or by the foreign parent, etc., (for imports).	1	2	3	4	/////	6	/////
150. Products of others – That part of item 136 that is products grown, extracted, processed, assembled, or manufactured by persons other than the shipper.	1	2	3	4	/////	6	/////
BY INTENDED USE:							
151. Capital equipment and other goods charged by U.S. affiliate to its fixed asset accounts	1	/////	/////	/////	5	6	7
152. Goods intended for further processing, assembly, or manufacture by this affiliate before resale to others	1	/////	/////	/////	5	6	7
153. Goods for resale without further processing, assembly, or manufacture by U.S. affiliate	1	/////	/////	/////	5	6	7
154. Other: Specify –	1	/////	/////	/////	5	6	7

* In the SITC, some parts that are shipped separately are included in SITC 78 and 79, respectively; however, others are included in SITC product categories appropriate to the type of part based, not on the part's end-use, but rather on the main type of material from which it is made or its general function. Major examples of such parts are gasoline and diesel engines (SITC 71); air conditioners for motor vehicles (SITC 74); tires and tubes (SITC 62); and lamps, batteries, and electrical parts for engines (SITC 77). For more complete information see the *Industry Classifications and Export and Import Trade Classifications Booklet*.

Part II – FINANCIAL AND OPERATING DATA OF U.S. AFFILIATE (Continued)

SECTION J   EXPORTS AND IMPORTS OF U.S. AFFILIATE – GOODS ONLY, DO NOT INCLUDE SERVICES (Continued)

MERCHANDISE TRADE OF U.S. AFFILIATE WITH ALL FOREIGNERS	BEA USE ONLY (1)	EXPORTS – Shipped by U.S. affiliate to foreigners (valued f.a.s. U.S. port)			IMPORTS – Shipped to U.S. affiliate by foreigners (valued f.a.s. foreign port)		
		TOTAL (2)	To foreign parent(s) and its (their) foreign affiliates (3)	To all other foreigners (4)	TOTAL (5)	By foreign parent(s) and its (their) foreign affiliates (6)	To all other foreigners (7)
		BIL. MIL. THOUS.	BIL. MIL. THOUS.	BIL. MIL. THOUS.	BIL. MIL. THOUS.	BIL. MIL. THOUS.	BIL. MIL. THOUS.
136. (Repeated) Bring forward amount from item 136, page 8, and beginning with item 155, must equal sum of all countries with entries and item 182.							
BY COUNTRY OF ULTIMATE DESTINATION OR ORIGIN	1	2	3	4	5	6	7
155. Australia							
156. Belgium and Luxembourg	1	2	3	4	5	6	7
157. Brazil	1	2	3	4	5	6	7
158. Canada	1	2	3	4	5	6	7
159. Denmark	1	2	3	4	5	6	7
160. France	1	2	3	4	5	6	7
161. Germany	1	2	3	4	5	6	7
162. Ireland	1	2	3	4	5	6	7
163. Italy	1	2	3	4	5	6	7
164. Japan	1	2	3	4	5	6	7
165. Mexico	1	2	3	4	5	6	7
166. Netherlands	1	2	3	4	5	6	7
167. New Zealand	1	2	3	4	5	6	7
168. Sweden	1	2	3	4	5	6	7
169. Switzerland	1	2	3	4	5	6	7
170. South Africa	1	2	3	4	5	6	7
171. United Kingdom	1	2	3	4	5	6	7
172. Venezuela	1	2	3	4	5	6	7
Other individual countries to which exports were $100,000.00 or more – Specify: (Use supplemental sheets, if necessary, to account for all such countries)							
173.	1	2	3	4	5	6	7
174.	1	2	3	4	5	6	7
175.	1	2	3	4	5	6	7
176.	1	2	3	4	5	6	7
177.	1	2	3	4	5	6	7
178.	1	2	3	4	5	6	7
179.	1	2	3	4	5	6	7
180.	1	2	3	4	5	6	7
181.	1	2	3	4	5	6	7
182. Sum of exports to all countries to which exports were less than $100,000.00 – The sum of this item and all countries with entries must equal item 136	1	2	3	4	5	6	7

Part II – FINANCIAL AND OPERATING DATA OF U.S. AFFILIATE (Continued)

SECTION K

SCHEDULE OF EMPLOYMENT, WAGES AND SALARIES, LAND AND
OTHER PROPERTY, PLANT, AND EQUIPMENT, BY LOCATION

Land and other property, plant, and equipment covers all such items, whether carried as investments, in fixed asset accounts, or in other balance sheet accounts. Include land held for resale, held for investment purposes, and all other land owned. Land and other property, plant, and equipment on capital lease from others should be included, but that on capital lease to others should be excluded.

In categorizing land and other property, plant, and equipment by use, classify by primary use. For land not in use, classify it by expected or intended use, if known; otherwise, include it in "other."

Do not include in the "foreign" category land and other property, plant, and equipment owned either by foreign business enterprises in which this U.S. affiliate has an equity interest or by foreign operations of this affiliate. The "foreign" category is primarily for use in reporting movable fixed assets temporarily outside the U.S. or for reporting any foreign fixed assets carried directly on the U.S. affiliate's books.

Location	BEA USE ONLY	State Code	Number of employees (Total must equal item 119)	Wages and salaries of employees listed in column 3 (Total must equal item 121)	Acres of mineral rights owned or leased from others, at close of FY 1980. Do not include acreage reported as land owned in column 6	All acres of land owned at close of FY 1980, by use					
						Total (Total must equal item 95, column 1)	Agriculture and forestry	Natural resources	Manu-facturing	Residential, office buildings, stores, and shopping centers	Other
	(1)	(2)	(3) Number	(4) Thous. Dols.	(5)	(6)	(7)	(8)	(9)	(10)	(11)
183. TOTAL for each column must equal sum of items 184 through 241											
184. Alabama		01		$							
185. Alaska		02		$							
186. Arizona		04		$							
187. Arkansas		05		$							
188. California		06		$							
189. Colorado		08		$							
190. Connecticut		09		$							
191. Delaware		10		$							
192. Florida		12		$							
193. Georgia		13		$							
194. Hawaii		15		$							
195. Idaho		16		$							
196. Illinois		17		$							
197. Indiana		18		$							
198. Iowa		19		$							
199. Kansas		20		$							
200. Kentucky		21		$							
201. Louisiana		22		$							
202. Maine		23		$							
203. Maryland		24		$							
204. Massachusetts		25		$							
205. Michigan		26		$							
206. Minnesota		27		$							
207. Mississippi		28		$							
208. Missouri		29		$							
209. Montana		30		$							
210. Nebraska		31		$							
211. Nevada		32		$							
212. New Hampshire		33		$							
213. New Jersey		34		$							
214. New Mexico		35		$							
215. New York		36		$							
216. North Carolina		37		$							
217. North Dakota		38		$							
218. Ohio		39		$							
219. Oklahoma		40		$							
220. Oregon		41		$							
221. Pennsylvania		42		$							
222. Rhode Island		44		$							
223. South Carolina		45		$							
224. South Dakota		46		$							
225. Tennessee		47		$							
226. Texas		48		$							
227. Utah		49		$							
228. Vermont		50		$							
229. Virginia		51		$							
230. Washington		53		$							
231. West Virginia		54		$							
232. Wisconsin		55		$							
233. Wyoming		56		$							
234. District of Columbia		11		$							
235. Puerto Rico		43		$							
236. Virgin Islands		52		$							
237. Guam		14		$							
238. American Samoa		03		$							
239. U.S. Offshore Oil and Gas Sites		65		$							
240. Other U.S. Territories and Possessions		60		$							
241. Foreign*		70		$							

* Include only that of U.S. business enterprises fully consolidated into the U.S. affiliate. No foreign business enterprises, incorporated or unincorporated, can be considered part of the reporting U.S. affiliate.

Page 10

Part II – FINANCIAL AND OPERATING DATA OF U.S. AFFILIATE (Continued)

SECTION K   SCHEDULE OF EMPLOYMENT, WAGES AND SALARIES, LAND AND OTHER PROPERTY, PLANT, AND EQUIPMENT, BY LOCATION (Continued)

Location	BEA USE ONLY	State Code	Gross book value (historical cost) of all land and other property, plant, and equipment, wherever carried on balance sheet, FY 1980 closing balance, by use — Total, column 3 must equal sum of item 95, column 2 plus column 3.							
			Total	Agriculture and forestry	Natural resources	Manufacturing			Residential, office buildings, stores, and shopping centers	Other
						Petroleum refining	Chemicals	Other		
			(3)	(4)	(5)	(6)	(7)	(8)	(9)	(10)
(1)		(2)	Thous. Dols.	Thous. Dols.	Thous. Dols.	Thous. Dols.	Thous. Dols.	Thous. Dols.	Thous. Dols.	Thous. Dols.
242. TOTAL for each column must equal sum of items 243 through 300.			$	$	$	$	$	$	$	$
243. Alabama		01	$	$	$	$	$	$	$	$
244. Alaska		02								
245. Arizona		04								
246. Arkansas		05								
247. California		06								
248. Colorado		08								
249. Connecticut		09								
250. Delaware		10								
251. Florida		12								
252. Georgia		13								
253. Hawaii		15								
254. Idaho		16								
255. Illinois		17								
256. Indiana		18								
257. Iowa		19								
258. Kansas		20								
259. Kentucky		21								
260. Louisiana		22								
261. Maine		23								
262. Maryland		24								
263. Massachusetts		25								
264. Michigan		26								
265. Minnesota		27								
266. Mississippi		28								
267. Missouri		29								
268. Montana		30								
269. Nebraska		31								
270. Nevada		32								
271. New Hampshire		33								
272. New Jersey		34								
273. New Mexico		35								
274. New York		36								
275. North Carolina		37								
276. North Dakota		38								
277. Ohio		39								
278. Oklahoma		40								
279. Oregon		41								
280. Pennsylvania		42								
281. Rhode Island		44								
282. South Carolina		45								
283. South Dakota		46								
284. Tennessee		47								
285. Texas		48								
286. Utah		49								
287. Vermont		50								
288. Virginia		51								
289. Washington		53								
290. West Virginia		54								
291. Wisconsin		55								
292. Wyoming		56								
293. District of Columbia		11								
294. Puerto Rico		43								
295. Virgin Islands		52								
296. Guam		14								
297. American Samoa		03								
298. U.S. Offshore Oil and Gas Sites		65								
299. Other U.S. Territories and Possessions		60								
300. Foreign*		70	$	$	$	$	$	$	$	$

* Include only that of U.S. business enterprises fully consolidated into the U.S. affiliate. No foreign business enterprises, incorporated or unincorporated, can be considered part of the reporting U.S. affiliate.

Page 11

Part III – INVESTMENT AND TRANSACTIONS BETWEEN U.S. AFFILIATE AND FOREIGN PARENT

A separate Part III, or Part III-ADDITIONAL, must be completed for each foreign parent that held a direct or indirect equity interest in the U.S. affiliate at <u>any time</u> during the reporting period.

301. Number of Part III schedules filed by the U.S. affiliate – If there is only one, enter "1" in the box below; if more than one, enter the number of Part III's to be filed.

☐ ◀ Number   If number is greater than "1," use Part III-ADDITIONAL schedules for the remaining foreign parents.

302. Name of foreign parent that this Part III, or Part III-ADDITIONAL is for:

Name:

The foreign parent named in item 302 holds: *(Mark either item 303 or 304):*

303. ☐ A direct equity interest in the U.S. affiliate

304. ☐ An indirect equity interest in the U.S. affiliate

(If a foreign parent holds both direct and indirect equity interests, then separate Part III's must be completed for each line of ownership. However, do not duplicate positions or transactions where multiple Part III's are filed. The marking of either 303 or 304 will indicate which is being reported on this Part III.)

305. If item 303 is marked, give percent of voting rights owned.

	Close FY 1980 (1)	Close FY 1979 (2)
(For the close of each year, the sum of this item from all Part III's filed for the U.S. affiliate must equal item 12.)	. %	. %

306. Country of location of foreign parent named in item 302.

_____

☐☐☐ **BEA USE ONLY**

307. Industry code* of foreign parent named in item 302:

☐☐☐ ◀ Code

308. Is the foreign parent named in item 302 the ultimate beneficial owner (UBO)? *(See definition)*

1 ☐ Yes

2 ☐ No

If the answer to item 308 is "No," complete the following:

309. Name of UBO *(if the UBO is an individual, a name is not required, complete only items 310 and 311):*

310. Country of UBO named in item 309:

_____

☐☐☐ **BEA USE ONLY**

311. Industry code* of UBO named in item 309:

☐☐☐ ◀ Code

NOTE: If item 304 is marked, then only the following items in the rest of this Part III need be completed to report direct transactions or positions, if any, between the U.S. affiliate and the foreign parent: 312, 313, 314, 315, 321, 322, 338, 339, 340, 341, 342, and 343.

SECTION A ▷ INVESTMENT BETWEEN U.S. AFFILIATE AND FOREIGN PARENT NAMED IN ITEM 302, ACCORDING TO BOOKS OF THE U.S. AFFILIATE

	Balance at Close FY 1980 (1)				Balance at Close FY 1979 (2)			
	Bil.	Mil.	Thous.	Dols.	Bil.	Mil.	Thous.	Dols.
● CURRENT ITEMS								
312. Current liabilities owed by U.S. affiliate to foreign parent – That portion of items 46 and 47 representing amounts owed to foreign parent	$				$			
313. Current receivables due to U.S. affiliate from foreign parent – That portion of items 35, 36, and 38 representing amounts due from foreign parent								
● LONG-TERM ITEMS								
314. Long-term debt owed by U.S. affiliate to foreign parent – That portion of item 48 representing amounts owed to foreign parent								
315. Long-term receivables due U.S. affiliate from foreign parent – That portion of items 42 and 43 representing amounts due from foreign parent								
● OWNERS' EQUITY ITEMS, INCORPORATED AFFILIATES ONLY – FOREIGN PARENT'S EQUITY IN:								
316. Capital stock, common and preferred, voting and nonvoting								
317. Additional paid-in capital								
318. Retained earnings (deficit)								
319. Treasury stock held by U.S. affiliate	(		)		(		)	
● FOREIGN PARENT'S SHARE OF TOTAL OWNERS' EQUITY OF INCORPORATED OR UNINCORPORATED U.S. AFFILIATE								
320. For incorporated U.S. affiliate, sum of items 316, 317, 318, and 319. For unincorporated U.S. affiliate, give no breakdown in items 316 through 319, but enter foreign parent's share of total owners' equity, item 55.								
● Net book value of property, plant, and equipment on lease and not reflected in items 312 to 319. Exclude operating leases of one year or less. (Net book value for operating leases of more than one year is the original cost less accumulated depreciation; for capital leases, it is the amount of principal payments remaining due at the specified time including payment called for by bargain purchase option, if any.)								
321. On lease from foreign parent to U.S. affiliate								
322. On lease from U.S. affiliate to foreign parent	$				$			
323. BEA USE ONLY ▶ Total direct investment position in the U.S. affiliate	$				$			

* Secure industry code for foreign parent or ultimate beneficial owner from page   of the Industry Classifications and Export and Import Trade Classifications Booklet.

Part III – INVESTMENT AND TRANSACTIONS BETWEEN U.S. AFFILIATE AND FOREIGN PARENT (Continued)

SECTION B   CHANGES IN FOREIGN PARENT'S EQUITY HOLDINGS IN U.S. AFFILIATE

Report in items 324 through 334 transactions during the reporting period by the foreign parent that changed its equity holdings in the U.S. affiliate. Exclude changes caused by carrying net income to the equity account, the payment of stock or cash dividends (other than liquidating dividends), or the distribution of earnings during the period. Exclude effect of treasury stock transactions with persons other than the foreign parent and reorganizations in capital structure that do not affect total equity. Report all amounts at transactions value, i.e., the value of the consideration given (received) by the foreign parent.

	Amount (1) Bil. Mil. Thous. Dols.
Transactions between foreign parent and U.S. affiliate:	
Increase in equity interest –	
324. Establishment of affiliate by foreign parent	$
325. Purchase by foreign parent of capital stock from incorporated affiliate	
326. Additional equity capital contributed by foreign parent (for an incorporated affiliate, report only those contributions not resulting in the issuance of stock)	
Decrease in equity interest –	
327. Total liquidation of affiliate by foreign parent	
328. Sale by foreign parent of capital stock to incorporated affiliate	
329. Return of contributed equity capital to foreign parent (for an incorporated affiliate, report here only those returns not resulting in a reduction of issued stock)	
Transactions between foreign parent and a person other than U.S. affiliate:	
Acquisition by foreign parent of equity interest in U.S. affiliate from –	
330. All U.S. persons	
331. All foreign persons	
Sale by foreign parent of equity interest in U.S. affiliate to –	
332. All U.S. persons	
333. All foreign persons	
334. Increase (decrease) at transactions value of changes in equity holdings –The consideration given (received) by the foreign parent in order to bring about the change in equity holdings; must equal sum of items 324, 325, 326, 330, and 331 minus sum of items 327, 328, 329, 332, and 333.	
335. Approximate book value on the date of the transaction(s), based on books of the U.S. affiliate, that is equivalent to the transactions value reported in item 334. (The amount given here should approximate the change in item 320, column 1 minus column 2, but allowance is made in item 320 to exclude changes caused by carrying net income to the equity account, payment of stock or cash dividends (other than liquidating dividends, distribution of earnings, and treasury stock transactions.)	$

SECTION C   PAYMENTS AND RECEIPTS OF DIVIDENDS, DISTRIBUTED EARNINGS, INTEREST, FEES, ROYALTIES, AND RENTALS BETWEEN U.S. AFFILIATE AND FOREIGN PARENT

Enter amounts paid, received, or entered into intercompany accounts. Include amounts for which payments were made in-kind. Amounts should be entered as of the date paid (received) by the affiliate, or entered into intercompany accounts with the foreign parent, whichever occurred first. For an item entered into intercompany account, in order to avoid duplication, any subsequent settlement of the account must not be reflected in one of the items below, but must be reflected only as a reduction in intercompany account.

	Payments or credits by U.S. affiliate to foreign parent		Receipts by or credits to U.S. affiliate from foreign parent	
	Net of U.S. tax withheld (1) Bil. Mil. Thous. Dols.	Amount of U.S. tax withheld (2) Bil. Mil. Thous. Dols.	Net of foreign tax withheld (3) Bil. Mil. Thous. Dols.	Amount of foreign tax withheld (4) Bil. Mil. Thous. Dols.
Incorporated U.S. affiliate:				
336. Dividends on the U.S. affiliate's common and preferred stock, paid out of current and past earnings, excluding stock dividends	$	$	/////////	/////////
Unincorporated U.S. affiliate:				
337. Earnings distributed, whether out of current or past earnings			/////////	/////////
All U.S. affiliates:				
338. Interest – Include interest on capital leases				
339. Royalties, license fees, and other fees for the use or sale of intangible property				
340. Payments and receipts for use of tangible property except film or television tape rentals – Include rentals for operating leases of one year or less and net rent on operating leases of more than one year. Net rent is the equivalent to the total lease payment less the return of capital (depreciation) component				
341. Film or television tape rentals				
342. Fees for services rendered – Include fees for management, professional or technical services, R&D assessments, and allocated expenses other than those given above				
343. TOTAL – Sum of items 336 through 342 ⟶	$	$	$	$

FOREIGN PARENT'S EQUITY IN U.S. AFFILIATE'S NET INCOME

Net income must be calculated in accordance with the all inclusive concept of the income statement.

	Amount (1) Bil. Mil. Thous. Dols.
344. Foreign parent's direct equity in U.S. affiliate's net income (loss) – Enter foreign parent's direct ownership share of net income, item 68.	$
Foreign parent's equity in U.S. affiliate's net realized and unrealized capital gains (losses):	
345. Foreign parent's share of item 60, net realized and unrealized capital gains included in net income	
346. Foreign parent's share of item 74, net realized and unrealized capital gains (losses) taken directly to retained earnings or owner's equity, after provision for income tax liability (benefit), if any, on the gains (losses).	$

Page 13

Part IV – DIRECT TRANSACTIONS OR ACCOUNTS BETWEEN U.S. AFFILIATE AND FOREIGN AFFILIATES OF THE FOREIGN PARENT(S)

Report all direct transactions or balances between the U.S. affiliate and foreign affiliates of the foreign parent(s). Do not include any direct transactions, accounts, or balances between U.S. affiliate and the foreign parent – they must be reported in Part III. Do not net payables against receivables.

In Section A, report payments and liabilities to, and in Section B report receipts and receivables due from foreign affiliates of the foreign parent(s), by country. Enter only one foreign country per line. If more lines than provided are needed in order to list all countries, use additional copied Part IV sheets as necessary, properly identified with the name and EI number of the U.S. affiliate. An item need not be reported by country only if it exceeds $250,000 for that country; for each item, the value not shown by country should be entered on the unallocated line.

347. Does the U.S. affiliate (as consolidated) have direct transactions or accounts with foreign affiliates of any foreign parent? (Mark one)

☐ Yes—If "Yes", complete Part IV

☐ No—If "No", skip Part IV

IMPORTANT EXAMPLE: *Report all dollars in thousands of U.S. dollars, as illustrated.*

EXAMPLE: If figure is $1,125,628,000.00

Bil.	Mil.	Thous.	Dols.
1	125	628	

SECTION A   U.S. AFFILIATE'S PAYMENTS AND LIABILITIES

Payments or accruals to foreign affiliates of the foreign parent (net of U.S. tax withheld) — Close FY 1980 / Liabilities of U.S. affiliate to foreign affiliates of the foreign parent — Close FY 1979

Country of foreign affiliate of foreign parent	BEA USE ONLY (1)	Interest, including interest on capital leases (2)	Royalties, license fees, and other fees for the use or sale of intangible property (3)	Rentals for use of tangible property (4)	Film or television tape rentals (5)	Fees for services rendered including fees for management, professional services, R&D assessments, and allocated expenses (6)	Current (include current portion of long-term debt) (7)	Long-term (Exclude current portion due) (8)	Current (include current portion of long-term debt) (9)	Long-term (Exclude current portion due) (10)
348. Canada										
349. United Kingdom										
350. Germany										
351. France										
352. Italy										
353. Japan										
354. Netherlands										
355. Switzerland										
Specify other countries:										
356.										
357.										
358.										
359.										
360.										
361. Unallocated by country – The amounts for countries for which entries are less than $250,000										
362. TOTAL, all countries Section A										

SECTION B   U.S. AFFILIATE'S RECEIPTS AND RECEIVABLES

Receipts or accruals from foreign affiliates of the foreign parent (net of foreign tax withheld) — Close FY 1980 / Receivables of U.S. affiliate from foreign affiliate of the foreign parent — Close FY 1979

Country	BEA USE ONLY (1)	(2)	(3)	(4)	(5)	(6)	(7)	(8)	(9)	(10)
363. Canada										
364. United Kingdom										
365. Germany										
366. France										
367. Italy										
368. Japan										
369. Netherlands										
370. Switzerland										
Specify other countries:										
371.										
372.										
373.										
374.										
375.										
376. Unallocated by country – The amounts for countries for which entries are less than $250,000										
377. TOTAL, all countries, Section B										

Page 14

FORM BE-12 Supplement A
(12-80)

U.S. DEPARTMENT OF COMMERCE
BUREAU OF ECONOMIC ANALYSIS

BEA USE ONLY ▶

Page No. ____ of ____
this Supplement A

LIST OF ALL U.S. BUSINESS ENTERPRISES FULLY CONSOLIDATED INTO THE REPORTING U.S. AFFILIATE

Name of U.S. affiliate as shown in Part I, item I, of Form BE-12

Supplement A — List of ALL U.S. Business Enterprises Fully Consolidated into the Reporting U.S. Affiliate, must be completed by the U.S. affiliate reporting consolidated financial and operating data to BEA; each U.S. business enterprise so fully consolidated must be more than 10 percent owned, directly or indirectly, by the foreign parent, and must also be more than 50 percent owned by the U.S. affiliate named in Part I, item I, of Form BE-12. The number of U.S. affiliates listed below plus the reporting U.S. affiliate must agree with item 5, Part I of Form BE-12. Continue listing onto as many additional copied pages as necessary.

Employer Identification Number of the above named U.S. affiliate used by affiliate to file income and payroll taxes (as given in item 4, Form BE-12) ▶

BEA USE ONLY Name and address of each U.S. business enterprise fully consolidated in this BE-12 Report (2)	Employer Identification Number used by U.S. business enterprise listed in column 2 to file income and payroll taxes (3)	Name of U.S. business enterprise which holds the direct equity interest in the U.S. business enterprise listed in column 2 (4)	Percentage of direct ownership which the U.S. business enterprise listed in column 4 has in the U.S. business enterprise listed in column 2 (Enter percentage to nearest tenth.) (5)
(1)			
			%
			%
			%
			%
			%
			%
			%
			%
			%
			%
			%
			%
			%
			%
			%
			%
			%
			%
			%

Page 15

FORM BE-12 Supplement B
(12-80)

U.S. DEPARTMENT OF COMMERCE
BUREAU OF ECONOMIC ANALYSIS

**LIST OF ALL U.S. AFFILIATES IN WHICH THE REPORTING U.S. AFFILIATE (AS CONSOLIDATED)
HAS A DIRECT EQUITY INTEREST BUT WHICH ARE NOT FULLY CONSOLIDATED ON THIS BE-12 REPORT**

BEA USE ONLY ►

IDENTIFICATION— Name of U.S. affiliate as shown in item 1 Part I of Form BE-12

Page No._____ of _____ —— pages of
this Supplement B.

List all other U.S. affiliates of the foreign parent(s) in which the fully consolidated U.S. affiliate named in item 1, Part I has a direct equity interest, but which are not fully consolidated on this BE-12 report. The number of such affiliates must agree with item 6, Part I of Form BE-12; use as many copied pages as needed.
NOTE: U.S. affiliates listed on Supplement B MUST NOT be listed on Supplement A.
The U.S. affiliate named in item 1, Part I MUST NOTIFY each U.S. affiliate listed below that it must file in its own name, a completed form BE-12 report or a BE-12 Supplement C, Claim for Not Filing a Form BE-12. Indicate in column 4 whether or not such notification has been given.

Employer Identification Number of the above named U.S. affiliate used by affiliate to file income and payroll taxes (as given in item 4, Form BE-12):

BEA USE ONLY (1)	Name of each U.S. affiliate in which a direct interest is held (2)	Address of each U.S. affiliate listed in column 2 Give number, street, city, State and ZIP Code (3)	Has affiliate been notified or previously been made aware of foreign ownership? (Check one) (4)	Employer Identification Number used by U.S. affiliate listed in Column 2 to file income and payroll taxes (5)	Percentage of direct ownership in the U.S. affiliate listed in Column 2, held by the reporting affiliate named in item 1, Part I of BE-12 (Enter percentage to nearest tenth) (6)
			☐ Yes ☐ No		%
			☐ Yes ☐ No		%
			☐ Yes ☐ No		%
			☐ Yes ☐ No		%
			☐ Yes ☐ No		%
			☐ Yes ☐ No		%
			☐ Yes ☐ No		%
			☐ Yes ☐ No		%
			☐ Yes ☐ No		%
			☐ Yes ☐ No		%
			☐ Yes ☐ No		%

Page 16

FORM BE-12 Supplement C
(12-80)

U.S. DEPARTMENT OF COMMERCE
BUREAU OF ECONOMIC ANALYSIS (BEA)

CLAIM FOR NOT FILING A BE-12
Benchmark Survey of Foreign Direct
Investment in the U.S. – 1980

The publication in the Federal Register of the notice implementing this survey is considered legal notice to covered U.S. business enterprises of their obligation to report. Therefore, a report is required from persons subject to the reporting requirements of the BE-12 survey, whether or not they are contacted by BEA. Also, a person, or their agent, contacted by BEA concerning their being subject to reporting either by sending them a report form or by written inquiry, must respond in writing pursuant to Section 806.4 of 15 CFR, Chapter VIII. For this survey, this may be accomplished by filing a completed Form BE-12 on a timely basis or, if applicable, by completing and returning this claim within 30 days of the date the BE-12 was sent by BEA.

If claim is disallowed, the original due date for the BE-12 remains in force.

Affiliate's 1980 fiscal year is defined to be the affiliate's financial reporting year that has an ending date in calendar year 1980.

See the Instruction Booklet for definitions and rules.

Name and address of U.S. business enterprise for which this claim is filed — If the business enterprise received a prelabeled BE-12 form — See Item I, Part I, Form BE-12 — Enter name, address and BEA Identification Number from that label into the blocks below; skip a single block between words. If a prelabeled form was not received, enter name and address as contained on letter transmitting the report forms to you, indicating any changes or corrections.

Name

Street or P.O. Box

City and State   ZIP Code

BEA Identification Number

[ ] **BEA USE ONLY**

BASIS OF CLAIM FOR NOT FILING *(Mark one and answer applicable questions)*

1. [ ] This U.S. business enterprise was not a U.S. affiliate of a foreign person at any time during its 1980 fiscal year but had been a U.S. affiliate of a foreign person at some time between January 1, 1974 and the beginning of its 1980 fiscal year.

   Give date foreign ownership ceased or went below 10 percent:

   Month | Day | Year

2. [ ] This U.S. business enterprise was not a U.S. affiliate of a foreign person at any time during its 1980 fiscal year and was not a U.S. affiliate of a foreign person at any time since January 1, 1974.

3. [ ] This U.S. business enterprise was a U.S. affiliate of a foreign person during its 1980 fiscal year but is fully consolidated into the BE-12 report for another U.S. affiliate — Give name, address, and BEA Identification Number of consolidated U.S. affiliate that is reporting to BEA, in the blocks below (Skip a single block between words):

   Name

   Street or P.O. Box

   City and State   ZIP Code

   BEA Identification Number

4. [ ] The U.S. business enterprise is not subject to the reporting requirements because the owners are citizens of the United States who are resident abroad as a result of official employment by the U.S. Government (including the immediate family of such persons), or the owners have been or expect to be resident abroad for less than one year.

5. [ ] This U.S. business enterprise was a U.S. affiliate of a foreign person during its 1980 fiscal year but is exempt because, on a fully consolidated, or, in the case of real estate investments, or an aggregated, basis:

   (a) Each of the following three items for the U.S. affiliate (not the foreign parent's share) was between –$1 million and +$1 million during its 1980 fiscal year:

   (1) Total assets,

   (2) Sales or gross operating revenues, excluding sales taxes, and

   (3) Net income after provision for U.S. income taxes;

   and

   (b) The U.S. affiliate did not own 200 acres or more of U.S. land during the reporting period (if the U.S. affiliate owned 200 acres or more of U.S. land, it must report regardless of the value of the three items listed above).

   Enter value or amount for each:

		Amount			
		Bil.	Mil.	Thous.	Dols.
i.	Total assets (do not net out liabilities)	$			
ii.	Sales or gross operating revenues, excluding sales taxes (do not give gross margin)	$			
iii.	Net income after provision for U.S. income taxes	$			

		Number
iv.	Number of acres of U.S. land owned	

   and complete the following:

   i. Country of foreign parent

   ii. Country of ultimate beneficial owner

   BEA USE ONLY

6. [ ] Other — Specify and include reference to section of regulations or instructions on which claim is based.

U.S. PERSON FOR BEA
TO CONSULT ABOUT
THIS CLAIM

Print name and address

U.S. TELEPHONE NUMBER
Area code | Number | Extension

▶ **CERTIFICATION** The undersigned official certifies that the information contained in this report is correct and complete to the best of his/her knowledge.

Authorized Official's signature | Please type Name and Title | Date

18 U.S.C. 1001 (Crimes and Criminal Procedure) makes it a criminal offense to make a willfully false statement or representation to any department or agency of the United States as to any matter within its jurisdiction. Any officer, director, employee, or agent of any corporation who knowingly participates in a willful failure to report, upon conviction, may be punished by a fine, imprisonment, or both (22 U.S.C. 3105). For a further citation of applicable statutes, see the Instruction Booklet to this form.

Form BE-12 BANK (Report for U.S. affiliate that is a bank)
(1-81)

U.S. DEPARTMENT OF COMMERCE
BUREAU OF ECONOMIC ANALYSIS (BEA)

MANDATORY – CONFIDENTIAL

BENCHMARK SURVEY OF
FOREIGN DIRECT INVESTMENT IN THE U.S.
1980

RETURN REPORTS TO: U.S. Department of Commerce, Bureau of Economic Analysis BE-50 (IN), Washington, D.C. 20230

Important

Read Instruction Booklet before completing form. The instructions given below are only a brief summary of certain ones relating to this form.

See SPECIAL NOTE: BANKS, before proceeding.

- **DEFINITIONS**

1. **Foreign direct investment in the United States** means the ownership or control, directly or indirectly, by one foreign person of 10 per centum or more of the voting securities of an incorporated U.S. business enterprise or an equivalent interest in an unincorporated U.S. business enterprise, including a branch.
2. **Business enterprise** means any organization, association, branch, or venture which exists for profitmaking purposes or to otherwise secure economic advantage, and any ownership of any real estate.
3. **Affiliate** means a business enterprise located in one country which is directly or indirectly owned or controlled by a person of another country to the extent of 10 per centum or more of its voting securities for an incorporated business enterprise or an equivalent interest for an unincorporated business enterprise, including a branch.
4. **U.S. affiliate** means an affiliate located in the United States in which a foreign person has a direct investment.
5. **U.S. affiliate's 1980 fiscal year** is the affiliate's financial reporting year that has an ending date in calendar year 1980.
6. **Banking** (industry code 600) includes business enterprises engaged in deposit banking, Edge Act corporations engaged in international or foreign banking, foreign branches and agencies of U.S. banks whether or not they accept deposits abroad, U.S. branches and agencies of foreign banks whether or not they accept deposits in the United States, and bank holding companies, i.e., holding companies for which over 50 percent of their total income is from banks which they hold.

- **REPORTING REQUIREMENTS**

1. **Who must report** – A BE-12 report is required from each U.S. affiliate, i.e., for each U.S. business enterprise in which one foreign person owned or controlled, directly or indirectly, 10 percent or more of the voting securities if an incorporated U.S. business enterprise, or an equivalent interest if an unincorporated U.S. business enterprise, at any time during the business enterprise's 1980 fiscal year.
2. **Consolidated reporting** – Except as specified in SPECIAL NOTE: BANKS, a U.S. affiliate shall file on a fully consolidated basis, including in the full consolidation all other U.S. affiliates in which it directly or indirectly owns more than 50 percent of the outstanding voting securities. Hereinafter, the fully consolidated entity is considered to be one U.S. affiliate. See *Instruction Booklet, page 3. Exemption criteria are applied to the consolidated entity.*
3. **Exemption** – A U.S. affiliate as consolidated is not required to file a report if:
   (a) Each of the following three items for the U.S. affiliate (not the foreign parent's share) was between –$1,000,000 and +$1,000,000 during the reporting period:
   (1) Total assets,
   (2) Sales or gross operating revenues, excluding sales taxes, and
   (3) Net income after provision for U.S. income taxes;
   and
   (b) The U.S. affiliate did not own 200 acres or more of U.S. land during the reporting period (if the U.S. affiliate owned 200 acres or more of U.S. land, it must report regardless of the value of the three items listed above).
4. A U.S. affiliate that is not required to file a completed Form BE-12 because it falls below the exemption levels, must complete and file a Claim for Not Filing a Form BE-12, with item 5 of the Claim marked, and furnish the information requested in item 5. (The Claim is on the last page of Form BE-12 and should be detached for filing.)
5. **Response required** – A person or their agent who is sent a report form by BEA and who claims to not be subject to the reporting requirements must file a completed "Claim for Not Filing a Form BE-12" which is printed on the last page of Form BE-12. The Claim must be filed within 30 days of the date the BE-12 was sent by BEA.
6. **Due date** – A completed report on Form BE-12 is due no later than

- ***ASSISTANCE – Telephone (202) 523–0547.***

- **GENERAL NOTES**

1. Number of employees and other non-monetary amounts must be reported to the nearest whole unit.
2. Monetary amounts must be reported in U.S. dollars rounded to the nearest thousand (omitting 000). Do not enter amounts in the shaded portions of any line.
   EXAMPLE: If amount is $1,334,615.00, report as:

Bil.	Mil.	Thous.	Dols.
	1	335	////

3. If an item is between +$500,000 or –$500,000, enter "0."
4. Use parentheses to indicate negative numbers.
5. All questions must be answered in the context of the reporting period delineated in items 8, 9, and 10.

Part I – IDENTIFICATION OF U.S. AFFILIATE

1. Name and principal mailing address

A mailing label, if affixed, shows, among other things, the name and address of this U.S. affiliate, as known to BEA. If there are no changes to the name and address, write "same" in spaces below. If there are any changes in name or address, enter correct name and address below in full.

If no mailing label is affixed, or if there is a change in the name and address as given on the mailing label, print name and address in blocks; skip a single block between words.

BEA USE ONLY

Name of U.S. Affiliate

Street or P.O. Box

City and State — ZIP Code

2. Is more than 50 percent of the ownership interest in this U.S. affiliate owned by another U.S. affiliate of your foreign parent?

1 1 ☐ Yes 1 2 ☐ No

If the answer is "Yes," do not complete this report unless this affiliate qualifies for filing separately and has obtained permission from BEA to do so. Note, however, that nonbank affiliates of a bank affiliate must file separately regardless of the ownership interest; see "SPECIAL NOTE: BANKS." Otherwise, the report must reflect information and data for, and be filed in the name of, the fully-consolidated U.S. business enterprise meeting the definition of U.S. affiliate. Please forward this Form BE-12 survey packet to the U.S. business enterprise owning your company to the extent of more than 50 percent, notify BEA of the action taken, and provide BEA the name and address of the U.S. business enterprise that is required to file for the fully-consolidated U.S. business enterprise.

(WHEREVER THE INSTRUCTION "MARK ONE" IS GIVEN BELOW, IF IT IS NECESSARY TO MARK MORE THAN ONE ANSWER, GIVE AN EXPLANATION.)

3. Form of organization of U.S. affiliate *(Mark one):*

1 1 ☐ Incorporated in U.S.
1 2 ☐ U.S. partnership
1 3 ☐ U.S. branch or agency of a foreign person
1 4 ☐ Business enterprise incorporated abroad, but whose head office is located in the U.S. and whose business activity is conducted in, or from, the United States
1 5 ☐ Other – *Specify:*

4. Enter primary Employer Identification Number used by U.S. affiliate to file U.S. income and payroll taxes

☐☐–☐☐☐☐☐☐☐ ← E.I. Number

SPECIAL NOTE: BANKS

A specialized report form, BE-12 BANK, has been adopted for banks (that is, a business enterprise for which over 50 percent of its total revenues are generated by activities classified in banking, industry code 600). Use of the specialized report form is at the discretion of BEA; in situations where its possible use is not clear-cut, permission must be secured from BEA in advance of filing.

The specialized report form, BE-12 BANK, is for reporting by a U.S. affiliate which is a bank or a bank holding company, and in which a foreign parent holds a direct or indirect ownership interest. It is not to be used by a U.S. affiliate which may technically be classified as a bank holding company because of an interest in a banking activity, but which has 50 percent or more of its revenues generated by non-bank activities. Activities of subsidiaries which may not be banks but which provide support to the parent company, such as real estate subsidiaries set up to hold office buildings occupied by the parent bank company, are considered bank activities.

A U.S. affiliate that is a bank holding company must fully consolidate on its BE-12 BANK report those of its majority-owned subsidiaries that are U.S. affiliates of its foreign parent that are normally consolidated, and that are engaged in banking (or provide support to bank activities of the U.S. bank holding company). Subsidiaries of a bank holding company that are non-bank U.S. affiliates must not be so consolidated, but must submit a standard Form BE-12 in their own name.

Each separately incorporated U.S. bank affiliate that does not meet the consolidation rules given in the Instruction Booklet must file a separate report on Form BE-12 BANK. Each unincorporated U.S. bank affiliate in which a foreign parent holds a direct ownership interest must file a BE-12 BANK. Two or more unincorporated U.S. bank affiliates owned by the same foreign person, and located in the same U.S. State or territory, may be aggregated on a single Form BE-12 BANK, provided that written permission has been obtained from BEA prior to such filing.

A U.S. affiliate that is a bank, but that has a non-bank foreign parent, must file a Form BE-12 BANK. A U.S. affiliate that is not a bank, but that has a bank foreign parent, must file a standard Form BE-12.

The BE-12 BANK form, where its use is permitted, stands in place of the standard form, and the instructions given herein and in the Instruction Booklet should be so construed, and references to Form BE-12 should be interpreted as also covering Form BE-12 BANK.

MANDATORY – This survey is being conducted pursuant to the International Investment Survey Act of 1976 (P.L. 94–472, 90 Stat. 2059, 22 U.S.C. 3101 to 3108 – hereinafter "the Act"), and the filing of reports is mandatory pursuant to Section 5(b)(2) of the Act (22 U.S.C. 3104).

PENALTIES – Whoever fails to report may be subject to a civil penalty not exceeding $10,000 and to injunctive relief commanding such person to comply, or both. Whoever willfully fails to report shall be fined not more than $10,000 and, if an individual, may be imprisoned for not more than one year, or both. Any officer, director, employee, or agent of any corporation who knowingly participates in such violations, upon conviction, may be punished by a like fine, imprisonment, or both. *(See Section 6 of the Act, 22 U.S.C. 3105.)*

CONFIDENTIALITY – The information filed in this report may be used only for analytical and statistical purposes and access to the information shall be available only to officials and employees (including consultants and contractors and their employees) of agencies designated by the President to perform functions under the Act. The President may authorize the exchange of the information between agencies or officials designated to perform functions under the Act, but only for analytical and statistical purposes. No official or employee (including consultants and contractors and their employees) shall publish or make available any information collected under the Act in such a manner that the person to whom the information relates can be specifically identified. Reports and copies of reports prepared pursuant to the Act are confidential and their submission or disclosure shall not be compelled by any person without the prior written permission of the person filing the report and the customer of such person where the information supplied is identifiable as being derived from the records of such customer (22 U.S.C. 3104).

U.S. PERSON FOR BEA TO CONSULT ABOUT THIS REPORT: Print name and address	U.S. TELEPHONE NUMBER		
	Area Code	Number	Extension

CERTIFICATION The undersigned official certifies that the information contained in this report is correct and complete to the best of his/her knowledge.

Authorized Official's Signature	Type Name and Title	Date

18 U.S.C. 1001 (Crimes and Criminal Procedure) makes it a criminal offense to make a willfully false statement or representation to any department or agency of the United States as to any matter within its jurisdiction. Any officer, director, employee, or agent of any corporation who knowingly participates in a willful failure to report, upon conviction, may be punished by a fine, imprisonment, or both (22 U.S.C. 3105). For a further citation of applicable statutes, see the Instruction Booklet to this form.

Part I – IDENTIFICATION OF U.S. AFFILIATE (Continued)

5. U.S. affiliates fully consolidated in this report:

If this report is for a single unconsolidated U.S. bank affiliate enter "1" in the box. If more than one U.S. affiliate is fully consolidated (or aggregated, in case of unincorporated U.S. bank affiliates) in this report, enter the number of U.S. affiliates fully consolidated or aggregated. (Hereinafter, they are considered to be one U.S. affiliate.) Exclude from full consolidation all foreign business enterprises (other than those mainly engaged in activities supportive of U.S. bank affiliates), all minority-owned U.S. business enterprises, and all foreign business enterprises owned by this U.S. affiliate; such affiliates must be included in this report on the equity basis, or cost basis if less than 20 percent owned. See consolidation instructions, page   of the *Instruction Booklet*. (Note that those U.S. affiliates not fully consolidated must file a separate Form BE-12.)

If number is greater than "1," attach a list referencing this Item 5 and the name of the U.S. affiliate given in Item 1, and give the name and U.S. mailing address of, and your percent ownership interest in each U.S. affiliate fully consolidated on this Form BE-12 BANK report.   ☐ ◄ Number

6. U.S. affiliates not fully consolidated in this report: /

Number of U.S. affiliates in which this U.S. affiliate has an ownership interest that ARE NOT fully consolidated (or aggregated, in case of unincorporated U.S. bank affiliates) in this report. The U.S. affiliate named in item 1 must include data for such U.S. affiliates in this report on an equity basis, or cost basis if less than 20 percent owned, and must notify such other U.S. affiliates of their obligation to file a Form BE-12 in their own name.

If figure is not zero, attach a list referencing this Item 6 and the name of the U.S. affiliate given in Item 1, and give the name and U.S. mailing address of, and your percent ownership interest in, such other U.S. affiliates   ☐ ◄ Number

7. Does this U.S. affiliate have an equity interest in a foreign business enterprise or conduct operations outside the United States?

1 ☐ Yes   *If "Yes," do not fully consolidate such enterprises in this report; include them in data on an equity basis, or cost basis if less than 20 percent owned.*

2 ☐ No

8. This U.S. affiliate's 1980 fiscal year ends on:

Month	Day	Year

NOTE: For a U.S. business enterprise that was a U.S. affiliate for all of FY 1980 – Data for the reporting period should be for the U.S. affiliate's 1980 fiscal year; data for close FY 1980 should be for the U.S. affiliate as it existed at the ending date of the 1980 fiscal year; and data for close FY 1979 should be for the U.S. affiliate as it existed one year prior to the 1980 fiscal year date. (Close FY 1979 data must not be restated due to changes in the entity during FY 1980.)

For a U.S. business enterprise that was a U.S. affiliate for only part of FY 1980 – if the enterprise became a U.S. affiliate during the reporting period, the Close FY 1979 data columns should all be zero. If the enterprise ceased to be an affiliate during the reporting period, the Close FY 1980 data columns should all be zero.

9. Was the U.S. business enterprise a U.S. affiliate for only part of FY 1980?

1 ☐ Yes

2 ☐ No

10. If the answer to item 9 is "YES," complete one of the following:

	Month	Day	Year
Date U.S. business enterprise became a U.S. affiliate:			
OR Date U.S. business enterprise ceased to be a U.S. affiliate:			

11. Was there a change in the entity during FY 1980 that caused prior-year data to be restated?

1 ☐ Yes   *If "Yes," please note that all Close FY 1979 data must be before restatement due to a change in the entity.*

2 ☐ No

Ownership – Enter percent of ownership, to a tenth of one percent, based on voting stock if an incorporated affiliate or an equivalent interest if an unincorporated affiliate, in this U.S. affiliate held directly by –

	Close FY 1980 (1)	Close FY 1979 (2)
12. All foreign parents of this affiliate – Give name of each (if more than 4, continue on separate sheet):	. %	. %
a.	////	////
b.	////	////
c.	////	////
d.	////	////
13. All U.S. affiliates of foreign parents of this affiliate	. %	. %
14. All other U.S. persons	. %	. %
15. All other foreign persons	. %	. %
16. TOTAL – Sum of items 12 through 15 ───────────►	100.0 %	100.0 %

If there is an entry in item 13, column 1 or column 2, give, beginning with item 17, the information requested for each U.S. affiliate holding a direct ownership interest in this U.S. affiliate (if more than 4, continue on separate sheet).

U.S. affiliate holding direct ownership interest in the U.S. affiliate named in item 1		Percent direct ownership in U.S. affiliate named in item 1 (For the close of each year, the sum of these percents for all direct owners must equal item 13)		U.S. affiliate in ownership chain which is directly owned by a foreign parent	
Name (1)	BEA Identification Number (2)	Close FY 1980 (3)	Close FY 1979 (4)	Name (5)	BEA Identification Number (6)
17.		. %	. %		
18.		. %	. %		
19.		. %	. %		
20.		. %	. %		

Industry classification of fully-consolidated U.S. affiliate (based on sales or gross operating revenues) – Enter the appropriate 3-digit industry code(s) and the sales (as defined for item 56 on the standard Form BE-12) associated with each code. For a full explanation of each code, see the *Industry Classifications and Export and Import Trade Classifications Booklet.* If you use fewer than eight codes you must account for total sales. For an inactive affiliate, show the industry classification(s) pertinent to the last active period; for "start-ups" with no sales, show the intended activity(ies). Bank holding companies must show percentage of total income (item 33 on this form).

	Industry code (1)	Sales (2) Bil. Mil. Thous. Dols.
21. Banking	600	$
22. Enter code with second largest sales		$
23. Enter code with third largest sales		
24. Enter code with fourth largest sales		
25. Enter code with fifth largest sales		
26. Enter code with sixth largest sales		
27. Enter code with seventh largest sales		
28. Enter code with eighth largest sales		
29. Sales accounted for (sum of items 21 through 28)	/////	
30. Sales not accounted for above	/////	
31. Total sales – Sum of items 29 and 30 ───────────►	/////	$

If the amount of sales as given in item 21 is not more than 50.0 percent of total sales as given in item 31, then the U.S. affiliate most likely does not qualify for using Form BE-12 BANK. *Before proceeding, call BEA for clarification (202) 523-0547.*

Part II – FINANCIAL AND OPERATING DATA OF U.S. AFFILIATE

- Use U.S. generally accepted accounting principles unless otherwise specified. All data must represent a full consolidation of domestic majority-owned U.S. affiliates that are banks; include other U.S. and foreign business enterprises on the equity basis, or cost basis if less than 20 percent owned.

IMPORTANT EXAMPLE: Report all dollar figures below in thousands of U.S. dollars, as illustrated:	Bil.	Mil.	Thous.	Dols.
EXAMPLE: If figure is $2,125,628,000.00	2	125	628	

	Amount (1)			
	Bil.	Mil.	Thous.	Dols.
32. Total assets at close FY 1980 – As defined for reporting on the U.S. bank affiliate's consolidated report of condition of its domestic offices and affiliates	$			
33. Total income – Include sales or gross operating revenues (excluding sales taxes), equity in net income of unconsolidated U.S. and foreign business enterprises, unrealized and realized capital gains (losses) which have been recognized, and other income. Use same basis as required by item 62 of standard Form BE-12				
34. Net income – Net income after provision for U.S. Federal, State, and local income taxes, but before dividends on common and preferred stock. Use same basis as required by item 68 of standard Form BE-12				
35. Net realized and unrealized capital gains (losses) – Include gains (losses) resulting from the sale or disposition of investment securities, property, plant, and equipment, or other assets; those resulting from changes in the dollar value of the affiliate's foreign currency denominated assets and liabilities due to changes in foreign exchange rates during the reporting period; and all other recognized capital gains (losses), including those resulting from revaluation of assets, whether or not realized. Equals sum of items 36 and 37.				
36. Those capital gains (losses) that are included in net income, item 34 above				
37. Those capital gains (losses) that are carried directly to an equity account and are not included in net income, item 34 above				

	Number
38. Total employment – Report the average number of employees for the year, as defined for item 119 of standard Form BE-12	

	Amount			
	Bil.	Mil.	Thous.	Dols.
39. Total employee compensation – For all employees, the sum of wages and salaries and employer expenditures for employee benefit plans, as defined for item 123 of standard Form BE-12	$			

If item 38, total employment, or item 39, total employee compensation, is zero, explain here.

Part III – INVESTMENT AND TRANSACTIONS BETWEEN U.S. AFFILIATE AND FOREIGN PARENT

A separate Part III, or Part III-ADDITIONAL, must be completed for each direct or indirect equity interest held by foreign parents in the U.S. affiliate at any time during the reporting period. Permanent debt and equity investment and related earnings, income, fees, and other items remitted or credited between the U.S. affiliate and the foreign parent, should be reported here on the appropriate lines. NOTE: In order to avoid duplication in U.S. Government statistics, permanent debt investment (item 52), and owners' equity (items 53 through 58), and changes in these items should not be reported on Treasury Department International Capital Forms. However, transactions and positions of the U.S. affiliate with foreign affiliates of the foreign parent are all assumed to be regular bank transactions and should be reported on the Treasury Department International Capital forms rather than here.

40. Number of Part III schedules filed by the U.S. affiliate – If there is only one, enter "1" in the box below; if more than one, enter the number of Part III's to be filed.

[ ] ◄— Number   If number is greater than "1", use Part III-ADDITIONAL schedules.

41. Name of foreign parent that this Part III is for:

Name
[   ]

The foreign parent named in item 41 holds (Mark either 42 or 43):

42.   [ ] A direct equity interest in the U.S. affiliate

43.   [ ] An indirect equity interest in the U.S. affiliate

If a foreign parent holds both direct and indirect equity interests, then separate Part III's must be completed for each line of ownership. The marking of either item 42 or 43 will indicate which is being reported on this Part III.

44. If item 42 is marked, give percent of voting rights directly owned (For the close of each year, the sum of this item from all Part III's filed for the U.S. affiliate must equal item 12.)	Close FY 1980 (1)	Close FY 1979 (2)	
	. %	. %	

45. Country of location of foreign parent named in item 41:

_____

[   ] ◄— BEA USE ONLY

46. Industry code* of foreign parent named in item 41:

[   ] ◄— Code

47. Is the foreign parent named in item 41 the ultimate beneficial owner (UBO) (See definition)?

1 [ ] Yes

2 [ ] No   If the answer to item 47 is "No," complete the following:

48. Name of UBO (if the UBO is an individual, a name is not required, complete only items 49 and 50):

[   ]

49. Country of UBO named in item 48:

_____

[   ] ◄—BEA USE ONLY

50. Industry code* of UBO named in item 48:

[   ] ◄— Code

* Secure industry code for foreign parent or ultimate beneficial owner from page   of the Industry Classifications and Export and Import Trade Classifications Booklet.

Part III – INVESTMENT AND TRANSACTIONS BETWEEN U.S. AFFILIATE AND FOREIGN PARENT (Continued)

NOTE: If item 43 is marked, then only the following items in the rest of this Part III need be completed to report direct transactions or positions, if any, related to permanent debt investment between the U.S. affiliate and the foreign parent: 51, 52, 73, 74, 75, 76, and 77. Do not duplicate data reported on other Part III's.

SECTION A > INVESTMENT BETWEEN U.S. AFFILIATE AND FOREIGN PARENT NAMED IN ITEM 41, ACCORDING TO BOOKS OF U.S. AFFILIATE

	Balance, Close FY 1980 (1) Bil. Mil. Thous. Dols.	Balance, Close FY 1979 (2) Bil. Mil. Thous. Dols.
● Debt to foreign parent		
51. Long-term debt to foreign parent, total – Debt with an original maturity of more than one year or with no stated maturity, and debt with an original maturity of one year or less which has been renewed, or with respect to which there is the intention and the means to renew, extend, or refinance, for more than one year. Exclude current portion due.	$	$
52. Foreign parent's permanent debt investment in the U.S. affiliate – That part of item 51 which is considered by the foreign parent to be permanent debt investment in the affiliate		
● Foreign parent's share in owners' equity		
Unincorporated affiliate:		
53. Permanent invested equity capital – That part of the foreign parent's investment in the U.S. affiliate, other than permanent debt investment reported in item 52, which the foreign parent considers to be permanent invested equity capital, including unremitted income. This would normally consist of capital allocated to the affiliate, special reserves out of net income, and net income not yet distributed		
Incorporated affiliate:		
54. Capital stock, common and preferred, voting and nonvoting		
55. Additional paid-in capital		
56. Retained earnings (deficit)		
57. Treasury stock held by U.S. affiliate	( )	( )
58. Total owners' equity – Sum of items 54, 55, 56, and 57 ————→	$	$
● BEA USE ONLY		

SECTION B > CHANGES IN FOREIGN PARENT'S EQUITY HOLDINGS IN U.S. AFFILIATE

Report in items 59 through 69 transactions during the reporting period by the foreign parent that changed its equity holdings, as given in item 53 or item 58, in the U.S. affiliate, but exclude changes caused by carrying net income to the equity account, the payment of stock or cash dividends (other than liquidating dividends), or the distribution of earnings during the period. Exclude effect of treasury stock transactions with persons other than the foreign parent and reorganizations in capital structure that do not affect total equity. Report all amounts at transactions value, i.e., the value of the consideration given (received) by the foreign parent. –

	Amount (1) Bil. Mil. Thous. Dols.
● Transactions between foreign parent and U.S. affiliate:	
Increase in equity interest –	
59. Establishment of affiliate by foreign parent	$
60. Purchase by foreign parent of capital stock from incorporated affiliate	
61. Additional equity capital contributed by foreign parent (for an incorporated affiliate, report only those contributions not resulting in the issuance of stock)	
Decrease in equity interest –	
62. Total liquidation of affiliate by foreign parent	
63. Sale by foreign parent of capital stock to incorporated affiliate	
64. Return of contributed equity capital to foreign parent (for an incorporated affiliate, report only those returns not resulting in a reduction of issued stock)	
● Transactions between foreign parent and a person other than U.S. affiliate:	
Acquisition by foreign parent of equity interest in U.S. affiliate from –	
65. U.S. persons other than the U.S. affiliate	
66. All foreign persons	
Sale by foreign parent of equity interest in U.S. affiliate to –	
67. U.S. persons other than the U.S. affiliate	
68. All foreign persons	
69. Increase (decrease) at transactions value of changes in equity holdings – The consideration given (received) by the foreign parent in order to bring about the change in equity holdings; must equal sum of items 59, 60, 61, 65, and 66 minus sum of items 62, 63, 64, 67, and 68.	
70. Approximate book value on the date of the transaction(s), based on books of the U.S. affiliate, that is equivalent to the transactions value reported in item 69. (The amount given here should approximate the change in item 53 or item 58, column 1 minus column 2, after allowance is made in item 53 or item 58 to exclude changes caused by carrying net income to the equity account, payment of stock or cash dividends (other than liquidating dividends), distribution of earnings, and treasury stock transactions.)	$

SECTION C > PAYMENTS AND RECEIPTS OF DIVIDENDS, DISTRIBUTED EARNINGS, INTEREST, FEES, ROYALTIES, AND RENTALS BETWEEN U.S. AFFILIATE AND FOREIGN PARENT

Enter amounts paid, received, or entered into intercompany accounts. Include amounts for which payments were made in-kind. Amounts should be entered as of the date paid (received) by the affiliate, or entered into intercompany accounts with the foreign parent, whichever occurred first. For an item entered into intercompany accounts, in order to avoid duplication, any subsequent settlement of the account must not be reflected in one of the items below, but must be reflected only as a reduction in intercompany account.

	Payments or credits by U.S. affiliate to foreign parent		Receipts by or credits to U.S. affiliate from foreign parent	
	Net of U.S. tax withheld (1) Bil. Mil. Thous. Dols.	Amount of U.S. tax withheld (2) Bil. Mil. Thous. Dols.	Net of foreign tax withheld (3) Bil. Mil. Thous. Dols.	Amount of foreign tax withheld (4) Bil. Mil. Thous. Dols.
Incorporated U.S. affiliate:				
71. Dividends on the U.S. affiliate's common and preferred stock, paid out of current and past earnings, excluding stock dividends	$	$	///////	///////
Unincorporated U.S. affiliate:				
72. Earnings distributed, whether out of current or past earnings			///////	///////
All U.S. affiliates:				
73. Interest on long-term debt considered to be permanent debt investment – Enter interest paid by U.S. affiliate on the affiliate's long-term debt to the foreign parent which is considered to be permanent debt investment in the affiliate, item 52			///////	///////
74. Royalties, license fees, and other fees for the use or sale of intangible property			$	$
75. Payments and receipts for use of tangible property – Include rentals for operating leases of one year or less and net rent on operating leases of more than one year. Net rent is due equivalent to the total lease payment less the return of capital (depreciation) component				
76. Fees for services rendered – Include fees for management, professional or technical services, R&D assessments, and allocated expenses other than those given above				
77. TOTAL – Sum of items 71 through 76 ————→	$	$	$	$

FOREIGN PARENT'S EQUITY IN U.S. AFFILIATE'S NET INCOME

Net income must be calculated in accordance with the all inclusive concept of the income statement.

	Amount (1) Bil. Mil. Thous. Dols.
78. Foreign parent's direct equity in U.S. affiliate's net income (loss) – Enter foreign parent's direct ownership share of net income, item 34	$
79. Foreign parent's share of item 36, net realized and unrealized capital gains (losses) included in net income	
80. Foreign parent's share of item 37, net realized and unrealized capital gains (losses) taken directly to retained earnings or owner's equity, after provision for income tax liability (benefit), if any, on the gains (losses)	$

Page 4

[FR Doc. 81-2367 Filed 1-21-81; 8:45 am]

BILLING CODE 3510-06-C

564

OMB No. 06-38-0015 Approval Expires March 1984

CONTROL NUMBER

FORM BE-13A
(REV. 2-81)

U.S. DEPARTMENT OF COMMERCE
BUREAU OF ECONOMIC ANALYSIS

FORM FOR A U.S. BUSINESS ENTERPRISE,
BUSINESS SEGMENT, OR OPERATING UNIT
THAT HAS BEEN ESTABLISHED OR ACQUIRED
BY A FOREIGN PERSON OR EXISTING
U.S. AFFILIATE OF A FOREIGN PERSON

MANDATORY – CONFIDENTIAL

Response to this inquiry is required by law. By the same law your report to this Bureau is CONFIDENTIAL. It may be used only for analytical or statistical purposes and CANNOT be used for purposes of taxation, investigation, or regulation. The law also provides that copies retained in your files are immune from legal process.

This form is to be completed either:

a) *by a U.S. business enterprise when a foreign person (hereinafter, the "foreign parent") establishes or acquires directly, or indirectly through an existing U.S. affiliate, a 10 percent or more voting interest in that enterprise, including an enterprise that results from the direct or indirect acquisition by a foreign person of a business segment or operating unit of an existing U.S. business enterprise that is then organized as a separate legal entity; or*

b) *by the existing U.S. affiliate of a foreign person (hereinafter, the "existing U.S. affiliate") when it acquires a U.S. business enterprise, or a business segment or operating unit of a U.S. business enterprise, that the existing U.S. affiliate merges into its own operations rather than continuing or organizing as a separate legal entity.*

RETURN
REPORT
TO

U.S. Department of Commerce
Bureau of Economic Analysis BE-50 (IN)
Washington, D.C. 20230

NOTE: A single original copy of the form is to be filed with the Bureau of Economic Analysis. To facilitate processing, it is preferred that the BE-13A and the BE-13B forms be filed together, or simultaneously. File copies should be retained for 3 years after the date on which the form is due.

Important Read instructions *before completing form.*

■ 1. EXCLUSIONS AND EXEMPTIONS:

a. Residential real estate held exclusively for personal use and not for profitmaking purposes is not subject to the reporting requirements. A U.S. residence which is an owner's primary residence that is then leased by the owner while outside the United States but which the owner intends to reoccupy, is considered real estate held for personal use. Ownership of residential real estate by a corporation whose sole purpose is to hold the real estate and where the real estate is for the personal use of the individual owner(s) of the corporation, is considered real estate held for personal use.

b. An existing U.S. affiliate is exempt from reporting the acquisition of a U.S. business enterprise, or a business segment or operating unit of a U.S. business enterprise, that it then merges into its own operations, if the total cost of the acquisition was $1,000,000 or less, and does not involve the purchase of 200 acres or more of U.S. land. (If the acquisition involves the purchase of 200 acres or more of U.S. land, it must be reported regardless of the total cost of the acquisition.)

c. An established or acquired U.S. business enterprise, as consolidated, is exempt if its total assets (not the foreign parent's or existing U.S. affiliate's share) at the time of acquisition or immediately after being established, were $1,000,000 or less and it does not own 200 acres or more of U.S. land. (If it owns 200 acres or more of U.S. land, it must report regardless of the value of total assets.)

If exempt under (b) or (c), an "Exemption Claim, Form BE-13A" must be filed to validate the exemption.

NOTE: See Section II.B. of Instructions concerning reporting on related forms that may be required when changes occur.

■ 2. EFFECTIVE DATE: A report on this revised form is required for each covered direct investment transaction occurring on or after January 1, 1981.

■ 3. ASSISTANCE – Telephone (202) 523–0547.

■ 4. DUE DATE: Form BE-13A is due no later than 45 days after the direct investment transaction occurs.
NOTE: Form CE-607, Industry Classification Questionnaire, must also be completed by a new U.S. affiliate and returned with Form BE-13A.

■ 5. GENERAL NOTES:

A. Figures such as the number of acres and the number of employees should be reported to the nearest unit.

B. Currency amounts should be reported in U.S. dollars rounded to thousands (omitting 000). Do not enter amounts in the shaded portions of each line.

EXAMPLE: If amount is $1,334,615.00, report as:

Bil.	Mil.	Thous.	Dols.
	1,	335	

C. If an item is between + or − $500.00 enter "0".
D. Use parentheses to indicate negative numbers.

PART I – Determination of Type of Transaction

The foreign parent or existing U.S. affiliate *(Mark one):*

1. 1001 `1` ☐ Created a new legal entity, either incorporated or unincorporated, including a branch, that it organized and began operating as a new U.S. business enterprise; or directly purchased real estate

2. `2` ☐ Secured a voting equity interest in a previously existing, separate legal entity that was already organized and operating as a U.S. business enterprise and that it continued to operate as a separate legal entity, either incorporated or unincorporated, including a branch

3. `3` ☐ Bought a business segment or operating unit of an existing U.S. business enterprise, that it organized as a new separate legal entity, either incorporated or unincorporated, including a branch

4. `4` ☐ The existing U.S. affiliate bought a U.S. enterprise, or business segment or operating unit of a U.S. business enterprise, and merged it into its own operations rather than continuing or organizing it as a separate legal entity

If 1, 2, or 3, is marked, the U.S. business enterprise acquired, or the new legal entity created, is hereinafter referred to as the "new U.S. affiliate" and Parts II, IV, and V below must be completed.

If 4 is marked, omit Part II and complete Parts III, IV, and V below.

NOTE: See Section II.E of Instructions concerning unusual reporting situations.

PART II – Identification and Capital Structure of the New U.S. Affiliate
(This Part is to be completed only if item 1, 2, or 3 is marked)

5. Name and address of new U.S. affiliate

Name of new U.S. affiliate
1002

Street or P.O. box
1003

City and State   ZIP Code
1004

6. Primary employer identification number to be used by the new U.S. affiliate to file income and payroll taxes.

1005 ⌐ ____ - ____ ____ ◄— E.I. Number

7. Form of organization of U.S. affiliate *(Mark one):*

1006 `1` ☐ Incorporated in U.S.   `5` ☐ Business enterprise incorporated abroad, but whose head office is located in the United States and whose business activity is conducted in, or from, the United States

`2` ☐ U.S. partnership

`3` ☐ U.S. branch of a foreign person   `6` ☐ Other – *Specify:*

`4` ☐ Real property not in 1–3 above

8. Is the investment primarily an investment in real estate, including agriculture and forestry land?

1007 `1` ☐ Yes

`2` ☐ No

9. *If the answer to item 8 is "YES," based on estimated current values, is this primarily an investment in (Mark one):*

1008 `1` ☐ Unimproved real estate

`2` ☐ Improved real estate

MANDATORY – This survey is being conducted pursuant to the International Investment Survey Act of 1976 (Pub. L. 94–472, 90 Stat. 2059, 22 U.S.C. 3101 to 3108 – hereinafter, "the Act"), and the filing of reports is mandatory pursuant to Section 5(b) (2) of the Act (22 U.S.C. 3104).

PENALTIES – Whoever fails to report may be subject to a civil penalty not exceeding $10,000 and to injunctive relief commanding such person to comply, or both. Whoever willfully fails to report shall be fined not more than $10,000 and, if an individual, may be imprisoned for not more than one year, or both. Any officer, director, employee, or agent of any corporation who knowingly participates in such violations, upon conviction, may be punished by a like fine, imprisonment or both. (See Section 6 of the Act, 22 U.S.C. 3105.)

CONFIDENTIALITY – The information filed in this report may be used only for analytical and statistical purposes and access to the information shall be available only to officials and employees (including consultants and contractors and their employees) of agencies designated by the President to perform functions under the Act. The President may authorize the exchange of information between agencies or officials designated to perform functions under the Act, but only for analytical and statistical purposes. No official or employee (including consultants and contractors and their employees) shall publish or make available any information collected under the Act in such a manner that the person to whom the information relates can be specifically identified. Reports and copies of reports prepared pursuant to the Act are confidential and their submission or disclosure shall not be compelled by any person without the prior written permission of the person filing the report and the customer of such person where the information supplied is identifiable as being derived from the records of such customer (22 U.S.C. 3104).

Print name and address

PERSON TO CONSULT
CONCERNING QUESTIONS
ABOUT THIS REPORT

U.S. TELEPHONE NUMBER		
Area Code	Number	Extension

▷ **CERTIFICATION** The undersigned official certifies that the information contained in this report is correct and complete to the best of his/her knowledge.

Authorized Official's Signature	Title	Date

Form BE-13A, Page 1

Form 3-C: BE-13A—Form for U.S. business enterprise, business segment, or operating unit that has been established or acquired by a foreign person or existing U.S. affiliate of a foreign person

PART II – Identification and Capital Structure of the New U.S. Affiliate (Continued)

10. Date on which the foreign person established or acquired directly, or indirectly through an existing U.S. affiliate, a 10 percent or more voting interest in the new U.S. affiliate. (If more than one foreign person or existing U.S. affiliate of a foreign person acquired a new interest on or about the same time, give date for each opposite their names and addresses in item 17 or item 18, as appropriate.)

	MONTH	DAY	YEAR
2009			

11. Did the foreign person own a voting interest, direct or indirect, in the new U.S. affiliate immediately prior to the date, as given in item 10, it acquired a 10 percent or more voting interest? *(Mark one)*
(If more than one foreign person or existing U.S. affiliate of a foreign person acquired a new interest on or about the same time, indicate a "Yes." or "No" to this item opposite each of their names and addresses in item 17 or item 18, as appropriate.)

2010   1 ☐ Yes
       2 ☐ No

Ownership of new U.S. affiliate – Number of voting shares, and percent of voting shares and equity interest for an incorporated U.S. affiliate, or an equivalent interest for an unincorporated U.S. affiliate, owned DIRECTLY by:

		Voting Shares		Total equity interest
		Number	Percent	Percent
12. All foreign parent(s), including the foreign parent(s) with a newly acquired direct investment ownership interest	2011	1	2	3
13. All U.S. affiliate(s) of foreign parent(s), including the existing U.S. affiliate(s) with a newly acquired ownership interest	2012	1	2	3
14. Other foreign persons	2013	1	2	3
15. Other U.S. persons	2014	1	2	3
16. Total – Sum of items 12 through 15	2015	1	100.0%	100.0%

17. Foreign parent(s) holding a newly acquired direct ownership interest included in item 12 – Give name, address, and percent of ownership directly held by each. If more than three, continue on a separate sheet. A Form BE-13B must be completed for or by each foreign parent with a newly acquired direct ownership interest. This item need not be filled out if a completed Form BE-13B for the foreign parent accompanies the filing of this Form BE-13A.

(1) Name and address of foreign parent   Percent of ownership

%

BEA USE ONLY
2016

(2) Name and address of foreign parent   Percent of ownership

%

BEA USE ONLY
2017

(3) Name and address of foreign parent   Percent of ownership

%

BEA USE ONLY
2018

18. Existing U.S. affiliate(s) holding a newly acquired direct ownership interest included in item 13 – Give name, address, and percent of ownership directly held by each. If more than two, continue on a separate sheet. A Form BE-13B must be filed by each existing U.S. affiliate with a newly acquired direct ownership interest. This item need not be filled out if a completed Form BE-13B for the existing U.S. affiliate accompanies the filing of this Form BE-13A.

(1) Name and address of existing U.S. affiliate   Percent of ownership

%

BEA USE ONLY
2036

(2) Name and address of existing U.S. affiliate   Percent of ownership

%

BEA USE ONLY
2037

19. Number of U.S. affiliates consolidated *(Enter number)*
If this report is for a single unconsolidated U.S. affiliate, enter "1" in the box. If the new U.S. affiliate owns subsidiaries that become U.S. affiliates and their data are included by consolidation in Part IV, enter the number of U.S. affiliates fully consolidated. (Hereinafter, they are considered to be one U.S. affiliate.) Exclude from the full consolidation all foreign business enterprises owned by this U.S. affiliate. See consolidation instructions, II.G. of Instructions.

If number is greater than one, Supplement A must be completed.

	NUMBER
2056	

20. U.S. affiliates not consolidated – Enter number of U.S. affiliates in which the new U.S. affiliate holds a direct equity interest but which ARE NOT fully consolidated in this report.

If an entry here, Supplement B must be completed.

	NUMBER
2057	

21. Does any U.S. affiliate fully consolidated in this report own, directly or indirectly, over 50 percent of the outstanding voting stock of a domestic corporation that is not a U.S. affiliate? (See definition of U.S. affiliate.) *(Mark one)*:

2058   1 ☐ Yes
       2 ☐ No

If yes, do not fully consolidate such domestic corporation in this report – include only by equity method of accounting.

22. Give the ending date for the new U.S. affiliate's fiscal year

	MONTH	DAY
2059		

Form BE-13A, Page 2

Form 3-C: BE-13A—Form for U.S. business enterprise, business segment, or operating unit that has been established or acquired by a foreign person or existing U.S. affiliate of a foreign person

PART II – Identification and Capital Structure of the New U.S. Affiliate (Continued)

Capital Structure of the New U.S. Affiliate: To be based on data from the books of the new U.S. affiliate immediately after the foreign person established or acquired a 10 percent or more, direct or indirect, voting interest or equivalent.

			MONTH	DAY	YEA*
23. Date data are as of:		2060			

		Total (1)	All foreign parent(s) (2)	All U.S. affiliate(s) of foreign parent(s) (3)	Other persons (4)
		Bil. Mil. Thou. Dols	Bil. Mil. Thou. Dols	Bil. Mil. Thou. Dols	Bil. Mil. Thou. D.
Incorporated U.S. affiliate:		1	2	3	4
24. Capital stock – voting	2061	$	$	$	$
25. Capital stock – nonvoting	2062		2	3	4
26. Additional paid-in capital	2063	1	2	3	4
27. Retained earnings	2064	1	2	3	4
28. Treasury stock	2065	( )			
29. Total – Sum of items 24 through 28	2066	$	2 $	3 $	4 $
Unincorporated U.S. affiliate:		1	2	3	4
30. Owners' equity	2067	$	$	$	$

GO DIRECTLY TO PART IV, AND ALSO COMPLETE PART V

PART III – Identification of a U.S. Business Enterprise, or a Business Segment or Operating Unit of a U.S. Business Enterprise, that has been Acquired by and Merged into an Existing U.S. Affiliate (*This Part is to be completed only if item 4, Part I, above is marked.*)

31. Name and address of existing U.S. affiliate that made acquisition.

Name of U.S. affiliate

Street or P.O. box

City and State   ZIP Code

32. Name and address of business enterprise acquired or main office or location of the operating facilities of the segment or operating unit acquired.

Name

Street or P.O. box

City and State   ZIP Code

33. If the enterprise, segment, or unit acquired had its own Employer Identification Number that it used to file income and payroll taxes, enter the number. Do not enter a number if it covered more than just the acquired entity.

3068 [ ] – [ ][ ][ ][ ][ ] ◄— E.I. Number

34. Name and address of person from whom acquired

Name

Street or P.O. box

City and State   ZIP Code

	MONTH	DAY	YEAR
35. Date on which the existing U.S. affiliate completed the purchase of the enterprise, segment, or operating unit that it then merged into its own operations. 3069			

ALSO COMPLETE PARTS IV AND V

BEA USE ONLY

3070

3071

3072

3073

3074

Form BE-13A, Page 3

Form 3-C: BE-13A—Form for U.S. business enterprise, business segment, or operating unit that has been established or acquired by a foreign person or existing U.S. affiliate of a foreign person

PART IV – Selected Financial and Operating Data
This Part is to be completed in the case of all types of transactions covered by items 1 through 4 above.

For items 36 through 42 and for items 44 through 51, column 2:

If item 1 above is marked: Where the investment represents the establishment of a new U.S. business enterprise, or the direct purchase of real estate, the data should be projections for or as of the end of the first full year of operations. Use projections made in the course of planning the investment if available; otherwise, give best estimate.

If item 2, 3, or 4 above is marked: Data should be for the fully consolidated U.S. business enterprise, or business segment or operating unit, acquired. Data should be for or as of the end of the most recent financial reporting year preceding acquisition. Exclude from full consolidation all foreign business enterprises owned by this U.S. affiliate; include such foreign enterprises only by the equity or cost method of accounting. (See Section II.G. of Instructions.)

For items 43 and for items 44 through 51, column 1:

If item 1, 2, or 3 above is marked: The data should show the number of acres owned by the new U.S. affiliate upon completion of the investment transaction.
If item 4 above is marked: The data should show the number of acres included in the purchase.

NOTE: *See special instructions regarding the reporting of employee compensation (item 41) and number of employees (item 42) in Section VIII of Instructions.*

		MONTH	DAY	YEAR
36. Give ending date for the year that these Part IV data are for, or as of	4120			

		Amount
		Bil. Mil. Thous. Dols.
37. Total assets	4121	$
38. Plant and equipment, net of accumulated depreciation, depletion, etc.	4122	$
39. Sales or gross operating revenues, excluding sales taxes (do not give gross margin)	4123	$
40. Net income after provision for U.S. Federal, State, and local income taxes	4124	$
41. Employee compensation – Include wages and salaries and cost of employee benefit plans	4125	$

		Number
42. Number of employees – Average for the reporting period, including part-time employees	4126	

43. Acres of mineral rights owned and leased from others – In those cases where both the land and the mineral rights to that land are owned, report the land only as land owned in items 44 through 51, column 1; do not also report it in this item. Include acres leased from others pursuant to both capital and operating leases.	4127

BEA USE ONLY ➤ 4128

Land and other property, plant, and equipment, total and by primary use. Items, including land, being leased from others pursuant to capital leases are to be considered as owned by the affiliate; items which the affiliate has sold on a capital lease basis are not to be considered as owned by the affiliate.		All land owned, whether carried in a fixed asset, investment, or other asset account (1) ACRES (To nearest whole acre)	Gross Book value (historical cost) of all land and other property, plant, and equipment, whether carried in a fixed asset, investment, or other asset account (2) Bil. Mil. Thous. Dols.
44. Agriculture and forestry	4129		$
45. Natural resources	4130		$
46. Manufacturing	Petroleum refining	4131		$
47.	Chemicals	4132		$
48.	Other	4133		$
49. Residential and office buildings, stores, and shopping centers	4134		$
50. Other – Specify	4135		$
51. Total	4136		$

PART V – Investment Incentives and Services Provided by State or Local Governments (Including Quasi-government Entities)
This Part to be completed in the case of all types of transactions covered by items 1 through 4 above.

52. Were any specific State or local government incentives or related services (such as those detailed in items 54 through 59 below) received in connection with this investment transaction?   5137   1 ☐ Yes   2 ☐ No

53. If the answer to item 52 is "Yes," were these incentives or services a significant factor in the decision to invest in (Mark as many categories as are applicable):

The United States as a whole?   5138   1 ☐ Yes   2 ☐ No

A region within the United States?   5139   1 ☐ Yes   2 ☐ No

A given State or local area?   5140   1 ☐ Yes   2 ☐ No

If the answer to item 52 is "Yes," indicate the category(ies) which most clearly describe the relevant State or local incentives or services and give, as accurately as possible for items 54 and 55, the monetary "value" of the incentives or services. The categories are not limited to the examples given. Mark as many categories as are applicable.	Applicable (1)	If Yes, value (2) (Thousands of Dollars)
54. Taxation – Such as investment tax credit; tax exemption; and tax reduction or holidays. If yes is marked, give estimate of average annual value of the tax savings over the first five years of the investment.	5141 1 ☐ Yes 2 ☐ No	$ _____
55. Financing programs – Such as industrial revenue bonds; direct loans or loan guarantees; and credits from development credit corporations. If yes is marked, give estimate of annual cost savings in relation to financing available at commercial rates over the life of the financing provided.	5142 1 ☐ Yes 2 ☐ No	$ _____
56. Labor programs – Such as recruiting programs; training programs; and State-financed relocation services	5143 1 ☐ Yes 2 ☐ No	
57. Information services – Such as State-funded site studies, area research, and feasibility studies; State university R&D assistance, and local marketing data	5144 1 ☐ Yes 2 ☐ No	
58. Special services – Such as State-funded road building or other services relating to construction or operation, and locally-owned industrial park sites	5145 1 ☐ Yes 2 ☐ No	
59. Other incentives or services – Describe	5146 1 ☐ Yes 2 ☐ No	

60. State, or State of location of local government unit, from which the incentives or services were received. (If more than one, enter all States from which received.)		BEA USE
	_____ 5147	
	_____ 5148	
	_____ 5149	

Form BE-13A, Page 4

Form 3-C: BE-13A—Form for U.S. business enterprise, business segment, or operating unit that has been established or acquired by a foreign person or existing U.S. affiliate of a foreign person

FORM BE-13A Supplement A
(REV. 2-81)

U.S. DEPARTMENT OF COMMERCE
BUREAU OF ECONOMIC ANALYSIS

OMB No. 0608-0035; Approval Expires March 1984

Page No. _____

LIST OF ALL U.S. SUBSIDIARIES FULLY CONSOLIDATED INTO THE NEW U.S. AFFILIATE

BEA USE ONLY △

Name of new U.S. affiliate as shown in item 5, Part II of BE-13A

Employer Identification Number as shown in item 6, Part II of BE-13A → 6148 –

Supplement A must be completed by a new U.S. affiliate which consolidates financial and operating data of any other U.S. affiliate(s). The number of U.S. affiliates listed below, in addition to the reporting U.S. affiliate, must agree with item 19, Part II of BE-13A. Continue listing onto as many additional copied pages as necessary.

BEA USE ONLY (1)	Name of each U.S. affiliate consolidated (as represented in item 19, Part II) (2)	Employer Identification Number used by U.S. affiliate listed in Column 2 to file income and payroll taxes (3)	Name of U.S. affiliate which holds the direct equity interest in the U.S. affiliate listed in Column 2 (4)	Percentage of direct ownership which the U.S. affiliate listed in Column 4 has in the U.S. affiliate listed in Column 2. (Enter percentage to nearest tenth.) (5)
6149				%
6150				%
6151				%
6152				%
6153				%
6154				%
6155				%
6156				%
6157				%
6158				%
6159				%
6160				%
6161				%
6162				%
6163				%
6164				%
6165				%
6166				%
6167				%
6168				%
6169				%
6170				%
6171				%

Form BE-13A, Page 5

Form 3-C: **BE-13A—Form for U.S. business enterprise, business segment, or operating unit that has been established or acquired by a foreign person or existing U.S. affiliate of a foreign person**

BE-13A Supplement A – LIST OF ALL U.S. SUBSIDIARIES FULLY CONSOLIDATED INTO THE NEW U.S. AFFILIATE – Continued

Page No. _____

BEA USE ONLY	Name of each U.S. affiliate consolidated (as represented in Item 19, Part II)	Employer Identification Number used by U.S. affiliate listed in Column 2 to file income and payroll taxes	Name of U.S. affiliate which holds the direct equity interest in the U.S. affiliate listed in Column 2	Percentage of direct ownership which the U.S. affiliate listed in Column 4 has in the U.S. affiliate listed in Column 2. (Enter percentage to nearest tenth.)
(1)	(2)	(3)	(4)	(5)
6172				%
6173				%
6174				%
6175				%
6176				%
6177				%
6178				%
6179				%
6180				%
6181				%
6182				%
6183				%
6184				%
6185				%
6186				%
6187				%
6188				%
6189				%
6190				%
6191				%
6192				%
6193				%
6194				%
6195				%
6196				%

Form BE-13A, Page 6

Form 3-C: BE-13A—Form for U.S. business enterprise, business segment, or operating unit that has been established or acquired by a foreign person or existing U.S. affiliate of a foreign person

OMB No. 0608—0035; Approval Expires March 1984

Form BE-13A Supplement B
(Rev. 2-81)

U.S. DEPARTMENT OF COMMERCE
BUREAU OF ECONOMIC ANALYSIS

BEA USE ONLY △

Page No. _____

LIST OF ALL U.S. AFFILIATES IN WHICH THE NEW U.S. AFFILIATE (AS CONSOLIDATED)
HAS A DIRECT EQUITY INTEREST BUT WHICH ARE NOT FULLY CONSOLIDATED

Name of new U.S. affiliate as shown in item 5 Part II of BE-13A

Supplement B must be completed by a new U.S. affiliate which files a BE-13A and has a direct ownership interest in a U.S. affiliate(s) which is (are) not fully consolidated.
The number of U.S. affiliates listed below must agree with item 20, Part II, of BE-13A. Continue listing onto as many additional copied pages as necessary.

Employer Identification Number as
shown in item 6, Part II of BE-13A /   7/97

BEA USE ONLY (1)	Name of each U.S. affiliate in which a direct interest is held but which is not listed in Supplement A (2)	Address of each U.S. affiliate listed in Column 2. Give number, street, city, State, and ZIP Code (3)	Employer Identification Number used by U.S. affiliate listed in Column 2 to file income and payroll taxes (4)	Percentage of direct ownership in the U.S. affiliate listed in Column 2 held by the new U.S. affiliate named in item 5, Part II of BE-13A. (Enter percentage to nearest tenth) (5)
7/98				%
7/99				%
7/200				%
7/201				%
7/202				%
7/203				%
7/204				%
7/205				%
7/206				%
7/207				%

Form BE-13A, Page 7

Form 3-C: BE-13A—Form for U.S. business enterprise, business segment, or operating unit that has been established or acquired by a foreign person or existing U.S. affiliate of a foreign person

BE-13A Supplement B — LIST OF ALL U.S. AFFILIATES IN WHICH THE NEW U.S. AFFILIATE (AS CONSOLIDATED) HAS A DIRECT EQUITY INTEREST BUT WHICH ARE NOT FULLY CONSOLIDATED — Continued

Page No. _____

BEA USE ONLY	Name of each U.S. affiliate in which a direct interest is held but which is not listed in Supplement A	Address of each U.S. affiliate listed in Column 2. Give number, street, city, State, and ZIP Code	Employer Identification Number used by U.S. affiliate listed in Column 2 to file income and payroll taxes	Percentage of direct ownership in the U.S. affiliate listed in Column 2 held by the new U.S. affiliate named in item 3, Part II of BE-13A. (Enter percentage to nearest tenth)
(1)	(2)	(3)	(4)	(5)
7209				%
7210				%
7211				%
7212				%
7213				%
7214				%
7215				%
7216				%
7217				%
7218				%
7219				%
7220				%

Form BE-13A, Page 8

Form 3–D: BE–13B—Form for foreign person, or existing U.S. affiliate of a foreign person that establishes or acquires a U.S. business enterprise, or a business segment or operating unit of a U.S. business enterprise

---

FORM BE-13B
(REV. 2-81)

U.S. DEPARTMENT OF COMMERCE
BUREAU OF ECONOMIC ANALYSIS

FORM FOR FOREIGN PERSON, OR EXISTING
U.S. AFFILIATE OF A FOREIGN PERSON,
THAT ESTABLISHES OR ACQUIRES A
U.S. BUSINESS ENTERPRISE, OR A BUSINESS
SEGMENT OR OPERATING UNIT
OF A U.S. BUSINESS ENTERPRISE

MANDATORY – CONFIDENTIAL

OMB No. 0608-0035, Approval Expires March 198_

CONTROL NO.

Response to this inquiry is required by law. By the same law your report to this Bureau is CONFIDENTIAL. It may be used only for analytical and statistical purposes and CANNOT be used for purposes of taxation, investigation, or regulation. The law also provides that copies retained in your files are immune from legal process.

This report is being completed for or by (mark one):

1. 01 ☐ 1 The foreign parent that directly established or acquired the new U.S. affiliate.

2. ☐ 2 The existing U.S. affiliate of a foreign person that established a new U.S. affiliate or acquired a direct voting interest in a U.S. business enterprise of such a magnitude that the established or acquired enterprise becomes a new U.S. affiliate of the existing U.S. affiliate's foreign parent

3. ☐ 3 The existing U.S. affiliate of a foreign person that acquired a U.S. business enterprise, or business segment or operating unit of a U.S. business enterprise, and merged it into its own operations

Reporting on this form should be as follows (see Section I of Instructions for definition of U.S. affiliate):

a) by a foreign person (hereinafter, the "foreign parent") when it establishes or acquires a direct voting interest in a U.S. business enterprise that becomes its U.S. affiliate (hereinafter, the "new U.S. affiliate"), or by the new U.S. affiliate for the foreign parent to the extent it has or can secure the information; or

b) by an existing U.S. affiliate of a foreign person (hereinafter, the "existing U.S. affiliate") when it establishes or acquires a direct voting interest in a U.S. business enterprise of such a magnitude that the established or acquired enterprise becomes a U.S. affiliate of the foreign person, i.e., the foreign person thereby acquires an indirect (or direct and indirect) voting interest of 10 percent or more in the established or acquired U.S. business enterprise (hereinafter, the "new U.S. affiliate") – see Section II.F. of Instructions for method for calculating indirect ownership; or

c) by an existing U.S. affiliate of a foreign person (hereinafter, the "existing U.S. affiliate") when it acquires a U.S. business enterprise, or a business segment or operating unit of a U.S. business enterprise, and merges it into its own operations.

A separate Form BE-13B must be completed by or for each foreign parent, or by each existing U.S. affiliate, that has secured a direct voting interest in a new U.S. affiliate.

RETURN REPORTS TO
U.S. Department of Commerce
Bureau of Economic Analysis BE-50 (IN)
Washington, D.C. 20230

NOTE: *A single original copy of the form is to be filed with the Bureau of Economic Analysis. To facilitate processing, it is preferred that the BE-13A and the BE-13B forms be filed together, or simultaneously. File copies should be retained for 3 years after the date on which the form is due.*

Important *Read instructions before completing form.*

■ 1. EXEMPTION:
The foreign parent or existing U.S. affiliate is exempt from filing a BE-13B if a BE-13A is not required to be filed.

■ 2. EFFECTIVE DATE:
A report on this revised form is required for each covered direct investment transaction occurring on or after January 1, 1981.

■ 3. ASSISTANCE – Telephone (202) 523-0547.

■ 4. DUE DATE:
Form BE-13B is due no later than 45 days after the direct investment transaction occurs.

■ 5. GENERAL NOTES:
A. Figures such as the number of voting shares held should be reported to the nearest whole unit.

B. Currency amounts should be reported in U.S. dollars rounded to thousands (omitting 000). Do not enter amounts in the shaded portions of each line.
EXAMPLE: If amount is $1,334,615.00, report as:

Bil.	Mil.	Thous.	Dols.
		1,335	

C. If an item is between + or – $500.00 enter "0".
D. Use parentheses to indicate negative numbers.

MANDATORY – This survey is being conducted pursuant to the International Investment Survey Act of 1976 (Pub. L. 94–472, 90 Stat. 2059, 22 U.S.C. 3101 to 3108 – hereinafter "the Act"), and the filing of reports is mandatory pursuant to Section 5(b)(2) of the Act (22 U.S.C. 3104).

PENALTIES – Whoever fails to report may be subject to a civil penalty not exceeding $10,000 and to injunctive relief commanding such person to comply, or both. Whoever willfully fails to report shall be fined not more than $10,000 and, if an individual, may be imprisoned for not more than one year, or both. Any officer, director, employee, or agent of any corporation who knowingly participates in such violations, upon conviction, may be punished by a like fine, imprisonment or both. (See Section 6 of the Act, 22 U.S.C. 3105.)

CONFIDENTIALITY – The information filed in this report may be used only for analytical and statistical purposes and access to the information shall be available only to officials and employees (including consultants and contractors and their employees) of agencies designated by the President to perform functions under the Act. The President may authorize the exchange of information between agencies or officials designated to perform functions under the Act, but only for analytical and statistical purposes. No official or employee (including consultants and contractors and their employees) shall publish or make available any information collected under the Act in such a manner that the person to whom the information relates can be specifically identified. Reports and copies of reports prepared pursuant to the Act are confidential and their submission or disclosure shall not be compelled by any person without the prior written permission of the person filing the report and the customer of such person where the information supplied is identifiable as being derived from the records of such customer (22 U.S.C. 3104).

4. Name and address of either the foreign parent (including country) or existing U.S. affiliate by, or for whom, the report is being completed

02 Name

03 Street or P.O. box

04 City and State | ZIP Code

05 Country

06 BEA USE ONLY

5a. If item 2 or 3 is marked, give the name and country of the foreign parent holding the direct, or indirect, ownership interest in the existing U.S. affiliate named in item 4. If more than one foreign parent, furnish, on a separate sheet, the information requested in items 5a and b and 6a through f for each additional foreign parent.

07 Name

08 Country

b. If item 2 or 3 is marked and if the existing U.S. affiliate named in item 4 is not directly owned by the foreign parent, give name and address of U.S. affiliate that is directly owned by the foreign parent and the percent of ownership by the foreign parent.

09 Name

10 Address | PERCENT

11

6a. Industry code of foreign parent named in either item 4 or item 5a*

12 ◄ Industry code

b. Is the foreign parent named in either item 4 or item 5a the ultimate beneficial owner (UBO)? (See definition of UBO)

13 ☐ 1 Yes
☐ 2 No If the answer to item 6b is "NO," complete items c, d, e, and f.

c. Is the UBO an individual?

14 ☐ 1 Yes If the answer to item 6c is "YES," then the name of the individual need not be given in item 6d, but the country of residence of the individual must be given in item 6e.
☐ 2 No

d. Name of UBO:

15

e. Country of UBO named in item 6d:

16

f. Industry code of UBO named in item 6d*:

17 ◄ Industry code

NOTE: *Failure to complete items 6a through 6f, to the extent required by the line instructions, will constitute an incomplete report, which will be returned to the reporter for completion.*

* For items 6a and 6f, secure foreign parent and UBO industry codes from page 2 of Form BE-607, which accompanies this BE-13 report.

18 BEA USE ONLY

7. If 1 or 2 was marked, give name and address of the new U.S. affiliate as it appears in item 5 of the BE-13A.

19 Name of new U.S. affiliate

20 Street or P.O. box

21 City and State | ZIP Code

22 BEA USE ONLY

Print name and address

PERSON TO CONSULT
CONCERNING QUESTIONS
ABOUT THIS REPORT

U.S. TELEPHONE NUMBER

Area Code	Number	Extension

► CERTIFICATION The undersigned official certifies that the information contained in this report is correct and complete to the best of his/her knowledge.

Authorized Official's Signature | Title | Date

Form BE-13B, Page 1

Form 3-D: **BE-13B—Form for foreign person, or existing U.S. affiliate of a foreign person that establishes or acquires a U.S. business enterprise, or a business segment or operating unit of a U.S. business enterprise**

8. *If 2 was marked, will data for the new U.S. affiliate be fully consolidated with that of the existing or another U.S. affiliate in other international investment reports filed with this Bureau?*

23   1 ☐ Yes   2 ☐ No.

If yes, give name under which consolidated report will be filed if it is not the name given in item 4.

(It must be consolidated if the ownership is more than 50 percent except that separate reports may be filed where the new U.S. affiliate will not normally be fully consolidated due to unrelated operations, in accordance with generally accepted accounting principles, or lack of control, provided written permission has been requested from and granted by BEA.)

For ownership interests in a U.S. business enterprise previously held by the foreign parent, or existing U.S. affiliate, but where the percentage ownership was insufficient to qualify the U.S. business enterprise as a U.S. affiliate *(see definition in Section I of the Instructions)* of the foreign parent, complete items 9 through 12 if the enterprise was incorporated, or complete only item 12 if the enterprise was unincorporated.

Enter data relating to previously held partial interest:

		Number
9.	Number of voting shares held 24	

		Amount
		Bil. Mil. Thous. Dols.
10.	Cost of voting shares held 25	
11.	Cost of other equity interest 26	
12.	Total cost of investment (item 10 plus item 11) 27	

For new ownership interests in a U.S. business enterprise that was <u>incorporated</u> prior to its acquisition, indicate how the new ownership interests were acquired (complete as appropriate):	Voting interest			Other equity interest (4)	Total cost of investment (Col. 3 + Col. 4) (5)
	Number of shares acquired (1)	Average price per share (2)	Total cost (3)		
	Number	Dollars and cents	Bil. Mil. Thous. Dols.	Bil. Mil. Thous. Dols.	Bil. Mil. Thous. Dols.
13. On open market without a tender offer 28		$.	$	$	$
14. By a tender offer 29		.			$
15. Directly from the new U.S. affiliate 30		.			$
16. For foreign parent only: From another of your U.S. affiliates 31					$
17. For existing U.S. affiliate only: From another U.S. affiliate of your foreign parent 32					$
18. Directly from other U.S. persons 33					$
19. Directly from other foreign persons 34					$
20. Other – *Specify* 35					$
21. Total – Sum of items 13 through 20 36			$	$	$

		Bil. Mil. Thous. Dols.
22.	For all new ownership interests other than those reported in items 13 through 21, enter total cost of new investment 37	$

		MONTH DAY YEAR
23.	Date on which the foreign person established or acquired directly, or indirectly through an existing U.S. affiliate, a 10 percent or more voting interest in the new U.S. affiliate. 38	

Sources of financing of the total cost of investment as shown in either item 21, col. 5, or item 22. (Funds that the investor borrowed specifically to finance the investment are to be included in the appropriate category of "borrowed" funds. Funds from other sources should be included in the appropriate category. Commingled funds that cannot be assigned to one category, or for which a reasonable allocation cannot be made, should be shown in "other.") Where the BE-13B is completed for an existing U.S. affiliate that is not directly foreign owned, the source of financing should be presented from the viewpoint of the consolidated U.S. affiliate as it normally reports on related direct investment forms.

		Amount
		Bil. Mil. Thous. Dols.
	For foreign parent only:	
24.	Funds from your other U.S. affiliates 39	$
	For existing U.S. affiliate only:	
25.	Funds from your foreign parent or other members of the affiliated foreign group 40	
26.	Funds from other U.S. affiliates of your foreign parent 41	
	For foreign parent or existing U.S. affiliate:	
27.	Your internally generated funds — For foreign parent, also include funds secured from other members of the affiliated foreign group 42	
	Incurrence of debt to sellers of ownership interests:	
28.	U.S. sellers 43	
29.	Foreign sellers 44	
30.	Your borrowings from other unaffiliated U.S. sources 45	
31.	Your borrowings from other unaffiliated foreign sources 46	
	Exchange of your shares for shares of the acquired U.S. business enterprise that were given in exchange to:	
32.	U.S. persons (give number _____) $ value ⟶ 47	
33.	Foreign persons (give number _____) $ value ⟶ 48	
34.	Other funds from U.S. sources – *Specify* 49	
35.	Other funds from foreign sources – *Specify* 50	
36.	Total – Sum of items 24 through 35 51	$
37.	If an entry was made in item 25, give amount of those funds that were borrowed by your foreign parent or other members of the affiliated foreign group from unaffiliated U.S. sources 52	$
38.	If an entry was made in item 26, give amount of those funds that were borrowed by the other U.S. affiliates of your foreign parent from unaffiliated U.S. sources 53	$

Form BE-13B, Page 2

Part III. INFORMATION RELATED TO JOINT VENTURE

DEFINITIONS

Part I - IDENTIFICATION OF PERSON FILING REPORT

Part II - INFORMATION RELATED TO PURCHASE OR SALE TRANSACTION

U.S. DEPARTMENT OF COMMERCE
BUREAU OF ECONOMIC ANALYSIS

REPORT BY A U.S. PERSON WHO ASSISTS
OR INTERVENES IN THE ACQUISITION OF
A U.S. BUSINESS ENTERPRISE BY,
OR WHO ENTERS INTO A JOINT VENTURE WITH,
A FOREIGN PERSON

CONTINUED ON REVERSE SIDE

Form Approved   OMB No 41-R299

FORM BE-15 (Report for U.S. Affiliate)
(REV. 5-80)

U.S. DEPARTMENT OF COMMERCE
BUREAU OF ECONOMIC ANALYSIS

**INTERIM SURVEY OF
FOREIGN DIRECT INVESTMENT IN THE U.S.**

1979

*(This form has been approved
for use as an annual report.)*

RETURN
REPORTS
TO

U.S. Department of Commerce
Bureau of Economic Analysis BE-50 (IN)
Washington, D.C. 20230

NOTE: *A single original copy of each form or supplement shall be filed with the Bureau of Economic Analysis; for Form BE-15, this should be the copy with the address label if such a labeled copy has been provided.*

Response to this inquiry is required by law. By the same law your report to this Bureau is CONFIDENTIAL. It may be used only for analytical or statistical purposes and CANNOT be used for purposes of taxation, investigation, or regulation. The law also provides that copies retained in your files are immune from legal process.

Important Read **Instructions** before completing form. The instructions given below are only a brief summary of certain ones relating to this form.

*Insurance companies – See the **Instructions**, page 10 before completing form.*

NOTE: *Data to be provided in this report should represent calendar year 1979.*

■ 1. DEFINITION OF FOREIGN DIRECT INVESTMENT IN THE U.S. – The ownership or control, directly or indirectly, by one foreign person of 10 per centum or more of the voting securities of an incorporated U.S. business enterprise or an equivalent interest in an unincorporated U.S. business enterprise, including a branch.

■ 2. DEFINITION OF AFFILIATE – A business enterprise located in one country which is directly or indirectly owned or controlled by a person of another country to the extent of 10 per centum or more of its voting stock for an incorporated business or an equivalent interest for an unincorporated business, including a branch.

■ 3. DEFINITION OF U.S. AFFILIATE – An affiliate located in the United States in which a foreign person has a direct investment.

■ 4. WHO MUST REPORT – Reports on Form BE-15 are required for each U.S. affiliate (except a bank), i.e., for each U.S. business enterprise in which a foreign person owned or controlled, directly or indirectly, 10 percent or more of the voting securities if an incorporated U.S. business enterprise, or an equivalent interest if an unincorporated U.S. business enterprise, at anytime during the year ending December 31, 1979.

■ 5. CONSOLIDATED REPORTING – A U.S. affiliate shall file on a fully consolidated basis, including in the consolidation all other U.S. affiliates in which it directly or indirectly owns more than 50 percent of the outstanding voting interest. Hereinafter, the fully consolidated entity is considered to be one U.S. affiliate. See Instructions, page 10.

■ 6. EXEMPTION – A U.S. affiliate as consolidated, is not required to file a report if:

(a) Each of the following three items for the U.S. affiliate not the foreign parent's share) was between –$5 million and +$5 million during the reporting period
    (1) Total assets,
    (2) Net sales or gross operating revenues, excluding sales taxes, and
    (3) Net income after provision for U.S. income taxes

and

(b) The U.S. affiliate did not own 200 acres or more of U.S. land during the reporting period (if the U.S. affiliate owned 200 acres or more of U.S. land, it must report regardless of the value of the three items listed above).

or

(c) The U.S. affiliate is a bank, i.e., a business enterprise in which over 50 percent of its total revenues are generated by activities classified in industry code 600

■ 7. ASSISTANCE – Telephone (202) 523-0547

■ 8. DUE DATE – A completed report on Form BE-15 shall be due no later than August 31, 1980.

■ 9. GENERAL NOTES

A. Figures such as the number of acres, the number of employees and hours worked should be reported to the nearest whole unit.

B. Currency amounts should be reported in U.S. dollars rounded to thousands (omitting 000). Do not enter amounts in the shaded portions of each line.

EXAMPLE: If amount is $1,334,615.00, report as:

BIL.	MIL.	THOU.	DOLS.
	1,	335	

C. If an item is between + or – $500.00 enter "0."

D. Use parentheses to indicate negative numbers.

E. All questions should be answered in the context of the reporting period given in items 4 and 5.

PERSON TO CONSULT
CONCERNING QUESTIONS
ABOUT THIS REPORT

Print name and address

Part I – IDENTIFICATION OF U.S. AFFILIATE

1. Name and address of U.S. affiliate *(Enter name and mailing address in blocks below. Skip a single block between words.)*

   001 ◄— BEA USE ONLY   BEA USE ONLY ►
   Name of U.S. Affiliate
   002
   Street or P.O. Box
   003
   City and State   ZIP Code
   004

2. Enter primary employer identification number used by U.S. affiliate to file income and payroll taxes.
   005 ◄— E.I. Number

3. Is the reported U.S. affiliate named in item 1 above separately incorporated in the United States, including its territories and possessions? *(Mark one)*
   006   1 ☐ Yes   2 ☐ No

REPORTING PERIOD

Report should be for the calendar year 1979; see **Instructions, Reporting Period.**   Month   Day   Year

4. The term "Opening balance" in this report always refers to data as of _____ 19__

5. The term "Closing balance" in this report always refers to data as of _____ 19__

			BEA USE ONLY	Reporting Period
				Closing	Opening

Direct Ownership of U.S. affiliate Named in Item 1 – Percent of voting stock, for an incorporated U.S. affiliate or an equivalent interest for an unincorporated U.S. affiliate, owned:

Directly by Foreign parent(s) of this U.S. affiliate – (if more than two, continue on a separate sheet) | Country of Location of Foreign Parent
Name of each foreign parent

6. _____ 1009

7. _____ 1010

Directly by another U.S. affiliate(s) of foreign parent(s) – (if more than two, continue on a separate sheet) | Country of Foreign Parent of each other U.S. Affiliate
Name of each other U.S. affiliate holding a direct interest in the U.S. affiliate identified in item 1 above.

8. _____ 1019

9. _____ 1020

10. Directly by other persons (do not list names); give percentage of direct interests held by all other persons   1029

TOTAL —► | 100.0 | 100.0 |

11. Complete this item only if a U.S. affiliate listed in 8 or 9 is not in turn directly 'foreign-owned to the extent of 10 percent or more. If it is not, give the name and address of the U.S. affiliate in the ownership chain which is directly foreign-owned (if more than two, continue on a separate sheet):

BEA USE ONLY | Country of Foreign Parent of each affiliate named here

Name of U.S. affiliate which is directly foreign-owned

Street or P.O. Box

City, State and ZIP Code
1030

Name of U.S. affiliate (additional) directly foreign-owned

Street or P.O. Box

City, State and ZIP Code
1030

12. Number of U.S. affiliates fully consolidated *(Enter number)*
If this report is for a single U.S. affiliate enter "1" in the box. If more than one U.S. affiliate is fully consolidated in this report, enter the number of U.S. affiliates fully consolidated. (Hereinafter they are considered to be one U.S. affiliate.) Exclude all foreign business enterprises owned by this U.S. affiliate from full consolidation. See consolidation instructions, page 10 of instructions.
1031
If number is greater than one, Supplement A must be completed.

13. U.S. Affiliates NOT fully consolidated – Number of U.S. affiliates in which this U.S. affiliate held a direct equity interest but which ARE NOT fully consolidated in this report.
1032
If an entry here, Supplement B must be completed.

TELEPHONE NUMBER
Area Code | Number | Extension

CERTIFICATION   The undersigned official certifies that the information contained in this report is correct and complete to the best of his/her knowledge.

Authorized Official's Signature | Type Name and Title | Date

USCOMM-DC 5980U-P79

Part I – IDENTIFICATION OF U.S. AFFILIATE (Continued)

14. Does any U.S. affiliate fully consolidated in this report own, directly or indirectly, over 50 percent of the outstanding voting stock of a domestic corporation that is not a U.S. affiliate? (See definition of U.S. affiliate) (Mark one)
If "Yes," do not fully consolidate them in this report — Include them on the equity basis only.   1034   1 ☐ Yes   2 ☐ No

15. Accounting changes and prior period adjustments — Has this reporting U.S. affiliate, as consolidated, restated the financial statements of the prior period (1978), resulting in opening balances in this report different from the closing balances as reported on the 1978 Form BE-15? (Mark one)
If "Yes," briefly describe the nature of and the reason for the restatement.   1035   1 ☐ Yes   2 ☐ No

16. Major activity of the U.S. affiliate (Mark one)
    - a. Extracting oil or minerals (including exploration and development) 1036   1 ☐
    - b. Manufacturing (fabricating, assembling, processing) . . . . 2 ☐
    - c. Selling or distributing goods . . . . 3 ☐
    - d. Providing a service . . . . 4 ☐
    - e. Real estate (investing in or engaging in as an operator, manager, developer, lessor, agent, or broker) . . . . 5 ☐
    - f. Other – (Specify) _____ 6 ☐

17. Major product or service involved in this activity
    See Instructions, II.G., regarding the filing of Form BE-607, Industry Classification Questionnaire, by a new affiliate or by an existing affiliate whose industry classification has changed.

    BEA USE ONLY
    1037
    1038
    1039
    1040

Part II – FINANCIAL AND OPERATING DATA OF U.S. AFFILIATE (Report all amounts in thousands of U.S. dollars)

SECTION A — BALANCE SHEET OF U.S. AFFILIATE

ASSETS		Balance Closing (1)				Balance Opening (2)			
		Bil.	Mil.	Thous.	Dols.	Bil.	Mil.	Thous.	Dols.
Current Assets:									
18. Trade accounts and notes receivable – Net of allowance for doubtful accounts	2041	$				$			
19. Other current receivables	2042								
20. Inventories – land development companies should exclude land held for resale (include in item 21); finance and insurance companies should exclude their inventories of marketable securities (include in item 23)	2043								
21. Other current assets, including cash	2044								
INVESTMENTS									
22. Investment in foreign affiliates and unconsolidated U.S. affiliates – Include, under the equity method of accounting, material investments in all foreign affiliates, both incorporated and unincorporated, and all unconsolidated U.S. affiliates owned 20 percent or more	2045								
23. Other investments	2046								
Fixed Assets:									
24. Property, plant and equipment at historical (gross) cost	2047								
25. Less: Accumulated depreciation, amortization and depletion	2048			)				)	
26. Property, plant and equipment, net – Item 24 less item 25	2049								
27. Other non-current assets	2050								
28. TOTAL ASSETS – Sum of items 18 thru 23 and 26 and 27 →	2051	$				$			
LIABILITIES AND OWNER'S EQUITY									
Current liabilities:									
29. Trade accounts and notes payable	2052	$				$			
30. Other current liabilities – Include current portion of long-term debt	2053								
Long-term debt and other non-current liabilities:									
31. Long-term debt – Exclude current portion, but include capitalized lease obligations	2054								
32. Other non-current liabilities – Items other than those identified as long-term debt, such as deferred taxes. Include minority interests in consolidated U.S. subsidiaries.	2055								
33. TOTAL LIABILITIES – Sum of items 29 thru 32 →	2056	$				$			
Owner's equity: **Incorporated in U.S. Only**									
34. Capital stock and additional paid-in-capital	2057	$				$			
35. Retained earnings (deficit)	2058								
36. Less: Treasury stock	2059			)				)	
Incorporated and unincorporated									
37. TOTAL OWNERS' EQUITY – Sum of items 34 + 35 – 36 for U.S. incorporated business enterprise or total equity for unincorporated business enterprise such as a branch, partnership, etc.	2060	$				$			
38. TOTAL LIABILITIES AND OWNER'S EQUITY – Item 33 plus item 37 →	2061	$				$			

SECTION B — INCOME STATEMENT OF U.S. AFFILIATE

Net income must be calculated in accordance with the "all inclusive" concept of the income statement

		Amount (1)			
		Bil.	Mil.	Thous.	Dols.
39. Net sales or gross operating revenues, excluding sales taxes – Gross sales and operating revenues less returns, allowances, and discounts, and excluding sales and excise taxes. All sales, and commissions thereon, should be included, whether or not physical possession was taken of the goods	2062	$			
40. Cost of goods sold and other expenses relating to operations	2063				
41. Income from operations – Items 39 less item 40	2064	$			
42. Equity in net income of unconsolidated business enterprises (domestic and foreign) in which this U.S. affiliate has equity investment – Equity in net income (distributed and undistributed) after income taxes	2065	$			
43. Other income – (Specify)	2066				
Other expenses:					
44. U.S. income taxes – Federal, state and local	2067				
45. Minority interests in net income (loss) of consolidated U.S. affiliates	2068				
46. Other – (Specify)	2069				
47. Net income – Equals items 41 + 42 + 43 – 44 – 45 – 46	2070	$			

FORM BE-13 (REV. 8-80)   Page 2

Part II – FINANCIAL AND OPERATING DATA OF U.S. AFFILIATE (Continued) *(Report all amounts in thousands of U.S. dollars)*

SECTION C	STATEMENT OF RETAINED EARNINGS		Amount (1)		
			Bil.	Mil. Thous.	Dols.

To be completed only be a U.S. affiliate that is incorporated in the U.S.

48.	Balance at beginning of period as previously reported	2071	$		
49.	Adjustments to opening balance – *Specify*	2072			
50.	Balance at beginning of period as restated – Same as item 35, column 2	2073			
51.	Net income – Same as item 47	2074			
52.	Less: Cash dividends declared	2075			
53.	Other changes, increase or (decrease), including stock dividends – *Specify*	2076			
54.	Retained earnings at end of period – Same as item 35, column 1. Equals items 50 + 51 – 52 + 53 ——→	2077	$		

SECTION D	MISCELLANEOUS ITEMS				

Expenditures for plant and equipment during the year – Include all acquisitions, improvements, and additions to plant and equipment which are part of fixed assets (item 24 above) on the balance sheet. Include capitalized exploration and development costs charged to plant and equipment. Do not include expenditures for land. Do not include as expenditures plant and equipment acquired as the result of the acquisition by, or the merger into, this U.S. affiliate of another U.S. business enterprise.

Amount (1) Bil. Mil. Thous. Dols.

55.	Amount for 1979 – Include capitalized portion of item 56 below, except charges for land	207d	$		
56.	Expenditures for new plant and equipment – Include that portion of item 55 which represents expenditures for new plant and equipment during 1979	2079	$		
57.	Exploration and development charges, total – Include capitalized E & D costs charged to fixed assets, including land considerations. Any shown in item 55 above should also be picked-up here.	2080	$		

Depreciation and like charges to income during the year for items included in fixed assets account, item 24, which is:

58.	Depletion, etc. – charge to the income statement for 1979 relating to gross costs of property	2081	$		
59.	Depreciation, etc. – charge to the income statement for 1979 relating to gross costs of plant and equipment	2082	$		
60.	Research and development (R & D) expenditures, calculated in accordance with FASB 2 – All R & D costs incurred, including depreciation, amortization, wages and salaries, taxes, costs of materials and supplies, allocated overhead, indirect R & D costs, and the cost of R & D conducted by others on behalf of the U.S. affiliate. Exclude costs incurred in R & D activities conducted for others under a contractual arrangement.	2083	$		
61.	Taxes (other than income and payroll taxes) and non-tax payments (other than production royalty payments) – Include amounts paid or accrued for the year, net of refunds or credits, to Federal, State, and local governments, their sub-divisions and agencies for sales, consumption, and excise taxes, property and other taxes on the value of assets and capital; any remaining taxes (other than income and payroll taxes), and all payments of non-tax liabilities (other than production royalty payments), such as import and export duties, license fees, fines, penalties, and similar items	2084	$		
62.	LAND: Total value, at historical (gross) costs, of all land owned at **end of 1979** – Sum of items 63 through 65	2085	$		
63.	Carried in investments, item 23, column 1	2086			
64.	Carried in fixed assets, item 24, column 1	2087			
65.	Carried elsewhere in the balance sheet, including land held for resale carried in item 21, or land carried in other noncurrent assets, item 27, among other places	2088			

66. Number of acres of land used at the end of 1979 for agricultural purposes, including timber growing, i.e., for one of the purposes included in codes 010, agricultural production-crops; 020, agricultural production – livestock, except beef cattle feedlots; 021, agricultural production – beef cattle feedlots; and 080, forestry. *(See Industry Classifications and Export and Import Trade Classifications Booklet.)*	Acres owned (1)	Acres leased from others (2)
2089		

SECTION E	EMPLOYMENT AND EMPLOYEE COMPENSATION *(See Instructions, page 11, for details of data requirements)*				

NOTE: CERTAIN ITEMS TO BE COMPLETED ONLY BY U.S. AFFILIATES CLASSIFIED IN THE MANUFACTURING INDUSTRY – The data cells in columns 2 and 3 of items 67, 68, and 70 are to be completed only by U.S. affiliates classified in manufacturing (i.e., in BEA industry codes 210 through 390). Column 1 must be completed by all U.S. affiliates. See page 11, Instructions, V.A., for determination of industry code. Production and related workers for manufacturing are those employees up to and including working foremen, but excluding other supervisory employees, who are involved in the physical production of goods, handling and storage of goods, related services (e.g., maintenance and repair), and auxiliary production for plant's own use (e.g., power plant). For affiliates classified in manufacturing which also have activities in industries outside manufacturing, consider as production workers only those employees, as defined, who are associated with manufacturing activities; all employees associated with non-manufacturing activities should be considered as non-production workers.

	To be completed by all U.S. affiliates	To be completed only by U.S. affiliates classified in manufacturing industry	
	Total (1)	Production and related workers *(Read note at left before completing)* (2)	Nonproduction workers *(Read note at left before completing)* (3)
	NUMBER	NUMBER	NUMBER
67. Number of employees – Average for the reporting period, including part-time employees 2090	1	2	3
68. Hours worked by production and related workers – See *Instructions*, page 11. 2091		2	

	Bil. Mil. Thous. Dols.	Bil. Mil. Thous. Dols.	Bil. Mil. Thous. Dols.
69. Employee compensation – For column (1), equals sum of items 70 and 71 2092	$		
70. Wages and salaries 2093	$	2 $	3 $
71. Employee benefit plans 2094	$		

SECTION F	COMPOSITION OF EXTERNAL FINANCING				

CLOSING BALANCES	Total – Sum of Columns (2) through (4) (1)	Position with		
		Foreign parent(s) and foreign affiliates of foreign parent(s) (2)	Other foreign persons (3)	All U.S. persons (4)
	Bil. Mil. Thous. Dols.	Bil. Mil. Thous. Dols.	Bil. Mil. Thous. Dols.	Bil. Mil. Thous. Dols.

Current Liabilities: Sum of items 72 and 73, col. 1, must equal sum of items 29 and 30, col. 1.

| 72. To banks 2095 | $ | $ | $ | 4 $ |
| 73. To other than banks 2096 | $ | $ | $ | 4 $ |

Long-term debt Sum of items 74 and 75, col. 1, must equal item 31, col. 1.

74. To banks 2097	1 $	2 $	3 $	4 $
75. To other than banks 2098	1 $	2 $	3 $	4 $
76. Current Receivables: Col. 1 must equal sum of items 18 and 19, col. 1 2099	1 $	2 $	3 $	4 $

BEA USE ONLY ▶ 2100

SECTION G	EXPORTS AND IMPORTS OF U.S. AFFILIATES (GOODS ONLY, DO NOT INCLUDE SERVICES)		

Note: The value of exports or imports requested in this section is not synonymous with sales to, or purchases from, a foreign person. Data in this section are to cover only goods which physically left or entered the U.S. customs area in 1979. Include capital goods.

See page 12, Instructions, V.B., for details of data requirements.	TOTAL (1)	Shipped to (by) foreign parent(s) and foreign affiliate(s) of foreign parent(s) (2)	Shipped to (by) all other foreigners (3)
	Bil. Mil. Thous. Dols.	Bil. Mil. Thous. Dols.	Bil. Mil. Thous. Dols.
77. Total exports, including capital goods – Shipped by U.S. affiliate to foreigners (valued f.a.s. U.S. port) 2101	1 $	2 $	3 $
78. Total imports, including capital goods – Shipped to U.S. affiliate by foreigners (valued f.a.s. foreign port) 2102	1 $	2 $	3 $

USCOMM-DC 58727-P80

Part III – SCHEDULE OF EMPLOYEES, LAND AND MINERAL RIGHTS, AND PROPERTY, PLANT AND EQUIPMENT, BY STATE OF LOCATION

State	BEA USE ONLY (1)	State Code (2)	Number of employees (Total must equal item 67 column 1) (3) NUMBER	Number of acres of land and mineral rights (Do not duplicate in column 5 acres reported as land owned in column 4) Owned — Land (4) NUMBER	Mineral rights (5) NUMBER	Land and mineral rights leased from others (6) NUMBER	Historical (gross) value of all land and other property, plant, and equipment: Land — Total must equal the total value given in item 62, column 1 (7) Bil. Mil. Thous. Dols.	Other property, plant and equipment — Total must equal item 24, column less item 64, column (8) Bil. Mil. Thous.
79. Total at end of year, or for number of employees, average for year – For each column, total must equal sum of data for all States and other geographic areas, items 80 through 138 3103							$	$
80. Alabama 3104		01	3	4	5	6	7 $	$
81. Alaska 3105		02	3	4	5	6	7 $	$
82. Arizona 3106		04	3	4	5	6	7 $	$
83. Arkansas 3107		05	3	4	5	6	7 $	$
84. California 3108		06	3	4	5	6	7 $	$
85. Colorado 3109		08	3	4	5	6	7 $	$
86. Connecticut 3110		09	3	4	5	6	7 $	$
87. Delaware 3111		10	3	4	5	6	7 $	$
88. Florida 3112		12	3	4	5	6	7 $	$
89. Georgia 3113		13	3	4	5	6	7 $	$
90. Hawaii 3114		15	3	4	5	6	7 $	$
91. Idaho 3115		16	3	4	5	6	7 $	$
92. Illinois 3116		17	3	4	5	6	7 $	$
93. Indiana 3117		18	3	4	5	6	7 $	$
94. Iowa 3118		19	3	4	5	6	7 $	$
95. Kansas 3119		20	3	4	5	6	7 $	$
96. Kentucky 3120		21	3	4	5	6	7 $	$
97. Louisiana 3121		22	3	4	5	6	7 $	$
98. Maine 3122		23	3	4	5	6	7 $	$
99. Maryland 3123		24	3	4	5	6	7 $	$
100. Massachusetts 3124		25	3	4	5	6	7 $	$
101. Michigan 3125		26	3	4	5	6	7 $	$
102. Minnesota 3126		27	3	4	5	6	7 $	$
103. Mississippi 3127		28	3	4	5	6	7 $	$
104. Missouri 3128		29	3	4	5	6	7 $	$
105. Montana 3129		30	3	4	5	6	7 $	$
106. Nebraska 3130		31	3	4	5	6	7 $	$
107. Nevada 3131		32	3	4	5	6	7 $	$
108. New Hampshire 3132		33	3	4	5	6	7 $	$
109. New Jersey 3133		34	3	4	5	6	7 $	$
110. New Mexico 3134		35	3	4	5	6	7 $	$
111. New York 3135		36	3	4	5	6	7 $	$
112. North Carolina 3136		37	3	4	5	6	7 $	$
113. North Dakota 3137		38	3	4	5	6	7 $	$
114. Ohio 3138		39	3	4	5	6	7 $	$
115. Oklahoma 3139		40	3	4	5	6	7 $	$
116. Oregon 3140		41	3	4	5	6	7 $	$
117. Pennsylvania 3141		42	3	4	5	6	7 $	$
118. Rhode Island 3142		44	3	4	5	6	7 $	$
119. South Carolina 3143		45	3	4	5	6	7 $	$
120. South Dakota 3144		46	3	4	5	6	7 $	$
121. Tennessee 3145		47	3	4	5	6	7 $	$
122. Texas 3146		48	3	4	5	6	7 $	$
123. Utah 3147		49	3	4	5	6	7 $	$
124. Vermont 3148		50	3	4	5	6	7 $	$
125. Virginia 3149		51	3	4	5	6	7 $	$
126. Washington 3150		53	3	4	5	6	7 $	$
127. West Virginia 3151		54	3	4	5	6	7 $	$
128. Wisconsin 3152		55	3	4	5	6	7 $	$
129. Wyoming 3153		56	3	4	5	6	7 $	$
130. District of Columbia 3154		11	3	4	5	6	7 $	$
131. Panama Canal Zone 3155		07	3	4	5	6	7 $	$
132. Puerto Rico 3156		43	3	4	5	6	7 $	$
133. Virgin Islands 3157		52	3	4	5	6	7 $	$
134. Guam 3158		14	3	4	5	6	7 $	$
135. American Samoa 3159		03	3	4	5	6	7 $	$
136. Other U.S. Territories and Possessions 3160		60	3	4	5	6	7 $	$
137. U.S. Offshore Oil and Gas Sites 3161		65	3	4	5	6	7 $	$
138. Foreign *(See below) 3162		70	3	4	5	6	7 $	$

* Include only that of U.S. business enterprises fully consolidated into the U.S. affiliate. No foreign affiliates, incorporated or unincorporated, can be considered part of the reporting U.S. affiliate.

FORM BE-13 (REV. 5-80)

Page 4

BE-13 SUPPLEMENT A — LIST OF ALL U.S. CORPORATIONS FULLY CONSOLIDATED INTO THE REPORTING U.S. AFFILIATE — Continued

Page No. _____

BEA USE ONLY (1)	Name of each U.S. affiliate consolidated (as represented in Item 12, Part I) (2)	Employer Identification Number used by U.S. affiliate listed in Column 2 to file income and payroll taxes (3)	Name of U.S. affiliate which holds the direct equity interest in the U.S. affiliate listed in Column 2 (4)	Percentage of direct ownership which the U.S. affiliate listed in Column 4 has in the U.S. affiliate listed in Column 2. (Enter percentage to nearest tenth) (5)
4187				%
4188				%
4189				%
4190				%
4191				%
4192				%
4193				%
4194				%
4195				%
4196				%
4197				%
4198				%
4199				%
4200				%
4201				%
4202				%
4203				%
4204				%
4205				%
4206				%
4207				%
4208				%
4209				%
4210				%

Form BE–15 Supplement B
(REV. 8-80)

U.S. DEPARTMENT OF COMMERCE
BUREAU OF ECONOMIC ANALYSIS

Form Approved OMB No. 41-R7991

Page No. _____

BEA USE ONLY ▶

Name of U.S. affiliate as shown in Item 1, Part I of BE-15

Employer Identification Number as shown in Item 2, Part I of BE-15 → 5211 –

LIST OF ALL U.S. AFFILIATES IN WHICH THE REPORTING AFFILIATE (AS CONSOLIDATED) HAS A DIRECT EQUITY INTEREST BUT WHICH ARE NOT FULLY CONSOLIDATED

NOTE: If you filed a Supplement B with your 1977 or 1978 report, in lieu of completing a new Supplement B, you may substitute a copy of the 1977 or 1978 Supplement B which has been updated to show any addition, deletion, or other changes.

Supplement B — List of All U.S. Affiliates in Which the Reporting Affiliate (as Consolidated) Has a Direct Equity Interest but Which Are Not Fully Consolidated must be completed by a reporting affiliate which files a BE-15 and has a direct ownership interest in a U.S. affiliate(s) which is (are) not fully consolidated. The number of U.S. affiliates listed below must agree with Item 13, Part I, of BE-15. Continue listing onto as many additional copied pages as necessary.

BEA USE ONLY (1)	Name of each U.S. affiliate in which a direct interest is held but which is not listed in Supplement A (2)	Address of each U.S. affiliate listed in Column 2. Give number, street, city, State, and ZIP Code (3)	Employer Identification Number used by U.S. affiliate listed in Column 2 to file income and payroll taxes (4)	Percentage of direct ownership in the U.S. affiliate listed in Column 2 held by the reporting affiliate named in Item 1, Part I of BE-15. (Enter percentage to nearest tenth) (5)
5212				%
5213				%
5214				%
5215				%
5216				%
5217				%
5218				%
5219				%
5220				%
5221				%
5222				%

USCOMM-DC 59727-P80

Page No. _____

BE-15 Supplement B – LIST OF ALL U.S. AFFILIATES IN WHICH THE REPORTING AFFILIATE (AS CONSOLIDATED) HAS DIRECT EQUITY INTEREST BUT WHICH ARE NOT FULLY CONSOLIDATED (Continued)

BEA USE ONLY (1)	Name of each U.S. affiliate in which a direct interest is held but which is not listed in Supplement A (2)	Address of each U.S. affiliate listed in Column 2. Give number, street, city, State, and ZIP Code. (3)	Employer Identification Number used by U.S. affiliate listed in Column 2 to file income and payroll taxes (4)	Percentage of direct ownership in the U.S. affiliate listed in Column 2 held by the reporting affiliate named in Item 1, Part I of BE-15. (Enter percentage to nearest tenth.) (5)
5223				%
5224				%
5225				%
5226				%
5227				%
5228				%
5229				%
5230				%
5231				%
5232				%
5233				%

FORM BE-15 (REV. 5-80)

INTERIM SURVEY
OF
FOREIGN DIRECT INVESTMENT IN THE U.S.
1979

INSTRUCTIONS

Purpose – Reports on this form are required in order to update the data reported in the Benchmark Survey of Foreign Direct Investment in the United States – 1974 on the operations of foreign-owned U.S. business enterprises, except banks. However, filing this report is not contingent upon having filed a report in the 1974 Benchmark Survey.

Authority – Reports on Form BE-15 are mandatory under Section 5(b) (2) of the International Investment Survey Act of 1976 (P.L. 94–472, 90 Stat. 2059, 22 U.S.C. 3101–3108 –– hereinafter "the Act"). In Section 3 of Executive Order 11961, the President designated the Department of Commerce as the federal agency responsible for collecting the required data on direct investment, and the Secretary of Commerce has assigned this responsibility to the Bureau of Economic Analysis. The implementing regulations are contained in Title 15, CFR, Part 806.

This report has been approved by the Office of Management and Budget under the Federal Reports Act (Public Law No. 831, 77th Congress).

Penalties – Whoever fails to report may be subject to a civil penalty not exceeding $10,000 and to injunctive relief commanding such person to comply, or both. Whoever willfully fails to report shall be fined not more than $10,000 and, if an individual, may be imprisoned for not more than one year, or both. Any officer, director, employee, or agent of any corporation who knowingly participates in such violation, upon conviction, may be punished by a like fine, imprisonment, or both. (See Section 6 of the Act, 22 U.S.C. 3105.)

Confidentiality – The information filed in this report may be used only for analytical and statistical purposes and access to the information shall be available only to officials and employees (including consultants and contractors and their employees) of agencies designated by the President to perform functions under the Act. The President may authorize the exchange of the information between agencies or officials designated to perform functions under the Act, but only for analytical and statistical purposes. No official or employee (including consultants and contractors and their employees) shall publish or make available any information collected under the Act in such a manner that the person to whom the information relates can be specifically identified. Reports and copies of reports prepared pursuant to the Act are confidential and their submission or disclosure shall not be compelled by any person without the prior written permission of the person filing the report and the customer of such person where the information supplied is identifiable as being derived from the records of such customer (22 U.S.C. 3104).

I. DEFINITIONS

A. United States, when used in a geographic sense, means the several States, the District of Columbia, the Commonwealth of Puerto Rico, the Canal Zone, and all territories and possessions of the United States.

B. Foreign, when used in a geographic sense, means that which is situated outside the United States or which belongs to or is characteristic of a country other than the United States.

C. Person means any individual, branch, partnership, association, estate, trust, corporation, or other organization (whether or not organized under the laws of any State), and any government (including a foreign government, the United States Government, a State or local government, and any agency, corporation, financial institution, or other entity or instrumentality thereof, including a government-sponsored agency).

D. Foreign person means any person resident outside the United States or subject to the jurisdiction of a country other than the United States.

E. Direct investment means the ownership or control, directly or indirectly, by one person of 10 per centum or more of the voting securities of an incorporated business enterprise or an equivalent interest in an unincorporated business enterprise.

F. Foreign direct investment in the United States means the ownership or control, directly or indirectly, by one foreign person of 10 per centum or more of the voting securities of an incorporated U.S. business enterprise or an equivalent interest in an unincorporated U.S. business enterprise, including a branch.

G. Branch means the operations or activities conducted by a person in a different location in its own name rather than through an incorporated entity.

H. Affiliate means a business enterprise located in one country which is directly or indirectly owned or controlled by a person of another country to the extent of 10 per centum or more of its voting stock for an incorporated business or an equivalent interest for an unincorporated business, including a branch.

I. U.S. affiliate means an affiliate located in the United States in which a foreign person has a direct investment.

J. Foreign parent means the foreign person, or the first person outside the United States in a foreign chain of ownership, which has direct investment in a U.S. business enterprise, including a branch.

K. Affiliated foreign group means (i) the foreign parent, (ii) any foreign person, proceeding up the foreign parent ownership chain, which owns more than 50 per centum of the person below it up to and including that person which is not owned more than 50 per centum by another foreign person, and (iii) any foreign person, proceeding down the ownership chain(s) of each of these members, which is owned more than 50 per centum by the person above it.

L. Foreign affiliate of foreign parent means, with reference to a given U.S. affiliate, any member of the affiliated foreign group owning the affiliate that is not a foreign parent of the affiliate.

M. U.S. corporation means a business enterprise incorporated in the United States.

N. Business enterprise means any organization, association, branch, or venture which exists for profitmaking purposes or to otherwise secure economic advantage, and any ownership of any real estate.

O. Lease is a contract by which one person gives another person the use and possession of tangible property (other than real estate) for a specified time in return for agreed-upon payments.

P. Banking includes business enterprises engaged in deposit banking, Edge Act corporations engaged in international or foreign banking, U.S. branches and agencies of foreign banks whether or not they accept domestic deposits, and bank holding companies, i.e., holding companies for which over 50 percent of their total income is from banks which they hold.

INSTRUCTIONS FOR BE-15 (Continued)

II. GENERAL INSTRUCTIONS

A. Who must report – Reports on Form BE-15 are required for each U.S. business enterprise (except a bank), in which a foreign person owned or controlled, directly or indirectly, 10 percent or more of the voting securities if an incorporated U.S. business enterprise, or an equivalent interest if an unincorporated U.S. business enterprise, at anytime during the year ending December 31, 1979. Reports are required even though the U.S. business enterprise may have been established, acquired, liquidated, sold, or inactivated during the reporting period.

B. Consolidated reporting by U.S. affiliates – A U.S. affiliate shall file on a fully consolidated basis, including in the consolidation all other U.S. affiliates in which it directly or indirectly owns more than 50 per cent of the outstanding voting interest. (Foreign subsidiaries of the U.S. affiliate are not to be included in the consolidation, except as provided below under the equity method of accounting.) However, separate reports may be filed where a given U.S. affiliate is not normally fully consolidated due to unrelated operations or lack of control, provided written permission has been requested from and granted by BEA. Hereinafter the fully consolidated entity is considered to be one U.S. affiliate.

A U.S. affiliate which is not fully consolidated into its U.S. parent's report and so noted on Supplement B must file its own Form BE-15.

C. Equity method of accounting – Investments by the U.S. affiliate in business enterprises not fully consolidated and which are 20 percent or more owned shall be accounted for following the equity method of accounting. However, for investments in foreign affiliates, intercompany items are not to be eliminated.

D. Reporting by unincorporated U.S. affiliates – A Form BE-15 shall be filed for each unincorporated U.S. affiliate, except a bank but including a branch, which is directly owned 10 percent or more by a foreign person. Two or more such directly owned U.S. affiliates may not be combined on a single BE-15. An indirectly owned unincorporated U.S. affiliate should be consolidated on the report with the U.S. affiliate which holds the equity interest in it, provided it meets the usual consolidation criterion of being more than 50 percent owned. Otherwise a separate report is required for each indirectly owned unincorporated U.S. affiliate.

E. Exemption – A U.S. affiliate as consolidated, is not required to file a report if:

    (a) Each of the following three items for the U.S. affiliate (not the foreign parent's share) was between −$5 million and +$5 million during the reporting period:

        (1) Total assets,

        (2) Net sales or gross operating revenues, excluding sales taxes, and

        (3) Net income after provision for U.S. income taxes;

    and

    (b) The U.S. affiliate did not own 200 acres or more of U.S. land during the reporting period (if the U.S. affiliate owned 200 acres or more of U.S. land, it must report regardless of the value of the three items listed above).

    or

    (c) The U.S. affiliate is a bank, i.e., a business enterprise in which over 50 percent of its total revenues are generated by activities classified in industry code 600.

F. Reporting period – Reports should be submitted on a calendar year basis for the year ending December 31, 1979. If the estimation of annual data based upon interim reports is necessary in order to present the data on or closely relating to a calendar year basis, such estimates are acceptable. If it would cause an undue burden on a company to provide data on a calendar year basis, a report may be submitted concerning a year ending between November 16, 1979 and February 15, 1980, inclusive, the actual date coinciding with the actual ending date of a fiscal year or a fiscal quarter within that period.

G. Industry Classification Questionnaire – A Form BE-607, Industry Classification Questionnaire, which is included in this mailing must be filed by an affiliate for which a prelabeled Form BE-15 has not been provided. If a prelabeled Form BE-15 has been provided for the affiliate, then no Form BE-607 must be filed unless the affiliate's industry classification has changed, i.e., unless the industry classification code of the affiliate as indicated following the "IND" on the bottom of the label does not accurately reflect the current industry classification of the affiliate.

See Form BE-607 for a list of industry classifications; for a detailed explanation of each classification see "Industry Classifications and Export and Import Trade Classifications Booklet," BE-799, which was previously furnished to you or which, for new affiliates, is included as part of this mailing.

H. Special instructions for U.S. affiliates that are insurance companies – When there is a difference, the Financial Schedules in Part II of this form are to be prepared on the same basis as an annual report to the stockholders, rather than on the basis of an annual statement to an insurance department. Valuation should be according to normal commercial accounting procedures, not at the rates promulgated by the National Association of Insurance Commissioners; include assets not acceptable for the annual statement to an insurance department.

Item

18   **Trade accounts and notes receivable** – Include current items such as agents' balances or uncollected premiums, amounts recoverable from reinsurers, and other current notes and accounts receivable (net of allowances for doubtful items) arising from the ordinary course of business.

29   **Trade accounts and notes payable** – Include current items such as loss liabilities, policy claims, commissions due, and other current liabilities arising from the ordinary course of business. Policy reserves are to be included in "Other noncurrent liabilities," item 32, unless they are clearly current liabilities.

39   **Net sales or gross operating revenues, excluding sales taxes** – Include items such as earned premiums, and annuity considerations, gross investment income, and items of a similar nature. Exclude income from unconsolidated affiliates that should be reported in item 42.

40   **Costs and expenses relating to operations** – Include costs relating to net sales or gross operating revenues, item 39, such as policy losses incurred, death benefits, matured endowments, other policy benefits, increases in liabilities for future policy benefits, other underwriting expenses, and investment expenses.

III. ACCOUNTING METHODS AND REPORTING PROCEDURES

A. Accounting methods and records – Generally accepted U.S. accounting principles should be followed. Corporations should generally use the same methods and records that are used to generate reports to stockholders except where the instructions indicate a variance.

B. Annual stockholder's report – Business enterprises issuing annual reports to stockholders are requested to furnish a copy of their annual reports to this Bureau.

C. Estimates – If actual figures are not available, estimates should be supplied and labeled as such. When a data item cannot be fully subdivided as required, a total and an estimated breakdown of the total should be supplied.

D. Space on form insufficient – When space on a form is insufficient to permit a full answer to any item, the required information should be submitted on supplementary sheets, appropriately labeled and referenced to the item number and the form.

INSTRUCTIONS FOR BE-15 (Continued)

IV. FILING REPORT

A. Due date – Form BE-15 is an annual report and shall be due no later than August 31, 1980.

B. Extension – Requests for an extension of the reporting deadline will not normally be granted. However, in a hardship case, a written request for an extension will be considered provided it is received at least 15 days prior to the due date of the report and enumerates substantive reasons necessitating the extension. BEA will provide a written response to such requests.

C. Assistance – If there are any questions concerning the report, telephone (202) 523-0547 for assistance.

D. Number of copies – A single original copy of each form or supplement shall be filed with the Bureau of Economic Analysis. For Form BE-15, this should be the copy with the address label if such a labeled copy has been provided. In addition, each U.S. affiliate must retain a copy of its report to facilitate resolution of any problems which may arise covering the data reported. (Both copies are protected by law, see statement on confidentiality in the Introduction.) File copies should be retained for 3 years after the date on which an annual report is due.

E. Where to send report – Return the report to U.S. Department of Commerce, Bureau of Economic Analysis, BE-50(IN), Washington, D.C. 20230.

V. INSTRUCTIONS FOR SPECIFIC PARTS OF THE REPORT FORM

A. Employment and Employee Compensation (Part II, Section E)

Employment and employee compensation data should be based on payroll records for the reporting period. They should relate, therefore, to activities during the reporting period regardless of whether the costs of such activities were charged as an expense on the income statement, charged to inventories, or capitalized. Do not include data related to activities taking place in periods prior to the reporting period, such as those whose costs were charged to inventories or capitalized in prior years.

NOTE: CERTAIN ITEMS TO BE COMPLETED ONLY BY AFFILIATES CLASSIFIED IN MANUFACTURING – The data cells in columns 2 and 3 for items 67, 68, and 70 are to be completed only by U.S. affiliates classified in manufacturing (i.e., in BEA industry codes 201 through 390). Items 64, 69, 70, and 71, column 1 must be completed for all affiliates. For those affiliates for which a pre-labeled BE-15 form is provided, the industry code is as appears at the bottom of the label following "IND=." For all other affiliates, the industry code may be determined by references to Form BE-607 (see Instructions II.G.). If, in the Form BE-607 completed in a given U.S. affiliate, a larger percentage of the affiliate's total sales is classified in manufacturing than in any other major industry group – mining, wholesale trade, services, etc. – then the affiliate's industry code is in manufacturing. If the information for production/non-production workers is not contained in the report as filed but it is subsequently determined that the affiliate is in manufacturing, you will be required to furnish the data retroactively. If you are unsure as to an affiliate's correct industry classification, call (202) 523-0547 for guidance.

Production and related workers for manufacturing are those employees, up to and including working foremen, but excluding other supervisory employees, who are involved in the physical production of goods, handling and storage of goods, related services (e.g., maintenance and repair), and auxiliary production for plant's own use (e.g., power plant). For affiliates classified in manufacturing which also have activities in industries outside manufacturing, consider as production workers only those employees, as defined, who are associated with manufacturing activities; all employees associated with non-manufacturing activities should be considered as non-production workers.

1. Employment is the average number of employees for the reporting period, including part-time employees but excluding home workers and independent sales personnel who are not employees. If possible, the average should be the average for the year of the number of persons on the payroll at the end of each payroll period, month, or quarter. If precise figures are not available, give your best estimate of the average number of employees for the annual reporting period. Employment at the end of the reporting period may be used as an estimate of average employment only if employment throughout the reporting period did not vary significantly due to seasonal operations, a strike, temporary shutdowns, etc. This definition of employment applies both to total employment and to its subdivisions, which are given below.

2. Employee compensation consists of wages and salaries of employees and employer expenditures for all employee benefit plans.

   a. Wages and salaries are the gross earnings of all employees before deduction of employees' payroll withholding tax, social insurance contributions, group insurance premiums, union dues, etc. Include basic time and piece-rate payments, cost of living adjustments, overtime pay and shift differentials, regularly paid bonuses, premiums, personal allowances, summer and yearend bonuses, profit-sharing allocations, and commissions. Exclude commissions paid to independent sales personnel and piece-rate payments made to home workers who are not employees. For incorporated business enterprises, include salaries of officers; for unincorporated business enterprises, exclude payments to proprietors or partners.

   Also include in wages and salaries any other direct payments by employers to employees, such as those for holiday and vacation pay, paid sick leave, severance (redundancy) pay, etc.

   If the employer contributes to benefit funds and also makes direct payments to employees, include the direct payments in "wages and salaries." However, exclude direct payments if the employer pays employees as an agent of benefit funds and is reimbursed for the payments by the funds. Exclude all payments made by benefit funds rather than by the employer. (Employer contributions to benefit funds are included in "employee benefit plans" as discussed below.)

   Also include wages and salaries paid in-kind, valued at the cost to the employer. Pay in-kind should include the actual cost to the employer of those goods and services furnished to employees free or at a significant discount which are clearly and primarily of benefit to employees as consumers, such as food, fuel, and housing. For goods sold to the employee below cost, include the difference between the cost of the goods to the employer and the prices paid by the employee. Housing costs should include depreciation of buildings and equipment; interest, taxes, insurance, repairs and maintenance, and other costs, less grants-in-aid or tax rebates received from public authorities and rent charged to workers. Allowances paid to employees in lieu of pay in-kind should also be included. Do not include expenditures that benefit employers as well as employees, such as for plant facilities, employee training programs, and reimbursements for business expenses.

   b. Employee benefit plans are employer expenditures for all employee benefit plans, including those required by government statute, those resulting from a collective-bargaining contract, or those that are voluntary. Employee benefit plans include retirement plans, life and disability insurance, guaranteed sick pay programs, workers' compensation insurance, medical insurance, family allowances, unemployment insurance, severance (redundancy) pay funds, etc. If plans are financed jointly by the employer and the employee, only the contributions of the employer should be included.

3. Hours worked by production and related workers – Report total number of hours worked during the reporting period by production and related workers included in item 67, column 2. Include stand-by or reporting time; exclude hours paid for holidays, vacations, sick leave, or other paid leave.

L & COMM-DC 59727-P80

Page 11

INSTRUCTIONS FOR BE-15 (Continued)

V. INSTRUCTIONS FOR SPECIFIC PARTS OF THE REPORT FORM   (Continued)

B. U.S. Exports and Imports (Part II, Section G)

The section of the report form on U.S. export and import trade between U.S. affiliates and foreigners attempts to obtain data on a "shipped" basis, i.e., on the basis of when, where, and to (or by) whom the goods were shipped. This is the basis used in compiling official U.S. trade statistics to which the data will be compared.

A. Definition of U.S. exports and imports – U.S. exports and imports refer to physical movements of goods, to include capital goods to be used in the business, between the customs area of the United States and the customs area of a foreign country. For purposes of this report, consigned goods that are shipped during the period must be included in the trade figures even though not normally recorded as sales or purchases, or entered into intercompany accounts when initially consigned.

B. Timing – Only goods actually shipped between the United States and a foreign country in calendar year 1979 should be included, regardless of when the goods were charged or consigned. For example, goods shipped by the U.S. affiliate to a foreign parent in 1979 that were charged or consigned to the foreign parent in 1980 should be included, but goods shipped to a foreigner in 1978 that were charged or consigned to the foreigner in 1979 should be excluded.

(Note: Goods shipped by an independent carrier or a freight forwarder at the expense of an entity are shipments by that entity.)

C. Valuation of exports – U.S. exports should be valued f.a.s. at the U.S. port of exportation. This includes all costs incurred up to the point of loading the goods aboard the export carrier at the U.S. port of exportation, including the selling price at the interior point of shipment (or cost if not sold), packaging costs, and inland freight and insurance. It excludes all subsequent costs, such as loading costs, foreign import duties, and freight and insurance from the U.S. port of exportation to the foreign port of entry.

D. Valuation of imports – U.S. imports should be valued at the actual contract price agreed upon between buyer and seller, adjusted to an f.a.s. foreign-port-of-exportation basis. This includes all costs incurred up to the point of loading the goods aboard the export carrier at the foreign port of exportation, including the selling price at the interior point of shipment (or cost if not sold), packaging costs, and inland freight and insurance. It excludes all subsequent costs, such as loading costs, U.S. import duties, and freight and insurance from the foreign port of exportation to the U.S. port of entry.

DO NOT RETURN INSTRUCTION PAGES WITH THE FORM

FORM BE-605
(REV. 3-79)

U.S. DEPARTMENT OF COMMERCE
BUREAU OF ECONOMIC ANALYSIS

O.M.B. No. 41-R0872; Approval Expires March 1981

TRANSACTIONS OF U.S. CORPORATION WITH FOREIGN PARENT

MANDATORY
CONFIDENTIAL QUARTERLY REPORT

This report is required by law — Section 5(b)(2), P.L. 94-472, 90 Stat. 2059, 22 U.S.C. 3104. Whoever fails to report may be subject to a civil penalty not exceeding $10,000 and to injunctive relief commanding such person to comply, or both. Whoever willfully fails to report shall be fined not more than $10,000 and, if an individual, may be imprisoned for not more than one year, or both.

RETURN TO ►
U.S. Department of Commerce
Bureau of Economic Analysis BE-50(IN)
Washington, D.C. 20230

NOTE: If item 6 is marked, only items 13 thru 22 should be completed (to report direct transactions of the U.S. Affiliate with the foreign parent) and Parts VII and VIII, as applicable.

IMPORTANT: This report covers items received from, paid to, or entered into intercompany accounts with the foreign parent. Report items according to books of U.S. affiliate. Read instructions before completing this form. REPORT ALL AMOUNTS IN THOUSANDS OF U.S. DOLLARS.

I. IDENTIFICATION

1. Report for quarter ending — MONTH / DAY / YEAR

If revised, mark here ☐

BEA USE ONLY

2. Name and address of U.S. affiliate (See instructions concerning consolidated reporting by U.S. affiliate)

3. Name of foreign parent of U.S. affiliate. (The foreign parent is that first person outside the U.S. which holds the direct investment interest; its ownership in the U.S. affiliate can be direct and/or indirect through another U.S. affiliate.)

4. Country of foreign parent of U.S. affiliate   004   BEA USE

Foreign parent named in Item 3 holds (Mark one):

5. Only a direct equity interest in the U.S. affiliate 05

6. Only an indirect equity interest in the U.S. affiliate (See NOTE at left) . . . .

7. Both a direct and an indirect equity interest in the U.S. affiliate . . . .

8. If either 6 or 7 is marked, give name of the U.S. affiliate which is directly foreign owned and which has a direct or indirect ownership interest in the U.S. affiliate identified in 2 above.

9. If U.S. affiliate's industry classification has changed, mark here ► ☐ and complete Form BE-607, Industry Classification Questionnaire   09   BEA USE

II. PAYMENTS TO AND RECEIPTS FROM FOREIGN PARENT BY U.S. AFFILIATE (AS CONSOLIDATED) OF DIVIDENDS, INTEREST, FEES AND ROYALTIES AND RENTALS. REPORT ALL DIRECT TRANSACTIONS WITH THE FOREIGN PARENT IDENTIFIED IN ITEM 3. REPORT ITEMS 13 THROUGH 16 AFTER ANY TAX WITHHELD.	Payments by U.S. Affiliate	Receipts by U.S. Affiliate
10. Dividends on common and preferred stock excluding stock dividends — gross amount: 10		
11. Tax withheld on dividends 11		
12. Dividends on common and preferred stock — net amount (Item 10 less Item 11) 12		
13. Interest, including interest on capital (financial) leases 13		
14. Royalties, license fees, and other fees for the use or sale of intangible property 14		
15. Charges for use of tangible property, and charges for film and television tape rentals 15		
16. Fees for services rendered, including fees for management, professional, or technical services, R&D assessments, and allocated expenses 16		

III. DEBT AND OTHER INTERCOMPANY ACCOUNT BALANCES BETWEEN THE U.S. AFFILIATE AND THE FOREIGN PARENT. Report all Direct Transactions with the Foreign Parent identified in Item 3.	End of quarter	Beginning of quarter
Current Items		
17. Owed to foreign parent by U.S. affiliate 17		
18. Due to U.S. affiliate from foreign parent 18		
Long-term Items		
19. Owed to foreign parent by U.S. affiliate 19		
20. Due to U.S. affiliate from foreign parent 20		
Net book value of property, plant, and equipment on lease and not reflected in Items 17-20 above:		
21. On lease from foreign parent to U.S. affiliate 21		
22. On lease by U.S. affiliate to foreign parent 22		

IV. FOREIGN PARENT'S EQUITY IN U.S. AFFILIATE'S:	Current quarter	Preceding quarter
23. Quarterly net income (loss) after provision for U.S. income taxes — foreign parent's share only 23		
Net unrealized and realized capital gains (losses) for the quarter, foreign parent's share only:		
24. Included in Item 23 24		
25. Taken directly to retained earnings or surplus account (not included in net income) 25		

V. CHANGE DURING THE QUARTER IN FOREIGN PARENT'S EQUITY IN U.S. AFFILIATE'S CAPITAL STOCK AND/OR ADDITIONAL PAID-IN CAPITAL, AT TRANSACTION VALUE	Amount Paid or Received
26. Establishment of U.S. affiliate 26	
Acquisition, partial or total, of an equity interest in this U.S. affiliate:	
27. From this U.S. affiliate 27	
28. From other U.S. persons 28	
29. From foreign persons 29	
30. Capital contributions not resulting in issuance of capital stock. Report return of such contributions in parentheses ( ). 30	
31. Distribution in liquidation of U.S. affiliate 31	
Sale, partial or total, of an equity interest in this U.S. Affiliate:	
32. To this U.S. affiliate 32	
33. To other U.S. persons 33	
34. To foreign persons 34	
35. Stock dividends 35	
36. Other change in capital not included above — Specify 36	

For Items 27 through 36, enter amount by which the transaction value	Amount
37. Exceeds the value carried on the books of the U.S. affiliate 37	
38. Is less than the value carried on the books of the U.S. affiliate 38	

VI. FOREIGN PARENT'S SHARE IN ANNUAL INCOME AND EQUITY POSITION OF THE U.S. AFFILIATE -- COMPLETE ONCE A YEAR. Complete Items 39-45 no later than the second report following the close of the calendar year or fiscal year, or if an initial report, complete Items 39, 40, and 42-45 as of the ending date of the quarter which the initial report is for

	MONTH	DAY	YEAR
39. U.S. affiliate's calendar (or fiscal) year ending 39			

40. Foreign parent's percentage of ownership of U.S. affiliate's voting stock at end of year. Enter to tenth of one percent.   40   _ _ . _

	Amount
41. Foreign parent's equity in U.S. affiliate's annual net income (loss) after provision for U.S. income taxes 41	
Foreign parent's equity in net worth of U.S. affiliate (the consolidated U.S. business enterprise)	
42. Total investment -- sum of Items 43 thru 45 42	
43. Common and preferred stock and additional paid-in capital of U.S. affiliate 43	
44. Retained earnings — compute on the equity basis consistent with Items 23 and 41 44	
45. Other equity accounts — Specify 45	

VII. 46. Does the U.S. affiliate (as consolidated) have direct transactions or accounts with foreign affiliates of the foreign parent identified in item 3? Mark one:

46 ☐ 1 Yes (If Yes, complete page 2 of this Form)
   ☐ 2 No   BEA USE ONLY   47

Name and Address for Mailing Purposes

PERSON TO CONSULT CONCERNING QUESTIONS ABOUT THIS REPORT

TELEPHONE — Area code / Number / Extension

► CERTIFICATION   The U.S. affiliate, and the official executing this certification on its behalf, hereby certify that the information contained in this report is correct and complete to the best of their knowledge and belief.

Authorized official's signature   Title   Date

VIII. DIRECT TRANSACTIONS OR ACCOUNTS BETWEEN U.S. AFFILIATE AND FOREIGN AFFILIATES OF THE FOREIGN PARENT

Do not include any direct financial transactions between U.S. affiliate and the foreign parent which are already included in Parts II and III of page one. Do not net out payables and receivables into one of the sections below. A U.S. affiliate which is a bank should have entries in this Part only if it has long-term liabilities to a foreign affiliate of the foreign parent and that capital is considered to be permanent investment capital in the U.S. affiliate. In this case, the affiliate would complete Section A, columns H and J, and if interest is paid on the debt, column C. REPORT ALL AMOUNTS IN THOUSANDS OF U.S. DOLLARS.

Country of Foreign Affiliate of Foreign Parent	COMMERCE USE ONLY	Interest, including interest on capital (financial) leases	Royalties, license fees, and other fees for the use or sale of intangible property	Charges for use of tangible property and charges for film and T.V. tape rentals	Fees for services rendered, including fees for management, professional, or technical services, R&D assessments, and allocated expenses	End of Quarter Balance		Beginning of Quarter Balance	
						Current	Long-term	Current	Long-term
(A)	(B)	(C)	(D)	(E)	(F)	(G)	(H)	(I)	(J)

A. Payments or Accruals to Foreign Affiliates of the Foreign Parent (net of tax withheld) — Liabilities of U.S. Affiliates to Foreign Affiliates of the Foreign Parent

48									
49									
50									
51									
52									
53									
54									
55									
56									
57									
58									
59									
60									
TOTAL ALL COUNTRIES (SECTION A) 61									

B. Receipts or Accruals from Foreign Affiliates of the Foreign Parent (net of tax withheld) — Receivables of U.S. Affiliate from Foreign Affiliates of the Foreign Parent

(A)	(B)	(C)	(D)	(E)	(F)	(G)	(H)	(I)	(J)
62									
63									
64									
65									
66									
67									
68									
69									
70									
TOTAL ALL COUNTRIES (SECTION B) 71									

FORM BE-605 (11-7-73)

INSTRUCTIONS

Purpose – Reports on this form are required in order to provide reliable and up-to-date information on foreign direct investment in the United States.

Authority – Reports on Form BE-605 are mandatory under Section 5(b)(2) of the International Investment Survey Act of 1976 (P.L. 94-472, 90 Stat. 2059, 22 U.S.C. 3104 – hereinafter "the Act"). In Section 3 of Executive Order 11961, the President designated the Department of Commerce as the federal executive agency responsible for collecting the required data on direct investment, and the Secretary of Commerce has assigned this responsibility to the Bureau of Economic Analysis. The implementing regulations are contained in Title 15, C.F.R., Part 806.

This report has been approved by the Office of Management and Budget under the Federal Reports Act (Public Law No. 831, 77th Congress).

Penalties – Whoever fails to report may be subject to a civil penalty not exceeding $10,000 and to injunctive relief commanding such person to comply, or both. Whoever willfully fails to report shall be fined not more than $10,000 and, if an individual, may be imprisoned for not more than one year, or both. Any officer, director, employee, or agent of any corporation who knowingly participates in such violation, upon conviction, may be punished by a like fine, imprisonment, or both. (See Section 6 of the Act, 22 U.S.C. 3105.)

Confidentiality – The information filed in this report may be used only for analytical and statistical purposes and access to the information shall be available only to officials and employees (including consultants and contractors and their employees) of agencies designated by the President to perform functions under the Act. The President may authorize the exchange of the information between agencies or officials designated to perform functions under the Act, but only for analytical and statistical purposes. No official or employee (including consultants and contractors and their employees) shall publish or make available any information collected under the Act in such a manner that the person to whom the information relates can be specifically identified. Reports and copies of reports prepared pursuant to the Act are confidential and their submission or disclosure shall not be compelled by any person without the prior written permission of the person filing the report and the customer of such person where the information supplied is identifiable as being derived from the records of such customer (22 U.S.C. 3104).

DEFINITIONS

United States, when used in a geographic sense, means the several States, the District of Columbia, the Commonwealth of Puerto Rico, the Canal Zone, and all territories and possessions of the United States.

Foreign, when used in a geographic sense, means that which is situated outside the United States or which belongs to or is characteristic of a country other than the United States.

Person means any individual, branch, partnership, associated group, association, estate, trust, corporation, or other organization (whether or not organized under the laws of any State), and any government (including a foreign government, the United States Government, a State or local government, and any agency, corporation, financial institution, or other entity or instrumentality thereof, including a government-sponsored agency).

Foreign person means any person resident outside the United States or subject to the jurisdiction of a country other than the United States.

Direct investment means the ownership or control, directly or indirectly, by one person of 10 per centum or more of the voting securities of an incorporated business enterprise or an equivalent interest in an unincorporated business enterprise.

Foreign direct investment in the United States means the ownership or control, directly or indirectly, by one foreign person of 10 per centum or more of the voting securities of an incorporated U.S. business enterprise or an equivalent interest in an unincorporated U.S. business enterprise, including a branch.

U.S. affiliate means an affiliate located in the United States in which a foreign person has a direct investment.

Foreign parent means the foreign person, or the first person outside the United States in a foreign chain of ownership, which has direct investment in a U.S. business enterprise, including a branch.

Affiliate means a business enterprise located in one country which is directly or indirectly owned or controlled by a person of another country to the extent of 10 per centum or more of its voting stock for an incorporated business or an equivalent interest for an unincorporated business, including a branch.

Affiliated foreign group means (i) the foreign parent, (ii) any foreign person, proceeding up the foreign parent ownership chain, which owns more than 50 per centum of the person below it up to and including that person which is not owned more than 50 per centum by another foreign person, and (iii) any foreign person, proceeding down the ownership chain of each of these members, which is owned more than 50 per centum by the person above it.

Foreign affiliate of foreign parent means, with reference to a given U.S. affiliate, any member of the affiliated foreign group owning the affiliate that is not a foreign parent of the affiliate.

U.S. corporation means a business enterprise incorporated in the United States.

Business enterprise means any organization, association, branch, or venture which exists for profitmaking purposes or to otherwise secure economic advantage, and any ownership of any real estate.

Lease is a contract by which one person gives another person the use and possession of tangible property (other than real estate) for a specified time in return for agreed-upon payments.

Banking includes business enterprises engaged in deposit banking, Edge Act corporations engaged in international or foreign banking, U.S. branches and agencies of foreign banks whether or not they accept domestic deposits, and bank holding companies, i.e., holding companies for which over 50 per cent of their total income is from banks which they hold.

GENERAL INSTRUCTIONS

Who must report – Except as exempted below, a Form BE-605 is required from every U.S. corporation in which a foreign person had a direct and/or indirect ownership interest of 10 percent or more of the voting stock at any time during the reporting period, provided there are direct transactions or positions between the U.S. corporation (U.S. affiliate) and the foreign parent. Related forms for reporting foreign direct investment in the United States are:

BE-606   Transactions of Unincorporated U.S. Business
         Enterprise (Except a Bank) with Foreign Parent

BE-606B Transactions of U.S. Banking Branch or Agency
         with Foreign Parent

BE-607   Industry Classification Questionnaire

Reports are required even though the U.S. affiliate may have been established, acquired, liquidated, sold, or inactivated during the reporting period.

Consolidated Reporting by U.S. Affiliates – A U.S. affiliate shall file on a fully consolidated basis, including in the consolidation all other U.S. affiliates in which it directly or indirectly owns more than 50 per centum of the outstanding voting stock. (Foreign subsidiaries of the U.S. affiliate are not to be included in the consolidation, except as provided under the equity method of accounting. However, separate reports may be filed where a given U.S. affiliate is not normally consolidated due to unrelated operations or lack of control, provided written permission has been requested from and granted by BEA.

A listing of the names and addresses of the U.S. affiliates included in the consolidation must be provided with the first filing and then updated as changed on a quarterly basis. The list should indicate each U.S. affiliate's direct owner and the percentage of direct ownership interest held.

NOTE: When any member of the consolidated group which is a subsidiary of a U.S. affiliate is also directly owned by the same foreign parent having the indirect interest, a separate BE-605 must be filed to present that direct equity interest. The separate BE-605 should be completed from the viewpoint of the subsidiary, U.S. affiliate and items 13 through 22 and Parts VII and VIII should NOT be completed since that data would normally be included in the consolidated report.

Equity method of accounting – Investments by the U.S. affiliates in business enterprises not included in the consolidation and which are 20 percent or more owned should be accounted for following the equity method of accounting. However, in these cases, intercompany items are not to be eliminated.

Multiple foreign parents – Where two or more foreign persons hold reportable equity interests in a U.S. affiliate, a separate report must be filed to report transactions or accounts with each foreign parent. Note, however, that transactions or accounts with foreign affiliates of a foreign parent, whether located in the same or in a different foreign country as the foreign parent, should not give rise to separate reports but should be entered in Part VIII (on page two) of the form for that foreign parent.

Exemption – A U.S. affiliate is not required to report if each of the following three items for the U.S. affiliate (not the foreign parent's share) is between –$5,000,000 and +$5,000,000.

   (1) Total assets,

   (2) Annual net sales of gross operating revenues,
        excluding sales taxes, and

   (3) Annual net income after provision for U.S. income taxes.

Quarterly reports for a year may be required retroactively when it is determined that the exemption level has been exceeded. If a U.S. affiliate's total assets, sales or net income exceed the exemption level in a given year, it is deemed that the exemption level will also be exceeded in the following year.

BE-605 (REV. 1/79)

U.S. COMM–DC 44137–P78

INSTRUCTIONS (Continued)

NOTE: If any one of the three items above exceeds the exemption level, either positive or negative, the U.S. affiliate must report. Since these items are not reported on Form BE-605, a U.S. affiliate claiming exemption from filing a given report must furnish a certification as to the levels of these three items.

Filing of report - Form BE-605 is a quarterly report. A single copy of each report should be sent to: U.S. Department of Commerce, Bureau of Economic Analysis, BE-50(N), Washington, D.C. 20230, within 30 days after the close of each calendar (or fiscal) quarter, except for the final quarter of the calendar (or fiscal) year, when reports may be filed within 45 days. Requests for extension of the filing date, additional forms, or clarification of the reporting requirements or instructions should be directed to the above address.

Special note for U.S. affiliates that are banks: Data to be reported on this form and relationships to other affiliated U.S. Foreign Exchange Forms B-1, B-2, and B-3.—For U.S. affiliates which are banks, items 17, 18, 20, and 22 should be blank, and items 19 and 21 should reflect only those amounts which the U.S. affiliate considers to be permanent invested debt capital by the foreign parent and any interest payments entered in item 13, column I, should relate only to this capital. Any entries in Part VIII, Section A, should also relate only to permanent invested debt capital by a foreign affiliate of the foreign parent, or the foreign parent's equity investment in the U.S. affiliate (Parts V and VI) must not be reported on Treasury Foreign Exchange Forms B-1, B-2, and B-3.

SPECIFIC INSTRUCTIONS

Currency amounts should be reported in U.S. dollars and rounded to the nearest thousand. If an amount is between -$500 enter "0". Use parentheses to indicate negative numbers.

Estimates may be provided where necessary in order to file a timely report.

A U.S. affiliate that is only indirectly foreign owned (item 6 must be marked), and which is required to file a separate report on Form BE-605 because it has direct transactions or positions with the foreign parent or foreign affiliates of the foreign parent, should complete only the following Parts as applicable:

Part I; Part II except items 10, 11, and 12; Part III; Part VII; and Part VIII.

Item 9. Industry classification refers to the BEA 3-digit industry codes as given in the Industry Classification Questionnaire, Form BE-607.

Items 10-16. Enter amounts as of the date they were either received, paid, or entered into intercompany accounts between the payor and payee, whichever occurred first. Include amounts for which payment was made in kind. For an item entered into intercompany account in, or prior to, the reporting period, in order to avoid duplication, any subsequent settlement of the account on the reporting period should not be reflected again in such item but should be reflected only as a reduction in intercompany account. Banks should exclude interest and fees relating to the items reportable on Treasury Foreign Exchange Forms B-1, B-2, and B-3. Stock dividends should be reported only in item 35.

Item 15. Receipts or payments for use of tangible property include rentals for operational leases of one year or less, net rent on operational leases of more than one year which have not been capitalized, and film and television tape rentals. Net rent is equivalent to the total lease payment less the return of capital (depreciation) component (see instruction for items 21 and 22.)

Items 17-20. Include all intercompany accounts or indebtedness of the U.S. affiliate with the foreign parent. Note that the current quarter's opening balance should be equal to the previous quarter's closing balance; therefore, if it is necessary to translate the balances to U.S. dollars, use the same exchange rate to translate the opening balance for the current quarter as was used to translate the closing balance on the previous quarter. If the closing balance on the preceding quarter's report was in error, note the correction. Entries in items 17-20 should be consistent with entries in items 10-16 insofar as they reflect the latter entries. For example, film rentals shown in item 15 and accrued but not paid by the U.S. affiliate in the current quarter should be included in item III. Banks should not include accounts reportable on Treasury Forms B-1, B-2, and B-3.

Items 17-18. Current items: Trade accounts and notes payable, current portion of long-term debt, overdrafts, and other current liabilities having an original maturity of one year or less, except debt with an original maturity of one year or less, which has been renewed, or with respect to which there is the intention and the means to renew, extend, or refinance for more than one year.

Items 19-20. Long-term items: Debt with an original maturity of more than one year or with no stated maturity, and debt with an original maturity of one year or less which has been renewed, or with respect to which there is the intention and the means to renew, extend, or refinance for more than one year.

If leases between the U.S. affiliate and the foreign parent are capitalized (in the manner, or in a manner similar to that, prescribed in FASB Statement No. 13), then the outstanding capitalized value amount should be shown here as an intercompany balance. Lease payments should be disaggregated into the amount, which is (a) a reduction in the intercompany balance, which would be reflected in one of these items, and (b) interest, which would be entered in item 13. Capital (financial) and operating leases of more than one year that are not capitalized should be entered in items 21 and 22.

Items 21 and 22. Enter here the value of capital (financial) leases and operating leases of more than one year that have not been capitalized. For the operating leases, the net book value of the leased plant and equipment is the original cost less accumulated depreciation. For capital (financial) leases, net book value is the amount of principal payments remaining due at the specified time including payment called for by a bargain purchase option, if any. Operating leases of one year or less should not be shown here. Lease payments should be disaggregated into (a) the return of capital, consisting of operational depreciation which should be reflected (as a reduction in these items entry) as your capital (financial) leases, which would be shown in item 13, and net rent for operational leases, which would be shown in item 15.

Item 23. Net income should be reported on a quarterly basis, NOT on a cumulative basis. Net income for the period shown in item I should be entered in column I. Column 2 should be used to correct data that were incorrect or were not given in the preceding report. Do not delay filing because current quarter data are not available. Estimates may be used where necessary.

The amount entered should represent the foreign parent's equity, based on its directly held equity interest, in the U.S. affiliate's net income (loss) for the quarter, before provision for common and preferred dividends and before any reduction for U.S. withholding taxes on dividends, but after provision for U.S. income taxes. The income statement underlying this and related items should be on that "all inclusive" basis. U.S. affiliates in extractive industries should report net income before depletion charges, except charges representing the amortization of the actual cost of capital's assets.

Net income should include, on an equity basis, the U.S. affiliate's share in the net income of all business enterprises owned by it.

If this report is for the U.S. affiliate's direct transactions or accounts with a foreign parent which does not hold a direct equity interest, the foreign parent's share in net income should be zero. If the foreign parent holds both a direct and an indirect equity interest, only the share representing the direct equity interest should be given in this item.

Items 24-25. Net unrealized and realized capital gains (losses) include net capital gains (losses) resulting from changes in U.S. affiliate's foreign currency denominated assets and liabilities due to changes in foreign exchange rates during the period, net unrealized capital gains (losses), which are recognized, resulting from revaluation of assets, and net realized capital gains (losses) resulting from disposition of assets such as the sale of investment securities or property, plant, or equipment items. All gains (losses) should be included in net income, item 23, and therefore, should be taken directly to retained earnings for some reason, they were not included in net income, but were taken directly to a surplus account, enter the amount in item 25.

Items 26-38. Entries in Section V are necessary to identify the cause of any changes in equity holdings by the foreign parent in the U.S. affiliate during the period, net unrealized capital gains (losses) which occurred first. This section must be completed on the report due within 30 days after the close of the first quarter, or April 30. Best estimates are permitted where necessary in order to file a timely report.

Item 41. Same instructions as for item 23, except that this refers to the annual figure for the year designated in item 39.

Items 42-45. Show the proportion of capital owned and equity in surplus accounts by the foreign parent as of the end of the year as shown in item 39. The retained earnings account underlying the foreign parent's share of retained earnings, item 44, must be computed on the equity basis consistent with items 23 and 41.

Part VIII — Report direct transactions during the quarter with foreign affiliates of the foreign parent in accordance with column headings. Do not include transactions already reported in previous sections of this form. In Section A, report payments and liabilities to, and in Section B report receipts and receivables due from, foreign affiliates of foreign parent. In column (A) enter only unit foreign country per line; if more lines than provided are needed in order to list all countries, use additional sheets. In column (B) report the Part VIII item number. Note however, only countries with an amount of $250 thousand or more must be reported on separate lines. Countries for which all amounts are less than $250 thousand may be combined on one line, the line should be designated as "unallocated" in column A.

TEAR OFF INSTRUCTIONS AFTER COMPLETION

USCOMM-DC 44137-P78

OMB No. 0608–0030, Approval Expires March 1981

| FORM BE-407 (REV. 3-81) | U.S. DEPARTMENT OF COMMERCE BUREAU OF ECONOMIC ANALYSIS | I. IDENTIFICATION |

INDUSTRY CLASSIFICATION QUESTIONNAIRE

MANDATORY

CONFIDENTIAL REPORT

This report is required by law — Section 5(b)(2), P.L. 94-472, 90 Stat. 2059, 22 U.S.C. 3104. Whoever fails to report may be subject to a civil penalty not exceeding $10,000 and to injunctive relief commanding such person to comply, or both. Whoever willfully fails to report shall be fined not more than $10,000 and, if an individual, may be imprisoned for not more than one year or both.

RETURN TO

U.S. Department of Commerce
Bureau of Economic Analysis, BE-50 (IN)
Washington, D.C. 20230

IMPORTANT — Read instructions on reverse side before completing this form.

1. Name and address of U.S. affiliate

2. Name of foreign parent holding either direct interest, or indirect interest through another U.S. affiliate, in the U.S. affiliate named in item 1.

3. Country of location of foreign parent named in 2.

4. Industry classification of foreign parent named in item 2. Determine code from list at bottom of page 2 and enter here:
☐☐ ← Code

5. This report represents: (Mark one)
a. ☐ The initial filing by the U.S. affiliate
b. ☐ A change in the 3-digit DI industry classification of this U.S. affiliate

6. If this report represents a change in industry classification of the U.S. affiliate, enter the period during which change took place.
MONTH   YEAR

II. U.S. AFFILIATE INDUSTRY CLASSIFICATION — If for an incorporated U.S. affiliate, this Part is to be completed from the viewpoint of the consolidated entity.

1. Activity and product or service of the U.S. affiliate

a. Major activity of this U.S. affiliate (Mark "X" one)

☐ Extracting of oil or minerals (including exploration and development)

☐ Manufacturing (fabricating, assembling, processing)

☐ Selling or distributing goods

☐ Real estate (investing in, or engaging in as an operator, manager, developer, lessor, agent, or broker)

☐ Providing a service

☐ Other — Specify

b. Major product or service involved in this activity: if a product, also state what is done to it; i.e., whether it is mined, manufactured, sold a wholesale, transported, packaged, etc.

2. In the area to the right, enter the appropriate 3-digit industry code(s) and the percent, to the nearest tenth of one percent, of sales associated with each code. The sales figures should be representative of the affiliate's most recent annual sales or gross operating revenue figures (excluding sales taxes). See the list of industry codes below. If you use fewer than eight codes you must account for one hundred percent of sales. In the case of a new or non-operating affiliate, show the projected breakdown of sales.

Line No.	DI code	Percent of sales (to tenth of one percent)
1		. %
2		. %
3		. %
4		. %
5		. %
6		. %
7		. %
8		. %
	BEA USE ONLY	
Total percentage accounted for 9		. %

SUMMARY OF DIRECT INVESTMENT (DI) INDUSTRY CLASSIFICATIONS

AGRICULTURE, FORESTRY, AND FISHING

010 Agricultural production — crops
020 Agricultural production — livestock, except beef cattle feedlots
021 Agricultural production — beef cattle feedlots
070 Agricultural services
080 Forestry
090 Fishing, hunting, and trapping

MINING

101 Iron ores
102 Copper, lead, zinc, gold, and silver ores
103 Bauxite and other aluminum ores
109 Other metallic ores and metal mining services
120 Coal
133 Crude petroleum extraction (no refining) and natural gas
138 Oil and gas field services
140 Nonmetallic minerals, except fuels

CONSTRUCTION

150 Construction

MANUFACTURING

201 Meat products
202 Dairy products
203 Preserved fruits and vegetables
204 Grain mill products
205 Bakery products
208 Beverages
209 Other food and kindred products
210 Tobacco manufactures
220 Textile mill products
230 Apparel and other textile products
240 Lumber and wood products
250 Furniture and fixtures
262 Pulp, paper, and board mills
264 Miscellaneous converted paper products
265 Paperboard containers and boxes
270 Printing and publishing
281 Industrial chemicals and synthetics
283 Drugs
284 Soap, cleaners, and toilet goods
285 Paints and allied products
287 Agricultural chemicals
289 Chemical products, nec
291 Integrated petroleum refining and extraction
292 Petroleum refining without extraction
299 Petroleum and coal products, nec
301 Rubber products
307 Miscellaneous plastics products
310 Leather and leather products
321 Glass products

MANUFACTURING — Continued

329 Stone, clay, concrete gypsum, and other nonmetallic mineral products
331 Primary metal industries, ferrous
335 Primary metal industries, non-ferrous
341 Metal cans and shipping containers
342 Cutlery, hand tools, and hardware
343 Metal plumbing fixtures and heating equipment, except electric
344 Fabricated structural metal products
345 Screw machine products, bolts, etc.
346 Metal forgings and stampings
349 Fabricated metal products, nec; ordnance; and metal services
351 Engines and turbines
352 Farm and garden machinery
353 Construction, mining, and materials handling machinery
354 Metalworking machinery
355 Special industry machinery
356 General industrial machinery
357 Office and computing machines
358 Refrigeration and service industry machinery
359 Machinery, except electrical, nec
363 Household appliances
364 Electric lighting and wiring equipment
366 Radio, television, and communication equipment
367 Electronic components and accessories
369 Electrical machinery, nec
371 Motor vehicles and equipment
379 Other transportation equipment
381 Scientific and measuring instruments
383 Optical and ophthalmic goods
384 Medical instruments and supplies
386 Photographic equipment and supplies
387 Watches, clocks, and watchcases
390 Miscellaneous manufacturing industries, nec

TRANSPORTATION, COMMUNICATION AND PUBLIC UTILITIES

401 Railroads
441 Petroleum tanker operations
449 Other water transportation
450 Transportation by air
461 Pipe lines, petroleum and natural gas
462 Pipe lines, except petroleum and natural gas
470 Petroleum storage for hire
478 Transportation, nec, warehousing, terminal facilities, travel agents, and related services
480 Communication
490 Electric, gas, and sanitary services

WHOLESALE TRADE

501 Motor vehicles and equipment
503 Lumber and construction materials
504 Farm and garden machinery and equipment
505 Metals and minerals, except petroleum
506 Electrical goods
507 Hardware, plumbing and heating equipment and supplies
508 Other machinery, equipment, and supplies
509 Durable goods, nec
511 Paper and paper products
512 Drugs, proprietaries, and sundries
513 Apparel, piece goods, and notions
514 Groceries and related products
515 Farm-product raw materials
517 Petroleum and petroleum products
519 Nondurable goods, nec

RETAIL TRADE

540 Food stores and eating and drinking places
554 Gasoline service stations
590 Retail trade, nec

FINANCE, INSURANCE, AND REAL ESTATE

600 Banking
610 Finance, except banking
630 Insurance
649 Lessors of agricultural and forestry real estate
650 Real estate, nec
671 Holding companies

SERVICES

700 Hotels and other lodging places
731 Advertising
732 Business services, nec
780 Motion pictures, including television tape and film
891 Engineering, architectural, and surveying services
893 Accounting, auditing, and bookkeeping services
898 Services, nec, provided on a commercial basis

NONBUSINESS ENTITIES

900 Government entities
905 Nonbusiness entities, except Government

NOTE: nec means not elsewhere classified.

Page 1

FORM BE-13 Supplement C
(2-81)

OMB No. 0608-0015, Approval Expires March 1984

CONTROL NUMBER

U.S. DEPARTMENT OF COMMERCE
BUREAU OF ECONOMIC ANALYSIS

EXEMPTION CLAIM, FORM BE-13
(Report on a Foreign Person's Establishment, Acquisition, or Purchase
of the Operating Assets of a U.S. Business Enterprise, Including Real Estate)
NOTE: Real estate purchased for other than personal use constitutes a "business enterprise".

Response to this inquiry is required by law. By the same law your report to this Bureau is CONFIDENTIAL. It may be used only for analytical or statistical purposes and CANNOT be used for purposes of taxation, investigation, or regulation. The law also provides that copies retained in your files are immune from legal process.

I have reviewed the instructions for the BE-13 Report and determined that we are not required to file a Form BE-13 for the following reason:

Mark one

1. 01 ☐ This U.S. business enterprise is not a U.S. affiliate of a foreign person, i.e., is not owned to the extent of 10 percent or more, directly or indirectly, by a foreign person.

2. 02 ☐ This acquisition is exempt from being reported because the U.S. business enterprise, or the business segment or operating unit of a U.S. business enterprise, was acquired by an existing U.S. affiliate who then merged it into its own operations and the total cost of the acquisition was $1,000,000 or less, and did not involve the purchase of 200 acres or more of U.S. land. (If it involves 200 acres or more of U.S. land, it must be reported regardless of the total cost of the acquisition.) Enter the total cost and number of acres of land involved at the right.

	Amount			
	Bil.	Mil.	Thous.	Dols.

Total cost 03 $

Number

Acres (to nearest whole acre) 04

3. 05 ☐ This acquisition is not required to be reported since it represents U.S. real estate acquired by a foreign person(s) held exclusively for personal use and not for profitmaking purposes.

4. 06 ☐ This U.S. business enterprise is a U.S. affiliate of a foreign person but is exempt because, on a fully consolidated basis:

(a) Each of the following three items for the U.S. affiliate (not the foreign parent's share) was between -$1 million and +$1 million:

(1) Total assets,

(2) Sales or gross operating revenues, excluding sales taxes, and

(3) Net income after provision for U.S. income taxes;

and

(b) The U.S. affiliate does not own 200 acres or more of U.S. land (if the U.S. affiliate owns 200 acres or more of U.S. land, it must report regardless of the value of the three items listed above).

Enter value or amount for each:

	AMOUNT			
	Bil.	Mil.	Thous.	Dols.

i.   Total assets (do not net out liabilities) 07 $

ii. Sales or gross operating revenues, excluding sales taxes (do not give gross margin) 08 $

iii. Net income after provision for U.S. income taxes 09 $

NUMBER

iv. Number of acres of U.S. land owned 10

and complete the following:

BEA USE ONLY

i. Country of foreign parent _____ 11

ii. Country of ultimate beneficial owner _____ 12

5. 13 ☐ Other – *Specify and include reference to section of regulations or instructions on which claim is based.*

Name and address of U.S. affiliate or U.S. business enterprise submitting this claim *(enter in blocks below, skip one block between words):*

Name

14

Street or P.O. Box

15

City and State   ZIP Code

16

▶ CERTIFICATION   The undersigned official certifies that the information contained in this report is correct and complete to the best of his/her knowledge.

Authorized Official's Signature   Please type Name and Title   Date

Print name and address

U.S. PERSON FOR BEA
TO CONSULT ABOUT
THIS CLAIM

U.S. TELEPHONE NUMBER		
Area code	Number	Extension

A foreign corporation ("Foreign Corp") and a United
States individual ("US Person") formed, on June 10, 1981,
a California corporation ("Cal Corp"). Foreign Corp is
owned by one foreign individual ("F.I."). On July 1, 1981,
Foreign Corp and US Person each purchased 150,000 shares of
the common stock of Cal Corp at a cost of $1 per share.

On October 1, 1981, Cal Corp acquired certain real
property in California for $1,600,000 with a $400,000
down payment. The remainder of the purchase price was
evidenced by a Note secured by a Deed of Trust.

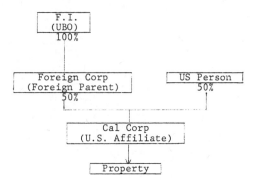

Form BE-13 Supplement C
(12-81)

OMB No. 0608-0035. Approval Expires March 1984

CONTROL NUMBER

U.S. DEPARTMENT OF COMMERCE
BUREAU OF ECONOMIC ANALYSIS

EXEMPTION CLAIM, FORM BE-13
(Report on a Foreign Person's Establishment, Acquisition, or Purchase
of the Operating Assets of a U.S. Business Enterprise, Including Real Estate)
NOTE: Real estate purchased for other than personal use constitutes a "business enterprise".

Response to this inquiry is required by law. By the same law your report to this Bureau is CONFIDENTIAL. It may be used only for analytical or statistical purposes and CANNOT be used for purposes of taxation, investigation, or regulation. The law also provides that copies retained in your files are immune from legal process.

I have reviewed the instructions for the BE-13 Report and determined that we are not required to file a Form BE-13 for the following reason:

Mark one

1. 01 ☐ This U.S. business enterprise is not a U.S. affiliate of a foreign person, i.e., is not owned to the extent of 10 percent or more, directly or indirectly, by a foreign person.

2. 02 ☒ This acquisition is exempt from being reported because the U.S. business enterprise, or the business segment or operating unit of a U.S. business enterprise, was acquired by an existing U.S. affiliate who then merged it into its own operations and the total cost of the acquisition was $1,000,000 or less, and did not involve the purchase of 200 acres or more of U.S. land. (If it involves 200 acres or more of U.S. land, it must be reported regardless of the total cost of the acquisition.) Enter the total cost and number of acres of land involved at the right.

		Amount			
		Bil.	Mil.	Thous.	Dols.
Total cost 03	$			300	
		Number			
Acres (to nearest whole acre) 04		1			

3. 05 ☐ This acquisition is not required to be reported since it represents U.S. real estate acquired by a foreign person(s) held <u>exclusively</u> for personal use and not for profitmaking purposes.

4. 06 ☐ This U.S. business enterprise is a U.S. affiliate of a foreign person but is exempt because, on a fully consolidated basis:

   (a) Each of the following three items for the U.S. affiliate (not the foreign parent's share) was between −$1 million and +$1 million:
   (1) Total assets,
   (2) Sales or gross operating revenues, excluding sales taxes, and
   (3) Net income after provision for U.S. income taxes;
   and
   (b) The U.S. affiliate does not own 200 acres or more of U.S. land (if the U.S. affiliate owns 200 acres or more of U.S. land, it must report regardless of the value of the three items listed above).

		AMOUNT			
		Bil.	Mil.	Thou.	Dols.
Enter value or amount for each: i. Total assets (do not net out liabilities) 07	$				
ii. Sales or gross operating revenues, excluding sales taxes (do not give gross margin) 08	$				
iii. Net income after provision for U.S. income taxes 09	$				
		NUMBER			
iv. Number of acres of U.S. land owned 10					

and complete the following:

		BEA USE ONLY
i. Country of foreign parent _____ 11		
ii. Country of ultimate beneficial owner _____ 12		

5. 13 ☐ Other − *Specify and include reference to section of regulations or instructions on which claim is based.*

Name and address of U.S. affiliate or U.S. business enterprise submitting this claim *(enter in blocks below, skip one block between words):*

Name
14 | C | A | L | | C | O | R | P | | | | | | | | | | | | | | | | | | |

Street or P.O. Box
15 | a | d | d | r | e | s | s | | | | | | | | | | | | | | | | | | | |

City and State   ZIP Code
16 | | | | | | | | | | | | | | | | | | | | | | | | | | |

▶ CERTIFICATION   The undersigned official certifies that the information contained in this report is correct and complete to the best of his/her knowledge.

Authorized Official's Signature	Please type Name and Title	Date
Cal Corp.		

Print name and address

U.S. PERSON FOR BEA TO CONSULT ABOUT THIS CLAIM   C/O preparer and/or corporate director

U.S. TELEPHONE NUMBER		
Area code	Number	Extension

Form BE-13A
(REV. 2-81)

OMB No. 0608-0035. Approval Expires March 1982

CONTROL NUMBER

U.S. DEPARTMENT OF COMMERCE
BUREAU OF ECONOMIC ANALYSIS

Response to this inquiry is required by law. By the same law your report to this Bureau is CONFIDENTIAL. It may be used only for analytical or statistical purposes and CANNOT be used for purposes of taxation, investigation, or regulation. The law also provides that copies retained in your files are immune from legal process.

FORM FOR A U.S. BUSINESS ENTERPRISE, BUSINESS SEGMENT, OR OPERATING UNIT THAT HAS BEEN ESTABLISHED OR ACQUIRED BY A FOREIGN PERSON OR EXISTING U.S. AFFILIATE OF A FOREIGN PERSON

MANDATORY – CONFIDENTIAL

PART I – Determination of Type of Transaction

The foreign parent or existing U.S. affiliate (Mark one):

1. 1001 ¹ [X] Created a new legal entity, either incorporated or unincorporated, including a branch, that organized and began operating as a new U.S. business enterprise; or directly purchased real estate

2. ² [ ] Secured a voting equity interest in a previously existing, separate legal entity that was already organized and operating as a U.S. business enterprise and that it continued to operate as a separate legal entity, either incorporated or unincorporated, including a branch

3. ³ [ ] Bought a business segment or operating unit of an existing U.S. business enterprise, that it organized as a new separate legal entity, either incorporated or unincorporated, including a branch

4. ⁴ [ ] The existing U.S. affiliate bought a U.S. enterprise, or business segment or operating unit of a U.S. business enterprise, and merged it into its own operations rather than continuing or organizing it as a separate legal entity

If 1, 2, or 3, is marked, the U.S. business enterprise acquired, or the new legal entity created, is hereinafter referred to as the "new U.S. affiliate" and Parts II, IV, and V below must be completed.

If 4 is marked, omit Part II and complete Parts III, IV, and V below.

NOTE:– See Section II.E of Instructions concerning unusual reporting situations.

This form is to be completed either:

(a) by a U.S. business enterprise when a foreign person (hereinafter, the "foreign parent") establishes or acquires directly, or indirectly through an existing U.S. affiliate, a 10 percent or more voting interest in that enterprise, including an enterprise that results from the direct or indirect acquisition by a foreign person of a business segment or operating unit of an existing U.S. business enterprise that is then organized as a separate legal entity; or

(b) by the existing U.S. affiliate of a foreign person (hereinafter, the "existing U.S. affiliate") when it acquires a U.S. business enterprise, or a business segment or operating unit of a U.S. business enterprise, that the existing U.S. affiliate merges into its own operations rather than continuing or organizing as a separate legal entity.

RETURN REPORT TO: U.S. Department of Commerce Bureau of Economic Analysis BE-50 (IN) Washington, D.C. 20230

PART II – Identification and Capital Structure of the New U.S. Affiliate
(This Part is to be completed only if item 1, 2, or 3 is marked)

NOTE: A single original copy of the form is to be filed with the Bureau of Economic Analysis. To facilitate processing, it is preferred that the BE-13A and the BE-13B forms be filed together, or simultaneously. File copies should be retained for 3 years after the date on which the form is due.

5. Name and address of new U.S. affiliate

or address that BEA will mail to if applicable

Name of new U.S. affiliate
1002 | C | a | l | C | o | r | p | - | R | e | a | l | | E | s | t | a | t | e |

Street or P.O. box
1003 | p | r | o | p | e | r | t | y | | a | d | d | r | e | s | s ** |

City and State   ZIP Code
1004

Important
Read instructions before completing form.

1. EXCLUSIONS AND EXEMPTIONS:

a. Residential real estate held exclusively for personal use and not for profitmaking purposes is not subject to the reporting requirements. A U.S. residence which is an owner's primary residence that is then leased by the owner while outside the United States but which the owner intends to reoccupy, is considered real estate held for personal use. Ownership of residential real estate by a corporation whose sole purpose is to hold the real estate and where the real estate is for the personal use of the individual owner(s) of the corporation, is considered real estate held for personal use.

b. An existing U.S. affiliate is exempt from reporting the acquisition of a U.S. business enterprise, or a business segment or operating unit of a U.S. business enterprise, that it then merges into its own operations, if the total cost of the acquisition was $1,000,000 or less, and does not involve the purchase of 200 acres or more of U.S. land. (If the acquisition involves the purchase of 200 acres or more of U.S. land, it must be reported regardless of the total cost of the acquisition.)

c. An established or acquired U.S. business enterprise, as consolidated, is exempt if its total assets (not the foreign parent's or existing U.S. affiliate's share) at the time of acquisition or immediately after being established, were $1,000,000 or less and it does not own 200 acres or more of U.S. land. (If it owns 200 acres or more of U.S. land, it must report regardless of the value of total assets.)

If exempt under (b) or (c), an "Exemption Claim, Form BE-13A" must be filed to validate the exemption.

NOTE: See Section II.B. of Instructions concerning reporting on related forms that may be required when changes occur.

2. EFFECTIVE DATE:
A report on this revised form is required for each covered direct investment transaction occurring on or after January 1, 1981.

3. ASSISTANCE – Telephone (202) 523-0547.

4. DUE DATE:
Form BE-13A is due no later than 45 days after the direct investment transaction occurs.
NOTE: Form CE-607, Industry Classification Questionnaire, must also be completed by a new U.S. affiliate and returned with Form BE-13A.

5. GENERAL NOTES:
A. Figures such as the number of acres and the number of employees should be reported to the nearest whole unit.
B. Currency amounts should be reported in U.S. dollars rounded to thousands (omitting 000). Do not enter amounts in the shaded portions of each line.
EXAMPLE: If amount is $1,334,615.00, report as:

Bil.	Mil.	Thous.	Dols.
	1	335	

C. If an item is between + or – $500.00 enter "0".
D. Use parentheses to indicate negative numbers.

6. Primary employer identification number to be used by the new U.S. affiliate to file income and payroll taxes.

1005 | | – | | | | | | ← E.I. Number **N/A Real Estate**

7. Form of organization of U.S. affiliate (Mark one):

1006 ¹ [ ] Incorporated in U.S.
² [ ] U.S. partnership
³ [ ] U.S. branch of a foreign person
⁴ [X] Real property not in 1–3 above

⁵ [ ] Business enterprise incorporated abroad, but whose head office is located in the United States and whose business activity is conducted in, or from, the United States
⁶ [ ] Other – Specify:

8. Is the investment primarily an investment in real estate, including agriculture and forestry land?

1007 ¹ [X] Yes
² [ ] No

9. If the answer to item 8 is "YES," based on estimated current values, is this primarily an investment in (Mark one):

1008 ¹ [X] Unimproved real estate
² [ ] Improved real estate

MANDATORY – This survey is being conducted pursuant to the International Investment Survey Act of 1976 (Pub. L. 94–472, 90 Stat. 2059, 22 U.S.C. 3101 to 3108 – hereinafter, "the Act"), and the filing of reports is mandatory pursuant to Section 5(b) (2) of the Act (22 U.S.C. 3104).

PENALTIES – Whoever fails to report may be subject to a civil penalty not exceeding $10,000 and to injunctive relief commanding such person to comply, or both. Whoever willfully fails to report shall be fined not more than $10,000 and, if an individual, may be imprisoned for not more than one year, or both. Any officer, director, employee, or agent of any corporation who knowingly participates in such violations, upon conviction, may be punished by a like fine, imprisonment or both. (See Section 6 of the Act, 22 U.S.C. 3105.)

CONFIDENTIALITY – The information filed in this report may be used only for analytical and statistical purposes and access to the information shall be available only to officials and employees (including consultants and contractors and their employees) of agencies designated by the President to perform functions under the Act. The President may authorize the exchange of information between agencies or officials designated to perform functions under the Act, but only for analytical and statistical purposes. No official or employee (including consultants and contractors and their employees) shall publish or make available any information collected under the Act in such a manner that the person to whom the information relates can be specifically identified. Reports and copies of reports prepared pursuant to the Act are confidential and their submission or disclosure shall not be compelled by any person without the prior written permission of the person filing the report and the customer of such person where the information supplied is identifiable as being derived from the records of such customer (22 U.S.C. 3104).

Print name and address

PERSON TO CONSULT CONCERNING QUESTIONS ABOUT THIS REPORT

**Cal Corp-Real Estate
c/o Preparer and/or corporate officer**

U.S. TELEPHONE NUMBER
Area Code	Number	Extension

CERTIFICATION — The undersigned official certifies that the information contained in this report is correct and complete to the best of his/her knowledge.

Authorized Official's Signature   Title   Date

Form BE-13A, Page 1

PART II – Identification and Capital Structure of the New U.S. Affiliate (Continued)

		MONTH	DAY	YEAR
10.	Date on which the foreign person established or acquired directly, or indirectly through an existing U.S. affiliate, a 10 percent or more voting interest in the new U.S. affiliate. (If more than one foreign person or existing U.S. affiliate of a foreign person acquired a new interest on or about the same time, give date for each opposite their names and addresses in item 17 or item 18, as appropriate.)	2009	10	01	81

11. Did the foreign person own a voting interest, direct or indirect, in the new U.S. affiliate immediately prior to the date, as given in item 10, it acquired a 10 percent or more voting interest? *(Mark one)*
(If more than one foreign person or existing U.S. affiliate of a foreign person acquired a new interest on or about the same time, indicate a "Yes," or "No" to this item opposite each of their names and addresses in item 17 or item 18, as appropriate.)

2010   1 ☐ Yes   2 ☒ No

Ownership of new U.S. affiliate – Number of voting shares, and percent of voting shares and equity interest for an incorporated U.S. affiliate, or an equivalent interest for an unincorporated U.S. affiliate, owned DIRECTLY by:		Voting Shares		Total equity interest
		Number	Percent	Percent
12.	All foreign parent(s), including the foreign parent(s) with a newly acquired direct investment ownership interest 2011	1	2	3
13.	All U.S. affiliate(s) of foreign parent(s), including the existing U.S. affiliate(s) with a newly acquired ownership interest 2012	1	2	3 100%
14.	Other foreign persons 2013	1	2	3
15.	Other U.S. persons 2014	1	2	3
16.	Total – Sum of items 12 through 15 2015	1	100.0%	100.0%

17. Foreign parent(s) holding a newly acquired direct ownership interest included in item 12 – Give name, address, and percent of ownership directly held by each. If more than three, continue on a separate sheet. A Form BE-13B must be completed for or by each foreign parent with a newly acquired direct ownership interest. This item need not be filled out if a completed Form BE-13B for the foreign parent accompanies the filing of this Form BE-13A.

(1) Name and address of foreign parent   Percent of ownership

See BE-13B   %

BEA USE ONLY
2016 | | | | | | | | | | | | | | | | | | | | | | | | | | | | | | | | | | | |

(2) Name and address of foreign parent   Percent of ownership

%

BEA USE ONLY
2017 | | | | | | | | | | | | | | | | | | | | | | | | | | | | | | | | | | | |

(3) Name and address of foreign parent   Percent of ownership

%

BEA USE ONLY
2018 | | | | | | | | | | | | | | | | | | | | | | | | | | | | | | | | | | | |

18. Existing U.S. affiliate(s) holding a newly acquired direct ownership interest included in item 13 – Give name, address, and percent of ownership directly held by each. If more than two, continue on a separate sheet. A Form BE-13B must be filed by each existing U.S. affiliate with a newly acquired direct ownership interest. This item need not be filled out if a completed Form BE-13B for the existing U.S. affiliate accompanies the filing of this Form BE-13A.

(1) Name and address of existing U.S. affiliate   Percent of ownership

%

BEA USE ONLY
2036 | | | | | | | | | | | | | | | | | | | | | | | | | | | | | | | | | | | |

(2) Name and address of existing U.S. affiliate   Percent of ownership

%

BEA USE ONLY
2037 | | | | | | | | | | | | | | | | | | | | | | | | | | | | | | | | | | | |

19. Number of U.S. affiliates consolidated *(Enter number)*
If this report is for a single unconsolidated U.S. affiliate, enter "1" in the box. If the new U.S. affiliate owns subsidiaries that become U.S. affiliates and their data are included by consolidation in Part IV, enter the number of U.S. affiliates fully consolidated. (Hereinafter, they are considered to be one U.S. affiliate.) Exclude from the full consolidation all foreign business enterprises owned by this U.S. affiliate. See consolidation instructions, II.G. of Instructions.

If number is greater than one, Supplement A must be completed.

NUMBER   2056   1

20. U.S. affiliates not consolidated – Enter number of U.S. affiliates in which the new U.S. affiliate holds a direct equity interest but which ARE NOT fully consolidated in this report.

N/A

If an entry here, Supplement B must be completed.

NUMBER   2057

21. Does any U.S. affiliate fully consolidated in this report own, directly or indirectly, over 50 percent of the outstanding voting stock of a domestic corporation that is not a U.S. affiliate? (See definition of U.S. affiliate.) *(Mark one)*:

2058   1 ☐ Yes   2 ☒ No

If yes, do not fully consolidate such domestic corporation in this report – include only by equity method of accounting.

22.	Give the ending date for the new U.S. affiliate's fiscal year		MONTH	DAY
		2059	12	31

Form BE-13A, Page 2

PART II – Identification and Capital Structure of the New U.S. Affiliate (Continued)

Capital Structure of the New U.S. Affiliate: To be based on data from the books of the new U.S. affiliate immediately after the foreign person established or acquired a 10 percent or more, direct or indirect, voting interest or equivalent.

23. Date data are as of: 2060

	MONTH	DAY	YEA
	1 0	0 1	8 1

		Total (1)	All foreign parent(s) (2)	All U.S. affiliate(s) of foreign parent(s) (3)	Other persons (4)
		Bil. Mil. Thou. Dols.	Bil. Mil. Thou. Dols.	Bil. Mil. Thou. Dols.	Bil. Mil. Thou. Do
Incorporated U.S. affiliate:					
24. Capital stock – voting	2061	$	$	$	$
25. Capital stock – nonvoting	2062				
26. Additional paid-in capital	2063				
27. Retained earnings	2064				
28. Treasury stock	2065	( )			
29. Total – Sum of items 24 through 28	2066	$	$	$	$
Unincorporated U.S. affiliate:					
30. Owners' equity	2067	$ 400	$	$ 400	$

GO DIRECTLY TO PART IV, AND ALSO COMPLETE PART V

PART III – Identification of a U.S. Business Enterprise, or a Business Segment or Operating Unit of a U.S. Business Enterprise, that has been Acquired by and Merged into an Existing U.S. Affiliate (*This Part is to be completed only if item 4, Part I, above is marked.*)

31. Name and address of existing U.S. affiliate that made acquisition.

Name of U.S. affiliate

Street or P.O. box

City and State   ZIP Code

32. Name and address of business enterprise acquired or main office or location of the operating facilities of the segment or operating unit acquired.

Name

Street or P.O. box

City and State   ZIP Code

33. If the enterprise, segment, or unit acquired had its own Employer Identification Number that it used to file income and payroll taxes, enter the number. Do not enter a number if it covered more than just the acquired entity.

3068 ☐ – ☐☐☐☐☐ ← E.I. Number

34. Name and address of person from whom acquired

Name

Street or P.O. box

City and State   ZIP Code

35. Date on which the existing U.S. affiliate completed the purchase of the enterprise, segment, or operating unit that it then merged into its own operations. 3069

MONTH	DAY	YEAR

ALSO COMPLETE PARTS IV AND V

BEA USE ONLY

3070
3071
3072
3073
3074

Form BE-13A, Page 3

PART IV – Selected Financial and Operating Data
This Part is to be completed in the case of all types of transactions covered by items 1 through 4 above.

For items 36 through 42 and for items 44 through 51, column 2:

If item 1 above is marked: Where the investment represents the establishment of a new U.S. business enterprise, or the direct purchase of real estate, the data should be projections for or as of the end of the first full year of operations. Use projections made in the course of planning the investment if available; otherwise, give best estimate.

If item 2, 3, or 4 above is marked: Data should be for the fully consolidated U.S. business enterprise, or business segment or operating unit, acquired. Data should be for or as of the end of the most recent financial reporting year preceding acquisition. Exclude from full consolidation all foreign business enterprises owned by this U.S. affiliate; include such foreign enterprises only by the equity or cost method of accounting. (See Section II.G. of Instructions.)

For items 43 and for items 44 through 51, column 1:

If item 1, 2, or 3 above is marked: The data should show the number of acres owned by the new U.S. affiliate upon completion of the investment transaction.

If item 4 above is marked: The data should show the number of acres included in the purchase.

NOTE: *See special instructions regarding the reporting of employee compensation (item 41) and number of employees (item 42) in Section VIII of Instructions.*

			MONTH	DAY	YEAR
36. Give ending date for the year that these Part IV data are for, or as of		4120	10	01	81

			Amount
			Bil. Mil. Thous. Dols.
37. Total assets		4121	$ 1,600
38. Plant and equipment, net of accumulated depreciation, depletion, etc.		4122	$ 0
39. Sales or gross operating revenues, excluding sales taxes (do not give gross margin)		4123	$ 0
40. Net income after provision for U.S. Federal, State, and local income taxes		4124	$ 0
41. Employee compensation – Include wages and salaries and cost of employee benefit plans		4125	$ 0

			Number
42. Number of employees – Average for the reporting period, including part-time employees		4126	0

43. Acres of mineral rights owned and leased from others – In those cases where both the land and the mineral rights to that land are owned, report the land only as land owned in items 44 through 51, column 1; do not also report it in this item. Include acres leased from others pursuant to both capital and operating leases.   4127

BEA USE ONLY ▷ 4128

Land and other property, plant, and equipment, total and by primary use Items, including land, being leased from others pursuant to capital leases are to be considered as owned by the affiliate; items which the affiliate has sold on a capital lease basis are not to be considered as owned by the affiliate.		All land owned, whether carried in a fixed asset, investment, or other asset account (1) ACRES (To nearest whole acre)	Gross book value (historical cost of all land and other property, plant, and equipment, whether carried in a fixed asset, investment, or other asset account (2) Bil. Mil. Thous. Dols.
44. Agriculture and forestry	4129		$
45. Natural resources	4130		$
46. Manufacturing	Petroleum refining	4131		$
47.	Chemicals	4132		$
48.	Other	4133		$
49. Residential and office buildings, stores, and shopping centers	4134		$
50. Other – *Specify* Land	4135	1	1,600 $
51. Total	4136	1	1,600 $

PART V – Investment Incentives and Services Provided by State or Local Governments (Including Quasi-government Entities)
This Part to be completed in the case of all types of transactions covered by items 1 through 4 above.

52. Were any specific State or local government incentives or related services (such as those detailed in items 54 through 59 below) received in connection with this investment transaction?   5137 1 ☐ Yes 2 ☒ No

53. If the answer to item 52 is "Yes," were these incentives or services a significant factor in the decision to invest in (Mark as many categories as are applicable):

The United States as a whole?	5138	1 ☐ Yes	2 ☐ No
A region within the United States?	5139	1 ☐ Yes	2 ☐ No
A given State or local area?	5140	1 ☐ Yes	2 ☐ No

If the answer to item 52 is "Yes," indicate the category(ies) which most clearly describe the relevant State or local incentives or services and give, as accurately as possible for items 54 and 55, the monetary "value" of the incentives or services. The categories are not limited to the examples given. Mark as many categories as are applicable.	Applicable (1)	If Yes, value (2) (Thousands of Dollars)
54. Taxation – Such as investment tax credit; tax exemption; and tax reduction or holidays. If yes is marked, give estimate of average annual value of the tax savings over the first five years of the investment. 5141	1 ☐ Yes 2 ☐ No	$ _____
55. Financing programs – Such as industrial revenue bonds; direct loans or loan guarantees; and credits from development credit corporations. If yes is marked, give estimate of annual cost savings in relation to financing available at commercial rates over the life of the financing provided. 5142	1 ☐ Yes 2 ☐ No	$ _____
56. Labor programs – Such as recruiting programs; training programs; and State-financed relocation services 5143	1 ☐ Yes 2 ☐ No	
57. Information services – Such as State-funded site studies, area research, and feasibility studies; State university R&D assistance, and local marketing data 5144	1 ☐ Yes 2 ☐ No	
58. Special services – Such as State-funded road building or other services relating to construction or operation, and locally-owned industrial park sites 5145	1 ☐ Yes 2 ☐ No	
59. Other incentives or services – Describe 5146	1 ☐ Yes 2 ☐ No	

60. State, or State of location of local government unit, from which the incentives or services were received. (If more than one, enter all States from which received.)

	BEA USE
_____ 5147	
_____ 5148	
_____ 5149	

Form BE-13A, Page 4

OMB No. 0608-0035. Approval Expires March 198_

FORM BE-13B
(REV. 2-81)

U.S. DEPARTMENT OF COMMERCE
BUREAU OF ECONOMIC ANALYSIS

FORM FOR FOREIGN PERSON, OR EXISTING U.S. AFFILIATE OF A FOREIGN PERSON, THAT ESTABLISHES OR ACQUIRES A U.S. BUSINESS ENTERPRISE, OR A BUSINESS SEGMENT OR OPERATING UNIT OF A U.S. BUSINESS ENTERPRISE

MANDATORY — CONFIDENTIAL

CONTROL NO.

Response to this inquiry is required by law. By the same law your report to this Bureau is CONFIDENTIAL. It may be used only for analytical and statistical purposes and CANNOT be used for purposes of taxation, investigation, or regulation. The law also provides that copies retained in your files are immune from legal process.

This report is being completed for or by (mark one):

1. 01 1 [ ] The foreign parent that directly established or acquired the new U.S. affiliate.

2. 2 [X] The existing U.S. affiliate of a foreign person that established a new U.S. affiliate or acquired a direct voting interest in a U.S. business enterprise of such a magnitude that the established or acquired enterprise becomes a new U.S. affiliate of the existing U.S. affiliate's foreign parent

3. 3 [ ] The existing U.S. affiliate of a foreign person that acquired a U.S. business enterprise, or business segment or operating unit of a U.S. business enterprise, and merged it into its own operations

Reporting on this form should be as follows (see Section I of Instructions for definition of U.S. affiliate):

a) by a foreign person (hereinafter, the "foreign parent") when it establishes or acquires a direct voting interest in a U.S. business enterprise that becomes its U.S. affiliate (hereinafter, the "new U.S. affiliate"), or by the new U.S. affiliate for the foreign parent to the extent it has or can secure the information; or

b) by an existing U.S. affiliate of a foreign person (hereinafter, the "existing U.S. affiliate") when it establishes or acquires a direct voting interest in a U.S. business enterprise of such a magnitude that the established or acquired enterprise becomes a U.S. affiliate of the foreign person, i.e., the foreign person thereby acquires an indirect (or direct and indirect) voting interest of 10 percent or more in the established or acquired U.S. business enterprise (hereinafter, the "new U.S. affiliate") — see Section II.F. of Instructions for method for calculating indirect ownership; or

c) by an existing U.S. affiliate of a foreign person (hereinafter, the "existing U.S. affiliate") when it acquires a U.S. business enterprise, or a business segment or operating unit of a U.S. business enterprise, and merges it into its own operations.

A separate Form BE-13B must be completed by or for each foreign parent, or by each existing U.S. affiliate, that has secured a direct voting interest in a new U.S. affiliate.

RETURN REPORTS TO U.S. Department of Commerce Bureau of Economic Analysis BE-50 (IN) Washington, D.C. 20230

NOTE: A single original copy of the form is to be filed with the Bureau of Economic Analysis. To facilitate processing, it is preferred that the BE-13A and the BE-13B forms be filed together, or simultaneously. File copies should be retained for 3 years after the date on which the form is due.

Important *Read instructions before completing form.*

■ 1. EXEMPTION: The foreign parent or existing U.S. affiliate is exempt from filing a BE-13B if a BE-13A is not required to be filed.

■ 2. EFFECTIVE DATE: A report on this revised form is required for each covered direct investment transaction occurring on or after January 1, 1981.

■ 3. ASSISTANCE — Telephone (202) 523-0547.

■ 4. DUE DATE: Form BE-13B is due no later than 45 days after the direct investment transaction occurs.

■ 5. GENERAL NOTES:
A. Figures such as the number of voting shares held should be reported to the nearest whole unit.

B. Currency amounts should be reported in U.S. dollars rounded to thousands (omitting 000). Do not enter amounts in the shaded portions of each line.
EXAMPLE: If amount is $1,334,615.00, report as:

Bil.	Mil.	Thous.	Dois.
		1,335	

C. If an item is between + or − $500.00 enter "0".
D. Use parentheses to indicate negative numbers.

MANDATORY — This survey is being conducted pursuant to the International Investment Survey Act of 1976 (Pub. L. 94–472, 90 Stat. 2059, 22 U.S.C. 3101 to 3108 — hereinafter "the Act"), and the filing of reports is mandatory pursuant to Section 5(b)(2) of the Act (22 U.S.C. 3104).

PENALTIES — Whoever fails to report may be subject to a civil penalty not exceeding $10,000 and to injunctive relief commanding such person to comply, or both. Whoever willfully fails to report shall be fined not more than $10,000 and, if an individual, may be imprisoned for not more than one year, or both. Any officer, director, employee, or agent of any corporation who knowingly participates in such violations, upon conviction, may be punished by a like fine, imprisonment or both. (See Section 6 of the Act, 22 U.S.C. 3105.)

CONFIDENTIALITY — The information filed in this report may be used only for analytical and statistical purposes and access to the information shall be available only to officials and employees (including consultants and contractors and their employees) of agencies designated by the President to perform functions under the Act. The President may authorize the exchange of information between agencies or officials designated to perform functions under the Act, but only for analytical and statistical purposes. No official or employee (including consultants and contractors and their employees) shall publish or make available any information collected under the Act in such a manner that the person to whom the information relates can be specifically identified. Reports and copies of reports prepared pursuant to the Act are confidential and their submission or disclosure shall not be compelled by any person without the prior written permission of the person filing the report and the customer of such person where the information supplied is identifiable as being derived from the records of such customer (22 U.S.C. 3104).

4. Name and address of either the foreign parent (including country) or existing U.S. affiliate by, or for whom, the report is being completed

02 Name: `Cal Corp`

03 Street or P.O. box: `address`

04 City and State: `Los Angeles CA` ZIP Code

05 Country: `USA`

06 BEA USE ONLY

5a. If item 2 or 3 is marked, give the name and country of the foreign parent holding the direct, or indirect, ownership interest in the existing U.S. affiliate named in item 4. If more than one foreign parent, furnish, on a separate sheet, the information requested in items 5a and b and 6a through f for each additional foreign parent.

07 Name:

08 Country:

b. If item 2 or 3 is marked and if the existing U.S. affiliate named in item 4 is not directly owned by the foreign parent, give name and address of U.S. affiliate that is directly owned by the foreign parent and the percent of ownership by the foreign parent.

09 Name: `Foreign Corp`

10 Address: `Address` PERCENT

11

6a. Industry code of foreign parent named in either item 4 or item 5a*

12 `6 05` ← Industry code

b. Is the foreign parent named in either item 4 or item 5a the ultimate beneficial owner (UBO)? (See definition of UBO)

13 1 [ ] Yes
2 [X] No If the answer to item 6b is "NO," complete items c, d, e, and f.

c. Is the UBO an individual?

14 1 [X] Yes If the answer to item 6c is "YES," then the name of the individual need not be given in item 6d, but the country of residence of the individual must be given in item 6e.
2 [ ] No

d. Name of UBO:

15

e. Country of UBO named in item 6d:

16 `Country`

f. Industry code of UBO named in item 6d*:

17 ← Industry code

NOTE: Failure to complete items 6a through 6f, to the extent required by the line instructions, will constitute an incomplete report, which will be returned to the reporter for completion.

* For items 6a and 6f, secure foreign parent and UBO industry codes from page 2 of Form BE-607, which accompanies this BE-13 report.

BEA USE ONLY
18

7. If 1 or 2 was marked, give name and address of the new U.S. affiliate as it appears in item 5 of the BE-13A.

19 Name of new U.S. affiliate: `Cal Corp Real Estate`

20 Street or P.O. box: `property address`

21 City and State: `Los Angeles Ca.` ZIP Code

BEA USE ONLY
22

Print name and address

PERSON TO CONSULT CONCERNING QUESTIONS ABOUT THIS REPORT

Cal Corp.-Real Estate
c/o Preparer and/or corporate officer

U.S. TELEPHONE NUMBER
Area Code | Number | Extension

▶ CERTIFICATION The undersigned official certifies that the information contained in this report is correct and complete to the best of his/her knowledge.

Authorized Official's Signature | Title | Date

Form BE-13B, Page I

8. *If it was merged, will data for the new U.S. affiliate be fully consolidated with that of the existing or another U.S. affiliate in other international investment reports filed with this Bureau?*

23 1 [X] Yes
    2 [ ] No.

If yes, give name under which consolidated report will be filed if it is not the name given in item 4.

(It must be consolidated if the ownership is more than 50 percent except that separate reports may be filed where the new U.S. affiliate will not normally be fully consolidated due to unrelated operations, in accordance with generally accepted accounting principles, or lack of control, provided written permission has been requested from and granted by BEA.)

For ownership interests in a U.S. business enterprise previously held by the foreign parent, or existing U.S. affiliate, but where the percentage ownership was insufficient to qualify the U.S. business enterprise as a U.S. affiliate *(see definition in Section I of the Instructions)* of the foreign parent, complete items 9 through 12 if the enterprise was incorporated, or complete only item 12 if the enterprise was unincorporated.

Enter data relating to previously held partial interest:

			Number
9.	Number of voting shares held	24	

			Amount Bil. Mil. Thous. Dols
10.	Cost of voting shares held	25	
11.	Cost of other equity interest	26	
12.	Total cost of investment (item 10 plus item 11)	27	

For new ownership interests in a U.S. business enterprise that was incorporated prior to its acquisition, indicate how the new ownership interests were acquired (complete as appropriate):	Voting interest			Other equity interest (4)	Total cost of investment (Col. 3 + Col. 4) (5)
	Number of shares acquired (1) Number	Average price per share (2) Dollars and cents	Total cost (3) Bil. Mil. Thous. Dols.	Bil. Mil. Thous. Dols.	Bil. Mil. Thous. Dols.
13. On open market without a tender offer 28		$	$	$	$
14. By a tender offer 29					$
15. Directly from the new U.S. affiliate 30					$
16. For foreign parent only: From another of your U.S. affiliates 31					$
17. For existing U.S. affiliate only: From another U.S. affiliate of your foreign parent 32					
18. Directly from other U.S. persons 33					$
19. Directly from other foreign persons 34					$
20. Other – *Specify* 35					
21. Total – Sum of items 13 through 20 36		$		$	$

			Bil. Mil. Thous. Dols.
22. For all new ownership interests other than those reported in items 13 through 21, enter total cost of new investment	37	$	1,600

			MONTH	DAY	YEAR
23. Date on which the foreign person established or acquired directly, or indirectly through an existing U.S. affiliate, a 10 percent or more voting interest in the new U.S. affiliate.	38		10	01	81

Sources of financing of the total cost of investment as shown in either item 21, col. 5, or item 22. (Funds that the investor borrowed specifically to finance the investment are to be included in the appropriate category of "borrowed" funds. Funds from other sources should be included in the appropriate category. Commingled funds that cannot be assigned to one category, or for which a reasonable allocation cannot be made, should be shown in "other.") Where the BE-13B is completed for an existing U.S. affiliate that is not directly foreign owned, the source of financing should be presented from the viewpoint of the consolidated U.S. affiliate as it normally reports on related direct investment forms.

			Amount Bil. Mil. Thous. Dols.
For foreign parent only:			
24. Funds from your other U.S. affiliates	39	$	
For existing U.S. affiliate only:			
25. Funds from your foreign parent or other members of the affiliated foreign group	40		200
26. Funds from other U.S. affiliates of your foreign parent	41		200
For foreign parent or existing U.S. affiliate:			
27. Your internally generated funds – For foreign parent, also include funds secured from other members of the affiliated foreign group	42		
Incurrence of debt to sellers of ownership interests:			
28. U.S. sellers	43		1200
29. Foreign sellers	44		
30. Your borrowings from other unaffiliated U.S. sources	45		
31. Your borrowings from other unaffiliated foreign sources	46		
Exchange of your shares for shares of the acquired U.S. business enterprise that were given in exchange to:			
32. U.S. persons (give number _____) $ value _____ →	47		
33. Foreign persons (give number _____) $ value _____ →	48		
34. Other funds from U.S. sources – *Specify*	49		
35. Other funds from foreign sources – *Specify*	50		
36. Total – Sum of items 24 through 35	51	$	1,600
37. If an entry was made in item 25, give amount of those funds that were borrowed by your foreign parent or other members of the affiliated foreign group from unaffiliated U.S. sources	52	$	0
38. If an entry was made in item 26, give amount of those funds that were borrowed by the other U.S. affiliates of your foreign parent from unaffiliated U.S. sources	53	$	0

Form BE-13B, Page 2

OMB No. 0608-0030, Approval Expires March 1931

FORM BE-607 (REV. 3-81) U.S. DEPARTMENT OF COMMERCE BUREAU OF ECONOMIC ANALYSIS	**I. IDENTIFICATION**

INDUSTRY CLASSIFICATION QUESTIONNAIRE

MANDATORY
CONFIDENTIAL REPORT

This report is required by law — Section 5(b)(2), P.L. 94–472, 90 Stat. 2059, 22 U.S.C. 3104. Whoever fails to report may be subject to a civil penalty not exceeding $10,000 and to injunctive relief commanding such person to comply, or both. Whoever willfully fails to report shall be fined not more than $10,000 and, if an individual, may be imprisoned for not more than one year or both.

RETURN TO
U.S. Department of Commerce
Bureau of Economic Analysis, BE-50 (IN)
Washington, D.C. 20230

IMPORTANT – Read instructions on reverse side before completing this form.

1. Name and address of U.S. affiliate

Cal Corp- Real Estate
Property Address
Los Angeles, CA

2. Name of foreign parent holding either direct interest, or indirect interest through another U.S. affiliate, in the U.S. affiliate named in item 1.

Foreign Corp

3. Country of location of foreign parent named in 2.

foreign country

4. Industry classification of foreign parent named in item 2. Determine code from list at bottom of page 2 and enter here:

650 ◄—— Code

5. This report represents: *(Mark one)*

a. [X] The initial filing by the U.S. affiliate

b. [ ] A change in the 3-digit DI industry classification of this U.S. affiliate

6. If this report represents a change in industry classification of the U.S. affiliate, enter the period during which change took place.

MONTH	YEAR
	N/A

II. U.S. AFFILIATE INDUSTRY CLASSIFICATION – If for an incorporated U.S. affiliate, this Part is to be completed from the viewpoint of the consolidated entity.

1. Activity and product or service of the U.S. affiliate

a. Major activity of this U.S. affiliate *(Mark "X" one)*

[ ] Extracting of oil or minerals (including exploration and development)

[ ] Manufacturing (fabricating, assembling, processing)

[ ] Selling or distributing goods

[X] Real estate (investing in, or engaging in as an operator, manager, developer, lessor, agent, or broker)

[ ] Providing a service

[ ] Other – *Specify*

b. Major product or service involved in this activity: If a product, also state what is done to it; i.e., whether it is mined, manufactured, sold a wholesale, transported, packaged, etc.

investment-commercial property

B. In the area to the right, enter the appropriate 3-digit industry code(s) and the percent, to the nearest tenth of one percent, of sales associated with each code. The sales figures should be representative of the affiliate's most recent annual sales or gross operating revenue figures (excluding sales taxes). If you use fewer than eight codes you must account for one hundred percent of sales. In the case of a new or non-operating affiliate, show the projected breakdown of sales.

Line No.	DI code	Percent of sales (to tenth of one percent)
1	650	100 %
2		. %
3		. %
4		. %
5		. %
6		. %
7		. %
8		. %
		BEA USE ONLY
Total percentage accounted for 9		. %

SUMMARY OF DIRECT INVESTMENT (DI) INDUSTRY CLASSIFICATIONS

AGRICULTURE, FORESTRY, AND FISHING

010	Agricultural production — crops
020	Agricultural production — livestock, except beef cattle feedlots
021	Agricultural production — beef cattle feedlots
070	Agricultural services
080	Forestry
090	Fishing, hunting, and trapping

MINING

101	Iron ores
102	Copper, lead, zinc, gold, and silver ores
103	Bauxite and other aluminum ores
109	Other metallic ores and metal mining services
120	Coal
133	Crude petroleum extraction (no refining) and natural gas
138	Oil and gas field services
140	Nonmetallic minerals, except fuels

CONSTRUCTION

150	Construction

MANUFACTURING

201	Meat products
202	Dairy products
203	Preserved fruits and vegetables
204	Grain mill products
205	Bakery products
206	Beverages
209	Other food and kindred products
210	Tobacco manufactures
220	Textile mill products
230	Apparel and other textile products
240	Lumber and wood products
250	Furniture and fixtures
262	Pulp, paper, and board mills
264	Miscellaneous converted paper products
265	Paperboard containers and boxes
270	Printing and publishing
281	Industrial chemicals and synthetics
283	Drugs
284	Soap, cleaners, and toilet goods
285	Paints and allied products
287	Agricultural chemicals
289	Chemical products, nec
291	Integrated petroleum refining and extraction
292	Petroleum refining without extraction
299	Petroleum and coal products, nec
305	Rubber products
307	Miscellaneous plastics products
310	Leather and leather products
321	Glass products

MANUFACTURING — Continued

329	Stone, clay, concrete gypsum, and other nonmetallic mineral products
331	Primary metal industries, ferrous
335	Primary metal industries, non-ferrous
341	Metal cans and shipping containers
342	Cutlery, hand tools, and hardware
343	Metal plumbing fixtures and heating equipment, except electric
344	Fabricated structural metal products
345	Screw machine products, bolts, etc.
346	Metal forgings and stampings
349	Fabricated metal products, nec; ordnance; and metal services
351	Engines and turbines
352	Farm and garden machinery
353	Construction, mining, and materials handling machinery
354	Metalworking machinery
355	Special industry machinery
356	General industrial machinery
357	Office and computing machines
358	Refrigeration and service industry machinery
359	Machinery, except electrical, nec
363	Household appliances
364	Electric lighting and wiring equipment
366	Radio, television, and communication equipment
367	Electronic components and accessories
369	Electrical machinery, nec
371	Motor vehicles and equipment
379	Other transportation equipment
381	Scientific and measuring instruments
383	Optical and ophthalmic goods
384	Medical instruments and supplies
386	Photographic equipment and supplies
387	Watches, clocks, and watchcases
390	Miscellaneous manufacturing industries, nec

TRANSPORTATION, COMMUNICATION AND PUBLIC UTILITIES

401	Railroads
441	Petroleum tanker operations
449	Other water transportation
450	Transportation by air
461	Pipe lines, petroleum and natural gas
462	Pipe lines, except petroleum and natural gas
470	Petroleum storage for hire
478	Transportation, nec, warehousing, terminal facilities, travel agents, and related services
480	Communication
490	Electric, gas, and sanitary services

WHOLESALE TRADE

501	Motor vehicles and equipment
503	Lumber and construction materials
504	Farm and garden machinery and equipment
505	Metals and minerals, except petroleum
506	Electrical goods
507	Hardware, plumbing and heating equipment and supplies
508	Other machinery, equipment, and supplies
509	Durable goods, nec
511	Paper and paper products
512	Drugs, proprietaries, and sundries
513	Apparel, piece goods, and notions
514	Groceries and related products
515	Farm-product raw materials
517	Petroleum and petroleum products
519	Nondurable goods, nec

RETAIL TRADE

540	Food stores and eating and drinking places
554	Gasoline service stations
590	Retail trade, nec

FINANCE, INSURANCE, AND REAL ESTATE

600	Banking
610	Finance, except banking
630	Insurance
649	Lessors of agricultural and forestry real estate
650	Real estate, nec
671	Holding companies

SERVICES

700	Hotels and other lodging places
731	Advertising
732	Business services, nec
780	Motion pictures, including television tape and film
891	Engineering, architectural, and surveying services
893	Accounting, auditing, and bookkeeping services
898	Services, nec, provided on a commercial basis

NONBUSINESS ENTITIES

900	Government entities
905	Nonbusiness entities, except Government

NOTE: nec means not elsewhere classified.

Page 1

OMB No. 0608–0030; Approval Expires March 1981

FORM BE-407 (REV. 3-81)	U.S. DEPARTMENT OF COMMERCE BUREAU OF ECONOMIC ANALYSIS

I. IDENTIFICATION

INDUSTRY CLASSIFICATION QUESTIONNAIRE

MANDATORY
CONFIDENTIAL REPORT

This report is required by law — Section 5(b)(2), P.L. 94–472, 90 Stat. 2059, 22 U.S.C. 3104. Whoever fails to report may be subject to a civil penalty not exceeding $10,000 and to injunctive relief commanding such person to comply, or both. Whoever willfully fails to report shall be fined not more than $10,000 and, if an individual, may be imprisoned for not more than one year or both.

RETURN TO
U.S. Department of Commerce
Bureau of Economic Analysis, BE-50 (IN)
Washington, D.C. 20230

IMPORTANT — Read instructions on reverse side before completing this form.

1. Name and address of U.S. affiliate

CAL CORP.
address

2. Name of foreign parent holding either direct interest, or indirect interest through another U.S. affiliate, in the U.S. affiliate named in item 1.

Foreign Corp.

3. Country of location of foreign parent named in 2.

foreign country

4. Industry classification of foreign parent named in item 2. Determine code from list at bottom of page 2 and enter here:

650 ◄— Code

5. This report represents: *(Mark one)*

a. ☒ The initial filing by the U.S. affiliate

b. ☐ A change in the 3-digit DI industry classification of this U.S. affiliate

6. If this report represents a change in industry classification of the U.S. affiliate, enter the period during which change took place.

MONTH	YEAR	
		N/A

II. U.S. AFFILIATE INDUSTRY CLASSIFICATION — If for an incorporated U.S. affiliate, this Part is to be completed from the viewpoint of the consolidated entity.

7. Activity and product or service of the U.S. affiliate

a. Major activity of this U.S. affiliate *(Mark "X" one)*

☐ Extracting of oil or minerals (including exploration and development)

☐ Manufacturing (fabricating, assembling, processing)

☐ Selling or distributing goods

☒ Real estate (investing in, or engaging in as an operator, manager, developer, lessor, agent, or broker)

☐ Providing a service

☐ Other – *Specify*

b. Major product or service involved in this activity: if a product, also state what is done to it; i.e., whether it is mined, manufactured, sold a wholesale, transported, packaged, etc.

investment-commercial property

8. In the area to the right, enter the appropriate 3-digit industry code(s) and the percent, to the nearest tenth of one percent, of sales associated with each code. The sales figures should be representative of the affiliate's most recent annual sales or gross operating revenue figures (excluding sales taxes). See the list of industry codes below. If you use fewer than eight codes you must account for one hundred percent of sales. In the case of a new or non-operating affiliate, show the projected breakdown of sales.

Line No.	DI code	Percent of sales (to tenth of one percent)
1	650	100 . %
2		. %
3		. %
4		. %
5		. %
6		. %
7		. %
8		. %
Total percentage accounted for 9	BEA USE ONLY	. %

SUMMARY OF DIRECT INVESTMENT (DI) INDUSTRY CLASSIFICATIONS

AGRICULTURE, FORESTRY, AND FISHING

010	Agricultural production — crops
020	Agricultural production — livestock, except beef cattle feedlots
021	Agricultural production — beef cattle feedlots
070	Agricultural services
080	Forestry
090	Fishing, hunting, and trapping

MINING

101	Iron ores
102	Copper, lead, zinc, gold, and silver ores
103	Bauxite and other aluminum ores
109	Other metallic ores and metal mining services
120	Coal
133	Crude petroleum extraction (no refining) and natural gas
138	Oil and gas field services
140	Nonmetallic minerals, except fuels

CONSTRUCTION

150	Construction

MANUFACTURING

201	Meat products
202	Dairy products
203	Preserved fruits and vegetables
204	Grain mill products
205	Bakery products
206	Beverages
209	Other food and kindred products
210	Tobacco manufactures
220	Textile mill products
230	Apparel and other textile products
240	Lumber and wood products
250	Furniture and fixtures
262	Pulp, paper, and board mills
264	Miscellaneous converted paper products
265	Paperboard containers and boxes
270	Printing and publishing
281	Industrial chemicals and synthetics
283	Drugs
284	Soap, cleaners, and toilet goods
285	Paints and allied products
287	Agricultural chemicals
289	Chemical products, nec
291	Integrated petroleum refining and extraction
292	Petroleum refining without extraction
299	Petroleum and coal products, nec
305	Rubber products
307	Miscellaneous plastics products
310	Leather and leather products
321	Glass products

MANUFACTURING — Continued

329	Stone, clay, concrete gypsum, and other nonmetallic mineral products
331	Primary metal industries, ferrous
335	Primary metal industries, non-ferrous
341	Metal cans and shipping containers
342	Cutlery, hand tools, and hardware
343	Metal plumbing fixtures and heating equipment, except electric
344	Fabricated structural metal products
345	Screw machine products, bolts, etc.
346	Metal forgings and stampings
349	Fabricated metal products, nec; ordnance; and metal services
351	Engines and turbines
352	Farm and garden machinery
353	Construction, mining, and materials handling machinery
354	Metalworking machinery
355	Special industry machinery
356	General industrial machinery
357	Office and computing machines
358	Refrigeration and service industry machinery
359	Machinery, except electrical, nec
363	Household appliances
364	Electric lighting and wiring equipment
366	Radio, television, and communication equipment
367	Electronic components and accessories
369	Electrical machinery, nec
371	Motor vehicles and equipment
379	Other transportation equipment
381	Scientific and measuring instruments
383	Optical and ophthalmic goods
384	Medical instruments and supplies
386	Photographic equipment and supplies
387	Watches, clocks, and watchcases
390	Miscellaneous manufacturing industries, nec

TRANSPORTATION, COMMUNICATION AND PUBLIC UTILITIES

401	Railroads
441	Petroleum tanker operations
449	Other water transportation
450	Transportation by air
461	Pipe lines, petroleum and natural gas
462	Pipe lines, except petroleum and natural gas
470	Petroleum storage for hire
478	Transportation, nec, warehousing, terminal facilities, travel agents, and related services
480	Communication
490	Electric, gas, and sanitary services

WHOLESALE TRADE

501	Motor vehicles and equipment
503	Lumber and construction materials
504	Farm and garden machinery and equipment
505	Metals and minerals, except petroleum
506	Electrical goods
507	Hardware, plumbing and heating equipment and supplies
508	Other machinery, equipment, and supplies
509	Durable goods, nec
511	Paper and paper products
512	Drugs, proprietaries, and sundries
513	Apparel, piece goods, and notions
514	Groceries and related products
515	Farm-product raw materials
517	Petroleum and petroleum products
519	Nondurable goods, nec

RETAIL TRADE

540	Food stores and eating and drinking places
554	Gasoline service stations
590	Retail trade, nec

FINANCE, INSURANCE, AND REAL ESTATE

600	Banking
610	Finance, except banking
630	Insurance
649	Lessors of agricultural and forestry real estate
650	Real estate, nec
671	Holding companies

SERVICES

700	Hotels and other lodging places
731	Advertising
732	Business services, nec
780	Motion pictures, including television tape and film
891	Engineering, architectural, and surveying services
893	Accounting, auditing, and bookkeeping services
898	Services, nec, provided on a commercial basis

NONBUSINESS ENTITIES

900	Government entities
905	Nonbusiness entities, except Government

NOTE: nec means not elsewhere classified.

Page 1

REPORTING REQUIREMENTS

Form Number	Title of Form	Who Must File	Exemptions
ASCS-153	Agricultural Foreign Investment Disclosure Act Report	A "foreign person" owning, acquiring or transfer-ring agricultural land. A "foreign person" includes a foreign individual, corporation or other entity, and also includes a U.S. corporation in which a significant interest is directly or indirectly held by a "foreign person".	Land held for personal use of under one acre where the agricultural products are produced for personal use. Leaseholds of under ten years; future interests, easements unrelated to agri-cultural production, and security interests in agricultural land are also exempt from reporting.

DUE DATE

90 days after date of acquisition or transfer; foreign persons holding an interest in agri-cultural land before February 2, 1979 were required to submit ASCS-153 by August 1, 1979.

PENALTY

Late reports will be assessed a penalty of one-tenth of one percent of the fair market value of the foreign person's interest in the reportable property, as determined by the ASCS for each week or portion thereof that the violation continues. However, the late filing penalty is not to exceed 25%.

OTHER CONSIDERATIONS

The information on this form is available for public inspection in the Washington, D.C. and the local Agricultural Stabilization and Conservation Service Office.

See Reiner. "The Agricultural Foreign Investment Disclosure Act and its Regulation", The Agri-cultural Law Journal, Winter 1981.

Instructions side

NOTE: P.L. 95-460 authorizes collection of the data on this form. The data will be used to determine the effects of foreign persons acquiring, transferring and holding agricultural land, and the effects of such activity on family farms and rural communities. Furnishing the data is mandatory. The data may be furnished to any Agency responsible for enforcing the provisions of the Act. Failure to comply or falsification of reporting is subject to civil penalty, not to exceed 25 percent of the fair market value of the interest held in the tract on the date of the assessment of such penalty.

IMPORTANT

DEFINITION: "Person" means any individual, corporation, company, association, firm, partnership, society, joint stock company, trust, estate, or any other legal entity.

You are a "foreign person" under the provisions of P.L. 95-460 and must complete the front side of this form (ASCS-153) if your answer to each of these three questions is "No":

	YES	NO
1. I AM a citizen of the United States		
2. I AM a citizen of the Northern Mariana Islands or the Trust Territories of the Pacific Islands.		
3. I AM lawfully admitted to the United States for permanent residence, or paroled into the United States, under the Immigration and Nationality Act.		

OR if your answer to any of these three questions is "Yes".

4. I AM a "person" other than an individual or government, which is created or organized under the laws of:
   a. A foreign government or which has its principal place of business located outside the United States.
   b. Any State of the United States, and in which any interest is held directly or indirectly, in that tract of agricultural land by any "foreign person".

5. I AM a foreign government.

INSTRUCTIONS

Complete this form in an original and three copies for each tract of land. Report as a tract all acreages under the same ownership in each county or parish. Land in different counties or parishes must be reported as separate tracts. Insertion of carbons is necessary.

Return the original and two copies to the Agricultural Stabilization and Conservation Service (ASCS) county office where the tract of land is located or administered. Retain the last copy (Foreign Person Copy) for your records.

After the original disclosure on ASCS-153 on the tract(s) of land owned by the same person within a county or parish, each subsequent change of ownership or use must be reported by filing another ASCS-153.

Item 1. ONLY ONE BOX MAY BE CHECKED. If the tract of land to be listed under item 2 was:
1. Owned on February 1, 1979, check A LAND HOLDING → [X] and return the completed form by August 2, 1979.

If the tract of land to be listed under item 2 was, on or after February 2, 1979:
2. Acquired, check B LAND ACQUISITION [X] ; or
3. Disposed of, check C LAND DISPOSITION [X] ; or
4. Changed from non-agricultural to agricultural use, check D LAND USE CHANGE TO AGRICULTURE [X] , or
5. Changed from agricultural to non-agricultural use, check E LAND USE CHANGE TO NON-AGRICULTURE [X] and return the completed form within ninety (90) days after the transaction.

Item 3E3c. If incorporated or formed in the United States as an independent, affiliate, or subsidiary company, show the State of incorporation or formation.
If the answers to 3E3 b and c are "United States" or any "state", list the name of all foreign persons who hold any interest in your organization and their address, citizenship of individual, country of government, and country of incorporation or principal place of business of organizations.

Item 8. This date would be as follows for activity checked in Item 1:
Box A and B - When acquired.
Box C - When disposed
Box D and E - When land use changed.

ADDITIONAL INFORMATION (Use additional sheets if more space is needed)

Front side (form)

ASCS-153 (1-12-79)
U.S. DEPARTMENT OF AGRICULTURE
Agricultural Stabilization and Conservation Service
AGRICULTURAL FOREIGN INVESTMENT DISCLOSURE ACT REPORT
NOTE: Read Instructions on Reverse Before Filling in Any Data Below. If Additional Space is Needed, Use Reverse.

Form Approved - OMB No. 40 R 4065

1. TYPE ACTIVITY (See reverse) (Check one)

A LAND HOLDING	B LAND ACQUISITION	C LAND DISPOSITION
D LAND USE CHANGE TO AGRICULTURE	E LAND USE CHANGE TO NON-AGRICULTURE	

ITEM	USE OFFICE ONLY	CHECK

2. Tract Location and Description
A. LEGAL DESCRIPTION OR ASCS TRACT NUMBER

6. Type of Interest Held by Foreign Person (Check one)
A. Fee Interest (ownership) Whole   WHAT %
B. Fee Interest (ownership) Partial
C. Life Estate
D. Trust Beneficiary
E. Option
F. Purchase Contract
G. Other (explain)

B. COUNTY OR PARISH   C. NO. ACRES
D. STATE

7. How was this Tract Acquired or Transferred?
A. Cash Transaction
B. Credit or Installment Transaction
C. Trade
D. Gift or Inheritance
E. Foreclosure
F. Other (explain)

E. F.P. TRACT ID (Office Use Only)
3. Foreign Person - Owner of Tract (in item 2A) (See Reverse)
A. NAME

7. Land Value, Including Improvements
A. Purchase Price of Land $

OR B. What is the estimated current value or if a land disposition, the selling price of the tract of land.

B. ID NO. (Nine digits)   CHECK IF NOT KNOWN [ ]

C. How much of purchase price in Item 7A remains to be paid

C. ADDRESS (Street, City, State/Province, Country)

8. Date of Acquisition or Transfer (see reverse)   MONTH   YEAR

D. Person Receiving This Tract. Complete ONLY if item 1C - Land Disposition - is checked.
1. NAME

9. Current Land Use (usual use: for idle, check "Other".) Report in Whole Numbers.
A. Crop (specify by acreage on reverse)   ACRES
B. Pasture
C. Forest or Timber
D. Other Agriculture
E. Other Non-Agriculture
F. Total (should equal 2C)

2. ADDRESS (Street, City, State/Province, Country)

10. Intended Use as of This Date (Check one)   CHECK
A. No Change
B. Other Agriculture
C. Other Non-Agriculture

E. Type of Owner (Check one)
1. Individual (including husband/wife)

3. CITIZENSHIP   U.S. [ ]   FOREIGN [ ]   UNKNOWN [ ]

11. Relationship of Foreign Owner to Producer
A. Producer is (check one):
1. Foreign owner
2. Manager
B. Rental agreement is (check one):
1. A crop share
2. Cash or fixed rent

2. Government (name of country)

3. Organization (list on the reverse the name, address and country of all other foreign persons holding an interest in this tract).

a. Type
1) Corporation
2) Partnership
3) Estate
4) Trust
5) Institution
6) Association
7) Other

12. Is the Producer on This Tract:
A. Same person as when the tract was acquired
B. A new person

b. Gov't. or country under whose law the organization is created
c. Principal place of business (for organization only) (see reverse)

4. Representative of Foreign Investor (completing form, if applicable)
A. NAME

B. ADDRESS (Street, State and Country)

C. TELEPHONE NO. (Area Code)

D. Relationship of Representative to Foreign Person
1. Attorney
2. Manager
3. Agent
4. Other (explain on reverse)

13. CERTIFICATION - I certify that the information entered above is complete and correct. I understand that falsification of reporting is subject to a civil penalty not to exceed 25% of the fair market value of the interest held in the tract of land.

SIGNATURE (Owner or legally authorized representative)   DATE

TITLE

ASCS-FOIA COPY

ASCS-153 (1-2-79)

U.S. DEPARTMENT OF AGRICULTURE
Agricultural Stabilization and Conservation Service

AGRICULTURAL FOREIGN INVESTMENT DISCLOSURE ACT REPORT

NOTE: Read Instructions on Reverse Before Filling In Any Data Below. If Additional Space Is Needed, Use Reverse.

Form Approved - OMB No. 40 R 4065

1. TYPE ACTIVITY (See reverse) (Check one)
A. LANDING → □ B. ACQUISITION ☒ C. LAND DISPOSITION □
D. LAND USE CHANGE TO AGRICULTURE □ E. LAND USE CHANGE TO NON-AGRICULTURE □

2. Tract Location and Description

A. LEGAL DESCRIPTION OR ASCS TRACT NUMBER

Sonoma County ASCA Tract A-152

B. COUNTY OR PARISH   Sonoma
D. California
C. NO. ACRES   200

E. F.P. TRACT ID (Office Use Only)

3. Foreign Person - Owner of Tract (in item 2A) (See Reverse)

A. NAME   Rein Co.

B. ID NO. (Nine digits)   15-449-7789   CHECK IF NO. NOT KNOWN □

C. ADDRESS (Street, City, State/Province, Country)
Amsterdam, Netherlands

D. Person Receiving This Tract. Complete ONLY if item 1C - Land Disposition - is checked.

1. NAME

2. ADDRESS (Street, City, State/Province, Country)

3. CITIZENSHIP   USA □   FOREIGN □   UNKNOWN □

E. Type of Owner (Check one)
1. Individual (including husband/wife)
   a. Citizenship of Individual
   2. Government (name of country)
   3. Organization (list on the reverse the name, address and country of all other foreign persons holding an interest in this tract).
      a. Type
         1) Corporation   X
         2) Partnership
         3) Estate
         4) Trust
         5) Institution
         6) Association
         7) Other
      b. Gov't or country under whose law the organization is created   Netherlands
      c. Principal place of business (for organizations only) (or reverse)   California, USA

4. Representative of Foreign Investor (completing form, if applicable)
A. NAME
B. ADDRESS (Street, State and Country)
One Main Street Tower
San Francisco, CA 94106
C. TELEPHONE NO. (Area Code)   (415) 111-1234

OFFICE USE ONLY

CHECK

ITEM	CHECK
5. Type of Interest Held by Foreign Person (Check one)	
A. Fee Interest (ownership) Whole	X
WHAT % B. Fee Interest (ownership) Partial	
C. Life Estate	
D. Trust Beneficiary	
E. Option	
F. Purchase Contract	
G. Other (explain)	
6. How was this Tract Acquired or Transferred?	
A. Cash Transaction	X
B. Credit or Installment Transaction	
C. Trade	
D. Gift or Inheritance	
E. Foreclosure	
F. Other (explain)	
7. Land Value, Including Improvements	
A. Purchase Price of Land	$ 1,000,000
OR B. Non-Purchase. Estimated Value at the Time of Acquisition	
What is the estimated current value or if a land disposition, the selling price of the tract of land.	1,000,000
C. How much of purchase price in Item 7A remains to be paid	500,000
8. Date of Acquisition or Transfer (see reverse) March 1980	
9. Current Land Use (usual use; for Idle, check "Other".) Report in Whole Number. ACRES	
A. Crop (specify by acreage on reverse)	
B. Pasture	200
C. Forest or Timber	
D. Other Agriculture	
E. Other Non-Agriculture	
F. Total (should equal 2C)	
10. Intended Use as of This Date (Check one) CHECK	
A. No Change	X
B. Other Agriculture	
C. Other Non-Agriculture	
11. Relationship of Foreign Owner to Producer	
A. Producer is (check one)	
1. Foreign owner	
2. Manager	X
3. Tenant or sharecropper	
B. Rental agreement is (check one)	
1. A crop share	
2. Cash or fixed rent	
12. Is the Producer on This Tract: CHECK	
A. Same person as when the tract was acquired	X
B. A new person	

13. CERTIFICATION - I certify that the information entered above is complete and correct. I understand that falsification of reporting is subject to civil penalty not to exceed 25% of the fair market value of the interest held in the tract of land.

SIGNATURE (Owner or legally authorized representative)   DATE

TITLE

ASCS-FOIA COPY

Rein Co. is an agricultural corporation owning 200 acres of farm land and is incorporated under the laws of the Netherlands. Its stock is in bearer form and is held by Jac Co., a Cayman corporation. The stock of Jac Co. is held by See Co., a Bahamian corporation. Rein Co. is a foreign person as defined by AFIDA and will be required to file a report on Form ASCS 153. Further, since Jac Co. is a legal entity other than an individual or foreign government, Rein Co. would be required to disclose certain information about Jac Co. Then after this information has been reviewed, the Secretary may make an official departmental request to require Jac Co. (since Jac Co.'s name was contained in the initial report) to submit an additional report for each person who holds an interest in Jac Co, thus disclosing See Co., the third-tier interest. However, the Secretary would not require disclosure beyond the third tier of ownership.

Appendix 4: Introduction to taxation of offshore companies in the Netherlands Antilles
including copies of treaties with the Netherlands and the Netherlands Antilles and related forms

---

Curaçao, June 1977.

Dear Reader,

Curaçao International Trust Company N.V. takes pleasure in presenting to you this booklet covering most aspects of operating an "offshore" company in the Netherlands Antilles. Should you have any queries in respect of its contents or subjects not dealt with, please contact us and we shall gladly answer your questions.

We have prepared this survey for your general information with respect to the tax situation in the Netherlands Antilles. Although every attempt has been made to be as accurate and reliable as possible, we suggest that you contact us before taking action on the basis of this booklet.

Sincerely yours,

CURAÇAO INTERNATIONAL TRUST COMPANY N.V.

- 1 -
(-2 - is blank)

NOTE P.L. 95-460 *authorizes collection of the data on this form. The data will be used to determine the effects of foreign persons acquiring, transferring and holding agricultural land, and the effects of such activity on family farms and rural communities. Furnishing the data is mandatory. The data may be furnished to any Agency responsible for enforcing the provisions of the Act. Failure to comply or falsification of reporting is subject to civil penalty, not to exceed 25 percent of the fair market value of the interest held in the tract on the date of the assessment of such penalty.*

IMPORTANT

DEFINITION: "Person" means any individual, corporation, company, association, firm, partnership, society, joint stock company, trust, estate, or any other legal entity.

You are a "foreign person" under the provisions of P.L. 95-460 and must complete the front side of this form (ASCS-153) if your answer to each of these three questions is "No".

	YES	NO
1. I AM a citizen of the United States		X
2. I AM a citizen of the Northern Mariana Islands or the Trust Territories of the Pacific Islands.		X
3. I AM lawfully admitted to the United States for permanent residence, or paroled into the United States, under the Immigration and Nationality Act.		X

OR if your answer to any of these three questions is "Yes".

	YES	NO
4. I AM a "person" other than an individual or government, which is created or organized under the laws of:		
a. A foreign government or which has its principal place of business located outside the United States.	X	
b. Any State of the United States, and in which any interest is held directly or indirectly, in that tract of agricultural land by any "foreign person".		X
5. I AM a foreign government.		X

INSTRUCTIONS

Complete this form in an original and three copies for each tract of land. Report as a tract all acreage under the same ownership in each county or parish. Land in different counties or parishes must be reported as separate tracts. Insertion of carbons is necessary.

Return the original and two copies to the Agricultural Stabilization and Conservation Service (ASCS) county office where the tract of land is located or administered. Retain the last copy (Foreign Person Copy) for your records.

After the original disclosure on ASCS-153 on the tract(s) of land owned by the same person within a county or parish, each subsequent change of ownership or use must be reported by filing another ASCS-153.

Item 1. ONLY ONE BOX MAY BE CHECKED. If the tract of land to be listed under item 2 was:

1. Owned on February 1, 1979, check A LAND HOLDING [X] and return the completed form by August 2, 1979.

If the tract of land to be listed under item 2 was, on or after February 2, 1979:

2. Acquired, check B LAND ACQUISITION [X] ; or
3. Disposed of, check C LAND DISPOSITION [X] ; or
4. Changed from non-agricultural to agricultural use, check D LAND USE CHANGE TO AGRICULTURE [X] ; or
5. Changed from agricultural to non-agricultural use, check E LAND USE CHANGE TO NON-AGRICULTURE [X]

and return the completed form within ninety (90) days after the transaction.

Item 3E3c. If incorporated or formed in the United States as an independent, affiliate, or subsidiary company, show the State of incorporation or formation.
If the answers to 3E3 b and c are "United States" or any "state", list the name of all foreign persons who hold any interest in your organization and their address, citizenship of individual, country of government, and country of incorporation or principal place of business or organizations.

Item 8. This date would be as follows for activity checked in Item 1:
Box A and B - When acquired.
Box C - When disposed of.
Box D and E - When land use changed.

ADDITIONAL INFORMATION (Use additional sheets if more space is needed)
INFORMATION REQUESTED BY QUESTION E(3) AND 7CFR 781.3(f)(1).

Name and Address   NATURE OF ENTITY
Hac. Co.   Corporation
P.O. Box 280
Grand Cayman   COUNTRY OF INCORPORATION & PRINCIPAL PLACE
British West Indies   OF BUSINESS
                     Grand Cayman, B.W.I.

A: CONTENTS:

B: LIST OF ABBREVIATIONS:

N.A. = Netherlands Antilles

Prot. = Protocol extending with modifications the Netherlands-U.S. tax treaty to the Netherlands Antilles, 1955, as amended.

P.T.O. = The National Profit Tax Ordinance of the Netherlands Antilles, 1940, as amended.

Treaty = Income Tax Convention between the Netherlands and the U.S., 1948, as amended.

U.K. = United Kingdom of Great Britain and Northern Ireland.

U.S. = United States of America.

C: THE NETHERLANDS ANTILLES:
SIX ISLANDS IN THE CARIBBEAN

The Netherlands Antilles are a group of six islands in the Caribbean Sea, consisting of the Leeward Islands (Curaçao, Aruba, Bonaire), not far from the coast of Venezuela, and the Windward Islands (St. Martin, St. Eustatius and Saba), about 100 miles east of Puerto Rico.

The Netherlands Antilles are a member of the Kingdom of the Netherlands and have internal autonomy. The form of government is democratic.

The climate in all six islands is tropical, but the nearly always blowing tradewinds cause an average daytime temperature of roughly 80° with little seasonal fluctuation.

The principal island of the group is Curaçao, situated approximately 20 miles north of the coast of Venezuela. It houses nearly two-thirds of the total population of the Netherlands Antilles of 230,000 inhabitants, and is also by far the largest island. Willemstad in Curaçao is the capital of the Netherlands Antilles accommodating the government, parliament and ministries.

The main sources of income of Curaçao are the huge oil refineries of the Royal Dutch/Shell, the harbour activities, the tourist trade. Curaçao further boasts the largest commercial dry-dock in the western hemisphere. The per capita income is high for the area.

There are excellent cable, telex and telephone connections between Curaçao and the rest of the world; daily flights connect the island with the U.S.A., South America and Europe. A number of international banks and reputable accounting firms have set up branches in Curaçao offering a variety of banking and accounting services.

Partly because of these high service standards, partly because of the special tax provisions and the various tax treaties, quite a large number of offshore investment, holding, finance, royalty and real estate companies have been established in the Netherlands Antilles, and especially on Curaçao. They provide an important source of tax income to the islands. There are several trust offices which have specialized in rendering services to such companies in respect of incorporation, bookkeeping, providing the registered office, filing tax returns, legal and tax advice, etc.

D: INCORPORATING A
NETHERLANDS ANTILLES COMPANY

1. Introduction

The Netherlands Antilles tax laws establish special low rates of 2.4% to 3% on net income (with capital gains tax free) for investment, holding, finance, royalty and copyrights, and real estate companies. This special tax treatment, together with the tax treaties concluded with the U.S.A., the

— 5 —

U.K. and the Netherlands, is the reason that the Netherlands Antilles have developed into a major offshore centre for investment, holding, finance and real estate purposes.

Except where we shall summarily discuss the shipping/airtransport and other special companies in the chapters J, K and L, we shall confine ourselves explicitly to the abovementioned companies. The standard tax rates of 31.05% and 39.1% applicable to companies doing trade or business within the Netherlands Antilles will therefore not be discussed.

The said low rates are laid down in the articles 14 and 14A of the Profit Tax Ordinance. Article 14 of this Ordinance defines the investment/holding/ finance companies as follows: Art. 14 P.T.O.

"a corporation......, which has the exclusive or almost exclusive purpose of investing its assets in securities, including shares and other certificates of participation and bonds, as well as other claims for interest bearing debts however denominated and in whatever form".

Article 14A of the Profit Tax Ordinance relates to the royalty/real estate companies, which it defines as follows: Art. 14A P.T.O.

"a corporation......, which exclusively or almost exclusively makes it its business to acquire:
a: revenues derived from the alienation or leasing of the right to use copyrights, patents, designs, secret processes or formulae, trademarks and other analogous property;
b: royalties, including rentals, in respect of motion picture films or for the use of industrial, commercial or scientific equipment, as well as to the operation of a mine or a quarry or of any other extraction of natural resources and other immovable properties;
c: considerations paid for technical assistance, received from outside the Netherlands Antilles".

The legal form most suited for the abovementioned purposes, and in practice the only one, is the "Naamloze Vennootschap", or abbreviated "N.V." This legal entity is the Dutch and Netherlands Antilles' equivalent of the U.S. Inc, the British Ltd., the German A.G. and the French, Spanish and South-American S.A.

Whenever the word Netherlands Antilles' company or corporation is used in this booklet it refers to the N.V.

2. Procedure

In order to incorporate a Netherlands Antilles company one has to go through several steps. First a draft Deed of Incorporation, containing the Company's articles of incorporation is prepared. This draft is then filed with the Minister of Justice to obtain his Declaration of No-objection to said articles, whereafter the actual incorporation is effected by at least two incorporators,* each subscribing for part of the capital of the company, appearing before a civil-law notary in the Netherlands Antilles, who then executes the original Deed of Incorporation. The company is in existence as of this moment. Thereafter the Deed of Incorporation must be published in the Official Gazette of the Netherlands Antilles.

* For practical purposes our trust company provides the services of incorporation through, Curaçao Corporation Company N.V., and Netherlands Antilles Corporation Company N.V., wholly owned subsidiaries of Curaçao International Trust Company N.V.

— 6 —

Each share of stock gives its owner the right to cast one vote. The articles of incorporation may however, within certain limits, provide that shares of a certain class give the right to cast more than one vote per share, and may also restrict the number of votes per shareholder. Non-voting stock is not permitted under Netherlands Antilles law.

Shares of stock rank equally for dividend and liquidation distributions, unless the articles of incorporation provide for cumulative or non-cumulative preferential shares.

6. Purposes of the company

The range of activities of the company is defined and limited by the purpose clause in the articles of incorporation. As said before, most offshore companies have a purpose clause that is covered by the articles 14 and 14A of the Profit Tax Ordinance of the Netherlands Antilles.

7. Name of the company

One is in principle free to choose the name of the company. The Department of Justice may however reject a certain name if same is indecent or misleading, or if a company with a similar name is already in existence.

8. Financial year

The articles of incorporation must specifically mention the company's financial year, which will also be its fiscal year. A change of the financial year can only be accomplished by amending the articles of incorporation.

9. Amendment of the articles of incorporation

The resolution to amend the articles of incorporation can only be taken by a general meeting of shareholders. The actual amendment is effectuated by a notarial deed along the same procedural lines as the deed of incorporation.

10. Registration and licenses

Every Netherlands Antilles company must be registered with the Commercial Register held by the local Chamber of Commerce; the registration includes the names and particulars of the company's managing directors, supervisory directors and general attorneys-in-fact (special attorneys-in-fact need not be registered). Further, a business license authorizing the company to do business should be obtained, and licenses for each of its managing directors authorizing him to act as such. Finally, a foreign exchange license should be obtained to exempt the company from foreign exchange control. All this is usually dealt with as a matter of routine.

In addition to the foreign exchange control exemption license finance companies need a special license to be issued by the Central Bank, authorizing such companies to engage in financing transactions. The Central Bank through these licenses maintains a control on the admittance of finance companies in the Netherlands Antilles.

E: MAINTAINING THE COMPANY

1. Annual tax-return

Every Netherlands Antilles company is required to file a tax-return with the Inspectorate of Taxes for each fiscal year, which need not be a calendar

— 8 —

3. Capital Requirements

There are no legal requirements in the Netherlands Antilles as to debt/equity ratio or minimum capitalization, and paid-in surplus is allowed. Consequently the authorized capital may be low in relation to the assets of the company. However, the Minister of Justice may refuse to issue his Declaration of No-objection to the Deed of Incorporation if he considers the authorized capital too low for the purposes of the company; in practice this means a minimum authorized capital of approximately US$ 10,000.— for investment and royalty companies, US$ 30,000.— for real estate companies, US$ 60,000.— for finance companies and US$ 600,000.— for offshore banks.

At least 20% of the authorized capital must be subscribed for at incorporation and must remain outstanding at all times.

Capital may be expressed in a foreign currency.

4. Management

Under Netherlands Antilles law a company is managed by a Board of Managing Directors, consisting of one or more managing directors ("Direktieren"). The powers of the Board are defined by the articles of incorporation of the company except in cases where the law grants certain powers explicitly to the General Meeting of Shareholders, e.g. the appointment of managing directors and supervisory directors, the approval of the financial statements, the amendment of the articles of incorporation, and the dissolution and liquidation of the company.

The Department of Social and Economic Affairs requires a Netherlands Antilles company to have at least one resident managing director. For offshore companies such resident managing director is usually provided by the local trust-offices.

Besides a Board of Managing Directors the company may, but is under no obligation to have a Supervisory Board ("Raad van Commissarissen"). Its structure and powers are defined by the articles of incorporation but again not where certain rights are reserved by law to the General Meeting of Shareholders.

Attorneys-in-Fact are appointed by the General Meeting of Shareholders unless the articles of incorporation provide that they are appointed by the Board of Managing Directors.

5. Shares

The articles of incorporation may provide that the shares of the company are in register and/or in bearer form. In case of registered shares, registration in the register of shareholders of the company is sufficient evidence of ownership, but sharecertificates may be issued, and must be issued if a shareholder so requests. For bearershares, sharecertificates must be issued.

After its formation there is no requirement as to the number of shareholders and the N.V. may therefore be wholly owned by one person or entity.

— 7 —

year. This tax-return should be accompanied by a profit & loss account, a balance-sheet and, in the case of an investment company, a specification of investments and income (See Appendix III). In case the company fails to file such tax-returns, the Inspector of Taxes may issue a tax-assessment ex officio.

Tax-assessments must be paid by the company within two months after the date of issue thereof on penalty of sheriff's charges and penalty-interest.

2. General meeting of shareholders

The financial statements must be submitted to the Annual General Meeting of Shareholders for approval. Such meeting must be held within nine months after the close of the financial year or earlier if the articles of incorporation so provide. Other items may be dealt with at the same meeting if the shareholders have been duly notified of such items. Voting by proxy is allowed; managing directors, supervisory directors and in general, persons in the service of the company may not act as proxy of shareholders. If the articles of incorporation do not provide otherwise, resolutions are adopted by an affirmative vote of the majority of the votes cast at the meeting and there is no quorum requirement.

Besides the Annual General Meeting of Shareholders, management may also call Extraordinary General Meetings of Shareholders for matters that have come up during the course of the year. The same rules as for the Annual General Meeting apply here.

The Commercial Code of the Netherlands Antilles provides that general meetings of shareholders must be held in its area of registration; for companies established in Curaçao this means that such meeting should be held in Curaçao.

As a rule, general meetings of shareholders are called by the management. However, on certain conditions, shareholders representing at least 10% of the issued capital may also call a general meeting.

If only registered shares are permitted, and the articles of incorporation so provide, valid shareholders' resolutions can also be adopted outside a General Meeting of Shareholders on the condition that all shareholders have declared themselves.

The net profits of the company are at the disposal of the General Meeting of Shareholders, which may declare a dividend or place such profits to reserve. During the year the management of the company may declare, if specifically authorized to do so under the articles of incorporation of the company in expectation of the final dividend, interim dividends, which should subsequently be ratified by the General Meeting of Shareholders.

F: TAXATION UNDER ART. 14 AND 14A PROFIT TAX ORDINANCE

1. Rates of taxation

As said before, the general tax rate under art. 14 and 14A Profit Tax Ordinance for investment, holding, finance, royalty and real estate companies is 2.4% on the first NAF. 100,000.— (= appr. US$ 56,000.—) net profit and 3% on the balance. Capital gains are tax exempt and capital losses are not taken into account, whether they are realized or not.

Profits derived from the trade in commodities, gold or currencies do not qualify for this special tax treatment. On the other hand, gains from shares,

— 9 —

bonds, U.S. Treasury bills, U.S. Treasury notes, commercial paper, bankers acceptances, goldcertificates, timedeposits etc. do qualify. The gains derived from the purchase and maturing of discount paper are treated in the Netherlands Antilles as taxable interest and not as a capital gain.

Not taxed are dividends received by an Article 14 or 14A company from another Netherlands Antilles company.

There is no requirement in the Netherlands Antilles as to how long the investments should be held by the Company.

2. The Guaranty Act

The tax rates of 2.4% and 3% have been guaranteed by law until and including the company's financial year that commenced before July 1, 1999. Two Guaranty Acts are presently in force in the Netherlands Antilles. The most recent Act covers the period of July 1, 1979 through July 1, 1999, while the prior Act guarantees the tax rates of 2.4% and 3% until July 1, 1979.

3. Calculation of taxable income

The taxable income is calculated by deducting the deductible expenses from gross income. In general, deductible expenses are all reasonable expenses incurred in the ordinary course of business, e.g. legal fees, accounting fees, management fees, salaries, necessary travelling expenses etc. Interest paid is deductible if paid to a recognized bank or similar financial institutions (pension funds, insurance companies etc.) The Tax Inspector determines whether interest payments to a certain financial institution should be considered as a deductible expense or tax purposes. Especially when such institution is located in one of the tax havens there may be doubt. Whenever there is uncertainty as to this point one is advised to obtain a tax ruling from the Tax Inspector.

When a company lends the funds borrowed from a bank on to a third party, such transaction should be on an arm's length basis. The Netherlands Antilles Tax Inspector will usually require that a taxable income of at least ¼ of one percent is reported on the basis of such transaction.

If the interest is not paid to a bank or similar financial institution, such interest is only deductible if a tax ruling from the N.A. Tax Inspector to that effect has been obtained. In such case the Tax Inspector usually requires a minimum taxable income of 1% of the face value of the loan.

The abovementioned spreads of ¼% and 1% are tax fictions for the determination of the minimum taxable income only; the actual spread may be less.

There is also a limitation on the deductibility of expenses in respect of royalty income. It is recommended to apply for a tax ruling clarifying which expenses are deductible, specifically where royalty payments to third parties (e.g. in the form of a license fee) are concerned.

As capital gains, increases in the value of the investment or source of royalty income, go taxfree in the Netherlands Antilles, capital losses are likewise not taken into account for the calculation of the company's taxable income and cannot be deducted.

There is a carry-forward of five years for losses, but no carry-back. The deductible expenses should be allocated proportionally to the various types of income unless they are specifically attributable to one type.

4. Stamptax

A stamptax of 0.4% is levied on the face value of share- and bondcertificates, but only if these are executed in the Netherlands Antilles. There is

— 10 —

the latter remain entitled to the reduced U.S. withholding tax of 15% while only being taxed in the N.A. at the low rates of 2.4 - 3.0% on the net. A further condition is that the U.S. corporation paying the dividends does not derive 60% or more of its income from interests, dividends royalties, rents from real property, or capital gains on securities or real property ("passive income"). A tax ruling should be obtained from the I.R.S. to secure the abovementioned special rates.

b. If the N.A. company that receives the U.S. source dividends is entirely owned by one or more corporations of the Netherlands or by one or more individuals residing in the Netherlands or Netherlands Antilles, the U.S. withholding tax rate is 15% and the Netherlands Antilles profit-tax rate is 2.4 - 3.0% (the VS-4 Status). Declarations from the Netherlands and Netherlands Antilles tax inspectors are required. [Art. 1 par. 2b Prot.]

c. If the Netherlands Antilles corporation controls directly or indirectly 95% or more of the voting power of the U.S. corporation, the U.S. withholding tax may be further reduced to 5%, provided that not more than 25% of the U.S. company's income is derived from interest and dividends (other than from its own subsidiary companies), and provided that the relationship of the two corporations has not been arranged or maintained primarily with the intention of securing such reduced rate. A tax ruling from the IRS should be obtained. [Art. VII Treaty]

The special rates mentioned under a, b and c are not necessarily mutually exclusive or inclusive. For example, a N.A. company controlling at least 95% of the voting power of a U.S. corporation may qualify under a or c or both, or under b or c or both. If it would qualify under both a and c, the U.S. withholding tax would be 5% and the N.A. profit tax 2.4 - 3.0%. The same rates apply if the N.A. company would qualify under both b and c. If, on the other hand, the company would only qualify under c, the U.S. withholding tax would be 5% and the N.A. profit-tax 15%. Whether or not the company will qualify depends on the aforementioned conditions and the willingness of the IRS to issue the necessary tax-ruling.

2. Interest and Royalties

Interest and royalties received by a N.A. corporation from U.S. sources are exempt from the 30% U.S. withholding tax if the company has waived its right to be taxed in the N.A. at the special low rates of 2.4 - 3.0% and instead will be taxed at the full rates or 24 - 30% on the net of such income (24% on the first US$ 56,000.— net profit and 30% on the balance). As explained in Chapter F paragraph 2, interest and royalties paid are deductible within certain limits. [Art. VIII + IX Treaty Art. 1 par. 1 Prot.]

Similar to the provisions in respect of dividends, discussed in the preceding paragraph, special rates are applicable to U.S. source interest and royalty income if:

a. the N.A. corporation owns 25% or more of the stock of the U.S. corporation and less than 60% of the U.S. corporation's income is passive income; a ruling from the IRS is required; or [Art. 1 par. 2a Prot.]

b. the N.A. company is entirely owned by one or more corporations of the Netherlands or one or more individuals resident in the Netherlands or Netherlands Antilles. [Art. 1 par. 2b Prot.]

— 12 —

---

also a stamptax on agreements signed in the Netherlands Antilles at the rate of NAF 1.— (about US$ 0.56) a page.

5. Personal income tax/withholding tax

Non-resident shareholders who are not engaged in a trade or business in the N.A., are not subject to any form of Netherlands Antilles personal income tax on dividends, interest or liquidation distributions received from the Netherlands Antilles company. Neither is there any form of withholding tax on such or other payments to a non-resident.

Remunerations paid to non-resident managing directors and supervisory directors are subject to the normal Netherlands Antilles personal income tax rates.

6. Other taxes

Non-resident shareholders not engaged in a trade or business in the N.A., are not subject to N.A. estate tax, property tax, gift tax or any other tax.

G: TAX-TREATY WITH THE U.S.A.

An Income Tax Convention between the United States and the Netherlands was concluded on April 29, 1948; this treaty was extended to the Netherlands Antilles in 1955 and subsequently modified by Protocol of October 23, 1963. The Treaty provides certain tax advantages in respect of income from U.S. sources to N.A. companies not engaged in trade or business in the U.S. through a permanent establishment. In the following paragraphs we will discuss the impact of the Treaty as modified by Protocol on the various types of income.

1. Dividends

Dividends received from a U.S. corporation by a foreign corporation are generally subject to 30% U.S. withholding tax on the gross amount of such dividends. Under the Treaty however, this U.S. withholding tax is reduced to 15% on the gross amount in case the dividends are received by a Netherlands Antilles corporation, provided that such income will not be taxed in the N.A. at the special low tax rates 2.4 - 3% of the arts. 14 and 14A of the Profit Tax Ordinance (this is the so-called Status VS-3). In other words, in order to qualify for the benefits of the Treaty, the company must waive its right to be taxed at the 2.4 - 3.0% rates as far as U.S. source dividend is concerned. Instead it will be taxed in the N.A. at the rate of 15% on the net amount of such income. i.e. after deduction of the 15% U.S. withholding tax and other deductible expenses. Consequently, the maximum effective combined rate is 27.75% on the gross amount of the dividends, instead of the 30% U.S. withholding tax; a saving of at least 2.25%. In this connection it should be emphasized again that capital gains are tax exempt. [Art. VII Treaty Art. I Par. 1 Prot.]

[Art. 8A P.T.O.]

The Treaty provides further benefits in the following cases:

a. If the Netherlands Antilles corporation owns directly or indirectly 25% or more of the stock of the U.S. corporation, dividends received from [Art. 1 par. 2A Prot.]

— 11 —

2.4 - 3.0%.

However: the exemption from the 30% U.S. withholding tax on interest (not royalties) does not apply in case the Netherlands Antilles corporation controls directly or indirectly more than 50% of the voting power of the U.S. corporation. On the other hand, whether the U.S. company controls the N.A. company or not, is irrelevant.

The question may arise what the Treaty understands by "royalties" to which the abovementioned rules apply. Article IX of the Treaty gives the following definition:

    "royalties for the right to use copyright, patents, designs, secret processes and formulae, trademarks and analogous property, and royalties, including rentals, in respect of motion picture films or for the use of industrial, commercial or scientific equipment." — *Art. VIII Treaty*

This is a slightly narrower definition of royalties than the one contained in art. 14A of the Profit Tax Ordinance because, unlike art. 14A, it leaves income from real estate out. Such income receives a separate tax treatment under Art. V of the Treaty (see the following paragraph of this Chapter).

3. Real Estate

Under the Treaty, income of whatever nature derived from real property and interest from mortgages secured by real property situated in the U.S., is taxable in the U.S. only. Consequently, such income will not be taxed in the N.A. at all. — *Art. V Treaty*

If the rental income of a foreign corporation from real estate is not effectively connected with the conduct of a trade or business in the U.S., the taxation in the U.S. will generally be on a gross income basis at a rate of 30%, unless the company elects to be taxed on a net income basis; if such election is made, capital gains from the sale of the property normally become taxable in the U.S. However, the N.A. - U.S. tax treaty provides that the company may elect for any given fiscal year to be taxed on its net income. In other words, it may elect to be taxed on its net income for the years that it is holding the property; in the year the company intends to sell the property it will not make the election and be taxed at 30% on its gross income, thusly securing a tax free capital gain. — *Art. X Treaty / Art. II Prot.*

If, on the other hand, the rental income of the company would be considered as income effectively connected with the conduct of a trade or business in the U.S. through a permanent establishment, the company would not have this advantageous choice; it would be taxed in the U.S. on a net basis including capital gains. This situation can be met by a two tier structure of a N.A. company and a fully owned N.A. or U.S. subsidiary which owns the property. When one wishes to dispose of his interests in the property, the N.A. parent sells the stock of its subsidiary instead of the property itself. Capital gains derived from this sale of stock are tax exempt both in the U.S. and the N.A. As long as the property is being held the subsidiary of course pays regular U.S. income taxes on a net basis, but no N.A. profit tax. Dividends paid by the subsidiary to its parent are taxed as normal dividends (par. 1 of this chapter).

— 13 —

In this connection we may remind the reader that dividends received by an art. 14 or 14A company from another N.A. company are not taxed.

The foregoing also applies to royalties in respect of the exploitation of mines, quarries or natural resources situated in the U.S.

4. Dividends paid by the N.A. company

Dividends paid by the N.A. company are exempt from U.S. income tax unless the payee is a United States citizen, resident or corporation. This is an important exception to the U.S. concepts in respect of extraterritorial taxation.

H: TREATY WITH THE UNITED KINGDOM

The Tax Convention between the United Kingdom and the Netherlands for the avoidance of double taxation and the prevention of fiscal evasion is dated October 31, 1967, and was extended, with some modifications, to the Netherlands Antilles in 1970.

1. Profits

Profits derived by a N.A. company from U.K. sources are only taxable in the N.A. unless the company carries on business in the U.K. through a permanent establishment.

2. Dividends

The provisions of the N.A.-U.K. Convention in respect of dividends are similar to the corresponding provisions of the N.A.-U.S. treaty. They have, however, become irrelevant as the U.K. no longer levies withholding tax on dividends paid by a U.K. company.

3. Interest and royalties

Interest and royalties derived by a N.A. company from U.K. sources are only taxable in the N.A. and are tax exempt in the U.K. provided that such income will not be taxed in the N.A. at the low rates of 2.4 - 3.0%; instead such income will be taxed in the N.A. at the rates of 24 - 30%, on the net amount; and further provided that such income is not effectively connected with a business carried on in the U.K. through a permanent establishment.

The word "royalties" is defined by the Convention as follows:

    "payments of any kind received as a consideration for the use of, or the right to use any copyrights of literary, artistic or scientific work (including cinematograph film and film or tapes for radio or television broadcasting), any patent, trademark, design or model, plan, secret formula or process, or for the use of, or the right to use, industrial, commercial or scientific equipment, or for information concerning industrial, commercial or scientific experience and shall include gains derived from the sale or exchange of any right or property giving rise to such royalties".

4. Real estate

Income from immovable property may be taxed in the state in which such property is situated.

— 14 —

5. Capital gains

Capital gains from the alienation by the N.A. company of any property that does not form part of the business property of a permanent establishment in the U.K., are tax exempt both in the U.K. and the N.A.

I: TAX REGULATION OF THE KINGDOM OF THE NETHERLANDS

The Tax Regulation of the Kingdom of the Netherlands of October 28, 1964, regulates the tax relations between the two parts of the Kingdom of the Netherlands: the Netherlands Antilles and the Netherlands.

Dividends paid by a Netherlands company are normally subject to a with-holding tax of 25%, which rate is reduced to 15% in case the payee is a N.A. company. If the N.A. company owns 25% or more of the nominally paid-in capital of the Netherlands company the said withholding tax is reduced to zero (except in certain instances).

J: SHIPPING AND AIRTRANSPORT COMPANIES

Art. 9A P.T.O.

In this chapter we shall discuss the shipping and air-transport companies which are entitled to a separate tax-treatment in the Netherlands Antilles under Art. 9A of the Profit Tax Ordinance.

1. Definitions

The Profit Tax Ordinance defines a shipping/air-transport company as a company, the purpose of which is the ocean-shipping or aviation business, including the letting and chartering of ocean-going vessels or aircrafts. In order to qualify under the special tax provisions, the company must further satisfy the following requirements:

1. the company must have been established under the laws of the Netherlands Antilles,

2. have its statutory seat within the Netherlands Antilles,

3. must conduct its daily management in the Netherlands Antilles if and in as far the company handles the actual transport itself,

4. and the vessels/aircrafts of the company must be registered in the Kingdom of the Netherlands, and must be owned by the company.

Chartered vessels not carrying the flag of the Kingdom of the Netherlands may also qualify in certain circumstances.

2. Tax treatment

In so far as the profits of the company have been derived from outside the N.A., 80% of such profits is subject to a tax rate of 2.76 - 3.45% and the

remaining 20% of the profits is subject to 27.6 - 34.5%. This means an average tax of about 7.7% - 9.6% on the aggregate amount of the profits (7.7% on the first ± US$ 56,000.— profit and 9.6% on the additional profit). Capital gains are included in the company's profit and capital losses are deductible.

The company is entitled to an investment allowance from profits of 8% of the investment in both the first and second year after the investment has been made. In order to take advantage of this provision, the investment should be held for at least ten years.

An accelerated depreciation of 1/3 of the purchase price of the vessel or aircraft is allowed. Losses may be carried forward for 6 years (instead of the general 5 years); losses incurred in the first 6 years of the company's operations can be carried forward for an unlimited period of time; there is no carry-back.

The company may form a reserve for replacement and reparation of vessels in case of loss, expropriation or damage.

The abovementioned preferential tax treatment of a shipping/air-transport company has been guaranteed by law until and including the company's financial year that commenced before July 1, 1981. It is to be expected that the guarantee will be extended until the year 2000. (See Chapter F, 3)

Charter income (bare-boat) does also qualify for the 2.4 - 3 percent rate of art. 14A P.T.O. If therefore the company does not satisfy the requirements of art. 9A P.T.O., it can still use art. 14A for its charter income (see Chapter F).

K: OFFSHORE BANKS

A limited number of offshore banks have been incorporated in the N.A. Mainly they are subsidiaries of major international banks set up for fiscal and/or foreign exchange reasons.

The net income of such offshore banks is taxed at the applicable rates of finance companies. However, income that cannot be classified as Article 14-14A P.T.O. income cannot qualify for the preferential rates.

Apart from the general foreign exchange license for the exemption from foreign exchange control, an offshore bank also needs a special license from the Central Bank authorizing it to conduct banking business. The Central Bank maintains a restricted policy in the issuance of these licenses.

L: OTHER TYPES OF OFFSHORE COMPANIES

1. Offshore Trading Companies:

Offshore trading companies are taxed at the 24 - 30% rates on their net income.

Capital gains will be taxable but capital losses, depreciation and all ordinary business expenses are deductible. Other deductions, such as assistance fees, are to be agreed upon with the Inspector of Taxes.

M: SCHEDULE OF TAX RATES

This schedule of tax rates is meant for your ready reference only. As it inevitably contains simplifications we suggest that you also consult the corresponding chapters of this booklet.

% TAX IN FOLLOWING SITUATIONS:	DIVIDENDS	INTEREST	ROYALTIES	RENTALS AND OTHER REAL ESTATE INCOME (not connected)	RENTALS AND OTHER REAL ESTATE INCOME (connected)	CAPITAL GAINS	OTHER INCOME
a: IN GENERAL (N.A. tax under art. 14 and 14A)	2.4-3%	2.4-3%	2.4-3%	2.4-3%	2.4-3%	0%	24-30%
b: VS3 STATUS 1. US. withh. tax (on gross)	15%	0%	0%	(election for normal corporate tax)	(normal corporate tax)	0% (except real estate)	—
2. N.A. tax (on net)	15%	24-30%	24-30%	0%	0%	0%	24-30%
c: VS4 STATUS 1. US withh. tax (on gross)	15%	0%	0%	(election for normal corporate tax)	(normal corporate tax)	0% (except real estate)	—
2. N.A. tax (on net)	2.4-3%	2.4-3%	2.4-3%	0%	0%	0%	24-30%
d: 25 - 50% of U.S. corp. owned by N.A. corp: 1. U.S. withh. tax (on gross)	15%	0%	0%	—	—	0%	—
2. N.A. tax (on net)	2.4-3%	2.4-3%	2.4-3%			0%	24-30%

— 18 —

A condition for this tax treatment is that the company will not engage in any trade or business within the Netherlands Antilles; the income of the company must therefore be fully derived from sources outside the N.A.

In case the offshore trading company is also receiving income in the form of dividends, interests or royalties (art. 14 and 14A income), it is often possible to obtain a tax ruling that the company may divide its income into art. 14 - 14A income, taxable at the 2.4 - 3.0% rates, and other (trading) income. taxable at the said 24 - 30% rates.

2. Article 12 companies

Art. 12 P.T.O.

Article 12 P.T.O. relates to N.A. companies with a permanent establishment or real property abroad. If in that other country a corporate profit tax exists that would in principal be levied on income from such permanent establishment or real estate, the applicable N.A. tax rate is 2.4 - 3 percent. This rate is levied on the net of such income. i.e. after deduction of expenses and foreign taxes. Capital gains are taxable but capital losses, amortization and depreciation are deductible for the determination of taxable income.

In case the permanent establishment or the real estate is situated in the Netherlands, the N.A. tax rate is zero.

Would certain income fall within art. 12 and arts. 14/14A the company may choose; this may be the case with e.g. real estate income.

— 17 —

Appendix 4: Introduction to taxation of offshore companies in the Netherlands Antilles

including copies of treaties with the Netherlands and the Netherlands Antilles and related forms

615

N: APPENDIX

I: Example of articles of incorporation of an investment/royalty/real estate company

II: Translated profit tax return

III: Form WB 14A

IV: Certificate of Status VS3

V: Certificate of Status VS4

VI: Form Profit Tax 92 NA

— 21 —
(-22- is blank)

TYPE OF INCOME: % TAX IN FOLLOWING SITUATIONS:	DIVIDENDS	INTEREST	ROYALTIES	RENTALS AND OTHER REAL ESTATE INCOME (not connected)	RENTALS AND OTHER REAL ESTATE INCOME (connected)	CAPITAL GAINS	OTHER INCOME
e: 50 - 95% of voting power of U.S. corp. owned by N.A. corp.:							
1. U.S. withh. tax (on gross)	15%	30%	0%	—	—	0%	—
2. N.A. tax (on net)	2.4-3%	2.4-3%	2.4-3%	—	—	0%	24-30%
f: More than 95% of voting power of U.S. corp. owned by N.A. corp.:							
1. U.S. withh. tax (on gross)	5%	30%	0%	—	—	0%	—
2. N.A. tax (on net)	2.4-3%	2.4-3%	2.4-3%	—	—	0%	24-30%
g: INCOME FROM THE NETHERLANDS:							
1. Neth. withh. tax (on gross)	15%	0%	0%	(taxed in the Neth.)	(taxed in the Neth.)	0%	—
2. N.A. tax (on net)	2.4-3%	2.4-3%	2.4-3%	0%	0%	0%	24-30%
h: Income from Netherlands corp. 25% or more of its stock owned by the N.A. corp.							
1. Neth. withh. tax (on gross)	0%	0%	0%	—	—	0%	—
2. N.A. tax (on net)	2.4-3%	2.4-3%	2.4-3%	0%	0%		24-30%

— 19 —
(-20- is blank)

APPENDIX I

Example of articles of incorporation for an investment/royalty/real estate company.

NAME AND DOMICILE

Article 1

1. The name of the company is:
2. The company is established in Curaçao.

PURPOSE

Article 2

1. The purpose of the company is:
a. to invest its assets in securities, including shares and other certificates of participation and bonds, as well as other claims for interestbearing debts however denominated and in any and all forms;
b. to acquire:
(i) revenues, derived from the alienation or leasing of the right to use copyrights, patents, designs, secret processes or formulae, trademarks and other analogous property;
(ii) royalties, including rentals, in respect of motion picture films or for the use of industrial, commercial or scientific equipment, as well as relating to the operation of a mine or a quarry or of any other extraction of natural resources and other immovable properties,
(iii) considerations paid for technical assistance;
c. to acquire, own, alienate, manage, rent, lease, mortgage or otherwise encumber real properties and/or any right or interest of the company in such real properties.

2. The company is entitled to do all that may be useful or necessary for the attainment of its object or that is connected therewith in the widest sense, including the participation in any other venture or company with a similar or corresponding purpose.

DURATION

Article 3

The company is constituted for an indefinite period of time.

CAPITAL AND SHARES

Article 4

The authorized capital of the company amounts to thirty thousand United States Dollars (US$ 30,000.—), divided into thirty thousand (30,000) shares of one United States Dollar (US$ 1.—) each, of which six thousand (6,000) shares are subscribed for.

Article 5

1. The shares, which shall be issued only if paid up in full, will be either registered or bearer shares.

— 23 —

2. The registered shares shall be entered in the stock register, which shall be kept by the Managing Board.
3. Shares shall be issued by the Managing Board.
4. On the request of a shareholder, share-certificates may be issued for registered shares. For bearer shares share-certificates shall be issued, which shall be provided with dividend-coupons and a talon in order to obtain new dividend-coupons. Share-certificates shall be signed by or on behalf of the Managing Board.
5. The transfer of registered shares is effected either by serving a deed of conveyance upon the company, or through written acknowledgement of the transfer by the company. The latter can only take place by an annotation on the share-certificate, if share-certificates have been issued.
6. The foregoing paragraph shall also apply in the case of an allocation resulting from a division and partition of community.
7. The company may acquire for its own account for a valid consideration fully paid up shares in its own capital stock up to such an amount that at least one/fifth part of the authorized capital remains outstanding with others than the company itself.
8. The company may not derive any rights from its treasury shares. For the purpose of establishing the issued capital such shares shall not be included as part of such capital.

MANAGEMENT

Article 6

1. The management of the company is commissioned to a Managing Board, consisting of one or more managing directors.
2. The managing directors shall be elected by the general meeting of shareholders and may be suspended or discharged by it at any time.
3. The company shall be represented in all matters, including court matters, by each of the managing directors, also in case of a conflict of interests between the company and one or more managing directors, either acting in private or ex officio, and provided that to issue debt obligation a resolution of the Managing Board is required in which case the Managing Board will decide on the terms and conditions thereof, including the price, the interest rate, the time of issuance and the time and manner of repayment.
4. The Managing Board is authorized to appoint attorneys-in-fact. It regulates their powers and the manner in which they will represent the company and sign for it and in general the conditions of their appointment.
5. The Managing Board is authorized to enter into such contracts as are referred to in Article 60 of the Commercial Code of the Netherlands Antilles without previous approval by the general meeting of shareholders.
6. In case one or more managing directors are prevented from or are incapable of acting as such, the management shall be left entirely to the remaining managing directors or remaining managing director.
7. In case all managing directors or the only managing director are (is) prevented from or are (is) incapable of acting as such, a person yearly appointed by the general meeting of shareholders, will be in charge of the management of the company.
8. The Managing Board may hold its meetings at such places, whether within or outside the Netherlands Antilles, as a majority of its members may from time to time determine.
9. Any managing director may be represented at any meeting of the

— 24 —

Managing Board by another managing director, who may vote as his proxy at such meeting.

10. Any managing director may waive notice of any meeting of the Managing Board by a writing signed by him or his representative either before, after or at the meeting. Every managing director present at the meeting in person or by proxy shall be deemed to have waived notice of the meeting.

11. The absolute majority of the members of the Managing Board present in person or by proxy shall constitute a quorum for taking resolutions.

12. All resolutions taken at a meeting of the Managing Board shall be taken by an absolute majority of the votes cast. In the event of an equality of votes, the chairman of the meeting shall have the deciding vote.

13. A written resolution signed by all of the members of the Managing Board without a meeting shall have the same effect as a resolution validly adopted at a meeting of the Managing Board duly called and held.

14. Minutes shall be kept of all meetings of the Managing Board, which shall be signed by the secretary or the chairman of the meeting or any other person thereunto authorized by the Managing Board.

15. Any resolution of the Managing Board may be evidenced as regards third persons by a written statement signed by one managing director.

GENERAL MEETINGS OF SHAREHOLDERS

Article 7

1. General meetings of shareholders shall be held on Curaçao.

2. The annual general meeting of shareholders shall be held within nine months of the close of the company's financial year.

3. In said meeting:

a. the Managing Board shall render a report on the business of the company and the conduct of its affairs during the preceding financial year;

b. the balance-sheet and the profit and loss account shall be adopted, after having been submitted together with an explanatory statement, stating by what standard the movable and immovable property of the company have been appraised;

c. the person, referred to in article 6, paragraph 7, shall be appointed;

d. such proposals shall be dealt with as shall have been included in the agenda specified in the notice of convocation of the meeting.

Article 8

1. General meetings of shareholders shall be convoked by means of registered airmail letters, mailed to the addresses of shareholders as stated in the register of shareholders kept by the Managing Board, and if bearer shares are outstanding, by means of an advertisement inserted in a newspaper, published in Curaçao.

2. The notice shall be mailed, respectively published at least twenty days prior to the date of the meeting. Said period may be reduced to ten days, excluding the day on which the notice is mailed, respectively published and the day on which the meeting is held, in case action of the shareholders' meeting is urgently required.

3. The agenda for the meeting shall be specified in the notice of convocation of the meeting or it shall be stated that the shareholders may take cognizance thereof at the office of the company.

4. General meetings shall be presided over by a person, designated thereto by such meeting.

— 25 —

5. All resolutions of the annual and special general meetings of shareholders shall be taken by absolute majority of votes, if not otherwise provided for by these articles of incorporation.

6. Shareholders may be represented at the meeting by proxy designated by letter or telegram.

7. Managing directors or in general persons employed by the company may not act as proxies of shareholders at a meeting.

8. One vote may be cast for each share.

9. Valid votes may also be cast for the shares of those who (otherwise than as shareholders of the company) would acquire any right or be discharged from any obligation towards the company, by the resolution to be adopted.

10. Proposals of items for an agenda to be made by shareholders, either for the annual or for the special general meetings can only be dealt with if presented to the Managing Board in writing at such time that they can be announced with observance of the term set and in the manner described for the convocation.

11. However, when the entire issued share capital is represented at any general meeting of shareholders, valid resolutions may be adopted, even if the provisions of these articles of incorporation with respect to convocation, specification of the agenda or place of the meeting have not or have only partially been observed, provided that such a resolution is unanimously adopted.

FINANCIAL YEAR

Article 9

1. The financial year of the company covers the period from January first to December thirty-first of each year.

2. The first financial year of the company runs from the date of the company's incorporation until the thirty-first day of December nineteenhundred and seventy.........., inclusive.

BALANCE-SHEET AND PROFIT AND LOSS ACCOUNT

Article 10

1. Within eight months after the close of the company's financial year, the balance-sheet and profit and loss account covering the preceding year, with the explanatory statement referred to in article 7, paragraph 3, shall be submitted to the general meeting of shareholders by the Managing Board.

2. The balance-sheet and profit and loss account shall be adopted by the annual meeting of shareholders.

3. The adoption of the balance-sheet and profit and loss account shall acquit and discharge the managing director(s) for his (their) management during the preceding financial year.

DISTRIBUTION OF PROFITS

Article 11

1. The profits, by which is to be understood the net profits according to the profit and loss account, may be accumulated or paid out in the form of dividends at the discretion of the general meeting of shareholders.

2. If and in so far as the profits of the company permit same, the Managing Board may resolve to declare one or more interim-dividends as an advance payment of expected dividends.

— 26 —

APPENDIX II

Translation of the profit tax return used for investment, royalty, finance and real estate companies (art. 8A, 14 and 14A Companies).

FISCAL YEAR:

PROFIT TAX

This form must be returned within 60 days after the date of issuance

TAX RETURN

For use by Curaçao International Trust Company N.V. only

Date of issuance:

Please mention the above code-number in all your correspondence

1. Division of profit (amounts of column no. 18 page 3)

A not taxable	B subject to 1/10 of the rate	C subject to 15% rate	D subject to full rate
f	*f*	*f*	*f*

2. Loss compensation (art. 10 of Profit Tax Ordinance 1940)

A Year	B Loss	C compensated in previous years	C To be compensated in year which this tax return covers	E Total of Column 2 C and 2 D
a. 19.......	*f*	*f*	*f*	*f*
b. 19.......	"	"	"	"
c. 19.......	"	"	"	"
d. 19.......	"	"	"	"
e. 19.......	"	"	"	"
Total	*f*	*f*	*f*	*f*

3. FOR OFFICIAL USE ONLY

FOR OFFICIAL USE ONLY

Article	Taxable income	Amount of assessment		Particulars
	f	Tax *f*		
		Surtax "		
		Total *f*		
	f	Tax *f*		
		Surtax "		
		Total *f*		

---

3. In the event that the profit and loss account shows a loss over any given year, which loss cannot be covered by the reserves or compensated in another manner, no profit shall be distributed in any subsequent year, so long as the loss has not been recovered.

AMENDMENT OF THE ARTICLES OF INCORPORATION AND LIQUIDATION OF THE COMPANY

Article 12

1. Resolutions to amend these articles of incorporation or to dissolve the company may only be passed in a general meeting of shareholders, at which at least three/fourths of the issued capital is represented.

2. If the required issued capital is not represented at said meeting, a second meeting shall be convened, to be held within two months after the first one, at which second meeting valid decisions may then be taken with respect to the foregoing, irrespective of the capital represented.

3. In the event of dissolution of the company, the liquidation shall take place under such provisions as the general meeting of shareholders shall determine.

WINSTBELASTING

APPENDIX III

Form WB 14A for specification of investment and income, to be filed with the Tax Inspectorate together with the corresponding balance sheet and profit and loss account.

Specificatie van beleggingen en opbrengsten (1)
Specification of investment and income

Maatschappij
Company

Boekjaar
Bookyear

Stamnummer
Code-number

	Aanwezige fondsen bij de aanvang van het boekjaar (Holdings at beginning of bookyear)		Aankopen in de loop van het boekjaar (2) (Acquirements during bookyear)			Verkopen in de loop van het boekjaar (Sales during bookyear)				Aanwezige fondsen per het einde van het boekjaar (Holdings at end of bookyear)				In het boekjaar ontvangen dividenden en interest (Earned dividends and interest in bookyear)		
Naam van het fonds (name of stock) (Voor obligaties met vermelding van de rentevoet) (For bonds indicate interest-rate)	Aantal stukken en/of nominaal bedrag (Number of shares and/or par value)	Kostprijs (Costprice)	Datum (Date)	Aantal stukken en/of nominaal bedrag (Number of shares and/or par value)	Kostprijs der aankopen (Costprice of acquirements)	Datum (Date)	Aantal stukken en/of nominaal bedrag (Number of shares and/or par value)	Opbrengst bij verkoop (Proceeds from sales)	Koerswinst of -verlies (Profit or loss from sales)	Aantal stukken en/of nominaal bedrag (Number of shares and/or par value)	Kostprijs (Costprice)	Koers per balansdatum (Closing-rates) (3)	Marktwaarde per balansdatum (Market-value) (3)	Bruto (Gross)	Belasting (tax)	Netto (Net)
A	B	C	D	E	F	G	H	I	J	K	L	M	N	O	P	Q
1																
2																
3																
4																
5																
6																
7																
8																
9																
10																
11																
12																
13																
14																
15																
16																
17																
18																
19																
20																
21																
22																
23																
24																
25																
26																
27																
28																
29																
30																
31																
32																
33																
34																
35																
36																
37																
38																
39																
40																
41																
42																
43																
44																
45																
46																

Totaal/Transport
(Total/Carry forward)

(1) Indien dit blad onvoldoende ruimte biedt, de opgave vervolgen op een extra blad.
(If this sheet offers insufficient space please continue on extra sheet).
W.B. 14a

(2) Stockdividenden en split-ups ook te vermelden.
(Stockdividends and stocksplits also to be mentioned).

(3) Invulling van de rubrieken M en N is niet verplicht
(Entries in column M and N are not required)

APPENDIX IV

Certificate of Status VS 3 for reducing the U.S. withholding tax on dividend, interest and royalty payments (Chapter G, par. 1 and par. 2).

Formulier W.B. 21

VS 3

GOVERNMENT OF THE NETHERLANDS ANTILLES

Income Tax Convention between the United States of America and the Netherlands Antilles.

Articles VII, VIII and IX of the Convention.

Protocol modifying and supplementing the Convention, effective September 28, 1964.

This is to certify that

Code-number:

is a legal entity organized in the Netherlands Antilles and that this entity with respect to any of its income from United States sources is not entitled to any of the special tax benefits as meant in article 1, paragraph 1 of the abovementioned Protocol.

This certificate shall be valid for a period of one year beginning on the first day of 19 unless cancelled prior to date of expiration. Notice of such cancellation will be sent to the withholding agent mentioned below.

Curaçao, 19

Official rubberstamp of the Inspectorate of Taxes

The Inspector of Taxes in the Netherlands Antilles, in his name: The Deputy Inspector of Taxes.

This certificate is issued on behalf of

(name)

(address)

as withholding agent for the abovementioned entity.

The duplicate copy is enclosed for filing with the U.S. Treasury Department.
W.B. 21

— 35 —
(—36— is blank)

19. Indicate under this heading by specifying the division of profit, how the balance of undivided profit at the end of the fiscal year connects with the balance of undivided profit at the end of the preceding fiscal year.

20. Further explanation (continue on separate sheet of paper when necessary see headings Nos. 10, 12, 13, 14 and 15)

19

21. Without reservation truthfully answered and signed

Regarding the obligation to submit copies of the balance sheet and Profit and Loss account or a substitute account reference is made to article 23 of the Profit Tax Ordinance of 1940

11. Division of Profit

	A Not taxable	B Subject to 1:10 of the rate	C Subject to 15% rate	D Subject to full rate
12. Income				
a. Securities (capital gains, etc.)				
1. not taxable				
2. taxable				
b. Interest				
c. Royalties				
d. Income/compensations art. 14A not being royalties				
e. Taxable income not mentioned under heading 12a through 12d				
f. Total				
g.				
h. Deduction of costs excluding profit tax paid (in case of interest paid indicate entity to which paid in heading no. 20) (Total costs:)				
Specify computation of allocation of costs under heading no. 20				
i. Profit **Article 11(1)**				
Article 11(1)				
13. Correction: Profit received share of profit of:				
a. Corporations, societies, companies or foundations as meant in sub paragraph a and b of paragraph 1 of article 1				
b. Entities as meant in sub paragraph of paragraph 1 of article 1 which derived at least 9/10 of the entire profit in the N.A. during the year to which the distributed profit applies				
Give specification under heading no. 20				
Article 11(3)				
14. Correction: Profit derived as interest on loans and/or compensation for the use or consumption of goods made available in whatever form to an entity meant in paragraph 1 of article 1 to which capital the body for which the return is filed is entitled.				
Give specification under heading no. 20				
Article 12(1)				
15. Correction: Profit derived from business conducted through a permanent establishment outside the N.A. or from real estate located outside the N.A. and which are subject to tax on				
a. of business or real estate in The Netherlands or Surinam				
b. of business or real estate elsewhere				
Give specification under heading no. 20				
16. Correction				
18. Corrected profit in N.A. currency (at)	f	f	f	f

---

4. a. The articles mentioned on this return without any further indication refer to articles of the Profit Tax Ordinance 1940.
   b. When in this return the word "Taxpayer" is used, this means a corporation, company, society or foundation in the sense of the paragraphs a and b of paragraph 1 article 1 of the Profit Tax Ordinance 1940

5. Person filing tax return
   a. Name
   b. Address
   c. Capacity

6. Managers and directors not residing in the Netherlands Antilles.
   a. Name
   b. Address
   c. Fees or salaries granted in the fiscal year

7. In case of liquidation:
   a. Name and address of persons in charge of liquidation within the Neth. Ant.
   b. Date of dissolution of the company

8. Tax return
   a. Name of person preparing return
   b. Address of such person

9. V.S. forms (Tax Treaty with the U.S.A.)
   a. Sort of form requested
   b. Last year for which form was requested (excluding year of this return)
   c. requested on behalf of (name legal entity, c.q. corporations see V.S. form)

10. The following questions are to be answered with yes or no. In case the answer is yes an explanation should be given under heading 20 or on a separate sheet of paper with reference to the number and letter of this heading.

Question	Answer		In case the answer is yes the following should be stated under heading 20:
	yes	no	
a. Has the purpose of the taxpayer been changed during the fiscal year?	yes	no	Year and number of articles of incorporation in which change has been laid down
b. Has the name of the taxpayer been changed during the fiscal year?	yes	no	The new name
c. Has the registered address of the taxpayer been changed during the fiscal year?	yes	no	The new place of residence
d. Has the fiscal year been changed since tax return of the preceding year?	yes	no	The amended fiscal year
e. Has the address to which the return is to be sent changed since the tax return of the preceding year?	yes	no	The new address
f. Does the tax payer conduct business through a permanent establishment on one of the other islands or does taxpayer own real estate on the other islands?	yes	no	Division of profit between the islands with a computation supporting such division
Article 6(2c)			
g. Has the profit and loss account been charged with the interest on borrowed money and/or payments made as consideration for the use of goods made available in whatever form, which interest and/or payments in question were received, directly or indirectly by persons or bodies who are wholly or partly entitled - directly or indirectly - to the capital of the body for which the return is filed, or who in another way have a special relation to the body concerning the division of profit?	yes	no	Name and address of persons and/or entities concerned as well as the amounts of interest and/or payments in question made
Article 7			
Publication sheet 1955 nr. 100			
h. Have gifts made to ecclesiastical, charitable, cultural and scientific institutions and institutions for the public benefit been charged to the profit and loss account?	yes	no	Name of institutions and amounts given

APPENDIX V

Certificate of Status VS 4 (Chapter G, par. 1 under b; par. 2 under b).

Formulier W.B. 22

VS 4

GOVERNMENT OF THE NETHERLANDS ANTILLES

Income Tax Convention between the United States of America and the Netherlands Antilles.

Articles VII, VIII and IX of the Convention.

Protocol modifying and supplementing the Convention, effective September 28, 1964.

This is to certify that

Code-number: ....

is a corporation organized in the Netherlands Antilles all of the stock of which is owned

(i) solely by one or more individual residents of the Netherlands Antilles in their individual capacities.

(ii) solely by one or more individual residents of the Netherlands in their individual capacities.

(iii) solely by one or more corporations of the Netherlands.

This certificate shall be valid for a period of three years beginning on the first day of .... 19 .... unless cancelled prior to date of expiration. Notice of such cancellation will be sent to the withholding agent mentioned below.

Official rubberstamp of the Inspectorate of Taxes

Curaçao, ... 19 ....

The Inspector of Taxes
in the Netherlands Antilles,
in his name:
The Deputy Inspector of Taxes,

This certificate is issued on behalf of

(name)

(address)

as withholding agent for the abovementioned corporation.

The duplicate copy is enclosed for filing with the U.S. Treasury Department.

W.B. 22

— 37 —

APPENDIX VI

Form Profit Tax 92 N.A. for reducing the Netherlands withholding tax (Chapter 1).

Formulier Inkomstenbelasting Nr. 92 N.A.

N.A.

VERZOEK OM GEDEELTELIJKE VRIJSTELLING OF TERUGGAAF VAN NEDERLANDSE DIVIDENDBELASTING

op grond van artikel 11 van de Belastingregeling voor het Koninkrijk

1. Volledige naam en adres van de verzoeker (natuurlijke persoon, maatschappij of ander lichaam):

....

....

(in blokletters)

2. De verzoeker maakt aanspraakt op vrijstelling / teruggaaf (1) van Nederlandse dividendbelasting tot het bedrag als vermeld in kolom (*f*), met betrekking tot de hieronder vermelde inkomsten:

Naam van het betalende lichaam Aantal en soort der aandelen of nominaal bedrag der obligaties	Nummer van het dividendbewijs of de coupon	Datum van betaalbaarstelling	Aantal dividendbewijzen of coupons	Totaal bruto bedrag van het dividend of de interest	Bedrag der belasting waarvoor vrijstelling / teruggaaf (1) wordt verzocht (2)
(a)	(b)	(c)	(d)	(e)	(*f*)
				f	*f*
				Totaal	*f*

3. De verzoeker verklaart dat hij uit hoofde van zijn eigendomsrechten met betrekking tot de hierboven in kolom (a) vermelde effecten, op de in kolom (c) vermelde datum(s) van betaalbaarstelling gerechtigd is (was) tot de in kolom (e) vermelde inkomsten.

(1) Doorhalen wat niet van toepassing is.

(2) De Nederlandse dividendbelasting bedraagt 25% (in een bepaald geval 20% van de bruto inkomsten. Ingevolge de Belastingregeling voor het Koninkrijk wordt zij met 10 (of 5) punten verminderd tot 15%.

Inkomstenbelasting nr. 92 N.A.

— 39 —

(-38- is blank)

dotam group

TO ESTABLISH A COMPANY IN THE NETHERLANDS (USUALLY A B.V.) AND/OR IN THE NETHERLANDS ANTILLES (N.V.)

1. To simplify communications, Dotam has developed a telex form which when completed, can be used to telex (or cable) Dotam. Dotam will, on receipt, commence formation procedures.

2. Directions for using attached telex form:

A) *Fill in:* H (Holland) NA (Netherlands Antilles)
If a particular address is required, please provide.

B) Dutch and Antillian company law distinguishes between the Board of Management and the Board of Supervisors (BoS), the so-called two-tier system.
Dotam advises installing a BoS whenever possible because a member of the BoS is allowed by law to inspect the books of the company, suspend and/or dismiss management, etc. This provides the ultimate shareholders with the opportunity to assume control should this action be deemed appropriate.
Fill in: BoS if desired or nil if a BoS is not required.

C) *Fill in:* Name of Shareholder(s)
If a Dutch Company is to have NA Shareholders — Please identify the 'ultimate beneficiary. Processing of the paperwork through the Dutch Ministry of Justice is less time consuming, when the Shareholder is a quoted company or is resident in a non-tax haven jurisdiction.

D) *Fill in:* Suggested name of company. Please provide two alternates. The name has to be checked out with the Chamber of Commerce in order to avoid confusion should two companies prove to have the same or a similar name.

E) *Fill in:* The objects of the company. In the event that the exact wording of the objects is important, please provide the exact wording. Otherwise a summary will suffice.

F) *Fill in:* Amount of paid-up capital. Minimum Dfl. 35,000, – for B.V. as well as N.V. If a high authorized capital is required, the following structure might be helpful:
paid-up capital: 10% of issued capital
issued capital: 20% of authorized capital.
In Holland a one-time 1% registration fee is payable on the paid-up capital (a tax deductible expense).

G) *Fill in:* The clients' appointee(s) if any. Data required for individuals:
1) full name
2) address
3) place of birth
4) date of birth
5) nationality
The above is in addition to the information that the Dotam Group will provide.

H) *Fill in:* Accounting year – This may run for a full 12 months starting at any date. Sometimes a short or long first year might be helpful, e.g. 3 months or 22 months.

I) *Fill in:* Names of BoS appointee(s) if any. Data required:
1) full name
2) address
3) place of birth
4) date of birth
5) nationality

Formulier Inkomstenbelasting nr. 92 N.A.

4. De verzoeker verklaart dat hij op de aan de ommezijde in kolom (c) vermelde datum(s) van betaalbaarstelling inwoner van de Nederlandse Antillen is (was) in de zin van de Belastingregeling voor het Koninkrijk.

5. De verzoeker verklaart dat hij de aan de ommezijde in kolom (a) vermelde effecten niet heeft verkregen ingevolge enige overeenkomst, optie of regeling, waarbij hij is overeengekomen of kan worden verplicht de effecten weer te verkopen of over te dragen of soortgelijke effecten te verkopen of over te dragen.

6. De verzoeker verklaart dat de effecten op de aan de ommezijde in kolom (c) vermelde datum(s) van betaalbaarstelling zich bevinden (bevonden) te:

onder berusting van: (1)

Datum: Handtekening: (2)

(1) Naam en adres van de bewaarnemer.
(2) Indien een gemachtigde tekent de machtiging bijvoegen. Indien de verzoeker een maatschappij of ander lichaam is, dient de hoedanigheid van de ondertekenaar te worden vermeld.

BEVESTIGING DOOR DE BEVOEGDE AANSLAGREGELENDE AUTORITEIT IN DE NEDERLANDSE ANTILLEN

De ondergetekende, ... (functie)
te .... bevestigt dat de verklaring onder
nr. 4 in bovenstaand verzoek juist is.

Datum: .... Handtekening:

(officieel stempel)

Article I

(1) The taxes which are the subject of the present Convention are:

(a) In the case of the United States: the Federal income taxes.

(b) In the case of the Netherlands:

(i) for the application of the provisions of the Convention other than Article XX, the income tax and the Netherlands taxes credited against it, the corporation tax and the Netherlands taxes credited against it, the property tax, and the tax on fees of directors and managers of corporations; and

(ii) for the application of Articles XX to XXVIII inclusive (except Articles XXIV and XXVII), the capital accretions tax and the extraordinary capital tax.

(2) The present Convention shall apply also to any other taxes of a substantially similar character imposed by either Contracting State subsequently to the date of signature of the present Convention, or, by the government of any overseas part of the Kingdom (in the case of the Netherlands) or overseas territory (in the case of the United States) to which the present Convention is extended under Article XXVII, subsequently to the date of the notification of extension.

(3) In the event of appreciable changes in the fiscal laws of either of the Contracting States the competent authorities of the Contracting States will consult together.

Article II

(1) In the present Convention, unless the context otherwise requires:

(a) The term "United States" means the United States of America, and when used in the geographical sense means the States thereof and the District of Columbia.

(b) The term "Netherlands" means only the Kingdom of the Netherlands in Europe.

(c) The term "United States corporation" means a corporation, association or other organization or juridical entity created in the United States or under the laws of the United States or of any State or territory of the United States.

(d) The term "Netherlands corporation" means a corporation, association or other organization or juridical entity created in the Netherlands or under the laws of the Netherlands.

(e) The terms "corporation of one Contracting State" and "corporation of the other Contracting State" mean a United States corporation or a Netherlands corporation, as the context requires.

(f) The term "United States enterprise" means an industrial or commercial enterprise or undertaking carried on in the United States by a citizen or resident of the United States or by a United States corporation.

(g) The term "Netherlands enterprise" means an industrial or commercial enterprise or undertaking carried on in the Netherlands by a citizen or resident of the Netherlands or by a Netherlands corporation.

(h) The terms "enterprise of one of the Contracting States" and "enterprise of the other Contracting State" mean a United States enterprise or a Netherlands enterprise, as the context requires.

(i)

(A) The term "permanent establishment" means a fixed place of business in which the business of an enterprise of one of the Contracting States is wholly or partly carried on.

---

dotam group

TELEX TO DOTAM – THE NETHERLANDS
Telex number 16791 (dotam nl)
attn: Dotrust

A) Situs of incorporation:

B) Board of Supervisors:

C) Shareholder(s):

D) Company Name and two alternates:

E) Object of the Company:

F) Capital:

  1) authorized:

  2) issued:

  3) paid-up:

G) Management [Dotam appointee(s)] and

H) Accounting year:

I) BoS appointee(s):

Article III

(1) Industrial or commercial profits of an enterprise of one of the Contracting States shall be exempt from tax by the other State unless the enterprise has a permanent establishment in such other State. If the enterprise has such a permanent establishment, tax may be imposed by such other State on the industrial or commercial profits of the enterprise, but only on so much of them as are attributable to the permanent establishment or are derived within such other State from sales of goods or merchandise of the same kind as those sold, or from other business transactions of the same kind as those effected, through the permanent establishment.

(2) Where an enterprise of one of the Contracting States has a permanent establishment in the other State, there shall in each Contracting State be attributed to such permanent establishment the industrial or commercial profits which it might be expected to derive if it were an independent enterprise engaged in the same or similar activities under the same or similar conditions and dealing at arm's length with the enterprise of which it is a permanent establishment. Where the enterprise, in addition to the profits derived through the permanent establishment, derives other profits of the kind referred to in paragraph (1), such other profits shall be treated as if they were derived through the permanent establishment.

(3) In determining the industrial or commercial profits of an enterprise of one of the Contracting States which are taxable in the other State in accordance with paragraphs (1) and (2), there shall be allowed as deductions all expenses, wherever incurred, which are reasonably connected with the profits so taxable, including executive and general administrative expenses.

(4) No profits shall be attributed to a permanent establishment merely by reason of the purchase by that permanent establishment or by the enterprise itself, of goods or merchandise for the account of the enterprise.

(5) The term "industrial or commercial profits" means income derived from the active conduct of a trade or business, but does not include income dealt with in Article VII (dividends), Article VIII (interest), Article IX (royalties), Articles V and X (income from real property and natural resources), Article XI (capital gains) and Article XVI (personal services), other than income described in Articles VII, paragraph 3, VIII, paragraph 2, IX, paragraph 3 and XI, paragraph 2. The term "industrial or commercial profits" includes profits derived by an enterprise from the furnishing of services of employees or other personnel.

Prior to amendment by supplementary convention signed December 30, 1965, Article III read as follows:

"(1) An enterprise of one of the Contracting States shall not be subject to taxation by the other Contracting State in respect of its industrial or commercial profits unless it is engaged in trade or business in the other Contracting State through a permanent establishment situated therein. If it is so engaged the other Contracting State may impose the tax only upon the income of such enterprise from sources within such other State.

"(2) Where an enterprise of one of the Contracting States is engaged in trade or business in the other Contracting State through a permanent establishment situated therein, there shall be attributed to such permanent establishment the industrial or commercial profits which it might be expected to derive if it were an independent enterprise engaged in the same or similar activities under the same or similar conditions and dealing at arm's length with the enterprise of which it is a permanent establishment, and the profits so attributed shall, subject to the law of such other Contracting State, be deemed to be income from sources within such other Contracting State.

"(3) In determining the industrial or commercial profits from sources within one of the Contracting States of an enterprise of the other Contracting State, no profits shall be deemed to arise from the mere purchase of goods or merchandise within the former Contracting State by such enterprise.

"(4) The competent authorities of the Contracting States may lay down rules by agreement for the apportionment of industrial or commercial profits."

Article IV

(1) Where a resident or corporation of a Contracting State and any other person are related and where such related persons make arrangements or impose conditions between themselves which are different from those which would be made between independent persons, then any income which, but for those arrangements or conditions, would have accrued to such resident or corporation, may be included in the income of such resident or corporation for purposes of the present Convention and taxed accordingly.

(2)

(a) A person other than a corporation is related to a corporation if such person participates directly or indirectly in the management, control or capital of the corporation.

(b) A corporation is related to another corporation if either participates directly or indirectly in the management, control, or capital of the other, or if any person or persons participate directly or indirectly in the management, control or capital of both corporations.

Prior to amendment by supplementary convention signed December 30, 1965, Article IV read as follows:

"Where an enterprise of one of the Contracting States, by reason of its participation in the management, control or capital of an enterprise of the other Contracting State, makes with or imposes on the latter enterprise, in their commercial or financial relations, conditions different from those which would be made with an independent enterprise, any profits which would, but for those conditions, have accrued to one of the enterprises, may be included in the taxable profits of that enterprise."

Article V

Income from real property (including gains derived from the sale of such property, but not including interest from mortgages or bonds secured by real property) and royalties from the operation of mines, quarries, or other natural resources may be taxed in

(B) A permanent establishment shall include especially:

(i) a branch;

(ii) an office;

(iii) a sales outlet;

(iv) a factory;

(v) a workshop;

(vi) a mine, quarry or other place of extraction of natural resources;

(vii) a building site or construction or assembly project which exists for more than twelve months.

(C) Notwithstanding sub-paragraph (i)(A) of this paragraph a permanent establishment shall not be deemed to include one or more of the following activities:

(i) the use of facilities for the purpose of storage, display or delivery of goods or merchandise belonging to the enterprise;

(ii) the maintenance of a stock of goods or merchandise belonging to the enterprise for the purpose of storage, display or delivery;

(iii) the maintenance of a stock of goods or merchandise belonging to the enterprise for the purpose of processing by another enterprise;

(iv) the maintenance of a fixed place of business for the purpose of purchasing goods or merchandise, or for collecting information, for the enterprise;

(v) the maintenance of a fixed place of business for the purpose of advertising, for the supply of information, for scientific research or for similar activities, if they have a preparatory or auxiliary character for the enterprise.

(D) Even if an enterprise of one of the Contracting States does not have a permanent establishment in the other State under sub-paragraph (i)(A) to (C) of this paragraph, nevertheless it shall be deemed to have a permanent establishment in the latter State if it is engaged in trade or business in that State through an agent who has an authority to conclude contracts in the name of the enterprise and regularly exercises that authority in that State, unless the exercise of authority is limited to the purchase of goods or merchandise for the account of the enterprise.

(E) An enterprise of one of the Contracting States shall not be deemed to have a permanent establishment in the other State merely because it is engaged in trade or business in that other State through a broker, general commission agent or any other agent of an independent status, where such persons are acting in the ordinary course of their business.

(F) The fact that a resident or a corporation of one of the Contracting States controls, is controlled by, or is under common control with:

(i) a corporation of the other State; or

(ii) a corporation which engages in trade or business in that other State (whether through a permanent establishment or otherwise)

shall not be taken into account in determining whether such resident or corporation has a permanent establishment in that other State."

(i) The term "competent authority" or "competent authorities" means, in the case of United States, the Commissioner of Internal Revenue or his duly authorized representative; and, in the case of the Netherlands, the Directeur-Generaal der Belastingen or his duly authorized representative; and, in the case of any part or territory to which provisions of the present Convention are extended under Article XXVII, the competent authority for the administration in such part or territory of the taxes to which such provisions apply.

(2) In the application of the provisions of the present Convention by either of the Contracting States, any term which is not defined in the present Convention shall, unless the context otherwise requires, have the meaning which that term has under the laws of such Contracting State relating to the taxes which are the subject of the present Convention.

Prior to amendment by supplementary convention signed December 30, 1965, clauses (1)(a) and (i) read as follows:

"(a) The term "United States" means the United States of America, and when used in a geographical sense means the States, the Territories of Alaska and of Hawaii, and the District of Columbia."

"(i) The term "permanent establishment", when used with respect to an enterprise of one of the Contracting States, means a branch, factory, or other fixed place of business, but does not include an agency unless the agent has, and habitually exercises, a general authority to negotiate and conclude contracts on behalf of such enterprise or has a stock of merchandise from which he regularly fills orders on behalf of such enterprise. An enterprise of one of the Contracting States shall not be deemed to have a permanent establishment in the other Contracting State merely because it carries on business dealings in such other Contracting State through a bona fide commission agent, broker or custodian acting in the ordinary course of his business as such. The fact that an enterprise of one of the Contracting States maintains in the other Contracting State a fixed place of business exclusively for the purchase of goods or merchandise shall not of itself constitute such fixed place of business a permanent establishment of such enterprise. When a corporation of one Contracting State has a subsidiary corporation which is a corporation of the other Contracting State or which is engaged in trade or business in such other Contracting State, such subsidiary corporation shall not, merely because of that fact, be deemed to be a permanent establishment of its parent corporation."

the Contracting State in which such property is situated.

Prior to amendment by supplementary convention signed December 30, 1965, Article V read as follows:

"Income of whatever nature derived from real property and interest from mortgages secured by real property shall be taxable only in the Contracting State in which the real property is situated."

Article VI

(1) Income which an enterprise of one of the Contracting States derives from the operation of ships or aircraft registered in that State shall be taxable only in the State in which such ships or aircraft are registered. Income derived by such an enterprise from the operation of ships or aircraft not so registered shall be subject to the provisions of Article III.

(2) The present Convention shall be deemed to suspend, for the duration of the Convention as between the United States and the Netherlands, the provisions of the arrangement effected by exchange of notes between the United States and the Netherlands, dated September 13, October 19, and November 27, 1926, providing for relief from double income taxation on shipping profits.

(3) In the event that the application of this Article is extended to the Netherland Indies in accordance with Article XXVII, the exchange of notes between the United States and the Netherlands, dated March 8, May 23, and November 8, 1939, relating to the arrangement referred to in paragraph (2) of this Article, shall be deemed to be suspended for so long as this Article continues to be applicable with respect to the Netherland Indies.

Article VII

(1) Dividends paid by a corporation of one of the Contracting States to a resident or corporation of the other Contracting State shall be taxed as follows in the former State:

(a) at a rate not exceeding 15 percent of the gross amount actually distributed; or

(b) at a rate not exceeding 5 percent of the gross amount actually distributed, if during the part of the paying corporation's taxable year which precedes the date of payment of the dividend and the whole of its prior taxable year (if any), the recipient is a corporation owning at least 25 percent of the voting stock of the paying corporation, either alone or in combination with another corporation of such other State, provided each recipient corporation owned at least 10 percent of such voting stock.

(2) The rules of subparagraph (b) shall not apply if more than 25 percent of the gross income of the paying corporation for such prior taxable year (if any) consisted of interest and dividends (other than interest derived in the conduct of a banking, insurance or financing business and dividends or interest received from subsidiary corporations, 50 percent or more of the voting stock of which was owned by the corporation at the time such dividends or interest were received).

(3) Paragraph (1) of this Article shall not apply if the recipient of the dividends has a permanent establishment in the former Contracting State and the shares with respect to which the dividends are paid are effectively connected with the permanent establishment. In such a case, the provisions of Article III shall apply.

Prior to amendment by supplementary convention signed December 30, 1965, Article VII read as follows:

"(1) The rate of United States tax on dividends derived from a United States corporation by a resident or corporation of the Netherlands not engaged in trade or business in the United States through a permanent establishment shall not exceed 15 percent: Provided that such rate of tax shall not exceed 5 percent if such Netherlands corporation controls, directly or indirectly, at least 95 percent of the entire voting power in the corporation paying the dividend, and not more than 25 percent of the gross income of such paying corporation is derived from interest and dividends, other than interest and dividends from its own subsidiary corporation. Such reduction of the rate to 5 percent shall not apply if the relationship of the two corporations has been arranged or is maintained primarily with the intention of securing such reduced rate.

"(2) Dividends derived from sources within the Netherlands by a resident or corporation of the United States not engaged in trade or business in the Netherlands through a permanent establishment shall be exempt from Netherlands tax.

"(3) Either of the Contracting States may terminate this Article, by giving written notice of termination to the other Contracting State through diplomatic channels, on or before the thirtieth day of June in any year after the first year for which the present Convention becomes effective. In such event this Article shall cease to be effective on and after the first day of January in the year next following that in which such notice is given."

Article VIII

(1) Interest on bonds, notes, debentures, securities, deposits or any other form of indebtedness (including interest from mortgages or bonds secured by real property) paid to a resident or corporation of one of the Contracting States shall be exempt from tax by the other Contracting State.

(2) Paragraph (1) of this Article shall not apply if the recipient of the interest has a permanent establishment in the other Contracting State and the indebtedness giving rise to the interest is effectively connected with the permanent establishment. In such a case, the provisions of Article III shall apply.

(3) Where any interest paid by a person to a related person, as defined in Article IV, exceeds a fair and reasonable consideration in respect of the indebtedness for which it is paid, paragraph (1) of this Article shall apply only to so much of such interest as represents such fair and reasonable consideration, and the excess payment shall be characterized and taxed according to the laws of each Contracting State, including the provisions of this Convention where applicable.

Prior to amendment by supplementary convention signed December 30, 1965, Article VIII read as follows:

"(1) Interest (on bonds, securities, notes, debentures, or on any other form of indebtedness), other than interest referred to in Article V of the present Convention, derived from sources within the United States by a resident or corporation of the Netherlands not engaged in trade or business in the United States through a permanent establishment, shall be exempt from United States tax; but such exemption shall not apply to such interest paid by a United States corporation to a Netherlands corporation controlling, directly or indirectly, more than 50 percent of the entire voting power in the paying corporation.

"(2) Interest (on bonds, securities, notes, debentures, or on any other form of indebtedness), other than interest referred to in Article V of the present Convention, derived from sources within the Netherlands by a resident or corporation of the United States not engaged in trade or business in the Netherlands through a permanent establishment, shall be exempt from Netherlands tax; but such exemption shall not apply to such interest paid by a Netherlands corporation to a United States corporation controlling, directly or indirectly, more than 50 percent of the entire voting power in the paying corporation."

Article IX

(1) Royalties paid to a resident or corporation of one of the Contracting States shall be exempt from tax by the other Contracting State.

(2) For the purposes of this Article, the term 'royalties' means any royalties, rentals or other amounts paid as consideration for the use of, or the right to use:

(a) copyrights, artistic or scientific works, patents, designs, plans, secret processes or formulae, trademarks, motion picture films, films or tapes for radio or television broadcasting, or other like property or rights, or

(b) information concerning industrial, commercial or scientific knowledge, experience or skill.

(3) Paragraph (1) of this Article shall not apply if the recipient of the royalties has a permanent establishment in the other Contracting State and the right or property giving rise to the royalties is effectively connected with the permanent establishment. In such a case, the provisions of Article III shall apply.

(4) Where any royalty paid by a person to a related person, as defined in Article IV, exceeds a fair and reasonable consideration in respect of the rights for which it is paid, paragraph (1) of this Article shall apply only to so much of the royalty as represents such fair and reasonable consideration, and the excess payment shall be characterized and taxed according to the laws of each Contracting State, including the provisions of this Convention where applicable.

Prior to amendment by supplementary convention signed December 30, 1965, Article IX read as follows:

"Royalties for the right to use copyrights, patents, designs, secret processes and formulae, trade marks, and other analogous property, and royalties, including rentals, in respect of motion picture films or for the use of industrial, commercial or scientific equipment, derived from sources within one of the Contracting States by a resident or corporation of the other Contracting State not engaged in trade or business in the former State through a permanent establishment, shall be exempt from tax imposed by the former State."

Article X

A resident or corporation of one of the Contracting States, deriving from sources within the other Contracting State royalties in respect of the operation of mines, quarries, or natural resources, or rentals from real property, may elect for any taxable year to be subject to the tax of such other Contracting State, on a net basis, as if such resident or corporation were engaged in trade or business within such other Contracting State through a permanent establishment therein during such taxable year.

Article XI

(1) Gains derived by a resident or corporation of one of the Contracting States from the alienation of a capital asset (other than gain from the alienation of real property to which Article V applies) shall be exempt from tax by the other Contracting State.

(2) If such resident or corporation has a permanent establishment in the other Contracting State, paragraph (1) of this Article shall not apply to gains derived by such resident or corporation from the alienation of a capital asset which is effectively connected with the permanent establishment. In such a case, the provisions of Article III shall apply.

(3) Paragraph (1) of this Article shall not apply if:

(a) the person deriving the gain is an individual who is a resident of the Netherlands and who is present in the United States for a period of 183 days or more during the taxable year, and

(b) the asset alienated was held by such person for six months or less.

(4) Paragraph (1) of this Article does not affect the right of the Netherlands to levy, according to its own law, a tax on the gains derived from the alienation of shares, or 'jouissance' shares, in a Netherlands joint stock corporation, by an individual who is a resident of the United States and who at the time of alienation:

(a) is a Netherlands citizen,

(b) has, at any time during the five-year period preceding such alienation, been a resident of the Netherlands, and

(c) owns, either alone or together with his close relatives, at least 25 percent of the voting stock of such corporation.

Article XI was added by supplementary convention signed December 30, 1965.

Prior Article XI was deleted by agreement of the two parties on ratification of the original treaty. It had read as follows:

"A resident or corporation of one of the Contracting States not engaged in trade or business in the other Contracting State shall be

exempt from tax in such other State on gains from the sale or exchange of capital assets.'

Dividends and interest paid by a Netherlands corporation shall be exempt from United States tax except where the recipient is a citizen, resident, or corporation of the United States.

Article XIII was deleted by agreement to U.S. Senate reservation on ratification of the original treaty. It had read as follows:

'A Netherlands corporation shall be exempt from United States tax on its accumulated or undistributed earnings, profits, income or surplus if it can prove to the satisfaction of the competent authorities of the United States that individuals who are residents of the Netherlands (other than citizens of the United States) control, directly or indirectly, throughout the last half of the taxable year, more than 50 percent of the entire voting power in such corporation.'

Article XIV

(1) The United States income tax liability for any taxable year beginning prior to January 1, 1936 of any individual (other than a citizen of the United States) resident in the Netherlands, or of any Netherlands corporation, or of any citizens or residents of the United States, may be adjusted on a basis satisfactory to the United States Commissioner of Internal Revenue: Provided that the amount to be paid in settlement of such liability shall not exceed the amount of the liability which would have been determined if

(a) the United States Revenue Act of 1936 (except in the case of a Netherlands corporation in which more than 50 percent of the entire voting power was controlled, directly or indirectly, throughout the latter half of the taxable year, by citizens or residents of the United States), and

(b) Articles XII and XIII of the present Convention, had been in effect for such year. If the taxpayer was a citizen of the Netherlands within the meaning of such Revenue Act, engaged in trade or business in the United States and had no office or place of business therein during the taxable year, the amount of interest and penalties shall not exceed 50 percent of the amount of the tax with respect to which such interest and penalties have been computed.

(2) The United States income tax unpaid on the effective date of the present Convention for any taxable year beginning after December 31, 1935 and prior to the effective date of the present Convention in the case of an individual (other than a citizen of the United States) resident of the Netherlands, or in the case of any Netherlands corporation, shall be determined as if the provisions of Articles XII and XIII of the present Convention had been in effect for such taxable year.

(3) The provisions of paragraph (1) of this Article shall not apply

(a) unless the taxpayer files with the Commissioner of Internal Revenue within a period of two years following the effective date of the present Convention a request that such tax liability be so adjusted and furnishes such information as the Commissioner may require; or

(b) in any case in which the Commissioner is satisfied that any deficiency in tax is due to fraud with intent to evade the tax.

A U.S. Senate reservation to Article XIII was deleted by the Netherlands. It eliminated (a) all references to Article XIII, and (b) any language which might prevent taxation by the United States of capital gains.

Article XV

(1) Wages, salaries and similar compensation and pensions, annuities or similar benefits paid by, or out of funds created by, one of the Contracting States or the political subdivisions thereof to an individual who is a citizen of that Contracting State for services rendered to that Contracting State or to any of its political subdivisions in the discharge of governmental functions shall be exempt from tax by the other Contracting State.

(2) Private pensions and life annuities derived from within one of the Contracting States and paid to individuals resident in the other Contracting State shall be exempt from taxation in the former State.

(3) The term "pensions" as used in this Article means periodic payments made in consideration for services rendered or by way of compensation for injuries received.

(4) The term "life annuities" as used in this Article means a stated sum payable periodically at stated times during life, or during a specified number of years, under an obligation to make the payments in return for adequate and full consideration in money or money's worth.

Prior to amendment by supplementary convention signed December 30, 1965, paragraph (1) read as follows:

'(1) Wages, salaries and similar compensation, and pensions and life annuities, paid either directly by, or from funds created by, one of the Contracting States or the political subdivision or territories thereof to individuals in the other Contracting State shall be exempt from taxation in the latter State.'

Article XVI

(1) An individual who is a resident of one of the Contracting States shall be exempt from tax by the other Contracting State with respect to income from personal services if—

(a) he is present within the latter Contracting State for a period or periods not exceeding in the aggregate 183 days during the taxable year, and

(b) in the case of employment income—

(i) such individual is an employee of a resident of a State other than the latter Contracting State or of a permanent establishment of a resident or corpora-

tion of the latter Contracting State located outside the latter Contracting State, and

(ii) such income is not deducted as such in computing the profits of a permanent establishment in the latter Contracting State.

(2) For purposes of paragraph (1), the term 'income from personal services' includes employment income and income earned by an individual from the performance of personal services in an independent capacity. The term 'employment income' includes income from services performed by officers and directors of corporations, but does not include income from personal services performed by partners.

Prior to amendment by supplementary convention signed December 30, 1965, Article XVI read as follows:

'(1) A resident of the Netherlands shall be exempt from United States tax upon compensation for labor or personal services performed within the United States if he is temporarily present within the United States for a period or periods not exceeding a total of one hundred eighty-three days during the taxable year and his compensation is received for labor or personal services performed as a worker or employee of, or under contract with, a resident of the Netherlands, or a Netherlands corporation, carrying the actual burden of the remuneration.

'(2) The provisions of paragraph (1) of this Article shall apply, mutatis mutandis, to a resident of the United States deriving compensation for labor or personal services performed within the Netherlands.'

Article XVII

(1) An individual who is a resident of one of the Contracting States at the beginning of his visit to the other Contracting State and who, at the invitation of a university or other accredited educational institution situated in the other Contracting State, visits the other Contracting State for the primary purpose of teaching or engaging in research, at a university or other accredited educational institution shall be exempt from tax by the other Contracting State on his income from personal services for teaching or research at such institutions, for a period not exceeding two years from the date of his arrival in the other Contracting State.

(2) This Article shall not apply to income from research if such research is undertaken not in the public interest but primarily for the private benefit of a specific person or persons.

Prior to amendment by supplementary convention signed December 30, 1965, Article XVII read as follows:

'Professors or teachers, residents of one of the Contracting States, who, in accordance with agreements between the Contracting States or between teaching establishments in the Contracting States for the exchange of professors and teachers, visit the other Contracting State to teach, for a maximum period of two years, in a university, college or other teaching establishment in such other Contracting State, shall not be taxed by such other State with respect to the remuneration which they receive for such teaching.'

Article XVIII

(1) An individual who is a resident of one of the Contracting States at the beginning of his visit to the other Contracting State and who is temporarily present in the other Contracting State for the primary purpose of:

(i) studying at a university or other accredited educational institution in that other Contracting State or otherwise engaging in research of an educational nature, or

(ii) securing training required to qualify him to practice a profession or professional specialty,

shall be exempt from tax by that other Contracting State with respect to:

(A) gifts from abroad for the purpose of his maintenance, education, study, research or training;

(B) a grant, allowance, or award by a government, educational institution, or non-profit organization; and

(C) income from personal services performed in the other Contracting State in an amount not in excess of $2,000 (in the case of services performed in the United States) or 3,600 guilders (in the case of services performed in the Netherlands) for any taxable year.

(b) The benefits under this paragraph shall only extend for such period of time as may be reasonably or customarily required to effectuate the purpose of the visit, but in no event shall any individual have the benefits of this paragraph for more than five taxable years.

(2) A resident of one of the Contracting States who is present in the other Contracting State as an employee of, or under contract with, a resident or corporation of the former State, for the primary purpose of:

(i) acquiring technical, professional, or business experience from a person other than that resident or corporation of the former State or a corporation 50 percent or more of the voting stock of which is owned by such corporation of the former State, or

(ii) studying at a university or other accredited educational institution in that other Contracting State,

shall be exempt from tax by that other Contracting State for one taxable year with respect to his income from personal services in an amount not in excess of $5,000 (in the case of services performed in the United States) or 18,000 guilders (in the case of services performed in the Netherlands).

Prior to amendment by supplementary convention signed December 30, 1965, Article XVIII read as follows:

'Students or business apprentices of one Contracting State residing in the other Contracting State exclusively for purposes of study or for acquiring business experience shall not be taxable by the

latter State in respect of remittances received by them from abroad for the purpose of their maintenance or studies."

Article XIX

(1) Notwithstanding any provisions of the present Convention (other than paragraph (1) of Article XV when applicable in the case of an individual who is deemed by each Contracting State to be a citizen thereof), each of the two Contracting States, in determining the taxes, including all surtaxes, of its citizens or residents or corporations, may include in the basis upon which such taxes are imposed all items of income taxable under its own revenue laws as though this Convention had not come into effect.

(2) The United States shall allow to a citizen, resident or corporation of the United States as a credit against its tax specified in subparagraph (1)(a) of Article I the appropriate amount of taxes paid to the Netherlands. Such appropriate amount shall be based upon the amount of tax paid to the Netherlands on income from sources within the Netherlands but shall not exceed that proportion of the United States tax which taxable income from sources within the Netherlands bears to the entire taxable income. For purposes of this paragraph, taxable income shall be computed without any deduction for personal exemptions. It is agreed that, by virtue of the provisions of paragraph (3) of this Article, the Netherlands has satisfied the similar credit requirement of the Internal Revenue Code with respect to taxes paid to the Netherlands.

(3) As far as may be in accordance with the provisions of Netherlands law, the Netherlands agrees to allow a deduction from Netherlands tax with respect to income from sources within the United States, in order to take into account the Federal income taxes paid to the United States, whether paid directly by the taxpayer or by withholding at the source. In addition, the Netherlands shall allow a deduction from the Netherlands tax, determined in conformity with paragraph (1), with respect to dividends received from a United States corporation by a resident or corporation of Netherlands. The amount of this deduction shall be the lesser of the following:

(a) an amount equal to 15 percent of the dividends; or

(b) an amount that is the same proportion of the Netherlands tax, determined in conformity with paragraph (1) of this Article, as the amount of the dividends bears to the income which forms the basis for the determination of the Netherlands tax.

Prior to amendment by supplementary convention signed December 30, 1965, Article XIX read as follows:

"(1) Notwithstanding any provisions of the present Convention (other than paragraph (1) of Article XV when applicable in the case of an individual who is deemed by each Contracting State to be a citizen thereof), each of the two Contracting States, in determining the taxes, including all surtaxes, of its citizens or residents or corporations, may include in the basis upon which such taxes are imposed all items of income taxable under its own revenue laws as though this Convention had not come into effect.

"(2) As far as may be in accordance with the provisions of the United States Internal Revenue Code, the United States agrees to allow as a deduction from the income taxes imposed by the United States the appropriate amount of taxes paid to the Netherlands, whether paid directly by the taxpayer or by withholding at the source.

"(3) As far as may be in accordance with the provisions of Netherlands law, the Netherlands agrees to allow a deduction from income from sources within the United States, in order to take into account the Federal income taxes paid directly by the taxpayer or by withholding at the source."

Article XX

(1) All persons who left the Netherlands between April 30, 1939 and December 31, 1945, inclusive (other than persons who were citizens of the United States or of the Netherlands or Netherlands subjects who by reason of their function as governmental officials in established service reside abroad and the members of their family living with them), and who are deemed to be taxpayers under the provisions of Netherlands law relating to the capital accretions tax or the extraordinary capital tax, and who became residents of the United States (according to the income tax law of the United States) during that period, and who did not return to the Netherlands on or before December 31, 1945 to resume residence in the Netherlands (according to the income tax law of the Netherlands), shall be taxable by the Netherlands:

(a) under the law relating to the capital accretions tax, only in respect of accretions arising from their property situated in the Netherlands (as defined in that law in the case of nonresidents) and from their activities in the Netherlands;

(b) under the law relating to the extraordinary capital tax, only in respect of their property situated in the Netherlands (as defined in that law in the case of nonresidents).

(2) All persons who left the Netherlands between April 30, 1939 and December 31, 1945, inclusive, and who were citizens of the United States at the time of leaving the Netherlands, and who are deemed to be taxpayers under the provisions of Netherlands law relating to the capital accretions tax or the extraordinary capital tax of the United States (according to the income tax law of the United States) on or before December 31, 1945, shall be taxable by the Netherlands:

(a) under the law relating to the capital accretions tax, only in respect of accretions arising from their property situated in the Netherlands (as defined in that law in the case of nonresidents) and from their activities in the Netherlands;

(b) under the law relating to the extraordinary capital tax, only in respect of their property situated in the Netherlands (as defined in that law in the case of nonresidents).

(3) The provisions of this Article shall be deemed to be effective as though the present Convention had entered into force on the effective date of the Netherlands law relating to the capital accretions tax or the extraordinary capital tax, as the case may be.

Article XXI

The competent authorities of the Contracting States shall exchange such information (being information which such authorities have in proper order at their disposal) as is necessary for carrying out the provisions of the present Convention or for the prevention of fraud or the administration of statutory provisions against legal avoidance in relation to the taxes which are the subject of the present Convention. Any information so exchanged shall be treated as secret and shall not be disclosed to any person other than those concerned with the assessment and collection of the taxes which are the subject of the present Convention. No information as aforesaid shall be exchanged which would disclose any trade, business, industrial or professional secret or trade process.

Article XXII

(1) The Contracting States undertake to lend assistance and support to each other in the collection of the taxes which are the subject of the present Convention, together with interest, costs, and additions to the taxes and fines not being of a penal character.

(2) In the case of applications for enforcement of taxes, revenue claims of each of the Contracting States which have been finally determined may be accepted for enforcement by the other Contracting State and collected in that State in accordance with the laws applicable to the enforcement and collection of its own taxes. The State to which application is made shall not be required to enforce executory measures for which there is no provision in the law of the State making the application.

(3) Any application shall be accompanied by documents establishing that under the laws of the State making the application the taxes have been finally determined.

(4) The assistance provided for in this Article shall not be accorded with respect to the citizens, corporations, or other entities of the State to which application is made, except as is necessary to insure that the exemption or reduced rate of tax granted under the convention to such citizens, corporations or other entities shall not be enjoyed by persons not entitled to such benefits.

Article XXIII

(1) In no case shall the provisions of Article XXI and XXII be construed so as to impose upon either of the Contracting States the obligation

(a) to carry out administrative measures at variance with the regulations and practice of either Contracting State, or

(b) to supply particulars which are not procurable under its own legislation or that of the State making application.

(2) The State to which application is made for information or assistance shall comply as soon as possible with the request addressed to it. Nevertheless, such State may refuse to comply with the request for reasons of public policy or if compliance would involve violation of a trade, business, industrial or professional secret or trade process. In such case it shall inform, as soon as possible, the State making the application.

Article XXIV

(1) Where a taxpayer shows proof that the action of the tax authorities of the Contracting States has resulted or will result in taxation not in accordance with the provisions of the present Convention, he shall be entitled to present his case to the State of which he is a citizen or a resident, or, if the taxpayer is a corporation of one of the Contracting States, to that State.

(2) Should the taxpayer's claim be deemed worthy of consideration, the competent authority of the State to which the claim is made shall endeavour to come to an agreement with the competent authority of the other State with a view to avoidance of taxation not in accordance with the provisions of the present Convention. In particular, the competent authorities of the Contracting States may consult together to endeavour to agree:

(a) to the same attribution of industrial or commercial profits to a permanent establishment situated in one of the States of an enterprise of the other State, or

(b) to the same allocation of profits between related enterprises as provided for in Article IV.

In the event· that the competent authorities reach such an agreement taxes shall be imposed, and refund or credit of taxes shall be allowed, by the Contracting States on such income in accordance with such agreement. If the taxpayer does not accept such agreement, the preceding sentence shall not be construed to deny a taxpayer the right to appeal to the courts the decision reached in such agreement.

(3) The competent authorities of the Contracting States may communicate with each other directly to implement the provisions of the present Convention. Should any difficulty or doubt arise as to the interpretation or application of the present Convention, the competent authorities shall endeavour to settle

the question as quickly as possible by mutual agreement.

Prior to amendment by supplementary convention signed December 30, 1965, Article XXIV read as follows:

"Where the action of the revenue authorities of the Contracting States has resulted or will result in double taxation contrary to the provisions of the present Convention, the taxpayer shall be entitled to lodge a claim with the State of which he is a citizen or subject or, if he is not a citizen or subject of either of the Contracting States, with the State of which he is a resident, or, if the taxpayer is a corporation, with the State in which it is created or organized. Should the claim be upheld, the competent authority of such State shall undertake to come to an agreement with the competent authority of the other State with a view to equitable avoidance of the double taxation in question."

Article XXV

(1) The provisions of the present Convention shall not be construed to restrict in any manner any exemption, deduction, credit or other allowance accorded by the laws of one of the Contracting States in the determination of the tax imposed by such State.

(2) A citizen of one of the Contracting States who is a resident in the other Contracting State shall not be subjected in that other Contracting State to more burdensome taxes than is a citizen of that other Contracting State who is a resident thereof.

(3) A permanent establishment which a citizen or corporation of one of the Contracting States has in the other Contracting State shall not be subjected in that other Contracting State to more burdensome taxes than is a citizen or corporation of that other Contracting State carrying on the same activities. This paragraph shall not be construed as obliging either Contracting State to grant to citizens of the other Contracting State who are not residents of the former Contracting State any personal allowances or deductions which are by its law available only to residents of that former Contracting State.

(4) A corporation of one of the Contracting States, the capital of which is wholly or partly owned by one or more citizens or corporations of the other Contracting State, shall not be subjected in the former Contracting State to more burdensome taxes than is a corporation of the former Contracting State, the capital of which is wholly owned by one or more citizens or corporations of that former Contracting State.

(5) As used in paragraphs 2, 3 and 4 of this Article the term "taxes" means taxes of every kind and whether imposed at the national, state or local level.

Prior to amendment by supplementary convention signed December 30, 1965, paragraphs (2) and (3) read as follows (there was no (4) or (5)):

"(2) Should any difficulty or doubt arise as to the interpretation or application of the present Convention, the competent authorities of the Contracting States shall undertake to settle the question by mutual agreement.

"(3) The citizens or subjects of one of the Contracting States shall not, while resident in the other Contracting State, be subjected therein to other or more burdensome taxes than are the citizens or subjects of such other Contracting State residing in its territory. The term "citizens" or "subjects" as used in this Article includes all legal persons, partnerships and associations deriving their status from, or created or organized under the laws in force in, the respective Contracting States. In this Article the word "taxes" means taxes of every kind or description whether national, federal, state, provincial or municipal."

Article XXVI

(1) The authorities of each of the Contracting States, in accordance with the practices of that State, may prescribe regulations necessary to carry out the provisions of the present Convention.

(2) With respect to the provisions of the present Convention relating to exchange of information and mutual assistance in the collection of taxes, the competent authorities may, by common agreement, prescribe rules concerning matters of procedure, forms of application and replies thereto, conversion of currency, disposition of amounts collected, minimum amounts subject to collection, and related matters.

Article XXVII

(1) Either of the Contracting States may, at the time of exchange of instruments of ratification or thereafter while the present Convention continues in force, by a written notification of extension given to the other Contracting State through diplomatic channels, declare the desire of the government of any overseas part of the Kingdom (in the case of the Netherlands) or overseas territory (in the case of the United States), which imposes taxes substantially similar in character to those which are the subject of the present Convention, that the operation of the present Convention, either in whole or as to such application, shall extend to such part or territory.

(2) In the event that a notification is given by one of the Contracting States in accordance with paragraph (1) of this Article, such provisions thereof as may be specified in the notification, shall apply to any part or territory named in such notification on and after the first day of January following the date of a written communication through diplomatic channels addressed to such Contracting State by the other Contracting State, after such action by the latter State as may be necessary in accordance with its own procedures, stating that such notification is accepted in respect of such part or territory. In the absence of such acceptance, none of the provisions of the present Convention shall apply to such part or territory.

(3) At any time after the expiration of one year from the effective date of an extension made by virtue of paragraphs (1) and (2) of this Article, either of the Contracting States may, by a written notice of termination given to the other Contracting State through diplomatic channels, terminate the application of the present Convention to any part or territory to which the Convention, or any of its provisions, has been extended. In that case, the present Convention, or the provisions thereof specified in the notice of termination, shall cease to be applicable to the part or territory named in such notice of termination on and after the first day of January following the expiration of a period of six months after the date of such notice; provided, however, that this shall not affect the continued application of the Convention, or any of the provisions thereof, to the United States, to the Netherlands, or to any part or territory (not named in the notice of termination) to which the Convention, or such provision thereof, applies.

(4) For the application of the present Convention in relation to any part or territory to which it is extended by notification given by the United States or the Netherlands, references to "the United States" or to "the Netherlands" or to one or the other Contracting State, as the case may be, shall be construed to refer to such part or territory.

Article XXVIII

(1) The present Convention shall be ratified and the instruments of ratification shall be exchanged at Washington as soon as possible.

(2) The present Convention shall become effective on the first day of January in the year last preceding the year in which the exchange of instruments of ratification takes place. It shall continue effective for a period of five years beginning with that date and indefinitely after that period, but may be terminated by either of the Contracting States at the end of the five-year period or at any time thereafter, provided that at least six months' prior notice of termination has been given, the termination to become effective on the first day of January following the expiration of the six-month period.

Supplementary convention signed 12/20/65 provided as follows:

"Article XV

"As respects the Kingdom of the Netherlands the Supplementary Convention shall only apply to the part of the Kingdom of the Netherlands that is situated in Europe.

"Article XVI

"(1) The present Supplementary Convention shall be ratified and the instruments of ratification shall be exchanged at The Hague as soon as possible.

"(2) The present Supplementary Convention shall come into force on the date of the exchange of instruments of ratification and, except as provided in paragraph (3), the articles shall have effect for taxable years beginning on or after the first day of January in the year following the year in which such exchange takes place.

"(3) Article VII shall have effect with respect to dividends paid beginning on the day after the date of exchange of instruments of ratification except that the rules of Article VII of the Convention of April 29, 1948, shall continue to apply for a period of two years beginning on the date of exchange of instruments of ratification of this Supplementary Convention with respect to dividends paid to

(a) a United States corporation or organization operated exclusively for a religious, charitable, scientific, educational or public purpose which is exempt from tax in the United States, or

(b) a trust created or organized in the United States and forming part of a stock bonus, pension, or profit sharing plan of an employer for the exclusive benefit of his employees or their beneficiaries which is exempt from tax in the United States

if such corporation, organization, or trust owned on April 30, 1965, the shares with respect to which such dividends are paid."

Article I

(1) The taxes which are the subject of the present Convention are:

(a) In the case of the United States: the Federal income taxes.

(b) In the case of the Netherlands:

(i) for the application of the provisions of the Convention other than Article XX, the income tax and the Netherlands taxes credited against it, the corporation tax and the Netherlands taxes credited against it, the property tax, and the tax on fees of directors and managers of corporations; and

(ii) for the application of Articles XX to XXVIII inclusive (except Articles XXIV and XXVII), the capital accretions tax and the extraordinary capital tax.

(2) The present Convention shall apply also to any other taxes of a substantially similar character imposed by either Contracting State subsequently to the date of signature of the present Convention, or, by the government of any overseas part of the Kingdom (in the case of the Netherlands) or overseas territory (in the case of the United States) to which the present Convention is extended under Article XXVII, subsequently to the date of the notification of extension.

(3) In the event of appreciable changes in the fiscal laws of either of the Contracting States the competent authorities of the Contracting States will consult together.

Article I (1) has application in the Netherlands Antilles only in respect of income taxes and profits taxes, since no property tax is levied in that jurisdiction.

Article II

(1) In the present Convention, unless the context otherwise requires:

(a) The term "United States" means the United States of America, and when used in a geographical sense means the States, the Territories of Alaska and of Hawaii, and the District of Columbia.

(b) The term "Netherlands" means only the Kingdom of the Netherlands in Europe.

(c) The term "United States corporation" means a corporation, association or other organization or juridical entity created in the United States or under the laws of the United States or of any State or territory of the United States.

(d) The term "Netherlands corporation" means a corporation, association or other organization or juridical entity created under the laws or under the laws of the Netherlands.

(e) The terms "corporation of one Contracting State" and "corporation of the other Contracting State" mean a United States corporation or a Netherlands corporation, as the context requires.

(f) The term "United States enterprise" means an industrial or commercial enterprise or undertaking carried on in the United States by a citizen or resident of the United States or by a United States corporation.

(g) The term "Netherlands enterprise" means an industrial or commercial enterprise or undertaking carried on in the Netherlands by a citizen or resident of the Netherlands or by a Netherlands corporation.

(h) The terms "enterprise of one of the Contracting States" and "enterprise of the other Contracting State" mean a United States enterprise or a Netherlands enterprise, as the context requires.

(i) The term "permanent establishment", when used with respect to an enterprise of one of the Contracting States, means a branch, factory, or other fixed place of business, but does not include an agency unless the agent has, and habitually exercises, a general authority to negotiate and conclude contracts on behalf of such enterprise or has a stock of merchandise from which he regularly fills orders on behalf of such enterprise. An enterprise of one of the Contracting States shall not be deemed to have a permanent establishment in the other Contracting State merely because it carries on business dealings in such other Contracting State through a *bona fide* commission agent, broker or custodian acting in the ordinary course of his business as such. The fact that an enterprise of one of the Contracting States maintains in the other Contracting State a fixed place of business exclusively for the purchase of goods or merchandise shall not of itself constitute such fixed place of business a permanent establishment of such enterprise. When a corporation of one Contracting State has a subsidiary corporation which is a corporation of the other Contracting State or which is engaged in trade or business in such other Contracting State, such subsidiary corporation shall not, merely because of that fact, be deemed to be a permanent establishment of its parent corporation.

(j) The term "competent authority" or "competent authorities" means, in the case of the United States, the Commissioner of Internal Revenue or his duly authorized representative; in the case of the Netherlands, the Directeur-Generaal der Belastingen or his duly authorized representative; and, in the case of any part or territory to which provisions of the present Convention are extended under Article XXVII, the competent authority for the administration in such part or territory of the taxes to which such provisions apply.

(2) In the application of the provisions of the present Convention by either of the Contracting States, any term which is not defined in the present Convention shall, unless the context otherwise requires, have the meaning which that term has under the laws of such Contracting State relating to the taxes which are the subject of the present Convention.

In the application of Article II(1)(j), the term "competent authority" would be taken to mean, in the case of the Netherlands Antilles, the Administrateur van Financien or his duly authorized representative.

Article III

(1) An enterprise of one of the Contracting States shall not be subject to taxation by the other Contracting State in respect of its industrial or commercial profits unless it is engaged in trade or business in the other Contracting State through a permanent establishment situated therein. If it is so engaged the other Contracting State may impose the tax only upon the income of such enterprise from sources within such other State.

(2) Where an enterprise of one of the Contracting States is engaged in trade or business in the other Contracting State through a permanent establishment situated therein, there shall be attributed to such permanent establishment the industrial or commercial profits which it might be expected to derive if it were an independent enterprise engaged in the same or similar activities under the same or similar conditions and dealing at arm's length with the enterprise of which it is a permanent establishment, and the profits so attributed shall, subject to the law of such other Contracting State, be deemed to be income from sources within such other Contracting State.

(3) In determining the industrial or commercial profits from sources within one of the Contracting States of an enterprise of the other Contracting State, no profits shall be deemed to arise from the mere purchase of goods or merchandise within the former Contracting State by such enterprise.

(4) The competent authorities of the Contracting States may lay down rules by agreement for the apportionment of industrial or commercial profits.

Article IV

Where an enterprise of one of the Contracting States, by reason of its participation in the management, control or capital of an enterprise of the other Contracting State, makes with or imposes on the latter enterprise, in their commercial or financial relations, conditions different from those which would be made with an independent enterprise, any profits which would, but for those conditions, have accrued to one of the enterprises, may be included in the taxable profits of that enterprise.

Article V

Income of whatever nature derived from real property and interest from mortgages secured by real property shall be taxable only in the Contracting State in which the real property is situated.

Article VI

(1) Income which an enterprise of one of the Contracting States derives from the operation of ships or aircraft registered in that State shall be taxable only in the State in which such ships or aircraft are registered. Income derived by such an enterprise from the operation of ships or aircraft not so registered shall be subject to the provisions of Article III.

Paragraphs (2) and (3) of Article VI have no application in the Netherlands Antilles, since the agreements of 1926 and 1939 referred to have no application in the Netherlands Antilles.

Article VII

(1) The rate of United States tax on dividends derived from a United States corporation by a resident or corporation of the Netherlands not engaged in trade or business in the United States through a permanent establishment shall not exceed 15 percent: Provided that such rate of tax shall not exceed 5 percent if such Netherlands corporation controls, directly or indirectly, at least 95 percent of the entire voting power in the corporation paying the dividend, and not more than 25 percent of the gross income of such paying corporation is derived from interest and dividends, other than interest and dividends from its own subsidiary corporation. Such reduction of the rate to 5 percent shall not apply if the relationship of the two corporations has been arranged or is maintained primarily with the intention of securing such reduced rate.

(2) Dividends derived from sources within the Netherlands by a resident or corporation of the

United States not engaged in trade or business in the Netherlands through a permanent establishment shall be exempt from Netherlands tax.

(3) Either of the Contracting States may terminate this Article, giving written notice of termination to the other Contracting State through diplomatic channels, on or before the thirtieth day of June in any year after the first year for which the present Convention becomes effective. In such event this Article shall cease to be effective on and after the first day of January in the year next following that in which such notice is given.

Article I, Protocol signed October 23, 1963, provided:

"(1) Articles VII, VIII, and IX of the Convention shall not apply to income derived from sources within the United States by any investment or holding company, corporation, limited partnership or other entity entitled to any of the special tax benefits provided under Article 13, Article 14, or Article 14A of the Netherlands Antilles' National Ordinance on Profit Tax of 1940, as in effect on September 1, 1963, or in substantially similar tax benefits granted under any law of the Netherlands Antilles enacted after such date."

Article VIII

(1) Interest (on bonds, securities, notes, debentures, or on any other form of indebtedness), other than interest referred to in Article V of the present Convention, derived from sources within the United States by a resident or corporation of the Netherlands not engaged in trade or business in the United States through a permanent establishment, shall be exempt from United States tax; but such exemption shall not apply to such interest paid by a United States corporation to a Netherlands corporation controlling, directly or indirectly, more than 50 percent of the entire voting power in the paying corporation.

(2) Interest (on bonds, securities, notes, debentures, or on any other form of indebtedness), other than interest referred to in Article V of the present Convention, derived from sources within the Netherlands by a resident or corporation of the United States not engaged in trade or business in the Netherlands through a permanent establishment, shall be exempt from Netherlands tax; but such exemption shall not apply to such interest paid by a Netherlands corporation to a United States corporation controlling, directly or indirectly, more than 50 percent of the entire voting power in the paying corporation.

Article IX

Royalties for the right to use copyrights, patents, designs, secret processes and formulae, trade marks, and other analogous property, and royalties, including rentals, in respect of motion picture films or for the use of industrial, commercial or scientific equipment, derived from sources within one of the Contracting States by a resident or corporation of the other Contracting State not engaged in trade or business in the former State through a permanent establishment, shall be exempt from tax imposed by the former State.

Article X

A resident or corporation of one of the Contracting States, deriving from sources within the other Contracting State royalties in respect of the operation of mines, quarries, or natural resources, or rentals from real property, may elect for any taxable year to be subject to the tax of such other Contracting State on such income on a net income basis.

Prior to amendments by Protocol signed October 23, 1963, Article X read as follows:

"A resident or corporation of one of the Contracting States, deriving from sources within the other Contracting State royalties in respect of the operation of mines, quarries, or natural resources, or rentals from real property, may elect for any taxable year to be subject to the tax of such other Contracting State, on a net basis, as if such resident or corporation were engaged in trade or business within such other Contracting State through a permanent establishment during such taxable year."

Article XII

Dividends and interest paid by a Netherlands corporation shall be exempt from United States tax except where the recipient is a citizen, resident, or corporation of the United States.

Article XIV

(1) The United States income tax liability for any taxable year beginning prior to January 1, 1936 of any individual (other than a citizen of the United States) resident in the Netherlands, or of any Netherlands corporation, remaining unpaid on the effective date of the present Convention, may be adjusted on a basis satisfactory to the United States Commissioner of Internal Revenue: Provided that the amount to be paid in settlement of such liability shall not exceed the amount of such liability which would have been determined if

(a) the United States Revenue Act of 1936 (except in the case of a Netherlands corporation of which more than 50 percent of the entire voting power was controlled, directly or indirectly, throughout the latter half of the taxable year, by citizens or residents of the United States), and

(b) Articles XII and XIII of the present Convention, had been in effect for such year. If the taxpayer was not, within the meaning of such Revenue Act, engaged in trade or business in the United States and had no office or place of business therein during the taxable year, the amount of interest and penalties shall not exceed 50 percent of the amount of the tax with respect to which such interest and penalties have been computed.

(2) The United States income tax unpaid on the effective date of the present Convention for any taxable year beginning after December 31, 1935 and prior to the effective date of the present Convention in the case of an individual (other than a citizen of the United States) resident of the Netherlands, or in the case of any Netherlands corporation, shall be

determined as if the provisions of Articles XII and XIII of the present Convention had been in effect for such taxable year.

(3) The provisions of paragraph (1) of this Article shall not apply

(a) unless the taxpayer files with the Commissioner of Internal Revenue within a period of two years following the effective date of the present Convention a request that such tax liability be so adjusted and furnishes such information as the Commissioner may require; or

(b) in any case in which the Commissioner is satisfied that any deficiency in tax is due to fraud with intent to evade the tax.

By agreement all references to Article XIII and to the nontaxability of capital gains are considered deleted.

Article XV

(1) Wages, salaries and similar compensation, and pensions and life annuities, paid either directly by, or from funds created by, one of the Contracting States or the political subdivisions or territories thereof to individuals in the other Contracting State shall be exempt from taxation in the latter State.

(2) Private pensions and life annuities derived from within one of the Contracting States and paid to individuals in the other Contracting State shall be exempt from taxation in the former State.

(3) The term "pensions" as used in this Article means periodic payments made in consideration for services rendered or by way of compensation for injuries received.

(4) The term "life annuities" as used in this Article means a stated sum payable periodically at stated times during life, or during a specified number of years, under an obligation to make the payments in return for adequate and full consideration in money or money's worth.

Article XVI

(1) A resident of the Netherlands shall be exempt from United States tax upon compensation for labor or personal services performed within the United States if he is temporarily present within the United States for a period or periods not exceeding a total of one hundred eighty-three days during the taxable year and his compensation is received for labor or personal services performed as a worker or employee of, or under contract with, a resident of the Netherlands, or a Netherlands corporation, carrying the actual burden of the remuneration.

(2) The provisions of paragraph (1) of this Article shall apply, mutatis mutandis, to a resident of the United States deriving compensation for labor or personal services performed within the Netherlands.

Article XVII

Professors or teachers, residents of one of the Contracting States, who, in accordance with agreements between the Contracting States or between teaching establishments in the Contracting States for the exchange of professors and teachers, visit the other Contracting State to teach, for a maximum period of two years, in a university, college or other teaching establishment in such other Contracting State, shall not be taxed by such other Contracting State with respect to the remuneration which they receive for such teaching.

Article XVIII

Students or business apprentices of one Contracting State residing in the other Contracting State exclusively for purposes of study or for acquiring business experience shall not be taxable by the latter State in respect of remittances received by them from abroad for the purpose of their maintenance or studies.

Article XIX

(1) Notwithstanding any provisions of the present Convention (other than paragraph (1) of Article XV when applicable in the case of an individual who is deemed by each Contracting State to be a citizen thereof), each of the two Contracting States, in determining the taxes, including all surtaxes, of its citizens or residents or corporations, may include all items of income taxable under its own revenue laws as though this Convention had not come into effect.

(2) As far as may be in accordance with the provisions of the United States Internal Revenue Code, the United States agrees to allow as a deduction from the income taxes imposed by the United States the appropriate amount of taxes paid to the Netherlands, whether paid directly by the taxpayer or by withholding at the source.

(3) The Netherlands Antilles shall allow a deduction (or the equivalent thereof) from its tax of the Federal income tax paid to the United States by citizens of the United States resident in the Netherlands Antilles with respect to income of such citizens from sources within the United States, but in an amount not in excess of that proportion of the entire Netherlands Antilles tax which such income bears to the entire income subject to such Netherlands Antilles tax.

Par. (3) was substituted by Protocol signed June 15, 1955.

Article XX

Article XX has no application in the Netherlands Antilles, since the provisions relating to certain Netherlands property taxes have no bearing on Netherlands Antilles taxes.

Article XXI

The competent authorities of the Contracting States shall exchange such information (being information which such authorities have in proper order at their disposal) as is necessary for carrying out the provisions of the present Convention or for the prevention of fraud or the administration of statutory provisions against legal avoidance in relation to the taxes which are the subject of the present Convention. Any information so exchanged shall be treated as secret and shall not be disclosed to any person other than those concerned with the assessment and collection of the taxes which are the subject of the present Convention. No information as aforesaid shall be exchanged which would disclose any trade, business, industrial or professional secret or trade process.

Article XXII

(1) The Contracting States undertake to lend assistance and support to each other in the collection of the taxes which are the subject of the present Convention, together with interest, costs, and additions to the taxes and fines not being of a penal character.

(2) In the case of applications for enforcement of taxes, revenue claims of each of the Contracting States which have been finally determined may be accepted for enforcement by the other Contracting State and collected in that State in accordance with the laws applicable to the enforcement and collection of its own taxes. The State to which application is made shall not be required to enforce executory measures for which there is no provision in the law of the State making the application.

(3) Any application shall be accompanied by documents establishing that under the laws of the State making the application the taxes have been finally determined.

(4) The assistance provided for in this Article shall not be accorded with respect to the citizens, corporations, or other entities of the State to which application is made, except as is necessary to insure that the exemption or reduced rate of tax granted under the convention to such citizens, corporations or other entities shall not be enjoyed by persons not entitled to such benefits.

The Governments will collect the other's tax only to the extent necessary to insure that the exemptions or reduced rates of tax provided under the convention would not be enjoyed by persons not entitled to such benefits.

Article XXIII

(1) In no case shall the provisions of Article XXI and XXII be construed so as to impose upon either of the Contracting States the obligation

(a) to carry out administrative measures at variance with the regulations and practice of either Contracting State, or

(b) to supply particulars which are not procurable under its own legislation or that of the State making application.

(2) The State to which application is made for information or assistance shall comply as soon as possible with the request addressed to it. Nevertheless, such State may refuse to comply with the request for reasons of public policy or if compliance would involve violation of a trade, business, industrial or professional secret or trade process. In such case it shall inform, as soon as possible, the State making the application.

Article XXIV

Where the action of the revenue authorities of the Contracting States has resulted or will result in double taxation contrary to the provisions of the present Convention, the taxpayer shall be entitled to lodge a claim with the State of which he is a citizen or subject or, if he is not a citizen or subject of either of the Contracting States, with the State of which he is a resident, or, if the taxpayer is a corporation, with the State in which it is created or organized. Should the claim be upheld, the competent authority of such State shall undertake to come to an agreement with the competent authority of the other State with a view to equitable avoidance of the double taxation in question.

Article XXV

(1) The provisions of the present Convention shall not be construed to restrict in any manner any exemption, deduction, credit or other allowance accorded by the laws of one of the Contracting States in the determination of the tax imposed by such State.

(2) Should any difficulty or doubt arise as to the interpretation or application of the present Convention, the competent authorities of the Contracting States shall undertake to settle the question by mutual agreement.

(3) The citizens or subjects of one of the Contracting States shall not, while resident in the other Contracting State, be subjected therein to other or more burdensome taxes than are the citizens or subjects of such other Contracting State residing in its territory. The term "citizens" or "subjects" as used in this Article includes all legal persons, partnerships and associations deriving their status from, or created or organized under the laws in force in, the respective Contracting States. In this Article the word "taxes" means taxes of every kind or description whether national, federal, state, provincial or municipal.

Article XXVI

(1) The authorities of each of the Contracting States, in accordance with the practices of that State, may prescribe regulations necessary to carry out the provisions of the present Convention.

(2) With respect to the provisions of the present Convention relating to exchange of information and mutual assistance in the collection of taxes, the competent authorities may, by common agreement, prescribe rules concerning matters of procedure, forms of application and replies thereto, conversion of currency, disposition of amounts collected, minimum amounts subject to collection, and related matters.

Article XXVII

(1) Either of the Contracting States may, at the time of exchange of instruments of ratification or thereafter while the present Convention continues in force, by a written notification of extension given to the other Contracting State through diplomatic channels, declare the desire of the government of any overseas part of the Kingdom (in the case of the Netherlands) or overseas territory (in the case of the United States), which imposes taxes substantially similar in character to those which are the subject of the present Convention, that the operation of the present Convention, either in whole or as to such provisions thereof as may be deemed to have special application, shall extend to such part or territory.

(2) In the event that a notification is given by one of the Contracting States in accordance with paragraph (1) of this Article, the present Convention, or such provisions thereof as may be specified in the notification, shall apply to any part or territory named in such notification on and after the first day of January immediately preceding the date of a written communication through diplomatic channels addressed to such Contracting State by the other Contracting State, after such action by the latter State as may be necessary in accordance with its own procedures, stating that such notification is accepted in respect of such part or territory. In the absence of such acceptance, none of the provisions of the present Convention shall apply to such part or territory.

(3) At any time after the expiration of one year from the effective date of an extension made by virtue of paragraphs (1) and (2) of this Article, either of the Contracting States may, by a written notice of termination given to the other Contracting State through diplomatic channels, terminate the application of the present Convention to any part or territory to which the Convention, or any of its provisions, has been extended. In that case, the present Convention, or the provisions thereof specified in the notice of termination, shall cease to be applicable to the part or territory named in such notice of termination on and after the first day of January following the expiration of a period of six months after the date of such notice; provided, however, that this shall not affect the continued application of the Convention, or any of the provisions thereof, to the United States, to the Netherlands, or to any part or territory (not named in the notice of termination) to which the Convention, or such provision thereof, applies.

(4) For the application of the present Convention in relation to any part or territory to which it is extended by notification given by the United States or the Netherlands, references to "the United States" or to "the Netherlands" or to one or the other Contracting State, as the case may be, shall be construed to refer to such part or territory.

"Immediately preceding" was substituted for "following" in par. (2) by Protocol signed June 15, 1955.

Article XXVIII

(1) The present Convention shall be ratified and the instruments of ratification shall be exchanged at Washington as soon as possible.

(2) The present Convention shall become effective on the first day of January in the year last preceding the year in which the exchange of instruments of ratification takes place.[1] It shall continue effective for a period of five years beginning with that date and indefinitely after that period, but may be terminated by either of the Contracting States at the end of the five-year period or at any time thereafter, provided that at least six months' prior notice of termination has been given, the termination to become effective on the first day of January following the expiration of the six-month period.

Article III, Protocol signed October 23, 1963, provided:

"(1) The present Protocol shall be ratified and the instruments of ratification shall be exchanged at Washington as soon as possible.

"(2) The present Protocol shall come into force on the date of exchange of instruments of ratification.

"(3) Article I of the present Protocol shall be applicable with respect to payments made on or after the first day of January of the year immediately following the year in which the exchange of instruments of ratification takes place. Article II of the present Protocol shall be applicable with respect to dividends and interest paid to a corporation or other entity which is organized in the Netherlands Antilles under a notarial deed of incorporation dated on or before May 14, 1963, if Articles VII and VIII of the Convention would not be applicable to such dividends and interest by reason of Article I of the present Protocol:

(a) In the case of a dividend

(i) paid during the period of two years beginning on the first day of January, 1964, the provisions of Article VII of the Convention shall continue to apply as though the present Protocol had not yet come into force;

(ii) paid during the year beginning on the first day of January, 1966, United States tax with respect to such dividend shall be imposed at a rate not exceeding 20 percent; and

"(4) Notwithstanding the provisions of paragraph (3) of this Article, the following provisions shall apply with respect to dividends and interest paid to a corporation or other entity which is organized in the Netherlands Antilles under a notarial deed of incorporation dated on or before May 14, 1963, if Articles VII and VIII of the Convention would not be applicable to such dividends and interest by reason of Article I of the present Protocol:

SAMPLE DUTCH PARTICIPATION EXEMPTION RULING

The Inspector of Corporate Taxes
Pantegoalstraat 5
Rotterdam

Dear Sir:

Re: ("BV")

The captioned corporation is presently in formation. The shares of BV will be held by a company called XYZ Holding N.V. which is incorporated under the laws of the Netherlands Antilles and managed in the Netherlands Antilles. The management of BV will be performed by Sample Trust BV, and BV will be registered at Rotterdam.

At the incorporation of BV, the share capital of DFL. XX,000 will be paid in cash, while the Articles of Incorporation will provide for the payment of capital surplus by way of the contribution of the share capital (or part of the share capital) of a company incorporated under the laws of the U.S., called ABC, Inc. ("ABC").

ABC is a general partner in a partnership called "The Partnership". The Partnership is engaged in a real estate project located in Beverly Hills, California. The Partnership has acquired an apartment building called "Casa de Howard" consisting of 500 units. After building has been upgraded and the apartments have been remodeled, the apartments will be converted into condominiums which will be sold out to the public.

It may be possible that BV sells its share holdings in ABC before the sale of the condominiums is completed.

In view of the foregoing, you are herewith respectfully requested to approve the following:

1. BV is not to be considered to hold the share in ABC as portfolio investment, and the participation exemption as meant in Article 13 of the Corporate Income Tax Act of 1969 will be applicable, while BV will be considered to hold the shares of ABC as from the beginning of its first bookyear.

2. Under the circumstances described here above, BV will be considered to be resident of the Netherlands according to Netherlands National Law and will accordingly be entitled to receive a Declaration of Residence.

3. BV will, as a result of the activities mentioned, not constitute a permanent establishment or a permanent representative for its shareholder.

4. As long as the participation exemption as meant in Article 13 of the Corporate Income Tax Act of 1969 shall apply with respect to said participations, BV shall report annually at least 25 pct. of its costs incurred in relation to its management and holding activities. The minimum amount to be reported, however, shall always amount to at least DFLS. 10,000, per twelve month period.

5. With respect to finance activities entered into by BV, the taxable amount generated from these activities will not be corrected as long as BV reports at least per twelve month period an amount equal to 1/8 of one pct. of the outstanding amount of borrowings on lend with a minimum of DFLS. 10,000. The taxable amount to be reported under this paragraph comes in addition to the amount mentioned in Paragraph 4.

6. The mentioned activities will be initiated within nine months after your approval to the above, while this arrangement will be applicable for the period ending December 31st, 1984. Thereafter, execution of this arrangement shall be granted unless severe arguments oppose such extension.

7. BV herewith appoints all its assets as assets mentioned in Paragraph 61 A 5 (M) of the Income Tax Act of 1964.

8. BV shall not engage in any activities substantially different than those mentioned here above or in any activities with respect to other real estate than the property described here above without advance consultation of the competent inspector of corporate income tax.

You are kindly requested to approve the above arrangement by signing and returning the attached copy of this letter to me.

Yours sincerely,

All orders and price inquiries should be made to:

CEB Publication Sales
2300 Shattuck Avenue
Berkeley, California 94704

PHONE: (415) 642-6810
For Books and for Tapes
(415) 642-8608

1. California Title Insurance Practice

CONTENTS

1. Title Insurance Industry
2. Title Search and Insurance
3. Title Policies, Reports, Guaranties, and Indorsements
4. Additional Title Company Services
5. Claims and Litigation

2. California Mortgage and Deed of Trust Practice

CONTENTS

1. Introduction
2. The Obligation
3. The Security Instrument
4. The One-Action and Antideficiency
5. Judicial Foreclosure
6. Trustee's Sales
7. Rents and Profits
8. Tax Consequences of Mortgage Foreclosure

3. Commercial Real Property Lease Practice

CONTENTS

1. Introduction to Commercial Real Property Lease Practice
2. Drafting a Commercial Real Property Lease
3. Commercial Real Property Lease Form With Comments
4. Income Tax Considerations of Specific Lease Clauses
5. General Income Tax Considerations of Commercial Real Property Leases
6. Ancillary Agreements

4. California Surety and Fidelity Bond Practice

CONTENTS

1. Introduction to Suretyship
2. Bonds Used in the Construction Industry
3. Fidelity Bonds
4. Litigation Bonds
5. Miscellaneous Bonds
Appendix: Chart of Undertakings and Bonds in Civil Actions

5. Landslide and Subsidence Liability

CONTENTS

1. Introduction
2. Assisting and Advising the Landslide Victim
3. Preparing for Litigation
4. Insurance Against Land Failure
5. Liability of Former Owner and His Agents
6. Liability of Land Developers
7. Liability of Adjoining Property Owners
8. Liability of Public Entities
9. Tax Considerations

7. Condemnation Practice in California

CONTENTS

1. Attorney's Initial Contact With Condemnation Action
2. Attorney's Role in Determining Facts
3. Selection of Valuation Experts
4. Just Compensation
5. Severance Damages
6. Public Use and Necessity Defenses
7. Negotiation and Arbitration
8. Pleadings
9. Trial Preparation and Trial
10. Apportionment, Judgment and Posttrial
11. Federal Condemnation Practice
12. Income Tax Consequences of Condemnation Awards
13. Inverse Condemnation

8. Attorney's Guide to California Construction Contracts and Disputes

CONTENTS

1. Contractors License Law
2. Construction Contracts
3. Private Contract Disputes
4. Public Contract Disputes
5. Arbitrating Construction Disputes
6. Construction Tort Litigation
7. Problems of Architects and Engineers
Appendixes: American Institute of Architects Standard Construction Contract Forms
Associated General Contractors' Standard Subcontract Forms
Sample Construction Contract Favoring the Owner

-4-

6. Ogden's Revised California Real Property Law, Volume 1 and Volume 2

CONTENTS - VOLUME 1

1. Nature of Real Property
2. Estates in Real Property
3. Transfer by Deed
4. Nondeed Methods of Transfer and Acquisition of Title
5. Transfer by Operation of Law
6. Who May Acquire and Convey
7. Joint Tenancy and Tenancy in Common
8. Community Property
9. Homesteads and Their Impact on Title
10. Recording and Constructive Notice
11. Land Sales Contracts
12. Leases
13. Easements
14. Descriptions
15. Boundaries
16. Condominiums and Forms of Multiple Ownership
Appendix: What is Title Insurance?

CONTENTS - VOLUME 2

17. Mortgages
18. Foreclosure Proceedings
19. Attachments, Judgments, and Other Liens
20. Mechanics' Liens
21. Real Property Taxes
22. Special Assessments and Other Levies
23. Covenants, Conditions, and Restrictions
24. Zoning Regulations and Other Governmental Controls
25. Land Subdivisions
26. Public Lands
27. Title Litigation
28. Bankruptcy and Its Impact on Title
29. Probate Proceedings and Their Impact on Title (Including Guardianship and Conservatorship)
30. Nature of Title Insurance
31. Types of Title Insurance Policies
32. Special Title Insurance Indorsements in Common Use
Appendix: Sample Title Insurance Policy

-3-

9. Guide to California Subdivision Sales Law

CONTENTS

1. Introduction
2. Applicability of the Subdivided Lands Act
3. Offering Requirements for All Subdivisions
4. Additional Requirements for Common Interest and Other Special Subdivision
5. The Public Report
6. Violations and Enforcement
7. Out-of-State Subdivisions

10. California Mechanics' Liens and Other Remedies

CONTENTS - PART 1: THE CLAIMANTS

1. Claimants' Rights and Remedies
2. Time Limitations
3. Claims on Private Works
4. Claims on Public Works
5. Complaint Form: Foreclosure of Mechanics' Lien

CONTENTS - PART 2: THE DEFENDERS

6. Owner
7. Prime Contractor
8. Construction Lender
9. Surety
10. Title Company
11. Government

11. California Zoning Practice

CONTENTS

1. History and Future Developments
2. Planning: The Relationship to Zoning
3. Land-Use Controls Related to Zoning
4. Sources of the Zoning Power
5. Zoning Purposes and Limitations
6. Types of Zones
7. Types of Zoning Relief
8. Accessory and Specialized Uses
9. Nonconforming Uses

11. California Zoning Practice - (Continued)

10. Relief: Organizations and Procedures
11. Enforcement
12. Methods of Judicial Review
Appendix A: Sources and Resources on Zoning and Planning
Appendix B: General Law and Charter Cities

12. Eminent Domain Law With Conforming Changes in Codified Sections and Official Comments

CONTENTS

1. Recommendations
2. Title 7: Eminent Domain Law
3. Conforming Revisions
Appendix: Disposition of Existing General Condemnation Statute
Recommendation Relating to Relocation Assistance by Private Condemnors
Recommendation Relating to Condemnation for Byroads and Utility Easements
Table Showing Session Law Chapter Source for Conforming Revisions

13. Ground Lease Practice

CONTENTS - PART I: CONSIDERATIONS UNIQUE TO GROUND LEASES

1. Function; Utility
2. Attorney's Role
3. Parties; Title; Interests
4. Premises
5. Term; Termination; Option fo Extend or Buy
6. Rent; Security; Other Payments
7. Uses; Purposes
8. Improvements; Construction; Maintenance;
9. Ownership
Condemnation
10. Financing; Encumbrance; Subordination
11. Assignment; Subletting
12. Liability; Insurance
13. Default; Remedies
14. Escrow; Execution; Recordation

13. Ground Lease Practice - (Continued)

PART 2 - GROUND LEASE FORM WITH COMMENTS

14. Income Tax Consequences in Real Property Transactions

This booklet covers basic income tax principles affecting real property transactions; nontaxable exchanges; financing the sale; leases; sale and leaseback; and entity selection for real property purchase. It also contains an appendix that contrasts the tax effects of capital improvements and repairs.

15. Introduction to Secured Real Property Transactions

A basic discussion for general practitioners who sometimes handle real property matters. This booklet covers antideficiency legislation, enforcement of deeds of trust, and negotiating and drafting security documents. The appendixes provide numerous sample forms and pertinent legislation.

16. Income Tax Aspects of Investment Real Property

Topics include tax aspects of condominium conversion (capital gains planning and ordinary income planning); unconventional real property disposition techniques (using an option, partnership used to acquire property, private annuity, and simultaneous use of two conventional techniques); and real estate as tax shelter investment (up-front, early-on, and depreciation deductions); leveraging; investment interests; tax preferences; min-max tax; special allocations; investment tax credits; rehabilitation of twenty-year or older commercial buildings; moderate income housing tax shelters; rehabilitation of historic property; vacation homes; and IRS audit manual instructions on real estate tax shelters.

17. Netotiating and Documenting Real Property Secured Transactions

Contains the following articles: "Selected Problems and Issues in Negotiating and Documenting Real Property Secured Transactions"; "What Lenders Look for When Reviewing Commercial Leases"; and "Drafting or Reviewing a Ground Lease To Make It Mortgageable". Contains 34 sample forms furnished by the American Land Title Association and the California Land Title Association, and a bibliography.

18. Current Developments in Insurance

Topics include a discussion of the evolving relationship between the bar and the title industry; increased participation of title insurance company in real estate closing; title insurance and the specialized interest--construction loans, leaseholds, oil and gas; business practices and economic considerations; recent cases of note; and abstractors' liability--the passing of an archaic theory. The booklet contains numerous American Land Title and California Land Title Association documents; insurance company documents; the Agreement between the State Bar of California and the California Land Title Association; State of California Department of Insurance Bulletins; and American Land Title Association Reports.

19. Major Real Property Acquisitions

Contains numerous illustrative documents, including purchase, management, and option agreements; assignment of contracts; certificate on warranties; certified rent roll; general assignment of rights and permits; estoppel certificates; assignment of leases; closing memorandum; opinion letter; joint venture agreement; ground lease; American Land Title Association loan policy; California Land Title Association Standard Coverage Policy and Preliminary Report Form; Interim Binder Form; and California Land Title Indorsement Form.

24. Real Estate Broker Practice

A guide to what you need to know when representing a real estate broker or salesperson, or a client who deals with a real estate broker. Topics include: definitions and services of brokers; selecting the business entity; employment of brokers; broker's claim for compensation of services; agency relationship duties; broker's duties and liabilities to principal; disciplinary actions by real estate commissioner; and the California Association of Realtors' standard forms.

25. Representing Residential Landlords and Tenants

Topics include nature of landlord-tenant relationship; beginning the landlord-tenant relationship; during the tenancy; ending the tenancy--unlawful detainer lawsuit; attorneys fees; lay "evictors"; ethical considerations; rental relief and control. Also contains the following forms and checklists: sample rental agreements and leases; notices and instructions for services of notices; unlawful detainer procedural checklists; sample unlawful detainer complaints; judicial council printed forms; sample transmittal letters; and rent control material.

26. Representing Parties to an Escrow and Escrow Litigation

Outlines the following topics: elements of escrow; consequences of escrow; escrow procedure; closing the sale; and remedies against the escrow agent. Contains a sample agreement of purchase and escrow instructions; various title insurance and trust company forms; lender's instructions and a sample complaint in interpleader.

27. Tax and Real Property Problems: Individual Ownership and Disposition of Substantial Properties

Presents text and outlines on "Estate Planning for Individuals Owning Substantial Real Property Assets" and "Tax and Real Property Problems in the Individual Ownership and Disposition of Substantial Properties". Also contains questionnaires and checklists, six sample forms and a bibliography.

-10-

20. Recent Developments in Real Property Law

Covers significant cases in public regulation of land use; real property financing; landlord/tenant law; real property sales; housing; attorneys' fees; taxation; and other pertinent topics. Also contains articles on "Caito v United California Bank", the new Bankruptcy Code and its impact on real property transactions, and "Wellenkamp v Bank of America" (invalidation of automatically enforceable due-on-sale clauses).

21. Selected Real Property Remedies

Covers reformation; rescission; restitution; quiet title; specific performance; breach of contract; cancellation of instruments; remedies in foreclosure; guarantors' remedies in foreclosure matters; receivership; the new Bankruptcy Code and its impact on real property transactions; and slander of title. This booklet also contains numerous procedural checklists, including a checklist for title insurance litigation.

22. Selected Problems in Ground Lease Practice

Features articles on "Ground Leasing Makes Dollars and Sense for Developers"; "Santa Anita Fashion Park: A Case Study"; "The Mortgaging of Long-Term Leases"; "Leasehold Mortgage Financing"; Drafting or Reviewing a Ground Lease to Make it Mortgageable"; and "The New Bankruptcy Act and Its Impact on Real Property Transactions". Also contains selected ground lease provisions; a sample memorandum of ground lease; a complete ground lease form; and a recognition and attornment agreement.

23. Condominiums in the 1980s

An important reference tool for attorneys who are advising owners, developers, and lenders confronted with the complex problems related to condominiums. Includes: Federal Home Loan Mortgage Corporation condominium warranties; Federal National Mortgage Association information and documents; Department of Housing and Urban Development condominium documentation; an all-inclusive note; an all-inclusive deed of trust; AITD financing documents; a declaration of covenants, conditions, and restrictions establishing a plan of condominium ownership; articles of incorporation of condominium owners association; an index for declaration of establishment of covenants, conditions and restrictions; and local condominium conversion ordinances.

-9-

Appendix 5: List of California Continuing Education of the Bar Publications relating to real estate and real estate tax matters

Appendix 6: Disclosure requirements under the Foreign Investment in Real Property Tax Act of 1980

28. Handling and Litigating Land Use Matters

Discusses inverse condemnation; preparing the
housing case; exhausting administrative remedies;
how to distinguish between quasi-legislative and
quasi-judicial administrative actions; presenting
the administrative case; and review by mandate
in California.

29. Preparing and Negotiating Commercial Leases

Contains sample forms, including: office building
lease; general lease; industrial lease agreement;
sublease; neighborhood shopping center leases;
ground lease; development agreement; restrictions
and easements; option to exchange real property;
and bylaws.

C.E.B. also produces a series of audio casette
tapes with reference material. For details
contact C.E.B. directly by mail or phone.

-11-

Table of Contents

FACTS

ISSUES

RECOMMENDATIONS

DISCUSSION

    I   FOREIGN INVESTMENT IN REAL PROPERTY TAX
        ACT OF 1980

        A. Overview of the Act

        B. Reporting Requirements

            (i) Returns by Foreign Corporations and
                 by a Foreign or Domestic Partner-
                 ship, Trust or Estate

           (ii) Returns by Foreign Persons Directly
                 Owning a USRPI

    II   RECENT DEVELOPMENTS

        A. Reporting

B. Technical Corrections Act

C. Proposed Regulations

III POTENTIAL LIMITATIONS ON THE REPORTING REQUIREMENTS

A. Treaties

B. Other Reporting Requirements

C. Foreign Secrecy Laws

D. The Attorney-Client Privilege

E. The Attorney's Professional Responsibility

CONCLUSION

FACTS

A nonresident client wishes to acquire a home in Southern California for a purchase price of $1.4 million.

Counsel is in the process of forming a Netherlands Antilles corporation (which will issue bearer shares) for that client. The Antilles company will acquire the real property.

ISSUE

The client is a prominent politician in his home country and has expressed a need to maintain secrecy concerning his U.S. home. He does not, however, object to paying U.S. tax.

In view of the current disclosure requirements, is there some method the client can utilize to avoid disclosing his identity?

RECOMMENDATIONS

Until the Treasury issues regulations under I.R.C. section 6039C (the reporting requirements), the recommendations made herein are tentative at best.

We suggest that the shares be issued in bearer form and that the only person who should know the identity of the shareholder should be Counsel. All statements for services should be sent to the corporation. As soon as the regulations have been issued, we will prepare a revised memorandum.

2.

Some specific preliminary planning suggestions are:

1. Post Adequate Security

If the Antilles company posts "adequate security", then only the Antilles company will be required to file an informational report and the anonymity of the ultimate shareholder is thus rather simply preserved. Unfortunately, Treasury has a number of details to resolve before the security system can be implemented.

2. Not Report Above the Antilles Level

The client can take the position that the United States does not have the authority to require the Antilles company to reveal the identity of its shareholder. Although the taxpayer might possibly be successful, such a position runs the risk of being costly in terms of potential penalties and legal fees.

3. Use of Pledge

It has been suggested that the shares of the Antilles company be owned by a third foreign person subject to an option or security interest in favor of your client. An option is treated as an interest in real property so ownership of the option would give rise to a report in itself. In theory, a security interest is a viable approach, (subject to a caveat of sham or fraud), however, until the regulations are issued there is no certainty that such an arrangement will be successful. There is case law which indicates a pledge is an interest in real property requiring reporting.

DISCUSSION

I FOREIGN INVESTMENT IN REAL PROPERTY TAX ACT OF 1980

A. Overview of the Act

For several years Congress has been concerned that foreign investors were buying real property, especially farmland, in the United States, and not paying taxes on the gain from the sale of the property. Congress, assuming that the inequality of the treatment between foreign investors and United States citizens was a fundamental cause of the inflation in the value of farm and urban real estate, considered legislation to tax the foreign investor on gains from United States real estate[1].

1 See "Taxation of Foreign Investment in U.S. Real Estate", Dept. of Treas., May 1979; Remarks of Senator Malcolm Wallop before the United States Senate on January 24, 1979.

3.

On December 5, 1980, President Carter signed the Foreign Investment in Real Property Tax Act of 1980. The Act adds two new sections to the Internal Revenue Code (sections 879 and 6039C).

Section 897 imposes a tax on the "disposition"[2] of a United States real property interest[3] (herein "USRPI"). Unlike the earlier Senate version[4], the Act is not enforced by a tax withheld by the buyer[5]; rather like a toothless tiger, the Act relies on the foreign investor to voluntarily file returns and pay the tax.

Section 6039C merely outlines the type of reporting and returns that will be required by domestic corporations, other "entities" and by the foreign investor. The section delegates extremely broad authority to the Treasury to require "such information...as the Secretary may by regulations prescribe,"[6] and that the returns "shall be made or furnished at such time and in such manner as the Treasury shall by regulations prescribe." A return will be due for the short taxable year between June 18, 1980 and December 31, 1980.

2   I.R.C. §897(a)(1). The term "disposition" apparently includes sales, exchanges, liquidations, dividends, gift, foreclosures, etc.

3   I.R.C. §§897(c)(1)(A), 897(c)(6)(A), 897(c)(6)[sic](8) [the correct cite should be §897(c)(6)(A)] (The Act contains numerous spelling and typographical errors). The Act defines a United States Real Property Interest as including fee and co-ownership, leaseholds, options, improvements, and associated personal property, as well as interests in mines, wells and other natural deposits, and the stock of a domestic corporation whose assets consist principally (50 percent or more) of the above.

4   S. 2939.

5   "[U]ntil and unless withholding provisions were adopted by a subsequent Congress, its tax should be enforced through information reporting as discussed below." H.R. Rept. No. 96-1479, 9th Cong., 2nd Sess., 189-196 (1980).

6   I.R.C. §6039C(a)(1)(A)(ii) and (iii); (b)(1)(B) and (C); (b)(3)(C); (c)(1)(C). The quote is I.R.C. §6039C(e)(2).

4.

B.   Reporting Requirements

Set forth below is a brief review of the relevant reporting requirements under the Act:

(i)   Returns by Foreign Corporations and by a Foreign or Domestic Partnership, Trust or Estate

Every "entity" (foreign corporation [e.g., the Antilles company] and any partnership, trust or estate, [whether foreign or domestic][7]) that holds a USRPI [e.g., the home], and that has a foreign investor as a shareholder or beneficiary who is a "substantial investor"[8] in the entity, must file an information return with the Service and furnish each such foreign and domestic investor a "statement"[9] unless adequate security is posted to assure payment of the foreign investor's tax liability[10].

A foreign investor is a "substantial investor" if his (its) prorata share of the USRPI held directly, or indirectly, by the entity has a fair market value of $50,000[11]. For example, if the foreign investor holds all of the shares of a foreign corporation which owns all of the shares of a USRPHC (a domestic corporation that owns real estate [USRPI]), then the value of the real property interest (USRPI) owned by the USRPHC (and not the value of the stock) will be attributed to the foreign investor as if the intervening corporate entities did not exist[12]. Therefore, no matter how many intervening entities are used, the identity of the ultimate beneficial owners is required to be disclosed.

In determining whether the prorata interest of the foreign investor in the entity exceeds $50,000, the foreign entity is attributed a prorata share of the assets of the partnership, trust or estate of which the entity is a member and any USRPI held by his spouse or minor child[13].

The entity is required to report the name and address of each substantiated investor[4], such information concerning the assets held by the entity during the calendar year[15] and such other information as the Secretary may by regulations prescribe[16].

7   I.R.C. §6039C(b)(4)(A)
8   I.R.C. §6039C(b)(4)(B)
9   I.R.C. §6039C(b)(1) and (3)
10   I.R.C. §6039C(b)(2)
11   I.R.C. §6039C(b)(4)(B)
12   I.R.C. §6039C(b)(4)(B)(i) and (ii)
13   I.R.C. §6039C(e)(1)(B). None of the other attribution rules of the Code make a distinction between a parent's child or his minor child.

14   I.R.C. §6039C(b)(1)(A)
15   I.R.C. §6039C(b)(1)(B)
16   I.R.C. §6039C(b)(1)(C)

5.

In addition to notifying the Treasury, the entity is required to furnish each substantial investor a statement showing the name and address of the entity making the return[17], the investor's prorata share of the USRPI held by such entity[18] and such other information as may be required in future regulations[19].

Since a substantial number of foreign investors may be reluctant to reveal their presence or identity to the Treasury, the Act provides that if the entity posts sufficient security to secure payment of all taxes that could result from the disposition of the USRPI (not just taxes from sales), then the entity will be excused from filing the required reports and from furnishing the foreign investor the required statement[20].

The Committee Report indicates that the re-gulations should apply a reasonable standard[21]. If, for example, the only asset which the entity owns is a parcel of real estate, the regulations might require a recorded security interest or a guarantee from some person the Service finds acceptable[22]. Conversely, if, e.g., a foreign corporation is engaged in business in the United States, with a variety of U.S. assets and where the circumstances indicate that it is improbable that the foreign corporation would attempt to remove its assets from the United States jurisdiction, the Service might only require an undertaking to pay the tax in a closing agreement or some similar security[22].

The current thinking of the Treasury is that the exact type, nature and amount of security to be posted will be up to the discretion of the District Director of the I.R.S. District in which the real property is located.

Treasury officials have stated that security such as a letter of credit or bond may be satisfactory, however, because they are concerned with whether the Treasury

17   I.R.C. §6039C(b)(3)(A)
18   I.R.C. §6039C(b)(3)(B)
19   I.R.C. §6039C(b)(3)(C)
20   I.R.C. §6039C(b)(2); H.R. Rept. No. 96-1479, 96th Cong., 2nd Sess., 191 (1980).
21   H.R. Rept. No. 96-1479, 96th Cong., 2nd Sess., 191 (1980).
22   IBID at 191-192.

6.

can legally take a mortgage or deed of trust on the under-lying real property in certain states, such as California it may take Treasury some time to issue regulations with respect to placing a lien against the real property. That issue arises because a tax lien does not technically come into existence until a tax liability is assessed; since an assessment is generally not made until after the close of the taxable year, to which the assessment relates, Treasury is concerned that the Government may have an invalid security interest or a security interest that has no priority over subsequent lienholders.

Though not reflected in statutory language, the Committee Report provides that where the foreign corporation is unable to supply the required information, e.g., because the stock is issued in bearer form, or was held by a nominee unwilling to disclose the identity of the beneficial owner, the foreign corporation will be required to provide security satisfactory to the Service[23].

Unless excused due to reasonable cause, the penalty for the entity's failure to file the required returns in a timely manner is $25 per day[24], up to a maximum of $25,000[25]. An additional penalty of $25 per day up to $25,000 is imposed if the entity (or nominee) fails to furnish the foreign investor the required statement[26].

(ii) Returns by Foreign Persons Directly Owning a USRPI

In a general catch-all provision, section 6039C provides that if a foreign person[27] is not engaged in a United States trade or business for the calendar year but owns a USRPI during the calendar year, the value of which is $50,000 or more, and he is not otherwise required to file an information return under the Act, he is required to file a return giving his name and address, a description of all USRPI held by him and such other information as the re-gulations, when issued, may require[28].

23   IBID at 192
24   I.R.C. §6652(g)(2)
25   I.R.C. §6652(g)(3)
26   I.R.C. §6652(g)(1)(B)
27   See fn. 14 above.
28   I.R.C. §6039C(c)

7.

security is posted by the foreign corporation, then the foreign person will have to file a return under this subsection because the corporation is not required to file. Treasury has indicated that the regulations will not take such a position. Treasury has stated that the holder of virtually any interest that is convertible into a USRPI (e.g., security interest, option, etc.) will be required to disclose their interest.

Note that the taxpayer is not allowed to post security to avoid reporting under this subsection. The regulations provide that the election, if made under the Code, does not cause the electing party to be treated as if he were engaged in business[29]; hence, the question of whether his (or the Antilles company) electing under either the Code[30] or any income tax treaty to be taxed on a net basis is sufficient to remove him from the obligation to file under the catch-all provision is unclear. Presumably, the regulations under the Act will indicate that an election to treat real property activities as a business is effective to avoid the catch-all reporting requirement under the Act.

The penalty for failing to file when required under the catch-all provision is to be the lesser of $25,000 or five percent of the aggregate of the fair market value of the USRPI held at any time during the calendar year by the taxpayer[31]. Value is to be determined as of the end of the year (or on the date of sale if a disposition is made of the property during the year).

is not a daily penalty. The penalty, unlike the other penalty provisions, If the return is not filed in a timely manner, that failure may generate an immediate penalty of $25,000. Why Congress chose such a harsh approach for the failure in the catch-all area that it did not select in the other reporting areas is not known.

II RECENT DEVELOPMENTS

A. Reporting

On March 3, 1981, the I.R.S. issued a news release stating that:

"Supplemental instructions for individual forms 1040NR, 1040C and 1030ES(OIO) will be available in IRS offices by mid-March. The IRS publication 519,

29 Treas. Reg. §1.871-10(c)(1)
30 I.R.C. §6039C(e)(1)(A) and (B)
31 I.R.C. §6039C(g)(3)(B)

8.

U.S. Tax Guide for Aliens, went to press before the law was signed and does not include these new rules, according to the I.R.S.

Corporations whose tax years ended after June 18, 1980, should see the supplemental instructions for Forms 990T, 1120T, 1120L and 1120M.

The new rules also require certain domestic and foreign businesses and certain nonresident aliens to file information returns. The IRS is currently working on these forms and will issue more information about them when the forms become available.

All nonresident aliens and foreign corporations affected by the new rules who have already filed their tax returns will have to file amended returns."

When we questioned the I.R.S. as to their authority to issue such instructions before the regulations are final, Mr. Fogarasi, Assistant International Tax Counsel, Internal Revenue Service, stated that the news release would be withdrawn within one week.

B. Technical Corrections Act

Congress and Treasury are now considering a technical corrections act. Messrs. David Brockway and Thomas Joyce of the Joint Tax Committee are working on a preliminary draft of a corrections act.

Mr. Joyce has informed us that they have not yet turned their attention to the reporting requirements, but that by mid-April they will be reviewing that area.

C. Proposed Regulations

Congress left all of the details of the reporting requirements to the regulations. Mr. Andre Fogarasi of International Tax Counsel's Office and Mr. Kenneth Klein of Legislation and Regulations are the two gentlemen with primary responsibility for drafting the regulations.

The regulations for the reporting requirements have the highest priority. They expect that the first draft of the proposed regulation will be furnished by April. Since, however, they then have to be reviewed by the Secretary of the Treasury's Office, they do not expect that proposed regulations will be published until mid-May.

Treasury has assured us that there will be adequate time given after the regulations are issued in order to post security and to file the appropriate tax returns.

9.

Furthermore, pursuant to Executive Order 12291 effective February 17, 1981, all regulations and rules that are legislative in nature must be reviewed by the Office of Budget and Management, and cannot take effect until such review is completed.

III POTENTIAL LIMITATIONS ON THE REPORTING REQUIREMENTS

A. Treaties

Under the Constitution, treaties are part of the "supreme law of the land".

There are two types of treaties that may limit the foreign investor's duty to report:

(i) FCN: The U.S. has entered into several treaties or friendship, commerce and navigation. To date we have over 40 such treaties. In general those treaties provide that a "national" of the foreign country must not be accorded treatment that is less favorable "than the treatment accorded...in like situations," to its residents (e.g., Japan, 4 U.S.T. 2063 (1953)). Some of the FCN treaties are applicable only to individuals.

(ii) Tax Treaties: Many of the U.S. tax treaties provide a nondiscrimination provision (e.g., U.S.- Netherlands Antilles Treaty, Article XXC).

Some attorneys have taken the position that if a domestic person is not required to report, then the FCN or income tax treaty overrides the reporting requirements thus the foreign person (entity) does not have to report.

(iii) Treaties have the same force and effect as law. In general, a treaty supersedes prior law. A law that is enacted after the treaty supersedes that treaty. Where the two are in conflict, the courts often endeavor to constitute the two as being compatible (e.g., the Foreign Investment in U.S. Real Estate Act provides that treaties take precedence over the Act until December 12, 1984; after that date the Act expressly overrides all income tax treaties to the extent the two are in conflict.) (Query: Can a 19th century treaty override a 1980 law?)

B. Other Reporting Requirements

Under the International Investment Survey Act (22 USC 3101), the Department of Commerce requires the filing

10.

of certain forms whenever a foreign investor acquires property in the United States. An exemption from the reporting requirements is provided for residences used exclusively by the investor. If your client rents the house, the Form BE-13B should be filed. In theory, the identity of the investor must be disclosed, however, the Department of Commerce has been accepting reports with only the nationality of the investor.

On January 22, 1981 the Department of Commerce issued proposed regulations concerning a new form (BE-12 [Fed. Reg. January 22, 1981]). Though the regulations are still in proposed form, the effective date of the regulations is January 1, 1981. Currently, the regulations are being reviewed by the Office of Management and Budget.

C. Foreign Secrecy Laws

Many countries have enacted strict secrecy laws, which in some instances make it a crime to disclose information restricted by the Secrecy Act, e.g., in a court proceeding in a "foreign" court.

Many of the secrecy laws have been enacted in retaliation for the extra-territorial application of U.S. laws (e.g., Australia, Cayman Islands, England, Japan, etc.).

The effect of foreign secrecy laws is far from settled (See, "Foreign Nondisclosure Law and Domestic Discovery," 88 Yale L.T. 612 (1979); "Compulsion of Alien's Testimony Contrary to the Mandate of the Laws of his Native Land," 26 Colum. J. Transnat. L. 357 (1977)).

D. The Attorney-Client Privilege

Confidential communications between an attorney and a client are "privileged" and are not subject to disclosure. However, the privilege may not be effective to prevent the U.S. courts (or Treasury) from requiring counsel to make appropriate disclosure if:

(a) The information is not "confidential," is on the "public record," or is known to third parties;

(b) The client intended to commit a crime or fraud, e.g., did not intent to report;

(c) The information requested is the identity of the client or his non-confidential "acts". (Jefferson, California Evidence Benchbook, §40 (1972)).

11.

CAYMAN ISLANDS

Supplement No. 4 published with Gazette No. 20 of 1976.

THE CONFIDENTIAL RELATIONSHIPS (PRESERVATION) LAW
(Law 16 of 1976)

Date of operation: 27th September, 1976.
Notice of non-disallowance published in Gazette No. 9 of 1977.

E.   The Attorney's Professional Responsibility

In addition to the substantive law, ethical con-siderations should also be reviewed, e.g.,

(a)   California Rule 7-101 of Professional Conduct. Rule 7-101. Advising the Violation of Law.

"A member of the State Bar shall not advise the violation of any law, rule or ruling of a tribunal unless he believes in good faith that such law, rule or ruling is invalid. A member of the State Bar may take appropriate steps in good faith to test the validity of any law, rule or ruling of a tribunal."

(b)   IRS Circular 230 provides

"§10.21   Knowledge of client's omission.-Each attorney, certified public accountant, or enrolled agent who, having been retained by a client with respect to a matter administered by the Internal Revenue Service, knows that the client has not complied with the revenue laws of the United States or has made an error in or omission from any return, document, affidavit, or other paper which the client is required by the revenue laws of the United States to execute, shall advise the client promptly of the fact of such non-compliance, error or omission.

"§10.22   Diligence as to accuracy.-Each attorney, certified public accountant, or enrolled agent shall exercise due diligence."

(c)   A.B.A. Committee on Professional Ethics Opinion 314 (April 27, 1965) provides that if a tax attorney informs his client of a violation of the law (e.g., failing to file a tax return) and the client does not comply with the law, the attorney should discontinue the professional relationship.

CONCLUSION

At this time, the only viable means of avoiding the reporting requirements is to post adequate security at such time as the Treasury issues regulations.

Dated: April, 1980

12.

CAYMAN ISLANDS

The Confidential Relationships (Preservation) Law — 3

Law 16 of 1976

I assent

————————
T. RUSSELL
Governor

15th September, 1976.

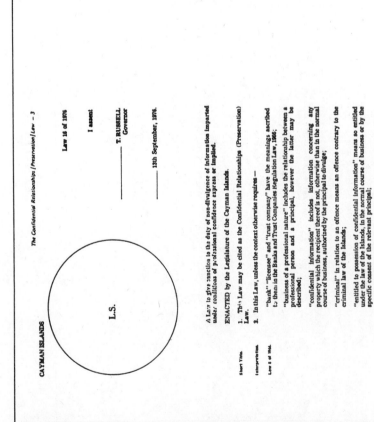

L.S.

A Law to give sanction to the duty of non-divulgence of information imparted under conditions of professional confidence express or implied.

ENACTED by the Legislature of the Cayman Islands.

Short Title.   1. This Law may be cited as the Confidential Relationships (Preservation) Law.

Interpretation.   2. In this Law, unless the context otherwise requires —

Law 8 of 1966.   "bank," "licensee" and "trust company" have the meanings ascribed to them in the Banks and Trust Companies Regulation Law, 1966;

"business of a professional nature" includes the relationship between a professional person and a principal, however the latter may be described;

"confidential information" includes information concerning any property which the recipient thereof is not, otherwise than in the normal course of business, authorized by the principal to divulge;

"criminal" in relation to an offence means an offence contrary to the criminal law of the Islands;

"entitled to possession of confidential information" means so entitled under the law of the Islands, in the normal course of business or by the specific consent of the relevant principal;

"Governor" means the Governor in Council;

"Inspector" means the Inspector of Banks and Trust Companies and to the extent of his authorization every person authorized by the Governor to

4 — *The Confidential Relationships (Preservation) Law*

perform his functions as such;

"normal course of business" means the ordinary and necessary routine involved in the efficient carrying out of the instructions of a principal including compliance with such laws and legal process as arises out of and in connection therewith and the routine exchange of information between licensees;

"principal" means a person who has imparted to another confidential information in the course of the transaction of business of a professional nature;

"professional person" includes a public or government official, a bank, trust company, an attorney-at-law, an accountant, an estate agent, an insurer, a broker and every kind of commercial agent and adviser whether or not answering to the above description and whether or not licensed or authorized to act in that capacity and every person subordinate to or in the employ or control of such person for the purpose of his professional activities;

"property" includes every present, contingent and future interest or claim, direct or indirect, legal or equitable, positive or negative, in any money, moneys worth, realty or personality, movable or immovable, rights and securities thereover and all documents and things evidencing or relating thereto.

Application and scope.   3. (1) This Law has application to all confidential information with respect to business of a professional nature which arises in or is brought into the Islands and to all persons coming into possession of such information at any time thereafter whether they be within the jurisdiction or thereout.

(2) This Law has no application, unless otherwise herein provided, to confidential information received or given —

(a) to any professional person acting in the normal course of business or with the consent, express or implied, of the relevant principal;

(b) to constables investigating offences committed or alleged to have been committed within the jurisdiction;

(c) to constables, specifically authorized by the Governor in that behalf, investigating an offence committed or alleged to have been committed outside the jurisdiction which if committed in the Islands would be a criminal offence;

(d) to the Financial Secretary or the Inspector.

Offences and penalties.   4. (1) Subject to the provisions of sub-section (2) of section 3, whoever —

(a) being in possession of confidential information however obtained;

(i) divulges it; or

(ii) attempts, offers or threatens to divulge it

to any person not entitled to possession thereof;

(b) wilfully obtains or attempts to obtain confidential information to

CAYMAN ISLANDS

Supplement No. 4 published with Gazette No. 21 of 1979

THE CONFIDENTIAL RELATIONSHIPS
(PRESERVATION) (AMENDMENT) LAW, 1979
(Law 26 of 1979)

Date of operation:
Notice of non-disallowance published in Gazette of 1979

The Confidential Relationships (Preservation) Law — 5

which he is not entitled,

is guilty of an offence and liable on summary conviction to a fine not exceeding $5,000 or to imprisonment for a term not exceeding 2 years or both.

(2) Whoever commits an offence under sub-section (1) and receives or solicits on behalf of himself or another any reward for so doing is liable to double the penalty therein prescribed and to a further fine equal to the reward received and also to forfeiture of the reward.

(3) Whoever, being in possession of confidential information, clandestinely, or without the consent of the principal, makes use thereof for the benefit of himself or another is guilty of an offence and on summary conviction liable to the penalty prescribed in sub-section (2) and for that purpose any profit accruing to any person out of any relevant transaction shall be regarded as a reward.

(4) Whoever being a professional person, entrusted as such with confidential information, the subject of the offence, commits an offence under subsections (1), (2) or (3) is liable to double the penalty therein prescribed.

(5) For the removal of doubt it is declared that, subject to subsection (2) of section 3, a Bank which gives a credit reference in respect of a customer without first receiving the authorization of that customer is guilty of an offence under subsections (1) and (4).

Savings. 5. Nothing in this Law shall by implication be deemed to derogate from the rule in Tournier v. National Provincial and Union Bank of England (1924) 1KB, 461, (which deals with the civil duty of banks to preserve the confidentiality of the business of their customers) which rule is declared to have application to the Islands

Regulations. 6. The Governor may make regulations for the administration of this Law.

Attorney General fiat. 7. No prosecution shall be instituted under this law without the consent of the Attorney General.

Passed the Legislative Assembly this 8th day of September, 1976.

T. RUSSELL
President

SYBIL McLAUGHLIN
Clerk of the Legislative Assembly.

The Confidential Relationships (Preservation) (Amdt.) Law, 1979. — 3

CAYMAN ISLANDS

Law 26 of 1979

I assent

T. RUSSELL
Governor

2nd October, 1979

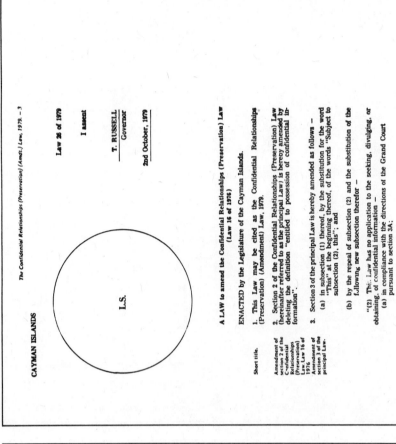

L.S.

A LAW to amend the Confidential Relationships (Preservation) Law (Law 16 of 1976)

ENACTED by the Legislature of the Cayman Islands.

Short title.   1. This Law may be cited as the Confidential Relationships (Preservation) (Amendment) Law, 1979.

Amendment of section 2 of the Confidential Relationships (Preservation) Law 16 of 1976   2. Section 2 of the Confidential Relationships (Preservation) Law (hereinafter referred to as the principal Law) is hereby amended by deleting the definition "entitled to possession of confidential information".

Amendment of section 3 of the principal Law.   3. Section 3 of the principal Law is hereby amended as follows –

(a) in subsection (1) thereof, by the substitution for the word "This" at the beginning thereof, of the words "Subject to subsection (2), this"; and

(b) by the repeal of subsection (2) and the substitution of the following new subsection therefor –

"(2) This Law has no application to the seeking, divulging, or obtaining, of confidential information –

(a) in compliance with the directions of the Grand Court pursuant to section 3A;

---

2 – The Confidential Relationships (Preservation) (Amdt.) Law, 1979

CAYMAN ISLANDS

THE CONFIDENTIAL RELATIONSHIPS (PRESERVATION) (AMENDMENT) LAW, 1979
ARRANGEMENT OF SECTIONS

Section
1. Short title
2. Amendment of section 2 of the Confidential Relationships (Preservation) Law. Law 16 of 1976
3. Amendment of section 3 of the principal Law
4. Addition of a new section 3A to the principal Law
5. Amendment of section 4 of the principal Law
6. Repeal of section 5 of the principal Law

The Confidential Relationships (Preservation) (Amdt.) Law, 1979 — 5

General may appear as *amicus curiae* at the hearing of any such application and any party on whom notice has been served as aforesaid shall be entitled to be heard thereon, either personally or by counsel.

(3) Upon hearing an application under subsection (2) a Judge shall direct —

(a) that the evidence be given; or

(b) that the evidence shall not be given; or

(c) that that evidence be given subject to conditions which he may specify whereby the confidentiality of the information is safeguarded.

(4) In order to safeguard the confidentiality of a statement, answer or testimony ordered to be given under subsection (3) (c) a Judge may order —

(i) divulgence of the statement, answer or testimony to be restricted to certain named persons;

(ii) evidence to be taken in camera; and

(iii) reference to the names, addresses and descriptions of any particular persons to be by alphabetical letters, numbers or symbols representing such persons the key to which shall be restricted to persons named by him.

(5) Every person receiving confidential information by operation of subsection (2) is as fully bound by the provisions of this Law as if such information had been entrusted to him in confidence by a principal.

(6) In considering what order to make under this section a Judge shall have regard to —

(a) whether such order would operate as a denial of the rights of any person in the enforcement of a just claim;

(b) any offer of compensation or indemnity made to any person desiring to enforce a claim by any person having an interest in the preservation of secrecy under this Law;

(c) in any criminal case, the requirements of the interests of justice.

(7) In this section, unless the context otherwise requires —

"court" bears the meaning ascribed to it in

---

4 — The Confidential Relationships (Preservation) (Amdt.) Law, 1979

(b) by or to —

(i) any professional person acting in the normal course of business or with the consent, express or implied, of the relevant principal;

(ii) a constable of the rank of Inspector or above investigating an offence committed or alleged to have been committed within the jurisdiction;

(iii) a constable of the rank of Inspector or above, specifically authorised by the Governor in that behalf, investigating an offence committed or alleged to have been committed outside the Islands which offence, if committed in the Islands, would be an offence against its laws; or

(iv) the Financial Secretary, the Inspector or, in relation to particular information specified by the Governor, such other person as the Governor may authorise;

(v) a bank in any proceedings, cause or matter when and to the extent to which it is reasonably necessary for the protection of the bank's interest, either as against its customers or as against third parties in respect of transactions of the bank for, or with, its customer;

(vi) the relevant professional person with the approval of the Financial Secretary when necessary for the protection of himself or any other person against crime; or

(c) in accordance with the provisions of this or any other Law."

Addition of a new section 3A to the principal Law:

4. The principal Law is hereby amended by the addition, immediately following section 3, of the following new section —

"Directions regarding the giving in evidence of confidential information.

3A. (1) Whenever a person intends or is required to give in evidence in, or in connection with, any proceeding being tried, inquired into or determined by any court, tribunal or other authority (whether within or without the Islands) any confidential information within the meaning of this Law, he shall before so doing apply for directions and any adjournment necessary for that purpose may be granted.

(2) Application for directions under subsection (1) shall be made to, and be heard and determined by, a Judge of the Grand Court sitting alone and in camera. At least seven days' notice of any such application shall be given to the Attorney General and, if the Judge so orders, to any person in the Islands who is a party to the proceedings in question. The Attorney

TAX RATE SCHEDULES FOR MARRIED INDIVIDUALS
FILING SEPARATE RETURNS

Taxable Income	1981* Pay +	% on Excess**	1982 Pay +	% on Excess**	1983 Pay +	% on Excess**	1984 Pay +	% on Excess**
0— $1,700	-0-	-0-	-0-	-0-	-0-	-0-	-0-	-0-
$1,700— 2,750	-0-	14	-0-	12	-0-	11	-0-	11
2,750— 3,800	$147	16	$126	14	$115	13	$115	12
3,800— 5,950	315	18	273	16	252	15	241	14
5,950— 8,000	702	21	617	19	574	17	542	16
8,000— 10,100	1,132.50	24	1,006	22	923	19	870	18
10,100— 12,300	1,636.50	28	1,468	25	1,322	23	1,248	22
12,300— 14,950	2,252.50	32	2,018	29	1,828	26	1,732	25
14,950— 17,600	3,100.50	37	2,787	33	2,517	30	2,395	28
17,600— 22,900	4,081	43	3,661	39	3,312	35	3,137	33
22,900— 30,000	6,360	49	5,728	44 .	5,167	40	4,886	38
30,000— 42,800	9,839	54	8,852	49	8,007	44	7,584	42
42,800— 54,700	16,751	59	15,124	50	13,639	48	12,960	45
54,700— 81,200	23,772	64	21,074	50	19,351	50	18,315	49
81,200—107,700	40,732	68	34,324	50	32,601	50	31,300	50
107,700—	58,752	70	47,574	50	45,851	50	44,550	50

* The CCH-prepared rate schedule shown above for 1981 is the same rate schedule that applied for 1980 taxes. A taxpayer may use this schedule to find the approximate taxes due for 1981 by computing the tax under the schedule and reducing the result by 1.25%. The IRS is expected to issue an official 1981 rate schedule that will incorporate the 1981 1.25% tax cut.

** The amount by which the taxpayer's taxable income exceeds the base of the bracket.

TAX RATE SCHEDULES FOR MARRIED INDIVIDUALS FILING
JOINT RETURNS AND SURVIVING SPOUSES

Taxable Income	1981* Pay +	% on Excess**	1982 Pay +	% on Excess**	1983 Pay +	% on Excess**	1984 Pay +	% on Excess**
0— $3,400	-0-	-0-	-0-	-0-	-0-	-0-	-0-	-0-
$3,400— 5,500	-0-	14	-0-	12	-0-	11	-0-	11
5,500— 7,600	$294	16	$252	14	$231	13	$231	12
7,600— 11,900	630	18	546	16	504	15	483	14
11,900— 16,000	1,404	21	1,234	19	1,149	17	1,085	16
16,000— 20,200	2,265	24	2,013	22	1,846	19	1,741	18
20,200— 24,600	3,273	28	2,937	25	2,644	23	2,497	22
24,600— 29,900	4,505	32	4,037	29	3,656	26	3,465	25
29,900— 35,200	6,201	37	5,574	33	5,034	30	4,790	28
35,200— 45,800	8,162	43	7,323	39	6,624	35	6,274	33
45,800— 60,000	12,720	49	11,457	44	10,334	40	9,772	38
60,000— 85,600	19,678	54	17,705	49	16,014	44	15,168	42
85,600—109,400	33,502	59	30,249	50	27,278	48	25,920	45
109,400—162,400	47,544	64	42,149	50	38,702	50	36,630	49
162,400—215,400	81,464	68	68,649	50	65,202	50	62,600	50
215,400—	117,504	70	95,149	50	91,702	50	89,100	50

* The CCH-prepared rate schedule shown above for 1981 is the same rate schedule that applied for 1980 taxes. A taxpayer may use this schedule to find the approximate taxes due for 1981 by computing the tax under the schedule and reducing the result by 1.25%. The IRS is expected to issue an official 1981 rate schedule that will incorporate the 1981 1.25% tax cut.

** The amount by which the taxpayer's taxable income exceeds the base of the bracket.

TAX RATE SCHEDULES FOR HEAD OF HOUSEHOLD

Taxable Income	1981*		1982		1983		1984	
	Pay +	% on Excess**	Pay +	% on Excess**	Pay +	% on Excess**	Pay +	% on Excess**
0— $2,300	–0–	–0–	–0–	–0–	–0–	–0–	–0–	–0–
$2,300— 4,400	–0–	14	–0–	12	–0–	11	–0–	11
4,400— 6,500	$294	16	$252	14	$231	13	$231	12
6,500— 8,700	630	18	546	16	504	15	483	14
8,700— 11,800	1,026	22	898	20	834	18	791	17
11,800— 15,000	1,708	24	1,518	22	1,392	19	1,318	18
15,000— 18,200	2,476	26	2,222	23	2,000	21	1,894	20
18,200— 23,500	3,308	31	2,958	28	2,672	25	2,534	24
23,500— 28,800	4,951	36	4,442	32	3,997	29	3,806	28
28,800— 34,100	6,859	42	6,138	38	5,534	34	5,290	32
34,100— 44,700	9,085	46	8,152	41	7,336	37	6,986	35
44,700— 60,600	13,961	54	12,498	49	11,258	44	10,696	42
60,600— 81,800	22,547	59	20,289	50	18,254	48	17,374	45
81,800—108,300	35,055	63	30,889	50	28,430	50	26,914	48
108,300—161,300	51,750	68	44,139	50	41,680	50	39,634	50
161,300—......	87,790	70	70,639	50	68,180	50	66,134	50

* The CCH-prepared rate schedule shown above for 1981 is the same rate schedule that applied for 1980 taxes. A taxpayer may use this schedule to find the approximate taxes due for 1981 by computing the tax under the schedule and reducing the result by 1.25%. The IRS is expected to issue an official 1981 rate schedule that will incorporate the 1981 1.25% tax cut.

** The amount by which the taxpayer's taxable income exceeds the base of the bracket.

TAX RATE SCHEDULES FOR SINGLE INDIVIDUALS

Taxable Income	1981*		1982		1983		1984	
	Pay +	% on Excess**	Pay +	% on Excess**	Pay +	% on Excess**	Pay +	% on Excess**
0— $2,300	–0–	–0–	–0–	–0–	–0–	–0–	–0–	–0–
$2,300— 3,400	–0–	14	–0–	12	–0–	11	–0–	11
3,400— 4,400	$154	16	$132	14	$121	13	$121	12
4,400— 6,500	314	18	272	16	251	15	241	14
6,500— 8,500	692	19	608	17	566	15	535	15
8,500— 10,800	1,072	21	948	19	866	17	835	16
10,800— 12,900	1,555	24	1,385	22	1,257	19	1,203	18
12,900— 15,000	2,059	26	1,847	23	1,656	21	1,581	20
15,000— 18,200	2,605	30	2,330	27	2,097	24	2,001	23
18,200— 23,500	3,565	34	3,194	31	2,865	28	2,737	26
23,500— 28,800	5,367	39	4,837	35	4,349	32	4,115	30
28,800— 34,100	7,434	44	6,692	40	6,045	36	5,705	34
34,100— 41,500	9,766	49	8,812	44	7,953	40	7,507	38
41,500— 55,300	13,392	55	12,068	50	10,913	45	10,319	42
55,300— 81,800	20,982	63	18,968	50	17,123	50	16,115	48
81,800—108,300	37,677	68	32,218	50	30,373	50	28,835	50
108,300—......	55,697	70	45,468	50	43,623	50	42,085	50

* The CCH-prepared rate schedule shown above for 1981 is the same rate schedule that applied for 1980 taxes. A taxpayer may use this schedule to find the approximate taxes due for 1981 by computing the tax under the schedule and reducing the result by 1.25%. The IRS is expected to issue an official 1981 rate schedule that will incorporate the 1981 1.25% tax cut.

** The amount by which the taxpayer's taxable income exceeds the base of the bracket.

TAX RATE SCHEDULES FOR ESTATES AND TRUSTS

Taxable Income	1981* Pay +	1981* % on Excess**	1982 Pay +	1982 % on Excess**	1983 Pay +	1983 % on Excess**	1984 Pay +	1984 % on Excess**
0— $1,050	–0–	14	–0–	12	–0–	11	–0–	11
$1,050— 2,100	$147	16	$126	14	$115	13	$115	12
2,100— 4,250	315	18	273	16	252	15	241	14
4,250— 6,300	702	21	617	19	574	17	542	16
6,300— 8,400	1,132.50	24	1,006	22	923	19	870	18
8,400— 10,600	1,636.50	28	1,468	25	1,322	23	1,248	22
10,600— 13,250	2,252.50	32	2,018	29	1,828	26	1,732	25
13,250— 15,900	3,100.50	37	2,787	33	2,517	30	2,395	28
15,900— 21,200	4,081	43	3,661	39	3,312	35	3,137	33
21,200— 28,300	6,360	49	5,728	44	5,167	40	4,886	38
28,300— 41,100	9,839	54	8,852	49	8,007	44	7,584	42
41,100— 53,000	16,751	59	15,124	50	13,639	48	12,960	45
53,000— 79,500	23,772	64	21,074	50	19,351	50	18,315	49
79,500—106,000	40,732	68	34,324	50	32,601	50	31,300	50
106,000—......	58,752	70	47,574	50	45,851	50	44,550	50

* The CCH-prepared rate schedule shown above for 1981 is the same rate schedule that applied for 1980 taxes. A taxpayer may use this schedule to find the approximate taxes due for 1981 by computing the tax under the schedule and reducing the result by 1.25%. The IRS is expected to issue an official 1981 rate schedule that will incorporate the 1981 1.25% tax cut.

** The amount by which the taxpayer's taxable income exceeds the base of the bracket.

INDEX

The text portion of this book was scanned on the Kurzweil Data Entry Machine, and composed Ticomp on the Autologic APS-5, in 11 and 10 point Stymie, leaded 2 points. Chapter numbers are 60 point Saul numerals; chapter titles are 18/20 Stymie Bold. The size of the type page is 35 by 56 picas.